MATHEMATICS WITH APPLICATIONS
IN MANAGEMENT AND ECONOMICS

MATHEMATICS WITH APPLICATIONS IN MANAGEMENT AND ECONOMICS

Gordon D. Prichett
John C. Saber

Both of Babson College

Seventh Edition

IRWIN

Burr Ridge, Illinois
Boston, Massachusetts
Sydney, Australia

 This symbol indicates that the paper in this book is made of recycled paper. Its fiber content exceeds the recommended minimum of 50% waste paper fibers as specified by the EPA.

© RICHARD D, IRWIN, INC., 1963, 1967, 1972, 1976, 1980, 1987, and 1994

All rights reserved. No part of this publication may be reproduced, stored in a retrieval system, or transmitted, in any form or by any means, electronic, mechanical, photocopying, recording, or otherwise, without the prior written permission of the publisher.

Senior sponsoring editor: Richard T. Hercher, Jr.
Developmental editor: Gail Korosa
Marketing manager: Robb Linsky
Project editor: Karen Smith
Production manager: Diane Palmer
Art coordinator: Mark Malloy
Compositor: J.M. Post Graphics, Book Division, Cardinal Communications Group, Inc.
Typeface: 10/12 Times Roman
Printer: R.R. Donnelley & Sons Company

Library of Congress Cataloging-in-Publication Data

Prichett, Gordon D.
   Mathematics with applications in management and economics / Gordon D. Prichett, John C. Saber.—7th ed.
      p.   cm.
   Rev. ed. of: Mathematics, with applications in management and economics / Earl K. Bowen, Gordon D. Prichett, John C. Saber. 6th ed.
   Includes index.
   ISBN 0-256-09237-0
   1. Business mathematics.   1. Saber, John C.   II. Bowen, Earl K. Mathematics, with applications in management and economics.
   III. Title.
HF5691.B69   1994
510—dc20   92-36042

Printed in the United States of America
1 2 3 4 5 6 7 8 9 0 DOC 0 9 8 7 6 5 4 3

TO
Jill, Reid, Trevor, and Glenn
Carol, John, Stephen, and Nicholas

PREFACE

The first edition of this text was written by Earl K. Bowen. His original objectives were to present mathematics to first-year college students of business and economics at a level appropriate to student preparation and directed specifically toward applications in management and economics. This seventh edition is motivated by the same objectives.

The systematic presentation in each chapter—motivation, explanation, example(s), and answered exercise(s)—which students and teachers have enthusiastically approved through six previous editions, is maintained and amplified in this edition. This approach provides a text easily adapted to self-study.

Many of the algebraic details omitted in most texts at this level have been included within the text to help students learn or recall the arithmetic and algebra needed to solve problems. In addition, we have added to this edition a preamble entitled "Refresher on the Essential Concepts of Algebra" to make available in a compact form the essential prerequisite tools needed for the text. This new section is organized as both a refresher section and a reference section; it is therefore quite terse. At the same time we have retained and revised the appendixes, which offer more in-depth coverage of the prerequisite material.

Our main concern in preparing this revision has remained: *Can students read and understand the text?* A second equally important concern has been to weave the use of calculators, software packages, and technological support comfortably into the fabric of the text. The following features have been added or retained with these objectives in mind.

New Features

Margin Notes. The basic core concepts in each section are summarized succinctly in the margins to facilitate content confirmation and review.

Vignettes. Each chapter contains one or two short descriptions called "From Theory to Practice" of an application or practical circumstance in which the topic under discussion plays an important role in everyday situations.

Examples. Many new examples that draw from contemporary issues or circumstances have been added.

Computer Applications. The use of LINDO in linear programming and Minitab in probability is integrated into the text as technique rather than alternative.

Extended Review Problems. Each chapter contains 10 extended review problems that are randomly numbered and can serve as examination questions or can be used for classroom review and discussion.

Enhanced Features

Examples. Several hundred worked examples are included in this text to demonstrate applications and techniques in problem solving.

Exercises. Each section contains answered exercises to allow students to reconfirm their understanding of the material while reading the text.

Applications. A greater number and selection of applications in management and economics than is customary are included in each chapter. Many chapters contain special application sections.

Calculator Applications. Calculator applications are presented where appropriate. Examples and exercises that involve the use of both standard features and preprogrammed functions are explained in detail.

Computer Applications. Computer applications in QBasic and computer exercises are included where appropriate. A disk with all of the QBasic programs used in the text is available from the publisher.

Theorems and Definitions. All theorems and definitions are boxed and highlighted to emphasize their importance. Care has been taken to state theorems and definitions simply but accurately.

Problems. The text contains over 1,500 numbered problems, with answers, and over 750 additional review problems that can serve as a basis for examination and lecture purposes. The Instructor's Solutions Manual includes solutions to the review problems that have been worked out in detail. In addition, there is a supplemental Student Solutions Manual that contains worked-out solutions to selected problems.

Organization

In this edition, we have divided the text into four parts to clarify how each part contributes to the whole.

Part I. Linear Relationships and Constrained Optimization. In this part, we cover the basics of linear equations, linear inequalities, linear functions, and systems of linear equations with an introduction to matrices and Gaussian Elimination. The concluding two chapters of this part deal with linear programming and the use and interpretation of LINDO.

Part II. Nonlinear Relationships with Applications in Business and Finance. The first chapter of this part reviews the fundamental properties of exponential and logarithmic functions. The second and final chapter is a comprehensive treatment of the basics of the mathematics of finance.

Part III. Introduction to Applied Calculus and Unconstrained Optimization. This part is an introductory treatment of the elementary concepts and applications of differential and integral calculus. Emphasis is given to the uses of calculus as a problem-solving tool. Special effort has been made to present the basic concepts in an intuitive fashion, and examples and problems have been chosen from a broad spectrum of management applications.

Part IV. Introduction to Probability with Applications. Much of this material has been rewritten so that it is more appropriate for a text at this level. Emphasis has been placed on the use and application of probability. Wherever applicable, examples and problems have been solved by using calculators and Minitab.

Pedagogical Philosophy

Students commonly ask "Why study mathematics?" and frequently follow this comment with "I can't do math." This question and comment really go hand in hand. The primary reason that students "can't do math" is because they have difficulty relating mathematics to their everyday experiences and thus have little inspiration to test their mathematical abilities.

The goal of this textbook is to answer the question and consequently change the comment. We first hope to convince students how to value mathematics. In other words, we want students to begin to understand that the techniques of mathematics can be looked at as a structured extension of their natural thinking process. Everyone loves to solve puzzles, but not everyone sees that the solution can be expressed as a mathematical model.

Next we want to help each student become confident in his/her own ability. Oftentimes, the student's first reaction to a mathematical problem is "I can't do it" before he or she even undertakes an attempt. Usually this is because the student has been unable to relate the problem to anything familiar or practical. Once a negative posture has been assumed, the student is more than likely doomed to failure. Rebuilding a student's confidence begins by relating problems to familiar real-life situations. An important step in this process is to have the student become adept at being a mathematical problem solver. Instead of just solving individual problems, emphasis should be placed on having the student get used to formulating an associated model. In other words, try to have the student recognize common patterns in problems and then translate these patterns into mathematical symbols. By doing this, the student sees a logical classification of problems and a systematic approach to problem solving rather than an unending set of problems.

At this stage the student should be learning how to communicate mathematically. The important point here is that the student becomes comfortable with estimating solutions and recognizing the proper magnitudes that the results should have. Thus a result that is way out of line should immediately send up a warning flag and cause the student to reevaluate his/her problem formulation and/or solution methodology. Further, once the mathematical solution has been achieved, it is critical that the student be able to translate the result back into the context of the original problem. Numbers alone are not sufficient. A proper translation and explanation of the numbers into real terms are needed for the numerical result to have any meaning.

The student must become comfortable with the translation from words to mathematical symbols and then from numerical results back into words.

When a student arrives at this point, solving problems in an analytical and structured way no longer is a tedious task but a pleasant and satisfying challenge. Students begin to see the value of a logical approach to problem solving and, in fact, soon realize that in the long run this approach is simpler, more efficient, and more fun.

One final factor needs to be added: The student needs to learn how to use technology effectively. While paper-and-pencil solutions remain at the core of the foundation that is needed for building a solid conceptual understanding of mathematics, slide rules (what were they?) and numerical tables have been replaced by calculators. Calculators are becoming more powerful and microcomputers are becoming faster and less expensive. It is therefore equally important to show the student how to properly use the calculator and the computer. Drilling in the basics of algebra is necessary and important, but once the student has mastered the fundamentals there is no practical value in focusing problem solving on endless and complicated manipulations that can easily be accomplished with modern technology. In our opinion, it is preferable to spend more time having the student learn about problem formulation, problem-solving techniques, and conceptualization and expression of ideas and results.

In way of summary, we hope this textbook will help to develop the problem-solving skills of students, encourage them to think analytically and critically, enhance their ability to communicate mathematically, and build or fortify their confidence in their own ability. Wherever appropriate, we try to illustrate the effective use of technology while at the same time emphasizing the need for mastering the standard analysis and solution techniques so that the student will always have a solid background in the fundamentals.

Supplementary Materials

Instructor's Solutions Manual. The Instructor's Solutions Manual contains detailed solutions to selected problems from each chapter. In addition, the manual contains detailed solutions to all review and extended review problems.

Student Solutions Manual. The Student Solutions Manual is a subset of the Instructor's Solutions Manual. It contains detailed solutions to the same selected problems from each chapter, but only those solutions for the odd review and extended review problems are provided.

Test Bank and Computest. The Test Bank contains over 500 additional problems broken down into true/false, multiple choice, and regular format. The level of difficulty of each problem is also indicated. In addition, the Test Bank is available on disk through Computest.

Transparency Masters. Transparency masters for the text material are available. These allow the careful planning, preparation, and presentation of each class session.

Math Applications Disk. The Math Applications Disk contains the QBasic programs that appear in the text material and problems. These programs can run on any DOS machine that supports QBasic.

About the Authors

Gordon D. Prichett has an undergraduate degree in mathematics from Williams College and an M.A. and Ph.D. in mathematics from the University of Wisconsin in Madison, Wisconsin. He is the author of numerous articles in mathematics and mathematics education. Together with John T. Anderson, he developed a successful self-paced calculus program at Hamilton College in the 1970s, the results of which culminated in a calculus textbook. His position paper in the 1987 conference "Calculus for a New Century," sponsored by the National Science Foundation and the Sloan Foundation, outlined the critical issues we face in calculus and general mathematics instruction for students of business in the 20th century. He has just returned to the faculty and classroom after serving as Vice President for Academic Affairs and Dean of the Faculty at Babson since 1987.

John C. Saber has an A.B. in mathematics and an A.M. in applied mathematics from Harvard University and a Ph.D. in mathematics from Brandeis University. He is the author of numerous books and articles in mathematics and computers. As Chairman of The Mathematics & Science Division of Babson since 1974, he has guided the growth and role of the division to include more than thirty full-time and part-time faculty members in Quantitative Methods, Probability and Statistics, Natural Sciences, and Information Systems. He has been a management consultant since 1970 and has designed and implemented management information systems in more than 30 companies ranging from Fortune 100 to small businesses. For the past four years, he has been developing classroom materials along with Joseph F. Aieta at Babson for the effective use of technology in the classroom. This work has led to a partnership with IBM whereby students learn and take examinations in a networked computer classroom in which each student has his/her own IBM workstation. Those interested in using these materials as they apply to the textbook can receive a disk from the authors.

Acknowledgments

Many reviewers have been a tremendous help in critiquing this textbook. Especially notable is the careful review written by Jerry Rubin of Marshall University. Other reviewers to whom we are indebted are Sufi Nazem and James Conway of the University of Nebraska at Omaha; Tom Obremski of the University of Denver; Roseanne Hofmann of Montgomery County Community College; Frank Jewett of Humboldt State University; Richard Levin of Western Washington University; Elton Lacey of Texas A&M University; Woo Bong Lee of Bloomsburg University; John Shannon of Suffolk University; William Marchal of the University of Toledo; David Ashley of the University of Missouri at Kansas City; Jean Clark of Virginia Commonwealth University; and John Spellman of Southwest Texas State University. Previous editions have benefited as well by suggestions over the years. Of special note are the comments by Christopher J. Toy of New Hampshire College. Others who have contributed to the text over its life include: R. Andres, P. Applebaum,

W. Beatty, F. Benn, T. Billesbach, G. Bloom, R. Borman, A. Brunson, R. Carlson, W. Cassidy, D. Chesnut, T. Church, D. Cleaver, C. Crell, R. Davis, W. Davis, E. Dawson, B. Dilworth, R. Dingle, D. Dixon, W. Etterbeek, J. Freigo, R. Fetter, J. Flaherty, J. Foster, R. Fox Jr., R. Friesen, H. Frisinger, H. Fullerton, W. Furman, E. Goldstein, L. Goldstein, M. Greenberg, V. Heeren, J. Hindle, A. Ho, A. Hoffman, G. Horcutt, J. Hudson, and D. Isaacson.

Also: R. Jaffa, C. I. Jones, R. J. Jones, H. King, R. Kizior, P. Latimer, R. Leezer, R. Leidig, J. Liff, S. Logan, G. Long, T. Lougheed, J. Lovell, T. Lupton, M. Malchow, E. Marrinan, Jr., P. McKeon, A. McLaury, E. Merrick, P. Merry, R. Moreland, J. Moreno, C. Murphy, D. Nichols, J. Papenfuss, R. Ralls, P. Randolph, G. Reeves, J. ReVelle, R. Salmon, F. Schwab, H. Sendek, P. Sgalla, R. Sheffield, L. Shumway, P. Siegel, B. Smith, J. Smith, W. Soule, Jr., M. Spinelli, H. Stein, D. Stoller, M. Tarrab, T. Taylor, O. Thomas, R. Tibrewalla, T. Tsukahara, E. Tyler, E. Underwood, B. Van Cor, T. Vasper, G. Waldron, B. Walker, and M. Williamson.

Many other reviewers were especially helpful in critiquing the sixth edition and their comments have been incorporated in this seventh edition. These include: Adelina S. Gomez of Nichols College, Judy Kay Hartzell of the University of Nebraska-Omaha, Robert V. High of Adelphi University, Kay C. Kriewald of Laredo Junior College, Gordon J. Landry of Nicholls State University, Norman F. Lindquist of Western Washington University, Stanley Lukawecki of Clemson University, Robert J. McManus of Algonquin College, and Gary Lee McGrath of Pittsburgh State University. We are indebted to their valuable suggestions.

Additionally, we wish to acknowledge the encouragement and contributions of our colleagues at Babson: W. Carpenter, I. Dambolena, D. Kopsco, H. Kriebel, J. McKenzie, W. Montgomery, M. Riskalla, A. Shah, and M. Weinblatt; in addition, Samuel C. Hanna of Boston University, who helped develop the authors' approach to linear programming and mathematics of finance.

Joseph F. Aieta and Stephen Turner, two other colleagues at Babson, reviewed the text and problems of the seventh edition; and their contributions helped to make the book as error free as possible.

We cannot let this opportunity pass to pay special recognition to Earl K. Bowen. It was his long and dedicated work through the first five editions that played an integral role in the development of this textbook. His fundamental ideas and individual mentoring are mirrored in the finished product available in this edition.

Finally, special recognition should go to our wives and children who gave up so many long winter nights and summer days with us so that this book could become a reality.

Gordon D. Prichett
John C. Saber

Contents in Brief

Refresher on the Essential Concepts of Algebra — 1

PART I Linear Relationships and Constrained Optimization — 14
1. Linear Equations and Functions — 16
2. Systems of Linear Equations and Matrices — 71
3. Introduction to Linear Programming and the Simplex Method — 151
4. Additional Topics in Linear Programming — 237

PART II Nonlinear Relationships with Applications in Business and Finance — 352
5. Exponential and Logarithmic Functions — 354
6. Introduction to the Mathematics of Finance — 387

PART III Introduction to Applied Calculus and Unconstrained Optimization — 458
7. Introduction to Differential Calculus — 460
8. Applications of Differential Calculus — 522
9. Additional Topics in Differential Calculus — 591
10. Introduction to Integral Calculus — 640

PART IV Introduction to Probability with Applications — 740
11. Counting and Probability — 742
12. Probability Distributions — 808

Appendix One   Elements of Algebra — 875

Appendix Two   Formulas, Equations, Inequalities, and Graphs — 926

Appendix Three   Sets — 969

Answers to Problem Sets — 983

Tables — 1050

Index — 1055

CONTENTS

Refresher on the Essential Concepts of Algebra ... 1

- R.1 The Real Numbers ... 1
- R.2 Order of Operations ... 1
- R.3 Variables, Equations, and Inequalities ... 3
- R.4 Properties of Zero ... 3
- R.5 Grouping Symbols and Factoring ... 4
- R.6 Rational Expressions ... 4
- R.7 Exponents ... 5
- R.8 Solving Equations and Inequalities ... 6
- R.9 Graphing ... 8
- R.10 Word Problems ... 10
- R.11 Sets ... 11

PART I Linear Relationships and Constrained Optimization ... 14

Chapter 1 Linear Equations and Functions ... 16

- 1.1 Introduction ... 16
- 1.2 Slope ... 20
- 1.3 Problem Set 1–1 ... 25
- 1.4 Equation of a Line: Slope-Intercept Form ... 26
- 1.5 Straight-Line Equation Given a Point and Slope ... 32
- 1.6 Straight-Line Equation from Two Points ... 33
- 1.7 Horizontal and Vertical Lines ... 34
- 1.8 Problem Set 1–2 ... 36
- 1.9 Parallel and Perpendicular Lines ... 38
- 1.10 Lines through the Origin ... 41
- 1.11 Piecewise Linear Functions ... 42
- 1.12 Problem Set 1–3 ... 47
- 1.13 Interpretive Exercise: Cost–Output ... 49
- 1.14 Problem Set 1–4 ... 51
- 1.15 Break-Even Interpretation: 1 ... 52
- 1.16 Break-Even Interpretation: 2 ... 56
- 1.17 Linear Demand Functions ... 61
- 1.18 Problem Set 1–5 ... 64
- 1.19 Review Problems ... 66
- 1.20 Extended Review Problems ... 69

Chapter 2 Systems of Linear Equations and Matrices ... 71

- 2.1 Introduction ... 71
- 2.2 Number of Solutions Possible in a System ... 71
- 2.3 Operations on Linear Systems ... 73
- 2.4 Elimination Procedure: Unique Solutions ... 75
- 2.5 Elimination Procedure: Nonunique Solutions ... 81
- 2.6 Problem Set 2–1 ... 88
- 2.7 Applications–1: Mixture Problems ... 89
- 2.8 Problem Set 2–2 ... 92
- 2.9 Applications–2: Supply and Demand Analysis ... 93
- 2.10 Applications–3: Two-Product Supply and Demand Analysis ... 96
- 2.11 Problem Set 2–3 ... 97
- 2.12 Matrices and Vectors ... 98
- 2.13 Matrix Operations ... 101
- 2.14 The Identity Matrix ... 107
- 2.15 Problem Set 2–4 ... 108
- 2.16 Row Operations and the Inverse of a Matrix ... 110
- 2.17 Problem Set 2–5 ... 119

2.18	Applications–4: Matrix Solution of n-by-n Linear Systems	121
2.19	Problem Set 2–6	131
2.20	Applications–5: Matrix Solution of m-by-n Linear Systems	132
2.21	Problem Set 2–7	138
2.22	Applications–6: Markov Chains	139
2.23	Problem Set 2–8	143
2.24	Review Problems	144
2.25	Extended Review Problems	148

Chapter 3 Introduction to Linear Programming and the Simplex Method   151

3.1	Introduction	151
3.2	Systems of Two Linear Inequalities	152
3.3	Nonnegativity Constraints	155
3.4	Problem Set 3–1	160
3.5	Maximization Examples: Product Mix	161
3.6	Minimization Examples: Ingredient Mix	174
3.7	Problem Set 3–2	181
3.8	Equality Constraints	184
3.9	Linear Programming with More Than Two Variables	186
3.10	Problem Set 3–3	191
3.11	More on Formulation	195
3.12	Problem Set 3–4	198
3.13	The Simplex Method	202
3.14	Problem Set 3–5	216
3.15	Introduction to LINDO	218
3.16	Problem Set 3–6	221
3.17	A Minimizing Problem with "≤" Constraints	222
3.18	Problem Set 3–7	228
3.19	Review Problems	229
3.20	Extended Review Problems	234

Chapter 4 Additional Topics in Linear Programming   237

4.1	Introduction	237
4.2	Tie for the Entering or Leaving Variable	237
4.3	Alternative Optimal Solutions	246
4.4	Unbounded Solutions	250
4.5	Negative Decision Variables	253
4.6	Problem Set 4–1	258
4.7	Sensitivity Analysis on ≤ Constraints: Shadow Prices and Right-Hand-Side Ranges	259
4.8	Problem Set 4–2	274
4.9	Two Penalty/Premium Examples with "≤" Constraints	276
4.10	Minimization by Maximizing the Dual	282
4.11	Problem Set 4–3	289
4.12	The Phase I–Phase II Method	291
4.13	Problem Set 4–4	300
4.14	No Feasible Solutions	302
4.15	An Example with "=" Constraints	306
4.16	Grand Summary of the Simplex Method	312
4.17	Problem Set 4–5	316
4.18	Sensitivity Analysis on "≥" and "=" Constraints	318
4.19	Sensitivity Analysis on the Objective Function and New Product Analysis	323
4.20	Problem Set 4–6	328
4.21	Review Problems	339
4.22	Extended Review Problems	348

PART II Nonlinear Relationships with Applications in Business and Finance   352

Chapter 5 Exponential and Logarithmic Functions   354

5.1	Introduction	354
5.2	Exponential Functions	354
5.3	Problem Set 5–1	362
5.4	The Need for Logarithms	362
5.5	Rules of Logarithms	364
5.6	Common Logarithms and Natural Logarithms	367
5.7	Problem Set 5–2	372
5.8	Application of Inverse Natural Logarithms	373
5.9	Graph of $y = \ln x$	377

5.10	Computing *e* and Natural Logarithms	380
5.11	Problem Set 5–3	384
5.12	Review Problems	384
5.13	Extended Review Problems	386

Chapter 6 Introduction to the Mathematics of Finance 387

6.1	Introduction	387
6.2	Simple Interest and the Future Value	388
6.3	Simple Discount: Present Value	393
6.4	Bank Discount	395
6.5	Effective Rate: Simple Interest	397
6.6	Problem Set 6–1	399
6.7	Compound Interest and the Future Value	401
6.8	The Conversion Period	404
6.9	Finding the Time and the Interest Rate	406
6.10	Problem Set 6–2	409
6.11	Compound Discount: Present Value	410
6.12	Problem Set 6–3	412
6.13	Effective Rate: Compound Interest	413
6.14	Problem Set 6–4	416
6.15	Continuous (Instantaneous) Compounding	416
6.16	Problem Set 6–5	423
6.17	Ordinary Annuities: Future Value	424
6.18	Ordinary Annuities: Sinking Fund	428
6.19	Problem Set 6–6	430
6.20	Ordinary Annuities: Present Value	431
6.21	Ordinary Annuities: Amortization	433
6.22	Problem Set 6–7	439
6.23	Summary of Financial Rules	440
6.24	Multistep Problems	444
6.25	Problem Set 6–8	447
6.26	Ordinary Annuities: Finding the Interest Rate and Time	449
6.27	Ordinary Annuities: Continuous Compounding	450
6.28	Problem Set 6–9	451
6.29	Review Problems	452
6.30	Extended Review Problems	455

PART III Introduction to Applied Calculus and Unconstrained Optimization 458

Chapter 7 Introduction to Differential Calculus 460

7.1	Introduction	460
7.2	Why Study Calculus?	460
7.3	Functional and Delta Notation	464
7.4	Problem Set 7–1	470
7.5	Limits	471
7.6	Problem Set 7–2	482
7.7	Continuity	483
7.8	Problem Set 7–3	486
7.9	The Difference Quotient	487
7.10	Definition of the Derivative	491
7.11	Problem Set 7–4	497
7.12	The Simple Power Rule	499
7.13	d/dx Notation and Rules of Operations	500
7.14	Problem Set 7–5	506
7.15	The Derivative of $[f(x)]^n$	507
7.16	Problem Set 7–6	511
7.17	Product and Quotient Rules	511
7.18	Problem Set 7–7	518
7.19	Review Problems	518
7.20	Extended Review Problems	520

Chapter 8 Applications of Differential Calculus 522

8.1	Introduction	522
8.2	Maxima and Minima of Functions: The First Derivative Test	522
8.3	Problem Set 8–1	539
8.4	The Second Derivative Test	540
8.5	Problem Set 8–2	548
8.6	Maxima and Minima: Applications	549
8.7	Problem Set 8–3	559
8.8	More Applications	561
8.9	Problem Set 8–4	568
8.10	An Inventory Model	570

8.11	Problem Set 8–5	575
8.12	Sketching Graphs of Polynomials	576
8.13	Problem Set 8–6	580
8.14	Sketching Rational Functions	581
8.15	Problem Set 8–7	586
8.16	Review Problems	587
8.17	Extended Review Problems	589

Chapter 9 Additional Topics in Differential Calculus   591

9.1	Introduction	591
9.2	Derivatives of Exponential Functions	591
9.3	Response Functions	602
9.4	Problem Set 9–1	603
9.5	Derivatives of Logarithmic Functions	605
9.6	Problem Set 9–2	607
9.7	The Chain Rule	608
9.8	Marginal Propensity to Consume and the Multiplier	612
9.9	Problem Set 9–3	616
9.10	Calculus of Two Independent Variables	617
9.11	Problem Set 9–4	621
9.12	Maxima and Minima: Two Independent Variables	622
9.13	Problem Set 9–5	635
9.14	Review Problems	636
9.15	Extended Review Problems	639

Chapter 10 Introduction to Integral Calculus   640

10.1	Introduction	640
10.2	Antiderivatives: The Indefinite Integral	640
10.3	Problem Set 10–1	659
10.4	Area and the Definite Integral: Riemann Sums	660
10.5	Problem Set 10–2	663
10.6	The Area Between Two Curves	666
10.7	Problem Set 10–3	672
10.8	Interpretive Applications of Area	672
10.9	Interpreting the Area Bounded by Two Functions	678
10.10	Consumers' and Producers' Surplus	680
10.11	Problem Set 10–4	685
10.12	The Integral of $(mx + b)^{-1}$	687
10.13	Problem Set 10–5	690
10.14	Integrals of Exponential Functions	690
10.15	Problem Set 10–6	695
10.16	Tables of Integrals	696
10.17	Problem Set 10–7	699
10.18	Asymptotic Areas: Improper Integrals	700
10.19	Problem Set 10–8	704
10.20	Numerical Integration	704
10.21	Problem Set 10–9	713
10.22	Integration by Parts	714
10.23	Problem Set 10–10	717
10.24	Differential Equations	718
10.25	Forms of the Constant	721
10.26	Problem Set 10–11	724
10.27	Applications of Differential Equations	725
10.28	Problem Set 10–12	732
10.29	Review Problems	733
10.30	Extended Review Problems	738

PART IV Introduction to Probability with Applications   740

Chapter 11 Counting and Probability   742

11.1	Introduction	742
11.2	Counting Techniques	742
11.3	Permutations and Combinations	752
11.4	Problem Set 11–1	758
11.5	More Counting Problems	760
11.6	The Binomial Theorem	764
11.7	Problem Set 11–2	767
11.8	Probability and Odds	769
11.9	Assigning Probabilities and Conditional Probabilities	771
11.10	Problem Set 11–3	781
11.11	Probability Rules	782
11.12	Practice with Probability Rules	787
11.13	Problem Set 11–4	793

11.14	Bayes' Rule	796	A1.6	Order of Operations	880
11.15	Problem Set 11–5	801	A1.7	Problem Set A1–1	882
11.16	Review Problems	802	A1.8	Representing Numbers by Letters	884
11.17	Extended Review Problems	806	A1.9	Importance of Fundamental Properties	885

Chapter 12 Probability Distributions 808

12.1	Introduction	808
12.2	Experiment, Event, Sample Space	808
12.3	Problem Set 12–1	811
12.4	Discrete Random Variables	812
12.5	Problem Set 12–2	819
12.6	The Binomial Probability Distribution	820
12.7	Cumulative Binomial Probabilities	826
12.8	Problem Set 12–3	831
12.9	Expected Monetary Value (EMV)	832
12.10	Problem Set 12–4	836
12.11	Continuous Probability Density Functions	837
12.12	Problem Set 12–5	842
12.13	Expected Value	842
12.14	Variance and Standard Deviation	846
12.15	Problem Set 12–6	848
12.16	The Normal Distribution	848
12.17	Problem Set 12–7	858
12.18	Estimating the Mean and the Standard Deviation	858
12.19	Problem Set 12–8	863
12.20	Applications	863
12.21	Problem Set 12–9	869
12.22	Review Problems	870
12.23	Extended Review Problems	873

A1.10	Problem Set A1–2	887
A1.11	Removing Grouping Symbols	889
A1.12	Definitions: Expression, Term, Factor	889
A1.13	Elementary Factoring	891
A1.14	Problem Set A1–3	894
A1.15	Properties of the Numbers Zero and One	896
A1.16	Product of Fractions	899
A1.17	Addition and Subtraction of Fractions	903
A1.18	Division of Fractions	905
A1.19	Problem Set A1–4	907
A1.20	Exponents	909
A1.21	Zero Exponent	910
A1.22	Negative Exponents	910
A1.23	Power to a Power	912
A1.24	Fractional Exponents	913
A1.25	Summary of Exponent Rules	916
A1.26	Practice Problem Set	917
A1.27	Problem Set A1–5	918
A1.28	Order of Operations Revisited	920
A1.29	Problem Set A1–6	923
A1.30	Review Problems	923

Appendix One Elements of Algebra 875

A1.1	Introduction	875
A1.2	The Real Numbers	875
A1.3	Rules of Sign	876
A1.4	Addition and Subtraction of Signed Numbers	877
A1.5	Multiplication and Division of Signed Numbers	879

Appendix Two Formulas, Equations, Inequalities and Graphs 926

A2.1	Introduction	926
A2.2	Some Axioms	927
A2.3	Solutions by Addition and Multiplication, with Inverses	928
A2.4	Problem Set A2–1	934
A2.5	Transposition	935
A2.6	Formulas	936
A2.7	Exact Evaluations	939
A2.8	Problem Set A2–2	940
A2.9	Coordinate Axes	942
A2.10	Plotting Observational Data	944

A2.11	Plotting Equations in Two Variables: Straight Lines	945	A3.4	Solution Sets for Equations	972
A2.12	Vertical Parabolas	946	A3.5	Relations and Functions	972
A2.13	Quadratic Equations	952	A3.6	Problem A3–1	975
A2.14	Problem Set A2–3	955	A3.7	Set Operations	976
A2.15	Definitions and Fundamental Properties of Inequalities	955	A3.8	Problem Set A3–2	980
A2.16	Fundamental Operations on Inequalities	957	A3.9	Review Problems	981
A2.17	Solving Single Equations	958			
A2.18	Problem Set A2–4	964			
A2.19	Review Problems	965			

Appendix Three   Sets   969

- A3.1 Introduction   969
- A3.2 Set Terminology   969
- A3.3 Set Specifications   971

Answers to Problem Sets   983

Tables   1050

Index   1055

REFRESHER ON THE ESSENTIAL CONCEPTS OF ALGEBRA

The following outline is presented as a review and easy reference on the essential concepts of algebra needed as a basis for this textbook. Use this outline to recall ideas, formulas, and techniques that may require a quick refresher. Appendixes 1, 2, and 3 at the end of the book contain a more extensive and detailed review. Table R–1 lists the concepts and references the corresponding sections of the appendixes. If you choose to do so, the appendixes will allow you to work with this review material in more detail before proceeding through the textbook.

TABLE R–1

Topic	Detailed Review in Appendixes
The real numbers	Sections A1.1–A1.5, A1.7, A1.15, and A1.19
Order of operations	Sections A1.6–A1.7 and A1.28–A1.29
Variables, equations, and inequalities	Sections A1.8, A1.10, A2.15–A2.16, and A2.18
Properties of zero	Sections A1.15 and A1.19
Grouping symbols and factoring	Sections A1.9–A1.14
Rational expressions	Sections A1.16–A1.19
Exponents	Sections A1.20–A1.27
Solving equations and inequalities	Sections A2.1–A2.8 and A2.13–A2.18
Graphing	Sections A2.9–A2.12 and A2.14
Word problems	Sections A1.6–A1.7 and A1.29 and A2.4
Sets	Sections A3.1–A3.8

R.1 THE REAL NUMBERS

The **real numbers** have three primary subcategories:

a. **Integers**, such as $0, 1, -1, 2, -2, 3$, and -3.
b. **Rational numbers** in the form p/q with p and q integers and $q \neq 0$, such as $2/7$, $-3/8$, and $5/1 = 5$.

c. **Irrational numbers** (real numbers that cannot be expressed as ratios of integers), such as $\sqrt{2}$ and π.

The real numbers can be plotted on a coordinate line, as shown in Figure R–1.

FIGURE R–1

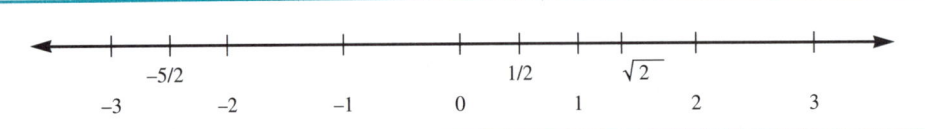

R.2 ORDER OF OPERATIONS

When an expression involves more than one operation, the order in which the operations are performed follows a very simple rule:

1st: **Parentheses**—expressions in parentheses are computed first.
↓
2nd: **Exponents** are computed left to right.
↓
3rd: **Multiplication** and **division** together are done left to right.
↓
4th: **Addition** and **subtraction** together are done left to right.

Note that parentheses are managed from the inside out and that the order of operations must be followed within each pair of parentheses and brackets. For example, to evaluate

$$17 - [5 + 2(6 \uparrow 2 / 4 - 5 \times 3)] \times 2,$$

we would proceed as follows:

$$17 - [5 + 2(36 / 4 - 5 \times 3)] \times 2$$
$$17 - [5 + 2(9 - 15)] \times 2$$
$$17 - [5 + 2(-6)] \times 2$$
$$17 - [5 - 12] \times 2$$
$$17 - [-7] \times 2$$
$$17 - (-14)$$
$$31.$$

R.3 VARIABLES, EQUATIONS, AND INEQUALITIES

A **variable** is a placeholder for an undetermined numerical value. It's treated algebraically as if it were a real number. Variables are denoted by letters, sometimes with subscripts (for example, a, x, y_2, c_1, T).

Equations are statements involving two or more expressions which are equal, whereas **inequalities** are statements involving two or more expressions which are not equal. Operations on equalities and inequalities follow the **order properties** of the real numbers.

Order Properties

1. Either $a < b$, $a > b$, or $a = b$. For example,
$$2 < 5 \text{ and } -1 > -3.$$

2. If $a < b$ and $b < c$, then $a < c$. For example,
$$-5 < -1 \text{ and } -1 < 7, \text{ so } -5 < 7.$$

3. If $a < b$ then $a + c < b + c$ for any real number c. For example,
$$1 < 8, \text{ so}$$
$$1 + (-10) < 8 + (-10), \quad \text{or} \quad -9 < -2.$$

4. If $a < b$ and $c > 0$, then $ac < bc$, but if $a < b$ and $c < 0$, then $ac > bc$. For example,
$$3 < 7, \text{ so}$$
$$3(4) < 7(4), \quad \text{or} \quad 12 < 28,$$
but
$$3(-4) > 7(-4), \quad \text{or} \quad -12 > -28.$$

R.4 PROPERTIES OF ZERO

For any real number a,
$$0 \times a = 0,$$
$$a + 0 = a - 0 = a,$$
$$a + (-a) = 0,$$
$$\frac{0}{a} = 0 \text{ if } a \neq 0,$$
$$\frac{a}{0} \text{ is } \textbf{not defined}.$$

For example,
$$\left(\frac{-5}{2}\right) \times 0 = 0,$$

$$\left(\frac{2}{3}\right) + 0 = \left(\frac{2}{3}\right) - 0 = \frac{2}{3},$$

$$15 + (-15) = 0,$$

$$\frac{0}{4} = 0,$$

$$\frac{4}{0} \text{ is not defined.}$$

Lastly,

$$\frac{0}{0} \text{ is ambiguous,}$$

and thus **not well defined**.

R.5 GROUPING SYMBOLS AND FACTORING

Factoring is based on the distributive law in reverse,

$$ab + ac = a(b + c).$$

We next list the most common factoring patterns with examples. First,

$$x^2 - (a + b)x + ab = (x - a)(x - b)$$
$$x^2 - 5x + 6 = (x - 2)(x - 3).$$

Also,

$$x^2 - y^2 = (x + y)(x - y)$$
$$x^2 - 16 = (x + 4)(x - 4),$$

and

$$x^3 - y^3 = (x - y)(x^2 + xy + y^2)$$
$$x^3 - 27 = (x - 3)(x^2 + 3x + 9),$$

and

$$x^3 + y^3 = (x + y)(x^2 - xy + y^2)$$
$$x^3 + 27 = (x + 3)(x^2 - 3x + 9).$$

R.6 RATIONAL EXPRESSIONS

Any expression of the form A/B is called a **rational expression**. A and B can be real numbers or polynomials in one or more variables. Addition, subtraction, multiplication, and division of rational expressions follow exactly the same rules as the operations for regular fractions.

= Rational Operations

$$\frac{A}{B} \pm \frac{C}{D} = \frac{AD \pm BC}{BD}.$$

$$\frac{A}{B} \times \frac{C}{D} = \frac{AC}{BD}.$$

$$\frac{A}{B} \div \frac{C}{D} = \frac{A}{B} \times \frac{D}{C} = \frac{AD}{BC}.$$

For example, to simplify

$$\left[2\left(\frac{b}{a} - \frac{b}{a-b}\right) - \frac{b+a}{b-a}\right] \div \left(\frac{a+2b}{a}\right),$$

we would proceed as follows:

$$\left[2\frac{b(a-b) - ab}{a(a-b)} - \frac{b+a}{b-a}\right] \times \left(\frac{a}{a+2b}\right)$$

$$\left[\frac{2(ba - b^2 - ab)}{a(a-b)} + \frac{b+a}{a-b}\right] \times \left(\frac{a}{a+2b}\right)$$

$$\left[\frac{-2b^2}{a(a-b)} + \frac{a(b+a)}{a(a-b)}\right] \times \left(\frac{a}{a+2b}\right)$$

$$\left(\frac{a^2 + ab - 2b^2}{\not{a}(a-b)}\right) \times \left(\frac{\not{a}}{a+2b}\right)$$

$$\frac{a^2 + ab - 2b^2}{(a-b)(a+2b)}$$

$$\frac{a^2 + ab - 2b^2}{a^2 + ab - 2b^2} = 1.$$

The basic rules of **exponents** can be applied for any **base** $a \neq 0$ and any rational numbers m and n.

R.7 EXPONENTS

1. $a^m a^n = a^{m+n}$. For example,

$$2^3 2^5 = 2^8 = 256$$

$$a^3 a^5 = a^8.$$

2. $a^{-n} = \frac{1}{a^n}$. For example,

$$3^{-2} = \frac{1}{3^2} = \frac{1}{9}$$

$$a^{-2} = \frac{1}{a^2}.$$

3. $\dfrac{a^m}{a^n} = a^{m-n} = \dfrac{1}{a^{n-m}}$. For example,

$$\dfrac{4^8}{4^9} = 4^{-1} = \dfrac{1}{4}$$

$$\dfrac{a^8}{a^9} = a^{-1} = \dfrac{1}{a}.$$

4. $(a^m)^n = a^{mn}$. For example,

$$(5^{1/2})^6 = 5^3 = 125$$

$$(a^{1/2})^6 = a^3.$$

5. $a^0 = 1$. For example,

$$\left(\dfrac{3}{5}\right)^0 = 1.$$

6. $a^{m/n} = (a^{1/n})^m = (a^m)^{1/n}$, where $a^{1/n} = \sqrt[n]{a}$. For example,

$$8^{4/3} = (8^{1/3})^4 = 2^4 = 16$$

$$a^{4/3} = (a^{1/3})^4 = (\sqrt[3]{a})^4.$$

R.8 SOLVING EQUATIONS AND INEQUALITIES

To solve an **equation** for a certain variable is to derive an expression that has the variable alone (coefficient of 1 and exponent of 1) on one side of the equal sign and an expression **not** involving this variable on the other side of the equal sign. The standard rules of arithmetic and algebra are applied to solve equations. Two basic formulas for solving simple polynomials are as follows.

= Equations

1. To solve the **linear equation** $ax = b$, we simply divide both sides of the equation by a to get

$$x = \dfrac{b}{a}.$$

For example, solving

$$2x + 5 = -8$$

we have

$$2x = -13$$

$$x = -13/2 = -6^1/_2.$$

2. To solve the **quadratic equation** $ax^2 + bx + c = 0$, we either factor the equation and solve for x or use the **quadratic formula**

$$x = \frac{-b \pm \sqrt{b^2 - 4ac}}{2a}.$$

For example, solving

$$2x^2 + 7x - 15 = 0$$

we would first factor the left-hand side:

$$(2x - 3)(x + 5) = 0.$$

Remember this is done by combining the factors of the coefficient a from the x^2 term (in this case the factors 2 and 1 from the term $2x^2$) with the factors of c from the constant term (in this case either 1 and 15, or 3 and 5 from the term -15), to form the coefficient b of the x term (in this case $+7$ from the term $+7x$). Now the last equation means

$$2x - 3 = 0 \quad \text{or} \quad x + 5 = 0$$

so that

$$x = \frac{3}{2} \quad \text{or} \quad x = -5.$$

As a second example suppose we want to solve the quadratic equation

$$3x^2 + 7x - 13 = 0.$$

This time we cannot factor the equation on the left-hand side. Why? The reason is that there is no combination of the factors 1 and 3 from the $3x^2$ term with the factors 1 and 13 from the constant term -13, which will result in the coefficient 7 of the $+7x$ term. So we use the quadratic formula with

$$a = 3, b = 7, \text{ and } c = -13$$

to get

$$x = \frac{-7 \pm \sqrt{7^2 - 4(3)(-13)}}{2(3)}$$

$$x = \frac{-7 \pm \sqrt{49 - (-156)}}{6} = \frac{-7 \pm \sqrt{205}}{6}$$

$$x = 1.220 \quad \text{or} \quad x = -3.553$$

to three-decimal place accuracy.

To solve an inequality, we apply the standard rules of arithmetic and algebra together with the order properties to derive an expression that has the intended variable alone on one side of the inequality. For example, to solve

= **Inequalities**

we would proceed as follows.

$$\frac{x^2 - x}{2} > 2x + 3$$

$$x^2 - x > 4x + 6$$

$$x^2 - 5x - 6 > 0$$

$$(x - 6)(x + 1) > 0.$$

The latter inequality means that either both terms on the left are positive or both are negative. Why? The reason is that the product of two terms, one of which is positive and the other of which is negative, will result in a negative number. So,

either

$$x - 6 > 0 \quad \text{and} \quad x + 1 > 0$$
$$x > 6 \quad \text{and} \quad x > -1$$

which means that

$$x > 6,$$

or

$$x - 6 < 0 \quad \text{and} \quad x + 1 < 0$$
$$x < 6 \quad \text{and} \quad x < -1$$

which this time means that

$$x < -1$$

In summary, the solution to our original inequality is

$$x < -1 \quad \text{or} \quad x > 6.$$

R.9 GRAPHING

When graphing **functions** on the **coordinate axes**, the **horizontal axis** represents the **independent variable** of the function while the **vertical axis** represents the **dependent variable**. For example, in

$$y = -2x^2 + 12x - 10,$$

x is the independent variable and y is the dependent variable, so y is a function of x. The table in Figure R–2 contains the coordinates of several arbitrarily selected points, and these points along with the associated graph of the function are plotted below the table. This graph is consistent with the fact that any function in the form

$$y = ax^2 + bx + c$$

represents a **vertical parabola** which

1. **Opens up** if $a > 0$ and **opens down** if $a < 0$, and
2. Has its **vertex** located at $x = -\dfrac{b}{2a}$.

In our example
$$a = -2, b = 12, \text{ and } c = -10,$$
so the parabola indeed opens down and has its vertex at
$$x = \frac{-12}{2(-2)} = \frac{-12}{-4} = 3.$$

What is the y coordinate of the vertex? Substituting $x = 3$ into the equation for y gives $y = 8$.

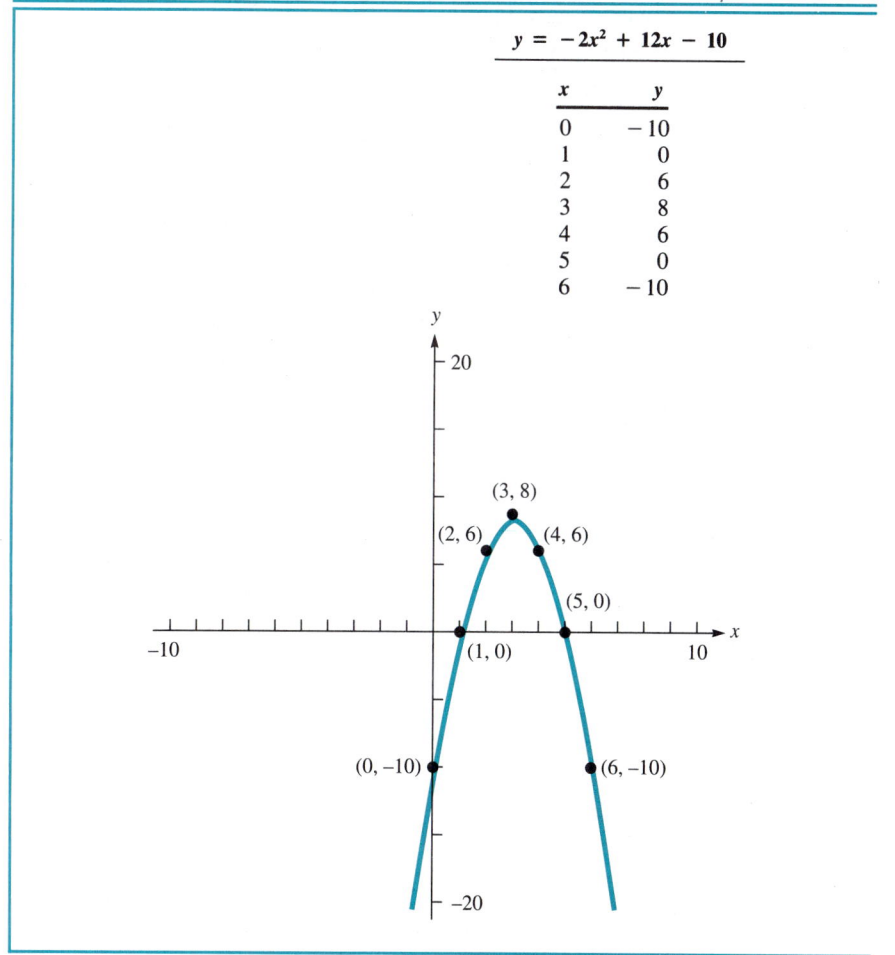

FIGURE R-2

R.10 WORD PROBLEMS

To solve a word problem it is necessary to first convert it from text into a **mathematical model** (often just a simple arithmetic or algebra problem) and then solve it by familiar techniques. The greatest difficulty usually is the conversion process which requires a thorough understanding of the original problem. The following steps are a guideline in solving word problems. If you always remember to focus on the **objective** of the problem (what is being asked for), word problems can become a less formidable task and perhaps even an enjoyable challenge.

Fundamental Steps

1. Read the problem.
2. Read the problem again, but more slowly this time.
3. Determine the objective of the problem (what is being asked for).
4. Draw a diagram or construct a table containing all the pertinent information in the problem.
5. Select the unknowns or **variables**.
6. Using these variables, convert the problem to one or more equations or inequalities to solve.
7. Solve the equations or inequalities.
8. Read the problem one last time.
9. Convert the numerical answer back into the context of the problem, and write your final answer in a carefully worded concluding statement.

Example. A little league baseball team has played 12 games and has won $83\frac{1}{3}\%$ of them. It has 16 remaining games on its schedule. If it should win $62\frac{1}{2}\%$ of the games left to be played, what would its win/loss standing be at the end of the season?

Object of the Problem: Determine the final win/loss standing.

The pertinent information is summarized in Table R–2. From the last **row** and last **column** of this table, the number of games won at season's end will be

$$\left(12 \times \frac{83\frac{1}{3}}{100}\right) + \left(16 \times \frac{62\frac{1}{2}}{100}\right) = 10 + 10 = 20.$$

TABLE R–2

	Number of Games	Percentage Won	Number of Games Won
Games to date	12	$83\frac{1}{3}\%$	$12 \times 83\frac{1}{3}\%$
Games to play	16	$62\frac{1}{2}\%$	$16 \times 62\frac{1}{2}\%$
End of season	28	?	$12 \times 83\frac{1}{3}\%$ + $16 \times 62\frac{1}{2}\%$

Since 28 games were played in total, the final win/loss standing of the team will be 20 wins and 8 losses for a winning percentage of

$$\frac{20}{28} \times 100 = 71.4\%.$$

Example. The cost of setting the type for a sales brochure is $12. In addition, the cost of paper and printing is 4 cents per copy. Write a formula (equation) that will give in dollars the total cost T of making n copies.

Object of the Problem: Write a formula for T, the total cost of n copies. The relationship between T and n can be expressed in words as

Total cost = Cost to set type + Cost of paper and printing.

This expression can be then converted to

$$T = \$12 + \frac{\$4}{100} \times n.$$

Simplifying this last expression, the total cost T in dollars of making n brochures is

$$T = \frac{n}{25} + 12.$$

R.11 SETS

A **set** is simply a collection of **objects**. Table R–3 contains the basic concepts and notation associated with sets. For example, if A is the collection of even integers (as usual, 0 is considered even) and B is the collection of odd integers, then the following set statements can be made:

$2 \in A$

$2 \notin B$

$\{4, 6, 8\} \subseteq A$

$A \cup B = \mathcal{U} = \{\text{all integers}\}$

$A \cap B = \emptyset$

$A' = B.$

TABLE R-3

Concept	Notation
The object x is in the set A (x is an **element** or **member** of A)	$x \in A$
The object x is not in the set A	$x \notin A$
Set A is a **subset** of set B (A is contained in B)	$A \subseteq B$
The **union** of two sets A and B (Collection of elements in either set)	$A \cup B$
The **intersection** of two sets A and B (Collection of elements in both sets)	$A \cap B$
The **empty set** (The set with no elements)	$\emptyset$
The **universal** set (Collection of all candidate elements)	$\mathcal{U}$
The **complement** of set A (Collection of elements in $\mathcal{U}$ but not in A)	A'
The set of all x for which property P holds	$\{x : P\}$

LINEAR RELATIONSHIPS AND CONSTRAINED OPTIMIZATION

CHAPTER 1
Linear Equations and Functions

CHAPTER 2
Systems of Linear Equations and Matrices

CHAPTER 3
Introduction to Linear Programming

CHAPTER 4
Additional Topics in Linear Programming

Mathematicians, economists, statisticians, and others have applied their skills to management problems for many years. The first concerted and dramatically successful effort in this area occurred during World War II when specialists were formed into operations analysis groups to assist in planning military operations. These analysts used mathematics and statistics extensively in their studies, and their resulting recommendations were an important contribution to the war effort. Following the war, analysts, soon joined by others, turned their attention and their new techniques to attacking problems of management operations. They accomplished major improvements in inventory control, quality control, warehouse location, oil industry operations, agriculture, purchasing decisions, scheduling of complex tasks such as building a shopping center, and a variety of other areas. Mathematics, old and newly created, was coupled with innovative applications of the rapidly evolving electronic computer and was directed toward business management problems. This resulted in a new field of study called *quantitative methods* (or *management science* or *operations research*), which has become a standard part of business colleges' curricula. The importance of quantitative approaches to management problems and decision making is now widely accepted, and a course in mathematics with management applications is critical to all management students' core of subjects. This text, which has been widely used in many hundreds of classrooms, develops the mathematics needed to understand the quantitative basis from which many management decisions and solutions are derived.

Linear relationships and constrained optimization are the subject matter of Part I of this book. Linear functions have a myriad of direct manage-

PART I

FROM THEORY TO PRACTICE
Quants on Wall Street

Quants are a new breed of investment managers, researchers, and executives that have invaded the Wall Street investment houses over the past decade. Before 1980 most mathematicians and "rocket scientists" working on "the street" were computer scientists and programmers in back offices developing data processing techniques to handle increased trading volume. In the late 1970s when interest rates were fluctuating wildly and deregulation of financial markets was becoming a reality, Wall Street houses were desperate for new ways to protect against catastrophic movements in bond prices that could wipe out their capital. They found that the old way of hedging one bond against another of a different maturity was often producing big losses. The problem was eventually solved using "convexity," a tool from calculus that describes bond prices' behavior when interest rates move wildly.

Using sophisticated mathematical strategies and analyses, these new denizens of Wall Street have created a collection of innovative products and techniques that have revolutionized the business of investment managers. Program trading, zero-coupon bonds, interest rate swaps, and collateralized mortgage obligations (CMOs) are only a few of the recent striking innovations.

Investment managers around the country are struggling to keep up with the latest techniques of the Quants. From MIT to Berkeley, big firms are actively courting students with strong quantitative and scientific skills. People wishing to enter the investment arena today should assure themselves of a solid quantitative background in fundamental mathematics and science.

Source: Z. Bodie, A. Kane, and A. Marcus, *Investments* (Homewood, Ill.: Richard D. Irwin; 1989).

ment applications. Indeed, at this very moment, lowest-cost and highest-profit decisions are being made somewhere with information generated by computers manipulating linear relationships. Linear functions are of special importance since they are easy to manipulate and understand both graphically and symbolically. Because of this, many nonlinear situations are analyzed using linear approximations (i.e., by replacing nonlinear functions with linear functions or combinations of linear functions that behave much the same as the original function). The intent of the approximation is to keep things as simple and as clear as possible. The mathematics of linear relationships as we develop it is quite easy. Only a minimal background, such as that provided in the appendixes, is required to get started and make progress. (For a review of the minimal background, read Appendix 1. In Appendix 2 read sections A2.1 through A2.5, A2.15 through A2.17, and the parts of A2.6 through A2.11 that deal with linear equations.) It would be useful to scan these appendixes. If needed, feel free to work through them systematically and refer to them as often as necessary.

LINEAR EQUATIONS AND FUNCTIONS

1.1 INTRODUCTION

In this chapter, we will consider in some detail the algebra and geometry of linear equations and functions in two variables, (that is, equations and functions whose graphs in a coordinate plane are straight lines).

> Linear equations are equations whose **terms** (the parts separated by plus, minus, and equal signs) are a constant, or a constant times **one** variable to the first power.

Thus,
$$2x - 3y = 7$$
is a linear equation because it consists of the constant 7, the term $2x$ (which is the constant 2 times x to the first power), and $-3y$, which is also a term consisting of a constant times one variable to the first power. From this example, it should be clear that the general form of a linear equation is
$$Ax + By = C$$
where A, B, and C are constants with A and B not both zero. Linear equations also appear in other forms. For example,
$$y = \frac{1}{2}x + 3$$
and
$$\frac{x}{3} + \frac{y}{2} = 1$$
are linear equations. On the other hand,
$$2x + 3xy = 7$$

is not linear because $3xy$ is a constant times the product of two variables. Also,

$$x^2 + y + 3x = 16$$

is not linear because of the presence of the second-power term, x^2.

Linear equations arise frequently in applied situations.

Example. Taxi fare from an airport to a nearby city is $1.25 per mile driven, plus $0.75 for a bridge toll. Let y represent the fare and x the number of miles driven on one trip, and write the equation for y in terms of x. Find the fare if the distance from the airport to the city is 22 miles.

The total fare will be

$$\text{Fare} = (1.25)(\text{number of miles driven}) + 0.75$$

or, using the specified symbols,

$$y = 1.25x + 0.75,$$

which is a linear equation. When the distance traveled is 22 miles, the fare is

$$y = 1.25(22) + 0.75$$
$$= \$28.25.$$

Exercise. Taxi fare from an airport to a nearby town is $0.80 per mile driven, plus $2 for tolls. Let y represent the fare and x the miles driven on one trip. Write the equation for y in terms of x. Find the fare when the distance driven is 17 miles.
Answer: $y = 0.80x + 2$. $15.60.

The equations of the last example and exercise,

$$y = 1.25x + 0.75 \quad \text{and} \quad y = 0.80x + 2,$$

are linear equations in the two **variables** x and y. These equations have graphs that are straight lines. To graph a straight line, you will recall that we need only to have the coordinates of two of its points (since there is precisely one line that can be drawn between two given points).[1] It does not matter which two points on the line are chosen, so we may arbitrarily select two values for x and obtain the corresponding values for y. For example, in

$$y = 1.25x + 0.75,$$

To graph a straight line, first determine the coordinates of two points, then draw the line between these points.

---

[1] See A2.11.

if we choose $x = 1$, then

$$y = 1.25(1) + 0.75 = 1.25 + 0.75 = \$2,$$

and we have the point $x = 1$, $y = 2$, which is designated in the conventional form (x, y) as $(1, 2)$. Again, choosing, say, $x = 5$, we find

$$y = 1.25(5) + 0.75 = 6.25 + 0.75 = \$7,$$

and we have the point $x = 5$, $y = 7$, or $(5, 7)$. Plotting $(1, 2)$ and $(5, 7)$ as points, then drawing a line through them, leads to Figure 1–1. Note that since the distance traveled must be nonnegative (i.e., $x \geq 0$), the graph is drawn only in the first quadrant. The accompanying Figure 1–2 shows the graph of $y = 0.80x + 2$.

Exercise. Verify the points shown in Figure 1–2.

Answer: In $y = 0.80x + 2$, if we choose $x = 0$, then $y = 2$, and if we choose $x = 5$, then $y = 6$.

FIGURE 1–1

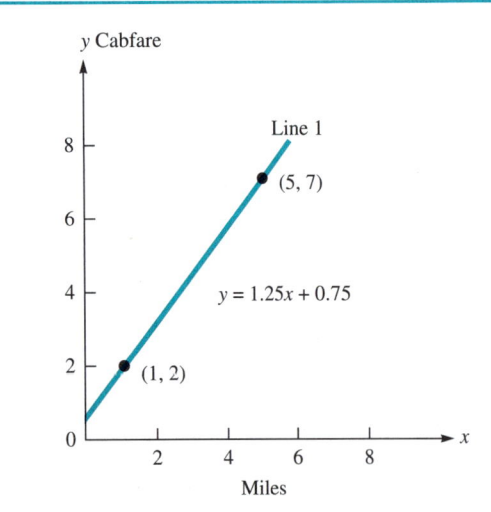

FIGURE 1–2

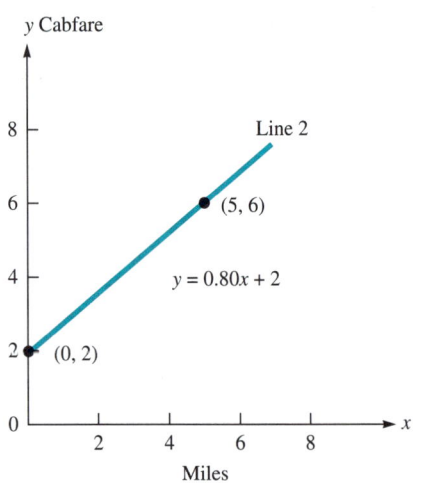

FROM THEORY TO PRACTICE
Calculators, Graphing Calculators, and Computer Algebra Systems

There is currently a strong trend toward incorporating technology into the teaching of mathematics. Electronic tools include basic calculators, programmable calculators, graphing calculators, and computer algebra systems (CAS). The effective use of this technology allows the individual to focus more on applications, problem formulation, and the interpretation of numerical and graphical results.

There is no need to flip through extensive tables (such as logarithms, exponentials, and interest) when all relevant computations can be done more efficiently on an inexpensive calculator. Wherever applicable, we will illustrate in the textbook how and when calculators can be appropriately used. We will also indicate where programmable calculators can enhance the solution process. This will allow us to concentrate more on problem formulation and problem solving rather than on the sometimes tedious mechanics which often confuse the issue and discourage people.

The advent of graphing calculators has added another dimension. Visual displays of equations and functions such as those in Figures 1–1 and 1–2 can easily be reproduced. Not only can we generate both numerical and graphical analyses of a problem, but we can do them at one and the same time in the palm of our hands. In addition, CAS technology is rapidly becoming available on microcomputers. This further enhances the problem-solving approach by expanding and extending the approach of the programmable and graphing calculators to more powerful, easy to use tools. Quick analysis of **what if** questions becomes readily available, and we can handle more complex problems with little, if any, additional effort.

Lastly, many problem-solving situations also lend themselves to solution by relatively small and easy computer programs. Examples of these written in QBasic will be provided at appropriate points in the textbook.

Linear Functions

The relationship between y and x expressed by

$$y = 1.25x + 0.75$$

is called a functional relationship because for each value of x, there is one, and only one, corresponding value for y. Notice that the expression states what y is (that is, $y =$) in terms of x, and we connote this by saying **y is a function of x**; of course, this is a **linear function**. If we write

$$y = \text{an expression involving } x \text{ and constants,}$$

y is a function of x means a relationship expressing a unique value of y for each value of x.

> The independent variable is plotted on the horizontal axis. The dependent variable is plotted on the vertical axis.

x is called the **independent** variable and is plotted on the horizontal axis. The value of y depends upon what value we assign to x, and so y is called the **dependent** variable, which is plotted on the vertical axis. Thus, when we plot points, the values of x can be chosen independently, but the corresponding values of y depend on the values chosen for x. Later in the text we will encounter situations where an expression has several letters, and we will want to be able to specify which is the independent variable. This is done by writing the independent variable as a function of the dependent variable denoted by $y = f(x)$, read **y equals f of x**. Thus, in our example, $y = 1.25x + .75$ is denoted by

$$f(x) = 1.25x + 0.75.$$

The need for identification of the independent variable can be seen if we write

$$y = kp + n.$$

It is impossible to treat this as a linear function because it is not clear which of the letters on the right is the independent variable. However, writing

$$y = f(p) = kp + n$$

specifies that p is the independent variable and, therefore, k and n are to be considered as being **constants**. In this chapter, the identity of the independent variable will be clear from the context, so we will use the parenthetical specification only in certain circumstances. However, **independent variable**, **dependent variable**, and **linear function** are phrases that should be a part of our vocabulary.

In summary, then, linear functions have the form

$$y = mx + b$$

> $y = mx + b$ is the general equation of a line.

where x is the independent variable, y is the dependent variable, and m and b are constants.

Returning to Figures 1–1 and 1–2, observe that both lines slant upward to the right, but that line 1, on the left, rises more rapidly (is steeper) than line 2. This means that for a **given** horizontal change, the vertical change on line 1 is greater than the vertical change on line 2. The ratio of vertical to horizontal change has numerous applied interpretations and so is discussed next.

1.2 SLOPE

The steepness of a ski slope, the pitch of a roof, and the steepness of the glide path of a descending airplane all are associated with the mathematical concept of the **slope** of a straight line or line segment. Numerically, the slope of a straight line is the ratio of the vertical change (**rise** or **fall**) to the horizontal change (**run**) between two points on the line, where the rise or fall is the vertical separation and the run is the horizontal separation of the two points. In Figure 1–3, the slope of the segment AB is the ratio

> $$\text{Slope} = \frac{\text{Vertical change}}{\text{Horizontal change}}$$

$$\text{Slope} = \frac{\text{Vertical change (rise)}}{\text{Horizontal change (run)}} = \frac{6}{2} = 3.$$

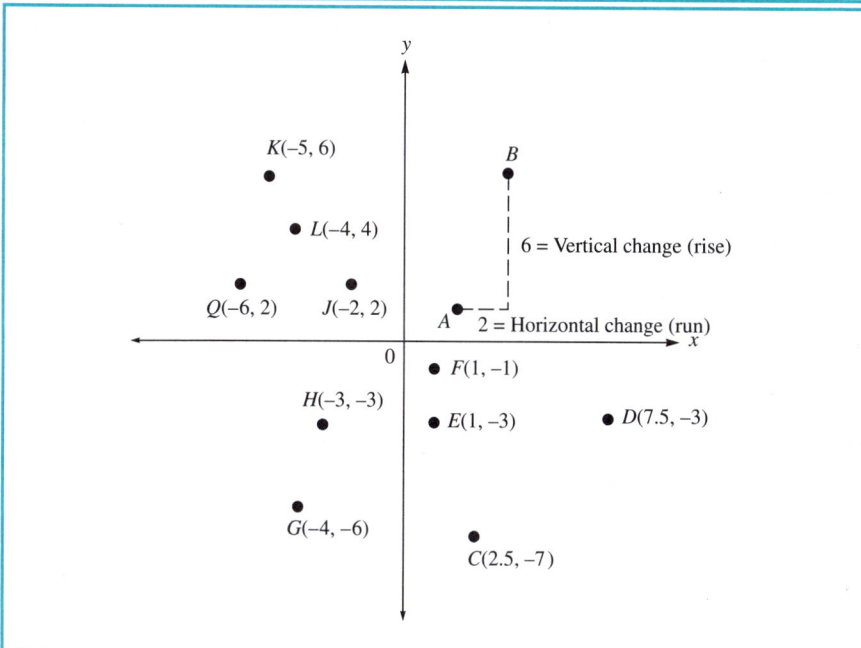

FIGURE 1-3

Clearly, the vertical change is the difference in the *y*-coordinates of the endpoints of the line segment, while the horizontal change is the difference in the endpoints' *x*-coordinates. We use the standard subscript notation to designate particular points: that is,

$$(x_1, y_1)$$

which is read as **x sub-one, y sub-one** or simply **x-one, y-one**. Hence the slope (generally called *m*) of a straight line or line segment joining the points (x_1, y_1) and (x_2, y_2) is

$$\text{Slope} = m = \frac{\text{Difference of } y\text{'s}}{\text{Difference of } x\text{'s}} = \frac{y_2 - y_1}{x_2 - x_1}.$$

Consider the segment *CD* connecting the points (2.5, 7) and (7.5, −3) in Figure 1-3:

$$m = \frac{\text{Rise}}{\text{Run}} = \frac{-3 - (-7)}{7.5 - 2.5} = \frac{4}{5} = 0.8.$$

It is important to distinguish between segments that rise to the right, such as *AB* in Figure 1–3, and those that fall to the right, such as *KL*. This is done by observing that lines that slant upward to the right have positive slope numbers and those slanting downward to the right have negative slope numbers. This requirement will be met if we **use the same point as the starting point** (x_1, y_1) when computing the rise or fall and the run. For example, the slope of $C(2.5, -7)$, $D(7.5, -3)$ computed above to be 0.8 by starting with point C as (x_1, y_1) for both the rise and the run, is also 0.8 if we designate point D as (x_1, y_1) for both the rise and the run. Thus,

$$m = \frac{-7-(-3)}{2.5-7.5} = \frac{-4}{-5} = 0.8.$$

> **Exercise.** See Figure 1–3. Verify that the slopes of *KL* and *GH* are, respectively, -2 and 3.

Returning to Figure 1–3, observe the horizontal segment *QJ*. If we substitute its coordinates into the slope formula we find

$$m = \frac{2-2}{-2-(-6)} = \frac{0}{4} = 0,$$

so the slope is zero. **All horizontal segments have a slope of zero** since if we were to pick any two points on a horizontal segment, their coordinates would be (x_1, y_1) and (x_2, y_1) where $x_1 \neq x_2$ and the y-coordinate of each point is the same value, y_1. Hence, the slope of any such segment is

The slope of any horizontal line segment is 0.

$$m = \frac{y_1 - y_1}{x_2 - x_1} = \frac{0}{x_2 - x_1} = 0.$$

The denominator, $x_2 - x_1$, is not zero here since $x_1 \neq x_2$. Consequently, the quotient is zero because zero divided by any nonzero number is zero.

Next, consider the vertical segment *EF* in Figure 1–3. From the slope formula we have

$$m = \frac{-1-(-3)}{1-1} = \frac{2}{0}.$$

The expression 2/0 is undefined since division by 0 is not permitted.[2] Thus, this vertical segment has no well-defined slope number. Saying a line has no slope number may not bring the image of a vertical line to mind. Some find it more

[2]See A1.15.

descriptive to say a vertical line has infinite slope because a straight up-and-down line is the steepest one we can imagine. However, in using the term **infinity**, which is symbolized as ∞, we must remember that ∞ is not a number, so saying a line has infinite slope means its slope is undefined.

In general, (x_1, y_1) and (x_1, y_2) represent two different points on a vertical segment because they have the same x-coordinate and the slope will be

$$m = \frac{y_2 - y_1}{x_1 - x_1} = \frac{y_2 - y_1}{0}$$

The slope of any vertical line segment is undefined.

which is undefined. Thus, in general, **all vertical segments have undefined or infinite slope.**

Exercise. Which of the following segments is horizontal and which is vertical?
a) The segment joining $(4, -6)$ and $(10, -6)$. b) The segment joining $(4, -6)$ and $(4, 10)$.

Answer: a) is horizontal and b) is vertical.

Exercise. Draw three segments through the point $(4, 7)$: one with infinite slope, one with the slope $m = 0$, and one with $m = 2/3$. (A slope of 2/3 is a rise of 2 for a run of 3.)

In applications, the slope of a line segment often is interpreted as the rate of change in the vertical for a unit change (that is, a change of one) in the horizontal. A number of such slopes have been given names.

Slope represents the dependent variable's rate of change with respect to the independent variable.

Example. This example uses the terms **disposable income, personal consumption expenditures**, and **savings**. It will be sufficient for our purposes here to think of disposable income as the amount of income left after taxes have been paid. The part of disposable income that is placed in a bank or otherwise invested is savings; the remainder, personal consumption expenditure, is spent on food, clothing, housing, luxuries, and so on.

A line segment fitted to points whose coordinates are in the order

(Disposable income, Consumption expenditures)

for the United States in recent years passes through

$(312, 295)$ and $(575, 537)$

where the numbers are in billions of dollars. The slope of the segment shown in Figure 1–4 is

$$\frac{\text{Change in consumption expenditures}}{\text{Change in disposable income}} = \frac{537 - 295}{575 - 312} = \frac{242}{263} = 0.92.$$

Thus an increase of $263 billion in disposable income resulted in an increase of $242 billion in consumption expenditures. On a proportionate basis,

$$\frac{\$242}{\$263} = \frac{\$0.92}{\$1} = 0.92,$$

so the slope of the segment, 0.92, when written with a denominator of 1, represents the rate of change in consumption expenditures per **one dollar of additional income**. Another way of saying this is that $0.92 out of every additional $1.00 in income will go to consumer expenditures. In economics, this change is called the **marginal propensity to consume**, or MPC for short, as shown in Figure 1–4. Here the word **marginal**, means **extra**, and MPC is the extra consumption that accompanies a $1 increase in income. Income not used for consumption expenditures is **saved**. We see from the preceding that $0.08 of each extra dollar of

FIGURE 1–4

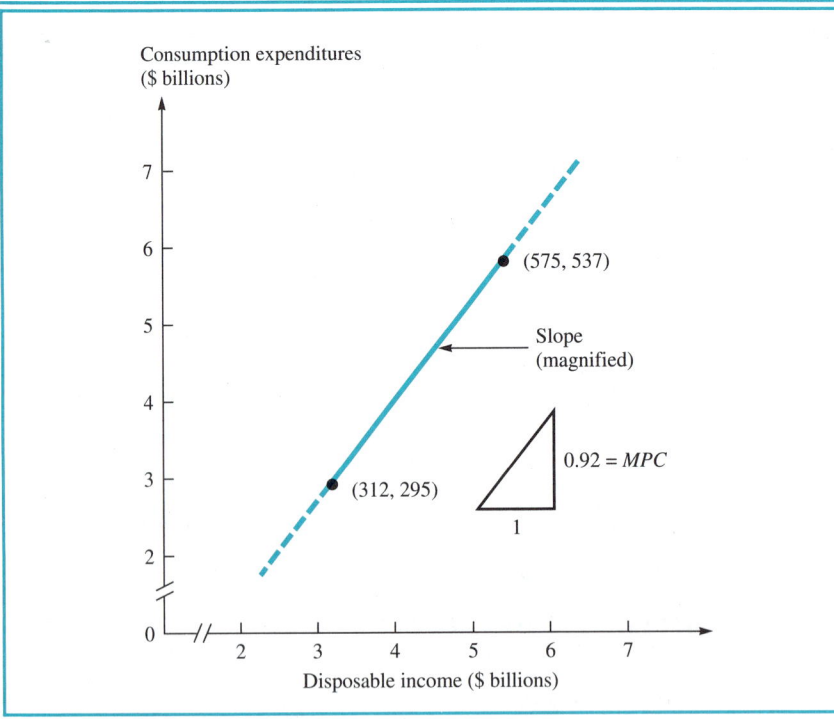

disposable income is saved, and 0.08 is called the **marginal propensity to save**, MPS. Clearly,

$$\text{MPS} = 1 - \text{MPC}.$$

The important bearing these two marginals have on the economic well-being of the nation can be understood by noting that savings are the source of investment in the factories and other economic activities that produce the income that becomes available to consumers. It is interesting to note that while many believe saving is a virtue, economics teaches us that when the nation has idle productive capacity, a high propensity to save (with the consequent low propensity to consume) is not necessarily a virtue for the national economy. What may be needed in such times is a high propensity to consume, for this could lead to the increased demand that will bring idle capacity back into use and increase national income. This is evidenced by the government lowering the interest rate it offers to stimulate the economy. Lower interest rates discourage savings and encourage borrowing and consumption.

1.3 PROBLEM SET 1-1

1. If (x_1, y_1) and (x_2, y_2) are the coordinates of two points on a line,
   a) How is the vertical change computed?
   b) How is the horizontal change computed?
   c) How is the rate of change of y with respect to x computed?

2. a) What is the nature of the steepest line that can be drawn through a point?
   b) Why does such a line not have a slope number?

3. If a set of stairs rises 8 inches for every horizontal run of 12 inches, what slope number (assumed positive) describes the steepness of the stairs?

4. If x is the ground path of an airplane and y is its altitude, and at one point in time the plane is at (500, 1,000) and soon after it is at (500, 0), what was the path of the airplane during the time interval?

5. A ski slope whose fall line makes a 45° angle with the horizontal is said to have a 100 percent grade. What slope number represents a 100 percent grade?

6. If the total manufacturing cost, y dollars, of producing x units of a product is $500 at 50 units output and $900 at 100 units output, and the cost-output relation is linear,
   a) What is the slope of the cost-output line?
   b) How much does the production of one unit add to total cost?

7. A line segment fitted to points whose coordinates are in the order (disposable income, personal consumption expenditures) for a nation passes through points (32, 30) and (57, 54), the numbers being in billions of dollars. What are the values, names, and interpretations of the slope and (1 − slope) of this line?

8. If x represents sales and y represents selling expense, then (30, 22) would mean $30 in sales were accompanied by $22 of selling expense. Suppose last month's figures were (14, 10) and this month's are (30, 22).
   a) How much did sales increase?
   b) How much did selling expense increase?
   c) Make a graph showing the points and labeling the increases.

Compute the slope of the segment joining each pair of points:

9. (0, 0), (2, 2).
10. (−3, 5), (4, −2).
11. (6, −1), (−2, 0).
12. (−3, −2), (−3, −4).

1.3 PROBLEM SET 1-1 (concluded)

13. (2, 3), (6, 3).
14. (1/2, −1/4), (2, −1/4).
15. (−4, 7), (−4, 2).
16. (1, 1), (3, 3).
17. (2/7, −1/3), (−2/9, −2/3).
18. (0, 3), (3, 0).
19. (12, −5), (3, 6).
20. (3, −7), (3, −15).
21. (−1, −2), (−3, −4).
22. (1.6, 3.8), (−3.6, 4.2).

23. Write the formula for the slope of a line segment; then discuss the formula by means of a numerical illustration.
24. Write the expression for the slope of the segment from $P(a, -2)$ to $Q(3, -b)$ in two equivalent forms.
25. Make and label sketches showing segments having positive slope, negative slope, zero slope, and no slope number.
26. Why is division by zero excluded from arithmetic calculations? (See Appendix 1.)

Mark (T) for true or (F) for false:

27. ( ) A line that rises to the right and is almost vertical does not have a slope number.
28. ( ) The slope of the x-axis is zero.
29. ( ) The segment $P(a, b) Q(a, c)$ is vertical.
30. ( ) A line segment of negative slope rises to the left.
31. ( ) The slope of the y-axis is not a number.
32. ( ) A line segment that is very, very close to the vertical has a slope number that has a large absolute value.
33. ( ) No matter how large a number we may write down, there is a line segment whose slope exceeds this number.
34. ( ) A line segment contained entirely in the second quadrant necessarily has a negative slope.
35. ( ) The quadrant in which a line segment lies has no necessary relation to the sign of the slope number of the segment.

36. Consider the QBasic program shown in Program 1–1 below.
    a) Describe what the program is doing line by line.
    b) Run the program for each pair of points in Problems 9 through 22.

```
REM PROGRAM 1-1
REM Slope Formula/P1(x1,y1),P2(x2,y2)
CLS
INPUT "Enter the coordinates of
    P1(x1,y1), then P2(x2,y2)"; x1,
    y1, x2, y2
IF x1 <> x2 THEN
    m = (y2 - y1) / (x2 - x1)
    PRINT "Slope is "; m
ELSE
    PRINT "Slope is infinite"
END IF
```

37. a) Modify Program 1–1 so that the printout will show the actual coordinates of the two points inputted.
    b) Run the program in (a) for each pair of points in Problems 9 through 22.

1.4 EQUATION OF A LINE: SLOPE-INTERCEPT FORM

In Section 1.2, we considered line segments and their slopes; we now turn to the infinite extension of a segment, which is a straight line. The first linear equation we wrote in Section 1.1

$$y = 1.25x + 0.75,$$

expressed the fare paid for a taxi ride, y, in terms of x, the number of miles driven, and the constant 0.75, which was a fixed charge for a bridge toll. For example, the fares for a one-mile ride and a five-mile ride are, respectively,

$$y = 1.25(1) + 0.75 = 2$$
$$y = 1.25(5) + 0.75 = 7,$$

giving us the two (x, y) points

$$(1, 2) \quad \text{and} \quad (5, 7).$$

If we now find the slope of the line between these points as

$$\frac{y_2 - y_1}{x_2 - x_1} = \frac{7 - 2}{5 - 1} = \frac{5}{4} = 1.25,$$

we find that the slope is precisely the **coefficient of x** in the equation

$$y = 1.25x + 0.75.$$

Exercise. If $y = 0.8x + 2$, a) Write the coordinates of the points where $x = 0$ and $x = 5$. b) Compute the slope from the points used in (a).
Answer: a) (0, 2) and (5, 6). b) Slope is 0.8, the coefficient of x in $y = 0.8x + 2$.

The last example and exercise suggest that if we write the equation of a line in the form y equals a constant times x, plus another constant, then the coefficient of x is the slope; that is, in

$$y = mx + b, \qquad (1)$$

m is the slope. To prove this is so, suppose we take any pair of points on the line (1), calling them (x_1, y_1) and (x_2, y_2). Then we must prove that

$$m = \frac{y_2 - y_1}{x_2 - x_1}.$$

We start by noting that because the points are on the line (1), their coordinates must satisfy Equation (1). That is, at (x_1, y_1),

$$y_1 = mx_1 + b \qquad (2)$$

and at (x_2, y_2),

$$y_2 = mx_2 + b. \qquad (3)$$

We can rewrite (2) and (3) as

$$y_1 - mx_1 = b \qquad (4)$$

$$y_2 - mx_2 = b. \qquad (5)$$

The left sides of (4) and (5) both equal b so they are themselves equal, and we have

$$y_1 - mx_1 = y_2 - mx_2$$

and, by transposing terms,

$$mx_2 - mx_1 = y_2 - y_1.$$

Factoring on the left yields

$$m(x_2 - x_1) = y_2 - y_1;$$

then, dividing both sides by $(x_2 - x_1)$, we have

$$\frac{m(x_2 - x_1)}{(x_2 - x_1)} = \frac{y_2 - y_1}{x_2 - x_1}$$

$$m = \frac{y_2 - y_1}{x_2 - x_1}$$

Since (x_1, y_1) and (x_2, y_2) were arbitrary points chosen on the line, we have shown what we set out to prove. Thus, if the equation of a line is written in the form

$$y = mx + b,$$

m is the slope. Moreover, if $x = 0$, then

$$y = m(0) + b = b,$$

and $(0, b)$ is the point where the line cuts the y-axis. This point (where $x = 0$) is called the **y-intercept**. Thus, we have

> On the line $y = mx + b$, m gives the value of the slope and b gives the value of the y-intercept.

Slope-Intercept Form

If the equation of a line is written in the form

$$y = mx + b,$$

then m is the slope and b is the y-intercept.

Example. Write $2y + 3x = 18$ in slope-intercept form and state the value of the slope and the y-intercept.

We must isolate y with a coefficient of 1 on the left-hand side of the equation. First we transpose the term $3x$ to the right-hand side:

$$2y = -3x + 18.$$

Then, dividing both sides by 2, we have

$$y = -\frac{3}{2}x + 9$$

as the desired $y = mx + b$ form. Hence, the slope is $-3/2$ and the y-intercept is 9. The line is shown in Figure 1–5. The point (4, 3) shown on the line was obtained by choosing x to be 4, arbitrarily, and computing

$$y = -\frac{3}{2}(4) + 9 = -3(2) + 9 = 3.$$

When a linear equation is not in slope-intercept form, the simplest points to find and use for plotting the line are its intercepts. To find the x-intercept, set $y = 0$ and solve for x; to find the y-intercept, set $x = 0$ and solve for y. For example, in the equation

$$2y + 3x = 18$$

x-intercept: $2(0) + 3x = 18$; $x = 6$. Point is (6, 0).

y-intercept: $2y + 3(0) = 18$; $y = 9$. Point is (0, 9).

This line and its intercepts are shown in Figure 1–5.

■ **Plotting by Intercepts**

The x-intercept occurs where the line intercepts the x-axis. The y-intercept occurs where the line intercepts the y-axis.

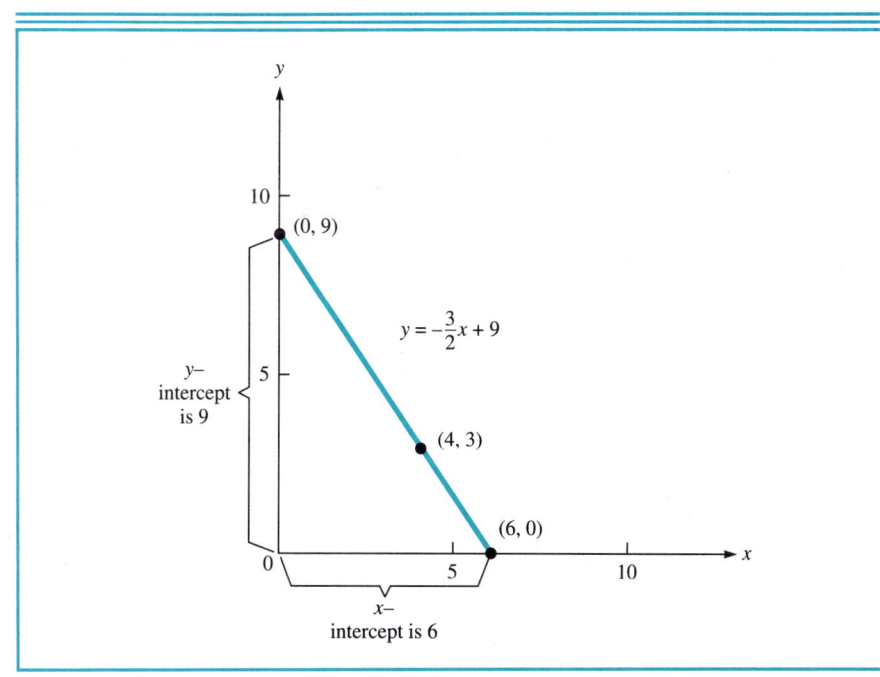

FIGURE 1–5

The slope-intercept form expresses y as a linear function of x and so from now on in this chapter we will write the final expression for all our linear equations in this form.

> **Exercise.** a) Write $3y - 2x = 24$ in slope-intercept form. b) What is the slope of the line? c) What is the y-intercept? d) What is the x-intercept? e) Write the coordinates of the points found in (c) and (d).
>
> **Answer:** a) $y = (\frac{2}{3})x + 8$. b) $\frac{2}{3}$. c) 8. d) -12. e) (0, 8) and $(-12, 0)$.

The next example illustrates one of the many interpretive applications that arise when a line is in slope-intercept form.

Example. It costs $2,500 to set up the presses and machinery needed to print and bind a paperback book. After setup, its costs $2 per book printed and bound. Let x represent the number of books made and y the total cost of making this number of books. a) Write the equation for y in terms of x. b) State the slope of the line, and interpret this number. c) State the y-intercept of the line, and interpret this number.

a) The total cost is made up of the $2,500 setup cost (often called the **fixed cost**) plus the cost to make x books (often called the **variable cost**). Since the cost per book is $2, the variable cost to make x books will be $2x$. Thus, the total cost function y is

$$y = 2x + 2,500,$$

a linear equation in slope-intercept form.

b) The slope, 2, means that every **additional** book printed, starting with the first copy, adds $2 to the total cost. Note that it would **not** be proper to say books cost $2 per copy. That is, for example, if $x = 100$ books are made, then total cost is

$$y = 2(100) + 2,500 = \$2,700$$

and $2,700 for 100 books is an **average cost** per copy of

$$\frac{2,700}{100} = \$27$$

not $2 per copy. It is because of this distinction—between average cost per copy and the slope of the line, which is variable cost per copy—that economists would call the slope the **marginal** cost, which is the extra cost when an **additional** copy is made.

> Marginal cost is the cost of making one additional unit.

c) The y-intercept, $2,500, is total cost when $x = 0$ books are made. That is, at $x = 0$,

$$y = 2(0) + 2,500 = \$2,500.$$

This means if the machines were made ready and then it was decided not to print the book, this cost would still be incurred. This is why we referred to it earlier as the **fixed cost**. Other examples of fixed cost are the cost of insurance on machinery whether or not it is used, and continuing rent on a building that is used only part-time.

Fixed cost is the cost of making no units (the overhead).

> **Exercise.** An agency rents cars for one day and charges $22 plus 20 cents per mile the car is driven.   a) Write the equation for the cost of one day's rental, y, in terms of x, the number of miles driven.   b) Interpret the slope and the y-intercept.   c) What is the renter's average cost per mile if a car is driven 100 miles? 200 miles?
>
> **Answer:**   a) $y = 0.20x + 22$.   b) The slope, 0.20, means that each additional mile driven adds 20 cents to total cost. The intercept, 22, is the fixed charge, which would be incurred even if the renter used the car only for a secret meeting with a friend and did not drive it out of the parking lot.   c) $0.42 per mile and $0.31 per mile.

Linear equations in the form

$$Ax + By = C,$$

also arise naturally in many applications. For example, suppose we have $31.50 to spend on pork and chicken. If we buy p pounds of pork at $2.25 per pound and c pounds of chicken at $1.80 per pound, our expenditures would be $2.25p + 1.80c$ dollars, and this must equal $31.50. Thus,

$$2.25p + 1.80c = 31.50.$$

In slope-intercept form, solving for p, this becomes

$$p = -\frac{1.80}{2.25}c + \frac{31.50}{2.25}, \quad \text{or} \quad p = -0.8c + 14.$$

The intercept tells us that we can buy 14 pounds of pork if we buy no chicken. The slope, -0.8, means that if we increase our purchase of chicken by one pound, we must decrease purchases of pork by 0.8 pounds. Thus, the **substitution rate** is 0.8 pounds of pork per pound of chicken.

> **Exercise.** Solve the preceding equation for c in terms of p in slope-intercept form, then interpret the intercept and the slope.
>
> **Answer:** $c = -1.25p + 17.5$. We can buy 17.5 pounds of chicken if we buy no pork. The substitution rate is 1.25 pounds of chicken per pound of pork.

1.5 STRAIGHT-LINE EQUATION GIVEN A POINT AND SLOPE

We have seen that the straight-line equation can be written directly if the slope m and a **particular point**, the y-intercept b, are given. The equation then is given by the slope-intercept form

$$y = mx + b.$$

If the given point is not the y-intercept, we can easily determine this intercept from the above slope-intercept form.

Example. Find the equation of the line with slope 0.75 that passes through the point (8, 10).

We first write the partially complete equation

$$y = 0.75x + b, \qquad (1)$$

and now we must find the value of b. Because the line passes through (8, 10), these coordinates must satisfy (1), so, substituting,

$$10 = 0.75(8) + b$$
$$10 = 6 + b$$
$$4 = b,$$

and the y-intercept is found to be $b = 4$. Hence substitution into (1) gives the desired equation

$$y = 0.75x + 4.$$

Exercise. Find the equation of the line that has a slope of -0.50 and passes through the point (4, 3).

Answer: $y = -0.5x + 5.$

An alternative approach is to let m represent the given slope and (x_1, y_1) represent the given point. The formula we want is the equation that is true not only for the point (x_1, y_1) but also for any other point (x, y) on the line. Thus, if we look at

$$(x_1, y_1) \quad \text{and} \quad (x, y)$$

as two points on the desired line, then the slope

$$m = \frac{y - y_1}{x - x_1}.$$

This must equal m for all pairs of points on the line. So, we have

> **Point-Slope Form**
>
> $$\frac{y - y_1}{x - x_1} = m, \quad \text{or} \quad y - y_1 = m(x - x_1).$$

Returning to the last example, where $m = 0.75$ and the given point (x_1, y_1) is $(8, 10)$, substitution into the point-slope form yields

$$y - 10 = 0.75(x - 8)$$
$$y - 10 = 0.75x - 6$$
$$y = 0.75x + 4$$

as before. For more practice, redo the last exercise using the point-slope form.

1.6 STRAIGHT-LINE EQUATION FROM TWO POINTS

Two points completely determine a straight line and, of course, they determine the slope of the line. We do not need a special two-point form since we can use the two points to first compute the slope, m, and then use this value of m together with either point in the point-slope form

$$y - y_1 = m(x - x_1)$$

to generate the equation of the line.

Example. The total cost, y, of producing x units is a linear function. Records show that on one occasion 100 units were made at a total cost of $200, and on another occasion, 150 units were made at a total cost of $275. Write the linear equation for total cost in terms of the number of units produced. What is the total cost if 250 units are made?

The information given consists of two points whose coordinates (x, y) are in the order (units made, total cost). These are

$$(100, 200) \quad \text{and} \quad (150, 275).$$

The slope of the line is then

$$m = \frac{275 - 200}{150 - 100} = \frac{75}{50} = 1.5$$

Now picking one of the points, say (100, 200), we substitute in the point-slope form to get

$$y - 200 = 1.5(x - 100$$

Solving this for y, we have the desired equation

$$y - 200 = 1.5x - 150$$
$$y = 1.5x + 50.$$

The total cost of making 250 units is then

$$y = 1.5(250) + 50 = \$425.$$

Exercise. A publisher asks a printer for quotations on the cost of printing 1,000 and 2,000 copies of a book. The printer quotes \$4,500 for 1,000 copies and \$7,500 for 2,000 copies. Assume that cost, y is linearly related to x, the number of books printed.   a) Write the coordinates of the given points.   b) Write the equation of the line.   c) What is the cost of printing 2,500 copies?

Answer: a) (1,000, 4,500); (2,000, 7,500).   b) $y = 3x + 1,500$.   c) \$9,000.

1.7 HORIZONTAL AND VERTICAL LINES

When the equation of a line is to be determined from two given points, it is a good idea to first compare corresponding coordinates. The reason is that if the y values are the same, the line is horizontal, but if the x values are the same, the line is vertical. For example, given the points

$$(3, 6) \quad \text{and} \quad (8, 6)$$

we see that the line through them is horizontal because both y-coordinates are 6. This line is shown in Figure 1–6. It is clear that y is 6 at every point on this line irrespective of the value assigned to the x-coordinate, and because

$$y = 6$$

describes this line, and this line only, we say $y = 6$ is the equation for the line.

If we had not noticed the quality of the y-coordinates of (3, 6) and (8, 6) and had proceeded with the slope-intercept determination of the equation by first finding

$$m = \frac{6 - 6}{8 - 3} = \frac{0}{5} = 0,$$

then using the point-slope form to get

$$y - 6 = 0(x - 3)$$
$$y - 6 = 0,$$

we would have obtained

$$y = 6$$

FIGURE 1-6 FIGURE 1-7

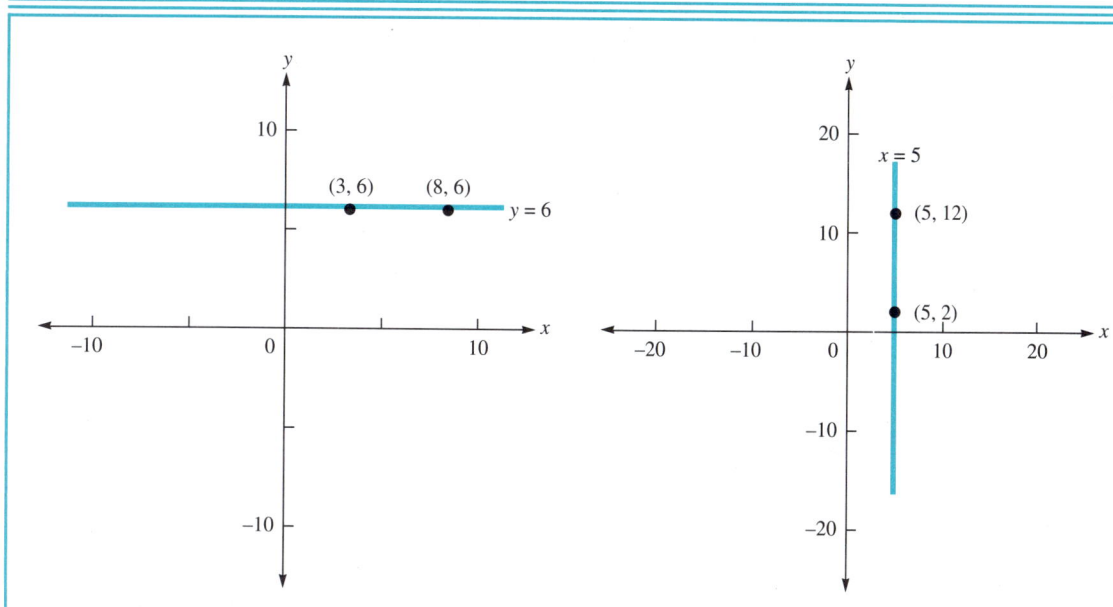

as the equation of the line. However, there is no need to proceed beyond the first step because **if the slope, m, turns out to be zero, the line is horizontal and has an equation of the form**

Horizontal lines have zero slope and equations

y = constant

$$y = \text{constant},$$

where the constant is the given y-coordinate.

If the x-coordinates of the two different points are equal, as in

$$(5, 2) \quad \text{and} \quad (5, 12),$$

the line through them is vertical, as shown in Figure 1-7, and its equation is

$$x = 5.$$

If we had proceeded to apply the point-slope procedure, we would obtain

$$m = \frac{12 - 2}{5 - 5} = \frac{10}{0}$$

which is undefined. We need not proceed further because **if the slope is undefined, the line is vertical and has an equation of the form**

Vertical lines have undefined slope and equations

x = constant

$$x = \text{constant},$$

where the constant is the given x-coordinate.

We have become accustomed to seeing both x and y in linear equations but, as we have just learned, the coefficient of x or the coefficient of y (but not both) can be zero, in which case we have a horizontal or a vertical line.

In summary:

The line through (x_1, y_1); (x_2, y_1) is $y = y_1$.
The line through (x_1, y_1); (x_1, y_2) is $x = x_1$.

> **Exercise.** What is the equation of the line through a) $(-4, 7)$ and $(-4, -3)$? b) $(3, 6)$ and $(2, 6)$?
> **Answer:** a) $x = -4$. b) $y = 6$.

1.8 PROBLEM SET 1-2

Find the equation (in slope-intercept form, if possible) of the line passing through the given point and having the given slope:

1. $(3, 4)$, slope 3.
2. $(-5, 6)$ slope -1.
3. $(-2, 6)$, slope $-2/3$.
4. $(1, -4)$, slope $1/2$.
5. $(-3, -8)$, slope 0.
6. $(2, 7)$, slope $-1/6$.
7. $(-5, -8)$, slope 13.
8. $(0, 0)$, slope 0.
9. $(5, 2)$, vertical.
10. $(0, 0)$, vertical.
11. $(3, 4)$, slope 0.
12. $(4, -3)$, slope 5.

Find the equation (in slope-intercept form, if possible) of the line passing through each of the given pairs of points:

13. $(4, 6), (-3, 7)$.
14. $(-5, 3), (2, 9)$.
15. $(1, 1), (3, 3)$.
16. $(-2, -4), (-1, 5)$.
17. $(0, 0), (2, 3)$.
18. $(2, 4), (-3, 4)$.
19. $(1/3, -1/2), (2, -3)$.
20. $(-7, 2), (-7, -8)$.
21. $(3, 5), (1, 4)$.
22. $(3, 5), (-4, 5)$.
23. $(6, 0), (10, 0)$.
24. $(-3, -2), (4, -7)$.

25. Write the equation of the x-axis.
26. Write the equation of the y-axis.
27. On the line passing through $(2, 3)$ and $(-5, 6)$, what is the y-coordinate of the point where $x = 17$?
28. On the line of slope -2 passing through $(3, 7)$, what is the x-coordinate of the point where $y = 17$?
29. What is the equation of the vertical line that passes through $(-6, 3)$?

1.8 PROBLEM SET 1-2 (continued)

30. a) What is the equation of the horizontal line that passes through $(-6, 3)$?
    b) A curve showing profit (vertical) and number of units produced and sold (horizontal) rises smoothly to a peak and then declines as we move to the right. The peak is at (100, 500). What is the equation of the tangent line at the peak? What is the significance of this equation? Hint: Make a sketch labeling the axes, showing a curve that has a rounded peak.

31. a) What is the equation of the line parallel to, and 5 units above, the x-axis?
    b) What is the equation of the line parallel to, and 10 units to the left of, the y-axis?

32. As sales (x) change from $100 to $400, selling expense (y) changes from $75 to $150. Assume that the given data establish the relationship between sales and selling expense as the two change, and assume that the relationship is linear. Find the equation of the relationship.

33. As the number of units manufactured increases from 100 to 200, manufacturing cost (total) increases from $350 to $650. Assume that the given data establish the relationship between cost (y) and number of units made (x), and assume that the relationship is linear. Find the equation of the relationship.

34. If the relationship between total cost and number of units made is linear, and if cost increases by $3 for each additional unit made, and if the total cost of 10 units is $40, find the equation of the relationship between total cost (y) and number of units made (x).

35. a) If taxi fare (y) is 50 cents plus 20 cents per quarter mile, write the equation relating fare to number of miles traveled, m.
    b) The weekly earnings of a salesman are $50 plus 10 percent of the retail value of the goods he sells. Write the equation for earnings, E, in terms of sales volume, V. What is the slope of this line called?

Mark (T) for true or (F) for false:

36. ( ) The horizontal line through (5, 6) has the equation $x = 5$.
37. ( ) The equation of the x-axis is $y = 0$.
38. ( ) The slope of the line through (4, 6) and (5, 9) is greater than the slope of the line through (0, 0) and (1, 2).
39. ( ) The equation of the x-axis is $x = 0$.
40. ( ) The x-intercept of $3x - 2y = 12$ is -6.
41. ( ) The slope of $2x + 3y = 6$ is $-2/3$.

Graph the following lines, using intercepts:

42. $y = -x + 6$.
43. $y = 1.5x - 6$.
44. $y = 0.4x + 1.2$.
45. $y = x - 4$.
46. $y = (-\frac{7}{6})x + \frac{1}{2}$.

What is the slope of each of the following lines?

47. $3x - 2y = 7$.
48. $x + y = 2$.
49. $2x - 6y = 5$.
50. $x - y = 0$.

1.8 PROBLEM SET 1-2 (concluded)

51. a) A pound of Food A contains 8 ounces of a nutrient, and a pound of Food B contains 12 ounces of the nutrient. Write the expression that must be satisfied if x pounds of A and y pounds of B are to provide 96 ounces of nutrient.
    b) What is the substitution rate of A per pound of B?
    c) What is the substitution rate of B per pound of A?

52. What is the equation of the line that has a slope of 2 and a y-intercept of -6?

53. If a straight-line equation is in the form
    $$Ax + By + C = 0$$
    and $B \neq 0$, then the slope is $-A/B$; that is, the negative of the ratio of the coefficient of x to the coefficient of y. Why is this statement true?

54. If total cost is y and number of units is x, what expression represents a constant cost per unit? What equation would replace the statement that cost per unit is $3? What is the slope and what are the intercepts of the line whose equation was just written?

55. A printer quotes the price of $1,400 for printing 100 copies of a report and $3,000 for printing 500 copies. Assuming a linear relationship, what would be the price for printing 300 copies?

56. Consider the QBasic program shown in Program 1-2.
    a) Describe what the program is doing line by line.
    b) Run the program for each pair of points in Problems 13 through 24.

```
REM PROGRAM 1-2
REM Equation of Line/P1(x1,y1),
  P2(x2,y2)
CLS
INPUT "Enter the coordinates of
  P1(x1,y1), then P2(x2,y2)"; x1, y1,
  x2, y2
PRINT "The equation of the line
  between P1 and P2 is ";
IF x1 = x2 THEN
  PRINT "x = "; x1
ELSE
  PRINT "y = ";
  IF y1 = y2 THEN
    PRINT y1
  ELSE
    m = (y2 - y1) / (x2 - x1)
    b = y1 - m * x1
    PRINT m; "x ";
    IF b > 0 THEN PRINT "+"; b; ELSE
      PRINT ; "-"; ABS(b)
  END IF
END IF
```

57. a) Modify Program 1-2 to print the slope, y-intercept, and equation of a line passing through the two points $P_1(x_1, y_1)$ and $P_2(x_2, y_2)$.
    b) Run the program in (a) for each pair of points in Problems 13 through 24.

58. a) Modify Program 1-2 to print the equation of a line passing through a given point $P_1(x_1, y_1)$ and having a given slope m.

1.9 PARALLEL AND PERPENDICULAR LINES

Lines that have the same slope are **parallel**. Thus,

$$y = \frac{1}{2}x + 5$$

$$y = \frac{1}{2}x + 2$$

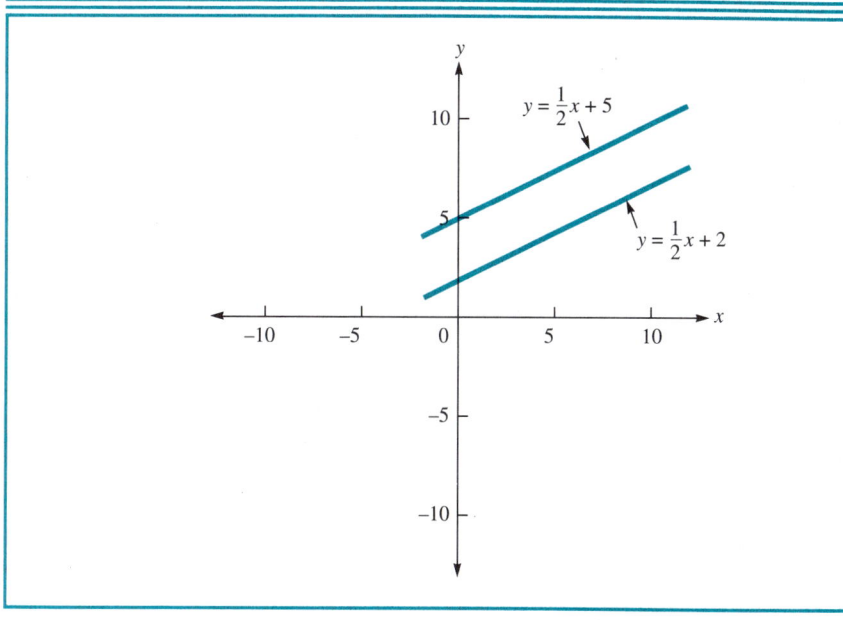

FIGURE 1-8

are parallel lines, as shown in Figure 1-8. We shall have occasion to be concerned about two lines in coming chapters where the equation of each line expresses a condition that must be satisfied, and we wish both conditions to be satisfied. This means that we will be seeking a point that is on **both** lines (that is, the point of intersection of the lines). Clearly, it is impossible to satisfy both conditions if the two lines are parallel because they do not intersect. The pair of equations associated with parallel lines is called **inconsistent**.

Parallel lines have the same slope. Their equations are inconsistent since no point lies on both lines.

Exercise. Which of the following pairs of lines are parallel?
a) $y = \frac{3}{2}x + 4$; $y = 1.5x + 5$; b) $y = -2x + 2$; $y = -1.5x + 5$.
Answer: The pair in (a).

We call a line a **slant line** if it is neither horizontal nor vertical. If two slant lines are perpendicular, the slope of one is the negative reciprocal of the slope of the other. Thus

Perpendicular Lines

$$y = \frac{2}{3}x + 5 \quad \text{and} \quad y = -\frac{3}{2}x + 10$$

Perpendicular lines have slopes which are negative reciprocals of each other.

are perpendicular, as shown in Figure 1–9, because the negative reciprocal of the slope of the first line is

$$-\frac{1}{\left(\frac{2}{3}\right)} = -1\left(\frac{3}{2}\right) = -\frac{3}{2},$$

and $-3/2$ is the slope of the second line. We could as easily say that the product of the slopes of two slant lines that are perpendicular is -1. Thus, for the last pair of lines

$$m_1 m_2 = \frac{2}{3}\left(-\frac{3}{2}\right) = -1.$$

Note that

$$y = 6 \quad \text{and} \quad x = 5$$

are perpendicular lines because the first is horizontal and the second is vertical. However, $x = 5$ has an undefined slope, so the $m_1 m_2 = -1$ relationship only applies if the lines are both slant lines.

Exercise. Given line 1 is $y = 2x - 3.5$ and line 2 is $y = -0.5x + 2$, to which of these is $y = 2x + 4$ a) parallel? b) perpendicular?

Answer: a) line 1. b) line 2.

FIGURE 1–9

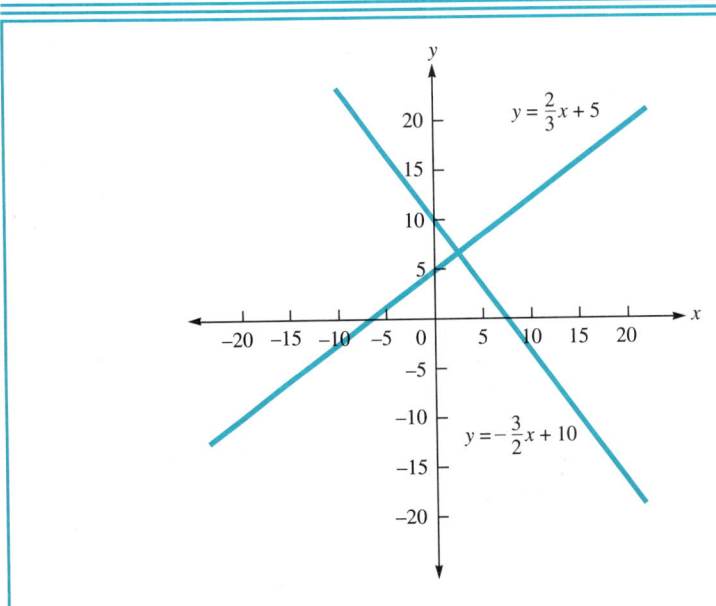

1.10 LINES THROUGH THE ORIGIN

Any equation in the variables x and y that has no constant term other than zero will have a graph that passes through the origin. For example, in the case of the straight line

$$y = \frac{2}{3}x,$$

it is obvious that (0, 0), the coordinates of the origin, satisfy the equation. To graph this line, we need to find a second point other than the origin. Choosing, for example, $x = 3$,

$$y = \frac{2}{3}(3) = 2,$$

so the point (3, 2) is on the line as shown in Figure 1–10.

From an applied point of view, such lines are of interest because they are the mathematical expression of **proportion.** That is, if we write the equation in the form

$$\frac{y}{x} = \frac{2}{3},$$

Lines passing through the origin have constant term 0 and represent a proportion between x and y.

we may read the statement as "y is to x as 2 is to 3." An assumption that, say, output per man-hour is 3 units would translate to $y/x = 3$, where y is number of

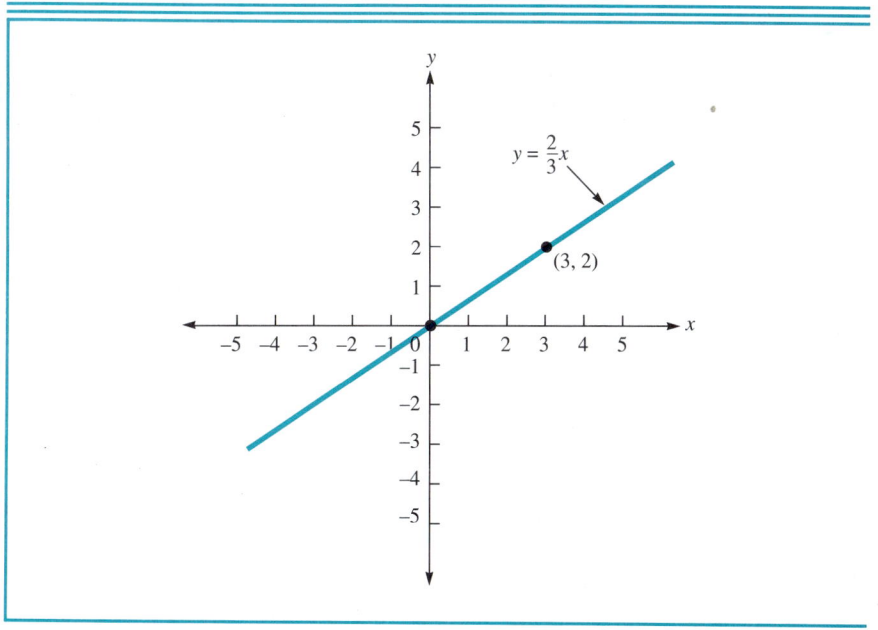

FIGURE 1–10

units of output and x is number of man-hours worked. Graphical expression of the assumption would be the straight line $y = 3x$, passing through the origin.

When considering revenue obtained from sale of a product, revenue, r, is 0 when the number of units sold, x, is 0. The revenue obtained by selling x units at a constant price of $5 per unit would be

$$r = 5x,$$

a line through the origin.

> **Exercise.** If it costs c dollars to maintain a factory and produce x units of product, would it be reasonable to assume the cost curve goes through the origin?
>
> **Answer:** It would not be reasonable because at $x = 0$ (no output) costs of insurance, security, interest payments, and other elements of fixed cost, which do not depend upon output, would still be incurred.

1.11 PIECEWISE LINEAR FUNCTIONS

Sometimes an equation will consist of more than one section or **piece**, each of which is linear. For example,

$$y = \begin{cases} x & x \leq 0 \\ 2x & x > 0 \end{cases}$$

describes a function composed of two linear pieces, the first being x for all values of $x \leq 0$, and the second being $2x$ for all values of $x > 0$. Such a function is called **a piecewise linear function** and its graph is shown in Figure 1–11.

Piecewise linear functions are composed of two or more pieces, all of which are linear.

Piecewise linear functions may be connected, as in Figure 1–11, or may have a **jump** as in

$$y = \begin{cases} x + 1 & x < 2 \\ x - 1 & x \geq 2 \end{cases}.$$

This function has a jump at $x = 2$ as indicated by the "o" at the right end of the left section of the graph in Figure 1–12.

Many practical situations give rise to piecewise linear functions.

Example. Boston Gas Company charges its customers according to their usage of gas as follows: a $6.71 customer charge, $0.7376 per "therm" for the first 160 therms, and $0.6800 per therm for each therm over 160. a) Determine the cost function and draw its graph. b) What is the charge for using 120 therms? c) What is the charge for using 200 therms? d) How many therms were used if the charge was $355.93.

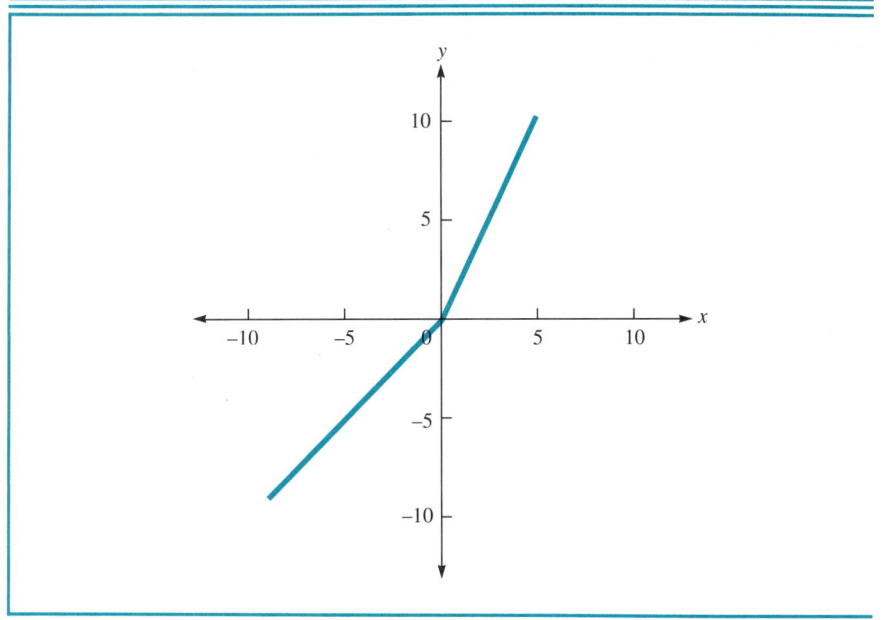

FIGURE 1-11

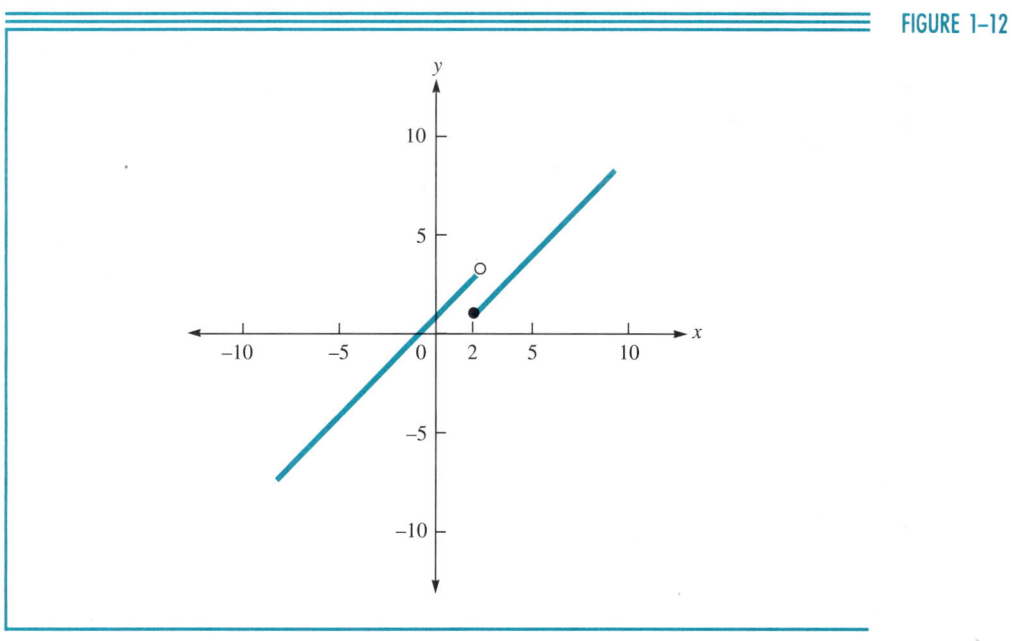

FIGURE 1-12

a) The charge for the first 160 therms consists of the $6.71 customer charge plus the $0.7376 charge per therm. Letting t represent the number of therms used, this charge becomes

$$6.71 + 0.7376t. \quad (1)$$

Now if the customer uses more than 160 therms, the charge from (1) for the first 160 therms will be

$$6.71 + 0.7376(160) = 124.726.$$

To this must be added the charge of $0.6800 for each therm over 160, resulting in a charge of

$$124.726 + 0.6800(t - 160) = 124.726 + 0.6800t - 108.8$$
$$= 15.926 + 0.6800t. \quad (2)$$

Putting (1) and (2) together, we get the cost function

$$C(t) = \begin{cases} 6.71 + 0.7376t & 0 \leq t \leq 160 \\ 15.926 + 0.6800t & t > 160. \end{cases}$$

Figure 1–13 graphs this function.

b) If the customer uses 120 therms, the charge is determined from the first piece since $120 < 160$. It is

FIGURE 1–13

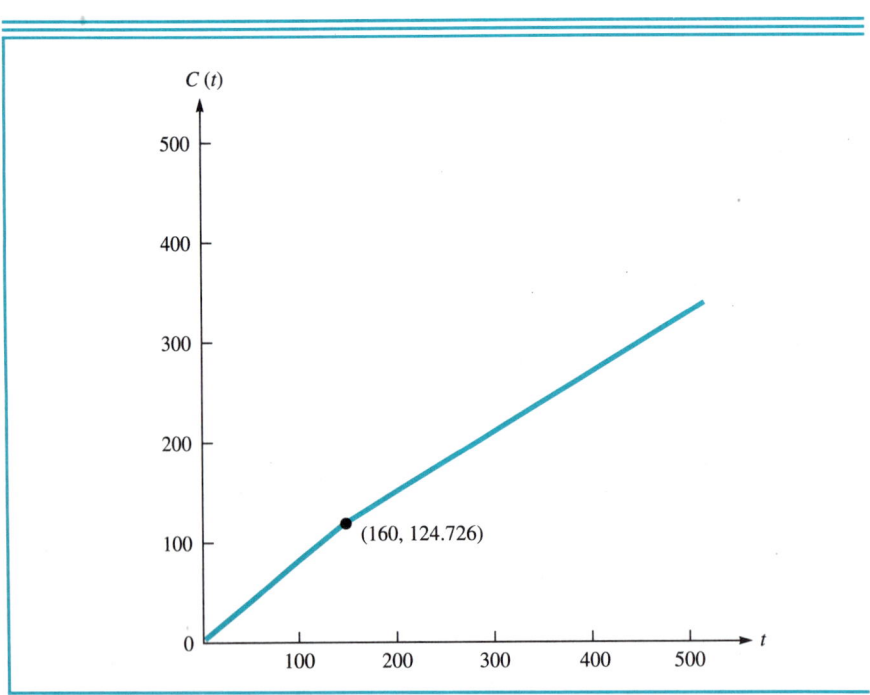

$$C(120) = 6.71 + 0.7376(120) = 95.222$$

or $95.22.

c) If the customer uses 200 therms, the charge is determined from the second piece (since 200 > 160) to be

$$C(200) = 15.926 + 0.6800(200) = 151.926$$

or $151.93.

d) Now if the charge is $355.93, the customer must have used more than 160 therms. (Remember the cost of the first 160 therms was determined to be 124.726.) So from the second piece of the cost function, we have

$$355.93 = 15.926 + 0.6800t$$

or

$$t = \frac{355.93 - 15.926}{0.6800} = 500.0059,$$

which means that 500 therms were used.

Before leaving this example, let's take a closer look at (b). In (b), the **total** charge for the 120 therms used was determined to be $95.22 resulting from a customer charge of $6.71 and a $0.7376 charge per therm used. On the other hand, the **average** charge per therm used is

$$\frac{\$95.22}{120 \text{ therms}} = \$0.7935.$$

Exercise. What is the average charge per therm in part (c) of the preceding example?

Answer: $0.75965.

Exercise. Boston Edison Company charges its customers according to their usage of electricity. One rate it charges a particular class of user is as follows: a basic monthly charge of $3.35, 3.380 cents per kilowatt hour (kwh) for the first 350 kwh, and 5.634 cents per kwh for any kwh in excess of 350. a) Determine the cost function and draw its graph. b) What are the total and average charges for using 200 kwh? c) What are the total and average charges for using 400 kwh? d) How many kwh were used if the total charge is $51.80?

Answer:

a) $C(k) = \begin{cases} 3.35 + 0.03380k & 0 \le k \le 350 \\ -4.539 + 0.05634k & k \ge 350. \end{cases}$

b) $10.11; $0.05055.   c) $18.00; $0.045.   d) 1,000 kwh.

FROM THEORY TO PRACTICE
Cash Flow Analysis

One of the most important measures of a company's present and future needs is the measure of cash flow. Since very few businesses have a constant influx or outflow of cash, meticulous planning is necessary. The company must be sure that it has sufficient cash on hand at any time to meet the monthly payroll. Also, the amount of cash a company needs to borrow must be minimal to keep down interest costs. Small companies selling services or products that are packaged as substantial contracts have cash flow projections that are tied directly to the lifetime of each contract. Many such contracts will pay the company a fixed amount during a set time frame over the life of the contract, and the graph of this cash inflow will be a straight-line segment of positive slope. Frequently, small companies will have time periods when there is little or no cash inflow, but the monthly or weekly payroll must continue to be met. The graph of this cash outflow will be a line segment of negative slope.

An example of such a cash flow diagram for Traffic Integration Inc., a small company (of about $4 million in annual sales) selling software engineering programs and hardware installations to large airports for airport traffic control is shown in Figure 1–14. Note that TII's cash flow is a piecewise linear function, each piece of which describes the cash flow during a given time period for 0, 1, 2, or more contracts in force. If there is no change in the company's circumstances, there is no change in the slope of the cash flow diagram. At each point where the diagram changes slope, there has been a new contract kicking in or an old one completed so that it is no longer paying cash into the company.

FIGURE 1–14
Traffic Integration Inc. Projected Cash Flow, January–December 1994

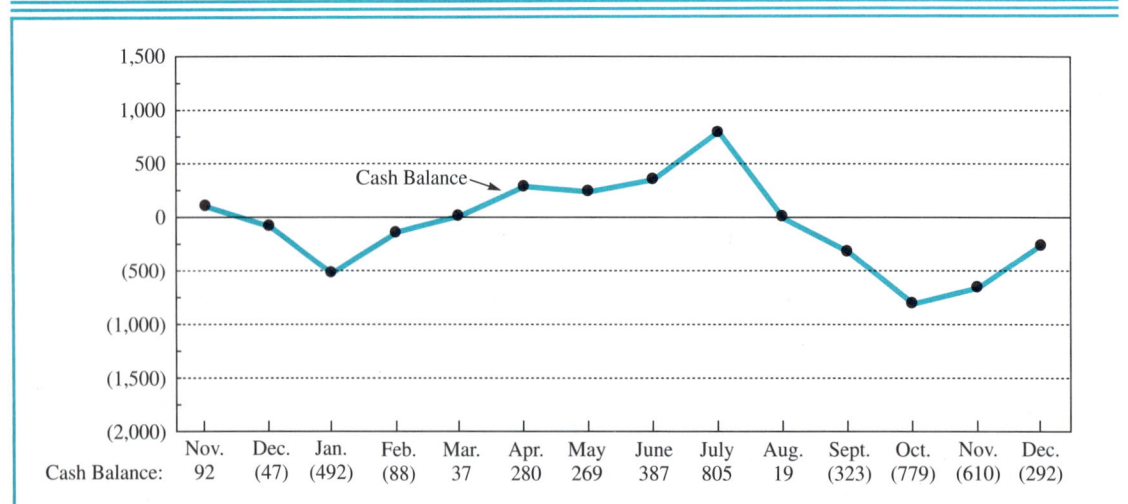

Cash Balance:	Nov.	Dec.	Jan.	Feb.	Mar.	Apr.	May	June	July	Aug.	Sept.	Oct.	Nov.	Dec.
	92	(47)	(492)	(88)	37	280	269	387	805	19	(323)	(779)	(610)	(292)

1.12 PROBLEM SET 1-3

1. a) Find the equation of the line through (2, 7) parallel to the line $y = 1.5x - 3.5$.
   b) Find the equation of the line through $(-2, -6)$ perpendicular to the line $y = (1/3)x + 4/3$.

2. What is the equation of the line on which the y-coordinate of any point is twice the x-coordinate?

3. Find the equation of the line through the origin parallel to $y = 0.8x - 2$.

4. Figure A shows an existing pipeline passing through two points. Plant A is in existence at the point (5, 6). A new plant, B, is to be located on the x-axis at a point such that the dotted pipeline that will be constructed to connect A and B to the existing line will be perpendicular to the existing line.
   a) Where should B be located?
   b) What is the advantage of having the new line meet the existing line at a right angle?

5. Prove that every line whose equation is of the form $Ax + By = 0$, where A and B are any number (not both zero), passes through the origin.

FIGURE A

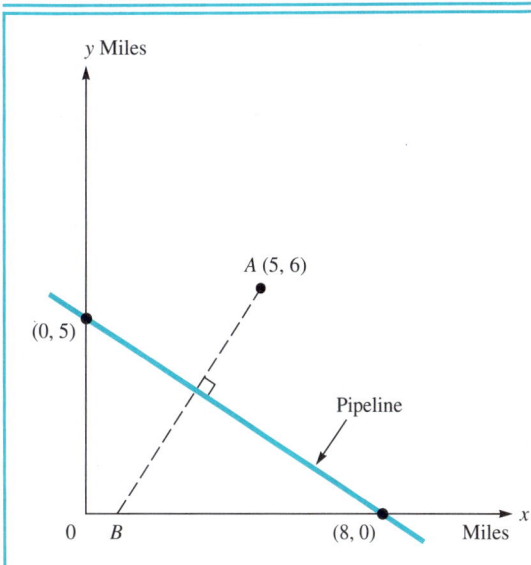

Mark (T) for true or (F) for false.

6. (　) The lines $x = 5$ and $x = 10$ are parallel to each other.

7. (　) The lines $x = 5$ and $y = 10$ are perpendicular to each other.

8. (　) If the graph of the equation $Ax + By + C = 0$ is to pass through the origin, C must be 0.

9. (　) If the ratio of y to x is constant for an equation, the graph of the equation must pass through the origin.

10. (　) $x + y = 6$ and $2x + 2y = 8$ are parallel but not identical lines.

11. (　) $x + y = 6$ and $2x + 2y = 12$ are identical lines.

12. (　) If the relationship between x and y can be expressed as $Ax + Dy = 0$, then x and y are in proportion.

13. (　) $x = 10$ has no y-intercept.

14. (　) Any line parallel to $x - 2y = 7$ must have a slope of 1/2.

15. (　) If y is units of output and x is man-hours worked, and if $y = 3x$, then output per man-hour is constant.

Draw the graphs of each of the following:

16. $y = \begin{cases} 3x - 1, & x \leq 1 \\ x + 1, & x > 1. \end{cases}$

17. $y = \begin{cases} x + 2, & x < -2 \\ x/2 + 1, & x \geq -2. \end{cases}$

18. $y = \begin{cases} 2x + 3, & x < -1 \\ 3x + 2, & x \geq -1. \end{cases}$

19. $y = \begin{cases} x - 2, & x \leq 3 \\ x - 1, & x > 3. \end{cases}$

1.12 PROBLEM SET 1-3 (concluded)

20. Colonial Gas Company charges its customers according to their usage of gas as follows: a $6.00 customer charge, $1.180 per unit (100 cubic feet) for the first 20 units, and $0.806 per unit for each unit over 20.
    a) Determine the cost function and draw its graph.
    b) What are the total and average charges for using 15 units?
    c) For using 50 units?
    d) How many units were used if the total charge is $73.93?

21. ComElectric charges its customers according to their usage of electricity. One rate it charges commercial users is as follows: a monthly customer charge of $6.00, $0.05973 energy charge per kwh for the first 2,300 kwh, $0.02505 energy charge per kwh in excess of 2,300 kwh, and $0.00048 conservation charge per kwh.
    a) Determine the cost function and draw its graph.
    b) What is the total and average charge for using 2,000 kwh?
    c) 4,000 kwh?
    d) How many kwh were used if the total charge is $254.26?

22. The 1990 U.S. federal tax rate for single individuals was as follows: 15 percent on an adjusted gross income (AGI) between $0 and $19,450; $2,917.50 plus 28 percent on the excess over $19,450 on an AGI between $19,450 and $47,050; and $10,645.50 plus 33 percent on the excess over $47,050 on an AGI between $47,050 and $97,620.
    a) Determine the tax function and draw its graph.
    b) How much tax would a single individual pay on an AGI of $15,000?
    c) On an AGI of $35,000?
    d) On an AGI of $85,000?
    e) What was the individual's AGI if taxes are $10,071.50?

23. The 1990 U.S. Federal tax rate for married couples was as follows: 15 percent on an AGI between $0 and $32,450; $4,867.60 plus 28 percent on the excess over $32,450 on an AGI between $32,450 and $78,400; and $17,733.50 plus 33 percent on the excess over $78,400 on an AGI between $78,400 and $162,770.
    a) Determine the tax function and draw its graph.
    b) How much taxes would a married couple pay on an AGI of $15,000?
    c) On an AGI of $35,000?
    d) On an AGI of $85,000?
    e) What was the couple's AGI if taxes are $8,381.50?

24. Micros Unlimited Corporation (a local distributor of microcomputers) sells one of its 486-based systems on a volume discount as follows: 1 to 5 units at a price of $2,495 per unit, units 6 to 10 at a price of $2,195 per unit, and any unit in excess of 10 at a price of $1,995 per unit.
    a) Determine the cost function and draw its graph.
    b) What are the total and average costs of 3 units?
    c) Of 8 units?
    d) Of 15 units?
    e) How many units were purchased if the total charge was $21,255?
    f) If the average charge was $2,382.50?

25. Fashion Designers Inc. sells each of its women's suits to retail stores based upon volume discount as follows: a $125 shipping and handling charge, $325 per suit for the first 50 suits, $275 per suit for the next 50 suits, and $195 per suit for each suit in excess of 100.
    a) Determine the cost function and draw its graph.
    b) What are the total and average costs of 30 suits?
    c) Of 80 suits?
    d) Of 150 suits?
    e) How many suits were purchased if the total charge was $49,625?
    f) If the average charge was $318.75?

1.13 INTERPRETIVE EXERCISE: COST–OUTPUT

In this section, we look at how the mathematical terminology of linear equations might be used in a real-world situation. Assume that C is the total factory (manufacturing) cost of production of a product when Q (for quantity) units of the product are made. We also assume that the relationship between C and Q is linear,[3] as is frequently the case, and show this in Figure 1–15 as the line segment LM.

When making interpretations from Figure 1–15, keep in mind that a vertical distance represents a cost while a horizontal distance represents a quantity (number of units). Thus, the segment PT represents the total cost of producing OP units of product, and UM is the total cost of producing OU units of product.

The distance OL, the vertical intercept, corresponds to the cost of operation when zero units are produced, the reasoning here being that some costs (such as insurance on the plant) exist even when no product is being made. Borrowing an accounting term, we interpret OL as **fixed cost**, that is, the component of cost that does not vary with the number of units made. (See Section 1.4.) In Figure 1–15, fixed cost is

$$OL = PS = UR.$$

If we make OP units of product, the total cost is PT. PT, in turn, is the sum of PS and ST. PS is fixed cost; ST we shall call the **variable cost** when OP units are made. The term variable cost refers to the component of cost that changes as the number of units produced changes (Again, see Section 1.4.) Thus, ST is variable cost when OP units are made; RM is the (larger) variable cost when OU units are made. At each level of output, total cost is the sum of fixed and variable costs.

Total cost is the sum of fixed cost plus variable cost.

Consider the ratio RM/LR. RM is the variable cost when LR (or OU) units are made. The ratio

$$\frac{\text{Variable cost}}{\text{Number of units made}}$$

is the variable cost per unit of product made. By definition, RM/LR is the slope of LM, and the slope of a straight-line segment is constant. Consequently, variable cost per unit is constant when cost and output are linearly related.[4]

Economic terminology leads us to another description of the slope of LM in Figure 1–15. Economists speak of the **extra** cost (the change in total cost) when one more unit is made as the **marginal cost** of that unit. This is the vertical change for a horizontal change of one. It is the slope of the line. We may say that when total cost is linearly related to output, marginal cost is constant. (Marginal cost, of course, will not be constant if the total cost function is not linear. As we will see in later chapters, though, the marginal cost will always be the slope of the total cost function.)

Marginal cost is the variable cost per unit or the slope of the total cost function; it is constant if the function is linear.

---

[3] When the output interval is wide, the cost–output relationship may well be curved rather than straight. We shall consider the case of a curve in later chapters.

[4] If, on a cost curve, variable cost is divided by number of units produced, the ratio is called **average variable cost** per unit and is **not** constant.

FIGURE 1–15

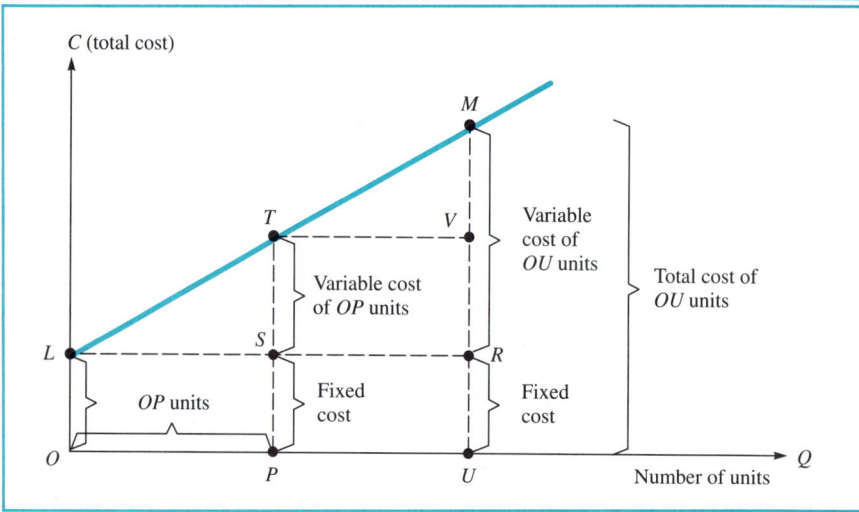

For further practice, observe that *UM* is *VM* greater than *PT*, which means that it costs *VM* more dollars to produce *OU* units than to produce *OP* units. *TV*, on the other hand, represents how many more units can be produced for *UM* dollars than for *PT* dollars.

We have said that when total cost is linearly related to output, then variable cost per unit is constant. Average cost per unit, defined as total cost over number of units produced, is not constant. Rather than argue this statement from Figure 1–15, suppose that we interpret the equation:

$$y = 3x + 2,$$

letting y be total cost of producing x units. The fixed cost is \$2 and the variable cost per unit (the slope) is \$3. However, by substitution, we find that total cost rises from \$17 to \$32 if x changes from 5 to 10 units. The average cost per unit

Average cost is the total cost per unit and is not constant.

Summary

Total cost = Variable cost + Fixed cost.

Also,

Marginal cost = Variable cost per unit

and is precisely the slope of the total cost function, while

Average cost = Total cost per unit.

declines from 17/5 to 32/10, that is, from $3.40 to $3.20. This reduction sometimes is referred to as being a consequence of **spreading fixed cost over a larger number of units**.

1.14 PROBLEM SET 1-4

Mark (T) for true or (F) for false. (Assume that cost means factory cost.) Given that total cost, y, of making x units is $y = 5x + 10$:

1. ( ) The total cost of making 20 units is $110.
2. ( ) Average cost per unit is $6 if 10 units are made.
3. ( ) The marginal cost of the 11th unit is greater than $5.
4. ( ) The marginal cost of the 20th unit is $5.
5. ( ) The variable cost per unit decreases as the number of units made increases.
6. ( ) The variable cost incurred when making 10 items is $50.
7. ( ) Average cost per unit decreases as the number of units made increases.
8. ( ) Variable cost increases as the number of units made increases.
9. ( ) The marginal cost of every unit is the same.
10. ( ) The slope of the line is the variable cost per unit.

11. If the total factory cost, y, of making x units of a product is given by $y = 3x + 20$, and if 50 units are made:
    a) What is the variable cost?
    b) What is the total cost?
    c) What is the variable cost per unit?
    d) What is the average cost per unit?
    e) What is the marginal cost of the 50th unit?

12. If total factory cost, y, of making x units of a product is $y = 10x + 500$ and if 1,000 units are made:
    a) What is the variable cost?
    b) What is the total cost?
    c) What is the variable cost per unit?
    d) What is the marginal cost of the last unit made?

13. A printer quotes a price of $7,500 for printing 1,000 copies of a book and $15,000 for printing 2,500 copies. Assuming a linear relationship and that 2,000 books are printed:
    a) Find the equation relating the total cost, y, to x, the number of books printed.
    b) What is the variable cost?
    c) What is the fixed cost?
    d) What is the variable cost per book?
    e) What is the average cost per book?
    f) What is the marginal cost of the last book printed?

14. If total factory cost, y, of making x units of a product is given by $y = 2x + 25$:
    a) Graph the cost–units equation.
    b) Draw a line representing fixed cost on the graph for (a).
    c) Erect a vertical line at $x = 10$; intersecting the x-axis at R, the fixed cost line at S, and the given equation at T.
    d) What are the numerical values and the interpretations of RS, ST, and RT?

15. In Figure A, the slant line represents the relation between total factory cost, C, of producing a number of units, and the number of units, Q, produced. What line segment(s), or ratios thereof, represent:
    a) Fixed cost?
    b) Total cost if OA units are made?
    c) Variable cost if OA units are made?
    d) Variable cost per unit made?
    e) Average cost per unit if OA units are made?
    f) Fixed cost per unit if OA units are made?
    g) How many more units can be made for AD dollars than for AF dollars?
    h) Marginal cost?

1.14 PROBLEM SET 1-4 (concluded)

FIGURE A

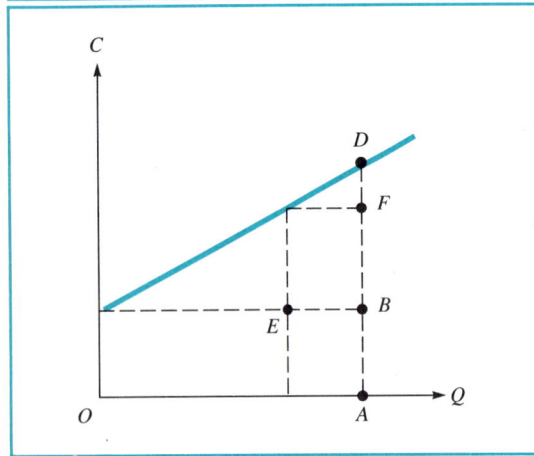

FIGURE B

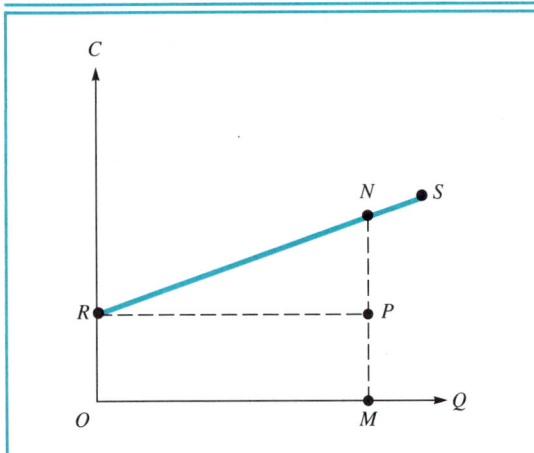

16. Prior to making a number of units of a certain part, a machine must be made ready, the cost incurred being called the **setup cost**. The total machine shop cost, C, of making Q units of the part is shown in Figure B as the segment RS. What interpretation would be given to:
   a) OR?
   b) PN?
   c) PN/OM?
   d) MN/OM?

1.15 BREAK-EVEN INTERPRETATION: 1

One way for a manager to make sure he or she is making a profit is to first analyze the circumstances necessary to **break-even** (i.e., neither make a profit nor suffer a loss). Then the manager can develop a plan to do better than break-even (i.e., make a profit). Now to break-even simply means that revenues must equal costs, so since

$$\text{Profit} = \text{Revenue} - \text{Cost},$$

then at break-even

$$\text{Revenue} = \text{Cost}$$

> Break-even occurs when Revenue = Cost so that Profit = 0.

means that

$$\text{Profit} = 0.$$

In this section and the next, we will present two break-even interpretations. The first will be from the point of view of a production manager and the second from that of a financial manager. The underlying principle, however, is the same in both situations (i.e., break-even occurs when Profit = 0).

On the production side, the cost of operation, as we have seen, is made up of the fixed cost plus the variable cost for the number of units produced. The revenue depends on the selling price and the number of units sold. For simplicity, we assume that the number of units made and sold is the same.

Example. A manufacturer of compact discs (CDs) has a fixed cost of $10,000 and variable cost of $7 per CD made. Selling price is $12 per CD. a) Find the revenue, cost, and profit functions. b) What is the profit if 2,800 CDs are made and sold? c) What is the profit if 1,000 CDs are made and sold? d) At what number of CDs made and sold will the manufacturer break even? e) At what sales volume (revenue) will break-even occur?

a) We denote the number (quantity) of CDs made and sold by q. Then since CDs are sold at $12 apiece, the revenue function is

$$R(q) = 12q.$$

Now since the variable cost per CD is $7, the variable cost of making q CDs will be $7q$. Adding the fixed cost of $10,000, the cost function becomes

$$C(q) = 7q + 10{,}000.$$

Lastly, since profit is revenue minus cost, the profit function is

$$\begin{aligned} P(q) &= R(q) - C(q) \\ &= 12q - (7q + 10{,}000) \\ &= 5q - 10{,}000. \end{aligned}$$

Notice that the coefficient 5 of q represents the profit per CD and is precisely the difference between the selling price per CD of $12 and the variable cost per CD of $7. Similarly, the constant term of $-10{,}000$ indicates that the manufacturer has to produce and sell enough CDs to compensate for the fixed cost of $10,000 before breaking even.

b) If 2,800 CDs are made and sold, then the profit is

$$P(2{,}800) = 5(2{,}800) - 10{,}000 = \$4{,}000.$$

c) On the other hand, if 1,000 CDs are made and sold, the profit is

$$P(1{,}000) = 5(1{,}000) - 10{,}000 = -\$5{,}000.$$

indicating a loss of $5,000.

d) At break-even, profit will be 0. Thus

$$P(q) = 0$$

$$5q - 10{,}000 = 0$$

$$q = \frac{10{,}000}{5} = 2{,}000 \text{ CDs}.$$

e) Finally, the break-even dollar volume of sales (revenue) is

$$R(2{,}000) = (12)(2{,}000) = \$24{,}000.$$

> **Exercise.** A manufacturer of cassette tapes has a fixed cost of $60,000 and a variable cost of $6 per cassette produced. Selling price is $9 per cassette. a) Find the revenue, cost, and profit functions. b) What is the profit if 25,000 cassettes are made and sold? c) What is the profit if 18,000 cassettes are made and sold? d) At what number of cassettes made and sold will the manufacturer break even? e) What is the break-even dollar volume of sales (revenue)?
>
> **Answer:** a) $R(q) = 9q$; $C(q) = 6q + 60,000$; $P(q) = 3q - 60,000$. b) $15,000. c) Loss of $6,000. d) 20,000 cassettes. e) $180,000.

Break-Even Charts

Returning to the revenue and cost functions of the last example,

$$R(q) = 12q \quad \text{and} \quad C(q) = 7q + 10,000,$$

and plotting these in the usual manner, we obtain the graphs in Figure 1–16. Observe that the revenue line goes through the origin and that the cost line has a y-intercept of $10,000. The dotted horizontal line shows that this fixed cost is constant at all

FIGURE 1–16

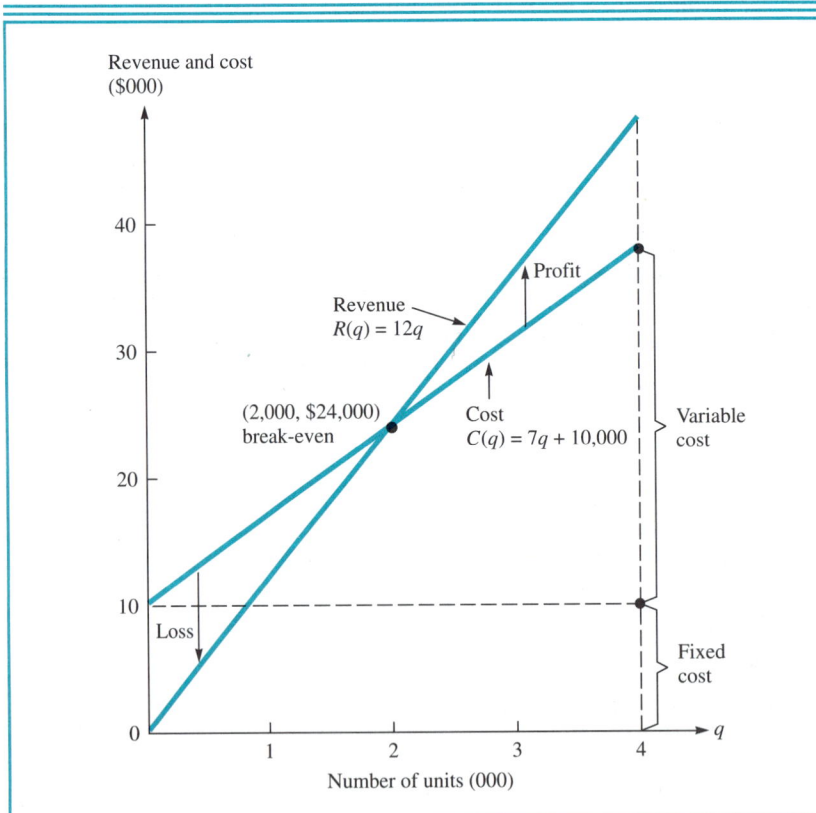

levels of operation. The variable cost, which is the $7q$ in the cost function (not the $7 **variable cost per unit**, which is constant) is the vertical distance from the fixed cost line to the total cost line; it of course increases as more units are produced. To the left of the break-even point (2,000, $24,000), the cost line is above the revenue line; the vertical separation at any point represents the associated loss. On the other hand, to the right of the break-even point, the vertical separation represents the associated profit. Break-even charts are a helpful graphic aid. They are frequently used in planning business operations.

> **Exercise.** Superimpose the profit function $P(q) = 5q - 10,000$ on the revenue and cost functions in Figure 1–16 and plot the break-even profit point (2,000, $0). Compare the profit to the left of (2,000, $0) with the preceding analysis of the cost and revenue functions to the left of the break-even point (2,000, $24,000). Do the same to the right of (2,000, $0).

The example of this section occurs often enough that it is useful to **parameterize** it (that is, to replace the numerical values by **arbitrary constants** called **parameters**). For this purpose, assume the manufacturer sells the q units of the product at a price of p per unit (instead of $12). The revenue function will then be

≡ Parameterizing a Model

A parameter is an arbitrary constant.

$$\text{Revenue} = (\text{Price per unit})(\text{Number of units sold})$$

or simply

$$R(q) = pq. \tag{1}$$

Next, if we assume the variable cost per unit is v (instead of $7), the variable cost will be

$$(\text{Variable cost per unit})(\text{Number of units made}) = vq.$$

Then if we assume the fixed cost is F (instead of $10,000) and add this to the variable cost, we have the cost function:

$$\text{Cost} = \text{Variable cost} + \text{Fixed cost}$$

or simply

$$C(q) = vq + F. \tag{2}$$

Finally, since

$$\text{Profit} = \text{Revenue} - \text{Cost},$$

we have the profit function

$$P(q) = R(q) - C(q)$$
$$= pq - (vq + F)$$

or simply

$$P(q) = (p - v)q - F. \qquad (3)$$

> **Exercise.** Substitute the numerical values of the example of this section and verify the revenue, cost, and profit functions in the preceding Equations (1), (2), and (3).

Now since break-even occurs when profit is zero, we have from Equation (3)

$$P(q) = 0$$
$$(p - v)q - F = 0$$
$$(p - v)q = F.$$

Solving this for q gives us a formula for the break-even quantity q_e

> **Break-Even Quantity**
>
> $$q_e = \frac{F}{p - v}. \qquad (4)$$

Using Equation (4) for our example where, as we saw, $p = \$12$, $v = \$7$, and $F = \$10{,}000$, we have

$$q_e = \frac{10{,}000}{12 - 7} = \frac{10{,}000}{5} = 2{,}000 \text{ records},$$

which is precisely the same result as before.

> **Exercise.** Use Equation (4) to verify the break-even quantity of the cassette tapes exercise of this section.

1.16 BREAK-EVEN INTERPRETATION: 2

Production managers and other operations executives tend to think of break-even analysis in the way it was presented in the previous section. Comptrollers and other financial managers are more likely to think in accounting terms. To illustrate this latter way of viewing break-even, we shall consider a company that purchases products and sells them at a price that is presumably above the cost. Suppose, for example, that an item that cost $130 is priced to sell at $200. The **markup** is therefore $70. That is,

$$\text{Cost} = \$130$$
$$\text{Retail price} = \$200$$
$$\text{Markup} = \text{Retail price} - \text{Cost} = \$200 - \$130 = \$70.$$

> Markup is the difference between the selling price and the cost.

From the manager's viewpoint, the dollar amounts of markup on numerous individual items, which will vary widely, are not very useful in planning and controlling operations. What is useful is the overall markup percentage on all items. For comparability in different items, markup is viewed in one of two ways: a function of the cost or a function of the retail price. In the current example, the markup as a function of cost is

$$\frac{\text{Markup}}{\text{Cost}} = \frac{70}{130} = 0.54 \text{ or } 54\%.$$

On the other hand, in financial statements, accountants use the concept of **margin**, which is the **markup percentage on retail price**. In our example, this is

> Margin is the markup as a percentage of the selling price.

$$\text{Margin} = \frac{\text{Markup}}{\text{Retail price}} = \frac{70}{200} = 0.35 \text{ or } 35\%.$$

This means that 35 percent of the retail price of $200 is margin, and the other 65 percent of $200, which is

$$0.65(200) = \$130,$$

is the cost.

We now suppose that the company in our illustration uses a margin of 35 percent on **all** items it purchases, so that if the firm sells $\$s$-worth of merchandise, 35 percent of this amount is margin and 65 percent is cost. Thus,

$$\text{Cost of goods sold} = 0.65s. \qquad (1)$$

Next the company incurs selling expenses, which it budgets at 10 percent of the volume of sales. Hence,

$$\text{Selling expense} = 0.10s. \qquad (2)$$

Finally, the company budgets fixed expense at $12,000, so that

$$\text{Fixed expense} = F = \$12,000. \qquad (3)$$

From Equations (1), (2), and (3), we see that the total cost function is

$$C(s) = 0.65s + 0.10s + 12,000.$$

or simply

$$C(s) = 0.75s + 12,000.$$

Now if the firm sells $\$s$ worth of merchandise, its revenue will clearly be the same $\$s$ so that the revenue function is

$$R(s) = s.$$

Since profit is still revenue minus cost, the profit function is

$$\begin{aligned} P(s) &= R(s) - C(s) \\ &= s - (0.75s + 12{,}000) \\ &= 0.25s - 12{,}000. \end{aligned}$$

Notice that the coefficient 0.25 of s represents the profit per dollar of sales; it is precisely the difference between each $1.00 of sales and the associated $0.75 cost per dollar of sales. Alternatively, the 0.25 can be viewed as the difference between the $0.35 margin per dollar of sales and the $0.10 selling expense per dollar of sales. As before, the constant term of $-12{,}000$ indicates that the company has to sell $12,000 worth of merchandise to compensate for the fixed expense of $12,000.

Now suppose the company has a sales volume of $60,000. Then its profit (before taxes) will be

$$P(60{,}000) = 0.25(60{,}000) - 12{,}000 = \$3{,}000.$$

On the other hand, if the company generates sales of $40,000, then its profit will be

$$P(40{,}000) = 0.25(40{,}000) - 12{,}000 = -\$2{,}000$$

indicating a loss of $2,000.

Break-even, as before, will occur when profit is 0. Here

$$P(s) = 0$$
$$0.25s - 12{,}000 = 0$$
$$s = \frac{12{,}000}{0.25} = \$48{,}000.$$

So the company must target sales of at least $48,000 just to be assured of breaking even.

Exercise. A toy company operates on a margin of 33 percent of retail, and estimates other variable cost at $0.13 per dollar of sales. Fixed expense is estimated at $4,000.
a) Find the revenue, cost, and profit functions.   b) Estimate profit if sales are $50,000.
c) Estimate profit if sales are $15,000.   d) What is the break-even sales volume?

Answer: a) $R(s) = s$; $C(s) = 0.8s + 4{,}000$; $P(s) = 0.2s - 4{,}000$.   b) $6,000.   c) Loss of $1,000.   d) $20,000.

The **break-even chart** for this example is shown in Figure 1-17. The point of intersection ($48,000, $48,000) of the revenue function $R(s)$ and the cost function $C(s)$ establishes the break-even level of sales. The separation of lines to the right of break-even indicates profit; to the left, it shows loss.

> **Exercise.** Superimpose the profit function $P(s) = 0.25s - 12,000$ on the revenue and cost functions in Figure 1-17 and plot the break-even profit point ($48,000, $0). Compare the profit to the left of ($48,000, $48,000) with the preceding analysis of the cost and revenue functions to the left of the break-even point ($48,000, $48,000). Do the same to the right of ($48,000, $48,000).

As in the previous section, the example of this section can be parameterized. Here, since revenue and sales dollars are synonymous, the revenue function is simply

$$R(s) = s. \qquad (1)$$

Next, if we assume the variable cost per dollar of sales is m, the variable cost will be

$$ms.$$

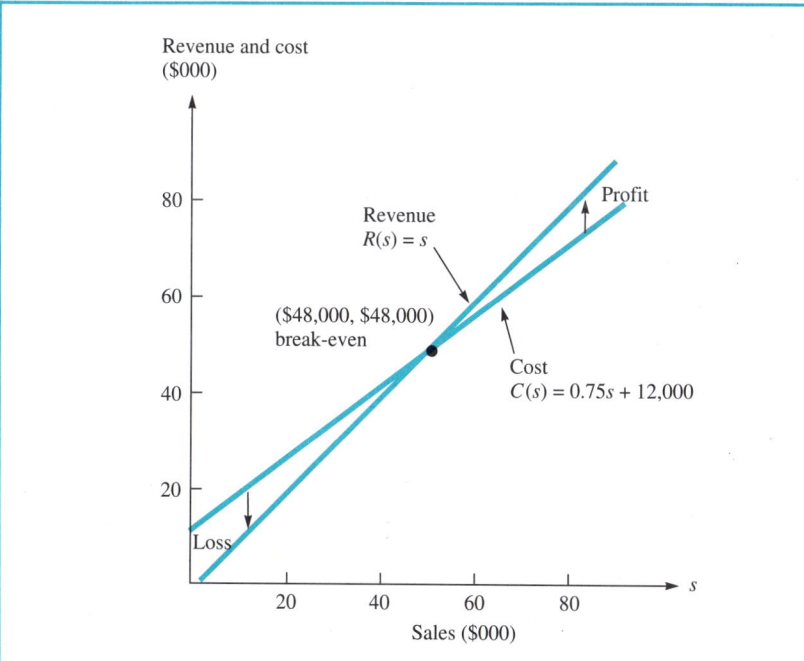

FIGURE 1-17

Then if we assume the fixed expense to be F and add this to the variable cost, we have the cost function:

$$C(s) = ms + F. \qquad (2)$$

Finally, we have the profit function:

$$P(s) = R(s) - C(s)$$
$$= s - (ms + F)$$

or simply

$$P(s) = (1 - m)s - F. \qquad (3)$$

> **Exercise.** Substitute the numerical values of the example of this section and verify the revenue, cost, and profit functions in the preceding Equations (1), (2), and (3).

Now since break-even occurs when profit is zero, we have from Equation (3)

$$P(s) = 0$$
$$(1 - m)s - F = 0$$
$$(1 - m)s = F.$$

Solving this for s gives us a formula for the break-even sales s_e.

> **Break-Even Sales**
>
> $$s_e = \frac{F}{1 - m}. \qquad (4)$$

Using Equation (4) for our example where, as we saw, $m = 0.65 + 0.10 = 0.75$, and $F = \$12{,}000$, we have

$$s_e = \frac{12{,}000}{1 - 0.75} = \frac{12{,}000}{0.25} = \$48{,}000,$$

which is precisely the same result as before.

> **Exercise.** Use Equation (4) to verify the break-even sales volume of the toy company exercise of this section.

Before leaving break-even analysis, we should note that the discussions in this and the previous section assumed that the total cost can be separated into two components: one fixed and the other varying directly in proportion to production or sales. These assumptions often are reasonably valid for a restricted range. It is not realistic, however, to assume fixed cost/expense will be constant over all ranges of production/sales. If production/sales are proving to be considerably below expected levels, management may reduce salaries or take other actions to reduce **fixed** cost/expense. It is not our purpose here to explore managerial action, but rather to introduce the tools, techniques, and models that a manager might use to make decisions needed to take the appropriate management action.

1.17 LINEAR DEMAND FUNCTIONS

In this section we introduce demand functions for products. Demand functions are an essential concept in the study of economics. Usually these functions are curves rather than straight lines, but lines provide good illustrations of demand characteristics. The demand for a product is the amount, q, of the product consumers are willing and able to buy at a given price per unit, p. Price per unit and quantity demanded are related; it is conventional in economics to plot price on the vertical and quantity demanded on the horizontal. For example, suppose the demand function for a product at one point in time is

Demand functions express price as a function of quantity demanded.

$$DD: \quad p = -0.2q + 20 \qquad (1)$$

where q is in millions of pounds per time period and p is in dollars per pound. The line is shown in Figure 1–18, together with the intercepts that were used to plot it, and is labeled in the conventional economic manner as DD.

From Equation (1), we compute that at quantity demanded $q = 25$ million pounds per time period, $p = -0.2(25) + 20 = \$15$ per pound. Similarly, at $q = 50$, $p = \$10$ per pound. Observe that

At $p = \$15$ per pound, demand $= 25$ million pounds.

At $p = \$10$ per pound, demand $= 50$ million pounds.

Thus, higher prices are associated with a lower quantity demanded, as we would expect, and this aspect of demand functions is present in Equation (1) because the line DD has a negative slope and, therefore, slants downward to the right, as shown in Figure 1–18.

Our purpose in this section is to discuss the idea of a parallel **shift** in the demand function DD. The basic idea involved is that as time goes on, various factors (such as changes in the prices of competing products, changes in population or family income, or changes in individual tastes) cause the demand function to shift position. Suppose, for example, that an increase in the price of competing product causes the demand function to shift. And suppose the new demand function, denoted by $D'D'$, is

Demand functions tend to shift as time goes on.

$$D'D': \quad p = -0.2q + 22,$$

FIGURE 1-18

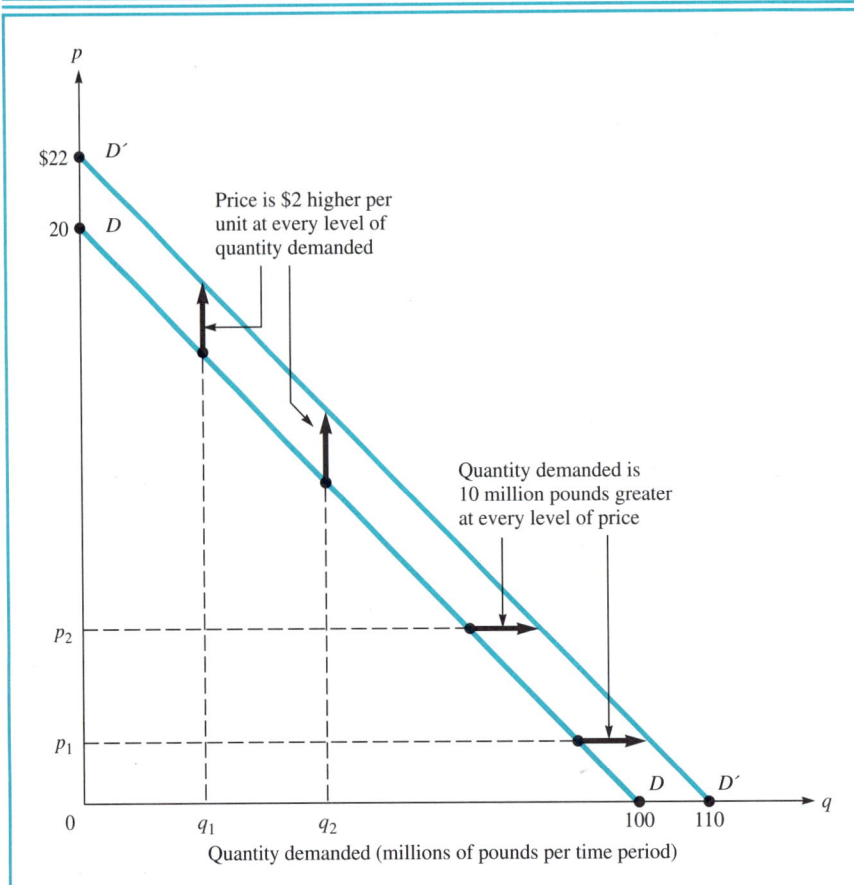

which is also plotted in Figure 1–18. Inasmuch as $D'D'$ is parallel to DD, the vertical separation of the lines is the same wherever it is measured. This separation is the difference in the intercepts on the vertical axis:

$$D'D' \text{ intercept} - DD \text{ intercept} = 22 - 20 = \$2.$$

We describe this **upward** shift by saying that **price per unit is $2 higher at every level of quantity demanded**. We can equally well describe the shift in terms of the constant horizontal separation of the lines, which is the difference of the intercepts on the horizontal axis:

$$D'D' \text{ intercept} - DD \text{ intercept} = 110 - 100 = 10 \text{ million pounds}.$$

This shift to the **right** is described by saying that after the shift, **quantity demanded is 10 million pounds greater at every level of price**.

> **Exercise.** Suppose that the demand functions just considered were interchanged, so that
>
> $$DD: \ p = -0.2q + 22, \quad D'D': \ p = -0.2q + 20,$$
>
> where $D'D'$ arose because of a decrease in the price of a competing product. In the manner of the previous boldface statements, describe: a) The vertical shift. b) The horizontal shift.
>
> **Answer:** a) Price per unit is $2 lower at every level of quantity demanded. b) Quantity demanded is 10 million pounds less at every price level.

The amount suppliers are willing to provide also is a function of price per unit, so there is a supply function that interacts with the demand function. We will return to this matter in the next chapter in our discussion of systems of linear equations.

= **Horizontal and Vertical Demand Functions**

The quantity of water demanded by consumers in a residential area probably remains nearly constant when the price of water varies over a limited range. This gives rise to the notion of a vertical demand function, such as

$$DD: \quad q = 10 \text{ billion cubic feet}$$

shown in Figure 1-19A, and we describe this by saying quantity demanded is constant at 10 billion cubic feet at different price levels. On the other hand, consider the small potato farmer who, because of the large competitive market, has no control over the demand price which is fixed at

$$p = \$5 \text{ per bushel}$$

no matter how many potatoes he has to sell. This gives rise to the horizontal demand line in Figure 1-19B. These cases are discussed in economics texts under the headings **perfectly inelastic** demand (Figure 1-19A) and **perfectly elastic** demand (Figure 1-19B).

Perfectly inelastic demand is a vertical line indicating a monopoly with total price control (i.e., pure price maker). Perfectly elastic demand is a horizontal line indicating a large competitive market (i.e., pure price taker).

FIGURE 1-19A

FIGURE 1-19B

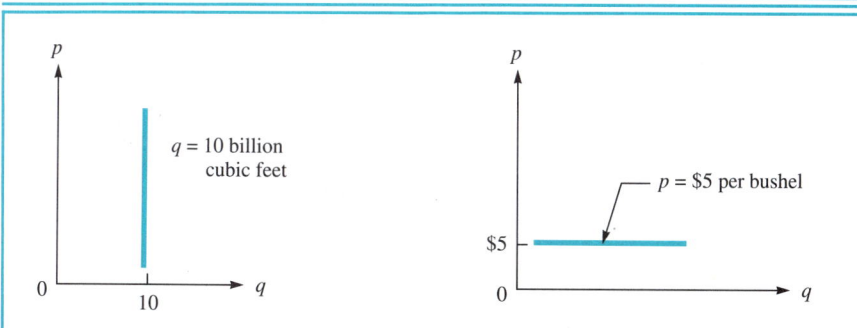

> **Exercise.** A college charges $75 per credit hour. If q is the number of credit hours supplied to students, write and interpret the equation of the supply line.
>
> **Answer:** $p = 75$, which means that the price per credit hour is $75 no matter how many credit hours are supplied to students.

1.18 PROBLEM SET 1-5

Given that total cost incurred in producing and selling q units of a product is $C(q) = 6q + 10,000$, and the q units are sold at a price of $46 per unit, mark (T) for true or (F) for false:

1. ( ) Total cost for 1,000 units is $16,000.
2. ( ) Average cost per unit is $6 no matter how many units are made and sold.
3. ( ) Average price is $46 per unit no matter how many units are made and sold.
4. ( ) Every additional unit made and sold increases total cost by $6.
5. ( ) Variable cost is the same at different values of q.
6. ( ) When 1,000 units are made and sold, variable cost will be $6,000.
7. ( ) Marginal cost is the same at all values of q.
8. ( ) Marginal cost is the same as average cost per unit.
9. ( ) A loss will be incurred if 200 units are made and sold.
10. ( ) A profit will be made if 250 units are made and sold.
11. ( ) Total cost is zero if no units are produced.
12. ( ) A total of 250 units must be made and sold in order to break-even.
13. A manufacturer has a fixed cost of $60,000 and a variable cost of $2 per unit made and sold. Selling price is $5 per unit.
    a) Find the revenue, cost, and profit functions using q for number of units.
    b) Compute profit if 25,000 units are made and sold.
    c) Compute profit if 10,000 units are made and sold.
    d) Find the break-even quantity.
    e) Find the break-even dollar volume of sales (revenue).
    f) Construct the break-even chart. Label the cost and revenue lines, the fixed cost line, and the break-even point.
14. A manufacturer has a fixed cost of $120,000 and a variable cost of $20 per unit made and sold. Selling price is $50 per unit.
    a) Find the revenue, cost, and profit functions using q for number of units.
    b) Compute profit if 10,000 units are made and sold.
    c) Compute profit if 1,000 units are made and sold.
    d) Find the break-even quantity.
    e) Find the break-even dollar volume of sales (revenue).
    f) Construct the break-even chart. Label the cost and revenue lines, the fixed cost line, and the break-even point.
15. A company has a linear total cost function and has determined that over the next three months it can produce 1,000 units at a total cost of $300,000. This same manufacturer can produce 2,000 units at a total cost of $400,000. The units sell for $180 each.
    a) Determine the revenue, cost, and profit functions using q for number of units.
    b) What is the fixed cost?
    c) What is the marginal cost?
    d) Find the break-even quantity.
    e) What is the break-even dollar volume of sales?
16. A company has a linear total cost function and has determined that over the next three months it can

1.18 PROBLEM SET 1-5 (continued)

produce 10,000 units at a total cost of $550,000. This same manufacturer can produce 20,000 units at a total cost of $600,000. The selling price per unit is $5.50.
  a) Determine the revenue, cost, and profit functions using q for number of units.
  b) What is the fixed cost?
  c) What is the marginal cost?
  d) Find the break-even quantity.
  e) What is the break-even dollar volume of sales?

17. (See Problem 15.)
  a) What would be the company's cost if it decided to shut down operations for the next three months?
  b) If, because of a strike, the most the company can produce is 1,000 units, should it shut down? Why or why not?

18. (See Problem 16.)
  a) What would be the company's cost if it decided to shut down operations for the next three months?
  b) If, because of a strike, the most the company can produce is 100,000 units, should it shut down? Why or why not?

Given that total cost, C is related to sales volume, s, by the equation $C(s) = 1{,}000 + 0.2s$, mark (T) for true or (F) for false:

19. (   ) Variable cost will be $200 on sales of $1,000.
20. (   ) Variable cost per dollar of sales is $0.20.
21. (   ) Fixed cost is $1,000.
22. (   ) A loss would occur if sales were $1,000.
23. (   ) Sales of $2,000 would lead to a profit of $600.
24. (   ) The cost–sales line rises $2 for each increase of $10 in sales volume.
25. (   ) Average cost per dollar of sales is the same at various sales levels.
26. (   ) The slope of the line is interpreted as variable cost.
27. (   ) Variable cost is a constant.
28. (   ) Variable cost per dollar of sales is constant.

---

29. A company expects fixed cost of $22,800. Margin is to be 55 percent of retail. Variable cost in addition to costs of goods is estimated at $0.17 per dollar of sales.
  a) Find the revenue, cost, and profit functions using s for sales volume.
  b) Find the break-even point.
  c) What will net profit before taxes be on sales of $75,000?
  d) Draw the break-even chart.

30. A company expects fixed cost of $36,000. Margin is to be 52 percent of retail, and variable cost in addition to cost of goods is estimated at $0.07 per dollar of sales.
  a) Find the revenue, cost, and profit functions using s for sales volume.
  b) Find the break-even point.
  c) What will net profit before taxes be on sales of $75,000?
  d) Draw the break-even chart.

31. A company has a linear total cost function and has determined that it has a total cost of $36,836 on sales of $15,000. This same company has a total cost of $41,536 on sales of $25,000. Find:
  a) The revenue, cost, and profit functions using s for sales volume.
  b) The variable cost per dollar of sales.
  c) The fixed cost.
  d) The variable cost on sales of $72,000?
  e) The total cost on sales of $72,000?
  f) The break-even dollar volume of sales.
  g) The net profit before taxes on sales of $80,000?

32. A company has a linear total cost function and has determined that it has a total cost of $30,200 on sales of $20,000. This same company has a total cost of $33,400 on sales of $30,000. Find:
  a) The revenue, cost, and profit functions using s for sales volume.
  b) The variable cost per dollar of sales.
  c) The fixed cost.
  d) The variable cost on sales of $40,000.
  e) The total cost on sales of $40,000.

1.18 PROBLEM SET 1–5 (concluded)

f) Find the break-even dollar volume of sales.
g) What is the net profit before taxes on sales of $30,000?

33. If variable cost per dollar of sales remains at last year's level, $0.40, but fixed cost this year is $3,600 compared to $3,000 last year, how much greater will this year's break-even point be than least year's?

34. Draw the break-even chart for the equation in
    a) Problem 31.   b) Problem 32.

35. The demand function for a product shifts from

$$DD: p = -0.10q + 40$$

to

$$D'D': p = -0.10q + 35.$$

Compute the horizontal and vertical shifts and write interpretive descriptions of these numbers.

36. The demand function for a product shifts from

$$DD: p = -0.05q + 40$$

to

$$D'D': p = -0.05q + 50.$$

Compute the horizontal and vertical shifts and write interpretive descriptions of the numbers.

37. Write a descriptive interpretation of a demand function that is
    a) Vertical.
    b) Horizontal.

38. The price of a particular raw material varies markedly from week to week. To be sure that it will be able to obtain this raw material, a company promises a supplier that it will buy 100 tons per week at whatever the going price is. Write the demand function implied by this promise.

39. An electric power company charges residential customers a fixed amount per kilowatt-hour of electricity used. What would be the graphical nature of the demand function in this case?

1.19 REVIEW PROBLEMS

1. If y and x represent, respectively, expenses and sales in thousands of dollars, and last week's operations are characterized as (10, 12), compared to this week's (13, 16), by how much did expenses and sales change from last week to this?

2. If sales increased from $12 thousand to $15 thousand, the **percent** increase was

   (100 percent) (15 − 12)/12 = 25 percent.

   a) Write the expression for percent change if sales go from S_1 to S_2.
   b) What would it mean if the answer to a calculation such as that in (a) was negative?

3. Find the slope of the segment joining the following pairs of points:
   a) (−4, 7), (−1, 3).
   b) (1, 2), (5, 6).
   c) (0, 0), (0, 5).
   d) (5, −1), (10, −1).
   e) (5, 0), (5, 3).
   f) (−2, −1), (2, −4).
   g) (1, −3), (4, −1).
   h) (−2, 5), (3, 5).

i) If personal consumption expenditures increased from $254 billion to $618 billion when disposable income (less consumer interest on loans) increased from $270 billion to $675 billion, compute the marginal propensities to consume and to save.

4. Find the equation of the line passing through each of the pairs of points in Problems 3(a) through 3(h). State answers in slope-intercept form where possible.

5. Find the equation of the line passing through the given point and having the stated slope. State answers in slope-intercept form where possible.
   a) (1, 3), slope 1/5.
   b) (0, 0), slope 0.
   c) (1, 1), slope 1.
   d) (1, 3), slope −2.
   e) (−2, −4), vertical.
   f) (−3, −4), slope 0.

6. What is the equation of the line parallel to and five units below the x-axis?

7. As sales, x, change from $300 to $600, selling expense changes from $250 to $400. Assume that the

1.19 REVIEW PROBLEMS (continued)

given data establish a linear relationship between sales and selling expense. Find the equation of the relationship in slope-intercept form.

8. If selling expense is $100 when sales are $150, and if expense increases $1 for each increase of $3 in sales, write the straight-line relationship between expense and sales in slope-intercept form.

9. If a man's weekly pay is computed at $50 (whether or not he works) plus $5 per hour worked, what equation relates weekly pay, y, to hours worked, x?

10. Explain why the lines $y = -6$ and $x = 15$ are perpendicular.

11. What are the slope and y-intercept of the line in Problem 9?

12. Graph the following lines using the intercepts:
    a) $y = (3/4)x - 6$.
    b) $y = -2x + 10$.
    c) $y = 15$.

13. Determine the slope of each of the following lines:
    a) $y = x - 4$.
    b) $y = (1/2)x - 2/3$.
    c) $y = (-3/4)x + 7/4$.

14. An ounce of bourbon contains 1/2 of an ounce of alcohol; an ounce of vermouth contains 1/8 of an ounce of alcohol. Write the relation that exists if b ounces of bourbon and v ounces of vermouth are to be mixed to make a drink containing two ounces of alcohol. What is the substitution rate of bourbon per ounce of vermouth?

15. What is the equation of the line that has a slope of $-2/3$ and a y-intercept of -4?

16. Find the equation of the line through (3, 4) that is parallel to the line $y = (1/2)x - 2$.

17. a) Find the equation of the line through $(-1, 15)$ that is perpendicular to the line
    $$y = (1/2)x - 2.$$
    b) If an existing pipeline is described by $y = x$ and a plant at (14, 26) wishes to connect to the pipeline on a perpendicular, what is the equation of the perpendicular?

18. If y and x are in proportion so that y is to x as 2 is to 5, then:
    a) Write the equation relating y and x.
    b) Graph the equation in (a).

19. If a company sells x units of a product at $4 per unit, write the expression for R, the total revenue received for the x units. Interpret the intercepts of this line.

20. If the first of two lines has the form $Ax + By + C = 0$, and the second the form $Dx + Ey + F = 0$, and if the first line is to pass through the origin and the second is to be parallel to the first, what relationships must exist among A, B, C, D, E, and F?

21. The **productivity** (as contrasted to **production**) of a factory is often measured by the ratio **output per labor-hour**. If a factory has a constant productivity of five units per labor-hour, what is the equation relating units of output, y, to number of labor-hours worked, x?

22. a) If y is a person's weekly pay in dollars and x is the number of hours the person worked, and if $y = 3.5x + 25$, interpret the numbers 3.5 and 25.
    b) A machine purchased now ($t = 0$) for $10,000 depreciates in value by a constant amount per year for 20 years to a scrap value of $1,000. Write the equation for D, the depreciated value of the machine at time t years. Interpret the slope and intercept of this line.

23. Graph each of the following:
    a) $y = \begin{cases} 4x - 5, & x \leq 0 \\ 8x - 5, & x > 0. \end{cases}$
    b) $y = \begin{cases} x + 6, & x < -3 \\ (1/3)x + 1, & x \geq -3. \end{cases}$

24. Boston Edison Company charges its customers according to their usage of electricity. One rate it charges a particular class of user is as follows: a basic monthly charge of $3.35, 4.129 cents per kwh for the first 350 kwh, and 6.882 cents per kwh for any kwh in excess of 350.
    a) Determine the cost function and graph it.
    b) What are the total and average charges for using 300 kwh?
    c) For using 500 kwh?
    d) How many kwh were used if the total charge was $131.35?

25. Micros Unlimited Corporation (a local distributor of microcomputers) sells one of its 586-based systems on a volume discount as follows: 1 to 5 units at a

1.19 REVIEW PROBLEMS (continued)

price of $4,495 per unit, units 6 through 10 at a price of $4,095 per unit, and any unit in excess of 10 at a price of $3,775 per unit.
a) Determine the cost function and graph it.
b) What are the total and average costs of 3 units?
c) Of 8 units?
d) Of 15 units?
e) How many units were purchased if the total charge was $58,050?
f) If the average charge was $4,035?

26. Fashion Designers Inc. sells each of its men's suits to retail stores based upon volume discount as follows: a $105 shipping and handling charge, $275 per suit for the first 50 suits, $185 per suit for the next 50 suits, and $125 per suit for each suit in excess of 100.
a) Determine the cost function and graph it.
b) What are the total and average costs of 40 suits?
c) Of 90 suits?
d) Of 200 suits?
e) How many suits were purchased if the total charge was $48,105?
f) If the average charge was $146.21?

27. If total factory cost, C, of making q units of a product is given by $C(q) = 2q + 40$, and if 100 units are made:
a) What is the variable cost?
b) What is total cost?
c) What is the variable cost per unit?
d) What is average cost per unit?
e) What is the marginal cost of the 100th unit?
f) What is the marginal cost of the 1st unit?

28. In Figure A, the slant line represents the total factory cost, C, of producing a number of units, q. Write an interpretation of each of the following:
a) OT.
b) PL/WP.
c) RW/OR.
d) PL.
e) SW.

29. A manufacturer has a fixed cost of $75,000 and a variable cost of $7 per unit made and sold. Selling price is $10 per unit.
a) Find the revenue, cost, and profit functions using q for number of units.
b) Compute profit if 40,000 units are made and sold.
c) Compute profit if 20,000 units are made and sold.

FIGURE A

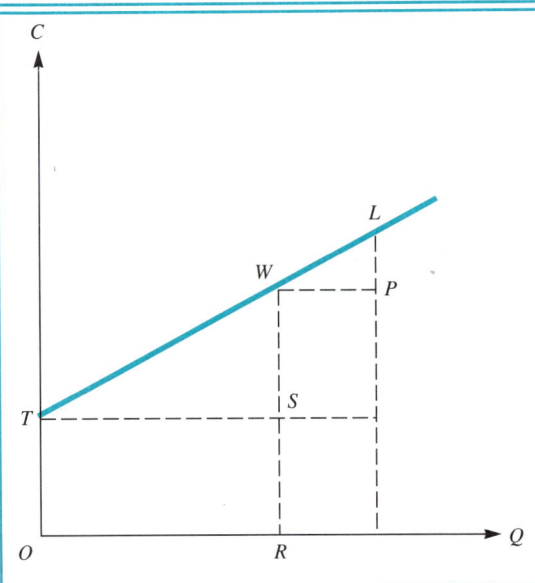

d) Find the break-even quantity.
e) Compute the break-even dollar volume of sales (revenue).
f) Construct the break-even chart. Label the cost, revenue, and fixed cost lines, and the break-even point.

30. A manufacturer has a fixed cost of $40,000 and a variable cost of $1.60 per unit made and sold. Selling price is $2 per unit.
a) Find the revenue, cost, and profit functions using q for number of units.
b) Compute profit if 150,000 units are made and sold.
c) Compute profit if 80,000 units are made and sold.
d) Find the break-even quantity.
e) Find the break-even dollar volume of sales (revenue).
f) Construct the break-even chart. Label the cost, revenue, and fixed cost lines, and the break-even point.

1.19 REVIEW PROBLEMS (concluded)

31. A company has a linear total cost function and has determined that over the next three months it can produce 12,000 units at a total cost of $224,000. This same manufacturer can produce 18,000 units at a total cost of $296,000. The selling price per unit is $13.25.
    a) Determine the revenue, cost, and profit functions using q for number of units.
    b) What is the fixed cost?
    c) What is the marginal cost?
    d) Find the break-even quantity.
    e) What is the break-even dollar volume of sales?
    f) What will profit be if the company shuts down operations?
    g) If, because of a strike, the company will be able to produce only 10,000 units, should it shut down for the next three months? Why or why not?

32. A company expects fixed cost of $25,000. It plans to work on a margin of 46 percent of retail, and to incur other variable costs of $0.06 per dollar of sales.
    a) Find the revenue, cost, and profit functions using s for sales volume.
    b) Find the break-even point.
    c) Make the break-even chart.
    d) What will net profit before taxes be if sales are $100,000?

33. A company has a linear total cost function and has determined that it has a total cost of $13,980 on sales of $6,000. This same company has a total cost of $18,620 on sales of $14,000. Determine:
    a) The revenue, cost, and profit functions using s for sales volume.
    b) Fixed cost.
    c) Variable cost on sales of $60,000.
    d) Total cost on sales of $60,000.
    e) The break-even point.
    f) Net profit before taxes on sales of $65,000.

34. Fixed cost is $10,000 and cost increases by $2 for each $3 increase in sales.
    a) Find the revenue, cost, and profit functions using s for sales volume.
    b) Find the break-even point.

35. A demand function shifts from

    $$DD: \ p = -0.2q + 50$$

    to

    $$D'D': \ p = -0.2q + 60.$$

    Compute the horizontal and vertical shifts and write an interpretive description of these numbers.

36. If p, price per unit, is vertical and q, number of units demanded, is horizontal, give the nature and interpretation of the demand functions $p = 2$ and $q = 100$.

1.20 EXTENDED REVIEW PROBLEMS

1. Winthrop Printing Company has estimated the cost of making new brochures for one of its major clients as follows: an initial cost of $2,500, $3 per brochure for the first 5,000 brochures, $2 per brochure for the next 10,000 brochures, and $1.50 per brochure for any brochure in excess of 15,000.
    a) Determine the cost function and graph it.
    b) What are the total and average costs of 4,000 brochures?
    c) Of 14,000 brochures?
    d) Of 24,000 brochures?
    e) How many brochures were printed if the total charge was $60,000?
    f) If the average charge was $2.75?

2. Hasbro Toy Company has determined that its fixed cost of retooling its machines to manufacture a new toy line is $15,000. The company has projected that cost will increase by $2 for each $5 increase in sales.
    a) Express revenue, cost, and profit as functions of sales volume.
    b) Find the break-even dollar volume of sales.
    c) What is net profit on sales of $20,000?

1.20 EXTENDED REVIEW PROBLEMS (concluded)

3. Ace Glass Company has found that its total factory cost of making eight-ounce tumblers is $C(q) = 5q + 250$. If it produces 10,000 eight-ounce tumblers, find
   a) The variable cost.
   b) The total cost.
   c) The variable cost per tumbler.
   d) The average cost per tumbler.
   e) The marginal cost of the 500th tumbler.
   f) The marginal cost of the 5th tumbler.

4. Economic analysis of the past 20 years has shown that personal consumption expenditures increased from $318 billion to $696 billion while disposable income increased from $355 billion to $739 billion.
   a) What is the marginal propensity to consume?
   b) What is the marginal propensity to save?

5. As sales change from $27,000 to $35,000, selling expense changes from $1,600 to $2,000. The relationship between sales and selling expense is known from past history to be linear. Find the equation describing this relationship.

6. On its line of extra-firm king-size mattresses, Mattress Discounters Company has a linear total cost function and has determined that it can produce 300 mattresses for a total cost of $130,000. The company can also produce 700 mattresses for a total cost of $210,000. The current sale price of these mattresses is $375 apiece.
   a) Find the revenue, cost, and profit functions using q for number of units.
   b) Compute profit if 200 mattresses are made and sold.
   c) Compute profit if 900 mattresses are made and sold.
   d) Find the break-even number of mattresses.
   e) What is the break-even dollar volume of sales?
   f) Draw the break-even chart. Label the cost, revenue, and fixed cost lines, and the break-even point.

7. An ounce of vodka contains 1/4 of an ounce of alcohol and an ounce of kahlua contains 1/10 of an ounce of alcohol.
   a) Write the equation that results if v ounces of vodka are mixed with k ounces of kahlua to make a drink containing five ounces of alcohol.
   b) What is the substitution rate of kahlua per ounce of vodka?

8. A new microcomputer system has been purchased for $75,000. For tax purposes, the company comptroller is depreciating the system by a constant amount over the next 15 years to a scrap value of $7,500.
   a) Write the equation for the depreciated value V of the system at time t years.
   b) Interpret the slope and intercept of the line.

9. The demand function for a certain product shifts from

   $$DD: p = -0.3q + 45$$

   to

   $$DD': p = -0.3q + 75.$$

   Compute the horizontal and vertical shifts, and write an interpretive description of these numbers.

10. A department store has overhead costs of $250,000 and a linear total cost function. The controller has set the store's margin policy using the example of a $140 markup on an item retailing for $500. The controller has also estimated that other variable costs on the same retail item selling for $500 are $15.
    a) Find the revenue, cost, and profit functions using s for sales volume.
    b) Find the break-even dollar volume of sales.
    c) Draw the break-even chart.
    d) What will net profit be if sales are $3,000,000?

SYSTEMS OF LINEAR EQUATIONS AND MATRICES

CHAPTER 2

2.1 INTRODUCTION

Often the variables encountered in a problem may have to fulfill more than one condition. In a production problem, for example, the numbers of units of various products made will be restricted by conditions such as time available and raw materials. When each of the conditions can be expressed in the form of a linear equation, the mathematical description of the problem becomes a **system of linear equations.** Procedures for finding the values of the variables that satisfy all equations of a system **simultaneously** are the subject of this chapter.

We will first explore operations that enable us to transform the equations in a system to an equivalent but much simpler system, and thereby find the solution values of the variables. We will then introduce the concept of a matrix and see how the use of matrices further simplifies the solution of a system of linear equations, especially when the system involves more than two variables.

The number of relevant variables in a system, and the number of equations representing conditions to be fulfilled, vary widely. The requirement that **all** conditions expressed by the system be satisfied sometimes cannot be met. In these cases, the system has no solution. In other cases, one set, or many sets, of values for the variables will satisfy all conditions. In this chapter, we shall learn (1) systematic procedures for solving systems with varying numbers of equations and variables, (2) how to determine if no solution is possible, and (3) how to express the solution if the system is satisfied by more than one set of values. We shall consider the effect of the requirement that values in the solution set not be negative (an important condition in many applied situations) and also show how the best set can be chosen when the system has more than one solution set. Two of the six sections on applications are concerned with supply and demand analysis.

2.2 NUMBER OF SOLUTIONS POSSIBLE IN A SYSTEM

The graphs of linear equations in the coordinate plane are straight lines. The first three parts of Figure 2–1 show the three intersection possibilities for such lines. If a system consists of two equations in two variables, either the corresponding lines:

1. Intersect in a single point (Figure 2–1A),
2. Are parallel and have no point of intersection (Figure 2–1B), or
3. Are coincident (are the same line) and have an unlimited number of points in common (Figure 2–1C).

FIGURE 2-1

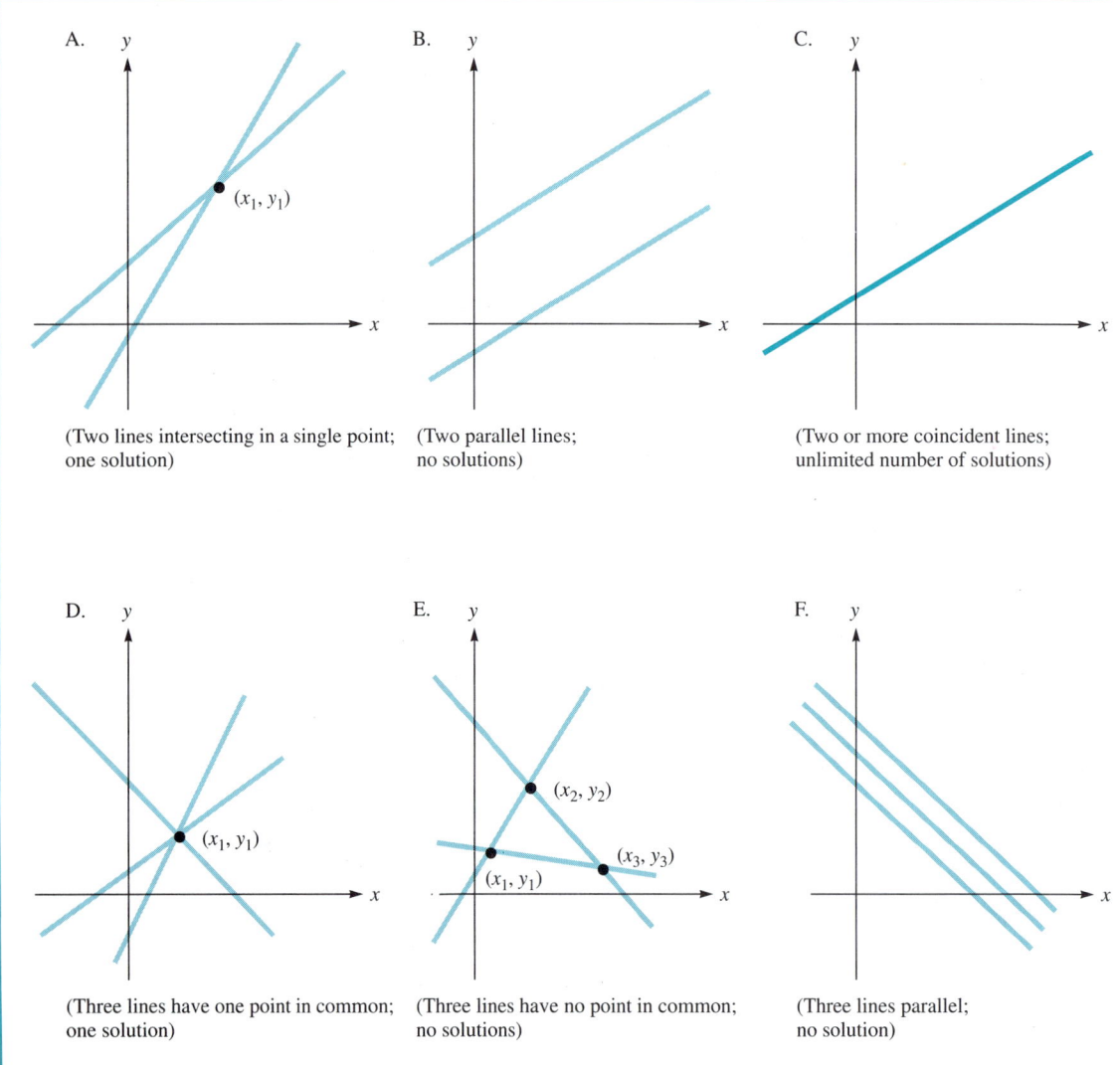

If a system consists of three equations in two variables, the associated graph will show three lines. These lines:

1. Can intersect in a single point (Figure 2–1D),
2. Might have no point that lies on all of them simultaneously (Figures 2–1E and 2–1F), or
3. Might have an unlimited number of points in common and therefore look exactly like Figure 2–1C since in such a case all three lines plot as precisely the same line.

The same three outcome possibilities hold when more than three lines are plotted. Hence, two or more lines give rise to precisely three possibilities:

1. All lines have exactly one point in common.
2. The lines have no point in common.
3. All the lines are coincident.

Two or more lines have either exactly one point in common, none in common, or an unlimited number in common.

The latter case occurs, of course, when the equations in the system are constant multiples of one another.

An m-by-n system of linear equations means a system of m linear equations in n variables (i.e., m is the number of equations and n is the number of variables). A specific solution of an m-by-n system of linear equations is a set of values, one for each variable, that simultaneously satisfy all equations of the system; that is, when the values of the n variables are substituted into **each** of the m equations, the left-hand and right-hand sides are identical in value. Geometrically, this set of values for the variables is represented by a point that lies on the graphs of **all** the equations (i.e., a solution is a point of intersection of all the graphs). We have seen that the intersections of two or more lines in the coordinate plane have only three outcomes—the lines have either one point in common, none in common, or an unlimited number in common. Correspondingly, the number of solutions of the associated m-by-2 linear system must be either one, zero, or unlimited.

An m-by-n system means m equations in n unknowns.

Number of Intersections of Two or More Lines	Number of Solutions to m-by-2 Linear System of Equations
One point in common	1
No points in common	0
Lines are coincident	Unlimited

An m-by-2 linear system has either one solution, no solution, or an unlimited number of solutions.

2.3 OPERATIONS ON LINEAR SYSTEMS

When a system of linear equations has a single solution, the solution is a point whose coordinates satisfy all the equations of the system. Specifically, if we have a 2-by-2 system that has a single solution, then, as illustrated in the previous section, the values of the x-coordinate and the y-coordinate must satisfy both equations.

For example, consider a system of two equations, the first of which is the line that passes through the points (2, 5) and (8, 3). The equation of this line, determined by methods in Chapter 1, is

$$e_1: \quad x + 3y = 17$$

where e_1 denotes that this is equation 1. Now suppose that the second line passes through the points (2, 5) and (4, 2) so it has the equation

$$e_2: \quad 3x + 2y = 16.$$

A solution to a system must satisfy all equations in the system.

The graphs of these two equations are shown in Figure 2–2. Notice that the point (2, 5) was used in constructing both e_1 and e_2. Hence $x = 2$ and $y = 5$ satisfies both equations and is a solution of the system. (In fact, from Figure 2–2, we see that it is the only solution.) We purposely chose (2, 5) to be a solution in order to

FIGURE 2-2

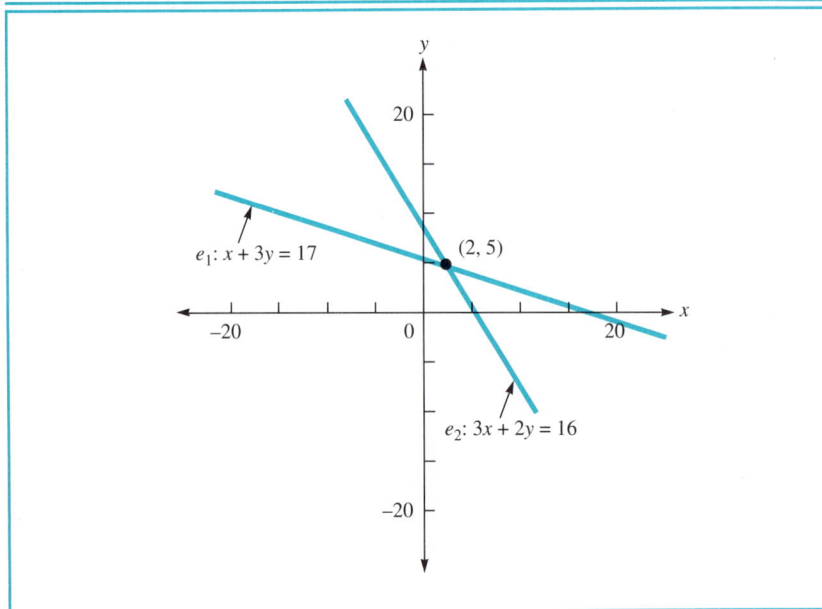

demonstrate the operations that can be performed on the equations of a system without changing the solution. We will number these operations as we proceed.

First, the solution of a system is not changed if both sides of an equation are multiplied by a constant. This is so, of course, because equals times equals are still equal. For example, multiplying both sides of e_1 by 3 gives

$$3e_1: \quad 3(x + 3y = 17) \quad \text{or} \quad 3x + 9y = 51$$

A solution of a system is unchanged if both sides of an equation are multiplied by a constant.

and the solution (2, 5) satisfies this equation (as well as the unchanged e_2) because

$$3(2) + 9(5) = 6 + 45 = 51.$$

Second, the solution of a system is not changed if an equation is replaced by a new equation that is the result of a nonzero constant times the original equation plus a nonzero constant times another equation in the system. The reason for this is that equals added to (or subtracted from) equals are still equal. For example, starting with the original system

The solution of a system is unchanged if an equation is replaced by a linear combination of equations.

$$\begin{aligned} e_1: & \quad x + 3y = 17 \\ e_2: & \quad 3x + 2y = 16, \end{aligned} \quad (1)$$

let us replace e_2 by $3e_1 - 1e_2$:

$$\begin{array}{rl} 3e_1: & 3x + 9y = 51 \\ 1e_2: & 3x + 2y = 16 \\ \hline e_3 = 3e_1 - 1e_2: & 0 + 7y = 35. \end{array}$$

Now observe that e_3 is also satisfied by the solution $(2, 5)$ because

$$0 + 7(5) = 35,$$

so the system

$$\begin{aligned} e_1: &\quad x + 3y = 17 \\ e_3: &\quad 0 + 7y = 35 \end{aligned} \quad (2)$$

has the same solution as the original system.

Third, the solution of a system is not changed if any pair of equations is interchanged. For example, it is obvious that interchanging e_1 and e_3 in (2) will have no effect on the solution.

The solution of a system is unchanged if equations are interchanged.

Inasmuch as the equations of a system are written horizontally, we often think of them as being **rows** and refer to the preceding operations as **row operations**. (More will be said on row operations in Section 2.16.) These three row operations can be summarized as:

Summary of the three row operations on systems of equations.

Row Operations

1. The solution of a system is not changed if both sides of one of the equations are multiplied by a constant.
2. The solution of a system is not changed if one of its equations is replaced by a linear combination of this and another equation in the system, where linear combination will mean a nonzero constant times the given equation plus a nonzero constant times another equation in the system.
3. The solution of a system is not changed if any pair of its equations are interchanged.

The manner in which row operations are used to systematically find an unknown solution is presented next.

2.4 ELIMINATION PROCEDURE: UNIQUE SOLUTIONS

The discussion in the previous section suggests a method of attack when seeking solutions of a linear system. Specifically, we form linear combinations of pairs of equations in a manner such that a variable can be **eliminated**. For example, recall the 2-by-2 system (1) of the previous section

$$\begin{aligned} e_1: &\quad x + 3y = 17 \\ e_2: &\quad 3x + 2y = 16. \end{aligned} \quad (1)$$

The elimination procedure forms linear combinations of equations that eliminate a variable.

We saw in the previous section that multiplying the first equation by 3 and the second by 1, followed by subtraction, resulted in the elimination of x. In other words,

$$3e_1: \quad 3x + 9y = 51$$
$$1e_2: \quad 3x + 2y = 16$$
$$e_3 = 3e_1 - 1e_2: \quad 0 + 7y = 35$$

so that the system

$$e_1: \quad x + 3y = 17$$
$$e_3: \quad 0 + 7y = 35 \tag{2}$$

has the same solution as the original system of e_1 and e_2. Now solving e_3, we have

$$7y = 35 \quad \text{or} \quad y = 5.$$

Rather than forming a linear combination eliminating y to obtain the required value of x, we may substitute 5 for y in e_1 and find that

$$x + 3(5) = 17$$
$$x = 2$$

so that the solution of the system is the point (2, 5), confirming what we saw in the previous section's text and in Figure 2–2.

Exercise. Show that the system

$$e_2: \quad 3x + 2y = 16$$
$$e_3: \quad y = 5$$

also has the same solution set (2, 5) as the original system e_1 and e_2.

Exercise. What linear combination would eliminate y from e_1 and e_2?
Answer: $2e_1 - 3e_2$.

Example. Solve the 2-by-2 system

$$e_1: \quad 2x + 3y = 2$$
$$e_2: \quad 5x + 4y = 12.$$

Suppose we choose to eliminate x. We would multiply e_1 by 5, multiply e_2 by 2, and then subtract the results to get

$$5e_1: \quad 10x + 15y = 10$$
$$2e_2: \quad 10x + 8y = 24$$
$$5e_1 - 2e_2: \quad 7y = -14$$

so that

$$y = -2.$$

Substituting this value into e_1 or e_2 yields $x = 4$, so the solution of the system is $(4, -2)$. The graphs of e_1 and e_2 along with the point of intersection $(4, -2)$ are shown in Figure 2–3.

Exercise. Show that the system

$$e_2: \quad 5x + 4y = 12$$
$$e_3: \quad \quad \quad y = -2$$

also has the same solution set $(4, -2)$ as the original system of e_1 and e_2.

Exercise. What linear combination would eliminate y from e_1 and e_2 in the preceding example?

Answer: $4e_1 - 3e_2$.

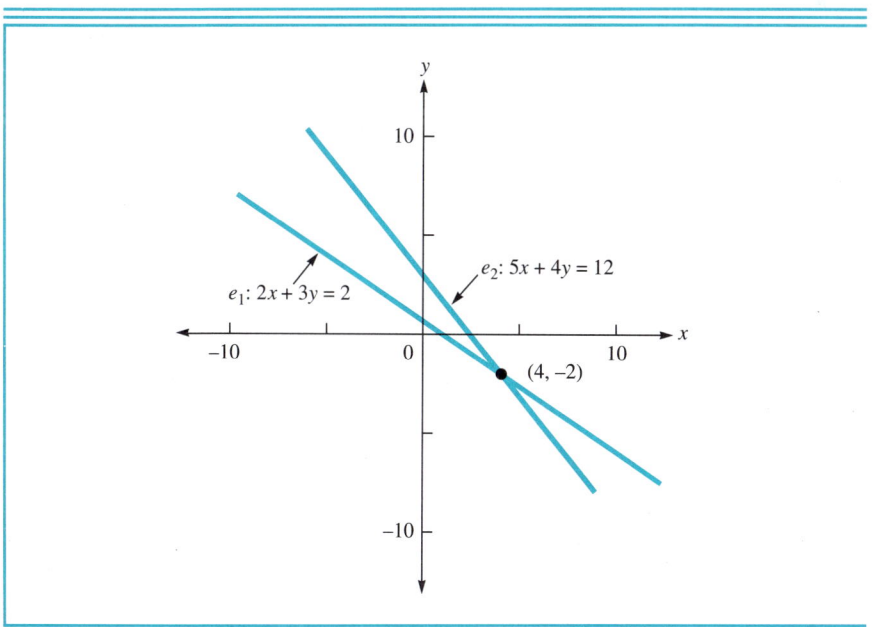

FIGURE 2–3

Example. Solve the 2-by-2 system

$$e_1: \quad 3x - 2y = 4$$
$$e_2: \quad 2x - 4y = 1.$$

Suppose here we choose to eliminate y. We would multiply e_1 by 2, multiply e_2 by 1, and then subtract the results to get

$$
\begin{array}{rl}
2e_1: & 6x - 4y = 8 \\
1e_2: & 2x - 4y = 1 \\
\hline
2e_1 - 1e_2: & 4x = 7
\end{array}
$$

so that

$$x = \frac{7}{4}.$$

Substitution of this value into e_1 or e_2 yields $y = 5/8$, so the solution of the system is (7/4, 5/8). The graphs of e_1 and e_2 along with the point of intersection (7/4, 5/8) are shown in Figure 2–4.

FIGURE 2–4

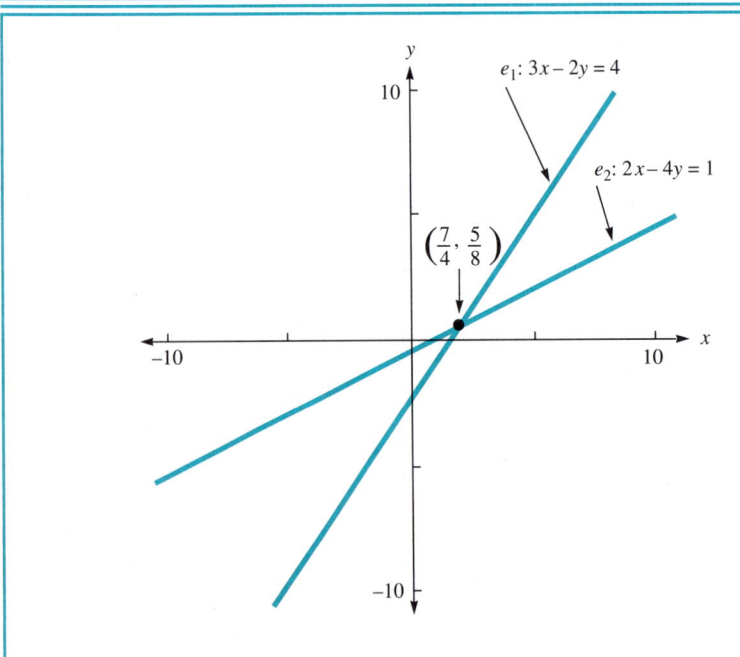

> **Exercise.** Find the solution of the following 2-by-2 system. Then graph the lines and label the coordinates of the point of intersection.
>
> $$4x - 3y = -3$$
> $$5x - y = 10.$$
>
> **Answer:** (3, 5).

As another example, suppose we add a third equation

$$e_3: \quad 16x + 8y = 33$$

to the system of the previous example, resulting in the following system of **three** linear equations in **two** variables (a 3-by-2 system)

$$e_1: \quad 3x - 2y = 4$$
$$e_2: \quad 2x - 4y = 1$$
$$e_3: \quad 16x + 8y = 33.$$

Superimposing the graph of e_3 on that of e_1 and e_2 from Figure 2–4, we get the result shown in Figure 2–5. Note that the third line e_3 also goes through the point (7/4, 5/8) so that the three lines intersect in a single point.

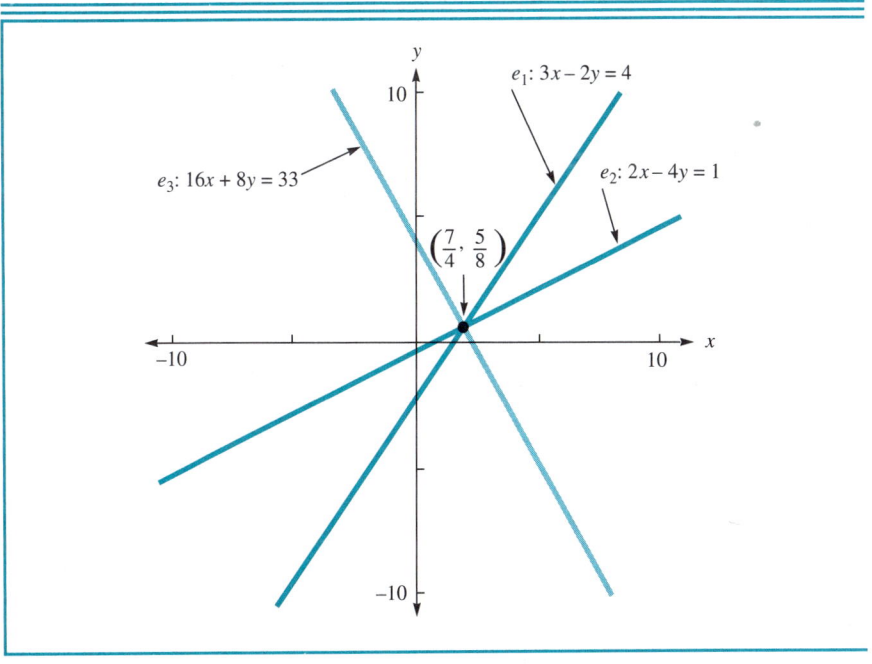

FIGURE 2-5

A 3-by-2 system is solved by eliminating one variable from any pair of equations and checking the result in the third equation.

To verify that the three equations do intersect in a single point, we can use the elimination method to eliminate y as before. A simple way to do this is to eliminate y from any two of the equations and then see if this plot satisfies the remaining third equation. In this example, we already have eliminated y from e_1 and e_2 in our previous example by forming $-2e_1 + e_2$ to get

$$x = \frac{7}{4} \quad \text{and} \quad y = \frac{5}{8}.$$

Substituting these values in e_3, we have

$$16\left(\frac{7}{4}\right) + 8\left(\frac{5}{8}\right) = 33$$
$$28 + 5 = 33$$
$$33 = 33$$

which checks. Thus, indeed, the point (7/4, 5/8) is the unique solution to all three equations in the system.

Exercise. Find the solution of the following 3-by-2 system. Then graph the lines and label the coordinates of the point of intersection.

$$4x - 3y = -3$$
$$5x - y = 10$$
$$2x + y = 11.$$

Answer: (3, 5).

A 3-by-3 system is solved by reducing the system to 2-by-2.

Now suppose we want to solve a system of three linear equations in three unknowns (a 3-by-3 system). We first use the elimination method to reduce the system to a 2-by-2 system. Then we solve the latter system in the usual way to obtain values for two of the three variables. Lastly we substitute these two values into any one of the three original equations to get the value of the third variable.

Example. Solve the 3-by-3 system

$$e_1: \quad 2x + y - z = 2$$
$$e_2: \quad x + 2y + z = 1$$
$$e_3: \quad 3x - y + 2z = 9.$$

We reduce this 3-by-3 system to a 2-by-2 system by eliminating x from e_1 and e_2 to get

$$e_4 = e_1 - 2e_2: \quad -3y - 3z = 0,$$

and **also** from e_2 and e_3 to get

$$e_5 = -3e_2 + e_3: \quad -7y - z = 6.$$

Now we proceed as usual for this 2-by-2 system e_4 and $\mathbf{e}_5$ to eliminate, say z, by

$$e_6 = -3e_5 + e_4: \quad 18y = -18$$

from which clearly

$$y = -1.$$

Substituting $y = -1$ in e_5, we find that

$$z = 1.$$

Lastly, substituting $y = -1$ and $z = 1$ in e_1, we have

$$x = 2$$

so that the solution to the system is the point $(2, -1, 1)$.

Exercise. Find the solution of the 3-by-3 system

$$x + y + z = 4$$
$$2x - y + z = 3$$
$$x - 2y + 3z = 5.$$

Answer: $(1, 1, 2)$.

Now the graphs of the three equations e_1, e_2, and e_3 of the example are planes in three dimensions. Since there is a single solution to the 3-by-3 system, these three planes must intersect in exactly one point. As is the case with systems of linear equations with two variables (m-by-2 systems), systems with three or more variables (m-by-n systems) can only have three outcomes: exactly one solution, no solutions, or an unlimited number of solutions. Although it becomes tedious, we can use the elimination procedure to solve any m-by-n system of linear equations regardless of the number m of equations or the number n of variables. We will soon see in this chapter that there are techniques (involving **matrices**) that greatly simplify solving these larger systems.

> The elimination procedure can be used to solve any m-by-n system, but it is easier done using matrices.

2.5 ELIMINATION PROCEDURE: NONUNIQUE SOLUTIONS

So far each system of equations we have considered has given rise to a unique solution. As stated in Section 2.1, it is also possible for a linear system of equations to have zero or an unlimited number of solutions. Our next example illustrates how the elimination procedure solves a system that has no solutions.

Example. Solve the 2-by-2 system

$$e_1: \quad 2x + 5y = 15$$
$$e_2: \quad 3.2x + 8y = 6.$$

Suppose we choose to eliminate y. Then we get

$$
\begin{array}{rrr}
8e_1: & 16y + 40z & = 120 \\
-5e_2: & -16y - 40z & = -30 \\
\hline
e_3 = 8e_1 - 5e_2: \quad 0 & & = 90.
\end{array}
$$

Thus, the original system will have the same solutions as the system

$$e_1: \quad 2x + 5y = 15$$
$$e_3: \quad 0 \quad\quad\quad = 90.$$

<u>A 2-by-2 system with no solution results in an equation that is impossible.</u>

However, equation e_3 is an impossibility! Zero cannot equal 90. We therefore conclude that the system has no solution. The reason for this is that a solution of a system must satisfy any linear combination of the original system. If a linear combination leads to a false or impossible statement, then the system must have a built-in contradiction and can have no solution. In this case, we say that the equations in the system are **inconsistent**. On the other hand, when there exists a unique solution or an unlimited number of solutions, the equations in the system are called **consistent**.

<u>A system with no solution is inconsistent.</u>

<u>A system with a solution(s) is consistent.</u>

The graphs of e_1 and e_2 are shown in Figure 2–6. Note that the two lines are parallel so that they will never intersect and, hence, there are no solutions common to both equations.

> **Exercise.** Prove that the following system is inconsistent:
>
> $$2x + 3y = 17$$
> $$9x + 13.5y = 25,$$
>
> and draw the associated graphs.

The elimination procedure will also tell us when a system of equations has an unlimited (or infinite) number of solutions.

Example. Solve the 2-by-2 system

$$e_1: \quad 2x + 5y = 15$$
$$e_2: \quad 3.2x + 8y = 24.$$

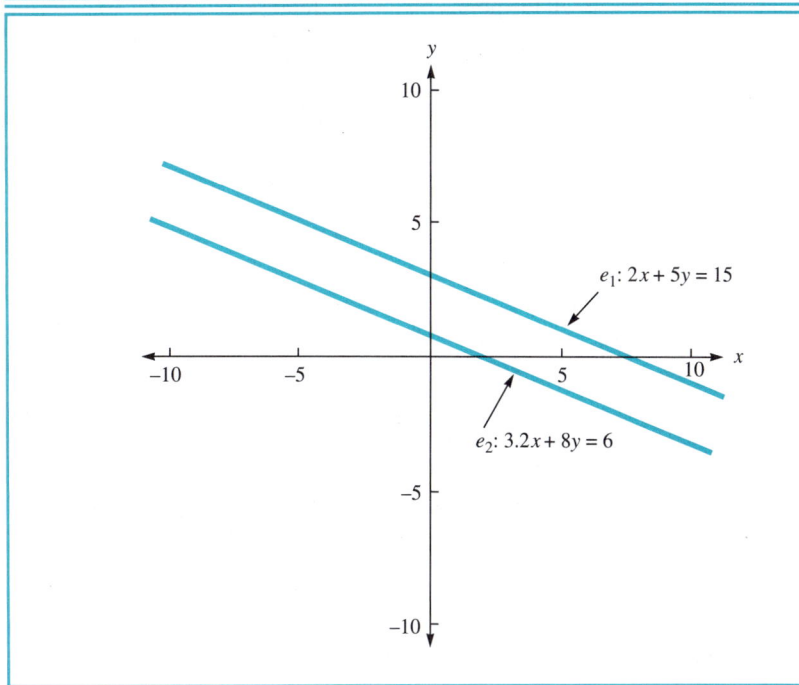

FIGURE 2-6

If we eliminate y, we get

$$
\begin{array}{rrr}
8e_1: & 16y + 40z & = 120 \\
-5e_2: & -16y - 40z & = -120 \\
\hline
e_3 = 8e_1 - 5e_2: & 0 & = 0.
\end{array}
$$

The original system will then have the same solutions as the system

$$
\begin{array}{rl}
e_1: & 2x + 5y = 15 \\
e_3: & 0 = 0.
\end{array}
$$

Now this last line is not a contradiction, since zero does indeed equal zero. In fact, since $0 = 0$ is always true, the original system will have the same solutions as the equation

$$e_1: \quad 2x + 5y = 15.$$

A 2-by-2 system with unlimited solutions results in the equation $0 = 0$.

The solution of a 2-by-2 system with unlimited solutions is described with one variable arbitrary in value (i.e., the solutions are expressed as functions of one of the variables).

These solutions are precisely all the points on the line represented by e_1. To describe this unlimited set of points, we solve e_1 for y and write the solution as

$$y = \left(-\frac{2}{5}\right)x + 3$$

x arbitrary.

This means that for each value of x that we arbitrarily choose, the corresponding value of y on the line

$$y = \left(-\frac{2}{5}\right)x + 3$$

gives a solution to the original 2-by-2 system e_1 and e_2.

Exercise. Prove that the following system has an unlimited number of solutions:

$$2x + 3y = 17$$
$$9x + 13.5y = 76.5.$$

Answer: x arbitrary, $y = (-2/3)x + 17/3$.

As before with systems that resulted in unique solutions, we can use the elimination method to solve 3-by-3 systems that result in zero or an unlimited number of solutions.

Example. Solve the 3-by-3 system

$$e_1: \quad x + y + z = 4$$
$$e_2: \quad 5x - y + 7z = 25$$
$$e_3: \quad 2x - y + 3z = 8.$$

Eliminating y from e_1 and e_2, and also from e_1 and e_3 leads to

$$e_4 = e_1 + e_2: \quad 6x + 8z = 29$$
$$e_5 = e_1 + e_3: \quad 3x + 4z = 12.$$

Next eliminating x or z from e_4 and e_5 leads to

$$e_6 = -2e_5 + e_4: \quad 0 + 0 = 5.$$

A 3-by-3 system with no solutions results in an equation that is impossible.

The last line is impossible. Zero cannot equal 5. We therefore conclude that the system has no solution and the equations in the system are inconsistent.

> **Exercise.** Prove that the following system is inconsistent:
> $$2x - y + 3z = 5$$
> $$x + 2y - z = 6$$
> $$3x + y + 2z = 8.$$

Our next example illustrates a 3-by-3 system that has an unlimited number of solutions. As was the case with 2-by-2 systems, we will see how to write the general solution in arbitrary-variable terminology.

Example. Solve the 3-by-3 system

$$e_1: \quad x + y + z = 4$$
$$e_2: \quad 5x - y + 7z = 20$$
$$e_3: \quad 2x - y + 3z = 8.$$

Proceeding in the usual manner, we find

$$e_4 = e_1 + e_2: \quad 6x + 8z = 24$$
$$e_5 = e_1 + e_3: \quad 3x + 4z = 12.$$

Eliminating x or z from these equations yields

$$e_6 = -2e_5 + e_4: \quad 0 + 0 = 0.$$

A 3-by-3 system with unlimited solutions results in the equation $0 = 0$.

The appearance of the true statement, zero equals zero, means simply, as we saw in the 2-by-2 case, that this linear combination arose from two equivalent equations. Looking back at

$$e_4: \quad 6x + 8z = 24$$
$$e_5: \quad 3x + 4z = 12$$

we see that e_4 could be divided by 2 and then would be identical to e_5. Any number pair satisfying one of these equations will satisfy the other. Moreover, any solution of the original system must satisfy these last equations. Solving either one, say e_5, for z yields

$$z = \frac{12 - 3x}{4}.$$

To repeat, any solution of the original system requires that z be related to x according to the last equation.

Returning to e_1, or any of the three original equations, and replacing z by

$$\frac{12 - 3x}{4},$$

we obtain

$$x + y + \frac{12 - 3x}{4} = 4.$$

Solving the last equation for y leads to

$$y = \frac{4 - x}{4}.$$

Both z and y have now been expressed in terms of x, and we state the **general solution** of the system as follows:

$$x \text{ arbitrary}$$

$$y = \frac{4 - x}{4}$$

$$z = \frac{12 - 3x}{4}.$$

> The solution of a 3-by-3 system with an unlimited number of solutions can be expressed as functions of one of the variables.

As with the 2-by-2 case, the general solution just written shows that the number of solutions is without limits because x may be assigned any arbitrary value whatsoever.

The general solution can be of use in actual problems to determine what conditions must be satisfied if the variables in solutions are not permitted to take on negative values. In the preceding general solution, for example, it is clear from the expressions for y and z that if x, y, and z are all to be nonnegative, then x must not exceed 4; that is, $0 \leq x \leq 4$.

The tactics of the previous example are worth reviewing. First, observation of the identity, zero equals zero, directed attention to the equations from which the statement arose. One of these equations was solved for z in terms of x. This automatically relegated x to the role of arbitrary variable, and we sought to express y also in terms of the same arbitrary variable. To do so, we returned to one of the original equations and replaced z by its x equivalent, leaving an expression that was solved for y in terms of x.

> **Exercise.** Start by eliminating z, then make y arbitrary and prove that the general solution of the system can be expressed as y arbitrary; $x = 2y + 3$; $z = y + 1$.
>
> e_1: $\quad x - 3y + z = 4$
> e_2: $\quad x - y - z = 2$
> e_3: $\quad 2x - 5y + z = 7$.

> **Exercise.** The general solution just obtained can be checked by substitution into the original equations. For example, substitution into e_1 yields
>
> $$(2y + 3) - 3y + (y + 1) = 4.$$
>
> Removing parentheses, we find the statement is the identity
>
> $$4 = 4.$$
>
> Show that substitution into e_2 and e_3 also leads to identities.

The arbitrary variable(s) in one general solution may be changed without solving the entire system again. For example, it may be verified that the general solution of

$$\begin{aligned} e_1: &\quad x + y + z = 6 \\ e_2: &\quad 4x - 2y + z = -9 \\ e_3: &\quad 3x - y + z = -4 \end{aligned}$$

= **Changing Arbitrary Variables**

can be written as

$$\begin{aligned} &x \text{ arbitrary} \\ &y = x + 5 \\ &z = 1 - 2x. \end{aligned}$$

If we wish to make y, rather than x, arbitrary, then solving the y-equation for x, we get

$$x = y - 5$$

and then obtain z by substituting into the z-equation:

$$\begin{aligned} z &= 1 - 2x \\ &= 1 - 2(y - 5) \\ &= 1 - 2y + 10 \\ z &= -2y + 11. \end{aligned}$$

The general solution now is

$$\begin{aligned} &y \text{ arbitrary} \\ &x = y - 5 \\ &z = -2y + 11. \end{aligned}$$

An unlimited solution set can be expressed as a function of any one of the variables.

> **Exercise.** Write the general solution of the preceding system with z arbitrary.
>
> **Answer:** z arbitrary; $x = (1 - z)/2$; $y = (11 - z)/2$.

2.6 PROBLEM SET 2–1

Solve the following systems of equations:

1. $x + y = 5$
   $2x + y = 7$.

2. $2x + 3y = 10$
   $3x + y = 1$.

3. $5x - 2y = 3$
   $2x + y = 3$.

4. $2x + 3y = 9$
   $4x - 2y = 2$.

5. $4x + 3y = 4$
   $2x + 6y = 5$.

6. $3x + 5y = 9$
   $4x + 2y = 5$.

7. $2x + 3y = 10$
   $3x + y = 1$
   $-5x + y = 9$.

8. $5x - 2y = 3$
   $2x + y = 3$
   $-4x + y = -3$.

9. $4x + 3y = 4$
   $2x + 6y = 5$
   $-6x + 6y = 1$.

10. $3x + 5y = 9$
    $4x + 2y = 5$
    $-4x + 2y = 1$.

11. $2x + y + 2z = 5$
    $x + y - z = 0$
    $3x - 2y + z = 1$.

12. $x - 2y + z = 7$
    $x - y + z = 4$
    $2x + y - 3z = -4$.

13. $2x + z = 5$
    $x + y = 3$
    $-y + z = 1$.

14. $2x - 5y + z = 7$
    $-3x + y - 2z = -7$
    $x + 2y + 3z = 14$.

15. $2x - 3y = 5$
    $6x - 9y = 8$.

16. $3x - 6y = 8$
    $-5x + 10y = 12$.

17. $2x + 3y = -15$
    $-(8/3)x - 4y = 25$.

18. $7x + 2y = 9$
    $17.5x + 5y = 14$.

19. $3x + 12y = -9$
    $-2x - 8y = 6$.

20. $5x + 3y = 15$
    $2x + 1.2y = 6$.

21. $2x + 3y = 15$
    $(8/3)x + 4y = 20$.

22. $6x - 15y = -3$
    $-10x + 25y = 5$.

23. $x + y + z = 10$
    $3x - y + 2z = 14$
    $2x - 2y + z = 8$.

24. $x = 4$
    $x - y - z = 7$
    $x + y + z = 2$.

25. $2x + y - 3z = 12$
    $x + 3y - 4z = 6$
    $x - 2y + z = 4$.

26. $2x - y + 2z = 5$
    $x + y + z = 2$
    $x - 2y + z = 1$.

27. $x + z = 5$
    $y + z = 3$
    $x - y = 2$.

28. $5x + y + z = 8$
    $x + 2y - z = 1$
    $2x + y = 3$.

2.6 PROBLEM SET 2-1 (concluded)

29. $2x - y + z = 5$
    $x + 4y - 3z = 2$
    $3x + 3y - 2z = 7.$

30. $x + y + z = 10$
    $3x - y + 2z = 14$
    $x - y + (1/2)z = 2.$

31. Consider the general system of two linear equations in two variables written in the form

    $a_1x + b_1y = c_1$
    $a_2x + b_2y = c_2.$

    Show by the elimination procedure that the solution to this system is

    $$x = \frac{b_2c_1 - b_1c_2}{b_2a_1 - b_1a_2}, \quad y = \frac{a_1c_2 - a_2c_1}{b_2a_1 - b_1a_2}.$$

    provided, of course, that $b_2a_1 - b_1a_2 \neq 0$. This technique is often called **Cramer's rule.**

32. Using the results of Problem 31, solve each of the systems in Problems 1 through 6.

33. Consider the QBasic program shown in Program 2-1.
    a) Describe what the program is doing line-by-line.
    b) Run the program for each of the systems in Problems 1 through 6.

    ```
    Program 2-1
    REM PROGRAM 2-1
    REM Two Linear Equations in Two
      Unknowns/Unique Solution
    CLS
    INPUT "Enter the coefficients and
        constant of Equation 1
        (a1,b1,c1)"; a1, b1, c1
    INPUT "Enter the coefficients and
        constant of Equation 2
        (a2,b2,c2)"; a2, b2, c2
    d = b2 * a1 - b1 * a2
    PRINT "The solution is x =";
        (b2 * c1 - b1 * c2) / d; " and
    y ="; (a1 * c2 - a2 * c1) / d
    ```

34. a) Modify Program 2-1 to handle the case of a 3-by-2 system that has a unique solution.
    b) Run the program in (a) for Problems 7 through 10.

35. a) Modify Program 2-1 to handle the case of a 3-by-3 system that has a unique solution.
    b) Run the program in (a) for Problems 11 through 14.

36. a) Modify Program 2-1 to handle the case of a 2-by-2 system that has no solutions.
    b) Run the program in (a) for Problems 15 through 18.

37. a) Modify Program 2-1 to handle the case of a 2-by-2 system that has an unlimited number of solutions.
    b) Run the program in (a) for Problems 19 through 22.

38. a) Modify Program 2-1 to handle the case of a 3-by-3 system that has no solutions.
    b) Run the program in (a) for Problems 23 through 26.

39. a) Modify Program 2-1 to handle the case of a 3-by-3 system that has an unlimited number of solutions.
    b) Run the program in (a) for Problems 27 through 30.

2.7 APPLICATIONS–1: MIXTURE PROBLEMS

Consider a buyer who wants to combine x liters of regular unleaded gasoline, which costs $0.30 per liter, with y liters of super unleaded gasoline, at $0.40 per liter, to obtain 2,000 liters of mixture worth $0.33 per liter. We find two equations by noting that the total number of liters is $x + y$, which must equal 2,000, and by noting that the value of x liters at $0.30 plus y liters at $0.40, which is $0.3x + 0.4y$, must equal the total value of 2,000 liters at $0.33, which is $660. Hence,

$$e_1: \quad x + y = 2000$$
$$e_2: \quad 0.3x + 0.4y = 660.$$

Eliminating x, we obtain

$$
\begin{array}{rl}
-0.3e_1: & -0.3x - 0.3y = -600 \\
e_2: & 0.3x + 0.4y = 660 \\
\hline
-0.3e_1 + e_2: & 0.1y = 60,
\end{array}
$$

so that

$$y = 600 \text{ liters},$$

and from e_1

$$x = 2{,}000 - y = 1{,}400 \text{ liters}.$$

The buyer should mix 1,400 liters of regular unleaded gasoline with 600 liters of super unleaded gasoline.

> A 2-by-2 system with one equation representing the total quantity and the other representing the total value is a mathematical model of the real application.

Exercise. We plan to invest x dollars in the bonds of Acme Company, which pay 7 percent interest, and y dollars in Star Company bonds, which pay 10 percent interest. We will invest $10,000 and require that we receive $820 interest. How much should be invested in each security?

Answer: The equations are $0.07x + 0.1y = 820$ and $x + y = 10{,}000$. The solution is $x = \$6{,}000$ and $y = \$4{,}000$.

Now let's look at a similar but more complicated mixture problem.

Example. A gasoline company wants to provide a customer with 2,000 liters of 85 octane gasoline with a vapor pressure index of 25. To do this, the supplier must mix three kinds of gasoline to form an appropriate mixture at a minimum cost. Regular unleaded gasoline costs $0.30 per liter and has an octane rating of 80 with a vapor pressure index of 30. Premium unleaded gasoline costs $0.33 per liter with an octane rating of 90 and a vapor pressure index of 20. Super unleaded gasoline costs $0.40 per liter and has an octane rating of 100 with a vapor pressure index of 10. What amount of each gasoline should be mixed?

Letting x, y, and z represent, respectively, the number of liters of regular, premium, and super, the cost function, C, is

$$C = 0.30x + 0.33y + 0.40z. \tag{1}$$

The first condition to be satisfied is that the mixture contain precisely 2,000 liters, so

$$e_1: \quad x + y + z = 2{,}000.$$

The second condition to be satisfied is that the octane rating be 85, so we get

$$80z + 90y + 100z = (85)(2{,}000)$$

or, dividing by 10,

$$e_2: \quad 8x + 9y + 10z = 17{,}000.$$

The last condition to be satisfied is that the vapor pressure index be 25, so we have

$$30x + 20y + 10z = 25(2{,}000)$$

or, again dividing by 10,

$$e_3: \quad 3x + 2y + z = 5{,}000.$$

Eliminating z from e_1, e_2, and e_3, we find

$$10e_1 - e_2 = e_4: \quad 2x + y = 3{,}000$$
$$e_1 - e_3 = e_5: \quad -2x - y = -3{,}000.$$

Now adding e_4 and e_5 we get

$$e_4 + e_5 = e_6: \quad 0 + 0 = 0$$

so that the system has an unlimited number of solutions. Letting x be arbitrary, we have from e_4

$$y = 3{,}000 - 2x$$

and then substituting into e_1

$$z = x - 1{,}000$$

x arbitrary.

Now clearly we cannot permit any of our variables to have a negative value. Inspecting the solution, we see that x can take on values from a low of 1,000 to prevent z from being negative (setting $z = 0$ yields $x = 1{,}000$) to a high of 1,500 to prevent y from being negative (setting $y = 0$ yields $x = 1{,}500$).

Our solution, then, becomes

$$1{,}000 \leq x \leq 1{,}500$$
$$y = 3{,}000 - 2x \tag{2}$$
$$z = x - 1{,}000. \tag{3}$$

Now we can express the cost function in terms of the arbitrary variable x by substituting (2) and (3) into (1). This yields

> A 3-by-3 system with one equation representing the total quantity, another representing the total octane, and the third representing the vapor index is a mathematical model of the real application.

> An unlimited number of solutions can be expressed as a function of a limited range of one of the variables.

$$C = 0.30x + 0.33(3{,}000 - 2x) + 0.40(x - 1{,}000)$$
$$= 0.30x + 990 - 0.66x + 0.40x - 400$$
$$= 0.04x + 590. \tag{4}$$

From (4) it is clear that cost increases when x increases, so to minimize cost we should use the lowest possible value of x. Because x is arbitrary in the range 1,000 to 1,500, we choose $x = 1{,}000$, and compute the corresponding values of y and z. We have

$$x = 1{,}000 \text{ liters of regular unleaded}$$
$$y = 1{,}000 \text{ liters of premium unleaded}$$
$$z = 0 \text{ liters of super unleaded}$$
$$\text{Minimum cost} = 0.04(1{,}000) + 590 = \$630.$$

> **Exercise.** a) Convert (2) and (3) of the preceding example into a solution with z arbitrary. b) What is the permissible interval for z? c) Write the cost function in terms of z. d) What value of z will minimize cost? e) What is the minimum cost?
>
> **Answer:** a) z arbitrary; $x = z + 1{,}000$; $y = 1{,}000 - 2z$. b) 0 to 500. c) Cost = $0.04z + 630$. d) $z = 0$. e) $630.

2.8 PROBLEM SET 2-2

1. If x liters of regular gasoline, which costs $0.50 per liter, are to be mixed with y liters of regular unleaded gasoline, at $0.66 per liter, to obtain 1,000 liters of mixture worth $0.60 per liter, how much of each gasoline should be used?

2. We plan to invest x dollars in Acme Company bonds, which pay 6.5 percent interest, and y dollars in Star Company bonds, which pay 9 percent interest. If $50,000 is to be invested and we require that $4,000 interest be received, how much should be invested in each bond?

3. It takes 20 minutes and costs $2 to make one double-edged razor blade, whereas it takes 30 minutes and costs $1 to make one single-edged razor blade. If 600 minutes and $40 are available, how many of each blade can be made?

4. It takes 10 minutes to make, and 20 minutes to paint, one captain's chair, whereas it takes 5 minutes to make, and 8 minutes to paint, one regular chair. If 300 minutes are available for making these products and 500 minutes are available for painting, how many of each chair can be made?

5. A mixture of pellets is to be made containing x regular pellets, y large pellets, and z extra large pellets. Cost, weight, and volume data for each type of pellet are shown in the table.

    Is it possible to make a mixture of 45 pellets at a cost of 85 cents if the mixture is to have 120 weight units and 130 volume units? If so, how many of each type of pellet should be in the mixture?

Pellet Type	Number of Pellets	Cost per Pellet in Cents	Weight Units per Pellet	Volume Units per Pellet
Regular	x	2	1	4
Large	y	3	2	2
Extra large	z	1	4	3

2.8 PROBLEM SET 2-2 (concluded)

6. Replace the volume data in the table for Problem 5 with the numbers 1.6, 2.8, and 3.6 for regular, large, and extra large pellets, respectively. Leaving the other data and the conditions of the problem unchanged, set up and solve the resultant system of equations.

7. Computer chips F, G, and H are each made using three different kinds of transistors: A, B, and C. The number of chips to be made along with their transistor requirements are shown in the table. How many of each kind could be made using all available transistors?

Chip	Number of Chips	Number of Transistors Required per Chip, by Type		
		A	B	C
F	x	1	2	2
G	y	2	7	1
H	z	1	3	1
Total transistors available		(12)	(34)	(14)

8. Solve Problem 7 if the requirement for transistor B in chip G is reduced from 7 to 6.

9. Solve Problem 7 if the requirement for transistor C in chip F is increased from 2 to 3.

10. The table shows the numbers of hours required in each of three departments to make a unit of various products named A, B, and C. For example, product B required 1 hour of time in Department I, 3 hours in Department II, and 7 hours in Department III.

   a) Find the numbers of units of A, B, and C that could be made if Department I has 75 hours available, Department II has 65 hours available, and Department III has 125 hours available.

Department	Hours Required per Unit of Product		
	A	B	C
I	1	1	9
II	1	3	7
III	2	7	13

   b) If profits per unit of A, B, and C are, respectively, $20, $30, and $40, what is the maximum profit and the composition of the maximum-profit combination of outputs?

11. Solve Problem 10(a) and (b) if Departments I and II each have 40 hours available and Department III has 80 hours available.

12. A mixture containing x pounds of macadamia nuts, y pounds of almonds, and z pounds of pecans is to be made. The mixture is to weigh 5 pounds and contain 1,500 units of vitamin and 2,500 calories. The vitamin and caloric contents of the three nuts are shown in the table.

Nut	Number of Pounds	Units of Vitamin per Pound	Calories per Pound
Macadamia	x	500	300
Almonds	y	200	600
Pecans	z	100	700

   a) Determine the number of pounds of each nut to be used in the 5-pound mixture.

   b) If the costs of nuts per pound are, respectively, $2, $3, and $1, what is the composition and cost of the minimum-cost mixture?

13. Solve Problem 12(a) and (b) if a 10-pound mixture is to be made containing 3,000 units of vitamin and 5,000 calories.

2.9 APPLICATIONS–2: SUPPLY AND DEMAND ANALYSIS

In Section 1.17, we introduced demand functions that relate the quantity of product consumers are willing and able to buy to the unit price of the product. Linear demand functions have negative slopes because demand decreases when price increases. A supply function, on the other hand, relates the quantity producers are willing and able to supply to the unit selling price of the product, and linear supply functions have positive slopes because producers increase the supply when the selling price increases. Consider Figure 2–7, which shows supply and demand functions as the straight lines labeled SS and DD, respectively. The equations are

$$e_1: \quad DD: p = -0.1q + 40 \text{ (negative slope, demand)}$$
$$e_2: \quad SS: p = 0.2q + 10 \text{ (positive slope, supply)}.$$

Point E, the intersection of DD and SS in Figure 2–7, is found by

$$\begin{array}{rl} e_1: & p + 0.1q = 40 \\ e_2: & p - 0.2q = 10 \\ \hline e_1 - e_2: & 0.3q = 30 \end{array}$$

so that

$$q = 100 \text{ units.}$$

From e_1,

$$p = -0.1(100) + 40 = \$30 \text{ per unit}$$

so we have $E(100, 30)$, the **equilibrium** point, which indicates the market price where the quantity consumers are willing and able to buy is equal to the quantity producers are willing and able to supply.

In this section, we show the effect of a change in the demand (but not the supply) function, and the effect of a change in the supply (but not the demand) function. This can be done by finding the new equilibrium point, E', after a change has

Supply and demand functions with price expressed as a function of quantity represent a mathematical model in economics.

Equilibrium occurs when supply equals demand.

FIGURE 2–7

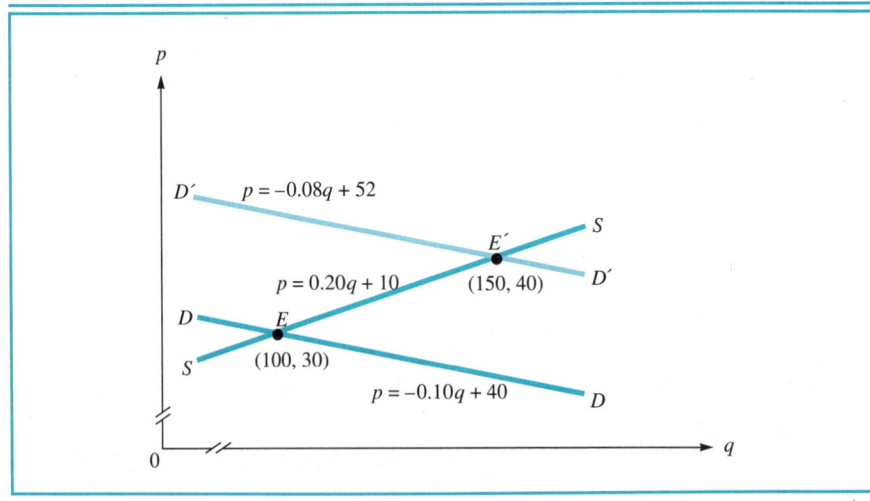

occurred. For example, suppose demand changes to the function $D'D'$ shown in Figure 2–7, with supply remaining at SS. The two functions now are

$$e_1: \quad D'D': p = -0.08q + 52$$
$$e_2: \quad SS: p = 0.2q + 10.$$

We now find

$$
\begin{array}{rl}
e_1: & p + 0.08q = 52 \\
e_2: & p - 0.2q = 10 \\
\hline
e_1 - e_2: & 0.28q = 42
\end{array}
$$

so that

$$q = 150$$

and, from e_1,

$$p = -0.08(150) + 52 = 40;$$

the new equilibrium point is $E'(150, 40)$, as shown in Figure 2–7. Comparing the equilibrium points whose coordinates are in the order (quantity, price),

$$E(100, 30) \quad \text{and} \quad E'(150, 40),$$

we see that the change in the demand function is an **increase** in demand, which results in a **higher** quantity and **higher** price at the new equilibrium. In economic terminology, the demand function shifted to the right so that a larger quantity is demanded at each price level.

The preceding discussion shows that to determine the effect of a change in a demand or supply function, we need only to compare the two equilibrium points and interpret the changes in q and p. Thus, if there is a change in a supply function, with the demand function unchanged, and the equilibrium points are

$$E(500, 15) \quad \text{and} \quad E'(400, 20),$$

the **decrease** in supply results in a lower quantity, but a **higher** price at equilibrium. Notice that in Figure 2–7, an **increase** in demand was accompanied by an **increase** in both quantity and price, so a demand change in one direction is accompanied by quantity and price changes in the **same** direction. The effect of a supply change, however, is **inverse** in the sense just illustrated. A decrease in supply lowers the quantity but increases the price, and an increase in supply will increase quantity but lower price.

> If demand changes in a certain direction, both quantity and price change in the same direction. If supply changes, quantity changes in the same direction, but price changes in the opposite direction.

Exercise. Interpret the results of the change in a supply function if the equilibrium points are $E(400, 50)$, $E'(500, 15)$.

Answer: Supply has increased, and at the new equilibrium point, quantity has increased and price has decreased.

2.10 APPLICATIONS—3: TWO-PRODUCT SUPPLY AND DEMAND ANALYSIS

Those planning to work through this section may wish to review the one-product discussion of Section 2.9. Here we consider the case of two products whose supply and demand expressions are interrelated. As an example consider the following expressions in which p_1 and q_1 are the price of product 1 and the quantity demanded of product 1, respectively, and similarly p_2 and q_2 are the price and quantity demanded for product 2.

Product	Demand	Supply
1	$p_1 = 2{,}000 - 3q_1 - 2q_2$	$p_1 = 100 + 2q_1 + q_2$
2	$p_2 = 2{,}800 - q_1 - 4q_2$	$p_2 = 200 + 3q_1 + 2q_2$

Two products with interrelated supply and demand functions give rise to two systems representing a mathematical model in economics.

To achieve equilibrium, the two price expressions for each product must be equal. Hence,

for product 1: $2{,}000 - 3q_1 - 2q_2 = 100 + 2q_1 + q_2$
for product 2: $2{,}800 - q_1 - 4q_2 = 200 + 3q_1 + 2q_2$

Rearranging the last two expressions, we have

$$e_1: \quad 5q_1 + 3q_2 = 1{,}900$$

$$e_2: \quad 4q_1 + 6q_2 = 2{,}600.$$

We obtain the equilibrium quantities supplied and demanded by solving the last pair of equations in the usual manner:

$$5e_2 - 4e_1 = e_3: \quad 18q_2 = 5{,}400.$$

Hence, $q_2 = 5{,}400/18 = 300$. Then from e_2 we find $q_1 = 200$. Using these quantities in the original supply (or demand) expressions, we find $p_1 = \$800$ and $p_2 = \$1{,}400$. The equilibrium prices and quantities are

$$E: \quad \begin{matrix} p_1 = \$800 & p_2 = \$1{,}400 \\ q_1 = 200 \text{ units} & q_2 = 300 \text{ units.} \end{matrix}$$

Now suppose the supply functions remain the same but a change occurs in the demand for product 1 and, since the two products are interrelated, there is a corresponding change in the demand for 2. Then suppose the outcomes are the new demand functions:

Product	Demand
1	$p_1 = 2{,}270 - 3q_1 - 2q_2$
2	$p_2 = 2{,}890 - q_1 - 4q_2$

Equating these new demand expressions with the corresponding original supply expressions leads to

$$5q_1 + 3q_2 = 2{,}170$$

$$4q_1 + 6q_2 = 2{,}690.$$

Solving the last pair, we find $q_1 = 275$ and $q_2 = 265$. Using these values in the new demand or the old supply expressions yields $p_1 = \$915$, $p_2 = \$1,555$. The new equilibrium is

$$E': \begin{array}{ll} p_1 = \$915 & p_2 = \$1,555 \\ q_1 = 275 \text{ units} & q_2 = 265 \text{ units}. \end{array}$$

> **Exercise.** Solve the preceding pair of equations. Then carry out the substitution necessary to verify the values at E'.

Comparing E' and E, we describe what occurred in the following manner. The demand for product 1 increased (from 200 to 275) and its price rose (from \$800 to \$915). At the same time, there was a decrease in demand for product 2 (from 300 to 265) but an increase in its price (from \$1,400 to \$1,555). To better understand these changes, let us think of product 1 as the standard model of an appliance and product 2 as the deluxe model. Then we can see that consumer response to rising prices of both appliances might well be to increase their demand for the standard model and decrease demand for the deluxe model, as was the outcome in this example. The outcome of supply and demand shifts depends on the nature of the products involved and relates directly to the constants in the mathematical expressions for supply and demand. Readers interested in pursuing this matter should refer to discussions of **complementary**, **competing** (or **substitute**), and **independent** products in economics textbooks.

The effect of supply and demand shifts depends on the model representing the economic situation.

2.11 PROBLEM SET 2-3

1. a) Graph the supply and demand functions

   $$SS: \ p = 0.1q + 8$$
   $$DD: \ p = -0.5q + 50.$$

   b) Find the equilibrium point, E, for (a).
   c) Plot the new demand function

   $$D'D': \ p = -0.6q + 36$$

   on the graph for (a).
   d) Find the new equilibrium point, E', and place its coordinates on the graph.
   e) Describe the change in the equilibrium points.

2. a) Graph the supply and demand functions

   $$SS: \ p = 0.20q + 10$$
   $$DD: \ p = -0.40q + 70.$$

   b) Find the equilibrium point, E, for (a).
   c) Plot the new supply functions

   $$S'S': \ p = 0.25q + 18$$

   on the graph for (a).
   d) Find the new equilibrium point, E', and place its coordinates on the graph.
   e) Describe the change in equilibrium points.

2.11 PROBLEM SET 2-3 (concluded)

3. (See Problem 2.) The equilibrium point for the functions in (a) is $E(100, 30)$. Find the new equilibrium point if the demand function changes to

$$D'D': \quad p = -0.44q + 90$$

and describe the change in the equilibrium points.

4. (See Problem 1.) The equilibrium point for the functions in (a) is $E(70, 15)$. Find the new equilibrium point if the supply function changes to

$$S'S': \quad p = 0.06q + 5.2$$

and describe the change in the equilibrium points.

Interpret the following supply and demand changes:

5. $E(100, 10)$ to $E'(125, 14)$ after a change in demand.
6. $E(200, 20)$ to $E'(150, 25)$ after a change in supply.
7. $E(150, 25)$ to $E'(200, 21)$ after a change in supply.
8. $E(200, 40)$ to $E'(180, 35)$ after a change in demand.
9. If either the supply or demand function (but not both) changed and the result was a shift $E(500, 15)$ to $E'(600, 10)$, which function changed? Explain why.
10. If either the supply or demand function (but not both) changed and the result was a shift from $E(500, 15)$ to $E'(400, 10)$, which function changed? Explain why.
11. The demand and supply expressions for products 1 and 2 are:

Demand	Supply
$p_1 = 1{,}000 - 5q_1 - 4q_2$	$p_1 = 90 + 2q_1 + 3q_2$
$p_2 = 900 - 2q_1 - 5q_2$	$p_2 = 120 + q_1 + 4q_2$

a) Find the prices and quantities at equilibrium.
b) If demands change to the following, with the same supply functions, find the new equilibrium point.

Product	Demand
1	$p_1 = 1{,}210 - 5q_1 - 4q_2$
2	$p_2 = 984 - 2q_1 - 5q_2$

12. The demand and supply expressions for products 1 and 2 are:

Demand	Supply
$p_1 = 1{,}500 - 4q_1 - 3q_2$	$p_1 = 400 + 3q_1 + q_2$
$p_2 = 700 - q_1 - 2q_2$	$p_2 = 200 + q_1 + q_2$

a) Find the prices and quantities at equilibrium.
b) If demands change to the following, with the same supply functions, find the new equilibrium point.

Product	Demand
1	$p_1 = 1{,}400 - 3q_1 - 3q_2$
2	$p_2 = 640 - q_1 - q_2$

2.12 MATRICES AND VECTORS

Numerical data arranged in a form that we shall come to call a matrix are very common in everyday life. For example, suppose that a company has six gasoline stations of three different types: one of each type in region 1 and in region 2. January sales volume, in thousands of gallons, is shown for each station in Table 2-1.

We note that sales of station type 1 in region 2 were 15 thousand gallons. The position of the **entry** (also called **element**) 15 is at the intersection of the first row

TABLE 2-1

Oil Company: Sales in Thousands of Gallons, January

Station Type	Region 1	Region 2
1	10	15
2	12	18
3	8	12

and second column, and we may symbolize the entry as a_{12} (read **a sub one two**)[1] where the first subscript refers to the row and the second to the column. To avoid having to specify which of a pair of subscripts specifies the row and which the column, we shall **always** use the row, column order convention.

Exercise. In Table 2-1, a) what are a_{11} and a_{32}? b) Write the symbol for the entry 8.

Answer: a) 10 and 12. b) a_{31}.

If we keep in mind that rows are station types and columns are regions, we can omit the stub and caption of the table and write the **matrix**:

Station type by region sales matrix

$$\begin{pmatrix} 10 & 15 \\ 12 & 18 \\ 8 & 12 \end{pmatrix} = \begin{pmatrix} a_{11} & a_{12} \\ a_{21} & a_{22} \\ a_{31} & a_{32} \end{pmatrix}. \quad (1)$$

Definition

A **matrix** is a rectangular array of numbers. Matrices are enclosed in grouping symbols such as parentheses or brackets.

If a matrix has m rows and n columns, the matrix is said to be of **order** m-by-n ($m \times n$) or of **dimension** m by n. Thus, a 5-by-4 matrix has the dimensions of a rectangle 5 (rows) down by 4 (columns) across.

An m-by-n matrix has m rows and n columns.

---

[1] A comma is required to avoid ambiguity if the number of rows or columns exceeds nine. For example, an entry in the 12th row, 3rd column would be $a_{12,3}$.

Matrices that have precisely one row or precisely one column are given special names.

A vector is a matrix with precisely one row or one column.

Definition

A 1-by-n matrix is called a **row vector of dimension** n. An m-by-1 matrix is called a **column vector of dimension** m.

Thus, the 1-by-3 matrix

$$(4 \quad 7 \quad 6)$$

is a row vector of dimension 3, while the 2-by-1 matrix

$$\begin{pmatrix} 5 \\ 7 \end{pmatrix}$$

is a column vector of dimension 2. The station type by region sales matrix (1) may be thought of as consisting of two column vectors, each of dimension 3, or three row vectors, each of dimension 2.

Exercise. Write the first row vector of the station type by region sales matrix (1).
Answer: (10 15).

Next, suppose Interstate Oil Company sells one grade of gasoline but, due to transportation costs, prices vary in the two regions as shown in Table 2–2.

We can represent the price matrix for Interstate Oil Company as a two-dimensional column or row vector. Thus,

Regional price vector

$$\begin{pmatrix} 1.10 \\ 1.20 \end{pmatrix} \quad \text{or} \quad (1.10 \quad 1.20). \tag{2}$$

TABLE 2–2
Interstate Oil Company: Regional Price Variation

Region	Price per Gallon
1	$1.10
2	$1.20

Finally, an *n*-by-*n* matrix has the same number of rows and columns and is called a **square matrix**. We may specify a square matrix simply by stating the order *n*. Thus, a 3-by-3 matrix is a square matrix of order 3.

2.13 MATRIX OPERATIONS

Scalar Multiplication

In matrix algebra, an ordinary number is called a **scalar**. To multiply a matrix by a scalar, we multiply each entry in the matrix by the scalar. For example,

$$12 \begin{pmatrix} 1 & 3 \\ 4 & 2 \end{pmatrix} = \begin{pmatrix} 12 & 36 \\ 48 & 24 \end{pmatrix}.$$

To see the origin of the word scalar, think of the entries 1, 3, 4, 2 in the left matrix as being in feet. Scaling these to inches requires that each entry be multiplied by 12. Similarly, Interstate Oil Company may wish to set February sales quota that are 10 percent higher than actual January sales. The February quota matrix will then be obtained by multiplying the January sales matrix by the scalar 1.1; thus,

Scalar multiplication:

$$k \begin{pmatrix} a & b \\ c & d \end{pmatrix} = \begin{pmatrix} ka & kb \\ kc & kd \end{pmatrix}$$

$$\begin{pmatrix} \text{Scaling} \\ \text{factor} \end{pmatrix} \times \begin{pmatrix} \text{January} \\ \text{sales} \end{pmatrix} = \begin{pmatrix} \text{February} \\ \text{quota} \end{pmatrix}$$

$$1.1 \begin{pmatrix} 10 & 15 \\ 12 & 18 \\ 8 & 12 \end{pmatrix} = \begin{pmatrix} 11 & 16.5 \\ 13.2 & 19.8 \\ 8.8 & 13.2 \end{pmatrix}. \quad (3)$$

Exercise. Interstate Oil Company's price vector is (1.10 1.20) in dollars per gallon. What would be the scaling factor and the resultant price vector if prices are to be in dollars per 1,000 gallons?
Answer: The scaling factor is 1,000. Hence, 1,000 (1.10 1.20) = (1,100 1,200).

Addition and Subtraction of Matrices

Matrices are added or subtracted by adding or subtracting **corresponding** entries. Since entries must correspond, the matrices involved must have the same dimensions. We cannot compute

$$\begin{pmatrix} 3 & 1 & 5 \\ 2 & 4 & 7 \end{pmatrix} + \begin{pmatrix} 5 & 2 \\ -3 & 6 \end{pmatrix}$$

because the first matrix is 2 by 3 and the second is 2 by 2. However,

$$\begin{pmatrix} 3 & 1 \\ 2 & 4 \end{pmatrix} + \begin{pmatrix} 5 & -6 \\ 2 & 0 \end{pmatrix} = \begin{pmatrix} 8 & -5 \\ 4 & 4 \end{pmatrix}$$

and

$$\begin{pmatrix} 5 & 8 \\ -1 & 3 \end{pmatrix} - 2 \begin{pmatrix} 1 & 0 \\ 3 & -2 \end{pmatrix} = \begin{pmatrix} 5 & 8 \\ -1 & 3 \end{pmatrix} - \begin{pmatrix} 2 & 0 \\ 6 & -4 \end{pmatrix} = \begin{pmatrix} 3 & 8 \\ -7 & 7 \end{pmatrix}.$$

Matrix addition (subtraction): Add (subtract) corresponding entries.

> **Exercise.** Compute
> $$3\begin{pmatrix} 4 & -1 \\ 2 & 5 \end{pmatrix} - 2\begin{pmatrix} 1 & 2 \\ -3 & 4 \end{pmatrix}.$$
>
> **Answer:** $\begin{pmatrix} 10 & -7 \\ 12 & 7 \end{pmatrix}.$

Returning to the affairs of Interstate Oil Company, recall its February sales quota matrix, (3). This is the middle matrix in the following. The left is the new matrix, (4) of **actual** February sales, and the difference between (3) and (4) appears in matrix (5), which shows the deviation of actual February sales from quota.

$$\begin{array}{ccc} (4) & (3) & (5) \\ \textit{February sales} & - \textit{February quota} & = \textit{Deviation from quota} \end{array}$$

$$\begin{pmatrix} 12 & 15.5 \\ 13 & 20 \\ 8.5 & 12.9 \end{pmatrix} - \begin{pmatrix} 11 & 16.5 \\ 13.2 & 19.8 \\ 8.8 & 13.2 \end{pmatrix} = \begin{pmatrix} 1 & -1 \\ -0.2 & 0.2 \\ -0.3 & -0.3 \end{pmatrix}.$$

From (5) we see, for example, that station type 1, region 2 sales were 1,000 gallons below quota.

> **Exercise.** In (5), interpret the entry a_{21}.
>
> **Answer:** Station type 2, region 1 sales were 0.2 thousand gallons below quota.

Two important properties of matrix addition are the **commutative** and **associative laws**.

> $$A + B = B + A \qquad \text{Commutative law}$$
> $$A + (B + C) = (A + B) + C \qquad \text{Associative law}$$

The commutative and associative laws of matrix addition follow from the corresponding laws of ordinary numbers.

These laws are valid for matrix addition because addition of matrices is accomplished by adding corresponding entries, and the commutative and associative laws hold for ordinary numbers. For example, we saw that

$$\begin{pmatrix} 3 & 1 \\ 2 & 4 \end{pmatrix} + \begin{pmatrix} 5 & -6 \\ 2 & 0 \end{pmatrix} = \begin{pmatrix} 8 & -5 \\ 4 & 4 \end{pmatrix},$$

and if we commute these matrices the result remains the same:

$$\begin{pmatrix} 5 & -6 \\ 2 & 0 \end{pmatrix} + \begin{pmatrix} 3 & 1 \\ 2 & 4 \end{pmatrix} = \begin{pmatrix} 8 & -5 \\ 4 & 4 \end{pmatrix}.$$

Just as with ordinary numbers, the associative law allows us to drop the parentheses and simply write $A + B + C$.

> **Exercise.** Compute $A + (B + C)$ and $(A + B) + C$ for
>
> $$A = \begin{pmatrix} 3 & 1 \\ 2 & 4 \end{pmatrix}, B = \begin{pmatrix} 5 & -6 \\ 2 & 0 \end{pmatrix}, \text{ and } C = \begin{pmatrix} 7 & 1 \\ -8 & 9 \end{pmatrix}.$$
>
> **Answer:** $\begin{pmatrix} 15 & -4 \\ -4 & 13 \end{pmatrix}.$

One special matrix is the **zero matrix**, in which all of the entries are zeros. For example,

$$\begin{pmatrix} 0 & 0 & 0 \\ 0 & 0 & 0 \end{pmatrix}$$

is a 2-by-3 zero matrix. Using O to denote the zero matrix, it is clear that O behaves like the number 0 in ordinary arithmetic. So we have the **identity law** for matrix addition:

> $A + O = A.$ Identity law

The identity law holds for matrix addition; i.e., $A + O = A.$

Of course, we also have the usual properties

$$A - O = A \quad \text{and} \quad O - A = -A,$$

where $-A$ means the matrix $(-1)A$. For example

$$\begin{pmatrix} 0 & 0 & 0 \\ 0 & 0 & 0 \end{pmatrix} - \begin{pmatrix} 2 & 3 & 4 \\ 5 & 2 & -3 \end{pmatrix} = \begin{pmatrix} -2 & -3 & -4 \\ -5 & -2 & 3 \end{pmatrix}.$$

Matrix multiplication is a specialized form of multiplication devised for very practical reasons. Consider the following:

= **Matrix Multiplication**

$$(3 \quad 2) \begin{pmatrix} 5 \\ 4 \end{pmatrix} = 23.$$

Inner product: A row vector times a column vector (same dimensions) resulting in a scalar.

We obtain the product, 23, as the sum of $3 \cdot 5 + 2 \cdot 4$. To fix this in mind, we may place our left index finger on the 3 and our right index finger on the 5. Multiply to obtain 15. Then move the **left finger across** to the 2 and the **right finger down** to the 4, multiply to obtain 8, then add this to 15 to get 23. A product obtained in this manner is called the **inner product.** Observe that the inner product of a row vector by a column vector is an ordinary number, a scalar. As another example,

$$(2 \quad -3 \quad 1 \quad 0) \begin{pmatrix} 4 \\ -2 \\ 3 \\ -1 \end{pmatrix} = 2(4) - 3(-2) + 1(3) + 0(-1)$$

$$= 8 + 6 + 3 + 0 = 17.$$

Exercise. Evaluate

$$(3 \quad -1) \begin{pmatrix} 4 \\ 2 \end{pmatrix}.$$

Answer: 10.

Now suppose we want to multiply two matrices in the general case where the matrices are not simply vectors. What we do is extend the scheme for the inner product of a row vector times a column vector. One obvious stipulation for using the **left finger across, right finger down** technique of the inner product is that there must be as many numbers across the first matrix as there are down the second matrix. That is, the first matrix must have as many columns as the second has rows. In our last example, we had a 1-by-4 matrix multiplied by a 4-by-1 matrix. If we indicate this as (1-by-4) · (4-by-1), observe that the two middle numbers are the same, 4. When the dimensions of two matrices are indicated in this manner and the middle numbers are the same, the two are said to be **conformable for multiplication**. Alternatively, we may say that two matrices are conformable for multiplication if the number of columns in the first is the same as the number of rows in the second. In the next example, we multiply a (2 by 2) and a (2 by 3).

Conformable for multiplication: The number of columns in the first matrix is the same as the number of rows in the second matrix.

$$\begin{pmatrix} 1 & 2 \\ 3 & 4 \end{pmatrix} \begin{pmatrix} 5 & 6 & 7 \\ 8 & 9 & 10 \end{pmatrix} = \begin{pmatrix} 21 & 24 & 27 \\ 47 & 54 & 61 \end{pmatrix}.$$

The calculations leading to the rightmost matrix are:

First row: $1(5) + 2(8) = 21$
$1(6) + 2(9) = 24$
$1(7) + 2(10) = 27.$
Second row: $3(5) + 4(8) = 47$
$3(6) + 4(9) = 54$
$3(7) + 4(10) = 61.$

> **Exercise.** Compute the following product:
>
> $$\begin{pmatrix} 1 & 2 & 3 \\ 4 & 5 & 6 \end{pmatrix} \begin{pmatrix} 0 & 1 \\ 2 & 3 \\ 4 & 5 \end{pmatrix}.$$
>
> **Answer:** $\begin{pmatrix} 16 & 22 \\ 34 & 49 \end{pmatrix}.$

Next let us take a look at how matrix multiplication might be put to use. Recall that the January gallons-sold matrix (entries in thousands of gallons) for the Interstate Oil Company was

$$\begin{array}{c} \text{Station} \\ \text{Type} \\ 1 \\ 2 \\ 3 \end{array} \begin{array}{c} \text{Region} \\ 1 \quad 2 \\ \begin{pmatrix} 10 & 15 \\ 12 & 18 \\ 8 & 12 \end{pmatrix}. \end{array}$$

Suppose that the price per thousand gallons vector is

$$\begin{array}{c} \\ \\ \text{Region} \\ 1 \\ 2 \end{array} \begin{array}{c} \text{Dollars per} \\ \text{Thousand} \\ \text{Gallons} \\ \begin{pmatrix} 1{,}100 \\ 1{,}200 \end{pmatrix}. \end{array}$$

Since the gallons-sold matrix is 3 by 2 and the price per thousand gallons vector is 2 b 1, they are conformable and can be multiplied to get

$$\begin{array}{c} \text{Station} \\ \text{Type} \\ 1 \\ 2 \\ 3 \end{array} \begin{array}{c} \text{Total Dollar Volume} \\ \text{of Sales by Station Type} \\ \begin{pmatrix} 10(1{,}100) + 15(1{,}200) \\ 12(1{,}100) + 18(1{,}200) \\ 8(1{,}100) + 12(1{,}200) \end{pmatrix} = \begin{pmatrix} \$29{,}000 \\ \$34{,}800 \\ \$23{,}200 \end{pmatrix}. \end{array}$$

Thus, if Mr. Jones owns both type 1 stations, his dollar volume of sales is computed from 10,000 gallons at $1,100 per thousand in region 1, plus 15,000 gallons at $1,200 per thousand in region 2 for a total of $29,000 in both regions. Similarly, type 2 stations gross $34,800 and type 3 stations gross $23,200. Hence, the product matrix represents gross revenues by station type, enabling us to compare revenues by type of station.

We saw that matrix addition has the associative and commutative properties of ordinary algebra. On the other hand, matrix multiplication has the associative property but the **commutative property does not hold in general for matrix multiplication.** Thus, it is possible that

$$A \cdot B \neq B \cdot A,$$

A commutative law for matrix multiplication does not hold.

PART I   LINEAR RELATIONSHIPS AND CONSTRAINED OPTIMIZATION

but it is always true that

> **An associative law for matrix multiplication does hold.**
>
> $A \cdot (B \cdot C) = (A \cdot B) \cdot C = A \cdot B \cdot C.$ Associative law

For example,

$$\begin{pmatrix} 1 & 2 \\ 3 & 4 \end{pmatrix} \begin{pmatrix} 5 & 6 \\ 7 & 8 \end{pmatrix} = \begin{pmatrix} 19 & 22 \\ 43 & 50 \end{pmatrix},$$

but if we interchange the matrices on the left we find

$$\begin{pmatrix} 5 & 6 \\ 7 & 8 \end{pmatrix} \begin{pmatrix} 1 & 2 \\ 3 & 4 \end{pmatrix} = \begin{pmatrix} 23 & 34 \\ 31 & 46 \end{pmatrix}.$$

Thus, if we **premultiply** (multiply on the left) by

$$\begin{pmatrix} 1 & 2 \\ 3 & 4 \end{pmatrix}$$

we get one result, but if we **postmultiply** (multiply on the right) by the same matrix we get a different result.

> **Exercise.** What do we obtain if we:
>
> a) Premultiply $\begin{pmatrix} 1 \\ 2 \end{pmatrix}$ by $(3 \quad 4)$?
>
> b) Postmultiply $\begin{pmatrix} 1 \\ 2 \end{pmatrix}$ by $(3 \quad 4)$?
>
> **Answer:**   a) 11.   b) $\begin{pmatrix} 3 & 4 \\ 6 & 8 \end{pmatrix}$.

We **can** design matrices that commute with each other in multiplication. For example,

$$\begin{pmatrix} 1 & 0 \\ 0 & 1 \end{pmatrix} \begin{pmatrix} 2 & 3 \\ 4 & 5 \end{pmatrix} = \begin{pmatrix} 2 & 3 \\ 4 & 5 \end{pmatrix} \begin{pmatrix} 1 & 0 \\ 0 & 1 \end{pmatrix} = \begin{pmatrix} 2 & 3 \\ 4 & 5 \end{pmatrix}.$$

However, as we have seen, the commutative property does not hold in general. On the other hand,

$$\begin{pmatrix} 1 & 2 \\ -2 & -1 \end{pmatrix} \left[\begin{pmatrix} 1 & 2 \\ 3 & 4 \end{pmatrix} \begin{pmatrix} 5 & 6 \\ 7 & 8 \end{pmatrix} \right] = \begin{pmatrix} 1 & 2 \\ -2 & -1 \end{pmatrix} \begin{pmatrix} 19 & 22 \\ 43 & 50 \end{pmatrix}$$

$$= \begin{pmatrix} 105 & 122 \\ -81 & -94 \end{pmatrix}$$

and

$$\left[\begin{pmatrix} 1 & 2 \\ -2 & -1 \end{pmatrix} \begin{pmatrix} 1 & 2 \\ 3 & 4 \end{pmatrix}\right] \begin{pmatrix} 5 & 6 \\ 7 & 8 \end{pmatrix} = \begin{pmatrix} 23 & 34 \\ 31 & 46 \end{pmatrix} \begin{pmatrix} 5 & 6 \\ 7 & 8 \end{pmatrix}$$

$$= \begin{pmatrix} 105 & 122 \\ -81 & -94 \end{pmatrix}.$$

PRE-multiply A by B → (B)(A)
POST-multiply A by B → (A)(B)

Here the two results are the same, and this will always be the case.

We repeat the suggestion that an *m*-by-*n* matrix can be postmultiplied by an *n*-by-*p* matrix (they are conformable), and the result will be an *m*-by-*p* matrix. Thus, we can postmultiply a 5-by-8 matrix by an 8-by-11 matrix, and the product matrix will be 5 by 11.

Exercise. a) What will be the dimensions of the product matrix if a 5-by-7 is postmultiplied by a 7-by-6? b) What happens if we premultiply the 5-by-7 by the 7-by-6?
Answer: a) 5-by-6. b) The matrices are not conformable for multiplication.

Of course, as the reader would expect, any matrix postmultiplied or premultiplied by the zero matrix results in the zero matrix. Thus,

The product of any matrix and the zero matrix is the zero matrix.

$$A \cdot O = O \cdot A = O.$$

2.14 THE IDENTITY MATRIX

An **identity** or **unit matrix** is a square matrix with 1 as the element in each position on the main diagonal (upper left to lower right) and 0 as the element in all other positions. Thus,

$$I = \begin{pmatrix} 1 & 0 & 0 \\ 0 & 1 & 0 \\ 0 & 0 & 1 \end{pmatrix}$$

is a 3-by-3 identity matrix or **the** identity matrix of order 3. We can call it **the** identity matrix since there is precisely one unit matrix for each square order.

The identity matrix of order 2 is

$$I = \begin{pmatrix} 1 & 0 \\ 0 & 1 \end{pmatrix}.$$

The most important property of the identity matrix is illustrated by the statements

$$A \cdot I = A \quad \text{and} \quad I \cdot A = A.$$

The role of the identity matrix is analogous to the role of the number 1.

That is, the product of any given matrix and the conformable identity matrix is the given matrix itself. Thus, the identity matrix behaves in matrix multiplication like the number 1 in ordinary arithmetic, where we say

$$(a)(1) = (1)(a) = a.$$

The reader may verify the unity property of I by carrying out the following multiplication, in which the first written matrix, I, when multiplied by the second matrix, yields the second matrix as the product:

$$\begin{pmatrix} 1 & 0 & 0 \\ 0 & 1 & 0 \\ 0 & 0 & 1 \end{pmatrix} \begin{pmatrix} 2 & 3 & 4 \\ -1 & -2 & 0 \\ 5 & 2 & -3 \end{pmatrix} = \begin{pmatrix} 2 & 3 & 4 \\ -1 & -2 & 0 \\ 5 & 2 & -3 \end{pmatrix}.$$

Exercise. Given

$$A = \begin{pmatrix} 2 & 3 & 4 \\ 5 & 2 & -3 \end{pmatrix},$$

verify that $A \cdot I = A$ and that $I \cdot A = A$. What is the dimension of the I matrices?
Answer: To postmultiply, I is 3-by-3; to premultiply, I is 2-by-2.

2.15 PROBLEM SET 2–4

Perform the following operations:

1. $(2 \quad 3 \quad 4) + (1 \quad -2 \quad 3)$.

2. $\begin{pmatrix} 1 \\ -3 \end{pmatrix} + \begin{pmatrix} -3 \\ 5 \end{pmatrix}$.

3. $\begin{pmatrix} 2 \\ 4 \end{pmatrix} + \begin{pmatrix} 5 \\ 7 \end{pmatrix} + \begin{pmatrix} 3 \\ 2 \end{pmatrix}$.

4. $(6 \quad -1 \quad 2) - (3 \quad -2 \quad 4) + (5 \quad -1 \quad 6)$.

5. $3 \begin{pmatrix} 7 \\ 2 \end{pmatrix}$.

6. $-2(5 \quad -9 \quad 3)$.

7. $(2 \quad 7) \begin{pmatrix} 3 \\ 5 \end{pmatrix}$.

8. $(1 \quad -3 \quad 6 \quad 2) \begin{pmatrix} 2 \\ 1 \\ 2 \\ -3 \end{pmatrix}$.

9. $\begin{pmatrix} 3 & 1 & 2 \\ 1 & 4 & 1 \end{pmatrix} + \begin{pmatrix} 1 & -5 & -2 \\ -3 & 2 & 4 \end{pmatrix}$.

2.15 PROBLEM SET 2-4 (continued)

10. $\begin{pmatrix} 4 & 7 \\ 1 & 3 \end{pmatrix} + \begin{pmatrix} 1 & -2 \\ 6 & -3 \end{pmatrix} - \begin{pmatrix} 2 & -4 \\ 5 & 7 \end{pmatrix}.$

11. $4\begin{pmatrix} 1 & -3 & 2 \\ 5 & 1 & -3 \end{pmatrix} - 3\begin{pmatrix} 2 & 5 & -3 \\ 1 & 2 & -1 \end{pmatrix}.$

12. $\begin{pmatrix} 1 & 2 \\ 3 & 5 \end{pmatrix}\begin{pmatrix} 3 & 0 & 5 \\ 1 & -2 & 0 \end{pmatrix}.$

13. $(5 \; 6 \; 7)\begin{pmatrix} 1 & 2 \\ 0 & 3 \\ 3 & 1 \end{pmatrix}.$

14. $\begin{pmatrix} 3 & 0 \\ -5 & 4 \end{pmatrix}\begin{pmatrix} 1 & 6 \\ 2 & 0 \end{pmatrix}.$

15. $\begin{pmatrix} 2 & 1 & 1 & 0 \\ 1 & 3 & 0 & 2 \\ -1 & -2 & 1 & 4 \end{pmatrix}\begin{pmatrix} 5 & 6 \\ 1 & 1 \\ 2 & 3 \\ 0 & -1 \end{pmatrix}.$

16. $\begin{pmatrix} 1 & -1 & 2 \\ 2 & 0 & 3 \end{pmatrix}\begin{pmatrix} 4 & 0 & 1 & 2 \\ -1 & 3 & 0 & 2 \\ 1 & 1 & 2 & 3 \end{pmatrix}.$

17. $\begin{pmatrix} 1 & 0 & 0 \\ 0 & 1 & 0 \\ 0 & 0 & 1 \end{pmatrix}\begin{pmatrix} 1 & 4 \\ 2 & 5 \\ 3 & 6 \end{pmatrix}.$

18. $\begin{pmatrix} 1 & 2 & 3 \\ 3 & 2 & 1 \end{pmatrix}\begin{pmatrix} 1 & 0 & 0 \\ 0 & 1 & 0 \\ 0 & 0 & 1 \end{pmatrix}.$

19. Given the following matrices:

$A = \begin{pmatrix} 4 & -2 \\ 1 & 8 \end{pmatrix} \quad B = \begin{pmatrix} 6 & 7 \\ 11 & 2 \end{pmatrix}$

$C = \begin{pmatrix} 5 & -1 & 9 \\ 6 & 0 & -11 \end{pmatrix} \quad D = \begin{pmatrix} 12 & 7 & 15 \\ 10 & 24 & 8 \end{pmatrix},$

find a) $6A - 5B$.   c) AB.   e) $AC + BD$.
b) $-3C + 2D$.   d) BA.   f) $CA + BD$.

20. Given the following matrices:

$A = \begin{pmatrix} -6 & 7 & 11 \\ 1 & 12 & 2 \\ 10 & -4 & -8 \end{pmatrix} \quad B = \begin{pmatrix} 20 & 15 & 5 \\ 6 & 8 & 10 \\ -4 & 3 & -1 \end{pmatrix}$

$C = \begin{pmatrix} 0 & -6 & 2 \\ 4 & -7 & 4 \\ 6 & 0 & -5 \end{pmatrix} \quad D = \begin{pmatrix} 5 & 8 & -7 \\ 6 & 3 & 2 \\ 15 & 12 & -4 \end{pmatrix}$

find a) $3A - 2B$.   c) AB.   e) $AC + BD$.
b) $-4C + 5D$.   d) BA.   f) $CA + DB$.

21. Interest at the rates 0.06, 0.07, and 0.08 is earned on respective investments of $3,000, $2,000, and $4,000.
   a) Express the total amount of interest earned as the product of a row vector by a column vector.
   b) Compute the total interest by matrix multiplication.

22. Two canned meat spreads, Regular and Superior, are made by grinding beef, pork, and lamb together. The numbers of pounds of each meat in a 15-pound batch of each brand are as follows:

	Pounds of		
Brand	Beef	Pork	Lamb
Superior	8	2	5
Regular	4	8	3

   a) Suppose we wish to make 10 batches of Superior and 20 of Regular. Multiply the meat matrix in the table and the batch vector (10 20) and interpret the result.
   b) Suppose that the per pound prices of beef, pork, and lamb are $2.50, $2.00, and $3.00, respectively. Multiply the price vector and the meat matrix and interpret the results.

23. Three jewelry salespeople each regularly buy a certain quantity of watches, rings, necklaces, and earrings from their respective wholesale supplier and sell certain other quantities of each item to a retailer. Their respective buying and selling transactions during a particular month are given by the following vectors:

$B_1 = (10 \; 20 \; 30 \; 40) \quad B_2 = (15 \; 25 \; 35 \; 45) \quad B_3 = (20 \; 10 \; 45 \; 35)$
$S_1 = (8 \; 20 \; 25 \; 35) \quad S_2 = (15 \; 20 \; 30 \; 40) \quad S_3 = (15 \; 10 \; 40 \; 35)$

where the first entry in each vector represents the number of watches, the second entry the number of

2.15 PROBLEM SET 2-4 (concluded)

rings, the third entry the number of necklaces, the fourth entry the number of sets of earrings. The buying prices were $50 per watch, $40 per ring, $25 per necklace, and $10 per set of earrings; whereas the selling prices were, respectively, $75, $55, $30, and $15.

a) Write the buying prices as a column vector B and the selling prices as a column vector S.
b) Find the amount of revenue each salesperson expended in buying.
c) Find the amount of revenue each salesperson collected in selling.
d) Find the amount of profit each salesperson realized (assuming, for simplicity, that the unsold jewelry cannot be returned or otherwise sold).

24. Ace Construction Company builds two kinds of driveways: asphalt and concrete. For a typical home, an asphalt driveway requires 2 tons of asphalt and 3 tons of gravel, whereas a concrete driveway requires 1 yard of concrete and 4 tons of gravel. Each ton of asphalt costs $50, each ton of gravel costs $25, and each yard of concrete costs $30. During the current month, it is expected that 100 asphalt driveways and 75 concrete driveways will be built.

a) Write the quantities of driveways to be build as a matrix.
b) Write the amounts of materials to be used per driveway as a matrix.
c) Write the materials costs as a matrix.
d) Using matrix multiplication, determine the total expected materials costs.

2.16 ROW OPERATIONS AND THE INVERSE OF A MATRIX

Recall in Section 2.4 that the elimination procedure for solving systems of linear equations utilized three **row operations**. This terminology arises from the fact that these operations usually appear as operations on the rows of a matrix. To better understand the connection between equations and matrices, let us look at the system of equations

$$\begin{aligned} e_1: & \quad 2x + 3y = 2 \\ e_2: & \quad 5x + 4y = 12 \end{aligned} \qquad (1)$$

from the first example of Section 2.4. Now, we will show how to express this system of equations in matrix form.

First, we see that the left side of e_1 can be written as the matrix product:

$$(2 \quad 3) \begin{pmatrix} x \\ y \end{pmatrix}. \qquad (2)$$

> **Exercise.** Using matrix multiplication from Section 2.13, show that (2) is the same as the left side of e_1.

In the same way, the left side of e_2 can be written as the matrix product

$$(5 \quad 4)\begin{pmatrix} x \\ y \end{pmatrix}. \tag{3}$$

Putting (2) and (3) together, we see that the left side of (1) can be written as the matrix product

$$\begin{pmatrix} 2 & 3 \\ 5 & 4 \end{pmatrix} \begin{pmatrix} x \\ y \end{pmatrix}. \tag{4}$$

The first matrix in (4) is the matrix of coefficients of (1), while the second is the matrix (vector) of unknowns. To complete the system in (1), we need to add to (4) the matrix (vector) of constants that appear on the right side of (1). Doing this, we get the matrix equation

$$\begin{pmatrix} 2 & 3 \\ 5 & 4 \end{pmatrix} \begin{pmatrix} x \\ y \end{pmatrix} = \begin{pmatrix} 2 \\ 12 \end{pmatrix}. \tag{5}$$

Note that when we multiply the left side of (5), we get

$$\begin{pmatrix} 2x + 3y \\ 5x + 4y \end{pmatrix} = \begin{pmatrix} 2 \\ 12 \end{pmatrix}$$

A system of equations can be represented by a matrix equation.

and, equating the first and second rows on both sides, we have precisely the original system of equations:

$$\begin{aligned} 2x + 3y &= 2 \\ 5x + 4y &= 12. \end{aligned} \tag{1}$$

Thus, each row of the matrix equation (5) represents the corresponding equation in the system of equations (1). From this example, we see that **row operations on the equations of a linear system are simply operations on the rows of the corresponding matrix equation.**

In summary, then, if we transform the row operations from Section 2.3 to the context of matrices, we have

---

Matrix Row Operations

1. Multiply or divide a row by a nonzero constant.
2. Add a multiple of one row to a multiple of another row.
3. Interchange two rows.

> **Exercise.** What row operation performed on
> $$\begin{pmatrix} 2 & 5 \\ 6 & 13 \end{pmatrix}$$
> will lead to another matrix that will have a 0 in place of the 6? What will the new matrix be?
>
> **Answer:** Multiply the first row of the given matrix by -3 and add to the second row, obtaining
> $$\begin{pmatrix} 2 & 5 \\ 0 & -2 \end{pmatrix}.$$

The Inverse of a Matrix

Any number times its multiplicative inverse equals 1.

In ordinary algebra, we have

$$a(a^{-1}) = (a^1)(a^{-1}) = a^{1-1} = a^0 = 1.$$

Thus,

$$aa^{-1} = 1,$$

and a^{-1} is called the **multiplicative inverse** of a because the product of a and a^{-1} is the identity. For example, 3^{-1} is the inverse of 3 because

$$3(3^{-1}) = 3 \cdot \frac{1}{3} = 1.$$

In matrix algebra, we have an analogous operation illustrated by

$$\begin{pmatrix} 3 & 2 \\ 1 & 1 \end{pmatrix} \begin{pmatrix} 1 & -2 \\ -1 & 3 \end{pmatrix} = \begin{pmatrix} 1 & 0 \\ 0 & 1 \end{pmatrix} = I.$$

That is, the product of the matrices at the left is the identity matrix I of order 2. If we call the leftmost matrix, A, that is,

$$A = \begin{pmatrix} 3 & 2 \\ 1 & 1 \end{pmatrix},$$

we define the second matrix as the **multiplicative inverse**, A^{-1}, and write

$$A^{-1} = \begin{pmatrix} 1 & -2 \\ -1 & 3 \end{pmatrix}.$$

Thus,

$$\begin{pmatrix} 3 & 2 \\ 1 & 1 \end{pmatrix} \cdot \begin{pmatrix} 1 & -2 \\ -1 & 3 \end{pmatrix} = I$$

$$A \quad \cdot \quad A^{-1} \quad = I.$$

Any matrix times its multiplicative inverse equals the identity matrix.

Definition

Two square matrices are inverses of each other if their product is the identity matrix, I.

Observe that the definition says **inverses of each other.** This means that either matrix can be called A and the other is A^{-1} or, more to the point, we may write the product as AA^{-1} or $A^{-1}A$ and still obtain

$$AA^{-1} = A^{-1}A = I.$$

Hence, any two square matrices that are inverses of one another will satisfy the rule of commutativity of multiplication.

For example, in the preceding, we have

$$A^{-1}A = \begin{pmatrix} 1 & -2 \\ -1 & 3 \end{pmatrix}\begin{pmatrix} 3 & 2 \\ 1 & 1 \end{pmatrix} = \begin{pmatrix} 1 & 0 \\ 0 & 1 \end{pmatrix} = I.$$

Exercise. Verify that the following matrices are inverses of each other:

$$\begin{pmatrix} 13 & 3 \\ 4 & 1 \end{pmatrix} \text{ and } \begin{pmatrix} 1 & -3 \\ -4 & 13 \end{pmatrix}.$$

We shall see later than not every square matrix has an inverse. However, if the inverse of A does exist, it is unique: that is, a matrix that has an inverse has exactly one inverse.[2]

We are now ready to present a method for computing the inverse of a given square matrix, if one exists. After we have learned the computational procedures, we shall discover that they are directly applicable to the solution of n-by-n systems of linear

= Gauss-Jordan Inversion

---

[2] The following is a simple proof: Suppose that the matrix A has two inverses: B and C. Then,
$$C = CI = C(AB) = (CA)B = IB = B.$$

equations. We present first the method attributed to Gauss and Jordan, which is the method we shall use as we continue our work.

Briefly, the Gauss-Jordan method starts by writing the given matrix at the left, and the corresponding identity matrix next to it, at the right. Then select and carry out the matrix row operations on page 111 that will convert the given matrix into the identity matrix, and **apply the same operations to the matrix at the right.** When the left (given) matrix becomes the identity matrix, the matrix on the right will be the desired inverse.

To illustrate this method, let us find the inverse of our earlier matrix[3]

$$A = \begin{pmatrix} 3 & 2 \\ 1 & 1 \end{pmatrix}.$$

> The Gauss-Jordan method for finding A^{-1} transforms the augmented matrix $(A \mid I)$ into the augmented matrix $(I \mid A^{-1})$.

We start by writing the given matrix to the left and the index matrix to the right, thus getting the **augmented matrix $(A \mid I)$**,

$$\begin{pmatrix} 3 & 2 & | & 1 & 0 \\ 1 & 1 & | & 0 & 1 \end{pmatrix}.$$

To change the left matrix A into the identity matrix I will require several steps (row operations that we perform on both matrices). We start by getting a 1 in the upper left corner. This could be accomplished by dividing the first row by 3. However, to avoid fractions and thus simplify the arithmetic, we simply interchange the first and second rows to obtain

$$\begin{pmatrix} 1 & 1 & | & 0 & 1 \\ 3 & 2 & | & 1 & 0 \end{pmatrix}.$$

Next, we get a 0 in the second row, first column of the left matrix by multiplying the new first row by -3 and adding it to the second row. We then have

$$\begin{pmatrix} 1 & 1 & | & 0 & 1 \\ 0 & -1 & | & 1 & -3 \end{pmatrix}$$

so that the first column of the left matrix is the first column of an identity matrix. Now we transform the second column of the new left matrix. First, we divide the second row by -1 to obtain a 1 in the second row, second column of the left matrix. Thus,

$$\begin{pmatrix} 1 & 1 & | & 0 & 1 \\ 0 & 1 & | & -1 & 3 \end{pmatrix}.$$

---

[3] Although simpler methods such as Cramer's Rule exist to find the inverse of a 2-by-2 matrix, the purpose of this example is to illustrate and develop the method with fewer computations than a larger square matrix would need.

Finally, multiply the new second row by -1 and add to the first to obtain a 0 in the first row, second column of the left matrix. This gives

$$\begin{pmatrix} 1 & 0 & | & 1 & -2 \\ 0 & 1 & | & -1 & 3 \end{pmatrix}$$

which completes the transformation to the identity matrix on the left. This augmented matrix is $(I \mid A^{-1})$, so the inverse of

$$A = \begin{pmatrix} 3 & 2 \\ 1 & 1 \end{pmatrix}$$

is the matrix at the right; namely,

$$A^{-1} = \begin{pmatrix} 1 & -2 \\ -1 & 3 \end{pmatrix}$$

which is precisely the same result as we found earlier.

Exercise. Apply the procedure of the previous example and find the inverse of the matrix

$$A = \begin{pmatrix} 7 & 3 \\ 2 & 1 \end{pmatrix}.$$

Answer: The inverse is the matrix

$$A^{-1} = \begin{pmatrix} 1 & -3 \\ -2 & 7 \end{pmatrix}.$$

In doing the exercise, interchanging of rows to avoid fractions was of no use. Another situation, where interchange is useful, occurs when the matrix is in a form that does not lend itself easily to the inversion process. For example, in

$$\begin{pmatrix} 0 & 1 & | & 1 & 0 \\ 2 & 3 & | & 0 & 1 \end{pmatrix}$$

we have an unwanted zero as the upper left diagonal element. Interchanging rows, we have

$$\begin{pmatrix} 2 & 3 & | & 0 & 1 \\ 0 & 1 & | & 1 & 0 \end{pmatrix}.$$

We can now proceed to the inverse in the usual manner. Thus, add -3 times row 2 to row 1:

$$\begin{pmatrix} 2 & 0 & | & -3 & 1 \\ 0 & 1 & | & 1 & 0 \end{pmatrix}.$$

Then, divide the first row by 2:

$$\begin{pmatrix} 1 & 0 & | & -3/2 & 1/2 \\ 0 & 1 & | & 1 & 0 \end{pmatrix}$$

and we have that

$$\text{if } A = \begin{pmatrix} 0 & 1 \\ 2 & 3 \end{pmatrix}, \text{ then } A^{-1} = \begin{pmatrix} -3/2 & 1/2 \\ 1 & 0 \end{pmatrix}.$$

Often, a matrix such as A^{-1} above is rewritten for convenience by factoring out the common denominator. Thus, we would write

$$A^{-1} = (1/2) \begin{pmatrix} -3 & 1 \\ 2 & 0 \end{pmatrix}.$$

We next illustrate the computation of the inverse of a square matrix of order 3, the left matrix in the following augmented matrix $(A \mid I)$:

$$\begin{pmatrix} 2 & 3 & 1 & | & 1 & 0 & 0 \\ 1 & 4 & 2 & | & 0 & 1 & 0 \\ 5 & 6 & 4 & | & 0 & 0 & 1 \end{pmatrix}.$$

First, we interchange rows 1 and 2 to obtain

$$\begin{pmatrix} 1 & 4 & 2 & | & 0 & 1 & 0 \\ 2 & 3 & 1 & | & 1 & 0 & 0 \\ 5 & 6 & 4 & | & 0 & 0 & 1 \end{pmatrix}.$$

Next we multiply the first row by -2 and add to the second row to obtain

$$\begin{pmatrix} 1 & 4 & 2 & | & 0 & 1 & 0 \\ 0 & -5 & -3 & | & 1 & -2 & 0 \\ 5 & 6 & 4 & | & 0 & 0 & 1 \end{pmatrix}.$$

Then we multiply the first row by -5 and add to the third row to obtain

$$\begin{pmatrix} 1 & 4 & 2 & | & 0 & 1 & 0 \\ 0 & -5 & -3 & | & 1 & -2 & 0 \\ 0 & -14 & -6 & | & 0 & -5 & 1 \end{pmatrix}.$$

The tactics we have followed are these: first, get a 1 in the first column, first row; then use combinations of this row with each of the other rows to get zeros in the first columns of these rows. We now repeat these tactics, starting by getting a 1 in the second column of the second row, and then using this row to get zeros in the second columns of the other rows.

Interchanging rows does not avoid fractions, so we divide the second row by -5 to obtain the new second row:

$$(0 \quad 1 \quad 3/5 \mid -1/5 \quad 2/5 \quad 0).$$

If we multiply this new second row by -4, add it to the first row, and then multiply the new second row by 14 and add it to the third row, we obtain

$$\begin{pmatrix} 1 & 0 & -2/5 & | & 4/5 & -3/5 & 0 \\ 0 & 1 & 3/5 & | & -1/5 & 2/5 & 0 \\ 0 & 0 & 12/5 & | & -14/5 & 3/5 & 1 \end{pmatrix}.$$

Finally, we repeat the tactics by getting a 1 in the third row of the third column and then using this row to get zeros in the third column of the other rows. The new third row, obtained by dividing the previous third row by 12/5, is

$$(0 \quad 0 \quad 1 \quad | \quad -7/6 \quad 1/4 \quad 5/12).$$

If we multiply this new third row by 2/5 and add it to the first row, and then multiply the new third row by $-3/5$ and add it to the second row, we find

$$\begin{pmatrix} 1 & 0 & 0 & | & 1/3 & -1/2 & 1/6 \\ 0 & 1 & 0 & | & 1/2 & 1/4 & -1/4 \\ 0 & 0 & 1 & | & -7/6 & 1/4 & 5/12 \end{pmatrix},$$

which is the augmented matrix $(I \mid A^{-1})$ with the identity matrix I to the left and the desired inverse A^{-1} to the right.

Exercise. a) Multiply the original matrix of the previous illustration by the inverse and verify that the product is I. b) Rewrite the inverse by factoring out the common denominator.

Answer:

$$A^{-1} = (1/12)\begin{pmatrix} 4 & -6 & 2 \\ 6 & 3 & -3 \\ -14 & 3 & 5 \end{pmatrix}.$$

The Gauss-Jordan method proceeds to obtain ones on the main diagonal and zeros for the off-diagonal elements. A variation on this procedure is to obtain the off-diagonal zeros first and, following this, obtain ones on the diagonal.[4] This **zeros-first** variation can simplify the work involved in hand calculation by avoiding fractions until the last step.

= **Zeros First**

The zeros-first method gets off-diagonal zeros first and then gets ones on the diagonal.

Example. By the zeros-first method, find the inverse of

$$A = \begin{pmatrix} 2 & 3 \\ 4 & 7 \end{pmatrix}.$$

[4]Suggested by Professor Van Cor of New Hampshire College.

We start in the usual manner by writing the augmented matrix $(A \mid I)$:

$$\begin{pmatrix} 2 & 3 & | & 1 & 0 \\ 4 & 7 & | & 0 & 1 \end{pmatrix}.$$

Multiplying the first row by -2 and adding to the second row, we have

$$\begin{pmatrix} 2 & 3 & | & 1 & 0 \\ 0 & 1 & | & -2 & 1 \end{pmatrix}.$$

We now have a zero as the lower off-diagonal element and proceed to obtain a zero as the upper off-diagonal element. Multiplying the second row by -3 and adding it to the first yields

$$\begin{pmatrix} 2 & 0 & | & 7 & -3 \\ 0 & 1 & | & -2 & 1 \end{pmatrix}.$$

The off-diagonal elements now are zero, and ones are obtained on the main diagonal by dividing the first row by 2 to give the augmented matrix $(I \mid A^{-1})$:

$$\begin{pmatrix} 1 & 0 & | & 7/2 & -3/2 \\ 0 & 1 & | & -2 & 1 \end{pmatrix}.$$

The desired inverse is

$$A^{-1} = \begin{pmatrix} 7/2 & -3/2 \\ -2 & 1 \end{pmatrix}.$$

As we stated earlier, this latter matrix is often rewritten for convenience by factoring out the common denominator to get

$$A^{-1} = (1/2) \begin{pmatrix} 7 & -3 \\ -4 & 2 \end{pmatrix}.$$

Exercise. Use the zeros-first method to find the inverse of

$$A = \begin{pmatrix} 3 & 2 & -1 \\ 1 & -1 & 0 \\ 2 & 0 & -1 \end{pmatrix}.$$

Answer:

$$A^{-1} = (1/3) \begin{pmatrix} 1 & 2 & -1 \\ 1 & -1 & -1 \\ 2 & 4 & -5 \end{pmatrix}.$$

The preceding example and exercise illustrates how the zeros-first method postpones the introduction of fractions until the final step. This is an advantage for hand calculation, and we recommend its use. Matrix inversion on high-speed computers, on the other hand, is usually carried out by programs following the Gauss-Jordan method. However, the computer program can be adapted to make use of the interchange of rows and/or the zeros-first method. In large-scale problems, these modifications can lead to significant improvements in speed and accuracy.

To better understand why the Gauss-Jordan method works, consider the true statement

$$A = IA.$$

Suppose that we carry out row operations on the left of the equal sign to change the left matrix to I, and maintain the equality by applying the same operations to the first matrix on the right of the equal sign (which starts out as I). The end result will be I on the left and something times A on the right; thus,

$$I = (?)A.$$

We indicated earlier that the inverse of a matrix is unique. Hence, there is only one appropriate entry for (?) in the preceding. It is A^{-1}. It follows that if we write a given square matrix A with I to its right, and then change the left to I by row operations that are applied also to the right, the end result will be A^{-1} on the right.

Of course, the Gauss-Jordan method will work only when there exists an inverse. Now clearly not every square matrix has an inverse. For example, the zero matrix O has no inverse since $O \cdot B = O$ for every matrix B.

Not every square matrix has an inverse.

Exercise: Use the Gauss-Jordan method to find the inverse of

$$\begin{pmatrix} 1 & 1 \\ 2 & 2 \end{pmatrix}.$$

Answer: There is no inverse, since we cannot proceed beyond the augmented matrix.

$$\left(\begin{array}{cc|cc} 1 & 1 & 1 & 0 \\ 0 & 0 & -2 & 1 \end{array} \right).$$

Matrices that have no inverse are said to be **singular**. In the matrix context, the word singular does not mean one or single but, rather, connotes that the matrix is special in that it has no inverse.

2.17 PROBLEM SET 2-5

Find the inverse of each of the following, if one exists:

1. $\begin{pmatrix} 7 & 3 \\ 2 & 1 \end{pmatrix}.$

2. $\begin{pmatrix} 9 & 4 \\ 2 & 1 \end{pmatrix}.$

3. $\begin{pmatrix} 2 & 2 \\ 3 & 5 \end{pmatrix}.$

4. $\begin{pmatrix} 1 & -1 \\ -1 & 2 \end{pmatrix}.$

2.17 PROBLEM SET 2-5 (continued)

5. $\begin{pmatrix} 2 & 2 \\ 6 & 6 \end{pmatrix}$.

6. $\begin{pmatrix} 3 & 3 \\ 2 & 2 \end{pmatrix}$.

7. $\begin{pmatrix} 1 & 3 \\ 2 & 0 \end{pmatrix}$.

8. $\begin{pmatrix} 2 & 5 \\ 3 & 4 \end{pmatrix}$.

9. $\begin{pmatrix} 0 & 1 \\ 2 & 3 \end{pmatrix}$.

10. $\begin{pmatrix} 0 & 3 \\ 2 & 5 \end{pmatrix}$.

11. $\begin{pmatrix} 2 & 8 & -11 \\ -1 & -5 & 7 \\ 1 & 2 & -3 \end{pmatrix}$.

12. $\begin{pmatrix} 2 & 2 & 3 \\ 0 & 1 & 1 \\ 4 & 0 & 3 \end{pmatrix}$.

13. $\begin{pmatrix} 1 & 1 & 1 \\ 1 & 1 & 1 \\ 2 & 2 & 2 \end{pmatrix}$.

14. $\begin{pmatrix} 0 & -1 & 1 \\ -1 & 1 & 2 \\ 1 & 0 & -2 \end{pmatrix}$.

15. $\begin{pmatrix} 2 & 1 & 4 \\ 3 & 0 & 2 \\ 1 & 2 & 3 \end{pmatrix}$.

16. $\begin{pmatrix} 1 & -1 & 0 \\ 2 & 1 & 3 \\ 3 & 0 & 3 \end{pmatrix}$.

17. Let

$$A = \begin{pmatrix} 2 & -1 & 0 \\ -1 & 1 & 3 \\ 2 & 1 & 4 \end{pmatrix}.$$

Find a matrix that:
a) Commutes multiplicatively with A.
b) Does not commute multiplicatively with A.

18. The inverse of the matrix in Problem 1 can be found using the elimination procedure of Section 2.4 as follows:
a) Designating the inverse matrix by

$$\begin{pmatrix} a & c \\ b & d \end{pmatrix}$$

results in the matrix equation

$$\begin{pmatrix} 7 & 3 \\ 2 & 1 \end{pmatrix} \begin{pmatrix} a & c \\ b & d \end{pmatrix} = \begin{pmatrix} 1 & 0 \\ 0 & 1 \end{pmatrix}.$$

Use matrix multiplication to transform this into four linear equations: two in a and b, and two in c and d.

b) Use the elimination procedure to find the inverse matrix by solving the equations in (a) for a, b, c, and d.

19. Repeat (a) and (b) of Problem 18 for Problems 2 through 10.

20. a) We can designate the inverse of a 3-by-3 matrix by

$$\begin{pmatrix} a & d & g \\ b & e & h \\ c & f & i \end{pmatrix}.$$

Use the matrix equation $AA^{-1} = I$ for the matrix in Problem 11 and to develop nine linear equations: three in a, b, and c, three in d, e, and f, and three more in g, h, and i.

b) Use the elimination procedure to find the inverse matrix by solving the equations in (a) for a, b, c, d, e, f, g, h, and i.

21. Repeat (a) and (b) of Problem 20 for Problems 12 through 16.

22. Consider the QBasic program shown in Program 2-2.
a) Describe what the program is doing line by line.

b) Run the program for Problems 1 through 8 and 11 through 16.

2.17 PROBLEM SET 2-5 (concluded)

23. a) Modify Program 2-2 to allow for the interchange of two rows.
    b) Run the program in (a) for Problems 1 through 16.
24. a) Modify Program 2-2 to perform the zeros-first method.
    b) Run the program in (a) for Problems 1 through 16.

```
REM PROGRAM 2-2
REM Inverse of an n-by-n matrix,
  n <= 10
CLS

Setup:
 INPUT "Enter the matrix
   dimension n"; n
 FOR row = 1 TO n
  PRINT "Enter the elements
   one-by-one in row"; row
  FOR col = 1 TO n
   INPUT A(row, col)
  NEXT col
  FOR col = n + 1 TO n + n
   IF col = row + n THEN A(row, col)
     = 1 ELSE A(row, col) = 0
  NEXT col
 NEXT row

Inversion:
 FOR diag = 1 TO n
  div = A(diag, diag)
  IF div = 0 THEN
   diag = n
  ELSE
   FOR col = 1 TO n + n
    A(diag, col) =
     A(diag, col) / div
   NEXT col
   FOR row = 1 TO n
    IF row <> diag THEN
     mul = -A(row, diag)
     FOR col = diagn TO n + n
      A(row, col) = mul * A(diag,
       col) + A(row, col)
     NEXT col
    END IF
   NEXT row
  END IF
 NEXT diag

Printout:
 IF div = 0 THEN
  PRINT "Diagonal element is 0, so
   program cannot proceed"
 ELSE
  PRINT " The inverse is"
  FOR row = 1 TO n
   FOR col = n + 1 TO n + n
    PRINT A(row, col),
   NEXT col
   PRINT
  NEXT row
 END IF
```

2.18 APPLICATIONS-4: MATRIX SOLUTION OF n-BY-n LINEAR SYSTEMS

In this section, we shall show how the solution of an n-by-n system of linear equations is accomplished by the Gauss-Jordan method. To set the stage, consider first the manner in which a simple linear equation such as

$$2x = 3$$

is solved for x. To bring out what we have in mind, two procedures using slightly different symbols are presented side by side.

Regular Solution Symbols	Inverse Solution Symbols
$2x = 3$	$2x = 3$
$\dfrac{1}{2}(2x) = \dfrac{1}{2}(3)$	$(2^{-1})(2x) = (2^{-1})(3)$
$(1)x = \dfrac{1}{2}(3)$	$(1)x = (2^{-1})(3)$
$x = \dfrac{1}{2}(3).$	$x = (2^{-1})(3).$

Notice on the right that the solution was obtained by multiplying both sides of the original equation by the multiplicative inverse of 2, which is 2^{-1}. More generally, if we start with

$$ax = b$$

and then multiply both sides of the equation by the inverse, a^{-1}, to obtain

$$(a^{-1})(a^1 x) = (a^{-1})b,$$

we have

$$(a^{-1+1})x = (a^{-1})b$$
$$a^0 x = a^{-1} b$$
$$(1)x = a^{-1} b$$
$$x = a^{-1} b.$$

The solution of a linear system proceeds in a manner analogous to that just illustrated for a single equation, except that now we multiply both sides of the matrix form of the system by the inverse of the coefficient matrix. To see how this works out, consider the 2-by-2 system

$$2x_1 + 3x_2 = 17$$
$$x_1 + 2x_2 = 10,$$

where we are now representing the unknowns by x_1 and x_2, instead of the usual x and y, for ease of extension to larger systems. As we saw in Section 2.16, the system can be written in matrix form as

$$\begin{pmatrix} 2 & 3 \\ 1 & 2 \end{pmatrix} \begin{pmatrix} x_1 \\ x_2 \end{pmatrix} = \begin{pmatrix} 17 \\ 10 \end{pmatrix},$$

or equivalently as the matrix equation

$$Ax = b.$$

In this equation, as in Section 2.16,

$$A = \begin{pmatrix} 2 & 3 \\ 1 & 2 \end{pmatrix}$$

In a matrix equation $Ax = b$ corresponding to a system of equations, A is the matrix of coefficients, x is the column vector of unknowns, and b is the column vector of constants.

is the matrix of coefficients while

$$x = \begin{pmatrix} x_1 \\ x_2 \end{pmatrix}$$

is the column vector of unknowns, and

$$b = \begin{pmatrix} 17 \\ 10 \end{pmatrix}$$

is the column vector of constants. If both sides of the matrix equation $Ax = b$ are multiplied by the inverse of the coefficient matrix, namely A^{-1}, we have

$$A^{-1}Ax = A^{-1}b,$$

from which it follows that

$$x = A^{-1}b.$$

> As in ordinary algebra the solution of a matrix equation $Ax = b$ is $x = A^{-1}b$.

Now recall that we solved for the inverse matrix A^{-1} by using row operations to transform the augmented matrix

$$(A \mid I)$$

into the augmented matrix

$$(I \mid A^{-1}).$$

If we then start with the augmented matrix

$$(A \mid b),$$

we can rewrite this in the form

$$(A \mid I \cdot b).$$

Using the row operations, we would be transforming the latter matrix into the augmented matrix

$$(I \mid A^{-1} \cdot b),$$

thereby giving us the solution to the system of equations.

For example, consider the system given earlier,

$$2x_1 + 3x_2 = 17$$
$$x_1 + 2x_2 = 10.$$

If we set this up in augmented form $(A \mid b)$, we have

$$\begin{pmatrix} 2 & 3 & | & 17 \\ 1 & 2 & | & 10 \end{pmatrix}.$$

Proceeding in the usual manner with the Gauss-Jordan method, we interchange rows to obtain

$$\begin{pmatrix} 1 & 2 & | & 10 \\ 2 & 3 & | & 17 \end{pmatrix}.$$

Then, we add -2 times row 1 to row 2:

$$\begin{pmatrix} 1 & 2 & | & 10 \\ 0 & -1 & | & -3 \end{pmatrix}.$$

Next, we divide row 2 by -1:

$$\begin{pmatrix} 1 & 2 & | & 10 \\ 0 & 1 & | & 3 \end{pmatrix}$$

and add -2 times row 2 to row 1:

$$\begin{pmatrix} 1 & 0 & | & 4 \\ 0 & 1 & | & 3 \end{pmatrix}.$$

From the last augmented matrix, we see that the solution is

$$\begin{pmatrix} x_1 \\ x_2 \end{pmatrix} = \begin{pmatrix} 4 \\ 3 \end{pmatrix}$$

so that $x_1 = 4$ and $x_2 = 3$.

Exercise. Graph the two lines in the system of the preceding example and show that they intersect in the single point (4, 3).

Exercise. If the system

$$7x_1 + 3x_2 = 5$$
$$2x_1 + x_2 = 7$$

is expressed in matrix form as $Ax = b$, what are A, x, and b; what is the solution? Verify the solution by drawing the associated graphs.

Answer: A is the coefficient matrix

$$\begin{pmatrix} 7 & 3 \\ 2 & 1 \end{pmatrix},$$

x is the solution vector

$$\begin{pmatrix} x_1 \\ x_2 \end{pmatrix},$$

> **Answer (concluded):** b is the vector of constants
> $$\begin{pmatrix} 5 \\ 7 \end{pmatrix},$$
> and the solution is
> $$x_1 = -16 \quad \text{and} \quad x_2 = 39.$$

Now consider the 3-by-3 system

$$\begin{aligned} 2x_1 + 2x_2 + 3x_3 &= 3 \\ x_2 + x_3 &= 2 \\ x_1 + x_2 + x_3 &= 4. \end{aligned}$$

This time, we start with the augmented matrix

$$\begin{pmatrix} 2 & 2 & 3 & | & 3 \\ 0 & 1 & 1 & | & 2 \\ 1 & 1 & 1 & | & 4 \end{pmatrix}.$$

We then interchange rows 1 and 3:

$$\begin{pmatrix} 1 & 1 & 1 & | & 4 \\ 0 & 1 & 1 & | & 2 \\ 2 & 2 & 3 & | & 3 \end{pmatrix}$$

and add -2 times row 1 to row 3:

$$\begin{pmatrix} 1 & 1 & 1 & | & 4 \\ 0 & 1 & 1 & | & 2 \\ 0 & 0 & 1 & | & -5 \end{pmatrix}.$$

At this point, we add -1 times row 2 to row 1:

$$\begin{pmatrix} 1 & 0 & 0 & | & 2 \\ 0 & 1 & 1 & | & 2 \\ 0 & 0 & 1 & | & -5 \end{pmatrix}.$$

Lastly, we add -1 times row 3 to row 2:

$$\begin{pmatrix} 1 & 0 & 0 & | & 2 \\ 0 & 1 & 0 & | & 7 \\ 0 & 0 & 1 & | & -5 \end{pmatrix}$$

so that the solution is given by

$$x_1 = 2, \quad x_2 = 7, \quad \text{and} \quad x_3 = -5.$$

An alternative approach to solving the system $Ax = b$ would be to use the Gauss-Jordan method to determine A^{-1} and then find the solution by multiplication

> An alternative solution technique for $Ax = b$ is to use the Gauss-Jordan method to find A^{-1}. This is not any shorter and works only for square systems.

of $A^{-1} \cdot b$. This method is no shorter than the one we just developed since the row operations would be the same; that is, instead of transforming

$$(A \mid b) \to (I \mid s)$$

where s is the solution vector, we would have transformed

$$(A \mid I) \to (I \mid A^{-1}).$$

In addition, matrix inversion is defined **only for square matrices** (n-by-n systems), whereas as we shall see in Section 2.20, the Gauss-Jordan method of transforming $(A \mid b) \to (I \mid s)$ works for any m-by-n system regardless of whether $m = n$ or $m \neq n$.

> The inverse approach is useful if we are solving the same system several times but with different constants.

One advantage, though, of using the inverse appears when we are trying to solve a system of equations whose coefficient matrix is A, for a variety of different constant vectors. As an example of this, suppose a company makes liquid products in three grades (Lowgrade, Midgrade, and Highgrade), which contain different amounts of additives, A_1, A_2, and A_3 per gallon, as shown in Table 2–3. The additives deteriorate if not used within a week, so each Saturday the company schedules production of $(x_1 \ x_2 \ x_3)$ gallons of Lowgrade, Midgrade and Highgrade product to use up the additives on hand. These amounts vary from week to week and are represented by the vector $(a_1 \ a_2 \ a_3)$. If we schedule $(x_1 \ x_2 \ x_3)$ gallons of the liquids, the pounds of additive A_1 used will be $x_1(1) + x_2(1) + x_3(2)$, and this should equal a_1, the amount available. Hence, $x_1 + x_2 + 2x_3 = a_1$. Combining this condition with the conditions on additives A_2 and A_3 leads us to the system

$$\begin{aligned} x_1 + x_2 + 2x_3 &= a_1 \\ x_1 + 2x_2 \phantom{{}+ 2x_3} &= a_2 \\ x_1 + x_2 + x_3 &= a_3. \end{aligned}$$

The coefficient matrix is

$$A = \begin{pmatrix} 1 & 1 & 2 \\ 1 & 2 & 0 \\ 1 & 1 & 1 \end{pmatrix}.$$

TABLE 2–3

Liquid	Gallons Made	Pounds of Additive per Gallon		
		A_1	A_2	A_3
Lowgrade	x_1	1	1	1
Midgrade	x_2	1	2	1
Highgrade	x_3	2	0	1

Using the techniques of Section 2.16, the inverse is

$$A^{-1} = \begin{pmatrix} -2 & -1 & 4 \\ 1 & 1 & -2 \\ 1 & 0 & -1 \end{pmatrix}.$$

Hence, the solution vector is

$$\begin{pmatrix} x_1 \\ x_2 \\ x_3 \end{pmatrix} = \begin{pmatrix} -2 & -1 & 4 \\ 1 & 1 & -2 \\ 1 & 0 & -1 \end{pmatrix} \begin{pmatrix} a_1 \\ a_2 \\ a_3 \end{pmatrix}.$$

Suppose that on a given Saturday the amounts of additives available are $a_1 = 20$ pounds of A_1, $a_2 = 30$ pounds of A_2, and $a_3 = 20$ pounds of A_3. To use up these additives, the production schedule should be

$$\begin{pmatrix} x_1 \\ x_2 \\ x_3 \end{pmatrix} = \begin{pmatrix} -2 & -1 & 4 \\ 1 & 1 & -2 \\ 1 & 0 & -1 \end{pmatrix} \begin{pmatrix} 20 \\ 30 \\ 20 \end{pmatrix} = \begin{pmatrix} 10 \\ 10 \\ 0 \end{pmatrix},$$

which is 10 gallons of Lowgrade product, 10 gallons of Midgrade product, and no Highgrade product.

> **Exercise.** If the additives available at a week's end are $(a_1 \ a_2 \ a_3) = (80 \ 100 \ 70)$, what should the production schedule be?
>
> **Answer:** $(x_1 \ x_2 \ x_3) = (20 \ 40 \ 10)$.

Of course, it may not be possible to schedule production to use all the additives available on a given Saturday. For example, if $(a_1 \ a_2 \ a_3) = (40 \ 60 \ 50)$, the solution vector is $(x_1 \ x_2 \ x_3) = (60 \ 0 \ -10)$, and the value $x_3 = -10$ is not possible. In such a case we might choose to maximize either the total amount of liquid made or the total amount of additive used, depending upon cost considerations. To do this, we would apply the linear programming techniques to be developed in Chapter 3 and continued in Chapter 4 to determine the optimum production schedule.

Finally, the Gauss-Jordan method can be used to solve systems of equations that have no solution or an unlimited number of solutions. For example, consider the system

The Gauss-Jordan method will indicate that a system has no solution.

$$2x_1 + 5x_2 = 15$$
$$3.2x_1 + 8x_2 = 6,$$

which was shown in Section 2.5 and Figure 2–6 to have no solutions. (Note we have changed the unknowns from x and y to x_1, and x_2.) Starting with the augmented matrix

$$\begin{pmatrix} 2 & 5 & | & 15 \\ 3.2 & 8 & | & 6 \end{pmatrix},$$

we first divide row 1 by 2 to obtain

$$\begin{pmatrix} 1 & 2.5 & | & 7.5 \\ 3.2 & 8 & | & 6 \end{pmatrix}$$

and add -3.2 times row 1 to row 2:

$$\begin{pmatrix} 1 & 2.5 & | & 7.5 \\ 0 & 0 & | & -18 \end{pmatrix}.$$

At this point, we can proceed no further! Why? To see exactly what has happened, we retranslate the latter augmented matrix back into equations to get

$$x_1 + 2.5x_2 = 7.5$$
$$0 + 0 = -18.$$

The last equation is impossible since $0 \neq -18$; so that, as we saw in Section 2.5, there can be no solution.

Exercise. Show that the following system has no solutions:

$$2x_1 + 3x_2 = 17$$
$$9x_1 + 13.5x_2 = 25,$$

and verify the result by drawing the associated graphs.

The Gauss-Jordan method will solve a system that has an unlimited number of solutions.

Now consider the system

$$2x_1 + 5x_2 = 15$$
$$3.2x_1 + 8x_2 = 24,$$

which we showed in Section 2.5 to have an unlimited number of solutions. This time, we start with the augmented matrix

$$\begin{pmatrix} 2 & 5 & | & 15 \\ 3.2 & 8 & | & 24 \end{pmatrix}$$

and obtain

$$\begin{pmatrix} 1 & 2.5 & | & 7.5 \\ 3.2 & 8 & | & 24 \end{pmatrix}$$

and then

$$\begin{pmatrix} 1 & 2.5 & | & 7.5 \\ 0 & 0 & | & 0 \end{pmatrix}.$$

The latter augmented matrix represents the system

$$x_1 + 2.5x_2 = 7.5$$
$$0 + 0 = 0,$$

which means we really have a single equation,

$$x_1 + 2.5x_2 = 7.5.$$

On a graph, the original two lines would be coincident, and hence the system has an unlimited number of solutions given by

$$x_2 \text{ arbitrary}$$
$$x_1 = -2.5x_2 + 7.5.$$

Exercise. Specify the solution set with x_1, arbitrary.

Answer: x_1 arbitrary, $x_2 = -0.4x_1 + 3$.

Exercise. Show that the following system has an unlimited number of solutions and specify the solution set:

$$2x_1 + 3x_2 = 17$$
$$9x_1 + 13.5x_2 = 76.5.$$

Answer: x_2 arbitrary, $x_1 = -1.5 x_2 + 8.5$.

> **Summary of the Gauss-Jordan method for solving an n-by-n system of linear equations.**
>
> Summarizing our results for solving an n-by-n system, we start with the matrix
>
> $$(A \mid b)$$
>
> and attempt to transform it into the matrix
>
> $$(I \mid s).$$
>
> One of three things will result:
>
> 1. An n-by-n matrix together with the unique solution; for example,
>
> $$\begin{pmatrix} 1 & 0 & 0 & | & 5 \\ 0 & 1 & 0 & | & -2 \\ 0 & 0 & 1 & | & 6 \end{pmatrix}.$$
>
> 2. A row that is all zeros **except for the value in the constant column**, indicating that there are no solutions; for example,
>
> $$\begin{pmatrix} 1 & 0 & 2 & | & -4 \\ 0 & 1 & 3 & | & 8 \\ 0 & 0 & 0 & | & 2 \end{pmatrix}.$$
>
> 3. A matrix in a form different from (1) and (2), indicating that there are an unlimited number of solutions. Note that for an n-by-n system, this case occurs when there is a row with all zeros, including the value in the constant column; for example,
>
> $$\begin{pmatrix} 1 & 0 & 2 & | & -4 \\ 0 & 1 & 3 & | & 8 \\ 0 & 0 & 0 & | & 0 \end{pmatrix}.$$

2.19 PROBLEM SET 2-6

1. Consider the system

    $$8x_1 + 5x_2 = 2$$
    $$3x_1 + 2x_2 = 1.$$

    a) Relating the system to $Ax = b$, what are A, x, and b?
    b) Solve the system using the Gauss-Jordan method.
    c) Compute A^{-1} using the Gauss-Jordan method.
    d) Write $x = A^{-1}b$ in expanded matrix form.
    e) Compute the solution from part (d).
    f) What would be the solution vector if the elements in the vector of constants, 2 and 1, were changed to each of the following:
    (1) 1, 0? (2) 0, 1? (3) 1, 1?
    (4) 3, 4? (5) -3, 1?

2. Answer parts (a) through (e) of Problem 1 for the system

    $$4x_1 + 3x_2 = 2$$
    $$9x_1 + 7x_2 = 3.$$

2.19 PROBLEM SET 2-6 (continued)

f) What would be the solution vector if the elements in the vector of constants, 2 and 3, were changed to each of the following:
(1) 1, 0?   (2) 0, 1?   (3) 1, 1?
(4) 2, 1?   (5) −1, 2?

3. Answer parts (a) through (e) of Problem 1 for the system
$$6x_1 + 8x_2 = 3$$
$$2x_1 + 3x_2 = 1.$$

f) What would be the solution vector if the elements in the vector of constants, 3 and 1, were changed to each of the following:
(1) 1, 1?   (2) 0, 1?   (3) 1, 0?
(4) 2, 3?   (5) −1, 1?

4. Given the system
$$8x_1 - 7x_2 = b_1$$
$$-5x_1 + 5x_2 = b_2$$

find the missing elements to complete the following equation:
$$\begin{pmatrix} x_1 \\ x_2 \end{pmatrix} = \begin{pmatrix} \quad \end{pmatrix} \begin{pmatrix} b_1 \\ b_2 \end{pmatrix}.$$

5. Answer parts (a) through (e) of Problem 1 for the system
$$3x_1 \quad\quad + 5x_3 = 3$$
$$2x_1 + 2x_2 + 5x_3 = 7$$
$$x_2 + x_3 = 2.$$

f) What would be the solution vector if the elements in the vector of constants, 3, 7, and 2, were changed to each of the following:
(1) 1, 2, 1?   (2) 2, 3, 4?   (3) 1, 0, −1?
(4) 1, 6, 2?   (5) 2, 10, 1?

6. Answer parts (a) through (e) of Problem 1 for the system
$$7x_1 + 3x_2 \quad\quad = 1$$
$$3x_2 + 5x_3 = 2$$
$$x_1 + x_2 + x_3 = 3.$$

f) What would be the solution vector if the elements in the vector of constants were changed from 1, 2, and 3 to each of the following:
(1) 1, −1, 1?   (2) 2, 3, 0?
(3) −1, 2, −2?   (4) 10, −1, 1?
(5) 0, −1, 0?

7. Given the system
$$2x_1 + 2x_2 + 3x_3 = b_1$$
$$x_2 + x_3 = b_2$$
$$4x_1 \quad\quad + 3x_3 = b_3.$$

find the missing elements to complete the following equation:
$$\begin{pmatrix} x_1 \\ x_2 \\ x_3 \end{pmatrix} = \begin{pmatrix} \quad \end{pmatrix} \begin{pmatrix} b_1 \\ b_2 \\ b_3 \end{pmatrix}.$$

8. Given the system
$$x_1 + 2x_2 + x_3 = b_1$$
$$2x_1 + x_2 + x_3 = b_2$$
$$3x_1 \quad\quad + 2x_3 = b_3.$$

a) Verify by multiplication that the inverse of the coefficient matrix is
$$A^{-1} = \begin{pmatrix} -2/3 & 4/3 & -1/3 \\ 1/3 & 1/3 & -1/3 \\ 1 & -2 & 1 \end{pmatrix}.$$

b) Compute the solution vector if the b's are, respectively,
(1) 3, 0, 3?   (2) 6, 3, 0?

9. Given the system
$$x_1 + x_2 + x_3 + x_4 = b_1$$
$$x_1 + 2x_2 + 2x_3 + 2x_4 = b_2$$
$$x_1 + 2x_2 + 3x_3 + 3x_4 = b_3$$
$$x_1 + 2x_2 + 3x_3 + 4x_4 = b_4$$

a) Verify by multiplication that the inverse of the coefficient matrix is
$$\begin{pmatrix} 2 & -1 & 0 & 0 \\ -1 & 2 & -1 & 0 \\ 0 & -1 & 2 & -1 \\ 0 & 0 & -1 & 1 \end{pmatrix}$$

2.19 PROBLEM SET 2-6 (concluded)

b) What is the solution vector if the b's are, respectively,
(1) 1, 1, 1, 1?   (2) 1, 0, 1, 0?

10. The table shows that we plan to make x_1 Primers. Making each Primer requires one hour on machine M_1 and one hour on M_3. Other entries in the table have corresponding interpretations. H_1, H_2, and H_3 are the total numbers of hours available on M_1, M_2, and M_3, respectively.

a) Set up the system of equations that must be solved if all available machine hours are to be used in making $(x_1 \ x_2 \ x_3)$ units of the products.

Product	Units Made	Machine Hours per Unit on Machine		
		M_1	M_2	M_3
Primer	x_1	1	0	1
Middler	x_2	0	1	2
Laster	x_3	2	3	0

b) Set up the coefficient matrix and find its inverse. What number of units can be made if the numbers of available hours, $(H_1 \ H_2 \ H_3)$, are:
c) (160 80 200)?   d) (400 400 400)?
e) (320 192 256)?

Solve the following systems:

11. $2x_1 - 3x_2 = 5$
    $6x_1 - 9x_2 = 8$.

12. $3x_1 - 6x_2 = 8$
    $-5x_1 + 10x_2 = 12$.

13. $2x_1 + 3x_2 = -15$
    $-(8/3)x_1 - 4x_2 = 25$.

14. $7x_1 + 2x_2 = 9$
    $17.5x_1 + 5x_2 = 14$.

15. $3x_1 + 12x_2 = -9$
    $-2x_1 - 8x_2 = 6$.

16. $5x_1 + 3x_2 = 15$
    $2x_1 + 1.2x_2 = 6$.

17. $2x_1 + 3x_2 = 15$
    $(8/3)x_1 + 4x_2 = 20$.

18. $6x_1 - 15x_2 = -3$
    $-10x_1 + 25x_2 = 5$.

19. a) Modify Program 2–2 (Section 2.17) to compute and print the solution of an n-by-n system of equations using the Gauss-Jordan method.
    b) Run the program in (a) for Problems 1 through 6 and Problems 11 through 18.

20. a) Modify the computer program in Problem 19(a) to allow for the interchange of two rows. (Hint: refer to Problem 23 of Problem Set 2–5 in Section 2.17.)
    b) Run the program in (a) for Problems 1 through 6 and Problems 11 through 18.

21. a) Modify the computer program in Problem 19(a) to perform the zeros-first method. (Hint: Refer to Problem 24 of Problem Set 2–5.)
    b) Run the program in (a) for Problems 1 through 6 and Problems 11 through 18.

2.20 APPLICATIONS–5: MATRIX SOLUTION OF m-BY-n LINEAR SYSTEMS

In this section, we will show how to use the Gauss-Jordan method to solve an m-by-n system of linear equations where $m \neq n$. For ease in understanding, we first present the case where the number of rows m is greater than the number of columns n (i.e., $m > n$).

Consider the 3-by-2 system.

$$4x_1 + 5x_2 = 30$$
$$3x_1 + 2x_2 = 19$$
$$2x_1 + 5x_2 = 20.$$

Proceeding in the usual manner, we start with the augmented matrix

$$\begin{pmatrix} 4 & 5 & | & 30 \\ 3 & 2 & | & 19 \\ 2 & 5 & | & 20 \end{pmatrix}.$$

Then, we divide row 1 by 4:

$$\begin{pmatrix} 1 & 5/4 & | & 15/2 \\ 3 & 2 & | & 19 \\ 2 & 5 & | & 20 \end{pmatrix}.$$

Next, we add -3 times row 1 to row 2 and -2 times row 1 to row 3:

$$\begin{pmatrix} 1 & 5/4 & | & 15/2 \\ 0 & -7/4 & | & -7/2 \\ 0 & 5/2 & | & 5 \end{pmatrix}.$$

Now we divide row 2 by $-7/4$:

$$\begin{pmatrix} 1 & 5/4 & | & 15/2 \\ 0 & 1 & | & 2 \\ 0 & 5/2 & | & 5 \end{pmatrix},$$

and then add $-5/4$ times row 2 to row 1 and $-5/2$ times row 2 to row 3:

$$\begin{pmatrix} 1 & 0 & | & 5 \\ 0 & 1 & | & 2 \\ 0 & 0 & | & 0 \end{pmatrix}.$$

> A 3-by-2 system with a unique solution results in a 2-by-2 identity matrix with the third row all zeros.

At this point, the method terminates since there is no entry in the third row and third column on the left-hand side of the augmented matrix. What does this last augmented matrix mean? The first row tells us

$$x_1 = 5,$$

the second row,

$$x_2 = 2,$$

and the third row,

$$0 = 0.$$

Thus, our solution is given by

$$x_1 = 5 \quad \text{and} \quad x_2 = 2.$$

Exercise. Graph the three lines in the preceding 3-by-2 system and verify that they intersect in the single point (5, 2).

Exercise. Solve the system

$$2x_1 + 3x_2 = 17$$
$$x_1 + 2x_2 = 10$$
$$4x_1 + x_2 = 19,$$

and verify the result by drawing the associated graphs.

Answer: $x_1 = 4$ and $x_2 = 3$.

Now consider the 3-by-2 system

$$4x_1 + 5x_2 = 30$$
$$3x_1 + 2x_2 = 19$$
$$2x_1 + 5x_2 = 30.$$

Here we start with

$$\begin{pmatrix} 4 & 5 & | & 30 \\ 3 & 2 & | & 19 \\ 2 & 5 & | & 30 \end{pmatrix},$$

and then obtain

$$\begin{pmatrix} 1 & 5/4 & | & 15/2 \\ 3 & 2 & | & 19 \\ 2 & 5 & | & 30 \end{pmatrix}$$

and

$$\begin{pmatrix} 1 & 5/4 & | & 15/2 \\ 0 & -7/4 & | & -7/2 \\ 0 & 5/2 & | & 15 \end{pmatrix}.$$

Next we have

$$\begin{pmatrix} 1 & 5/4 & | & 15/2 \\ 0 & 1 & | & 2 \\ 0 & 5/2 & | & 15 \end{pmatrix}$$

and finally

$$\begin{pmatrix} 1 & 0 & | & 5 \\ 0 & 1 & | & 2 \\ 0 & 0 & | & 10 \end{pmatrix}.$$

> A 3-by-2 system with no solution results in a 2-by-2 identity matrix with the third row all zeros except in the constant column.

Again the method terminates, but this time the final matrix gives

$$x_1 = 5$$
$$x_2 = 2$$
$$0 = 10.$$

Of course, the statement $0 = 10$ is impossible, so that the system has no solution. By the way, the preceding result still tells us something about the system. Indeed, $x_1 = 5$ and $x_2 = 2$ is a solution to the first two equations of the system but not the third. How much is the third equation off by? If you guessed precisely the 10 in the previous absurd statement, $0 = 10$, you were correct.

Exercise. Graph the three lines in the preceding 3-by-2 system and verify that the lines have no points in common. Verify also that the first two lines intersect in the point (5,2).

Lastly, it is possible but rare that a 3-by-2 system (in general, m by n with $m > n$) will have an unlimited number of solutions. The Gauss-Jordan method will identify this situation, as indicated by the summary of all three possibilities on the next page.

Note the similarity between this summary and that for n-by-n systems at the end of Section 2.18.

Now let us consider the case where the number of rows m is less than the number of columns n (i.e., $m < n$). This time, the system has either no solutions or else an unlimited number of solutions. There cannot be just one common solution! Why? Picture the situation where $m = 2$ and $n = 3$ so that we have two planes in three-dimensional space. What can happen? The planes are parallel, intersect in a line, or are coincident. They can never intersect in a single point. Can you guess, then, how the Gauss-Jordan method will identify the two possibilities?

Summary of the Gauss-Jordan method for solving an *m*-by-*n* system of linear equations where $m > n$.

To solve an m-by-n system of equations with $m > n$, we start with the matrix

$$(A \mid b)$$

and attempt to transform it into the matrix

$$(I \mid s).$$

One of three things will result:

1. An n-by-n identity matrix above $m - n$ bottom rows that are all zeros, giving the unique solution; for example,

$$\begin{pmatrix} 1 & 0 & 0 & \mid & 5 \\ 0 & 1 & 0 & \mid & -2 \\ 0 & 0 & 1 & \mid & 6 \\ 0 & 0 & 0 & \mid & 0 \\ 0 & 0 & 0 & \mid & 0 \end{pmatrix}.$$

2. A row that is all zeros **except in the constant column,** indicating that there are no solutions; for example,

$$\begin{pmatrix} 1 & 0 & 0 & \mid & 5 \\ 0 & 1 & 0 & \mid & -2 \\ 0 & 0 & 1 & \mid & 6 \\ 0 & 0 & 0 & \mid & 2 \\ 0 & 0 & 0 & \mid & 0 \end{pmatrix}.$$

3. A matrix in a form different from (1) and (2), indicating that there are an unlimited number of solutions; for example,

$$\begin{pmatrix} 1 & 0 & 2 & \mid & -4 \\ 0 & 1 & 3 & \mid & 8 \\ 0 & 0 & 0 & \mid & 0 \\ 0 & 0 & 0 & \mid & 0 \\ 0 & 0 & 0 & \mid & 0 \end{pmatrix}.$$

Summary of the Gauss-Jordan method for solving an *m*-by-*n* system of linear equations where $m < n$.

Our attempt to transform $(A \mid b)$ into $(I \mid s)$ in the case where $m < n$ will result in

1. A row that is all zeros except in the constant column, indicating that there are no solutions; or
2. A matrix in a form different from (1), indicating that there are an unlimited number of solutions.

Typically, the latter situation occurs. Don't two planes in three-dimensional space intersect in a line more often than not? Let us look at an example of this; namely, the 2-by-3 system

$$2x_1 + 2x_2 + x_3 = 36$$
$$x_1 + 3x_2 + 2x_3 = 30.$$

Starting with the augmented matrix

$$\begin{pmatrix} 2 & 2 & 1 & | & 36 \\ 1 & 3 & 2 & | & 30 \end{pmatrix},$$

we interchange rows 1 and 2, obtaining

$$\begin{pmatrix} 1 & 3 & 2 & | & 30 \\ 2 & 2 & 1 & | & 36 \end{pmatrix},$$

and then add -2 times row 1 to row 2:

$$\begin{pmatrix} 1 & 3 & 2 & | & 30 \\ 0 & -4 & -3 & | & -24 \end{pmatrix}.$$

Next, we divide row 2 by -4:

$$\begin{pmatrix} 1 & 3 & 2 & | & 30 \\ 0 & 1 & 3/4 & | & 6 \end{pmatrix}$$

and add -3 times row 2 to row 1:

$$\begin{pmatrix} 1 & 0 & -1/4 & | & 12 \\ 0 & 1 & 3/4 & | & 6 \end{pmatrix}.$$

At this point, the method terminates. Why? There is no entry in the third row and third column. In fact, there is no third row at all. Thus, we have an unlimited number of solutions given by

$$x_1 + 0 - \frac{1}{4}x_3 = 12$$

$$0 + x_2 + \frac{3}{4}x_3 = 6,$$

or, solving both equations in terms of x_3,

$$x_1 = \frac{1}{4}x_3 + 12$$

$$x_2 = -\frac{3}{4}x_3 + 6$$

x_3 arbitrary.

> A 2-by-3 system with an unlimited number of solutions does not have a row that is all zeros except in the constant column.

> **Exercise.** Solve the system
>
> $$x_1 + 3x_2 + x_3 = 6$$
> $$-x_1 + x_2 + x_3 = 2.$$
>
> **Answer:** $x_1 = (1/2)x_3$; $x_2 = (-1/2)x_3 + 2$; x_3 arbitrary.

2.21 PROBLEM SET 2-7

Solve each of the following systems of equations:

1. $2x_1 - 3x_2 = 6$
   $x_1 + 5x_2 = 29$
   $3x_1 - 4x_2 = 11.$

2. $-3x_1 + 4x_2 = -11$
   $4x_1 - 5x_2 = 13$
   $x_1 + 2x_2 = -13.$

3. $2x_1 + x_2 = 30$
   $x_1 + 2x_2 = 24$
   $4x_1 + 5x_2 = 72.$

4. $6x_1 + 5x_2 = 20$
   $9x_1 + (15/2)x_2 = 30$
   $(36/5)x_1 + 6x_2 = 24.$

5. $3x_1 + 2x_2 + x_3 = 23$
   $x_1 + 3x_2 + 2x_3 = 26$
   $2x_1 + x_2 + 2x_3 = 19$
   $4x_1 + 5x_2 + 3x_3 = 49.$

6. $2x_1 - 5x_2 + x_3 = 7$
   $-3x_1 + x_2 - 2x_3 = -7$
   $x_1 + 2x_2 + 3x_3 = 14$
   $-x_1 + 3x_2 - 4x_3 = -25.$

7. $3x_1 + 4x_2 - 6x_3 = 10$
   $12x_1 + 16x_2 - 24x_3 = 7$
   $x_1 + 2x_2 + 3x_3 = 8$
   $5x_1 + 3x_2 + 2x_3 = 12.$

8. $3x_1 + 2x_2 + x_3 = 6$
   $2x_1 + (4/3)x_2 + (2/3)x_3 = 4$
   $(9/2)x_1 + 3x_2 + (3/2)x_3 = 9$
   $(15/2)x_1 + 5x_2 + (5/2)x_3 = 15.$

9. $-2x_1 + x_2 - 3x_3 = 0$
   $x_1 + 3x_2 - 4x_3 = 34$
   $3x_1 + 4x_2 - x_3 = 44$
   $2x_1 - 2x_2 + x_3 = 1$
   $-4x_1 + 2x_2 - 2x_3 = -12.$

10. $-3x_1 + 4x_2 + 2x_3 = 16$
    $2x_1 + 2x_2 - 5x_3 = 24$
    $x_1 + 3x_2 + 6x_3 = 47$
    $-x_1 + x_2 - 3x_3 = -5$
    $4x_1 - 2x_2 + x_3 = 16.$

11. $-3x_1 + x_2 - 2x_3 = 9$
    $-5x_1 + (5/3)x_2 - (10/3)x_3 = 15$
    $-2x_1 + (2/3)x_2 - (4/3)x_3 = 18$
    $-7x_1 + (7/3)x_2 - (14/3)x_3 = 21$
    $4x_1 - (4/3)x_2 + (8/3)x_3 = -12.$

12. $-3x_1 + x_2 - 2x_3 = 9$
    $-5x_1 + (5/3)x_2 - (10/3)x_3 = 15$
    $-2x_1 + (2/3)x_2 - (4/3)x_3 = 6$
    $7x_1 - (7/3)x_2 + (14/3)x_3 = -21$
    $6x_1 - 2x_2 + 4x_3 = -18.$

13. $4x_1 + 6x_2 - 3x_3 = 12$
    $6x_1 + 9x_2 - (9/2)x_3 = 20.$

14. $3x_1 - 2x_2 + 4x_3 = 15$
    $4x_1 - (8/3)x_2 + (16/3)x_3 = 20.$

15. $2x_1 + 4x_2 + 3x_3 - 2x_4 = 12$
    $3x_1 + 6x_2 + (9/2)x_3 - 3x_4 = 18$
    $5x_1 + 10x_2 + (15/2)x_3 - 5x_4 = 25.$

16. $3x_1 + 5x_2 - 6x_3 + 4x_4 = 36$
    $2x_1 + (10/3)x_2 - 4x_3 + (8/3)x_4 = 24$
    $5x_1 + (25/3)x_2 - 10x_3 + (20/3)x_4 = 60.$

17. Stay Trim Bakery makes two kinds of diet candy: Luscious and Delicious. To make one dozen of Luscious Candy requires 1 gallon of milk, 2 pounds of butter, and 1 pint of cream. To make one dozen of Delicious Candy requires 3 gallons of milk, 1 pound of butter, and 1 pint of cream. Find the number of

2.21 PROBLEM SET 2-7 (concluded)

dozens of each candy to be made in the coming week if exactly 24 gallons of milk, exactly 13 pounds of butter, and exactly 10 pints of cream are to be consumed.

18. A special food for athletes is to be developed from two foods: food X and food Y. The new food is to be designed so that it contains exactly 16 ounces of vitamin A, exactly 44 ounces of vitamin B, and exactly 12 ounces of vitamin C. Each pound of food X contains 1 ounce of vitamin A, 5 ounces of vitamin B, and 1 ounce of vitamin C. On the other hand, each pound of food Y contains 2 ounces of A, 1 ounce of B, and 1 ounce of C. Find the number of pounds of each food to be used in the mixture in order to meet the above requirements.

19. A candy manufacturer regularly makes three kinds of candy, each of which requires milk and butter as follows: candy 1 requires 3 gallons of milk and 1 pound of butter per dozen, candy 2 requires 2 gallons of milk and 3 pounds of butter per dozen, and candy 3 requires 1 gallon of milk and 2 pounds of butter per dozen. The purchasing department buys a variable amount of milk and butter each week, depending upon the market prices; the production department must then determine each week the amounts of each candy to be made in order to consume the quantities of milk and butter bought. If in the current week 23 gallons of milk and 26 pounds of butter are purchased, how many dozens of each candy are to be made?

20. Safety Tire Company makes four kinds of tires: model SS, the super sport; model P, the premium; Model S, the second line; and Model E, the economy. Each tire must be processed on three machines as follows: Each model SS tire requires two hours on machine I, one hour on machine II, and three hours on machine III. Each model P tire requires three hours on I, two hours on II, and one hour on III. Each model S tire requires four, three, and one hour, respectively; whereas each model E tire requires one, two, and three hours, respectively. Find the number of each tire to be made in the coming week if exactly 37 hours on machine I, exactly 24 hours on machine II, and exactly 33 hours on machine III are to be utilized.

21. a) Modify the computer program in Problems 19(a), 20(a), and 21(a) of Problem Set 2–6 in Section 2.19 to solve m-by-n systems of equations in which $m \neq n$.

    b) Run the program in (a) for Problems 1 through 16.

2.22 APPLICATIONS-6: MARKOV CHAINS

To set the stage for this section, suppose that a restaurant chain notes that 30 percent of the dinners it sells each week are beef dinners, and 70 percent are other dinners. The chain manager has a special arrangement for volume buying of beef at relatively low prices, and would like to raise the proportion of beef dinners sold. He carries out a promotional campaign to increase beef sales and collects the information shown in Table 2–4.

TABLE 2-4

Transition Proportions, One Week to the Next Week

One Week	Next Week	
	Beef	Other
Beef	0.8	0.2
Other	0.6	0.4

> A transition matrix is a matrix of proportions.

The matrix of proportions is called the **transition matrix**. The number 0.8 means that 80 percent of those buying beef dinners one week buy beef dinners again the next week. Similarly, 20 percent of those buying beef one week buy other dinners the next week.

> **Exercise.** Interpret the second row of Table 2–4.
>
> **Answer:** 60 percent of those buying other dinners one week change to beef dinners the next week, and the remaining 40 percent buy other dinners again the next week.

> A state vector is a vector of current values.

The state of affairs at the beginning of the section was 30 percent beef and 70 percent other. We shall call the vector (0.3 0.7) the **state vector**. Writing the state vector to the left of the transition matrix, we have

$$\begin{array}{cc} \text{Beef} \quad \text{Other} \\ (0.3 \quad 0.7) \end{array} \quad \begin{array}{c} \\ \text{Beef} \\ \text{Other} \end{array} \begin{pmatrix} \text{Beef} & \text{Other} \\ 0.8 & 0.2 \\ 0.6 & 0.4 \end{pmatrix}.$$

If we wish to find what proportion will buy beef after a one-week transition, we note that 80 percent of the 30 percent who bought beef one week will buy it the next and an additional 60 percent of the 70 percent who bought other dinners one week will buy beef the next week. The sum is $0.3(0.8) + 0.7(0.6) = 0.66$, which we found by the usual inner product matrix multiplication procedure of Section 2.13. In the same manner $0.3(0.2) + 0.7(0.4) = 0.34$ is the proportion buying other dinners next week, and the new state vector is

$$\begin{array}{cc} \text{Beef} & \text{Other} \\ (0.66 & 0.34). \end{array}$$

In summary,

> A new state vector is the matrix product of the current state vector times the transition matrix.

$$\begin{array}{ccc} \text{Current} & \text{Transition} & \text{New} \\ \text{State Vector} & \text{Matrix} & \text{State Vector} \\ (0.3 \quad 0.7) & \begin{pmatrix} 0.8 & 0.2 \\ 0.6 & 0.4 \end{pmatrix} = & (0.66 \quad 0.34). \end{array}$$

Now suppose the promotion activity is maintained and the transition matrix remains constant from week to week. Then the state vector for week 1, (0.66 0.34) can be used as a premultiplier of the transition matrix to obtain the state vector for week 2.

> **Exercise.** What proportions will buy beef and other in week 2?
>
> **Answer:** $(0.66 \quad 0.34) \begin{pmatrix} 0.8 & 0.2 \\ 0.6 & 0.4 \end{pmatrix} = (0.732 \quad 0.268),$
>
> which is 73.2 percent beef and 26.8 percent other dinners.

If we continue this procedure forming a chain (called a **Markov chain**[5]), we may examine the successive state vectors as shown in Table 2–5.

Observe that the components of each state vector sum to 1, as must be the case because they are proportions of a whole. Also, for the same reason, the rows of any transition matrix must each sum to 1. Note also that the state vector appears to be approaching (0.75 0.25). What would happen if we used this state vector as a multiplier of the transition matrix? We would obtain

$$(0.75 \quad 0.25) \begin{pmatrix} 0.8 & 0.2 \\ 0.6 & 0.4 \end{pmatrix} = (0.75 \quad 0.25).$$

We see that the transition of (0.75 0.25) leads to the same state, (0.75 0.25), and we call this vector the **steady state**. The actual calculation of successive state vectors will never yield exactly (0.75 0.25), so it is a matter of importance to learn how to find the steady state by a method other than tabulating successive state vectors and guessing the steady state from the sequence of results. In our problem, let us call the steady state $(v_1 \quad v_2)$. Then it must be true that

A steady state vector is the state vector that remains unchanged by the transition matrix.

$$(v_1 \quad v_2) \begin{pmatrix} 0.8 & 0.2 \\ 0.6 & 0.4 \end{pmatrix} = (v_1 \quad v_2),$$

where, of course, $v_1 + v_2 = 1$. The matrix multiplication yields

$$\begin{array}{ll} e_1: & 0.8v_1 + 0.6v_2 = v_1 \\ e_2: & 0.2v_1 + 0.4v_2 = v_2 \end{array} \quad \text{or} \quad \begin{array}{l} -0.2v_1 + 0.6v_2 = 0 \\ 0.2v_1 - 0.6v_2 = 0. \end{array}$$

TABLE 2–5

Successive State Vectors

Week	Beef	Other
Beginning	(0.30	0.70)
1	(0.66	0.34)
2	(0.732	0.268)
3	(0.7464	0.2536)
4	(0.74928	0.25072)
5	(0.749856	0.250144)

---

[5]Markov chains are named after the Russian mathematician A. A. Markov (1856–1922).

Clearly, e_1 and e_2 are the same equation, so we need only one of them. Taking e_1 with $v_1 + v_2 = 1$ we have

$$e_1: \quad -0.2v_1 + 0.6v_2 = 0$$
$$e_3: \quad v_1 + v_2 = 1.$$

Eliminating v_1, we obtain

$$e_4: \quad 0.8v_2 = 0.2.$$

From the last statement, $v_2 = 0.25$ and from e_3, $v_1 = 0.75$, so we have the steady state vector (0.75 0.25) that we obtained by guessing from the sequence in Table 2–5.

Exercise. Find the steady state for the transition matrix

$$\begin{pmatrix} 0.5 & 0.5 \\ 1 & 0 \end{pmatrix}.$$

Answer: (2/3 1/3).

Next, let us suppose that once a customer buys beef she is so satisfied that she will buy beef the next time. This results in a 1 in the upper left corner of the transition matrix. Thus,

	Beef	Other
(0.3	0.7)	

	Beef	Other
Beef	1.0	0.0
Other	0.6	0.4

An absorbing Markov chain is one that leads to a steady state that is impossible to leave, such as (1 0).

Inasmuch as 60 percent of those buying other meals change to beef and then continue to buy beef, it is reasonable to expect that ultimately all customers will buy beef and the steady state will be (1 0). In this situation, beef has absorbed all the business, and the chain leading to this steady state is called an **absorbing Markov chain**.

Exercise. Verify that the steady state for the last written beef–other matrix is (1 0).

Markov processes are those in which the future state depends only on the present state. The process is stationary if the transition matrix is constant.

We have used 2-by-2 transition matrices to illustrate the concept of Markov chains. Clearly, the methodology can be applied to n-by-n matrices. All that would change is the complexity of the calculations, so we shall not pursue this topic further. We should mention that Markov was a mathematician whose name has been given to processes of the type discussed in this section; namely, processes in which the future state is completely determined by the present state and not at all by the way in which the present state arose. Finally, we should call attention to the fact that the transition matrices in our discussion have been constant as we changed from state to state, and this fact can be made explicit by referring to the processes as **stationary Markov processes**.

2.23 PROBLEM SET 2-8

1. Lotus and Microsoft each have 50 percent of the market for a certain software product. Because of a promotion campaign, buyers are switching between Lotus and Microsoft according to the following transition matrix.

$$\begin{array}{c} \\ \text{Lotus} \\ \text{Microsoft} \end{array} \begin{array}{c} \text{Lotus} \quad \text{Microsoft} \\ \begin{pmatrix} 0.6 & 0.4 \\ 0.5 & 0.5 \end{pmatrix}. \end{array}$$

   a) What do the numbers 0.6 and 0.4 mean?
   b) What will be the market shares after the first and second transitions?
   c) What are the steady state market shares?

2. At a point in time, 95 percent of the population were spenders of copper pennies and 5 percent were savers. Because of the increasing value of pennies, only 30 percent of the spenders remain spenders, and 10 percent of the savers become spenders.
   a) What will be the (spender saver) state vector after one transition?
   b) What is the steady state vector?

3. At a point in time, 1 percent of the population use a drug and 99 percent do not. In a year, 1/10 of one percent of nonusers become users, but all users remain users.
   a) What will be the percentages of users and nonusers after one transition?
   b) What is the steady state?

4. A recent survey showed that 60 percent of the population own some kind of microcomputer and 40 percent do not. Market experts predict that in a year 10 percent of the nonowners will become owners, and 1/100 of one percent of the owners will become nonowners.
   a) What are the predicted percentages of owners and nonowners for next year?
   b) What is the predicted steady state?

5. Currently, it is known that 85 percent of the population own an automobile and 15 percent do not. Based upon past experience, in a year $1\frac{1}{4}$ percent of the nonowners will become owners, and 1/1,000 of one percent of the owners will become nonowners.
   a) What are the expected percentages of owners and nonowners for next year?
   b) What is the expected steady state?

6. Florida Power and Light researched homeowners' preferences of heating. It found that of the people who have oil heat, 60 percent stay with oil heat, 30 percent change to gas heat, and the rest change to electric heat. Of the homeowners with gas heat, 80 percent stay with gas heat, 15 percent change to electric heat, and 5 percent change to oil heat. Of the homeowners with electric heat, 75 percent stay with electric heat and 25 percent change to gas heat. Currently, 45 percent of the homes in Miami are heated by oil, 40 percent by gas, and 15 percent by electricity.
   a) What are the expected market shares next year?
   b) What is the predicted steady state?

7. The mayor of San Francisco has obtained data on the people's tendencies for renting an apartment, buying a condominium, or buying a home. Of the people who rent, 40 percent continue to rent, 25 percent move to a condominium, and the rest buy homes. Of the people who own condominiums, 60 percent stay in a condominium and the rest buy homes. Of the people who own homes, 80 percent stay in a home and the rest split evenly between rental property and a condominium. Currently, 55 percent of the people in San Francisco rent, 15 percent own a condominium, and 30 percent own a home.
   a) What percentage will rent year after next? Own a condominium? Own a home?
   b) What are the long-run percentages?

2.23 PROBLEM SET 2-8 (concluded)

8. The undergraduate admissions office at Babson College analyzed where children of Babson, Bentley College, and Bryant College alumni apply. From the pool of children that apply to exactly one of the three schools, research indicates that of the children of Babson alumni, 85 percent apply to Babson, 10 percent apply to Bentley, and the rest apply to Bryant. Of the children of Bentley alumni, 40 percent apply to Bentley, 35 percent apply to Babson, and the rest apply to Bryant. Of the children of Bryant alumni, 40 percent apply to Bryant, and the rest split evenly between Babson and Bentley.
   a) What percentage of the grandchildren of each college's alumni will apply to that college?
   b) What percentage of the great-grandchildren of each college's alumni will apply to that college?

9. In the current presidential election year, the Democratic party chairperson in Illinois has done an analysis of the voting preferences of the state's residents. The data indicate that every year 25 percent of the registered Democrats change to Republican and 5 percent change to independent. Also, 30 percent of the registered Republicans change to Democrat and 10 percent change to independent, while 45 percent of the registered independents change to Democrat and 15 percent change to Republican.
   a) In the gubernatorial election two years from now, what percentage of each party will remain unchanged?
   b) In the presidential election four years from now, what percentage of each party will remain unchanged?

10. Carry out the multiplication and interpret the result.

$$\begin{array}{cc} \text{State} & \text{State} \\ 1 \quad 2 & \end{array}$$
$$\begin{array}{cc} 1 & 2 \\ (a \quad b) & \end{array} \begin{array}{c} 1 \\ 2 \end{array} \begin{pmatrix} 1 & 0 \\ 0 & 1 \end{pmatrix}$$

11. The following chain is cyclical, meaning that it returns periodically to the same state. Write the successive state vectors until the initial one, (0.6 0.3 0.1), reappears.

$$(0.6 \quad 0.3 \quad 0.1) \begin{pmatrix} 0 & 0 & 1 \\ 1 & 0 & 0 \\ 0 & 1 & 0 \end{pmatrix}$$

2.24 REVIEW PROBLEMS

Solve each of the following systems by the elimination method.

1. $x + 10y = 25$
   $3x - 7y = 1.$

2. $6x + 8y = 15$
   $9x + 12y = 25.$

3. $2x + 3y = 9$
   $4x - y = 4$
   $6x - 5y = -1.$

4. $3x + 5y = 9$
   $4x + 2y = 5$
   $5x + 3y = 7.$

5. $x + 2y - 3z = 11$
   $3x + 2y + z = 1$
   $2x + y - 5z = 11.$

6. $3x + y + z = 4$
   $x - 2y - 3z = 0$
   $2x + 3y + 4z = 6.$

7. $2x \quad\quad + z = 4$
   $\quad\quad 3y + 2z = 6$
   $4x - 3y \quad\quad = 2.$

8. $x - y \quad\quad = 1$
   $2x + y - 3z = 2$
   $x + y - 2z = 1.$

2.24 REVIEW PROBLEMS (continued)

9. The table shows, for example, that a pound of cashews contains two ounces of nutrient P, three ounces of Q, and one ounce of R. Similar relations are shown for walnuts and almonds. If a mixture of x pounds of cashews, y pounds of walnuts, and z pounds of almonds is to contain exactly 9 ounces P, 13 ounces of Q, and 4 ounces of R, find the permissible values for x, y, and z.

Ounces per Pound of Nuts

Nut	Nutrient P	Nutrient Q	Nutrient R
Cashews	2	3	1
Walnuts	1	2	1
Almonds	1	1	0

Write the solution in arbitrary-variable form, and state the permissible ranges of values for the variables.

10. See Problem 9. If the per-pound costs are 20, 10, and 5 cents for cashews, walnuts, and almonds, respectively, find the cost and composition of the minimum-cost mixture.

11. We wish to mix x liters of regular unleaded gasoline with y liters of premium unleaded and z liters of super premium unleaded to obtain 1,000 liters of 90 octane gasoline with a vapor pressure index of 27.5. Costs per liter are $0.50, $0.55, and $0.65, respectively. Octane ratings are 84, 92, and 100, respectively. Vapor pressure indices are 20, 30, and 40, respectively.
    a) Write the solution in arbitrary-variable form.
    b) What is the composition and cost of the minimum-cost mixture?

12. The table below shows the number of hours required to make one unit of various products (A, B, and C) in each of three departments (I, II, and III). For example, it takes one hour of department I time,

Hours to Make One Unit of:

Department	Product A	Product B	Product C
I	1	1	1
II	2	1	3
III	3	2	4

three hours of department II time, and four hours of department III time to make one unit of product C.
  a) Find the numbers of units, x, y, and z of products A, B, and C that can be made if exactly 8 hours of department I time, 14 hours of department II time, and 22 hours of department III time are to be utilized.
  b) If the maximum possible number of units of C are made, how many hours of each department's time will be spent on making C?
  c) It is possible to utilize the hours exactly if no units of B are made? Explain.

13. The demand and supply expressions for products 1 and 2 are

Demand	Supply
$p_1 = 1{,}700 - 3q_1 - q_2$	$p_1 = 100 + 2q_1 + q_2$
$p_2 = 1{,}650 - q_1 - 2q_2$	$p_2 = 50 + q_1 + 2q_2$

  a) What will be the prices and quantities at equilibrium?
  b) If the demand functions change to the following and the supply functions are unchanged, find the new equilibrium point.

Product	Demand
1	$p_1 = 1{,}730 - 3q_1 - q_2$
2	$p_2 = 1{,}710 - q_1 - 2q_2$

14. The demand and supply expressions for products 1 and 2 are

Demand	Supply
$p_1 = 2{,}300 - 30q_1 - 10q_2$	$p_1 = 180 + 5q_1 + 2q_2$
$p_2 = 2{,}000 - 10q_1 - 20q_2$	$p_2 = 120 + q_1 + 4q_2$

  a) What will be the prices and quantities at equilibrium?
  b) If the demand functions change to the following and the supply functions remain the same, find the new equilibrium point.

Product	Demand
1	$p_1 = 4{,}424 - 30q_1 - 10q_2$
2	$p_2 = 2{,}708 - 10q_1 - 20q_2$

2.24 REVIEW PROBLEMS (continued)

Perform the following operations:

15. $(1 \quad 4 \quad 6) + (3 \quad -1 \quad 0) - 5(3 \quad 5 \quad -4)$.

16. $\begin{pmatrix} 8 \\ 2 \end{pmatrix} - 3\begin{pmatrix} 4 \\ 6 \end{pmatrix} + 2\begin{pmatrix} 1 \\ 5 \end{pmatrix}$.

17. $\begin{pmatrix} 3 & 2 & 0 \\ 1 & 5 & 4 \end{pmatrix} + \begin{pmatrix} 1 & -3 & 6 \\ 2 & 4 & 5 \end{pmatrix} - 2\begin{pmatrix} 1 & 1 & 3 \\ 4 & 0 & -1 \end{pmatrix}$.

18. $\begin{pmatrix} 3 & -2 \\ 1 & 7 \end{pmatrix} - \begin{pmatrix} -3 & 4 \\ 6 & 0 \end{pmatrix} - 3\begin{pmatrix} 1 & 2 \\ 1 & 3 \end{pmatrix}$
    $+ 5\begin{pmatrix} 1 & -1 \\ -2 & 2 \end{pmatrix}$.

19. $(1 \quad 0 \quad 2)\begin{pmatrix} 2 & -1 & 3 & 5 \\ 0 & 2 & -2 & 1 \\ 1 & 4 & 2 & 3 \end{pmatrix}$.

20. $\begin{pmatrix} 1 & 3 & 2 \\ 2 & 0 & 1 \\ 0 & 1 & 2 \end{pmatrix}\begin{pmatrix} 2 & 3 & 4 \\ -1 & 2 & 0 \\ 3 & -1 & 5 \end{pmatrix}$.

21. $\begin{pmatrix} 2 & 3 \\ 1 & -1 \end{pmatrix}\begin{pmatrix} 1 & 3 & 5 \\ 2 & 4 & 6 \end{pmatrix}$.

22. $\begin{pmatrix} 4 & 1 & -1 \\ 2 & 0 & 3 \\ 0 & -2 & 4 \end{pmatrix}\begin{pmatrix} 0 & 1 & -1 \\ 1 & -1 & 0 \\ -1 & 0 & 1 \end{pmatrix}$.

23. Given the following matrices:

$$A = \begin{pmatrix} -1 & 12 & 16 \\ 6 & 17 & 7 \\ 15 & 1 & -3 \end{pmatrix} \quad B = \begin{pmatrix} 18 & 13 & 3 \\ 4 & 6 & 8 \\ -6 & 1 & -3 \end{pmatrix}$$

$$C = \begin{pmatrix} 7 & 1 & 9 \\ 11 & 0 & 11 \\ 13 & 7 & 2 \end{pmatrix} \quad D = \begin{pmatrix} 1 & 4 & -11 \\ 2 & -1 & -2 \\ 11 & 8 & -8 \end{pmatrix},$$

find a) $3A - 2B$. c) AB. e) $AC + BD$.
     b) $-4C + 5D$. d) BA. f) $CA + DB$.

---

24. The number of trees, bushes, and shrubs used in landscaping small, medium, and large lots are shown as the requirements matrix in the table. Costs per unit are shown at the left.
    a) A contractor orders plantings for 6 small, 10 medium, and 5 large lots. Multiply the planting vector and the requirements matrix then interpret the results.
    b) Multiply the cost vector and the requirements matrix. Then interpret the results.

		Requirements Matrix Number Needed to Landscape a		
Unit Cost	Item	Small Lot	Medium Lot	Large Lot
$30	Red maple	0	1	2
20	Hard maple	1	1	1
20	Yew	2	4	5
40	Arborvitae	0	2	2
50	Spruce	0	2	3
20	Rhododendron	2	3	6
10	Laurel	2	2	4
20	Azalea	2	5	8

Find the inverse of each of the following matrices (if an inverse exists):

25. $\begin{pmatrix} 0 & 1 \\ 1 & 0 \end{pmatrix}$.

26. $\begin{pmatrix} 3 & 1 \\ 0 & 2 \end{pmatrix}$.

27. $\begin{pmatrix} 1 & 2 \\ 3 & 3 \end{pmatrix}$.

28. $\begin{pmatrix} 1 & 1 \\ 2 & 1 \end{pmatrix}$.

29. $\begin{pmatrix} 5 & 3 \\ 2 & 2 \end{pmatrix}$.

30. $\begin{pmatrix} 1 & 2 \\ 3 & 4 \end{pmatrix}$.

2.24 REVIEW PROBLEMS (continued)

31. $\begin{pmatrix} 1 & 0 & 1 \\ 0 & 1 & 2 \\ 2 & 3 & 0 \end{pmatrix}$.

32. $\begin{pmatrix} 1 & 2 & -1 \\ 1 & 0 & 1 \\ 0 & 5 & -5 \end{pmatrix}$.

33. $\begin{pmatrix} 1 & 0 & 2 \\ 0 & 1 & 3 \\ 1 & 2 & 0 \end{pmatrix}$.

34. $\begin{pmatrix} 0 & 0 & 1 \\ 0 & 1 & 0 \\ 1 & 0 & 0 \end{pmatrix}$.

35. $\begin{pmatrix} 60 & 30 & 20 \\ 30 & 20 & 15 \\ 20 & 15 & 12 \end{pmatrix}$.

36. $\begin{pmatrix} 1 & 1 & 1 \\ 2 & 1 & 1 \\ 1 & 2 & 2 \end{pmatrix}$.

37. $\begin{pmatrix} 1 & 2 & 1 \\ 2 & 1 & 1 \\ 1 & 2 & 2 \end{pmatrix}$.

38. $\begin{pmatrix} 2 & 4 & 1 \\ 3 & 1 & 2 \\ 0 & 5 & 6 \end{pmatrix}$.

39. $\begin{pmatrix} 2 & 0 & 1 \\ 3 & 1 & 3 \\ 0 & 1 & 4 \end{pmatrix}$.

40. Consider the system

$$7x_1 + 11x_2 = 3$$
$$5x_1 + 8x_2 = 5.$$

a) Relating the system to $Ax = b$, what is A? x? b?
b) Solve the system using the Gauss-Jordan method.
c) Compute A^{-1}.
d) Write $x = A^{-1}b$ in expanded matrix form.
e) Compute the solution from part (d).
f) What would be the solution vector if the elements in the vector of constants, 3 and 5, were changed to:
(1) 1, 1? (2) 0, 1? (3) 1, 0? (4) 2, −3?

41. Answer parts (a) through (e) of Problem 40 for the systems

$$2x_1 + 4x_2 = 4$$
$$5x_1 + 6x_2 = 8.$$

f) What would be the solution vector if the elements in the vector of constants, 4 and 8, were changed to:
(1) 4, 12? (2) 12, 16? (3) 20, 40? (4) 0, 4?

42. Answer parts (a) through (e) of Problem 40 for the system

$$3x_1 + 2x_3 = 1$$
$$5x_1 + 2x_2 + 5x_3 = 2$$
$$ x_2 + x_3 = 3.$$

f) What would be the solution vector if the elements in the vector of constants, 1, 2, and 3, were changed to.
(1) 1, 1, 1? (2) 1, 0, 1? (3) 1, 1, 0?

43. Answer parts (a) through (e) of Problem 40 for the system

$$2x_1 + 3x_2 - 15x_3 = 3$$
$$-5x_1 - 7x_2 + 35x_3 = 2$$
$$3x_1 + 4x_2 - 21x_3 = 1.$$

f) What would be the solution vector if the elements in the vector of constants, 3, 2, and 1, were changed to:
(1) 1, 1, 1? (2) 0, 1, 1? (3) 1, 1, 0?

44. The table shows the x_1 units of product X_1 are to be made and that a unit of X_1 requires one hour of time

2.24 REVIEW PROBLEMS (concluded)

on machine M_1, three hours on M_2, and two hours on M_3. For $i = 1, 2, 3$, machine M_i has H_i hours of time available. Similar interpretations apply to other entries.

Product	Units to Be Made	Hours of Machine Time per unit of Product on		
		M_1	M_2	M_3
X_1	x_1	1	3	2
X_2	x_2	2	1	3
X_3	x_3	3	2	1

Find the number of units that can be made if the machine time availability vector $(H_1\ H_2\ H_3)$ is:
a) (180 540 360).
b) (180 180 180).
c) (270 360 360).

45. Consider the system

$$x_1 + x_2 + x_3 = 3$$
$$2x_1 + 3x_2 + 2x_3 = 5$$
$$x_1 + 2x_2 + x_3 = 2.$$

a) Show that the matrix of coefficients does not have an inverse.
b) Find the solution of the system.
c) Change the constant in the first equation from 3 to 4.
   (1) Does the change in the constant have an effect upon the matrix of coefficients?
   (2) Does the change have an effect upon the solution in part (b)?
   (3) Our example illustrates what it means if the matrix of coefficients in an n-by-n system has no inverse. What does it mean if the coefficient matrix has no inverse?

46. In a section of the country, 35 percent live in urban areas and 65 percent in rural areas at a point in time. Urban–rural movement each year is described by the transition matrix

$$\begin{array}{c} \\ \text{Urban} \\ \text{Rural} \end{array} \begin{array}{cc} \text{Urban} & \text{Rural} \\ \begin{pmatrix} 0.8 & 0.2 \\ 0.4 & 0.6 \end{pmatrix} \end{array}$$

a) What will be the proportions in urban and rural areas after one year?
b) After two years?
c) After three years?
d) What is the steady state?

47. Brand X has 25 percent of the market. Other brands share the rest of the market. Because of a promotional effort, 50 percent of those buying other brands shift to Brand X each month, while 70 percent of those buying Brand X continue to buy this brand.
a) What percentage of the market will Brand X have after one month?
b) What is the steady state?

2.25 EXTENDED REVIEW PROBLEMS

1. The demand and supply function for brown eggs and white eggs are:

	Demand	Supply
Brown eggs:	$p_b = 2{,}200 - 4q_b - 3q_w$	$p_b = 300 + 3q_b + 2q_w$
White eggs:	$p_w = 1{,}300 - 2q_b - 3q_w$	$p_w = 100 + 2q_b + q_w.$

a) What will be the prices and quantities at equilibrium?
b) If the supply functions change to the following and the demand functions are unchanged, find the new equilibrium point.

	Supply
Brown eggs:	$p_b = 150 + q_b + 4q_w$
White eggs:	$p_w = 25 + q_b + 3q_w.$

2.25 EXTENDED REVIEW PROBLEMS (continued)

2. The following table shows the number of blouses, skirts, and dresses to be made and the time required for each on the cutting, stitching, and finishing machines.

		Hours of Machine Time per Unit Made		
Product	Quantity	C	S	F
Blouses	b	4	7	3
Skirts	s	3	5	2
Dresses	d	5	6	4

Find the number of each item that can be made if the machine time availability vector is:

a) (230 355 170).
b) (175 290 130).
c) (180 262 136).

3. Given the following matrices:

$$A = \begin{pmatrix} 17 & 3 & -4 \\ -2 & 10 & 15 \\ 7 & -3 & 11 \end{pmatrix} \quad B = \begin{pmatrix} -5 & 12 & 2 \\ 3 & -1 & -3 \\ 6 & 0 & 8 \end{pmatrix}$$

$$C = \begin{pmatrix} 2 & -1 & -9 \\ 4 & 0 & 4 \\ 10 & 5 & -1 \end{pmatrix} \quad D = \begin{pmatrix} 5 & 2 & -10 \\ 3 & -4 & 6 \\ 10 & 7 & -7 \end{pmatrix},$$

find a) $3A - 2B$. c) AB. e) $AC + BD$.
b) $-4C + 5D$. d) BA. f) $CA + DB$.

Solve each of the following systems by the elimination method:

4. $2x - 3y = -14$
$5x - 2y = -13$
$3x + y = 1.$

5. $3x - 2y + 4z = 50$
$-x + 3y - 5z = -54$
$2x + y - 3z = -18.$

6. Find the inverse of each of the following matrices (if an inverse exists):

a) $\begin{pmatrix} 2 & -1 & -9 \\ 4 & 0 & 4 \\ 10 & 5 & -1 \end{pmatrix}$. b) $\begin{pmatrix} 5 & 2 & -10 \\ 3 & -4 & 6 \\ 10 & 7 & -7 \end{pmatrix}$.

7. Florida Juice Company wants to make a new 30-gallon mixture of apple, cranberry, and grapefruit juice for its restaurant clients. The new mixture should have a sugar content of 11 percent and an acidity rating of 3 percent. Each gallon of apple juice costs $1.25 and has a sugar content of 12 percent and an acidity rating of 4 percent. The per-gallon cost of cranberry juice is $1.00 with a sugar content of 10 percent and an acidity rating of 2 percent, while the per-gallon cost of grapefruit juice is $0.90 with a sugar content of 9 percent and an acidity rating of 1 percent.
a) What is the solution in arbitrary-variable form?
b) If the new mixture should be made at a minimum cost, how much of each juice should be used and what is the cost?

8. The following table shows the number of hours required to make one silk, polyester, and cotton shirt in the cutting, stitching, and finishing departments.
a) Find the number of each shirt that can be made if exactly 30 hours of cutting time, 15 hours of stitching time, and 20 hours of finishing time are available.
b) If the maximum number of cotton shirts are made, how many hours of each department's time will be spent on making cotton shirts?

	Hours to Make One Shirt		
Department	Silk	Polyester	Cotton
Cutting	2	1	4
Stitching	1	0.5	2
Finishing	1	1	3

c) Is it possible to utilize the hours if no polyester shirts are made?

2.25 EXTENDED REVIEW PROBLEMS *(concluded)*

9. In a small town just outside of Portland, Oregon, 80 percent of the people live in condominiums and 20 percent live in houses. The yearly transition matrix is

$$\begin{array}{c} \\ \text{Condo} \\ \text{Home} \end{array} \begin{array}{cc} \text{Condo} & \text{Home} \\ \begin{pmatrix} 0.7 & 0.3 \\ 0.6 & 0.4 \end{pmatrix}. \end{array}$$

   a) What will be the proportions in condominiums and homes after one year?
   b) After two years?
   c) After three years?
   d) What is the steady state?

10. Consider the system

$$3x_1 + 2x_2 - 7x_3 = 4$$
$$4x_1 - 5x_2 - 8x_3 = -15$$
$$-2x_1 + 6x_2 + x_3 = 12.$$

   a) Relating to the system $Ax = b$, what is A? x? b?
   b) Solve the system using the Gauss-Jordan method.
   c) Compute A^{-1}.
   d) Write $x = A^{-1}b$ in expanded matrix form.
   e) Compute the solution from part (d).
   f) What would be the solution vector if the elements in the vector of constants (4 −15 12) were changed to:
      (1) −2, −9, 5?   (2) −13, −21, 5?
      (3) 12, 2, 3?

Introduction to Linear Programming and the Simplex Method

3.1 INTRODUCTION

In our everyday lives, we are often confronted with a number of different ways of accomplishing a certain objective, some ways being better in certain senses than others. For example, many different combinations of foods will provide a satisfactory diet, but some combinations are more costly than others. We may be interested in finding the **minimum cost** of providing dietary requirements. Again, there are many combinations of products a plant can manufacture, and we may be interested in finding the combination that leads to the **maximum profit.**

The variables in real-life situations are subject to restrictions called **constraints.** In most instances, it is required that the variables not take on negative values. (How can you make a negative number of automobiles?) Furthermore, certain combinations of variables are not permissible. (For example, a manufacturing plant cannot operate more than 24 hours a day.) Also, production is restricted by plant capacity and raw material availability. Each of these constraints (or restrictions) gives rise to a mathematical inequality or equality. Our discussion will be limited to the case where the constraints are **linear.** When all the constraints are taken together for a given problem, then, we will have a **system of linear inequalities and/or equalities.**

We will first investigate how to solve systems of linear inequalities and systems with **nonnegativity constraints.** We will then examine situations that give rise to constraints that can be formulated as a system of linear inequalities and/or equalities. In the formulation, we will derive an expression called the **objective function** which will state how the objective (profit or cost) is computed. The problem is then reduced to **optimizing** this objective function (maximizing the profit or minimizing the cost) subject to the constraints. If the constraints and the objective function are linear, we have a problem in **linear programming.**

The remainder of the chapter will be devoted to solution techniques for linear programming problems. We will present a **three-step graphical procedure** for problems in two variables. We will then use this procedure to motivate and introduce the **Simplex Method,** (an algorithmic approach for solving problems with any number of variables). Along the way, we will show how to use a computer package, **LINDO,** to quickly solve linear programming problems.[1]

---

[1]**LINDO** stands for Linear Interactive and Discrete Optimizer and was developed by Linus Schrage at the Graduate School of Business, University of Chicago.

3.2 SYSTEMS OF TWO LINEAR INEQUALITIES[2]

The system of inequalities

$$x > 4$$
$$x \leq 9$$

requires that x be greater than 4 but less than or equal to 9. Hence, x is in an interval with the smaller number, 4, at the left and the larger number, 9, at the right. This may be written as

$$4 < x \leq 9.$$

Again, the statement

$$0 \leq x \leq 10$$

says that x is greater than or equal to 0 but less than or equal to 10.

> **Exercise.** Write the statement that specifies that y is less than 0 but greater than or equal to -3.
> **Answer:** $-3 \leq y < 0$.

A system of inequalities is inconsistent if no point satisfies all the inequalities simultaneously. An inequality is redundant in a system if it holds automatically when another inequality (or combination of other inequalities) holds.

Two inequalities are said to be **inconsistent** if both cannot be true at the same time, and one of a pair is **redundant** if it is true automatically when the other is true. Thus, if company policy states that workers may not work more than 10 hours a day ($x \leq 10$) and the union contract specifies that workers must not work more than 8 hours a day ($x \leq 8$), company policy is redundant.

> **Exercise.** How would the system $x < 5$ and $x > 8$ be described? Why?
> **Answer:** The inequalities are inconsistent because if x is less than 5, it cannot be greater than 8.

Two linear inequalities are used in describing the space between two lines.

Example. Graph the solution space described by the inequalities

$$i_1: \quad y \geq 2x - 1$$
$$i_2: \quad y \leq x + 2.$$

---

[2] For a review of single linear inequalities, see A2.15 through A2.17.

CHAPTER 3 INTRODUCTION TO LINEAR PROGRAMMING AND THE SIMPLEX METHOD

Recall from Appendix A2.17 that to graph an inequality we first graph the corresponding equality and then determine the half-space that satisfies the strict inequality. So, we first graph

$$e_1: \quad y = 2x - 1$$

in the usual way as shown in Figure 3–1A and then check the origin (0, 0) in the inequality to find

$$0 > 2(0) - 1 \quad \text{or} \quad 0 > -1$$

so that we want to include the half-space containing the origin. We indicate this by the direction of the arrows on line e_1.

In the same way, we graph

$$e_2: \quad y = x + 2$$

and find that

$$0 < 0 + 2 \quad \text{or} \quad 0 < 2$$

as indicated by directions of the arrows on line e_2.

The shaded area in Figure 3–1A then represents the solution space satisfying the two inequalities i_1 and i_2. Now the lines are found in the usual manner to intersect at (3, 5). Hence for any point in the solution space, the x-coordinate must be less than or equal to 3.

Exercise. Suppose that we let x have the permissible value 0. What y values are permissible if $x = 0$? (See Figure 3–1A.)
Answer. $-1 \leq y \leq 2$.

The Exercise and Figure 3–1A show that for a given permissible value of x, the permissible values of y are those that are greater than or equal to $2x - 1$ but less than or equal to $x + 2$. That is, the solution space is completely described by

$$x \leq 3; \quad 2x - 1 \leq y \leq x + 2.$$

This last result says, for example, that if $x = -1$, then both i_1 and i_2 will be true for any y value in the closed interval

$$-3 \leq y \leq 1.$$

Example. Graph the solution space described by the inequalities

$$i_1: \quad y \leq 2x - 1$$
$$i_2: \quad y \geq x + 2.$$

This time we get the solution space represented by the shaded space in Figure 3–1B. Note here that the origin (0, 0) does not satisfy either inequality.

FIGURE 3–1A

FIGURE 3–1B

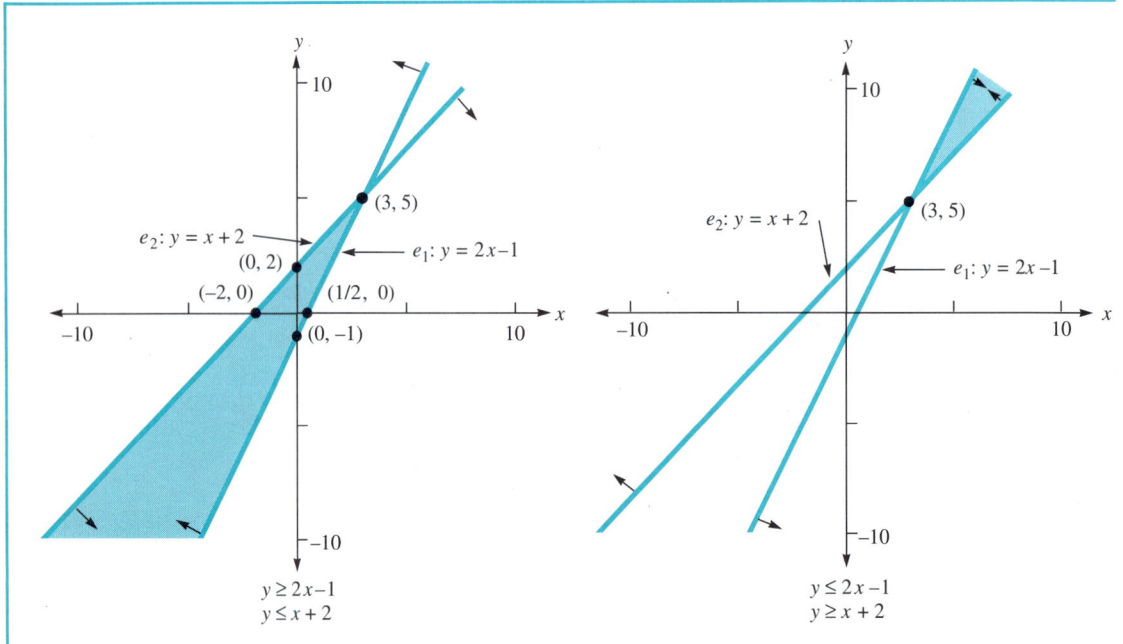

Exercise. Describe the preceding example's solution space algebraically.

Answer: $x \geq 3$; $x + 2 \leq y \leq 2x - 1$.

Example. Graph the solution space described by the inequalities

$$i_1: \quad y \leq 2x - 1$$
$$i_2: \quad y \leq x + 2$$

and describe the space algebraically.

This time we get the solution space represented by the shaded space in Figure 3–1C. Note here that the origin $(0, 0)$ satisfies inequality i_2 but does not satisfy i_1.

Now from Figure 3–1C we see that to the left of $(3, 5)$ we have points with $x < 3$ that are below e_1 (i.e., $y \leq 2x - 1$). On the other hand, to the right of $(3, 5)$ we have points with $x > 3$ that are below line e_2 (i.e., $y \leq x + 2$). So the solution set is described algebraically by

$$x \leq 3; \quad y \leq 2x - 1$$
$$x \geq 3; \quad y \leq x + 2.$$

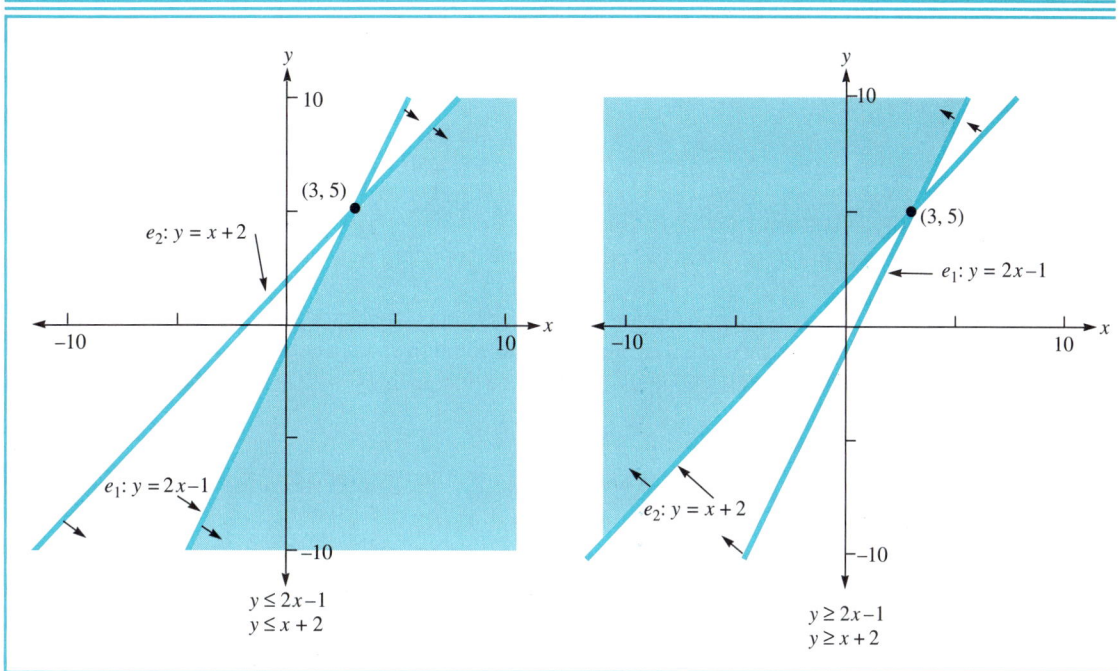

FIGURE 3-1C

FIGURE 3-1D

> **Exercise.** Graph the solution space described by the inequalities
>
> i_1: $y \geq 2x - 1$
> i_2: $y \geq x + 2$
>
> and describe the solution space algebraically.
>
> **Answer:** See Figure 3-1D.
>
> $x \leq 3$; $y \geq x + 2$ or $x \geq 3$; $y \geq 2x - 1$.

3.3 NONNEGATIVITY CONSTRAINTS

In the work to come, we shall deal often with quantities and prices of goods, and other variables that cannot take on negative values. In the case of two variables, x and y, this restriction is expressed by writing

$$x \geq 0$$
$$y \geq 0$$

> Nonnegativity restricts us to points in the first quadrant.

along with the other inequalities at hand. **Nonnegativity** means that only points in the first quadrant, including the axes, are under consideration.

The system

$$x \geq 0$$
$$y \geq 0$$
$$x \leq 4$$
$$y \leq 2$$

has as its solution the points on the boundary and inside the rectangle shown in Figure 3–2.

The algebraic solution of 2-by-2 systems of inequalities with nonnegativity constraints is facilitated by graphing the solution space and determining from the graph what algebraic manipulations of the inequalities will lead to the correct general solution.

Example. Assuming nonnegativity for x and y, graph the solution space described by the inequalities

$$i_1: \quad x + 2y \leq 8$$
$$i_2: \quad 7x + 4y \geq 28$$

and describe the space algebraically.

The nonnegativity constraints on x and y restrict us to the first quadrant. Restricting the graphs of i_1 and i_2, then, to the first quadrant, we get the solution space shown in Figure 3–3A. The point of intersection is found by the usual method to be (2.4, 2.8).

FIGURE 3–2

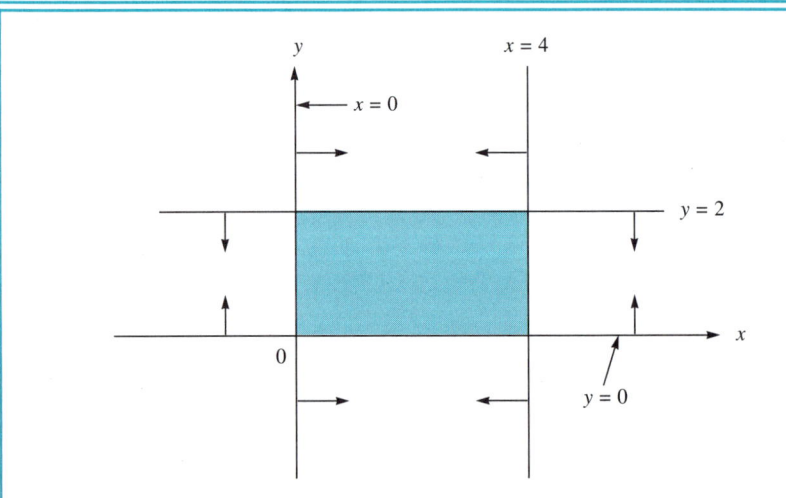

From Figure 3–3A we see that y is restricted to the interval between 0 and 2.8, inclusively. In this interval, the value of x is restricted between e_2 on the lower end and e_1 on the upper end. Solving i_2 and i_1 for x, then, we get

$$\frac{28 - 4y}{7} \leq x \leq 8 - 2y$$

so the solution set is

$$0 \leq y \leq 2.8; \quad \frac{28 - 4y}{7} \leq x \leq 8 - 2y.$$

Exercise. Express the algebraic solution by putting a numeric limit on the values of x.

Answer: $2.4 \leq x \leq 4; \quad \frac{28 - 7x}{4} \leq y \leq \frac{8 - x}{2}$

$4 \leq x \leq 8; \quad 0 \leq y \leq \frac{8 - x}{2}.$

Exercise. Assuming nonnegativity for x and y, graph the solution space described by the inequalities

$i_1: \quad x + 2y \geq 8$
$i_2: \quad 7x + 4y \leq 28$

and describe the space algebraically.

Answer: See Figure 3–3B.

$2.8 \leq y \leq 4; \quad (8 - 2y) \leq x \leq \frac{28 - 4y}{7}$

$4 \leq y \leq 7; \quad 0 \leq x \leq \frac{28 - 4y}{7}$

or

$0 \leq x \leq 2.4; \quad \frac{8 - x}{2} \leq y \leq \frac{28 - 7x}{4}.$

Example. Assuming nonnegativity for x and y, graph the solution space described by the inequalities

$i_1: \quad x + 2y \geq 8$
$i_2: \quad 7x + 4y \geq 28$

and describe the space algebraically.

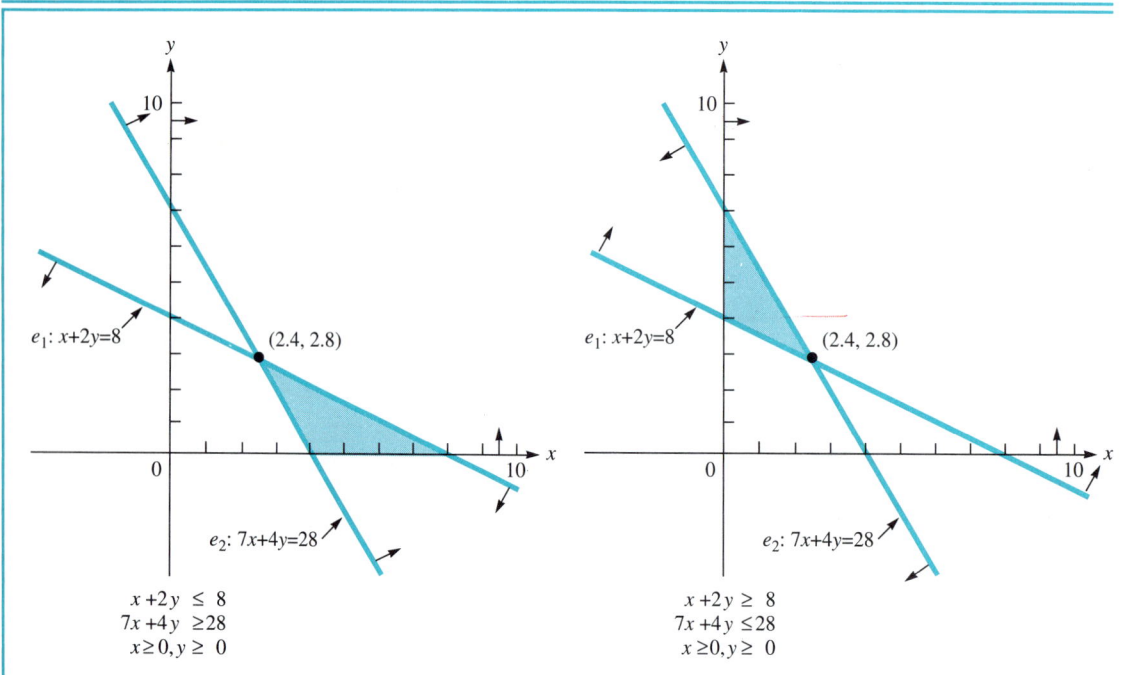

FIGURE 3–3A

FIGURE 3–3B

This time, we get the solution space shown in Figure 3–3C. From this figure, we see that to the left of the point (2.4, 2.8) we must remain above line e_2 and to the right of the y-axis, while to the right of (2.4, 2.8) we must remain above line e_1 and above the x-axis. The first part is represented by

$$0 \leq x \leq 2.4; \quad y \geq \frac{28 - 7x}{4},$$

and the second part by

$$2.4 \leq x \leq 8; \quad y \geq \frac{8 - x}{2},$$

together with

$$x \geq 8; \quad y \geq 0.$$

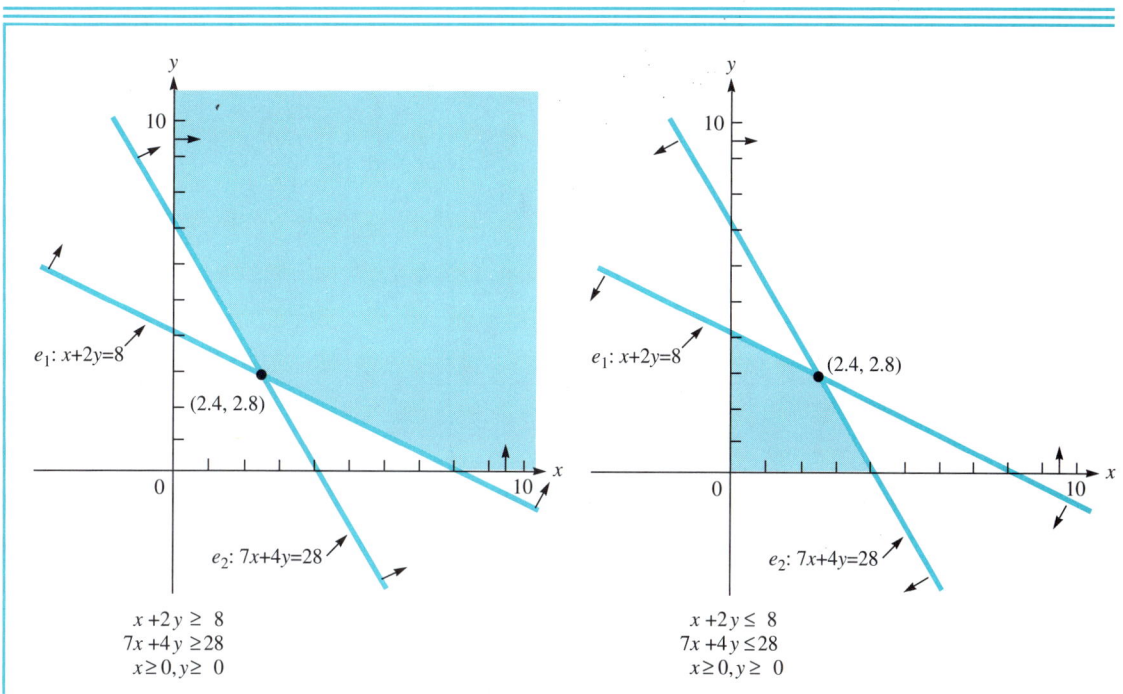

FIGURE 3-3C

FIGURE 3-3D

Exercise. Assuming nonnegativity for x and y, graph the solution space described by the inequalities

$$i_1: \quad x + 2y \leq 8$$
$$i_2: \quad 7x + 4y \leq 28$$

and describe the space algebraically.

Answer: See Figure 3-3D.

$$0 \leq x \leq 2.4; \quad 0 \leq y \leq \frac{8-x}{2}$$

$$2.4 \leq x \leq 4; \quad 0 \leq y \leq \frac{28-7x}{4}$$

or

$$0 \leq y \leq 2.8; \quad 0 \leq x \leq \frac{28-4y}{7}$$

$$2.8 \leq y \leq 4; \quad 0 \leq x \leq 8 - 2y.$$

3.4 PROBLEM SET 3-1

Graph the solution space:

1. $y \geq -1$
   $x \leq 4$.
2. $x \geq -2$
   $y \leq -1$.
3. $x \leq 3$
   $x \leq y$.
4. $y \geq -3$
   $y \geq -x$.
5. $x \leq 3$
   $y \leq 1$
   $x + 3y \geq 3$.
6. $x \leq 2$
   $y \geq -4$
   $2x - y \geq 4$.

In each of the following,
(a) Graph the solution space and
(b) Describe the solution space algebraically:

7. $2x + y \geq 6$
   $x + 4y \leq 8$.
8. $2x + y \leq 6$
   $x + 4y \geq 8$.
9. $2x + y \geq 6$
   $x + 4y \geq 8$.
10. $2x + y \leq 6$
    $x + 4y \leq 8$.
11. $x - 2y \leq 8$
    $x + y \geq 2$.
12. $x - 2y \geq 8$
    $x + y \leq 2$.
13. $x - 2y \leq 8$
    $x + y \leq 2$.
14. $x - 2y \geq 8$
    $x + y \geq 2$.
15. $4x + 9y \geq 130$
    $2x + 3y \leq 50$
    $x \geq 5$.
16. $x + 2y \geq 20$
    $3x + 2y \leq 40$
    $y \leq 15$.

Assuming $x \geq 0$ and $y \geq 0$ in each of the following,
(a) Graph the solution space and
(b) Describe the solution space algebraically:

17. $2x + 3y \leq 12$
    $x - 2y \geq 2$.
18. $2x + 3y \geq 12$
    $x - 2y \leq 2$.
19. $2x + 3y \leq 12$
    $x - 2y \leq 2$.
20. $2x + 3y \geq 12$
    $x - 2y \geq 2$.
21. $4x + y \geq 12$
    $x + 5y \leq 8$.
22. $4x + y \leq 12$
    $x + 5y \leq 8$.
23. $4x + y \geq 12$
    $x + 5y \geq 8$.
24. $4x + y \leq 12$
    $x + 5y \geq 8$.

3.4 PROBLEM SET 3-1 (concluded)

25. $4x + 3y \leq 120$
    $x + y \leq 40$
    $6x + 7y \leq 190.$

26. $4x + 3y \leq 120$
    $x + y \leq 40$
    $6x + 7y \geq 190.$

3.5 MAXIMIZATION EXAMPLES: PRODUCT MIX

Table 3-1 shows that Lounge Chairs and Swivel Chairs are made using the equipment of two departments: I and II. It requires one hour in each department to make a Lounge Chair, but making a Swivel Chair takes one hour in Department I and two hours in Department II. Department I has four hours of time available, and II has six hours available. Each Lounge Chair made and sold contributes $1 to profit, and each Swivel Chair contributes $0.50 to profit.

The problem is to determine the maximum profit that can be achieved, keeping in mind the four- and six-hour time limitations in the departments. The profit achieved from x Lounge Chairs and y Swivel Chairs is

(Profit per Lounge Chair)(Number of Lounge Chairs)
+ (Profit per Swivel Chair)(Number of Swivel Chairs),

which is

$$\$1x + \$0.5y.$$

The last expression is the **objective function**, which we shall denote by θ (theta) for simplicity[3]

$$\text{Profit} = \theta = x + 0.5y.$$

TABLE 3-1

Chair	Number of Units Made	Profit per Unit	Hours Required per Unit in	
			Department I (4 Hours Available)	Department II (6 Hours Available)
Lounge	x	$1.00	1	1
Swivel	y	0.50	1	2

---

[3] Z is another variable used for the objective function. We choose θ to avoid ambiguity later when z might be used as a variable.

From Table 3–1, we see that to make x Lounge Chairs and y Swivel Chairs will require $x + y$ hours in Department I and $x + 2y$ hours in Department II. The time limitations, 4 hours available in I and 6 hours available in II, therefore are

$$x + y \leq 4$$
$$x + 2y \leq 6.$$

These conditions, taken together with nonnegativity constraints on x and y,

$$x \geq 0$$
$$y \geq 0,$$

> Many real-world problems can be formulated as linear programming problems with a linear objective function subject to linear inequality constraints plus nonnegativity.

lead to the following statement of the problem:

Maximize the objective function

$$\theta = x + 0.5y$$

subject to the constraint inequalities labeled i_1 through i_4:

Department I i_1: $x + y \leq 4$
Department II i_2: $x + 2y \leq 6$
Nonnegativity i_3, i_4: $x, y \geq 0$

where the last expression combines the two nonnegativity constraints in a simplified form. Clearly, we can find nonnegative values of x and y (that is, values satisfying i_3 and i_4) that also satisfy i_1 and i_2. The obvious values are $x = 0$ and $y = 0$. However, if we substitute $(0, 0)$ into the objective function, we find that the profit is 0. We must make some product to achieve a profit. If we make one Lounge Chair and one Swivel Chair ($x = 1$ and $y = 1$), we find $\theta = 1.5$ and all the inequalities are satisfied.

Exercise. Is it possible to make two units of each product? If so, what profit will be achieved?

Answer: Yes, $x = 2$, $y = 2$ satisfy all constraints in the problem. The profit will be $3.

Exercise. Is it possible to make three units of each product?

Answer: No; $x = 3$, $y = 3$ satisfy neither i_1 nor i_2.

Our goal is not simply to list all the various profits that might be achieved but, rather, to find the **maximum profit** that can be achieved.

The solution space for the inequalities i_1 through i_4, commonly called the **feasible solution set**, is shown in Figure 3–4 as the area bounded by lines whose intersections (which we shall call **corners**) are at O, A, B, and C. The coordinates of $A(0, 3)$ and $C(4, 0)$, of course, are found as a result of graphing the equalities e_1 and e_2. $O(0, 0)$ is precisely the origin, while $B(2, 2)$ is found by solving the equalities e_1 and e_2 by the elimination procedure.

> The feasible solution set is the collection of points satisfying all the constraints simultaneously.

Now each point in the shaded solution space has a pair of coordinates (x, y) that, when substituted into the objective function, yield the value of θ associated with that point. For example, the point $P(1, 2)$ is in the solution space. At P, we find

$$\theta = 1 + 0.5(2) = 2.$$

Again, point $A(0, 3)$ is in the solution space. At A,

$$\theta = 0 + 0.5(3) = 1.5.$$

Clearly, the value of θ varies from point to point in the solution space. But observe that for a given x, we obtain the largest value of θ, for this given x, by making y as large as possible, that is, by going all the way to the boundary of the solution space. We see, therefore, that any point that will maximize θ for this problem must lie on the boundary of the solution space.

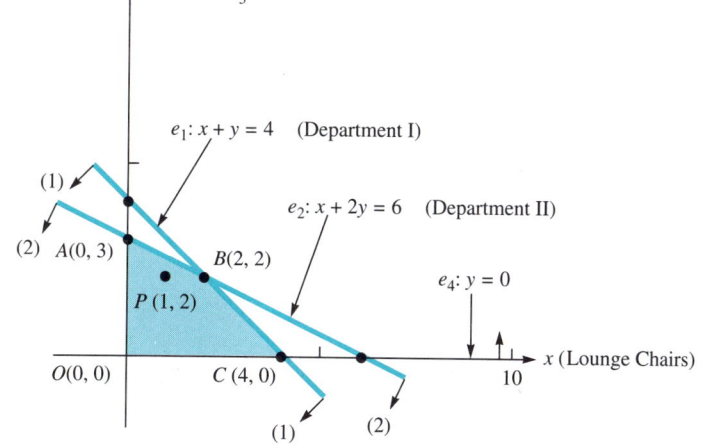

FIGURE 3–4

Consider next the boundary segment from $A(0, 3)$ to $B(2, 2)$:

$$\text{at } A, \quad \theta = 1.5$$
$$\text{at } B, \quad \theta = 3.$$

This implies that as we go from A toward B on the boundary AB, θ is increasing. Clearly, therefore, in seeking the maximum θ on this segment, we should go as far as possible in this direction, that is, to corner B.

Consider next the boundary segment from $B(2, 2)$ to $C(4, 0)$:

$$\text{at } B, \quad \theta = 3$$
$$\text{at } C, \quad \theta = 4.$$

Following the preceding reasoning, we move along the boundary to corner C, and then consider the segment from C to O. Obviously, θ decreases along this boundary. Whichever direction we move from C (toward O or toward B), we find θ decreases. Hence we conclude that the maximum value occurs at $C(4, 0)$ and is

$$\theta_{max} = 4.$$

The solution of our problem is to make four Lounge Chairs and no Swivel Chairs. This schedule will provide a profit of $4, the maximum possible with the stated constraints.

A graphical aid that helps us visualize the analysis just described on the objective function can be accomplished through the use of **isovalue lines**. The prefix **iso** means **same** as in the term **isobar** (often used in weather forecasts). Isobars are drawn on a weather map by connecting points that have the **same bar**ometric pressure. In our example, let us examine the **isoprofit** lines associated with our objective function

$$\theta = x + 0.5y.$$

> Each point on an isoprofit line results in the same profit value for the objective function.

As we saw, the smallest profit would be $0 occurring at the origin $(0, 0)$. Now suppose we wanted to find all points where profit would be $0. Substituting 0 for θ, we would get the equation

$$0 = x + 0.5y.$$

Superimposing the graph of this line on the feasible solution set from Figure 3–4, we get the result in Figure 3–5A. Notice that only the single point $(0, 0)$ on this isoprofit line is a feasible solution.

In an analogous way, the points where profit would be $1 are represented by the isoprofit line

$$1 = x + 0.5y$$

as shown in Figure 3–5B. Here we see that there are an infinite number of feasible points where profit would be $1; namely, all points on the line segment from $(1, 0)$ to $(0, 2)$.

Continuing in this manner, for the isoprofit lines for profits of $2, $3, $4, and $5, which are

$$\$2 \text{ profit:} \quad 2 = x + 0.5y,$$
$$\$3 \text{ profit:} \quad 3 = x + 0.5y,$$
$$\$4 \text{ profit:} \quad 4 = x + 0.5y,$$
$$\$5 \text{ profit:} \quad 5 = x + 0.5y,$$

we get the results shown in Figure 3–5C. Note that the isoprofit lines in Figures 3–5A, 3–5B, and 3–5C form a **family of parallel lines**. Why? Note also that the isoprofit line for $5 is **outside the feasible solution set**. From these figures, we see that any profit value greater than $4 would result in an isoprofit line outside the feasible solution set. Thus, as before, the maximum profit would be $4 which occurs at the point (4, 0) where the company would make four Lounge Chairs and no Swivel Chairs.

> The isoprofit lines for a specific objective function form a family of parallel lines intersecting the feasible solution set.

Exercise. Suppose the profit per Lounge Chair was changed to $2.00, and the profit per Swivel Chair was changed to $3.00. a) Find the new profit function. b) Find the values of the profit function at each of Figure 3–5's corners O, A, B, and C and draw the four associated isoprofit lines. c) How many of each chair should be made to maximize the profit? d) What is the maximum profit?

Answer: (a) $\theta_{max} = 2x + 3y$. (b) $0, $9, $10, $8. (c) Two Lounge Chairs and two Swivel Chairs. (d) $10.

FIGURE 3–5A   **FIGURE 3–5B**

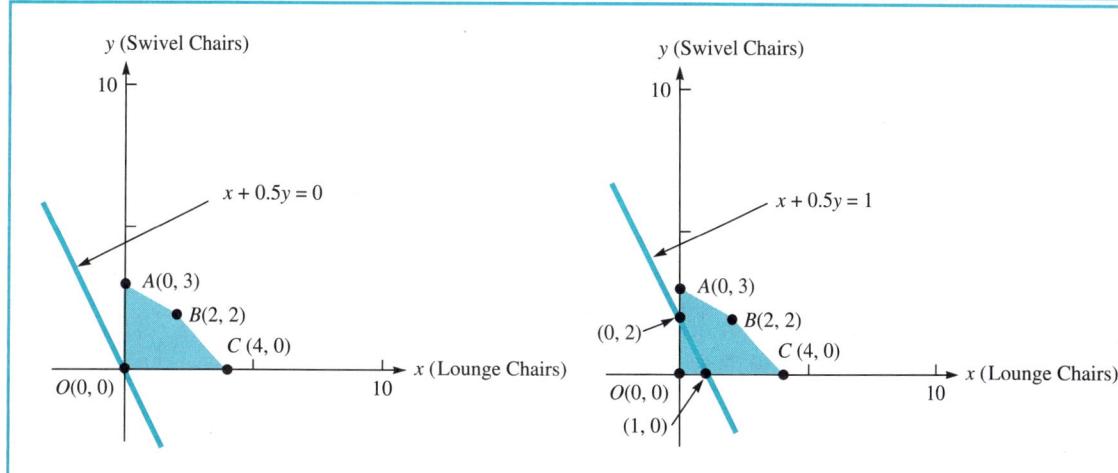

FIGURE 3-5C

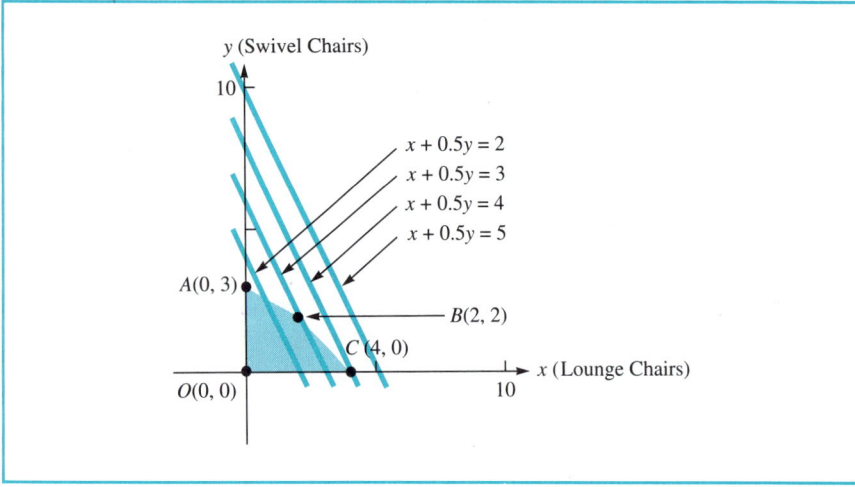

Now suppose that the profit per Lounge Chair in our original example remained at $1.00, but the profit per Swivel Chair was increased from $0.50 to $1.00. Then, the objective function would become

$$\theta_{max} = x + y.$$

Evaluating this profit function at each of the four corners, we get

$$(0, 0): \quad \theta = 0$$
$$(0, 3): \quad \theta = 3$$
$$(4, 0): \quad \theta = 4$$
$$(2, 2): \quad \theta = 4.$$

Thus there is a **tie** for the maximum value of $4.00 at both (4, 0) and (2, 2). Superimposing the profit function on our original feasible solution set from Figure 3-4, we get the result shown in Figure 3-6. Note in this figure that the isoprofit line for $\theta = 4$ is parallel to the constraint line e_1, $x + y = 4$. Thus the objective function is coincident with the line segment between the two corners at (4, 0) and (2, 2). In this case, then, the maximum profit of $4.00 can be attained not only at each of these corners, but at any point on the line segment joining them; that is, **at any point on the line segment from (4, 0) to (2, 2).** Although there are an infinite number of points on this line segment, for practical reasons we must restrict ourselves to those with integral coordinates. Why? Since this line segment is given by the equation

$$x + y = 4,$$

When there is a tie for the maximum at two corners, every point on the line segment between these corners results in the maximum value.

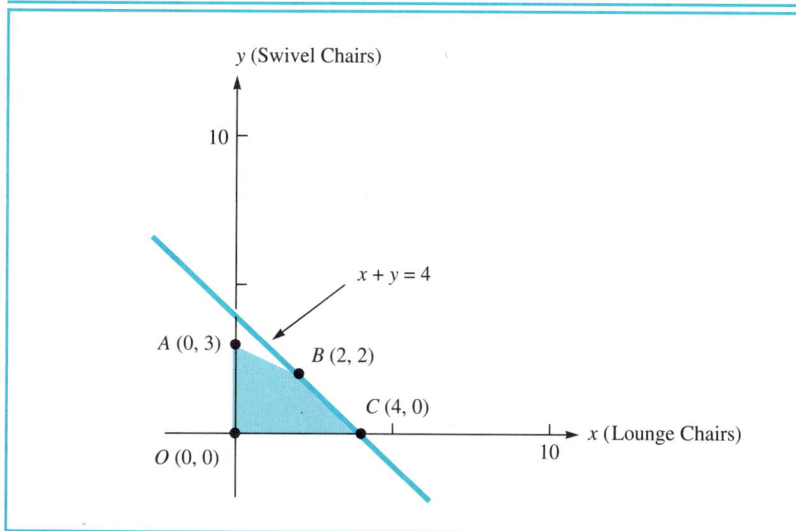

FIGURE 3-6

it is easy to see that the only other point with integral coordinates would be (3, 1). So, the company has a choice of manufacturing either four Lounge Chairs and no Swivel Chairs, three Lounge Chairs and one Swivel Chair, or two of each chair, with all three choices resulting in the maximum profit of $4.00. On what basis should the company decide among these three options?

Exercise. Draw a graph superimposing the isoprofit lines for $0, $1, $2, and $3 on Figure 3–4.

As another variation, suppose we return to our original example but introduce an additional constraint. Specifically, suppose the company has determined that the number of Swivel Chairs made should be at least 1/3 the number of Lounge Chairs. Since there are y Swivel Chairs and x Lounge Chairs, this new constraint becomes

$$y \geq \frac{1}{3}x \quad \text{or} \quad 3y \geq x.$$

We will adopt the convention of keeping all the variables on the left-hand side and so rewrite this inequality as

$$-x + 3y \geq 0.$$

Superimposing this on the original solution space in Figure 3–4, we get the feasible solution set shown in Figure 3–7. Note here that since the corresponding equality

$$e_3: \quad -x + 3y = 0$$

goes through the origin, we cannot use $(0, 0)$ as a test point. As an alternative, we could test the point $(0, 1)$ on the y-axis

$$-0 + 3(1) \geq 0 \quad \text{or} \quad 3 \geq 0,$$

thus indicating that we want to include $(0, 1)$ and thus all points above e_3.

> **Exercise.** What happens if we test the point $(1, 0)$ on the x-axis?
>
> **Answer:** We get $-1 \geq 0$, which is impossible, so we do not want to include $(1, 0)$.

As can be seen from Figure 3–7, we have three of the original four corners, but the fourth corner $(4, 0)$ has been replaced by the new corner $(3, 1)$, found in the usual way by the elimination method on e_1 and e_3. Why? Evaluating the original profit function

$$x + 0.5y,$$

FIGURE 3–7

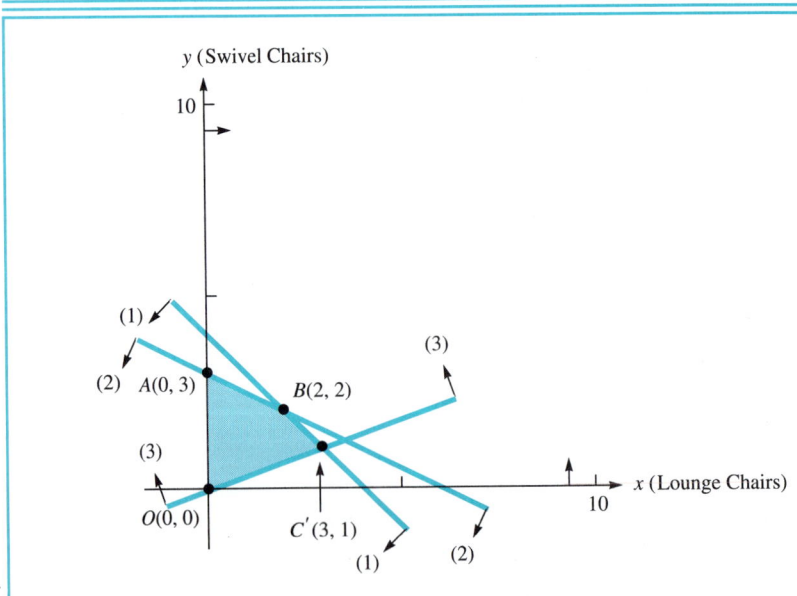

then, we get

$$(0, 0): \quad \theta = 0$$
$$(0, 3): \quad \theta = 1.5$$
$$(3, 1): \quad \theta = 3.5$$
$$(2, 2): \quad \theta = 3,$$

so the maximum profit is $3.50 when three Lounge Chairs and one Swivel Chair are made. Note the solution is not as good as the original problem which attained a maximum profit of $4.00 at the point (4, 0). Why?

Exercise. Draw a graph superimposing the isoprofit lines for $0, $1, $2, $3, and $4 on Figure 3–7.

Exercise. a) How many of each chair should be made to maximize the profit if the profit on each chair were $1? b) What is this maximum profit?

Answer: (a) Any combination on the line segment from (3, 1) to (2, 2). Note these are the only two points with integral coordinates. (b) $4.00.

At this point, we would like to discuss the technique of formulation, whereby a word problem is transformed into a mathematical model that can subsequently be solved by some algorithm such as the graphical method we have just seen.

Example. Ace Rubber Company manufactures two types of tires: Model P (the premium) and Model R (the regular). Model P sells for $95 per tire and costs $85 per tire to make, whereas Model R sells for $50 per tire and costs $42 per tire to make. To make one Model P tire, it requires two hours on Machine A and four hours on Machine B. On the other hand, to make one Model R tire, it takes nine hours on Machine A and three hours on Machine B. Production scheduling indicates that during the coming week Machine A will be available for at most 36 hours and Machine B for at most 42 hours. How many of each tire should the company make in the coming week in order to maximize its profit? What is this maximum profit?

The first step in the formulation of a linear programming problem is to determine what our specific objective is. In this example, we can see that we are being asked to find the respective number of Model P and Model R tires to be made in the coming week that will maximize the company's profit, keeping in mind, of course, the limited resources available on Machines A and B.

> The first step in the formulation is to determine the objective.

> The second step in the formulation is to assign variables to each unknown quantity.

The second step is to assign variables to each of the unknown quantities for which we wish to solve. Thus, in our example, we let

$$x = \text{Number of Model P tires to be made in the coming week}$$

and

$$y = \text{Number of Model R tires to be made in the coming week.}$$

(Note that x and y are the customary variable names, although any other letters would do just as well.)

> The third step in the formulation is to express the objective as a function of the variables.

The third step is to find a mathematical expression or function that represents our objective in terms of the unknowns just chosen. Since in our example we wish to maximize the profit made by the company, we now examine the profit data given in the statement of the example for each of the two types of tires. First, since each Model P tire sells for $95 and costs $85 to make, the company clearly makes a profit of $95 − $85 = $10 on each tire made and sold. Similarly, since each Model R tire sells for $50 and costs $42 to make, the company makes a profit of $50 − $42 = $8 on each tire made and sold. These facts are summarized, for convenience, in Table 3–2. We now make the simplifying assumption that the company can sell all the tires it manufactures. (We will adopt the convention of assuming that a company can sell all that it produces. In actuality, of course, it is the responsibility of the marketing division of a company to set production levels and any associated restrictions.) Thus, the profit from the Model P line is

$$(\$10/\text{tire}) \cdot (x \text{ tires}) = \$10x$$

and the profit from the Model R line is

$$(\$8/\text{tire}) \cdot (y \text{ tires}) = \$8y,$$

so that the total profit for the company is

$$\$10x + \$8y.$$

Therefore, the company would like to choose x and y in such a way as to maximize the objective or profit function

$$\theta = 10x + 8y.$$

TABLE 3–2

	Tire Model	
	P	R
Selling price	$95/tire	$50/tire
Cost	$85/tire	$42/tire
Profit	$10/tire	$8/tire

CHAPTER 3 INTRODUCTION TO LINEAR PROGRAMMING AND THE SIMPLEX METHOD

> **Exercise.** Suppose each Model P tire sells for $120 and costs $88 to make, and each Model R tire sells for $67 and costs $49 to make. What is the objective function?
> **Answer:** $\theta = 32x + 18y$.

The fourth step in the formulation of a linear programming problem is to find mathematical expressions that represent any limited resources or constraints in terms of our unknowns. In our example, we see that the company is not free to select just any values of x and y since each tire must be processed on the two Machines A and B, both of which have limited availability. In particular, the resource data can be summarized, for convenience, as shown in Table 3-3. From this table, we can see that because each Model P tire (x) requires 2 hours on Machine A, each Model R tire (y) requires 9 hours on Machine A, and because there are at most 36 hours available on Machine A, we must have

The fourth step in the formulation is to express the constraints as inequalities or equalities in terms of the variables.

$$(2 \text{ hours/tire}) \cdot (x \text{ tires}) + (9 \text{ hours/tire}) \cdot (y \text{ tires}) \leq 36 \text{ hours}.$$

Similarly, since each Model P tire takes 4 hours on Machine B, each Model R tire takes 3 hours on Machine B, and since there are at most 42 hours available on Machine B, we must also have

$$(4 \text{ hours/tire}) \cdot (x \text{ tires}) + (3 \text{ hours/tire}) \cdot (y \text{ tires}) \leq 42 \text{ hours}.$$

Thus, the constraints on x and y resulting from the limited resources of Machines A and B, respectively, are

$$\text{Machine A:} \quad 2x + 9y \leq 36$$
$$\text{Machine B:} \quad 4x + 3y \leq 42.$$

> **Exercise.** What would the constraints be if the availabilities on Machines A and B were 41 and 38, respectively?
> **Answer:** $2x + 9y \leq 41$ and $4x + 3y \leq 38$.

TABLE 3-3

Resources	Tire Model		Total
	P	R	
Machine A	2 hours/tire	9 hours/tire	at most 36 hours
Machine B	4 hours/tire	3 hours/tire	at most 42 hours

> The fifth step in the formulation is to include any additional implicit constraints.

The fifth and last step is to include any additional constraints on our unknowns that are not explicitly stated in the problem but are implicit from the context of the problem. In our case, we have the obvious requirements that x and y must both be nonnegative since we cannot make a negative number of tires:

$$x, y \geq 0.$$

It is important to realize that, in practice, we would also have to require that x and y both be integers since we cannot make a fractional number of tires. Doing this, though, would lead us to the concept of integer programming, which is beyond the scope of our text, and hence, the integer constraints are omitted. We will, however, only accept integer solutions in practical problems unless otherwise noted. For the sake of accuracy, all the practical problems in our text have been designed so that the integer constraints can be omitted without affecting the final solution.

In summary, then, the linear programming problem the company has is:

Maximize the profit function

$$\theta = 10x + 8y$$

subject to the constraints

$$\text{Machine A:} \quad 2x + 9y \leq 36$$
$$\text{Machine B:} \quad 4x + 3y \leq 42$$
$$\text{Nonnegativity:} \quad x, y \geq 0.$$

The solution space for this problem is shown in Figure 3–8. Evaluating the objective function at each corner, we have

$$(0, 0): \quad \theta = 0$$
$$(0, 4): \quad \theta = 32$$
$$(21/2, 0): \quad \theta = 105$$
$$(9, 2): \quad \theta = 106,$$

so the maximum profit is $106 which is obtained when the company makes nine Model P tires and two Model R tires.

> **Exercise.** Draw a graph superimposing the isoprofit lines for $0, $32, $105, and $106 on Figure 3–8.

At this point, we summarize our five-step procedure for formulating a linear programming problem as we have just seen in our preceding example as follows:

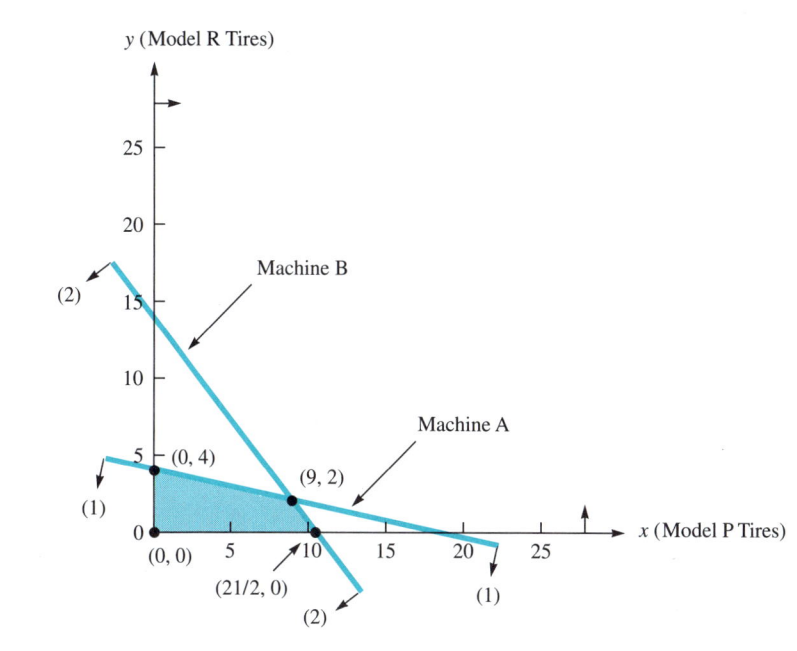

FIGURE 3-8

1. Determine what the specific objective is.
2. Assign variables to each of the unknown quantities for which we are solving.
3. Express the desired objective in terms of the chosen variables as an objective function and state how it is to be optimized (maximized or minimized). If helpful, use a table to summarize the appropriate data.
4. Express the limited resources or constraints in terms of the chosen variables. Again, if helpful, use a table to summarize the appropriate data.
5. Add any additional constraints that are implicit in the nature of the problem.

Lastly we wish to point out that the constraints in the preceding Steps 4 and 5 take on one of three forms: a mathematical expression involving the variables can be **at most** ($\leq$) some number, must be **at least** ($\geq$) some number, or is precisely **equal to** ($=$) some number. We saw the first two kinds of constraints in our examples in this section, and we will see the third kind of constraint later on in this chapter.

3.6 MINIMIZATION EXAMPLES: INGREDIENT MIX

Our next example illustrates a minimization linear programming problem.

Example. Pure Gasoline Company operates two refineries with different production capacities. Refinery A can produce 4,000 gallons per day of Super Unleaded gasoline, 2,000 gallons per day of Regular Unleaded gasoline, and 1,000 gallons per day of Diesel Fuel. On the other hand, Refinery B can produce 1,000 gallons per day of Super Unleaded, 3,000 gallons per day of Regular Unleaded, and 4,000 gallons per day of Diesel Fuel. The company has made a contract with an automobile manufacturer to provide 24,000 gallons of Super Unleaded, 42,000 gallons of Regular Unleaded, and 36,000 gallons of Diesel Fuel. Determine (1) the number of days the company should operate each refinery in order to meet the terms of the contract most economically, (2) the minimum cost, and (3) what grade(s) of fuel would be overproduced if the cost of running Refinery A is $1,500 per day and Refinery B is $2,400 per day.

Step 1: Determine the objective.

Following the format of the previous section, our first step in the formulation of this problem is to determine our specific objective. In this case, we can see that we want to find the respective number of days that Refineries A and B are to be operated to minimize the company's cost associated with producing the required number of gallons of Super Unleaded gasoline, Regular Unleaded gasoline, and Diesel Fuel.

Step 2: Assign the variables.

Now our second step is to assign variables to each of the unknown quantities. In our example, an obvious choice is to let

$$x = \text{Number of days Refinery A is operated}$$

and

$$y = \text{Number of days Refinery B is operated}.$$

Step 3: Formulate the objective function.

Then our third step is to determine the objective function to be optimized. Since in our example we want to minimize the cost incurred by the company, we now examine the cost data for each refinery. In particular, since Refinery A costs $1,500 per day to operate and since it is operated x days, the cost for Refinery A is

$$\$1,500x;$$

and since Refinery B costs $2,400 per day to operate and since it is operated y days, the cost for Refinery B is

$$\$2,400y.$$

Thus, since the company's objective is to minimize the total cost of operation, we want to minimize the objective or cost function

$$\theta = 1,500x + 2,400y.$$

(Note that we did not use a table to summarize the cost figures because the data were straightforward.)

Next our fourth step is to determine the constraints on the variables. This time we do not have limited resources to be concerned about, but rather contractual obligations that we must meet. For convenience, we summarize this data as shown in Table 3–4. From this table, we can see that since Refinery A can produce 4,000 gallons per day of Super Unleaded for each of the x days that it is operated, Refinery B can produce 1,000 gallons of Super Unleaded for each of the y days that it is operated, and since at least 24,000 gallons of Super Unleaded are needed, we must have

Step 4: Formulate the constraints.

$$(4{,}000 \text{ gallons/day}) \cdot (x \text{ days}) + (1{,}000 \text{ gallons/day}) \cdot (y \text{ days})$$
$$\geq 24{,}000 \text{ gallons.}$$

Similarly since Refinery A can produce 2,000 gallons per day of Regular Unleaded, since Refinery B can produce 3,000 gallons per day of Regular Unleaded, and since at least 42,000 gallons of Regular Unleaded are required, we must also have

$$(2{,}000 \text{ gallons/day}) \cdot (x \text{ days}) + (3{,}000 \text{ gallons/day}) \cdot (y \text{ days})$$
$$\geq 42{,}000 \text{ gallons.}$$

In the same way, the requirement on the Diesel Fuel becomes

$$(1{,}000 \text{ gallons/day}) \cdot (x \text{ days}) + (4{,}000 \text{ gallons/day}) \cdot (y \text{ days})$$
$$\geq 36{,}000 \text{ gallons.}$$

Thus our constraints on x and y due to the contractual obligations are

$$\text{Super Unleaded:} \quad 4{,}000x + 1{,}000y \geq 24{,}000$$
$$\text{Regular Unleaded:} \quad 2{,}000x + 3{,}000y \geq 42{,}000$$
$$\text{Diesel Fuel:} \quad 1{,}000x + 4{,}000y \geq 36{,}000.$$

Lastly, simplifying the preceding constraints and introducing the nonnegativity or real constraints, we see that the linear programming problem is:

Step 5: Formulate any implicit constraints.

TABLE 3–4

Grade	Refinery A	Refinery B	Total
Super Unleaded	4,000 gallons/day	1,000 gallons/day	At least 24,000 gallons
Regular Unleaded	2,000 gallons/day	3,000 gallons/day	At least 42,000 gallons
Diesel Fuel	1,000 gallons/day	4,000 gallons/day	At least 36,000 gallons

Minimize the cost function

$$\theta = 1{,}500x + 2{,}400y$$

subject to constraints

$$\begin{aligned}\text{Super Unleaded:} &\quad 4x + y \geq 24 \\ \text{Regular Unleaded:} &\quad 2x + 3y \geq 42 \\ \text{Diesel Fuel:} &\quad x + 4y \geq 36 \\ \text{Nonnegativity:} &\quad x, y \geq 0,\end{aligned}$$

where, of course, there are two nonnegativity constraints specified by the last expression.

> **Exercise.** a) What would the objective function become if the cost of running Refinery A is $1,600 per day and Refinery B is $2,400 per day? b) What additional constraints are needed if the automobile manufacturer wants delivery in no more than 14 days?
> **Answer:** a) $\theta_{min} = 1{,}600x + 2{,}400y$; b) $x \leq 14$ and $y \leq 14$.

The solution space for this example is shown in Figure 3–9A. Note in this figure that the origin does not satisfy any of the three fuel constraints so that the solution space is the area going away from (0, 0). Note also that there are four corners; namely,

$$(0, 24),$$
$$(36, 0),$$
$$(3, 12) \text{ from } e_1 \text{ and } e_2, \text{ and}$$
$$(12, 6) \text{ from } e_2 \text{ and } e_3.$$

Each point on an isocost line results in the same cost value for the objective function.

Now suppose we superimpose **isocost** lines on the feasible solution set; for example,

$$\begin{aligned}\$60{,}000 \text{ cost:} &\quad 60{,}000 = 1{,}500x + 2{,}400y, \\ \$50{,}000 \text{ cost:} &\quad 50{,}000 = 1{,}500x + 2{,}400y, \\ \$40{,}000 \text{ cost:} &\quad 40{,}000 = 1{,}500x + 2{,}400y, \\ \$30{,}000 \text{ cost:} &\quad 30{,}000 = 1{,}500x + 2{,}400y.\end{aligned}$$

Isocost lines form a family of parallel lines intersecting the feasible solution set.

Again we have a family of lines, but, this time, moving toward the origin as the cost decreases as shown in Figure 3–9B. Using the same analysis as before, then, the minimum cost will occur at one of the corners of the solution space. Evaluating the objective function at each corner, we have

$(0, 24)$: $\theta = 57,600$
$(36, 0)$: $\theta = 54,000$
$(3, 12)$: $\theta = 33,300$
$(12, 6)$: $\theta = 32,400$,

so the minimum cost is $32,400 which occurs when Refinery A is operated 12 days and Refinery B is operated 6 days.

It is possible, however, that this solution allows an overproduction of fuel. To check this, we simply substitute the optimum point (12, 6) back into the constraints and check for any overage. For Super Unleaded

$$4(12) + 1(6) = 54,$$

which is larger than our requirement of 24,000 gallons by $54,000 - 24,000 = 30,000$ gallons. Note that in practice any overproduction should be taken into consideration in the final decision-making process. For example, if the excess can be utilized, then this fact should be used to **reduce** the cost function appropriately. On the other hand, if the excess cannot be utilized, then the cost of storage should be **added** to the cost function.

Overproduction should be incorporated into the objective function.

Exercise. Are either Regular Unleaded or Diesel Fuel overproduced?

Answer: No, since $2(12) + 3(6) = 42$ and $1(12) + 4(6) = 36$.

FIGURE 3–9A   FIGURE 3–9B

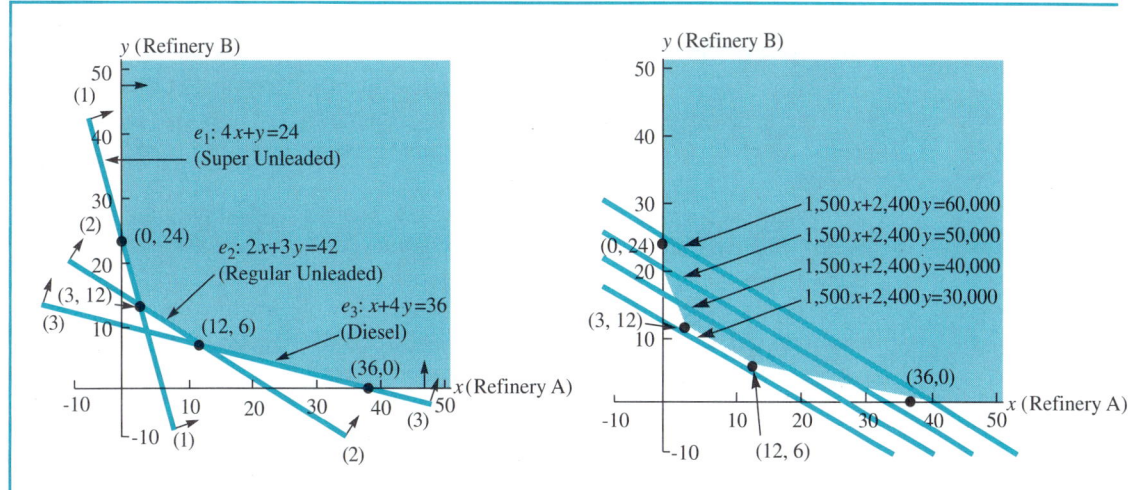

Overproduction can be checked graphically.

The preceding results concerning overproduction can be verified directly from Figure 3–9A by noting that the corner (12, 6) lies **precisely on** e_2 and e_3 so that Regular Unleaded and Diesel Fuel are not overproduced. Of course, (12, 6) lies above e_1 so that Super Unleaded is overproduced.

> **Exercise.** a) What should be the minimum if the cost of running Refinery A is $1,600 per day and the cost of running Refinery B is $2,400 per day? b) What grade(s) of fuel would be overproduced?
>
> **Answer:** (a) $33,600 at any point on the line segment joining (3, 12) and (12, 6). (b) At (3, 12), Diesel Fuel is overproduced; at (12, 6) Super Unleaded is overproduced; at any other point, both Super Unleaded and Diesel Fuel are overproduced. Note there are only two other points with integral coordinates; namely, (9, 8) and (6, 10).

Summarizing our graphical results from this section and the previous section, we can now see that

The optimum of an objective function always occurs at a corner of the solution space. Sometimes, additional optima occur on the line segment joining two corners.

> An optimum (maximum or minimum) value of an objective function in the two-variable case occurs at one corner of the solution space (feasible solution set) or at two corners and all points along a line segment joining these two corners.

Thus the solution of a linear programming problem does occur at a corner. In the case where the isovalue lines of the objective function are parallel to a constraint line, the solution can occur at an unlimited number of points (including corner points) which then must be interpreted in terms of the practical nature of the problem at hand.

Furthermore, we can in principle solve a two-variable linear programming problem by changing all the constraints to equalities, finding the intersection point of each of inequalities to obtain all the possible corners, checking for the feasible corners and substituting these into the objective function, and then choosing a corner that optimizes the objective function. This procedure, however, involves unnecessary work since not every intersection point is feasible. A more efficient method would be to sketch the constraining lines, identify the solution space (feasible solution set), and calculate only the intersections that are on the boundary of the solution space. This **three-step graphical procedure** can be summarized as:

> 1. Graph the constraints in the plane.
> 2. Use the graph as a visual aid to identify the corners and determine the coordinates of these corners either from the graphing procedure or by the elimination procedure.
> 3. Evaluate the objective function at each corner. The largest value is the maximum (if a maximum exists) and the smallest value is the minimum (if a minimum exists). If two corners have the same optimal value, then the optimum occurs at every point on the line segment joining the respective corners.

One caution is in order. **A maximum and/or minimum need not exist.** For example, in Figure 3–9A we saw that the minimum occurred at (3, 12), but looking at the isolines in Figure 3–9B we see that there would be no maximum. However, in Figure 3–8 the maximum occurred at (9, 2) and the minimum, if desired, would occur at (0, 0). The distinction between the two configurations is that Figure 3–8 is **bounded in both optimizing directions**, whereas Figure 3–9 is **bounded in the minimizing direction but unbounded in the maximizing direction.**

An optimum will not exist if the solution space is unbounded in the optimizing direction.

Example. As one last example, suppose we combine the Pure Gasoline Company example and exercise in this section, so that subject to the constraints

$$\begin{aligned}
\text{Super Unleaded:} &\quad 4x + y \geq 24 \\
\text{Regular Unleaded:} &\quad 2x + 3y \geq 42 \\
\text{Diesel Fuel:} &\quad x + 4y \geq 36 \\
\text{Refinery A:} &\quad x \leq 14 \\
\text{Refinery B:} &\quad y \leq 14 \\
\text{Nonnegativity:} &\quad x, y \geq 0,
\end{aligned}$$

we want to minimize two objective functions

a) $\theta = 1{,}500x + 2{,}400y$

b) $\theta = 1{,}600x + 2{,}400y.$

We shall solve the two parts of this example together by using the three-step graphical procedure. Figure 3–10 shows the solution space for this system of constraints.

The boundary lines are plotted in the usual manner, using intercepts. Of course, the lines obtained by plotting equations e_4 and e_5 are parallel to the y-axis and x-axis, respectively.

FIGURE 3-10

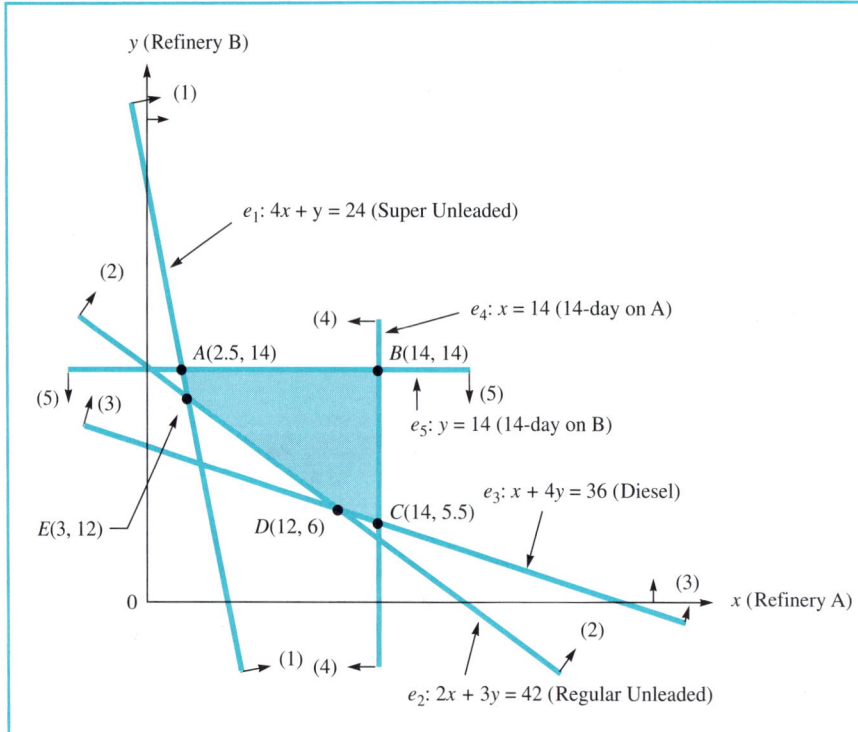

Using the symbol 1#2 to designate the corner where lines e_1 and e_2 intersect, and similarly for the other corners, we see from Figure 3–10 that the only corners A, B, C, D, and E that are part of the solution space are 1#5, 4#5, 3#4, 2#3, and 1#2. The coordinates of these corners are found in the usual manner by elimination and substitution. Thus, for 1#5,

$$e_1: \quad 4x + y = 24$$
$$e_5: \quad\quad\quad y = 14,$$

we simply substitute $y = 14$ into e_1 to get the point (2.5, 14). The coordinates of the other corners are shown in Table 3–5.

Exercise. Verify the coordinates of the other corners in Table 3–5.

TABLE 3-5

Corner	Coordinates	Objective Function, θ	
		$1,500x + 2,400y$	$1,600x + 2,400y$
A: 1#5	(2.5, 14)	37,350	37,600
B: 4#5	(14, 14)	54,600	56,000
C: 3#4	(14, 5.5)	34,200	35,600
D: 2#3	(12, 6)	32,400*	33,600*
E: 1#2	(3, 12)	33,300	33,600*

*Indicates the minimum.

Also shown in Table 3–5 are the values of the two objective functions at each of the five corners. From this table, we see that for (a), θ_{min} = $32,400 when Refinery A is operated 12 days and Refinery B is operated 6 days. On the other hand for (b), θ_{min} = $33,600 at any point on the line segment from (12, 6) to (3, 12). Note that both of these solutions are precisely the same as before. The reason for this is that the two 14-day constraints are satisfied by the previous optimal solutions in the example and exercise, and hence, these additional constraints are unnecessary or **redundant**.

Lastly, since the optimal solutions have not changed, the question of overproduction of fuel for either (a) or (b) has not changed. As before, the precise results can be determined either algebraically or from the graph in Figure 3–10.

> A constraint is redundant if it has no effect on the optimal solution.

3.7 PROBLEM SET 3–2

Use the three-step graphical procedure to find the optimum, as required, assuming $x \geq 0$ and $y \geq 0$:

1. Subject to
   $4x + 3y \leq 24$
   $x + 2y \leq 11$,
   find θ_{max} if:
   a) $\theta = x + y$.
   b) $\theta = x + 3y$.
   c) $\theta = 3x + y$.
   d) $\theta = 2x + 1.5y$.

2. Subject to
   $3x + 7y \leq 42$
   $x + 5y \leq 22$,
   find θ_{max} if:
   a) $\theta = 4x + 10y$.
   b) $\theta = 2x - 3y$.
   c) $\theta = -3x + 10y$.
   d) $\theta = 1.5x + 3.5y$.

3. Subject to
   $2x + 3y \geq 12$
   $5x + y \geq 17$,
   find θ_{min} if:
   a) $\theta = x + 2y$.
   b) $\theta = 5x + 7y$.
   c) $\theta = 8x + y$.
   d) $\theta = 5x + y$.

3.7 PROBLEM SET 3-2 (continued)

4. Subject to
   $4x + 5y \geq 30$
   $3x + 2y \geq 19$,
   find θ_{min} if:
   a) $\theta = 2x + 8y$.
   b) $\theta = 4x + 2y$.
   c) $\theta = 2x + 2y$.
   d) $\theta = 8x + 10y$.

5. Subject to
   $3x + y \leq 9$
   $x + y \leq 5$
   $x \leq 4$
   $y \leq 4$,
   find θ_{max} if:
   a) $\theta = 0.3x + 0.5y$.
   b) $\theta = 2x + y$.
   c) $\theta = 5x + y$.
   d) $\theta = 3x + 3y$.

6. Subject to
   $x + y \leq 13$
   $x + 2y \leq 22$
   $2x + y \leq 20$
   $x \leq 4$,
   find θ_{max} if:
   a) $\theta = 5x + 8y$.
   b) $\theta = 4x - y$.
   c) $\theta = -2x + 7y$.
   d) $\theta = 5x + 10y$.

7. Subject to
   $x + 3y \geq 24$
   $2x + y \geq 18$
   $3x + 4y \geq 52$,
   find θ_{min} if:
   a) $\theta = x + y$.
   b) $\theta = 4x + 3y$.
   c) $\theta = 6x + 2y$.
   d) $\theta = 6x + 8y$.

8. Subject to
   $4x + y \geq 16$
   $3x + 2y \geq 24$
   $x - y \leq 0$,
   find θ_{min} if:
   a) $\theta = 2x + y$.
   b) $\theta = x + 2y$.
   c) $\theta = 8x + 2y$.
   d) $\theta = 6x + 4y$.

9. Subject to
   $2x + y \geq 8$
   $6x + 10y \leq 60$,
   find θ_{max} and θ_{min} if:
   a) $\theta = 3x + 2y$.
   b) $\theta = 10x + y$.

10. Subject to
    $0.15x + 0.10y \geq 15$
    $x + y \leq 120$
    $0.4x \leq 32$,
    find θ_{max} and θ_{min} if:
    a) $\theta = 0.20x + 0.15y$.
    b) $\theta = 0.15x + 0.20y$.
    c) $\theta = 0.1x + 0.1y$.

11. Subject to
    $2x + 4y \geq 36$
    $x + y \leq 12$,
    find θ_{max} and θ_{min} if:
    a) $\theta = 3x + 5y$.
    b) $\theta = 6x + 2y$.
    c) $\theta = 3x + 3y$.

12. Subject to
    $2x + 4y \geq 36$
    $x + y \leq 12$
    $-2x + y \geq 0$,
    find θ_{max} and θ_{min} if:
    a) $\theta = 3x + 5y$.
    b) $\theta = 6x + 2y$.
    c) $\theta = 3x + 3y$.

13. Subject to
    $2x + 4y \geq 36$
    $x + y \leq 12$
    $x - 2y \leq 0$,
    find θ_{max} and θ_{min} if:
    a) $\theta = 3x + 5y$.
    b) $\theta = 6x + 2y$.
    c) $\theta = 3x + 3y$.

14. Subject to
    $2x + 4y \geq 36$
    $x + y \leq 12$
    $x - 2y \geq 0$,
    find θ_{max} and θ_{min} if:
    a) $\theta = 3x + 5y$.
    b) $\theta = 6x + 2y$.
    c) $\theta = 3x + 3y$.

3.7 PROBLEM SET 3-2 (continued)

15. Subject to
    $2x + 3y \leq 24$
    $2x - y \leq 8$
    $-2x + 3y \leq 12$,
    find θ_{max} and θ_{min} if:
    a) $\theta = 6x + y - 7$.
    b) $\theta = -3x + 7y + 10$.
    c) $\theta = -x - 3y + 25$.
    d) $\theta = 8x - 4y + 18$.

16. Subject to
    $0.15x + 0.10y \geq 15$
    $x + y \leq 120$
    $0.4x \geq 32$,
    find θ_{max} and θ_{min} if:
    a) $\theta = 0.3x - 0.2y + 0.75$.
    b) $\theta = -0.6x + 0.5y - 0.80$.
    c) $\theta = -0.7x - 0.9y + 2.50$.
    d) $\theta = 0.4x + 0.4y - 0.30$.

17. Star Insulating Company manufactures two types of storm windows: Model H (the heavy duty) and Model R (the regular). Model H sells for $45 per window and costs $36 per window to make, whereas Model R sells for $35 per window and costs $27 per window to make. To make one Model H window, it requires 4 hours on Machine A and 3 hours on Machine B. On the other hand, to make one Model R window, it takes 5 hours on Machine A and 2 hours on Machine B. Production scheduling indicates that during the coming week Machine A will be available for at most 30 hours and Machine B for at most 19 hours. How many of each window should the company make in the coming week in order to maximize its profit? What is this maximum profit?

18. Safety Lock Company makes two kinds of locks: Model SS (the super safe) and Model S (the safe). Each Model SS lock sells for $24 and costs $19 to make, while each Model S lock sells for $18 and costs $15 to make. Each of the locks must be processed on two machines: Model SS requires 3 hours on Machine A and 2 hours on Machine B, whereas Model S requires 7 hours on A and 1 hour on B. During the coming week Machine A will be free for no more than 42 hours and Machine B for no more than 17 hours. Determine the number of each kind of lock to be made in the coming week for the company to maximize its profit. What is this maximum profit?

19. XYZ Steel Company manufactures two kinds of wrought-iron rails: Model E (the elegant) and Model D (the distinctive). Model E rails sell for $59 and cost $50 to make, whereas Model D rails sell for $48 and cost $41 to make. To make one Model E rail requires 2 hours on Machine A, 1 hour on Machine B, and 4 hours on Machine C. On the other hand, to make one Model D rail requires 1 hour on A, 2 hours on B, and 5 hours on C. Production scheduling indicates that during the coming week Machine A will be available for at most 30 hours, Machine B for at most 24 hours, and Machine C for at most 72 hours. Find the number of each kind of rail to be made in the coming week in order for the company to maximize its profit. What is this maximum profit? At the maximum, which machines, if any, are not fully utilized?

20. A special food for athletes is to be developed from two foods: Food X and Food Y. The new food is to contain at least 16 milligrams of Vitamin A, at least 20 milligrams of Vitamin B, and at least 12 milligrams of Vitamin C. Each pound of Food X costs $1.50 and contains 1 milligram of Vitamin A, 5 milligrams of Vitamin B, and 1 milligram of Vitamin C. On the other hand, each pound of Food Y costs $2.50 and contains 2 milligrams of A, 1 milligram of B, and 1 milligram of C. How many pounds of each food should be used in the mixture in order to meet the preceding requirements at a minimum cost? What is this minimum cost?

21. Repeat Problem 20 if, in addition, the amount of Food Y in the mixture must be no more than one-half the amount of Food X.

22. Strong Steel Company operates two steel mills with different production capacities. Mill I can produce 1,000 tons per day of AAA steel, 3,000 tons per day of AA steel, and 5,000 tons per day of A steel. Mill F can produce 2,000 tons per day of each grade of steel. The company has made a contract with the construction firm to provide 24,000 tons of AAA steel, 32,000 tons of AA steel, and 40,000 tons of

3.7 PROBLEM SET 3-2 (concluded)

A steel. For each of the following costs, determine the number of days the company should operate each mill in order to meet the terms of the preceding contract most economically, the minimum cost, and also what grade(s) of steel would be overproduced:
a) The cost of running Mill I is $1.400 per day and Mill F is $1,000 per day.
b) The cost of running Mill I is $1,500 per day and Mill F is $3,000 per day.

23. ABC Dairy Company wishes to make a new cheese from two of its current cheeses: Cheese X and Cheese Y. The mixture is to weigh no more than four pounds and is to contain at least six ounces of the sharpness ingredient S. Each pound of X costs $4 and contains three ounces of S, whereas each pound of Y costs $1 and contains one ounce of S. How many pounds of each cheese should be used in the mixture in order to meet these requirements at a minimum cost? What is this minimum cost?

24. Repeat Problem 23 if, in addition, the amount of Cheese Y cannot exceed the amount of Cheese X by more than one pound.

3.8 EQUALITY CONSTRAINTS

Our next example illustrates a linear programming problem that has an "=" constraint.

Example. Klean Soap Company wishes to make a new detergent from two of its current soaps: Soap A and Soap B. The company wants the new detergent to contain at least 20 ounces of cleaning ingredient D. Each pound of Soap A costs $0.20 and contains five ounces of D, whereas each pound of Soap B costs $0.25 and contains one ounce of D. Furthermore, for ecological reasons, the amount of Soap A must be no more than that of Soap B. Finally, the new mixture must weigh exactly 12 pounds. How many pounds of each soap should be used in the mixture in order to meet these requirements at a minimum cost? What is this minimum cost?

In this example, we wish to determine the respective number of pounds of Soaps A and B to be mixed together to minimize the company's cost associated with making a new mixture that not only satisfies the cleaning ingredient and ecological constraints, but also weighs precisely 12 pounds. Thus we assign our variables as follows: We let

$$x = \text{Number of pounds of Soap A in the mixture}$$

and

$$y = \text{Number of pounds of Soap B in the mixture.}$$

Next since Soap A costs $0.20 per pound and Soap B costs $0.25 per pound, the cost of the new mixture will be

$$\$0.20x + \$0.25y;$$

so that the company wants to minimize the objective or cost function

$$\theta = 0.2x + 0.25y.$$

Turning now to our constraints, we first see that the new detergent is to contain at least 20 ounces of cleaning ingredient D. Since each pound of Soap A (x) contains 5 ounces of D while each pound of Soap B (y) contains 1 ounce of D, we must have

$$(5 \text{ oz/lb of A}) \cdot (x \text{ lbs of A}) + (1 \text{ oz/lb of B}) \cdot (y \text{ lbs of B}) \geq 20 \text{ oz}$$

or simply

$$5x + y \geq 20.$$

Also, since the amount of Soap A must be no more than that of Soap B, we get

$$x \leq y$$

or

$$x - y \leq 0.$$

Lastly, since the mixture is to weigh exactly 12 pounds, we have

$$x + y = 12.$$

Adding the nonnegativity constraints, then, the linear programming problem is:

Minimize the cost function

$$\theta = 0.2x + 0.25y$$

subject to the constraints

Ingredient D:	$5x + y \geq 20$		(1)
Ecology:	$x - y \leq 0$		(2)
Weight:	$x + y = 12$		(3)
Nonnegativity:	$x, y \geq 0.$		(4),(5)

Figure 3–11 shows the solution space for the system of constraints.

Note that our third constraint is an **equality** so that our solution space is limited to points on this line itself. From Figure 3–11, we see that there are two corners: 1#3 and 2#3. Thus we get the results shown in Table 3–6, from which we see that the minimum cost is $2.70 when six pounds of each soap are mixed together to form the new product.

> The equality constraint limits the solution to a line rather than a half-plane.

Exercise. Suppose the company decided that the new detergent should weigh exactly 16 pounds. In addition, suppose that each soap cost $0.40 per pound. Find the new minimum-cost mixture and the new minimum cost.

Answer: $6.40 at any point on the line segment from (1, 15) to (8, 8). Note that in this case there are an infinite number of mixtures possible. Why?

FIGURE 3-11

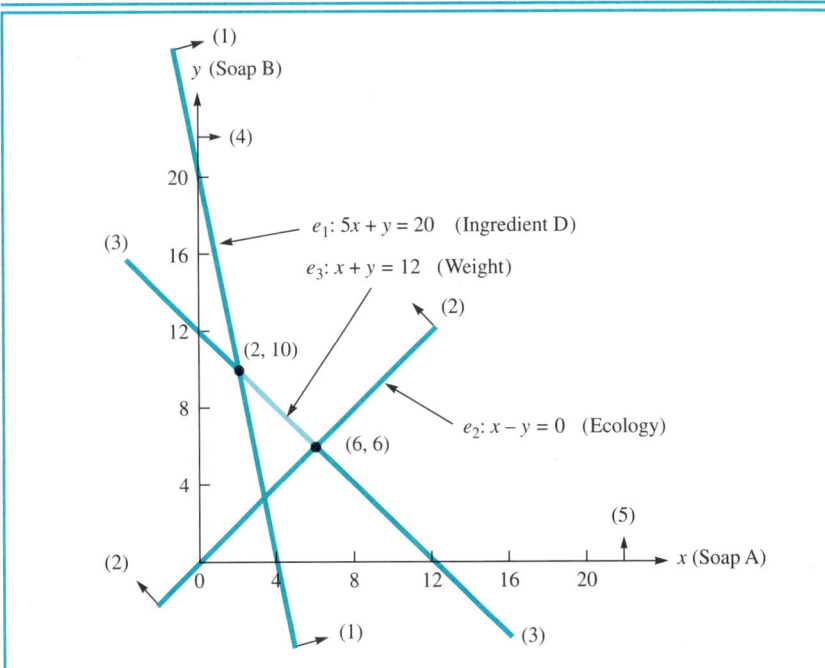

TABLE 3-6

Corner	Coordinates	$\theta = 0.2x + 0.25y$
1#3	(2, 10)	2.9
2#3	(6, 6)	2.7*

*Indicates the minimum.

3.9 LINEAR PROGRAMMING WITH MORE THAN TWO VARIABLES

In real-world situations, most linear programming problems will have more than two variables. Now if there are three variables, it is possible to extend the three-step graphical procedure to three-dimensional space. However, sketching the three-dimensional planes on a flat (two-dimensional) piece of paper and trying to identify the solution space is too complex to be practical. If there are more than three variables, it is impossible to graph the solution space. In Section 3.13, we will show how to use a computer package to solve linear programming problems with any number of variables. The technique used for solution is an advanced application of the systematic procedure which we will present in Chapter 4. **The underlying principle is to proceed from corner to corner of the solution set, constantly**

improving the value of the objective function. When no permissible corner improving the solution exists, the current corner provides the optimum value. Those who plan to study Chapter 4 need only scan the remainder of this chapter, first, to see the need for a procedure that eliminates the extensive computation of nonpermissible corners and, second, to fix in mind the key principle that if a system has m constraints on n variables ($m < n$) in addition to the nonnegativity constraints on the variables, then at every corner **at least** $(n - m)$ of the variables have the value zero.

First, consider the Lounge and Swivel Chair example of Section 3.5, which was

Maximize the objective function

$$\theta = x + 0.5y$$

subject to the constraints

Department I $\quad i_1:\quad x + y \leq 4$

Department II $\quad i_2:\quad x + 2y \leq 6$

Nonnegativity $i_3, i_4:\quad\quad x,\ y \geq 0$.

Recall that we graphed the solution space in Figure 3–4 and determined that there were four permissible corners: (0, 0), (0, 3), (4, 0), and (2, 2). In using the graph as a visual aid, we were able to eliminate two corners that were not permissible; namely (0, 4) from e_1 and e_3 plus (6, 0) from e_2 and e_4. If we did not have the graph available as a visual aid, we could determine these facts as follows: Each corner is the solution of a two-by-two system of equations. Since there are four equations in all (e_1, e_2, e_3, and e_4), the number of corners can be found using the formula for counting the number of combinations of four equations taken two at a time. This is

$$\text{Number of corners} = \frac{4!}{2!2!},$$

where the factorial symbol, !, means, for example,

$$4! = 4(3)(2)(1)$$
$$2! = 2(1)$$

so

$$\text{Number of corners} = \frac{24}{(2)(2)} = 6.$$

In general, if there are c constraints (including nonnegativity) and n variables, then

$$\text{Number of corners} = \frac{c!}{n!(n - c)!}.$$

> Each corner in a two-variable linear programming problem is the solution of a two-by-two system of equations.

> The number of corners in a two-variable linear programming problem with c total constraints is found by counting the number of combinations of c equations taken two at a time.

> With c constraints and n variables, there are
> $$\frac{c!}{n!(n - c)!}$$
> possible corners of the solution set.

> **Exercise.** How many corners would there be if the problem had 5 constraints and 2 variables?
> **Answer:** 10.

The results of calculating and checking the six corners in our example are shown in Table 3-7. Note that each pair of equations is solved and then the resultant solution is checked against the remaining constraints. For example, at 1#4 we check (4, 0) in i_2 and i_3:

$$i_2: \quad x + 2y = 4 + 2(0) = 4 \leq 6$$
$$i_3: \qquad\qquad\qquad x = 4 \geq 0,$$

so that (4, 0) is a permissible corner. However, at 1#3 we see that for (0, 4)

$$i_2: \quad x + 2y = 0 + 2(4) = 8 \nleq 6,$$

so that (0, 4) is not a permissible corner.

> **Exercise.** Which constraint does (6, 0) not satisfy?
> **Answer:** i_1.

Our next example illustrates the situation where the number of constraints (not counting nonnegativity) is less than the number of variables.

Example. Solve the following three-variable linear programming problem:

Minimize

$$\theta = x + 4y + 3z$$

subject to:

TABLE 3-7

Corner	Coordinates	Check	$\theta = x + 0.5y$
1#2	(2, 2)	Yes	3
1#3	(0, 4)	No	
1#4	(4, 0)	Yes	4*
2#3	(0, 3)	Yes	1.5
2#4	(6, 0)	No	
3#4	(0, 0)	Yes	0

*Indicates the maximum.

$$i_1: \quad 0.5x + y + 0.2z \geq 600$$
$$i_2: \quad 2x + 3y + z \leq 2{,}000$$
$$i_3, i_4, i_5: \quad x, y, z \geq 0.$$

The problem has three variables, so each corner is the solution of a three-by-three system of equations. For example, writing the equality part of i_1, i_2, and i_3, we have

> Each corner in a three-variable linear programming problem is the solution of three-by-three system of equations.

Corner 1#2#3

$$e_1: \quad 0.5x + y + 0.2z = 600$$
$$e_2: \quad 2x + 3y + z = 2{,}000$$
$$e_3: \quad x = 0.$$

Substituting $e_3(x = 0)$ into e_1 and e_2, we have

$$y + 0.2z = 600$$
$$3y + z = 2{,}000,$$

which we can solve for z to get

$$z = 500.$$

Substituting $z = 500$, we find $y = 500$, so the desired corner is $(0, 500, 500)$. These coordinates satisfy all inequalities, i_1 through i_5.

On the other hand,

Corner 1#3#4

$$e_1: \quad 0.5x + y + 0.2z = 600$$
$$e_3: \quad x = 0$$
$$e_4: \quad y = 0.$$

Substitution of $x = y = 0$ into e_1 yields $z = 3{,}000$. However, $(0, 0, 3{,}000)$ does not satisfy i_2 and so is not a permissible corner at which to evaluate the objective function.

Exercise. Find and check the corner 1#2#4.

Answer: $x = 2{,}000$, $y = 0$, $z = -2{,}000$ does not check because z is negative, contrary to constraint i_5.

For the system at hand we have

$$c = 5 \text{ constraints}$$
$$n = 3 \text{ variables}$$
$$c - n = 5 - 3 = 2,$$

so that

$$\text{Number of corners} = \frac{5!}{3!2!} = \frac{5(4)(3)(2)(1)}{(3)(2)(1)(2)(1)} = 10.$$

The results of calculating and checking these 10 corners are shown in Table 3–8. The desired minimum is seen to be 2,000 and occurs at $x = 400$, $y = 400$, and $z = 0$.

> Each corner has at least one zero coordinate since one of the three equations in the system corresponds to a nonnegativity constraint, which translates to an equality with the associated variable equal to zero.

In Table 3–8, each corner is the solution of a three-by-three system of equations because there are $n = 3$ variables, and each set of coordinates has **at least one zero value.** The reason for this is that, of the total number of constraints, $c = 5$, three of them are nonnegativity constraints that become

$$x = 0, \quad y = 0, \quad z = 0$$

when written as equalities. The number of remaining constraints is $n = 2$, and written as equalities these are

$$0.5x + y + 0.2z = 600$$
$$2x + 3y + z = 2,000.$$

Clearly, any three-by-three system formed from the five equalities has to include at least one of the first three ($x = 0$, $y = 0$, $z = 0$), and this accounts for the presence of at least one zero in the coordinates of every corner shown in Table 3–8. In linear programming, nonnegativity constraints are always assumed to be present. Consequently, when we say that the problem has $m = 2$ constraints on $n = 3$ variables, it is to be understood that there are three nonnegativity constraints and $m = 2$ means two constraints in addition to nonnegativity. In our example,

$$n = 3, \quad m = 2, \quad n - m = 3 - 2 = 1$$

tells us that every corner will have **at least one zero coordinate**. Similarly, every corner for a problem that has $m = 4$ constraints on $n = 7$ variables will have zero

TABLE 3–8

Corner	Coordinates	Check	$\theta = x + 4y + 3z$
1#2#3	(0, 500, 500)	Yes	3,500
1#2#4	(2000, 0, −2000)	No	
1#2#5	(400, 400, 0)	Yes	2,000*
1#3#4	(0, 0, 3000)	No	
1#3#5	(0, 600, 0)	Yes	2,400
1#4#5	(1200, 0, 0)	No	
2#3#4	(0, 0, 2000)	No	
2#3#5	(0, 2000/3, 0)	Yes	8,000/3
2#4#5	(1000, 0, 0)	No	
3#4#5	(0, 0, 0)	No	

*Indicates the minimum.

values for at least three variables because

$$n - m = 7 - 4 = 3.$$

The fact just illustrated is a key principle in the procedure to be developed in Chapter 4, so we highlight it here.

> If a linear programming problem has m constraints[4] (not counting nonnegativity constraints) on n variables, where $n \geq m$, then the coordinates of every corner of the solution space will contain at least $n - m$ zeros.

Each corner has at least $n - m$ zero coordinates (m constraints, n variables, $n \geq m$).

Exercise. A linear programming problem has a **total** number of 16 constraints on $n = 10$ variables. (a) How many nonnegativity constraints are there? (b) What is m? (c) How many zeros will every corner have?

Answer: (a) 10. (b) $m = 6$. (c) At least 4.

3.10 PROBLEM SET 3-3

Use the three-step graphical procedure to find the optimum, as required, assuming $x \geq 0$ and $y \geq 0$:

1. Subject to
   $x + 3y \leq 24$
   $x + y \geq 10$
   $2x + y = 18,$
   find θ_{max} and θ_{min} if:
   a) $\theta = 5x + 2y.$
   b) $\theta = x + 7y.$
   c) $\theta = 4x + 2y.$

2. Subject to
   $2x + 4y \geq 36$
   $x + y \leq 12$
   $-2x + y = 0,$
   find θ_{max} and θ_{min} if:
   a) $\theta = 7x + 4y.$
   b) $\theta = 3x + 8y.$
   c) $\theta = 4x + 2y.$

3. Subject to
   $x + 3y \leq 24$
   $x + y \geq 10$
   $2x + y = 18$
   $4x - 3y = 16,$
   find θ_{max} and θ_{min} if:
   a) $\theta = 5x + 2y.$
   b) $\theta = x + 7y.$
   c) $\theta = 4x + 2y.$

4. Subject to
   $2x + 4y \geq 36$
   $x + y \leq 12$
   $-2x + y = 0$
   $-x + 2y = 12,$
   find θ_{max} and θ_{min} if:

---

[4]This assumes the constraints are linearly independent, that is, that no constraint is a linear combination of other constraints. If, for example, one constraint is a linear combination of two others (in the simplest case, one is a constant times another), this constraint is not counted in specifying m.

3.10 PROBLEM SET 3-3 (continued)

a) $\theta = 7x + 4y$.
b) $\theta = 3x + 8y$.
c) $\theta = 4x + 2y$.

5. Subject to
$x + 3y \leq 24$
$x + y \geq 10$
$2x + y = 18$
$5x + y = 20$,
find θ_{max} and θ_{min} if:
a) $\theta = 5x + 2y$.
b) $\theta = x + 7y$.
c) $\theta = 4x + 2y$.

6. Subject to
$2x + 4y \geq 36$
$x + y \leq 12$
$-2x + y = 0$
$-x + y = 10$,
find θ_{max} and θ_{min} if:
a) $\theta = 7x + 4y$.
b) $\theta = 3x + 8y$.
c) $\theta = 4x + 2y$.

7. Slim Soda Company wishes to make a new drink from two of its current sodas: Soda A and Soda B. The new drink is to contain at least six ounces of the taste ingredient T. Each quart of A costs $0.20 and contains one ounce of T, whereas each quart of B costs $0.30 and contains three ounces of T. Furthermore, for dietary reasons, the amount of B must not exceed the amount of A. Finally, the volume of the new drink must be exactly four quarts. How many quarts of each soda should be used in the mixture in order to meet the preceding requirements at a minimum cost? What is this minimum cost?

8. Suppose the company in Problem 7 decided that the new drink should contain exactly six quarts. In addition, suppose that each soda cost $0.40 per quart. Find the new minimum-cost mixture and the new minimum cost.

Assuming $x \geq 0$, $y \geq 0$, and $z \geq 0$:

9. Find θ_{max} if:
$\theta = 0.5x + y + 0.2z$
subject to
$x + 4y + 3z \leq 1,800$
$2x + 3y + z \leq 2,000$.

10. Find θ_{min} if:
$\theta = 0.4x + 1.2y + 0.5z$
subject to
$x + 2y + 3z \geq 1,200$
$2x + y + z \geq 600$.

11. Find θ_{max} if:
$\theta = 1.5x + 2.5y + 2z$
subject to
$x + 1.5y \leq 4$
$y + 2.5z \leq 5$
$1.5x + 5y + z \leq 7.5$.

12. Find θ_{min} if:
$\theta = 4x + 2y + 3z$
subject to
$x + 2y + 4z \geq 29$
$3x + 2y + z \geq 23$
$10x + 4y + 3z \geq 62$.

13. A wholesaler has 9,600 feet of space available and $5,000 to buy merchandise of types A, B, and C. Type A costs $4 per unit and requires 4 feet of storage space in the warehouse. B costs $10 per unit and requires 8 feet of space. C costs $5 per unit and requires 6 feet of space. Only 500 units of type A are available to the wholesaler. Assuming that the wholesaler expects to make a profit of $1 on each unit of A bought and stocked, $3 per unit on B, and $2 per unit on C, how many units of each should be bought and stocked in order to maximize his profit?

14. A diet is to contain at least 10 ounces of nutrient P, 12 ounces of R, and 20 ounces of S. These nutrients are to be obtained from foods A, B, and C. Each

3.10 PROBLEM SET 3-3 (concluded)

pound of A costs 3 cents and contains 4 ounces of P, 2 ounces of R, and 1 ounce of S. Each pound of B costs 6 cents and contains 1 ounce of P, 3 ounces of R, and 3 ounces of S. Each pound of C costs 9 cents and contains 1 ounce of P, 1 ounce of R, and 5 ounces of S. How many pounds of each food should be purchased if the stated dietary requirements are to be met at minimum cost?

15. Products A, B, and C are sold door-to-door. A costs $3 per unit, takes 10 minutes to sell (on the average), and costs $0.50 to deliver to a customer. B costs $5, takes 15 minutes to sell, and is left with the customer at the time of sale. C costs $4, takes 12 minutes to sell, and costs $1 to deliver. During any week, a salesperson is allowed to draw up to $500 worth of A, B, and C (at cost) and is allowed delivery expenses not to exceed $75. If a salesperson's selling time is not expected to exceed 30 hours (1,800 minutes) in a week, and if the salesperson's profit (net after all expenses) is $1 each on a unit of A or B and $2 on a unit of C, what combination of sales of A, B, and C will lead to maximum profit, and what is this maximum profit?

16. AAA Electrical Company makes three kinds of automobile batteries: Model S (the super), Model N (the normal), and Model E (the economy). Each battery must be processed on three machines: Machine I, Machine II, and Machine III. To make one Model S battery requires 2 hours on I, 1 hour on II, and 3 hours on III; whereas to make one Model N battery requires 2 hours on I, 4 hours on II, and 1 hour on III; while to make one Model E battery requires 5 hours on I, 2 hours on II, and 3 hours on III. Production scheduling indicates that during the coming week Machine I will be available for at most 40 hours, Machine II for at most 26 hours, and Machine III for at most 27 hours. If the company makes an $8 profit on each Model S battery, a $6 profit on each Model N battery, and a $12 profit on each Model E battery, how many of each kind should be made in the coming week in order to maximize profit? What is this maximum profit?

17. A special food for athletes is to be developed from three foods: Food X, Food Y, and Food Z. The new food is to contain at least 66 milligrams of Vitamin A, at least 48 milligrams of Vitamin B, at least 40 milligrams of Vitamin C, and at least 58 milligrams of Vitamin D. Each pound of Food X costs $1.50 and contains 2 milligrams of Vitamin A, 4 milligrams of Vitamin B, 1 milligram of Vitamin C, and 6 milligrams of Vitamin D. On the other hand, each pound of Food Y costs $2.50 and contains 9 milligrams of A, 3 milligrams of B, 4 milligrams of C, and 2 milligrams of D; whereas each pound of Food Z costs $2.00 and contains 7 milligrams of A, 2 milligrams of B, 8 milligrams of C, and 1 milligram of D. How many pounds of each food should be used in the mixture in order to meet these requirements at a minimum cost? What is the minimum cost?

18. Safety Lock Company makes three kinds of locks: Model SS (the super safe) Model S (the safe), and Model O (the economy). Each Model SS lock sells for $16 and costs $11 to make, whereas each Model S lock sells for $9 and costs $6 to make, and each Model O lock sells for $7 and costs $3 to make. Each of the locks must be processed on five machines: Model SS requires 3 hours on Machine A, 1 hour on Machine B, 2 hours on Machine C, 4 hours on Machine D, and 3 hours on machine E. On the other hand, Model S requires 2 hours on A, 3 hours on B, 1 hour on C, 5 hours on D, and 4 hours on E; while Model O requires 1 hour on A, 2 hours on B, 2 hours on C, 3 hours on D, and 4 hours on E. During the coming week Machine A will be free for no more than 23 hours, Machine B for no more than 26 hours, Machine C for no more than 19 hours, Machine D for no more than 49 hours, and Machine E for no more than 45 hours. Determine the number of each kind of lock to be made in the coming week in order for the company to maximize its profit. What is this maximum profit?

19. a) Write a computer program that will locate all the permissible corners of the solution space of a linear programming problem with two variables, evaluate each of these corners at any given objective function, and then print the associated optimum.

b) Run the program in (a) for Problems 1 through 16 of Problem Set 3-2.

c) Run the program in (a) for Problems 1 through 6 of Problem Set 3-3.

FROM THEORY TO PRACTICE
Linear Programming Models in Business and Government

The techniques of linear programming are applicable to a wide variety of problems in business and government. Problems 8 through 12 of Problem Set 3–4 which follows illustrate some typical business situations that lend themselves to linear programming models. These problems are examples of what might be called minicases. We next present an example of an application in government based on a Harvard University case.

The Ganges–Brahmaputra River Basin*

The lower Ganges and Brahmaputra rivers in Northeastern India flow through a region that is dominated by rain-fed agriculture and that is chronically short of electric power. Moreover, each year the rivers flood during the monsoon season, causing loss of life plus damage to crops and property.

To tame the river waters, as well as to harness them for power generation and irrigation, the government of India is considering building two dams, one on each river. For the sites chosen, the Brahmaputra dam cannot exceed 17.5 million acre-feet and the Ganges dam 20 million acre-feet. Furthermore, it is not technically feasible to construct a dam of less than 5 million acre-feet in capacity.

Because of the immediate benefits of the dams, the government has decided to build them with no foreign assistance. It has commissioned a team of engineers to estimate the costs. The team discovered that the two sites differ markedly in their topographic structures and hence in the quantity and type of materials required. As an overall figure, they estimate the annualized cost of constructing, maintaining, and operating the Ganges reservoir to be 21 rupees (Rs. 21) per acre-foot; the analogous figure for the site on the Brahmaputra River is Rs. 15 per acre-foot. These costs diverge even more in their foreign exchange content [since different materials will be purchased in different currencies for each project]: 12 percent for the Ganges dam and 40 percent for the Brahmaputra project. In addition to draining the government treasury, it is feared that construction and operation of the dam may strain the already scarce supply of skilled labor in the area. Experts project that no more than 500 trained technicians, engineers, and managers will be available for the next few years. Again, the labor requirements of the two dams are different: 17 per million acre-feet for the Ganges site and 20 per million acre-feet for the Brahmaputra dam.

While both projects will yield at least three types of benefits—power generation, irrigation, and flood control—the latter two are difficult to quantify. Power generation will be greater in the Brahmaputra than in the Ganges site: 33.3 units per acre-foot versus 14.3 units per acre-foot. However, because of greater industrialization in the area surrounding the Ganges, the government places a 50 percent premium on electricity generation there over the Brahmaputra River area.

The Indian government is anxious to keep the total costs of the two dams combined below Rs. 1,050 million, and the foreign exchange costs below Rs. 125 million.

What advice should be given the Indian government on the construction of the two dams? Using linear programming, it is possible to determine the most profitable strategy to pursue in completing this project.

*Source: Prepared by Rajiv Chaudhri under the supervision of Professor Shantayanan Devarajan of the John F. Kennedy School of Government, Harvard University. It is based on a more detailed study by Professor Peter Rogers of the Kennedy School.

3.11 MORE ON FORMULATION

As we have already seen, one of the most important phases in the solution of a linear programming problem is the formulation, which translates the verbiage into an objective function together with a set of constraints. The more complicated the problem, of course, the more involved the formulation itself. Our next example will help to illustrate this fact.

Example. A certain professor likes to give weekly quizzes composed of multiple-choice questions divided into two groups: A and B. By closely observing the format of the first few quizzes, one rather clever student has determined that although there are always 30 questions of each type, the student is allowed to answer at most 40 total questions. In addition, the student is prohibited from answering more than 25 A questions but is required to answer at least as many B questions as A questions. Furthermore, while each A question counts two points, each B question counts three points. Lastly, the student is always restricted by having the number of B questions answered not exceed the number of A questions answered by more than 8; and, indeed, is penalized 1/2 point each for the number of B questions answered over the number of A questions answered. After some deliberation, the student has worked out a scheme for the number of each kind of question that should be answered to attain the best possible grade and finds that there are five alternative combinations. What is the scheme and what will be the grade?

In this example, we clearly want to maximize the student's grade. Thus, we first let

$$x = \text{Number of A questions that the student answers}$$

and

$$y = \text{Number of B questions that the student answers.}$$

Steps 1 and 2: Determine the objective and assign the variables.

Now since each A question counts two points while each B question counts three points, the student's grade is given by

$$2x + 3y.$$

Step 3: Formulate the objective function.

However, the student is penalized 1/2 point each for the number of B questions answered over the number of A questions answered. In other words, we must deduct 1/2 point for the difference between y and x. This penalty, of course, is meaningful only if $y \geq x$, which we will see later on is actually one of the constraints. Thus the goal is to maximize the objective or grade function

$$2x + 3y - \left(\frac{1}{2}\right)(y - x)$$

or simply

$$\theta = 2.5x + 2.5y.$$

> **Exercise.** What would the objective function be if the student were awarded one point for the number of B questions answered in excess of the number of A questions answered?
>
> **Answer:** $\theta_{max} = x + 4y$.

Step 4: Formulate the constraints.

Turning now to our constraints, we first see that there are always 30 questions of each type and that the student is allowed to answer at most 40 questions. These conditions give rise to the three constraints

$$x \leq 30, \tag{1}$$

$$y \leq 30, \tag{2}$$

$$x + y \leq 40. \tag{3}$$

Next, we see that the student is prohibited from answering more than 25 A questions but is required to answer at least as many B questions as A questions. Thus we have the two additional constraints

$$x \leq 25 \tag{4}$$

$$y \geq x.$$

As stated in Section 3.5, we rewrite the latter constraint with all the variables on the left-hand side to get

$$-x + y \geq 0. \tag{5}$$

(Alternatively, of course, this constraint could have been written as $x - y \leq 0$ simply by multiplying through by -1.)

Lastly we see that the student is always restricted by having the number of B questions that she answers not exceed the number of A questions by more than 8. This gives rise to the constraint

$$y \leq x + 8,$$

which, again, we rewrite as

$$-x + y \leq 8. \tag{6}$$

> **Exercise.** Can we rewrite the last constraint in the form $x - y \geq -8$? Why?
>
> **Answer:** No, since we want the constant on the right-hand side to be nonnegative.

Adding the nonnegativity constraints, then, the linear programming problem becomes:

Step 5: Formulate any implicit constraints.

Minimize the grade function

$$\theta = 2.5x + 2.5y$$

subject to the constraints

$$x \leq 30 \quad (1)$$
$$y \leq 30 \quad (2)$$
$$x + y \leq 40 \quad (3)$$
$$x \leq 25 \quad (4)$$
$$-x + y \geq 0 \quad (5)$$
$$-x + y \leq 8 \quad (6)$$
$$x, y \geq 0. \quad (7), (8)$$

Although we could stop with the formulation at this point, an inspection of the constraints will show that some are redundant. It would clearly simplify the solution process if these redundancies were removed.

To simplify the solution, check for and eliminate any redundant constraints.

Examining the constraints, then, we first see that constraint (1), $x \leq 30$, is clearly unnecessary because of constraint (4), $x \leq 25$.

Secondly, constraint (4), $x \leq 25$, is itself unnecessary because of constraint (3), $x + y \leq 40$, together with constraint (5), $-x + y \geq 0$ (or $y \geq x$). In other words, if the two variables x and y can sum to no more than 40 and if y must be at least as large as x, then x must in fact be no larger than 20.

Thirdly, constraint (2), $y \leq 30$, is unnecessary because of constraint (6), $-x + y \leq 8$ (or $y \leq x + 8$), together with constraint (3), $x + y \leq 40$. This last redundancy is not so evident, but becomes clear upon some reflection of the numbers involved or alternatively upon adding the two constraints; i.e.,

$$\begin{aligned} y &\leq x + 8 \\ y &\leq -x + 40 \\ \hline 2y &\leq 48 \end{aligned}$$

which means, of course, that

$$y \leq 24.$$

Thus, in summary, the linear programming problem is:

Maximize the grade function

$$\theta = 2.5x + 2.5y$$

subject to the constraints

$$x + y \leq 40$$
$$-x + y \geq 0$$
$$-x + y \leq 8$$
$$x, y \geq 0.$$

> **Exercise.** Solve the preceding problem by the graphical procedure. How many practical solutions are there? Why?
>
> **Answer:** The maximum is 100 at any point on the line segment from (16, 24) to (20, 20). Only (16, 24), (17, 23), (18, 22), (19, 21), and (20, 20) are practical since the student cannot answer a fractional number of questions.

3.12 PROBLEM SET 3-4

1. To introduce its new economy automobile to the public, the marketing department of Guarantee Motors, Inc., has decided to sponsor a 90-minute television special featuring the world-famous comedian I. M. Hilarious. From past experience, it is known that to reach a maximum number of viewers, a delicate balance must be maintained between the number of minutes devoted to commercials and the number of minutes that the comedian is on the air. In fact, although Hilarious's popularity is such that he attracts 15,000 viewers for every minute that he is on the air, any television program tends to lose about 150 viewers for each minute devoted to commercials. Furthermore, the time devoted to commercials should be no more than 25 percent of the time Hilarious is on the air. On the other hand, the president of Guarantee insists that the commercial time be at least 20 percent of the comedian's time. Under all of these conditions, what is the optimum strategy for allotting the 90 minutes between commercials and Hilarious? What is the maximum number of viewers that Guarantee will reach?

2. Lifetime Siding Company sells both aluminum and vinyl siding for homes with a 30-year guarantee on all materials and labor. The company has to order its stock at least six months in advance, but must pay the manufacturer within 15 days of delivery. Since business in the current economic times is slow, management wants to place its next order very carefully so as to minimize its cost. Aluminum siding costs the company $75 per square (10-foot by 10-foot section), while vinyl siding costs the company $100 per square. The company has to carry the inventory in stock until sold and has determined that the carrying cost is $5 per square (aluminum or vinyl) for the average number of squares in the inventory (the average being typically one-half of the number originally acquired). On the basis of past experience, the sales department of the company has projected that for the period to be covered by the order, its needs will be at most 4,000 but at least 2,000 total squares. Furthermore, no more than 3,000 but at least 1,000 squares of aluminum will be needed; and, in addition, the number of vinyl squares should be at least 20 percent of the total.
   a) What order should the company place and what will be its cost?
   b) If the company had, by mistake, maximized its cost, what would the results be?

3. In the last days before the election, the political prospects of I. M. Hopeful look rather dim unless he can reach a very large part of his constituency immedi-

3.12 PROBLEM SET 3-4 (continued)

ately. His campaign manager has hit upon an idea of staging a rally highlighted by performances by the leading male and female singers in the area. Unfortunately, there are a few complications. First of all, the two singers dislike each other intensely and so will not do a song together but only sing solos. In addition, the female singer insists on having at least equal time, while the male singer will not perform for less than 30 minutes. Also, the rally is to last two hours with at least 20 minutes devoted to political speeches. Finally, the two singers' personalities not only attract large audiences, but also tend to drive some people away. In fact, for every minute the male singer is on the stage alone he ordinarily draws 300 people, while for every minute the female singer is on stage alone she ordinarily draws 200 people. However, the male singer's presence in the program drives away 10 percent of the people who would have come to see the female singer perform solo, whereas the female singer's presence in the program drives away 5 percent of the people who would have come to see the male singer perform solo.

a) How should the two hours be divided up to maximize the number of people drawn to the rally? What is this maximum number?

b) If the male singer charges $100 per minute and the female singer charges $90 per minute, what is the cost of the results of (a)?

c) If the campaign manager decided to minimize the total cost rather than maximize the size of the audience, how would the time be divided up and what would the cost be?

4. Premium Brewing Company has to decide the optimal mix of two blending processes for making rye whiskey and bourbon. Each unit of Process A uses 25 pounds of malted grain and 50 pounds of unmalted grain to make 100 gallons of rye whiskey and 1,500 gallons of bourbon. On the other hand, each unit of Process B needs 40 pounds of malted grain and 20 pounds of unmalted grain to make 120 gallons of rye whiskey and 400 gallons of bourbon. The company has only 500 pounds of malted grain and only 400 pounds of unmalted grain on hand. Furthermore, the sales department has projected that it will need a minimum of 1,200 gallons of rye whiskey and 7,500 gallons of bourbon. If the company makes a profit of $1,500 per unit of Process A and $2,000 per unit of Process B, find the blending mix that maximizes that total profit. What is this maximum profit?

In Problems 5 through 7, formulate the problem and then determine the number of corners in the feasible solution space.

5. The brothers of XYZ fraternity have kept a record of a certain logic professor's final examinations and have determined the following interesting facts: The examination is always divided into three categories of questions: T/F (true–false), M/C (multiple-choice), and S/E (short-essay). Now the student is given a choice of 50 T/F questions each counting one point, 50 M/C questions each counting two points, and 10 S/E questions each counting four points. However, the student must select at least 40 questions but no more than 60 questions, and must answer at least 5 S/E questions. In addition, the student must answer more M/C questions than T/F questions, but the student's score is penalized one point each for the number of M/C questions answered over the number of T/F questions answered. Finally, the number of T/F questions answered must be smaller by at least 10 than the difference between the number of M/C questions answered and twice the number of S/E questions answered. The president of the fraternity, now enrolled in the logic professor's course, has decided that one phase of the initiation of the new pledges will be to find all possible combinations of the number of each kind of question that should be answered to attain the best possible grade on the upcoming final examination. Determine the maximum score and all alternative combinations.

6. Superior Paint Company sells three kinds of exterior finishes: oil-base paint, water-base paint, and stain. In order to keep all its distributors properly supplied, the company must manufacture and store at least three months' sales in advance. Oil-base paint costs the company $5.50 per gallon to make, whereas water-base paint costs $4.50 per gallon, and stain costs $3.50 per gallon. The company has determined that

3.12 PROBLEM SET 3-4 (continued)

the carrying costs for all three finishes is $0.50 per gallon for the average number of gallons in the inventory (the average being typically one-half of the number originally manufactured). On the basis of past experience, the sales department of the company has projected that its needs for the next three months will be at most 10,000 but at least 6,000 total gallons. Furthermore, no more than 2,000 gallons of stain but at least 1,000 gallons of each finish will be needed. In addition, the number of gallons of paint should be at least 75 percent of the total. How many gallons of each finish should the company make and what will be the cost?

7. Mideast Tobacco Company makes three kinds of cigarettes: filter regulars, filter kings, and filter super kings. Management has to decide the optimal production mix of three blending processes for making each cigarette: Process X, Process Y, and Process Z. Each unit of Process X uses 4 pounds of tobacco, 1 ream of paper, and 3 ounces of charcoal to make 800 filter regulars, 700 filter kings, and 600 filter super kings. On the other hand, each unit of Process Y uses 5 pounds of tobacco, 2 reams of paper, and 4 ounces of charcoal to make 1,000 filter regulars; 800 filter kings, and 600 filter super kings; whereas each unit of Process Z uses 3 pounds of tobacco, 1 ream of paper, and 3 ounces of charcoal to make 900 filter regulars, 400 filter kings, and 700 filter super kings. The company has only 425 pounds of tobacco, 140 reams of paper, and 350 ounces of charcoal on hand. Furthermore, the sales department has projected that it will need a minimum of 50,000 filter regulars, 40,000 filter kings, and 30,000 filter super kings. If the company makes a profit of $18 per unit of Process X, $23 per unit of Process Y, and $15 per unit of Process Z, find the production mix that maximizes the total profit. What is this maximum profit?

In Problems 8 through 12, formulate the problem only.

8. Growth Investment Company is planning a pension fund of $10,000,000 for one of its valued clients. Federal and state regulations require that, for the workers' protection, the fund must be made up of stocks, bonds, and a reserve in the form of bank notes or savings accounts. After much investigation, the company has decided upon the following combination: three stocks (S_1, S_2, and S_3), two bond issues (B_1 and B_2), and a particular bank note (N). Their study shows that the expected yield from S_1 will be 8 percent, S_2 will be 9 percent, S_3 will be 7 percent, B_1 will be 10 percent, B_2 will be 11 percent, and N will be 6 percent. There are, however, stringent limitations on the investment possibilities written in the regulations on pension funds. First, the amount invested in stocks must be no more than 40 percent of that invested in bonds. Second, a minimum of 25 percent of the total fund must be held in reserve. Third, no more than 35 percent of the total fund can be invested in stocks. Finally, no single investment other than a bank note or savings account can constitute more than 30 percent of the total fund. What portfolio will the company recommend for the pension fund and what will be its expected yield?

9. True Sound Radio Company makes four kinds of radios for automobiles: AM, AM/FM, AM/FM stereo, and AM/FM stereo tape. Each radio can be manufactured by either of two methods. Method I involves two processes: P_1 and P_2. Method II involves three processes: P_3, P_4, and P_5. Revenue and cost data on the radios are shown in Table A, while manufacturing data are shown in Table B. What is the optimal

TABLE A

	Radio			
	AM	AM/FM	AM/FM Stereo	AM/FM Stereo Tape
Unit selling price ($)	100	150	250	300
Unit cost, Method I	70	90	150	225
Unit cost, Method II	95	70	185	190
Maximum quantity that can be sold	5,000	3,000	2,000	1,000

3.12 PROBLEM SET 3-4 (continued)

TABLE B

	\multicolumn{4}{c}{Manufacturing Time (Hours)}	
	AM	AM/FM	AM/FM Stereo	AM/FM Stereo Tape	Maximum Hours Available
Method I					
Process P_1	4	4	3	0	2,100
Process P_2	8	10	6	7	14,000
Method II					
Process P_3	1	0	5	5	1,500
Process P_4	3	8	0	6	2,400
Process P_5	1	1	11	20	2,500

number of each kind of radio for the company to make and what is the associated profit? (Hint: Let x_{1A}, x_{1F}, x_{1S}, and x_{1T} be the number of AM, AM/FM, AM/FM stereo, and AM/FM stereo tape radios made by Method I. Similarly, use x_{2A}, x_{2F}, x_{2S}, and x_{2T} for Method II).

10. Precision Instruments, Inc., has a contract to supply Electronic Calculator Company with 600 minicircuits in July and 500 minicircuits in August. Precision makes and tests the minicircuits on an assembly line, using people on both a regular- and second-shift basis. In July, because of other commitments, only 650 minicircuits can be produced during regular time and only 200 during the second shift. On the other hand, only 450 minicircuits can be produced during regular time in August and only 150 in the second shift. The problem is that production costs differ not only for each shift, but also for each of the two months. Specifically, in the month of July the regular-shift cost is $250 per minicircuit, while the second-shift cost is $350 per minicircuit. The respective costs for August are $300 and $375. Of course, Precision can make more than the 600 minicircuits required by Electronic in July; but, in this case, Precision must store the difference over from July to August at a unit inventory cost of $25. What should Precision's production schedule be and what is the associated cost?

   a) Formulate the problem with the following variables: x_{JR} and x_{JS} are the number of minicircuits produced in July during regular and second shift, respectively; x_{AR} and x_{AS} in August; and x_1 the inventory from July to August. (Hint: Be careful to remember that, for consistency, the inventory must be the excess over the 600.)

   b) Formulate the problem with the following variables: x_{JRJ} and x_{JRA} are the numbers of minicircuits produced in July, regular shift, for use in July and August, respectively; x_{JSJ} and x_{JSA} the numbers of minicircuits produced in July, second shift; x_{AR} and x_{AS} as in (a).

11. The intensive care unit of City Hospital has to schedule the shifts for its nursing staff on a round-the-clock basis to ensure that a certain minimum number of nurses are on duty at various times. The supervisor of nurses has broken the day into six slots of four hours each and has determined that in order to maintain efficiency at least 12 nurses must be on duty from 8 A.M. to 12 noon, at least 14 from 12 noon to 4 P.M., at least 16 from 4 P.M. to 8 P.M., at least 10 from 8 P.M. to 12 midnight, at least 6 from 12 midnight to 4 A.M., and at least 9 from 4 A.M. to 8 A.M. Of course, the nurses work eight-hour shifts, but they are scheduled to arrive (and depart) every four hours starting at 8 A.M. That is, Shift 1 works from 8 A.M. to 4 P.M., Shift 2 from 12 noon to 8 P.M., Shift 3 from 4 P.M. to 12 midnight, and so on. Find the optimal schedule that meets the preceding requirements and, at the same time, employs the smallest total number of nurses. What is this total? (Hint: Let x_i, be the number of nurses who are scheduled to work Shift i where $i = 1, 2, 3, 4, 5, 6$).

12. Fine Paper Mill produces paper in reels having a standard width of 60 inches and a fixed length. The mill receives orders from its customers for reels of the same fixed length but smaller widths. One customer's order calls for 50 reels of width 10, 75 reels of width 16, and 85 reels of width 23; all of which the mill cuts from the standard size reel. The mill wants to meet the customer's needs in such a way as to minimize the total trim waste. This trim waste occurs, of course, when the standard reel is cut into smaller reels; that is, if one 60-inch reel is cut into

3.12 PROBLEM SET 3-4 (concluded)

one 10-inch reel and two 23-inch reels, then there is a trim waste of $60 - [10(1) + 23(2)] = 4$ inches.

a) Find every possible combination of cutting the standard 60-inch reel into combinations of 10-inch, 16-inch, and 23-inch reels, and calculate the trim waste for each such combination. (Hint: There are eight such combinations.)

b) Formulate the problem minimizing the total trim waste, assuming that the mill ignores the extra 10-inch, 16-inch, and 23-inch reels made. What is this total waste?

c) Formulate the problem minimizing the total trim waste assuming that the extra reels are also waste. What is this total waste?

3.13 THE SIMPLEX METHOD

The Simplex Method is a step-by-step solution technique for linear programming problems.

Linear programming problems can be solved by a procedure called the **Simplex Method**. The word **simplex** is derived from two mathematical terms used in n-space geometry and is not a synonym for "simple." The important attribute of the Simplex Method is that it provides a step-by-step solution of linear programming problems in which each step brings us closer to the optimal value of the objective function.

We will now develop the Simplex Method as it pertains to "$\leq$" constraints. The extensions to other types of constraints as well as other advanced analyses in linear programming will be done in Chapter 4.

The example we choose as our starting point is the Lounge and Swivel Chair example of Section 3.5. There our linear programming problem was:

Maximize
$$\theta = x_1 + 0.5x_2$$

subject to:

$$
\begin{array}{lll}
\text{Department I} & i_1: & x_1 + x_2 \leq 4 \\
\text{Department II} & i_2: & x_1 + 2x_2 \leq 6 \\
\text{Nonnegativity } i_3, i_4: & & x_1, x_2 \geq 0
\end{array}
\tag{1}
$$

For reasons that will become clear later, we now have changed x and y to x_1 and x_2, respectively.

Step 1. Conversion of the Constraints and Objective Function. The first step in the Simplex Method is to convert the inequalities in the problem statement to equalities, thus creating a system of equations. To do this, we need to introduce one new variable for each constraint. Thus,

$$x_1 + x_2 \leq 4$$

requires that a **nonnegative** quantity be added to the left side to increase its value to 4. Let us call this quantity s_1 and write

$$x_1 + x_2 + s_1 = 4.$$

For example, if we do not make any Lounge or Swivel Chairs, then

$$x_1 = x_2 = 0$$

so that

$$s_1 = 4.$$

Remembering that the inequality at hand is the Department I constraint, the last equation says that if we do not make any Lounge or Swivel Chairs, then four hours of available time in I are not used. This unused time is called **slack.**

In a similar manner, we convert

$$x_1 + 2x_2 \leq 6$$

to

$$x_1 + 2x_2 + s_2 = 6$$

by adding the nonnegative slack variable s_2.

> Slack variables are added to "≤" constraints, transforming them into equalities.

Exercise. What does s_2 represent?

Answer: Unused time in Department II.

Inasmuch as slack time does not produce any product, the slack variables ordinarily contribute nothing to profit, so our objective function is now

$$\theta = x_1 + 0.5x_2 + 0s_1 + 0s_2.$$

At the moment, we shall not bother to write the slack variables in the objective function, θ. We will see later on in Chapter 4 how to handle problems where the slack variables do actually contribute something to the objective function. Thus the formulation of the problem is:

> Slack variables do not usually contribute to profit (or cost).

$$\begin{aligned} e_1 &: \quad x_1 + x_2 + s_1 = 4 \\ e_2 &: \quad x_1 + 2x_2 + s_2 = 6 \\ e_3 &: \quad \theta = x_1 + 0.5x_2 \end{aligned} \quad (2)$$

$$x_1, x_2, s_1, s_2 \geq 0.$$

> The original problem has been reformulated as a system of equations.

The original problem, (1), had **two constraints** (i_1 and i_2) which have been converted to the **two equalities** e_1 and e_2. However, in the conversion we introduced two more variables, s_1 and s_2, so that we now have **$m = 2$ constraints on $n = 4$ variables** ($x_1, x_2, s_1,$ and s_2) and, hence, four nonnegativity constraints. According to the principle illustrated and stated in Section 3.9, in any solution of the system **at least $n - m$ of the variables must have the value zero.** Here,

$$n - m = 4 - 2 = 2,$$

so **at least two of the variables must be zero** in a solution of system (2). The critical question, now, is which two are zero in the optimal solution.

> Each corner has at least $n - m$ zero coordinates (m constraints, n variables, $n \geq m$).

Step 2. Finding an Initial Solution. We start our search by making sure that we have a **permissible** or **feasible solution**. The easiest starting point when all constraints are $\leq$ is the origin, where $x_1 = x_2 = 0$. To be clear on this point, refer to Figure 3–12 (a reproduction of Figure 3–4 of Section 3.5). Any point on the boundary of the shaded space, or within it, is a feasible solution, and the corner (0, 0) is indeed feasible.

> The easiest initial solution when all constraints are "$\leq$" is the origin.

Our next step is to write the system (2) with the zero-valued variables (x_1 and x_2) as independent variables. Thus,

$$x_1 + x_2 + s_1 = 4$$

becomes

$$s_1 = 4 - x_1 - x_2.$$

FIGURE 3–12

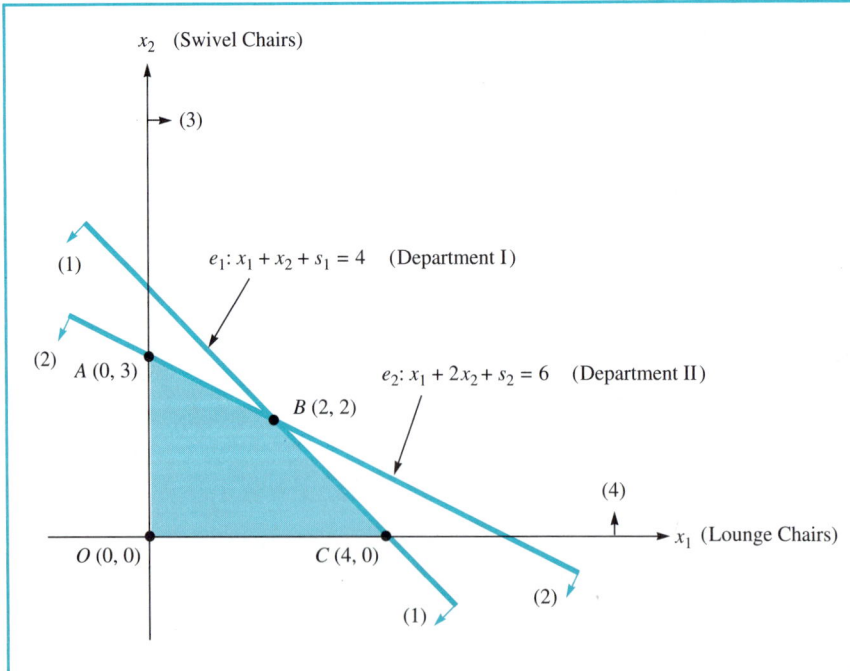

Similarly,

$$x_1 + 2x_2 + s_2 = 6$$

becomes

$$s_2 = 6 - x_1 - 2x_2.$$

The variable θ is already expressed in terms of x_1 and x_2. We have

$$\begin{aligned} s_1 &= 4 - x_1 - x_2 \\ s_2 &= 6 - x_1 - 2x_2 \\ \theta &= x_1 + 0.5x_2. \end{aligned} \qquad (3)$$

Remembering that the variables x_1 and x_2 on the **right side** take on the value zero at the origin, we have the feasible solution:

$$x_1 = x_2 = 0; \quad s_1 = 4; \quad s_2 = 6; \quad \theta = 0. \qquad (4)$$

Now for more terminology. The variables that are **in the solution**, the ones on the **left side** of (3), s_1 and s_2, are called **basic variables**. The basic variables, all of them, form the **basis**. Thus, currently, s_1 is in the basis and s_2 is in the basis. Together, s_1 and s_2 are the basis. The variables that are **out of the solution**, the ones on the **right side** of (3) that have the value zero, are called **nonbasic variables**, that is, x_1 and x_2 are nonbasic variables at the present time. The solution, (4), which is **on the boundary** of the feasible solution space exhibited in Figure 3–12 is called a **basic feasible solution** to distinguish it from feasible solutions that are not on the boundary. Our interest centers on the corners of the feasible solution space, so we will confine our attention to the basic feasible solutions.

> Variables in the solution are basic; variables not in the solution are nonbasic. A basic feasible solution is one on the boundary of the feasible solution space.

The basic feasible solution (4), in which $x_1 = x_2 = 0$, means, of course, that no Lounge or Swivel Chairs are produced, so Department I has $s_1 = 4$ hours of unused time (slack time) and Department II has $s_2 = 6$ hours of slack. No product is made, so the profit $\theta = 0$. **This vertex serves the important purpose of providing an initial basic feasible solution.** It is, however, merely a starting point.

At this point, we use the techniques of Chapter 2 to introduce an **augmented matrix** which summarizes the Simplex Method and will simplify subsequent steps. We first rewrite our starting equations (2) by moving all the variables to the left-hand side and viewing the system as consisting of three equations in the five unknowns (x_1, x_2, s_1, s_2, and θ):

$$\begin{aligned} 0 + x_1 + x_2 + s_1 + 0 &= 4 \\ 0 + x_1 + 2x_2 + 0 + s_2 &= 6 \\ \theta - x_1 - 0.5x_2 + 0 + 0 &= 0. \end{aligned} \qquad (5)$$

> The original problem is reformulated as a system of three equations in five unknowns.

Here we have filled out the equations with zeros in the appropriate places. Now, using the techniques of Chapter 2, (5) can be written as the augmented matrix

$$\begin{pmatrix} 0 & | & 1 & 1 & | & 1 & 0 & | & 4 \\ 0 & | & 1 & 2 & | & 0 & 1 & | & 6 \\ 1 & | & -1 & -0.5 & | & 0 & 0 & | & 0 \end{pmatrix}$$

and summarized as shown in the **Preliminary Tableau** of Table 3–9. In this Preliminary Tableau, the starting basic variables s_1 and s_2 are contained in the leftmost column. The fact that we are maximizing the variable θ, representing the objective function, is entered at the bottom of this column. The rest of the tableau is precisely the preceding matrix with the last column containing the **current values** of our basis and θ; namely

$$s_1 = 4, \quad s_2 = 6, \quad \text{and} \quad \theta = 0.$$

Recall that the nonbasic variables x_1 and x_2 were assigned the value zero, so that

$$x_1 = x_2 = 0.$$

Step 3. Choosing the Entering Variable. We now wish to choose an improved corner of the feasible solution space (i.e., a corner with a larger profit). To do this, we need to replace a basic variable with another variable. What we plan to do at this point is decide which corner we should move to next. Examining

$$\theta = 1x_1 + 0.5x_2,$$

which currently is zero, we note that if we **increase** x_1, from its zero value, then every increase of 1 in x_1 (every Lounge Chair made) will add \$1 to profit, but another Swivel Chair (increasing x_2 by 1) will add only \$0.50 to profit. We now plan to bring **only one new variable** into the basis (and subsequently **take one out**). Because a Lounge Chair provides more profit than a Swivel Chair, it is reasonable to choose to bring in all the Lounge Chairs we can, leaving the number of Swivel Chairs at zero. Thus we want to **increase** x_1 **as much as possible**. Note in the Preliminary Tableau of Table 3–9 that these coefficients of 1 and 0.5 have become -1 and -0.5, respectively, in the θ row. Why? How did we get from

The Preliminary Tableau represents the matrix equivalent of the system of three equations in five unknowns.

The solution is changed one variable at a time.

TABLE 3–9

Basic Variables	θ	Coefficient of				Current Values
		x_1	x_2	s_1	s_2	
s_1	0	1	1	1	0	4
s_2	0	1	2	0	1	6
(max) θ	1	-1	-0.5	0	0	0

system (2) in Step 1 to system (5) in Step 2? What happened is that when we transposed x_1 and x_2 to the left-hand side of the θ-equation, their coefficients became negative. **Thus the entering-variable column or pivot column for a maximizing problem is always the one that has the most negative value in the θ-row**. So our tableau becomes that shown in Table 3–10, where the ↑ indicates the entering variable. By the way, if there are no negative values in the θ-row, we would stop the procedure, since then we would be at the maximum.

The entering variable for a maximizing problem is the one with the most negative value in the θ-row.

Step 4. Choosing the Leaving Variable. If we look at the first two equations of (3), we see

$$e_4: \quad s_1 = 4 - x_1 - x_2$$
$$e_5: \quad s_2 = 6 - x_1 - 2x_2.$$

Covering up the x_2 terms (which remain at zero), we see from e_4 that

$$s_1 = 4 - x_1$$

so that x_1 must not be increased to more than 4, otherwise s_1 will become negative. Similarly, from e_5 with $x_2 = 0$, we see that

$$s_2 = 6 - x_1$$

Bring in as much of the entering variable as possible without another variable becoming negative.

and x_1 cannot be increased to more than 6. The controlling condition, therefore, is that x_1 **not be increased by more than 4** (which in turn guarantees that it will not be increased by more than 6). Thus, we have found that x_1 **should be brought into the basis and that it should be brought in at e_4, so that s_1 must go out of the basis.**

Now notice from Table 3–10 that if we divide the coefficients in the pivot column for x_1 into the corresponding current values in the last column, we have

$$s_1\text{-row:} \quad \frac{4}{1} = 4$$

$$s_2\text{-row:} \quad \frac{6}{1} = 6.$$

TABLE 3–10

Basic Variables	θ	Coefficient of				Current Values
		x_1	x_2	s_1	s_2	
s_1	0	1	1	1	0	4
s_2	0	1	2	0	1	6
(max) θ	1	−1	−0.5	0	0	0
		↑				

The ratios, then, represent the upper limits on the number of units of x_1 we can introduce, and we obviously must select the controlling one. **Thus, the leaving-variable row or point row is the one which corresponds to the smallest non-negative ratio of the current values to the corresponding pivot column values.** This procedure for selection is shown in the **Initial Tableau** of Table 3–11. Here we have boxed in the entries that are used to compute the ratios, shown the ratios to the right of the tableau, and indicated the leaving variable with the usual arrow. We call this tableau the Initial Tableau since it contains the initial solution together with the optimality analysis on test solution.

The leaving variable is the one with the smallest nonnegative ratio.

Exercise. What would the ratios be if x_2 were the entering variable? What would the leaving variable be?

Answer: $\frac{4}{1} = 4$ and $\frac{6}{2} = 3$; s_2.

At this point, it suffices to say that we ignore negative ratios since a negative ratio indicates no limiting value. An example of such an occurrence, with a more detailed explanation, will be seen later on in Section 3.17. Since the current values are always nonnegative, a negative ratio can occur only when an entry in the pivot column is negative. Thus we need not even compute the ratio if the pivot column entry is negative. What if the pivot column entry were 0? In this case, the ratio is not finite and again produces no limiting value. Obviously, then, the ratios need be computed only for positive entries in the pivot column.

Negative ratios are ignored, so we need only compute ratios for positive entries in the pivot column.

Step 5. Determining the New Solution. To perform the change of basis indicated in Table 3–11, we use the techniques of Chapter 2 to **first get a 1 in the pivot entry**, where the entering-variable column (x_1-column) intersects with the leaving-variable row (s_1-row). By chance, this is already the case:

$$\begin{pmatrix} 0 & | & 1^* & 1 & | & 1 & 0 & | & 4 \\ 0 & | & 1 & 2 & | & 0 & 1 & | & 6 \\ 1 & | & -1 & -0.5 & | & 0 & 0 & | & 0 \end{pmatrix} \rightarrow .$$
$$\uparrow$$

This 1* in the pivot row and pivot column is called the **pivot element**. To find the new solution, we must now **change all other values in the pivot column to 0**. To do this, we add -1 times row 1 to row 2 and $+1$ times row 1 to row 3 to obtain

To obtain the new solution (basis), we transform the pivot element into a "1" and all other entries in the pivot column into "0"s.

$$\begin{pmatrix} 0 & | & 1 & 1 & | & 1 & 0 & | & 4 \\ 0 & | & 0 & 1 & | & -1 & 1 & | & 2 \\ 1 & | & 0 & 0.5 & | & 1 & 0 & | & 4 \end{pmatrix}.$$

TABLE 3-11
Initial Tableau

Basic Variables	θ	Coefficient of				Current Values	
		x_1	x_2	s_1	s_2		
s_1	0	[1]	1	1	0	[4]	4/1 = 4 →
s_2	0	[1]	2	0	1	[6]	6/1 = 6
(max) θ	1	−1	−0.5	0	0	0	

↑

This process is summarized in tableau form as shown in Table 3-12, where, for ease of understanding, we have included the steps necessary to perform the change of basis in a **Working Tableau** and boxed in the first column and pivot row operations. As we did above, we first get a 1 in the asterisked pivot entry of the pivot column. Then we add −1 times the new pivot row to the old s-row and +1 times the new pivot row to the old θ-row, thus transforming all other entries in the pivot column to 0. The purpose of the Working Tableau is to indicate the values used to change from the Initial Tableau to the **Second Tableau**. The resultant Second Tableau is shown in Table 3-12.

From the Second Tableau in Table 3-12, we see that the current solution is

$$x_1 = 4, \quad s_2 = 2, \quad x_2 = s_1 = 0, \quad \theta = 4,$$

which means a profit of \$4 when four Lounge Chairs ($x_1 = 4$) and no Swivel Chairs ($x_2 = 0$) are made. There is no slack in Department I ($s_1 = 0$) and 2 hours of slack in Department 2 ($s_2 = 2$). Note that this solution corresponds to the corner C (4,0) in Figure 3-12.

Exercise. What system of equations is summarized in the Second Tableau of Table 3-12?

Answer:

$$0 + x_1 + x_2 + s_1 + 0 = 4$$
$$0 + 0 + x_2 - s_1 + s_2 = 2$$
$$\theta + 0 + 0.5x_2 + s_1 + 0 = 4,$$

or solving for our basic variables x_1 and s_2 together with θ,

$$x_1 = 4 - x_2 - s_1$$
$$s_2 = 2 - x_2 + s_1$$
$$\theta = 4 - 0.5x_2 - s_1.$$

TABLE 3-12

Initial Tableau

Basic Variables	θ	Coefficient of				Current Values	
		x_1	x_2	s_1	s_2		
s_1	0	1*	1	1	0	4	4/1 = 4 →
s_2	0	1	2	0	1	6	6/1 = 6
(max) θ	1	-1	-0.5	0	0	0	

↑

Working Tableau

Order	Operation
(1)	Pivot row = (Old s_1 row) ÷ 1
(2)	$(-1) \cdot$ (Pivot row)
(3)	$(+1) \cdot$ (Pivot row)

θ	Coefficient of				Current Values	Use
	x_1	x_2	s_1	s_2		
0	1	1	1	0	4	replaces old s_1-row
0	-1	-1	-1	0	-4	is added to old s_2-row
0	1	1	1	0	4	is added to old θ-row

Second Tableau

Basic Variables	θ	Coefficient of				Current Values
		x_1	x_2	s_1	s_2	
x_1	0	1	1	1	0	4
s_2	0	0	1	-1	1	2
(max) θ	1	0	0.5	1	0	4

The optimal solution is reached in a maximizing problem when there are no negative entries in the θ-row.

Returning to Step 3. We now look again at the objective function in the θ-row for improvement. Since there are no negative values in the θ-row of the Second Tableau of Table 3–12, we have reached the maximum. Note that the current optimal solution is precisely the one we found in Section 3.5.

> **Exercise.** In the optimal solution, how many hours are being utilized in each department?
>
> **Answer:** Four hours in each.

The procedure just illustrated is summarized in Figure 3–13 and what follows, using the word constraint to refer to constraints other than nonnegativity constraints.

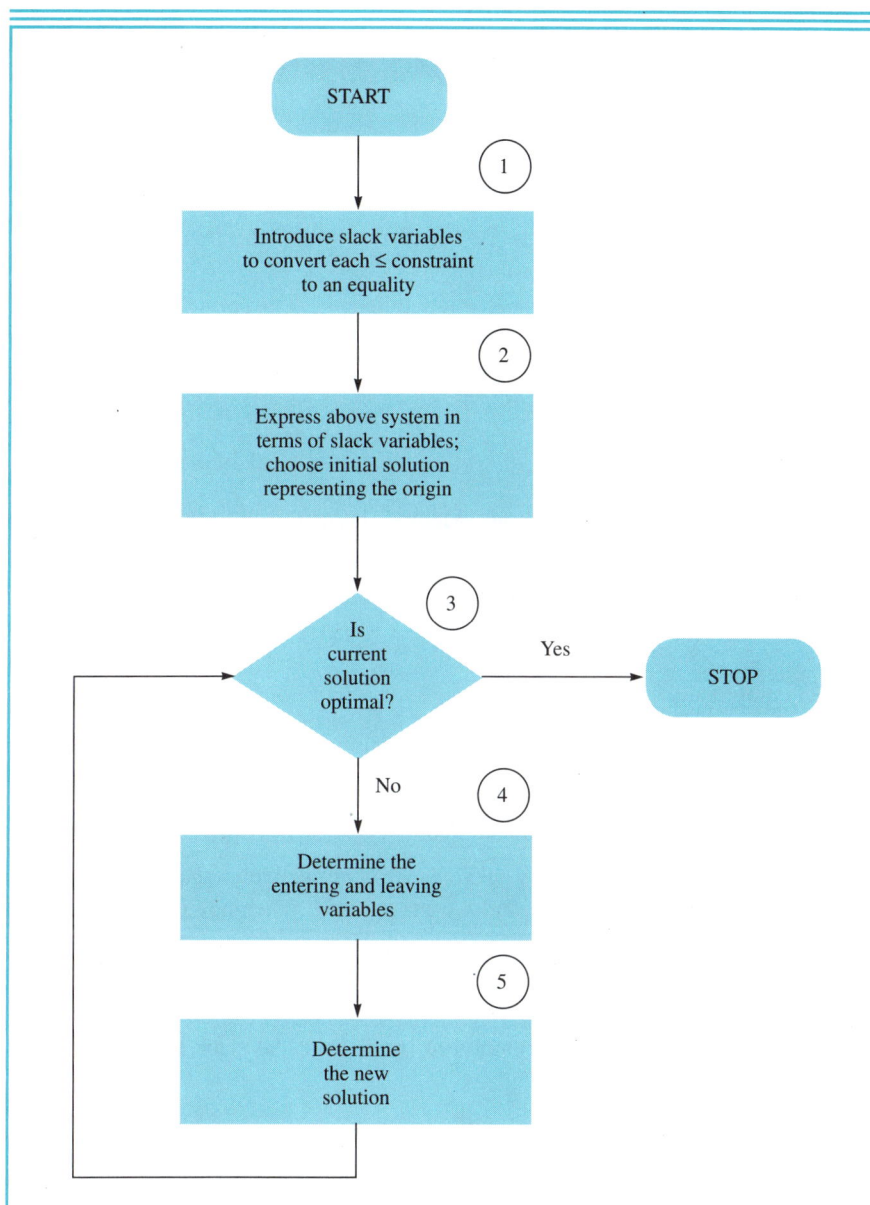

FIGURE 3-13

An Outline of the Simplex Method

1. Introduce a nonnegative slack variable to convert each $\leq$ constraint to an equality.
2. Write the first system with the slacks as the basic variables (on the left).
3. a) If θ can be improved by bringing in a new basic variable and taking one out, determine which variable is to be brought in. Go to Step 4.
   b) If at any juncture θ cannot be improved, the present solution is optimal. Stop.
4. Determine which variable is to come out.
5. Adjust the equations to bring in the new variable, taking one out (See Step 4.) Write the new system. Return to Step 3.

As another example of the Simplex Method, let us recall the Ace Rubber Company example of Section 3.5:

Maximize

$$\theta = 10x_1 + 8x_2$$

subject to

Machine A: $\quad 2x_1 + 9x_2 \leq 36$

Machine B: $\quad 4x_1 + 3x_2 \leq 42$

Nonnegativity: $\quad x_1, x_2 \geq 0.$

Again we have changed x and y to x_1 and x_2, respectively. Our first step is to introduce two slack variables, s_1 and s_2, one for each machine. Thus we have

Step 1: Convert the constraints and objective function into a system of equations.

Machine A: $\quad 2x_1 + 9x_2 + s_1 = 36$

Machine B: $\quad 4x_1 + 3x_2 + s_2 = 42.$

Since there is no specified contribution to profit from the slack times, θ remains unchanged

$$\theta = 10x_1 + 8x_2.$$

Step 2: Represent the initial solution by the origin.

The Preliminary Tableau, then, is as shown in Table 3–13.

Exercise. What is the current solution?

Answer: $x_1 = x_2 = 0, \quad s_1 = 36, \quad s_2 = 42,$ and $\theta = 0.$

TABLE 3-13
Preliminary Tableau

Basic Variables	θ	Coefficient of x_1	x_2	s_1	s_2	Current Values
s_1	0	2	9	1	0	36
s_2	0	4	3	0	1	42
(max) θ	1	−10	−8	0	0	0

TABLE 3-14
Initial Tableau

Basic Variables	θ	Coefficient of x_1	x_2	s_1	s_2	Current Values	
s_1	0	[2]	9	1	0	[36]	36/2 = 18
s_2	0	[4]	3	0	1	[42]	42/4 = 21/2 →
(max) θ	1	−10	−8	0	0	0	

↑

TABLE 3-15
Preliminary Second Tableau

Basic Variables	θ	Coefficient of x_1	x_2	s_1	s_2	Current Values
s_1	0	0	15/2	1	−1/2	15
x_1	0	1	3/4	0	1/4	21/2
(max) θ	1	0	−1/2	0	5/2	105

Examining the θ-row of Table 3–13, we see that the maximum has not been reached. Why? We see also that x_1 should now enter the solution. Why? To determine the leaving variable, we perform the ratio analysis on the x_1 (pivot) column, as shown in Table 3–14.

Step 3: Choose the entering variable.

From this Initial Tableau, we see that the smallest nonnegative ratio is the 21/2 for s_2, so that s_2 should now leave the solution.

Step 4: Choose the leaving variable.

We next perform the change of basis specified in Table 3–14, bringing x_1 into the solution (making x_1 basic) and taking s_2 out of the solution (making s_2 nonbasic), as shown in Table 3–15. Note that we have omitted the Working Tableau.

Step 5: Change the basis to get the new solution.

> **Exercise:** What is the current solution?
>
> **Answer:** $s_1 = 15$, $x_1 = 21/2$, $x_2 = s_2 = 0$, and $\theta = 105$.

> **Exercise.** Why is the tableau in Table 3–15 labeled "Preliminary Second Tableau?"
>
> **Answer:** Because it represents the second solution without any optimality analysis.

Return to Step 3 and check for optimality.

Inspecting the tableau in Table 3–15, we see that we still have not reached the maximum. Why? So, as usual, we perform the entering and leaving variable analysis to get the Second Tableau, shown in Table 3–16.

> **Exercise.** Why do we select x_2 as the entering variable? Why do we select s_1 as the leaving variable?
>
> **Answer:** The most (in fact, only) negative value in the θ-row is $-1/2$, while 2 is the smallest nonnegative ratio.

Performing the change of basis specified in Table 3–16, we obtain the result shown in the Third Tableau of Table 3–17. From this tableau, we see that we have reached the maximum. Why? The optimal solution, as seen from this tableau, is

$$x_1 = 9, \quad x_2 = 2, \quad s_1 = s_2 = 0, \quad \text{and} \quad \theta = 106,$$

so that the maximum profit is $\theta = \$106$, which is attained when $x_1 = 9$ Model P tires and $x_2 = 2$ Model R tires are made. Furthermore, both Machines A and B are fully utilized, since $s_1 = s_2 = 0$.

Now before we go on, take a look at the θ-column in Tables 3–12 through 3–17. You should notice that the θ-column never changes from its original form of

$$\begin{pmatrix} 0 \\ 0 \\ 1 \end{pmatrix}.$$

The θ-column never changes, so it is omitted from here on.

Why? The reason is that the entry in the pivot row of the θ-column is always a zero. So, no matter what number we multiply the pivot row by, the entry in the θ-column will always be 0. (Zero times any number is still zero.) Since this will always be the case, we no longer include the θ-column in our tableaus.

TABLE 3-16 Second Tableau

Basic Variables	θ	Coefficient of				Current Values	
		x_1	x_2	s_1	s_2		
s_1	0	0	[15/2]	1	−1/2	15	15/(15/2) = 2 →
x_1	0	1	[3/4]	0	1/4	21/2	(21/2)/(3/4) = 14
(max) θ	1	0	−1/2	0	5/2	105	

↑

Repeating Steps 3 and 4.

TABLE 3-17 Third Tableau

Basic Variables	θ	Coefficient of				Current Values
		x_1	x_2	s_1	s_2	
x_2	0	0	1	2/15	−1/15	2
x_1	0	1	0	−1/10	3/10	9
(max) θ	1	0	0	1/15	37/15	106

Repeating Step 5.

Lastly, it should be clear that the Simplex Method will handle minimizing problems with all ≤ constraints (except for nonnegativity constraints) in the same way as a maximizing problem, but with one change. Can you guess what that is? Since we are trying to improve our objective function by **reducing** it rather than increasing it, we will look for **positive values** rather than negative values in the θ-row. Another way to look at this is to note that **minimizing θ** is equivalent to **maximizing (−θ)** so we look for the opposite sign in the θ-row. With this in mind, we present a summary of the Simplex Method for ≤ constraints on the next page.

Referring to the summary, note that it is possible to have a **tie** for the entering or leaving variable, or both, in Steps 3 and 4. We will discuss both of these cases in detail in Chapter 4, where we will see that, for all practical purposes, we can arbitrarily choose either one of the tied variables. In addition, it is possible to have negative ratios in Step 4 of the solution of a problem. As stated earlier, the reason that negative ratios are ignored will be explained in detail in Section 3.17 where we will see how such a ratio occurs.

Finally, we want to reemphasize the following two properties of the Simplex Method:

1. The current values of all nonbasic variables are zero **by choice**.
2. The coefficients of the basic variables in the θ-row are zero **by design**.

In a minimizing problem, we look for positive entries in the θ-row. All other steps in the Simplex Method are identical.

In any solution, nonbasic variables are zero as are the coefficients of the basic variables in the θ-row (equation).

Summary of the Simplex Method for "≤" Constraints

Step 1. Convert each "≤" constraint into an equality by introducing one slack variable for each such constraint, and also convert the objective function into a θ-equation containing these slack variables.

Step 2. For the system derived in Step 1, set up the associated tableau that represents the initial solution at the origin together with the corresponding θ value by choosing the slack variables as the initial basic variables.

Step 3. Determine whether the current solution is the maximum (minimum) by examining the θ-row for negative (positive) entries. If there are no negative (positive) entries in the θ-row, then the maximum (minimum) has been obtained. Otherwise, choose as the entering variable in a maximizing (minimizing) problem the one corresponding to the most negative (positive) entry in the θ-row.

Step 4. Determine the leaving variable (in both maximizing and minimizing problems) by examining the ratios of the current values to the respective coefficients of the entering variable and choosing as the leaving variable the one corresponding to the smallest nonnegative ratio.

Step 5. Use the row operations to transform the pivotal entry in the column of the entering variable and row of the leaving variable to a 1 and transform all other entries in the pivot column to 0. Then return to Step 3.

In each of the following, find the maximum value of θ by the Simplex Method, and state the values of the variables that make θ maximum. It is to be assumed that all variables must be nonnegative.

1. $\theta = x_1 + 2x_2$
   subject to
   $x_1 + x_2 \leq 5$
   $2x_1 + 3x_2 \leq 12$.

2. $\theta = 2x_1 - 3x_2$
   subject to
   $3x_1 + 7x_2 \leq 42$
   $x_1 + 5x_2 \leq 22$.

3. $\theta = 5x_1 + 8x_2$
   subject to
   $x_1 + x_2 \leq 13$
   $x_1 + 2x_2 \leq 22$
   $2x_1 + x_2 \leq 20$.

4. $\theta = 5x_1 + 8x_2$
   subject to
   $x_1 + x_2 \leq 13$
   $x_1 + 2x_2 \leq 22$
   $2x_1 + x_2 \leq 20$
   $x_1 \leq 4$.

3.14 PROBLEM SET 3-5 (continued)

5. $\theta = x_1 + 2x_2 + 4x_3$
   subject to
   $x_1 + 2x_2 + 3x_3 \leq 50$
   $x_1 + 3x_2 + 5x_3 \leq 60.$

6. $\theta = 2x_1 + 4x_2 + 3x_3$
   subject to
   $x_1 + 3x_2 + 4x_3 \leq 30$
   $x_1 + 5x_2 + 2x_3 \leq 40.$

7. $\theta = x_1 + 4x_2 + 6x_3$
   subject to
   $x_1 + 3x_2 + 6x_3 \leq 48$
   $x_1 + 6x_2 + 3x_3 \leq 90$
   $x_1 + 9x_2 + 10x_3 \leq 137.$

8. $\theta = 0.5x_1 + 6x_2 + x_3$
   subject to
   $x_1 + 5x_2 + 2x_3 \leq 30$
   $x_1 + 7x_2 \leq 40$
   $2x_1 + x_2 + 3x_3 \leq 70.$

9. $\theta = 3x_1 + 7x_2 + 6x_3$
   subject to
   $x_1 + x_2 + x_3 \leq 4$
   $x_1 + x_2 \leq 3.$

10. $\theta = 1.5x_1 + 2.5x_2 + 2x_3$
    subject to
    $1.5x_1 + x_2 + x_3 \leq 7.5$
    $x_1 + x_2 + x_3 \leq 4$
    $x_2 + 2.5x_3 \leq 5.$

11. $\theta = 3x_1 + 5x_2 + 3x_3$
    subject to
    $2x_1 + 3x_2 + 6x_3 \leq 50$
    $3x_1 + 4x_2 + x_3 \leq 40$
    $3x_1 + 5x_2 + 2x_3 \leq 20.$

12. $\theta = 2x_1 + 3x_2 + x_3$
    subject to
    $2x_1 + x_2 + 3x_3 \leq 10$
    $x_1 + 3x_2 + 2x_3 \leq 20.$

13. $\theta = x_1 + 2x_2 + x_3$
    subject to
    $2x_1 + x_2 + 3x_3 \leq 12$
    $x_1 + 2x_2 \leq 6$
    $2x_1 + x_3 \leq 4.$

14. $\theta = x_1 + x_2 + x_3$
    subject to
    $x_1 + 2x_2 + x_3 \leq 12$
    $2x_1 + x_2 + x_3 \leq 20$
    $x_1 + x_2 + 3x_3 \leq 15.$

---

15. Star Insulating Company manufactures two types of storm windows: Model H (the heavy duty) and Model R (the regular). Model H sells for $35 per window and costs $26 per window to make, whereas Model R sells for $28 per window and costs $20 per window to make. To make 1 Model H window, it requires 4 hours on Machine A and 3 hours on Machine B. On the other hand, to make 1 Model R window, it takes 5 hours on Machine A and 2 hours on Machine B. Production scheduling indicates that during the coming week Machine A will be available for at most 30 hours and Machine B for at most 19 hours. How many of each window should the company make in the coming week in order to maximize its profit? What is this maximum profit?

16. Ace Rubber Company manufactures two types of tires: Model P (the premium) and Model S (the second line). Each tire must be processed on three machines: A, B, and C. To make one Model P tire requires 0.5 hours on Machine A, 1 hour on Machine B, and 2 hours on Machine C. To make one Model S tire requires 0.5 hours on A, 2 hours on B, and 1 hour on C. Production scheduling indicates that during the coming week Machine A will be free for at most 6.5 hours, B for at most 22 hours, and C for at most 20 hours. In addition, no more than eight Model S tires may be made. If the company makes a $5 profit on each Model P tire and an $8 profit on each Model S tire, determine the number of each model to be made in the coming week in order for the company to maximize its profit. What is this maximum profit? At the maximum, which machines, if any, are not fully utilized?

17. A wholesaler has 9,600 feet of space available, and $5,000 to buy merchandise of types A, B, and C. Type A costs $4 per unit and requires 4 feet of storage space in the warehouse. B costs $10 per unit and requires 8 feet of space. C costs $5 per unit and

3.14 PROBLEM SET 3–5 (concluded)

requires 6 feet of space. Only 500 units of type A are available to the wholesaler. Assuming that the wholesaler expects to make a profit of $1 on each unit of A bought and stocked, $3 per unit on B, and $2 per unit on C, how many units of each should be bought and stocked in order to maximize his profit, and what is this maximum profit?

18. Products A, B, and C are sold door-to-door. A costs $3 per unit, takes 10 minutes to sell (on the average), and costs $0.50 to deliver to a customer. B costs $5, takes 15 minutes to sell, and is left with the customer at the time of sale. C costs $4, takes 12 minutes to sell, and costs $1 to deliver. During any week, a salesperson is allowed to draw up to $500 worth of A, B, and C (at cost) and is allowed delivery expenses not to exceed $75. If a salesperson's selling time is not expected to exceed 30 hours (1,800 minutes) in a week, and if the salesperson's profit (net after all expenses) is $1 each on a unit of A or B and $2 on a unit of C, what combination of sales of A, B, and C will lead to maximum profit, and what is this maximum profit?

3.15 INTRODUCTION TO LINDO

Computer solutions reduce the amount of time required to solve large-scale linear programming packages.

The Simplex Method introduced in Section 3.13 is the basis for a number of computer packages that handle linear programming problems with various numbers of variables and constraints. These packages are available on most mainframes, minicomputers, and microcomputers and use more advanced techniques to speed up the solution and reduce the amount of time required to solve some large-scale problems. Our purpose in this section is to illustrate one of these packages, LINDO, on problems with "≤" constraints other than nonnegativity.[5] In Chapter 4, we will continue to illustrate LINDO for other types of constraints.

We use the Ace Rubber Company example of Sections 3.5 and 3.13 to introduce LINDO. Recall that our problem was:

Maximize

$$\theta = 10x_1 + 8x_2$$

subject to

Machine A: $\quad 2x_1 + 9x_2 \leq 36$

Machine B: $\quad 4x_1 + 3x_2 \leq 42$

Nonnegativity: $\quad x_1, x_2 \geq 0.$

Table 3–18 shows the LINDO solution as generated on a VAX™ 6000-410, where the information entered by the user has been underlined for ease of understanding.[6]

---

[5]For a detailed explanation of LINDO, see L. Schrage, *Linear, Integer, and Quadratic Programming with LINDO* (Palo Alto, Cal.: Scientific Press, 1984).

[6]VAX is a trademark of Digital Equipment Corporation.

TABLE 3-18

```
Username: SABER
Password:
        Welcome to VAX/VMS version V5.4-2 on node X

$ lindo
LINDO (7 OCTOBER 88 CHICAGO)
: max 10x1 + 8x2
 ?st
 ?2x1 + 9x2 <=36
 ?4x1 + 3x2 <=42
 ?end

: go
LP OPTIMUM FOUND AT STEP      2

       OBJECTIVE FUNCTION VALUE
       1)    106.000000

  VARIABLE         VALUE            REDUCED COST
       X1          9.000000             0.000000
       X2          2.000000             0.000000

       ROW    SLACK OR SURPLUS       DUAL PRICES
       2)          0.000000             0.066667
       3)          0.000000             2.466667

NO. ITERATIONS=      2

DO RANGE (SENSITIVITY) ANALYSIS?
 ?no
: quit
FORTRAN STOP
$ lo
```

As can be seen from Table 3–18, the first prompt from LINDO is the "**:**" to which we responded with the type of optimization together with the objective function, namely,

$$: \text{max } 10x1 + 8x2.$$

Note that the computer does not accept subscripts. Next we respond to the first "**?**" query with "**st**":

$$?\text{st}$$

(meaning **subject to**) to indicate that the constraints are forthcoming. To each of the next queries we input the constraints one by one, **with the exception of the nonnegativity constraints** since LINDO assumes nonnegativity for all variables

$$?2x1 + 9x2 <= 36$$
$$?4x1 + 3x2 <= 42.$$

Computer packages assume nonnegativity for the variables.

To the next query, we respond with **"end"** to signify that we have finished the constraint set

$$? \, \text{end}$$

to which the computer responds with the "**:**" prompt. At this point, we respond with **"go"** to instruct LINDO to proceed with the optimization process

$$: \, \text{go}$$

and LINDO then prints the optimum solution, which is

$$\theta = 106, \quad x_1 = 9, \quad x_2 = 2, \quad \text{and} \quad s_1 = s_2 = 0$$

as seen from the OBJECTIVE FUNCTION VALUE and the first two columns under VARIABLE and VALUE and then ROW and SLACK OR SURPLUS. We will see in Chapter 4 the meaning of the term **surplus** as well as the meaning of the third columns REDUCED COST and DUAL PRICES. Finally, LINDO asks if we want to perform SENSITIVITY ANALYSIS. Since we will discuss this topic also in Chapter 4, we will delay any explanation here. So we respond to the query with **"no"**:

$$\text{DO RANGE (SENSITIVITY) ANALYSIS?}$$
$$? \, \text{no}$$

at which point LINDO prompts us again with "**:**". Since we are done with the current session, we respond with **"quit"**

$$: \, \text{quit}$$

and then log off the computer

$$\$ \, \text{lo.}$$

Exercise. What would be the format to run LINDO for the Lounge and Swivel Chair example of Section 3.5?

Maximize

$$\theta = x_1 + 0.5x_2$$

subject to

$$x_1 + x_2 \leq 4$$
$$x_1 + 2x_2 \leq 6$$
$$x_1, x_2 \geq 0.$$

Answer:
```
max x1 + 0.5x2
st
x1 + x2 <= 4
x1 + 2x2 <= 6
end
go
```

3.16 PROBLEM SET 3-6

Use a computer program such as LINDO to solve each of the following, assuming all variables to be nonnegative.

1. Maximize
$$\theta = 5x_1 + 7x_2$$
subject to
$$x_1 + x_2 \leq 5$$
$$2x_1 + 3x_2 \leq 12.$$

2. Maximize
$$\theta = 4x_1 + 10x_2$$
subject to
$$3x_1 + 7x_2 \leq 42$$
$$x_1 + 5x_2 \leq 22.$$

3. Maximize
$$\theta = 4x_1 - x_2$$
subject to
$$x_1 + x_2 \leq 13$$
$$x_1 + 2x_2 \leq 22$$
$$2x_1 + x_2 \leq 20.$$

4. Repeat Problem 1 with the additional constraint that $x_1 \leq 4$.

5. Repeat Problem 2 with the additional constraint that $x_2 \leq 3$.

6. Repeat Problem 3 with the additional constraints that $x_1 \leq 8$ and $x_2 \leq 8$.

7. Maximize
$$\theta = 6x_1 + x_2 - 7$$
subject to
$$2x_1 + 3x_2 \leq 24$$
$$2x_1 - x_2 \leq 8$$
$$-2x_1 + 3x_2 \leq 12.$$

8. Repeat Problem 7 but, this time, minimize the objective function.

9. Maximize
$$\theta = 5x_1 + 6x_2 + 10x_3$$
subject to
$$x_1 + 2x_2 + 3x_3 \leq 24$$
$$2x_1 + x_2 + x_3 \leq 18.$$

10. Maximize
$$\theta = -2x_1 + 5x_2 + 9x_3$$
subject to
$$x_1 + x_2 + 4x_3 \leq 36$$
$$2x_1 + 2x_2 + 3x_3 \leq 42.$$

11. Maximize
$$\theta = 2x_1 + 5x_2 + 8x_3 - 10$$
subject to
$$x_1 + x_2 + 4x_3 \leq 36$$
$$x_1 + 2x_2 + 3x_3 \leq 42.$$

12. Maximize
$$\theta = 3x_1 + 5x_2 + 12x_3$$
subject to
$$x_1 + 2x_2 + 3x_3 \leq 36$$
$$x_2 + 2x_3 \leq 12.$$

13. Repeat Problem 9 with the additional constraint that $x_2 \leq 5$.

14. Repeat Problem 9 with the additional constraint that $x_3 \leq 5$.

15. Repeat Problem 10 with the additional constraint that $x_1 \leq 4$.

16. Maximize
$$\theta = 3x_1 + 4x_2 + 10x_3$$
subject to
$$x_1 + x_2 + 4x_3 \leq 42$$
$$x_1 + 2x_2 + 3x_3 \leq 40$$
$$2x_1 + x_2 + 2x_3 \leq 30.$$

17. Maximize
$$\theta = 10x_1 + 8x_2 + 14x_3$$
subject to
$$2x_1 + 2x_2 + 5x_3 \leq 40$$
$$3x_1 + x_2 + 3x_3 \leq 27$$
$$x_1 + 4x_2 + 2x_3 \leq 26.$$

18. Ace Rubber Company manufactures three types of tires: Model P (the premium), Model S (the second line), and Model E (the economy). Model P sells for $96 per tire and costs $86 per tire to make; Model S sells for $79 per tire and costs $73 per tire to make; Model E sells for $76 per tire and costs $64 per tire to make. To make one Model P tire, it requires one hour on Machine A, one hour on Machine B, and

3.16 PROBLEM SET 3-6 (concluded)

two hours on Machine C. To make one Model S tire, it takes one hour on Machine A, two hours on Machine B, and one hour on Machine C; to make one Model E tire requires four hours on A, three hours on B, and two hours on C. Production scheduling indicates that during the coming week Machine A will be available for at most 42 hours, Machine B for at most 40 hours, and Machine C for at most 30 hours. How many of each tire should the company make in the coming week in order to maximize its profit? What is this maximum profit?

19. New Sound Radio Company makes four kinds of radios for automobiles: AM, AM/FM, AM/FM stereo, and AM/FM stereo tape. Each radio can be manufactured by either two methods: Method I (which involves two processes: P_1 and P_2) and Method II (which involves three processes: P_3, P_4, and P_5). Revenue and cost data on the radios are shown in Table A, while manufacturing data are shown in Table B. What is the optimal number of each kind of radio for the company to make and what is the associated profit? (Hint: Let x_{1A}, x_{1F}, x_{1S}, x_{1T} be the number of AM, AM/FM, AM/FM stereo, and AM/FM stereo tape radios made by Method I, and similarly x_{2A}, x_{2F}, x_{2S}, x_{2T} for Method II.)

TABLE A

	\multicolumn{4}{c}{Radio}
	AM	AM/FM	AM/FM Stereo	AM/FM Stereo Tape
Unit selling price ($)	100	150	250	300
Unit cost, Method I	70	90	150	225
Unit cost, Method II	95	70	185	190
Maximum quantity that can be sold	5,000	3,000	2,000	1,000

TABLE B

	\multicolumn{4}{c}{Manufacturing Time (Hours)}	
	AM	AM/FM	AM/FM Stereo	AM/FM Stereo Tape	Maximum Hours Available
Method I					
Process P_1	4	4	3	0	2,100
Process P_2	8	10	6	7	14,000
Method II					
Process P_3	1	0	5	5	1,500
Process P_4	3	8	0	6	2,400
Process P_5	1	1	11	20	2,500

3.17 A MINIMIZING PROBLEM WITH "≤" CONSTRAINTS

We now reinforce the Simplex Method by presenting the solution of the following minimizing linear programming problem, all of whose constraints other than the nonnegativity constraints are "≤."

Example. Clear Film Company has won a much-desired contract with the CIA to supply Standard Microfilm Dots for its agents. The contract, in addition, requires the company to provide a second specially designed kind of microfilm dot whose cost, because of its unusual requirements, is actually subsidized by the government.

CHAPTER 3 INTRODUCTION TO LINEAR PROGRAMMING AND THE SIMPLEX METHOD

In fact, whereas the Standard Microfilm Dot costs the company $1 apiece to make, the company is given $2 apiece above its cost for the Special Microfilm Dot. Each dot is processed for one hour on a single Machine A, which has no more than seven hours available during the coming week. Furthermore, the fixed or setup cost for the processing is $8 per week. Finally, the CIA has specified that the number of Special Dots cannot exceed the number of Standard Dots by more than one and that the number of Standard Dots must be limited to no more than five per week. Find the number of each kind of dot the company should make in the coming week in order to minimize its cost. What is this minimum cost?

If we let x_1 and x_2 be the number of Standard and Special Microfilm dots, respectively, to be made in the coming week, then the total cost function to be minimized is simply

$$\theta = x_1 - 2x_2 + 8.$$

Note that the negative coefficient, -2, of x_2 is due to the fact that the cost of the Special Microfilm Dots is subsidized at the rate of $2 apiece. Note also that the constant term, 8, is the fixed or setup cost.

The constraints for this problem are

$$\text{Machine A:} \quad x_1 + x_2 \leq 7,$$

together with

$$\text{Relative quantities:} \quad x_2 \leq x_1 + 1$$

which, as usual, we rewrite in the form

$$-x_1 + x_2 \leq 1,$$

and

$$\text{Production limit:} \quad x_1 \leq 5.$$

Thus our problem is to minimize the objective function

$$\theta = x_1 - 2x_2 + 8$$

subject to the five constraints

Machine A:	$x_1 + x_2 \leq 7$	(1)
Relative quantities:	$-x_1 + x_2 \leq 1$	(2)
Production limit:	$x_1 \leq 5$	(3)
Nonnegativity:	$x_1, x_2 \geq 0.$	(4), (5)

The graph of these constraints gives rise to the feasible solution set shown in Figure 3–14.

FIGURE 3-14

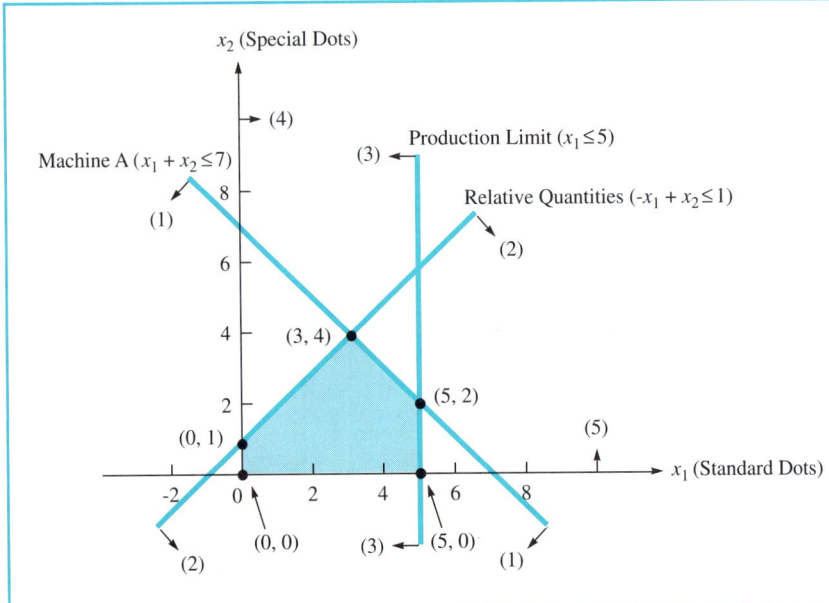

Proceeding in the usual manner, we first add a slack variable to each of the three ≤ constraints (1), (2), and (3) to get

Step 1: Convert the constraints and the objective function.

$$x_1 + x_2 + s_1 + 0 + 0 = 7$$
$$-x_1 + x_2 + 0 + s_2 + 0 = 1$$
$$x_1 + 0 + 0 + 0 + s_3 = 5,$$

where, of course, s_1 is the slack on Machine A, s_2 is the slack on the relative quantities, and s_2 is the slack on the production limit of Standard Microfilm Dots. Next, we assign the coefficient zero to each slack variable (since no penalty or premium was specified for any of them) to get the θ-equation

$$\theta = x_1 - 2x_2 + 0s_1 + 0s_2 + 0s_3 + 8$$

or

$$\theta - x_1 + 2x_2 + 0 + 0 + 0 = 8.$$

Step 2: Set up the associated tableau that represents the initial solution.

At this point, then, we can generate our Initial Tableau, as shown in Table 3-19.

Exercise. What point in Figure 3-14 is represented by the Initial Tableau?

Answer: The origin (0, 0), where $x_1 = 0$, $x_2 = 0$, $s_1 = 7$, $s_2 = 1$, $s_3 = 5$, and $\theta = 8$.

TABLE 3–19

Initial Tableau

Basic Variables	Coefficient of					Current Values	
	x_1	x_2	s_1	s_2	s_3		
s_1	1	1	1	0	0	7	7
s_2	−1	1	0	1	0	1	1 →
s_3	1	0	0	0	1	5	∞
(min) θ	−1	2	0	0	0	8	

↑

Second Tableau

Basic Variables	Coefficient of					Current Values	
	x_1	x_2	s_1	s_2	s_3		
s_1	2	0	1	−1	0	6	3 →
x_2	−1	1	0	1	0	1	−1
s_3	1	0	0	0	1	5	5
(min) θ	1	0	0	−2	0	6	

↑

Third Tableau

Basic Variables	Coefficient of					Current Values
	x_1	x_2	s_1	s_2	s_3	
x_1	1	0	1/2	−1/2	0	3
x_2	0	1	1/2	1/2	0	4
s_3	0	0	−1/2	1/2	1	2
(min) θ	0	0	−1/2	−3/2	0	3

Now from the Initial Tableau of Table 3–19, we see that x_2 enters first. Why? Since we are **minimizing θ**, the entering variable corresponds to the **most positive** entry in the θ-row and the coefficient 2 of x_2 is the most (in fact, only) positive entry in the θ-row.

Step 3: The entering variable for a minimum is the most positive one in the θ-row.

Exercise: What variable would have entered if we had been maximizing θ?
Answer: x_1.

Step 4: The leaving variable is the one with the smallest nonnegative ratio.

Step 5: Change the basis to get the new solution.

Now the ratio analysis in the Initial Tableau of Table 3–19 shows that s_2 is to leave the solution since the ratio 1 for s_2 is the smallest nonnegative ratio. Note that, for simplicity, we are no longer computing the ratios on the right of the tableau, but simply stating the results. Note also that the ratio for s_3 is $5/0 = \infty$ or unbounded and, hence, is ignored. Performing the change of basis in the usual manner, then, we find the result shown in the Second Tableau of Table 3–19, which corresponds to the solution:

$$x_1 = 0, \quad x_2 = 1, \quad s_1 = 6, \quad s_2 = 0, \quad s_3 = 5, \quad \text{and} \quad \theta = 6.$$

> **Exercise.** What point in Figure 3–14 is represented by the Second Tableau? How did we get there from the origin?
>
> **Answer:** (0, 1). We moved from (0, 0) along the x_2-axis to (0, 1).

Return to Step 3 to check for optimality.

A negative ratio corresponds to an increase in a potential leaving variable, which is in the wrong direction and so is ignored.

From the Second Tableau of Table 3–19, we see that we should now bring x_1 into the solution and remove s_1. Note here that the negative ratio $1/(-1) = -1$ for x_2 comes from its negative exchange coefficient and indicates that increasing x_1 by 1 unit actually results in an **increase** in x_2 of 1 unit; hence, x_2 **would never decrease to 0.** Specifically, we see from the x_2-row of this tableau that the constraint equation is

$$-x_1 + x_2 + 0 + s_2 + 0 = 1$$

so that if we increase x_1 by 1 unit from 0 to 1 while keeping $s_2 = 0$, we get

$$-(+1) + x_2 + 0 + (0) + 0 = 1$$

or simply

$$x_2 = 2;$$

which, of course, is an **increase** of 1 from the current value of $x_2 = 1$. This fact can be confirmed graphically in Figure 3–14, where we see that as we move along boundary line (2), $-x_1 + x_2 = 1$, increasing x_1 by 1 unit from (0, 1) takes us to the point (1, 2); **this is precisely the reason why the Simplex Method ignores negative ratios.** Changing the basis, then, as indicated in the Second Tableau of Table 3–19, we get the result shown in the Third Tableau of that table, which corresponds to the solution

Repeat Steps 3, 4, and 5 until the optimum is reached.

$$x_1 = 3, \quad x_2 = 4, \quad s_1 = 0, \quad s_2 = 0, \quad s_3 = 2, \quad \text{and} \quad \theta = 3.$$

> **Exercise.** What point in Figure 3–14 is represented by the Third Tableau? How did we get there from (0, 1)?
>
> **Answer:** (3, 4). We moved out from (0, 1) along line (2) to (3, 4).

We can see from the Third Tableau of Table 3–19 that the optimal solution is to make three Standard and four Special Microfilm Dots for a total cost of $3 ($x_1 = 3$, $x_2 = 4$, and $\theta = 3$). Doing this would fully utilize Machine A ($s_1 = 0$), would result in one more Special Dot than Standard ($s_2 = 0$), and would be two fewer than the production limit of Standard Dots ($s_3 = 2$).

The LINDO printout for this example is shown in Table 3–20. Note that the objective function

$$\theta = x_1 - 2x_2 + 8$$

is entered simply as

$$\max x1 - 2x2.$$

The reason for this is that LINDO does not accept any constant terms in the objective function. So we will have to add 8 to the LINDO answer to get the actual value

TABLE 3–20

```
Username: SABER
Password:
          Welcome to VAX/VMS version V5.4-2 on node X

$ lindo
LINDO (7 OCTOBER 88 CHICAGO)
: min x1 - 2x2
? st
? x1 + x2 <=7
? -x1 + x2 <=1
? x1 <=5
? end

: go
LP OPTIMUM FOUND AT STEP          2

        OBJECTIVE FUNCTION VALUE
     1)     -5.00000000

VARIABLE              VALUE                REDUCED COST
    X1              3.000000                0.000000
    X2              4.000000                0.000000

       ROW       SLACK OR SURPLUS           DUAL PRICES
       2)            0.000000                0.500000
       3)            0.000000                1.500000
       4)            2.000000                0.000000

NO. ITERATIONS=        2

DO RANGE (SENSITIVITY) ANALYSIS?
? no
: quit
FORTRAN STOP
$ lo
```

of the objective function. The constraints are then entered in the usual manner, resulting in the optimal solution

$$\theta = -5, \quad x_1 = 3, \quad x_2 = 4, \quad s_1 = s_2 = 0, \quad \text{and} \quad s_3 = 2.$$

Adding 8 to the objective function results in precisely the same result as before; namely, a minimum cost of \$3 when three Standard and four Special Microfilm Dots are made. Of course, Machine A is fully utilized ($s_1 = 0$), the number of Special Dots is one more than the number of Standard Dots ($s_2 = 0$), and the number of Standard Dots is two less than the production limit ($s_3 = 2$).

3.18 PROBLEM SET 3–7

In each of the following, find the minimum value of θ by the Simplex Method, and state the values of the variables that make θ minimum. It is to be assumed that all variables must be nonnegative.

1. $\theta = 2x_1 - 3x_2 + 14$
   subject to
   $3x_1 + 7x_2 \leq 42$
   $x_1 + 5x_2 \leq 22$.

2. $\theta = 2x_1 - 3x_2 + 14$
   subject to
   $3x_1 + 7x_2 \leq 42$
   $x_1 + 5x_2 \leq 22$
   $x_2 \leq 3$.

3. $\theta = 8x_1 - 12x_2 + 150$
   subject to
   $-x_1 + x_2 \leq 10$
   $x_1 + x_2 \leq 20$.

4. $\theta = 8x_1 - 12x_2 + 150$
   subject to
   $-x_1 + x_2 \leq 10$
   $x_1 + x_2 \leq 20$
   $x_2 \leq 8$.

5. $\theta = 4x_1 - 3x_2 + 50$
   subject to
   $x_1 + x_2 \leq 13$
   $x_1 + 2x_2 \leq 22$
   $2x_1 + x_2 \leq 20$.

6. $\theta = 4x_1 - 3x_2 + 50$
   subject to
   $x_1 + x_2 \leq 13$
   $x_1 + 2x_2 \leq 22$
   $2x_1 + x_2 \leq 20$
   $x_1 \leq 8$
   $x_2 \leq 8$.

7. $\theta = 3x_1 - 5x_2 + 24$
   subject to
   $2x_1 + 3x_2 \leq 24$
   $2x_1 - x_2 \leq 8$
   $-2x_1 + 3x_2 \leq 12$.

8. $\theta = 3x_1 - 5x_2 + 24$
   subject to
   $2x_1 + 3x_2 \leq 24$
   $2x_1 - x_2 \leq 8$
   $-2x_1 + 3x_2 \leq 12$
   $x_1 \leq 5$
   $x_2 \leq 5$.

9. Remington Powder Company, one of several subsidiaries of Sure Fire Munitions, Inc., supplies the parent company with most of its gunpowder. The management of Sure Fire requires all of its subsidiaries to make dynamite, whose production is subsidized by the parent company. Specifically, each company is given \$5 per dozen sticks above its cost of manufacturing dynamite. The management of Remington Powder has determined that its cost for making gunpowder is \$3 per pound and that its fixed

3.18 PROBLEM SET 3-7 (concluded)

production costs for all manufacturing in any given week are $24. The gunpowder and dynamite are both processed on a single Machine A, which has at most 24 hours available during the coming week. The production of the gunpowder requires two hours per pound on A while the dynamite requires three hours per dozen sticks on A. Sure Fire has further stipulated that twice the number of pounds of gunpowder must not exceed the number of dozens of sticks of dynamite by more than eight. On the other hand, Sure Fire insists that three times the number of dozens of sticks of dynamite must not exceed twice the number of pounds of gunpowder by more than 12. How many pounds of gunpowder and dozens of sticks of dynamite should the company make in the coming week in order to minimize its total cost? What is this minimum cost?

10. Studemaker Motor Company, a truck manufacturer, has been ardently pursuing a long-term exclusive contract with Near East Oil Company, located in Asia, to supply tractors and tractor bodies. The oil company has asked the truck manufacturer to produce a sample of such tractors and tractor bodies. The tractors themselves are fairly standard items and cost $8,000 each to manufacture. The tractor bodies, on the other hand, are very specialized items, since they have to meet stringent temperature, humidity, and corrosion requirements due to the climate; and, indeed, the oil company has agreed to subsidize these units by giving the truck manufacturer $12,000 per tractor body above its actual cost. The truck manufacturer, in addition, has estimated that the cost of negotiations to date, together with the subsequent tractor body design specifications, amount to $150,000. There are certain restrictions accompanying the oil company's request. First, the oil company wants to see no more than eight tractors. Second, the oil company does not want the number of tractor bodies to exceed the number of tractors by more than 10. Third and last, the oil company wants the total number of pieces of equipment (tractors together with tractor bodies) not to exceed 20. Determine the number of tractors and tractor bodies the truck manufacturer should make in order to minimize its total cost. What is this minimum cost?

3.19 REVIEW PROBLEMS

Graph the solution space for each of the following, assuming in each system that the nonnegativity constraints $x \geq 0$ and $y \geq 0$ prevail, and write the algebraic statement of the solution space:

1. $x - 2y \leq 0$
   $x + y \leq 2$.
2. $x + y \geq 2$
   $x + 2y \leq 4$.
3. $x - 2y \leq 0$
   $x + 2y \leq 4$.
4. $x - 2y \geq 0$
   $x + 2y \geq 4$
   $x \geq 3$.
5. $x + y \geq 2$
   $x - 2y \leq 0$
   $x + 2y \leq 4$.

6. a) We plan to invest x dollars at 6 percent and y dollars at i percent and require that the combined investment yield at least 8 percent. Express the restriction on i in terms of x and y, and state the restrictions on x and y.
   b) If $x = \$2{,}000$ and $y = \$1{,}000$, what is the

3.19 REVIEW PROBLEMS (continued)

minimum interest rate that must be obtained on the $1,000?

7. A mixture of nuts is to weigh no more than 5 pounds and contain at least 24 ounces of nutrient. Spanish nuts contain 6 ounces of nutrient per pound and beer nuts contain 4 ounces of nutrient per pound. Write the general solution showing the permissible mixtures of the two nuts.

8. See Problem 7. If, in addition to the stated constraints, the mixture must contain at least three pounds of Spanish nuts, write the general solution showing the permissible nut mixtures.

9. See Problem 7. If, in addition to the stated constraints in Problem 7 it is required that the mixture not cost more than 21 cents, and if Spanish nuts cost 6 cents a pound and beer nuts cost 2 cents a pound, write the general solution showing the permissible nut mixtures.

10. A high-quality batch of a substance contains 3 ounces of butter and 4 ounces of margarine. A low-quality batch contains 1 ounce of butter and 3 ounces of margarine. If 70 ounces of butter and 110 ounces of margarine are available, write the general solution showing permissible combinations of numbers of high- and low-quality batches.

11. See Problem 10. Write the solution if a high-quality batch contributes $1 to profit and a low-quality batch contributes $2 to profit, and total profit is to be at least $65.

12. If, in addition to the conditions and facts stated in Problems 10 and 11, it is required that at least 5 percent of total output be high-quality batches, write the solution showing permissible combinations of the numbers of batches of each quality.

Solve each of the following two-variable linear programming problems, assuming $x \geq 0$ and $y \geq 0$:

13. $x + 2y \leq 40$
    $3x + y \leq 45$
    a) Find θ_{max} if $\theta = 2x + 3y$.
    b) Find θ_{max} if $\theta = 6x + 2y$.

14. $x + 2y \geq 40$
    $3x + y \geq 45$
    a) Find θ_{min} if $\theta = 4x + y$.
    b) Find θ_{min} if $\theta = 2x + 4y$.

15. $-x + y \leq 1$
    $3x + 2y \leq 17$
    $x + 4y \geq 9$
    Find θ_{max} if $\theta = 2x + y$.

16. $-x + y \leq 1$
    $3x + 2y \geq 17$
    $x + 4y \geq 9$
    Find θ_{min} if $\theta = 2x + y$.

17. $x \geq 2$
    $x + y \geq 7$
    $3x + 4y \geq 24$
    Find θ_{min} if $\theta = 3x + 2y$.

18. $x + y \leq 13$
    $x + 2y \leq 22$
    $2x + y \leq 20$
    Find θ_{max} if $\theta = 10x + 10y$.

19. $x - y \leq 7$
    $-x + y \geq 2$
    $-5x + y = 0$
    Find θ_{min} if $\theta = 3x + 4y$.

20. $x + y \leq 10$
    $3x + y = 18$
    Find θ_{max} if $\theta = 2x + y$.

---

21. One pound of Food A costs $1 and contains 2 ounces of Nutrient I and 4 ounces of Nutrient II. One pound of Food B costs $2 and contains 3 ounces of I and 1 ounce of II. A mixture is to contain at least 90 ounces of I and 80 ounces of II. Find the minimum-cost mixture.

3.19 REVIEW PROBLEMS (continued)

22. (See Problem 21.) Suppose the mixture must weigh not more than 40 pounds. What will be the minimum-cost mixture now?

23. (See Problem 21.) What will be the minimum-cost mixture if at least 80 percent of the mixture must be Food B?

24. To make 1 unit of Product A requires 3 minutes each in Departments I and II. One unit of Product B requires 2 minutes in I and 4 minutes in II. A unit of either product contributes $1 to profit. If Departments I and II have 900 and 1,200 minutes available, respectively, for making A and B, find the numbers of each that should be made to maximize profit, and find what the maximum profit is.

25. (See Problem 24.) Solve the problem if the number of units of A must be at least as great as the number of units of B.

Solve each of the following three-variable linear programming problems, assuming $x \geq 0$, $y \geq 0$, and $z \geq 0$:

26. $x + 3y + 4z \leq 30$
    $x + 4y + 2z \leq 40$
    Find θ_{max} if $\theta = x + 4y + 3z$.

27. $4x + 8y + z \leq 52$
    $8x + 28y + 3z \leq 168$
    Find θ_{max} if $\theta = 3x + 9y + z$.

28. $x + 3y + 3z \leq 50$
    $x + 4y + 2z \leq 60$
    $z \leq 10$
    Find θ_{max} if $\theta = x + 4y + 2z$.

29. $x + 2y + 7z \leq 21$
    $5x + 17y + 28z \leq 140$
    $x + 9y + 10z \leq 66$
    Find θ_{max} if $\theta = x + 3y + 7z$.

30. $x + 2y + z \leq 14$
    $0.5x + 2y + 0.5z \leq 10$
    $x + 5y + 4z \leq 26$
    Find θ_{max} if $\theta = x + 3y + 3z$.

31. $x + 2y + 3z \leq 25$
    $x + 3y + 2z \leq 30$
    Find θ_{max} if $\theta = x + 3y + 2z$.

32. A person sells and installs products A, B, and C. The table shows, for example, that it takes 3 hours to sell a unit of B, it takes 4 hours to install it, and net profit per unit is $40.

Product	Number of Units	Selling Hours per Unit	Installation Hours per Unit	Profit per Unit
A	x	1	1	$10
B	y	3	4	40
C	z	2	1	10

During a 38-hour week, the person allots no more than 18 hours to selling and no more than 20 hours to installation. Find the combination of numbers of units of A, B, and C that would yield maximum profit.

33. The table shows, for example, that 2 labor-hours are needed to sell a unit of B, 3 labor-hours to deliver it, and 3 labor-hours to install it. Profit per unit of B is $60.

Product	Number of Units	Selling Hours per Unit	Delivery Hours per Unit	Installation Hours per Unit	Profit per Unit
A	x	1	1	2	$20
B	y	2	3	3	60
C	z	3	2	5	40

If 220 labor-hours are available, of which not more than 50 are to be used for selling, not more than 60 for delivery, and not more than 110 for installation, find the combination of A, B, and C that yields maximum profit and state what this maximum is.

3.19 REVIEW PROBLEMS (continued)

In Problems 34 through 36, formulate the problem and then determine the number of corners in the feasible solution space.

34. Strong Steel Company operates three steel mills with different production capacities: Mill I can produce 4,000 tons per day of AAAA steel, 1,000 tons per day of AAA steel, 3,000 tons per day of AA steel, and 10,000 tons per day of A steel. Mill F can produce 3,000 tons per day of AAAA steel, 2,000 tons per day of AAA steel, 2,000 tons per day of AA steel, and 4,000 tons per day of A steel. Mill S can produce 2,000, 4,000, 1,000, and 3,000 tons per day, respectively. The company has made a contract with a construction firm to provide 35,000 tons of AAAA steel, 29,000 tons of AAA steel, 23,000 tons of AA steel, and 62,000 tons of A steel. If it costs $1,400 per day to run Mill I, $1,000 per day to run Mill F, and $1,200 per day to run Mill S, determine the number of days the company should operate each mill in order to meet the terms of the preceding contract most economically. What is this minimum cost?

35. Ace Rubber Company manufactures three types of tires: Model P (the premium), Model S (the second line), and Model E (the economy). Model P sells for $95 per tire and costs $60 per tire to make, whereas Model S sells for $75 per tire and costs $45 to make, while Model E sells for $55 per tire and costs $30 to make. To make one Model P tire, it requires 1 hour on Machine A, 1 hour on Machine B, 2 hours on Machine C, and 3 hours on Machine D. On the other hand, to make one Model S tire, it takes 1 hour on A, 2 hours on B, 1 hour on C, and 4 hours on D. Model E requires 4 hours on A, 3 hours on B, 2 hours on C, and 1 hour on D. Production scheduling indicates that during the coming week Machine A will be available for at most 42 hours, Machine B for at most 40 hours, Machine C for at most 30 hours, and Machine D for at most 44 hours. How many of each tire should the company make in the coming week in order to maximize its profit? What is this maximum profit?

36. The Hickory Desk Company, an office furniture manufacturer, produces two types of desks: executive desks and secretary/stenographer desks. The company has two plants at which desks are made. Plant 1, which is an older plant, operates on a double shift of 80 hours per week. Plant 2 is a newer plant and is not running at full capacity. However, since management plans to operate the second plant on a double-shift basis similar to Plant 1, operators have been employed to work two shifts. Currently each shift at Plant 2 works 25 hours per week. No premium is paid to second-shift workers. The following table shows production time (in hours/unit) and standard costs (in dollars/unit) at each plant.

Type of Desk	Production Time (hours/unit)		Standard Costs (dollars/unit)	
	Plant 1	Plant 2	Plant 1	Plant 2
Executive	7.0	6.0	250	260
Sec./steno.	4.0	5.0	200	180

The company has been competitive in the past by pricing the executive desks at $350. However, it appears the company will have to drop the price on the secretary/stenographer desks to $275 in order to be competitive. The company has been experiencing cost overruns in the past 8 to 10 weeks; therefore, the management has set a weekly budget restraint on production costs. The weekly budget for the total production of executive desks is $2,000, while the budget for the secretary/stenographer desks is $2,200. Management would like to determine the number of each type of desk that should be produced at each plant in order to maximize profit.

3.19 REVIEW PROBLEMS (continued)

Use a computer program such as LINDO to solve Problems 37 through 52, assuming all variables to be nonnegative.

37. Maximize
$$\theta = 2x_1 + x_2$$
subject to
$$x_1 + x_2 \leq 5$$
$$2x_1 + 3x_2 \leq 12.$$

38. Maximize
$$\theta = -3x_1 + 10x_2$$
subject to
$$3x_1 + 7x_2 \leq 42$$
$$x_1 + 5x_2 \leq 22.$$

39. Maximize
$$\theta = -2x_1 + 7x_2$$
subject to
$$x_1 + x_2 \leq 13$$
$$x_1 + 2x_2 \leq 22$$
$$2x_1 + x_2 \leq 20.$$

40. Repeat Problem 37 with the additional constraint that $x_1 \leq 4$.

41. Repeat Problem 38 with the additional constraint that $x_2 \leq 3$.

42. Repeat Problem 39 with the additional constraints that $x_1 \leq 8$ and $x_2 \leq 8$.

43. Maximize
$$\theta = 3x_1 + 5x_2 - 4x_3$$
subject to
$$x_1 + 2x_2 + 3x_3 \leq 24$$
$$2x_1 + 2x_2 + x_3 \leq 18.$$

44. Maximize
$$\theta = 4x_1 + 3x_2 + 7x_3$$
subject to
$$x_1 + x_2 + 4x_3 \leq 36$$
$$2x_1 + x_2 + 3x_3 \leq 42.$$

45. Maximize
$$\theta = 4x_1 + 3x_2 + 2x_3 - 10$$
subject to
$$x_1 + x_2 + 4x_3 \leq 36$$
$$x_1 + 2x_2 + 3x_3 \leq 42.$$

46. Maximize
$$\theta = 3x_1 + 5x_2 + 8x_3$$
subject to
$$x_1 + 2x_2 + 3x_3 \leq 36$$
$$x_1 + 3x_2 \leq 18.$$

47. Repeat Problem 43 with the additional constraint that $x_2 \leq 5$.

48. Repeat Problem 43 with the additional constraint that $x_3 \leq 3$.

49. Repeat Problem 44 with the additional constraint that $x_1 \leq 4$.

50. Southeast Tobacco Company makes three kinds of cigarettes: filter regulars, filter kings, and filter super kings. Management has to decide the optimal production mix of three blending processes for making each cigarette: Process X, Process Y, and Process Z. Each unit of Process X uses 4 pounds of tobacco, 1 ream of paper, and 3 ounces of charcoal to make 800 filter regulars, 700 filter kings, and 600 filter super kings. Each unit of Process Y uses 5 pounds of tobacco, 2 reams of paper, and 4 ounces of charcoal to make 1,000 filter regulars, 800 filter kings, and 600 filter super kings. Each unit of Process Z uses 3 pounds of tobacco, 1 ream of paper, and 3 ounces of charcoal to make 900 filter regulars, 400 filter kings, and 700 filter super kings. The company has only 425 pounds of tobacco, 140 reams of paper, and 350 ounces of charcoal on hand. Furthermore, the sales department has projected that they will need a minimum of 50,000 filter regulars, 40,000 filter kings, and 30,000 filter super kings. If the company makes a profit of $18 per unit of Process X, $23 per unit of Process Y, and $15 per unit of Process Z, find the production mix that maximizes the total profit. What is this maximum profit?

51. Growth Investment Company is planning a pension fund of $10 million for one of its valued clients. Federal and state regulations require that, for the

3.19 REVIEW PROBLEMS (concluded)

workers' protection, the fund must be made up of stocks, bonds, and a reserve in the form of bank notes or savings accounts. After much investigation, the company has decided upon the following combination: three stocks (S_1, S_2, and S_3), two bond issues (B_1 and B_2), and a particular bank note, N. Their study shows that the expected yield from S_1 will be 8 percent, S_2 will be 9 percent, S_3 will be 7 percent, B_1 will be 10 percent, B_2 will be 11 percent, and N will be 6 percent. There are, however, stringent limitations on the investment possibilities written in the regulations on pension funds. First, the amount invested in stocks must be no more than 40 percent of that invested in bonds. Second, a minimum of 25 percent of the total fund must be held in reserve. Third, no more than 35 percent of the total fund can be invested in stocks. Finally, no single investment other than a bank note or savings account can constitute more than 30 percent of the total fund. What portfolio will the company recommend for the pension fund and what will be its expected yield?

52. During the Gulf War crisis, the oil refinery companies were asked by the government to increase their production of jet fuel and tank fuel. Because of the unusual demands, the government subsidized the production of tank fuel at the rate of $2.90 above direct cost. In the production of each fuel, there is a by-product in the way of sludge which is strictly controlled by the government under the hazardous waste regulations enforced by the Environmental Protection Agency (EPA). All companies must adhere to the EPA regulations or risk a stiff fine as well as the closing of their refineries. Star Oil Company has determined that its setup cost to meet government demands in the next cycle will be $500,000. The company has determined that each gallon of jet fuel costs $2.00 and produces two pounds of sludge. On the other hand, each gallon of tank fuel produces four pounds of sludge. To properly process the sludge according to EPA regulations costs the company $0.25 per pound. Government demands for the next production cycle indicate that the company should produce no more than 100,000 gallons of jet fuel and no more than 80,000 gallons of tank fuel. In addition, the amount of tank fuel should not be more than four times the amount of jet fuel. Finally, the amount of jet fuel should not exceed the amount of tank fuel by more than 60,000 gallons. How many gallons of each type of fuel should the company produce in the next cycle to minimize its total cost? What is this cost?

3.20 EXTENDED REVIEW PROBLEMS

1. Craft Dairy Company wishes to make a new gourmet cheese from two of its current gourmet cheeses: Sharp and Extra Sharp. The mixture is to weigh exactly four pounds and should contain at least six ounces of the taste ingredient T. Each pound of Sharp Cheese costs $1.75 and contains three ounces of T, whereas each pound of Extra Sharp Cheese costs $1.95 and contains one ounce of T. In addition, the amount of Extra Sharp Cheese should not exceed the amount of Sharp Cheese. What mixture should the company use to make the new cheese at a minimum cost? What is this cost?

2. The Hickory Desk Company, an office furniture manufacturer, produces two types of desks: executive desks and secretary/stenographer desks. The company has two plants at which desks are made. Plant 1, an older plant, operates on a double shift of 80 hours per week. Plant 2, a newer plant is not running at full capacity. However, since management plans to operate the second plant on a double-shift basis similar to Plant 1, operators have been employed to work two shifts. Currently each shift at Plant 2 works 25 hours per week. No premium is paid to second-shift workers. The following table

3.20 EXTENDED REVIEW PROBLEMS (continued)

shows production time (in hours/unit) and standard costs (in dollars/unit) at each plant.

Type of Desk	Production Time (hours/unit)		Standard Costs (dollars/unit)	
	Plant 1	Plant 2	Plant 1	Plant 2
Executive	7.0	6.0	250	260
Sec./steno.	4.0	5.0	200	180

The company has been competitive in the past by pricing the executive desks at $350. However, it appears the company will have to drop the price on the secretary/stenographer desks to $275 in order to be competitive. The company has been experiencing cost overruns in the pat 8 to 10 weeks; therefore, the management has set a weekly budget restraint on production costs. The weekly budget for the total production of executive desks is $2,000, while the budget for the secretary/stenographer desks is $2,200. Management would like to determine the number of each type of desk that should be produced at each plant in order to maximize profit.

3. The accompanying table shows, for example, that in making a unit of B, 3 minutes are required for stamping, 13 minutes for forming, and 5 minutes for painting, and each unit of B contributes $4 to profit.

Product	Number of Units	Minutes per Unit for			Profit per Unit
		Stamping	Forming	Painting	
A	x	1	3	1	$1
B	y	3	13	5	4
C	z	2	2	5	2

Minutes available for stamping, forming, and painting are 40, 144, and 70, respectively. Find the combination of numbers of units of A, B, and C that leads to maximum profit. (Note: Assume that fractional units are permissible and that a fractional unit contributes its fraction to profit.)

4. Make a graph showing the solution space, assuming that the nonnegativity constraints prevail, and write the algebraic statement of the solution space:

$$x + y \geq 2$$
$$x - 2y \geq 0$$
$$x \leq 3$$
$$x + 2y \leq 4.$$

5. The accompanying table shows, for example, that it takes two hours in Department I, one hour in II, and one hour in III to make a premium tire. If hours available in I, II, and III are, respectively, 12, 7, and 15, write the solution showing the permissible combinations of the two products.

Department	Hours Required to Make One Tire	
	Premium	Regular
I	2	1
II	1	1
III	1	3

6. Assuming all the variables to be nonnegative, use a computer program such as LINDO to maximize and minimize

$$\theta = -3x_1 + 7x_2 + 10$$

subject to

$$x_1 + x_2 \leq 13$$
$$2x_1 - x_2 \leq 8$$
$$-2x_1 + 3x_2 \leq 12.$$

7. A custom molder has one injection molding machine and two different dies to fit the machine. Due to differences in number of cavities and cycle times, with the first die she can produce 100 cases of 6-ounce juice glasses in 6 hours, while with the second die she can produce 100 cases of 10-ounce fancy cocktail glasses in 5 hours. She prefers to operate on a schedule of no more than 60 hours of production per week. She stores the week's production in her own stockroom which has an effective capacity of 15,000 cubic feet. A case of 6-ounce juice glasses requires 10 cubic feet. A case of 10-ounce fancy cocktail glasses requires 20 cubic feet. The contribution of the 6-ounce juice glasses is $6.00 per case; however, the only customer available will not accept more than 800 cases per week. The contribution of the 10-ounce cocktail glasses is $4.50 per case, and there is no limit on the amount that can be sold. Find the number of cases of each type of glass the custom

3.20 EXTENDED REVIEW PROBLEMS (concluded)

molder should produce each week in order to maximize the total contribution.

8. Solve the Ganges–Brahmaputra River Basin problem of Section 3.11.

9. Kentucky Farms, Inc., raises cattle for producing milk and also for sale to slaughterhouses for meat for fast-food restaurants. In addition, the company breeds Arabian horses for thoroughbred racing. The government presently subsidizes cattle so that the company receives $500 per head above its cost each year. On the other hand, the company has determined that the annual cost for breeding Arabian horses is $1,500 each. Overhead cost for running the farm has been calculated at $750,000 per year. The company has 5,000 acres of grazing land to utilize but, because of the special nature of the horses, must keep them separated from the cattle. Past experience has shown that each head of cattle requires 5 acres for grazing, while each horse requires 10 acres for pasture and various training activities. To be entitled to government subsidies, the number of horses must be no more than 25 percent of the total number of animals. In addition, the company has decided for profit reasons that 5 times the number of cattle should not exceed 18 times the number of horses by more than 1,500. What mix of animals should the company choose this year to minimize its total cost? What is this cost?

10. Ace Rubber Company manufactures three types of tires: Model P (the premium), Model S (the second line), and Model E (the economy). Model P sells for $95 per tire and costs $85 per tire to make, whereas Model S sells for $78 per tire and costs $72 to make, while Model E sells for $75 per tire and costs $63 to make. To make one Model P tire requires 1 hour on Machine A, 1 hour on Machine B, 2 hours on Machine C, and 3 hours on Machine D. On the other hand, to make one Model S tire, it takes 1 hour on A, 2 hours on B, 1 hour on C, and 4 hours on D. Model E requires 4 hours on A, 3 hours on B, 2 hours on C, and 1 hour on D. Production scheduling indicates that during the coming week Machine A will be available for at most 42 hours, Machine B for at most 40 hours, Machine C for at most 30 hours, and Machine D for at most 44 hours. How many of each tire should the company make in the coming week in order to maximize its profit? What is this maximum profit?

ADDITIONAL TOPICS IN LINEAR PROGRAMMING

4.1 INTRODUCTION

The previous chapter introduced the topic of linear programming. There we learned the graphical procedure for solving problems that had two variables, and then developed the Simplex Method for solving problems with all $\leq$ constraints (other than nonnegativity) and any number of variables. We also showed how to use the computer package LINDO to solve such problems.

In this chapter, we discuss some additional aspects of linear programming. We first present four special cases and show how they are handled by the Simplex Method. Next we introduce **sensitivity analysis** for $\leq$ constraints, and begin the discussion of **shadow prices** and **right-hand-side ranges.** We then give an example of a **penalty/premium** problem where the slack variables have nonzero coefficients in the objective function. After this, we show how to change a minimization problem with $\geq$ constraints into a maximization problem with $\leq$ constraints and then apply the **Dual Theorem** to solve both problems simultaneously. After introducing the **Phase I–Phase II Method** for solving problems with $\geq$ and $=$ constraints, one last special case is discussed followed by a comprehensive summary of the Simplex Method. The last part of this chapter deals with sensitivity analysis of $\geq$ and $=$ constraints as well as sensitivity analysis on the objective function and **new product analysis**. Wherever applicable, we show how to use LINDO to handle each special situation.

FROM THEORY TO PRACTICE
Management Science in Practice

The topics in linear programming presented in this chapter and the previous chapter are all part of the subject area known as **management science.** The discussions could be extended to other topics such as **integer programming, goal programming, quadratic programming, dynamic programming, and assignment and transportation methods.** These are the subject matter of a course in management science or operations research.

The problems of Section 3.12 were intended to give some examples of how linear programming techniques are used in practice. The following "Municipal Bond Bidding Problem" from Schrage[1] illustrates how Wall Street uses the methods we have developed.

(continued)

Each year many millions of dollars worth of bonds are sold by U.S. municipalities. In many instances, the municipality sells its bonds through a competitive bidding process to intermediaries known as *underwriters*. The request for bids usually stipulates at least the following parameters:

- The amount of money to be raised by the sale (e.g., $50 million).
- The number of maturities in the sale (e.g., four).
- The maturity dates and the amount coming due on each maturity (e.g., $10 million coming due in 1995, $10 million in 2005, and $20 million in 2015).
- Restrictions on the interest rates or coupon amounts (e.g., the interest rates corresponding to the coupon payments must be in multiples of 1/8; there can be at most three different coupon rates).

This model was introduced by Weingarter and elaborated upon by Nauss and Keller.[2]

An underwriter bids by specifying the interest payments (coupon amounts). The lower the coupon amount, the more appealing the bid is to the municipality. A second option usually available for making a bid appealing is to offer a premium to the municipality or issuer in excess of the face value of the bonds. For example, the bonds may have a total face value of $50 million, but the underwriter may offer $50.5 million. Historically municipalities have used a **naive** method for determining the **lowest** bid, and therein lies the complexity that makes this an interesting integer programming problem. The municipality simply sums the coupon or interest payments over all years for all maturities, subtracts any premium offered, and then awards the sale to the bid minimizing this value. Thus the **time value of money** is disregarded. It is the total cost of all interest payments, regardless of timing, that the municipality considers in selecting the winning bid.

In selecting its bid or coupon amounts, the underwriter considers how it must sell bonds to the market. Once it has won the auction, the coupon amounts are fixed and other investors purchase the bonds from the underwriter by offering an initial payment for a bond that need not be the same as the face value of the bond. For each maturity the underwriter estimates what this lumpsum bid will be as a function of the coupon amount.

The underwriter has two conflicting objectives: it wants to make a low bid (in terms of interest cost) to increase its chances of winning but, on the other hand, the bid should be high enough so that if it wins, the underwriter still makes a reasonable profit. The approach usually taken by the underwriter is to incorporate its profit desires (e.g., $8 per $1,000 of bond face value) into the problem as a constraint and then minimize the net cost so as to maximize the bid's chances of winning.

Those interested in the solution of this problem are referred to Schrage (see footnote 1).

---

[1]Schrage, L., *Linear, Integer, and Quadratic Programming with LINDO* (Palo Alto, Calif.: Scientific Press, 1984), pp. 197–200.

[2]Weingarter, H. M., "Municipal Bond Coupon Schedules with Limitations on the Number of Coupons," *Management Science* 19, no. 4 (Dec. 1972), pp. 369–78; and Nauss, R. M., and B. R. Keller, "Minimizing Net Interest Cost in Municipal Bond Bidding," *Technical Report* (University of Missouri, St. Louis, 1978).

4.2 TIE FOR THE ENTERING OR LEAVING VARIABLE

In the summary of the Simplex Method in Section 3.13, we pointed out that it was possible to have a tie for the entering and/or leaving variable in one of the tableaus. The following example shows that when there is a tie for the entering variable, we can choose either one of the tied variables without affecting the optimal solution.

Example. Let us return to the Ace Rubber Company example of Sections 3.5 and 3.13, but change the objective function to

$$\theta = 10x_1 + 10x_2,$$

so that we are to maximize this objective function subject to

$$2x_1 + 9x_2 \leq 36$$
$$4x_1 + 3x_2 \leq 42$$
$$x_1, x_2 \geq 0.$$

The Preliminary Tableau, then, is as shown in Table 4–1A. In this table, the entry in the θ-row for both x_1 and x_2 is -10, so that we have a **tie for the entering variable;** that is, the **unit gain** in introducing either x_1 or x_2 is the same, so we can choose either one. The resultant tableaus for entering x_1 are shown in Table 4–1B, on page 240, whereas those for entering x_2 are shown in Table 4–1C, on page 241. Note that, although the Second Tableaus are different, the Third Tableaus are identical, with the maximum value of $\theta = 110$ occurring at

$$x_1 = 9, \quad x_2 = 2, \quad \text{and} \quad s_1 = s_2 = 0.$$

Thus the maximum profit is $110 when nine Model P tires and two Model R tires are made. At this optimal solution, both machines are fully utilized ($s_1 = s_2 = 0$).

It is interesting to note in the preceding example that, although the **unit gains** in moving from the origin along the x_1-axis and the x_2-axis are the same, the **total gains** are different. The total gain, of course, is the **unit gain times the maximum**

> A tie for the entering variable indicates unit gains are the same, so we can choose either one.

> Although the unit gains may be the same, the total gains may be different.

TABLE 4–1A
Preliminary Tableau

Basic Variables	Coefficient of				Current Values
	x_1	x_2	s_1	s_2	
s_1	2	9	1	0	36
s_2	4	3	0	1	42
(max) θ	-10	-10	0	0	0

TABLE 4–1B

Initial Tableau

Basic Variables	Coefficient of				Current Values	
	x_1	x_2	s_1	s_2		
s_1	[2]	9	1	0	36	18
s_2	[4]	3	0	1	42	21/2 →
(max) θ	−10	−10	0	0	0	

↑

Second Tableau

Basic Variables	Coefficient of				Current Values	
	x_1	x_2	s_1	s_2		
s_1	0	[15/2]	1	−1/2	15	2 →
x_1	1	[3/4]	0	1/4	21/2	14
(max) θ	0	−5/2	0	5/2	105	

↑

Third Tableau

Basic Variables	Coefficient of				Current Values
	x_1	x_2	s_1	s_2	
x_2	0	1	2/15	−1/15	2
x_1	1	0	−1/10	3/10	9
(max) θ	0	0	1/3	7/3	110

number of units that can be introduced. Thus, as can be seen from the Initial Tableau of Table 4–1B, the total gain in moving along the x_1-axis is

($10/unit of x_1)(21/2 units of x_1) = $105;

whereas, as can be seen from the Initial Tableau of Table 4–1C, the total gain in moving along the x_2-axis is

($10/unit of x_2)(4 units of x_2) = $40.

Exercise. Compare the unit and total gains for the Second Tableaus.

Answer: In Table 4–1B, the unit gain for x_2 is $2.50 and the total gain is $5. In Table 4–1C, the unit gain for x_1 is $7.78 and the total gain is $70.

TABLE 4-1C

Initial Tableau

Basic Variables	Coefficient of				Current Values	
	x_1	x_2	s_1	s_2		
s_1	2	[9]	1	0	[36]	4 →
s_2	4	[3]	0	1	[42]	14
(max) θ	-10	-10	0	0	0	
		↑				

Second Tableau

Basic Variables	Coefficient of				Current Values	
	x_1	x_2	s_1	s_2		
x_2	[2/9]	1	1/9	0	[4]	18
s_2	[10/3]	0	$-1/3$	1	[30]	9 →
(max) θ	$-70/9$	0	10/9	0	40	
	↑					

Third Tableau

Basic Variables	Coefficient of				Current Values
	x_1	x_2	s_1	s_2	
x_2	0	1	2/15	$-1/15$	2
x_1	1	0	$-1/10$	3/10	9
(max) θ	0	0	1/3	7/3	110

Since, as we saw above, any tied variable may be selected without affecting the final solution, we henceforth adopt the **convention of choosing the left-most entering variable.**

The LINDO printout for this example is shown in Table 4–2. Note that the objective function and the constraints are entered in the usual manner. Note also the optimal solution

$$\theta = 110, \quad x_1 = 9, \quad x_2 = 2, \quad \text{and} \quad s_1 = s_2 = 0;$$

namely, a maximum profit of $110 when nine Model P tires and two Model R tires are made. Of course, Machines A and B are fully utilized ($s_1 = s_2 = 0$).

Now suppose that there is a tie for the leaving variable in one of the tableaus. This tie indicates that the associated basic variables are **decreasing to zero simultaneously.** Thus, after one of these basic variables is chosen to leave the basis to become zero as a nonbasic variable, the other(s) will remain basic but, nevertheless, have its (their) current value(s) decreased to zero. Moreover, such an occurrence of a basic variable with a current value of zero in a tableau is called

> Convention: When there is a tie for the entering variable, simply choose the left-most one.

> A tie for the leaving variable indicates variables are decreasing to zero simultaneously. One will become nonbasic (zero); the other will have a current value of zero. This case is called **degeneracy**.

TABLE 4-2

```
$ lindo
LINDO (7 OCTOBER 88 CHICAGO)
: max 10x1 + 10x2
?st
?2x1 + 9x2 < =36
?4x1 + 3x2 < =42
?end

: go
LP OPTIMUM FOUND AT STEP        2

        OBJECTIVE FUNCTION VALUE
     1)      110.000000

    VARIABLE        VALUE         REDUCED COST
       X1         9.000000          0.000000
       X2         2.000000          0.000000

       ROW    SLACK OR SURPLUS     DUAL PRICES
        2)        0.000000          0.333333
        3)        0.000000          2.333333

NO. ITERATIONS=        2

DO RANGE(SENSITIVITY) ANALYSIS?
?no
: quit
FORTRAN STOP
$ lo
```

degeneracy and arises, as we will see, in two dimensions when three or more constraints intersect in a single point, in three dimensions when four or more constraints intersect in a single point, and so on.

When a tie for the leaving variable does occur in a tableau, one way to handle the tie is simply to choose any one of the tied basic variables. However, as will be seen in the problems, in so doing, there is a slight chance that the Simplex Method may not converge or lead to an answer (i.e., the solution of the problem may begin to cycle by returning to a previously generated tableau). One **sure** way to avoid cycling is by applying the following simple rule (developed by Charnes, Cooper, and Henderson[3]):

> Divide each coefficient in the tied rows by the respective coefficient of the entering variable. Compare the resultant ratios from left to right, ignoring negative ratios, until they are not equal. At that point, select the variable corresponding to the smallest nonnegative ratio as the leaving variable.

Convention: When there is a tie for the leaving variable, simply choose either one.

[3] A. Charnes, W. W. Cooper, and A. Henderson, *An Introduction to Linear Programming* (New York: John Wiley & Sons, 1953).

The following example illustrates this rule.

Example. Resolve the Ace Rubber Company example, but with the additional constraint that

$$2x_1 + x_2 \leq 21$$

(arising, for example, if each tire had to be processed on a third machine), so that we are to maximize the objective function

$$\theta = 10x_1 + 8x_2$$

subject to

$$2x_1 + 9x_2 \leq 36 \tag{1}$$
$$4x_1 + 3x_2 \leq 42 \tag{2}$$
$$2x_1 + x_2 \leq 21 \tag{3}$$
$$x_1, x_2 \geq 0. \tag{4},(5)$$

The feasible solution set for this set of constraints is shown in Figure 4–1. Note that constraints (2), (3), and (5) all intersect in the single point (21/2, 0), so that, as stated before, we have a case of degeneracy. Note also that the third constraint (3) that we added is, in fact, redundant since it does not affect the feasible solution

---

Degeneracy in two variables indicates that more than two constraint lines intersect in the same point.

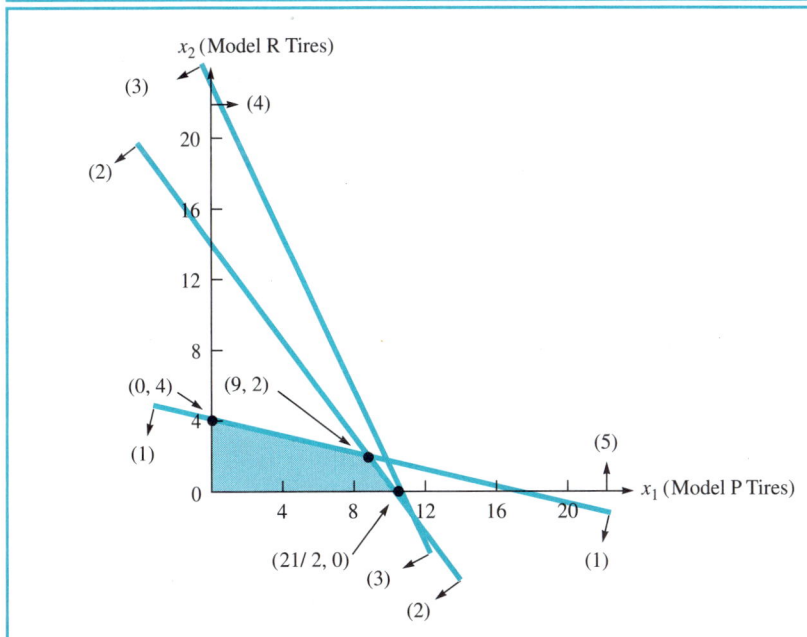

FIGURE 4–1

set resulting from the other constraints. Thus the solution of this problem will be the same as before except, of course, that here we will have another row and column in each of the tableaus to reflect the additional constraint (3).

Specifically, the Preliminary Tableau is as shown in Table 4–3A, where we have introduced the slack variable s_3 to handle the additional third constraint (3). Note in this tableau that x_1 is the entering variable and that there is a tie between s_2 and s_3 for the leaving variable. Using the preceding rule, then, we now divide each coefficient in the s_2-row by 4 and each coefficient in the s_3-row by 2 to get

s_2-row ÷ 4: | 1 | 3/4 | 0 | 1/4 | 0 | 21/2 |

and

s_3-row ÷ 2: | 1 | 1/2 | 0 | 0 | 1/2 | 21/2 |.

Next, comparing the corresponding entries from left to right, we see that the tie is broken in the second column, where the entry 1/2 for s_3 is smaller than the entry 3/4 for s_2. Thus, as shown in the Initial Tableau of Table 4–3B, we now select s_3 as the leaving variable.

In the usual manner, then, we get the remaining three tableaus in Table 4–3B. Note in the Second Tableau that, consistent with our earlier discussion, the current value of the basic variable s_2 (which was tied with the leaving variable s_3 in the Initial Tableau) now equals zero; of course, the nonbasic variables x_2 and s_3 also equal zero.

Next in the Third Tableau, we see that the same three variables s_2, x_2, and s_3 are still zero, but s_2 is now nonbasic whereas x_2 is now basic. Furthermore, the values of s_1, x_1, and θ are the same as those in the Second Tableau, since we are still at the **same point of intersection** of Figure 4–1; namely, the point (21/2, 0). Lastly, note in the Third Tableau that we have asterisked the ratio $0/(-2) = -0$

Degeneracy results in a current value of zero for a basic variable.

Degeneracy can result in two successive tableaus representing the same point with, of course, different variables being basic.

TABLE 4–3A
Preliminary Tableau

Basic Variables	Coefficient of					Current Values	
	x_1	x_2	s_1	s_2	s_3		
s_1	2	9	1	0	0	36	18
s_2	4	3	0	1	0	42	21/2
s_3	2	1	0	0	1	21	21/2
(max) θ	−10	−8	0	0	0	0	

↑

TABLE 4-3B

Initial Tableau

Basic Variables	Coefficient of					Current Values	
	x_1	x_2	s_1	s_2	s_3		
s_1	[2]	9	1	0	0	[36]	18
s_2	[4]	3	0	1	0	[42]	21/2
s_3	[2]	1	0	0	1	[21]	21/2 →
(max) θ	−10	−8	0	0	0	0	

↑

Second Tableau

Basic Variables	Coefficient of					Current Values	
	x_1	x_2	s_1	s_2	s_3		
s_1	0	[8]	1	0	−1	[15]	15/8
s_1	0	[1]	0	1	−2	[0]	0 →
x_1	1	[1/2]	0	0	1/2	[21/2]	21
(max) θ	0	−3	0	0	5	105	

↑

Third Tableau

Basic Variables	Coefficient of					Current Values	
	x_1	x_2	s_1	s_2	s_3		
s_1	0	0	1	−8	[15]	[15]	1 →
x_2	0	1	0	1	[−2]	[0]	−0*
x_1	1	0	0	−1/2	[3/2]	[21/2]	7
(max) θ	0	0	0	3	−1	105	

↑

Fourth Tableau

Basic Variables	Coefficient of					Current Values
	x_1	x_2	s_1	s_2	s_3	
s_3	0	0	1/15	−8/15	1	1
x_2	0	1	2/15	−1/15	0	2
x_1	1	0	−1/10	3/10	0	9
(max) θ	0	0	1/15	37/15	0	106

to indicate that, although it is 0, it should be interpreted as negative (since the exchange rate, -2, is negative) and hence it is to be ignored.

Finally, we see that the Fourth Tableau of Table 4–3B corresponds to the solution

$$x_1 = 9, \; x_2 = 2, \; s_1 = s_2 = 0, \; s_3 = 1, \;\; \text{and} \;\; \theta = 106.$$

This solution is exactly the same as that obtained earlier, except, of course, that we now have the additional result that $s_3 = 1$, reflecting that the third machine has one hour of slack time.

At this point, we wish to emphasize that although in the preceding example we had both a degeneracy and a redundancy, these two concepts are independent of one another.

Degeneracy is different from redundancy, and the two concepts are independent.

Exercise. Graph each of the following sets of constraints and determine whether there is a degeneracy or a redundancy.

a) $x_1 + x_2 \leq 3$
   $x_2 \leq 4$
   $x_1, x_2 \geq 0.$

b) $x_1 + x_2 \leq 3$
   $x_1 + x_2 \geq 3$
   $x_1, x_2 \geq 0.$

c) $x_1 + x_2 = 3$
   $x_1, x_2 \geq 0.$

d) What is the relationship between the constraint sets in (b) and (c)?

Answer: a) Redundancy, but no degeneracy. b) Degeneracy, but no redundancy. c) No degeneracy and no redundancy. d) They are equivalent.

The LINDO printout for this example is shown in Table 4–4. Once again, the objective function and the constraints are entered in the usual manner. Note the optimal solution

$$\theta = 106, \; x_1 = 9, \; x_2 = 2, \; s_1 = s_2 = 0, \;\; \text{and} \;\; s_3 = 1,$$

indicating a maximum profit of \$106 when nine Model P tires and two Model R tires are made. In addition, there is a slack of one hour on the third machine ($s_3 = 1$).

4.3 ALTERNATIVE OPTIMAL SOLUTIONS

The existence of an alternative optimal solution is indicated by a zero in the θ-row for a nonbasic variable.

We saw in Section 3.5 that alternative optimal solutions can result when the objective function is parallel to one of the constraints. In such a case, there will be a **zero in the θ-row for one or more of the nonbasic variables in the last simplex tableau.** (Recall from Section 3.13 that the **coefficients of the basic variables in the θ-row are always zero.**) The next example shows that the way to find an alternative optimum (maximum or minimum) is simply to introduce into the solution the nonbasic variable that has the zero coefficient in the θ-row.

TABLE 4-4

```
$ lindo
LINDO (7 OCTOBER 88 CHICAGO)
: max 10x1 + 8x2
?st
?2x1 + 9x2 < =   36
?4x1 + 3x2 < =   42
?2x1 +  x2 < =   21
?end

: go
LP OPTIMUM FOUND AT STEP       2

        OBJECTIVE FUNCTION VALUE
     1)    106.000000
   VARIABLE        VALUE         REDUCED COST
       X1         9.000000          0.000000
       X2         2.000000          0.000000

        ROW    SLACK OR SURPLUS    DUAL PRICES
         2)        0.000000         0.066667
         3)        0.000000         2.466667
         4)        1.000000         0.000000

 NO. ITERATIONS=      2

DO RANGE (SENSITIVITY) ANALYSIS?
?no
: quit
FORTRAN STOP
$ lo
```

Example. Resolve the Ace Rubber Company example, but change the objective function to

$$\theta = 4x_1 + 18x_2,$$

so that we are to maximize this objective function subject to

$$2x_1 + 9x_2 \leq 36$$
$$4x_1 + 3x_2 \leq 42$$
$$x_1, x_2 \geq 0.$$

This time, the simplex tableaus are as shown in Table 4–5A. Note that the Second Tableau corresponds to the solution

$$x_1 = 0, \ x_2 = 4, \ s_1 = 0, \ s_2 = 30, \ \text{and} \ \theta = 72,$$

TABLE 4–5A
Initial Tableau

Basic Variables	Coefficient of				Current Values	
	x_1	x_2	s_1	s_2		
s_1	2	[9]	1	0	[36]	4 →
s_2	4	[3]	0	1	[42]	14
(max) θ	−4	−18	0	0	0	

↑

Second Tableau

Basic Variables	Coefficient of				Current Values
	x_1	x_2	s_1	s_2	
x_2	2/9	1	1/9	0	4
s_2	10/3	0	−1/3	1	30
(max) θ	0	0	2	0	72

A zero in the θ-row for a nonbasic variable means introducing that variable has no effect on the objective function value.

which is optimal since there are no negative entries in the θ-row. Thus an optimal solution occurs at a maximum profit of $72 when no Model P tires and four Model R tires are made. In this case, there are 30 hours of slack time on Machine B ($s_2 = 30$).

At this point, we can see from the Second Tableau of Table 4–5A that the θ-entry for the nonbasic variable x_1 is 0. The zero value here means that we can bring x_1 into the solution without any gain or loss (i.e., without changing the value of $\theta = 72$). Doing this in the usual manner, we get the Third Tableau shown in Table 4–5B. Note that, as expected, the θ-row of this tableau is precisely the same as that of the Second Tableau. Note also that this tableau corresponds to the solution

$$x_1 = 9, \ x_2 = 2, \ s_1 = s_2 = 0, \quad \text{and} \quad \theta = 72,$$

or a maximum of $72 when nine Model P tires and two Model R tires are made. In this case, both machines are fully utilized. Combining this with our previous solution, we see that the maximum profit of $72 can be obtained at any point on the line segment between (0, 4) and (9, 2).

It is important to realize in the preceding example that the Simplex Method only determined the **two alternative optimal solution points** (0, 4) and (9, 2). The reason that we were able to state that the maximum occurred at every point on the line segment between these two points was that we had previously seen in Section 3.5 that whenever there are alternative optimal solutions in two dimensions, they must occur on a line segment. Hence we can always use the Simplex Method as we did in the preceding example to determine the two endpoints. In more than two dimensions, however, alternative optimal solutions do not necessarily occur only

TABLE 4-5B
Second Tableau

Basic Variables	Coefficient of				Current Values	
	x_1	x_2	s_1	s_2		
x_2	2/9	1	1/9	0	4	18
s_2	10/3	0	−1/3	1	30	9 →
(max) θ	0	0	2	0	72	

↑

Third Tableau

Basic Variables	Coefficient of				Current Values
	x_1	x_2	s_1	s_2	
x_2	0	1	2/15	−1/15	2
x_1	1	0	−1/10	3/10	9
(max) θ	0	0	2	0	72

on a line segment. There are techniques for determining the set of all possible alternative solutions in these cases, but they are rather complicated and so are omitted. In any case, though, **we can always determine the alternative optimal solution points by bringing into the solution any nonbasic variables that have a coefficient of zero in the θ-row.**

To determine an alternative optimal solution, simply bring in any variable with a value of zero in the θ-row.

Exercise. Resolve the preceding example if the objective function is changed to $\theta = 8x_1 + 6x_2$.

Answer: 84 at any point on the line segment between (21/2, 0) and (9, 2).

The LINDO printout for this example is shown in Table 4–6. The optimal solution is

$$\theta = 72, \quad x_1 = 0, \quad x_2 = 4, \quad s_1 = 0, \quad \text{and} \quad s_2 = 30,$$

indicating a maximum profit of $72 when no Model P tires and four Model R tires are made. Of course, in this case there is a slack of 30 hours on Machine B ($s_2 = 30$). The fact that the variable x_1 has both a VALUE of zero and a REDUCED COST of zero (the shaded row of Table 4–6) indicates that there are alternative optimal solution points. An alternate optimum point can be generated in LINDO using the TABLE and PIVOT commands, or using **sensitivity analysis**, which is discussed later in this chapter. Those interested in a more detailed discussion are referred to Schrage (see footnote 1).

Computer packages find only a single solution point. Alternative optimal solutions require sensitivity analysis.

TABLE 4-6

```
$ lindo
LINDO (7 OCTOBER 88 CHICAGO)
: max 4x1 + 18x2
? st
? 2x1 + 9x2 <= 36
? 4x1 + 3x2 <= 42
? end

: go
LP OPTIMUM FOUND AT STEP        1

        OBJECTIVE FUNCTION VALUE
    1)      72.0000000

    VARIABLE        VALUE           REDUCED COST

        X1          0.000000        0.000000

        X2          4.000000        0.000000

        ROW     SLACK OR SURPLUS    DUAL PRICES
        2)          0.000000        2.000000
        3)         30.000000        0.000000

NO. ITERATIONS=     1

DO RANGE(SENSITIVITY) ANALYSIS?
? no
: quit
FORTRAN STOP
$ lo
```

4.4 UNBOUNDED SOLUTIONS

Another special case that can occur with linear programming problems is to have **an unbounded feasible solution set in the "optimizing direction."** This case gives rise to a tableau in which the ratios of the current values of the basic variables to the respective coefficients of the entering variable will all be either negative or undefined, so that no leaving variable can be selected. Recall from Section 3.17 that a negative ratio corresponds to increasing the associated current basic variable away from zero rather than decreasing it toward zero. Thus if all the ratios are negative or undefined, then we can bring in an unlimited amount of the proposed entering variable without any of the current basic variables ever decreasing to zero, indicating, therefore, that the solution set is unbounded in the direction of that proposed entering variable.

The following example illustrates an unbounded solution set.

When all the ratios for possible leaving variables are negative or undefined, there is an unbounded solution set.

Example. Maximize the objective function

$$\theta = x_1 + x_2$$

subject to

$$-x_1 + x_2 \leq 1 \quad (1)$$

$$x_2 \leq 3 \quad (2)$$

$$x_1, x_2 \geq 0. \quad (3),(4)$$

The feasible solution set for this set of constraints is shown in Figure 4–2. Note that this feasible solution set is unbounded in the x_1-direction.

The Initial Tableau is as shown in Table 4–7. Note in this tableau that we have a tie for the entering variable between x_1 and x_2; as is our convention, stated in Section 4.2, we have chosen x_1 (the left-most variable). At this point, then, no leaving variable can be chosen since the ratio for s_1 is negative (i.e., -1) while that for s_2 is undefined (i.e., ∞). Thus the solution is unbounded in the x_1-direction; that is, as we saw in Figure 4–2, if we proceed out from the origin (0, 0) along the x_1-axis, then the feasible solution set is unbounded in this direction.

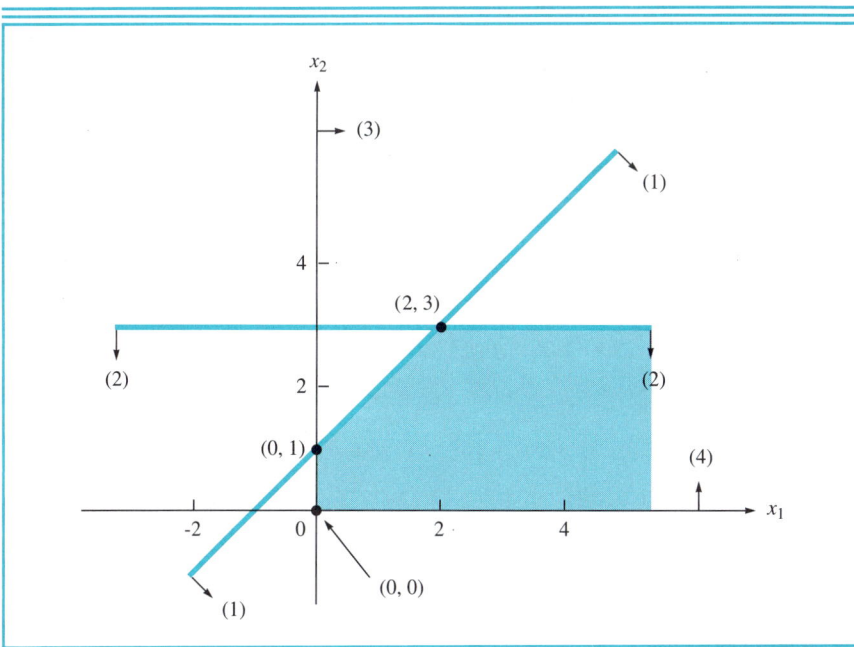

FIGURE 4–2

TABLE 4-7
Initial Tableau

Basic Variables	Coefficient of				Current Values	
	x_1	x_2	s_1	s_2		
s_1	$\boxed{-1}$	1	1	0	$\boxed{1}$	-1
s_2	$\boxed{0}$	1	0	1	$\boxed{3}$	∞
(max) θ	-1	-1	0	0	0	

↑

Exercise. Choose x_2 as the entering variable in Table 4–7. In which tableau is it impossible to find a leaving variable? What is the entering variable?

Answer: Third. s_1

We need not compute ratios associated with coefficients that are negative or zero.

Now it is interesting to note in the Initial Tableau of Table 4–7 that we need not have computed the actual ratios, since all the coefficients of the entering variable were negative or zero. Thus the ratios themselves would have to be negative or undefined, since the current values of the basic variables are always nonnegative. This fact will hold in general; that is, the only way for all the ratios to be negative or undefined, so that there is an unbounded solution, is for **all the coefficients of the entering variable to be nonpositive.**

Finally, we wish to emphasize that if we were to encounter an unbounded solution in a real-world problem, then we should carefully reexamine the formulation of the problem to determine whether or not it is an accurate model.

The LINDO printout for this example is shown in Table 4–8. Note here that there is no optimal solution, but an

UNBOUNDED SOLUTION AT STEP 2.

Note also the message

UNBOUNDED VARIABLES ARE:
SLK   2
X1,

indicating that the solution is unbounded in the x_1-direction and also that the slack variable s_2 is unbounded. Both of these results are consistent with the ratio analysis of Table 4–7.

TABLE 4-8

```
$ lindo
LINDO (7 OCTOBER 88 CHICAGO)
: max x1 + x2
?st
?-x1 + x2 <= 1
?x2 <= 3
?end

: go
UNBOUNDED SOLUTION AT STEP     2
 UNBOUNDED VARIABLES ARE:
 SLK    2
        X1

       OBJECTIVE FUNCTION VALUE
    1)       99999904

  VARIABLE        VALUE          REDUCED COST
       X1      99999904.000000       0.000000
       X2             3.000000       0.000000

       ROW     SLACK OR SURPLUS    DUAL PRICES
        2)          0.000000       -1.000000
        3)          0.000000        2.000000
NO. ITERATIONS=      2
: quit
FORTRAN STOP
$ lo
```

4.5 NEGATIVE DECISION VARIABLES

It is possible to have a linear programming problem where one or more of the decision variables may be **negative**. Such negativity can arise, for example, when one of the variables represents an inventory level; of course, negative inventory indicates a **shortage**. Although it is possible to have negative decision variables in the formulation of a linear programming problem, we saw in Section 3.13 that the Simplex Method requires that all variables be nonnegative. One way to handle problems with variables that may be negative is to **replace each such variable by the difference of two variables both of which are nonnegative.**

The following example illustrates how to handle negative decision variables.

Negative decision variables are replaced by the difference of two nonnegative variables.

Example. Maximize the objective function

$$\theta = 8x_1 + 10x_2$$

subject to

$$-x_1 + x_2 \leq 4 \quad (1)$$
$$x_1 + x_2 \leq 6 \quad (2)$$
$$x_1 \geq 0 \quad (3)$$

x_2 unrestricted in sign. (4)

First, we note that constraint (4) is really a **pseudoconstraint** that allows x_2 to be nonnegative or negative. As already stated, negative variables are not permissible in the Simplex Method but are acceptable as constraints of a linear programming problem.

The graph of the feasible solution set for the preceding set of constraints is as shown in Figure 4-3. Note that this graph is unbounded in the negative x_2-direction and, as a consequence, there are only two extreme points: (0, 4) and (1, 5).

At this point, we must overcome the difficulty of the possible negativity of the

FIGURE 4-3

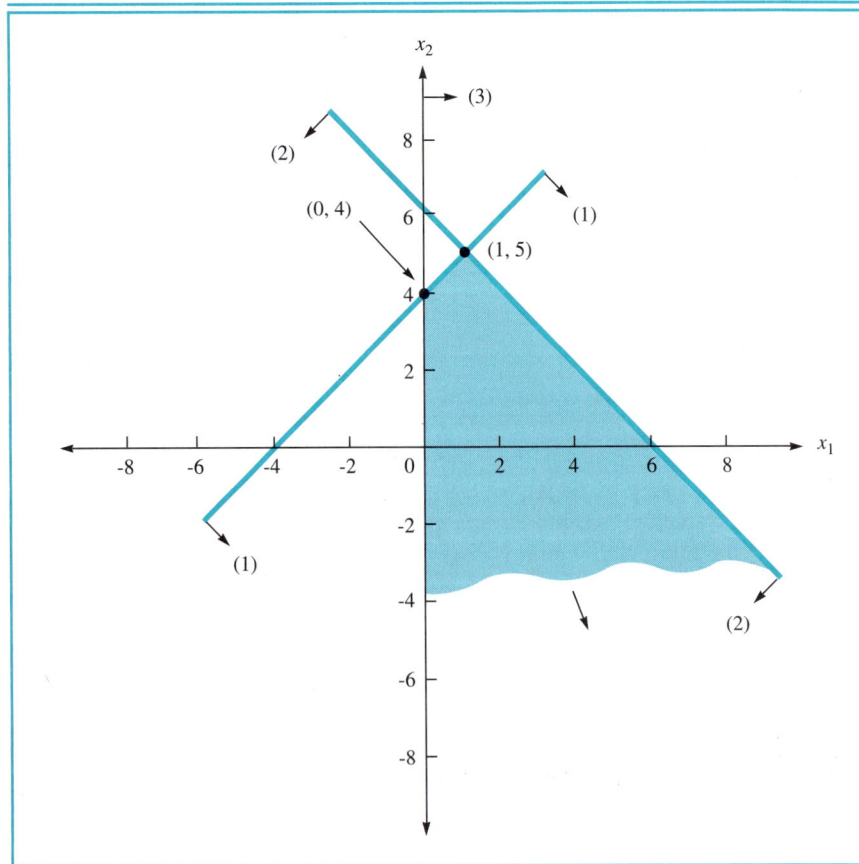

x_2-variable insofar as the Simplex Method is concerned. We do this simply by making the substitution

$$x_2 = x_{2p} - x_{2n}$$

in the objective function and in all the constraints where, now, x_{2p} and x_{2n} are both nonnegative variables; that is

$$x_{2p}, x_{2n} \geq 0.$$

The purpose of the preceding substitution is to break the value of x_2 up into **its positive portion, represented by x_{2p}, and its negative portion, represented by x_{2n}**; for example, if $x_2 = 4$, then $x_{2p} = 4$ and $x_{2n} = 0$, whereas if $x_2 = -4$, then $x_{2p} = 0$ and $x_{2n} = 4$. In general, as will be seen shortly, one of the two variables x_{2p} and x_{2n} will be zero and the other will be nonnegative.[4]

> Negative decisions variables are separated into their positive and negative components.

Making the preceding substitution, then, our modified problem is to maximize

$$\theta = 8x_1 + 10x_{2p} - 10x_{2n}$$

subject to

$$-x_1 + x_{2p} - x_{2n} \leq 4$$
$$x_1 + x_{2p} - x_{2n} \leq 6$$
$$x_1, x_{2p}, x_{2n} \geq 0.$$

The simplex tableaus for this modified problem are as shown in Table 4–9 on page 256. From the last tableau, we see that the maximum is 58, which occurs when

$$x_{2n} = s_1 = s_2 = 0,$$

(nonbasic variables) while

$$x_1 = 1 \quad \text{and} \quad x_{2p} = 5$$

(basic variables). Now since

$$x_2 = x_{2p} - x_{2n},$$

we have

$$x_2 = 5 - 0 = 5,$$

so that, in terms of our original variables, the optimal solution is

$$x_1 = 1, x_2 = 5, s_1 = s_2 = 0, \quad \text{and} \quad \theta = 58.$$

It is interesting to see how the Simplex Method forced one of the two variables x_{2p} and x_{2n} to equal zero. First, we note that, by reason of the substitution $x_2 = x_{2p} - x_{2n}$, the x_{2p}- and x_{2n}-columns start off in the Initial Tableau of Table 4–9 as negatives of each other. Then, by reason of the diagonalization process, these

> The Simplex Method forces one of the pseudovariables to zero.

---

[4]Note that $x_{2p} = \max\{0, x_2\}$ and $x_{2n} = -\min\{0, x_2\}$ so that $x_2 = x_{2p} - x_{2n}$ and $|x_2| = x_{2p} + x_{2n}$.

TABLE 4-9

Initial Tableau

Basic Variables	Coefficient of					Current Values	
	x_1	x_{2p}	x_{2n}	s_1	s_2		
s_1	−1	[1]	−1	1	0	[4]	4 →
s_2	1	[1]	−1	0	1	[6]	6
(max) θ	−8	−10	10	0	0	0	

↑

Second Tableau

Basic Variables	Coefficient of					Current Values	
	x_1	x_{2p}	x_{2n}	s_1	s_2		
x_{2p}	[−1]	1	−1	1	0	[4]	−4
s_2	[2]	0	0	−1	1	[2]	1 →
(max) θ	−18	0	0	10	0	40	

↑

Third Tableau

Basic Variables	Coefficient of					Current Values
	x_1	x_{2p}	x_{2n}	s_1	s_2	
x_{2p}	0	1	−1	1/2	1/2	5
x_1	1	0	0	−1/2	1/2	1
(max) θ	0	0	0	1	9	58

two columns remain negatives of each other in the subsequent tableaus of Table 4–9. Thus when both are nonbasic, as in the Initial Tableau, both are equal to zero. When one becomes basic, however, as does x_{2p} in the Second Tableau, the other (nonbasic) variable x_{2n} will always have a single −1 and then zeros in its column. This, in turn, prevents the variable from subsequently entering the basis as long as the former variable is in the basis since, in computing the appropriate ratios, the exchange rates of −1 and zero will always result in negative and undefined ratios. Therefore, the two variables cannot be basic at the same time; hence, at least one must be nonbasic; that is, at least one must be equal to zero.

As a consequence of the preceding analysis, when either variable has a θ-coefficient of zero, then they both must. This can be seen in the Second and also the Third Tableaus of Table 4–9. However, if in either of these two tableaus we tried to introduce the nonbasic variable x_{2n} (e.g., for an alternative optimal solution in the Third Tableau), then, as stated before, we would find only negative or undefined ratios. This means, as we saw in the previous section, that the feasible solution set is unbounded in the x_{2n}-direction. This latter fact is consistent, of course, with the fact that the original variable x_2 was unrestricted in sign and that

TABLE 4-10

```
$ lindo
LINDO (7 OCTOBER 88 CHICAGO)
: max 8x1 + 10x2p - 10x2n
 ?st
 ?-x1 + x2p - x2n <=  4
 ?x1 + x2p -x2n <=  6
 ?end

: go
LP OPTIMUM FOUND AT STEP        2

        OBJECTIVE FUNCTION VALUE
     1)     58.0000000

  VARIABLE         VALUE         REDUCED COST
       X1          1.000000          0.000000
      X2P          5.000000          0.000000
      X2N          0.000000          0.000000

      ROW    SLACK OR SURPLUS     DUAL PRICES
       2)          0.000000          1.000000
       3)          0.000000          9.000000

NO. ITERATIONS=        2

DO RANGE(SENSITIVITY) ANALYSIS?
 ?no
: quit
FORTRAN STOP
$ lo
```

x_{2n} represented the **negative portion** of x_2; this was previously noted in Figure 4–3, where we saw that the feasible solution set was **unbounded in the negative x_2 direction.**

Exercise. Reformulate the preceding example if x_1 were unrestricted in sign and $x_2 \geq 0$.

Answer: Maximize
$$\theta = 8x_{1p} - 8x_{1n} + 10x_2$$
subject to
$$-x_{1p} + x_{1n} + x_2 \leq 4$$
$$x_{1p} - x_{1n} + x_2 \leq 6$$
$$x_{1p}, x_{1n}, x_2 \geq 0.$$

The LINDO printout for this example is shown in Table 4–10, indicating the optimal solution of

$$\theta = 58, x_1 = 1, x_{2p} = 5, x_{2n} = 0, s_1 = s_2 = 0.$$

4.6 PROBLEM SET 4–1

In each of the following, assume that all variables must be nonnegative unless otherwise indicated.

1. Maximize
$$\theta = 2x_1 + 2x_2$$
subject to
$$3x_1 + 7x_2 \leq 42$$
$$x_1 + 5x_2 \leq 22.$$

2. Minimize
$$\theta = -3x_1 - 3x_2 + 45$$
subject to
$$x_1 + x_2 \leq 13$$
$$x_1 + 2x_2 \leq 22$$
$$2x_1 + x_2 \leq 20.$$

3. Maximize
$$\theta = 6x_1 + 6x_2 - 4$$
subject to
$$x_1 + 2x_2 \leq 8$$
$$-x_1 + x_2 \leq 1$$
$$x_1 \leq 6.$$

4. Minimize
$$\theta = -3x_1 - 4x_2 + 25$$
subject to
$$x_1 - 2x_2 \leq 4$$
$$2x_1 + 3x_2 \leq 15$$
$$x_2 \leq 5.$$

5. Maximize
$$\theta = x_1 + 2x_2$$
subject to
$$-x_1 + x_2 \leq 0$$
$$x_1 + x_2 \leq 18$$
$$x_1 \leq 12.$$

6. Maximize
$$\theta = 5x_1 + 6x_2 + 10x_3$$
subject to
$$x_1 + 2x_2 + 3x_3 \leq 24$$
$$2x_1 + x_2 + x_3 \leq 18$$
$$x_1 + 2x_2 + 4x_3 \leq 32.$$

7. This problem illustrates that cycling can occur if an arbitrary rule is used to break ties for the leaving variable; namely, choose the variable in the uppermost row:
Maximize
$$\theta = (3/4)x_1 - 150x_2 + (1/50)x_3 - 6x_4$$
subject to
$$(1/4)x_1 - 60x_2 - (1/25)x_3 + 9x_4 \leq 0$$
$$(1/2)x_1 - 90x_2 - (1/50)x_3 + 3x_4 \leq 0$$
$$x_3 \leq 1.$$

8. Maximize
$$\theta = 4x_1 + 6x_2$$
subject to
$$x_1 + x_2 \leq 5$$
$$2x_1 + 3x_2 \leq 12.$$

9. Maximize
$$\theta = 1.5x_1 + 3.5x_2$$
subject to
$$3x_1 + 7x_2 \leq 42$$
$$x_1 + 5x_2 \leq 22.$$

10. Maximize
$$\theta = x_1 + x_2$$

4.6 PROBLEM SET 4-1 (concluded)

subject to
$$x_1 + x_2 \leq 7$$
$$-x_1 + x_2 \leq 1$$
$$x_1 \leq 5.$$

11. Maximize
$$\theta = x_1 - x_2$$
subject to
$$x_1 - x_2 \leq 4$$
$$x_1 \leq 5.$$

12. Maximize
$$\theta = 3x_1 + 3x_2 + 12x_3$$
subject to
$$x_1 + x_2 + 4x_3 \leq 36$$
$$2x_1 + 2x_2 + 3x_3 \leq 42.$$

13. Maximize
$$\theta = 2x_1 + 3x_2$$
subject to
$$-2x_1 + x_2 \leq 2$$
$$x_2 \leq 6.$$

14. Maximize
$$\theta = x_1 + x_2$$
subject to
$$x_1 - x_2 \leq 4$$
$$x_1 \leq 5.$$

15. Maximize
$$\theta = -5x_1 + x_2$$
subject to
$$x_1 - 4x_2 \leq 8$$
$$-7x_1 + x_2 \leq 7.$$

16. Maximize
$$\theta = 20x_1 + 12x_3$$
subject to
$$5x_1 - x_2 + x_3 \leq 1/5$$
$$x_1 + x_2 + x_3 \leq 1/4$$
x_3 unrestricted in sign.

17. Maximize
$$\theta = -24x_1 + 10x_2 + 18x_3$$
subject to
$$-x_1 + x_2 + 2x_3 \leq 1$$
$$-3x_1 + x_2 + x_3 \leq 7$$
x_3 unrestricted in sign.

18. Maximize
$$\theta = 6x_1 + 4x_3$$
subject to
$$x_1 + x_2 + x_3 \leq 1/5$$
$$3x_1 - x_2 + x_3 \leq 3/10$$
x_3 unrestricted in sign.

4.7 SENSITIVITY ANALYSIS ON ≤ CONSTRAINTS: SHADOW PRICES AND RIGHT-HAND-SIDE RANGES

In practice, the constants and coefficients of the constraints and/or the objective function in a linear programming problem cannot be determined precisely. In other words, statements such as "Machine A will be available for at most 36 hours" are actually educated guesses and management must have the flexibility to **vary the numerical values slightly one way or the other.** The purpose of **postoptimality analysis** or **sensitivity analysis** is to determine the effects of such changes on the solution to the linear programming problem. Of course, we could reformulate the problem and resolve it in its entirety. As we will see, this procedure is not only inefficient but also unnecessary. Rather, we can start from the optimal solution to

> Sensitivity analysis assesses the effect that small changes in the problem have on the optimal solution.

the original linear programming problem, determine the effects of the proposed modifications, and then, if necessary, proceed from there to the optimal solution of the modified problem. In this way, we can save all of the work done in solving the original problem.

The following illustration will give us a better understanding of sensitivity analysis and the associated concept of shadow prices. Recall the Ace Rubber Company example:

Maximize
$$\theta = 10x_1 + 8x_2$$
subject to

$$\text{Machine A:} \quad 2x_1 + 9x_2 \leq 36$$
$$\text{Machine B:} \quad 4x_1 + 3x_2 \leq 42$$
$$\text{Nonnegativity:} \quad x_1, x_2 \geq 0.$$

We saw in Section 4.2 that the optimal solution was

$$x_1 = 9, \ x_2 = 2, \ s_1 = s_2 = 0, \ \text{and} \ \theta = 106,$$

where s_1 and s_2 represented the slack time on Machines A and B, respectively. We shall say that **when a slack variable is zero in an optimal solution, the associated constraint is binding.** The binding constraints in the present case mean simply that no more Model P or R tires can be manufactured because all of the available resources (Machine A and B time) have been used. Consequently, the only way to increase output, all other things remaining unchanged, is to increase the amount of available time on the machines. By way of contrast, a slack that turns out to be greater than zero in the optimal solution is associated with a nonbinding constraint because the corresponding available resource is not fully utilized.

> A binding constraint indicates the optimal solution cannot be changed unless the limiting value of the constraint is changed.

The management of Ace Rubber Company, noting that the binding constraints on resources limit the number of tires that can be made and consequently limit profit, wishes to know the effect of freeing up machine time. What if, for example, Machine A could be available for 66 hours instead of 36? The only change to the original problem would be to raise the right-hand side of the Machine A constraint to a new limit of 66:

$$\text{Machine A:} \quad 2x_1 + 9x_2 \leq 66;$$

the effect of this new Machine A constraint is shown in Figure 4-4.

Exercise. What would be the change in the original problem if Machine B could be available for 76 hours? Draw the graph showing both the old and new constraints.

Answer: The right-hand side of the Machine B constraint would change from 42 to 76:

$$\text{Machine B:} \quad 4x_1 + 3x_2 \leq 76.$$

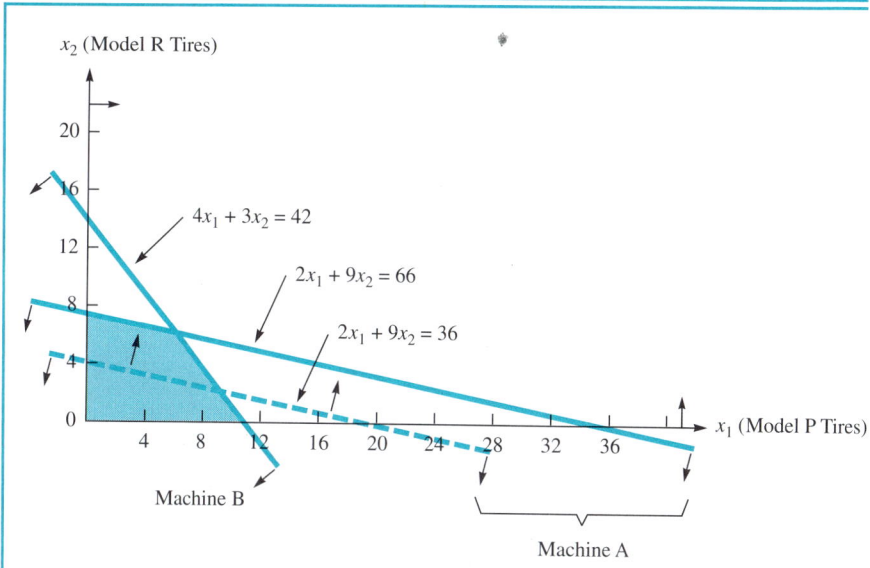

FIGURE 4-4

Using the Simplex Method with the new Machine A constraint, we get the results shown in Table 4–11. From the last tableau in this table, we see that the new optimal solution is

$$x_1 = x_2 = 6, s_1 = s_2 = 0, \text{ and } \theta = 108,$$

or a profit of $108 when six of each model tire are made. Once again, there is no slack on either machine.

Now compare Table 4–11 with Tables 3–14, 3–16, and 3–17 for the original problem. What do you notice? In both Initial Tableaus, x_1 entered the basis and s_2 left. In both Second Tableaus, x_2 entered the basis and s_1 left. Thus exactly the same row operations were performed in both solutions. **The fact that we changed the right-hand side of the Machine A constraint from 36 to 66 shows up only in the current values column.**

Changing the limiting value of a constraint affects only the current values column in the tableaus.

Exercise. What would be the entering and leaving variables in the Initial Tableau if the original problem were changed so that Machine B became available for 76 hours?

Answer: x_1 would enter and s_1 would leave.

TABLE 4-11

Initial Tableau

Basic Variables	Coefficient of				Current Values	
	x_1	x_2	s_1	s_2		
s_1	[2]	9	1	0	[66]	33
s_2	[4]	3	0	1	[42]	21/2 →
(max) θ	−10	−8	0	0	0	
	↑					

Second Tableau

Basic Variables	Coefficient of				Current Values	
	x_1	x_2	s_1	s_2		
s_1	0	[15/2]	1	−1/2	[45]	6 →
x_1	1	[3/4]	0	1/4	[21/2]	14
(max) θ	0	−1/2	0	5/2	105	
		↑				

Third Tableau

Basic Variables	Coefficient of				Current Values
	x_1	x_2	s_1	s_2	
x_2	0	1	2/15	−1/15	6
x_1	1	0	−1/10	3/10	6
(max) θ	0	0	1/15	37/15	108

When performing sensitivity analysis, we use the optimal solution as a starting point to reduce the subsequent number of calculations.

The matchup of Tables 3–14, 3–16, and 3–17 with Table 4–11 suggests an alternative way of solving a modified problem. Why not go directly to the last tableau and compute the effect of the change? Maybe, as in the present situation, the tableau will still be optimal, so we will be done. Even if the tableau is not optimal, we can continue on without repeating all the calculations done to that point. How, then, can we determine the new tableau directly? One way is to look at the tableaus in terms of their column vectors. For example, in the Initial Tableau of Table 4–11 the x_1 column vector, $\boldsymbol{x}_1$, is

$$\boldsymbol{x}_1 = \begin{pmatrix} 2 \\ 4 \\ -10 \end{pmatrix}.$$

> **Exercise.** What is the x_2 column vector in this tableau?
> **Answer:**
> $$x_2 = \begin{pmatrix} 9 \\ 3 \\ -8 \end{pmatrix}.$$

Now notice that the column vectors for our initial basic variables s_1 and s_2 are

$$s_1 = \begin{pmatrix} 1 \\ 0 \\ \hline 0 \end{pmatrix} \quad \text{and} \quad s_2 = \begin{pmatrix} 0 \\ 1 \\ \hline 0 \end{pmatrix},$$

respectively. Recall also that in the solution of the original problem in Tables 3–14, 3–16, and 3–17 there was a never-changing θ column of

$$\theta = \begin{pmatrix} 0 \\ 0 \\ \hline 1 \end{pmatrix},$$

which we subsequently dropped from the solution. Now then we can express x_1 in terms of s_1, s_2, and θ as

$$x_1 = \begin{pmatrix} 2 \\ 4 \\ \hline -10 \end{pmatrix} = 2 \cdot \begin{pmatrix} 1 \\ 0 \\ \hline 0 \end{pmatrix} + 4 \cdot \begin{pmatrix} 0 \\ 1 \\ \hline 0 \end{pmatrix} - 10 \cdot \begin{pmatrix} 0 \\ 0 \\ \hline 1 \end{pmatrix}$$

or

$$x_1 = 2 \cdot s_1 + 4 \cdot s_2 - 10 \cdot \theta.$$

> **Exercise.** Express x_2 in terms of s_1, s_2, and θ.
> **Answer:** $x_2 = 9 \cdot s_1 + 3 \cdot s_2 - 8 \cdot \theta.$

For the current values (or CV) column of the Initial Tableau, we have a column vector that we symbolize by

$$CV = \begin{pmatrix} 66 \\ 42 \\ \hline 0 \end{pmatrix}$$

or

$$CV = 66 \cdot s_1 + 42 \cdot s_2 + 0 \cdot \theta. \tag{1}$$

Now look at the CV-column in the last tableau of Table 4–11:

$$CV = \begin{pmatrix} 6 \\ 6 \\ 108 \end{pmatrix}.$$

Does the preceding vector relationship (1) still hold?

$$66 \cdot s_1 + 42 \cdot s_2 + 0 \cdot \theta = 66 \cdot \begin{pmatrix} 2/15 \\ -1/10 \\ 1/15 \end{pmatrix} + 42 \cdot \begin{pmatrix} -1/15 \\ 3/10 \\ 37/15 \end{pmatrix} + 0 \cdot \begin{pmatrix} 0 \\ 0 \\ 1 \end{pmatrix}$$

$$= \begin{pmatrix} 6 \\ 6 \\ 108 \end{pmatrix}.$$

It does; indeed this will always be the case.

Every column in a tableau can be expressed in terms of the accompanying initial basic variable column vectors.

Every column vector of the Initial Tableau can be expressed in terms of the initial basic variable column vectors together with the θ-column vector. Furthermore, the same vector relationship holds throughout all the tableaus.

Exercise. Verify that $x_1 = 2 \cdot s_1 + 4 \cdot s_2 - 10 \cdot \theta$ and $x_2 = 9 \cdot s_1 + 3 \cdot s_2 - 8 \cdot \theta$ in all the tableaus of Table 4–11.

Now we return to the original problem and consider a different modification. What if the hours available on Machine A must remain at 36, but Machine B can be made available for 72 hours instead of 42? This time, the only change to the original problem will affect the right-hand side of the Machine B constraint; the new limit will be 72:

Machine B: $4x_1 + 3x_2 \leq 72.$

Once again, the Initial Tableau of Table 3–14 would be affected only in the CV-column, which would become

$$CV = \begin{pmatrix} 36 \\ 72 \\ 0 \end{pmatrix}.$$

Expressing this column vector in terms of the initial basic vectors s_1 and s_2 together with θ, we have

$$CV = 36 \cdot s_1 + 72 \cdot s_2 + 0 \cdot \theta.$$

Thus the only change in the Third Tableau of Table 4–11 would be a new CV-column

$$CV = \begin{pmatrix} x_2 \\ x_1 \\ \theta \end{pmatrix} = 36 \cdot s_1 + 72 \cdot s_2 + 0 \cdot \theta$$

$$= 36 \cdot \begin{pmatrix} 2/15 \\ -1/10 \\ 1/15 \end{pmatrix} + 72 \cdot \begin{pmatrix} -1/15 \\ 3/10 \\ 37/15 \end{pmatrix} + 0 \cdot \begin{pmatrix} 0 \\ 0 \\ 1 \end{pmatrix}$$

$$= \begin{pmatrix} 0 \\ 18 \\ 180 \end{pmatrix},$$

so that the tableau would be as shown in Table 4–12.

From the table, we see that the new optimal solution is

$$x_1 = 18, \quad x_2 = s_1 = s_2 = 0, \quad \text{and} \quad \theta = 180,$$

or a profit of $180 when 18 Model P tires and no Model R tires are made. As before, there is no slack on either machine.

Exercise. Suppose the management of Ace Rubber Company is forced to reduce the availability on both machines from their original levels to 15 hours each. a) What would be the change to the original problem? b) What is the new CV-column for the Initial Tableau? c) What is the CV-column for the Third tableau? d) What is the new optimal solution?

Answer: a) The original constraints on Machine A and B become

Machine A: $2x_1 + 9x_2 \leq 15$

Machine B: $4x_1 + 3x_2 \leq 15$.

b) $CV = \begin{pmatrix} 15 \\ 15 \\ 0 \end{pmatrix}$. c) $CV = \begin{pmatrix} 1 \\ 3 \\ 38 \end{pmatrix}$.

d) $38 profit when three Model P tires and one Model R tire are made.

TABLE 4–12
Third Tableau

Basic Variables	Coefficient of				Current Values
	x_1	x_2	s_1	s_2	
x_2	0	1	2/15	−1/15	0
x_1	1	0	−1/10	3/10	18
(max) θ	0	0	1/15	37/15	180

Now let us generalize the previous discussion by returning to the original problem and assuming that the availability of Machine A is changed by an amount of c hours from its original value of 36. This time, the constraint on Machine A becomes

$$\text{Machine A:} \quad 2x_1 + 9x_2 \leq 36 + c \tag{2}$$

so that the CV-column of the Initial Tableau would be

$$CV = \begin{pmatrix} 36 + c \\ 42 \\ 0 \end{pmatrix}.$$

Thus in our Third Tableau, we would have

$$CV = (36 + c) \cdot s_1 + 42 \cdot s_2 + 0 \cdot \theta$$

$$= (36 + c) \cdot \begin{pmatrix} 2/15 \\ -1/10 \\ 1/15 \end{pmatrix} + 42 \cdot \begin{pmatrix} -1/15 \\ 3/10 \\ 37/15 \end{pmatrix} + 0 \cdot \begin{pmatrix} 0 \\ 0 \\ 1 \end{pmatrix} \tag{3}$$

$$= \begin{pmatrix} 2 + 2c/15 \\ 9 - c/10 \\ 106 + c/15 \end{pmatrix}$$

so that the tableau would be as shown in Table 4–13.
The new solution is

$$x_1 = 9 - c/10, \quad x_2 = 2 + 2c/15, \quad s_1 = s_2 = 0, \tag{4}$$
$$\text{and} \quad \theta = 106 + c/15,$$

where c is the change in the number of hours available on Machine A. Recall our first modification in this section was to increase the availability from 36 to 66 hours. In this case, then, the change is

$$c = 66 - 36 = 30$$

so our solution would be

TABLE 4–13
Third Tableau

Basic Variables	Coefficient of				Current Values
	x_1	x_2	s_1	s_2	
x_2	0	1	2/15	−1/15	$2 + 2c/15$
x_1	1	0	−1/10	3/10	$9 - c/10$
(max) θ	0	0	1/15	37/15	$106 + c/15$

$$x_1 = 9 - \frac{30}{10} = 6$$

$$x_2 = 2 + \frac{2(30)}{15} = 6$$

$$s_1 = s_2 = 0$$

$$\theta = 106 + \frac{30}{15} = 108,$$

which is precisely the same answer as before.

On the other hand, what if there had been an increase from the original 36 to 37 hours? The new profit would be

$$\theta = 106 + \frac{c}{15}$$
$$= 106 + \frac{1}{15},$$

or an increase of 1/15 ≈ $0.07. This particular value is called the **shadow price** of an hour of Machine A time. It is also called the **marginal value** of an hour of Machine A time, because it is the **additional profit when the available amount of the resource is increased by one unit.** Finally, it may be referred to as the **imputed price** of an hour of Machine A time, because the original problem statement did not provide a dollar value for Machine A time, and the $0.07 per hour was imputed from the analysis.

By the way, where did the $c/15$ come from in the new value of $\theta = 106 + c/15$? Looking back at (3), we see that it came from multiplying c times the θ-row entry 1/15 for s_1. This 1/15, of course, is precisely the θ-row entry of the s_1-column in the Third Tableau of Table 4–13 (or the original Table 3–17 of Section 3–13. Recall that s_1 is the slack variable for Machine A.

≡ Shadow Price

The shadow price associated with a resource indicates the associated change in the objective function value for each unit change in the availability of the resource.

> **Exercise.** a) What is the shadow price of an hour of Machine B time? b) Which entry in Table 4–13 gives us this value? c) Why?
>
> **Answer:** a) 37/15 or $2.47. b) The 37/15 in the θ-row of the s_2-column. c) s_2 is the slack variable for Machine B.

Right-Hand-Side Ranges

The solutions we just considered were still optimal because the change c did not alter the basis. Clearly, if a change of c caused x_1 or x_2 to be negative in (4), the Simplex Method would not have produced (3), because adherence to the simplex rules ensures that basic variables will not be negative. Thus it follows that in (4), the values x_1 and x_2 must be greater than or equal to zero:

$$x_1 = 9 - \frac{c}{10} \geq 0 \quad \text{and} \quad x_2 = 2 + \frac{2c}{15} \geq 0.$$

Working first with x_1, we find

$$9 - \frac{c}{10} \geq 0$$

$$-\frac{c}{10} \geq -9$$

$$\frac{c}{10} \leq 9$$

$$c \leq 90. \tag{5}$$

Working next with x_2, we have

$$2 + \frac{2c}{15} \geq 0$$

$$\frac{2c}{15} \geq -2$$

$$2c \geq -30$$

$$c \geq -15. \tag{6}$$

Taking (5) and (6) together gives

$$-15 \leq c \leq 90. \tag{7}$$

Recalling our time constraint (2) on Machine A,

Machine A: $2x_1 + 9x_2 \leq 36 + c$,

the result (7) means that we can decrease the right-hand side by as much as 15 to $36 - 15 = 21$, that is,

$$2x_1 + 9x_2 \leq 21,$$

or increase it by as much as 90 to 36 + 90 = 126, that is

$$2x_1 + 9x_2 \leq 126,$$

without changing the variables that are in the basis. In summary, then, the shadow price of an hour of Machine A time is $0.07 for available Machine A times in the range 21 to 126 hours.

The price we have found in the shadows, $0.07 per hour of Machine A time, is an important value because it shows that profit can be increased by $0.07 for each hour of increased Machine A time made available. It follows that it would be profitable to increase Machine A time availability if the cost per additional hour is less than $0.07.

An alternative way to determine the right-hand-side range is to compute the ratios in the last tableau of the original problem. For example, the last tableau in our present example from Table 3–17 of Section 3–13 is repeated for convenience in Table 4–14. If we were to try to change the availability of Machine A time by bringing s_1 (the slack variable for Machine A) into this optimal solution, we see the ratios are 15 and −90, respectively. Recall that the **original constraint equation** for Machine A is

$$\text{Machine A:} \quad 2x_1 + 9x_2 + s_1 = 36$$

or

$$2x_1 + 9x_2 = 36 - s_1.$$

So, **subtracting the two limiting ratios** for s_1 of 15 and −90, we have

$$36 - 15 = 21$$

and

$$36 - (-90) = 126,$$

which is precisely the same result as before. Note that if there were more than one positive (negative) ratio, we would select the one with the smallest magnitude.

Shadow prices are valid for a limited range on the resource availability.

TABLE 4–14

Basic Variables	Coefficient of				Current Values	
	x_1	x_2	s_1	s_2		
x_2	0	1	2/15	−1/15	2	15
x_1	1	0	−1/10	3/10	9	−90
(max) θ	0	0	1/15	37/15	106	

> **Exercise.** Using Table 4–14, determine a) the ratios for Machine B and b) the associated right-hand-side range.
>
> **Answer:** a) -30 and 30. b) $42 - 30 = 12$ and $42 - (-30) = 72$, so the constraint ranges between $4x_1 + 3x_2 \leq 12$ and $4x_1 + 3x_2 \leq 72$.

LINDO has the ability to perform sensitivity analysis. For our preceding example, the associated LINDO printout is shown in Table 4–15 where we have rerun the Ace Rubber Company example but, this time, responded **yes** to the query about sensitivity analysis

$$\text{DO RANGE (SENSITIVITY) ANALYSIS?}$$
$$?yes.$$

In the section headed by RIGHTHAND SIDE RANGES, we see for s_1 the value 36 under the CURRENT RHS column together with an ALLOWABLE INCREASE of 90.000000 and an ALLOWABLE DECREASE of 14.999999. This means, then, that the right-hand-side range for s_1 is from

$$36 - 15 = 21$$

(replacing 14.999999 with 15) to

$$36 + 90 = 126,$$

which is precisely the same result as before.

> **Exercise.** Use the LINDO printout in Table 4–15 to find the right-hand-side range for s_2.
>
> **Answer:** From $42 - 30 = 12$ to $42 + 30 = 72$, using 30 instead of 29.999998.

Sensitivity on the constraint coefficients can be accomplished using vector analysis.

At this point, we present an example illustrating how the vector relationship approach can be used to perform sensitivity analysis on the coefficients of the constraints.

Example. Suppose that the management of Ace Rubber Company is forced to change the Machine A time requirement for Model R tires from the original nine hours per tire to three hours per tire. What is the optimal solution of the modified problem?

TABLE 4-15

```
$ lindo
LINDO (7 OCTOBER 88 CHICAGO)
: max 10x1 + 8x2
 ? st
 ? 2x1 + 9x2 <= 36
 ? 4x1 + 3x2 <= 42
 ? end

: go
LP OPTIMUM FOUND AT STEP        2

        OBJECTIVE FUNCTION VALUE
     1)     106.000000

  VARIABLE        VALUE          REDUCED COST
      X1         9.000000          0.000000
      X2         2.000000          0.000000

     ROW    SLACK OR SURPLUS      DUAL PRICES
      2)        0.000000           0.066667
      3)        0.000000           2.466667

 NO. ITERATIONS=        2

DO RANGE (SENSITIVITY) ANALYSIS?
 ? yes

RANGES IN WHICH THE BASIS IS UNCHANGED:

                         OBJ COEFFICIENT RANGES
  VARIABLE      CURRENT         ALLOWABLE          ALLOWABLE
                 COEF           INCREASE            DECREASE
      X1       10.000000         0.666667           8.222222
      X2        8.000000        37.000000           0.500000

                         RIGHTHAND SIDE RANGES
     ROW       CURRENT         ALLOWABLE           ALLOWABLE
                 RHS            INCREASE            DECREASE
      2        36.000000       90.000000           14.999999
      3        42.000000       29.999998           29.999998

: quit
FORTRAN STOP
$ lo
```

The only change to the original problem is to the coefficient of x_2 in the Machine A constraint so we want to

maximize
$$\theta = 10x_1 + 8x_2$$

subject to

$$\text{Machine A:} \quad 2x_1 + 3x_2 \leq 36$$
$$\text{Machine B:} \quad 4x_1 + 3x_2 \leq 42$$
$$\text{Nonnegativity:} \quad x_1, x_2 \geq 0.$$

Thus the only change to the Initial Tableau would be a new x_2-column:

$$x_2 = \begin{pmatrix} 3 \\ 3 \\ \hline -8 \end{pmatrix}$$

$$= 3 \cdot s_1 + 3 \cdot s_2 - 8 \cdot \theta.$$

Hence in our Third Tableau we would have

$$x_2 = 3 \cdot s_1 + 3 \cdot s_2 - 8 \cdot \theta$$

$$= 3 \cdot \begin{pmatrix} 2/15 \\ -1/10 \\ 1/15 \end{pmatrix} + 3 \cdot \begin{pmatrix} -1/15 \\ 3/10 \\ 37/15 \end{pmatrix} - 8 \cdot \begin{pmatrix} 0 \\ 0 \\ 1 \end{pmatrix}$$

or

$$x_2 = \begin{pmatrix} 1/5 \\ 3/5 \\ \hline -2/5 \end{pmatrix}$$

so that the Third Tableau would be as shown in Table 4–16.

TABLE 4–16 Third Tableau

Basic Variables	Coefficient of				Current Values
	x_1	x_2	s_1	s_2	
x_2	0	1/5	2/15	−1/15	2
x_1	1	3/5	−1/10	3/10	9
(max) θ	0	−2/5	1/15	37/15	106

Is this tableau optimal? Certainly not, because of the negative entry $-2/5$ in the θ-row for x_2. But something else is wrong with this tableau. It does not have the proper form for a simplex tableau. Why not? Look at the x_2-column. x_2 is part of the basis, so the column should be

$$\begin{pmatrix} 1 \\ 0 \\ 0 \end{pmatrix}.$$

Thus we cannot even begin to consider the question of optimality until the tableau is transformed into its proper form. We do this in the usual way, as shown in Table 4–17. From the New Third Tableau, we see that we have the optimal solution

$$x_1 = 3, \quad x_2 = 10, \quad s_1 = s_2 = 0, \quad \theta = 110,$$

or a profit of $110 when 3 Model P and 10 Model R tires are made.

It should be clear, at this point, that the vector relationship approach can be used to perform sensitivity analysis on any combination of coefficients and/or constants of the $\leq$ constraints. We will see later that this same approach also works for $\geq$ and $=$ constraints. What we will do is use the vector relationship(s) to modify the last tableau of the original problem. Then we examine the new tableau as follows:

All types of sensitivity analysis can be done by the vector approach.

TABLE 4–17
Third Tableau

Basic Variables	Coefficient of				Current Values
	x_1	x_2	s_1	s_2	
x_2	0	1/5	2/15	$-1/15$	2
x_1	1	3/5	$-1/10$	3/10	9
(max) θ	0	$-2/5$	1/15	37/15	106

New Third Tableau

Basic Variables	Coefficient of				Current Values
	x_1	x_2	s_1	s_2	
x_2	0	1	2/3	$-1/3$	10
x_1	1	0	$-1/2$	1/2	3
(max) θ	0	0	1/3	7/3	110

> **Three steps for analyzing the tableau resulting from sensitivity analysis.**
>
> **Step 1.** Check that all the basic variable columns are in the proper form. If not, transform them as we did in the previous example.
>
> **Step 2.** Check that the current values column is feasible, that is, has no negative entries. If not, then a special technique known as the Dual Simplex Method (which is beyond the scope of our work) must be used.[5]
>
> **Step 3.** Check that the θ-row is optimal. If not, proceed in the usual manner, starting from the new tableau.

Lastly, the simplest way to use LINDO for the previous example is by means of the ALTER command on the original problem. Those interested in this approach are referred to the Schrage book.

4.8 PROBLEM SET 4-2

1. If we were to maximize

$$\theta = 5x_1 + 8x_2$$

   subject to

$$x_1 + x_2 \leq 13$$
$$x_1 + 2x_2 \leq 22$$
$$2x_1 + x_2 \leq 20$$
$$x_1, x_2 \geq 0,$$

   the Final Tableau would be

Basic Variables	Coefficient of					Current Values
	x_1	x_2	s_1	s_2	s_3	
x_1	1	0	2	-1	0	4
x_2	0	1	-1	1	0	9
s_3	0	0	-3	1	1	3
(max) θ	0	0	2	3	0	92

   Find the new optimal solution if
   a) Only the right-hand side of the first constraint is changed from 13 to 14.
   b) Only the right-hand side of the second constraint is changed from 22 to 20.
   c) Only the right-hand side of the third constraint is changed from 20 to 18.

2. Find the right-hand-side ranges of each of the first three constraints in Problem 1.

3. Consider the original Problem 1.
   a) Find the new optimal solution if the right-hand sides of the first three constraints were simultaneously changed to 14, 20, and 24, respectively.
   b) Find the Preliminary Final Tableau if the right-hand sides of the first three constraints were simultaneously changed to 14, 20, and 18, respectively. Explain why this tableau does not represent the optimal solution.

---

[5]See any textbook in management science or operations research for a discussion of the Dual Simplex Method; for example, H. M. Wagner, *Principles of Management Science* (Englewood Cliffs, N.J.: Prentice Hall, 1975), or F. S. Hillier and G. J. Lieberman, *Introduction to Operations Research* (San Francisco: Holden-Day, 1986).

4.8 PROBLEM SET 4-2 (continued)

4. If we were to maximize

$$\theta = 3x_1 + 2x_2$$

subject to

$$x_1 + 3x_2 \leq 24$$
$$2x_1 + x_2 \leq 18$$
$$x_1 + x_2 \leq 10$$
$$x_1, x_2 \geq 0,$$

the Final Tableau would be

Basic Variables	Coefficient of					Current Values
	x_1	x_2	s_1	s_2	s_3	
s_1	0	0	1	2	−5	10
x_1	1	0	0	1	−1	8
x_2	0	1	0	−1	2	2
(max) θ	0	0	0	1	1	28

a) Find the right-hand-side ranges of each of the first three constraints.
b) Find the new optimal solution if the right-hand side of the first constraint was decreased to 21, simultaneously the second was increased to 22, and also the third was increased to 11.

5. If we were to maximize

$$\theta = 5x_1 + 6x_2 + 10x_3$$

subject to:

$$x_1 + 2x_2 + 3x_3 \leq 24$$
$$2x_1 + x_2 + x_3 \leq 18$$
$$x_1, x_2, x_3 \geq 0,$$

then the Final Tableau would be

Basic Variables	Coefficient of					Current Values
	x_1	x_2	x_3	s_1	s_2	
x_3	0	3/5	1	2/5	−1/5	6
x_1	1	1/5	0	−1/5	3/5	6
(max) θ	0	1	0	3	1	90

a) Find the right-hand-side ranges of each of the first two constraints.
b) Find the new optimal solution if the right-hand sides of the first two constraints were simultaneously changed to 30 and 20, respectively.

6. Find the new optimal solution to the Ace Rubber Company example if the requirement on Machine A for Model R tires were again changed to three hours per tire and simultaneously the requirement on Machine B for Model R tires were changed to one hour per tire.

7. Find the new optimal solution to Problem 4 if the original problem were changed so that each unit of x_1 were to require two units of the first resource and simultaneously each unit of x_2 were to require four units of the first resource.

8. Find the new optimal solution to Problem 4 if the original problem were changed so that each unit of x_1 were to require two units of the first resource, simultaneously each unit of x_2 were to require four units of the first resource, and also the number of available units of the first resource were increased to 36.

9. A glass manufacturer is making x_1 4-ounce, x_2 8-ounce, and x_3 12-ounce glasses, with each glass made contributing to profit. Resources available are 80 labor-hours of moulding time (slack is s_1), 40 labor-hours of grinding time (slack is s_2), and 24 labor-hours of polishing time (slack is s_3). Suppose the optimal profit-maximizing tableau is the following, where θ is dollars of profit.

Basic Variables	Coefficient of						Current Values
	x_1	x_2	x_3	s_1	s_2	s_3	
x_1	1	−2	0	0	20	25	100
s_1	0	3	0	1	−1	5	5
x_3	0	−5	1	0	40	−20	80
(max) θ	0	3	0	0	30	50	1,500

a) How many of each type of glass should be made to maximize profit? What is the maximum profit?

4.8 PROBLEM SET 4-2 (concluded)

b) Find the shadow price of any resource for which the constraint is binding and state the meaning of this price.

c) Find the right-hand-side ranges for the constraints in (b).

10. A contractor plans to build x_1 Superdeluxe, x_2 Deluxe, and x_3 Standard houses, each of which contributes to θ, the profit function. Resources available are the amounts of money a bank will loan for land purchase, building, and landscaping. Maximum amounts that will be loaned are \$100,000 for land (slack is s_1), \$500,000 for building (slack is s_2), and \$40,000 for landscaping (slack is s_3). Suppose the optimal tableau is as follows:

Basic Variables	x_1	x_2	Coefficient of x_3	s_1	s_2	s_3	Current Values
x_1	1	0	2/3	−1	0	2	4
x_2	0	1	−1/4	−3	0	1/3	9
s_2	0	0	0	1	1	−1/2	5
(max) θ	0	0	2	1/5	0	1/20	125

a) How many of each type of house should be built to maximize profit? What is the maximum profit?

b) Find the shadow price of any resource for which the constraint is binding and state the meaning of this price.

c) Find the right-hand-side ranges for the constraints in (b).

11. The table shows, for example, that making one unit of Product A requires one minute for stamping, three minutes for forming, and one minute for painting and contributes \$1 to profit.

Product	Number of Units	Minutes per Unit for Stamping	Forming	Painting	Profit per Unit
A	x_1	1	3	1	\$1
B	x_2	3	10	5	\$4
C	x_3	2	5	5	\$2

Minutes available for stamping, forming, and painting are, respectively, 48, 150, and 70.

a) How many units of each product should be made to maximize profit? What is the maximum profit?

b) Find the shadow price of any resource for which the constraint is binding and state the meaning of this price.

c) Find the right-hand-side range for constraints in (b).

4.9 TWO PENALTY/PREMIUM EXAMPLES WITH ≤ CONSTRAINTS

In Section 3.13, we stated that there were situations where the slack variables may contribute (positively or negatively) to the objective function. Obviously then, the coefficient of such a variable in the θ-equation will not be zero. The following two examples will illustrate linear programming problems in which penalties and/or premiums are assigned to the slack variables.

Example. Star Insulating Company manufactures three types of storm windows: Model H (the heavy duty), Model R (the regular), and Model E (the economy). Model H sells for \$25 per window and costs \$16 per window to make, Model R sells for \$22 per window and costs \$10 per window to make, and Model E sells for \$17 per window and costs \$7 per window to make. To make one Model H window requires two hours on Machine A and one hour on Machine B. To make one Model R window takes two hours on Machine A and three hours on Machine B. To make one Model E window requires one hour on A and two hours on B. Production scheduling indicates that during the coming week Machine A will be available for at most 36 hours and Machine B for at most 30 hours. **However, any unused time on Machine A creates an expense (penalty) of \$2 per hour allocated for idle time for an operator, but any unused time on Machine B can be rented to another firm at a rate (premium) of \$2 per hour.** How many of each window should the company make in the coming week in order to maximize its profit? What is this maximum profit?

The constraints for this problem are

$$\text{Machine A:} \quad 2x_1 + 2x_2 + x_3 \leq 36$$
$$\text{Machine B:} \quad x_1 + 3x_2 + 2x_3 \leq 30$$
$$\text{Nonnegativity:} \quad x_1, x_2, x_3 \geq 0,$$

where x_1, x_2, and x_3 represent the respective numbers of Model H, Model R, and Model E windows to be made in the coming week. Ignoring the unused time for the moment, the objective function is

$$\theta = 9x_1 + 12x_2 + 10x_3.$$

If we now let s_1 and s_2 be the slack times on Machines A and B, respectively, we can modify θ for the unused times. Since any unused time s_1 on Machine A has an associated expense (penalty) of \$2 per hour, while any unused time s_2 on Machine B has an associated rental (premium) of \$2 per hour, the new θ-equation is

$$\theta = 9x_1 + 12x_2 + 10x_3 - 2s_1 + 2s_2.$$

Thus the Preliminary Tableau is as shown in Table 4–18A.

Do you notice anything peculiar about this tableau? Look at the coefficients of the basic variables s_1 and s_2 in the θ-row. They should both be zero. In addition, if we start out at the origin with $x_1 = x_2 = x_3 = 0$, $s_1 = 36$, and $s_2 = 30$, then we should have

$$\theta = 9(0) + 12(0) + 10(0) - 2(36) + 2(30)$$
$$= -12.$$

When a penalty or premium is involved, the Preliminary Tableau will not be a proper starting tableau.

TABLE 4–18A
Preliminary Tableau

Basic Variables	Coefficient of					Current Values
	x_1	x_2	x_3	s_1	s_2	
s_1	2	2	1	1	0	36
s_2	1	3	2	0	1	30
(max) θ	−9	−12	−10	2	−2	0

But what is the value of θ in Table 4–18A? The tableau indicates $\theta = 0$. So we do not have a proper starting tableau.

To transform the θ-row coefficients of s_1 and s_2, we use the usual row operations as shown in Table 4–18B. We add -2 times the s_1-row and 2 times the s_2-row to get the new θ-row. Note that we now do have a correct value of $\theta = -12$.

> **Exercise.** Why is $\theta = -12$?
>
> **Answer:** We pay a penalty of $2 per hour on Machine A for $s_1 = 36$ hours, gain a value of $2 per hour on Machine B for $s_2 = 30$ hours, and $(-2)(36) + (2)(30) = -\$12$.

We now continue in Table 4–18B to generate the simplex tableaus in the usual manner. From the Third Tableau, we see that the optimal solution is

$$x_1 = 14, \quad x_2 = 0, \quad x_3 = 8, \quad s_1 = s_2 = 0, \quad \text{and} \quad \theta = 206$$

for a profit of $206 when 14 Model H and 8 Model E windows are made. Since $s_1 = s_2 = 0$, there are no unused hours on either machine and so no penalty or value occurs in the optimal solution.

To solve the preceding example using LINDO, we must rewrite the objective function with zero coefficients on the slack variables. This is done simply by using the θ-row of the Initial Tableau of Table 4–18B which alternatively expresses the objective function as

$$\theta = 11x_1 + 10x_2 + 8x_3 - 12.$$

Computer packages usually do not accept constant terms in the objective function.

We then proceed as shown in Table 4–19 where, of course, we are unable to include the "-12" in the objective function.[6] From this table, we see that the optimal solution is

$$\theta = 218, \quad x_1 = 14, \quad x_2 = 0, \quad x_3 = 8, \quad s_1 = s_2 = 0$$

where, of course, the θ is adjusted to $218 + (-12) = 206$.

Our second example illustrates a minimizing linear programming problem with penalties or premiums; it is simply a modification of the previous example.

Example. Suppose in the preceding example that instead of **maximizing the profit** the supervisor of the machine shop of the company wished to **minimize the cost of operation.** Suppose also that the cost of operating Machine A is $15 per hour and Machine B is $10 per hour. Suppose finally that the supervisor places an **opportunity cost** (i.e., cost due to lost opportunities) on the slack time for each machine because of the special nature of the respective machines and the skill of

---

[6] An alternate method is to introduce an additional variable x_4 with a coefficient of -12 in the objective function ($-12x_4$) and an additional constraint requiring the variable to be 1 ($x_4 = 1$).

TABLE 4–18B
Preliminary Tableau

Basic Variables	Coefficient of					Current Values
	x_1	x_2	x_3	s_1	s_2	
s_1	2	2	1	1	0	36
s_2	1	3	2	0	1	30
(max) θ	-9	-12	-10	2	-2	0

Working Rows for θ

	x_1	x_2	x_3	s_1	s_2	
$(-2) \cdot (s_1\text{-row})$	-4	-4	-2	-2	0	-72
$(2) \cdot (s_2\text{-row})$	2	6	4	0	2	60

Initial Tableau

Basic Variables	Coefficient of					Current Values	
	x_1	x_2	x_3	s_1	s_2		
s_1	[2]	2	1	1	0	[36]	18 →
s_2	[1]	3	2	0	1	[30]	30
(max) θ	-11	-10	-8	0	0	-12	

↑

Second Tableau

Basic Variables	Coefficient of					Current Values	
	x_1	x_2	x_3	s_1	s_2		
x_1	1	1	[1/2]	1/2	0	[18]	36
s_2	0	2	[3/2]	$-1/2$	1	[12]	8 →
(max) θ	0	1	$-5/2$	11/2	0	186	

↑

Third Tableau

Basic Variables	Coefficient of					Current Values
	x_1	x_2	x_3	s_1	s_2	
x_1	1	1/3	0	2/3	$-1/3$	14
x_3	0	4/3	1	$-1/3$	2/3	8
(max) θ	0	13/3	0	14/3	5/3	206

the corresponding operators. In particular, the supervisor feels that each slack hour on Machine A gives rise to an opportunity cost of $12 while each slack hour on Machine B creates an opportunity cost of $14 (the latter machine being an uncommon and rather expensive device that, in addition, requires a skilled operator). Now find

TABLE 4-19

```
$ lindo
LINDO (7 OCTOBER 88 CHICAGO)
: max 11x1 + 10x2 + 8x3
?st
?2x1 + 2x2 + x3 <= 36
?x1 + 3x2 + 2x3 <= 30
?end

: go
LP OPTIMUM FOUND AT STEP        2

        OBJECTIVE FUNCTION VALUE
    1)      218.000000

    VARIABLE        VALUE           REDUCED COST
      X1           14.000000         0.000000
      X2            0.000000         4.333333
      X3            8.000000         0.000000

      ROW      SLACK OR SURPLUS      DUAL PRICES
      2)            0.000000         4.666667
      3)            0.000000         1.666667

NO. ITERATIONS=       2

DO RANGE (SENSITIVITY) ANALYSIS?
?no
: quit
FORTRAN STOP
$ lo
```

how many of each window model the supervisor recommends be made in the coming week in order to minimize the cost of operation. What is this minimum cost?

The constraints for this problem are clearly the same as those for the previous problem; namely,

$$\text{Machine A:} \quad 2x_1 + 2x_2 + x_3 \leq 36 \quad (1)$$
$$\text{Machine B:} \quad x_1 + 3x_2 + 2x_3 \leq 30 \quad (2)$$
$$\text{Nonnegativity:} \quad x_1, x_2, x_3 \geq 0 \quad (3),(4),(5)$$

so that we still need the two slack variables s_1 and s_2. The objective function, this time, is given by

$$\theta = 15(2x_1 + 2x_2 + x_3) + 10(x_1 + 3x_2 + 2x_3) + 12s_1 + 14s_2.$$

Opportunity costs result in penalties on the objective function.

In this equation, the coefficients 15 and 10 are the respective costs per hour on Machines A and B, the parenthetical expressions are the respective hours required

TABLE 4-20

Preliminary Tableau

Basic Variables	Coefficient of					Current Values
	x_1	x_2	x_3	s_1	s_2	
s_1	2	2	1	1	0	36
s_2	1	3	2	0	1	30
(min) θ	−40	−60	−35	−12	−14	0

Initial Tableau

Basic Variables	Coefficient of					Current Values	
	x_1	x_2	x_3	s_1	s_2		
s_1	2	|2|	1	1	0	|36|	18
s_2	1	|3|	2	0	1	|30|	10 →
(min) θ	−2	6	5	0	0	852	

↑

Second Tableau

Basic Variables	Coefficient of					Current Values	
	x_1	x_2	x_3	s_1	s_2		
s_1	4/3	0	|−1/3|	1	−2/3	|16|	−48
x_2	1/3	1	|2/3|	0	1/3	|10|	15 →
(min) θ	−4	0	1	0	−2	792	

↑

Third Tableau

Basic Variables	Coefficient of					Current Values
	x_1	x_2	x_3	s_1	s_2	
s_1	3/2	1/2	0	1	−1/2	21
x_3	1/2	3/2	1	0	1/2	15
(min) θ	−9/2	−3/2	0	0	−5/2	777

on each machine, as can be seen from constraints (1) and (2), and the coefficients 12 and 14 are the respective opportunity costs per slack hour on each machine. Simplifying the preceding expression, we have

$$\theta = 40x_1 + 60x_2 + 35x_3 + 12s_1 + 14s_2.$$

This time the simplex tableaus are as shown in Table 4–20. From the Third Tableau in this table, we see that the optimal solution is

$$x_1 = x_2 = 0, x_3 = 15, s_1 = 21, s_2 = 0, \text{ and } \theta = 777$$

for a profit of $777 when 15 Model E windows are made. Note that since $s_1 = 21$, there is an opportunity cost of $(12) \cdot (21) = \$252$ associated with the optimal solution.

Exercise. What is the value of θ in the Initial Tableau? Why?

Answer: $\theta = 852$. This represents a cost of (\$12/hour of A) $\cdot$ ($s_1 = 36$ hours) + (\$14/hour of B) $\cdot$ ($s_2 = 30$ hours) = \$852.

Exercise. What would be the format to run LINDO for Example 2? How would the value of θ have to be adjusted?

Answer:
```
min 2x1 - 6x2 - 5x3
st
    2x1 + 2x2 +  x3 <= 36
     x1 + 3x2 + 2x3 <= 30
end
go
```

Add 852 to the value of θ.

4.10 MINIMIZATION BY MAXIMIZING THE DUAL

Our discussion to this point has involved only problems with $\leq$ constraints. In this section, we will learn how to change a minimization problem with $\geq$ constraints into a maximization problem with $\leq$ constraints, so that the solution method already developed can be applied to either problem. Thus we shall solve a **less than or equal to max or min** by the methods already shown, but change a **greater than or equal to min** to a **less than or equal to max** and then solve by the methods already shown. Later on, we shall develop a method to solve problems with mixes of $\leq$ and $\geq$ constraints and/or equality constraints.

The original **greater than or equal to min** will be called the **primal problem**. The **less than or equal to max** to which we change will be called the **dual problem**. We illustrate how the primal is converted to the dual, and then solve the dual problem and give the necessary rules for reading the solution of the primal from the solution of the dual.

The dual of a minimizing problem with all $\geq$ constraints is a maximizing problem with all $\leq$ constraints.

Example. Let us return to the Pure Gasoline Company example of Section 3.6 which was to

minimize
$$\theta = 1{,}500x_1 + 2{,}400x_2$$
subject to
$$i_1: \quad 4x_1 + x_2 \geq 24$$
$$i_2: \quad 2x_1 + 3x_2 \geq 42$$
$$i_3: \quad x_1 + 4x_2 \geq 36$$
$$i_4, i_5: \quad x_1, x_2 \geq 0.$$

First, observe in i_1, if $4x_1 + x_2$ is, say 27, the inequality is satisfied because **27 is 3 more than 24**; that is, there is a **surplus of 3 units.** Hence, to convert i_1, i_2, and i_3 to equalities, **positive variables would be subtracted,** and these are called **surplus variables** rather than slack variables. We denote the surplus variables here by p_1, p_2, and p_3, and indicate them next to their respective constraints. We also rewrite the primal for ease of manipulation with the nonnegativity constraints first and the objective function last, as follows:

> Surplus variables are subtracted from $\geq$ constraints, transforming them into equalities.

Primal

$$x_1, x_2 \geq 0$$
$$p_1: \quad 4x_1 + x_2 \geq 24$$
$$p_2: \quad 2x_1 + 3x_2 \geq 42$$
$$p_3: \quad x_1 + 4x_2 \geq 36$$
$$\text{Minimize:} \quad 1{,}500x_1 + 2{,}400x_2 = \theta.$$

To formulate the **dual problem,** which is a maximization problem with $\leq$ constraints, we look at the x_1-column in the primal, make 4 the coefficient of the new variable p_1, make 2 the coefficient of the new variable p_2, and make 1 the coefficient of the new variable p_3 to obtain

$$4p_1 + 2p_2 + p_3.$$

Next change $\geq$ to $\leq$, use the coefficient 1,500 of x_1 in θ as the right-hand-side constant, and write

$$4p_1 + 2p_2 + p_3 \leq 1{,}500.$$

Now repeat the process with the x_1-column to get

$$p_1 + 3p_2 + 4p_3 \leq 2{,}400.$$

Finally, the new objective function is formed in a similar manner from the right-hand-side column of constants; namely,

$$24p_1 + 42p_2 + 36p_3 = \theta.$$

> The direction of the constraints in the dual is the opposite of those in the primal. The dual right-hand-side limits come from the primal objective function coefficients. The coefficient rows of the dual constraints are the columns of the primal.

> The coefficients of the objective function in the dual are the right-hand-side limits of the primal.

The dual problem is thus

maximize
$$\theta = 24p_1 + 42p_2 + 36p_3$$

subject to

$$x_1: \quad 4p_1 + 2p_2 + p_3 \leq 1{,}500$$
$$x_2: \quad p_1 + 3p_2 + 4p_3 \leq 2{,}400$$
$$p_1, p_2, p_3 \geq 0.$$

Note that the dual is a **less than or equal to max problem and has x_1 and x_2 as slack variables,** as indicated at the left of the first two inequalities.

Exercise. a) Construct the dual of the following, using p_1 and p_2 as surplus variables: Minimize $\theta = 4x_1 + 3x_2$ subject to $2x_1 + x_2 \geq 10$; $x_1 + 5x_2 \geq 20$; $x_1, x_2 \geq 0$.
b) What are the slack variables in the dual?

Answer: a) Maximize $\theta = 10p_1 + 20p_2$ subject to $2p_1 + p_2 \leq 4$; $p_1 + 5p_2 \leq 3$; $p_1, p_2 \geq 0$.
b) x_1 and x_2.

We have formed the dual of a primal **greater than or equal to min** problem because the dual is a **less than or equal to max** problem that can be solved by the Simplex Method we have already developed. We should mention, however, that a **greater than or equal to max** can be considered the primal, in which case the dual is a **less than or equal to min** and it is clear that whichever problem is the primal, the dual of the dual is the original problem itself. In any event, the **dual theorem** proves that all of the information contained in the solution of the primal (dual) is present in the solution of the dual (primal). The development of the Dual Theorem is outside the scope of this text, so we will state without proof the part of the theorem that we want to use.

The Dual Theorem states that the optimal values of the primal and dual are the same.

If a minimization problem with $\geq$ constraints has an optimum (minimum) value, this value equals the maximum of the dual problem.

Thus to solve a primal **greater than or equal to min,** we set up the dual and find its maximum in the usual manner. The Dual Theorem then assures us that this maximum of the dual is the minimum of the primal.

Returning to our Pure Gasoline Company example, we solve the dual by the Simplex Method in the usual manner as shown in Table 4–21. From the Third Tableau of this table, we have for the **dual,**

$$\theta_{max} = 32{,}400.$$

TABLE 4-21

Initial Tableau

Basic Variables	Coefficient of					Current Values	
	p_1	p_2	p_3	x_1	x_2		
x_1	4	[2]	1	1	0	1,500	750 →
x_2	1	[3]	4	0	1	2,400	800
(max) θ	−24	−42	−36	0	0	0	

↑

Second Tableau

Basic Variables	Coefficient of					Current Values	
	p_1	p_2	p_3	x_1	x_2		
p_2	2	1	[1/2]	1/2	0	750	1,500
x_2	−5	0	[5/2]	−3/2	1	150	60 →
(max) θ	60	0	−15	21	0	31,500	

↑

Third Tableau

Basic Variables	Coefficient of					Current Values
	p_1	p_2	p_3	x_1	x_2	
p_2	3	1	0	4/5	−1/5	720
p_3	−2	0	1	−3/5	2/5	60
(max) θ	30	0	0	12	6	32,400

The Dual Theorem states that the minimum of the primal must equal the maximum of the dual, so for the **primal**

$$\theta_{min} = 32,400.$$

The values for x_1 and x_2 at the minimum can also be obtained from the solution of the dual by the following rules:

> To obtain the values of the variables in the solution of the primal, set the basic variables of the optimal dual tableau equal to zero and set the values of the nonbasic variables equal to the number under their respective columns in the θ-row. The nonbasic variables in the dual are the basic variables in the primal.

Applying these rules, we see from the Third Tableau of Table 4–21 that

$$p_2 = p_3 = 0, \quad p_1 = 30, \quad x_1 = 12, \quad \text{and} \quad x_2 = 6$$

which is the same result as in Section 3.6; namely, the company should operate Refinery A for 12 days and Refinery B for 6 days with an associated minimum cost of \$32,400. In addition, the fact that $p_1 = 30$ means there is a surplus of 30 thousand gallons of Super Unleaded gasoline. Of course, there is no surplus of Regular Unleaded gasoline or Diesel fuel since $p_2 = p_3 = 0$.

Now the LINDO printout for the solution of the dual problem is shown in Table 4–22. Note that the REDUCED COST and DUAL PRICES columns correspond precisely to the θ-row of the Third (and final) Tableau of Table 4–21. Thus the optimal solution to the primal problem can be read directly from these columns.

In Section 3.9, we stated a minimization problem in 3 variables and proceeded to solve it by the laborious method of finding all 10 intersections, eliminating 6 vertices as infeasible, then determining the optimum from the remaining 4 basic

Using the Dual Theorem can simplify the solution of certain minimization problems.

TABLE 4–22

```
$ lindo
LINDO (7 OCTOBER 88 CHICAGO)
: max 24p1 + 42p2 + 36p3
? st
? 4p1 + 2p2 + p3 <= 1500
? p1 + 3p2 + 4p3 <= 2400
? end

: go
LP OPTIMUM FOUND AT STEP         2

         OBJECTIVE FUNCTION VALUE
    1)       32400.0000

     VARIABLE         VALUE          REDUCED COST
         P1         0.000000           30.000000
         P2       720.000000            0.000000
         P3        60.000000            0.000000

       ROW     SLACK OR SURPLUS     DUAL PRICES
        2)         0.000000           12.000000
        3)         0.000000            6.000000

 NO. ITERATIONS=        2

DO RANGE (SENSITIVITY) ANALYSIS?
? no
: quit
FORTRAN STOP
$ lo
```

CHAPTER 4   ADDITIONAL TOPICS IN LINEAR PROGRAMMING

feasible solutions. We shall now illustrate how to solve such a problem by maximizing the dual.

Example.   Three variables. A diet is to contain at least 10 ounces of Nutrient R, 12 ounces of Nutrient S, and 20 ounces of Nutrient T. These nutrients are to be obtained by some combination of foods A, B, and C. Each pound of A costs 4 cents and has 4 ounces of R, 3 of S, and no T. Each pound of B costs 7 cents and has 1 ounce of R, 2 of S, and 4 of T. Each pound of C costs 5 cents and has no R, 1 ounce of S, and 5 of T. How many pounds of A, B, and C should be combined to provide the required amount of nutrient at minimum cost?

Letting x_1, x_2, and x_3 represent, respectively, the number of pounds of A, B, and C, the data of the problem lead to the following:

Minimize
$$\theta = 4x_1 + 7x_2 + 5x_3$$
subject to

$$\begin{aligned}
p_1: \quad & 4x_1 + x_2 && \geq 10 \quad \text{(Nutrient R constraint)} \\
p_2: \quad & 3x_1 + 2x_2 + x_3 && \geq 12 \quad \text{(Nutrient S constraint)} \\
p_3: \quad & \phantom{3x_1 + {}} 4x_2 + 5x_3 && \geq 20 \quad \text{(Nutrient T constraint)} \\
& x_1, x_2, x_3 \geq 0,
\end{aligned}$$

where p_1, p_2, and p_3 are surplus variables in the primal, and x_1, x_2, and x_3 will become slack variables in the dual.

We first write the dual as follows:

Maximize
$$\theta = 10p_1 + 12p_2 + 20p_3$$
subject to

$$\begin{aligned}
x_1: \quad & 4p_1 + 3p_2 && \leq 4 \\
x_2: \quad & p_1 + 2p_2 + 4p_3 && \leq 7 \\
x_3: \quad & \phantom{p_1 + {}} p_2 + 5p_3 && \leq 5 \\
& p_1, p_2, p_3 \geq 0.
\end{aligned}$$

Introducing x_1, x_2, and x_3 as slacks, we change the constraints and the θ-equation to

$$\begin{aligned}
4p_1 + 3p_2 + 0 + x_1 + 0 + 0 &= 4 \\
p_1 + 2p_2 + 4p_3 + 0 + x_2 + 0 &= 7 \\
0 + p_2 + 5p_3 + 0 + 0 + x_3 &= 5 \\
\theta - 10p_1 - 12p_2 - 20p_3 + 0 + 0 + 0 &= 0.
\end{aligned}$$

Using the Simplex Method, we get the results shown in Table 4–23.

TABLE 4-23
Initial Tableau

Basic Variables	Coefficient of						Current Values	
	p_1	p_2	p_3	x_1	x_2	x_3		
x_1	4	3	[0]	1	0	0	[4]	∞
x_2	1	2	[4]	0	1	0	[7]	7/4
x_3	0	1	[5]	0	0	1	[5]	1 →
(max) θ	−10	−12	−20	0	0	0	0	

↑

Second Tableau

Basic Variables	Coefficient of						Current Values	
	p_1	p_2	p_3	x_1	x_2	x_3		
x_1	[4]	3	0	1	0	0	[4]	1 →
x_2	[1]	6/5	0	0	1	−4/5	[3]	3
p_3	[0]	1/5	1	0	0	1/5	[1]	∞
(max) θ	−10	−8	0	0	0	4	20	

↑

Third Tableau

Basic Variables	Coefficient of						Current Values	
	p_1	p_2	p_3	x_1	x_2	x_3		
p_1	1	[3/4]	0	1/4	0	0	[1]	4/3 →
x_2	0	[9/20]	0	−1/4	1	−4/5	[2]	40/9
p_3	0	[1/5]	1	0	0	1/5	[1]	5
(max) θ	0	−1/2	0	5/2	0	4	30	

↑

Fourth Tableau

Basic Variables	Coefficient of						Current Values
	p_1	p_2	p_3	x_1	x_2	x_3	
p_2	4/3	1	0	1/3	0	0	4/3
x_2	−3/5	0	0	−2/5	1	−4/5	7/5
p_3	−4/15	0	1	−1/15	0	1/5	11/15
(max) θ	2/3	0	0	8/3	0	4	92/3

Following the rules for writing the minimum of the primal from the last tableau (which provides the maximum of the dual), we have for the minimum cost of the mixture,

$$\theta_{min} = 92/3 \text{ cents;}$$

and for the contents of the minimum-cost mixture,

$$x_1 = 8/3 \text{ pounds of Food A}$$
$$x_2 = 0 \text{ pounds of Food B}$$
$$x_3 = 4 \text{ pounds of Food C.}$$

Exercise. What are the values of p_1, p_2, and p_3 in the optimal solution? What do these values mean?

Answer: $p_1 = 2/3, p_2 = p_3 = 0$. There is a surplus of 2/3 ounce of Nutrient R, but no surplus of either Nutrient S or Nutrient T.

From this example, we can see the superiority of the Simplex Method to the algebraic method of Section 3.7. Indeed, the method of Section 3.7 is an unthinkable procedure to apply to problems with numerous variables and constraints. The Simplex Method is a general procedure that can solve any linear programming problem efficiently. It is true, of course, that an extensive amount of arithmetic has to be done in applying the Simplex Method to large problems, but, as we have seen, computer packages exist that handle the computations.

The Simplex Method can solve any linear programming problem efficiently.

Exercise. What would be the format to run LINDO for the previous example?

Answer:
```
max 10p1 + 12p2 + 20p3
st
4p1 + 3p2        <=  4
 p1 + 2p2 + 4p3  <=  7
      p2  + 5p3  <=  5
end
go
```

4.11 PROBLEM SET 4–3

1. a) Suppose in Example 1 of Section 4.9 that the storm windows had to be processed on a third Machine C as follows: Each Model H window and each Model R window require one hour on C; each Model E window requires two hours on C. Suppose also that during the coming week

4.11 PROBLEM SET 4-3 (continued)

Machine C will be available for at most 24 hours. Now find the number of each window the company should make in the coming week in order to maximize its profit, assuming no penalties or premiums for any unused time. What is this maximum profit?

b) Resolve (a) if, this time, any unused time on Machine A creates an expense of $1 per hour allocated for idle time for an operator, while any unused time on Machines B and C can be rented to other firms at a rate of $1 per hour.

c) Resolve (a) if, this time, the company wished to minimize its cost of operation where the cost of operating Machine A is $15 per hour, Machine B is $10 per hour, and Machine C is $9 per hour; while each slack hour on A creates an opportunity cost of $16, each slack hour on B creates an opportunity cost of $11, and each slack hour on C creates an opportunity cost of $8.

2. Ace Rubber Company makes two types of tires: Model P (the premium) and Model S (the second line). Each tire must be processed on three machines: A, B, and C. To make one Model P tire requires one hour on Machines A and B and two hours on Machine C. To make one Model S tire requires one hour on Machines A and C and two hours on Machine B. Production scheduling indicates that during the coming week Machine A will be free for at most 13 hours, Machine B for at most 22 hours, and Machine C for at most 20 hours. In addition, no more than eight Model S tires may be made.

a) If the company makes a $25 profit on each Model P tire and a $30 profit on each Model S tire, find the number of each kind of tire to be made in the coming week in order to maximize the profit. What is this maximum profit?

b) Resolve (a) if, this time, any unused time on Machine A creates an expense of $1 per hour allocated for idle time for an operator, while any unused time on Machines B and C can be rented to another firm at a rate of $3 per hour.

c) Resolve (a) if, this time, the company wishes to minimize its cost of operation where the cost of operating Machine A is $8 per hour, Machine B is $6 per hour, and Machine C is $9 per hour; while each slack hour on A creates an opportunity cost of $6, each slack hour on Machine B creates an opportunity cost of $10, and each slack hour on Machine C creates an opportunity cost of $7.

Convert each of the primal problems into its dual and write the **first** tableau for the dual. It is not necessary to carry out iterations. All variables are assumed to be nonnegative.

3. Given $\theta = 5x_1 + 3x_2$, find θ_{min} subject to

$$4x_1 + 2x_2 \geq 20$$
$$6x_1 + x_2 \geq 10.$$

4. Given $\theta = 4x_1 + 2x_2$, find θ_{min} subject to

$$3x_1 + 2x_2 \geq 10$$
$$x_1 + 2x_2 \geq 20.$$

5. Given $\theta = x_1 + x_2 + x_3$, find θ_{min} subject to

$$3x_1 + 3x_2 + x_3 \geq 2$$
$$2x_1 + x_2 \geq 4$$
$$4x_1 + 2x_2 + 2x_3 \geq 6.$$

6. Given $\theta = 2x_1 + 3x_2 + x_3$, find θ_{min} subject to

$$x_1 + x_2 + x_3 \geq 10$$
$$2x_1 + 3x_2 + x_3 \geq 15$$
$$3x_1 + x_2 + 2x_3 \geq 20.$$

Find the minimum value of θ by maximizing the dual, assuming all variables are nonnegative.

7. $\theta = 3x_1 + 2x_2$
subject to

$$4x_1 + 3x_2 \geq 24$$
$$x_1 + 2x_2 \geq 11.$$

8. $\theta = 5x_1 + 4x_2$
subject to

$$3x_1 + 2x_2 \geq 24$$
$$x_1 + x_2 \geq 9.$$

4.11 PROBLEM SET 4-3 (concluded)

9. $\theta = x_1 + x_2 + 3x_3$
   subject to
   $$x_1 + 2x_2 + 3x_3 \geq 1{,}200$$
   $$2x_1 + x_2 + x_3 \geq 600.$$

10. $\theta = 18x_1 + 30x_2 + 4x_3$
    subject to
    $$x_1 + 2x_2 - x_3 \geq 2$$
    $$2x_1 + 3x_2 + 8x_3 \geq 6.$$

11. A special food for athletes is to be developed from two foods: Food R and Food S. The new food is to be designed so that it contains at least 16 milligrams of Vitamin A, at least 20 milligrams of Vitamin B, and at least 12 milligrams of Vitamin C. Each pound of Food R costs $1.50 and contains 1 milligram of Vitamin A, 5 milligrams of Vitamin B, and 1 milligram of Vitamin C. Each pound of Food S costs $2.50 and contains 2 milligrams of A, 1 milligram of B, and 1 milligram of C. How many pounds of each food should be used in the mixture in order to meet these requirements at a minimum cost? What is this minimum cost?

12. Strong Steel Company operates two steel mills with different production capacities. Mill I can produce 1,000 tons per day of AAA steel, 3,000 tons per day of AA steel, and 5,000 tons per day of A steel. Mill F can produce 2,000 tons per day of each grade of steel. The company has made a contract with a construction firm to provide 24,000 tons of AAA steel, 32,000 tons of AA steel, and 40,000 tons of A steel. Determine the number of days the company should operate each mill in order to meet the terms of the contract most economically, the minimum cost, and also what grade(s) of steel would be overproduced, if the cost of running Mill I is $1,400 per day and Mill F is $1,000 per day.

13. A special food for athletes is to be developed from three foods: Food R, Food S, and Food T. The new food is to contain at least 66 milligrams of Vitamin A, at least 48 milligrams of Vitamin B, and at least 40 milligrams of Vitamin C. Each pound of Food R costs $1.50 and contains 2 milligrams of Vitamin A, 4 milligrams of Vitamin B, and 1 milligram of Vitamin C. Each pound of Food S costs $2.50 and contains 9 milligrams of Vitamin A, 3 milligrams of Vitamin B, and 4 milligrams of Vitamin C. Each pound of Food T costs $2.00 and contains 7 milligrams of A, 2 milligrams of B, and 8 milligrams of C. How many pounds of each food should be used in the mixture in order to meet the requirements at a minimum cost? What is this minimum cost?

14. Strong Steel Company operates three steel mills with different production capacities. Mill I can produce 1,000 tons per day of AAA steel, 3,000 tons per day of AA steel, and 10,000 tons per day of A steel. Mill F can produce 2,000 tons per day of AAA steel, 2,000 tons per day of AA steel, and 4,000 tons per day of A steel. Mill S can produce 4,000, 1,000, and 3,000 tons per day, respectively. The company has made a contract with a construction firm to provide 29,000 tons of AAA steel, 23,000 tons of AA steel, and 62,000 tons of A steel. If it costs $1,400 per day to run Mill I, $1,000 per day to run Mill F, and $1,200 per day to run Mill S, determine the number of days the company should operate each mill in order to meet the terms of the contract most economically. What is this minimum cost?

4.12 THE PHASE I– PHASE II METHOD

In Section 4.10 we saw how to solve a **minimization problem with all $\geq$ constraints** by transforming the problem into its dual, a **maximization problem with all $\leq$ constraints** (other than nonnegativity). This technique, as we noted, will not work if the problem has a **mix of $\geq$ and $\leq$ constraints and/or equality constraints.**

In this section, we develop the general technique used to handle $\geq$ and $=$ constraints.

Let us return once again to the Pure Gasoline Company example:

Minimize
$$\theta = 1{,}500x_1 + 2{,}400x_2$$

subject to

Super Unleaded:	$4x_1 + x_2 \geq 24$	(1)
Regular Unleaded:	$2x_1 + 3x_2 \geq 42$	(2)
Diesel Fuel:	$x_1 + 4x_2 \geq 36$	(3)
Nonnegativity:	$x_1, x_2 \geq 0.$	(4),(5)

Now the preceding constraints give rise to the feasible solution set shown in Figure 4–5. As can be seen from this figure, the feasible solution set consists of the four extreme points (0, 24) from boundary lines (1) and (4), (3, 12) from boundary lines (1) and (2), (12, 6) from boundary lines (2) and (3), and (36, 0) from boundary lines (3) and (5).

The Simplex Method selects the path indicated by the best unit gain, so it does not always take the shortest path to the optimum.

We will see that the Simplex Method will start at the point of intersection at the origin (0, 0), will then proceed along the x_2-axis to the point of intersection at (0, 9) of Figure 4–5, next along boundary line (3) to the point of intersection at (4, 8), after this along boundary line (1) to the point of intersection (extreme point) at (3, 12), and finally along boundary line (2) to the point of intersection (extreme

FIGURE 4–5

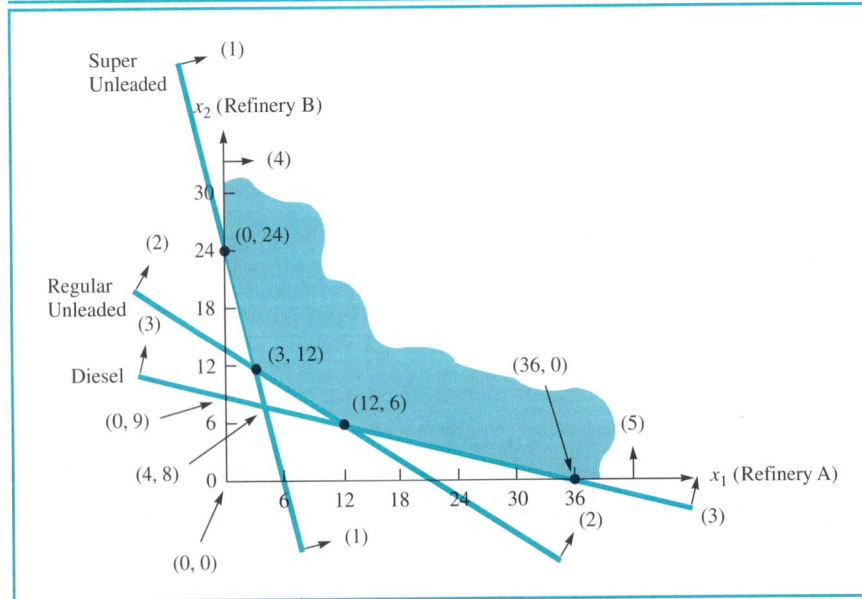

point) at (12, 6). We wish to point out that the Simplex Method does not proceed directly from the point of intersection at (4, 8) along boundary line (3) to the final solution at (12, 6), as we might expect. The reason for this is that the Simplex Method **selects the best unit gain at each step and so it does not always take the shortest possible path to the optimum.** In solving this problem, then, the Simplex Method will examine five points of intersection before finding the optimum; and furthermore, the first three solution points are nonfeasible, whereas the last two are feasible (extreme).

> **Exercise.** In Figure 4–5, how many points of intersection (feasible and nonfeasible) are there?
>
> **Answer:** 10.

As in Section 4–10, we convert the $\geq$ constraints, other than nonnegativity, into equalities by introducing a surplus variable to take up the surplus or excess gallons of each grade of gasoline:

p_S = surplus variable (excess in 1,000 gallons) of Super Unleaded,

p_R = surplus variable (excess in 1,000 gallons) of Regular Unleaded,

p_D = surplus variable (excess in 1,000 gallons) of Diesel.

Thus constraints (1), (2), and (3) become

$$4x_1 + x_2 - p_S + 0 + 0 = 24 \qquad (1')$$

$$2x_1 + 3x_2 + 0 - p_R + 0 = 42 \qquad (2')$$

$$x_1 + 4x_2 + 0 + 0 - p_D = 36. \qquad (3')$$

Now, to choose an initial solution from equations (1'), (2'), and (3') corresponding to the origin, we have to choose $x_1 = x_2 = 0$ so that

$$p_S = -24, \; p_R = -42, \text{ and } \; p_D = -36.$$

These three values are obviously impossible since negative values are not allowed for the variables used in the Simplex Method. **Therefore, for each surplus variable we now add an associated artificial variable that will allow us to circumvent the problem of negative values.** In particular, we respectively add the artificial variables a_S, a_R, and a_D to equations (1'), (2'), and (3') to get

Artificial variables are added to $\geq$ constraints to generate a starting solution.

$$4x_1 + x_2 - p_S + 0 + 0 + a_S + 0 + 0 = 24 \qquad (1'')$$

$$2x_1 + 3x_2 + 0 - p_R + 0 + 0 + a_R + 0 = 42 \qquad (2'')$$

$$x_1 + 4x_2 + 0 + 0 - p_D + 0 + 0 + a_D = 36, \qquad (3'')$$

so that we now have a system of three equations in eight unknowns.

In the initial solution, surplus variables are zero while artificial variables are nonzero.

To see how the artificial variables allow us to circumvent the negative surpluses, let us reconsider the origin where $x_1 = x_2 = 0$. At this point, we operate both Refineries A and B zero days, so that no fuel is produced and hence, we have no surpluses; that is,

$$p_S = p_R = p_D = 0.$$

This, in turn, means from equations (1″), (2″), and (3″) that

$$a_S = 24, \quad a_R = 42, \quad \text{and} \quad a_D = 36;$$

that is, we have (positive) **shortages** (in terms of meeting the contract) of 24,000 gallons of Super Unleaded gasoline, 42,000 gallons of Regular Unleaded gasoline, and 36,000 gallons of Diesel fuel.

Either surplus and artificial variables are both zero together, or one is zero while the other is positive.

> **Exercise.** Using Figure 4–5, verify the following three facts for constraining lines (1), (2), and (3):
>
> 1. Below each constraining line, the corresponding surplus variable is zero while the artificial variable is greater than zero; there is no surplus, but there is a shortage.
> 2. On each constraining line, both the corresponding surplus variable and artificial variable are zero; that is, there is no surplus and no shortage.
> 3. Above each constraining line, the corresponding surplus variable is greater than zero but the artificial variable is zero; that is, there is a surplus so there is, of course, no shortage.

Now that we have introduced the surplus and artificial variables, we must redefine our objective function,

$$\theta = 1{,}500x_1 + 2{,}400x_2,$$

in terms of all eight variables x_1, x_2, p_S, p_R, p_D, a_S, a_R, and a_D rather than in terms of simply x_1 and x_2. The surplus variables p_S, p_R, and p_D represent the numbers of excess gallons of Super Unleaded gasoline, Regular Unleaded gasoline, and Diesel fuel, respectively. Thus they clearly do not contribute anything directly to the cost function being minimized. Therefore, as with slack variables in Chapter 4, we assign a coefficient of zero to p_S, p_R, and p_D in the objective function. So our objective function now becomes

$$\theta = 1{,}500x_1 + 2{,}400x_2 + 0p_S + 0p_R + 0p_D. \tag{6}$$

Artificial variables must be driven out of the solution since they represent shortages.

Of course, just as with slack variables, there are cases where there is a penalty or premium associated with surplus variables. In these situations, as will be seen in the problems, the coefficients would not be zero.

Now what about the artificial variables a_S, a_R, and a_D? As we saw already, these variables represent shortages of each respective fuel, so we would like to literally

drive them out of the solution. One way to do this is to **define an additional objective function**

$$W = a_S + a_R + a_D \tag{7}$$

and then **minimize W all the way down to zero.** This will then force

$$a_S = a_R = a_D = 0$$

since all the variables are nonnegative.

Using this analysis, we can break our minimizing problem into **two phases** for (6) and (7) as follows:

Phase I: Minimize W to zero.
Phase II: Minimize θ.

Of course, if we cannot complete Phase I then we terminate the procedure since, as we will see in Section 4.14, there will be no solution to the problem.

This two-phase procedure is begun as shown in the Preliminary Tableau of Table 4–24A. Note that this tableau represents the system (1″), (2″), and (3″) of three equations in eight unknowns. Note also that the θ-row and the W-row represent (6) and (7), expanded to include all eight variables.

Now Phase I consists of minimizing the W-row while including the θ-row in all the calculations. After Phase I is completed, Phase II consists of subsequently omitting the W-row and also the artificial variable columns from the tableaus, and then proceeding to minimize the θ-row as it appears at that stage. We wish to point out, as will be seen shortly, that since the θ-row itself is included in all the calculations of Phase I and since it is in the proper form for the initial basis, then it will necessarily be expressed in terms of the proper basis for the start of Phase II.

To start Phase I of the solution, then, we first examine the W-row of Table 4–24A. We can see immediately that this tableau is **not in the proper form for W.** Why?

> The Phase I–Phase II Method minimizes the artificial-variable row and simultaneously optimizes the objective function row.

TABLE 4–24A Preliminary Tableau

Basic Variables	Coefficient of								Current Values
	x_1	x_2	p_S	p_R	p_D	a_S	a_R	a_D	
a_S	4	1	−1	0	0	1	0	0	24
a_R	2	3	0	−1	0	0	1	0	42
a_D	1	4	0	0	−1	0	0	1	36
(min) θ	−1,500	−2,400	0	0	0	0	0	0	0
(min) W	0	0	0	0	0	−1	−1	−1	0

> **Exercise.** How would the W-row be transformed into the proper form?
> **Answer:** Add 1 · (a_S-row) plus 1 · (a_R-row) plus 1 · (a_D-row) to the W-row.

The transformation of the W-row into proper form is shown in Table 4–24B. Note that, for ease in understanding, we have included the Working Rows for W in an intermediate tableau.

At this point, we minimize W in the usual manner. Therefore, we now examine the new W-row of Table 4–24B for positive entries. The coefficient 8 for x_2 is the most positive entry in the new W-row; and hence, as shown in the Initial Tableau of Table 4–25, x_2 enters the basis first. Next computing the ratios, we see that the smallest nonnegative ratio is the 9 for a_D, so that a_D now leaves the basis. Performing the change of basis in the usual way, we get the Second Tableau shown in Table 4–25. Note that, once more for ease in understanding, we have included the Working Tableau. Note also that the θ-row is included in the process.

Continuing with Phase I, we then see from the Second Tableau of Table 4–25 that x_1 enters next while a_S leaves. The result of this change of basis is as shown in the Third Tableau of Table 4–25.

Working Tableaus can be helpful in performing changes of basis.

TABLE 4–24B Preliminary Tableau

Basic Variables	Coefficient of								Current Values
	x_1	x_2	p_S	p_R	p_D	a_S	a_R	a_D	
a_S	4	1	−1	0	0	1	0	0	24
a_R	2	3	0	−1	0	0	1	0	42
a_D	1	4	0	0	−1	0	0	1	36
(min) θ	−1,500	−2,400	0	0	0	0	0	0	0
(min) W	0	0	0	0	0	−1	−1	−1	0

Working Rows for W

	x_1	x_2	p_S	p_R	p_D	a_S	a_R	a_D	
1 · (a_S-row)	4	1	−1	0	0	1	0	0	24
1 · (a_R-row)	2	3	0	−1	0	0	1	0	42
1 · (a_D-row)	1	4	0	0	−1	0	0	1	36

New W-Row

	x_1	x_2	p_S	p_R	p_D	a_S	a_R	a_D	
(min) W	7	8	−1	−1	−1	0	0	0	102

Again continuing with Phase I, we see from the Third Tableau of Table 4–25 that we should introduce p_D into the basis, while a_R should leave. Performing this change of basis in the usual manner, we get the Fourth Tableau shown in Table 4–25.

Once more continuing with Phase I, we see from the W-row of the Fourth Tableau of Table 4–25 that we are done with Phase I since there are no positive entries.

TABLE 4–25

Preliminary Tableau

Basic Variables	Coefficient of								Current Values	
	x_1	x_2	p_S	p_R	p_D	a_S	a_R	a_D		
a_S	4	[1]	−1	0	0	1	0	0	[24]	24
a_R	2	[3]	0	−1	0	0	1	0	[42]	14
a_D	1	[4]	0	0	−1	0	0	1	[36]	9 →
(min) θ	−1,500	−2,400	0	0	0	0	0	0	0	
(min) W	7	8	−1	−1	−1	0	0	0	102	

Working Tableau

	x_1	x_2	p_S	p_R	p_D	a_S	a_R	a_D	
(−1) · (pivotal row)	−1/4	−1	0	0	1/4	0	0	−1/4	−9
(−3) · (pivotal row)	−3/4	−3	0	0	3/4	0	0	−3/4	−27
pivotal row = (a_D-row) ÷ 4	1/4	1	0	0	−1/4	0	0	1/4	9
2,400 · (pivotal row)	600	2,400	0	0	−600	0	0	600	21,600
(−8) · (pivotal row)	−2	−8	0	0	2	0	0	−2	−72

(↑ under x_2)

Second Tableau

Basic Variables	Coefficient of								Current Values	
	x_1	x_2	p_S	p_R	p_D	a_S	a_R	a_D		
a_S	[15/4]	0	−1	0	1/4	1	0	−1/4	[15]	4 →
a_R	[5/4]	0	0	−1	3/4	0	1	−3/4	[15]	12
x_2	[1/4]	1	0	0	−1/4	0	0	1/4	[9]	36
(min) θ	−900	0	0	0	−600	0	0	600	21,600	
(min) W	5	0	−1	−1	1	0	0	−2	30	

(↑ under x_1)

TABLE 4–25 (concluded)

Third Tableau

Basic Variables	x_1	x_2	Coefficient of						Current Values	
			p_S	p_R	p_D	a_S	a_R	a_D		
x_1	1	0	−4/15	0	1/15	4/15	0	−1/15	4	60
a_R	0	0	1/3	−1	2/3	−1/3	1	−2/3	10	15 →
x_2	0	1	1/15	0	−4/15	−1/15	0	4/15	8	−30
(min) θ	0	0	−240	0	−540	240	0	540	25,200	
(min) W	0	0	1/3	−1	2/3	−4/3	0	−5/3	10	

Fourth Tableau

↑

Basic Variables	x_1	x_2	Coefficient of						Current Values
			p_S	p_R	p_D	a_S	a_R	a_D	
x_1	1	0	−3/10	1/10	0	3/10	−1/10	0	3
p_D	0	0	1/2	−3/2	1	−1/2	3/2	−1	15
x_2	0	1	1/5	−2/5	0	−1/5	2/5	0	12
(min) θ	0	0	30	−810	0	−30	810	0	33,300
(min) W	0	0	0	0	0	−1	−1	−1	0

Abbreviated Fourth Tableau

Basic Variables	x_1	x_2	Coefficient of			Current Values	
			p_S	p_R	p_D		
x_1	1	0	−3/10	1/10	0	3	−10
p_D	0	0	1/2	−3/2	1	15	30 →
x_2	0	1	1/5	−2/5	0	12	60
(min) θ	0	0	30	−810	0	33,300	

Fifth Tableau

↑

Basic Variables	x_1	x_2	Coefficient of			Current Values
			p_S	p_R	p_D	
x_1	1	0	0	−4/5	3/5	12
p_S	0	0	1	−3	2	30
x_2	0	1	0	1/5	−2/5	6
(min) θ	0	0	0	−720	−60	32,400

Note that, as mentioned earlier, the minimum value of W is indeed zero and the artificial variables a_S, a_R, and a_D have been removed from the basis.

Now we start Phase II, as we stated earlier, by omitting the W-row and the a_S, a_R, and a_D columns from the Fourth Tableau of Table 4–25 to get the Abbreviated Fourth Tableau shown in Table 4–25. Note, also as we stated earlier, that the θ-row of this tableau is in the proper form. Proceeding to minimize θ, then, we can see from the Abbreviated Fourth Tableau that p_S enters next and p_D leaves. The result of this change of basis is as shown in the Fifth Tableau of Table 4–25.

Continuing with Phase II, now, we see that there are no positive entries in the θ-row of the Fifth Tableau of Table 4–25. Thus we are done with Phase II and, consequently, with the solution of the entire problem. The minimum from this tableau is

$$x_1 = 12, \quad x_2 = 6, \quad p_S = 30, \quad p_R = p_D = 0, \quad \text{and} \quad \theta = 32{,}400.$$

TABLE 4–26

```
$ lindo
LINDO (7 OCTOBER 88 CHICAGO)
: min 1500x1 + 2400x2
? st
? 4x1 + x2 >= 24
? 2x1 + 3x2 >= 42
? x1 + 4x2 >= 36
? end

: go
LP OPTIMUM FOUND AT STEP        3

            OBJECTIVE FUNCTION VALUE
        1)      32400.0000
    VARIABLE        VALUE           REDUCED COST
        X1          12.000000        0.000000
        X2           6.000000        0.000000

        ROW     SLACK OR SURPLUS    DUAL PRICES
        2)          30.000000         0.000000
        3)           0.000000      -720.000000
        4)           0.000000       -60.000000
NO. ITERATIONS=         3

DO RANGE (SENSITIVITY) ANALYSIS?
? no
: quit
FORTRAN STOP
$ lo
```

This is precisely the extreme point (12, 6) of Figure 4–5 and the minimum cost is $32,400 when Refinery A is operated 12 days and Refinery B is operated 6 days. Furthermore, since $p_S = 30$ the company has a surplus of 30,000 gallons of Super Unleaded gasoline. Note that this is also the same result as in Sections 4.10 and 3.6.

Before leaving this example, take a closer look at the p- and a-columns of the tableaus in Table 4–25. Except for the W-rows, **the a-columns are precisely the negatives of the corresponding p-columns.** Why? Remember we replaced $-p_S$ in (1') by $a_S - p_S$ in (1"), replaced $-p_R$ in (2') by $a_R - p_R$ in (2"), and replaced $-p_D$ in (3') by $a_D - p_D$ in (3"). **This relationship will always hold** and will be useful later when we do sensitivity analysis on $\geq$ constraints. Also, look back in Section 4.5 where we saw how to handle negative decision variables. **This same type of substitution was made there.**

The LINDO printout for the solution of this example is shown in Table 4–26 (page 299). Note that the LINDO solution uses only three steps or four tableaus rather than the five tableaus used by Phase I–Phase II in Table 4–25. The reason for this, as was stated in Section 3.15, is that LINDO uses advanced solution techniques.

The a-columns are precisely the negatives of the p-columns, similar to the handling of negative decision variables.

Computer packages use advanced solution techniques.

4.13 PROBLEM SET 4-4

Use the Phase I–Phase II Method to solve each of the following, assuming that all variables are nonnegative.

1. Minimize
$$\theta = 5x_1 + 7x_2$$
   subject to
$$2x_1 + 3x_2 \geq 12$$
$$5x_1 + x_2 \geq 17.$$

2. Minimize
$$\theta = 2x_1 + 8x_2$$
   subject to
$$4x_1 + 5x_2 \geq 30$$
$$3x_1 + 2x_2 \geq 19.$$

3. Minimize
$$\theta = 6x_1 + 2x_2$$
   subject to
$$x_1 + 3x_2 \geq 24$$
$$2x_1 + x_2 \geq 18$$
$$3x_1 + 4x_2 \geq 52.$$

4. Minimize
$$\theta = 3x_1 + 5x_2 + 4x_3$$
   subject to
$$2x_1 + x_2 + 2x_3 \geq 30$$
$$x_1 + x_2 + 2x_3 \geq 20.$$

5. Minimize
$$\theta = 5x_1 + 2x_2 + 6x_3 + 8$$
   subject to
$$2x_1 + 2x_2 + 5x_3 \geq 30$$
$$3x_1 + x_2 + 3x_3 \geq 27.$$

6. Minimize
$$\theta = 2x_1 + 5x_2 + 8x_3 - 15$$
   subject to
$$x_1 + x_2 + 4x_3 \geq 36$$
$$3x_1 + 2x_2 + 2x_3 \geq 48.$$

4.13 PROBLEM SET 4-4 (continued)

7. Minimize

$$\theta = 4x_1 + 2x_2 + 5x_3 - 20$$

subject to

$$x_1 + 2x_2 + 3x_3 \geq 36$$
$$x_1 \qquad + 2x_3 \geq 16.$$

8. Minimize

$$\theta = 5x_1 + 2x_2 + 3x_3 - 24$$

subject to

$$2x_1 + x_2 + 3x_3 \geq 36$$
$$x_2 \qquad \geq 18.$$

9. Strong Steel Company operates three steel mills with different production capacities. Mill I can produce 1,000 tons per day of AAA steel, 3,000 tons per day of AA steel, and 10,000 tons per day of A steel. Mill F can produce 2,000 tons per day of AAA steel, 2,000 tons per day of AA steel, and 4,000 tons per day of A steel. Mill S can produce 4,000, 1,000, and 3,000 tons per day, respectively. The company has made a contract with a construction firm to provide 29,000 tons of AAA steel, 23,000 tons of AA steel, and 62,000 tons of A steel. If it costs $1,400 per day to run Mill I, $1,000 per day to run Mill F, and $1,200 per day to run Mill S, determine the number of days the company should operate each mill in order to meet the terms of the contract most economically. What is this minimum cost?

10. A special food for athletes is to be developed from three foods: Food X, Food Y, and Food Z. The new food is to contain at least 66 milligrams of Vitamin A, at least 48 milligrams of Vitamin B, and at least 40 milligrams of Vitamin C. Each pound of Food X costs $1.50 and contains 2 milligrams of Vitamin A, 4 milligrams of Vitamin B, and 1 milligram of Vitamin C. Each pound of Food Y costs $2.50 and contains 9 milligrams of Vitamin A, 3 milligrams of Vitamin B, and 4 milligrams of Vitamin C; each pound of Food Z costs $2.00 and contains 7 milligrams of A, 2 milligrams of B, and 8 milligrams of C. How many pounds of each food should be used in the mixture in order to meet the requirements at a minimum cost? What is this minimum cost?

11. The intensive care unit of City Hospital has to schedule the shifts for its nursing staff on a round-the-clock basis so as to ensure that a certain minimum number of nurses are on duty at various times. The supervisor of nurses has broken the day into six slots of four hours each and has determined that in order to maintain efficiency, at least 12 nurses must be on duty from 8 A.M. to 12 noon, at least 14 from 12 noon to 4 P.M., at least 16 from 4 P.M. to 8 P.M., at least 10 from 8 P.M. to 12 midnight, at least 6 from 12 midnight to 4 A.M., and at least 9 from 4 A.M. to 8 A.M.. The nurses work eight-hour shifts, but they are scheduled to arrive (and depart) every four hours starting at 8 A.M.; that is, Shift 1 works from 8 A.M. to 4 P.M., Shift 2 from 12 noon to 8 P.M., Shift 3 from 4 P.M. to 12 midnight, and so on. Find the optimal schedule that meets the requirements and, at the same time, employs the fewest total nurses. What is this total? (Hint: Let x_i be the number of nurses who are scheduled to work shift i where $i = 1, 2, 3, 4, 5, 6$.)

12. Fine Paper Mill produces paper in reels having a standard width of 60 inches and a fixed length. The mill receives orders from its customers for reels of the same fixed length but smaller widths. One customer's order calls for 50 reels of width 10 inches, 75 reels of width 16, and 85 reels of width 23, all of which the mill cuts from the standard-size reel. The mill wants to meet the customer's needs in such a way as to minimize the total trim waste. This trim waste occurs when the standard reel is cut into narrower reels; that is, if one 60-inch reel is cut into one 10-inch reel and two 23-inch reels, then there is a trim waste of $60 - [10(1) + 23(2)] = 4$ inches.

a) Find every possible combination of cutting the standard 60-inch reel into combinations of 10-inch, 16-inch, and 23-inch reels, and calculate the trim waste for each such combination. (Hint: There are eight such combinations.)

4.13 PROBLEM SET 4-4 (concluded)

b) Formulate the problem of minimizing the total trim waste, assuming that the mill ignores the extra 10-inch, 16-inch, and 23-inch reels made. What is this total waste?

c) Formulate the problem of minimizing the total trim waste, assuming that the extra reels are also waste. What is this total waste?

4.14 NO FEASIBLE SOLUTIONS

When the constraints are contradictory, the feasible solution set is empty. Phase I will not be completed.

There is one last special case that can occur in linear programming problems—the empty feasible solution set. This occurs when no point satisfies all the constraints simultaneously, so that the constraints contradict themselves. If this happens the associated objective function can have no optimum (maximum or minimum). When we try to solve such a problem by the Simplex Method, we will find that **we are unable to complete Phase I;** that is, we will not be able to get $W = 0$ and hence, an artificial variable will be left in the basis. Recall from Section 4.12 that when an artificial variable is not zero (so that it is still in the basis), then the constraint corresponding to that artificial variable is not satisfied; that is, we have a shortage.

The following modification of the Ace Rubber Company example will serve to illustrate a linear programming problem with no feasible solutions.

Example. Maximize

$$\theta = 10x_1 + 8x_2$$

subject to

$$\text{Machine A:} \quad 2x_1 + 9x_2 \leq 36 \qquad (1)$$

$$\text{Machine B:} \quad x_1 + x_2 \geq 20 \qquad (2)$$

$$x_1, \ x_2 \geq 0. \qquad (3),(4)$$

The graph of the constraint set is shown in Figure 4-6. Note that the feasible solution set is indeed empty.

We begin the Simplex Method solution, as usual, by converting the constraints (1) and (2) into equalities. Thus we introduce the **slack variable** s_A into the $\leq$ constraint (1), while we introduce the **surplus variable** p_B together with the **artificial variable** a_B into the $\geq$ constraint (2). Doing this, we get

$$2x_1 + 9x_2 + s_A + 0 + 0 = 36 \qquad (1')$$

$$x_1 + x_2 + 0 - p_B + a_B = 20. \qquad (2')$$

Next we convert the objective function into the θ-equation for the nonartificial variables x_1, x_2, s_A, and p_B, together with the W-equation for the artificial variable a_B. The θ-equation becomes

FIGURE 4-6

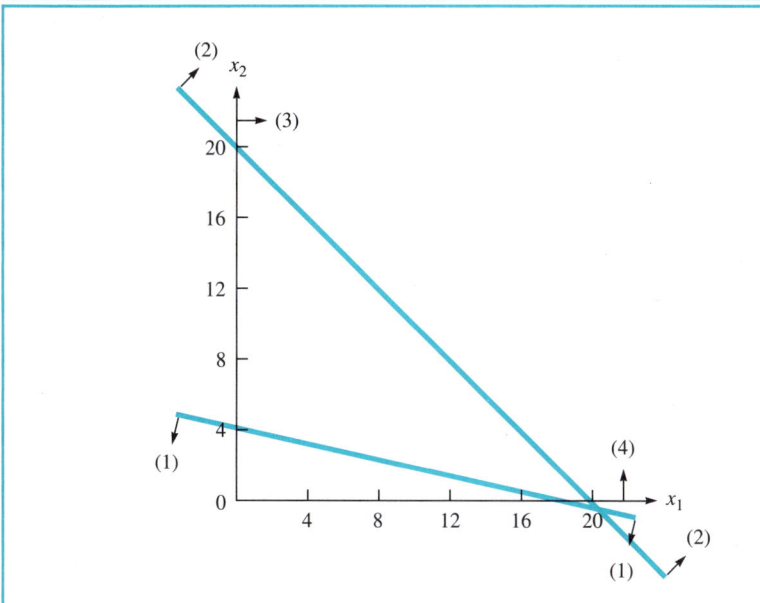

$$\theta = 10x_1 + 8x_2 + 0s_A + 0p_B \tag{5}$$

(since there are no penalties and/or premiums for the slack or surplus variables), whereas the W-equation becomes

$$W = a_B \tag{6}$$

so that, as always, W is simply the sum of the artificial variables.

The initial solution to the system of equations (1'), (2'), (5), and (6) representing the origin is

$$x_1 = x_2 = p_B = 0$$

so that

$$s_A = 36 \quad \text{and} \quad a_B = 20$$

and hence,

$$\theta = 0 \quad \text{and} \quad W = 20.$$

Thus the **slack variable** s_A and the **artificial variable** a_B are our initial basic variables, and our Preliminary Tableau is as shown in Table 4–27. This tableau, however, is not in the proper diagonalized form for W because of the -1 coefficient in the W-row for the basic variable a_B. Therefore we add 1 times the a_B-row to the W-row, as shown in the Working row for W, to get the new W-row also shown in Table 4–27. Note that we did not use the row corresponding to the basic variable

s_A since the coefficient of s_A is already (and will always be) zero in the W-row of the Preliminary Tableau. Note also that the Preliminary Tableau with its new W-row corresponds to the point of intersection (0, 0) on boundary lines (3) and (4) of Figure 4–6.

Now, as usual, we perform the initial optimality analysis to get the Initial Tableau

TABLE 4–27

Preliminary Tableau

Basic Variables	Coefficient of					Current Values
	x_1	x_2	s_A	p_B	a_B	
s_A	2	9	1	0	0	36
a_B	1	1	0	−1	1	20
(max) θ	−10	−8	0	0	0	0
(min) W	0	0	0	0	−1	0

Working Row for θ

	x_1	x_2	s_A	p_B	a_B	
1 · (a_B-row)	1	1	0	−1	1	20

New W-Row

	x_1	x_2	s_A	p_B	a_B	
(min) W	1	1	0	−1	0	20

Initial Tableau

Basic Variables	Coefficient of					Current Values	
	x_1	x_2	s_A	p_B	a_B		
s_A	[2]	9	1	0	0	[36]	18 →
a_B	[1]	1	0	−1	1	[20]	20
(max) θ	−10	−8	0	0	0	0	
(min) W	1	1	0	−1	0	20	
	↑						

Second Tableau

Basic Variables	Coefficient of					Current Values
	x_1	x_2	s_A	p_B	a_B	
x_1	1	9/2	1/2	0	0	18
a_B	0	−7/2	−1/2	−1	1	2
(max) θ	0	37	5	0	0	180
(min) W	0	−7/2	−1/2	−1	0	2

of Table 4–27. From this tableau, we see that we have a tie for the entering variable between x_1 and x_2. As we saw in Section 4.2, we can choose either one and the end result will be identical. However, as we agreed for conformity, we bring the left-most entering variable, x_1, into the basis so that s_A leaves. Performing this change of basis, then, we get the result shown in the Second Tableau of Table 4–27, which corresponds to the point of intersection (18, 0) on boundary lines (1) and (4) of Figure 4–6.

From the second Tableau of Table 4–27, we see that there are no positive entries left in the W-row, indicating that W has been minimized. However, at this "minimum," $W = 2$ and, furthermore, $a_B = 2$ is still in the basis. Therefore, Phase I cannot be completed; and hence, as stated earlier in our graphical analysis of Figure 4–6, the feasible solution set is empty.

TABLE 4–28

```
$ lindo
LINDO (7 OCTOBER 88 CHICAGO)
: max 10x1 + 8x2
? st
? 2x1 + 9x2 <= 36
? x1 + x2 >= 20
? end

: go

NO FEASIBLE SOLUTION AT STEP      1
SUM OF INFEASIBILITIES=    2.00000

VIOLATED ROWS HAVE NEGATIVE SLACK,
OR (EQUALITY ROWS) NONZERO SLACKS.
ROWS CONTRIBUTING TO INFEASIBILITY HAVE
NONZERO DUAL PRICE.

           OBJECTIVE FUNCTION VALUE
       1)      180.000000

  VARIABLE         VALUE         REDUCED COST
        X1      18.000000           0.000000
        X2       0.000000           3.500000

       ROW    SLACK OR SURPLUS     DUAL PRICES
        2)       0.000000           0.500000
        3)      -2.000000          -1.000000

NO. ITERATIONS=       1

: quit
FORTRAN STOP
$ lo
```

> **Exercise.** Which constraint is violated by the last solution point (18, 0)? Why? Verify this fact by substitution into the constraint itself.
>
> **Answer:** 2. a_B corresponds to constraint (2). $x_1 + x_2 = 18 + 0 = 18$, which is not greater than or equal to 20.

The LINDO printout for this example is shown in Table 4–28 on page 305. Note in this table the line

SUM OF INFEASIBILITIES = 2.000000,

which corresponds precisely to our result in Table 4–27.

Linear programming problems with all ≤ constraints have nonempty feasible solution sets, and only Phase II is needed.

Lastly, we wish to emphasize that **a linear programming problem with all ≤ constraints (and nonnegative right-hand-side constants) other than the nonnegativity constraints would always have a nonempty feasible solution set.** Algebraically, this makes sense since we would not need to introduce any artificial variables and hence, the Phase I portion of the Phase I–Phase II Method is not even necessary.

4.15 AN EXAMPLE WITH = CONSTRAINTS

We now complete the discussion of the Simplex Method by illustrating the solution of a linear programming problem that has = constraints. The Klean Soap example of Section 3.8 will serve as our example and we repeat it here.

Example. Klean Soap Company wishes to make a new detergent from two of its current soaps: Soap A and Soap B. The company wants the new detergent to contain at least 20 ounces of Cleaning Ingredient D. Each pound of Soap A costs $0.20 and contains 5 ounces of D, whereas each pound of Soap B costs $0.25 and contains 1 ounce of D. Furthermore, for ecological reasons, the amount of Soap A must be no more than that of Soap B. Finally, the new mixture must weigh exactly 12 pounds. How many pounds of each soap should be used in the mixture in order to meet the preceding requirements at a minimum cost? What is this minimum cost?

We saw in Section 3.8 that the linear programming problem is to minimize

$$\theta = 0.2x_1 + 0.25x_2$$

subject to

$$\text{Ingredient D:} \quad 5x_1 + x_2 \geq 20 \quad (1)$$
$$\text{Ecology:} \quad x_1 - x_2 \leq 0 \quad (2)$$
$$\text{Weight:} \quad x_1 + x_2 = 12 \quad (3)$$
$$\text{Nonnegativity:} \quad x_1, x_2 \geq 0. \quad (4),(5)$$

(Once again, we have changed the unknowns from x and y to x_1 and x_2, respectively.) Recall that these constraints gave rise to the feasible solution set shown in Figure 4–7, which is nothing more than Figure 3–11 of Section 3.8 repeated here for convenience. From this figure, we see that there are two extreme points: namely, (2, 10) from boundary lines (1) and (3), and (6, 6) from boundary lines (2) and (3). Recall also that the minimum value was \$2.70 at (6, 6).

We begin the Simplex Method solution, as usual, by converting the constraints (1), (2), and (3) into equalities. For convenience, we reorder the constraints with the $\leq$ constraints first, then the $\geq$ constraints, and lastly the $=$ constraints; that is,

$$\text{Ecology:} \quad x_1 - x_2 \leq 0 \tag{6}$$

$$\text{Ingredient D:} \quad 5x_1 + x_2 \geq 20 \tag{7}$$

$$\text{Weight:} \quad x_1 + x_2 = 12. \tag{8}$$

Now, as usual, we introduce the **slack variable** s_E into the $\leq$ constraint (6), and next the **surplus variable** p_D together with the **artificial variable** a_D into the $\geq$ constraint (7). At this point, we note that although constraint (8) is already an equality, we cannot at one and the same time satisfy this constraint and select an

An artificial variable is added to $=$ constraints to generate a starting solution.

FIGURE 4–7

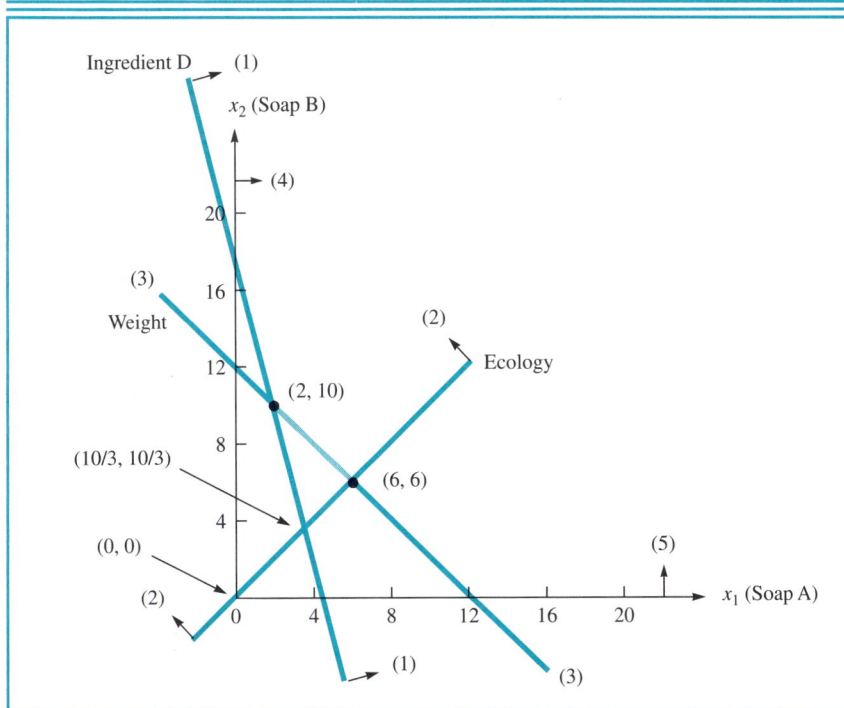

initial solution representing the origin; that is, substituting $x_1 = x_2 = 0$ in equation (8) gives $0 = 12$, **which is impossible.** Thus we now introduce an **artificial variable** a_W into constraint (8) so that our constraints become

$$x_1 - x_2 + s_E + 0 + 0 + 0 = 0 \qquad (6')$$

$$5x_1 + x_2 + 0 - p_D + a_D + 0 = 20 \qquad (7')$$

$$x_1 + x_2 + 0 + 0 + 0 + a_W = 12. \qquad (8')$$

Next we convert the objective function

$$\theta = 0.2x_1 + 0.25x_2$$

into a θ-equation and a W-equation in the usual manner to get

$$\theta = 0.2x_1 + 0.25x_2 + 0s_E + 0p_D \qquad (9)$$

and

$$W = a_D + a_W. \qquad (10)$$

The initial solution to the system of equations (6'), (7'), (8'), (9), and (10) representing the origin (0, 0) is

$$x_1 = x_2 = p_D = 0$$

so that

$$s_E = 0, \quad a_D = 20, \quad a_W = 12$$

and hence

$$\theta = 0 \quad \text{and} \quad W = 32.$$

Note that we have a basic variable, s_E, which **equals** zero. Do you remember what this means? In Section 4.2, we saw that this meant that the problem had a degeneracy. Recall that this presented no difficulty in the Simplex Method solution.

Exercise. Refer to Figure 4–7 and identify the degeneracy.

Answer: Ecology constraint (2) passes through the origin (0, 0), where two other constraints (4), $x_1 = 0$, and (5), $x_2 = 0$, intersect.

The Preliminary Tableau, then, is as shown in Table 4–29, where, for ease in computation, we have converted the decimals in the θ-equation to their fractional equivalents. As usual, this tableau must be properly converted to begin the Simplex Method. Doing this by means of the working rows for W as shown in Table 4–29

TABLE 4-29 Preliminary Tableau

Basic Variables	Coefficient of						Current Values
	x_1	x_2	s_E	p_D	a_D	a_W	
s_E	1	−1	1	0	0	0	0
a_D	5	1	0	−1	1	0	20
a_W	1	1	0	0	0	1	12
(min) θ	−1/5	−1/4	0	0	0	0	0
(min) W	0	0	0	0	−1	−1	0

Working Rows for W

	x_1	x_2	s_E	p_D	a_D	a_W	
1 · (a_D-row)	5	1	0	−1	1	0	20
1 · (a_W-row)	1	1	0	0	0	1	12

New W-row

	x_1	x_2	s_E	p_D	a_D	a_W	
(min) W	6	2	0	−1	0	0	32

Initial Tableau

Basic Variables	Coefficient of						Current Values	
	x_1	x_2	s_E	p_D	a_D	a_W		
s_E	[1]	−1	1	0	0	0	[0]	0 →
a_D	[5]	1	0	−1	1	0	[20]	4
a_W	[1]	1	0	0	0	1	[12]	12
(min) θ	−1/5	−1/4	0	0	0	0	0	
(min) W	6	2	0	−1	0	0	32	

↑

Second Tableau

Basic Variables	Coefficient of						Current Values	
	x_1	x_2	s_E	p_D	a_D	a_W		
x_1	1	[−1]	1	0	0	0	[0]	−0*
a_D	0	[6]	−5	−1	1	0	[20]	10/3 →
a_W	0	[2]	−1	0	0	1	[12]	6
(min) θ	0	−9/20	1/5	0	0	0	0	
(min) W	0	8	−6	−1	0	0	32	

↑

TABLE 4–29 (concluded)

Third Tableau

Basic Variables	Coefficient of						Current Values	
	x_1	x_2	s_E	p_D	a_D	a_W		
x_1	1	0	1/6	−1/6	1/6	0	10/3	20
x_2	0	1	−5/6	−1/6	1/6	0	10/3	−4
a_W	0	0	2/3	1/3	−1/3	1	16/3	8 →
(min) θ	0	0	−7/40	−3/40	3/40	0	3/2	
(min) W	0	0	2/3	1/3	−4/3	0	16/3	

↑

Fourth Tableau

Basic Variables	Coefficient of						Current Values
	x_1	x_2	s_E	p_D	a_D	a_W	
x_1	1	0	0	−1/4	1/4	−1/4	2
x_2	0	1	0	1/4	−1/4	5/4	10
s_E	0	0	1	1/2	−1/2	3/2	8
(min) θ	0	0	0	1/80	−1/80	21/80	29/10
(min) W	0	0	0	0	−1	−1	0

Abbreviated Fourth Tableau

Basic Variables	Coefficient of				Current Values	
	x_1	x_2	s_E	p_D		
x_1	1	0	0	−1/4	2	−8
x_2	0	1	0	1/4	10	40
s_E	0	0	1	1/2	8	16 →
(min) θ	0	0	0	1/80	29/10	

↑

Fifth Tableau

Basic Variables	Coefficient of				Current Values
	x_1	x_2	s_E	p_D	
x_1	1	0	1/2	0	6
x_2	0	1	−1/2	0	6
p_D	0	0	2	1	16
(min) θ	0	0	−1/40	0	27/10

(again using only the rows corresponding to the artificial variables), we get the new W-row also shown in Table 4–29. The Preliminary Tableau, then, with its new W-row corresponds to the point of intersection (0, 0) on boundary lines (2), (4), and (5) of Figure 4–7.

Our initial optimality analysis now leads us to the Initial Tableau shown in Table 4–29. From this tableau, we see that x_1 enters the basis first, while s_E leaves. This change of basis gives the Second Tableau shown in Table 4–29. Note that s_E and x_1 are both still zero, but s_E is now nonbasic whereas x_1 is now basic. Note also that the values of a_D, a_W, θ, and W, as well as x_2, are the same as in the Initial Tableau since we are still at the **same point of intersection** (0, 0) of Figure 4–7.

Next, as shown in the Second Tableau of Table 4–29, x_2 is brought into the basis and a_D is removed. Note that, as usual, we have asterisked (*) the ratio $0/(-1) = -0$ to indicate that, although it is zero, it should be interpreted as negative and hence is to be ignored. Performing the change of basis indicated in the Second Tableau, then, we get the result shown in the Third Tableau of Table 4–29. This solution corresponds to the point of intersection (10/3, 10/3) on boundary lines (1) and (2) of Figure 4–7. **Thus, this time, we did not move from the origin out along either the x_1- or x_2-axis, but rather we did move up along the ecology constraint (2).**

Now from the Third Tableau of Table 4–29, we see that s_E enters next, while a_W leaves. This change of basis gives us the Fourth Tableau of Table 4–29, which corresponds to the extreme point (2, 10) on boundary lines (1) and (3) of Figure 4–7.

At this point, then, we find in the Fourth Tableau of Table 4–29 that Phase I is done; and hence, as always, we begin Phase II by omitting the W-row and the a_D- and a_W-columns to get the Abbreviated Fourth Tableau shown in Table 4–29. Continuing with Phase II, we now see from the latter tableau that p_D enters next and s_E leaves. Doing this, we get the result shown in the Fifth Tableau of Table 4–29, which corresponds to the extreme point (6, 6) on boundary lines (2) and (3) of Figure 4–7.

From the Fifth Tableau of Table 4–29, we see that Phase II is now completed so that the minimum is (6, 6) = 27/10 (or 2.7) with p_D = 16, which is precisely the same result as in Section 3.8. Specifically, the minimum cost is $2.70, which arises from a mixture of six pounds each of Soaps A and B with a surplus of 16 ounces of Cleaning Ingredient D.

Degeneracy occurs at the origin—three constraints intersect in (0, 0).

> **Exercise.** Substitute the optimum solution of (6, 6) into the original constraint set (1), (2), (3) and verify the surplus of 16 ounces of D.

The LINDO printout for this example is shown in Table 4–30.

TABLE 4-30

```
$ lindo
LINDO (7 OCTOBER 88 CHICAGO)
: min .2x1 + .25x2
? st
? x1 - x2 <= 0
? 5x1 + x2 >= 20
? x1 + x2 = 12
? end

: go
LP OPTIMUM FOUND AT STEP        2

         OBJECTIVE FUNCTION VALUE
     1)     2.70000005

    VARIABLE         VALUE          REDUCED COST
        X1         6.000000           0.000000
        X2         6.000000           0.000000

       ROW    SLACK OR SURPLUS     DUAL PRICES
        2)        0.000000           0.025000
        3)       16.000000           0.000000
        4)        0.000000          -0.225000

    NO. ITERATIONS=        2

    DO RANGE(SENSITIVITY) ANALYSIS?
    ? n
    : quit
    FORTRAN STOP
$ lo
```

4.16 GRAND SUMMARY OF THE SIMPLEX METHOD

At this point, it is helpful to collect all our techniques of this chapter and the previous chapter into a grand summary of the Simplex Method. Before doing so, however, we wish to reemphasize three important points associated with using the method. The first point concerns the constraints of the linear programming problem being solved, the second concerns the objective function (specifically, the θ-equation and the W-equation), while the third concerns the Phase I–Phase II Method; namely:

> Three-step grand summary of the Simplex Method.

1. We always convert the constraints into equalities where
   a. We add a slack variable to each $\leq$ constraint.
   b. We subtract a surplus variable and simultaneously add an artificial variable to each $\geq$ constraint (other than the nonnegativity constraints).
   c. We add an artificial variable to each $=$ constraint.
2. The objective function is always separated into a θ-equation and a W-equation where
   a. The θ-equation contains all the original decision variables together with all the slack and surplus variables. (Slack and surplus variables are given a coefficient of zero unless there is an associated penalty or premium.)
   b. The W-equation is simply the sum of all the artificial variables.
3. a. Phase I always consists of **minimizing the W-row,** the initial basic variables being the slack variables (if any) together with the artificial variables.
   b. Phase II consists of **optimizing (maximizing or minimizing) the θ-row** depending upon the original objective of the problem.

Of course, as we have seen in this chapter, the W-row must be transformed into the proper form before beginning Phase I. Also, as we saw in the previous chapter, if there is a penalty and/or premium for the slack variables, then the θ-row too will have to be put into the proper form before starting Phase I. (We need not be concerned about surplus variables since they are never in the initial basis.) Furthermore, Phase I is completed when there are no positive entries left in the W-row and $W = 0$; but if Phase I cannot be completed, then, as we saw in Section 4.14, the feasible solution set is empty. Lastly, we wish to point out that if initially there are no artificial variables, then obviously Phase I is not needed and only Phase II must be performed. This was the case, of course, in the previous chapter where we treated problems with all $\leq$ constraints (other than the nonnegativity constraints); that is, **the method used in the previous chapter was precisely Phase II.**

The grand summary of the Simplex Method can be viewed as shown in the self-explanatory flowchart of Figure 4–8. Note that this flowchart is broken into four separate sections: Preliminaries, Phase I, Phase II, and Improving the Solution.

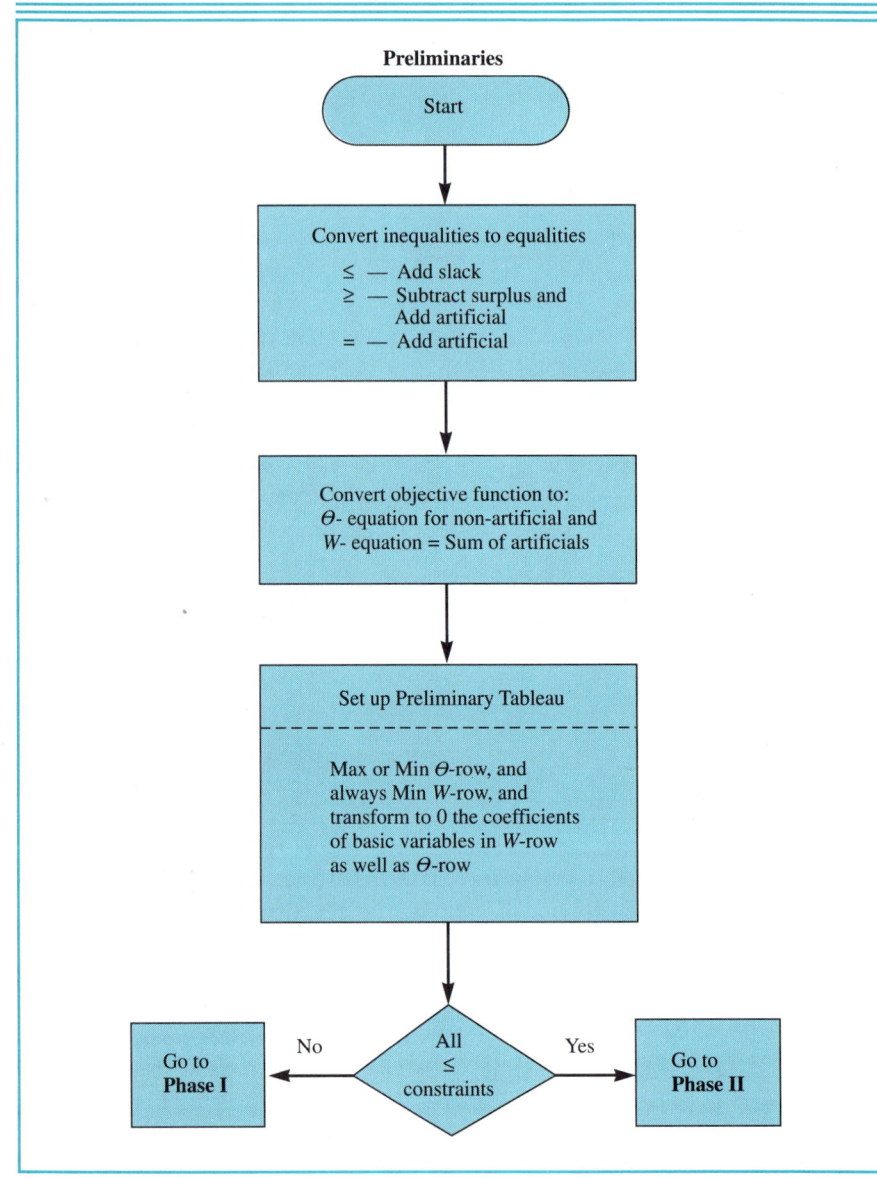

FIGURE 4–8

Grand Summary of the Simplex Method

FIGURE 4–8 (*concluded*)

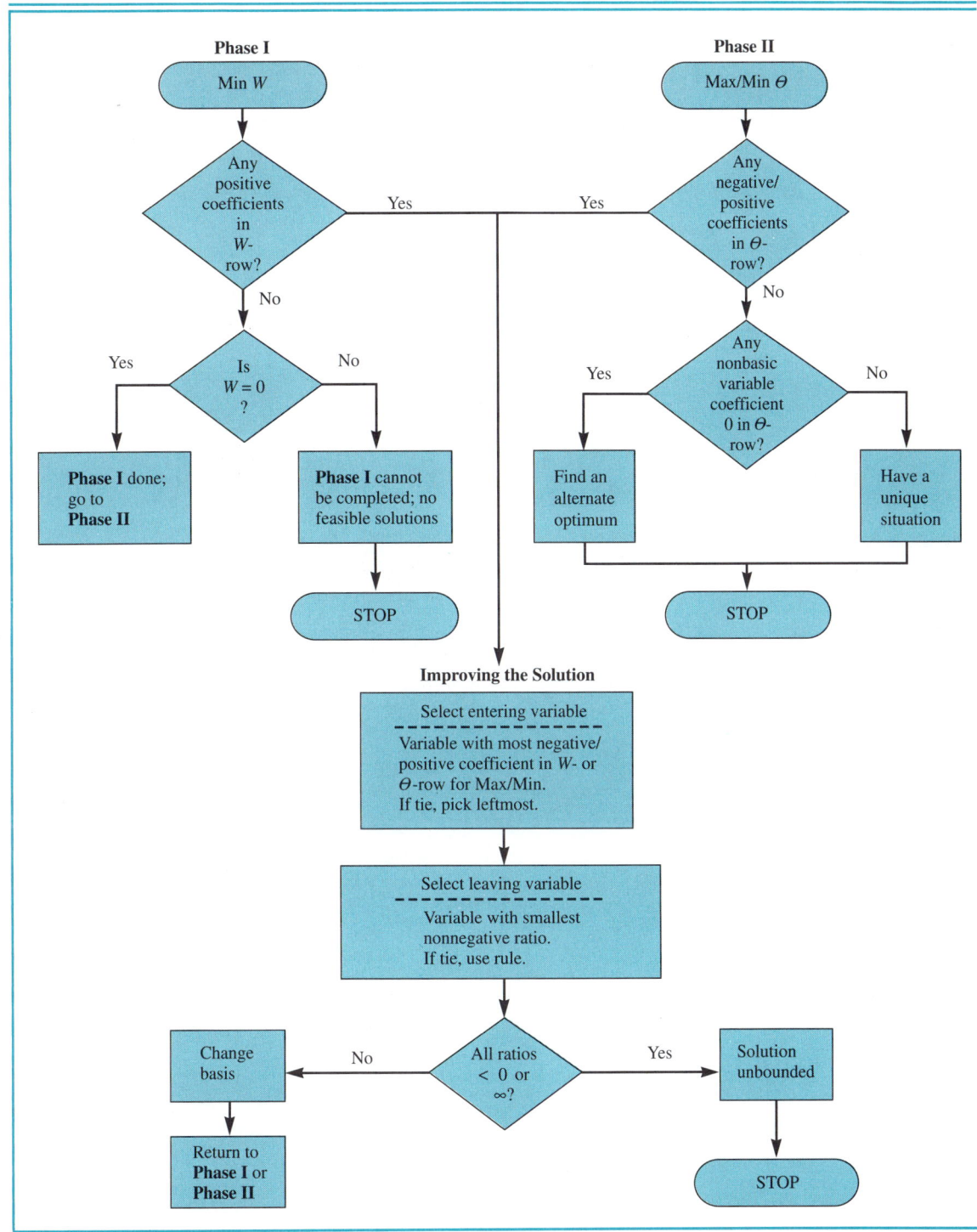

4.17 PROBLEM SET 4-5

Use the Phase I–Phase II Method to solve each of the following, assuming that all variables are nonnegative.

1. Maximize
$$\theta = 3x_1 + 5x_2$$
subject to
$$x_1 + x_2 \leq 12$$
$$2x_1 + 4x_2 \geq 36$$
$$x_1 - 2x_2 \geq 0.$$

2. Maximize
$$\theta = 5x_1 + 2x_2$$
subject to
$$x_1 + 3x_2 \leq 24$$
$$x_1 + x_2 \geq 10$$
$$2x_1 + x_2 = 18$$
$$5x_1 + x_2 = 20.$$

3. Minimize
$$\theta = 2x_1 + 3x_2$$
subject to
$$x_1 + x_2 \leq 10$$
$$2x_1 + x_2 \geq 12$$
$$x_2 \geq 10.$$

4. Minimize
$$\theta = 5x_1 + 6x_2$$
subject to
$$x_1 + x_2 \leq 15$$
$$-x_1 + x_2 \geq 3$$
$$x_1 \geq 9.$$

5. Minimize
$$\theta = 6x_1 + 2x_2$$
subject to
$$x_1 + x_2 \leq 10$$
$$3x_1 + x_2 = 18$$
$$x_2 = 9.$$

6. Maximize
$$\theta = 4x_1 + 2x_2$$
subject to
$$x_1 + 3x_2 \leq 24$$
$$x_1 + x_2 \geq 10$$
$$2x_1 + x_2 = 18$$
$$x_2 = 8.$$

7. Minimize
$$\theta = 3x_1 + 3x_2$$
subject to
$$x_2 \leq 6$$
$$-x_1 + 3x_2 \geq 0$$
$$x_1 + x_2 = 12$$
$$x_1 = 10.$$

8. Minimize
$$\theta = 5x_1 + 2x_2$$
subject to
$$x_1 \leq 5$$
$$2x_1 + 3x_2 \geq 12$$
$$5x_1 + x_2 \geq 17.$$

9. Minimize
$$\theta = 8x_1 + 10x_2$$
subject to
$$x_2 \leq 8$$
$$4x_1 + 5x_2 \geq 30$$
$$3x_1 + 2x_2 \geq 19.$$

10. Maximize and minimize
$$\theta = 3x_1 + 5x_2$$
subject to
$$x_1 + x_2 \leq 12$$
$$2x_1 + 4x_2 \geq 36.$$

4.17 PROBLEM SET 4-5 (concluded)

11. Repeat Problem 10 with the additional constraint that $-2x_1 + x_2 \geq 0$.

12. Repeat Problem 10 with the additional constraint that $x_1 - 2x_2 \leq 0$.

13. Maximize and minimize
$$\theta = x_1 + 5x_2$$
subject to
$$x_1 \leq 8$$
$$x_1 + x_2 \geq 12$$
$$-x_1 + x_2 \geq 0.$$

14. Maximize and minimize
$$\theta = 2x_1 + 3x_2$$
subject to
$$x_1 + x_2 \leq 10$$
$$2x_1 + x_2 \geq 12$$
$$x_2 \geq 4.$$

15. Maximize and minimize
$$\theta = 5x_1 + 6x_2$$
subject to
$$x_1 + x_2 \leq 15$$
$$-x_1 + x_2 \geq 3$$
$$x_1 \geq 4.$$

16. Maximize and minimize
$$\theta = 2x_1 + x_2$$
subject to
$$x_1 + x_2 \leq 10$$
$$3x_1 + x_2 = 18.$$

17. Maximize and minimize
$$\theta = 5x_1 + 2x_2$$

subject to
$$x_1 + 3x_2 \leq 24$$
$$x_1 + x_2 \geq 10$$
$$2x_1 + x_2 = 18.$$

18. Maximize and minimize
$$\theta = 6x_1 + 3x_2$$
subject to
$$x_2 \leq 6$$
$$-x_1 + 3x_2 \geq 0$$
$$x_1 + x_2 = 12.$$

19. Subject to
$$3x_1 + x_2 \leq 18$$
$$x_1 + x_2 \geq 12,$$
maximize
$$\theta = 5x_1 + 2x_2,$$
where there is both a premium of $3 per unit of slack associated with the first constraint and a penalty of $2 per unit of surplus associated with the second constraint.

20. Subject to
$$4x_1 + 3x_2 + x_3 \leq 36$$
$$2x_1 + 3x_2 + 2x_3 \geq 24,$$
minimize
$$\theta = 8x_1 + 6x_2 + 2x_3,$$
where we treat θ as a cost function and, furthermore, there is both a premium of $3 per unit of slack associated with the first constraint and a penalty of $2 per unit of surplus associated with the second constraint.

4.18 SENSITIVITY ANALYSIS ON ≥ AND = CONSTRAINTS

In Section 4.7, we developed a vector relationship approach to performing sensitivity analysis on ≤ constraints. This same approach can be used to perform sensitivity analysis on ≥ and = constraints. Before illustrating how to do this, though, we will show how to interpret the associated LINDO output for ≥ and = constraints, as we did in Section 4.7 for ≤ constraints.

The Pure Gasoline Company example will serve as a starting point, and the LINDO solution from Table 4-26 is repeated here in Table 4–31 with its associated sensitivity analysis. Examining the right-hand-side ranges in this table, we see that the right-hand-side 24 of the Super Unleaded constraint can be increased by 30 to 54, and decreased by ∞, indicating that there is no lower limit. Why is there no lower limit? Recall that the surplus variable p_s associated with Super Unleaded was basic in the optimal solution at a value of $p_s = 30$, indicating that the lower limit of 24 is not really a restricting value. Similarly, the right-hand-side 42 of the Regular Unleaded constraint can be increased by 30 to 72 and decreased by 10 to 32.

If a surplus (slack) variable is basic in the optimal solution, then there is no lower (upper) limit on the right-hand side of the associated constraint.

> **= Exercise.** What is the right-hand-side range for Diesel Fuel?
> **Answer:** 21 to 51.

In Section 4.7, we saw that the initial basic variable column vectors and the θ-column vector were all that were needed to develop the vector relationship approach. We also saw that the right-hand-side ranges could easily be computed by the usual ratio analysis on these initial basic variables in the optimal tableau. In our current example, the artificial variables a_S, a_R, and a_D form our initial basis. If we examine the optimal tableau in Table 4–25, repeated on page 320 as Table 4–32, we see that there are no a-columns. But remember from Section 4.12 the relationship between the a- and p-columns. **They are simply negatives of each other.** So using the negatives of the p-columns in Table 4–32, the ratios for Super Unleaded from the p_S-column are

$$\frac{12}{0} = \infty$$

$$\frac{30}{-1} = -30$$

$$\frac{6}{0} = \infty.$$

Remember that $-0 = 0$. Thus our limiting ratios are ∞ and -30, meaning that the original right-hand-side 24 can range from

$$24 - \infty = -\infty,$$

TABLE 4-31

```
$ lindo
LINDO (7 OCTOBER 88 CHICAGO)
: min 1500x1 + 2400x2
?st
?4x1 + x2 >= 24
?2x1 + 3x2 >= 42
?x1 + 4x2 >= 36
?end

: go
LP OPTIMUM FOUND AT STEP       2

        OBJECTIVE FUNCTION VALUE
     1)     32400.0000

   VARIABLE        VALUE          REDUCED COST
         X1     12.000000            0.000000
         X2      6.000000            0.000000

       ROW   SLACK OR SURPLUS      DUAL PRICES
        2)      30.000000             0.000000
        3)       0.000000          -720.000000
        4)       0.000000           -60.000000

NO. ITERATIONS=       2

DO RANGE(SENSITIVITY) ANALYSIS?
?yes

RANGES IN WHICH THE BASIS IS UNCHANGED:

                     OBJ COEFFICIENT RANGES
                 CURRENT      ALLOWABLE       ALLOWABLE
   VARIABLE        COEF        INCREASE        DECREASE
         X1   1500.000000     99.999992      900.000000
         X2   2400.000000   3600.000000      150.000000

                     RIGHTHAND SIDE RANGES
                 CURRENT      ALLOWABLE       ALLOWABLE
       ROW        RHS          INCREASE        DECREASE
         2      24.000000     30.000000        INFINITY
         3      42.000000     30.000000       10.000000
         4      36.000000     15.000000       15.000000

: quit
FORTRAN STOP
$ lo
```

TABLE 4-32
Fifth Tableau

Basic Variables	Coefficient of					Current Values
	x_1	x_2	p_S	p_R	p_D	
x_1	1	0	0	$-4/5$	$3/5$	12
p_S	0	0	1	-3	2	30
x_2	0	1	0	$1/5$	$-2/5$	6
(min) θ	0	0	0	-720	-60	32,400

(meaning no lower limit) to

$$24 - (-30) = 54.$$

This is precisely the same result as we had with LINDO.

In the same way, the ratios for Regular Unleaded from the negatives of the p_R-column of Table 4-32 are

$$\frac{12}{-(-4/5)} = 15$$

$$\frac{30}{-(-3)} = 10$$

$$\frac{6}{-1/5} = -30.$$

Here, our limiting ratios are 10 and -30, meaning that the original right-hand side of 42 can range from

$$42 - 10 = 32$$

to

$$42 - (-30) = 72.$$

Again, this result coincides precisely with our previous LINDO analysis.

Exercise. What are the ratios for Diesel fuel? What is the right-hand-side range?

Answer: $-20, -15, 15.$ 21 to 51.

Now what about = constraints? For example, the LINDO solution of the Klean Soap Company example of Sections 4.15 and 3.8 was given in Table 4-30 and is repeated here in Table 4-33 with its associated sensitivity analysis. Examining the right-hand-side range for the = constraint of Weight, we see that the

TABLE 4-33

```
$ lindo
LINDO (7 OCTOBER 88 CHICAGO)
: min .2x1 + .25x2
 ?st
 ?x1 - x2 <= 0
 ?5x1 + x2 >= 20
 ?x1 + x2 = 12
 ?end

: go
LP OPTIMUM FOUND AT STEP        2

        OBJECTIVE FUNCTION VALUE
    1)      2.70000005

 VARIABLE         VALUE          REDUCED COST
      X1        6.000000          0.000000
      X2        6.000000          0.000000

      ROW    SLACK OR SURPLUS     DUAL PRICES
       2)       0.000000           0.025000
       3)      16.000000           0.000000
       4)       0.000000          -0.225000

 NO. ITERATIONS=        2

DO RANGE(SENSITIVITY) ANALYSIS?
 ?yes

RANGES IN WHICH THE BASIS IS UNCHANGED:

                      OBJ COEFFICIENT RANGES
                CURRENT       ALLOWABLE       ALLOWABLE
 VARIABLE        COEF          INCREASE        DECREASE
      X1       0.200000        0.050000        INFINITY
      X2       0.250000        INFINITY        0.050000

                      RIGHTHAND SIDE RANGES
                CURRENT       ALLOWABLE       ALLOWABLE
      ROW        RHS           INCREASE        DECREASE
       2        0.000000       12.000000        8.000000
       3       20.000000       16.000000        INFINITY
       4       12.000000        INFINITY        5.333333

: quit
FORTRAN STOP
$ lo
```

right-hand-side 12 can be increased by ∞ (indicating that there is no upper limit) and decreased by 5.333333 or 16/3 to 20/3.

Exercise. Using Table 4–33, determine the right-hand-side ranges for Ecology and Ingredient D.

Answer: -8 to 12, and 36 with no lower limit.

When doing sensitivity analysis on = constraints, it is necessary to carry the associated artificial-variable columns throughout Phase II.

Now the initial basic variable for the = constraint in this example was the artificial variable a_W. Examining the optimal tableau in Table 4–29, repeated here as Table 4–34, we see that again there is no column for the artificial variable a_W. This time, though, there is no p_W-column either, since there was no p_W variable. If we had carried the a_W-column throughout, then it would have been

$$\begin{pmatrix} 0.50 \\ 0.50 \\ 3.00 \\ 0.23 \end{pmatrix}.$$

Thus the ratios for weight are

$$\frac{6}{0.5} = 12$$

$$\frac{6}{0.5} = 12$$

$$\frac{16}{3} = \frac{16}{3},$$

so the only limiting ratio is 16/3. This means that the original right-hand-side 12 can range from

$$12 - \frac{16}{3} = \frac{20}{3}$$

with no upper limit, since there are no negative ratios. Again, this is precisely the same result that we had with LINDO.

Exercise. Using ratios from Table 4–34, determine the right-hand-side ranges for Ecology and Ingredient D.

Answer: -8 to 12, and 36 with no lower limit.

TABLE 4-34
Fifth Tableau

Basic Variables	Coefficient of				Current Values
	x_1	x_2	s_E	p_D	
x_1	1	0	1/2	0	6
x_2	0	1	-1/2	0	6
p_D	0	0	2	1	16
(min) θ	0	0	-1/40	0	27/10

4.19 SENSITIVITY ANALYSIS ON THE OBJECTIVE FUNCTION AND NEW PRODUCT ANALYSIS

Now let's return to the Ace Rubber Company example and discuss sensitivity analysis on the objective function coefficients. Management might like to know how much the profit coefficients 10 for Model P tires and 8 for Model R tires can be changed **without affecting the optimal solution point of (9, 2).** This range is contained in the LINDO solution of Table 4-15. Under the columns headed

OBJ COEFFICIENT RANGES

we see that the coefficient 10 for Model P tires can be increased by 0.666667 to $10.67, and decreased by 8.222222 to $1.78. Similarly, the coefficient 8 for Model R tires can be increased by 37 to $45, and decreased by 0.5 to $7.50.

LINDO contains sensitivity analysis on the objective function under the columns headed OBJ COEFFICIENT RANGES.

Exercise. Verify the ranges by running a computer program for the Ace Rubber Company example with the objective function coefficients of 5 and 8, next 10 and 40, and then 5 and 40. What are the new optimal solutions? What happened in the last case?

Answer: $61 at (9, 2). $170 at (9, 2). $160 at (0, 4). We moved away from the original optimal solution point of (9, 2), since the range analysis applies only when changing precisely one coefficient at a time.

Exercise. Using the LINDO solution of the Pure Gasoline Company example in Table 4-31, determine the ranges for the objective function coefficients of Refinery A and Refinery B.

Answer: $600 to $1,600. $2,250 to $6,000.

Sensitivity on the objective function can be accomplished using vector analysis.

The vector relationship analogy carries over to this type of sensitivity analysis also. However, the mechanics are somewhat cumbersome and hence are omitted.[7]

As another example, suppose we were to maximize

$$\theta = 9x_1 + 12x_2 + 10x_3$$

subject to

$$\text{Resource 1:} \quad 2x_1 + 2x_2 + x_3 \leq 36$$
$$\text{Resource 2:} \quad x_1 + 3x_2 + 2x_3 \leq 30$$
$$x_1, x_2, x_3 \geq 0.$$

The LINDO solution of this example, together with the associated sensitivity analysis, is shown in Table 4–35. Here we can see that the original objective function coefficient 9 of x_1 can be increased by 11 to $20, and decreased by 4 to $5. Similarly, the objective function coefficient 12 of x_2 can be increased by 4.333333 to $16.33 with no lower limit.

> **Exercise.** What is the range for the objective function coefficient 10 of x_3 in this example?
>
> **Answer:** $6.75 to $18.

Now let's take a closer look at this example. Note that x_2 is nonbasic in the optimal solution. Why? Note also that the REDUCED COST of 4.333333 is the same as the allowable increase. This will always be true.

The θ-row coefficients of the nonbasic variables indicate the limiting change to the corresponding objective function coefficients.

> In a maximizing (minimizing) linear programming problem, the θ-row coefficients of the **final nonbasic variables** represent the largest increase (decrease) of the original objective function coefficients that will leave the optimal solution unaffected. Any decrease (increase) in these coefficients has no effect on the optimal solution.

---

[7] For a full treatment showing that the vector relationship approach can be used to do any type of sensitivity analysis, see *Linear Programming and Matrix Algebra* by S. Hanna and J. Saber (Babson Park, Mass.: Babson College Press, 1978).

TABLE 4-35

```
$ lindo
LINDO (7 OCTOBER 88 CHICAGO)
: max 9x1 + 12x2 + 10x3
? st
? 2x1 + 2x2 + x3 <= 36
? x1 + 3x2 + 2x3 <= 30
? end

: go
LP OPTIMUM FOUND AT STEP        2

        OBJECTIVE FUNCTION VALUE
    1)      206.000000

    VARIABLE        VALUE           REDUCED COST
        X1          14.000000       0.000000
        X2          0.000000        4.333333
        X3          8.000000        0.000000

        ROW     SLACK OR SURPLUS    DUAL PRICES
        2)          0.000000        2.666667
        3)          0.000000        3.666667

NO. ITERATIONS=         2

DO RANGE(SENSITIVITY) ANALYSIS?
? yes

RANGES IN WHICH THE BASIS IS UNCHANGED:
```

	OBJ COEFFICIENT RANGES		
VARIABLE	CURRENT COEF	ALLOWABLE INCREASE	ALLOWABLE DECREASE
X1	9.000000	11.000000	4.000000
X2	12.000000	4.333333	INFINITY
X3	10.000000	8.000000	3.250000

	RIGHTHAND SIDE RANGES		
ROW	CURRENT RHS	ALLOWABLE INCREASE	ALLOWABLE DECREASE
2	36.000000	24.000000	21.000000
3	30.000000	42.000000	12.000000

```
: quit
FORTRAN STOP
$ lo
```

> **Exercise.** In Table 4–35, what other variables are nonbasic? What were the original objective function coefficients of these variables? What are their respective ranges?
>
> **Answer:** The slack variables s_1 and s_2. Both were zero. The variable s_1 can be increased to $2.67, s_2 can be increased to $3.67.

One final type of sensitivity analysis that can be performed is the **introduction of a new product.** In this case, management is interested in the level at which it makes sense to introduce such an item. For example, let's go back to our previous maximization example, where

$$\theta = 9x_1 + 12x_2 + 10x_3$$

subject to

Resource 1: $\quad 2x_1 + 2x_2 + x_3 \leq 36$

Resource 2: $\quad x_1 + 3x_2 + 2x_3 \leq 30.$

Now suppose that a new product is proposed that would contribute $P to θ while using R_1 units of the first resource and R_2 units of the second resource. This modification would simply result in one additional initial column,

$$\begin{pmatrix} R_1 \\ R_2 \\ P \end{pmatrix}.$$

Why? In terms of our vector relationship, this column is

$$R_1 \cdot s_1 + R_2 \cdot s_2 - P \cdot \theta$$

and would remain so throughout all the tableaus. The θ-row entries in the last tableau are simply the DUAL PRICES in LINDO, so from Table 4–35, we would get

$$R_1 \cdot (2.666667) + R_2 \cdot (3.666667) - P \cdot 1. \qquad (1)$$

Why is the θ-row coefficient a 1 for θ itself? Simplifying (1), we get a θ-row coefficient of

$$R_1 \cdot \left(\frac{8}{3}\right) + R_2 \cdot \left(\frac{11}{3}\right) - P. \qquad (2)$$

Since we have a maximizing problem, **we would bring this new product into the solution only if its θ-row coefficient were less than zero.** From (2), then, we would want

$$R_1 \cdot \left(\frac{8}{3}\right) + R_2 \cdot \left(\frac{11}{3}\right) - P < 0$$

or

$$8R_1 + 11R_2 - 3P < 0$$
$$8R_1 + 11R_2 < 3P. \qquad (3)$$

Suppose, then, that the new product required one unit of R_1 and three units of R_2. From (3), we have

$$8(1) + 11(3) < 3P$$
$$41 < 3P$$
$$\frac{41}{3} < P,$$

so that the product would have to contribute at least 41/3 or $13.67 to θ before it would be introduced into the solution.

As another example, suppose that the new product contributed $13 to θ and used three units of Resource 2. Then from (3), we have

$$8R_1 + 11(3) < 3(13)$$
$$8R_1 + 33 < 39$$
$$8R_1 < 6$$
$$R_1 < \frac{3}{4}.$$

Thus the new product can use no more than 3/4 units of Resource 1.

Exercise. Suppose that the new product contributed $15 to θ and used two units of resource 1. How many units of resource 2 can the product use if it is to be introduced into the solution?

Answer: No more than 29/11.

Finally, as stated in Section 4.7, there are commands in LINDO that will allow changes to the constraints and/or objective function as well as the introduction of a new product. Those interested in this approach are referred to the Shrage book.

4.20 PROBLEM SET 4-6

Solve each of the following problems, using the accompanying LINDO printout and/or the accompanying computer printout of the optimal tableau.

1. $ lindo
   LINDO (7 OCTOBER 88 CHICAGO)
   : min 6x1 + 2x2
   ?st
   ?x1 + 3x2 >= 24
   ?2x1 + x2 >= 18
   ?3x1 + 4x2 >= 52
   ?go

   LP OPTIMUM FOUND AT STEP   1

          OBJECTIVE FUNCTION VALUE
       1)   36.000000

   VARIABLE   VALUE   REDUCED COST
       X1   0.000000   2.000000
       X2   18.000000   0.000000

       ROW   SLACK OR SURPLUS   DUAL PRICES
       2)   30.000000   0.000000
       3)   0.000000   -2.000000
       4)   20.000000   0.000000

   NO. ITERATIONS=   1

   DO RANGE(SENSITIVITY) ANALYSIS?
   ?yes

   RANGES IN WHICH THE BASIS IS UNCHANGED:

                        OBJ COEFFICIENT RANGES
                  CURRENT   ALLOWABLE   ALLOWABLE
   VARIABLE   COEF   INCREASE   DECREASE
       X1   6.000000   INFINITY   2.000000
       X2   2.000000   1.000000   2.000000

                        RIGHTHAND SIDE RANGES
                  CURRENT   ALLOWABLE   ALLOWABLE
       ROW   RHS   INCREASE   DECREASE
        2   24.000000   30.000000   INFINITY
        3   18.000000   INFINITY   5.000000
        4   52.000000   20.000000   INFINITY

4.20 PROBLEM SET 4-6 (continued)

Simplex Tableau Number 5

2.00	1.00	0.00	-1.00	0.00	0.00	1.00
0.00	18.00					
5.00	0.00	0.00	-4.00	1.00	0.00	4.00
-1.00	20.00					
5.00	0.00	1.00	-3.00	0.00	-1.00	3.00
0.00	30.00					
-2.00	0.00	0.00	-2.00	0.00	0.00	2.00
0.00	36.00					

a) Find the right-hand-side ranges of each of the first three constraints.
b) Find the new optimal solution if the right-hand sides of the first three constraints were simultaneously changed to 18, 20, and 48, respectively.
c) Find the new optimal solution to the original problem if only the third constraint were changed to $3x_1 + 3x_2 \geq 48$.
d) Find the Preliminary Final Tableau if in the original problem only the third constraint were changed to $3x_1 + 2x_2 \geq 48$. Explain why this tableau does not represent the optimal solution.

2. ```
$ lindo
LINDO (7 OCTOBER 88 CHICAGO)
: min x1 + 5x2
?st
?x1 <= 8
?x1 + x2 >= 12
?-x1 + x2 >= 0
?end

: go
LP OPTIMUM FOUND AT STEP   2

        OBJECTIVE FUNCTION VALUE
    1)   36.000000

 VARIABLE   VALUE   REDUCED COST
       X1   6.000000   0.000000
       X2   6.000000   0.000000

      ROW   SLACK OR SURPLUS   DUAL PRICES
       2)   2.000000   0.000000
       3)   0.000000   -3.000000
       4)   0.000000   -2.000000

 NO. ITERATIONS=   2

DO RANGE (SENSITIVITY) ANALYSIS?
?yes
```
```

4.20 PROBLEM SET 4-6 (continued)

RANGES IN WHICH THE BASIS IS UNCHANGED:

OBJ COEFFICIENT RANGES

VARIABLE	CURRENT COEF	ALLOWABLE INCREASE	ALLOWABLE DECREASE
X1	1.000000	4.000000	6.000000
X2	5.000000	INFINITY	4.000000

RIGHTHAND SIDE RANGES

ROW	CURRENT RHS	ALLOWABLE INCREASE	ALLOWABLE DECREASE
2	8.000000	INFINITY	2.000000
3	12.000000	4.000000	12.000000
4	0.000000	12.000000	4.000000

Simplex Tableau Number 3

0.00	0.00	1.00	0.50	−0.50	−0.50	0.50
2.00						
1.00	0.00	0.00	−0.50	0.50	0.50	−0.50
6.00						
0.00	1.00	0.00	−0.50	−0.50	0.50	0.50
6.00						
0.00	0.00	0.00	−3.00	−2.00	3.00	2.00
36.00						

a) Find the right-hand-side ranges of each of the first three constraints.
b) Find the new optimal solution if the right-hand sides of the first three constraints were simultaneously changed to 12, 16, and 2, respectively.
c) Find the new optimal solution to the original problem if only the first constraint were changed to $x_1 + 2x_2 \leq 32$.
d) Find the Preliminary Final Tableau if in the original problem only the first constraint were changed to $x_1 + 8x_2 \leq 32$. Explain why this tableau does not represent the optimal solution.

3. ```
$ lindo
LINDO (7 OCTOBER 88 CHICAGO)
: max 2x1 + 3x2
? st
? x1 + x2 <= 10
? 2x1 + x2 <= 12
? x1 <= 2
? end

: go
LP OPTIMUM FOUND AT STEP   2
```
```

4.20 PROBLEM SET 4-6 (continued)

```
            OBJECTIVE FUNCTION VALUE
       1)      28.000000

  VARIABLE           VALUE              REDUCED COST
     X1            2.000000               0.000000
     X2            8.000000               0.000000

     ROW     SLACK OR SURPLUS            DUAL PRICES
      2)          0.000000                4.000000
      3)          0.000000               -1.000000
      4)          0.000000                0.000000

 NO. ITERATIONS=     2

 DO RANGE(SENSITIVITY) ANALYSIS?
 ?yes

 RANGES IN WHICH THE BASIS IS UNCHANGED:

                         OBJ COEFFICIENT RANGES
                 CURRENT          ALLOWABLE         ALLOWABLE
  VARIABLE         COEF           INCREASE          DECREASE
     X1          2.000000         1.000000          INFINITY
     X2          3.000000         INFINITY          1.000000

                         RIGHTHAND SIDE RANGES
                 CURRENT          ALLOWABLE         ALLOWABLE
    ROW            RHS            INCREASE          DECREASE
     2          10.000000         0.000000          4.000000
     3          12.000000         8.000000          0.000000
     4           2.000000         0.000000          INFINITY

 Simplex Tableau Number   5

    0.00      0.00      1.00      1.00     -1.00     -1.00      1.00
    0.00
    0.00      1.00      1.00      0.00      1.00      0.00     -1.00
    8.00
    1.00      0.00      0.00      0.00     -1.00      0.00      1.00
    2.00
    0.00      0.00      3.00      0.00      1.00      0.00     -1.00
   28.00
```

a) Find the right-hand-side ranges of each of the first three constraints.

b) Find the new optimal solution if the right-hand sides of the first three constraints were simultaneously changed to 6, 1, and 2, respectively.

c) Find the new optimal solution to the original problem if only the first constraint were changed to $x_1 + 2x_2 \leq 16$.

d) Find the new optimal solution to the original problem if only the first constraint were changed to $3x_1 + x_2 \geq 18$ and the objective function were to be minimized.

4.20 PROBLEM SET 4-6 (continued)

4. ```
$ lindo
LINDO (7 OCTOBER 88 CHICAGO)
: min 5x1 + 2x2
?st
?x1 + 3x2 <= 24
?x1 + x2 >= 10
?2x1 + x2 = 18
?end

: go
LP OPTIMUM FOUND AT STEP   2

        OBJECTIVE FUNCTION VALUE
    1)   42.000000

VARIABLE   VALUE   REDUCED COST
    X1   6.000000   0.000000
    X2   6.000000   0.000000

    ROW   SLACK OR SURPLUS   DUAL PRICES
    2)   0.000000   0.200000
    3)   2.000000   0.000000
    4)   0.000000   -2.600000

NO. ITERATIONS=   2

DO RANGE(SENSITIVITY) ANALYSIS?
?yes

RANGES IN WHICH THE BASIS IS UNCHANGED

                    OBJ COEFFICIENT RANGES
             CURRENT   ALLOWABLE   ALLOWABLE
VARIABLE   COEF   INCREASE   DECREASE
    X1   5.000000   INFINITY   1.000000
    X2   2.000000   0.500000   INFINITY

                    RIGHTHAND SIDE RANGES
             CURRENT   ALLOWABLE   ALLOWABLE
    ROW   RHS   INCREASE   DECREASE
    2   24.000000   30.000000   10.000000
    3   10.000000   2.000000   INFINITY
    4   18.000000   30.000000   5.000000

Simplex Tableau Number   4
    0.00   0.00   0.20   1.00   -1.00   0.40   2.00
    0.00   1.00   0.40   0.00   0.00   -0.20   6.00
    1.00   0.00   -0.20   0.00   0.00   0.60   6.00
    0.00   0.00   -0.20   0.00   0.00   2.60   42.00
```
```

4.20 PROBLEM SET 4-6 (continued)

a) Find the right-hand-side ranges of each of the first three constraints.
b) Find the new optimal solution if the right-hand sides of the first three constraints were simultaneously changed to 30, 12, and 20, respectively.
c) Find the new optimal solution to the original problem if only the first constraint were changed to $x_1 + 20x_2 \leq 30$.
d) Find the maximum corresponding to the changes in (c).

5.
```
$ lindo
LINDO (7 OCTOBER 88 CHICAGO)
: min 6x1 + 3x2
?st
?x2 <= 6
?-x1 + 3x2 >= 0
?x1 + x2 = 12
?end

: go
LP OPTIMUM FOUND AT STEP       2

        OBJECTIVE FUNCTION VALUE
    1)      54.000000

  VARIABLE        VALUE         REDUCED COST
      X1         6.000000         0.000000
      X2         6.000000         0.000000

      ROW    SLACK OR SURPLUS    DUAL PRICES
       2)       0.000000          3.000000
       3)      12.000000          0.000000
       4)       0.000000         -6.000000

 NO. ITERATIONS=      2

 DO RANGE(SENSITIVITY) ANALYSIS?
 ?yes

 RANGES IN WHICH THE BASIS IS UNCHANGED:
```

	OBJ COEFFICIENT RANGES		
VARIABLE	CURRENT COEF	ALLOWABLE INCREASE	ALLOWABLE DECREASE
X1	6.000000	INFINITY	3.000000
X2	3.000000	3.000000	INFINITY

	RIGHTHAND SIDE RANGES		
ROW	CURRENT RHS	ALLOWABLE INCREASE	ALLOWABLE DECREASE
2	6.000000	6.000000	3.000000
3	0.000000	12.000000	INFINITY
4	12.000000	12.000000	6.000000

4.20 PROBLEM SET 4-6 (continued)

Simplex Tableau Number 4

0.00	0.00	4.00	1.00	−1.00	−1.00	12.00
0.00	1.00	1.00	0.00	0.00	0.00	6.00
1.00	0.00	−1.00	0.00	0.00	1.00	6.00
0.00	0.00	−3.00	0.00	0.00	6.00	54.00

a) Find the right-hand-side ranges of each of the first three constraints.

b) Find the new optimal solution if the right-hand sides of the first three constraints were simultaneously changed to 8, 4, and 16, respectively.

c) Find the new optimal solution to the original problem if only the first constraint were changed to $(1/2)x_1 + x_2 \leq 9$.

d) Repeat (c), but, this time, with the constraint changed to the equivalent restraint $x_1 + 2x_2 \leq 18$. Compare the slack variable column in the Final Tableau of this problem with that in (c) and explain the difference.

6. ```
$ lindo
LINDO (7 OCTOBER 88 CHICAGO)
: max 3x1 + 2x2
?st
?x1 + 3x2 <= 24
?2x1 + x2 <= 18
?x1 + x2 <= 10
?end

: go
LP OPTIMUM FOUND AT STEP   2

        OBJECTIVE FUNCTION VALUE
    1)   28.000000

 VARIABLE   VALUE   REDUCED COST
       X1   8.000000   0.000000
       X2   2.000000   0.000000

      ROW   SLACK OR SURPLUS   DUAL PRICES
       2)   10.000000   0.000000
       3)   0.000000   1.000000
       4)   0.000000   1.000000

 NO. ITERATIONS=   2

DO RANGE (SENSITIVITY) ANALYSIS?
?yes

RANGES IN WHICH THE BASIS IS UNCHANGED:
```
```

4.20 PROBLEM SET 4-6 (continued)

OBJ COEFFICIENT RANGES

VARIABLE	CURRENT COEF	ALLOWABLE INCREASE	ALLOWABLE DECREASE
X1	3.000000	1.000000	1.000000
X2	2.000000	1.000000	0.500000

RIGHTHAND SIDE RANGES

ROW	CURRENT RHS	ALLOWABLE INCREASE	ALLOWABLE DECREASE
2	24.000000	INFINITY	10.000000
3	18.000000	2.000000	5.000000
4	10.000000	2.000000	1.000000

Simplex Tableau Number   3

0.00	0.00	1.00	2.00	−5.00	10.00
1.00	0.00	0.00	1.00	−1.00	8.00
0.00	1.00	0.00	−1.00	2.00	2.00
0.00	0.00	0.00	1.00	1.00	28.00

a) What is the range for the objective function coefficient 3 of x_1?

b) What is the range for the objective function coefficient 2 of x_2?

c) What is the range for the objective function coefficient 0 of s_2?

d) What is the range for the objective function coefficient 0 of s_3?

---

7. The following are the computer printouts for the first example of Section 4.9, where

$$\theta_{max} = 9x_1 + 12x_2 + 10x_3 - 2s_1 + 2s_2$$

was transformed into

$$\theta_{max} = 11x_1 + 10x_2 + 8x_3 - 12.$$

```
$ lindo
LINDO (7 OCTOBER 88 CHICAGO)
: max 11x1 + 10x2 + 8x3
?st
?2x1 + 2x2 + x3 <= 36
?x1 + 3x2 + 2x3 <= 30
?end

: go
LP OPTIMUM FOUND AT STEP     2

      OBJECTIVE FUNCTION VALUE
   1)    218.000000

  VARIABLE        VALUE          REDUCED COST
       X1        14.000000          0.000000
       X2         0.000000          4.333333
       X3         8.000000          0.000000
```

4.20 PROBLEM SET 4-6 (continued)

ROW	SLACK OR SURPLUS	DUAL PRICES
2)	0.000000	4.666667
3)	0.000000	1.666667

NO. ITERATIONS=   2

DO RANGE (SENSITIVITY) ANALYSIS?
?yes

RANGES IN WHICH THE BASIS IS UNCHANGED

OBJ COEFFICIENT RANGES

VARIABLE	CURRENT COEF	ALLOWABLE INCREASE	ALLOWABLE DECREASE
X1	11.000000	5.000000	7.000000
X2	10.000000	4.333333	INFINITY
X3	8.000000	13.999999	2.500000

RIGHTHAND SIDE RANGES

ROW	CURRENT RHS	ALLOWABLE INCREASE	ALLOWABLE DECREASE
2	36.000000	24.000000	21.000000
3	30.000000	42.000000	12.000000

Simplex Tableau Number   3

1.00	0.33	0.00	0.67	-0.33	14.00
0.00	1.33	1.00	-0.33	0.67	8.00
0.00	4.33	0.00	4.67	1.67	218.00

a) What is the optimal solution?
b) What is the range for the objective function coefficient 9 of x_1?
c) What is the range for the objective function coefficient 12 of x_2?
d) What is the range for the objective function coefficient 10 of x_3?
e) What is the range for the objective function coefficient -2 of s_1?
f) What is the range for the objective function coefficient 2 of s_2?

8. In Problem 1,
   a) What is the range for the objective function coefficient 6 of x_1?
   b) What is the range for the objective function coefficient 2 of x_2?
   c) What is the range for the objective function coefficient 0 of p_2?

9. The following are the computer printouts for the second example in Section 4.9, where

$$\theta_{\min} = 40x_1 + 60x_2 + 35x_3 + 12s_1 + 14s_2$$

was transformed into

$$\theta_{\min} = 2x_1 - 6x_2 - 5x_3 + 852.$$

4.20 PROBLEM SET 4-6 (continued)

```
$ lindo
LINDO (7 OCTOBER 88 CHICAGO)
: min 2x1 - 6x2 - 5x3
?st
?2x1 + 2x2 + x3 <= 36
?x1 + 3x2 + 2x3 <= 30
?end

: go
LP OPTIMUM FOUND AT STEP      1

        OBJECTIVE FUNCTION VALUE
    1)     -75.0000000

 VARIABLE         VALUE          REDUCED COST
    X1          0.000000            4.500000
    X2          0.000000            1.500000
    X3         15.000000            0.000000

    ROW     SLACK OR SURPLUS       DUAL PRICES
    2)         21.000000            0.000000
    3)          0.000000            2.500000

NO. ITERATIONS=       1

DO RANGE(SENSITIVITY) ANALYSIS?
?yes

RANGES IN WHICH THE BASIS IS UNCHANGED:

                    OBJ COEFFICIENT RANGES
                CURRENT        ALLOWABLE       ALLOWABLE
VARIABLE         COEF          INCREASE        DECREASE
    X1        2.000000         INFINITY        4.500000
    X2       -6.000000         INFINITY        1.500000
    X3       -5.000000         1.000000        INFINITY

                    RIGHTHAND SIDE RANGES
                CURRENT        ALLOWABLE       ALLOWABLE
    ROW          RHS           INCREASE        DECREASE
     2         36.000000       INFINITY        21.00000
     3         30.000000       42.000000       30.000000

Simplex Tableau Number   3
        1.50      0.50      0.00      1.00     -0.50     21.00
        0.50      1.50      1.00      0.00      0.50     15.00
       -4.50     -1.50      0.00      0.00     -2.50    -75.00
```

4.20 PROBLEM SET 4–6 (concluded)

a) What is the optimal solution?
b) What is the range for the objective function coefficient 40 of x_1?
c) What is the range for the objective function coefficient 60 of x_2?
d) What is the range for the objective function coefficient 35 of x_3?
e) What is the range for the objective function coefficient 14 of s_2?

10. In Problem 6,
   a) Find the inequality relating the profit P associated with the introduction of a new product and its corresponding resource requirements R_1, R_2, and R_3.
   b) Suppose the new product utilized 2 units of Resource 1, 3 units of Resource 2, and 1 unit of Resource 3. How much would it have to contribute to the profit for it to be introduced into the solution?
   c) Suppose the new product utilized 3 units of Resource of 1 plus 1 unit of Resource 2, and contributed $5 to the profit. How many units of Resource 3 can the product use if it is to be introduced into the solution?
   d) What is the restriction on the number of units the new product can use of Resource 1 if it is to be introduced into the solution?

11. In Problem 1,
   a) Find the inequality relating the cost C associated with the introduction of a new product and its corresponding resource requirements R_1, R_2, and R_3.
   b) Suppose the new product utilized 4 units of Resource 1, 3 units of Resource 2, and 5 units of Resource 3. How much could it add to the cost for it to be introduced into the solution?
   c) Suppose the new product added $14 to the cost? How many units of Resource 2 can the product use if it is to be introduced into the solution? Resource 1? Resource 3?

12. In Problem 7,
   a) Find the inequality relating the profit P associated with the introduction of a new product and its corresponding resource requirements R_1 and R_2.
   b) Suppose the new product utilized 2 units of Resource 1 and 1 unit of Resource 2. How much would it have to contribute to the profit for it to be introduced into the solution?
   c) Suppose the new product utilized 3 units of Resource 1 and contributed $19 to the profit. How many units of Resource 2 can the product use if it is to be introduced into the solution?
   d) Suppose the new product utilized 4 units of Resource 2 and contributed $20 to the profit. How many units of Resource 1 can the product use if it is to be introduced into the solution?

13. In Problem 9,
   a) Find the inequality relating the cost C associated with the introduction of a new product and its corresponding resource requirements R_1 and R_2.
   b) Suppose the new product utilized 2 units of Resource 1 and 2 units of Resource 2. How much could it add to the cost for it to be introduced into the solution?
   c) Suppose the new product utilized 1/8 unit of Resource 1 and added $36 to the cost. How many units of Resource 2 can the product use if it is to be introduced into the solution?
   d) Suppose the product utilized 2 units of Resource 2 and added $35 to the cost. How many units of Resource 1 can the product use if it is to be introduced into the solution?

4.21 REVIEW PROBLEMS

Solve by the Simplex Method:

1. Given $\theta = x_1 + 6x_2 + 3x_3$, find θ_{max} subject to $x_1, x_2, x_3 \geq 0$ and

$$x_1 + 5x_2 + 4x_3 \leq 39$$
$$2x_1 + 13x_2 + 5x_3 \leq 90$$
$$x_1 + 2x_2 + 3x_3 \leq 40.$$

2. Given $\theta = 2x_1 + 3x_2 + x_3$, find θ_{max} subject to $x_1, x_2, x_3 \geq 0$ and

$$3x_1 + 2x_2 + x_3 \leq 8$$
$$2x_1 + 3x_2 + x_3 \leq 10$$
$$5x_1 + 3x_2 + 2x_3 \leq 17.$$

3. Given $\theta = 3x_1 + 2x_2 + x_3$, find θ_{max} subject to $x_1, x_2, x_3 \geq 0$ and

$$3x_1 + x_2 + x_3 \leq 35$$
$$2x_1 + 10x_2 + 3x_3 \leq 140$$
$$4x_1 + 4x_2 + x_3 \leq 50.$$

4. Given $\theta = 2x_1 + x_2 + 2x_3$, find θ_{max} subject to $x_1, x_2, x_3 \geq 0$ and

$$x_1 + x_2 + 2x_3 \leq 8$$
$$2x_1 + x_2 + x_3 \leq 10$$
$$3x_1 + x_2 + 3x_3 \leq 15.$$

5. Maximize

$$\theta = 3x_1 + 3x_2 + 2x_3$$

subject to

$$2x_1 + 2x_2 + x_3 \leq 36$$
$$x_1 + 3x_2 + 2x_3 \leq 30$$
$$x_1, x_2, x_3 \geq 0.$$

6. Safety Lock Company makes three kinds of locks: Model SS (the super safe), Model S (the safe), and Model O (the economy). Each Model SS lock sells for $16 and costs $11 to make, each Model S lock sells for $9 and costs $6 to make, and each Model O lock sells for $7 and costs $3 to make. Each of the locks must be processed on five machines: Model SS requires three hours on Machine A, one hour on Machine B, two hours on Machine C, four hours on Machine D, and three hours on Machine E. Model S requires two hours on A, three hours on B, one hour on C, five hours on D, and four hours on E. Model O requires one hour on A, two hours on B, two hours on C, three hours on D, and four hours on E. During the coming week Machine A will be free for no more than 23 hours, Machine B for no more than 26 hours, Machine C for no more than 19 hours, Machine D for no more than 49 hours, and Machine E for no more than 45 hours. Determine the number of each kind of lock to be made in the coming week in order for the company to maximize its profit. What is this maximum profit?

7. Subject to

$$x_1 + x_2 + 4x_3 \leq 36$$
$$2x_1 + 2x_2 + 3x_3 \leq 42$$
$$x_1, x_2, x_3 \geq 0,$$

maximize

a) $\theta = 3x_1 + 3x_2 + 12x_3$.
b) $\theta = 6x_1 + 6x_2 + 7x_3$.

8. Subject to

$$-x_1 + x_2 \leq 4$$
$$x_1 + x_2 \leq 6$$
$$x_1 \geq 0$$

x_2 unrestricted in sign,

a) Maximize $\theta = 10x_1 + 10x_2$.
b) Maximize $\theta = 10x_1 + 8x_2$.
c) Minimize $\theta = 8x_1 + 10x_2$.

9. Ace Rubber Company makes two types of tires: Model P (the premium) and Model S (the second line). Each tire must be processed on three machines: A, B, and C. To make one Model P tire requires one hour on Machines A and B plus two hours on Machine C. To make one Model S tire requires one hour on Machines A and C plus two hours on Machine B. Production scheduling indicated that during the coming week Machine A will be free for at most 13 hours,

4.21 REVIEW PROBLEMS (continued)

Machine B for at most 22 hours, and Machine C for at most 20 hours. In addition, no more than eight Model S tires may be made. The cost of operating Machine A is $10 per hour, Machine B is $4 per hour, and Machine C is $8 per hour; while each slack hour on A creates an opportunity cost of $8, each slack hour on B creates an opportunity cost of $9, and each slack hour on C creates an opportunity cost of $6. Find the number of each type of tire to be made in the coming week for the company to minimize its cost of operation.

Solve Problems 10 through 14 by the dual procedure.

10. Given $\theta = 6x_1 + 24x_2 + 12x_3$, find θ_{min} subject to $x_1, x_2, x_3 \geq 0$ and

$$x_1 + 2x_2 + x_3 \geq 1$$
$$x_1 + x_2 + 3x_3 \geq 2$$
$$x_1 + 3x_2 + x_3 \geq 3.$$

11. Given $\theta = 2x_1 + x_2 + x_3$, find θ_{min} subject to $x_1, x_2, x_3 \geq 0$ and

$$2x_1 + 3x_2 + 2x_3 \geq 10$$
$$x_1 + 4x_2 + 3x_3 \geq 20.$$

12. Given $\theta = 12x_1 + 6x_2 + 4x_3$, find θ_{min} subject to $x_1, x_2, x_3 \geq 0$ and

$$2x_1 + x_2 + 2x_3 \geq 1$$
$$x_1 + 2x_2 \geq 2$$
$$3x_1 + x_3 \geq 1.$$

13. Given $\theta = 8x_1 + 10x_2 + 15x_3$, find θ_{min} subject to $x_1, x_2, x_3 \geq 0$ and

$$x_1 + 2x_2 + 3x_3 \geq 2$$
$$x_1 + x_2 + x_3 \geq 1$$
$$2x_1 + x_2 + 3x_3 \geq 2.$$

14. Given $\theta = 5x_1 + 7x_2 + 6x_3$, find θ_{min} subject to $x_1, x_2, x_3 \geq 0$ and

$$x_1 + x_3 \geq 3$$
$$x_1 + x_2 \geq 2$$
$$x_2 + x_3 \geq 1.$$

---

15. If we were to maximize

$$\theta = 2x_1 + x_2$$

subject to

$$x_1 + x_2 \leq 7$$
$$-x_1 + x_2 \leq 1$$
$$x_1 \leq 5$$
$$x_1, x_2 \geq 0,$$

the final tableau would be as shown at the top of the right column.

a) Find the right-hand-side ranges for each of the first three constraints.
b) Find the new optimal solution to the original problem if the right-hand sides of the first three constraints were simultaneously changed to 8, 6, and 4, respectively.

Basic Variables	Coefficient of					Current Values
	x_1	x_2	s_1	s_2	s_3	
x_2	0	1	1	0	-1	2
s_2	0	0	-1	1	2	4
x_1	1	0	0	0	1	5
(max) θ	0	0	1	0	1	12

16. Find the new optimal solution to Problem 15 if only the first constraint were changed to $2x_1 + x_2 \leq 10$.

4.21 REVIEW PROBLEMS (continued)

Use a computer program such as LINDO to solve Problems 17 through 23, assuming all variables to be nonnegative.

17. Maximize and minimize
$$\theta = -3x_1 + 7x_2 + 10$$
subject to
$$2x_1 + 3x_2 \le 24$$
$$2x_1 - x_2 \le 8$$
$$-2x_1 + 3x_2 \le 12.$$

18. Minimize
$$\theta = 2x_1 + 5x_2 + 6x_3$$
subject to
$$4x_1 + 3x_2 + 2x_3 \ge 48$$
$$x_1 + 4x_2 + 8x_3 \ge 40$$
$$2x_1 + 9x_2 + 7x_3 \ge 66.$$

19. Ace Rubber Company manufactures three types of tires: Model P (the premium), Model S (the second line), and Model E (the economy). Model P sells for $95 per tire and costs $85 per tire to make; Model S sells for $78 per tire and costs $72 per tire to make; Model E sells for $75 per tire and costs $63 per tire to make. To make one Model P tire requires one hour on Machine A and one hour on Machine B. To make one Model S tire takes one hour on Machine A and two hours on Machine B. To make one Model E tire requires four hours on A and three hours on B. Production scheduling indicates that during the coming week Machine A will be available for at most 42 hours and Machine B for at most 40 hours. How many of each tire should the company make in the coming week to maximize its profit? What is this maximum profit?

20. Suppose in Problem 19 that each tire must be processed on two additional machines C and D as follows: Model P requires two hours on C and three hours on D, Model S requires one hour on C and four hours on D, and Model E requires two hours on C and one hour on D. Suppose also that during the coming week Machine C will be available for at most 30 hours and Machine D at for at most 44 hours. Find the number of each tire the company should make in the coming week to maximize its profit. What is this maximum profit?

21. The brothers of XYZ fraternity have kept a record of a certain logic professor's final examinations and have determined the following interesting facts: The examination is always divided into three categories of questions: T/F (true-false), M/C (multiple-choice), and S/E (short-essay). Now the student is given a choice of 50 T/F questions, each counting one point, 50 M/C questions, each counting two points, and 10 S/E questions, each counting four points. However, the student must select at least 40 questions but no more than 60 questions, and must answer at least five S/E questions. In addition, the student must answer more M/C questions than T/F questions, but the student's score is penalized one point each for the number of M/C questions answered over the number of T/F questions answered. Finally, the number of T/F questions answered must be smaller by at least 10 than the difference between the number of M/C questions answered and twice the number of S/E questions answered. The president of the fraternity, now enrolled in the logic professor's course, has decided that one phase of the initiation of the new pledges will be to find all possible combinations of the number of each kind of question that should be answered to attain the best possible grade on the upcoming final examination. Determine the maximum score and all alternative combinations.

22. Superior Paint Company sells three kinds of exterior finishes: oil-base paint, water-base paint, and stain. In order to keep all its distributors properly supplied, the company must manufacture and store at least three months' sales in advance. Since consumers' color preferences tend to change rapidly and since warehousing costs are high, management wishes to carefully select its next manufacturing choices. Oil-base paint costs the company $5.50 per gallon to make, water-base paint costs $4.50 per gallon, and stain costs $3.50 per gallon. The company has determined that the carrying cost for all three finishes is $0.50 per gallon for the average number of gallons in the inventory (the average being typically one-half

4.21 REVIEW PROBLEMS (continued)

of the number originally manufactured). Based on past experience, the sales department of the company has projected that its needs for the next three months will be at most 10,000 but at least 6,000 total gallons. Furthermore, no more than 2,000 gallons of stain but at least 1,000 gallons of each finish will be needed. In addition, the number of gallons of paint should be at least 75 percent of the total. How many gallons of each finish should the company make and what will be the cost?

23. Precision Instruments, Inc. has a contract to supply Electronic Calculator Company 600 minicircuits in July and 500 minicircuits in August. Precision makes and tests the minicircuits on an assembly line, using people on both a regular- and second-shift basis. In July, because of other commitments, only 650 minicircuits can be produced during regular time and only 200 during the second shift. On the other hand, only 450 minicircuits can be produced during regular time in August and only 150 in the second shift. The problem is that production costs differ not only for each shift, but also for each of the two months.

Specifically, in the month of July the regular-shift cost is $250 per minicircuit, while the second-shift cost is $350 per minicircuit. The respective costs for August are $300 and $375. Of course, Precision can make more than the 600 minicircuits required by Electronic in July; but, in this case, Precision must store the excess from July to August at a unit inventory cost of $25. What should Precision's production schedule be and what is the associated cost?

a) Formulate the problem with the following variables: x_{JR} and x_{JS} are the number of minicircuits produced in July during regular and second shift, respectively; x_{AR} and x_{AS} in August; and x_1 the inventory from July to August. (Hint: Be careful to remember that, for consistency, the inventory must be the excess over the 600.)

b) Formulate the problem with the following variables: x_{JRJ} and x_{JRA} are the number of minicircuits produced in July, regular shift, for use in July and August, respectively; x_{JSJ} and x_{JSA}, the number of minicircuits produced in July, second shift; x_{AR} and x_{AS} in (a).

Use the Phase I–Phase II Method or a computer program such as LINDO to solve Problems 24 through 49, assuming all variables to be nonnegative.

24. Minimize

$$\theta = 5x_1 + x_2$$

subject to

$$2x_1 + 3x_2 \geq 12$$
$$5x_1 + x_2 \geq 17.$$

25. Minimize

$$\theta = 8x_1 + 10x_2$$

subject to

$$4x_1 + 5x_2 \geq 30$$
$$3x_1 + 2x_2 \geq 19.$$

26. Minimize

$$\theta = 6x_1 + 8x_2$$

subject to

$$x_1 + 3x_2 \geq 24$$

$$2x_1 + x_2 \geq 18$$
$$3x_1 + 4x_2 \geq 52.$$

27. Minimize

$$\theta = 2x_1 + x_2 + 3x_3$$

subject to

$$2x_1 + 2x_2 + 5x_3 \geq 30$$
$$3x_1 + x_2 + 3x_3 \geq 27.$$

28. Minimize

$$\theta = 3x_1 + 4x_2 + 6x_3 + 10$$

subject to

$$x_1 + x_2 + 4x_3 \geq 36$$
$$3x_1 + 2x_2 + 2x_3 \geq 48.$$

29. Minimize

$$\theta = 3x_1 + x_2 + 4x_3 - 5$$

4.21 REVIEW PROBLEMS (continued)

subject to

$$x_1 + 2x_2 + 3x_3 \geq 36$$
$$x_1 \phantom{{}+ 2x_2} + 2x_3 \geq 16.$$

30. Maximize and minimize

$$\theta = 4x_1 + 6x_2 + 5x_3$$

   subject to

$$x_1 + 2x_2 + 3x_3 \leq 18$$
$$x_1 + x_2 + x_3 \geq 12.$$

31. Maximize and minimize

$$\theta = 8x_1 + 6x_2 + 2x_3$$

   subject to

$$x_1 + 3x_2 + x_3 \leq 36$$
$$2x_1 + x_2 + 2x_3 \geq 24.$$

32. Strong Steel Company operates three steel mills with different production capacities. Mill I can produce 4,000 tons per day of AAAA steel, 1,000 tons per day of AAA steel, 3,000 tons per day of AA steel, and 10,000 tons per day of A steel. Mill F can produce 3,000 tons per day of AAAA steel, 2,000 tons per day of AAA steel, 2,000 tons per day of AA steel, and 4,000 tons per day of A steel. Mill S can produce 2,000, 4,000, 1,000, and 3,000 tons per day, respectively. The company has made a contract with a construction firm to provide 35,000 tons of AAAA steel, 29,000 tons of AAA steel, 23,000 tons of AA steel, and 62,000 tons of A steel. If it costs $1,400 per day to run Mill I, $1,000 per day to run Mill F, and $1,200 per day to run Mill S, determine the number of days the company should operate each mill in order to meet the terms of the contract most economically. What is this minimum cost?

33. Maximize

$$\theta = 6x_1 + 2x_2$$

   subject to

$$x_1 + x_2 \leq 12$$
$$2x_1 + 4x_2 \geq 36$$
$$x_1 - 2x_2 \geq 0.$$

34. Maximize

$$\theta = x_1 + 7x_2$$

   subject to

$$x_1 + 3x_2 \leq 24$$
$$x_1 + x_2 \geq 10$$
$$2x_1 + x_2 = 18$$
$$5x_1 + x_2 = 20.$$

35. Minimize

$$\theta = 3x_1 + 2x_2$$

   subject to

$$x_1 + x_2 \leq 10$$
$$2x_1 + x_2 \geq 12$$
$$x_2 \geq 9.$$

36. Minimize

$$\theta = 4x_1 + 5x_2$$

   subject to

$$x_1 + x_2 \leq 15$$
$$-x_1 + x_2 \geq 3$$
$$x_1 \geq 8.$$

37. Maximize

$$\theta = 5x_1 + 2x_2$$

   subject to

$$x_1 + 3x_2 \leq 24$$
$$x_1 + x_2 \geq 10$$
$$2x_1 + x_2 = 18$$
$$x_2 = 6.$$

38. Minimize

$$\theta = 5x_1 + 7x_2$$

   subject to

$$x_1 \leq 5$$
$$2x_1 + 3x_2 \geq 12$$
$$5x_1 + x_2 \geq 17.$$

4.21 REVIEW PROBLEMS (continued)

39. Minimize
$$\theta = 2x_1 + 8x_2$$
subject to
$$x_2 \le 8$$
$$4x_1 + 5x_2 \ge 30$$
$$3x_1 + 2x_2 \ge 19.$$

40. Minimize
$$\theta = 3x_1 + 5x_2 + 4x_3$$
subject to
$$x_1 + 2x_2 + x_3 \le 24$$
$$2x_1 + x_2 + 2x_3 \ge 30$$
$$x_1 + x_2 + 2x_3 \ge 20.$$

41. Maximize and minimize
$$\theta = 6x_1 + 2x_2$$
subject to
$$x_1 + x_2 \le 12$$
$$2x_1 + 4x_2 \ge 36.$$

42. Repeat Problem 41 with the additional constraint that $-2x_1 + x_2 \ge 0$.

43. Repeat Problem 41 with the additional constraint that $x_1 - 2x_2 \le 0$.

44. Maximize and minimize
$$\theta = 2x_1 + 3x_2$$
subject to
$$x_1 \le 8$$
$$x_1 + x_2 \ge 12$$
$$-x_1 + x_2 \ge 0.$$

45. Maximize and minimize
$$\theta = 3x_1 + 4x_2$$
subject to
$$x_1 + x_2 \le 10$$
$$2x_1 + x_2 \ge 12$$
$$x_2 \ge 4.$$

46. Maximize and minimize
$$\theta = 4x_1 + 5x_2$$
subject to
$$x_1 + x_2 \le 15$$
$$-x_1 + x_2 \ge 3$$
$$x_1 \ge 4.$$

47. Maximize and minimize
$$\theta = x_1 + 2x_2$$
subject to
$$x_1 + x_2 \le 10$$
$$3x_1 + x_2 = 18.$$

48. Maximize and minimize
$$\theta = 6x_1 + 5x_2$$
subject to
$$x_1 + 3x_2 \le 24$$
$$x_1 + x_2 \ge 10$$
$$2x_1 + x_2 = 18.$$

49. Subject to
$$3x_1 + x_2 \le 18$$
$$x_1 + x_2 \ge 12,$$
minimize
$$\theta = 5x_1 + 2x_2$$
where there is both a premium of $3 per unit of slack associated with the first constraint and a penalty of $2 per unit of surplus associated with the second constraint.

4.21 REVIEW PROBLEMS (continued)

Solve Problems 50 through 53, using the accompanying LINDO printout and/or the accompanying computer printout of the optimal tableau:

50. ```
    $ lindo
    LINDO (7 OCTOBER 88 CHICAGO)
    : min 1500x1 + 2400x2
    ?st
    ?4x1 + x2 >= 24
    ?2x1 + 3x2 >= 42
    ?x1 + 4x2 >= 36
    ?end

    : go
    LP OPTIMUM FOUND AT STEP     2

            OBJECTIVE FUNCTION VALUE
         1)    32400.0000

    VARIABLE        VALUE           REDUCED COST
        X1        12.000000           0.000000
        X2         6.000000           0.000000

        ROW     SLACK OR SURPLUS    DUAL PRICES
         2)       30.000000           0.000000
         3)        0.000000        -720.000000
         4)        0.000000         -60.000000

    NO. ITERATIONS=       2


    DO RANGE (SENSITIVITY) ANALYSIS?
     ?yes

    RANGES IN WHICH THE BASIS IS UNCHANGED:


                            OBJ COEFFICIENT RANGES
                    CURRENT        ALLOWABLE       ALLOWABLE
    VARIABLE         COEF          INCREASE        DECREASE
        X1        1500.000000      99.999992      900.000000
        X2        2400.000000    3600.000000      150.000000


                            RIGHTHAND SIDE RANGES
                    CURRENT        ALLOWABLE       ALLOWABLE
        ROW          RHS           INCREASE        DECREASE
         2         24.000000       30.000000        INFINITY
         3         42.000000       30.000000       10.000000
         4         36.000000       15.000000       15.000000
    ```
    ```

4.21 REVIEW PROBLEMS (continued)

Simplex Tableau Number 5

1.00	0.00	0.00	−0.80	0.60	0.00	0.80
−0.60	12.00					
0.00	0.00	1.00	−3.00	2.00	−1.00	3.00
−2.00	30.00					
0.00	1.00	0.00	0.20	−0.40	0.00	−0.20
0.40	6.00					
0.00	0.00	0.00	−720.00	−60.00	0.00	720.00
60.00	32,400.00					

a) Find the right-hand-side ranges of each of the first three constraints.

b) Find the new optimal solution if the right-hand sides of the first three constraints were simultaneously changed to 10, 20, and 15, respectively.

c) Find the new optimal solution to the original problem if only the first constraint were changed to $3x_1 + x_2 \geq 24$.

d) Find the Preliminary Final Tableau if in the original problem only the third constraint were changed to $3x_1 + 4x_2 \geq 36$. Explain why this tableau does not represent the optimal solution.

51. ```
    $ lindo
    LINDO (7 OCTOBER 88 CHICAGO)
    : max 3x1 + 5x2 −4x3
    ? st
    ? x1 + 2x2 + 3x3 <= 24
    ? 2x1 + x2 + x3 <= 18
    ? x1 >= 3
    ? end

    : go
    LP OPTIMUM FOUND AT STEP      3

            OBJECTIVE FUNCTION VALUE
         1)     28.0000000

    VARIABLE         VALUE           REDUCED COST
        X1          5.000000            0.000000
        X2          5.000000            0.000000
        X3          3.000000            0.000000

         ROW    SLACK OR SURPLUS     DUAL PRICES
         2)         0.000000           2.333333
         3)         0.000000           0.333333
         4)         0.000000         −11.333333

     NO. ITERATIONS=        3

    DO RANGE (SENSITIVITY) ANALYSIS?
    ? yes
    ```
    ```

4.21 REVIEW PROBLEMS (concluded)

RANGES IN WHICH THE BASIS IS UNCHANGED:

OBJ COEFFICIENT RANGES

VARIABLE	CURRENT COEF	ALLOWABLE INCREASE	ALLOWABLE DECREASE
X1	3.000000	7.000000	0.500000
X2	5.000000	1.000000	3.500000
X3	-4.000000	11.333333	INFINITY

RIGHTHAND SIDE RANGES

ROW	CURRENT RHS	ALLOWABLE INCREASE	ALLOWABLE DECREASE
2	24.000000	15.000000	7.500000
3	18.000000	15.000000	7.500000
4	3.000000	3.000000	3.000000

Simplex Tableau Number 4

0.00	1.00	0.00	0.67	-0.33	1.67	-1.67
5.00						
1.00	0.00	0.00	-0.33	0.67	-0.33	0.33
5.00						
0.00	0.00	1.00	0.00	0.00	-1.00	1.00
3.00						
0.00	0.00	0.00	2.33	0.33	11.33	-11.33
28.00						

a) Find the right-hand-side ranges of each of the first three constraints.
b) Find the new optimal solution if the right-hand sides of the first three constraints were simultaneously changed to 27, 15, and 6, respectively.
c) Find the new optimal solution to the original problem if only the first constraint were changed to $x_1 + 2x_2 + 4x_3 \le 24$.
d) Find the Preliminary Final Tableau if in the original problem only the third constraint were changed to $x_2 + x_3 \ge 3$. Explain why this tableau does not represent the optimal solution.

---

52. In Problem 50,
    a) What is the range for the objective function coefficient 1,500 of x_1?
    b) What is the range for the objective function coefficient 2,400 of x_2?
    c) What is the range for the objective function coefficient 0 of p_2?

53. In Problem 50,
    a) Find the inequality relating the cost C associated with the introduction of a new product and its corresponding resource requirements R_1, R_2, and R_3.
    b) Suppose the new product utilized 5 units of Resource 1, 2 units of Resource 2, and 3 units of Resource 3. How much could it add to the cost for it to be introduced into the solution?
    c) Suppose the new product used 10 units of Resource 1 plus 1 unit of Resource 2, and added $1,800 to the cost. How many units of Resource 3 can the product use if it is to be introduced into the solution?
    d) Suppose the new product added $2,100 to the cost. How many units of Resource 1 can the product use if it is to be introduced into the solution?

4.22 EXTENDED REVIEW PROBLEMS

1. Given $\theta = 2x_1 + 3x_2 + x_3$, use the dual procedure to find the minimum value of θ subject to $x_1, x_2, x_3 \geq 0$ and

$$x_1 + x_2 + x_3 \geq 10$$
$$2x_1 + 3x_2 + x_3 \geq 15$$
$$3x_1 + x_2 + 2x_3 \geq 20.$$

   a) What is the range for the objective function coefficient 5 of x_1?
   b) What is the range for the objective function coefficient 6 of x_2?
   c) What is the range for the objective function coefficient 10 of x_3?
   d) What is the range for the objective function coefficient 0 of s_1?
   e) What is the range for the objective function coefficient 0 of s_2?

2. Using the accompanying computer printouts:

```
$ lindo
LINDO (7 OCTOBER 88 CHICAGO)
: max 5x1 + 6x2 + 10x3
?st
?x1 + 2x2 + 3x3 <= 24
?2x1 + x2 + x3 <= 18
?end

: go
LP OPTIMUM FOUND AT STEP        2

        OBJECTIVE FUNCTION VALUE
    1)      90.0000000

    VARIABLE        VALUE           REDUCED COST
        X1          6.000000            0.000000
        X2          0.000000            1.000000
        X3          6.000000            0.000000

        ROW     SLACK OR SURPLUS    DUAL PRICES
        2)          0.000000            3.000000
        3)          0.000000            1.000000

NO. ITERATIONS=         2

DO RANGE (SENSITIVITY) ANALYSIS?
?yes

RANGES IN WHICH THE BASIS IS UNCHANGED:

                        OBJ COEFFICIENT RANGES
                CURRENT         ALLOWABLE       ALLOWABLE
    VARIABLE    COEF            INCREASE        DECREASE
        X1      5.000000        15.000000       1.666667
        X2      6.000000        1.000000        INFINITY
        X3      10.000000       4.999999        1.666667
```

4.22 EXTENDED REVIEW PROBLEMS (continued)

RIGHTHAND SIDE RANGES

ROW	CURRENT RHS	ALLOWABLE INCREASE	ALLOWABLE DECREASE
2	24.000000	30.000000	15.000000
3	18.000000	30.000000	10.000000

Simplex Tableau Number 3

0.00	0.60	1.00	0.40	-0.20	6.00
1.00	0.20	0.00	-0.20	0.60	6.00
0.00	1.00	0.00	3.00	1.00	90.00

3. Minimize
$$\theta = 2x_2 + x_2$$
subject to
$$x_1 + x_2 \leq 10$$
$$3x_1 + x_2 = 18$$
$$x_2 = 7.$$

4. A certain professor likes to give weekly quizzes composed of multiple-choice questions divided into two groups: A and B. By closely observing the format of the first few quizzes, one rather clever student has determined that although there are always 30 questions of each type, the student is allowed to answer at most 40 total questions. In addition, the student is prohibited from answering more than 25 A questions but is required to answer at least as many B questions as A questions. Furthermore, while each A question counts two points, each B question counts three points. Lastly, the student is always restricted by having the number of B questions answered not exceed the number of A questions by more than 8; and, indeed, is penalized 1/2 point each for the number of B questions answered over the number of A questions answered. After some deliberation, the student has worked out a scheme for the number of each kind of question that should be answered to attain the best possible grade and finds five alternative combinations. What is his scheme and what will be his score?

5. A doll manufacturer makes x_1 dresses, x_2 hats, and x_3 gloves a day, each of which contributes to the profit function θ. Resources available are 100 hours of cutting time (slack is s_1), 40 hours of assembly time (slack time is s_2), and 50 hours of stitching time (slack is s_3). The optimal profit-maximizing tableau is:

Basic Variables	Coefficient of						Current Values
	x_1	x_2	x_3	s_1	s_2	s_3	
s_1	1	0	2	50	-40	0	200
x_3	0	0	-1	-1	-1	1	10
s_2	0	1	-3	20	50	0	300
(max) θ	0	0	5	60	30	0	800

a) How many of each item should be made to maximize profit? What is the maximum profit?
b) Find the shadow price of any resource for which the constraint is binding. State the meaning of this price.
c) Find the right-hand-side ranges for the constraints in (b).

6. Maximize and minimize
$$\theta = 5x_1 + x_2$$
subject to
$$x_2 \leq 6$$
$$-x_1 + 3x_2 \geq 0$$
$$x_1 + x_2 = 12.$$

7. Subject to
$$x_1 + 2x_2 + 3x_3 \leq 18$$
$$x_1 + x_2 + x_3 \geq 12,$$
maximize the objective function
$$\theta = 4x_1 + 6x_2 + 5x_3$$

4.22 EXTENDED REVIEW PROBLEMS (continued)

where there is both a premium of $3 per unit of slack associated with the first constraint and a penalty of $2 per unit of surplus associated with the second constraint.

8. XYZ Steel Company manufactures two kinds of wrought-iron rails: Model E (the elegant) and Model D (the distinctive). Model E rails sell for $84 and cost $75 to make; Model D rails sell for $73 and cost $66 to make. To make one Model E rail requires two hours on Machine A, one hour on Machine B, and four hours on Machine C. On the other hand, to make one Model D rail requires one hour on A, two hours on B, and five hours on C. Production scheduling indicates that during the coming week Machine A will be available for at most 30 hours, Machine B for at most 24 hours, and Machine C for at most 72 hours. In addition, each unused hour on Machine A is worth $2, on Machine B is worth $2, and on Machine C is worth $1. Find the number of each kind of rail to be made in the coming week in order for the company to maximize its profit.

9. In Problem 2,
   a) Find the inequality relating the profit P associated with the introduction of a new product and its corresponding resource requirements R_1 and R_2.
   b) Suppose the new product utilized 2 units of Resource 1 plus 3 units of Resource 2. How much would it have to contribute to the profit for it to be introduced into the solution?
   c) Suppose the new product utilized 4 units of Resource 1 and contributed $18 to profit. How many units of Resource 2 can the product use if it is to be introduced into the solution?
   d) Suppose the new product utilized 5 units of Resource 2 and contributed $14 to profit. How many units of Resource 1 can the product use if it is to be introduced into the solution?

10. Using the accompanying computer printouts:

```
$ lindo
LINDO (7 OCTOBER 88 CHICAGO)
: max -2x1 + 5x2 + 9x3
 ? st
 ? x1 + x2 + 4x3 <= 36
 ? 2x1 + 2x2 + 3x3 <= 42
 ? x1 = 4
 ? end

: go
LP OPTIMUM FOUND AT STEP        2

        OBJECTIVE FUNCTION VALUE
        1)      86.0000000

VARIABLE        VALUE           REDUCED COST
    X1          4.000000        0.000000
    X2          8.000000        0.000000
    X3          6.000000        0.000000

    ROW     SLACK OR SURPLUS    DUAL PRICES
    2)          0.000000        0.600000
    3)          0.000000        2.200000
    4)          0.000000       -7.000000

NO. ITERATIONS=         2
```

4.22 EXTENDED REVIEW PROBLEMS (concluded)

```
DO RANGE (SENSITIVITY) ANALYSIS?
?yes

RANGES IN WHICH THE BASIS IS UNCHANGED:

                         OBJ COEFFICIENT RANGES
                CURRENT         ALLOWABLE        ALLOWABLE
VARIABLE         COEF           INCREASE         DECREASE
   X1          -2.000000        INFINITY         INFINITY
   X2           5.000000        1.000000         2.750000
   X3           9.000000       11.000000         1.500000

                      RIGHTHAND SIDE RANGES
                CURRENT         ALLOWABLE        ALLOWABLE
   ROW           RHS            INCREASE         DECREASE
    2          36.000000       13.333333        15.000000
    3          42.000000       30.000000        10.000000
    4           4.000000        8.000000         4.000000

Simplex Tableau Number   4
    0.00      0.00      1.00      0.40     -0.20      0.00      6.00
    0.00      1.00      0.00     -0.60      0.80     -1.00      8.00
    1.00      0.00      0.00      0.00      0.00      1.00      4.00
    0.00      0.00      0.00      0.60      2.20     -7.00     86.00
```

a) Find the right-hand-side ranges of each of the first three constraints.
b) Find the new optimal solution if the right-hand sides of the first three constraints were simultaneously changed to 35, 40, and 5, respectively.
c) Find the new optimal solution to the original problem if only the first constraint were changed to $x_1 + 3x_2 + 4x_3 \leq 36$.
d) Find the Preliminary Final Tableau if in the original problem only the third constraint were changed to $x_1 + 2x_2 = 4$. Explain why this tableau does not represent the optimal solution.

NONLINEAR RELATIONSHIPS WITH APPLICATIONS IN BUSINESS AND FINANCE

CHAPTER 5
Exponential and Logarithmic Functions

CHAPTER 6
Introduction to Mathematics of Finance

In Part I, we studied the uses and applications of linear relationships and constrained optimization. We noted that in many situations linear functions are used as approximations to nonlinear functions to simplify computation and modeling. It is important, however, to understand the basic nonlinear functions that describe many critical phenomena in business and nature. The most notable of these phenomena is that of growth.

Growth of populations, contamination, epidemics, money, etc., is described using exponential and logarithmic functions. In Part II, we will study the fundamental properties of these functions and then look closely at how these mystical functions continually reappear as the driving descriptive force of many monetary instruments and events.

The background needed for Part II is only a basic understanding of the rules of exponents. Those who want to refresh their memories are referred to the appendixes.

FROM THEORY TO PRACTICE
The Plight of the Borrower

Many years ago, the decisions that borrowers had to make were quite limited. On secured loan transactions such as home mortgages, the choice was simply to find the best interest rate. Today, the choices are many and oftentimes bewildering. Whereas previously the borrower had to put 20% down, now the down payment can be 10% or even 5%. If the down payment is only 5%, then the borrower must take out Property Mortgage Insurance or PMI. In addition, there are vastly different rates for mortgages on owner-occupied property versus investment property. Also, the term of the loan can be 15, 20, 25, or 30 years. Finally, there are special mortgages with adjustable rates, biweekly payments, etc.

How does the borrower make a decision? Clearly, there are two considerations: monthly cash-flow and total cash outlay. The borrower must be careful not to select a mortgage that has payments that amount to a significant portion of monthly take-home pay. Of course, lenders have reasonably tight guidelines as to the percentage that is available for debt amortization, but borrowers should be comfortable with the ratio of their payments to their take-home pay.

But what about the total cash outlay? As we will see in this part, this is very sensitive to the interest rate, term, and method of payment. Suppose we take a very common example. You have just purchased a $70,000 home. You are able to put $10,000 down and can then get a mortgage at 9.75%. You have the option of selecting a 15-year mortgage with payments of $635.62 per month, a 20-year mortgage with payments of $569.11 per month, or a 30-year mortgage with payments of $515.49 per month. What should you do? First, you must decide which of the three monthly payment options you can afford. Let us say for the sake of argument that you are able to stretch your budget to make any of them. Now let us look at the total cash outlay. The 15-year mortgage results in total payments of about $114,411.60. This means that the total interest on the $60,000 borrowed was $54,411.60. On the other hand, the 20-year mortgage results in total payments of about $136,586.40 with an interest amount of $76,586.40, and the 30-year mortgage is about $185,576.40 with an interest amount of $125,576.40. This example with its various choices clearly indicates the so-called **time value of money.**

5 EXPONENTIAL AND LOGARITHMIC FUNCTIONS
CHAPTER

5.1 INTRODUCTION

The object of this chapter is to review the nature and properties of exponents, exponential functions, logarithms, and logarithmic functions. We will look at some of the many applications of these very important functions, and in Chapter 6 we will see useful applications of both exponential and logarithmic functions in the mathematics of finance. Until the 1970s, students labored with extensive tables of logarithms and exponential values, but today we are fortunate to have these numerical values at our fingertips via the calculator and computer. We shall include in our discussion important techniques in the use of the calculator and the computer.

5.2 EXPONENTIAL FUNCTIONS

We are familiar with the functions

$$s(x) = x^2, \quad t(x) = \sqrt{x}, \quad \text{and} \quad u(x) = x^{-1}.$$

Each of these is of the same form as the function

$$f(x) = x^n,$$

where we have chosen a particular value of the **exponent** n and allowed the **base** x to vary over all appropriate real values. What if we were to choose a particular value for the base and allow the exponent to vary over all real values? We then obtain functions such as

$$w(x) = 2^x \quad \text{or} \quad z(x) = \left(\frac{1}{2}\right)^x.$$

The general form of these functions is

$$f(x) = a^x \quad (a > 0 \text{ and } a \neq 1),$$

In an exponential function, the base is fixed and the exponent varies.

where the value of the **base**, a, is fixed and the **exponent**, x, varies over all real numbers. Such a function is called an **exponential function** since the variable now appears as an exponent.

It is helpful to review the important properties of exponents before we continue our discussion of exponential functions.[1] The following seven properties are the most important.

---
[1] A more detailed review of exponents is given in Appendix 1.

> **Properties of Exponents** ($a, b > 0$)
>
> 1. $a^0 = 1$.
> 2. $a^x \cdot a^y = a^{x+y}$.
> 3. $a^x/a^y = a^{x-y}$.
> 4. $(a^x)^y = a^{xy}$.
> 5. $(ab)^x = a^x b^x$.
> 6. $(a/b)^x = a^x/b^x$.
> 7. $a^{-x} = 1/a^x$.

Seven important properties of exponents.

1. Any number to the power 0 is 1; $a^0 = 1$.
2. Always add exponents when multiplying two powers of the same base; $a^x \cdot a^y = a^{x+y}$.
3. When dividing a^x by a^y, subtract exponents; $a^x/a^y = a^{x-y}$.
4. The quantity a^x to the power y is equal to a^{xy}; $(a^x)^y = a^{xy}$.
5. The base ab to the power x is equal to a^x times b^x; $(ab)^x = a^x \cdot b^x$.
6. The base a/b to the power x is equal to a^x over b^x; $(a/b)^x = a^x/b^x$.
7. A base to the power $-x$ is equivalent to one over that base to the power x; $a^{-x} = 1/a^x$.

The graph of an exponential function is easy to sketch. Consider the function

$$f(x) = 2^x.$$

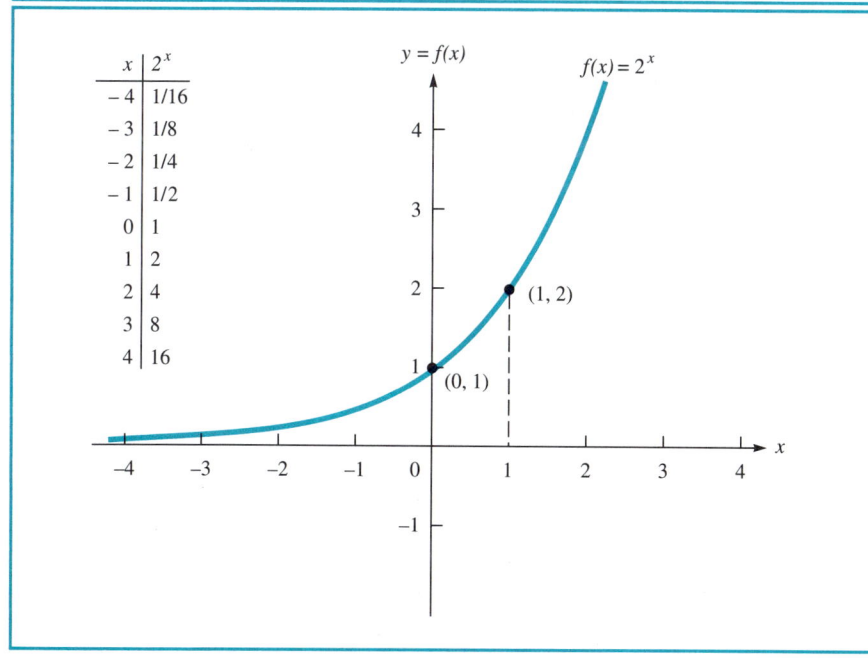

FIGURE 5-1

The graph of an exponential function is always positive.

Since $2^0 = 1$, the point $(x, f(x)) = (0, 1)$ is on the graph. Looking at the values displayed in Figure 5–1, we see that $2^x > 0$ for all values of x. In addition, as x becomes large positively, 2^x increases rapidly; and as x takes on values more and more negative, 2^x seems to decrease to zero. This is indeed the case, as shown in the graph in Figure 5–1.

Some more graphs of exponential functions are given in Figure 5–2. Notice how these graphs all look like the one in Figure 5–1. When the base a is between 0 and 1, however, the graphs look like those shown in Figure 5–3. Why?

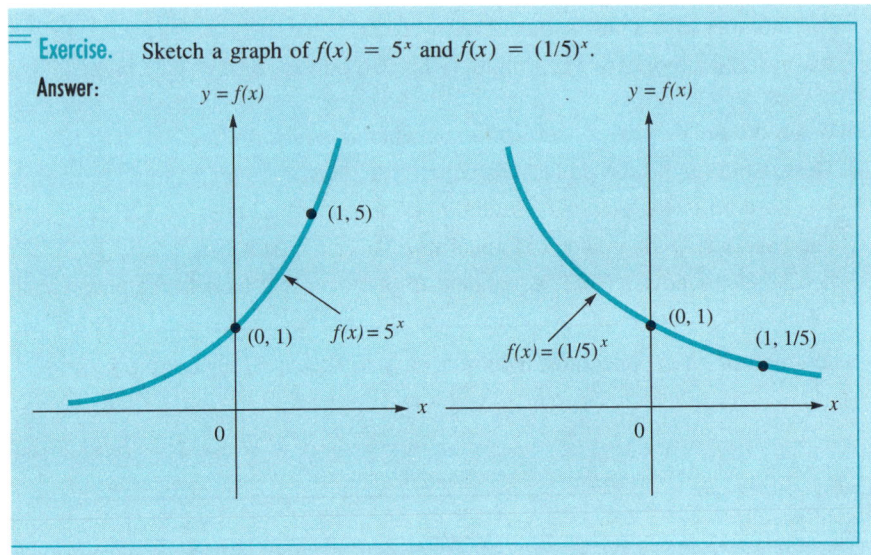

Exercise. Sketch a graph of $f(x) = 5^x$ and $f(x) = (1/5)^x$.

Answer:

From these sketches we can see that exponential functions come in two forms; those with $a > 1$ increase to the right and those with $0 < a < 1$ decrease to the right. All exponential functions of the form a^x

Three properties of exponential functions.

1. Pass through $(0, 1)$ since $a^0 = 1$;
2. Are positive for all values of x; and
3. Tend to infinity in one direction and to zero in the other.

If you remember these three basic properties, you can easily sketch any exponential function.

The Function e^x

Now that we have recalled the general properties of exponential functions and exponents, we wish to look at a particularly important exponential function for a specific base a. It turns out that in many applications the most natural (and hence convenient) choice for a base is the irrational number e, approximated by decimals as

$$e \approx 2.718281829 \ldots$$

FIGURE 5-2

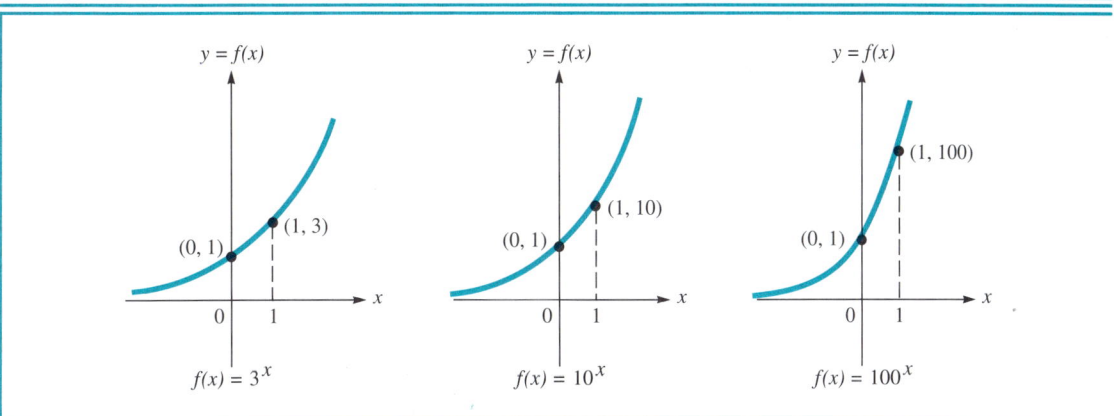

FIGURE 5-3

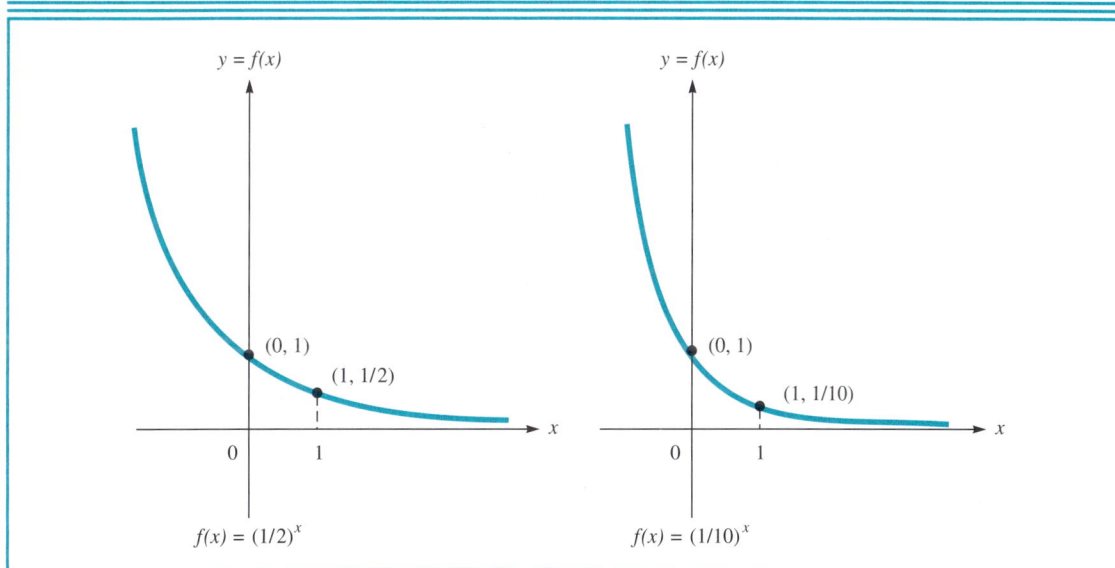

This number appears to be anything but convenient, and in fact we cannot express e in a simple form since it is an irrational number. In Chapter 6, we will see how this base evolves naturally out of the formulas for compound interest. Notice that the graph of $y = e^x$ in Figure 5-4 displays the fundamental properties of all exponential functions just described.

FIGURE 5–4

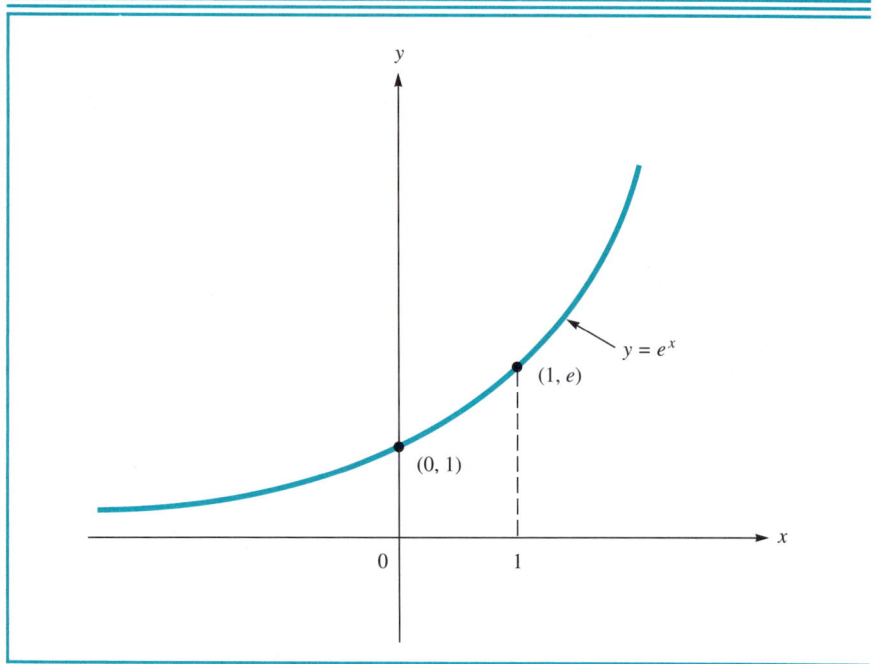

Exercise. Graph $y = e^{-x}$.
Answer:

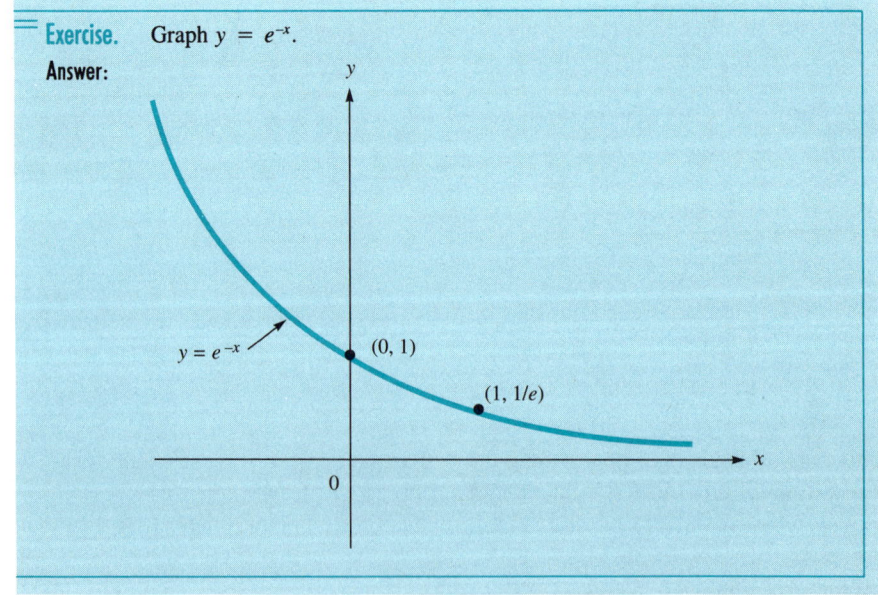

Applications abound in finance, the social sciences, and the natural sciences for the exponential function $f(x) = a^x$.

≡ **Applications**

Example. If $1 is deposited in an account earning 6 percent compounded annually, then after n years the account will contain

$$F = 1(1 + 0.06)^n = (1.06)^n$$

dollars. (The derivation of this expression will be shown in Chapter 6.) Suppose Cathy deposits $1,000.00 in a 12-month CD (certificate of deposit) which yields 6 percent per annum. How much money will she have after one year? If she reinvests the total amount for another 12 months at the same yield, what will Cathy have after two years?

From the stated formula for F, in one year each dollar will earn $(1.06)^1$ or $1.06. So after one year the CD will have the value

$$1,000 \times \$1.06 = \$1,060.$$

Now, after two years, Cathy will have

$$1,000 \times (1.06)^2 = \$1,123.60.$$

This example indicates clearly that the **time value of money** in the business world is very dependent upon exponential functions.

The time value of money is an exponential function.

≡ **FROM THEORY TO PRACTICE**
The Magic and the Tragedy of Exponential Growth

The problem in forecasting exponential trends results from the nonintuitive nature of exponential growth. A long-standing tale relates a chess game between an ancient emperor of China and one of his most revered advisors. They are said to have played a game where the stakes could be named by the winner after the game. When the emperor lost, he offered his advisor anything he wished. Being a humble subject, the advisor asked only for some rice. He asked that the quantity of rice be determined as follows:

Take the chessboard and place 1 grain of rice on the first square, 2 grains on the second, $4 (= 2^2)$ grains on the third, $8 (= 2^3)$ grains on the fourth, and continue in this way to place 2^n grains on the $(n + 1\text{st})$ square. The emperor was pleased that his loss cost him so little and ordered that the rice be delivered immediately. To his surprise, this turned out to be an impossible request! Why? A closer look will show that the Emperor had to deliver

$$(2^0 + 2^1 + 2^2 + \ldots + 2^{63}) = 2^{64} - 1$$

grains of rice. **This is a sufficient amount of grains to cover the entire surface of the earth with grains of rice more than twice!**

(continued)

The previous discussion illustrates the astonishing power of exponential growth and its nonintuitive nature. Unfortunately, exponential growth also drives such phenomena as the spread of an epidemic or the spread of rumors. If we look at the data of the total cumulative number of reported AIDS cases in the United States by year since 1983 (of course, nowhere near all cases are actually reported), we see the following trend:[2]

1983	1984	1985	1986	1987	1988	1989	1990
2,059	6,494	14,676	27,800	48,917	79,775	113,489	155,633

Plotting these data points in the coordinate plane and connecting them, we get the graph in Figure 5–5A. This graph resembles the graphs of $y = a^x$ that we saw earlier. Given the experience of the emperor of China, we would be well advised to take the AIDS epidemic seriously, for clearly no one can hide from the effect of its exponential growth. Figure 5–5B shows a table and graph with similar projections that appeared in *The Boston Globe*.

[2]*Statistical Abstract of the United States*, 1991, Table 192.

FIGURE 5–5A

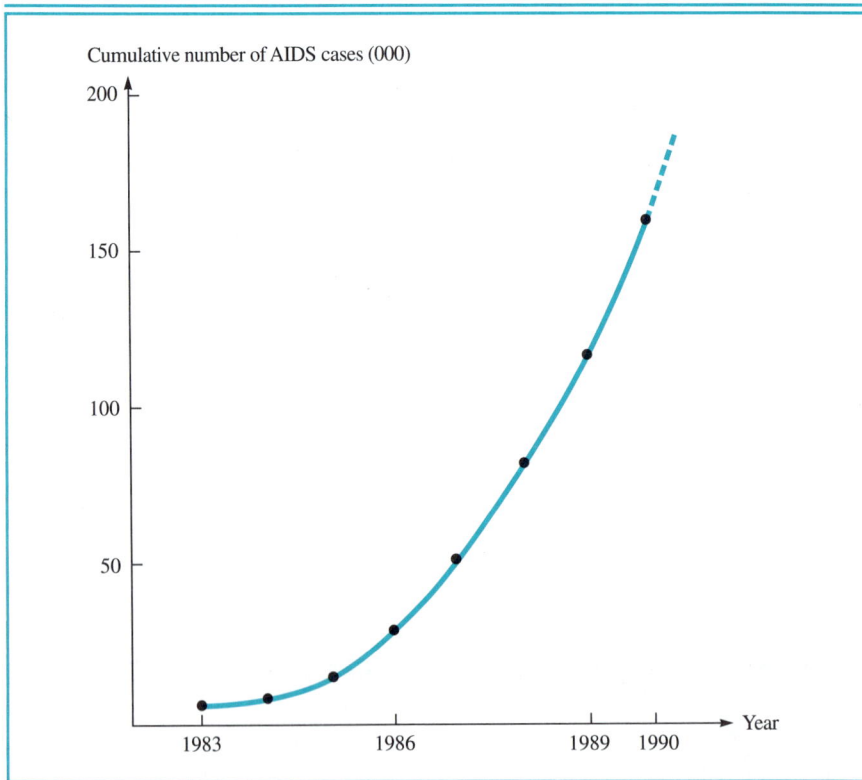

FIGURE 5-5B

AIDS around the world*

Geographic area	HIV infections 1992 (estimated)	HIV infections 1995 (projected)	AIDS 1992 (estimated)	AIDS 1995 (projected)
North America	1,167,000	1,495,000	257,500	534,000
Western Europe	718,000	1,186,000	99,000	279,500
Australia/Oceania	28,000	40,000	4,500	11,500
Latin America	995,000	1,407,000	173,000	417,500
Sub-Saharan Africa	7,803,000	11,449,000	1,367,000	3,277,500
Caribbean	310,000	474,000	43,000	121,000
Eastern Europe	27,000	44,000	2,500	9,500
S.E. Mediterranean	35,000	59,000	3,500	12,500
Northeast Asia	41,000	80,000	3,500	14,500
Southeast Asia†	675,000	1,220,000	65,000	240,500
Total	11,799,000	17,454,000	2,018,500	4,918,000

* A new study predicts that almost 5 million adults will have AIDS, and almost 17.5 million will be HIV-infected by 1995.
† Minimum estimate.

AIDS in the year 2000*

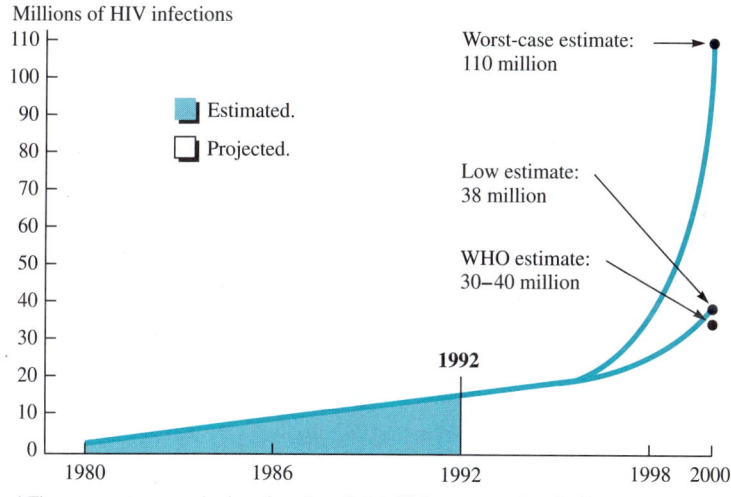

* The new worst-case projection of number of adult HIV cases more than doubles earlier estimates by WHO.

Source: *The Boston Globe,* June 8, 1992. (Source of original data: Global AIDS Policy Coalition.) Used with permission.

Exercise. In the preceding example, how much would Cathy's CD be worth if reinvested at 6 percent for a third year? A fourth year?

Answer: $1,191.02; $1,262.48.

5.3 PROBLEM SET 5-1

Evaluate each of the expressions in Problems 1 through 10:

1. $4(4^3)$.
2. $64^{1/2}$.
3. $27^{2/3}$.
4. $(8^{1/2})(2^{1/2})$.
5. $(1/5)^{-2}$.
6. $[(9^{1/2})(9^2)]^{1/5}$.
7. $[(3^{-1})(3^{2/3})]^3$.
8. $(e^2)(e^4)$.
9. $(e^3)^{-2}$.
10. $(1/e)^{-4}$.

Sketch a graph of the exponential functions in Problems 11 through 28:

11. $f(x) = 3^x$.
12. $f(x) = 12^x$.
13. $f(x) = 4^{-x}$.
14. $f(x) = (1/5)^x$.
15. $f(x) = (1/4)^{-x}$.
16. $f(x) = 2^{-x}$.
17. $f(x) = 3^{-x}$.
18. $f(x) = 2^x + 1$.
19. $f(x) = 2^{-x} + 3$.
20. $f(x) = 2^x/2$.
21. $f(x) = e^{2x}$.
22. $f(x) = e^x/e$.
23. $f(x) = 2^{x+1}$.
24. $f(x) = 3^{x-1}$.
25. $f(x) = (1/3)^{-x}$.
26. $f(x) = 4^{x/2}$.
27. $f(x) = 2^{x^2}$.
28. $f(x) = 2^{-x^2}$.

29. a) What is the value of an account with an initial deposit of $1 and an annual return of 5 percent after 5 years? After 10 years?
    b) Make a table that shows the account value after each of the first 10 years.

30. Find the value of $25,000 invested in an account yielding 7 percent annually after 3 years. After 5 years.

31. Take a piece of paper .001 inches thick, tear it in half, and stack the two pieces. Now take the stack and tear it in half, stacking the resulting pieces. Guess how thick the pile will be if this is repeated for a total of 10 times. 25 times. 50 times. Now compute the actual values and compare them with your guesses.

32. Explain the difficulty in predicting exponential growth and the relative ease in predicting linear growth.

5.4 THE NEED FOR LOGARITHMS

The concept of logarithms was introduced by a Scot, John Napier (1550–1617), and independently by J. Burgi (1552–1632) of Switzerland in the beginning of the 17th century. From then until the early part of this century, logarithms greatly reduced both the time and the effort required for the many computations in such areas as finance, astronomy, navigation, and engineering. Now such calculations are made accurately and rapidly by calculators and computers. However, the appearance of calculators and computers has not outmoded the importance of logarithms.

Logarithms were originally used for computational ease.

For one thing, logarithms are used extensively in numerical calculations. For example, calculations such as

$$1{,}000 \, (1.005)^{60}$$

are performed many times daily by banks using either calculators or computers.

In addition to their calculational use, logarithms are **helpful in the solution of certain types of equations.** For example, the solution of exponential equations such as

Logarithms are helpful in solving exponential equations.

$$3^x = 8 \quad \text{and} \quad (1 + i)^{10} = 2$$

where the unknown is in either the **base** or the **exponent** requires the use of logarithms.

To fully understand how best to use logarithms, it is necessary to be thoroughly familiar with the definition of a logarithm and the rules that apply to operations with logarithms. We start by recalling that the **logarithm to the base a of a number x is the exponent to which you must raise a to obtain x.** So

---

For $a > 0$ and $a \neq 1$,

$$\log_a x = y \quad \text{means} \quad a^y = x.$$

Logarithms are an alternative way of expressing exponents.

The arrows below show a technique for remembering this relationship

$$\log_a x = y \quad \text{means} \quad a^y = x.$$

Example.
a) $\log_2 8 = 3$ means $2^3 = 8$.
b) $\log_5 125 = 3$ means $5^3 = 125$.
c) $\log_2 (1/2) = -1$ means $2^{-1} = 1/2$.
d) $\log_b M = N$ means $b^N = M$.

Notice in this example that the expressions on the left are in logarithmic form while the equivalent expressions on the right are in exponential form. For this reason, logarithms and exponentials are called **inverse forms** of one another.

Logarithms and exponentials are inverse forms of each other.

Example. Write $\log_9 3 = 1/2$ and $2^5 = 32$ in inverse form.

For the first part,

$$\log_9 3 = 1/2,$$

we use the arrow technique to identify 9 as the base of the exponent, 1/2 as the exponent, and 3 as the resulting calculation so that the inverse form is

$$9^{1/2} = 3.$$

For the second part,

$$2^5 = 32,$$

we identify 2 as the base of the logarithm, 32 as the number whose logarithm we are taking, and 5 as the resultant value of the logarithm so that the inverse form is

$$\log_2 32 = 5.$$

> **Exercise.** Write the following in inverse form. a) $\log_{10} 100 = 2$. b) $\log_a N = x$. c) $(0.5)^2 = 0.25$. d) $x^2 = 10$. e) $a^z = M$.
> **Answer:** a) $10^2 = 100$. b) $a^x = N$. c) $\log_{0.5} (0.25) = 2$. d) $\log_x 10 = 2$. e) $\log_a M = z$.

5.5 RULES OF LOGARITHMS

Logarithms, as we stated, are an alternative way of expressing exponents and therefore must obey rules corresponding to exponent rules. Three of the exponent rules we reviewed in Section 5.2 are

$$a^x \cdot a^y = a^{x+y}$$

$$\frac{a^x}{a^y} = a^{x-y}$$

$$(a^x)^y = a^{xy}.$$

Briefly, the preceding say that when the bases are the same, exponents of the powers are added in multiplication, subtracted in division, and multiplied when a power is raised to a power. The corresponding rules for logarithms are:

> **Logarithm Rules**
>
> Product: $\log_a xy = \log_a x + \log_a y$.
>
> Quotient: $\log_a \left(\frac{x}{y}\right) = \log_a x - \log_a y$.
>
> Power: $\log_a x^y = y(\log_a x)$.

Warning. Logarithms of sums and differences **cannot be taken term by term**. That is, $\log_a(x + y)$ **cannot be written as** $\log_a x + \log_a y$, and similarly for $\log_a(x - y)$.

Thus the logarithm of a product is the sum of the logarithms of the factors, the logarithm of a quotient is the logarithm of the numerator minus the logarithm of the denominator, and the logarithm of a number to a power is the power times the logarithm of the number. These rules apply whenever the base of the logarithm is a positive real number not equal to 1 ($a \neq 1$).

In addition, there are two other rules of logarithms that are very useful and come from the exponential rules that

$$a^0 = 1$$
$$a^1 = a.$$

Translating these into logarithms, we have

Additional Logarithm Rules

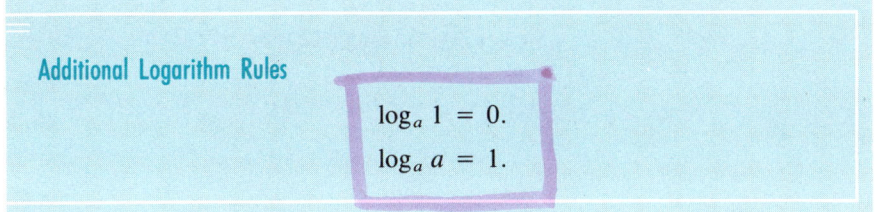

$$\log_a 1 = 0.$$
$$\log_a a = 1.$$

The first rule of logarithms says that the logarithm of 1 is always 0. The second rule says that the logarithm of any number to the same base as the number itself is always 1.

Let us prove the product rule. To do this, we assume the base is some number a, and let

$$\log_a x = m \quad \text{so that} \quad a^m = x$$
$$\log_a y = n \quad \text{so that} \quad a^n = y.$$

The proof of the product rule for logarithms comes from the product rule for exponents.

If we multiply x by y, at the right, the result is the same as multiplying the equivalent values, a^m and a^n. Hence,

$$(a^m)(a^n) = xy$$
$$a^{m+n} = xy.$$

Writing the inverse of the last statement gives

$$\log_a xy = m + n.$$

Now, remembering that $m = \log_a x$ and $n = \log_a y$, we have

$$\log_a xy = \log_a x + \log_a y,$$

which proves the product rule. Similar proofs can be written for the quotient and power rules, but we shall leave these for the next problem set.

Example. Assume that for some base a, $\log_a x = 0.3000$, $\log_a y = 2.8642$, and $\log_a z = 1.7642$. Find

$$\log_a \left(\frac{x^3 y^{1/2}}{z} \right).$$

The purpose of this example is to fix the rules of logarithms in mind. If we apply the product and quotient rules and then the power rule, we have

$$\log_a \left(\frac{x^3 y^{1/2}}{z} \right) = \log_a x^3 + \log_a y^{1/2} - \log_a z$$

$$= 3 \log_a x + \frac{1}{2} \log_a y - \log_a z$$

$$= 3(0.3000) + \frac{1}{2}(2.8642) - 1.7642$$

$$= 0.9000 + 1.4321 - 1.7642$$

$$= 0.5679.$$

Exercise. Assume that, for some base a, $\log_a x = 0.5$, $\log_a y = 1.5$, and $\log_a z = 3$. Compute the value of $\log_a (xy/z^{1/3})$.
Answer: 1.

Example. Rewrite the following using the log symbol only once:

$$\log_a x - 2 \log_a y + \frac{1}{2} \log_a z.$$

We proceed to use the power rule first and then apply the product and quotient rules. Doing this, we obtain

$$\log_a x - 2 \log_a y + \frac{1}{2} \log_a z$$

$$= \log_a x - \log_a y^2 + \log_a z^{1/2}$$

$$= (\log_a x + \log_a z^{1/2}) - \log_a y^2$$

$$= \log_a (xz^{1/2}) - \log_a y^2$$

$$= \log_a \left(\frac{xz^{1/2}}{y^2} \right).$$

> **Exercise.** Rewrite $2\log_a x - \log_a y - 0.5\log_a z$ using the log symbol only once.
> **Answer:** $\log_a (x^2/yz^{0.5})$.

$\log_a x$ Requires That x Be Positive. There are no logarithms for 0 or for negative numbers, and an attempt to obtain logarithms for such numbers on a calculator will lead to an error signal. This is because the base of a logarithm system, which must be positive, when raised to any power, is always positive. For example, for base 10,

$$\log_{10} x = n \quad \text{means} \quad 10^n = x.$$

Only logarithms of positive numbers make sense.

If we examine various values of 10^n, we can see that these values are always positive. Thus

$$10^2 = 100$$
$$10^0 = 1$$
$$10^{-1} = 0.1$$
$$10^{-5} = 0.00001,$$

and, in general,

$$10^n > 0$$
$$10^{-n} = \frac{1}{10^n} > 0.$$

Hence, for every value of n in

$$\log_{10} x = n,$$

x must be strictly positive; that is, x cannot be zero or negative.

5.6 COMMON LOGARITHMS AND NATURAL LOGARITHMS

Logarithms to the base 10 are called **common logarithms** since they were the most convenient to use on numbers in the base-10 (decimal) system. Because common logarithms were used so frequently in practice, the base was omitted.

*Base-10 logarithms are called **common** logarithms.*

> **Definition.** $\log x$ means $\log_{10} x$.

The absence of a base means base-10.

Thus

$$\log 1 = 0.$$
$$\log 10 = 1.$$
$$\log 100 = \log 10^2 = 2(\log 10) = 2.$$
$$\log 0.1 = \log (1/10) = \log 10^{-1} = -1(\log 10) = -1.$$

Base-e logarithms are called natural logarithms.

Today most applications of logarithms use the base e. These logarithms are called **natural logarithms** or **Napierian logarithms**, even though John Napier did not discover them. To simplify the notation, the natural logarithm $\log_e x$ is abbreviated to $\ln x$.

Definition. $\ln x$ means $\log_e x$.

Thus

$$\ln 1 = 0.$$
$$\ln e = 1.$$
$$\ln e^2 = 2(\ln e) = 2.$$
$$\ln(1/e) = \ln e^{-1} = -1(\ln e) = -1.$$

Example. If $y = x(x - \ln x)$, compute y when $x = 1$.

Substituting $x = 1$, we find

$$y = 1(1 - \ln 1)$$
$$= 1(1 - 0)$$
$$= 1.$$

Most calculators have keys for both common and natural logarithms. Calculators that have only one logarithm key usually provide for natural logarithms. For example, to find the value of $\ln 2$, just press the sequence of keystrokes on your calculator shown in Table 5–1.[3]

TABLE 5–1

Keystroke	Calculator Display
2	2
$\ln x$	0.693147181

[3] Some calculators apply the keystrokes in reverse.

Now use a calculator to verify the following (use three-place accuracy):

$$\ln 6.7 = 1.902,$$
$$\ln 0.1 = -2.303,$$
$$\ln 6.14 = 1.815,$$
$$\ln 603 = 6.402.$$

Henceforth, we will use three-place accuracy unless otherwise specified.

Example. Solve for x:

$$e^{-0.1x} = 0.2.$$

Inasmuch as the base of the exponential is e, taking the natural logarithm of both sides of the equation is the simplest way to proceed. Thus

$$\ln (e^{-0.1x}) = \ln 0.2$$
$$(-0.1x)(\ln e) = \ln 0.2$$
$$(-0.1x)(1) = \ln 0.2$$
$$x = \frac{\ln 0.2}{-0.1}$$
$$x = 16.094.$$

> The first step in solving an exponential equation is to take the ln of both sides.

Exercise. a) Evaluate $\ln (x^2 - 3)$ when $x = 2$. b) Solve $e^{3x} = 0.5$ for x.
Answer: a) 0. b) -0.231.

Example. Suppose that Jan has $1,000 to invest and finds that interest can be earned at the rate of 6 percent compounded annually. Jan wants to know how many years it will take for her investment of $1,000 to grow to $2,000.

From Section 5.2, we know that the equation to solve is

$$1,000(1.06)^n = 2,000$$

where n is the number of years. Here the unknown is an exponent, and so logarithms are needed to determine the value. First, dividing both sides by 1,000, we have

$$(1.06)^n = 2.$$

Next, we can take the natural logarithm of both sides of the equation and apply the rules of logarithms to get

$$\ln (1.06)^n = \ln 2$$
$$n(\ln 1.06) = \ln 2$$

$$n = \frac{\ln 2}{\ln 1.06}$$

$$n = 11.896,$$

so it will take 11.896 years (about 12 years) for Jan's investment of $1,000 to grow to $2,000.

Money will double at 6 percent interest in about 12 years.

The keystrokes involved in solving this example using a calculator are shown in Table 5–2.

Whenever you use a calculator, you want to keep all values in the calculator to avoid round-off error. **Don't write down values from the display and reenter them at a later point in the computation.** With a little practice, you will be able to choose the right starting point and perform almost all calculations with a single continuous sequence of keystrokes as shown in Table 5–2. It would be helpful to review the order of operations in Appendix 1 to help you with the sequence. When you have the final result, then you can round off to the number of decimal places desired. (As we said earlier, we use three-place accuracy unless otherwise stated.)

When doing calculations on a calculator, do not round off until the final step.

In the solution of the previous example, we chose to use natural logarithms. We could just as easily have used common logarithms to obtain the same result.

> **Exercise.** Solve the example using common logarithms instead of natural logarithms. What is the difference?
>
> **Answer:** The logarithms are different, but the result is the same; that is, $n = (\log 2)/(\log 1.06) = 11.896$.

Any base logarithm can be used to solve exponential equations. We will use ln.

The preceding example and exercise show that it does not matter whether common logarithms or natural logarithms are used in the solution of exponential equations. On the other hand, in the previous example and exercise it was beneficial to use natural logarithms since the base of the exponent in the equation was e. For consistency, and since all calculators that compute logarithms have an ln x key, we

TABLE 5–2

Keystroke	Calculator Display
2	2
ln x	0.693147181
÷	0.693147181
1.06	1.06
ln x	0.058268908
=	11.89566104

will adopt the convention of using natural logarithms unless otherwise stated. If, for some reason, we have a logarithm in one base and want to find the corresponding logarithm in the other base, the conversion is simple. Using four decimal places

---

Ln to Log Conversion

$$\ln x = (\ln 10)(\log x) = 2.3026(\log x).$$
$$\log x = (\log e)(\ln x) = 0.4343(\ln x).$$

Exercise. A calculator shows that $\ln 5 = 1.609437912$. How can $\log 5$ be computed if there is no $\log x$ key?

Answer: $\log 5 = 0.4343(\ln 5) = 0.699$.

Our final example and exercise of this section will give us additional practice in solving exponential equations where the unknown is in the exponent itself.

Example. Solve for x: $3^{x+2} = 8$.

As usual, we first take the logarithm of both sides to obtain

$$\ln 3^{x+2} = \ln 8.$$

Next we apply the rule for the power giving

$$(x + 2)(\ln 3) = \ln 8$$

$$x + 2 = \frac{\ln 8}{\ln 3}$$

$$x = \frac{\ln 8}{\ln 3} - 2$$

$$x = -0.107.$$

If you solve this using your calculator, the sequence of keystrokes would be those shown in Table 5–3. Note that the order of operations used for the keystrokes is precisely that specified in Appendix 1.

Exercise. Solve for x: $5^{x+3} = 9$.

Answer: -1.635.

TABLE 5-3

Keystroke	Calculator Display
8	8
ln x	2.079441542
÷	2.079441542
3	3
ln x	1.098612289
=	1.892789261
−	1.892789261
2	2
=	−0.107210739

5.7 PROBLEM SET 5-2

Note: Remember that $\log x = \log_{10} x$ and $\ln x = \log_e x$. Write the following in inverse form:

1. $3^2 = 9$.
2. $2^5 = 32$.
3. $\log_3 N = x$.
4. $\log_2 N = y$.
5. $(1/2)^3 = 0.125$.
6. $(0.2)^2 = 0.04$.
7. $\log_{16} 4 = 1/2$.
8. $\log_{27} 3 = 1/3$.
9. $2^{-3} = 0.125$.
10. $3^{-2} = 1/9$.
11. $\log_5 0.04 = -2$.
12. $\log_2 0.0625 = -4$.
13. $\ln 20 = 2.9957$.
14. $\ln 10 = 2.3026$.
15. $\log 0.5 = -0.3010$.
16. $\ln 0.5 = -0.6931$.

What is the value of x in Problems 17 through 24?

17. $\ln e = x$.
18. $\log 10 = x$.
19. $\log_2 4 = x$.
20. $\log_3 27 = x$.
21. $\log_7 7 = x$.
22. $\log_{0.5} (0.5) = x$.
23. $\log_4 2 = x$.
24. $\log_{64} 4 = x$.

Given that $\log_a x = 4.2$, $\log_a y = 1.4$, $\log_a z = -1.2$, compute the value of each of the following:

25. $\log_a (xyz)$.
26. $\log_a \sqrt{z}$.
27. $\log_a (x/z)$.
28. $\log_a (xy/z)$.
29. $\log_a (z^{3/2})$.
30. $\log_a z^2$.
31. $\log_a \sqrt{xy}$.
32. $\log_a (xz)^{1/3}$.

5.7 PROBLEM SET 5-2 (concluded)

Using the rules of logarithms, write the following in a different, but equivalent form:

33. $2 \ln x + 3 \ln y$.
34. $3 \ln x - 2 \ln y$.
35. $0.2 \ln x^5$.
36. $(1/2) \ln x^4$.
37. $(\ln y)/x$.
38. $(1/y) \ln x$.

39. Using the ln symbol only once, rewrite
$$\frac{\ln x}{0.5} - 2 \ln y + 3 \ln z.$$

40. Using the log symbol only once, rewrite
$$\frac{\log x}{0.2} + (1/2)\log y - 2 \log z.$$

Solve the following for x:

41. $2^x = 3$.
42. $3^x = 2$.
43. $10^x = 5$.
44. $2^x = 1.08$.
45. $5^x = 1.02$.
46. $1.06^x = 3$.
47. $1.08^x = 2$.
48. $0.5^x = 8$.
49. $0.25^x = 10$.
50. $1.08^x = 3$.
51. $1.03^x = 5$.
52. $4^{x+6} = 7$.
53. $9^{x-5} = 6$.
54. $12^{3x+5} = 250$.
55. $15^{4x-7} = 475$.

56. Jim has $1,500 to invest and would like his investment to grow to $4,500. If he can earn interest at the rate of 6 percent compounded annually, how many years it will take?

57. Janet has $2,000 to invest and would like her investment to grow to $8,000. If she can earn interest at the rate of 6 percent compounded annually, how many years it will take?

58. Using the rules of exponents, prove the following logarithm rules:
   a) The quotient rule: $\log_a (x/y) = \log_a x - \log_a y$.
   b) The power rule: $\log_a x^y = y(\log_a x)$.

5.8 APPLICATION OF INVERSE NATURAL LOGARITHMS

Recall from Section 5.4 that

For $a > 0$ and $a \neq 1$,

$$\log_a x = y \quad \text{means} \quad a^y = x.$$

374   PART II NONLINEAR RELATIONSHIPS WITH APPLICATIONS IN BUSINESS AND FINANCE

Another way to write this is that

$$a^{\log_a x} = x.$$

Logarithms and exponents are inverses of each other.

The last expression says that $\log_a x$ and a^x are **inverse functions** to one another. In other words, for any number x, if we take the logarithm base a of x and then exponentiate this result to the base a, we will be right back to x. In the same way,

$$\log_a a^x = x$$

so that if we exponentiate the base a to any number x and then take the logarithm base a of this result, we again will be right back to x.

In particular,

$$10^{\log x} = x \quad \text{and} \quad \log 10^x = x;$$

and also

$$e^{\ln x} = x \quad \text{and} \quad \ln e^x = x.$$

Positive and negative powers of e can be obtained from a calculator having an e^x key by simply entering the value of x and depressing the e^x key. Some calculators do not have a separate e^x key but have a ln x key and an INV key designating inverse. Since e^x and ln x are inverse functions the sequence shown in Table 5–4 will produce the value e^2 on these calculators. Remember to push the key marked 2nd when the operation you desire is shown above the key.

Exercise. Find a) e^5. b) e^{-5}. c) $e^{0.05}$. d) $e^{-0.1}$. e) $e^{\ln 3}$. f) $\ln e^3$.
Answer: a) 148.413. b) 0.007. c) 1.051. d) 0.905. e) 3. f) 3.

Antilogarithm is another way of saying exponentiation.

Occasionally, the symbol *antiln x* is used instead of e^x.

Definition. antiln $x = e^x$.

TABLE 5–4

Keystroke	Calculator Display
2	2
INV	2
ln x	7.389056099

Since we just saw that ln x and e^x are inverse functions, this definition means that ln x and antiln x are inverse functions. In summary, then

Rule

antiln (ln x) = x or $e^{\ln x} = x$.
ln (antiln x) = x or $\ln e^x = x$.

Exercise. Find a) antiln 5. b) antiln -5. c) antiln 0.05. d) antiln -0.1. e) antiln(ln 3). f) ln (antiln 3).

Answer: a) 148.413. b) 0.007. c) 1.051. d) 0.905. e) 3. f) 3.

Example. One dollar has been deposited in a bank account. At time n years later, the expression relating F, the amount in the account, to the time n is

$$\ln F = 0.08n.$$

Find the amount in the account at time $n = 20$ years.

Substituting $n = 20$, we have

$$\ln F = 0.08(20) = 1.6.$$

Hence,

$$e^{\ln F} = e^{1.6}$$
$$F = e^{1.6} = \$4.95.$$

Example. A $1,000 deposit in a bank account grows to $2,000 in 10 years at an interest rate of i, where i must be computed from

$$1{,}000(1 + i)^{10} = 2{,}000;$$

find i.

We first divide by 1,000, giving

$$(1 + i)^{10} = 2.$$

One way to proceed is to isolate $(1 + i)$ by raising both sides of the equation to the 0.1 power; that is, by taking the tenth root. Thus

$$[(1 + i)^{10}]^{0.1} = 2^{0.1}$$
$$(1 + i)^1 = 2^{0.1}$$

because, on the left, we multiply exponents when a power is raised to a power. Consequently,

$$1 + i = 2^{0.1}$$
$$i = 2^{0.1} - 1.$$

With a calculator we find 2 to the 0.1 power is 1.071773463. Hence,

$$i = 1.071773463 - 1 = 0.071773463$$

or 7.177 percent.

An alternate way of solving

$$(1 + i)^{10} = 2$$

is to take the logarithms of both sides of the equation. This approach is useful if your calculator cannot compute $2^{0.1}$ or if the exponent is not a simple decimal (e.g., $2^{1/3}$). Using natural logarithms, then,

$$\ln (1 + i)^{10} = \ln 2$$
$$10 \ln (1 + i) = 0.693147181$$
$$\ln (1 + i) = 0.069314718.$$

The last, in inverse form, says

$$1 + i = e^{0.069314718}$$

and, by calculator, e to the 0.069314718 power is 1.071773463, so

$$1 + i = 1.071773463$$
$$i = 1.071773463 - 1 = 0.071773463,$$

or 7.177 percent as before.

The precise steps to use when solving this example on a calculator are shown in Table 5–5. Note in this table that, for simplicity, the process of finding ln 2 has been simplified from two steps to the single step "2, *then* ln *x*" (two keystrokes). What two steps are combined in the single step "2nd, *then* e^x"?

The preceding example illustrates a commonly occurring problem in finance, that of determining an unknown interest rate. The answer 0.07177, or 7.177 percent, means that $1,000 at this interest rate, applied in the compounding procedure described in the next chapter, will grow to $2,000 (i.e., double) in 10 years.

Money will double in 10 years at an interest rate of 7.177 percent.

Exercise. a) If $\ln F = 3 + 0.1n$, find F when $n = 5$. b) Find the interest rate i at which $10,000 will grow to $30,000 in 10 years.

Answer: a) $33.12. b) 0.11612 or 11.612 percent.

TABLE 5-5

Keystroke	Calculator Display
2, then ln x	0.693147181
÷	0.693147181
10	10
=	0.069314718
2nd, then e^x	1.071773463
−	1.071773463
1	1
=	0.071773463

5.9 GRAPH OF $y = \ln x$

To sketch the graph of

$$y = \ln x,$$

we start at $x = 1$, where $y = \ln 1 = 0$, and move to the right (x increasing) to

$$x = 2 \quad \text{and} \quad y = \ln 2 = 0.693,$$

then to

$$x = 3, \quad y = \ln 3 = 1.099,$$

and so on. We see that as we move to the right, $\ln x$ increases, and the curve of $y = \ln x$ rises. If we move to the left of $x = 1$ to

$$x = 0.5, \quad y = \ln 0.5 = -0.693$$

then to

$$x = 0.1, \quad y = \ln 0.1 = -2.303,$$

and so on, the curve of $y = \ln x$ falls even further below the x-axis. Figure 5–6 illustrates the behavior of $y = \ln x$. The curve rises slowly, but always rises, to the right of $x = 1$. Recalling that x cannot be zero or negative, we conclude that to the left of $x = 1$ the curve falls indefinitely as x gets closer to zero, but never touches the y-axis (where $x = 0$). It is not important to graph $y = \ln x$ carefully, but it is useful to know its characteristics, including the intercept point, $(1, 0)$.

There is an easy way to remember the graph of $y = \ln x$; we only need to remember that e^x and $\ln x$ are inverse functions. This method is based on the geometric fact that the point (b, a) is the reflection across the line $y = x$ of the point (a, b) as shown in Figure 5–7. Since $y = \ln x$ is inverse to $y = e^x$, the graph of $y = \ln x$ is the reflection across the line $y = x$ of $y = e^x$, as shown in Figure 5–8. Notice that $(0, 1)$ is on the graph of $y = e^x$ since $e^0 = 1$, and $(1, 0)$ is on the graph of $y = \ln x$ since $\ln 1 = 0$. Hence if you can sketch the graph of $y = e^x$, then you can sketch the graph of $y = \ln x$.

> The graph of $y = \ln x$ passes through $(1, 0)$ and rises continually to the right.

FIGURE 5-6
(not to scale)

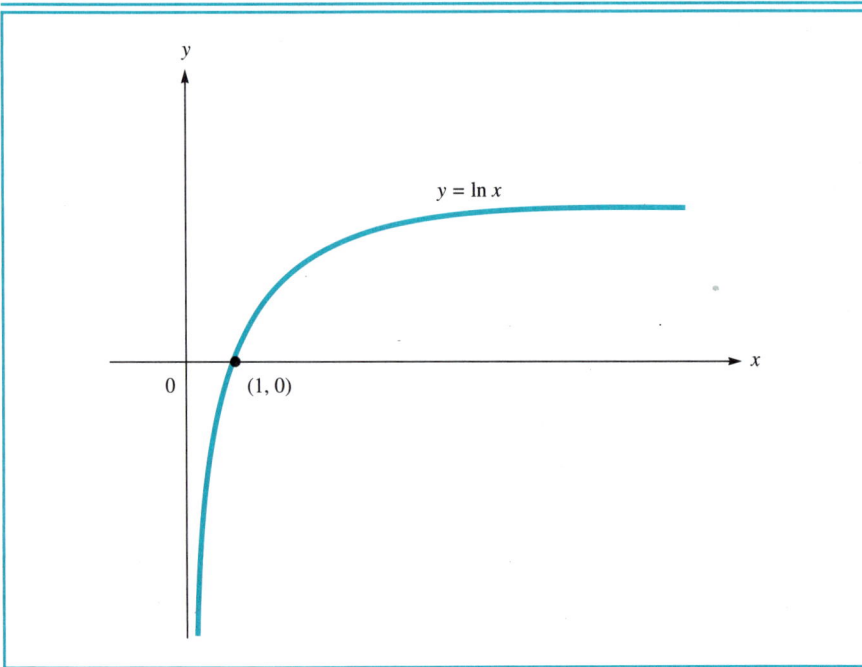

FIGURE 5-7

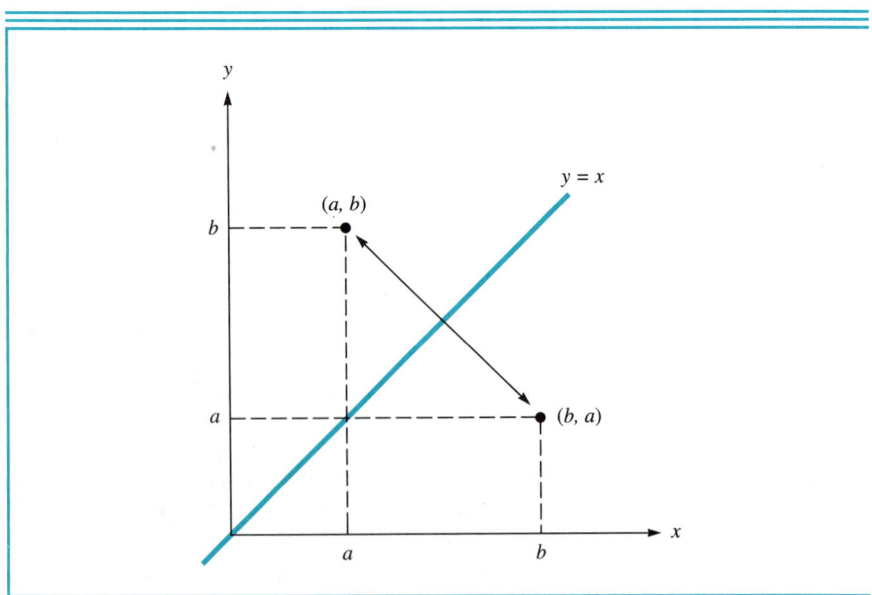

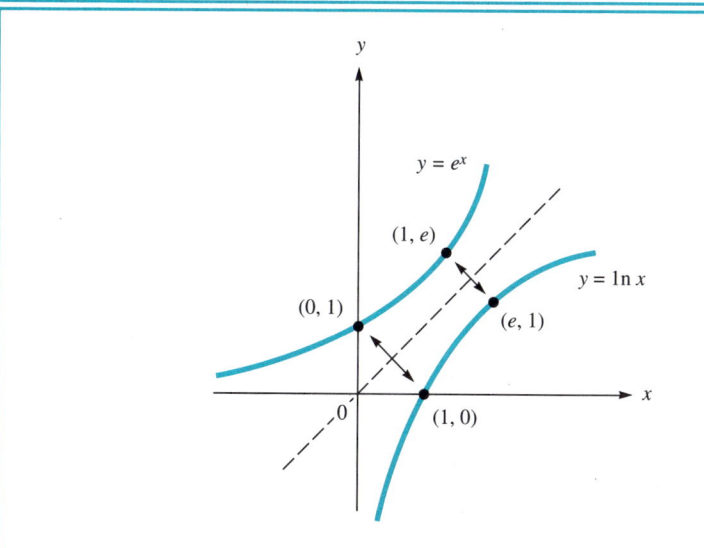

FIGURE 5-8

FIGURE 5-9

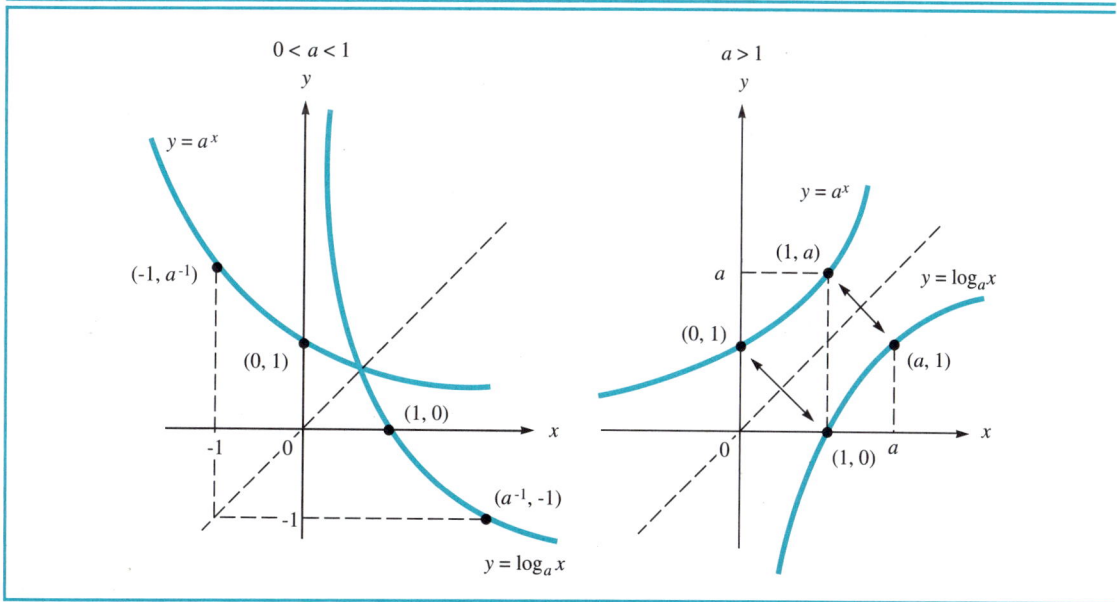

This technique will work for the sketch of the graph of any pair of functions that are inverses of each other. For example, consider

$$y = \log_a x.$$

Since $y = \log_a x$ and $y = a^x$ are inverse functions, we can sketch both graphs as shown in Figure 5–9.

5.10 COMPUTING e AND NATURAL LOGARITHMS

e can be approximated by an exponential.

The number e can be calculated to any desired degree of accuracy. One such way to approximate e, discovered and proved by mathematicians, is to compute

$$(1 + 1/n)^n$$

using a **sufficiently large value** of n. But how large is sufficiently large? With a calculator, we find that for $n = 10$

$$(1 + 1/10)^{10} = 2.593742461$$

as shown in Table 5–6. Of course, the calculator also shows directly from the e^x key with $x = 1$ that

$$e = 2.718281829,$$

so clearly $n = 10$ is not sufficiently large. Table 5–7 shows calculations of

$$(1 + 1/n)^n$$

for $n = 1,000$ through 10,000. The same results are obtained from running a QBasic program on a microcomputer as shown in Table 5–8. Obviously we need n to be much larger than 10,000 just to have four-place accuracy.

TABLE 5–6

Keystroke	Calculator Display
10	10
1/x	0.1
+	0.1
1	1
=	1.1
2nd, then y^x	1.1
10	10
=	2.593742461

> **Exercise.** Compute $(1 + 1/n)^n$ for $n = $ 20,000, 50,000, and 100,000.
> **Answer:** 2.718213875; 2.718254646; 2.718268237.

An alternate and more precise way to approximate e is by the **series factorial approximation**

$$1 + \frac{1}{1!} + \frac{1}{2!} + \frac{1}{3!} + \cdots + \frac{1}{n!}.$$

e can be approximated by a factorial series.

Here the factorial symbol ! is illustrated by

$$4! = 4 \text{ factorial} = 4 \times 3 \times 2 \times 1 = 24$$
$$3! = 3 \text{ factorial} = 3 \times 2 \times 1 = 6.$$

TABLE 5-7

n	$(1 + 1/n)^n$
1,000	2.716923973
2,000	2.717602658
3,000	2.717828748
4,000	2.717942316
5,000	2.718010286
6,000	2.718056101
7,000	2.718087163
8,000	2.718112213
9,000	2.718130908
10,000	2.718146298

TABLE 5-8

```
REM PROGRAM 5-1
REM Approximation of e, using (1 + 1/n)^n
CLS
Print "n", "(1 + 1/n)^n"
PRINT
FOR n = 1000 TO 10000 STEP 1000
  PRINT n, (1 + 1 / n)^n
NEXT n
```

n	$(1 + 1/n)\char`\^n$
1000	2.716924
2000	2.717602
3000	2.717829
4000	2.717942
5000	2.71801
6000	2.718055
7000	2.718088
8000	2.718112
9000	2.718131
10000	2.718146

Now computing the factorial approximation for e with $n = 4$, we have

$$1 + \frac{1}{1!} + \frac{1}{2!} + \frac{1}{3!} + \frac{1}{4!}$$

$$1 + 1 + \frac{1}{2} + \frac{1}{6} + \frac{1}{24}$$

or simply

$$2.708333333.$$

Using a calculator with an $n!$ key, we would proceed as shown in Table 5–9. Table 5–10 shows the factorial calculation for $n = 5$ through 10. Note that $n = 9$ already gives six-place accuracy, a decided advantage over the exponential approximation.

> **Exercise 13.** Compute the series factorial approximation for e with $n = 11$, 12, and 13.
>
> **Answer:** 2.718281826; 2.718281828; 2.718281828.

ln x can be approximated by an alternating series.

Mathematicians have also derived a set of series approximation formulas for computing natural logarithms of numbers. One of them is

$$\ln(1 + x) = x - \frac{x^2}{2} + \frac{x^3}{3} - \frac{x^4}{4} + \frac{x^5}{5} - \frac{x^6}{6} \cdots ; \quad 0 < x \le 1,$$

where the signs of the terms alternate. This series will settle in (**converge**) on a value for a logarithm only if x is positive and not greater than 1, but other formulas and the rules of logarithms can be applied to obtain logarithms for all nonnegative numbers. To illustrate a logarithm calculation, we compute

$$\ln 1.2 = \ln(1 + 0.2).$$

This is

$$\ln(1 + x)$$

with $x = 0.2$. Hence, using the first six terms,

$$\ln 1.2 \approx 0.2 - \frac{(0.2)^2}{2} + \frac{(0.2)^3}{3} - \frac{(0.2)^4}{4} + \frac{(0.2)^5}{5} - \frac{(0.2)^6}{6}$$
$$= 0.18232,$$

where, as usual, $\approx$ means equals approximately. Your calculator will show that

$$\ln 1.2 = 0.182321557$$

so that the value calculated is $\ln 1.2$ correct to five decimal places.

CHAPTER 5 EXPONENTIAL AND LOGARITHMIC FUNCTIONS

TABLE 5-9

Keystroke	Calculator Display
1	1
+	1
1	1
÷	1
1	1
2nd, then n!	1
=	2
+	2
1	1
÷	1
2	2
2nd, then n!	2
=	2.5
+	2
1	1
÷	1
3	3
2nd, then n!	6
=	2.666666667
1	1
÷	1
4	4
2nd, then n!	24
=	2.708333333

TABLE 5-10

n	$1+(1/1!)+(1/2!)+\ldots+(1/n!)$
5	2.716666667
6	2.718055556
7	2.718253968
8	2.718278770
9	2.718281526
10	2.718281801

Exercise. a) Approximate ln 1.01 using only the first two terms of the preceding series. b) By how much does the result in (a) differ from the calculator value for ln 1.01?

Answer: a) 0.00995. b) No difference in the first five decimal places.

5.11 PROBLEM SET 5-3

1. By taking natural logarithms and antilogarithms of both sides, prove that $x = 2$ if
$$e^{\ln x} = 2.$$

2. By taking common logarithms and antilogarithms of both sides, prove that $x = 3$ if
$$10^{\log x} = 3.$$

3. What value must x have if
$$10^{\log 5} = x?$$

4. What value must x have if
$$e^{\ln 4} = x?$$

5. Find the value of x:
$$7^{\log_7 6} = x.$$

6. Find the value of x:
$$4^{\log_4 5} = x.$$

Solve for x:

7. $\ln x = 0.42$.
8. $\ln x = 1.2$.
9. $\ln x = -1.1$.
10. $\ln x = -0.01$.
11. $\ln (1 + x) = 0.3$.
12. $\ln (2 + x) = 1$.
13. $\ln (0.5x - 2) = -0.5$.
14. $\ln (1 - 0.1x) = -0.65$.

Use the compound interest formula, $F = P(1 + i)^n$, to solve the following:

15. Compute n if $F = 5{,}000$, $P = 2{,}000$, and $i = 0.085$.
16. Compute n if $F = 10{,}000$, $P = 5{,}000$, and $i = 0.12$.
17. Compute i if $F = 4{,}000$, $P = 1{,}000$, and $n = 10$.
18. Compute i if $F = 2{,}500$, $P = 1{,}000$, and $n = 5$.

Compute the following by summing five terms of the series approximation,
$$\ln (1 + x) = x - \frac{x^2}{2} + \frac{x^3}{3} - \frac{x^4}{4} + \frac{x^5}{5} \cdots \quad 0 < x \leq 1.$$

19. $\ln 1.1$
20. $\ln 1.3$
21. Write a computer program to approximate e, using 5, 6, 7, 8, 9, and 10 terms of the series factorial approximation.

5.12 REVIEW PROBLEMS

Find the following:

1. $\ln 8.46$.
2. $\ln 33$.
3. $\ln 0.08$.
4. $\ln 0.1$.
5. $\ln 2.27$.
6. $\ln 3.36$.

5.12 REVIEW PROBLEMS (concluded)

7. ln 58.
8. ln 425.
9. ln 786.
10. $e^{0.25}$.
11. $e^{0.01}$.
12. $e^{-0.25}$.
13. $e^{1.6}$.
14. $e^{2.3}$.
15. e^{-2}.
16. e^{-3}.

Write the following in inverse form:

17. $5^2 = 25$.
18. $2^3 = 8$.
19. $\log_7 49 = 2$.
20. $\log_5 125 = 3$.
21. $27^{1/3} = 3$.
22. $64^{1/2} = 8$.
23. $\log_8 2 = 1/3$.
24. ln $e = 1$.

What is the value of x in each of the following?

25. $\log_2 32 = x$.
26. $\log_3 81 = x$.
27. $\log_{0.2} (0.04) = x$.
28. $\log_3 x = 3$.
29. $\log_2 x = 4$.
30. $e^{\ln e} = x$.
31. $3^{\log_3 5} = x$.
32. $5^{\log_5 4} = x$.

33. If, for base a, $\log_a x = 0.6$, $\log_a y = 1.8$, and $\log_a z = 1.2$, compute the value of
$$\log_a \left[\frac{x^2}{(yz)^{1/3}} \right].$$

34. Rewrite the following, using the ln symbol only once:
$$2 \ln x - (1/2) \ln y^2 + \ln z.$$

Solve the following for x:

35. ln $x = 0.84$.
36. ln $x = 2.4$.
37. ln $x = -2.3$.
38. ln $x = -0.08$.
39. ln $(1 + x) = 1.2$.
40. ln $(1 + x) = -0.5$.
41. $(6.75)^x = 4$.
42. $(25)^{2x+5} = 127$.
43. $(0.23)^{3x-6} = 0.15$.
44. $3^{-x} = 2$.
45. $4^{-x} = 8$.
46. $(0.2)^{-4x+3} = 0.7$.
47. $(0.8)^{-5x+2} = 0.5$.
48. $(4/x)^{-5} = 0.26$.
49. $(x/5)^{2.1} = 8$.
50. $e^x = 25$.
51. $x^{10} - 1 = 0$.
52. $x^{10} - 2 = 0$.
53. $(1 + x)^{15} = 2.5$.
54. $(1 + x)^{-10} = 0.5$.
55. $x[1 + (1.01)^{50}] = 5$.
56. $2,500[1 + (1.02)^{-x}] = 3,000$.

5.13 EXTENDED REVIEW PROBLEMS

1. If, for base a, $\log_a x = -1.3$, $\log_a y = 2.5$, and $\log_a z = -3.4$, compute the value of
$$\log_a \frac{z^{1/4}}{x^{1/3} y^{1/6}}.$$

2. a) What is the value of an account with an initial deposit of $1,800 invested in an account yielding 9% annually after 3 years? After 5 years? After 8 years?
   b) Make a table which shows the account value after each of the first ten years.

3. Rewrite the following using the ln symbol only once
$$3 \ln x^{1/3} - (1/2)\ln y - 2 \ln z.$$

4. Find the value of ln 8.18.

5. Find the value of $e^{-0.01}$.

6. Solve for x: $(0.55)^{4x-7} = 1.8$.

7. Write in inverse form: $\log_{81} 3 = 1/4$.

8. Solve for x: $\log_{0.2} 5 = x$.

9. A cardboard cover .05 inches thick is cut into four equal parts and the pieces are then stacked on top of each other. Then the stack is cut in four equal pieces and the resultant pieces are stacked on top of each other. How thick will the pile be if this is repeated for a total of 5 times? 10 times? 20 times? Now compute the actual values and compare them with your guesses.

10. Solve for x: $(7/x)^{-3} = 0.67$.

Introduction to the Mathematics of Finance

CHAPTER 6

6.1 INTRODUCTION

Just about everyone becomes involved in transactions where interest rates affect the amount to be paid or received. For many, the largest such transaction is the purchase of a home. As we shall learn, a person who borrows $150,000 for such a purchase and cancels the debt by making monthly payments over a period of 30 years, will pay back about $284,502 if the interest rate is 9 percent per year, compounded monthly. Not very many years ago, when the interest rate was about 12 percent, the corresponding payback would have been about $405,440. The size of these paybacks serves to show both the effect of compound interest and the effect of changes in interest rates. In this chapter, we first look at simple interest calculation. We then turn to the major objective of the chapter, which is to develop and apply formulas for financial transactions that involve compound interest calculations. In so doing, we shall ask and answer questions such as the following, for various interest rates and frequencies of compounding:

1. If $5,000 is deposited in a bank account now, what will be the amount in the account 10 years from now?
2. How much must be deposited in a bank account now if the amount in the account 5 years from now is to be $10,000?
3. If $1,000 is added to an account every year, to what amount will the account grow in 15 years?
4. How much must be deposited in an account each year if the amount in the account at the end of 10 years is to be $15,000?
5. What sum deposited now will provide an income of $10,000 per year each year for the next 20 years?
6. If $100,000 is borrowed now to pay for a home, how much must be paid back each month if the debt is to be cancelled in 20 years?

We shall also answer questions like the preceding if interest is compounded instantaneously (continuously) rather than at discrete points in time such as the end of each day, month, four months, six months, or one year.

Extensive tabulations are available to aid in carrying out the calculations involved in financial tabulations. However we shall show how these calculations are easily carried out on a calculator and/or computer. We prefer this approach because even the most extensive tabulations provide a limited cross section of interest rates and time periods. It is important, however, to understand that the chapter has been designed so that it is possible to learn the subject matter and do practice calculations using either approach. Also, we should point out that compound interest calculations involve exponents and, as a consequence, logarithms play a role in some of these calculations.

6.2 SIMPLE INTEREST AND THE FUTURE VALUE

Interest rates are generally quoted in percentage form and, for use in calculations, must be converted to the equivalent decimal value by dividing the percentage by 100; that is, by moving the decimal point in the percentage two places to the left. For example,

$$i = 8\frac{1}{4}\% = 8.25\% = 0.0825.$$

Interest rates are converted to decimals by dividing the rate by 100.

Unless otherwise stated, a **quoted rate is a rate per year**. Thus $1 at 8 percent means that interest of $0.08 will be earned in a year, and $100 at this rate provides

$$100(0.08) = \$8$$

of interest in one year. Interest on $100 at 8 percent for 9 months is interest for 9/12 year; that is,

$$\text{Interest} = 100 \quad (0.08) \quad \left(\frac{9}{12}\right) = \$6.00.$$

$$\uparrow \qquad \uparrow \qquad \uparrow$$

$$\text{Interest} = (\text{Principal})(\text{Rate})(\text{Time in years}).$$

Interest (I) equals Principal (P) times Rate (i) times Time (n).

The last line introduces the following definitions, which apply in simple interest calculations:

Definitions

I = Interest, in dollars.
P = Principal, the sum of money on which interest is being earned.
i = Rate of interest per period (assumed to be one year).
n = Number of years, or fraction of one year.

Simple interest formula: $I = Pin$.

Thus interest on $600 at 7½ percent for 10 months is computed using $P = 600$, $i = 0.075$, and $n = 10/12$ year. This is

$$I = 600(0.075)\left(\frac{10}{12}\right) = \$37.50.$$

> **Exercise.** Compute the interest on $480 at $6\frac{1}{4}$ percent for 9 months.
> **Answer:** $22.50.

The simple interest formula $I = Pin$ involves four variables. Given any three of the four variables, we can solve the formula for the remaining fourth variable.

The simple interest formula can be solved for any one of its variables given the other three.

Example. Find the interest rate if $1,000 earns $45 interest in 6 months.

Here, $I = 45$, $P = 1,000$, and $n = 6/12 = 0.5$. Hence

$$I = Pin$$
$$45 = 1,000(i)(0.5)$$
$$45 = 500i$$
$$\frac{45}{500} = i$$
$$0.09 = i.$$

To obtain the percent rate, the decimal rate, $i = 0.09$, is multiplied by 100. Thus

$$i = 0.09 = 100(0.09)\% = 9\%.$$

The **yield** on the common stock of a company is a percentage obtained by dividing the amount (called the **dividend**) that a shareholder receives per share of stock held by the price of a share of the stock. Thus yield is like an interest rate with the dividend analogous to the interest for $n = 1$ year and the price per share analogous to the principal. A stock market report showing

GenElec   2.20   76

means that at the time of the quotation, a share of General Electric stock sold for $76.00 and the annual dividend was estimated to be $2.20 per share.

> **Exercise.** Compute the yield for General Electric from the market report in the preceding.
> **Answer:** 2.895 percent.

When time is given in days, there are two ways of computing the interest: the **exact method** and the **ordinary method** (often called the **Banker's Rule**). If the exact method is used, then the time is

> The exact method divides the number of days by 365 (366 in a leap year); the ordinary method divides by 360.

$$n = \frac{\text{Number of days}}{365};$$

but if the ordinary method is used, then

$$n = \frac{\text{Number of days}}{360}.$$

Banks, for convenience, often count a year as twelve 30-day months, 360 days for a year.

Example. Find the interest on $1,460 for 72 days at 10 percent interest using (a) the exact method and (b) the ordinary method.

In both methods, $P = 1,460$ and $i = 0.1$. For (a),

$$I = Pin$$
$$= (1,460)(0.1)\left(\frac{72}{365}\right)$$
$$= \$28.80.$$

On the other hand, for (b)

$$I = Pin$$
$$= (1,460)(0.1)\left(\frac{72}{360}\right)$$
$$= \$29.20.$$

As you can see from this example, the ordinary interest is more than the exact interest. This will always be the case. Why? In fact,

$$\frac{\text{Ordinary interest}}{\text{Exact interest}} = \frac{Pi(\text{Number of days}/360)}{Pi(\text{Number of days}/365)}$$
$$= \frac{365}{360}$$
$$= \frac{73}{72}.$$

So

> Ordinary interest is 73/72 of exact interest.

$$\text{Ordinary interest} = \left(\frac{73}{72}\right)(\text{Exact interest}).$$

We will adopt the common practice of using ordinary interest unless otherwise specified.

> **Exercise.** Find the exact and ordinary interest on $2,190 for 75 days at 12 percent interest.
>
> **Answer:** $54.00, $54.75.

The Future Value

If interest on $1,000 at 9 percent for 8 months is computed as

$$I = Pin = 1,000(0.09)\left(\frac{8}{12}\right) = \$60$$

and the interest is added to the principal, the sum is called the **future value**, F. Thus

Future value is the sum of principal plus interest.

$$F = 1,000 + 1,000(0.09)\left(\frac{8}{12}\right)$$
$$= 1,000 + 60$$
$$= \$1,060.$$

> **Definition.** Future value: $F = P + Pin = P(1 + in)$.

Example. Find the future value if $20,000 is invested at 6 percent for 3 months.

Here, 3 months is $3/12 = 1/4$ of a year, so $n = 1/4$. Hence

$$F = 20,000\left[1 + 0.06\left(\frac{1}{4}\right)\right]$$
$$= 20,000(1 + 0.015)$$
$$= \$20,300.$$

It is often helpful to visualize money transactions in a **time diagram**. In our current example, such a diagram is shown in Figure 6–1. Here we have started at the present with $P = \$20,000$, drawn a line pointing out to the unknown F in the future three months hence, and indicated the 6 percent interest rate over the line.

Time diagrams are a useful visual aid in money transactions.

FIGURE 6-1

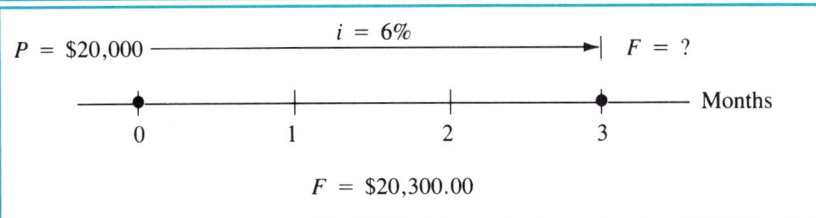

> **Exercise.** Find the future value of $5,000 at 10 percent for 9 months.
> **Answer:** $5,375.00.

Table 6–1 shows a QBasic program to compute the future value, along with the results of running the program for the preceding example.

The future value formula can be solved for any one of its variables given the other three.

The future value formula $F = P(1 + in)$ also involves four variables. As with the simple interest formula, given any three of the four variables, we can solve for the remaining fourth variable.

Example. Jan received $50 for a diamond at a pawn shop and a month later paid $53.50 to get the diamond back. Find the percent interest rate.

Here,

$$P = \$50, \quad F = \$53.50, \quad n = \frac{1}{12} \text{ year}$$

and the associated time diagram is shown in Figure 6–2.

TABLE 6-1

```
REM PROGRAM 6-1
REM Future Value -- Simple Interest
CLS
INPUT "Enter P, i, and n"; P, i, n
F = P * (1 + i * n)
PRINT "The Future Value F = ";
PRINT USING "$###,###.##"; F

Enter P, i, and n? 20000,.06,.25
The Future Value F = $ 20,300.00
```

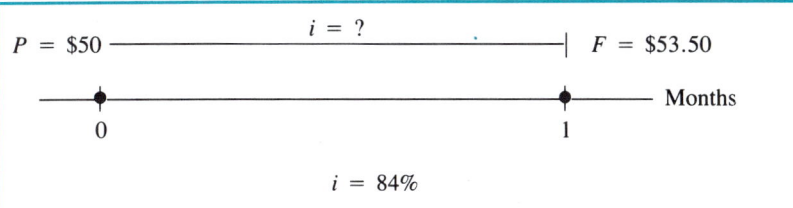

FIGURE 6-2

Therefore

$$53.50 = 50\left[1 + i\left(\frac{1}{12}\right)\right].$$

Dividing both sides by 50 yields

$$\frac{53.50}{50} = 1 + \frac{i}{12}.$$

Multiplying both sides by 12, we find

$$12\left(\frac{53.50}{50}\right) = 12 + i$$

$$12.84 = 12 + i$$

$$0.84 = i.$$

The last is the **decimal rate**. The **percent rate** is 100 times the decimal rate:

$$0.84 = 100(0.84)\% = 84\%.$$

The percent rate is 100 times the decimal rate.

> **Exercise.** Fran has placed $500 in an employees' savings account that pays 8 percent simple interest. How long will it be, in months, until the investment amounts to $530?
> **Answer:** 3/4 of a year = 9 months.

In the previous exercise, $500 now amounts to $530 nine months from now if the interest rate is 8 percent. In reverse, we say that the **present value** of $530 receivable in 9 months is $500 now if the interest rate is 8 percent. This present value is analogous to a principal, so we shall denote it by P. Inasmuch as

$$F = P(1 + in),$$

6.3 SIMPLE DISCOUNT: PRESENT VALUE

The present value is the worth in present-day dollars.

we do not really need a separate formula for calculating the present value. However, in practice, accountants and financiers use the present value concept so often that it is convenient to have such a formula. We obtain the present value formula by dividing both sides of the preceding expression by $(1 + in)$. Thus

$$\frac{F}{1 + in} = P.$$

Definition. Present value: $P = \dfrac{F}{1 + in}$.

Thus the present value of $530 receivable 9 months from now if the interest rate is 8 percent is

$$P = \frac{530}{1 + 0.08(9/12)}$$
$$= \frac{530}{1.06}$$
$$= \$500.$$

The time diagram for this example is shown in Figure 6–3.

Exercise. How much will Fran have to invest now in the employees' 8 percent savings account in order to have $600 a year from now?
Answer: $600/1.08 = \$555.56$.

It is important in this chapter to keep in mind that a future amount of money, F, is worth less than F now. The sense of this is that certainly, in a business

FIGURE 6–3

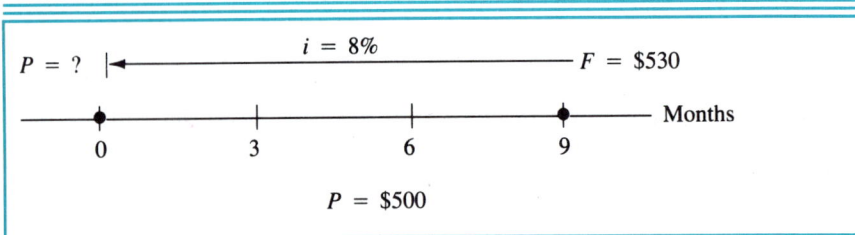

TABLE 6-2

```
REM PROGRAM 6-2
REM Present Value -- Simple Interest
CLS
INPUT "Enter F, i, and n"; F, i, n
P = F / (1 + i * n)
PRINT "The Present Value P = ";
PRINT USING "$###,###.##"; P

Enter F, i, and n? 530,.08,.75
The Present Value P = $   500.00
```

transaction, a person who promises to pay back $1,000 to a lender at some time in the future cannot expect to receive as much as $1,000 now. This principle is often referred to as the **time value of money**.

> The time value of money is important in financial transactions.

> **Exercise.** Find the present value of $1,000 at 9 percent due 8 months from now.
> **Answer:** $943.40.

Table 6-2 shows a QBasic program to compute the present value, along with the results of running the program for our previous example.

6.4 BANK DISCOUNT

In many loans, the interest charge is computed not on the amount the borrower receives, but on the amount that is repaid later. A charge for a loan computed in this manner is called the **bank discount**, and the amount the borrower receives is called the **proceeds** of a loan. Proceeds begins with P and it is an amount received now. The future amount to be paid back is F, now called the **maturity value** of the loan. If $1,000 is borrowed at 12 percent for 6 months, the borrower receives the proceeds, P, and pays back $F = \$1,000$. The proceeds will be $1,000 minus the interest on $1,000. This will be

> Loan transactions involve maturity value rather than future value and proceeds rather than present value.

$$P = 1{,}000 - 1{,}000(0.12)\left(\frac{6}{12}\right)$$

$$P = F - F \quad (d) \quad (n)$$
$$ = 1{,}000 - 60$$
$$ = \$940.$$

Note that the $60 interest was **subtracted** from the maturity value of $1,000 to get the proceeds of $940. This is quite different from a future value transaction where the $60 interest would be **added** to the principal of $1,000 to get a future value of $1,060. To emphasize this difference, the interest rate was designated as d and is called the **bank discount rate**. This method is also called **interest deducted-in-advance** because the interest amount is deducted from the maturity value F before the proceeds P are given to the borrower.

> Loan transactions often involve interest deducted in advance.

Definition. Proceeds: $P = F(1 - dn)$.

The example just completed shows that the borrower receives $940 but pays interest on the maturity value $1,000. If the borrower wants to receive proceeds of $P = \$1,000$, then

$$1{,}000 = F\left[1 - 0.12\left(\frac{6}{12}\right)\right]$$

$$1{,}000 = F(1 - 0.06)$$

$$1{,}000 = 0.94F$$

$$\frac{1{,}000}{0.94} = F$$

$$\$1{,}063.83 = F.$$

Thus the borrower who wants $1,000 now will pay back $1,063.83 six months from now.

> **Exercise.** a) A borrower signs a note promising to pay a bank $5,000 ten months from now. How much will the borrower receive if the discount rate is 8.4 percent? b) How much would the borrower have to repay in order to receive $5,000 now?
> **Answer:** a) $4,650. b) $5,376.34.

> Proceeds are less than present value.

Proceeds are an amount received now for repayment in the future, so they are analogous to present value, which was discussed in the previous section. However proceeds are not equal to present value because the proceeds from a future obligation to pay are always **less than** the present value of the obligation if, of course, the same rate of interest is used in both calculations.

> **Exercise.** What would be the present value of $1,000 payable in 6 months at 12 percent simple interest?
>
> **Answer:** $943.40.

In general, **proceeds should be computed when the interest rate is stated as a discount rate or a bank discount or interest deducted-in-advance, and present value should be computed where the interest rate is given without the qualifier, discount.**

6.5 EFFECTIVE RATE: SIMPLE INTEREST

We have just seen the difference between the bank discount (proceeds) and the simple discount (present value). These two methods can be compared from an **effective** or **true** interest rate point of view. By the effective interest rate we mean the actual true simple interest rate for one year:

> The effective rate is the actual simple interest rate paid or received for one year.

Effective Interest Rate

$$i_e = \frac{\text{Interest amount for one year}}{\text{Amount borrower receives}}.$$

In the simple discount (present value) exercise of Section 6.4, we had $F = \$1,000$, $i = 12\%$, $n = 6/12$, and computed $P = \$943.40$. So the interest amount for one year is

$$(1{,}000.00 - 943.40)\left(\frac{12}{6}\right) = (56.60)\left(\frac{12}{6}\right)$$
$$= \$113.20,$$

and

$$i_e = \frac{113.20}{943.40} = 0.12,$$

or 12 percent. It will always be the case with the simple discount that $i_e = i$. Why? Because the interest amount is charged against the actual amount (present value):

$$i_e = \frac{(P)(i)(1\text{ year})}{P}$$
$$= \frac{Pi}{P}$$
$$= i.$$

In present value transactions, the quoted rate is the effective interest rate.

Thus **the effective interest rate for a simple discount (present value) transaction is precisely the quoted rate**.

On the other hand, for the bank discount (proceeds) example of Section 6.4, we had $F = \$1,000$, $d = 12\%$, $n = 6/12$, and computed $P = \$940$. Here the interest for one year is

$$(1,000 - 940)\frac{12}{6} = (60)(2)$$
$$= \$120.00,$$

and

$$i_e = \frac{120}{940} = 0.12766,$$

In bank discount transactions, the quoted rate is less than the effective interest rate.

or 12.766 percent. This is more than the quoted rate of 12 percent, and this will always be the case. Why? Because here the interest amount is charged against the amount to be paid back (maturity value), not the actual amount received (proceeds). Writing i_e as a function of F, d, and n, we have

$$i_e = \frac{(F)(d)(1 \text{ year})}{F(1 - dn)}$$

$$i_e = \frac{Fd}{F(1 - dn)}$$

$$i_e = \frac{d}{1 - dn}. \qquad (1)$$

Exercise. Use the preceding Equation (1) to calculate i_e for our previous example where $d = 12$ percent and $n = 6/12$.

Answer: 12.766 percent.

Exercise. a) Find the present value and effective rate of $1,000 due in 4 months at 12 percent interest. b) Find the proceeds and effective rate of $1,000 due in 4 months at a discount rate of 12 percent.

Answer: a) $961.54, 12 percent. b) $960.00, 12.5 percent.

An interesting application of (1) occurs when a lender wishes to determine the discount rate d that should be quoted in order to receive a desired effective rate i_e. Solving (1) for d, we have

$$i_e = \frac{d}{1 - dn}$$

$$i_e(1 - dn) = d$$

$$i_e - i_e dn = d$$

$$i_e = d + i_e dn$$

$$i_e = d(1 + i_e n)$$

$$d = \frac{i_e}{1 + i_e n}. \qquad (2)$$

Returning to our example where $F = \$1,000$ and $n = 6/12$, if the lender only wants to earn 12 percent true interest, then from (2) the discount rate should be

To earn a particular effective rate, the associated quoted discount rate will be smaller.

$$d = \frac{0.12}{1 + (0.12)(6/12)}$$

$$= 0.11321,$$

or 11.321 percent.

Exercise. Suppose a lender wishes to earn 15 percent true interest on a 4-month transaction using interest deducted-in-advance. What discount rate should be quoted?

Answer: 14.286 percent.

6.6 PROBLEM SET 6–1

In Problems 1 through 10, find a) the interest and b) the amount for each of the principals for the stated simple interest rate and time period:

1. $500; 7 percent; 1 year.
2. $1,000; 8 percent; 1 year.
3. $1,000; 9 percent; 6 months.
4. $2,000; 6 percent; 6 months.
5. $100; 36 percent; 4 months.
6. $500; 24 percent; 3 months.
7. $200; 12 percent; 18 months.
8. $500; 18 percent; 16 months.
9. $5,000; 24 percent; 3 years.
10. $4,000; 30 percent; 2 years.

11. How many months will it take until the interest on $900 at 12 percent will be $135?

12. A credit card holder has owed the credit card company $200 for a month and receives a bill containing an interest charge of $3. Find the interest rate.

6.6 PROBLEM SET 6-1 *(concluded)*

13. Compute the yield of New England Electric Company stock from the following stock market report:

    New Eng Elec   2.16   32.

14. How much must be deposited in an account paying 7 percent if interest of $100 is to be earned in 24 months?

In solving Problems 15 through 26, draw the associated time diagram.

15. How many months will it take at 8 percent interest for $2,000 to grow to an amount of $2,400?

16. Fran deposits $1,000 in an employees' savings account at 6 percent. How many months will it be until the amount in the account is $1,100?

17. Dan buys a TV set priced at $500 and is to pay this amount, plus interest, 3 months later. The total bill was $520. Compute the interest rate.

18. At what rate of interest will an investment of $1,000 for 2 years grow to the amount of $1,100?

19. Find the present value of $460 receivable 18 months from now if the interest rate is 10 percent.

20. Find the present value of $1,000 receivable 2 years from now if the interest rate is 8.5 percent.

21. How much will Sam have to invest now in an employees' savings account at 7 percent in order to have $1,000 in the account 18 months from now?

22. (See Problem 21.) How much would Sam have to invest if the interest rate were 10 percent?

23. Find the proceeds of a $2,000, 18-month loan from a bank if the discount rate is 12 percent.

24. Find the proceeds of a $500, 9-month loan from a bank if the discount rate is 9 percent.

25. Dan wants $2,000 now from a bank, to be repaid 18 months from now. How much will the repayment be if the discount rate is 15 percent?

26. Fran signs a note promising to pay a bank $1,000 ten months from now and receives $900. Find the discount rate.

---

27. Find the effective interest rate in Problem 23.
28. Find the effective interest rate in Problem 24.
29. Find the effective interest rate in Problem 25.
30. What discount rate should a lender quote to earn 9 percent true interest on a 90-day transaction?
31. What discount rate should a lender quote to earn 11 percent true interest on a 6-month transaction?
32. What discount rate should a lender quote to earn 15 percent true interest on a 9-month transaction?

---

33. Run the computer program in Section 6.2 for Problems 1 through 10.
34. Run the computer program in Section 6.3 for Problems 19 through 22.
35. a) Modify the computer programs in Sections 6.2 and 6.3 into a single program that will compute any one of the four parameters F, P, i, and n, given the other three. Include a modification that will allow n to be entered directly in terms of days, months, or years.
    b) Run the program in (a) for Problems 1 through 10 and 15 through 22.
36. a) Modify the computer program in Problem 35(a) for the bank discount.
    b) Run the program in (a) for Problems 23 through 26.
37. a) Write a computer program to determine the effective interest rate for a quoted discount rate.
    b) Run the program in (a) for Problems 27 through 29.
38. a) Write a computer program to determine the quoted discount rate for a given effective rate.
    b) Run the program in (a) for Problems 30 through 32.

6.7 COMPOUND INTEREST AND THE FUTURE VALUE

To see how compound interest works and develop a formula for computing the future value, suppose $5,000 is invested at 10 percent interest compounded each year. The amount at the end of the first year would be

$$F_1 = 5,000 + 5,000(0.10)(1)$$
$$= 5,000 + 500$$
$$= \$5,500.$$

This $5,500 becomes the principal at the beginning of the second year, and the amount at the end of the second year is

$$F_2 = 5,500 + 5,500(0.10)(1)$$
$$= 5,500 + 550$$
$$= \$6,050.$$

Thus in the second year, interest is earned on not only the $5,000 invested, but also on the $500 of interest earned in the first year. This common practice of **computing interest on interest** is called **compounding interest**.

To obtain a formula for computing the future value, we will again use **i as the interest rate per period.** It will suffice for the moment to think of the period as being a year, and we will adjust our formula accordingly later when the period is something other than a year.

Compound interest includes interest on the interest.

Definition. i = Interest rate per period.

Assuming, then, that the period is one year, a principal of P will amount to

$$F_1 = P(1 + i)^1$$

at the end of the first year. At the beginning of the second year, $P(1 + i)$ becomes the new beginning principal, which is multiplied by $(1 + i)$ to find the future value at the end of the second year. Thus

$$F_2 = P(1 + i)(1 + i) = P(1 + i)^2$$

after two years. At the beginning of the third year, the new principal is $P(1 + i)^2$, and to obtain the future value at the end of the third year, this must be multiplied by $(1 + i)$. Thus

$$F_3 = P(1 + i)^2(1 + i) = P(1 + i)^3$$

after three years. Similarly the future value at the end of 10 years would be

$$F_{10} = P(1 + i)^{10}.$$

In general, at the end of n years, the future value will be

$$F_n = P(1 + i)^n.$$

Conventionally the subscript n on F_n is not written.

> **Definition.** Future value: $F = P(1 + i)^n$.

This last expression is the **future value of P for n periods at an interest rate of i per period.**

Example. Find the future value of $1,000 at 7 percent per year for 10 years.

We have $P = \$1{,}000$, $i = 0.07$, and $n = 10$, so that

$$F = 1{,}000(1 + 0.07)^{10}$$
$$= 1{,}000(1.07)^{10}$$

FIGURE 6–4

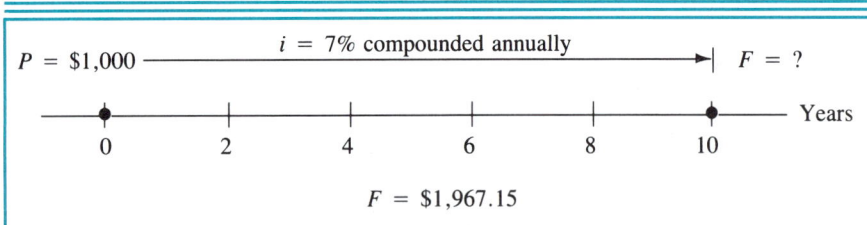

$P = \$1{,}000$ $i = 7\%$ compounded annually $F = ?$

0   2   4   6   8   10   Years

$F = \$1{,}967.15$

TABLE 6–3

Keystroke	Calculator Display
1.07	1.07
2nd, then y^x (or just y^x)	1.07
10	10
=	1.967151358
×	1.967151358
1000	1000
=	1967.151358

$$= 1{,}000(1.96715)$$
$$= \$1{,}967.15.$$

The time diagram for this example is shown in Figure 6–4.

There are two ways to compute the answer to this example on a calculator. One way is to calculate $(1.07)^{10}$ and then multiply this by 1,000, as shown in Table 6–3.

On the other hand, some calculators are programmed with the financial functions, and then this example is solved as shown in Table 6–4.

Exercise. If $500 is invested at 6 percent compounded annually, what will be the future value 30 years later?

Answer: $2,871.75.

Table 6–5 shows a QBasic program to compute the future value, along with the results of running the program for our preceding example.

TABLE 6–4

Keystroke	Calculator Display
1000, then PV	1000
7, then % i	7
10, then n	10
CPT, then FV	1967.151358

TABLE 6–5

```
REM PROGRAM 6-3
REM Future Value -- Compound Interest
CLS
INPUT "Enter P, i, and n"; P, i, n
F = P * (1 + i) ^ n
PRINT "The Future Value F = ";
PRINT USING "$###,###.##"; F

Enter P, i, and n? 1000,.07,10
The Future Value F = $  1,967.15
```

6.8 THE CONVERSION PERIOD

Quoted interest rates are rates **per year** if not accompanied by a qualifying statement such as 1½ percent per month. In the absence of a qualifier, the quoted annual rate is called the **nominal rate** and it is symbolized by j.

The nominal rate is the quoted annual rate.

Definition. Nominal rate = Rate per year = j.

Although the quoted nominal rate is per year, it is common practice to compound interest more frequently than once a year. Many banks compound interest on savings accounts on a daily basis (365 times a year). In other transactions, interest is compounded monthly, quarterly, or semiannually as shown in Table 6–6.

Definition. Number of conversions per year = m.

Example. Find the future value of $500 at 8 percent compounded quarterly for 10 years.

There are four quarters in one year and

$$4(10) = 40$$

quarters in 10 years. Thus we multiply the number of years by the number of conversions per year. We shall now use this number of periods (40 quarters) as n in the future value formula.

TABLE 6–6

Conversion	Number of Conversions per Year, m
Daily	365
Monthly	12
Quarterly	4
Semiannually	2

Inasmuch as the quoted 8 percent is a nominal or per-year rate, we divide 8 percent by the number of conversions per year to obtain

$$i = \frac{8\%}{4} = 2\% \text{ per period.}$$

Using a calculator, we then have

$$F = 500\left(1 + \frac{0.08}{4}\right)^{10(4)}$$
$$= 500(1.02)^{40}$$
$$= 500(2.208039665)$$
$$= \$1,104.02.$$

On a calculator with preprogrammed financial functions, we would proceed as shown in Table 6–7.

In summary, **when interest is compounded more often than once a year, n is the total number of conversion periods**, so that

$$n = (\text{Number of years})(\text{Number of conversions per year})$$

and

$$i = \frac{\text{Nominal rate per year}}{\text{Number of conversions per year}} = \frac{j}{m}.$$

The interest rate per period is the nominal rate divided by the number of periods per year. The total number of periods is the number of years times the number of periods per year.

TABLE 6–7

Keystroke	Calculator Display
500, then PV	500
8	8
÷	8
4	4
=, then % i	2
10	10
×	10
4	4
=, then n	40
CPT, then FV	1104.019832

> **Exercise.** If $800 is invested at 6 percent compounded semiannually, what will be the amount in 5 years?
> **Answer:** $1,075.13.

Example. Compute the future value of $5,000 at 9 percent compounded monthly for 10 years.

Here we have

$$n = (10 \text{ years})(12 \text{ months per year}) = 120$$

and

$$i = \frac{0.09}{12}.$$

Hence

$$F = 5{,}000\left(1 + \frac{0.09}{12}\right)^{120}$$
$$= \$12{,}256.79.$$

> **Exercise.** A bank pays 7.25 percent compounded daily on 90-day notice accounts. If $500 is deposited in such an account, what will be the amount in 90 days? (Use 365 days per year.)
> **Answer:** $509.02

6.9 FINDING THE TIME AND THE INTEREST RATE

The future value formula can be solved for the time n given F, P, and i.

As with simple interest, the compound interest formula

$$F = P(1 + i)^n$$

involves four variables. Thus, once again, given any three of the variables, we can solve the formula for the remaining fourth variable.

In particular, we can determine n if F, P, and i are given; that is, we can find how many periods it will take for P dollars deposited now at i percent to grow to an amount of F dollars.

Example. At 8 percent compounded annually, how many years will it take for $2,000 to grow to $3,000?

We have

$$3{,}000 = 2{,}000(1 + 0.08)^n$$

$$\frac{3{,}000}{2{,}000} = (1.08)^n$$

$$1.5 = (1.08)^n.$$

Taking the natural logarithm of both sides,

$$\ln 1.5 = \ln (1.08)^n = n(\ln 1.08).$$

Thus

$$\frac{\ln 1.5}{\ln 1.08} = n$$

$$5.268 = n,$$

so n is a bit more than $5\frac{1}{4}$ years.

To solve the preceding example on a calculator, we would proceed as shown in Table 6–8. If the calculator has preprogrammed financial functions, then we would proceed as shown in Table 6–9.

> **Exercise.** Find how many years it will take at 9 percent compounded annually for $1,000 to grow to $2,000.
>
> **Answer:** About 8.043 years.

TABLE 6–8

Keystroke	Calculator Display
1.5, then ln x	0.405465108
÷	0.405465108
1.08, then ln x	0.076961041
=	5.268446243

TABLE 6–9

Keystroke	Calculator Display
8, then % i	8
2000, then PV	2000
3000, then FV	3000
CPT, then n	5.268446243

The future value formula can be solved for the interest rate i given F, P, and n.

The next example illustrates how to determine an unknown compound interest rate i given F, P, and n.

Example. At what interest rate compounded annually will a sum of money double in 10 years?

Here double means $100 grows to $200, $25 grows to $50, $1 grows to $2, and so on, and the time required is the same in any doubling. We shall use

$$P = \$1, \quad F = \$2.$$

Hence in

$$F = P(1 + i)^n$$

or

$$P(1 + i)^n = F,$$

we have

$$(1)(1 + i)^{10} = 2$$
$$(1 + i)^{10} = 2.$$

Then, taking the natural logarithm of both sides,

$$\ln (1 + i)^{10} = \ln 2$$
$$10 \ln (1 + i) = \ln 2$$
$$\ln (1 + i) = \frac{\ln 2}{10}.$$

To obtain $(1 + i)$, we must take the antilogarithm of both sides. Thus

$$1 + i = e^{(\ln 2)/10}$$
$$i = e^{(\ln 2)/10} - 1$$
$$= 1.071773463 - 1$$
$$= 0.071773463$$
$$i = 7.177\%.$$

To solve the preceding example on a calculator, we would proceed as shown in Table 6–10, which is precisely Table 5–5 of Section 5.8 repeated here for convenience. If the calculator has preprogrammed financial functions, then we would proceed as shown in Table 6–11.

Exercise. Find the rate of interest that, compounded annually, will result in tripling a sum of money in 10 years.

Answer: 11.612 percent.

TABLE 6-10

Keystroke	Calculator Display
2, then ln x	0.693147181
÷	0.693147181
10	10
=	0.069314718
2nd, then e^x	1.071773463
−	1.071773463
1	1
=	0.071773463

TABLE 6-11

Keystroke	Calculator Display
1, then PV	1
2, then FV	2
10, then n	10
CPT, then % i	7.17734625

6.10 PROBLEM SET 6-2

In Problems 1 through 4, find the future value at the stated nominal interest rate compounded annually (once a year):

1. $200; 20 years; 5 percent.
2. $300; 10 years; 6 percent.
3. $400; 40 years; 8 percent.
4. $500; 15 years; 7 percent.

In Problems 5 through 8, find the future value using the appropriate interest rate and number of periods:

5. $150; 8 years; 8 percent compounded quarterly.
6. $250; 3 years; 12 percent compounded monthly.
7. $600; 20 years; 8 percent compounded semiannually.
8. $1,000; 10 years; 16 percent compounded quarterly.

9. How many years will it take at 7 percent compounded annually for $5,000 to amount to $20,000?
10. How many years will it take for a sum of money to double at 10 percent compounded annually?
11. Find the rate of interest compounded annually at which a sum of money will double in 20 years.
12. Find the rate of interest compounded semiannually at which $5,000 will grow to $12,000 in 8 years.
13. A bank pays 5.25 percent compounded daily on certificate accounts running for 6 years. Using 365 days per year, compute the future value of a deposit of $5,000 for 6 years.

6.6 PROBLEM SET 6-2 (concluded)

14. A bank pays 5.25 percent compounded daily on certain accounts. Find the future value of a deposit of $2,000 for 45 days.

15. How many years will it take at 9 percent compounded annually for $5,000 to grow to $10,000?

16. At what rate of interest compounded annually will $1,000 grow to $5,000 in 10 years?

17. Run the computer program in Section 6.7 for Problems 1 through 4.

18. a) Modify the computer program in Section 6.7 so that it will compute any one of the three parameters F, i, and n, given P and the other two parameters.
    b) Run the program in (a) for Problems 5 through 16.
    c) Modify the program in (a) so that you can enter j and m into the program instead of i and n.
    d) Run the program in (c) for Problems 5 through 16.

6.11 COMPOUND DISCOUNT: PRESENT VALUE

The future value formula can be solved for the present value P, given F, i and n.

As with simple interest, we do not really need a separate formula for calculating the present value. However, it is convenient to have such a formula. So, dividing both sides of the future value formula

$$F = P(1 + i)^n$$

by $(1 + i)^n$, we have

$$\frac{F}{(1 + i)^n} = P \quad \text{or} \quad P = \frac{F}{(1 + i)^n}.$$

By the definition of a negative exponent, then,

$$P = \frac{F}{(1 + i)^n} = F(1 + i)^{-n}.$$

Definition. Present value: $P = F(1 + i)^{-n}$.
Compound discount factor = $(1 + i)^{-n}$.

Example. What is the present value of $2,500 payable 4 years from now at 8 percent compounded quarterly?

Here the amount 4 years hence is $F = \$2,500$. With quarterly compounding,

$$n = (4 \text{ periods per year})(4 \text{ years}) = 16 \text{ periods}.$$

$$i = \frac{0.08}{4} = 0.02.$$

Therefore

$$P = 2,500(1 + 0.02)^{-16}$$
$$= 2,500(0.728445814)$$
$$= \$1,821.11$$

On a calculator with preprogrammed financial functions, we would proceed as shown in Table 6–12.

Exercise. What is the present value of $4,000 payable in 20 years at 8 percent compounded semiannually?

Answer: $833.16.

Example. How much must be deposited now in an account paying 7.3 percent compounded daily in order to have just enough in the account 3 years from now to make $10,000 available for investment in a business enterprise?

TABLE 6–12

Keystroke	Calculator Display
2500, then FV	2500
4	4
×	4
4	4
=, then n	16
8	8
÷	8
4	4
=, then % i	2
CPT, then PV	1821.114534

TABLE 6-13

```
REM PROGRAM 6-4
REM Present Value -- Compound Interest
CLS
INPUT "Enter F, i, and n"; F, i, n
P = F * (1 + i) ^ (-n)
PRINT "The Present Value P = ";
PRINT USING "$###,###.##"; P

Enter F, i, and n? 2500,.02,16
The Present Value P = $   1,821.11
```

With one day as a period,

$$n = (365 \text{ days per year})(3 \text{ years}) = 1{,}095 \text{ periods}$$

and

$$i = \frac{0.073 \text{ per year}}{365 \text{ conversions per year}}.$$

Hence

$$P = 10{,}000 \left(1 + \frac{0.073}{365}\right)^{-1095}$$

$$= \$8{,}033.39.$$

> **Exercise.** How much must be deposited now in an account paying 8 percent compounded monthly in order to have just enough in the account 5 years from now to make a $10,000 down payment on a home?
>
> **Answer:** $6,712.10.

Table 6–13 shows a QBasic program to compute the present value, along with the results of running the program for our first example of this section.

6.12 PROBLEM SET 6-3

In Problems 1 through 4, compute the present value:

1. $1,000 at 8 percent compounded annually, due in 20 years.

2. $2,000 at 7 percent compounded annually, due in 10 years.

6.12 PROBLEM SET 6-3 (concluded)

3. $5,000 at 10 percent compounded semiannually, due in 5 years.

4. $4,000 at 12 percent compounded monthly, due in 3 years.

5. What sum of money deposited now at 8 percent compounded quarterly will provide just enough money to pay a $1,000 debt due 7 years from now?

6. What sum of money invested now at 12 percent compounded monthly will provide just enough to pay a debt of $2,500 due in 3 years?

7. If output per laborhour increases by 5 percent compounded annually and is currently 100 units per laborhour, what was output per laborhour 5 years ago?

8. An account bearing interest at 6 percent compounded semiannually was established 10 years ago. The account balance now is $9,030.55. What was the initial amount when the account was established?

9. Find the present value of $1,000 due in 2 years at 8 percent compounded daily. (Use 365 days in a year).

10. Find the present value of $2,000 due in 10 years at 9 percent compounded monthly.

11. Run the computer program in Section 6.11 for Problems 1 and 2.

12. a) Modify the computer program in Problem 18a of Problem Set 6-2 (Section 6.10) so that it will compute any one of the four parameters F, P, i, and n, given the other three.

    b) Run the program in (a) for Problems 3 through 10.

6.13 EFFECTIVE RATE: COMPOUND INTEREST

Because of lack of comparability, it is hard to judge whether interest quoted at 8 percent compounded semiannually results in more or less interest than would be the case if the rate was 7.9 percent compounded monthly. To make the comparison possible, we change both to their equivalent annual rates; these equivalents are called **effective rates** as in Section 6.5. For example, $1 at 8 percent compounded quarterly for **one year** would amount to

$$F = 1\left(1 + \frac{0.08}{4}\right)^4$$
$$= (1.02)^4$$
$$= 1.08243216,$$

which is the same as the amount of $1 at a rate of 0.08243, or 8.243 percent for one year. Similarly, by calculator, $1 at 7.9 percent compounded monthly for *one* year would amount to

$$F = 1\left(1 + \frac{0.079}{12}\right)^{12}$$
$$= 1.081924169,$$

which is equivalent to the amount of $1 at a rate of 8.192 percent for one year.

In general, at nominal (annual) rate j compounded m times a year, $1 grows to

$$F = (1)(1 + i)^m, \quad i = \frac{j}{m},$$

The effective rate is the equivalent annual simple interest rate.

in one year. At the **effective rate**, r_e, $1 grows to

$$F = 1 + r_e$$

in a year. Hence

$$1 + r_e = (1 + i)^m$$
$$r_e = (1 + i)^m - 1.$$

Effective Rate of i Compounded m Times a Year

$$r_e = (1 + i)^m - 1; \quad i = \frac{j}{m}.$$

Example. Find the effective rate of 24 percent compounded monthly.

Here, as usual,

$$i = \frac{24\%}{12} = 2\%$$

$$m = 12 \text{ months in a year.}$$

Consequently

$$r_e = (1 + 0.02)^{12} - 1$$
$$= 1.268241795 - 1$$
$$= 0.268241795$$
$$= 26.824\%.$$

On a calculator with preprogrammed financial functions, we would proceed as shown in Table 6–14.

Exercise. Find the effective rate of 16 percent compounded quarterly.
Answer: 16.986 percent.

TABLE 6-14

Keystroke	Calculator Display
1, then PV	1
24	24
÷	24
12	12
=, then % i	2
12, then n	12
CPT, then FV	1.268241795
−	1.268241795
1	1
=	0.268241795

Example. Find the effective rate of 12 percent compounded annually, semiannually, quarterly, monthly, semimonthly, weekly, and daily.

In this case,

$$i = \frac{12\%}{m},$$

where $m = 1, 2, 4, 12, 24, 52,$ and 365. The results for

$$r_e = (1 + i)^m - 1$$

are shown in Table 6–15. Note that r_e increases as m increases, but the amount of increase in r_e is gradually diminishing, especially after $m = 12$. What do you think will happen if we compounded by the hour, minute, or second? More will be said about this in Section 6.15.

Exercise. Find the effective rate of 15 percent compounded annually, semiannually, quarterly, monthly, semimonthly, weekly, and daily.

Answer: 15 percent, 15.563 percent, 15.865 percent, 16.075 percent, 16.129 percent, 16.158 percent, 16.180 percent.

TABLE 6-15

m	1	2	4	12	24	52	365
r_e	12%	12.36%	12.551%	12.683%	12.716%	12.734%	12.747%

6.14 PROBLEM SET 6-4

In Problems 1 through 10, find the effective interest rate:

1. 8 percent, compounded quarterly.
2. 10 percent, compounded semiannually.
3. 12 percent, compounded monthly.
4. 16 percent compounded quarterly.
5. 10 percent, compounded monthly.
6. 7 percent, compounded quarterly.
7. 18 percent, compounded monthly.
8. 9 percent, compounded quarterly.
9. 9 percent, compounded monthly.
10. 9 percent, compounded daily (365 days).

11. Find the effective rate of 11 percent compounded annually, semiannually, quarterly, monthly, semi-monthly, weekly, and daily.

12. Find the effective rate of 14 percent compounded annually, semiannually, quarterly, monthly, semi-monthly, weekly, and daily.

13. a) Write a computer program that will compute the effective rate of interest.

    b) Run the program in (a) for Problems 1 through 12.

6.15 CONTINUOUS (INSTANTANEOUS) COMPOUNDING

Before the appearance of modern high-speed data processing computers, calculation and recording of interest for even a few thousand bank accounts was too costly in time to be done at frequent intervals. Consequently the common practice was to compound quarterly—once every three months—and depositors who withdrew money from their accounts between interest dates did not receive interest for the time between the last interest calculation and the date of withdrawal. Now, with high-speed computers, it is possible to calculate and add interest whenever any account transaction takes place. A common practice currently is to compute interest from the day of deposit to the day of withdrawal, with interest compounded daily. The number of compoundings in a year would then be 365 (366 for a leap year). However, as stated in Section 6.2, banks may, for convenience, count a year as twelve 30-day months, 360 days for a year.

We start on our way toward **continuous**, or **instantaneous**, compounding by recalling the number e, which is the base of the system of natural logarithms (Chapter 5). This constant, like the constant π, is a nonrepeating decimal and therefore cannot be expressed exactly as a fraction. However e can be expressed as accurately as needed for any applied problem. To 12 decimal places,

$$e = 2.7182\ 8182\ 8459^+.$$

As we saw in Section 5.10, the value of e can be computed to any desired degree of accuracy by calculating

$$\left(1 + \frac{1}{m}\right)^m$$

using a **sufficiently large value of m.** For example, with $m = 200{,}000$

$$\left(1 + \frac{1}{200{,}000}\right)^{200{,}000} = 2.718281829,$$

which is e correct to nine decimal places. The important point to note is that the expression

$$\left(1 + \frac{1}{m}\right)^m$$

can be interpreted as the future value, F, of \$1 at 100 percent interest ($i = 1.00$) for one year, compounded m times a year. Thus, for example, \$1 at 100 percent compounded monthly for a year would yield

$$F = 1\left(1 + \frac{1}{12}\right)^{12} = \$2.61.$$

This is illustrated in Figure 6–5, which shows 12 discrete points (that is, separated points) representing the 12 compoundings that make \$1 at 100 percent grow to \$2.61 in a year.

If we compound \$1 at 100 percent for a year with daily compoundings, $m = 365$ and

$$F = 1\left(1 + \frac{1}{m}\right)^m = 1\left(1 + \frac{1}{365}\right)^{365} = \$2.71,$$

as shown in Figure 6–6, which has a discrete set of 365 points representing the daily compoundings. Note that in the result, \$2.71, we have the first two decimal

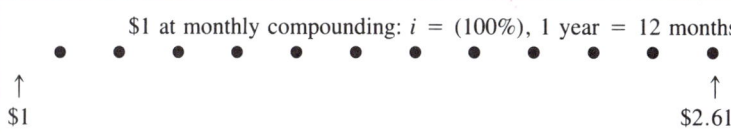

FIGURE 6–5

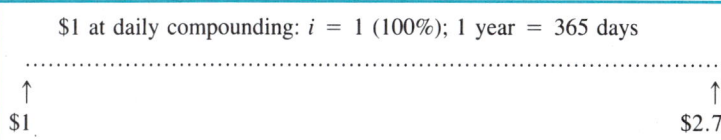

FIGURE 6–6

digits of *e*. Note also that the discrete set of 365 points is beginning to look like a **continuous line** (that is, a line drawn without lifting the pencil from the paper). Now, going one step further, suppose we compound every hour for a year so that

$$m = (365 \text{ days})(24 \text{ hours per day}) = 8{,}760.$$

Then

$$F = \left(1 + \frac{1}{m}\right)^m = \left(1 + \frac{1}{8{,}760}\right)^{8{,}760} = 2.718128098,$$

a result that has the first four decimal digits of *e*. It might be possible with the aid of a magnifying glass and a very sharp point to make a figure like Figure 6–6 showing these 8,760 compoundings, but if the magnifying glass were removed, the result would appear to be a continuous line without gaps, but the set of points is discrete, and the gaps are there.

To approach the core concept of instantaneous compounding, we now contemplate compounding every minute ($m = 525{,}600$ compoundings per year), every second ($m = 31{,}536{,}000$ compoundings a year), and so on, with the duration of the compounding period getting smaller and the number of compounding points increasing. There is no limit to the number of compounding periods but, as it grows, the **duration of a period approaches zero,** and this leads us to the concept of a **point in time of zero duration,** which is connoted by the word **instant**. The nature of time in the real world forces us to attach meaning to a point in time—an instant—because, for example, the time from 9 A.M. to 11 A.M. goes through all times in the interval, and at some point the time must be precisely 10 o'clock. We cannot, of course, mark a clock dial in instants. However, real time does not progress in discrete jumps—it is **continuous**. A real time line, then, is not a discrete set of points, but a continuous line with no gaps. It is a line we represent on paper by drawing a pencil along a straight edge without removing the pencil from the paper, as shown in Figure 6–7, which represents instantaneous compounding. As this figure shows, instantaneous compounding of $1 at 100 percent for one year yields a compound amount of $*e*. For present purposes, we state that **the sequence of digits generated by calculating**

$$\left(1 + \frac{1}{m}\right)^m$$

> Continuous compounding measures the effect of computing interest at every instant of time.

FIGURE 6–7

$1 at instantaneous compounding: $i = 1$ (100%); 1 year

↑
$1

↑
$e = \$2.71828^+$

using larger and larger values of m becomes closer and closer to the sequence of digits representing e. Of course, the letter m is arbitrary, and we can say equally well that e is generated by

$$\left(1 + \frac{1}{x}\right)^x \quad \text{or} \quad \left(1 + \frac{1}{p}\right)^p$$

as x, on the left, or p, on the right, becomes larger and larger.

We have demonstrated that \$1 at 100 percent for one year, compounded continuously (instantaneously), yields \$$e$. If we have \$1 at nominal rate j per year for t years, the future value is

$$F = 1e^{jt}$$

as shown in the footnote.[1] If \$$P$ rather than \$1 is the principal, we have:

Future Value with Continuous Compounding

$$F = Pe^{jt}.$$

Note: We shall use the symbol t to denote a **number of years.** This number can be a fraction or a decimal. We do this to distinguish t from n because n has been defined to be a discrete **number of periods.**

Example. Find the future value of \$500 at 8 percent compounded continuously for 9 years and 3 months.

Remembering that t is the number of years, we find

$$t = 9 + \frac{3}{12} = 9.25 \text{ years.}$$

---

[1]The compound amount of \$1 at rate j compounded m times a year for t years is

$$\left(1 + \frac{j}{m}\right)^{mt}. \tag{1}$$

Now let $p = m/j$ so that $j/m = 1/p$ and $m = pj$, and substitute these into (1), giving

$$\left(1 + \frac{1}{p}\right)^{pjt} = \left[\left(1 + \frac{1}{p}\right)^p\right]^{jt}. \tag{2}$$

Now as m becomes larger and larger, p (which is m/j) becomes larger and larger, the bracketed expression in (2) generates e, and we obtain e^{jt}.

Hence
$$F = 500e^{0.08(9.25)}$$
$$= 500e^{0.74}$$
$$= \$1,047.97.$$

> **Exercise.** Find the future value of $200 at 6 percent compounded continuously for 30 months.
> **Answer:** $232.37.

If both sides of the formula
$$F = Pe^{jt}$$
are divided by the exponential term, we have
$$\frac{F}{e^{jt}} = P$$
or, using the negative exponent,
$$Fe^{-jt} = P.$$
This is the present value, P, of a future amount, F.

> **Present Value with Continuous Compounding**
> $$P = Fe^{-jt}.$$

> **Exercise.** How much must be deposited now in an account earning 7.5 percent compounded continuously if the amount in the account 8 years from now is to be $10,000?
> **Answer:** $5,488.12.

The effective continuous compounding rate is the true annual simple interest rate earned or paid.

An interesting problem is to determine the **effective rate** for continuous compounding. For example, what is the effective rate of 8 percent compounded continuously? At a nominal rate $j = 0.08$, $1 compounded continuously for one year amounts to

$$F = e^{0.08} = 1.083287068,$$

so the interest earned is

$$1.083287068 - 1 = 0.083287068 \quad \text{or} \quad 8.329\%.$$

Generalizing this result, we have

Effective Rate of Nominal Rate j

$$r_e = e^j - 1.$$

Exercise. Find the effective rate of 10 percent compounded continuously.

Answer: 10.517 percent.

There are legal limits on the interest rates banks can offer for various types of accounts. In the past decade, these limits have not compared favorably with interest rates that can be obtained from nonbank investments and, in an effort to attract more deposits, some banks have adopted not only the ultimate in compounding, continuous compounding, but also the **modified year.** Although banks customarily use a 360-day year, they sometimes give the investor the advantage of the full 365-day year by using the multiplier,

$$\frac{365}{360},$$

which is greater than one. For example, we might read a newspaper advertisement that states that the effective rate on 8 percent is 8.449 percent. To obtain this result, we replace the exponent in

$$e^{0.08} - 1$$

by

$$\frac{365}{360}(0.08) \quad \text{or} \quad 0.081111111$$

to obtain

= Current Banking Practice

Sometimes the interest rate is adjusted by 365/360 to reflect the exact versus ordinary days in a year.

$$r_e = e^{0.081111111} - 1$$
$$= 1.084491389 - 1$$
$$= 0.084491389$$

or 8.449 percent.

Exercise. Using the modified year, what is the effective rate of 6 percent compounded continuously?

Answer: 6.272 percent.

In passing, we note that going from daily to continuous compounding contributes very little to interest earned, but the modified year makes a significant contribution when large sums of money are involved. **We shall use one year as $t = 1$ unless specifically instructed to use the modified year.**

We return now to the nominal rate j compounded continuously, for which the effective rate is

$$r_e = e^j - 1.$$

If we solve this for j we have the nominal rate, which, compounded continuously, yields a **given effective rate**, r_e. Rearranging the terms of the previous equation, we have

$$e^j = 1 + r_e.$$

Taking the natural logarithm of both sides,

$$\ln e^j = \ln (1 + r_e).$$

By the power rule of logarithms,

$$j \ln e = \ln (1 + r_e),$$

where $\ln e = 1$. Hence

Continuous j Equivalent of r_e Effective

$$j = \ln (1 + r_e).$$

Example. A bank states that the effective interest on savings accounts that earn continuous interest is 7 percent. Find the nominal rate.

Here,

$$r_e = 0.07,$$

so

$$j = \ln(1 + r_e)$$
$$= \ln(1.07)$$
$$= 0.67658648$$

or 6.766 percent.

Exercise. What nominal rate compounded continuously gives an effective rate of 8 percent?

Answer: 7.696 percent.

6.16 PROBLEM SET 6–5

In Problems 1 through 4, find the future value if interest is compounded continuously:
1. $1,000; 6 percent; 5 years.
2. $500; 8 percent; 10 years.
3. $5,000; 8 percent; 4 years and 6 months.
4. $4,000; 6 percent; 5 years and 8 months.

In Problems 5 through 8, find the present value if interest is compounded continuously:
5. $800; 8.5 percent; due in 10 years.
6. $2,500; 9.5 percent; due in 12 years.
7. $1,000; 12 percent; due in 9 months.
8. $3,000; 10 percent; due in 18 months.

The rates in Problems 9 through 12 are nominal rates. Find the effective rate if interest is compounded continuously:
9. $j = 0.05$.
10. $j = 0.06$.
11. $j = 0.07$.
12. $j = 0.08$.

What nominal rate compounded continuously will yield the effective rates in Problems 13 through 16?
13. $r_e = 0.12$.
14. $r_e = 0.09$.
15. $r_e = 0.05$.
16. $r_e = 0.10$.

6.16 PROBLEM SET 6–5 (concluded)

In Problems 17 through 25, use continuous compounding:

17. How much will a deposit of $5,000 grow to in 20 years at 6.8 percent interest compounded continuously?
18. How much should be deposited now at 8.4 percent compounded continuously if the amount in the account 10 years from now is to be $10,000?
19. Sam invests $10,000 in a bank account paying 7.6 percent compounded continuously for 15 years. How much will the account amount to at the end of this time?
20. How much must be deposited now in an account paying 7.5 percent interest compounded continuously if the amount in the account 6 years from now is to be $7,500?
21. History tells us that Peter Minuit purchased Manhattan Island in New York from the Indians for $24 about 370 years ago. If the $24 had been invested at 5 percent compounded continuously, what would be its amount after 370 years?
22. How much should be deposited now in an account paying 7.6 percent compounded continuously if the account is to grow to $10,000 in 8 years?
23. What is the effective rate of 7.9 percent compounded continuously?
24. What nominal rate compounded continuously will yield an effective rate of 8.22 percent?
25. A bank offers 7.6 percent compounded continuously and uses the modified year. Find the effective rate.

6.17 ORDINARY ANNUITIES: FUTURE VALUE

Annuities are series of periodic payments.

Annuities certain begin and end on specific dates.

The payment interval for a simple annuity coincides with the interest interval.

In an ordinary annuity, payments are made at the end of each period.

An **annuity** is a **series of periodic payments,** usually made in equal amounts. Annuities can be classified by when they begin and end, by when the payments are made, and by whether or not the payment intervals coincide with the interest intervals. We will discuss the most common type of annuity, ordinary annuities; people interested in a more complete discussion are referred to any standard textbook on mathematics of finance.[2]

An annuity that begins and ends on designated dates is called an **annuity certain.** Examples include loan transactions and rent payments. Second, an annuity whose payment intervals coincide with the interest intervals is called a **simple annuity.** An example is a transaction whose payments are made monthly and whose interest is charged monthly. (When the two intervals do not coincide, the annuity is called **complex.**) Lastly, an annuity whose payment is made at the end of each payment interval is called an **ordinary annuity.** Loan transactions are such an annuity. (An annuity whose payment is made at the beginning of each payment interval is called an **annuity due.**)

We will investigate **simple ordinary annuities certain,** usually just called **ordinary annuities.** In our work, we shall use the following symbols:

n = Number of periods

i = Interest rate per period

---

[2] For example, see Stephen P. Shao and Stephen P. Shao, Jr. *Mathematics for Management and Finance* (Cincinnati: Southwestern Publishing Co., 1986).

R = Payment per period

F = Future value of the annuity.

Figure 6–8 illustrates the ordinary annuity. Here we see that the first payment of $R accumulates interest for $n - 1$ periods, the second payment R for $n - 2$ periods, and so on. The next-to-last payment R accumulates one period of interest, and the last payment R accumulates no interest. So using the future value formula for compound interest from Section 6.7, we get the future value of the annuity:

$$F = R(1 + i)^{n-1} + R(1 + i)^{n-2} + \cdots + R(1 + i)^1 + R. \qquad (1)$$

All but the last payment of an ordinary annuity accumulate interest for varying lengths of time.

To simplify (1), we multiply both sides by $(1 + i)$ to get

$$F(1 + i) = R(1 + i)^n + R(1 + i)^{n-1} + \cdots + R(1 + i)^2 + R(1 + i). \qquad (2)$$

The future value of an annuity is the sum of all the payments plus their associated interest.

Next we subtract (1) from (2),

$$\begin{aligned} F(1+i) - F &= [R(1+i)^n + R(1+i)^{n-1} + \cdots + R(1+i)] \\ &\quad - [R(1+i)^{n-1} + \cdots + R(1+i) + R] \\ &= R(1+i)^n - R. \end{aligned}$$

This last operation becomes

$$F + Fi - F = R(1 + i)^n - R$$

or

$$Fi = R(1 + i)^n - R,$$

which gives us

Future Value of Ordinary Annuity

$$F = R\left[\frac{(1 + i)^n - 1}{i}\right]. \qquad (3)$$

Example. If $100 is deposited in an account at the end of every quarter for the next 5 years, how much will be in the account at the time of the final deposit if interest is 8 percent compounded quarterly?

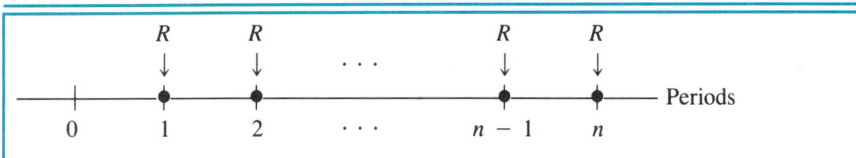

FIGURE 6–8

First, this annuity transaction is simple since payments are made quarterly and interest is accrued quarterly. Second, this is an ordinary annuity since the payments are made at the end of each quarter. Third, this is an annuity certain since it begins now and ends 5 years from now. From the information given, we have

$$R = \$100,$$

$$i = \frac{0.08}{4} = 0.02, \text{ and}$$

$$n = (5 \text{ years})(4 \text{ quarters per year}) = 20 \text{ periods}.$$

The associated time diagram is shown in Figure 6–9. Using the annuity future value formula

$$F = R\left[\frac{(1+i)^n - 1}{i}\right]$$

and substituting the preceding values, we get

$$F = 100\left[\frac{(1 + 0.02)^{20} - 1}{0.02}\right]$$

$$= 100(24.29736982)$$

$$= \$2,429.74.$$

Observe that 20 payments of $100 each amount to $2,000. The $2,429.74 amount is this $2,000 plus interest for varying lengths of time on all payments except the last one.

On a calculator with preprogrammed financial functions, we would proceed as shown in Table 6–16.

Exercise. Sums of $500 are deposited in an account at the end of each 6-month period for 8 years. Find the amount in the account after the last deposit has been made if interest is earned at the rate of 10 percent compounded semiannually.

Answer: $11,828.75.

Example. If $100 is deposited in an account each month for 10 years and the account earns 7 percent compounded monthly, how much will be in the account after the last deposit is made?

We have

$$R = \$100,$$

$$i = \frac{0.07}{12}, \text{ and}$$

$$n = 10 \text{ years } (12 \text{ months per year}) = 120 \text{ periods}.$$

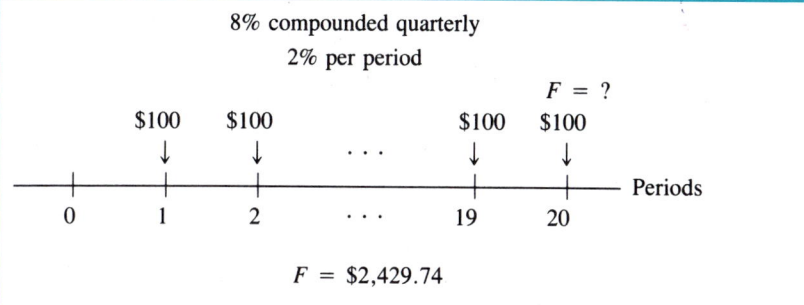

FIGURE 6-9

Keystroke	Calculator Display
100, then PMT	100
8	8
÷	8
4	4
=, then % i	2
5	5
×	5
4	4
=, then n	20
CPT, then FV	2429.736982

TABLE 6-16

Hence

$$F = 100\left[\frac{(1 + 0.07/12)^{120} - 1}{0.07/12}\right]$$
$$= 100(173.0848066)$$
$$= \$17,308.48.$$

Exercise. Sums of $500 are deposited in an account at the end of each 6-month period for 25 years. Find the amount in the account after the last deposit is made if interest is computed at 6 percent compounded semiannually.
Answer: $56,398.43.

6.18 ORDINARY ANNUITIES: SINKING FUNDS

To generate the future value of an annuity, periodic payments are made into a sinking fund.

The future value formula can be solved for the payment R, given F, i, and n.

A **sinking fund** is a fund into which periodic payments are made in order to accumulate a specified amount at some point in the future. For example, say a corporation needs money to expand so it sells $1 million worth of bonds payable in 10 years. The firm must pay interest to bondholders (usually semiannually) while the bonds mature and, at maturity 10 years later, must pay $1 million to redeem the bonds. To be sure that the $1 million is available 10 years hence, the corporation may set up a sinking fund to accumulate this amount. The problem is to determine R, the required periodic payment into the sinking fund. The n payments constitute an ordinary annuity of R per period, and the known future value of this annuity is

$$F = R\left[\frac{(1 + i)^n - 1}{i}\right].$$

Solving this for the unknown periodic payment R, we have

Sinking Fund Payment

$$R = F\left[\frac{i}{(1 + i)^n - 1}\right].$$

Example. How much should be deposited in a sinking fund at the end of each quarter for 5 years to accumulate $10,000 if the fund earns 8 percent compounded quarterly?

We have

$$F = \$10{,}000,$$

$$i = \frac{0.08}{4} = 0.02, \text{ and}$$

$$n = (5 \text{ years})(4 \text{ quarters per year}) = 20 \text{ periods}.$$

Hence

$$R = 10{,}000\left[\frac{0.02}{(1 + 0.02)^{20} - 1}\right]$$

$$= 10{,}000(0.041156718)$$

$$= \$411.57.$$

Over the life of the sinking fund, the sum of the deposits will be

$$20(411.57) = \$8{,}231.40.$$

This sum, plus interest earned, will provide the desired $10,000.

TABLE 6-17

Keystroke	Calculator Display
10000, then FV	10000
8	8
÷	8
4	4
=, then % i	2
5	5
×	5
4	4
=, then n	20
CPT, then PMT	411.5671809

On a calculator with preprogrammed financial functions, we would proceed as shown in Table 6–17.

Exercise. Instead of creating a sinking fund at a bank, a company has its controller create a reserve fund in the company's accounts to which a contribution is made each quarter. By so doing, the company can realize a return of 12 percent compounded quarterly. What should be the amount transferred quarterly to the reserve fund to accumulate $10,000 in 5 years?

Answer: $372.16.

Example. A company wants to accumulate $100,000 to purchase replacement machinery 8 years from now. To accomplish this, equal semiannual payments are made to a fund that earns 7 percent compounded semiannually. Find the amount of each payment.

We have

$$F = 100{,}000,$$

$$i = \frac{0.07}{2} = 0.035, \text{ and}$$

$$n = 8(2) = 16.$$

From

$$R = F\left[\frac{i}{(1+i)^n - 1}\right],$$

we have

$$R = 100{,}000 \left[\frac{0.035}{(1.035)^{16} - 1} \right]$$

$$= 100{,}000(0.047684831)$$

$$= \$4{,}768.48.$$

> **Exercise.** A company issues $1 million of bonds and sets up a sinking fund at 8 percent compounded quarterly to accumulate $1 million 15 years hence to redeem the bonds. Find the quarterly payment to the sinking fund.
>
> **Answer:** $8,767.97.

6.19 PROBLEM SET 6-6

Find the future value of the ordinary annuities in Problems 1 through 4:

1. $500 per month for 3 years at 12 percent compounded monthly.

2. $1,000 every 3 months for 10 years at 8 percent compounded quarterly.

3. $2,000 per year for 20 years at 7 percent compounded annually.

4. $2,500 a year for 34 years at 8 percent compounded annually.

5. When Kathy was born, her parents decided to deposit $500 every 6 months thereafter for 15 years in an account earning 6 percent compounded semiannually. How much will be in the account after the last deposit is made?

6. Greg has $100 deducted from his salary at the end of each month and invested in an employees' fund that, because of company contributions, pays 12 percent interest compounded monthly. How much will Greg's account amount to when he retires 3 years from now after receiving his last salary check?

7. What amount should be deposited at the end of each quarter in a sinking fund earning 8 percent compounded quarterly if the amount in the fund after 4 years is to be $90,000?

8. What amount should be deposited at the end of each 6-month period in a sinking fund earning 6 percent compounded semiannually if the amount in the fund after 15 years is to be $75,000?

9. New Venture Corporation has decided to transfer a sum of money to a reserve account at the end of each year to accumulate $100,000 to be used to replace machinery 10 years from now. How much should be transferred each year if interest at 8 percent compounded annually is credited to the reserve?

10. In order to accumulate $15,000 for a down payment on a home 8 years from now, the Joneses are going to deposit a sum of money at the end of each 6-month period in an account earning 8 percent compounded semiannually. What should be the amount of each deposit?

11. Find the future value of an ordinary annuity of $1,000 per quarter for 25 years at 8 percent compounded quarterly.

12. Septech Corporation has issued $10 million worth of bonds to obtain money now for expanding its corporate activities. To redeem the bonds, which fall

6.19 PROBLEM SET 6-6 (concluded)

due in 30 years, Septech will transfer an amount to a reserve fund at the end of each 6-month period. How much should be transferred if the account earns 7 percent compounded semiannually?

13. a) Write a computer program that will compute the future value F of an ordinary annuity given R, i, and n. (Hint: Refer to the program in Section 6.7.)
    b) Run the program in (a) for Problems 1 through 6, and 11.

14. a) Modify the program in Problem 13(a) to print out the period-by-period amounts under the headings Period, Current Balance, Interest, Payment, and New Balance.

15. a) Write a computer program that will compute the sinking fund payment R of an ordinary annuity given F, i, and n. (Hint: Refer to Problem 13a.)
    b) Run the program in (a) for Problems 7 through 10, and 12.

16. a) Modify the program in Problem 15(a) to print out the period-by-period amounts under the headings Period, Present Fund, Interest, Payment, Accumulated Fund, and Sinking Fund.

6.20 ORDINARY ANNUITIES: PRESENT VALUE

We learned in Section 6.11 that the present value of any amount due n periods from now is

$$P = F(1 + i)^{-n}.$$

If we replace F by the future value of an annuity

$$F = R\left[\frac{(1 + i)^n - 1}{i}\right],$$

we have

$$P = R\left[\frac{(1 + i)^n - 1}{i}\right](1 + i)^{-n}$$

$$= R\left[\frac{(1 + i)^n(1 + i)^{-n} - 1(1 + i)^{-n}}{i}\right]$$

$$= R\left[\frac{(1 + i)^0 - (1 + i)^{-n}}{i}\right]$$

$$= R\left[\frac{1 - (1 + i)^{-n}}{i}\right].$$

The present value formula of an annuity can be generated from the compound present value formula together with the annuity future value formula.

Present Value of Ordinary Annuity

$$P = R\left[\frac{1 - (1 + i)^{-n}}{i}\right].$$

> Present value represents the lump sum needed today to equate to a future series of periodic payments.

Present value annuity calculations arise when we wish to determine what lump sum must be deposited in an account now if this sum and the interest it earns are to provide equal payments for a stated number of periods, with the last payment making the account balance zero.

Example. What sum deposited now in an account earning 8 percent interest compounded quarterly will provide quarterly payments of $1,000 for 10 years, the first payment to be made 3 months from now?

Here we have

$$R = \$1,000,$$
$$i = \frac{0.08}{4} = 0.02, \text{ and}$$
$$n = (10 \text{ years})(4 \text{ quarters per year}) = 40 \text{ periods}.$$

Hence

$$P = 1,000 \left[\frac{1 - (1 + 0.02)^{-40}}{0.02} \right]$$
$$= 1,000(27.35547925)$$
$$= \$27,355.48.$$

On a calculator with preprogrammed financial functions, we would proceed as shown in Table 6–18.

Exercise. a) A sum of money invested now at 10 percent compounded semiannually is to provide payments of $1,500 every 6 months for 8 years, with the first payment due 6 months from now. How much should be invested? b) How much interest will the investment earn?

Answer: a) $16,256.65 b) $7,743.35.

Example. a) The directors of a company have voted to establish a fund that will pay a retiring accountant or his estate $1,000 per month for the next 10 years, with the first payment to be made a month from now. How much should be placed in the fund if it earns interest at 7 percent compounded monthly? b) How much interest will the fund earn during its existence?

Here, for part (a)

$$R = \$1,000,$$
$$i = \frac{0.07}{12}, \text{ and}$$
$$n = (10 \text{ years})(12 \text{ months per year}) = 120 \text{ periods}.$$

TABLE 6-18

Keystroke	Calculator Display
1000, then PMT	1000
8	8
÷	8
4	4
=, then % i	2
10	10
×	10
4	4
=, then n	40
CPT, then PV	27355.47925

Hence

$$P = 1{,}000 \left[\frac{1 - (1 + 0.07/12)^{-120}}{0.07/12} \right]$$
$$= 1{,}000\,(86.12635393)$$
$$= \$86{,}126.35.$$

For part (b) we have

$$(120 \text{ payments})(\$1{,}000 \text{ per payment}) = \$120{,}000.00.$$
$$\text{Interest earned} = \$120{,}000.00 - \$86{,}126.35 = \$33{,}873.65.$$

Exercise. Answer (a) and (b) of the previous example if the interest rate is 8 percent compounded monthly.

Answer: a) $82,421.48. b) $37,578.52.

6.21 ORDINARY ANNUITIES: AMORTIZATION

In many financial transactions, a current obligation is discharged by making a series of payments in the future. After the last payment, the obligation ceases to exist—it is dead—and it is said to have been **amortized by the payments.** Prominent examples of amortization are loans taken to buy a home or a car and amortized over a period of 20 to 30 years in the case of a home mortgage and over 2, 3, or 4 years in the case of a car purchase loan. Given the amount of the loan (the current principal, P), the number of periods (n), and the interest rate (i), the quantity to be calculated is R, the amount of the periodic payment. The n payments of R dollars

The amortization formula computes the periodic payments needed to discharge a present-day debt. It is obtained by solving the annuity present value formula for the payment R, given P, i, and n.

each constitute an ordinary annuity whose present value is P, and we have learned that

$$P = R\left[\frac{1 - (1 + i)^{-n}}{i}\right].$$

Solving this for the unknown R, we have

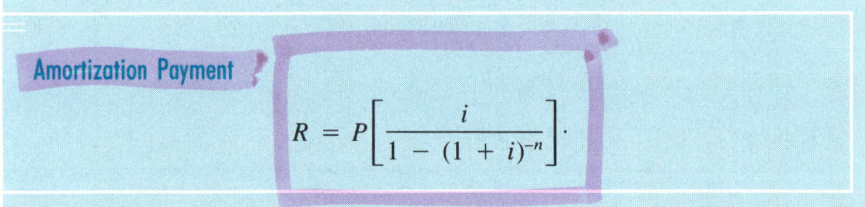

Amortization Payment

$$R = P\left[\frac{i}{1 - (1 + i)^{-n}}\right].$$

Example. Sam borrowed $5,000 to buy a car. He will amortize the loan by monthly payments of $R each over a period of 3 years. a) Find the monthly payment if interest is 12 percent compounded monthly. b) Find the total amount Sam will pay.

For part (a) we have

$$P = \$5{,}000,$$

$$i = \frac{0.12}{12} = 0.01 \text{ per month, and}$$

$$n = (3 \text{ years})(12 \text{ months per year}) = 36 \text{ periods}.$$

Hence,

$$R = 5{,}000\left[\frac{0.01}{1 - (1 + 0.01)^{-36}}\right]$$

$$= 5{,}000(0.03321431)$$

$$= \$166.07.$$

b) Sam pays $166.07 a month for 36 months. The total paid will be

$$36(166.07) = \$5{,}978.52,$$

of which $978.52 is interest.

On a calculator with preprogrammed financial functions, we would proceed as shown in Table 6–19.

TABLE 6–19

Keystroke	Calculator Display
5000, then PV	5000
12	12
÷	12
12	12
=, then % i	1
3	3
×	3
12	12
=, then n	36
CPT, then PMT	166.0715489

Exercise. (See the preceding example). Sam paid for his car, but more than once was late in making payments because of financial reverses, one being an accident that badly damaged the car. He now wishes to buy another car and receives a 3-year loan for $5,000, but the interest charge is 24 percent compounded monthly. a) What will Sam's monthly payment be for the new car? b) How much interest will he pay on this loan?

Answer: a) $196.16.   b) $2,061.76.

Example. A company has borrowed $50,000 at 10 percent compounded quarterly. The debt is to be amortized by equal payments each quarter over 15 years. a) Find the quarterly payment.   b) How much interest will be paid?

a) We have $P = 50{,}000$, $i = 0.10/4$, and $n = 15(4) = 60$. Hence

$$R = 50{,}000 \left[\frac{0.10/4}{1 - (1 + 0.10/4)^{-60}} \right]$$

$$= \$1{,}617.67 \text{ per quarter.}$$

b) Payments for 60 quarters will be

$$60(1{,}617.67) = \$97{,}060.20.$$

Interest paid will be

$$\$97{,}060.20 - \$50{,}000.00 = \$47{,}060.20.$$

> **Exercise.** A real estate developer borrows $100,000 at 12 percent compounded monthly. The debt is to be discharged by monthly payments for the next 6 years. a) Find the monthly payment. b) How much interest will be paid?
>
> **Answer:** a) $1,955.02. b) $40,761.44.

Mortgage Payments

Mortgages are amortizations secured by a piece of property.

In a typical home purchase transaction, the homebuyer pays part of the cost in cash and borrows the remainder needed, usually from a bank or a savings and loan institution. As security for the loan, the lending agency ordinarily obtains a **mortgage** (conditional title to the property). The buyer amortizes the indebtedness by periodic payments over a period of time. Typically payments are monthly and the time period is long—30 years is not unusual.

Example. A $70,000 condominium is to be purchased by paying $10,000 in cash and a $60,000 mortgage for 30 years at 9.75 percent compounded monthly. a) Find the monthly payment on the mortgage. b) What will be the total amount of interest paid?

a) For a principal amount of $60,000,

$$P = \$60{,}000,$$
$$i = 0.0975/12, \text{ and}$$
$$n = 30(12) = 360.$$

So

$$R = 60{,}000 \left[\frac{.0975/12}{1 - (1 + .0975/12)^{-360}} \right]$$
$$= 60{,}000(0.008591544)$$
$$= \$515.49.$$

b) The total amount paid in 360 months will be

$$360(515.49) = \$185{,}576.40.$$

Interest paid will be

$$\$185{,}576.40 - \$60{,}000.00 = \$125{,}576.40.$$

The amount of interest just calculated is very large, but it must be remembered that the buyer has a home to live in for 30 years and, moreover, real estate values have risen, and are predicted to continue to rise. If the experience of the past 30 years is repeated, the value of the home when the mortgage has been paid off could easily be three times its purchase cost.

FROM THEORY TO PRACTICE
A New Kind of Mortgage Instrument: The Biweekly Mortgage

Home buyers have always looked for the most cost-effective way to service a mortgage. Historically the options were limited; the interest rate was fixed and the term was either 20 or 25 years. Later the term became more flexible with many lending institutions offering mortgages of 15, 20, 25, or 30 years. Finally adjustable-rate mortgages (ARMs) arrived on the scene with the interest rate adjusted annually and several points of up-front interest charged to initiate the transaction. ARMs begin with a lower interest rate than standard mortgages, so that the initial cash flow is eased, but the rate is tied to the bank's cost of money (usually the bank's prime lending rate) and can increase within specified limits at certain well-defined intervals. Currently 1-year, 3-year, and 5-year ARMs are the most popular. Selecting an appropriate mortgage instrument (given this wide range of choices, estimates of future interest rates, and degrees of risk aversion) is a complicated problem.

Now a popular, new option has appeared—the **biweekly mortgage.** With a biweekly mortgage based on a standard 30-year mortgage, the borrower makes payments every two weeks in an amount equal to one-half of the monthly payment on the standard 30-year mortgage. Because of the accelerated payment schedule, the borrower amortizes the mortgage sooner, resulting in savings in thousands of dollars in interest over the standard mortgage. Of course, the amount of savings depends on the usual parameters, namely, the amount borrowed, the interest rate, and the term of the loan.

But is the borrower really saving money and thus decreasing the cost of the mortgage? It is true enough that an accelerated payment schedule reduces the principal balance quicker and so reduces the total amount of interest paid. But what is this acceleration's cost to the borrower? A detailed analysis can be found in a Teaching Series Note coauthored by one of the authors.* For purposes of illustration, let us look at the effect of a biweekly mortgage on our amortization example.

In our present standard 30-year amortization of the $60,000 mortgage at 9.75 percent, we had monthly payments of $515.49 resulting in a total payment amount of $185,582.74 and associated total interest of $125,582.74. If the borrower secured a biweekly mortgage, the biweekly payment would be $257.75, which is one-half of the original $515.49 **rounded up** to the next cent. A computer analysis of the biweekly transaction would show an amortization in about 21 years with a total payment amount of $141,170.56 and associated total interest of $81,170.56. Thus the biweekly mortgage amortizes in about two-thirds of the time of a standard mortgage and results in less than two-thirds of the total interest. The cost for this substantial savings is the requirement of making 26 biweekly payments, which is equivalent to requiring one extra monthly payment per year, but spread out over 26 installments.

One last question. Since the biweekly amortizes in 21 years, how does it compare to a standard 20-year mortgage? Calculations would show that a 20-year mortgage would require 240 monthly payments of $569.11. This mortgage would result in total payments of $136,586.56 and associated total interest of $76,586.56. Clearly, if you can qualify for the standard 20-year mortgage (which requires only $53.62 more each month than the standard 30-year mortgage), you will be better off in the long run with it than with even the biweekly mortgage.

*Steven R. Gordon and John C. Saber, *Biweekly Mortgages: Do They Really Decrease Costs?* (Babson College Teaching Note Series TN-89-4, November 1989).

> **Exercise.** A manufacturer has a 15-year, 8.5 percent, mortgage for $100,000 on a building. Payments are made monthly. a) Find the monthly payment. b) How much interest will be paid?
>
> **Answer:** a) $984.74. b) $77,253.20

≡ Amortization Schedules

When a mortgage payment is made, the interest due is subtracted first and the remainder is then applied to the outstanding balance.

When a debt is amortized, part of each payment is interest on the balance outstanding, and the remainder is used to reduce the balance outstanding. The largest interest charge occurs at the first payment because then interest is due on the entire principal and, of course, the smallest reduction of principal occurs at the time of the first payment. To see how this works, recall the $60,000, 9.75 percent, 30-year mortgage of the previous example. The monthly payment is $515.49. At the time the first payment is due, one month has passed and the interest on the $60,000 is

$$I = 60{,}000(0.0975)\left(\frac{1}{12}\right) = \$487.50.$$

The amount applied to reduce the balance outstanding is

$$\$515.49 - \$487.50 = \$27.99,$$

so the new balance is

$$\$60{,}000.00 - \$27.99 = \$59{,}972.01.$$

It is clear that the first payment is almost entirely absorbed by the interest charge, with little left to reduce the balance still owed. Each month, of course, the interest charge decreases and the reduction of the amount owed increases. However, in financial jargon, early payments do not increase the homeowner's equity very much.

Continuing to the second payment, the beginning balance is now $59,972.01, and we proceed as follows:

Beginning balance owed		$59,972.01
Payment	$515.49	
Interest charge (59,972.01)(.0975)$\left(\frac{1}{12}\right)$:	487.27	
Reduction of balance owed	28.22	28.22
Ending balance owed		$59,943.79

A schedule of payments amortizing a mortgage has a last payment adjusted to precisely zero out the outstanding balance.

When the process just described is repeated for the entire period of the loan (360 months for the example) and the results tabulated, the table is called an **amortization schedule.** The process is simple, but it must be repeated many times, and the chore is best left to a computer that can be programmed to do the process once and then instructed to repeat it over and over again, printing out a line of entries in an amortization schedule at the end of each repetition. When this is done, the last payment is adjusted to precisely zero out the remaining balance, so it may be different from the rest of the payments. For example, a computer program for our preceding example would show payment number 360 to be $521.83, not $515.49, resulting in a total interest paid of $125,582.74, not $125,576.40.

> **Exercise.** For the $100,000, 15-year, 8.5 percent mortgage of the previous exercise, the monthly payment is $984.74. For the first and second payments, find the
> a) Interest charge. b) Reduction in balance owed. c) Ending balance owed.
>
> **Answer:** First month: a) $708.33. b) $276.41. c) $99,723.59. Second month: a) $706.38. b) $278.36. c) $99,445.23.

6.22 PROBLEM SET 6–7

Find the present value of the ordinary annuities in Problems 1 through 4:

1. $400 every 3 months for 5 years at 8 percent compounded quarterly.

2. $1,000 per month for 3 years at 12 percent compounded monthly.

3. $2,000 every 6 months for 18 years at 8 percent compounded semiannually.

4. $1,000 every year for 40 years at 6 percent compounded annually.

5. A company offers its salespeople a bonus of $500 per quarter for 3 years. To win a bonus, a salesperson must have sold at least $1 million worth of the company's products in the period January 1 through December 31, and the first bonus payment is made at the end of the first quarter following. The company funds each bonus on December 31 by a lump-sum deposit in a bank account that pays 8 percent compounded quarterly, and the bank sends out the bonus checks. a) What total sum is received by each bonus winner? b) How much does it cost the company to fund each bonus?

6. A college alumni club has decided to establish a scholarship fund that will provide grants of $5,000 a year for 25 years, with the first grants to be made a year from now. a) What should be the sum placed in the fund if interest on it is earned at the rate of 8 percent compounded annually? b) What is the total amount of scholarship aid the fund will provide over its life?

7. What payment at the end of each month for 2 years will discharge a current debt of $1,000 if the interest charge on the debt balance at any time is 12 percent compounded monthly?

8. What payment at the end of each 6-month period for 10 years will discharge a current debt of $2,500 if the interest charge on the debt balance is 10 percent compounded semiannually?

9. A company borrows $100,000 at 12 percent compounded semiannually. The debt is amortized by making equal payments at the end of each 6 months for 7 years.
   a) Find the amount of each payment.
   b) How much of the first payment is for interest, and by how much does it reduce the balance owed?
   c) How much of the second payment is for interest, and by how much does it reduce the balance owed?

10. Fran borrowed $6,000 at 24 percent compounded monthly to buy a car. The debt is to be discharged

6.22 PROBLEM SET 6–7 (concluded)

by equal payments at the end of each month for 3 years.
a) Find the amount of each payment.
b) How much of the first payment is for interest, and by how much does it reduce the balance owed?
c) How much of the second payment is for interest, and by how much does it reduce the balance owed?

11. First Realty Development Corporation has taken out a $1,500,000, 25-year mortgage on its new office building, with interest at 9 percent compounded monthly.
a) Find the monthly payment.
b) How much of the first payment is for interest, and by how much does it reduce the balance owed?

12. The Smiths have taken out a $35,000, 30-year mortgage on their home, with interest at 8.75 percent compounded monthly.
a) Find the monthly payment.
b) How much of the first payment is for interest, and by how much does it reduce the balance owed?

13. Find the present value of an ordinary annuity of $1,000 per month for 10 years at 7 percent compounded monthly.

14. New Venture Corporation has borrowed $5,000,000 at 7 percent compounded semiannually. The debt is discharged by equal payments at the end of each 6-month period for 30 years. Find the amount of each payment.

---

15. a) Write a computer program that will compute the present value P of an ordinary annuity given R, i, and n. (Hint: Refer to the program in Section 6.11.)
b) Run the program in (a) for Problems 1 through 6, and 13.

16. a) Write a computer program that will compute the amortization payment R of an ordinary annuity given P, i, and n. (Hint: Refer to Problem 15a.)
b) Run the program in (a) for Problems 7 through 12, and 14.

17. a) Modify the program in Problem 16(a) to print out the period-by-period amounts under the headings Period, Current Balance, Interest, Payment, Principal, and New Balance.
b) Run the program in (a) for Problems 7 through 12, and 14.

6.23 SUMMARY OF FINANCIAL RULES

The purpose of this section and the subsequent problem set is to provide guidance in identifying the type of problem at hand and the proper rule or rules to be selected to solve the problem. We shall use time diagrams to analyze problems, and you are encouraged to do the same.

Example. How much money should be deposited now in an account earning 8 percent compounded quarterly if the amount in the account 10 years from now is to be $10,000?

The time diagram, Figure 6–10, demonstrates that the $10,000 is a future value, and the unknown amount, P, is the **present value** of the future amount. Using the compound present value formula

$$P = F(1 + i)^{-n},$$

we have

$$P = 10{,}000 \left[1 + \frac{0.08}{4}\right]^{-(10)(4)} = \$4{,}528.90.$$

Example. How much will be accumulated at the end of 10 years by depositing $1,000 at the end of each 6-month period in an account paying 6 percent compounded semiannually?

Figure 6–11 shows the given $1,000 deposits at the end of each 6-month period, with the unknown **future value**, F, at the end of 10 years. Using the annuity future value formula

$$F = R\left[\frac{(1+i)^n - 1}{i}\right],$$

we have

$$F = 1{,}000\left[\frac{(1 + 0.06/2)^{(10)(2)} - 1}{0.06/2}\right] = \$26{,}870.37.$$

Example. Ms. Smith borrows $5,000 from a bank at 12 percent compounded monthly and promises to discharge the debt by equal payments at the end of each month for 3 years. Find the amount of each payment.

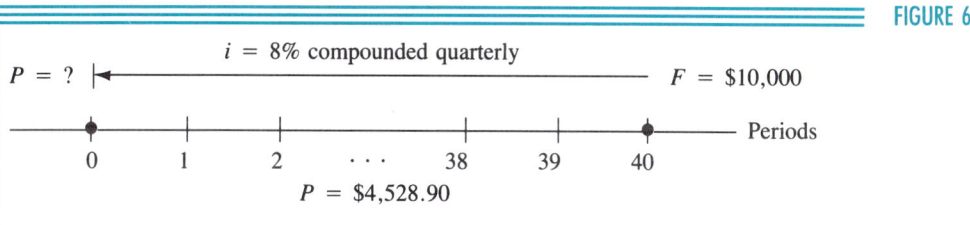

FIGURE 6–10

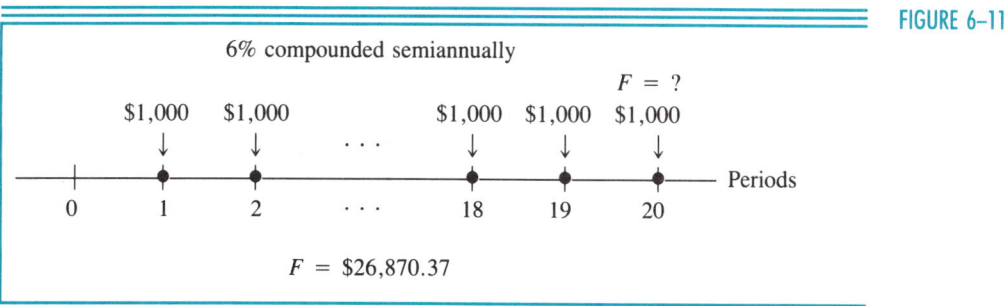

FIGURE 6–11

Figure 6–12 shows the present debt is $5,000, and the $R **payments** are the per-period equivalent of the $5,000 plus interest. Using the annuity amortization formula

$$R = P \left[\frac{i}{1 - (1 + i)^{-n}} \right],$$

we have

$$R = 5{,}000 \left[\frac{0.12/12}{1 - (1 + 0.12/12)^{-(3)(12)}} \right] = \$166.07.$$

Example. Sue will start college 6 months from now, and her parents have decided to establish a bank account now to provide $2,500 every 6 months for tuition payments. If 8 tuition payments are to be made and the account earns 6 percent compounded semiannually, how much should be deposited?

Figure 6–13 shows the unknown **deposit**, P, to be made now, is the present value of $2,500 per period. Using the annuity present value formula

$$P = R \left[\frac{1 - (1 + i)^{-n}}{i} \right],$$

FIGURE 6–12

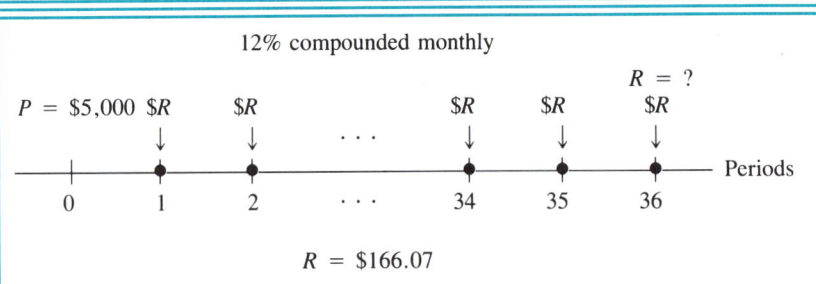

FIGURE 6–13

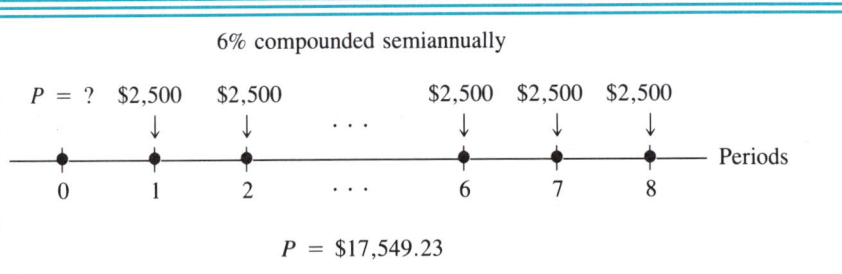

we have

$$P = 2{,}500 \left[\frac{1 - (1 + 0.06/2)^{-8}}{0.06/2} \right] = \$17{,}549.23.$$

Example. If the gross national product now is $1,683.5 billion and is growing at a rate of 6 percent compounded annually, what will the GNP be 20 years from now?

Figure 6–14 shows that we want the **future value** of the single value, $1,683.5 billion. Using the compound future value formula

$$F = P(1 + i)^n,$$

we have

$$F = 1{,}683.5(1 + 0.06)^{20} = \$5{,}399.2 \text{ billion.}$$

Example. Sam plans to buy a new car 2 years from now and decides to accumulate $3,000 to help pay for it by having a deduction made from his monthly salary at the end of each month and deposited in an employees' savings account that, because of employer contributions, earns 12 percent interest compounded monthly. How much will be deducted each month?

Figure 6–15 shows the amount Sam desires as a future value. The **periodic payment**, $R, needed to accumulate this amount is the per-period equivalent of

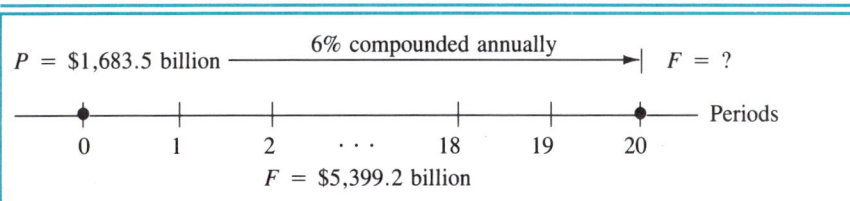

FIGURE 6–14

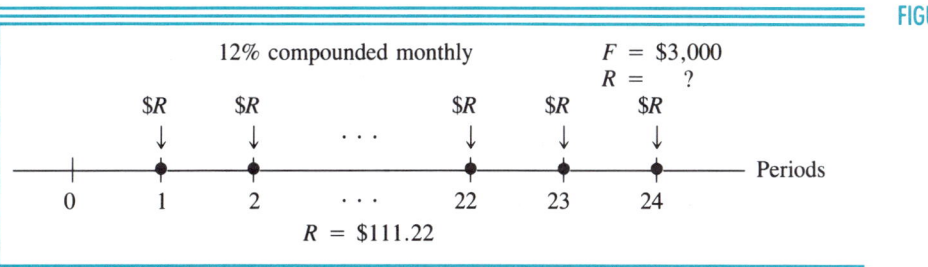

FIGURE 6–15

$3,000 future value. Using the annuity sinking fund formula

$$R = F\left[\frac{i}{(1+i)^n - 1}\right],$$

we have

$$R = 3{,}000\left[\frac{0.12/12}{(1+0.12/12)^{(2)(12)} - 1}\right] = \$111.22.$$

6.24 MULTISTEP PROBLEMS

The solution of a problem may require more than one step and involve more than one interest rate, as illustrated by the following examples.

Example. Sam wants to determine how much he should deposit in a retirement account now at 8 percent compounded quarterly so that the amount in the account 10 years from now will provide an income of $5,000 every 6 months for 12 years, with the first $5,000 to be received in $10\tfrac{1}{2}$ years. Sam estimates that 10 years from now he should be able to earn 6 percent compounded semiannually on the account when it is used to provide his semiannual income of $5,000. How much should Sam deposit now?

Figure 6–16 shows the structure of the problem. Sam's goal is to have $\$P_1$ in his account at the point shown, where P_1 must be the then **present value** of $5,000 per period. Using the annuity present value formula, we find

$$P_1 = 5{,}000\left[\frac{1 - (1 + 0.06/2)^{-(12)(2)}}{0.06/2}\right] = \$84{,}677.71,$$

FIGURE 6–16

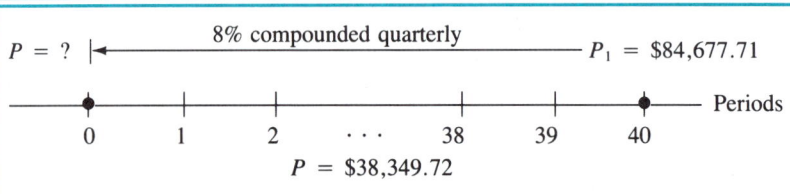

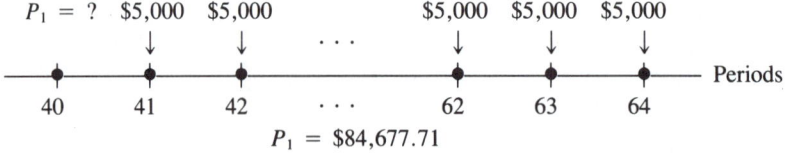

as shown in the lower portion of Figure 6–16. The current deposit now, at time zero, is the **present value** of P_1. Using the compound present value formula, we then get

$$P = 84{,}677.71(1 + 0.08/4)^{-(10)(4)} = \$38{,}349.72,$$

as shown in the upper portion of Figure 6–16.

The previous example was an illustration of a **deferred annuity**; that is, an annuity purchased now with the annuity payments being deferred so that they start at a time later than would be the case for an ordinary annuity.

> A deferred annuity does not begin until some specified condition is met.

Example. Fran borrowed $2,000 from Silverbank and signed a note promising to discharge the debt with interest at 12 percent compounded monthly at a maturity date 2 years from now. Six months later, Silverbank needed more cash and sold Fran's note to Goldbank. Goldbank computed the maturity amount of Fran's note and gave Silverbank the present value of this amount, computed at 8 percent compounded quarterly. How much did Silverbank receive?

Figure 6–17 shows the structure of the problem. The maturity value of the note, F, is the **future value** of $2,000, which, using the compound future value formula, is

$$F = 2{,}000\left(1 + \frac{0.12}{12}\right)^{(2)(12)} = \$2{,}539.47.$$

When Goldbank buys the note, it still has 1½ years (6 quarters) until maturity. Thus the amount Silverbank receives, P_1, is the **present value** of $F = \$2{,}539.47$, which, using the compound present value formula, is

$$P_1 = 2{,}539.47\left(1 + \frac{0.08}{4}\right)^{-(1\frac{1}{2})(4)} = \$2{,}254.98.$$

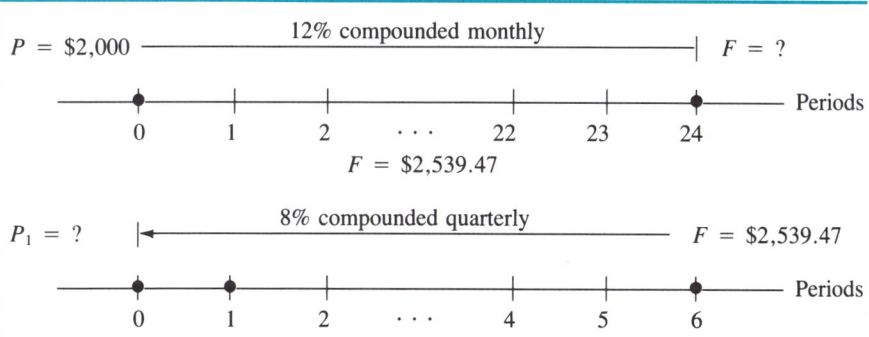

FIGURE 6–17

> Notes can be discounted using either compound or simple interest.

The previous example illustrated the **compound discounting of a note**. Simple interest calculations are frequently used to discount notes, but we shall not use simple interest in this section.

Example. Sam wishes to provide himself (or his estate) with an income of $5,000 every 6 months, starting 15½ years from now and continuing for 20 years. He deposits $25,000 in the account now, and he has a guaranteed inheritance of $10,000, which he will receive 10 years from now and add to the account. He knows these sums will not provide the income he wants, so he plans to make periodic deposits to the account at the end of every 6 months for 15 years to make up the difference. How much should the periodic deposits be if all interest is computed at 6 percent compounded semiannually?

Figure 6–18 brings all amounts back to **time zero**. There, from diagram (a), Sam has available $P_1 = \$25,000$ plus the **present value**, $\$P_2$, of the $10,000 inheritance, which by the compound present value formula is

$$P_2 = 10,000\left(1 + \frac{0.06}{2}\right)^{-(10)(2)} = \$5,536.76.$$

FIGURE 6–18

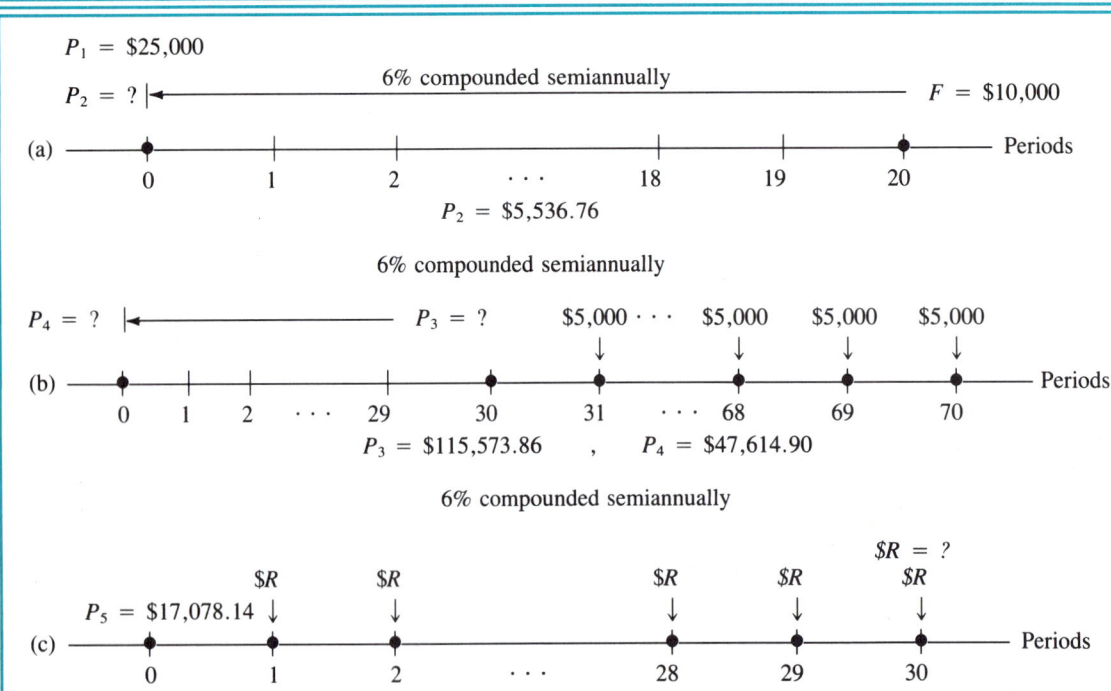

Thus the total amount available so far is $P_1 + P_2 = \$30{,}536.76$. Now from diagram (b), the **deferred annuity** Sam wants to establish has a **principal** of $\$P_3$, and it is an annuity of \$5,000 for 20 years at 6 percent compounded semiannually. Hence, using the annuity present value formula,

$$P_3 = 5{,}000 \left[\frac{1 - (1 + 0.06/2)^{-(20)(2)}}{0.06/2} \right] = \$115{,}573.86.$$

The **present value** P_4, then, of $\$P_3$ is the amount Sam needs. Using the compound present value formula, this is

$$P_4 = 115{,}573.86 \left(1 + \frac{0.06}{2} \right)^{-(15)(2)} = \$47{,}614.90,$$

as shown in diagram (b). The annuity Sam must provide by his additional payments to the acccount must make up the difference between the amount needed and the amount available, which is

$$P_5 = \$47{,}614.90 - \$30{,}536.76 = \$17{,}078.14.$$

Consequently, as shown in diagram (c), Sam needs to know the **per-period equivalent** of \$17,078.14 present value for 15 years at 6 percent compounded semiannually which, by the amortization formula, is

$$R = 17{,}078.14 \left[\frac{0.06/2}{1 - (1 + 0.06/2)^{-(15)(2)}} \right] = \$871.31$$

Hence Sam should deposit \$871.31 into the account every 6 months for the next 15 years.

6.25 PROBLEM SET 6–8

Solve the following assuming all periodic payments are in the form of ordinary annuities:

1. If \$100 is deposited at the end of every 6 months for 5 years at 6 percent compounded semiannually, what will be the amount in the account after the last deposit?

2. Sue borrowed \$7,000 at 12 percent compounded monthly for 3 years to buy a car. How much will she have to pay at the end of each month to discharge the debt?

3. At 8 percent compounded quarterly, what will be the amount of a current deposit of \$5,000 in 10 years?

4. How much should be deposited at the end of each year into an account earning 8 percent compounded annually in order to accumulate \$10,000 at the time of the last deposit 9 years from now?

5. What sum of money deposited now at 8 percent compounded annually will grow to \$10,000 in 20 years?

6. How much should be deposited now at 7 percent compounded annually to provide an income of \$20,000 at the end of each year for the next 22 years?

7. The population of a town now is 52,000. Population five years ago is unknown, but it is estimated that population has increased at the rate of 6 percent compounded annually. Estimate the population 5 years ago.

6.25 PROBLEM SET 6-8 (concluded)

8. Sam borrowed $4,000 at 24 percent compounded monthly to pay for construction of a garage. The debt is to be discharged by payments at the end of each month for 30 months. Find the amount of the monthly payment.

9. Jill has $250 taken from her salary at the end of each quarter and deposited in an employees' fund that earns 8 percent compounded quarterly. What will be the amount in the account after the last deposit is made 5 years from now?

10. The board of directors of a company has voted to establish a fund that will provide a retiring executive with an income of $5,000 at the end of each quarter for 10 years. The fund will be invested in the company, which earns 12 percent compounded quarterly. Find the amount that should be invested.

11. The real estate tax on a piece of property now is $2,000 per year. If taxes increase at the rate of 5 percent compounded annually, what will the tax on this property be 10 years from now?

12. Sam wants to accumulate $10,000 for a down payment on a home 8 years from now. He will do this by making a deposit at the end of each quarter in an account earning 8 percent compounded quarterly. How much should he deposit each quarter?

13. A note for $3,000 with interest at 12 percent compounded monthly is payable 40 months from now. Find the (then present) value of the note 19 months from now if this value is computed at 8 percent compounded quarterly.

14. Sue has purchased $20,000 worth of securities earning 10 percent compounded semiannually. Ten years from now, she plans to use the securities and interest to establish an account earning 7 percent compounded annually, and to exhaust this account by equal withdrawals at the end of each year for 5 years. How much will each withdrawal be?

15. How much should be deposited now at 8 percent compounded semiannually to make possible equal withdrawals of $5,000 at the end of each year for 5 years, the first withdrawal to be made 10 years from now? Interest during the withdrawal period is to be 7 percent compounded annually.

16. Nine years from now, Sam wants to have an amount available to deposit into an account that earns 6 percent compounded annually. This account is to provide Sam with an income of $10,000 at the end of each year for 10 years. To accomplish this, Sam invests in an 8-year bank certificate that pays 8 percent compounded semiannually, and he will use this certificate, plus its interest, to establish his income account. What should the principal value of the certificate be?

17. Fran will make 20 equal semiannual deposits to an account earning 8 percent compounded semiannually. Then, after the last deposit, she will use the amount in the account to establish an ordinary annuity earning 6 percent compounded annually which will provide her with $10,000 at the end of each year for 5 years. How much should Fran's semiannual deposit be?

18. During a 3-year period when his business was prospering, Jack was able to deposit $1,000 at the end of each month in an account earning 12 percent compounded monthly. The business slackened, and Jack could not continue the deposits. Moreover, the interest rate on his accumulated deposits fell to 8 percent compounded quarterly and remained at this level for 10 years, at which time Jack decided to exhaust the account by withdrawing equal amounts at the end of every 6 months for 5 years. The interest rate remained at 8 percent compounded semiannually over the time of the withdrawals. How much did Jack withdraw every 6 months?

19. Jill wishes to provide herself, or her estate, with an income of $10,000 at the end of each year for 10 years. She will make a lump sum deposit when the account is established and add $3,000 at the end of each year for 12 years. The income is to start at the end of the year following the year in which the last deposit was made. Compute the lump sum deposit. (All interest rates are 7 percent compounded annually.)

6.26 ORDINARY ANNUITIES: FINDING THE INTEREST RATE AND TIME

An unknown interest rate i can be approximated by interpolation in periodic payment tables, or by calculator. However the annuity formulas cannot be solved for i, so a precise value is not easily attainable. The annuity formulas also cannot be solved for an unknown time n, and in this case, interpolation is not even useful. We prefer not to burden the reader with the interpolation approach. Rather, we will show how a calculator with preprogrammed financial functions can be used to determine an unknown interest rate or an unknown time.

Annuity formulas cannot be solved for precise values of i or n, but can be approximated.

Example. Sam purchased a piece of property by making a down payment and signing an agreement to pay the remaining amount, $5,000, by making equal year-end payments of $700 for 10 years. Find the rate of annually compounded interest that Sam is paying.

In this example, we know that $700 is the per-period equivalent of the $5,000 plus interest at an unknown interest rate i. So we proceed as shown in Table 6-20. From this table, we see that the desired interest rate is $i = 6.637$ percent.

> **Exercise.** At what interest rate, compounded semiannually, will an ordinary annuity of $100 every 6 months amount to $2,500 in 8 years?
> **Answer:** 11.353 percent.

The next example illustrates how to compute an unknown time.

Example. Mary bought a new sports car for $26,000. She was able to put 10 percent down and wanted to finance the rest with payments of $500 per month. If she is charged 12 percent interest, how many payments must she make?

Mary is putting down 10 percent of $26,000,

$$(0.10)(26,000) = \$2,600,$$

TABLE 6-20

Keystroke	Calculator Display
5000, then PV	5000
700, then PMT	700
10, then n	10
CPT, then % i	6.637325947

TABLE 6-21

Keystroke	Calculator Display
23400, then PV	23400
500, then PMT	500
1, then % i	1
CPT, then n	63.42621146

and so her balance will be

$$\$26,000 - \$2,600 = \$23,400.$$

Thus she has to make a series of $500 payments every month at 12 percent interest (1 percent per month) until the $23,400 is amortized. From Table 6–21, we see that the desired number of payments n turns out to be 63.426 periods or months. What does this mean? One interpretation is 63 payments of $500 each, and then a final (64th) payment equal to 0.426 times $500 for a total of

$$(63)(500) + (0.426)(500) = 31,500 + 213$$
$$= \$31,713.$$

> **Exercise.** George buys a chalet in the mountains for $250,000. He puts 20 percent down and finances the balance with payments of $3,000 per month at 15 percent interest. a) How many payments does he make? b) What is the total amount paid to the nearest dollar?
>
> **Answer:** a) 145 (actually 144.235). b) $432,705.

6.27 ORDINARY ANNUITIES: CONTINUOUS COMPOUNDING

In this section we present without development the continuous compounding counterparts of the formulas developed earlier in the chapter for periodic compounding. Table 6–22 contains the formulas for periodic payments of $R each, where payment is made at the end of the period. Between payments the amount in the account is compounded continuously.

The annuity formulas can be extended to continuous compounding.

Example. How much must be deposited at the end of each quarter for 5 years at 8 percent compounding continuously to accumulate $10,000 at the time of the last deposit?

Here we have to find the per-period equivalent of $10,000 future value, so Formula 2 of Table 6–22 applies with $t = 5$, $j = 0.08$, $m = 4$, and $F = 10,000$.

TABLE 6-22

Continuous Compounding Formulas (t = number of years; j = nominal rate; m = number of periods per year)

Quantity	Formula
1. Amount of $R per period	$F = R\left[\dfrac{e^{jt} - 1}{e^{j/m} - 1}\right]$
2. Per-period equivalent of $F future value	$R = F\left[\dfrac{e^{j/m} - 1}{e^{jt} - 1}\right]$
3. Present value of $R per period	$P = R\left[\dfrac{1 - e^{-jt}}{e^{j/m} - 1}\right]$
4. Per-period equivalent of $P present value	$R = P\left[\dfrac{e^{j/m} - 1}{1 - e^{-jt}}\right]$

$$\frac{j}{m} = \frac{0.08}{4} = 0.02; \quad jt = 0.08(5) = 0.4.$$

Substituting into Formula 2 yields

$$R = 10,000\left[\frac{e^{0.02} - 1}{e^{0.4} - 1}\right]$$

$$= \$410.74.$$

Exercise. How much should be deposited now at 6 percent compounded continuously to provide payments of $2,000 at the end of each 6 months for 8 years?

Answer: (Formula 3 of Table 6-22). $25,035.13.

6.28 PROBLEM SET 6-9

1. At what rate of interest compounded annually will payments of $2,000 at the end of each year for 8 years amount to $20,000?

2. At what rate of interest compounded annually will $50,000 be accumulated by payments of $2,000 at the end of each year for 15 years?

3. At what rate of interest will a principal of $20,000 provide payments of $2,000 at the end of each year for 20 years?

4. At what rate of interest compounded annually will $5,000 payments at the end of each year for 11 years be provided by a principal investment now of $40,000?

5. Joan deposits $500 in her savings account at the end of every 6 months until she has $5,800. If she is

6.28 PROBLEM SET 6-9 (concluded)

getting 12 percent interest compounded semiannually, how many deposits will she make? What will be the amount of her last deposit?

6. Chris wants to accumulate $10,000 and is able to put $300 into his credit union monthly. If he is getting 15 percent interest compounded monthly, how long will it take him? What is his last contribution?

7. Nick has a chance to buy a new power boat for $14,000. His uncle, who owns the boat, has agreed to allow Nick to pay $600 per month and will charge him 10 percent interest compounded monthly. How many payments will Nick make? What is the total amount paid to the nearest dollar?

8. Rita wants to buy a vacation condominium for $75,000. She is able to put 10 percent down and wants to pay $800 per month to amortize the balance. If she is charged 11 percent interest compounded monthly, how many payments will she make? What is the total amount paid to the nearest dollar?

9. Sam deposits $500 at the end of each 6 months for 10 years in an account earning 6 percent. How much will be in the account after the last payment?

10. Bill wants to accumulate $5,000 to buy a boat 5 years from now by making deposits at the end of each quarter to an account earning 8 percent. How much should Bill deposit each quarter?

11. George has $100 deducted from his salary at the end of each month and invested in an employees' fund that earns 12 percent interest. How much will he have after the last payment 10 years from now?

12. A company wants to accumulate $15,000 to replace a machine 5 years from now. To do this, equal payments are to be made at the end of each 6-month period to an account earning 10 percent interest. Find the periodic payment.

13. Fran has an opportunity to lend a growing company a sum of money and earn 10 percent interest. The company will discharge its debt to Fran by sending her equal amounts every 6 months for 5 years. How much should Fran lend if she wants to receive $2,000 every 6 months?

14. How much invested now at 8 percent will provide an income of $1,000 per quarter for the next 7 years?

15. Jan has lent a new company $10,000 at 12 percent. The company will discharge its debt by sending Jan checks of equal amounts, one each month, for 6 years. How much will Jan receive each month?

16. Bill has borrowed $5,000 at 24 percent to purchase a car. He will discharge the debt by equal end-of-the-month payments for 3 years. Find the payment.

17. Fran deposits $150 at the end of each month for 6 years in an account earning 7.2 percent compounded continuously. What will be the amount in the account after the last deposit?

18. How much should be deposited at the end of each month for 10 years to accumulate $20,000 if the account earns 8 percent compounded continuously?

19. What sum of money deposited at 7.5 percent compounded continuously will yield an income of $1,500 at the end of each month for 6 years?

20. Bill borrowed $6,000 at 18 percent compounded continuously to buy a car. He will discharge the debt by equal end-of-the-month payments for 3 years. Find the amount of the payment.

6.29 REVIEW PROBLEMS

1. Compute the simple interest at 9 percent on $500 for 15 months.

2. Compute the future value of $1,500 at 8 percent simple interest for 10 months.

3. How many months will it take for the simple interest on $2,000 at 7 percent to be $175?

4. A credit card holder has owed the card company $400 for one month and receives a bill for $405. Find the simple rate of interest.

5. Compute the yield of the stock of Detroit Edison Company from the following stock market report.

    DetEd   1.98   31¼

6.29 REVIEW PROBLEMS *(continued)*

6. How much must be deposited in an account paying 8.5 percent simple interest if $210 interest is to be earned in 30 months?

7. At what rate of simple interest will $500 grow to $560 in 9 months?

8. How many months will it take at 8.4 percent simple interest for $2,000 to grow to $2,280?

9. Find the present value of $1,500 due 2 years from now with simple interest at 10 percent.

10. How much will Fran have to deposit now in an employees' savings account earning 10 percent simple interest in order to have $2,500 in the account $2\frac{1}{2}$ years from now?

11. Find the proceeds of a $1,000 two-year loan from a bank if the simple bank discount rate is 18 percent.

12. Bill receives $2,000 from a bank now, to be repaid in 30 months. If the bank discount rate is 12 percent, how much will Bill have to pay back?

13. Sam signs a note promising to pay a bank $3,000 in 2 years. If Sam receives $2,400 when he signs the note, what is the bank's discount rate?

14. Find the future value of $10,000 at 12 percent compounded monthly for 3 years and 4 months.

15. Find the future value of $4,000 at 8 percent compounded quarterly for 7 years.

16. Find the future value of $5,000 at 7 percent compounded annually for 20 years.

17. An employees' Credit Union Fund pays interest at 12 percent compounded monthly. How much will an employee who invests $2,500 now have 3 years from now?

18. How many years will it take at 8 percent compounded annually for $2,000 to grow to $10,000?

19. How many years will it take for a sum of money to double at 9 percent compounded annually?

20. Find the rate of interest compounded annually at which $1,000 will grow to $2,500 in 10 years.

21. A company sold 125,000 machines 5 years ago and this year sold 350,000 machines. Find the annually compounded percentage rate of increase in sales over the 5-year period.

22. Find the present value of $5,000 payable 10 years from now with interest at 10 percent compounded semiannually.

23. A town's population now is about 500,000. If it has increased at the rate of 7 percent compounded semiannually, estimate the population 20 years ago.

24. What sum invested now at 8 percent compounded quarterly will grow to $10,000 in 9 years?

25. Find the future value of an ordinary annuity of $500 per quarter for 10 years at 8 percent compounded quarterly.

26. Sam deposits $250 at the end of every 3 months for 10 years to an account earning 8 percent compounded quarterly. How much will he have in the account after the last deposit?

27. Sue plans to accumulate $8,000 for a trip around the world 5 years from now. Find how much she should deposit to the trip fund at the end of each quarter if the fund earns 8 percent compounded quarterly.

28. How much should be deposited now in an account earning 6 percent compounded semiannually to provide an income of $5,000 at the end of each 6-month period for $17\frac{1}{2}$ years?

29. Sam has borrowed $12,000 at 12 percent, compounded monthly, from a bank. He will discharge the debt by end-of-the-month payments for the next 30 months. Find the monthly payment.

30. a) New Venture Corporation has taken out a $5 million, 30-year, 10 percent mortgage on its new manufacturing facility. How much will New Venture pay each month to discharge this mortgage?
    b) How much of the first payment is for interest, and by how much does it reduce the balance owed?
    c) How much of the second payment is for interest, and by how much does it reduce the balance owed?

31. a) The Browns have taken out a $50,000, 20-year, 8 percent mortgage on their home. How much will they pay each month to discharge this mortgage?
    b) How much of the first payment is for interest, and by how much does it reduce the balance owed?
    c) How much of the second payment is for interest, and by how much does it reduce the balance owed?

32. A note for $3,000 with interest at 12 percent compounded monthly is payable 30 months from now.

6.29 REVIEW PROBLEMS (continued)

Find the (then present) value of the note 12 months from now if this value is computed at 8 percent compounded quarterly.

33. Bill promises to pay off a current debt of $10,000 at 7 percent compounded annually by making equal end-of-the-year payments for the next 10 years. Compute the payment.

34. How much should be deposited now at 7 percent compounded annually to make possible withdrawals of $7,500 at the end of each year for 10 years, with the first withdrawal to be made 15 years from now? Interest during the withdrawal period is 6 percent compounded annually.

35. If fuel is now consumed by a plant at the rate of 25,000 barrels a year, and the rate increases by 7 percent compounded annually, what will yearly fuel consumption be 15 years from now?

36. Septech Corporation is setting up a reserve account earning 10 percent compounded semiannually. At the end of each 6-month period, equal sums are transferred to this account. The purpose of the account is to provide $20,000 after the last transfer 8 years from now to be used to replace equipment. Compute the seminannual transfer to the account.

37. A businessman has an obligation to pay $8,000 four years from now, and another obligation to pay $12,000 nine years from now. The money needed is to be provided by setting up an account into which equal deposits are made at the end of each year for 9 years. Find the annual deposit. (All interest is at 7 percent compounded annually.)

38. Sam wants to buy a boat for $10,000 nine years from now. How much should he deposit now at 8 percent compounded quarterly in order to have the desired amount available?

39. A company will need 1,500 barrels of fuel at the end of this month, and its needs will increase at the rate of 1 percent per month (12 percent compounded monthly). The company plans to take advantage of a currently favorable price situation and purchase a 3-year supply of fuel. How many barrels should be purchased?

40. How much should be deposited now in an account at 7 percent compounded annually to provide an income of $10,000 at the end of each year for 22 years?

41. Sue has an investment that will pay her $20,000 plus interest at 5 percent in 10 years. She can obtain the present value of this investment, computed at 6 percent, and deposit this amount in an account paying 8 percent. If she does so, what will be the amount of the account in 10 years? (All interest is compounded annually.)

42. At what rate of interest compounded annually will payments of $1,000 per year for 15 years discharge a current debt of $10,000?

43. At what rate of interest compounded annually will a series of end-of-the-year deposits of $2,500 amount to $41,000 in 12 years?

44. At what rate of interest compounded annually will a series of end-of-the-year deposits of $1,000 amount to $25,000 in 15 years?

45. How many monthly payments will it take to amortize a debt of $150,000 with payments of $1,800 per month at an interest rate of 14 percent compounded monthly? What is the total amount paid to the nearest dollar?

46. How many monthly payments will it take to amortize a debt of $125,000 with payments of $1,500 per month at an interest rate of 13 percent compounded monthly? What is the total amount paid to the nearest dollar?

47. Find the effective interest rate of 12 percent compounded quarterly.

48. Find the effective interest rate of 24 percent compounded monthly.

49. Find the effective interest rate for 6 percent compounded daily, using 365 days per year.

50. Find the future value of $5,000 for 9 years at 7 percent compounded continuously.

51. How much should be deposited now at 8 percent compounded continuously to have $10,000 seven years from now?

52. What is the effective rate of 12 percent compounded continuously?

53. What nominal rate of interest compounded continuously will yield an effective rate of 12 percent?

54. Fran wants to have $4,000 available 3 years from now. She makes equal deposits at the end of each

6.29 REVIEW PROBLEMS (concluded)

quarter in an employees' fund earning 12 percent compounded continuously. Compute the amount of the deposit.

55. Bill has lent a company $20,000 at 14 percent compounded continuously. The company will discharge the debt by sending Bill a check at the end of each 6-month period for 10 years. Compute the amount of the check.

56. How much should be deposited now in an account earning 6.6 percent compounded continuously in order to have $12,000 fifteen years from now?

57. Sam has an opportunity to invest in an income account at 12 percent compounded continuously. The amount invested plus interest come back to Sam in the form of a check at the end of each month for 8 years. How much should Sam invest if he wants the monthly income check to be $1,000?

58. How much will a deposit of $2,500 amount to in 10 years at 8.3 percent compounded continuously?

59. Sue deposits $400 at the end of each 6-month period for 12 years in an account earning 8 percent compounded continuously. What will the amount in the account be after the last payment?

6.30 EXTENDED REVIEW PROBLEMS

1. Carol has joined an employees' savings plan. She has $200 withheld monthly from her paycheck and placed in her account in the company credit union. To encourage employees to save, the company contributes an additional 10 percent to these savings accounts, with the company's contribution not to exceed $50 per month per employee. The company's contributions, however, do not become available to the employee unless the account is maintained for at least 5 years. If the credit union guarantees an interest rate of 8 percent compounded monthly, how much will Carol have in her account after 3 years? After 10 years?

2. Nick has calculated his retirement needs. He would like to receive $1,000 per month for 20 years after retirement. His plan is to retire in 15 years. He is trying to compute the amount he must put away now at 8 percent compounded semiannually to generate the sum needed for retirement. After checking with some financial planners, he finds that the typical risk-free interest he can expect to receive on his retirement income is about 7 percent compounded monthly. How much does Nick have to put away now?

3. Rita is planning ahead for a 3-month world tour to celebrate completing graduate school. The trip's estimated cost is $7,000. Rita would like to accumulate that sum over the next 4 years. She plans to make monthly deposits into her school's minibank which gives 5 percent interest compounded monthly. How much does she have to contribute monthly?

4. Joan signs a promissory note for $2,400 from a bank charging a discount rate of 12 percent. If Joan receives $1,968 now, how long will she have to pay back the note? What is the effective interest rate?

5. Robert has $10,000 he would like to invest for 10 years. What rate of interest compounded quarterly will he have to get if he wishes his money to double? Triple? Quadruple?

6. Bill and his wife have found their dream house. It sits on 2 acres of land in a suburb of Houston, 20 minutes from downtown and within 15 minutes of each of their offices. The purchase price they have agreed upon is $175,000 and they have 20 percent to use as a down payment. They can secure a 30-year mortgage from one bank at 9.25 percent and a 25-year mortgage from another bank at 9.125 percent. What are their respective monthly payments and what is the approximate difference in total payments?

7. What is the effective interest rate of 13 percent compounded quarterly, monthly, daily, hourly, and continuously?

8. In going through some old belongings of his ancestors, John found papers indicating that they sold several acres in the town of Plymouth, Massachusetts,

6.30 EXTENDED REVIEW PROBLEMS (concluded)

in 1720 for $22. If they had invested this money at 4.5 perent compounded continuously, how much would it amount to in the year 1995?

9. Michael is updating his estate plan for himself and his family. He would like to provide an income of $3,000 every month starting 10½ years from now and continuing for the next 20 years. He has started his account with an initial deposit of $10,000; and he knows his life insurance, maturing in 5 years, will have a cash value of $150,000. To make up the difference, Michael has decided to make monthly deposits in the account. How much should each deposit be if all interest is computed at 6 percent compounded monthly?

10. Joseph added a $4,500 Jacuzzi to his condominium's bathroom. He signed a bank promissory note with a maturity date 3 years from the transaction date at 11 percent compounded monthly. One year later, the bank holding the note was taken over by an international financial organization that demanded payment in full of the then present value computed at 5 percent compounded semiannually. What was the amount demanded?

INTRODUCTION TO APPLIED CALCULUS AND UNCONSTRAINED OPTIMIZATION

CHAPTER 7
Introduction to Differential Calculus

CHAPTER 8
Applications of Differential Calculus

CHAPTER 9
Additional Topics in Differential Calculus

CHAPTER 10
Introduction to Integral Calculus

Calculus is the mathematical tool used to measure changes in physical quantities. The subject matter was developed in the 17th century to resolve several mathematical problems of the time, most notably:

1. Finding the tangent to a curve at a point.
2. Finding the area of a region enclosed by a curve(s).
3. Finding the optimum (maximum or minimum) value of a function.

In the next four chapters we will study how these problems were resolved using calculus. The first three chapters are devoted to **differential calculus**. Here we will introduce the **derivative** which measures the slope or rate of change of a curve. We will then illustrate its use in **unconstrained optimization** of business-related problems. The fourth chapter is devoted to **integral calculus**. There we will introduce the **indefinite integral** which is nothing more than the **inverse** of the derivative. Then we will show how the **definite integral** measures areas associated with curves, and we will illustrate its use in business-related problems.

Throughout Part III we shall see applications of the techniques developed in differential and integral calculus to solve problems such as the maximization of profit, the minimization of cost, the determination of an optimal management strategy for inventory, the determination of the optimal time an advertising promotion should be run, and the

construction of a **predictor function** to estimate future values of a set of data from known present values.

Although almost always a behind-the-scene player, the calculus is critical to the development of many procedures and techniques used to solve day-to-day problems. Indeed, successes in modern transportation and even space travel are dependent on advanced techniques in both differential and integral calculus.

FROM THEORY TO PRACTICE
Who Created Calculus?

History evolves in seemingly unexpected ways. Historians study history not only for its cultural value, but also for the lessons that can be learned from the past and to better understand the nature of historical evolution. One perplexing question historians wrestle with concerns how important historical discoveries and inventions are made. Were these discoveries or inventions a product of a great mind ahead of his or her time? On the other hand, were they crying out to be made because of the knowledge of the time? In other words, was it inevitable that someone (not necessarily a genius ahead of her or his time) would have made the discovery or invention in question the way a seed germinates in the spring due to conditions around it?

The creation of the calculus is fertile ground for such a discussion. Two men, both considered geniuses of their time, simultaneously created the calculus while working on major scientific and mathematical problems. The first, Isaac Newton (1642–1727), was an Englishman considered in his time to be the leading intellect of his nation. His major discoveries were published in his masterpiece, *Philosophae Naturalis Principia Mathematica* in 1687, considered to be the most important and influential scientific book ever written. His work on calculus, however, was not published until 1705. Gottfried Wilhelm Leibniz (1646–1716), perhaps the last of the great humanists, simultaneously developed the fundamental concepts of the calculus in Germany. In fact, in 1685 Leibniz became the first to publish his discoveries, although Newton's notes and letters indicate that his discoveries were made in 1675.

A tremendous controversy arose between scholars of England and scholars of the Continent as to who was the true creator of the calculus. Both Newton and Leibniz managed to stay above the controversy, most likely because there were other things far more important to each of these great men. One thing is for certain: neither man could have dreamed of the far-reaching implications of their discoveries.

CHAPTER 7
INTRODUCTION TO DIFFERENTIAL CALCULUS

7.1 INTRODUCTION

This and the next two chapters discuss elementary differential calculus and its applications. One of our major objectives is to present these concepts with a minimum of prerequisite study. Only algebra and a study of straight lines and slopes (Chapter 1) are needed for Chapters 7 and 8. In Chapter 9 we introduce and apply exponential and logarithmic functions that have the material in the first part of Chapter 5 (the modern treatment of logarithms) as an additional prerequisite.

The present chapter introduces the basic concepts of differential calculus including the definition of the derivative, limits, continuity, and the fundamental rules of taking derivatives. Chapter 8 shows how to use the derivative to solve optimization problems (for example, to determine how to maximize profit or minimize cost). We also present a simple technique to help in sketching graphs of polynomials and rational functions. Chapter 9 includes the chain rule and introduces the calculus of two independent variables.

7.2 WHY STUDY CALCULUS?

Many real-world problems can be solved using calculus.

The answer to the question posed in the title of this section has several parts, but we select the part we consider most significant; namely, that **the tools of calculus can be used to solve applied problems**. The purpose of this section is to document the last statement by first posing a simple applied problem and showing how it can be solved approximately by **brute force** without calculus. Then we shall explain what tools are needed to obtain an **exact** solution in a **simple** manner. The tools, of course, are the procedures of calculus.

Example. The United Parcel Service operates a fleet of trucks that pick up and deliver packages. UPS charges extra for packages whose length plus girth[1] exceeds 108 inches. Seafare Fruit Company ships a fresh product that requires as much ventilation as possible, and its boxes are made of a perforated material. To obtain maximum ventilation, Seafare Fruit wants the boxes to have as large a surface area as possible. The problem then is to find what box dimensions will utilize the entire 108 inches allowed **and** provide maximum surface area. The box is to be rectangular,

[1] For example, the length of this book is the vertical (longer) dimension of the cover, and the girth is the distance around the book in the horizontal direction.

with square ends, as shown in Figure 7–1. The length of the box is L, and its girth is $4x$. Thus

$$\text{Length plus girth} = L + 4x.$$

When all 108 inches are utilized,

$$L + 4x = 108$$

so that

$$L = 108 - 4x. \qquad (1)$$

To find the expression for the surface area, which is to be maximized, we note first that the area of each square end is x^2, and there are two such ends. Hence

$$\text{Area of the two ends} = 2x^2.$$

The area of the rectangle forming one side is $x \cdot L$, and there are four such sides, so that

$$\text{Side area} = 4xL.$$

Thus

$$\text{Total area} = A(x, L) = 2x^2 + 4xL,$$

a function of the **two** variables: x and L.

The mathematical model associated with maximizing the surface area gives rise to a function of two variables.

Substituting the expression (1) and L into the last expression, we can write the total area in terms of the **single** variable x as

$$\begin{aligned} A(x) &= 2x^2 + 4x(108 - 4x) \\ &= 2x^2 + 432x - 16x^2 \\ &= 432x - 14x^2. \end{aligned} \qquad (2)$$

Known information is used to transform the given function of two variables into a function of one variable.

Our objective, then, is to find the value of x that makes $A(x)$ as large as possible. This value can then be substituted back into (1) to get the required value of L. In the **brute force** approach to the solution, we let $x = 1$, then 2, 3, 4, and so on. For each value of x, the area is computed using Equation (2) and tabulated. For example,

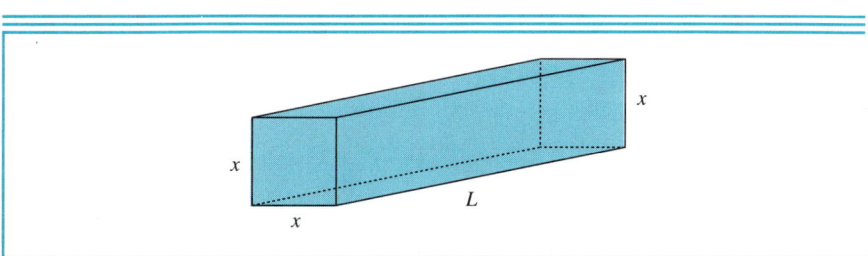

FIGURE 7–1

$$x = 1: \quad A(1) = 432(1) - 14(1)^2 = 418 \text{ square inches.}$$
$$x = 2: \quad A(2) = 432(2) - 14(2)^2 = 808 \text{ square inches.}$$

We see that $x = 2$ provides a larger area than $x = 1$, so we try $x = 3$.

$$x = 3: \quad A(3) = 432(3) - 14(3)^2 = 1{,}170 \text{ square inches.}$$

Continuing in this manner, we obtain the results shown in Table 7–1. Observe that as x increases, the area increases, until the point marked with * at the bottom of the fourth column. When x went from 15 to 16, the area decreased from 3,330 to 3,328. We conclude that the maximum area occurs near $x = 15$. In the right section of Table 7–1 we find that $x = 15.1$ gives a larger area than $x = 15$ so we continue by steps of 0.1 until 15.5 where the area once again decreases. Now we change to steps of 0.01 until we encounter a decrease at 15.44. Clearly we could proceed to steps of 0.001 and so on to get a more exact value for x. However we have demonstrated that this time-consuming procedure, even if we use a computer, is a brute force attack on the problem.

The **brute force** method is time-consuming and gives only an approximate result.

We leave the preceding work with the conclusion that the area is maximized when x is approximately 15.4 inches. Of course, we have no absolute assurance, without looking at the graph, that $A(x)$ does not take on a larger value at some value of x quite a bit larger than 16. We can only assume that once $A(x)$ begins to decrease at $x = 16$ it continues to do so.

The calculus method of solving this problem can be understood by reference to the graph of

$$A(x) = 432x - 14x^2$$

shown in Figure 7–2. Observe that the graph is a parabola opening downward and that the largest possible value of the area $A(x)$ occurs at the vertex.[2]

TABLE 7–1

x	Area	x	Area	x	Area
1	418	9	2754	15.1	3331.06
2	808	10	2920	15.2	3331.84
3	1170	11	3058	15.3	3332.34
4	1504	12	3168	15.4	3332.56
5	1810	13	3250	15.5	3332.50*
6	2088	14	3304	15.6	3332.16
7	2338	15	3330	15.41	3332.5666
8	2560	16	3328*	15.42	3332.5704
		17	3298	15.43	3332.5714
				15.44	3332.5696*
				15.45	3332.5650

*Marks a point in a sequence where area decreases.

[2] For a review of parabolas, see Section A2.12 in Appendix Two at the end of this book.

> **Exercise.** a) Why does the parabola in the preceding equation open downward?
> b) What is the x-coordinate of the vertex?
>
> **Answer:** a) Because the coefficient -14 of x^2 is negative.
>
> b) $x = \dfrac{-b}{2a} = \dfrac{-432}{2(-14)} = \dfrac{108}{7}.$

Now suppose that we did not know that the graph was a parabola opening downward. How then would we locate the peak of the curve? From Figure 7–1, we can see that the line tangent to the curve at the peak is horizontal so this tangent has a slope of 0. In this chapter we shall develop the techniques of differential calculus showing that the tangent to

$$A(x) = 432x - 14x^2$$

is horizontal when

$$28x = 432$$

$$x = \frac{432}{28}$$

$$= \frac{108}{7},$$

The maximum of the function occurs at the point where the tangent line is horizontal and has slope 0.

exactly, or 15.437 inches, correct to three decimal places. Note that since this is the **only** value of x, there can be no other candidate for a maximum value. The corresponding value for L, computed from $L = 108 - 4x$ is $324/7$ inches exactly, or 46.286 inches, correct to three decimals. The question, of course, is how we

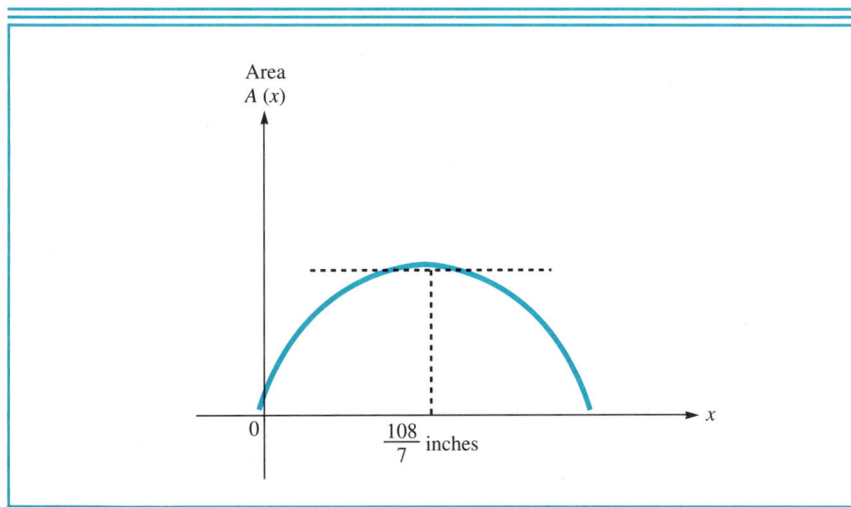

FIGURE 7–2

obtained $28x = 432$, and that is the question we shall answer in this chapter. In the course of developing the tools needed to answer the question, and in the application of these tools, functional notation will be used extensively, so we shall review functions before proceeding.

7.3 FUNCTIONAL AND DELTA NOTATIONS

In Chapter 1 the expression

$$y = mx + b$$

was called the slope-intercept form of the equation of a straight line. The quantities m (the slope) and b (the y-intercept) for any specific line are constants, as in

$$y = 2x + 5,$$

whereas x and y are variables. Thus, even though

$$y = mx + b$$

Parameters are placeholders for constant values.

contains four letters (y, m, x, b), we know from the context that x and y are to be considered as the variables, while m and b are called **parameters** since they represent constant rather than variable values. The first advantage of functional notation is to ensure that the variable in any expression is stated specifically. To do this for $y = mx + b$, we write, as we saw in Chapter 1,

$$f(x) = mx + b,$$

The independent variable is explicitly stated in the definition of a function.

and read $f(x)$ as **the function f of x** or, more briefly, **f of x**. In the symbol $f(x)$, recall x is called the **independent variable**. Similarly in

$$C(L) = \frac{NF}{L} + \frac{iL}{2},$$

L is the independent variable and, this being the case N, F, and i are parameters as are m and b in

$$f(x) = mx + b.$$

If we write

$$g(x) = 3x^3 - 2x + 10,$$

g is the name of the function, x is the independent variable, and $g(x)$ represents values of the function. To find the value of the function when $x = 2$, written as $g(2)$, we evaluate

$$g(x) = 3x^3 - 2x + 10$$

at $x = 2$ to find

$$g(2) = 3(2^3) - 2(2) + 10$$
$$= 30.$$

Exercise. Given $h(q) = 2q - \dfrac{10}{q}$, find a) $h(1)$. b) $h(5)$. c) $h(100)$.

Answer: a) -8. b) 8. c) 199.9.

The preceding exercise shows a second advantage of functional notation; namely, brevity of statement. That is, the instruction "Find $h(1)$" replaces the longer instruction "Find the value of the function $h(q)$ when the independent variable q equals 1." For emphasis, we note that if

$$f(k) = k^2 - 2kg$$

then

$$f(5) = 25 - 10g,$$

but if, for the same expression, g is the independent variable as in

$$h(g) = k^2 - 2kg,$$

then

$$h(5) = k^2 - 10k.$$

Functional notation allows us to abbreviate statements.

Exercise. If $p(q) = q^2 - r^2 + 5$ and $h(r) = q^2 - r^2 + 5$, what is a) $p(2)$? b) $h(2)$?

Answer: a) $9 - r^2$. b) $q^2 + 1$.

It is helpful to think of a function as a rule that specifies how to find the value of the function for a stated value of the independent variable. For example, given

$$f(x) = x^2 - 6,$$

the rule, $x^2 - 6$, tells us to square the value of the independent variable and then subtract 6. Thus $f(5)$ is obtained by squaring 5 and then subtracting 6, and the resulting function value is 19. Similarly

$$f(x + a)$$

will be obtained by squaring $(x + a)$ and subtracting 6, so

$$f(x + a) = (x + a)^2 - 6$$
$$= x^2 + 2ax + a^2 - 6.$$

Example. Find $g(a) - g(x - a)$ if $g(x) = x^2 + 10$.

We find

$$g(a) = a^2 + 10$$
$$g(x - a) = (x - a)^2 + 10.$$

Hence

$$\begin{aligned} g(a) - g(x - a) &= (a^2 + 10) - [(x - a)^2 + 10] \\ &= a^2 + \cancel{10} - (x - a)^2 - \cancel{10} \\ &= a^2 - (x^2 - 2ax + a^2) \\ &= \cancel{a^2} - x^2 + 2ax - \cancel{a^2} \\ &= 2ax - x^2. \end{aligned}$$

Exercise. Find $f(x + a) - f(x)$ if $f(x) = x^2 - 3$.
Answer: $2ax + a^2$.

A Function Must Be Single-Valued

A function has a single value for each permissible value of the independent variable.

To avoid ambiguity in the meaning of the value of a function, we require that a function shall have one, and only one, value for each permissible value of the independent variable. In particular, in

$$f(x) = x^{1/2} = \sqrt{x}$$

we define $f(x)$ to be the **nonnegative square root** of x. That is,

$$f(4) = 4^{1/2} = 2.$$

This does not mean that

$$y^2 = 4$$

has only $y = 2$ as a solution, because $y^2 = 4$ is a **conditional equality**, not a function, and both $y = 2$ and $y = -2$ satisfy the conditional equality.

What has been said for

$$f(x) = x^{1/2}$$

applies also to any other fractional power that has an even denominator, such as

$$g(x) = x^{3/4}, \quad h(x) = x^{-5/6}.$$

An even root can be taken only for nonnegative numbers; an odd root can be taken for any number.

That is, **the function value for such even roots is the nonnegative value**. Note also that for even roots, x must not be negative, so only positive numbers (or 0 if the exponent is positive) are permissible values for x. An odd root, such as

$$p(x) = x^{2/3},$$

raises no question of ambiguity because such roots are single-valued. Thus

$$p(8) = 8^{2/3}$$
$$= (8^{1/3})^2$$
$$= (2)^2$$
$$= 4$$

and

$$p(-8) = (-8)^{2/3}$$
$$= (-8^{1/3})^2$$
$$= (-2)^2$$
$$= 4.$$

We note in passing that while odd roots of negative numbers are permissible, we shall not use them in our work.

Exercise. For

$$g(x) = \frac{x^{3/2}}{32} - 16x^{-1/2} + 2x^{1/3},$$

find a) $g(64)$. b) $g(-1)$.
Answer: a) 22. b) $x = -1$ is not permissible.

Calculus has been described as the mathematics of change because it was invented to solve problems involving rates of change. We now show how to find the general expression for the change in the value of a function when its independent variable changes value. Conventionally the symbol Δ, delta, is taken to mean **the change in**. Thus Δx, read as delta x, is the change in x; that is, the change in the value of the independent variable. In summary:

= **Delta Notation**

Δ **means the change in.**
Δx **means the change in x.**

Example. Given the function

$$g(z) = z^2 + 3z,$$

find (a) Δg when z changes from 5 to 5.5 and (b) the general expression for Δg.

For (a), we want to find $g(5.5) - g(5)$ which is

$$g(5.5) - g(5) = [(5.5)^2 + 3(5.5)] - [5^2 + 3(5)]$$

$$= (30.25 + 16.5) - (25 + 15)$$
$$= 46.75 - 40$$
$$= 6.75.$$

For (b), Δg means the change in $g(z)$ when z changes by Δz. Assuming that Δz is positive, we can picture the change in z as

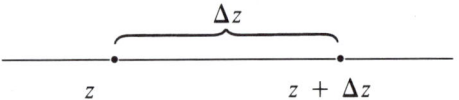

so that g changes from $g(z)$ to $g(z + \Delta z)$ and

$$\Delta g = g(z + \Delta z) - g(z). \qquad (1)$$

Of course, if Δz were negative then $z + \Delta z$ would be to the left of z in the preceding picture, but equation (1) would still give Δg. Now to find the expression for Equation (1), we simplify the algebra by replacing Δz with h so that the preceding picture becomes

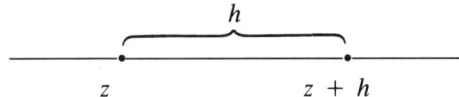

and

$$\begin{aligned}
\Delta g &= g(z + h) - g(z) \\
&= [(z + h)^2 + 3(z + h)] - [z^2 + 3z] \\
&= [z^2 + 2zh + h^2 + 3z + 3h] - z^2 - 3z \\
&= 2zh + h^2 + 3h \\
&= h(2z + h + 3). \qquad (2)
\end{aligned}$$

The general expression for the change in a function allows us to evaluate various changes by simple substitution.

Note that Equation (2) now allows us to find Δg for any change in z by simple substitution. Indeed, to solve part (a) of the preceding example where z changed from 5 to 5.5 we would substitute $z = 5$ and $h = 0.5$ into Equation (2) to get

$$\begin{aligned}
\Delta g &= 0.5[2(5) + 0.5 + 3] \\
&= 0.5(13.5) \\
&= 6.75
\end{aligned}$$

which is the same result as before. What if we want to find Δg when z changes from 8 to 8.1? Then we would simply substitute $z = 8$ and $h = 0.1$ into Equation (2) to get

$$\begin{aligned}
\Delta g &= 0.1[2(8) + 0.1 + 3] \\
&= 0.1(19.1) \\
&= 1.91.
\end{aligned}$$

Henceforth we will use the general definition

> **Definition.** For any function $f(x)$, the change in f is
> $$\Delta f = f(x + h) - f(x).$$

The change in $f(x)$ is $f(x+h) - f(x)$.

> **Exercise.** a) Find the general expression for Δf if $f(x) = 2x^2 - 5$. b) Find Δf if x goes from 2 to 3. c) Find Δf if x goes from 5 to 5.2.
> **Answer:** a) $2h(2x + h)$. b) 10. c) 4.08.

As an application to help fix the preceding in mind, recall that in Chapter 1 the marginal cost of a unit of production was defined as the change in total cost when that unit is produced. Thus if the total cost of making g gallons of olive oil is $C(g)$, then the marginal cost of the 10th gallon is

$$C(10) - C(9),$$

which is the total cost of 10 gallons minus the total cost of 9 gallons. In general, the marginal cost of the gth gallon is

$$\Delta C = C(g) - C(g - 1)$$

where ΔC is the change in the total cost when going from the $(g-1)$st gallon to the gth gallon. Now suppose we have the cost function

If $C(g)$ is the total cost function, then the marginal cost of the gth gallon is
$\Delta C = C(g) - C(g-1)$.

$$C(g) = 1{,}000 + 5g + 0.01g^2$$

and we want the expression for the marginal cost of the gth gallon:

$$\begin{aligned}\Delta C &= C(g) - C(g - 1) \\ &= [1{,}000 + 5g + 0.01g^2] - [1{,}000 + 5(g - 1) + 0.01(g - 1)^2] \\ &= 1{,}000 + 5g + 0.01g^2 - [1{,}000 + 5g - 5 + 0.01(g^2 - 2g + 1)] \\ &= 1{,}000 + 5g + 0.01g^2 - 1{,}000 - 5g + 5 - 0.01g^2 + 0.02g - 0.01 \\ &= 5 + 0.02g - 0.01 \\ &= 4.99 + 0.02g.\end{aligned}$$

Thus

$$\text{Marginal cost of the } g\text{th gallon} = 4.99 + 0.02g.$$

> **Exercise.** For the cost function of the preceding example, find the marginal cost of the a) 10th gallon. b) 50th gallon.
> **Answer:** a) $5.19. b) $5.99.

In the answer to the preceding exercise, note that the marginal cost of the 50th gallon is greater than that of the 10th gallon. In Chapter 1, where **linear** cost functions were considered, marginal cost was the **constant** slope of a straight line. The cost function of the exercise has a second-degree term ($0.01g^2$) and is a curve. After we have discussed slope as it applies to a curve, we will see the reason for the increase in marginal cost observed in the answer to the last exercise.

7.4 PROBLEM SET 7-1

1. If $f(x) = 3x - 2$, find the value of or the algebraic expression for
    a) $f(3)$.
    b) $f(-2)$.
    c) $f(a)$.
    d) $[f(a)]^2$.
    e) $f(ab)$.
    f) $f(3y + 4)$.
    g) $f(x + 1)$.
    h) $f(x + 1) - f(x)$.

2. If $h(x) = x^2 + 3x$, find the value of or the algebraic expression for
    a) $h(2)$.
    b) $h(-3)$.
    c) $h(1/2)$.
    d) $h(2/a)$.
    e) $h(x + 0.5)$.
    f) $h(a + 1)$.
    g) $h(a - 1)$.
    h) $h(x) - h(x - 1)$.

3. a) If $g(x) = x^2y - y^2$, write the expression for $g(a)$.
   b) If $f(y) = x^2y - y^2$, write the expression for $f(a)$.

4. a) If $h(y) = 2x + 5y$, write the expression for $h(3)$.
   b) If $p(x) = 2x + 5y$, write the expression for $p(3)$.

5. If $p(x) = 2x^{-1} - 3x^{-2}$, write the value of or the algebraic expression for
   a) $p(2)$. b) $p(3)$. c) $p(a)$. d) $p(x + 1)$.

6. If $f(x) = 2x^{1/3} + 3x^{-2/3}$, find the value of
   a) $f(1)$.   b) $f(64)$.   c) $f(1/8)$.

7. What is the meaning of
    a) Δx?
    b) $f(x + \Delta x)$?
    c) $f(x + \Delta x) - f(x)$?

8. Given $f(x) = x^2 - 3x + 5$, find Δf if x changes from 2 by 0.5.

9. Given $f(x) = 2x^2 - 10x + 8$, find Δf if x changes from 0 by 0.1.

10. Find the expression for Δf if $f(x) = 10 - 3x$.

11. Find the expression for Δg if $g(x) = mx + b$.

12. Find the expression for
    a) Δf if $f(x) = x^2$.
    b) Δg if $g(x) = 2x^2 - 3x + 5$.

13. Find the expression for
    a) Δf if $f(x) = 2x^2$.
    b) Δg if $g(x) = x^2 + 2x - 10$.

14. If the total cost of making g gallons of olive oil is $C(g)$ dollars and
    $$C(g) = 100 + 3g + 0.01g^2,$$
    a) Find the expression for the marginal cost of the gth gallon, which is $C(g) - C(g - 1)$.
    b) Find the marginal cost of the 10th gallon.
    c) Find the marginal cost of the 50th gallon.

15. If the total cost of making g gallons of corn oil is $C(g)$ dollars and
    $$C(g) = 50 + g + 0.1g^2,$$

7.4 PROBLEM SET 7-1 (concluded)

a) Find the expression for the marginal cost of the gth gallon, which is $C(g) - C(g-1)$.

b) Find the marginal cost of the 10th gallon.

c) Find the marginal cost of the 50th gallon.

7.5 LIMITS

Limits are the core concept in the development of calculus. We shall not pursue the theory of limits in detail in this text, but in this section you will become familiar enough with the limit concept to use it when needed as we proceed. We start by observing that the function

$$g(x) = \frac{x^2}{x}$$

does not have a value at $x = 0$, because at $x = 0$ the resultant expression 0/0 is ambiguous (not well defined) so we shall say **$g(x)$ is not defined at $x = 0$.** Those who think this ratio has the value 1 should review Appendix Section A1.15 where it is shown why we cannot divide any number, including 0, by 0. To emphasize this exception, we can write

$$g(x) = \frac{x^2}{x}, \quad x \neq 0.$$

It is true, though, that

$$g(x) = \frac{x^2}{x} = x, \quad x \neq 0$$

since we can cancel the nonzero term x in the numerator and denominator. Thus $g(x) = x$ for any value of x except 0. Because this is true, it is correct to state that **$g(x)$ is close to 0 whenever x is close to zero** or that **$g(x)$ approaches 0 if x approaches 0.** We describe this behavior of $g(x)$ by saying that $g(x)$ approaches 0 as a limiting value as x approaches 0 and that as **x goes to 0, the limit of $g(x)$ is 0.** This is expressed symbolically as

$$\lim_{x \to 0} g(x) = 0,$$

where the symbol "$x \to 0$" means x approaches 0 or gets closer and closer to 0 without ever equalling 0. Thus in the case of $g(x)$ we are able to state that a limit exists. It is especially important to note that $\lim_{x \to 0} g(x)$ is not always related to the value of $g(x)$ at $x = 0$. In this particular example, $g(0)$ does not exist but $\lim_{x \to 0} g(x) = 0$.

For any number $a \neq 0$, we have $\frac{0}{a} = 0$, $\frac{a}{0}$ is not defined, and $\frac{0}{0}$ is ambiguous.

$\lim_{x \to 0} \frac{x^2}{x} = 0$ means that as x approaches (but never equals) 0, the function $\frac{x^2}{x}$ approaches 0.

The limit of a function is not always related to the value of the function at the point in question.

By way of contrast, consider the function

$$f(x) = \frac{x}{x^2}, \quad x \neq 0.$$

Like the earlier $g(x)$, $f(x)$ at $x = 0$ results in the ambiguous expression 0/0 and so $f(x)$ is not defined at $x = 0$. It is true, of course, that

$$f(x) = \frac{x}{x^2} = \frac{1}{x}, \quad x \neq 0.$$

That is, $f(x) = 1/x$ for any value except $x = 0$. But $f(x)$, unlike $g(x)$, does not have a limit as x approaches 0. For example, if x takes on the sequence of values

$$1, 0.1, 0.01, 0.001,$$

and so on, approaching 0 **from above**, then

$$f(1) = \frac{1}{1} = 1$$

$$f(0.1) = \frac{1}{0.1} = 10$$

$$f(0.01) = \frac{1}{0.01} = 100$$

$$f(0.001) = \frac{1}{0.001} = 1{,}000$$

and so on, and this last sequence of values becomes larger and larger and approaches $+\infty$ as x gets closer and closer to 0. Similarly if we took $x = -1, -0.1, -0.01, -0.001$, and so on, as a sequence approaching 0 **from below**, then

$$f(-1) = \frac{1}{-1} = -1$$

$$f(-0.1) = \frac{1}{-0.1} = -10$$

$$f(-0.01) = \frac{1}{-0.01} = -100$$

$$f(-0.001) = \frac{1}{-0.001} = -1{,}000$$

$\lim_{x \to 0} \frac{x}{x^2}$ d.n.e. means that as x approaches (but never equals) 0, the function $\frac{x}{x^2}$ does not approach a limit.

and so on. Again, the sequence $-1, -10, -100, -1{,}000$ continues indefinitely and approaches $-\infty$. Hence

$$\lim_{x \to 0} \frac{x}{x^2} \text{ does not exist (abbreviated as d.n.e.)}$$

because there is no single value that $f(x)$ approaches as x approaches 0.

Comparing

$$g(x) = \frac{x^2}{x}, \quad x \neq 0$$

and

$$f(x) = \frac{x}{x^2}, \quad x \neq 0,$$

we see that they are alike at $x = 0$ in that both become the ambiguous expression 0/0. However they have the important difference that $g(x)$ has a limit as x approaches 0 and $f(x)$ does not. The distinction is important because, as we shall see, the central definition of the differential calculus always leads to 0/0, but we can attach a meaningful interpretation to the expression that leads to 0/0 when this expression has a limit.

The limits we shall use in the major part of the chapter are easily found. We start by stressing the real meaning of the limit concept, and then we will show an easy way to find the limits without formally applying the concept. The real meaning of the concept is embodied in the proper interpretation of $x \to a$. This is that x **gets closer and closer to, but never reaches (and thus never equals), a.**

Sometimes a picture is worth a thousand words. Study Figure 7–3. Do you see any source of confusion when we say that x approaches a? Let us take a closer look at the behavior of x as it approaches a. The value of x could remain larger than a (to the right of a on the x-axis) or smaller than a (to the left of a on the x-axis), or it could jump back and forth, taking values alternately larger and smaller

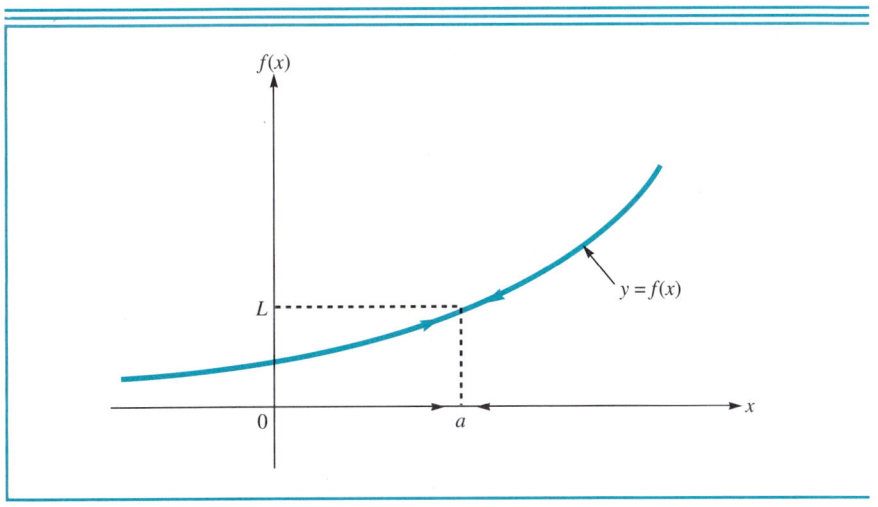

FIGURE 7–3

than a as it approaches a. Think first of x as approaching a from the right side only, always remaining greater than a. We designate the process by

$$x \to a^+,$$

read x **approaches a from above.** Similarly as x approaches a from the left side only, we write

$$x \to a^-$$

and say x **approaches a from below.** In each of these expression, a is called a **one-sided limit.**

What happens to $f(x)$ in Figure 7–3 while this is going on? As x approaches a from above, $f(x)$ approaches L from above, while as x approaches a from below, $f(x)$ approaches L from below. Clearly if

$$\lim_{x \to a} f(x) = L,$$

then as x approaches a in any fashion the height of the function curve $f(x)$ must approach the height L. Note in Figure 7–3 that $f(a) = L$ so that the limit is precisely the value of the function at the point in question. However, as we will see shortly, this is not always the case. Furthermore, as we saw earlier, often the function is not even defined at the point in question. With this discussion in mind we are ready for a definition.

$\lim_{x \to a} f(x) = L$ means that as x approaches a from above or below, the function $f(x)$ approaches L.

Definition. The limit of $f(x)$ as x approaches a is L,

$$\lim_{x \to a} f(x) = L,$$

if and only if $f(x)$ approaches L as x approaches a along any sequence of values.

Example. Find

$$\lim_{x \to 2} (x + 3).$$

Keeping in mind that $x \to 2$ means x must not equal 2, we set up any sequence of x values approaching 2, and compute the corresponding values of the function $x + 3$. For example,

x	1.9	1.99	1.999	1.9999	$\to$	2
$f(x) = x + 3$	4.9	4.99	4.999	4.9999	$\to$	?

or

x	1.5	2.25	1.875	2.0625	$\rightarrow$	2
$f(x) = x + 3$	4.5	5.25	4.875	5.0625	$\rightarrow$	?

All indications seem to be that the "?" at the right of the sequence for $f(x) = x + 3$ is 5, so that we can conclude

$$\lim_{x \to 2} (x + 3) = 5.$$

There are many more (in fact, an infinite number) of such sequences. For every one of these sequences $x + 3$ must approach 5 as x approaches 2.

> **Exercise.** Use a calculator or write a computer program to generate some of these sequences and to reconfirm this fact.

Note in the preceding example that the limit of 5 is precisely the same as the value of the function $x + 3$ at $x = 2$. This result, together with our earlier discussion, suggests that for **some** functions the limit can be found by simple substitution. Indeed this is true for an **polynomial function**[3] so we have

> **Property.** For any polynomial function $f(x)$,
> $$\lim_{x \to a} f(x) = f(a).$$

The limit of a polynomial function can be found by substitution.

> **Exercise.** a) Can we find $\lim_{x \to 3}(x^2 + 5x - 7)$ by substitution? b) What is the limit?
>
> **Answer:** a) Yes. b) 17.

---

[3] Recall that a polynomial function is one of the form

$$a_n x^n + a_{n-1} x^{n-1} + \cdots + a_1 x + a_0.$$

Example. Not all functions are as easy to handle as the last example. Let's try another one. Let

$$f(x) = \begin{cases} 1 & \text{if } x \geq 2 \\ -1 & \text{if } x < 2. \end{cases}$$

What is $\lim_{x \to 2} f(x)$?

The function in this example is defined in two pieces: one for $x \geq 2$ and the other for $x < 2$. When working with such functions, it is often helpful to draw a graph, as shown in Figure 7–4 where the o indicates that the lower piece is not defined at $x = 2$. Now observe the following sequences:

x	3	2.5	2.25	2.125	→	2
$f(x)$	1	1	1	1	→	1

and

x	1	1.5	1.75	1.875	→	2
$f(x)$	-1	-1	-1	-1	→	-1

In the first instance

$$\lim_{x \to 2^+} f(x) = 1$$

as x approaches 2 from above. But in the second instance

$$\lim_{x \to 2^-} f(x) = -1$$

FIGURE 7–4

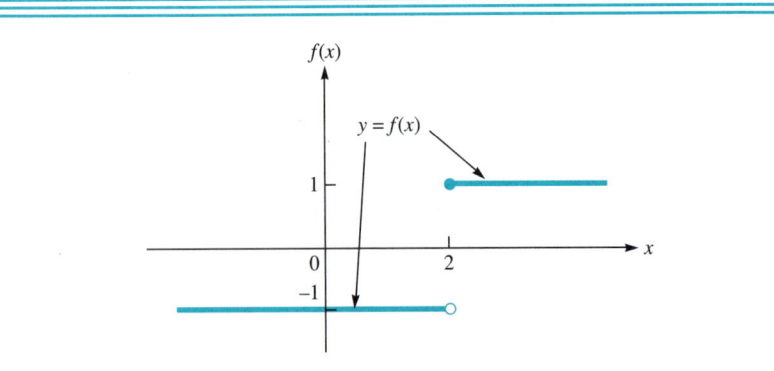

as x approaches 2 from below. For

$$\lim_{x \to 2} f(x)$$

to exist, we must have

$$\lim_{x \to 2^+} f(x) = \lim_{x \to 2^-} f(x) = \lim_{x \to 2} f(x).$$

The only logical conclusion to be drawn in this case is that

$$\lim_{x \to 2} f(x)$$

does not exist (d.n.e.).

This technique of examining the limits of the function as the variable approaches its limit from the left and from the right is important for nonpolynomial functions and is especially useful in showing that limits do not exist.

For a limit to exist at a point, the limit from above the point must equal the limit from below the point.

Exercise. If

$$f(x) = \begin{cases} x \text{ if } x > 0 \\ -1 \text{ if } x \leq 0, \end{cases}$$

find $\lim_{x \to 0} f(x)$.

Answer: The limit does not exist since

$$\lim_{x \to 0^-} f(x) = -1 \text{ and } \lim_{x \to 0^+} f(x) = 0.$$

Example. Find, if it exists,

$$\lim_{x \to 2} \frac{x}{x - 2}.$$

The graph of $x/(x - 2)$ is shown in Figure 7–5. Utilizing the new-found significance of left-hand-side and right-hand-side limits, let us check

$$\lim_{x \to 2} \frac{x}{x - 2}$$

as x approaches 2 from above and from below. To check the right-hand limit, we can use the sequence in the following table:

x	3	2.5	2.25	2.125	2.0625	$\to$	2
$x - 2$	3	5	9	17	33	$\to$	$+\infty$

FIGURE 7-5

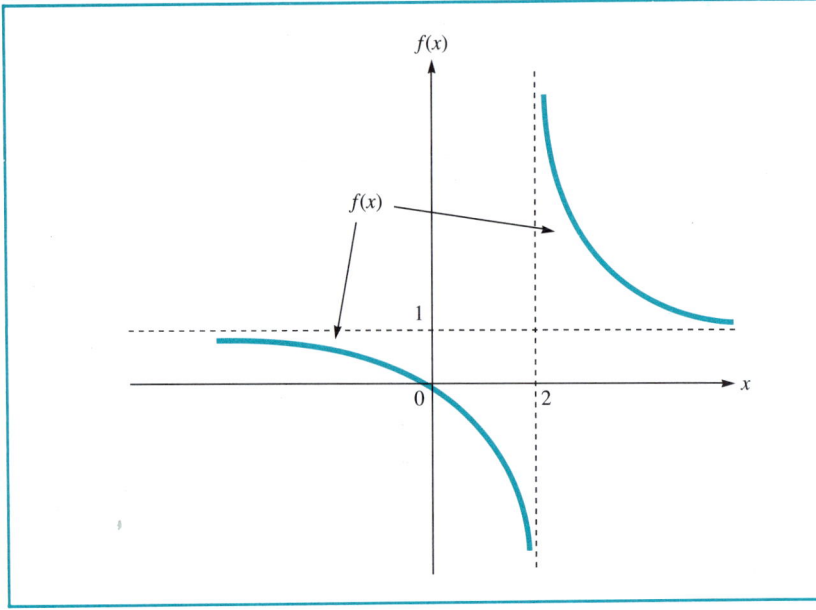

We conclude that

$$\lim_{x \to 2^+} \frac{x}{x-2} = +\infty.$$

Exercise. Choose a sequence to show that

$$\lim_{x \to 2^-} \frac{x}{x-2} = -\infty.$$

Using either of the sequences, we conclude that

$$\lim_{x \to 2} \frac{x}{x-2}$$

> If evaluation of the function results in
> $$\frac{n}{0}$$
> where $n \neq 0$, then the limit does not exist.

does not exist.

What would have happened in the preceding example if we tried to evaluate the function $x/(x-2)$ at $x = 2$? We would get 2/0, which is not defined. This then is an alternative way to determine that the limit does not exist.

A few more examples will help us fully understand the limits we need in this text.

CHAPTER 7 INTRODUCTION TO DIFFERENTIAL CALCULUS

Example. Find, if it exists,
$$\lim_{x \to 2} \frac{x^2 - 4}{x - 2}.$$

A graph of the function is again useful. First, we see that the function is not defined for $x = 2$ since the denominator would be 0. Also if we substitute $x = 2$ in the function, we get 0/0, which is ambiguous. But the latter expression indicates that the numerator and denominator have a common factor that can be canceled. Indeed, when $x \neq 2$, then $x - 2$ is not 0, and we can cancel $x - 2$ with a factor of $x^2 - 4$; that is,

$$\lim_{x \to 2} \frac{x^2 - 4}{x - 2} = \lim_{x \to 2} \frac{(x + 2)(x - 2)}{x - 2} = \lim_{x \to 2} (x + 2).$$

> If evaluation of the function results in
> $$\frac{0}{0},$$
> then there is a common factor in the numerator and denominator that can be canceled.

We emphasize the fact that we can perform the preceding cancellation because the value of x is never equal to 2 when we let x approach 2, hence $x - 2$ is never 0 in the preceding limit. Thus the graph of $(x^2 - 4)/(x - 2)$ must look just like the graph of $x + 2$ everywhere except at $x = 2$, as shown in Figure 7–6.

Now it is easy to see that
$$\lim_{x \to 2} \frac{x^2 - 4}{x - 2} = \lim_{x \to 2} (x + 2) = 4.$$

This technique of cancellation occurs frequently in limit problems so be alert. Think before you jump to the limit.

Exercise. Find, if it exists, a) $\lim_{x \to 5} \frac{x^2 - 25}{x - 5}$. b) $\lim_{x \to 1} \frac{x + 1}{x^2 - 1}$.

Answer: a) 10. b) Limit does not exist.

Example. Find, if it exists,
$$\lim_{a \to b} (3a + 2b).$$

Since the function is a polynomial, we can evaluate it at $a = b$ to get
$$\lim_{a \to b} (3a + 2b) = 3b + 2b = 5b.$$

Example. Find, if it exists,
$$\lim_{b \to a} \frac{a^2 - b^2}{a - b}.$$

FIGURE 7-6

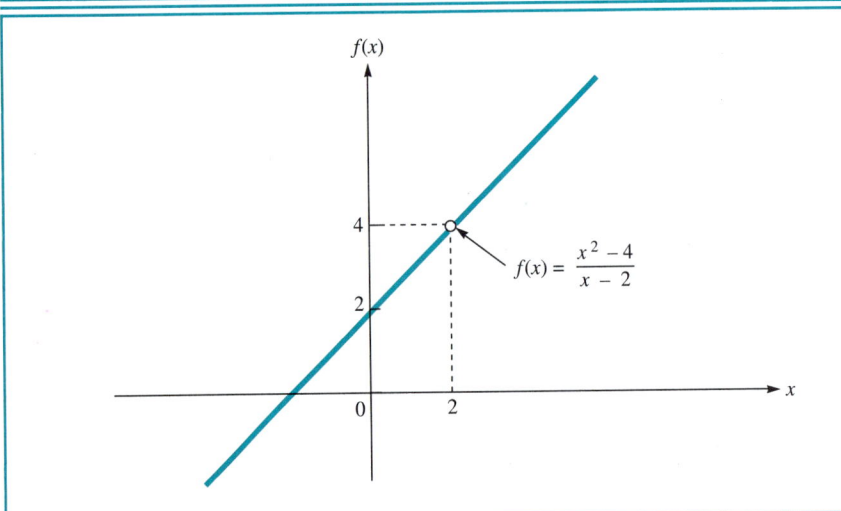

Evaluation of the function at $b = a$ results in

$$\frac{b^2 - b^2}{b - b} = \frac{0}{0},$$

so we have a common term to be canceled.

Factoring leads to

$$\lim_{b \to a} \frac{a^2 - b^2}{a - b} = \lim_{b \to a} \frac{(a + b)(a - b)}{a - b}$$

$$= \lim_{b \to a} (a + b)$$

$$= 2a.$$

Note that in this example b approaches a, whereas in the preceding example a approaches b.

Exercise. Find, if it exists, a) $\lim_{y \to x} (2x + y)$. b) $\lim_{x \to y} \frac{x^2 - y^2}{x - y}$.

Answer: a) $3x$. b) $2y$.

Limit Theorems

We now state and illustrate limit theorems we shall refer to from time to time as our work progresses. These theorems are intuitively reasonable, but their proof requires attention to details that are not appropriate for this text. The following are true if all of the indicated limits exist.

1. If k is any constant, $\lim_{x \to a} k = k$.

   Here note that $x \to a$ specifies that x is changing and approaching a. The constant k does not change. (It does not involve x.) Thus **the limit of a constant is the constant.**

   Examples: $\lim_{x \to 5} 10 = 10$, $\lim_{a \to b} c = c$.

2. $\lim_{x \to a} k f(x) = k \lim_{x \to a} f(x)$.

   That is, **a constant, here k, may be factored out of a limit or we may say that a constant may be placed inside or outside the limit symbol.**

   Example: $\lim_{x \to a} 3x^2 = 3\left(\lim_{x \to a} x^2\right) = 3(a^2) = 3a^2$.

3. $\lim_{x \to a} [f(x) \pm g(x)] = \lim_{x \to a} f(x) \pm \lim_{x \to a} g(x)$.

   That is, the limit of a sum or difference is the sum or difference of the limits. Or we can say that **the limit of an expression can be taken term by term.**

   Example: $\lim_{x \to a} (x^2 - 2x + 3) = \lim_{x \to a} x^2 - 2 \lim_{x \to a} x + \lim_{x \to a} 3$

   $= a^2 - 2a + 3$.

4. $\lim_{x \to a} [f(x)g(x)] = \left[\lim_{x \to a} f(x)\right]\left[\lim_{x \to a} g(x)\right]$.

   That is, **the limit of a product is the product of the limits.**

   Example: $\lim_{x \to 2} (x + 3)(x - 2) = \left[\lim_{x \to 2} (x + 3)\right]\left[\lim_{x \to 2} (x - 2)\right]$

   $= [5][0]$

   $= 0$.

5. $\lim_{x \to a} [f(x)]^n = \left[\lim_{x \to a} f(x)\right]^n$.

   That is, **the limit of a power of $f(x)$ is the power of the limit of $f(x)$.**

   Example: $\lim_{x \to 3} (x - 1)^5 = \left[\lim_{x \to 3} (x - 1)\right]^5 = 2^5 = 32$.

6. If $\lim_{x \to a} f(x) = L$ and $\lim_{x \to a} g(x) = M$, then

   (a) if $M \neq 0$, then $\lim_{x \to a} [f(x)/g(x)] = L/M$.

   (b) if $M = 0$, and $L \neq 0$, then $\lim_{x \to a} [f(x)/g(x)]$ does not exist (d.n.e.).

   (c) if $M = 0$ and $L = 0$, then $f(x)$ and $g(x)$ have a common factor and the limit can be evaluated after employing the process of cancellation.

As we have seen, the effect of these limit theorems is that for functions defined in a single piece, evaluation at the point in question results in:

Summary of the evaluation technique for determining limits of single-piece functions.

1. An expression or a number n, which is then the limit (remember that $0/n = 0$ for any $n \neq 0$);
2. The expression $n/0$ where $n \neq 0$, indicating that the limit does not exist; or
3. The expression $0/0$, indicating that a common term should be canceled from the numerator and denominator, after which evaluation will result in either (1) or (2).

7.6 PROBLEM SET 7-2

Find each of the following, if it exists:

1. $\lim_{x \to 1} (x^2 + 2x - 2)$.
2. $\lim_{x \to 2} (x^3 - 5x^2 - 1)$.
3. $\lim_{x \to b} ax^2$.
4. $\lim_{b \to a} a^2 b^2$.
5. $\lim_{x \to 1} \dfrac{x^2 - 1}{x + 1}$.
6. $\lim_{x \to 1} \dfrac{x^2 + 1}{x + 1}$.
7. $\lim_{x \to 2} \dfrac{x^2 + 5}{x - 2}$.
8. $\lim_{x \to 1} \dfrac{x^2 + 1}{x - 1}$.
9. $\lim_{x \to a} (x - 1)^{1/3}$.
10. $\lim_{x \to 24} (x + 1)^{1/2}$.
11. $\lim_{b \to a} (3a + 5b)$.
12. $\lim_{a \to b} (5a - b)$.
13. $\lim_{x \to 3/2} \dfrac{4x^2 - 9}{2x - 3}$.
14. $\lim_{x \to 5/3} \dfrac{9x^2 - 25}{3x - 5}$.
15. $\lim_{x \to 0} \dfrac{x^4}{x^3}$.
16. $\lim_{x \to 0} \dfrac{x^3}{x^4}$.
17. $\lim_{x \to 1/2} \dfrac{2x + 1}{2x - 1}$.
18. $\lim_{x \to 1/3} \dfrac{3x - 1}{3x + 1}$.
19. $\lim_{h \to 0} \dfrac{(h)(2x + 3h)}{h}$.
20. $\lim_{h \to 0} \dfrac{(h)(3x^2 + 2xh)}{h}$.
21. $\lim_{a \to 0} \dfrac{\dfrac{1}{2 + a} - \dfrac{1}{2}}{a}$.
22. $\lim_{a \to 0} \dfrac{\dfrac{1}{5 + a} - \dfrac{1}{5}}{a}$.
23. $\lim_{x \to 1} \dfrac{x^3 - 1}{x - 1}$.
24. $\lim_{x \to 2} \dfrac{x^3 - 2}{x - 2}$.

7.6 PROBLEM SET 7-2 (concluded)

25. $\lim_{x \to 2} \left(\dfrac{x}{x-2} - \dfrac{2}{x-2} \right)$.

26. $\lim_{x \to 1} \left(\dfrac{x^2}{x-1} - \dfrac{1}{x-1} \right)$.

27. $\lim_{x \to 3} \left(\dfrac{x^3}{x-3} + \dfrac{27}{x-3} \right)$.

28. $\lim_{x \to 2} \left(\dfrac{x^2}{x-2} + \dfrac{4}{x-2} \right)$.

29. $\lim_{x \to 2} \dfrac{x^2 + x - 6}{x^2 - 4}$.

30. $\lim_{x \to -1} \dfrac{x^3 + 1}{x + 1}$.

31. $\lim_{x \to -2} \dfrac{x - 3}{x^2 + x - 2}$.

---

32. The QBasic program shown in Program 7-1 generates the values of

$$f(x) = \dfrac{x^3 - 2}{x}$$

corresponding to the x values in the sequence

$$x: \ 1, \ 1/2, \ 1/2^2, \ 1/2^3, \ldots, 1/2^{10}.$$

Program 7-1
```
REM PROGRAM 7-1
REM Limit
CLS
PRINT TAB(7); "x", TAB(27); "f(x)"
FOR n = 0 TO 10
  X = 1 / 2 ^ n
  PRINT x, TAB(25); (x ^ 3 - 2) / x
NEXT n
```

a) Describe what the program is doing line by line.
b) Run the program.
c) What is $\lim_{x \to 0^+} f(x)$?

33. a) Modify Program 7-1 for

$$f(x) = \dfrac{x^2 - 4\sqrt{x} + 2}{x - 1}.$$

b) Run the program in (a).
c) What is $\lim_{x \to 0^+} f(x)$?

34. a) Modify Program 7-1 for

$$f(x) = \begin{cases} 1/x, & x < 0 \\ x, & x \geq 0. \end{cases}$$

b) Run the program in (a).
c) What is $\lim_{x \to 0^+} f(x)$?

7.7 CONTINUITY

It is often useful to consider sets of functions with a common property. **Continuity** is such a property. In simple terms, **continuous functions are functions with graphs that are unbroken.** Let us sketch a graph of

$$f(x) = \begin{cases} x + 1, & x \geq 0 \\ x - 1, & x < 0 \end{cases}$$

as shown in Figure 7-7. This graph is fragmented in that we cannot draw the graph in one continuous stroke without having to lift our pencil from the paper. Roughly speaking, a function is called continuous if its graph can be drawn without lifting the pencil from the paper. In what circumstances do we have to lift the pencil from the paper while drawing? As we see in Figures 7-7 and 7-8, if there is a jump in the graph (or, as in Figure 7-9, a gap or hole in the graph) at $x = a$, we then

A continuous function is one that can be drawn without lifting the pencil from the paper.

A jump or a hole in the graph means the function is *not* continuous.

must lift the pencil. In the first instance, the jump in Figure 7–8, we notice that $\lim_{x \to a} f(x)$ does not exist at the jump point *a* since the right-hand limit does not equal the left-hand limit. Think about this a moment and it will become clear that to avoid a jump at a point *a*, $\lim_{x \to a} f(x)$ must exist.

In the second instance (the gap in Figure 7–9), the function $f(x)$ does not have a value at $x = a$. Clearly $f(x)$ must have a value $f(a)$ if we are to draw the graph in one continuous motion. Are these two conditions enough? Before you answer,

FIGURE 7–7

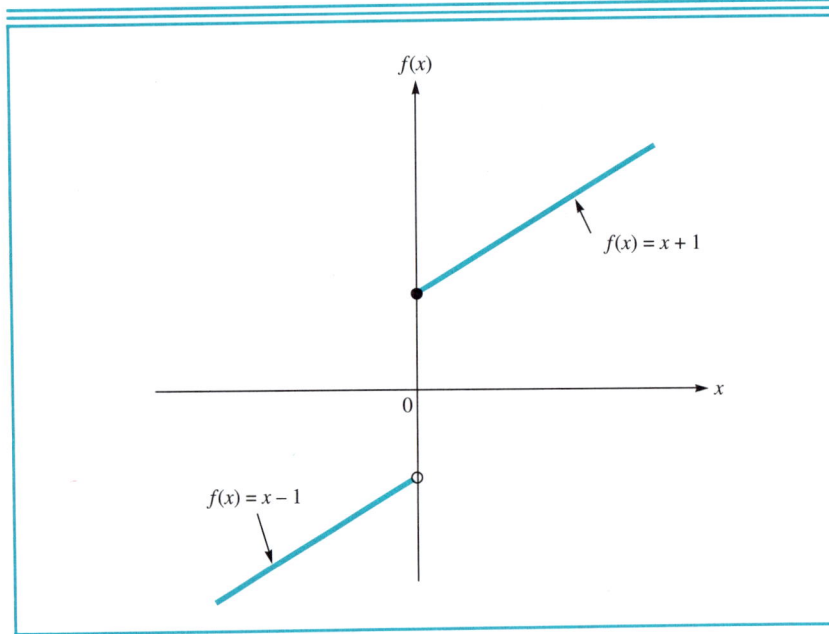

FIGURE 7–8

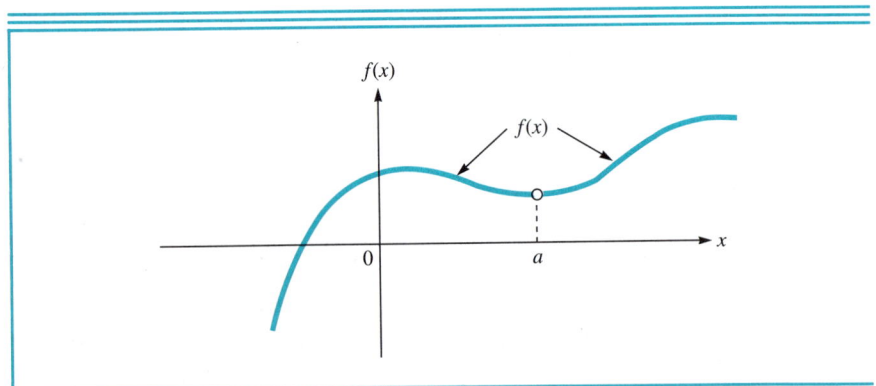

let us look at one more special case in Figure 7–10. In this picture, $\lim_{x \to a} f(x)$ exists and $f(a)$ is defined, but $\lim_{x \to a} f(x) \neq f(a)$.

Now with all this in mind, we are ready for a formal definition of continuity.

Definition. A function $f(x)$ is said to be **continuous** at a point a if the following three conditions are met:

1. $f(a)$ is defined.
2. $\lim_{x \to a} f(x)$ exists.
3. $\lim_{x \to a} f(x) = f(a)$.

If a function is not continuous at a point a, we say it is **discontinuous** at a or has a discontinuity at a.

For a function to be continuous at a point, the function must be defined at that point, the limit must exist, and these two values must be the same.

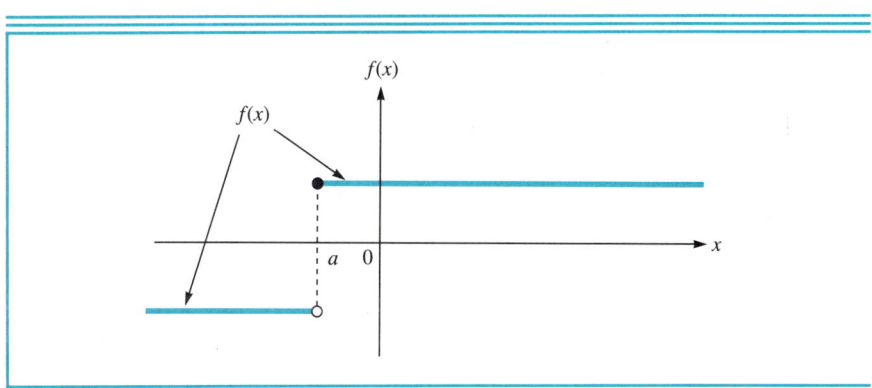

FIGURE 7–9

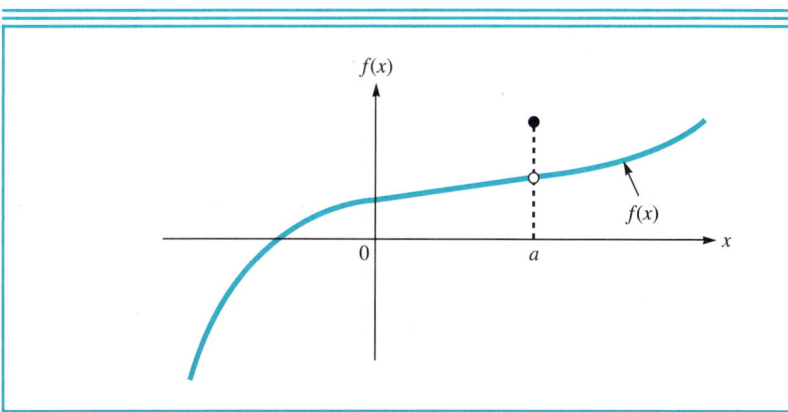

FIGURE 7–10

Example. Discuss the continuity of

$$f(x) = \frac{x + 2}{x^2 - 3x + 2}.$$

First, we factor the denominator

$$f(x) = \frac{x + 2}{(x - 1)(x - 2)}.$$

Now we can go through the three conditions of our definition to check for points of discontinuity. Once we have found these points of discontinuity, if any, then the function will clearly be continuous at all other points.

Condition 1: $f(x)$ is defined for all x except $x = 1$ and $x = 2$.
Condition 2: By Limit Theorem 6 of Section 7.5, $\lim_{x \to a} f(x)$ exists for all x except $x = 1$ and $x = 2$.
Condition 3: Again by Limit Theorem 6, we see that $\lim_{x \to a} f(x) = f(a)$ for all x except $x = 1$ and $x = 2$.

Hence $f(x)$ is continuous at all x except $x = 1$ and $x = 2$, where it has discontinuities.

Exercise. Find the discontinuities, if any, for

$$f(x) = \frac{3x - 7}{6x^2 - 19x + 15}.$$

Answer: $x = 3/2$ and $x = 5/3$.

The concepts of continuity and discontinuity can be simplified by recognizing that certain classes of function are always continuous. For our purposes, the following list, presented without justification, will be very helpful in determining the continuity of functions.

1. All polynomial functions are continuous.
2. If $f(x)$ is continuous and $g(x)$ is continuous, then
   a) $f(x) \pm g(x)$ is continuous.
   b) $f(x) \cdot g(x)$ is continuous.
   c) $f(x)/g(x)$ is continuous when $g(x) \neq 0$.

7.8 PROBLEM SET 7-3

In Problems 1 through 10, find the discontinuities, if any, for each function

1. $f(x) = x^3 + 2x - 4$.
2. $f(x) = \dfrac{1}{x - 1}$.

7.8 PROBLEM SET 7-3 (concluded)

3. $f(x) = \dfrac{x}{x^2 + 1}$.

4. $f(x) = \dfrac{x - 2}{x^2 - 4}$.

5. $f(x) = \dfrac{x^2 - 4}{x - 2}$.

6. $f(x) = \dfrac{x + 2}{x^2 - 5x + 6}$.

7. $f(x) = \begin{cases} x + 1, & x > 1 \\ x, & x \leq 1. \end{cases}$

8. $f(x) = \begin{cases} x + 1, & x \geq 1 \\ 2, & x < 1. \end{cases}$

9. $f(x) = \begin{cases} x^2 + 1, & x \geq 2 \\ x + 3, & x < 2. \end{cases}$

10. $f(x) = \begin{cases} \dfrac{x}{2} + 1, & x \geq -2 \\ x + 2, & x < -2. \end{cases}$

11. The QBasic program shown in Program 7-2 generates the values of $f(x)$ for Problem 7.

    Program 7-2
    ```
    REM PROGRAM 7-2
    REM Continuity
    CLS
    PRINT " x",  "f(x) "
    FOR x = 0 to 1.1 STEP .1
      PRINT x, x
    NEXT x
    PRINT "*****",  "*****"
    FOR x = 2 TO 1 STEP -.1
      PRINT x, x + 1
    NEXT x
    ```
    a) Describe what the program is doing line by line.
    b) Run the program and verify the answer to Problem 7.

12. a) Modify Program 7-2 for each function in Problems 8 through 10.
    b) Run the program in (a) and verify the answers to Problems 8 through 10.

13. A direct-dial long-distance call between Boston and New York costs $0.49 for the first three minutes and $0.21 for each additional minute or fraction thereof. Sketch a graph of this function and discuss its continuity.

14. An electric utility company used to make the following charges for usage of electricity: $8.50 flat charge for 0 to 70 kilowatt hours (kwh) of usage, 10 cents per kwh for the next 380 kwh, and 8 cents per kwh for the excess over 450 kwh. Sketch a graph of this function and discuss its continuity.

7.9 THE DIFFERENCE QUOTIENT

As we saw in Chapter 1, the function

$$f(x) = mx + b$$

is a **linear function** represented graphically by a **straight line**. Thus

$$f(x) = 0.8x + 3$$

is a linear function. Conventionally when we graph functions, the function values, $f(x)$, are on the vertical axis, and the independent variable values are on the horizontal axis. The graph of $f(x)$, which has a slope of 0.8 and a vertical intercept of 3, is shown in Figure 7-11. If the independent variable changes from x to $x + h$, the value of the function changes from $f(x)$ to $f(x + h)$ so the change in the function, Δf, is

$$\Delta f = f(x + h) - f(x),$$

FIGURE 7-11

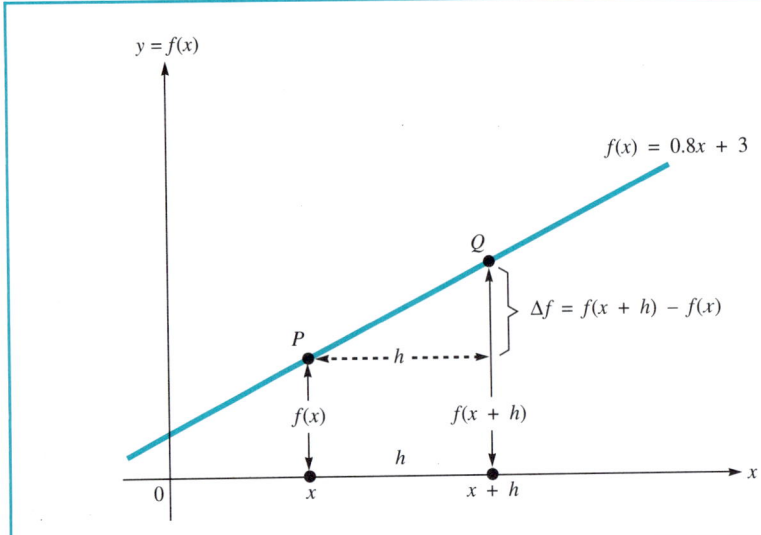

as shown in Figure 7–11. The slope of the line can be determined from any two of its points, such as P and Q. It is the vertical change Δf, divided by the horizontal change Δx, that is, the change in the function divided by the change in x, which is

$$\frac{\Delta y}{\Delta x} = \frac{\Delta f}{h} = \frac{f(x+h) - f(x)}{h}.$$

The difference quotient is simply the slope; that is

$$\frac{\Delta y}{\Delta x} = \frac{f(x+h) - f(x)}{h}.$$

This expression is called the **difference quotient**. Thus the difference quotient is simply the slope of a straight line. For our function,

$$f(x) = 0.8x + 3,$$

we find

$$\Delta f = f(x+h) - f(x) = [0.8(x+h) + 3] - [0.8x + 3]$$
$$= \cancel{0.8x} + 0.8h + \cancel{3} - \cancel{0.8x} - \cancel{3}$$
$$= 0.8h.$$

Hence the difference quotient is

$$\frac{\Delta y}{\Delta x} = \frac{\Delta f}{h} = \frac{\Delta f}{x} = \frac{0.8h}{h} = 0.8.$$

The result, a constant, is not surprising, of course, because $f(x)$ is a straight line and we know that a given line has the same slope number for any pair of its points.

> **Exercise.** If $g(x) = mx + b$, what will the difference quotient be?
> **Answer:** m, the slope of the line specified by $g(x)$.

Consider next the function x^3, a section of which is shown in Figure 7–12 (p. 492). A line, called a **secant line**, has been drawn through two points, P and Q, on the curve. The difference quotient for this pair of points we shall call m_s, where m stands for slope and s for secant. We have

$$m_s = \frac{\Delta f}{h} = \frac{f(x+h) - f(x)}{h} = \frac{(x+h)^3 - x^3}{h}.$$

First we find $(x + h)^3$:

$$\begin{aligned}(x+h)^3 &= (x+h)(x+h)^2 \\ &= (x+h)(x^2 + 2xh + h^2) \\ &= x^3 + 2x^2h + xh^2 + x^2h + 2xh^2 + h^3 \\ &= x^3 + 3x^2h + 3xh^2 + h^3.\end{aligned}$$

Hence

$$\begin{aligned} m_s &= \frac{(x+h)^3 - x^3}{h} \\ &= \frac{x^3 + 3x^2h + 3xh^2 + h^3 - x^3}{h} \\ &= \frac{3x^2h + 3xh^2 + h^3}{h} \\ &= \frac{h(3x^2 + 3xh + h^2)}{h} \\ &= 3x^2 + 3xh + h^2 \\ &= 3x^2 + h(3x + h). \end{aligned}$$

Here the difference quotient, m_s, is not constant as it is in the case of a straight line, but depends instead upon the size of h and the particular value of x at hand. We could call m_s the **average rate of change** of $f(x)$ over the interval $(x, x + h)$. For example, over the interval $(2, 2.5)$, $x = 2$ and $h = 0.5$ so

$$m_s = 3(2)^2 + (0.5)(6 + 0.5) = 15.25.$$

On the other hand, over the interval $(2, 2.4)$,

$$m_s = 3(2)^2 + (0.4)(6 + 0.4) = 14.56.$$

FIGURE 7-12

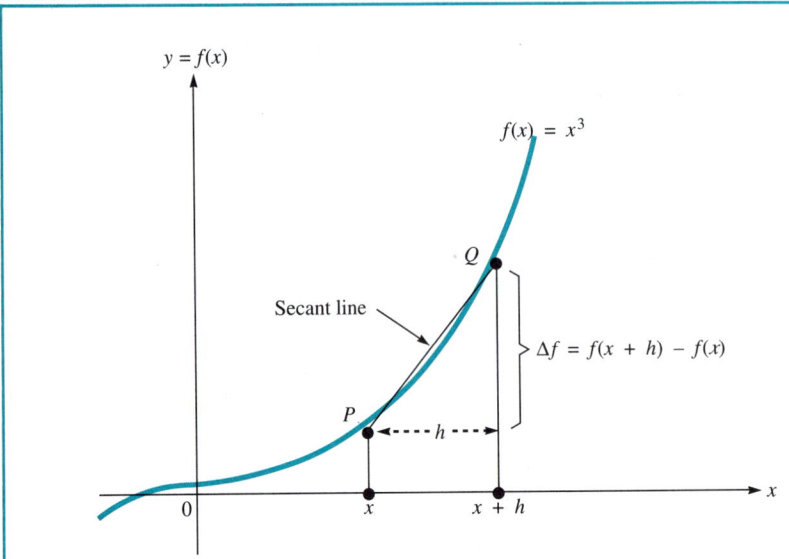

> **Exercise.** Find m_s for the preceding function x^3 over the interval $(1, 1.7)$.
> **Answer:** 5.59.

Example. Compute the average rate of change m_s for $f(x) = x^2$ over the interval $(x, x + h)$ when $h = 0.1, 0.01, 0.001$ and $x = 1$.

First, we compute

$$m_s = \frac{\Delta f}{h} = \frac{(x+h)^2 - x^2}{h} = \frac{x^2 + 2xh + h^2 - x^2}{h}$$

$$= \frac{2xh + h^2}{h} = 2x + h.$$

So we have

h	$(x, x+h)$	m_s
0.1	(1, 1.1)	2.1
0.01	(1, 1.01)	2.01
0.001	(1, 1.001)	2.001

Do you see a pattern?

> **Exercise.** Find the average rate of change m_s, for $f(x) = 2x^2 + 1$.
> **Answer:** $4x + 2h$.

7.10 DEFINITION OF THE DERIVATIVE

We now have the tools needed to obtain the rules of differential calculus. The problem at hand can be thought of as that of **determining the slope of a line tangent to a curve at a point on the curve.** This is a new problem because until now it has been necessary to have **two** points to compute a slope and here we have only one point. But we also have the function that determines the shape of the graph, and this shape governs the slopes of the tangents.

We start, as shown in Figure 7–13 (p. 494), by taking the stated point on a curve, P, and a nearby point, Q. The secant line through these points has the slope m_s. We will take the slope of the secant line,

$$m_s = \frac{\Delta f}{h},$$

as an approximation of the slope of the tangent line. Clearly the closer Q is to P, the more closely will the secant slope approximate the tangent slope. Thus if we move Q down the curve toward P (as indicated by the arrowheads on the curve) so that Q **approaches** P, secant slopes will change and **approach** the slope of the tangent line at P.[4] Thus as Q approaches P,

$$\text{Secant line} \to \text{Tangent line at } P$$
$$\text{Secant slope} \to \text{Tangent slope at } P$$
$$m_s = \frac{\Delta f}{h} \to \text{Tangent slope at } P.$$

> The secant slope m_s approaches the tangent slope at the point in question as $h \to 0$.

The next step is to find a mathematical procedure that can be used to make Q approach P. Returning to Figure 7–13, note the points at the arrowheads on the x-axis. As $x + h$ approaches x, it passes through each of these points, getting closer and closer to x itself. Consequently, h is getting smaller and smaller, and so h approaches 0. The corresponding points above on the curve then move from Q toward P as h approaches 0. Hence as

---

[4] To see this clearly, construct a curve on a full sheet of paper, and use a ruler to sketch a tangent line at a point P. Then take a piece of thread and stretch it across P and another point Q to represent the secant line in Figure 7–13. Now, holding the thread fixed at point P, rotate the stretched thread so that it cuts the curve at points successively closer to P. Observe that as the thread (which represents the secant line) moves downward, it approaches the tangent line.

FIGURE 7-13

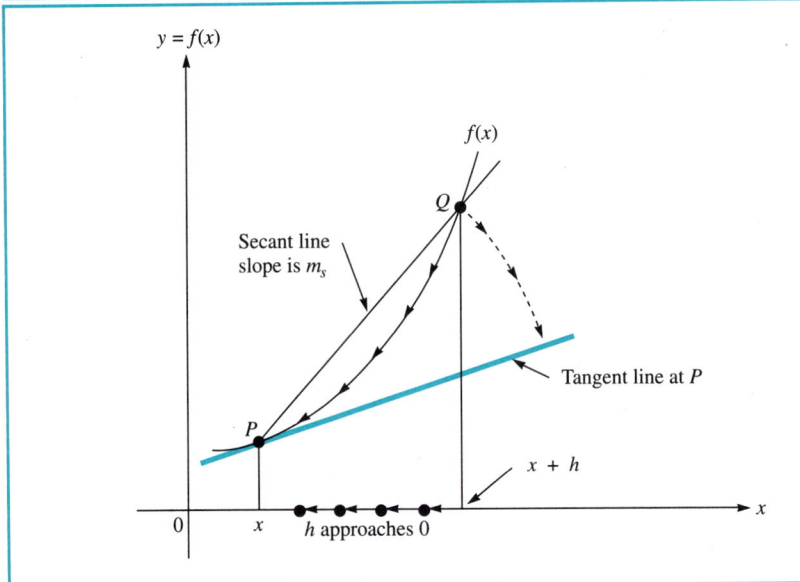

$$h \to 0$$
$$Q \to P$$
$$\frac{\Delta f}{h} \to \text{Tangent slope at } P.$$

The smaller h is, the closer the secant slope is to the tangent slope at P. As a consequence, it is intuitively reasonable to define the tangent slope at P to be the limit of the secant slope as h approaches 0.

$$\text{Tangent slope} = \lim_{h \to 0} \frac{\Delta f}{h}.$$

The function derived when this limit is obtained is called the **derivative** of $f(x)$ and is symbolized by $f'(x)$.

The derivative of $f(x)$ is

$$f'(x) = \lim_{h \to 0} \frac{f(x + h) - f(x)}{h}$$

and measures the slope of the line tangent to the function of the point in question.

Definition. $f'(x)$ = the derivative of $f(x)$.

$$f'(x) = \lim_{h \to 0} \frac{\Delta f}{h} = \lim_{h \to 0} \frac{f(x + h) - f(x)}{h}.$$

The definition just stated is the fundamental definition of differential calculus, and all rules for finding derivatives are developed by starting from this definition. Its statement requires the use of functions, delta procedures, and limits, which we have studied earlier in the chapter. It is worth noting in particular that the need for the limit concept arises because the secant slope in Figure 7–13 is

$$m_s = \frac{\Delta f}{h} = \frac{f(x+h) - f(x)}{h}.$$

If h is set equal to 0, m_s becomes

$$m_s = \frac{f(x+0) - f(x)}{0} = \frac{f(x) - f(x)}{0} = \frac{0}{0},$$

so m_s is not defined at $h = 0$. What has happened here, of course, is that $h = 0$ means that in Figure 7–13, points P and Q are the same point and the slope of a line cannot be determined from one of its points. But if we let $h \to 0$, rather than set $h = 0$, and a limit exists, then this limit has an important interpretation; namely, the limit is the slope of a tangent line at a (one) point on the curve. Thus the problem that is solved by finding $f'(x)$ is that of finding the expression that gives the slope of a tangent line when only one point on such a line is specified. **A function that has a derivative at a point P is said to be differentiable at P. If a function $f(x)$ has a derivative at all points for which it is defined, we merely say that $f(x)$ is differentiable.**

Before going on to an example, we state the following definition in order to simplify statements:

Definition. The slope of a curve at a point means the slope of the line tangent to the curve at that point.

The slope of a curve at a particular point is the slope of the tangent line at that point which is precisely the derivative at that point.

Example. Find the slope of $f(x) = x^3$ at the point where $x = 0.5$.

First we must find the expression for the derivative, $f'(x)$. This will be done in steps that we shall number so that the reader can refer to them. For convenience and to emphasize the use of the **three-step procedure,** we repeat the algebra done in Section 7.9.

1. Find $f(x + h)$. For $f(x) = x^3$,

$$f(x + h) = (x + h)^3$$
$$= (x + h)(x + h)^2$$

The three-step procedure for finding $f'(x)$ is:

1. Find $f(x + h)$.
2. Find
$$m_s = \frac{f(x+h) - f(x)}{h}.$$
3. Find
$$f'(x) = \lim_{h \to 0} \frac{f(x+h) - f(x)}{h}.$$

$$= (x + h)(x^2 + 2xh + h^2)$$
$$= x^3 + 2x^2h + xh^2 + x^2h + 2xh^2 + h^3$$
$$= x^3 + 3x^2h + 3xh^2 + h^3.$$

2. Set up the difference quotient. This is

$$m_s = \frac{f(x + h) - f(x)}{h}$$
$$= \frac{\cancel{x^3} + 3x^2h + 3xh^2 + h^3 - \cancel{x^3}}{h}$$
$$= \frac{3x^2h + 3xh^2 + h^3}{h}$$
$$= \frac{h(3x^2 + 3xh + h^2)}{h}$$
$$= 3x^2 + 3xh + h^2.$$

3. Find $f'(x)$, which is the limit of the difference quotient as $h \to 0$, if a limit exists. Here we have

$$f'(x) = \lim_{h \to 0} \frac{f(x + h) - f(x)}{h} = \lim_{h \to 0} (3x^2 + 3xh + h^2) = 3x^2.$$

Observe in the last line that h is the changing quantity and the terms with h as a factor vanish as h approaches 0. However the first term does not involve h so it will not change, and

$$f'(x) = 3x^2.$$

This says the slope of

$$f(x) = x^3$$

at any point is computed as three times the square of the x-coordinate of the point. Thus for the point where $x = 0.5$,

$$f'(0.5) = 3(0.5)^2 = 3(0.25) = 0.75.$$

Figure 7–14 shows $f(x)$ and the tangent line at the point P where

$$x = 0.5; \quad f(x) = f(0.5) = (0.5)^3 = 0.125.$$

Exercise. Given $f(x) = x^2$, follow the preceding three steps and write the results of a) Step 1. b) Step 2. c) Step 3. d) Compute the slope of $f(x)$ at the point where $x = 1$.

Answer: a) $x^2 + 2xh + h^2$. b) $2x + h$. c) $2x$. d) 2.

FIGURE 7–14

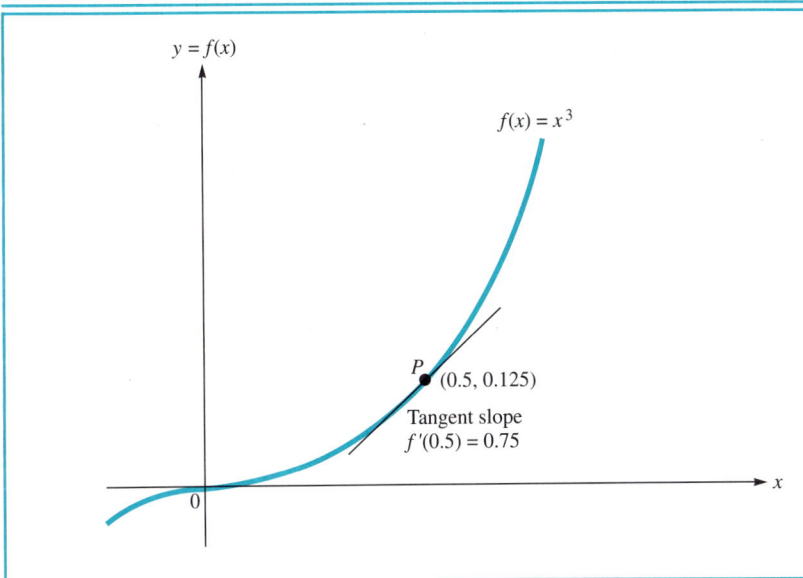

As another example we now return to the UPS example in Section 7.2. There the problem was that of finding box dimensions that provided a box of maximum surface area. The problem, illustrated in Figure 7–2, was to find x so that the slope of the tangent to

$$A = A(x) = 432x - 14x^2$$

was 0. This horizontal tangent marked the peak (highest value) of the area function in Figure 7–2. Applying the three-step procedure to find $A'(x)$, we have

1. $A(x + h) = 432(x + h) - 14(x + h)^2$
    $= 432x + 432h - 14(x^2 + 2xh + h^2)$
    $= 432x + 432h - 14x^2 - 28xh - 14h^2.$

2. $m_s = \dfrac{A(x + h) - A(x)}{h}$

    $= \dfrac{(432x + 432h - 14x^2 - 28xh - 14h^2) - (432x - 14x^2)}{h}$

    $= \dfrac{432h - 28xh - 14h^2}{h}$

    $= \dfrac{h(432 - 28x - 14h)}{h}$

    $= 432 - 28x - 14h.$

3. $A'(x) = \lim\limits_{h \to 0} (432 - 28x - 14h)$

$= 432 - 28x,$

where, as before, terms with h as a factor vanish when $h \to 0$. Now we wish to know where the slope of the curve is 0. This is where $A'(x) = 0$.

$$A'(x) = 0 \text{ where } 432 - 28x = 0$$
$$432 = 28x$$
$$\frac{432}{28} = x$$
$$\frac{108}{7} = x,$$

which is the result stated in Section 7.2.

With practice, this three-step procedure will become second nature and problem solutions will appear as in the next example.

Example. Find the slope of $f(x) = x^2 + 1$ at $x = -1, 0,$ and 1.

First we must find the difference quotient

$$m_s = \frac{[(x+h)^2 + 1] - (x^2 + 1)}{h}$$

$$= \frac{x^2 + 2xh + h^2 + 1 - x^2 - 1}{h}$$

$$= \frac{2xh + h^2}{h}$$

$$= 2x + h.$$

Now we find $f'(x)$:

$$f'(x) = \lim\limits_{h \to 0} (2x + h) = 2x.$$

Thus we have

x	$y = f(x) = x^2 + 1$	$f'(x) = 2x$
-1	2	-2
0	1	0
1	2	2

Figure 7–15 shows the three tangent lines at the three designated values of x.

We shall pause now for a brief problem set that will serve to fix in your mind the fundamental definition of the derivative. Then we shall return to develop a simple rule that can be applied to take derivatives quickly.

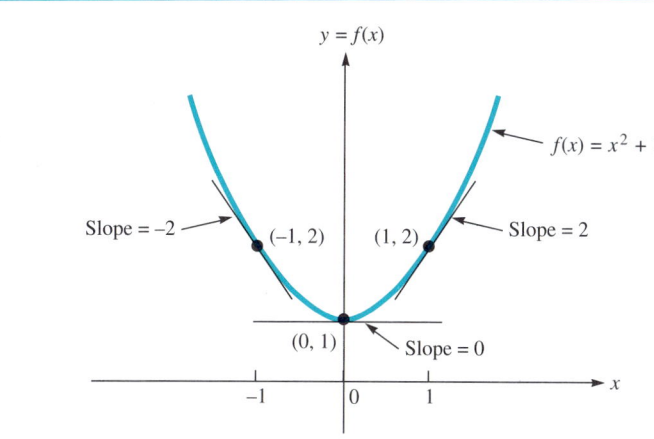

FIGURE 7-15

7.11 PROBLEM SET 7-4

Apply the three steps of the delta method to determine $f'(x)$ for each of the following. Then find the slope of the curve of $f(x)$ for the stated value of x.

1. $f(x) = 3x + 2$, at $x = 1$.
2. $f(x) = 2 - 0.5x$, at $x = 1$.
3. $f(x) = x^2 - 2x - 1$, at $x = 1$.
4. $f(x) = 3x^2 - 12x + 2$, at $x = 3$.
5. $f(x) = 1/x$, at $x = 2$.
6. $f(x) = 1/x^2$, at $x = -1$.
7. $f(x) = x^3 + 2x$, at $x = 2$.
8. $f(x) = x^3 - (1/2)x^2 + x + 1$, at $x = -1$.
9. $f(x) = x^4$, at $x = -1$.
10. $f(x) = \sqrt{x}$, at $x = 1$.

The definition of the derivative of $f(x) = x^2$ is

$$f'(x) = \lim_{h \to 0} \frac{(x+h)^2 - x^2}{h}.$$

Write the corresponding definition of the derivative of the following. Do not continue beyond writing the definition.

11. $f(x) = x^5 - 2x^4$.
12. $f(x) = 3x^6 + 2x^3$.
13. $f(x) = x^{1/3}$.
14. $f(x) = x^{1/2}$.

15. The QBasic program shown in Program 7-3 computes the derivative in Problem 1.

    Program 7-3

    ```
    REM PROGRAM 7-3
    REM Derivative
    CLS
    PRINT " x", "f'(x)"
    FOR x = 2 TO 1 STEP -.1
    PRINT x, ((3 * x + 2) - (3 * 1 + 2)) / (x - 1)
    NEXT x
    ```

7.11 PROBLEM SET 7-4 (concluded)

a) Describe what the program is doing line by line.
b) Run the program and verify the answer to Problem 1.

16. a) Modify Program 7-3 for each function in Problems 2 through 10.
b) Run the program in (a) and verify the answers to Problems 2 through 10.

7.12 THE SIMPLE POWER RULE

There is a simple rule that can be applied to find the derivative of any power of x. To see where the rule comes from, we state some results obtained earlier. Namely,

$$\text{for } f(x) = x^2, \quad \frac{f(x+h) - f(x)}{h} = 2x + h;$$

$$\text{for } f(x) = x^3, \quad \frac{f(x+h) - f(x)}{h} = 3x^2 + h(3x + h).$$

Omitting the algebra, we state the further results that

$$\text{for } f(x) = x^4, \quad \frac{f(x+h) - f(x)}{h} = 4x^3 + h(\ ),$$

$$\text{for } f(x) = x^5, \quad \frac{f(x+h) - f(x)}{h} = 5x^4 + h(\ ),$$

where, in the last two lines, $h(\ )$ means that all remaining terms have h as a factor and hence will vanish in the limit,

$$f'(x) = \lim_{h \to 0} \frac{f(x+h) - f(x)}{h}.$$

Thus taking the limit of each of the preceding, we find:

if $f(x) = x^2, \quad f'(x) = 2x;$
if $f(x) = x^3, \quad f'(x) = 3x^2;$
if $f(x) = x^4, \quad f'(x) = 4x^3.$

We see that in each case

$$f'(x) = (\text{power})(x \text{ to the power minus 1}),$$

and this can be proved to be true for x to any power that is a constant, for all values of x where the derivative is defined. To see the need for the last clause, which implies a restriction on values of x, observe that

if $f(x) = x^{1/2},$

then by the rule just stated

$$f'(x) = \frac{1}{2}x^{1/2-1}$$
$$= \frac{1}{2}x^{-1/2}$$
$$= \frac{1}{2x^{1/2}}$$

and note that $f'(x)$ is not defined at $x = 0$ because

$$f'(0) = \frac{1}{2(0)^{1/2}} = \frac{1}{0}$$

is not defined. **To avoid endless repetition, we shall follow convention and omit the necessary qualification that a derivative rule holds only for values of the independent variable where the derivative is defined.**

Simple Power Rule

If $f(x) = x^n$, then $f'(x) = nx^{n-1}$.

The derivative of x raised to any constant power is the power times x to the power minus 1; that is, the derivative of x^n is $n \cdot x^{n-1}$.

Example. Leaving no negative exponents, find $f'(x)$ if a) $f(x) = x^{10}$. b) $f(x) = x^{2/3}$. c) $f(x) = \frac{1}{x^3}$.

We have the following:

a) $n = 10$ so $f'(x) = 10x^{10-1} = 10x^9$.

b) $n = \frac{2}{3}$ so $f'(x) = \frac{2}{3}x^{2/3-1} = \frac{2}{3}x^{-1/3} = \frac{2}{3x^{1/3}}$.

c) We first rewrite the function as x raised to a power

$$f(x) = \frac{1}{x^3} = x^{-3}.$$

Then, using the Simple Power Rule with $n = -3$, we have

$$f'(x) = -3x^{-3-1} = -3x^{-4} = -\frac{3}{x^4}.$$

> **Exercise.** Find $g'(x)$ for: a) $g(x) = x^7$. b) $g(x) = x^{6.5}$. c) $g(x) = x^{4/3}$. d) $g(x) = x^{1/2}$. e) $g(x) = x$. f) $g(x) = \dfrac{1}{x}$.
>
> **Answer:** a) $7x^6$. b) $6.5x^{5.5}$. c) $\dfrac{4}{3}x^{1/3}$. d) $\dfrac{1}{2x^{1/2}}$. e) 1. f) $-\dfrac{1}{x^2}$.

We have called the rule at hand the **simple power rule** to distinguish it from the **function power rule** we shall develop later in Section 7.15 and apply to cases where the base of the power is a function of x other than simply x itself. Thus the derivative of

$$f(x) = x^9$$

is found by the simple power rule, but the derivative of

$$g(x) = (3x^2 + 2x - 7)^9$$

will be found later by the function power rule.

7.13 d/dx NOTATION AND RULES OF OPERATIONS

The two-part statement,

$$\text{if } f(x) = x^3, \quad \text{then} \quad f'(x) = 3x^2,$$

is awkward, and it will be convenient to use a symbol that means to take the derivative with respect to an independent variable.

Leibniz notation is an alternative way of writing the derivative; that is,

$$\frac{d}{dx} f(x) = f'(x).$$

> **Definition.** $\dfrac{d}{dx}$ means take the derivative with respect to x.
>
> $\dfrac{df(x)}{dx}$ means $f'(x)$.

Thus the symbol d/dx, often called **Leibniz notation,** is a one-piece symbol and should never be read as d over d times x. Instead it means **the derivative with respect to x.** The symbol may be written apart from the function, as in

$$\frac{d}{dx} f(x),$$

or it may appear as

$$\frac{df(x)}{dx}.$$

Using the Simple Power Rule we now can make simple one-part statements such as

$$\frac{d}{dx}x^3 = 3x^2; \quad \frac{d(x^4)}{dx} = 4x^3.$$

Next we state the rules that govern operations with derivatives. We give an example of each. We shall prove the first two rules and leave the third one for the reader to prove in the coming problem set.

1. If k is any constant, $\frac{d}{dx}(k) = 0.$

   That is, **the derivative of any constant is 0.** Thus if we have

   $$f(x) = 10, \quad \frac{df(x)}{dx} = \frac{d}{dx}(10) = 0.$$

   Graphically this means simply that $f(x) = 10$, or $f(x) = k$, is a **horizontal straight line,** and the slope of a horizontal line is 0.

   Proof: a) If $f(x) = k$, meaning $f(x)$ is the same no matter what the value of x is, then $f(x + h) = k.$

   b) $\frac{f(x + h) - f(x)}{h} = \frac{k - k}{h} = 0.$

   c) $f'(x) = \lim_{h \to 0}(0) = 0$ because the limit of a constant is the constant.

   > The derivative of any constant is 0; that is,
   >
   > $$\frac{d}{dx}(k) = 0.$$

2. If k is any constant, $\frac{d}{dx}[kf(x)] = k\frac{df(x)}{dx} = kf'(x).$

   That is, a constant (multiplier) may be factored out of the derivative or, we may say, a constant factor may be placed inside or outside of the derivative symbol.

   > A constant may be factored out of a derivative; that is,
   >
   > $$\frac{d}{dx}[k\,f(x)]$$
   >
   > $$= k \cdot \frac{d}{dx}[f(x)].$$

   Examples

   $$\frac{d}{dx}(2x) = 2\frac{d}{dx}(x) = 2(1) = 2.$$

   $$\frac{d}{dx}(3x) = 3\frac{d}{dx}(x) = 3.$$

   $$\frac{d}{dx}(3x^2) = 3\frac{d}{dx}(x^2) = 3(2x) = 6x.$$

> The derivative of a coefficient times x raised to a power is the coefficient times the power times x raised to the power minus 1; that is,
>
> $$\frac{d}{dx}(kx^n) = (k \cdot n)x^{n-1}.$$

This last example illustrates a useful extension of the Simple Power Rule:

$$\frac{d}{dx}(kx^n) = (k \cdot n)x^{n-1}.$$

Proof: Let $g(x) = kf(x)$ and apply steps a, b, and c of the preceding to $g(x)$.

a) $g(x + h) = kf(x + h)$.

b) $\dfrac{g(x + h) - g(x)}{h} = \dfrac{kf(x + h) - kf(x)}{h}$

$= \dfrac{k[f(x + h) - f(x)]}{h}.$

c) $\lim\limits_{h \to 0} \dfrac{g(x + h) - g(x)}{h} = \lim\limits_{h \to 0} \dfrac{k[f(x + h) - f(x)]}{h}$

$= k \lim\limits_{h \to 0} \dfrac{f(x + h) - f(x)}{h}$

$= kf'(x),$

which is rule number 2. Note in the next to the last step that we applied the limit theorem that states that a constant factor may be placed inside or outside of the limit symbol.

> The derivative may be taken term by term; that is,
>
> $$\frac{d}{dx}[f(x) \pm g(x)]$$
> $$= \frac{d}{dx}f(x) \pm \frac{d}{dx}g(x).$$

3. $\dfrac{d}{dx}[f(x) \pm g(x)] = \dfrac{df(x)}{dx} \pm \dfrac{dg(x)}{dx}.$

That is, **the derivative of an expression may be taken term by term.** This follows from the limit theorem which says the limit may be taken term by term. (See the last problem in Section 7.14.)

Example

$$\frac{d}{dx}(5x^4 + 3x^2 + 2x + 7)$$

$$= \frac{d}{dx}(5x^4) + \frac{d}{dx}(3x^2) + \frac{d}{dx}(2x) + \frac{d}{dx}(7)$$

$$= 20x^3 + 6x + 2.$$

Summary of Rules

1. The derivative of a constant is 0.
2. The derivative of a constant times a function equals the constant times the derivative of the function.
3. The derivative of an expression may be taken term by term.

Because the point seems unclear to some students, we call special attention to the fact that

$$f(x) = kx \text{ is } f(x) = kx^1.$$

By the Simple Power Rule,

$$\frac{df(x)}{dx} = k(1)x^{1-1} = kx^0 = k.$$

(Of course, $y = kx$ is a straight line with slope equal to k.)

For example,

$$\frac{d}{dx}\left(\frac{x}{3}\right) = \frac{1}{3}, \quad \frac{d}{dx}(5x) = 5, \quad \frac{d}{dx}(0.2x) = 0.2, \quad \text{and} \quad \frac{d}{dx}(-2x) = -2.$$

Note also that in

$$\frac{d}{dx}(3x^2 + ax - b),$$

the derivative is with respect to x. This means that **other letters are treated as constants** because x is the independent variable. Thus

$$\frac{d}{dx}(3x^2 + ax - b) = 6x + a.$$

Similarly

$$\frac{d}{dq}(3q^2 - pq + 4r) = 6q - p.$$

Exercise. Find a) $\dfrac{d}{dx}(2x^{3/2} - 4x^3 + 5x - 10)$. b) $\dfrac{d}{dp}(2q^3 - 4p^2q^2 + 3p)$.

Answer: a) $3x^{1/2} - 12x^2 + 5$. b) $-8pq^2 + 3$.

Suppose the total cost, in dollars, of producing g gallons of olive oil can be represented on the interval $0 \le g \le 150$ by the cost function

$$C(g) = 0.1g^2 + 2g + 30.$$

This function is sketched as the vertical parabola in Figure 7–16. In Chapter 1 and earlier in this chapter we determined the marginal cost of, say, the 51st gallon as

$$C(51) - C(50);$$

that is, the additional cost incurred when the 51st gallon is produced. In Figure 7–16 this will be the slope of the secant line joining the points where $g = 50$

= Parabolic Cost Functions: Marginal Cost

FIGURE 7-16
(not to scale)

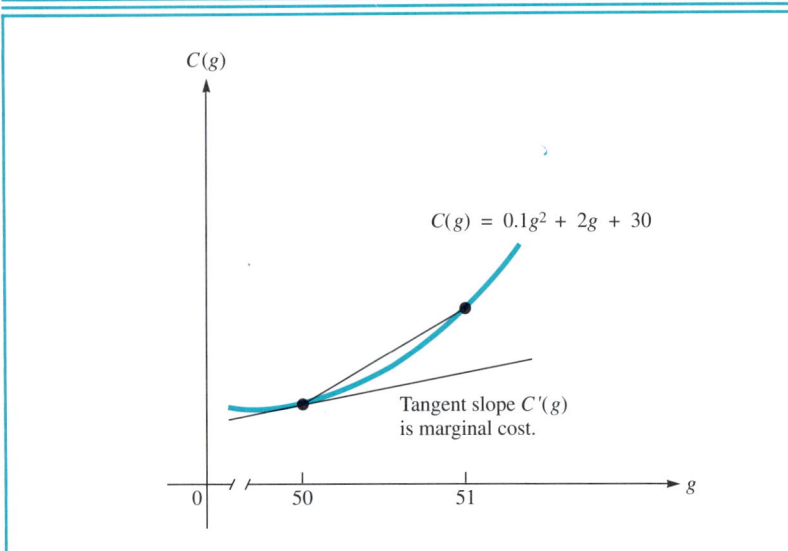

> Since units may lead to confusion, we define the marginal cost at a point to be the derivative of the cost function; that is, if $C(g)$ is the total cost function,
>
> Marginal cost = $C'(g)$.

and $g = 51$. However we should realize that a gallon is an arbitrary unit and we can as easily deal with quarts, in which case the interval from 50 to 51 gallons becomes 200 to 204 quarts. Now we can compute the marginal cost of the 201st, 202nd, 203rd, and 204th quarts. These again will be secant slopes, all of which will be different because our cost function curves, and all of which will be different from the marginal cost of the 51st gallon, $C(51) - C(50)$. Again, quarts are an arbitrary unit, and we could think in terms of pints, in which case each of the 8 pints in the 51st gallon would have a different marginal cost. The way out of the confusion caused by the fact that measuring units is arbitrary is to **define marginal cost at a point; that is, to use the slope of the tangent line, $C'(g)$, as marginal cost.**

Definition. If $C(x)$ is the total cost of producing x units of a product, $C'(x)$ is the point marginal cost.

Hereafter in this text, **marginal cost will mean point marginal cost.**

Example. If $C(g) = 0.1g^2 + 2g + 30$, find the marginal cost at 50 and 51 gallons of output.

Using the Simple Power Rule, the derivative is $C'(g) = 0.2g + 2$, so

Marginal cost $= C'(g) = 0.2g + 2$.
$C'(50) = 0.2(50) + 2 = \$12$ per gallon.
$C'(51) = 0.2(51) + 2 = \$12.20$ per gallon.

FROM THEORY TO PRACTICE
Instantaneous Velocity

Much of your previous work in mathematics concerned **static** situations. With the calculus, you will start to handle **dynamic** situations. Whereas before you were asked to find the area of a rectangle with fixed dimensions (say, 25 feet by 40 feet), you will soon be able to find the dimensions of the **rectangle of greatest area** that has a perimeter of 130 feet.

The first question to ask about a dynamic situation is just what is changing. Change is always measured relative to some known quantity. For example, what does a speed of 60 miles per hour (mph) mean? Suppose you made a trip of 120 miles in two hours. Then your **average speed** was 60 mph. To accomplish this, you did not have to travel 60 mph for the entire two hours. In fact, your **instantaneous velocity** most likely vacillated between speeds greater than and less than 60 mph. It is interesting to note that at **some instant** in the two-hour period you must have been traveling **exactly** 60 mph. For if you had traveled the entire time at speeds less than 60 mph, you would not have gone 120 miles; and if you had traveled only at speeds greater than 60 mph, you would have arrived too early. Thus some time during the trip you must have accelerated from a speed below 60 mph to a speed above, or vice versa. This fact follows from a famous theorem in calculus known as the **Intermediate Value Theorem**.

Physicists and engineers use the calculus and theorems such as the Intermediate Value Theorem regularly in designing vehicles and complex machinery. The derivative plays an important role in understanding any motion. If you have a mathematical expression describing the position of an object as a function of time, then it is a well-known result of the calculus that the **derivative of this expression describes the instantaneous velocity of the object.** In fact, the **derivative of the derivative then describes the instantaneous acceleration.**

Have you ever traveled on a turnpike where the tolls are printed on a ticket? Did you wonder why the time is also stamped on the ticket? If you travel between two exits 120 miles apart and arrive in 1 1/2 hours, your average speed must have been 80 mph. By the Intermediate Value Theorem, a state trooper at the second exit can give a ticket for exceeding the speed limit. Calculus techniques are also used in the fundamental theory behind modern radar guns which shoot a microwave or infrared beam at your car and measure the time it takes for the beam to return to the gun.

Only with mathematical tools such as those just described could scientists have designed automobiles that travel 200 mph, airplanes that fly 1,000 mph, and space vehicles capable of landing on the moon.

> **Exercise.** If the total cost of producing p pounds of pepper is $C(p) = 0.0015p^3 - 0.9p^2 + 200p + 60,000$, compute the marginal cost at outputs of a) 100 pounds. b) 200 pounds. c) 300 pounds.
> **Answer:** a) $65 per pound. b) $20 per pound. c) $65 per pound.

7.14 PROBLEM SET 7-5

In Problems 1 through 18, find $f'(x)$. Do not leave negative exponents in answers.

1. $f(x) = 2 + k$.
2. $f(x) = x$.
3. $f(x) = x/2$.
4. $f(x) = 2x + 3$.
5. $f(x) = x/3 + 4$.
6. $f(x) = 2/3 - 3(x/2)$.
7. $f(x) = 3x^2 + 2x - 5$.
8. $f(x) = x^3/3 - x^2/2 + x + 12$.
9. $f(x) = 0.01x^2 + 2x + 100$.
10. $f(x) = 0.5x^3 - x^2/2 + 7$.
11. $f(x) = mx + b$.
12. $f(x) = ax^2 + bx + c$.
13. $f(x) = 2/x - 1/x^2$.
14. $f(x) = 1/(2x) + 1/x^3$.
15. $f(x) = 2x^{3/2} - 4x^{1/2} + 3x^{2/3} + 2x - 7$.
16. $f(x) = 2x^{1/3} + x^{4/3} + 5x^{1.2} + x - 1$.
17. $f(x) = 1/(3x) + 2/x^{1/2}$.
18. $f(x) = 3/x^{1/3} - 12/x^{1/4}$.

Find each of the following:

19. $\dfrac{d}{dx}(3x^2 - 2x + 5)$.
20. $\dfrac{d}{dy}(10y^2 - 4x + 7)$.
21. $\dfrac{d}{dz}(az + b)$.
22. $\dfrac{d}{dx}(3pw^2 - 2p^3)$.
23. $\dfrac{d}{dh}(kh^2 - ah^{1/3} + 5ak)$.
24. $\dfrac{d}{dm}\left(\dfrac{a}{m} - 3m^2 + 5a^3\right)$.

Find the slope of the tangent to each of the following curves at the indicated value of x:

25. $f(x) = 3; x = 1$.
26. $f(x) = -5; x = 4$.
27. $f(x) = 2x + 6; x = -0.5$.
28. $f(x) = 3 - 4x; x = -3$.
29. $f(x) = 3x^2 - 2x + 5; x = 0.5$.
30. $f(x) = 10x - 2x^2 + 3; x = 2.5$.
31. $f(x) = 3x + 12/x; x = 2$.
32. $f(x) = 12x^{1/2} - 3x; x = 9$.
33. $f(x) = 8x^{1/3} + x; x = 8$.
34. $f(x) = 1/x^2 - 1/x + x; x = 2$.

7.14 PROBLEM SET 7-5 (concluded)

In Problems 35 through 40, find the value of x for which the slope is 0.

35. $f(x) = 10 - 3x^2 + 3x$.
36. $f(x) = 0.2x^2 - 40x + 50$.
37. $f(x) = 3x^{1/3} - 4x; x > 0$.
38. $f(x) = 3x^{1/2} - 2x$.
39. $f(x) = x + 9/x; x > 0$.
40. $f(x) = 3x + 48/x; x > 0$.

41. If the total cost of producing y yards of Yardall is
$$C(y) = 0.001y^2 + 2y + 500,$$
find the marginal cost at outputs of
a) 1,000 yards.
b) 2,000 yards.

42. If the total cost of producing t tons of Tonal is
$$C(t) = 0.0005t^3 - 0.3t^2 + 100t + 30,000$$
compute marginal cost at outputs of
a) 100 tons.
b) 200 tons.
c) 300 tons.

43. Prove from the definition of derivatives and limit theorems that
$$\frac{d}{dx}[f(x) + g(x)] = f'(x) + g'(x).$$

7.15 THE DERIVATIVE OF $[f(x)]^n$

Now that we are familiar with the use of the Simple Power Rule,
$$\frac{d}{dx}(x^n) = nx^{n-1},$$
we wish to learn how to expand this rule to take the derivative of expressions such as
$$\frac{d}{dx}(2x - 7)^{10}$$
$$\frac{d}{dx}(3x^2 - 2x + 5)^{3/2}$$
where the base of the power is something other than simply x; that is, we want a rule for finding
$$\frac{d}{dx}[f(x)]^n.$$
The rule is easily learned and applied. We shall state it, give illustrations, and then show its source.

> The derivative of a function raised to a power is the power times the function raised to the power minus 1 times the derivative of the function (what's inside); that is
>
> $$\frac{d}{dx}[f(x)]^n = n[f(x)]^{n-1} \cdot f'(x).$$

Function Power Rule

$$\frac{d}{dx}[f(x)]^n = n[f(x)]^{n-1}\frac{df(x)}{dx}$$
$$= n[f(x)]^{n-1} f'(x).$$

Thus the new rule starts out as does the simple rule with the (power) times the (function to the power minus 1), then is completed by **multiplying by the derivative of the function** (often called **the derivative of what's inside the parentheses**).

Example. Find the derivative of $g(x) = (2x - 7)^{10}$.

Here we could expand $g(x)$ by raising $(2x - 7)$ to the 10th power and take the derivative of the result term by term using the Simple Power Rule—but this is almost unthinkable. By the Function Power Rule, we have

$$\frac{d}{dx}(2x - 7)^{10} = 10(2x - 7)^9 \frac{d}{dx}(2x - 7)$$
$$= 10(2x - 7)^9 (2)$$
$$= 20(2x - 7)^9.$$

Exercise. Find $h'(x)$ if $h(x) = (3x^2 + 5)^{100}$.
Answer: $600x(3x^2 + 5)^{99}$.

Example. Find $f'(x)$ if $f(x) = (3x^2 - 2x + 5)^{3/2}$.

We have

$$\frac{d}{dx}(3x^2 - 2x + 5)^{3/2} = \frac{3}{2}(3x^2 - 2x + 5)^{1/2}\frac{d}{dx}(3x^2 - 2x + 5)$$
$$= \frac{3}{2}(3x^2 - 2x + 5)^{1/2}(6x - 2)$$
$$= \frac{3}{2}(3x^2 - 2x + 5)^{1/2}(2)(3x - 1)$$
$$= 3(3x^2 - 2x + 5)^{1/2}(3x - 1).$$

> **Exercise.** Find $f'(x)$ if $f(x) = (2x^3 - 3x^2 - 10)^{4/3}$.
> **Answer:** $8(2x^3 - 3x^2 - 10)^{1/3}(x)(x - 1)$.

Example. Find $f'(x)$ if $f(x) = \dfrac{50}{0.2x + 5}$.

We first rewrite the function as an expression raised to a power:

$$f(x) = \frac{50}{0.2x + 5} = 50(0.2x + 5)^{-1}.$$

Then, using the Function Power Rule, we have

$$\begin{aligned} f'(x) &= -50(0.2x + 5)^{-2} \frac{d}{dx}(0.2x + 5) \\ &= -50(0.2x + 5)^{-2}(0.2) \\ &= -10(0.2x + 5)^{-2} \\ &= -\frac{10}{(0.2x + 5)^2}. \end{aligned}$$

Example. Find $f'(1)$ if $f(x) = 10x - \dfrac{54}{(5x^2 + 4)^{1/2}}$.

Changing to proper form, we have

$$\begin{aligned} f(x) &= 10x - 54(5x^2 + 4)^{-1/2} \\ f'(x) &= 10 + 27(5x^2 + 4)^{-3/2} \frac{d}{dx}(5x^2 + 4) \\ &= 10 + 27(5x^2 + 4)^{-3/2}(10x) \\ &= 10 + \frac{270x}{(5x^2 + 4)^{3/2}}. \end{aligned}$$

Then

$$\begin{aligned} f'(1) &= 10 + \frac{270 \cdot 1}{(5 \cdot 1^2 + 4)^{3/2}} = 10 + \frac{270}{9^{3/2}} \\ &= 10 + \frac{270}{27} = 20. \end{aligned}$$

Source of the Function Power Rule

This, like all derivative rules, starts with the limit definition of a derivative. For a function $g(x)$ this is

$$\frac{d}{dx} g(x) = g'(x) = \lim_{h \to 0} \frac{\Delta g}{h} = \lim_{h \to 0} \frac{g(x+h) - g(x)}{h}.$$

Here we shall use

$$[f(x)]^n \quad \text{as} \quad g(x)$$

so

$$\frac{d}{dx} [f(x)]^n = \lim_{h \to 0} \frac{\Delta f^n}{h}$$

where, as usual, f stands for $f(x)$.

Next we apply a device often used by mathematicians to change a form at hand into a different, but equivalent, form that is wanted. The device is to multiply and divide the given form by the **same** quantity, which, in this case, is Δf. Thus

$$\frac{\Delta f^n}{h} = \frac{\Delta f^n}{h} \left(\frac{\Delta f}{\Delta f}\right) = \frac{\Delta f^n}{\Delta f} \left(\frac{\Delta f}{h}\right),$$

where, at the right, the factors have been rearranged as permitted by the commutative property for multiplication. Then we take the limit as h approaches 0 to obtain the derivative:

$$\lim_{h \to 0} \frac{\Delta f^n}{h} = \lim_{h \to 0} \frac{\Delta f^n}{\Delta f} \left(\frac{\Delta f}{h}\right).$$

Limit Theorem 4 of Section 7.5 says the limit of a product is the product of the limits so

$$\lim_{h \to 0} \frac{\Delta f^n}{h} = \left[\lim_{h \to 0} \frac{\Delta f^n}{\Delta f}\right] \left[\lim_{h \to 0} \frac{\Delta f}{h}\right]. \tag{1}$$

We know that the term in the right-hand bracket of Equation (1) is $f'(x)$ since

$$\lim_{h \to 0} \frac{\Delta f}{h} = f'(x).$$

Using some more complicated algebra and limit techniques, we can show that the other term of Equation (1) is

$$\lim_{h \to 0} \frac{\Delta f^n}{\Delta f} = nf^{n-1}.$$

Hence we can rewrite Equation (1) as

$$\lim_{h \to 0} \frac{\Delta f^n}{h} = [nf^{n-1}] [f'(x)]. \tag{2}$$

Finally recalling that f stands for $f(x)$, Equation (2) becomes

$$\lim_{h \to 0} \frac{\Delta[f(x)]^n}{h} = n[f(x)]^{n-1} f'(x),$$

which is the Function Power Rule.

We pause now for a problem set.

7.16 PROBLEM SET 7-6

Find $f'(x)$. Simplify where possible. Leave no negative exponent in answers.

1. $f(x) = (6x - 5)^5$.
2. $f(x) = (2x + 6)^5$.
3. $f(x) = (2x)^3$.
4. $f(x) = (6x)^{1/3}$.
5. $f(x) = (4x)^{1/2}$.
6. $f(x) = (9x)^{4/3}$.
7. $f(x) = (8x - 3)^{3/2}$.
8. $f(x) = (12x - 9)^{5/3}$.
9. $f(x) = (3x^2 - 6x + 2)^{5/2}$.
10. $f(x) = (x^3 - 3x^2 + 6x)^{4/3}$.
11. $f(x) = (2x - 3)^{1/2}$.
12. $f(x) = (3x^2 + 5)^{2/3}$.
13. $f(x) = \dfrac{4}{2x - 3}$.
14. $f(x) = \dfrac{6}{3x - 5}$.
15. $f(x) = (1/x - 2)^2$.
16. $f(x) = (5 - 1/x^2)^3$.
17. $f(x) = \dfrac{9}{(3x - 5)^2}$.
18. $f(x) = \dfrac{12}{(2x + 10)^3}$.
19. $f(x) = 5x + \dfrac{10}{3x + 2}$.
20. $f(x) = 0.1x + \dfrac{5}{5 - 0.2x}$.
21. $f(x) = 3x + \dfrac{1}{(5 + 2x)^{1/2}}$.
22. $f(x) = \dfrac{1}{(3x - 7)^{1/2}} - 2x$.

23. Find $g'(2)$ if $g(x) = 10x + \dfrac{18}{(5 + 2x)^{1/2}}$.

24. Find $h'(3)$ if $h(x) = 7x + \dfrac{4}{(x^2 - 1)^{1/3}}$.

7.17 PRODUCT AND QUOTIENT RULES

We now extend our list of rules to include the derivative of the product of two functions and the quotient of two functions; that is, for example, to find

$$\frac{d}{dx}(x - 1)(x^2 + 2)^{4/3} \quad \text{and} \quad \frac{d}{dx}\left(\frac{2x^2 + 3}{x + 1}\right),$$

or, more generally,

$$\frac{d}{dx}[f(x)g(x)] \quad \text{and} \quad \frac{d}{dx}\left[\frac{f(x)}{g(x)}\right].$$

= **The Product Rule**

The derivative of the product of two functions is **not** the product of the two individual derivatives.

The natural inclination when asked to find the derivative of the product of two functions is to simply multiply the two individual derivatives together. A quick example will illustrate why this approach is **incorrect.** Consider

$$x^5 \cdot x^3 = x^8. \tag{1}$$

We know by the Simple Power Rule that the derivative of the right-hand side is $8x^7$. Now the product of the derivatives on the left-hand side of Equation (1) is

$$(5x^4) \cdot (3x^2) = 15x^6,$$

which is clearly different from the correct result, $8x^7$, given by the Simple Power Rule.

To find the proper rule for taking the derivative of the product of two functions, we start with the definition that the derivative is the limit of the difference quotient as $h \to 0$. For

$$f(x)g(x),$$

the difference quotient is

$$\frac{f(x+h)g(x+h) - f(x)g(x)}{h}. \tag{2}$$

Now

$$\Delta f = f(x+h) - f(x)$$

so

$$f(x+h) = f(x) + \Delta f.$$

For clarity we shall abbreviate the last expression as

$$f(x+h) = f + \Delta f.$$

Similarly

$$g(x+h) = g + \Delta g.$$

The difference quotient, Equation (2), then is

$$\frac{(f+\Delta f)(g+\Delta g) - fg}{h} = \frac{\cancel{fg} + f(\Delta g) + g(\Delta f) + (\Delta f)(\Delta g) - \cancel{fg}}{h}$$

$$= \frac{f(\Delta g) + g(\Delta f) + (\Delta f)(\Delta g)}{h}$$

$$= f\left(\frac{\Delta g}{h}\right) + g\left(\frac{\Delta f}{h}\right) + \Delta f\left(\frac{\Delta g}{h}\right).$$

The derivative is the limit of the last expression as h approaches 0, and the limit may be taken term by term. Thus

$$\frac{d}{dx}[f(x)g(x)] = \frac{d}{dx}[fg]$$

$$= \lim_{h \to 0} f\left(\frac{\Delta g}{h}\right) + \lim_{h \to 0} g\left(\frac{\Delta f}{h}\right) + \lim_{h \to 0} \Delta f\left(\frac{\Delta g}{h}\right). \quad (3)$$

Now f and g are to be thought of as function values (at a **given** point x) that do not vary as we approach the point by letting h approach 0, so f and g may be placed outside the limit symbols. And, of course, as h approaches 0, so also do Δf and Δg approach 0. Finally the limit of the product at the right end of Equation (3) is the product of the limits. Hence, Equation (3) may be written as

$$\frac{d}{dx}[fg] = f \lim_{h \to 0}\left(\frac{\Delta g}{h}\right) + g \lim_{h \to 0}\left(\frac{\Delta f}{h}\right) + \left[\lim_{\Delta f \to 0} \Delta f\right]\left[\lim_{h \to 0}\left(\frac{\Delta g}{h}\right)\right]. \quad (4)$$

Now, because

$$\lim_{h \to 0}\left(\frac{\Delta g}{h}\right) = g' = g'(x),$$

$$\lim_{h \to 0}\left(\frac{\Delta f}{h}\right) = f' = f'(x)$$

and

$$\left[\lim_{\Delta f \to 0} \Delta f\right]\left[\lim_{h \to 0}\left(\frac{\Delta g}{h}\right)\right] = 0(g') = 0.$$

Equation (4) becomes

$$\frac{d}{dx}[fg] = fg' + gf'.$$

Replacing the independent variable, we have

Product Rule

$$\frac{d}{dx}[f(x)g(x)] = f(x)g'(x) + g(x)f'(x).$$

The derivative of the product of two functions is the first times the derivative of the second, plus the second times the derivative of the first; that is,

$$\frac{d}{dx}[f \cdot g] = f \cdot g' + g \cdot f'.$$

In words, **the derivative of the product of two functions is the first times the derivative of the second, plus the second times the derivative of the first.**

PART III INTRODUCTION TO APPLIED CALCULUS AND UNCONSTRAINED OPTIMIZATION

To show that the Product Rule works, recall our simple example of $x^3 \cdot x^5$ which had a derivative of $8x^7$ by the Simple Power Rule. If we now think of

$$f(x) = x^3 \quad \text{as the first function}$$

and

$$g(x) = x^5 \quad \text{as the second function,}$$

then by the Product Rule

$$\frac{d}{dx}(x^3)(x^5) = x^3 \frac{d}{dx}(x^5) + x^5 \frac{d}{dx}(x^3)$$
$$= x^3(5x^4) + x^5(3x^2)$$
$$= 5x^7 + 3x^7$$
$$= 8x^7,$$

as it should be.

Exercise. a) By the Simple Power Rule, find

$$\frac{d}{dx}(2x + 1)(x - 1) = \frac{d}{dx}(2x^2 - x - 1).$$

b) Do (a) by the Product Rule.

Answer: a) $4x - 1$. b) $(2x + 1)(1) + (x - 1)(2) = 4x - 1$.

Example. Find

$$\frac{d}{dx}(x - 1)(x^3 + 2)^{4/3}.$$

Here the first function is $(x - 1)$ and the second is $(x^3 + 2)^{4/3}$.

$$\frac{d}{dx}(x - 1)(x^3 + 2)^{4/3} = (x - 1)\frac{d}{dx}(x^3 + 2)^{4/3} + (x^3 + 2)^{4/3} \frac{d}{dx}(x - 1)$$
$$= (x - 1)(4/3)(x^3 + 2)^{1/3}(3x^2)^* + (x^3 + 2)^{4/3}(1)$$
$$= 4x^2(x - 1)(x^3 + 2)^{1/3} + (x^3 + 2)^{4/3},$$

where * on the equation's second line calls attention to application of the Function Power Rule. The expression last written has $(x^3 + 2)^{1/3}$ as a common factor so it can be rewritten as

$$(x^3 + 2)^{1/3}[4x^2(x - 1) + (x^3 + 2)^1]$$
$$= (x^3 + 2)^{1/3}(4x^3 - 4x^2 + x^3 + 2)$$
$$= (x^3 + 2)^{1/3}(5x^3 - 4x^2 + 2).$$

Note that we wrote the expression $(x^3 + 2)^1$ with an exponent of 1 to emphasize the fact that when factoring out the common term $(x^3 + 2)^{1/3}$, we are left with a power of 1. The reason for this is that in taking the derivative of $(x^3 + 2)^{4/3}$, we reduced the power by 1.

Exercise. Find $\dfrac{d}{dx}(x^2 + 3)(2x + 5)^{3/2}$.

Answer: $3(x^2 + 3)(2x + 5)^{1/2} + 2x(2x + 5)^{3/2}$. Factoring this expression yields $(2x + 5)^{1/2}(7x^2 + 10x + 9)$.

The Quotient Rule

Since we know that the Product Rule does not allow us to find the derivative of the product of two functions simply by multiplying the two individual derivatives together, we would not expect the Quotient Rule to allow us simply to divide the derivatives. A quick example will again illustrate why this approach is **incorrect**. Consider

> The derivative of the quotient of two functions is not the quotient of the two individual derivatives.

$$\frac{x^5}{x^3} = x^2. \tag{5}$$

We know by the Simple Power Rule that the derivative of the right-hand side of Equation (5) is

$$2x. \tag{6}$$

Now the quotient of the derivatives on the left-hand side of Equation (5) is

$$\frac{5x^4}{3x^2} = \frac{5}{3}x^2$$

which is clearly different from the correct result given by Equation (6).

To find the proper rule for taking the derivative of the quotient of two functions, we need not use the difference-quotient definition. Rather, the quotient rule can be derived easily from the Product Rule if we remember that by the Function Power Rule

> The Quotient Rule can be easily derived from the Product Rule.

$$\frac{d}{dx}\left[\frac{1}{g(x)}\right] = \frac{d}{dx}[g(x)]^{-1} = -1[g(x)]^{-2}\, g'(x).$$

We start by changing the quotient to a product, and then apply the Product Rule.

$$\frac{d}{dx}\left[\frac{f(x)}{g(x)}\right] = \frac{d}{dx}(f(x)[g(x)]^{-1})$$

$$= f(x)\frac{d}{dx}[g(x)]^{-1} + [g(x)]^{-1}\frac{d}{dx}f(x)$$

$$= f(x)(-1)[g(x)]^{-2} g'(x) + [g(x)]^{-1} f'(x)$$
$$= \frac{-f(x)g'(x)}{[g(x)]^2} + \frac{f'(x)}{g(x)}$$
$$= \frac{-f(x)g'(x)}{[g(x)]^2} + \frac{f'(x)}{g(x)} \left[\frac{g(x)}{g(x)}\right]$$
$$= \frac{-f(x)g'(x) + f'(x)g(x)}{[g(x)]^2},$$

where in the next to the last step we multiplied the rightmost term by $g(x)/g(x)$ to obtain a common denominator. Rearranging the last expression, we have

> The derivative of the quotient of two functions is the denominator times the derivative of the numerator, minus the numerator times the derivative of the denominator, all over the denominator squared; that is,
>
> $$\frac{d}{dx}\left[\frac{f}{g}\right] = \frac{g \cdot f' - f \cdot g'}{g^2}.$$

Quotient Rule

$$\frac{d}{dx}\left[\frac{f(x)}{g(x)}\right] = \frac{g(x)f'(x) - f(x)g'(x)}{[g(x)]^2}.$$

In words, **the derivative of a quotient is the denominator times the derivative of the numerator, minus the numerator times the derivative of the denominator, all over the denominator squared.**

To show that the Quotient Rule works, recall our simple example of

$$\frac{x^5}{x^3} = x^2$$

which had a derivative of $2x$. Now by the Quotient Rule,

$$\frac{d}{dx}\frac{x^5}{x^3} = \frac{(x^3)(5x^4) - (x^5)(3x^2)}{(x^3)^2}$$
$$= \frac{5x^7 - 3x^7}{x^6} = \frac{2x^7}{x^6}$$
$$= 2x,$$

as it should be.

As another example,

$$\frac{d}{dx}\left(\frac{2x + 5}{3x - 7}\right) = \frac{(3x - 7)(2) - (2x + 5)(3)}{(3x - 7)^2}$$
$$= \frac{6x - 14 - (6x + 15)}{(3x - 7)^2}$$
$$= -\frac{29}{(3x - 7)^2}.$$

Exercise. Find $\dfrac{d}{dx}\left(\dfrac{5x}{3-4x}\right)$.

Answer: $\dfrac{15}{(3-4x)^2}$.

Example. Find the derivative of $x^2/(3x+2)^{1/2}$.

We have

$$\dfrac{d}{dx}\left[\dfrac{x^2}{(3x+2)^{1/2}}\right] = \dfrac{(3x+2)^{1/2}(2x) - x^2(1/2)(3x+2)^{-1/2}(3)}{[(3x+2)^{1/2}]^2}$$

$$= \dfrac{(3x+2)^{1/2}(2x) - \dfrac{3x^2(3x+2)^{-1/2}}{2}}{3x+2}.$$

To remove the divisor, 2, and the negative exponent in the numerator, we multiply the numerator and denominator by

$$2(3x+2)^{1/2}$$

as follows:

$$\left[\dfrac{(3x+2)^{1/2}(2x) - \dfrac{3x^2(3x+2)^{-1/2}}{2}}{3x+2}\right]\left[\dfrac{2(3x+2)^{1/2}}{2(3x+2)^{1/2}}\right]$$

$$= \dfrac{4x(3x+2) - 3x^2}{2(3x+2)^{3/2}} = \dfrac{9x^2 + 8x}{2(3x+2)^{3/2}} = \dfrac{x(9x+8)}{2(3x+2)^{3/2}}.$$

Exercise. Find the derivative of

$$\dfrac{x^3}{(2x+3)^{1/3}}.$$

Answer: $\dfrac{(2x+3)^{1/3}(3x^2) - \dfrac{2x^3(2x+3)^{-2/3}}{3}}{(2x+3)^{2/3}} = \dfrac{x^2(16x+27)}{3(2x+3)^{4/3}}$.

It may help to refer to the preceding examples and exercises when working on the next set of problems.

7.18 PROBLEM SET 7-7

Find the first derivative of each of the following. Simplify results and factor where possible. Do not leave negative exponents or complex fractions (fractions containing fractions) in answers.

1. $f(x) = (3x - 2)(2x + 5)$.
2. $f(x) = (7x + 3)(4 - 3x)$.
3. $f(x) = (x^2 + 2)(3x - 5)$.
4. $f(x) = (3 - x^2)(5x + 6)$.
5. $f(x) = x(x - 1)^4$.
6. $f(x) = x^2(x + 5)^3$.
7. $f(x) = x^2(x + 3)^{3/2}$.
8. $f(x) = x^3(6x - 1)^{2/3}$.
9. $f(x) = 2x(3x^2 + 7)^{1/3}$.
10. $f(x) = 3x(2x^3 + 5)^{1/2}$.
11. $f(x) = \dfrac{x}{x - 1}$.
12. $f(x) = \dfrac{x - 2}{x + 1}$.
13. $f(x) = \dfrac{x^2}{2x + 3}$.
14. $f(x) = \dfrac{x^3}{3x + 5}$.
15. $f(x) = \dfrac{x}{3 + 2x^2}$.
16. $f(x) = \dfrac{3x}{1 - 2x^2}$.
17. $f(x) = \dfrac{x}{(3x + 2)^{1/2}}$.
18. $f(x) = \dfrac{2x}{(2x + 3)^{1/2}}$.
19. $f(x) = \dfrac{2x + 1}{(x^2 + 5)^{1/3}}$.
20. $f(x) = \dfrac{3 - 5x}{(x^3 + 2)^{1/3}}$.

7.19 REVIEW PROBLEMS

1. If $f(x) = 3x^2 + 2x + 5$, find the value of, or the algebraic expression for
   a) $f(0)$.
   b) $f(1)$.
   c) $f(-1)$.
   d) $f(5)$.
   e) $f(2a)$.
   f) $f\left(\dfrac{1}{x + 1}\right)$.
   g) $f(x + 1) - f(x)$.
   h) $f(x) - f(x - a)$.

2. a) If $f(x) = 2xy$, write the expression for $[f(a)]^2$.
   b) If $g(y) = 2xy$, write the expression for $g(a - 1)$.

3. If $f(x) = 32x^{-1} - 2x^{-2/3} + 24x^{-1/2}$, find $f(64)$.

4. If $f(x) = 3x^2 - 2x + 4$,
   a) Write the expression for Δf.
   b) Compute Δf if x changes from 2 by the amount 0.1.

5. The total cost of making p pounds of pepper is $C(p)$ dollars where
   $$C(p) = 50 + 1.5p + 0.02p^2.$$
   a) Write the expression for the marginal cost of the pth pound.
   b) Find the marginal cost of the 5th pound.
   c) Find the marginal cost of the 40th pound.

Find each of the following, if it exists:

6. $\lim\limits_{x \to 0} (3x^2 - 2x + 5)$.

7. $\lim\limits_{b \to a} (a^3 + 3a^2b + 3ab^2 + b^3)$.

7.19 REVIEW PROBLEMS (continued)

8. $\lim_{x \to 1} \dfrac{x^2 + 1}{x - 1}$.

9. $\lim_{x \to 4} \dfrac{3x}{0.5x - 2}$.

10. $\lim_{x \to 8} 2x^{-2/3}$.

11. $\lim_{x \to 0} \dfrac{x^{3/2}}{x}$.

12. $\lim_{a \to b} (a^2 + 2ab + b^2)$.

13. $\lim_{x \to 1.25} \dfrac{16x^2 - 25}{4x - 5}$.

14. $\lim_{x \to 0} \dfrac{x}{x^{1/3}}$.

15. $\lim_{h \to 0} \dfrac{h(x - 1)}{h}$.

16. $\lim_{x \to 0} \left(8 + \dfrac{x^2}{x} \right)^{1/3}$.

Apply the delta definition to find the derivatives for Problems 17 through 21.

17. $f(x) = 2x^2 + 3$.
18. $f(x) = x^2 + 3x - 2$.
19. $f(x) = \dfrac{1}{1 - x}$.
20. $f(x) = \dfrac{2}{3x - 5}$.
21. $f(x) = x^{1/2}$. [Hint: After the difference quotient has been set up, multiply its numerator and denominator by $(x + h)^{1/2} + x^{1/2}$ and proceed.]

---

22. Find the derivative by the delta limit definition. Then find the slope of the curve at the point where $x = 2$ if $f(x) = x^2 - 5x$.

23. Find the derivative by the delta limit definition. Then find the slope of the curve at the point where $x = 2$ if $f(x) = 12/x$.

In Problems 24 through 34, find $f'(x)$. Do not leave negative exponents in answers.

24. $f(x) = 2x - 3$.
25. $f(x) = 5 - 4x$.
26. $f(x) = 1.5x^2 - 2x^3 - 4x + 5$.
27. $f(x) = 0.25x^4 - 2.5x^2 + x - 6$.
28. $f(x) = ax^3 - bx + 1$.
29. $f(x) = xy - ax^2$.
30. $f(x) = 3/(2x^2) - 5/x$.
31. $f(x) = 1/(3x)^2 - 1/x$.
32. $f(x) = 3x^{1/2} + 2x^{1/3} + 1$.
33. $f(x) = 6x^{4/3} - 3x^{2/3} - 2x + 6$.
34. $f(x) = x^{-1/2} - x^{-1/3} + 4x - 25$.

Find each of the following:

35. $\dfrac{d}{dx}(ax^3 - bx^2 + cx - d)$.

36. $\dfrac{d}{dy}(xy^2 - 2y + 3x^2y - 2x + 3)$.

Find the slope of the line tangent to each curve at the indicated value of x.

37. $f(x) = 2 - 0.5x$; $x = 2$.
38. $f(x) = x^3/6 - 18/x + 2x - 1$; $x = 2$.
39. $f(x) = 18x^{1/3}$; $x = 8$.
40. $f(x) = x + 12/x^{1/2}$; $x = 4$.

7.19 REVIEW PROBLEMS (concluded)

Find the value(s) of x for which the slope is 0 for the following:

41. $f(x) = 0.25x^2 - x + 4$.
42. $f(x) = 2x + 72/x$.
43. $f(x) = 4x^3 - 3x^2$.
44. $f(x) = x^3 - 12x$.
45. $f(x) = x - 3x^{1/2}$.
46. $f(x) = 0.1x + 12.8/x^{1/2}$.

In Problems 47 through 53, find $f'(x)$. Simplify where possible. Leave no negative exponents in answers.

47. $f(x) = (3x - 2)^{15}$.
48. $f(x) = (2x^3 + 3x^2 + 4x - 50)^{3/2}$.
49. $f(x) = (x^3 - 3x^2 + 5)^{1/3}$.
50. $f(x) = (10x)^{1/2}$.
51. $f(x) = \dfrac{1}{4(8x - 6)}$.
52. $f(x) = \dfrac{2}{27(10 - 3x)^{3/2}}$.
53. $f(x) = x - \dfrac{1}{(5 - 0.3x)^{1/3}}$.

54. Find the slope of the curve at the point where $x = 1$ for
$$f(x) = \left(5 + \frac{3}{x}\right)^{1/3}.$$

55. Find the value of x at the points on the curve where the tangent line is horizontal for
$$f(x) = x + \frac{50}{2 + 0.5x}.$$

Find the first derivative for Problems 56 through 61. Simplify results where possible. Do not leave negative exponents or complex fractions (fractions containing fractions) in answers.

56. $f(x) = x(2x - 1)^6$.
57. $f(x) = 2x(x^3 - 5x)^{1/2}$.
58. $f(x) = (2x + 1)(4x - 5)^{1/2}$.
59. $f(x) = \dfrac{3x + 2}{2 - 3x}$.
60. $f(x) = \dfrac{x}{1 - 0.5x^2}$.
61. $f(x) = \dfrac{2x - 1}{(2x + 3)^{1/2}}$.

7.20 EXTENDED REVIEW PROBLEMS

1. Leaving no negative exponents, find $f'(x)$ if
$$f(x) = \frac{12}{x^{2/3}} - \frac{16}{x^{3/4}} + x.$$

2. Leaving no negative exponents, find $f'(x)$ if
$$f(x) = 2x^2(3x^2 + 5)^{1/2}.$$

3. Find the slope of the line tangent to
$$f(x) = \frac{x^2}{9} - \frac{5}{x^{1/3}}$$
at $x = 27$.

7.20 EXTENDED REVIEW PROBLEMS (concluded)

4. Find the expression for Δf if
   a) $f(x) = 7 - 2x$.   b) $f(x) = x^2 + 3x - 6$.

5. The total cost of making v vats of milk is $C(v)$ dollars where
   $$C(v) = 4.5v^3 + 3.2v^2 - 0.8v - 5.9.$$
   a) Write the expression for the marginal cost of the vth vat.
   b) What is the marginal cost of the 33rd vat?
   c) What is the marginal cost of the 65th vat?

6. Find the value(s) of x for which the slope is 0 for
   $$f(x) = 4.5x^2 + \frac{10}{x^{1/5}}.$$

7. Find the following limit, if it exists:
   $$\lim_{a \to 0} \frac{\frac{1}{(x+a)^2} - \frac{1}{x^2}}{a}; \quad x \neq 0.$$

8. Using the three-step delta method, find the derivative of
   $$f(x) = x^{3/2}.$$

9. Leaving no negative exponents, find $f'(x)$ if
   $$f(x) = \frac{3x + 2}{(6x^2 + 5)^{1/3}}.$$

10. Leaving no negative exponents, find $f'(x)$ if
    $$f(x) = \left(5 - \frac{2}{x}\right)^3.$$

8 CHAPTER
APPLICATIONS OF DIFFERENTIAL CALCULUS

8.1 INTRODUCTION

In this chapter we will show how to apply the techniques of differential calculus to solve optimization problems and sketch curves. We will begin by illustrating maxima and minima of simple polynomial functions and develop the concept of critical points along with the first derivative test. Next we will use concavity to introduce the second derivative test and illustrate how to use this test in many different applications. Lastly we will give a detailed presentation of curve sketching including both polynomial and rational functions.

8.2 MAXIMA AND MINIMA OF FUNCTIONS: THE FIRST DERIVATIVE TEST

One of the most useful applications of calculus in management and economics is finding the maximum and minimum values for a function. To find these **optimum values,** we need to develop a keener sense of the behavior of the graph of a function. This section is intended to help us develop that sense.

> In interval notation, a bracket is used to include an endpoint, whereas a parenthesis is used to exclude an endpoint.

Consider the graph of the function $f(x)$ shown in Figure 8–1. First we note that $f(x)$ is defined only on the interval $[a, \infty)$. When we use the brackets [and] to enclose an interval, we indicate that the endpoint of the interval next to the bracket is included in the interval. The parentheses (and) mean that the interval contains all points except the endpoints next to the parentheses. Certainly no interval can contain ∞ so when ∞ or $-\infty$ appears in place of a finite endpoint we always use a parenthesis.

> **Exercise.** What points are indicated by the following intervals? a) $[-2, 5]$. b) $(-2, 5]$. c) $[-2, 5)$. d) $(-2, 5)$.
> **Answer:** a) All points between -2 and 5, inclusively. b) All points between -2 and 5, including 5 but excluding -2. c) All points between -2 and 5, including -2 but excluding 5. d) All points between -2 and 5, excluding -2 and 5.

Returning to Figure 8–1, where are the maxima and minima of our function $f(x)$? If you look carefully at the graph you will see three optima: one at a (an

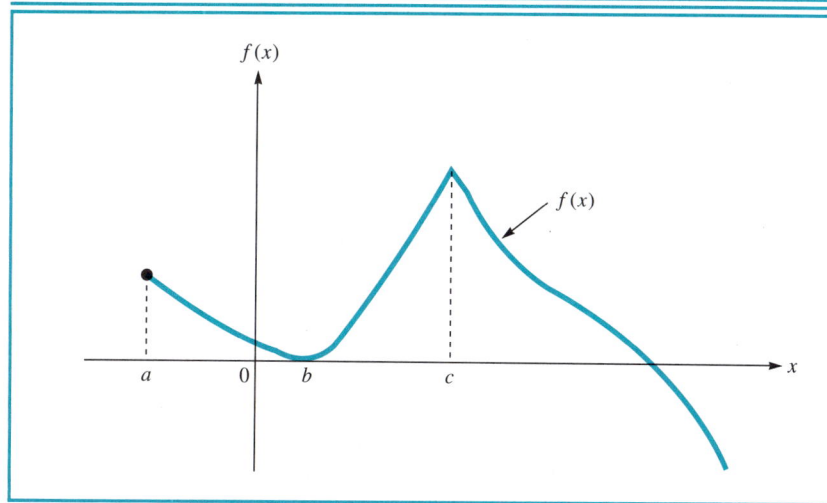

FIGURE 8-1

endpoint maximum), one at b (a **local minimum**), and one at c (a **local and global or absolute maximum**). You probably already have gleaned that a local maximum or minimum point p is a point where $f(x)$ takes on a maximum or minimum value for all points in the **immediate vicinity** of p. An absolute (or global) maximum for $f(x)$ would be the largest value of $f(x)$ over all values of $f(x)$. Notice that the function in Figure 8-1 has no absolute minimum. We shall now show how to test whether a point is a maximum or minimum (or neither) for most functions. We lead up to the tests by discussing **critical points** and **increasing and decreasing properties**.

Critical points are those points that are **candidates** for maximum and minimum values. There are three kinds of critical points: **stationary points, cusps,** and **endpoints**.

In Figure 8-1 $f(x)$ has a stationary point at $x = b$ (a local minimum), a cusp at $x = c$ (the absolute maximum), and an endpoint at $x = a$ (an endpoint maximum). A cusp occurs at a point where the function is defined, but the derivative is not defined. Since we will not encounter any functions with cusps in this textbook, we now limit our analysis to stationary points and endpoints.

> A local maximum (minimum) at a point is the largest (smallest) value of the function in the immediate vicinity of that point; an absolute maximum (minimum) is the largest (smallest) value of the function over all values for which the function is defined.

The slope of a line tangent to a curve at a point is, by definition, the value of the first derivative at that point. Hence when the first derivative is 0, the tangent line is horizontal. Points where this occurs are called **stationary points**.

= **Stationary Points**

Definition. A stationary point on $f(x)$ is a point where $f'(x) = 0$.

> A stationary point occurs when the first derivative is 0; that is, $f'(x) = 0$.

Figure 8–2 shows the graph of
$$f(x) = x^3 - 6x^2 + 37.$$
To find the stationary points, we start with the first derivative,
$$f'(x) = 3x^2 - 12x,$$
and then set it equal to 0:
$$f'(x) = 0 \text{ when } 3x^2 - 12x = 0$$
$$x(3x - 12) = 0.$$
The values of x are determined by setting each factor of the last expression equal to 0. Thus
$$x = 0; \quad 3x - 12 = 0$$
$$3x = 12$$
$$x = 4.$$
The function values for $x = 0$ and $x = 4$ are
$$f(0) = 0^3 - 6(0)^2 + 37 = 37 \quad \text{and}$$
$$f(4) = 4^3 - 6(4)^2 + 37 = 5,$$
and the stationary points $P(0, 37)$ and $Q(4, 5)$ are shown in Figure 8–2. P is a **local maximum** but not an absolute maximum because it is the highest point in its neighborhood, but not the highest point on the curve. Similarly Q is a **local minimum**. By way of contrast, the stationary point on a vertical parabola is the highest

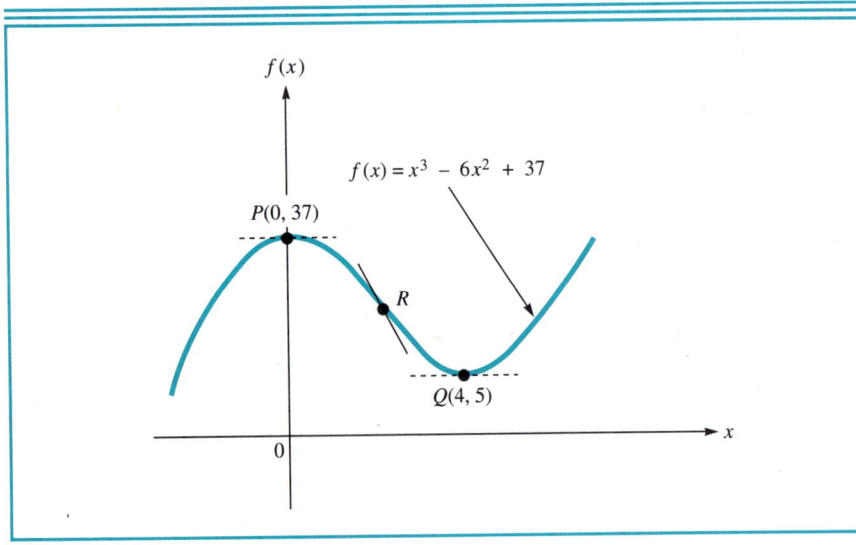

FIGURE 8–2
(not to scale)

or lowest point on the entire curve so it is an absolute as well as a local maximum or minimum.

> **Exercise.** Find the stationary points for
> $$f(x) = 2x^2 + 8x - 7.$$
> Then use the graph to determine what these points represent.
>
> **Answer:** There is only one stationary point, $(-2, -15)$, that is a local and absolute minimum.

In the preceding example and exercise, we were able to determine that a stationary point is a maximum or minimum by referring to the graphs of the functions. How can we determine what a stationary point represents analytically? Inspection of Figure 8–2 will help us answer this question. We can see that just to the left of the local maximum $P(0, 37)$ the function is **increasing**, at $P(0, 37)$ the function is **stationary**, and just to the right of $P(0, 37)$ the function is **decreasing**. On the other hand, just to the left of the local minimum $Q(4, 5)$ the function is **decreasing**, at $Q(4, 5)$ the function is **stationary**, and just to the right of $Q(4, 5)$ the function is **increasing**. So if we had a way of determining when a function is increasing or decreasing, we could identify whether a stationary point represented a local maximum or a local minimum. This determination can be made using the following:

1. A function $f(x)$ is **increasing** if $f'(x) > 0$.
2. A function $f(x)$ is **decreasing** if $f'(x) < 0$.

> At a local maximum, the function is increasing just to the left and decreasing just to the right; at a local minimum, the function is decreasing just to the left and increasing just to the right.

To better understand why these statements are true, consider the graphs in Figures 8–3A and 8–3B. If $f'(x) > 0$, then the slope of the tangent line must be positive as shown in the three graphs in Figure 8–3A. In all three cases the function is increasing as we proceed from left to right. Note that strictly speaking the function is not increasing at a specific point but in an **interval**, since the concept of increasing requires you to compare at least two points. In other words, if we have two points, x_1 and x_2, with $x_1 < x_2$ so that x_1 is to the left of x_2, then "$f(x)$ is increasing" means $f(x_1) < f(x_2)$ or $f(x_1)$ is below $f(x_2)$. (Verify this in Figure 8–3A.) In a similar manner if $f'(x) < 0$, the slope of the tangent line must be negative as shown in the three graphs in Figure 8–3B. In these three cases the function is decreasing as we proceed from left to right. Here for two points, x_1 and x_2, with $x_1 < x_2$ so that x_1 is to the left of x_2, "$f(x)$ is decreasing" means $f(x_1) > f(x_2)$ or $f(x_1)$ is above $f(x_2)$. (Verify this in Figure 8–3B.)

Suppose we apply the preceding analysis to our earlier example where

$$f(x) = x^3 - 6x^2 + 37$$

gave rise to a local maximum at $P(0, 37)$ and a local minimum at $Q(4, 5)$ as shown

FIGURE 8-3A

FIGURE 8-3B

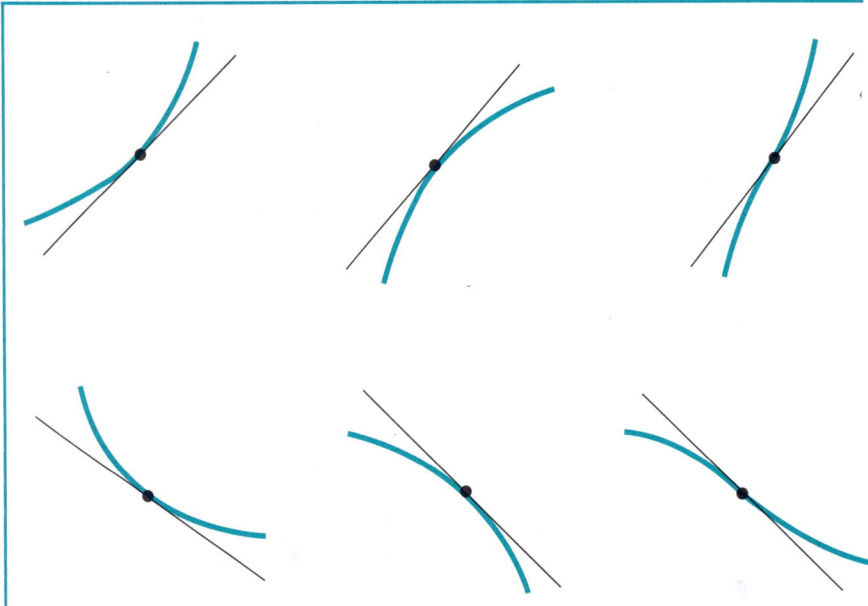

in Figure 8-2. Recall that

$$f'(x) = 3x^2 - 12x$$

so that if we tested points near the first stationary point, we would see that to the **left** of $x = 0$

$$f'(-1) = 15,$$

which is positive, so the function is increasing, while to the **right** of $x = 0$

$$f'(1) = -9,$$

which is negative, so the function is decreasing. This shows analytically that the stationary point $P(0, 37)$ is a local maximum. For the second stationary point, we find that to the left of $x = 4$

$$f'(3) = -9,$$

which means the function is decreasing, while to the right of $x = 4$

$$f'(5) = 15,$$

which means that the function is increasing. This shows analytically that the stationary point $Q(4, 5)$ is a local minimum.

It is often helpful to represent the preceding analysis graphically as shown in Figure 8-4 where we use the upward arrow ↑ to indicate the function is increasing,

CHAPTER 8 APPLICATIONS OF DIFFERENTIAL CALCULUS

FIGURE 8–4

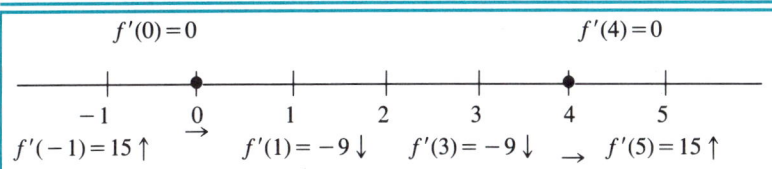

the sideways arrow → to indicate the function is stationary, and the downward arrow ↓ to indicate the function is decreasing. Note also that we chose points **just to the left** and **just to the right** of the stationary point being analyzed. Thus we test for increasing and decreasing near a stationary point **being careful not to go beyond another critical point.**

> When testing to the left and right of a stationary point, be careful to choose points close to the stationary point without going beyond another critical point.

Exercise. Use the preceding approach for the function

$$f(x) = 2x^2 + 8x - 7$$

of the previous exercise to verify that the stationary point $(-2, -15)$ is a local minimum.

Answer: $f'(-3) = -4$ so the function is decreasing to the left of $x = -2$, while $f'(-1) = 4$ so the function is increasing to the right of $x = -2$.

Now what happens if the function does not change from increasing to decreasing, or vice versa, in the vicinity of a stationary point? Figure 8–5A illustrates a function that is **increasing to the left and right** of a stationary point, while Figure 8–5B illustrates a function which is **decreasing to the left and right** of a stationary point. Clearly neither of these stationary points represents a local maximum or a local minimum. They are both **inflection points.** To better understand points of inflection, go back to Figure 8–2 and examine the curve at the two stationary points, $P(0, 37)$ and $Q(4, 5)$. At $P(0, 37)$ the local maximum, the shape of the curve is **concave down** (like a cup upside down). On the other hand at $Q(4, 5)$, the local minimum, the shape of the curve is **concave up** (like a cup rightside up).

> If a function is increasing (decreasing) on both sides of a stationary point, then the stationary point is an inflection point.

Definition. An **inflection point** is one where the curve **changes concavity.**

> An inflection point occurs where the curve changes concavity.

Indeed in Figure 8–2 the point R is an inflection point that is *not* a stationary point. Nonstationary inflection points will be discussed fully in Section 8.4.

FIGURE 8–5A **FIGURE 8–5B**

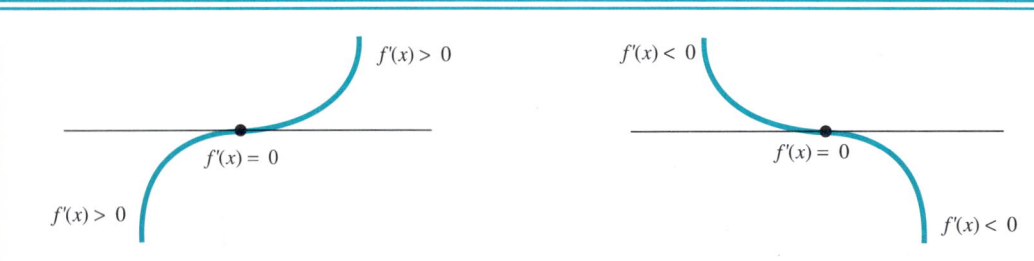

Returning to Figure 8–5A, the curve is concave down to the left of the stationary point and concave up to the right, indicating an inflection point. Similarly in Figure 8–5B the curve is concave up to the left of the stationary point and concave down to the right, again indicating an inflection point.

Summarizing the analysis developed to this point results in the **First Derivative Test** for local maxima, local minima, and stationary inflection points.

First Derivative Test for Local Maxima, Local Minima, and Stationary Points of Inflection

1. Set $f'(x) = 0$ and solve for x to determine the **stationary** points.
2. Test a point just to the left, x_l, and a point just to the right, x_r, of each stationary point.

    a) If $f'(x_l) > 0$ and $f'(x_r) < 0$,

    $$\underset{f'(x_l) > 0 \ \uparrow \rightarrow \downarrow \ f'(x_r) < 0}{\underline{\bullet \ f'(x) = 0 \ }},$$

    then the stationary point is a **local maximum**.

    b) If $f'(x_l) < 0$ and $f'(x_r) > 0$,

    $$\underset{f'(x_l) < 0 \ \downarrow \rightarrow \uparrow \ f'(x_r) > 0}{\underline{\bullet \ f'(x) = 0 \ }},$$

    then the stationary point is a **local minimum**.

    c) If $f'(x_l) > 0$ and $f'(x_r) > 0$, or $f'(x_l) < 0$ and $f'(x_r) < 0$,

    $$\underset{f'(x_l) > 0 \ \uparrow \rightarrow \uparrow \ f'(x_r) > 0}{\underline{\bullet \ f'(x) = 0 \ }} \quad \underset{f'(x_l) < 0 \ \downarrow \rightarrow \downarrow \ f'(x_r) < 0}{\underline{\bullet \ f'(x) = 0 \ }},$$

    then the stationary point is an **inflection point**.

Example. Find the coordinates of all local maxima, local minima, and stationary inflection points of

$$f(x) = \frac{x^3}{3} + x^2 - 8x + 4.$$

We use the First Derivative Test as follows.

Step 1. We start by finding the first derivative,

$$f'(x) = x^2 + 2x - 8.$$

We then set the first derivative equal to 0,

$$f'(x) = 0,$$

and solve for x to find the stationary points:

$$x^2 + 2x - 8 = 0$$
$$(x + 4)(x - 2) = 0$$
$$x = -4, 2.$$

Step 2. We test the first stationary point, $x = -4$, on the left,

$$f'(-5) = 7 \uparrow,$$

and then on the right,

$$f'(-3) = -5 \downarrow.$$

Since the function is increasing on the left and decreasing on the right, then by Step 2a we have a local maximum at $x = -4$. Of course, to find the value of the function we substitute $x = -4$ into the original function to get

$$f(-4) = \frac{92}{3}$$

so that there is a local maximum at the point $(-4, 92/3)$.

Analyzing the second stationary point at $x = 2$, we see that on the left

$$f'(1) = -5 \downarrow$$

and then on the right

$$f'(3) = 7 \uparrow.$$

Since the first derivative is decreasing on the left and increasing on the right, then by Step 2b we have a local minimum at $x = 2$. This time to find the value of the function we substitute $x = 2$ into the original function to get

$$f(2) = -\frac{16}{3}$$

so there is a local minimum at the point $(2, -16/3)$.

Finally since there are no other stationary points to consider, there are no stationary inflection points. The graph of the function (Figure 8–6), verifies that there is a local maximum at $(-4, 92/3)$, a local minimum at $(2, -16/3)$, and no stationary inflection points.

Exercise. Find the coordinates of all local maxima, local minima, and stationary inflection points of

$$f(x) = \frac{x^3}{3} - x^2 - 3x + 7.$$

Answer: A local maximum at $(-1, 26/3)$, a local minimum at $(3, -2)$, and no stationary inflection points.

FIGURE 8–6

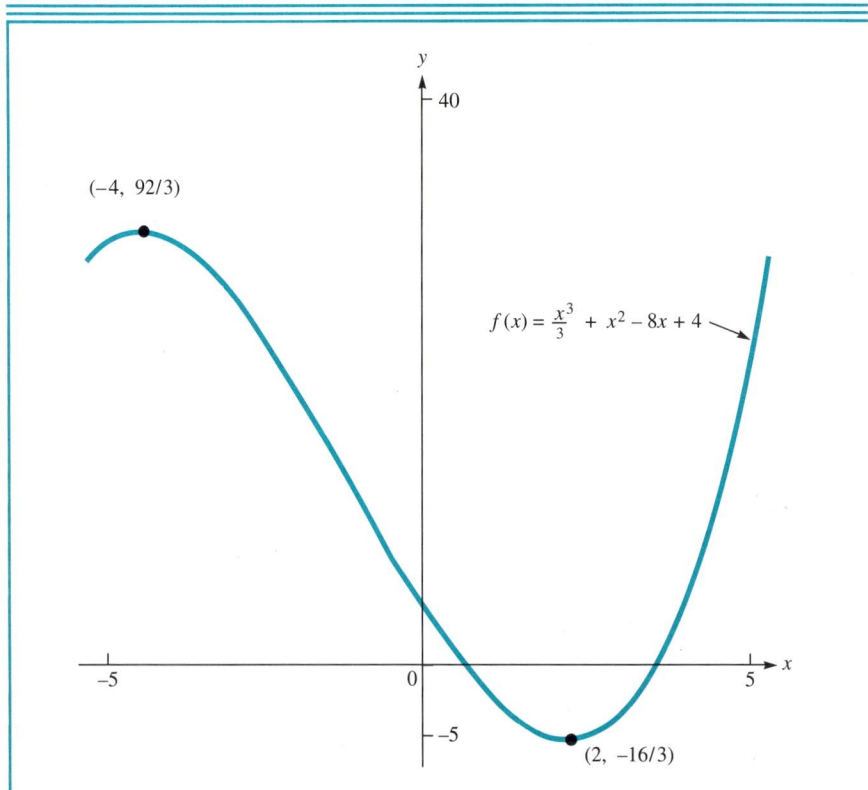

Example. Find the coordinates of all local maxima, local minima, and stationary inflection points of

$$f(x) = x^3 - 6x^2 + 12x - 3.$$

Using the same approach as in the preceding example and exercise, we proceed as follows.

Step 1. We start by finding the first derivative,

$$f'(x) = 3x^2 - 12x + 12,$$

and then set it equal to 0:

$$3x^2 - 12x + 12 = 0$$
$$3(x^2 - 4x + 4) = 0$$
$$3(x - 2)(x - 2) = 0$$
$$x = 2.$$

Thus there is only the one stationary point, $x = 2$.

Step 2. Testing on the left of $x = 2$,

$$f'(1) = 3 \uparrow,$$

so the function is increasing. On the right

$$f'(3) = 3 \uparrow$$

so the function is again increasing. Thus by Step 2c we have a stationary inflection point at $x = 2$. Substituting $x = 2$ into the original function we have

$$f(2) = 5$$

so the function has a stationary inflection point at (2, 5) but no local maxima and no local minima. This fact is verified by the graph in Figure 8–7.

Exercise. Find the coordinates of all local maxima, local minima, and stationary inflection points of

$$f(x) = x^3 - 3x^2 + 3x + 5.$$

Answer: There is a stationary inflection point at (1, 6), with no local maxima and no local minima.

FIGURE 8–7

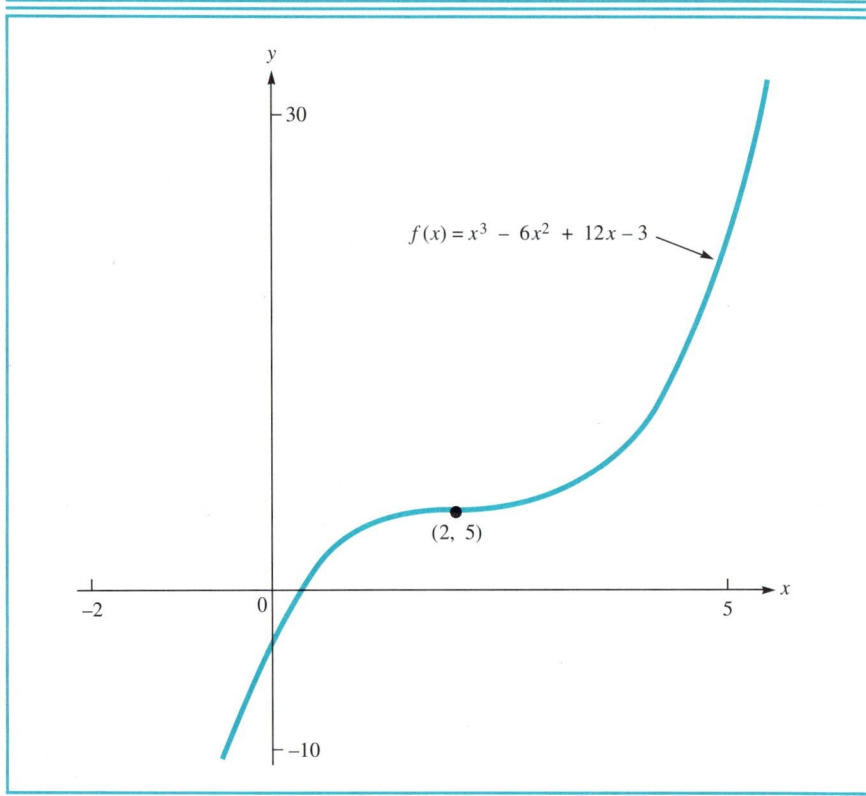

Endpoints

If a function is defined only in an interval, then the endpoints of the interval, if included, are usually endpoint maxima or minima.

When a function is defined only for a restricted set of points, then if the endpoints are included in the definition, they will usually be **endpoint maxima** or **endpoint minima**. For example, suppose that for our earlier function

$$f(x) = x^3 - 6x^2 + 37$$

we restricted the x values to the interval $[-3, 7]$. **Then the graph would appear as shown in Figure 8–8. From this graph we can see that the function has an endpoint minimum at $x = -3$ where**

$$f(-3) = -44$$

since the value of the function at this endpoint is the **smallest value in the vicinity just to the right of the endpoint**. (Note that the function is not defined to the left of this endpoint.) In the same way we see that the function has an endpoint maximum at $x = 7$ where

$$f(7) = 86$$

FIGURE 8-8

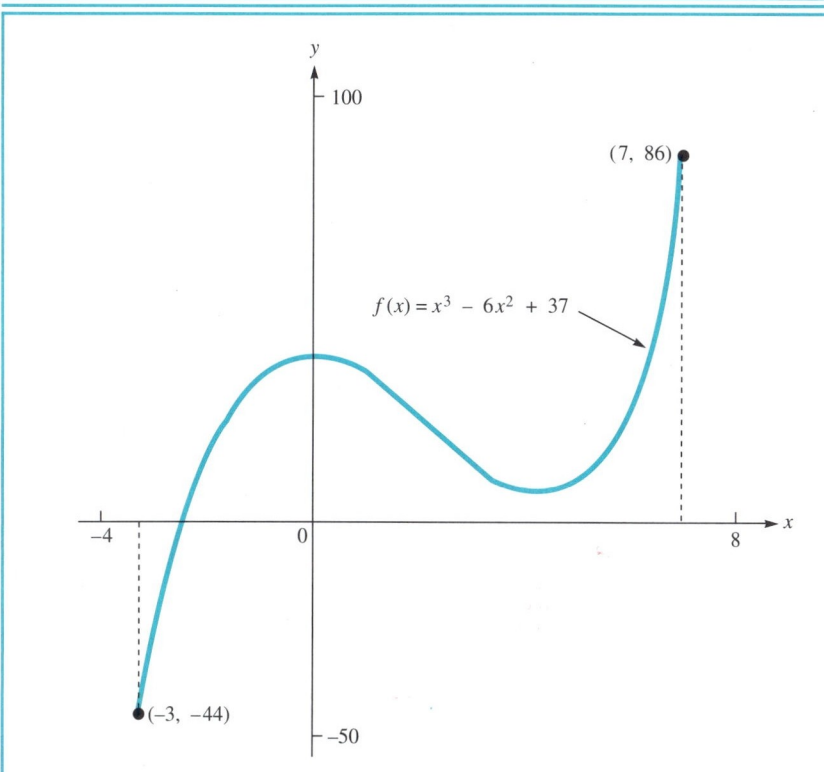

since the value of the function at this endpoint is the **largest value in the vicinity just to the left of the endpoint.** (In this case the function is not defined to the

Now, how can we determine these endpoint optima analytically? Inspection of Figure 8–8 will help us answer this question. We can see that the function is **increasing just to the right of the left-hand endpoint** where $x = -3$ which means that the first derivative should be positive. Indeed

$$f'(-2) = 36 \uparrow.$$

Similarly the function is **increasing just to the left of the right-hand endpoint** where $x = 7$ which means that again the derivative should be positive. In this case

$$f'(6) = 36 \uparrow.$$

Thus we have shown analytically that there is an endpoint minimum at $(-3, -44)$ and an endpoint maximum at $(7, 86)$.

> When testing a left-hand endpoint, choose a point just to the right.

> When testing a right-hand endpoint, choose a point just to the left.

> **Exercise.** Use the preceding approach to check the endpoints of the function
> $$f(x) = 2x^2 + 8x - 7$$
> in the interval $[-5, 3]$.
>
> **Answer:** $f'(-4) = -8 \downarrow$ so there is an endpoint maximum at $(-5, 3)$, while $f'(2) = 16 \uparrow$ so there is an endpoint maximum at $(3, 35)$.

Summarizing the analysis illustrated in the preceding example and exercise, we have the **endpoint test** for maxima and minima.

> **First Derivative Test for Endpoint Maxima and Endpoint Minima**
>
> If $f(x)$ is restricted to the interval $[a, b]$, then
>
> 1. Test a point just to the right, x_r, of $x = a$.
>   a) If $f'(x_r) < 0$, then there is an **endpoint maximum** at $x = a$.
>   b) If $f'(x_r) > 0$, then there is an **endpoint minimum** at $x = a$.
> 2. Test a point just to the left, x_l, of $x = b$.
>   a) If $f'(x_l) < 0$, then there is an **endpoint minimum** at $x = b$.
>   b) If $f'(x_l) > 0$, then there is an **endpoint maximum** at $x = b$.

If a function is not defined at an endpoint, that point cannot be an endpoint optimum.

It is possible to have a function restricted to an interval where the function is not defined at one or both of the endpoints. What if in the preceding example the function

$$f(x) = x^3 - 6x^2 + 37$$

were restricted to the interval $[-3, 7)$? In this case there would still be an endpoint minimum at the left-hand endpoint $(-3, -44)$, but there would no longer be a right-hand endpoint so there could be no right-hand endpoint optimum.

Example. Find all local and endpoint maxima, all local and endpoint minima, and all stationary inflection points of

$$f(x) = x^2 + 1$$

on the interval $[-1, 2)$.

We begin by taking the first derivative,

$$f'(x) = 2x,$$

and setting it equal to 0:

$$2x = 0$$
$$x = 0.$$

Then we check the stationary point $x = 0$ on the left,

$$f'(-1) = -2 \downarrow,$$

and then on the right

$$f'(1) = 2 \uparrow,$$

thus indicating that we have a local minimum at $x = 0$ where

$$f(0) = 1.$$

Now at the left-hand endpoint where $x = -1$ we check the first derivative just to the right,

$$f'(-1/2) = -1 \downarrow,$$

indicating that the function is decreasing so that there is an endpoint maximum at $x = -1$ where

$$f(-1) = 2.$$

There is no right-hand endpoint since $x = 2$ is not included in the interval so there can be no right-hand endpoint optimum. The graph of this function is shown in Figure 8–9, verifying that there is indeed an endpoint maximum at $(-1, 2)$ and a local minimum at $(0, 1)$. Note from this figure that the local minimum is also an absolute minimum, but there is no absolute maximum since the function is not defined at $x = 2$.

Answer: Local minimum at $(2, 0)$ and endpoint maximum at $(3, 1)$.

In applied problems endpoint tests are needed when there is a restriction on the range of permissible values the independent variable may have. Typically x must not be negative ($x \geq 0$) or x must be strictly positive ($x > 0$). Again if x is the number of hours a machine is operated during a day, then

$$\text{Range: } 0 \leq x \leq 24.$$

When we find a local optimum point by setting the derivative equal to 0, the x obtained may be outside the range. For example, if

$$f(x) = 0.01x^2 - 1.2x + 100; \quad 0 \leq x \leq 50,$$

In real-world situations the variables will usually be restricted by practical considerations such as nonnegativity or hours in a day.

FIGURE 8-9

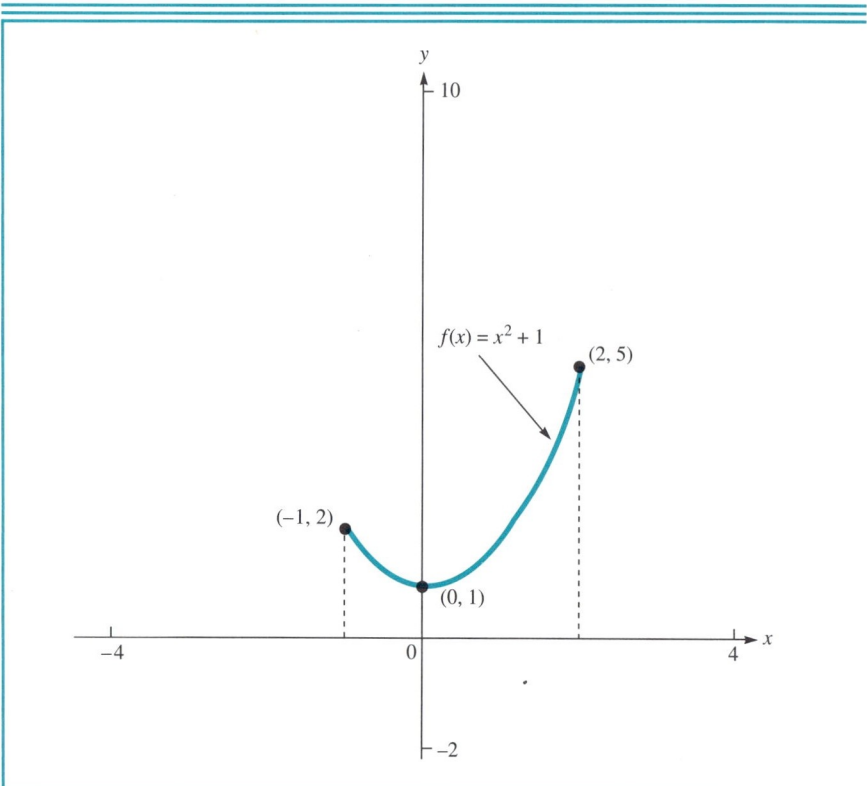

it may be verified that (60, 64) would be a local minimum, but $x = 60$ is outside the range, and the minimum (absolute) value of the function occurs at the right-hand endpoint, (50, 65).

Second, the value of a function at the endpoint of the range may be greater (less) than the value found at a local maximum (minimum) and, finally, a function may have no local optimum points, in which case its absolute maximum and minimum occur at the endpoints of the range.

It follows that in working with an unfamiliar function it would be wise to keep endpoint considerations in mind. However in this book problems have been designed so that we need not be preoccupied with endpoints, and we shall call attention to these considerations on the rare occasion where they are relevant.

A function may have several local maxima and minima, as we previously saw. However a function will never have more than one absolute maximum or minimum. The absolute maximum (minimum) of a function is the largest (smallest) value of the function over all points for which it is defined. In applied problems these are almost always the values we seek, and we find them by enumerating every optimum value and choosing the appropriate absolute optima.

Example. Find all local and endpoint optimum points and all stationary points of inflection of the function

$$f(x) = 20x^{1/2} - 2x.$$

First, we notice that $x^{1/2}$ is defined only for nonnegative values of x so that $f(x)$ is defined over the interval $[0, \infty)$. With this in mind we first find $f'(x)$:

$$f'(x) = 10x^{-1/2} - 2.$$

Next we find that $f'(x) = 0$ when

$$10x^{-1/2} - 2 = 0$$

or

$$\frac{10}{x^{1/2}} - 2 = 0$$

$$\frac{10}{x^{1/2}} = 2$$

$$10 = 2x^{1/2}$$

$$5 = x^{1/2}, \text{ or}$$

$$x^{1/2} = 5.$$

To obtain x we must square both sides:

$$(x^{1/2})^2 = 5^2$$

$$x = 25.$$

We then check this stationary point on the left

and on the right,

$$f'(36) = -\frac{1}{3} \downarrow,$$

thus indicating that we have a local maximum at $x = 25$ where

$$f(25) = 50.$$

Now at the left-hand endpoint where $x = 0$, we check the first derivative just to the right,

$$f'(1) = 8 \uparrow,$$

indicating that the function is increasing so that there is an endpoint minimum at $x = 0$ where

$$f(0) = 0.$$

The graph of the function (Figure 8–10) verifies that there is indeed an endpoint minimum at (0, 0) and a local maximum at (25, 50). Note from this figure that the local maximum is also an absolute maximum, but there is **no absolute minimum** since the function continues down indefinitely to the right.

Exercise. Find all local and endpoint optimum points and all stationary inflection points of

$$f(x) = 3x - 18x^{1/2}.$$

Answer: There is a local minimum at (9, −27) and an endpoint maximum at (0, 0).

FIGURE 8–10

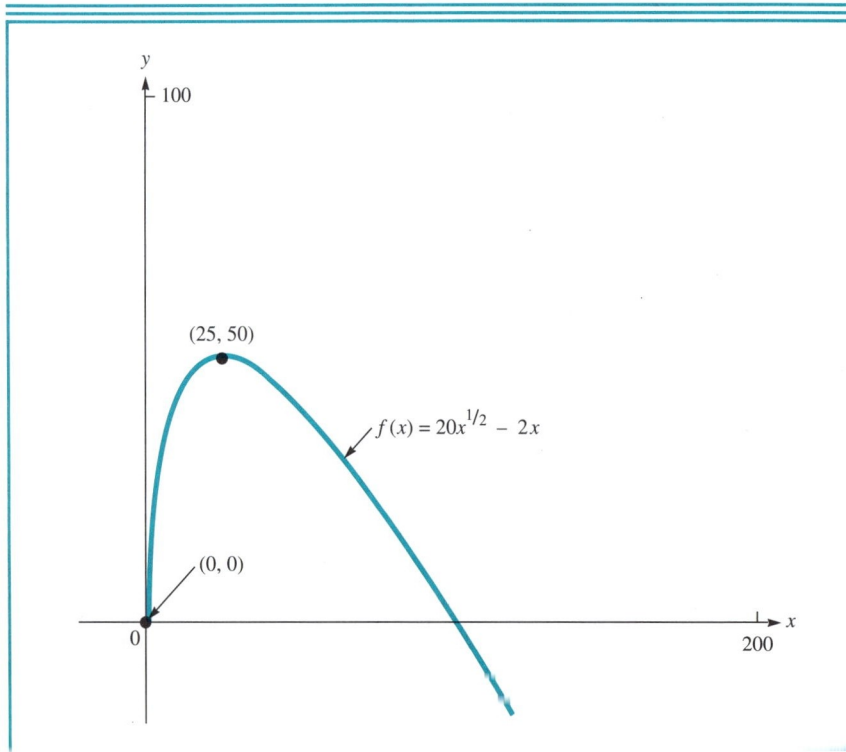

8.3 PROBLEM SET 8-1

For each of the following, find the coordinates of all local and endpoint optimum points, and all stationary inflection points.

1. $f(x) = 5x - x^2$.
2. $f(x) = 2x^2 - 12x + 20$.
3. $f(x) = 3 - x^2$.
4. $f(x) = 2x^2 + 20$.
5. $f(x) = 30x - 3x^2 + 10$.
6. $f(x) = x^2 - x + 1$.
7. $f(x) = x^3 - 12x^2 + 12$.
8. $f(x) = x^3 - 3x^2 + 2$.
9. $f(x) = 3x^3 + 27$.
10. $f(x) = 14 - 2x^3$.
11. $f(x) = 21x^2 - 2x^3 - 60x + 20$.
12. $f(x) = 6x^2 - x^3 - 9x$.
13. $f(x) = 2x - 8x^{1/2}$.
14. $f(x) = 9x^{2/3} - 2x$.
15. $f(x) = x^{3/2} - 12x^{1/2}$.
16. $f(x) = 10x^{1/3} - x^{2/3}$.
17. $f(x) = 4x + 64/x$.
18. $f(x) = 4x + 250/x^2$.
19. $f(x) = x^3 - 9x^2 + 27x$ on $[-1, 6]$.
20. $f(x) = x^3 + 15x^2 + 75x$ on $[-8, 2]$.
21. $f(x) = x^4 - 32x + 100$ on $[-2, 4]$.
22. $f(x) = 108x - x^4$ on $[-1, 5]$.
23. $f(x) = 4x^3 - 3x^4 + 4$ on $[-1, 2)$.
24. $f(x) = x^4 - 4x^3 + 30$ on $[-2, 4)$.

25. When x gallons of antifreeze are produced, the average cost per gallon is $A(x)$ where

$$A(x) = 100/x + 0.04x + 1.$$

  a) How many gallons should be produced if average cost per gallon is to be minimized?
  b) Prove (a) is a minimum.
  c) Compute the minimum average cost per gallon.

26. If we use 100 linear feet of fence to enclose a rectangular plot (using x feet for one pair of sides, so x feet for the other pair of sides (or $b = x$ feet for one of these sides). The rectangle is then x feet by $(50 - x)$ feet and its area, $A(x)$, is

$$A(x) = x(50 - x) = 50x - x^2.$$

  a) Find the value of x that maximizes the area of the plot.
  b) Prove (a) is a maximum.
  c) What are the dimensions of the maximum-area rectangle?
  d) What is the maximum area?

27. In many sampling surveys only a small number n of a large population of people are interviewed. Published survey results state what proportion, p, of the n people interviewed answered yes to a particular question. Inherently, because only a fraction of the population is interviewed, the proportion p is expected to be in error. Statisticians measure this error by $V(p)$, where V stands for *variance,* and

$$V(p) = \frac{p}{n} - \frac{p^2}{n}.$$

Thus variance, or error, is a function of p for a given expected error.

  b) Prove (a) is a maximum.
  c) Taking $n = 10$, find $V(0.5)$ and $V(0.1)$.

28. The profit realized when y gallons of distilled water are made and sold is

$$P(y) = 20y - 0.005y^2.$$

  a) Find the number of gallons that should be made to maximize profit.
  b) Prove (a) is a maximum.
  c) Compute the maximum profit.

8.4 THE SECOND DERIVATIVE TEST

In this section we introduce a new test that is simple to use and is very helpful in optimization problems and curve sketching. Recall from Section 8.2 the function

$$f(x) = x^3 - 6x^2 + 37$$

and its graph which we have redrawn in Figure 8–11. As we saw, the curve is concave down (like a cup upside down so that the curve always lies below the tangent line) at the local maximum $P(0, 37)$ and concave up (like a cup rightside up so that the curve always lies above the tangent line) at the local minimum $Q(4, 5)$. We also saw that the curve had a nonstationary point of inflection at R. We will now develop a technique using the **second derivative** of the function that will help us to effectively determine when a function is concave up or concave down. From this we will generate an alternative test for local optima as well as a test for inflection points (stationary or nonstationary).

The derivative of a function, $f'(x)$, is itself a function—the slope function. The derivative of the derivative is

$$\frac{d}{dx} f'(x) = f''(x),$$

where $f''(x)$ is called the **second derivative**.[1] If the derivative of $f'(x)$, which is $f''(x)$, is positive (negative), the **slope function** is increasing (decreasing). Now look at points A and B in Figure 8–11. The slope at B is less than the slope at A because the curve is concave down. When the slopes decrease in this way, it means that the slope function is decreasing so its derivative, $f''(x)$, must be negative. In general, a curve is concave down at a point where the second derivative is negative. This will be true, for example, at $x = -1$, $x = 0$, and $x = +1$ for the function plotted in Figure 8–11, that is,

$$f(x) = x^3 - 6x^2 + 37$$
$$f'(x) = 3x^2 - 12x$$
$$f''(x) = 6x - 12$$

and

$$f''(-1) = -18$$
$$f''(0) = -12$$
$$f''(1) = -6.$$

> When a curve is concave down (up), the curve lies below (above) the tangent line.

> A curve is concave down if the second derivative is negative; that is, $f''(x) < 0$.

---

[1] The second derivative may also be symbolized as

$$\frac{d^2 f(x)}{dx^2},$$

which is read as "d second f of x, dx second."

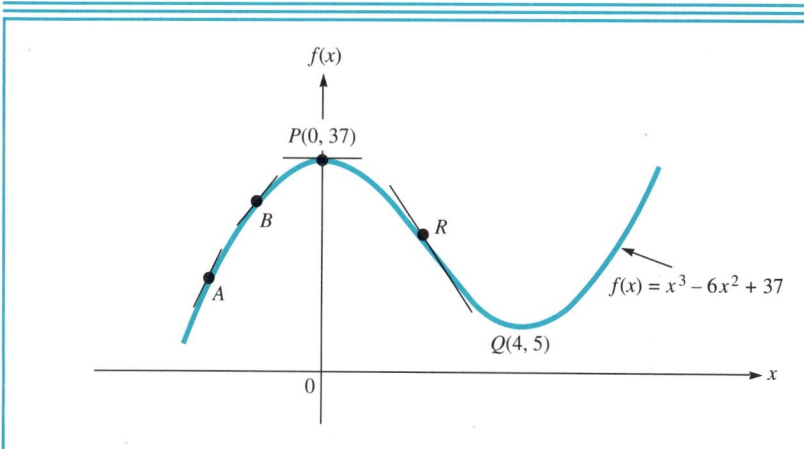

FIGURE 8–11
(not to scale)

Moreover we have

$f'(0) = 0$: Stationary point at $x = 0$.
$f''(0) = -12$: Curve concave down at $x = 0$.
Conclusion: There is a local maximum at $x = 0$.

Turning next to the point $Q(4, 5)$ in Figure 8–11, we first note that a curve is concave up at a point where the second derivative is positive. Thus we find

> A curve is concave up if the second derivative is positive; that is, $f''(x) > 0$.

$f'(4) = 0$: Stationary point at $x = 4$.
$f''(4) = +12$: Curve concave up at $x = 4$.
Conclusion: There is a local minimum at $x = 4$.

In summary, if x is a value such that $f'(x) = 0$ (stationary point), the point is a

timum points and testing to determine whether they are local maxima or minima.

Second Derivative Test for Local Maxima and Local Minima

1. Set $f'(x) = 0$ and solve for x to determine the **stationary** points.
2. a) If $f''(x) > 0$ (concave up), then the stationary point is a **local minimum**.
   b) If $f''(x) < 0$ (concave down), then the stationary point is a **local maximum**.
   c) If $f''(x) = 0$, then the test fails and we go back to Step 2 of the First Derivative Test.

> A local minimum occurs at a stationary point where the curve is concave up; that is, $f'(x) = 0$ and $f''(x) > 0$.
> A local maximum occurs at a stationary point where the curve is concave down; that is, $f'(x) = 0$ and $f''(x) < 0$.

Note that Step 1 of the Second Derivative Test is the same as Step 1 of the First Derivative Test. The reason for this, of course, is that in both tests, we start by finding the stationary points where $f'(x) = 0$. Note also that Steps 2a and 2b of the Second Derivative Test require one fewer test than Steps 2a and 2b of the First Derivative Test so the second derivative test is more efficient when $f''(x) \neq 0$.

The reason the test fails when $f''(x) = 0$ can be seen by examining Figures 8–12A, B, and C. All of the stationary points in these figures $S(0, 8)$, $T(0, 5)$, and $V(0, 6)$, have $x = 0$ and the second derivative is also 0 at these points.

Exercise. Write the expression for the second derivatives of the functions under consideration and compute the values of these derivatives at $x = 0$. The functions are: a) $g(x) = x^3 + 8$. b) $h(x) = x^4 + 5$. c) $k(x) = 6 - x^4$.

Answer: a) $g''(x) = 6x$; $g''(0) = 0$. b) $h''(x) = 12x^2$; $h''(0) = 0$. c) $k''(x) = -12x^2$; $k''(0) = 0$.

Thus we see that if both first and second derivatives are 0, the point at hand could be a stationary inflection point (Figure 8–12A), a minimum (Figure 8–12B), or a maximum (Figure 8–12C). These three figures show us that the Second Derivative Test gives us no help in determining the type of point at hand if both derivatives are 0 at the point. Notice that in this case we can always rely on the First Derivative Test. Fortunately the Second Derivative Test does work in a majority of the problems we will encounter.

Exercise. Use Step 2 of the First Derivative Test to prove the results shown in Figures 8–12A, B, and C.

Answer: a) $g'(x) = 3x^2$; $g'(-1) = 3 \uparrow$ and $g'(1) = 3 \uparrow$ so $(0, 8)$ is a stationary inflection point. b) $h'(x) = 4x^3$; $h'(-1) = -4 \downarrow$ and $h'(1) = 4 \uparrow$ so $(0, 5)$ is a local minimum. c) $k'(x) = -4x^3$; $k'(-1) = 4 \uparrow$ and $k'(1) = -4 \downarrow$ so $(0, 6)$ is a local maximum.

Example. Find all local optimum points of

$$f(x) = 2x^2 - 12x + 50.$$

We start with this example to illustrate the Second Derivative Test because we know the answer. The curve is a vertical parabola opening upward, and its optimum point is the vertex, which is a local (and absolute) minimum. Applying the Second Derivative Test, we would proceed as follows.

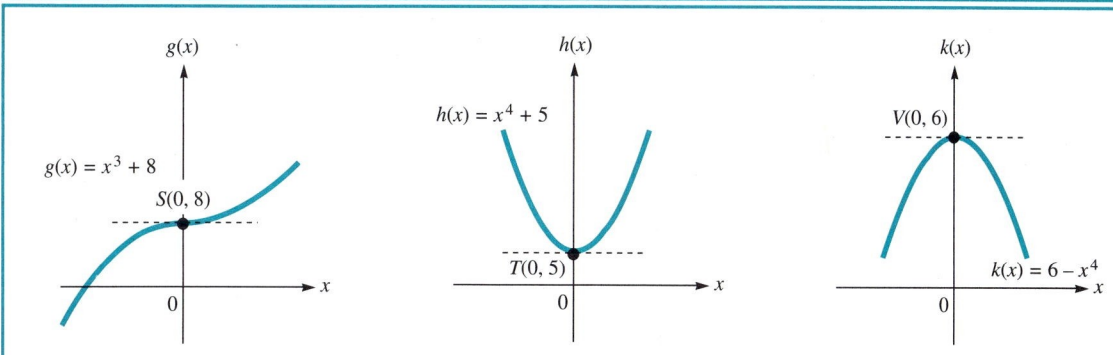

FIGURE 8–12A
(not to scale)

FIGURE 8–12B
(not to scale)

FIGURE 8–12C
(not to scale)

Step 1. We begin, as usual, by finding the first derivative,

$$f'(x) = 4x - 12,$$

and checking for stationary points:

$$f'(x) = 0 \quad \text{when} \quad 4x - 12 = 0 \quad \text{or} \quad x = 3.$$

Step 1 consists of using the first derivative to determine the stationary points.

Step 2. Now we find the second derivative,

$$f''(x) = 4,$$

and test the stationary point at $x = 3$. We see that

Step 2 consists of using the second derivative to check each stationary point for a local optimum.

since the second derivative does not depend on x and is 4 for all values of x. Because the second derivative is positive, then by Step 2a we have a local minimum at $x = 3$. To find the value of the function we substitute $x = 3$ into the original function to get

$$f(3) = 32,$$

so that there is a local minimum at the point $(3, 32)$. Note as we stated earlier the second derivative,

$$f''(x) = 4,$$

is a positive constant not depending on x. This means that the curve is concave up at all points, which of course is the case for an upward-opening parabola so the local minimum $(3, 32)$ is also the absolute minimum.

> **Exercise.** Find all local optimum points of the following:
> a) $f(x) = 30x - 3x^2 + 25$. b) $g(x) = x - 6x^{1/2} + 20$.
>
> **Answer:** a) Local maximum at (5, 100). b) Local minimum at (9, 11).

As we know, inflection points occur where a curve changes concavity. Since concavity is measured by the second derivative and changes in the second derivative are measured by the **third derivative,** we have the following test for determining inflection points (stationary and nonstationary).

Candidates for inflection points are identified by the second derivative and checked in the third derivative.

> **Third Derivative Test for Inflection Points**
> 1. Set $f''(x) = 0$ and solve for x. (Also determine where $f''(x)$ is undefined.)
> 2. a) If $f'''(x) \neq 0$, then we have an inflection point.
>   b) If $f'''(x) = 0$, then test the second derivative just to the left and right. If the second derivative changes sign (from **positive to negative** or from **negative to positive**), then we have an inflection point.

The third derivative test for inflection points is analogous to the second derivative test for local optimum points, but uses one higher derivative at each step.

Note the similarities between this Third Derivative Test for inflection points and the Second Derivative Test for local optimum points. Step 1 of the Second Derivative Test sets the **first derivative** equal to 0 to locate stationary points, whereas Step 1 of the Third Derivative Test sets the **second derivative** equal to 0 to locate candidate points. Steps 2a and 2b of the Second Derivative Test check the stationary points in the **second derivative,** whereas Step 2a of the Third Derivative Test checks the candidate points in the **third derivative.** Lastly, when the Second Derivative Test fails, we revert back to testing the **first derivative** just to the left and right of the stationary point, whereas the Third Derivative Test reverts back to testing the **second derivative** just to the left and right of the candidate point. Note also that when an inflection point is found, whether or not it is also stationary depends on whether or not the first derivative is also 0.

Example. Determine all local optimum points and all inflection points of
$$f(x) = 0.1x^3 - 1.8x^2 + 8.1x + 2.$$

Since we will use the second and third derivative tests, we start by finding the first three derivatives:

$$f'(x) = 0.3x^2 - 3.6x + 8.1,$$
$$f''(x) = 0.6x - 3.6,$$
$$f'''(x) = 0.6.$$

Be careful! Always double-check each of your derivatives because if any one is incorrect, all subsequent ones will be wrong so the rest of your work will be useless.

Determining Local Optimum Points. We start in the usual way by setting the first derivative equal to 0 to find the stationary points:

$$f'(x) = 0 \quad \text{when} \quad 0.3x^2 - 3.6x + 8.1 = 0$$
$$0.3(x^2 - 12x + 27) = 0$$
$$0.3(x - 9)(x - 3) = 0$$

so

$$x = 9, 3.$$

Then we test each of these points in the second derivative:

$$f''(x) = 0.6x - 3.6,$$
$$f''(9) = 1.8 \quad \text{so there is a local minimum at } x = 9,$$
$$f''(3) = -1.8 \quad \text{so there is a local maximum at } x = 3.$$

Evaluating the original function $f(x)$ at these optimum points, we have

$$f(9) = 2$$

so there is a local minimum at the point (9, 2), and

$$f(3) = 12.8$$

so there is a local maximum at the point (3, 12.8).

Determining Inflection Points. This time we set the second derivative equal to 0 to

$$f''(x) = 0 \quad \text{when} \quad 0.6x - 3.6 = 0$$
$$0.6x = 3.6$$
$$x = 6.$$

Then testing this point in the third derivative,

$$f'''(x) = 0.6$$
$$f'''(6) = 0.6 \neq 0$$

so there is an inflection point at $x = 6$. Evaluating the original function $f(x)$ at this point,

$$f(6) = 7.4,$$

so there is an inflection point at (6, 7.4).

FIGURE 8–13
(not to scale)

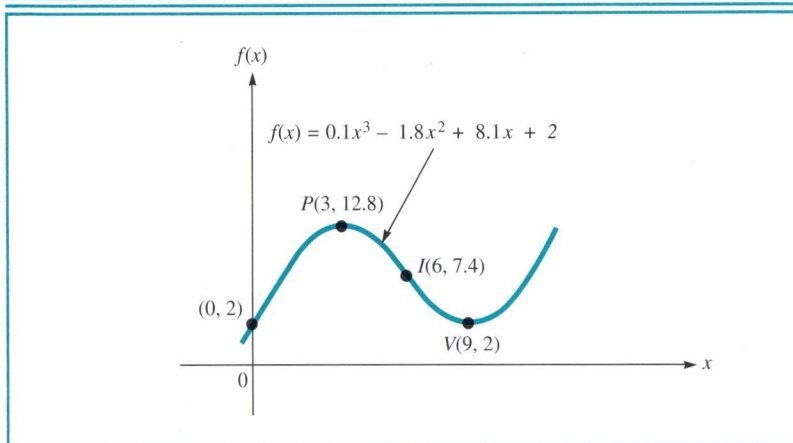

The graph of this function is shown in Figure 8–13 where we see that indeed there is a local maximum at $P(3, 12.8)$, a local minimum at $V(9, 2)$, and an inflection point (nonstationary) at $I(6, 7.4)$.

Note in the preceding example that once we determined there was a local maximum (where the curve is concave down) and a local minimum (where the curve is concave up), we would expect to find an inflection point (where the concavity changes) in between. Note also that all inflection points occur at points where the second derivative is 0 (or is undefined), but **not all points where the second derivative is 0 are inflection points.** (Refer back to Figures 8–12B and 8–12C.)

Example. Determine all local optimum points and all inflection points of

$$f(x) = 15x^4 + 8x^3 - 18x^2 + 1.$$

We begin by finding the first three derivatives:

$$f'(x) = 60x^3 + 24x^2 - 36x,$$
$$f''(x) = 180x^2 + 48x - 36,$$
$$f'''(x) = 360x + 48.$$

Determining Local Optimum Points. We now set the first derivative equal to 0 to find the stationary points:

$$60x^3 + 24x^2 - 36x = 0$$
$$12x(5x^2 + 2x - 3) = 0$$
$$x(5x^2 + 2x - 3) = 0$$
$$x(x + 1)(5x - 3) = 0$$

or
$$x = 0, \ x = -1, \ \text{ and } \ x = \frac{3}{5}.$$

Then checking the second derivative,
$$f''(0) = -36, \ f''(-1) = 96, \ f''\left(\frac{3}{5}\right) = \frac{288}{5},$$

so we have a local maximum at $x = 0$ and local minima at $x = -1$ and $x = 3/5$. The corresponding values of $f(x)$ are
$$f(0) = 1, \ f(-1) = -10, \ \text{ and } \ f\left(\frac{3}{5}\right) = -\frac{226}{125};$$

hence there is a local maximum at $(0, 1)$, and local minima at $(-1, -10)$ and $(3/5, -226/125)$.

Determining Inflection Points. Now to locate the inflection points we set the second derivative equal to 0 to find the candidate points,
$$180x^2 + 48x - 36 = 0$$
$$12(15x^2 + 4x - 3) = 0$$
$$15x^2 + 4x - 3 = 0$$
$$(5x + 3)(3x - 1) = 0,$$

so that
$$x = -\frac{3}{5} \ \text{ and } \ x = \frac{1}{3}.$$

Then testing these points in the third derivative,

$$f'''\left(\frac{1}{3}\right) = 168,$$

so we have inflection points at both $x = -3/5$ and $x = 1/3$. Next, evaluating the original function $f(x)$ at these points, we have
$$f\left(-\frac{3}{5}\right) = -\frac{658}{125}$$
$$f\left(\frac{1}{3}\right) = -\frac{14}{27}.$$

Hence there are inflection points at $(-3/5, -658/125)$ and $(1/3, -14/27)$.
The graph of this function is shown in Figure 8–14.

FIGURE 8-14
(not to scale)

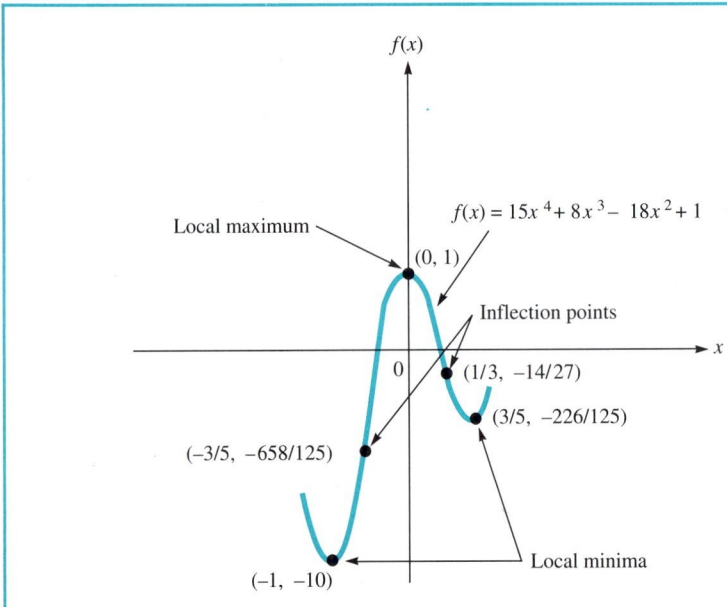

> **Exercise.** Find all local optimum points and all inflection points of
> $$f(x) = x^3 - 6x^2 + 37.$$
> **Answer:** Local maximum at (0, 37), local minimum at (4, 5), and inflection point at (2, 21).

8.5 PROBLEM SET 8-2

In Problems 1 through 10, find the first three derivatives of the function.

1. $f(x) = x^5 - 2x^4 + x^3 + 3$.
2. $f(x) = x^3 - x^2 - x - 1$.
3. $f(x) = 8x^3 - 2x^2$.
4. $f(x) = x^6 - x^4 + 3x^2 + 7$.
5. $f(x) = 3x^4 - 5x^3 + 2x^2$.
6. $f(x) = x^{10} \sqrt{x} - 3x^7 + x$.
7. $f(x) = (x + 5)^3$.
8. $f(x) = (x^2 + 1)^{1/2}$.
9. $f(x) = \dfrac{3x + 4}{x - 3}$.
10. $f(x) = \dfrac{x + 2}{x - 2}$.

8.5 PROBLEM SET 8–2 (concluded)

In Problems 11 through 20, determine all local optimum points and all inflection points.

11. $f(x) = x^2 - 4x + 3$.
12. $f(x) = x^2 + 10x - 9$.
13. $f(x) = x^3 - 6x^2 + 9x + 1$.
14. $f(x) = x^3 + 9x$.
15. $f(x) = x^3 - 2x^2 - 4x + 3$.
16. $f(x) = x^3 + 3x^2 - 9x - 3$.
17. $f(x) = -x^3 - 12x^2 - 45x + 2$.
18. $f(x) = x^4 - 8x^3 + 24x^2$.
19. $f(x) = 0.1(x - 10)^4 - 25.6x + 340.8$.
20. $f(x) = x^4 - 8x^3 + 18x^2 - 27$.

8.6 MAXIMA AND MINIMA: APPLICATIONS

In this section we present a series of examples that involve the application of calculus rules and procedures developed in earlier sections. The technique we will employ will be to find all local and endpoint optimum points. The absolute maximum (minimum) will then be the largest (smallest) of all the local and endpoint maxima (minima).

Example. A rectangular warehouse with a flat roof is to have a floor area of 9,600 square feet. The interior is to be divided into storeroom and office space by an interior wall parallel to one pair of the sides of the building. The roof and floor areas will be 9,600 square feet for any building, but the total wall length will vary for different dimensions. For example, a 96-foot by 100-foot building could have a 96-foot interior wall plus two 96-foot and two 100-foot exterior walls for a total length of $3(96) + 2(100) = 488$ feet.

Answer: $3(40) + 2(240) = 600$ feet.

The problem is to find the dimensions that minimize the total amount of wall. Letting x and y be the dimensions as in Figure 8–15, we see that the total amount of wall, w, is

$$w = 3x + 2y,$$

subject to the constraint that

$$xy = 9600 \quad \text{or} \quad y = \frac{9,600}{x}.$$

As first stated, w depends upon *two* variables, x and y, and our calculus to this point deals with only *one* independent variable. However, since $xy = 9,600$, we

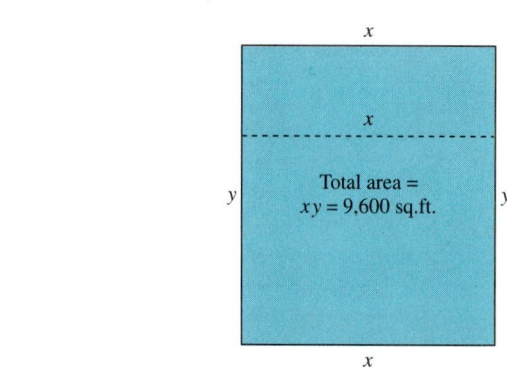

FIGURE 8–15

can replace y by $9{,}600/x$ and write w as a function of the single variable, x. Thus

$$w(x) = 3x + 2\left(\frac{9{,}600}{x}\right), \quad x > 0.$$

The condition that x be positive holds because x is the length of a wall.

We next find the first two derivatives:

$$w'(x) = 3 - \frac{2(9{,}600)}{x^2} \quad \text{and}$$

$$w''(x) = \frac{4(9{,}600)}{x^3}.$$

We then determine stationary points by setting $w'(x) = 0$:

$$3 - \frac{2(9{,}600)}{x^2} = 0 \quad \text{so} \quad x^2 = \frac{2(9{,}600)}{3} = 6{,}400.$$

$$x = \pm 80.$$

We discard $x = -80$ because x must be positive in this problem. To determine the type of stationary point at $x = 80$, we test the second derivative at $x = 80$,

$$w''(80) = \frac{4(9{,}600)}{80^3} = \frac{3}{40},$$

which is positive, so we have a local minimum. Recalling that

$$y = \frac{9{,}600}{x} = \frac{9{,}600}{80} = 120,$$

we find that the building dimensions should be 80 × 120, with the interior wall being 80 feet long. The minimum total wall length is

$$w = 3x + 2y = 3(80) + 2(120) = 480 \text{ feet.}$$

> **Exercise.** Suppose the floor area is to be 10,000 square feet, with no interior wall.
> a) What is the function $w(x)$?   b) What dimensions minimize $w(x)$?
>
> **Answer:**   a) $w(x) = 2x + 20,000/x$.   b) A square building, 100 by 100 feet.

Example. A rectangular plot of land is to be enclosed by a fence. Fence for the east-west (E–W) sides costs $10 per running foot, while that for the north-south (N–S) sides costs $5 per running foot. What is the maximum area that can be enclosed if $1,500 is available for purchasing the fence?

We shall carry through the solution of this problem by listing questions and answers in a step-by-step sequence in order to provide a reference framework for solving optimization problems. We shall use x and y, respectively, for E–W and N–S dimensions, and A for the area.

1. What quantity is to be maximized? Answer: The area, A.
2. What is the formula for this quantity? Answer: $A = xy$.
3. How can this quantity be made a function of a single variable? Answer: By expressing y in terms of x, or vice versa, and substituting into Step 2.
4. What information is available to accomplish Step 3? Answer: We know the total amount to be spent is $1,500 and this must equal the cost of the two E–W sides, which will be $2x(\$10)$, plus the cost of the two N–S sides, which will be $2y(\$5)$; hence

$$2x(10) + 2y(5) = 1,500 \quad \text{or} \quad 20x + 10y = 1,500.$$

Therefore

$$y = \frac{1,500 - 20x}{10}$$

5. Express the quantity to be optimized as a function of a single variable. Answer: $A(x) = x(150 - 2x) = 150x - 2x^2$.
6. Find the first derivative, set it equal to 0, and solve. Answer: $A'(x) = 150 - 4x$ is 0 when $x = 150/4 = 37.5$.
7. Test the result in (6) by the second derivative. Answer: $A''(x) = -4$ is always negative so we have a local maximum.
8. Evaluate the remaining variable and find the optimum. Answer: $y = 150 - 2(37.5) = 75$. $A = (37.5)(75) = 2,812.5$.
9. Write a concluding statement directly answering the original problem. Answer: The dimensions of the maximum area enclosure are 37.5 feet by 75 feet, and the maximum area is 2,812.5 square feet.

Example. **Parameterizing a model.** When we write $y = mx + b$ to represent the equation of a straight line, the arbitrary letters m and b represent constant values (slope and y-intercept) that distinguish one line from another. Letters used as placeholders in this fashion (that is, letters standing for constants) are called **parameters**. Now return to Example 2 and let $e (instead of $10) be the cost per E–W foot, and let $n (instead of $5) be the cost per N–S foot.

Similarly let $C (instead of $1,500) represent the total cost. We would then have

$$C = 2x(e) + 2y(n)$$

from which

$$y = \frac{C - 2xe}{2n} \qquad (1)$$

and

$$A(x) = x\left(\frac{C - 2xe}{2n}\right). \qquad (2)$$

The model for $A(x)$ has now been parameterized, and we seek the optimal solution in terms of the parameters, C, e, and n. We have from (2)

$$A(x) = \frac{xC}{2n} - \frac{x^2 e}{n}.$$

Remembering that the parameters represent constants, we find

$$A'(x) = \frac{C}{2n} - \frac{2xe}{n} \qquad (3)$$

and $A'(x) = 0$ when

$$\frac{C}{2n} - \frac{2xe}{n} = 0.$$

Multiplying by $2n$, we have

$$C - 4xe = 0 \quad \text{or} \quad x = \frac{C}{4e}. \qquad (4)$$

From (1) we obtain

$$y = \frac{C - 2xe}{2n} = \frac{C - 2(C/4e)e}{2n} = \frac{C - C/2}{2n}$$

and, multiplying numerator and denominator of the last by 2, we find

$$y = \frac{2C - C}{4n} = \frac{C}{4n}. \qquad (5)$$

The parameterized expression for the area is from (4) and (5),

$$A = xy = \left(\frac{C}{4e}\right)\left(\frac{C}{4n}\right) = \frac{C^2}{16en}.$$

To show that we have a local maximum, we start with the first derivative (3) and take the second derivative, which is

$$A''(x) = \frac{-2e}{n}.$$

$A''(x)$ is negative because e and n, which are costs, are positive, so we have a local maximum.

The obvious advantage of using parameters instead of specific numbers in solving a problem of a given type is that the solution of the parameterized model is a **general solution** that covers all specific cases. For the problem type under discussion, we see that if $C = \$1{,}500$ is to be spent, with $e = \$10$, and $n = \$5$ then from (4) and (5), the optimal dimensions are

$$x = \frac{C}{4e} = \frac{1{,}500}{4(10)} = 37.5 \text{ feet}$$

and

$$y = \frac{C}{4n} = \frac{1{,}500}{4(5)} = 75 \text{ feet}.$$

Exercise. If, in Example 2, the E–W and N–S costs per foot are $2 and $3, and $2,400 is to be spent, what dimensions will maximize the area?

Answer: 300 by 200 feet.

Example. A rectangular manufacturing plant with a floor area of 16,875 square feet is to be built on a straight road. The front of the plant must be set back

high cost of land, builders seek to minimize the total area (plant plus buffers). This area is

$$A = (x + 80)(y + 60).$$

Since the *plant area* is 16,875 square feet, we have

$$xy = 16{,}875 \quad \text{so} \quad y = \frac{16{,}875}{x}.$$

Hence

$$A(x) = (x + 80)\left(\frac{16{,}875}{x} + 60\right)$$

$$= 16{,}875 + 60x + \frac{80(16{,}875)}{x} + 4{,}800.$$

FIGURE 8-16

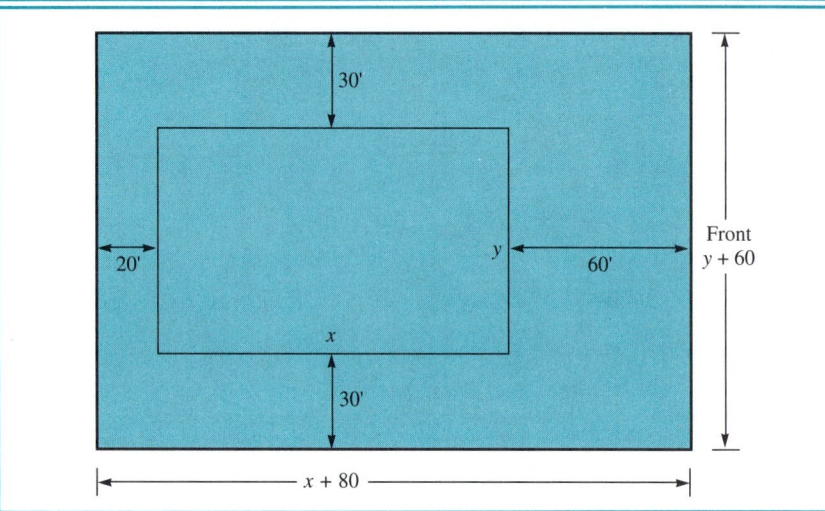

We next find the first two derivatives:

$$A'(x) = 60 - \frac{80(16,875)}{x^2} \quad \text{and}$$

$$A''(x) = \frac{160(16,875)}{x^3}.$$

Now $A'(x)$ is 0 when

$$60 - \frac{80(16,875)}{x^2} = 0$$

$$x^2 = \frac{80(16,875)}{60} = 22,500$$

$$x = \pm 150.$$

Again we discard $x = -150$ because x must be positive.

Testing $x = 150$ in $A''(x)$, we have

$$A''(150) = \frac{160(16,875)}{150^3} = \frac{4}{5},$$

which is positive so we have a local minimum.

It follows that

$$y = \frac{16,875}{x} = \frac{16,875}{150} = 112.5 \text{ ft.}$$

The plant dimensions should be 112.5 feet at the front by 150 feet deep. The total land dimensions will then be

$$x + 80 = 230 \text{ feet} \quad \text{by} \quad y + 60 = 172.5 \text{ feet}.$$

The minimal total land area is $(230)(172.5) = 39{,}675$ square feet.

Example. Figure 8–17 shows a box with square top and bottom and rectangular sides. The total surface area of this box is $2x^2$ for top and bottom, plus $4xy$ for the four sides. Thus

$$A = 2x^2 + 4xy.$$

The volume of the box is the area of the base times the height. Thus

$$V = x^2 y.$$

Suppose that we require a box of volume 2,592 cubic inches, and we seek to minimize the cost of materials for the sides, top, and bottom. Side material costs 6 cents per square inch, and top and bottom material costs 9 cents per square inch. Total cost, C, will be

$$C = \text{(Top and bottom area) at 9 cents} + \text{(Side areas) at 6 cents}$$
$$C = (2x^2)(9) + (4xy)(6) = 18x^2 + 24xy.$$

From

$$V = x^2 y$$

or

$$2{,}592 = x^2 y$$

we have

$$y = \frac{2{,}592}{x^2}.$$

$$C(x) = 18x^2 + \frac{24(2{,}592)}{x}.$$

The first two derivatives are

$$C'(x) = 36x - \frac{(24)(2{,}592)}{x^2} \quad \text{and}$$

$$C''(x) = 36 + \frac{(48)(2{,}592)}{x^3}.$$

Now $C'(x) = 0$ when

$$36x = \frac{(2{,}592)(24)}{x^2}.$$

FIGURE 8–17

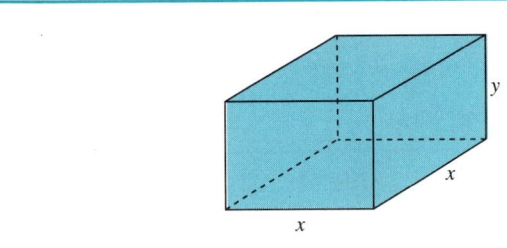

Multiplying by x^2 we find

$$36x^3 = (2{,}592)(24)$$

or

$$x^3 = 1{,}728.$$

Hence

$$x = (1{,}728)^{1/3} = 12 \text{ inches.}$$

It follows that

$$y = \frac{2{,}592}{x^2} = \frac{2{,}592}{144} = 18 \text{ inches.}$$

As the following exercise shows, the cost function has a local minimum at $x = 12$ inches and $y = 18$ inches.

Exercise. For the preceding: a) Find the cost of a 12-by 12-by 18-inch box. b) Prove this cost is a minimum.

Answer: a) 7,776 cents or $77.76. b) $C''(12) = 108$.

Example. According to United Parcel Service requirements stated at the opening of Chapter 7, the length plus girth of a package must not exceed 108 inches. Suppose packages are to be cylinders, as shown in Figure 8–18, and we seek the dimensions (length L and radius r) that will yield maximum volume. The volume of a cylinder is the circular base area, πr^2, times the height, L, so

$$V = \pi r^2 L.$$

The girth of the cylinder is the perimeter of the circular cross section, $2\pi r$, so length plus girth is $L + 2\pi r$ and

$$L + 2\pi r = 108 \quad \text{or} \quad L = 108 - 2\pi r.$$

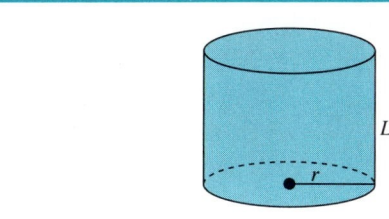

FIGURE 8-18

Hence by substituting
$$V(r) = \pi r^2(108 - 2\pi r) = 108\pi r^2 - 2\pi^2 r^3.$$

The first two derivatives are
$$V'(r) = 216\pi r - 6\pi^2 r^2 \quad \text{and}$$
$$V''(r) = 216\pi - 12\pi^2 r.$$

Setting $V'(r) = 0$,
$$6\pi r(36 - \pi r) = 0$$

from which
$$r = 0 \quad \text{and} \quad r = \frac{36}{\pi}.$$

Of course, we discard $r = 0$ since this value would be impractical. Testing $r = 36/\pi$ in the second derivative,

$$V''\left(\frac{36}{\pi}\right) = 216\pi - 12\pi^2\left(\frac{36}{\pi}\right) = -216\pi,$$

which is negative, so $r = 36/\pi$ yields a local maximum. Next

so the optimal dimensions for maximum volume are a radius of $36/\pi$ (about 11.5 inches) and a height of 36 inches. The maximum volume will be

$$V = \pi\left(\frac{36}{\pi}\right)^2(36) = \frac{(36)^3}{\pi} = \frac{46{,}656}{\pi} \approx 14{,}851 \text{ cubic inches.}$$

Exercise. In the preceding example, suppose the limitation on length plus girth is the parameter, M inches. Express the dimensions r and L for maximum volume in terms of M.

Answer: $r = M/(3\pi)$ and $L = M/3$.

Example. In normal operations, a plant employs 100 workers working eight hours a day for a total of 100(8) = 800 labor-hours of work per day. In normal operations, productivity averages 30 units per labor-hour worked. Thus in a normal day, production is

$$P = \text{(Labor-hours worked)(Output per labor-hour)}$$
$$= (800)(30) = 24{,}000 \text{ units.}$$

If the work level (labor-hours) is raised above 800, management estimates that average output per labor-hour falls off at the rate of 2.5 units for each extra 100 labor-hours or by 0.025 units for each labor-hour in excess of 800. For example, if 840 labor-hours are worked, the excess would be 840 − 800 = 40 and average productivity would be 30 − 40(0.025) = 29 units per labor-hour. Total output would then be

$$P = 840(29) = 24{,}360 \text{ units.}$$

The problem is to find the work level, x labor-hours, that maximizes output. Reviewing the illustrative calculations, we find that for $x = 840$ labor hours,

$$P(840) = 840[30 - (840 - 800)(0.025)].$$

In general, if $x \geq 800$,

$$P(x) = x[30 - (x - 800)(0.025)]$$
$$= 30x - 0.025x^2 + 20x$$
$$= 50x - 0.025x^2.$$

We find the first two derivatives:

$$P'(x) = 50 - 0.05x \text{ and}$$
$$P''(x) = -0.05.$$

Now

$$P'(x) = 0 \quad \text{when} \quad x = 1{,}000 \text{ labor-hours.}$$

Also, since $x = 1{,}000$ is feasible for the output function, and

$$P''(1{,}000) = -0.05$$

we have a local maximum, which is

$$P(1{,}000) = 50(1{,}000) - 0.025(1{,}000)^2 = 25{,}000 \text{ units.}$$

Note that if the stationary point had been at an x-value, which was less than 800, then productivity would have been maximized at the end point where $x = 800$.

8.7 PROBLEM SET 8-3

1. A rectangular warehouse is to have 3,300 square feet of floor area and is to be divided into two rectangular rooms by an interior wall. Cost per running foot is $125 for exterior walls and $80 for the interior wall.
   a) What dimensions will minimize total wall cost?
   b) What is the minimum cost?

2. (Similar to Problem 1, but the area is to be found.) If $49,500 has been allocated for walls,
   a) What are the dimensions of the largest warehouse that can be built?
   b) What is the floor area of this warehouse?

3. (Problem 1 in parameterized form.) The floor area is to be A square feet and the cost per running foot is e for exterior walls and i for the interior wall. Let x and y be the warehouse dimensions, with x being the length of the interior wall.
   a) Write the expression for total wall cost $C(x)$.
   b) Find the expression for x that minimizes $C(x)$.

4. (Problem 2 in parameterized form.) If D are allocated for wall construction then, using the parameters in Problem 3,
   a) Write the expression for the enclosed area, $A(x)$.
   b) Find the expression for x that will maximize $A(x)$.

5. Both interior and exterior walls of a 13,500-square-foot rectangular warehouse cost $100 per running foot. The warehouse is to be divided into eight rooms by three interior walls running in the x direction and one running in the y direction.

   b) What is this minimal cost?

6. A rectangular area of 1,050 square feet is to be enclosed by a fence, then divided down the middle by another piece of fence. The fence down the middle costs $0.50 per running foot, and the other fence costs $1.50 per running foot. Find the minimum cost for the required fence.

7. Fence is required on three sides of a rectangular plot. Fence for the two ends costs $1.25 per running foot; fence for the third side costs $2 per running foot. Find the maximum area that can be enclosed with $100 worth of fence.

8. A rectangular cardboard poster is to have a 96-square-inch rectangular section of printed material, a 2-inch border top and bottom, and a 3-inch border on each side. Find the dimensions and area of the smallest poster that meets these specifications. (Note: Let x and y be the dimensions of the 96-square-inch area.)

9. A rectangular-shaped manufacturing plant with a floor area of 600,000 square feet is to be built in a location where zoning regulations require buffer strips 50 feet wide front and back, and 30 feet wide at either side. (A buffer strip is a grass and tree belt that must not be built upon.) What plot dimensions will lead to minimum total area for plant and buffer strips? What is this minimum total area? (Note: Let x and y be the dimensions of the 600,000-square-foot area.) If the plant dimensions were made 1,500 by 400 feet rather than the dimensions leading to minimum area, by how much would the total plot area exceed the minimum area?

10. In the United Parcel Service example at the beginning of Chapter 7, the length plus girth of a package was restricted to 108 inches. Suppose a shipper uses rectangular boxes with square ends made of a perforated material to provide ventilation to the box contents. To secure maximum ventilation, the shipper wants the total surface area to be as large as possible. Use x as the side of the square base and L as the length.
    a) Write the expression for the area, A, in terms of L and x.
    b) Express $A(x)$ as a function of x alone.

11. (See Problem 10.) Suppose the maximum length plus girth is M. Express the optimal x and L in terms of M.

12. A box with a square top and bottom is to be made to contain a volume of 64 cubic inches. What should be the dimensions of the box if its surface area is to be a minimum? What is this minimum surface area?

13. A box with a square bottom and no top is to be made to contain a volume of 500 cubic inches. What should be the dimensions of the box if its surface area is to be a minimum? What is this minimum surface area?

14. A box with a square top and bottom is to be made to contain 250 cubic inches. Material for top and

8.7 PROBLEM SET 8–3 (concluded)

bottom costs $2 per square inch and material for the sides costs $1 per square inch. What should be the dimensions of the box if its cost is to be a minimum? What is the minimum cost?

15. A box with a square bottom and no top is to be made to contain 100 cubic inches. Bottom material costs five cents per square inch and side material costs two cents per square inch. Find the cost of the least expensive box that can be made.

16. A box with a square bottom and no top is to be made from a 6-by 6-inch piece of material by cutting equal-sized squares from the corners and then turning up the sides. What should the dimensions of the squares be if the box is to have maximum volume?

17. A box with a rectangular bottom and no top is to be made from a rectangular piece of material with dimensions 16 by 30 inches by cutting equal-sized squares from the corners and then turning up the sides. What should the dimensions of the squares be if the box is to have maximum volume?

18. A cylindrical storage tank is to contain $V = 16{,}000\pi$ cubic feet (about 400,000 gallons). The cost of the tank is proportional to its area, so the minimal-cost tank will be the one with minimum area. The volume (V) of a cylinder of radius r and height h is $\pi r^2 h$. Its surface area is the area of top and bottom, $2\pi r^2$, plus the side area, $2\pi rh$. Find the dimensions, r and h, of the minimal-area tank.

19. Suppose the tank in Problem 18 is to be built into the ground to catch runoff water so it needs no top. Suppose, further, that the cost of the base of the tank is $10 per square foot and the sides $8.64 per square foot. What dimensions will lead to the minimal-cost tank?

20. A consulting firm conducts training sessions for employees of various companies. The charge to a company sending employees to a session is $50 per employee, less $0.50 for each employee in excess of 10. That is, for example, if 12 employees are sent, the charge per employee would be $49.00 and the total prorated charge to the company would be $12(49.00) = \$588.00$. The consulting firm further has a fixed total charge for groups of x or more, where x is the number that maximizes the prorated group charge. What should x be, and what is the maximum total group charge to a company?

21. A household appliance service organization has a parts stockroom and a garage at its central office. Its trucks and drivers service customers in a roughly circular area of radius r around the central office. The number of customers per square mile is approximately $80/\pi$ (about 25) in any circular area around the office. Therefore the number of calls in a month is found by multiplying the number of customers per square mile by the number of square miles in the service area.
    a) What is the expression for the number of calls in a month?
    b) The company figures travel cost at $2 per mile and computes mileage per call at $r/2$ miles out from the garage plus $r/2$ miles back in, for a total of r miles per call, on the average. The travel charge per call, excluding parts and labor, is fixed at $24. What is the expression for the net travel income per call? (*Net* means after deducting mileage cost.)
    c) What is the expression for the total net monthly travel income?
    d) What service area radius will maximize total net monthly travel income?
    e) What is the maximum net monthly travel income?

22. When State College charges $195 for a continuing education class in the uses of microcomputers, it attracts 125 students. For each $10 decrease in the charge, an additional eight students will attend the class. Find the tuition value State should charge to maximize revenue. Then find this maximum revenue.

8.8 MORE APPLICATIONS

In this section we present applications using some more complicated functions.

Example. When x gallons of alcohol are produced, the average cost per gallon is $A(x)$ dollars, where

$$A(x) = \frac{200}{0.1x + 5} + 0.05x, \quad x > 0.$$

a) Find the value of x where $A(x)$ has a stationary point.
b) Prove that this value of x occurs at a local minimum of $A(x)$.
c) Compute the minimum average cost per gallon.

a) We start by rewriting $A(x)$ as

$$A(x) = 200(0.1x + 5)^{-1} + 0.05x.$$

Differentiating $A(x)$, we obtain

$$A'(x) = 200(-1)(0.1x + 5)^{-2}(0.1) + 0.05$$
$$= -20(0.1x + 5)^{-2} + 0.05.$$

$$A'(x) = \frac{-20}{(0.1x + 5)^2} + 0.05.$$

Continuing, we set $A'(x)$ equal to 0 and solve for x:

$$\frac{-20}{(0.1x + 5)^2} + 0.05 = 0$$

$$0.05 = \frac{20}{(0.1x + 5)^2}.$$

$$(0.1x + 5)^2 = \frac{20}{0.05} = 400.$$

Taking the square root of both sides (the 1/2 power),

$$[(0.1x + 5)^2]^{1/2} = (400)^{1/2}$$
$$0.1x + 5 = \pm 20$$

$$0.1x + 5 = 20 \qquad 0.1x + 5 = -20$$
$$0.1x = 15 \qquad 0.1x = -25$$
$$x = 150. \qquad x = -250.$$

We discard $x = -250$ because it is negative and the problem statement requires that x be greater than 0.

b) To show $x = 150$ yields a local minimum, we start with
$$A'(x) = -20(0.1x + 5)^{-2} + 0.05$$
and find the second derivative,
$$A''(x) = -20(-2)(0.1x + 5)^{-3}(0.1)$$
$$= \frac{4}{(0.1x + 5)^3},$$
then
$$A''(150) = \frac{4}{(15 + 5)^3} = \frac{1}{2,000}$$
so there is a local minimum where $x = 150$.

c) To find the minimum average cost per gallon of alcohol, we write
$$A(x) = \frac{200}{0.1x + 5} + 0.05x.$$
Then
$$A(150) = \frac{200}{0.1(150) + 5} + 0.05(150)$$
$$= \frac{200}{20} + 7.5$$
$$= \$17.50 \text{ per gallon.}$$

Example.

a) Find the slope of the line tangent to the curve representing
$$f(x) = (169 - x^2)^{1/2}$$
at the point where $x = 12$.

b) Find the y-intercept of the tangent line in (a).

A meaningful application of the method of solving this problem appears in the next problem set.

a) We first find the slope function, which is the derivative
$$f'(x) = \frac{1}{2}(169 - x^2)^{-1/2}(-2x)$$
$$f'(x) = \frac{-x}{(169 - x^2)^{1/2}}.$$

Hence the tangent slope where $x = 12$ is
$$f'(12) = \frac{12}{(169 - 12^2)^{1/2}} = \frac{12}{(169 - 144)^{1/2}} = \frac{-12}{(25)^{1/2}} = \frac{-12}{5} = -2.4.$$

b) The function value at $x = 12$ is

$$f(12) = (169 - 12^2)^{1/2} = (25)^{1/2} = 5$$

so the point at hand has coordinates $(12, 5)$. The intercept of the tangent line we seek has coordinates $(0, b)$ as shown in Figure 8–19. If we now set the slope of the line through $(12, 5)$ and $(0, b)$ equal to -2.4, from (a), we have

$$\frac{b - 5}{0 - 12} = -2.4$$
$$b - 5 = (-12)(-2.4)$$
$$b - 5 = 28.8$$
$$b = 33.8,$$

which is the desired intercept.

Example. Based on historical data, a bus company uses the function

$$P(x) = (3 + 0.6x)^{1/2} - 0.1x, \quad x > 0,$$

to estimate the net weekly profit, in hundreds of dollars, if a particular bus route is x miles long. How long should the route be to maximize the net profit, and what is the maximum net profit?

First, we obtain

$$P'(x) = \frac{1}{2}(3 + 0.6x)^{-1/2}(0.6) - 0.1 = 0.3(3 + 0.6x)^{-1/2} - 0.1.$$

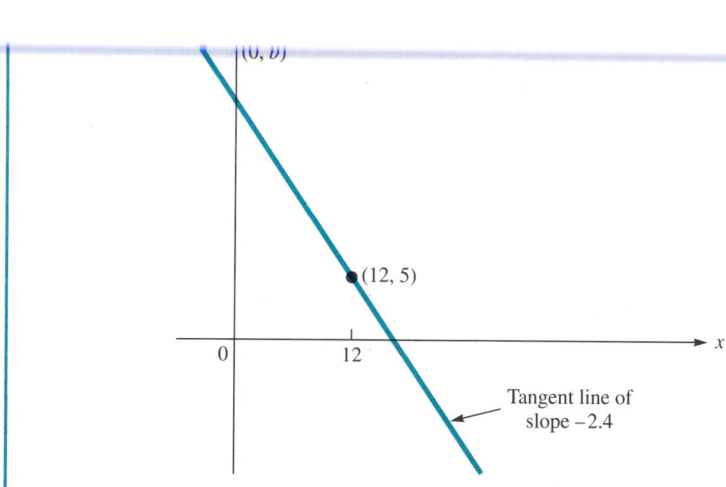

FIGURE 8–19

Continuing,

$$P'(x) = \frac{0.3}{(3 + 0.6x)^{1/2}} - 0.1$$

and $P'(x) = 0$ where

$$\frac{0.3}{(3 + 0.6x)^{1/2}} - 0.1 = 0$$

$$\frac{0.3}{(3 + 0.6x)^{1/2}} = 0.1.$$

Multiplying by the denominator leads to

$$0.3 = (0.1)(3 + 0.6x)^{1/2}$$

so

$$3 = (3 + 0.6x)^{1/2}.$$

Then squaring both sides, we have

$$3^2 = [(3 + 0.6x)^{1/2}]^2$$
$$9 = 3 + 0.6x$$
$$6 = 0.6x$$
$$\frac{6}{0.6} = x$$
$$10 = x$$

so a stationary point exists at $x = 10$ miles. To test this point, we return to

$$P'(x) = 0.3(3 + 0.6x)^{-1/2} - 0.1$$

and find the second derivative,

$$P''(x) = (0.3)(-1/2)(3 + 0.6x)^{-3/2}(0.6)$$
$$= -0.09(3 + 0.6x)^{-3/2}$$
$$= -\frac{0.09}{(3 + 0.6x)^{3/2}},$$

and

$$P''(10) = -\frac{0.09}{(3 + 6)^{3/2}} = -\frac{1}{300},$$

proving there is a maximum at $x = 10$. From

$$P(x) = (3 + 0.6x)^{1/2} - 0.1x,$$

the maximum profit is

$$P_{max} = P(10) = [3 + 0.6(10)]^{1/2} - (0.1)(10)$$
$$= (9)^{1/2} - 1$$
$$= 2,$$

which means $200 per week.

Example. Points A and D on Figure 8–20 are to be connected by highways. Construction cost above BD is $200,000 per mile and cost along BD is $160,000 per mile. Consequently it would be more costly to run a highway directly from A to D, the shortest distance, than to run a section from A to a point C, and another section from C to D. The problem is to find where the intersection, C, should be if cost is to be minimized. As shown in Figure 8–20, AB is 6 miles and BD is 20 miles. If we let BC be x miles, then CD is $20 - x$ miles. Also, because ABC is a right triangle,

$$AC = \sqrt{x^2 + 6^2} = (x^2 + 36)^{1/2} \text{ miles.}$$

Total highway cost then will be, in hundreds of thousands of dollars,

$$2(AC) + 1.6(CD)$$

so

$$C(x) = 2(x^2 + 36)^{1/2} + 1.6(20 - x).$$

Proceeding to the derivative, we have

$$C'(x) = 2\left(\frac{1}{2}\right)(x^2 + 36)^{-1/2}(2x) - 1.6$$
$$= \frac{2x}{(x^2 + 36)^{1/2}} - 1.6.$$

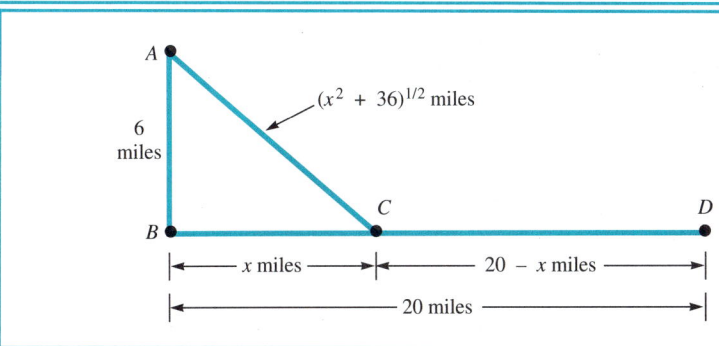

FIGURE 8–20

Setting $C'(x)$ equal to 0 yields

$$\frac{2x}{(x^2 + 36)^{1/2}} - 1.6 = 0$$

$$\frac{2x}{(x^2 + 36)^{1/2}} = 1.6.$$

Now multiply both sides by the denominator, then square both sides to obtain

$$2x = 1.6(x^2 + 36)^{1/2}$$
$$(2x)^2 = (1.6)^2[(x^2 + 36)^{1/2}]^2$$
$$4x^2 = 2.56(x^2 + 36)$$
$$4x^2 = 2.56x^2 + 92.16$$
$$4x^2 - 2.56x^2 = 92.16$$
$$1.44x^2 = 92.16$$
$$x^2 = \frac{92.16}{1.44}$$
$$x^2 = 64$$
$$x = 8, x = -8 \text{ miles.}$$

We discard $x = -8$ because x must be in the interval $0 \leq x \leq 20$ in this problem. To test $x = 8$ by the second derivative, we have to find the derivative of

$$C'(x) = \frac{2x}{(x^2 + 36)^{1/2}} - 1.6.$$

Using the quotient rule, we find

$$C''(x) = \frac{(x^2 + 36)^{1/2} \cdot (2) - (2x) \cdot (1/2)(x^2 + 36)^{-1/2} \cdot 2x}{[(x^2 + 36)^{1/2}]^2}$$

$$= \frac{2(x^2 + 36)^{1/2} - \frac{2x^2}{(x^2 + 36)^{1/2}}}{(x^2 + 36)}$$

$$= \frac{2(x^2 + 36)^{1/2}(x^2 + 36)^{1/2} - 2x^2}{(x^2 + 36)^{1/2}(x^2 + 36)}$$

$$= \frac{2(x^2 + 36) - 2x^2}{(x^2 + 36)^{3/2}}$$

$$= \frac{\cancel{2x^2} + 72 - \cancel{2x^2}}{(x^2 + 36)^{3/2}}$$

$$= \frac{72}{(x^2 + 36)^{3/2}}$$

so

$$C''(8) = \frac{72}{(64 + 36)^{3/2}} > 0,$$

and hence a minimum occurs at the stationary point $x = 8$ miles.
The cost at $x = 8$ is

$$C(8) = \$39.2 \text{ hundred thousand}$$
$$= \$3,920,000.$$

We have two endpoint considerations at $x = 0$ and $x = 20$. A direct road from A to D, that is when $x = 20$, in Figure 8–20 would have a length of

$$[(20)^2 + (6)^2]^{1/2} = (436)^{1/2} = 20.880613$$

and the cost would be

$$\$2(20.880613) = \$41.76123 \text{ hundred thousand}$$
$$= \$4,176,123.$$

This exceeds the cost at $x = 8$, \$3,920,000, found in the preceding by

$$\$4,176,123 - \$3,920,000 = \$256,123.$$

Solve the following exercise to prove that

$$C_{\min} = C(8) = \$3,920,000.$$

Exercise. a) Compute the cost when $x = 0$. b) By how much does this exceed the cost at $x = 8$?
Answer: a) \$4,400,000. b) \$480,000.

We might have been better off to use the first derivative test to determine the behavior of $C(x)$ at $x = 8$. Let's try it. Recall that

$$C'(x) = 2x/(x^2 + 36)^{1/2} - 1.6$$

so testing on the left of $x = 8$,

$$C'(7) = -0.081 \downarrow,$$

and testing on the right,

$$C'(9) = 0.064 \uparrow.$$

Thus we can conclude, with much less work, that (8, 39.2) is a minimum. Through practice, you will learn to recognize the easiest route to the final solution of most problems.

8.9 PROBLEM SET 8-4

1. When y gallons of crude oil are produced the average cost per barrel is $A(y)$, where

$$A(y) = \frac{2{,}500}{0.04y + 9} + 0.16y, \quad y > 0.$$

   a) Find the value of y that minimizes average cost per barrel.
   b) Compute the minimum average cost per barrel.

2. When x gallons of olive oil are produced, the average cost per barrel is $A(x)$, where

$$A(x) = \frac{4{,}000}{0.1x + 20} + 0.25x, \quad x > 0.$$

   a) Find the value of x that minimizes average cost per barrel.
   b) Compute the minimum average cost per barrel.

3. Profit realized when x thousand gallons of antifreeze are produced and sold is $P(x)$ thousand dollars, where

$$P(x) = (100 + 10x)^{1/2} - 0.2x.$$

   a) Find the value of x that leads to maximum profit.
   b) Compute the maximum profit.

4. The output of a chemical process that is applied for t hours is $k(t)$ hundreds of pounds, where

$$k(t) = (6 + 0.3t)^{1/2} - 0.05t.$$

   a) Find the value of t that leads to maximum output.
   b) Compute the maximum output.

5. The section of circular roadway in Figure A is part of the graph of the function

$$f(x) = (10{,}000 - x^2)^{1/2}.$$

   An exit is planned at $P(60, 80)$ and the straight exit path is to be tangent to the circular roadway at point P. Find the vertical intercept, b, of the intersection point, Q.

6. (See Problem 5.) Find the vertical intercept if the circular section is

$$f(x) = (225 - x^2)^{1/2}$$

   and the point on this section is $P(12, 9)$.

7. In Figure B, points B, C, and D are on a horizontal line and A is three miles above B on a perpendicular to BD. Straight-line sections of road are to be con-

FIGURE A

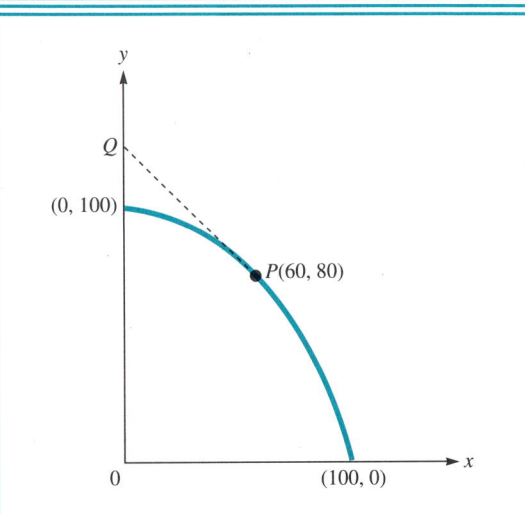

FIGURE B

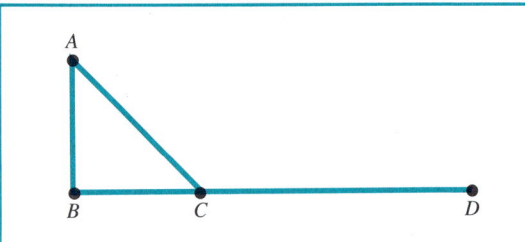

structed from A to C and then from C to D. Construction cost along BD is \$200,000 per mile, but the cost above BD is \$250,000 per mile. The distance BD is 10 miles.

   a) How many miles from B should the intersection C be located if cost is to be minimized?
   b) Compute the minimum cost.
   c) How much more than the minimum would be the cost of a single segment from A to D?

8. Answer (a), (b), and (c) of Problem 7 if A is 8.4 miles above B, BD is 15 miles, cost along BD is

8.9 PROBLEM SET 8-4 (continued)

$200,000 per mile, and cost above BD is $290,000 per mile.

9. a) Find the expression for x at the stationary point on
    $$f(x) = \frac{a}{bx + c} + kx.$$
    b) If a, b, c, k, and x are all positive, determine by the second derivative test whether x is at a local maximum or a local minimum.

10. a) Find the expression for x at the stationary point on
    $$f(x) = (ax + b)^{1/2} - kx.$$
    b) If a, b, and k are all positive, determine by the second derivative test whether x is at a local maximum or a local minimum.

11. A company operates a fleet of delivery trucks. Study shows that gallons of fuel consumed per mile of driving, $F(x)$, is related to the speed at which a truck is driven, x miles per hour, by the function
    $$F(x) = \frac{k_1}{x} + k_2 x; \quad 10 \leq x \leq 80,$$
    where k_1 and k_2 are parameters that vary somewhat from truck to truck.
    a) Find and write the expression for the speed, x, that will lead to minimal fuel consumption per mile of driving.
    b) What speed will provide minimal fuel consumption?

12. (See Problem 11.) Fuel cost is d dollars per gallon and truck drivers are paid p dollars per hour of driving.
    a) Write the expression for the value of x that will minimize the combined cost of fuel and driver, per mile driven, in terms of the parameters d, p, k_1, and k_2.
    b) With $k_1 = 4.9$ and $k_2 = 0.004$, what speed will minimize the cost in (a) if fuel is $0.52 per gallon and drivers are paid $9 per hour?

13. United Parcel Service (UPS) will pick up and deliver packages whose length plus girth does not exceed 108 inches. Fisher Corporation ships a granular grinding abrasive in rectangular boxes with square ends. What is the largest volume of abrasive Fisher can ship in a box? (Neglect the volume of the materials of which the box is made.)

14. When a 3-ton truck is driven at a speed of x miles per hour, it travels $m(x)$ miles per gallon of fuel consumed, where
    $$m(x) = \frac{x}{5.76 + 0.0036x^2}.$$
    At what speed should a truck be driven if $m(x)$ is to be maximized?

15. Answer Problem 14 for a 2-ton truck for which
    $$m(x) = \frac{x}{4.5 + 0.005x^2}.$$

16. Answer Problem 14 in terms of the parameters k_1 and k_2 if
    $$m(x) = \frac{x}{k_1 + k_2 x^2}.$$

17. If the proportion of defective transistors in a very large stock of transistors is p, then the proportion of good transistors is $1 - p$. For example, if 5 percent (0.05 as a proportion) are defective, then 95 percent (0.95) are good. Now suppose that p is unknown. One transistor is selected at random and inspected; then a second is selected and inspected, and so on until the first defective is found, and this is the 10th one, $C(p)$, where
    $$C(p) = p(1 - p)^9.$$
    What value of p will maximize $C(p)$, the chance that the first defective will be the 10th one inspected?

18. (See Problem 17.) The chance that the first defective found is the nth transistor inspected is
    $$C(p) = p(1 - p)^{n-1},$$
    where, of course, n is a parameter. In terms of this parameter, what value of p maximizes $C(p)$?

19. In one run of a process, the number of pounds of brass screws that can be produced is x, where

8.9 PROBLEM SET 8-4 (concluded)

$0 < x \le 300$. The production cost per pound is, in dollars,

$$\frac{100}{40 - 0.1x}.$$

Brass screws sell for $10 per pound.
a) Find the number of pounds that should be made in a run of the process if profit (revenue from sales, minus cost) is to be maximized.
b) Compute the maximum profit.

20. (See Problem 19.) A new process has been designed to make an improved product, self-tapping brass screws, which sells at $15 per pound. In one run of this process, x pounds are produced at a per-pound cost of

$$\frac{100}{60 - 0.05x}; \quad 0 < x \le 750.$$

a) Find the number of pounds to be made in a run if profit is to be maximized.
b) Compute the maximum profit.

8.10 AN INVENTORY MODEL

We all have seen advertisements featuring inventory clearance sales. Such sales serve to emphasize that it costs money to carry a stock in inventory. **Carrying costs** include the cost of warehouse space, record keeping, insurance, damage losses, and obsolescence. Additionally inventory often is acquired with borrowed money, and interest charges on this money can be a significant cost. In this model we consider the case of a manufacturer who produces a product in batches, or lots, periodically, places the produced lot in inventory, and then sells from this inventory until it is exhausted and a new lot is produced. On the production side, the manufacturer can achieve the cost economies of mass production if large lots are produced, but large lots will incur higher inventory carrying costs than small lots. The problem at hand, then, is to determine what lot size, L, should be produced to obtain an estimate of the optimal (minimum-cost) balance between production costs and inventory carrying costs.

To make the problem more specific, suppose that a manufacturer plans to produce 98,000 units of a product during a year. A lot, of size L, to be determined, is to be made periodically, and every time a lot is made it is necessary to set up the appropriate machinery and other production facilities before production starts. The **setup cost** is then a fixed cost incurred for each lot produced. Let us suppose this setup cost is $500. When production commences, the cost of making a unit is constant at $5 per unit. Inventory cost is to be determined on the basis that it costs $0.50 per year to carry one unit in inventory. However when a lot is made and placed in inventory, there are L units in inventory, but as the product is sold during the interval until production of the next lot, the number of units in inventory decreases to 0. Thus the largest and smallest numbers of units in inventory are, respectively, L and 0, and we shall assume that on the average

$$\frac{L+0}{2} = \frac{L}{2}$$

units are carried in inventory during the year. We assign parameters as follows:

Number of units to be made in a year:	$N = 98{,}000$
Number of units to be made in each lot:	L
Fixed setup cost per lot:	$F = \$500$
Variable cost per unit made:	$v = \$5$
Average annual inventory carrying cost per unit:	$i = \$0.50$
Average inventory during a year:	$\dfrac{L}{2}.$

We now determine the expressions for costs incurred. First we note that if, for example, each lot contains 14,000 units, then to make 98,000 units in a year, the number of lots required would be

$$\text{Lots per year} = \frac{\text{Units per year}}{\text{Units per lot}} = \frac{98{,}000}{14{,}000} = 7.$$

Consequently if the optimal lot size (to be determined) is L, we would have

$$\text{Lots per year} = \frac{98{,}000}{L} = \frac{N}{L}.$$

Each time a lot is made, the setup cost is $F = \$500$, so the total setup cost for a year will be

$$\text{Total setup cost per year} = (\text{Lots per year})(\text{Setup cost per lot})$$

$$= \frac{N}{L}(F) = \frac{98{,}000(500)}{L}. \qquad (1)$$

$$\text{Inventory carrying cost for year} = \left(\frac{L}{2}\right)i = \frac{0.50L}{2}. \qquad (2)$$

Finally, no matter what the lot size, 98,000 units will be made after setups during the year, and add a cost of 98,000 units times $v = \$5$ per unit to total cost. Thus

$$\text{Total variable cost for year} = vN = 5(98{,}000). \qquad (3)$$

The sum of the costs (1), (2), and (3) is the total cost for the year, and this, a function of L, is

$$C(L) = \frac{98{,}000(500)}{L} + \frac{0.50L}{2} + 5(98{,}000)$$

or, in parameterized form,

$$C(L) = \frac{NF}{L} + \frac{iL}{2} + vN. \tag{4}$$

Seeking to minimize $C(L)$ in (4), we find

$$C'(L) = -\frac{NF}{L^2} + \frac{i}{2}$$

and $C'(L) = 0$ when

$$-\frac{NF}{L^2} + \frac{i}{2} = 0 \quad \text{so} \quad L = \sqrt{\frac{2NF}{i}}.$$

Inasmuch as

$$C''(L) = \frac{2NF}{L^3}$$

is positive for any applied problem (that is, N, F, and L are positive), we have a local minimum. For the illustrative parameter values,

$$L = \sqrt{\frac{2(98,000)(500)}{0.5}} = \sqrt{196,000,000} = 14,000 \text{ units/lot}.$$

It follows that the firm would make $98,000/14,000 = 7$ lots each year or a lot every $365/7$ days, that is, a lot every 52 days.

Exercise. The annual requirement for another product made by the preceding firm is 7,200 units. The setup cost per batch is $100 and the inventory cost is $1 per unit in average inventory. a) What batch size will minimize total annual cost? b) How often should a lot be made?

Answer: a) 1,200 per lot b) Six lots will be made in a year, or a lot every two months.

In the model

$$C(L) = \frac{NF}{L} + \frac{iL}{2} + vN,$$

note that vN is constant, so its derivative is 0. Consequently the parameter v does not appear in the optimal solution. Notice also that when L is small, the setup cost term NF/L is large but the inventory cost $iL/2$ is small; the reverse holds when L is large. The optimal balance of the cost terms occurs when

$$L = \sqrt{\frac{2NF}{i}}.$$

Finally observe that the optimal L is not proportional to N. That is, if the annual requirement was reduced by 19 percent to 81 percent of its old value, so that the new requirement is $0.81N$, then

$$L = \sqrt{\frac{2(0.81N)F}{i}} = 0.9\sqrt{\frac{2NF}{i}}$$

so the optimal lot size is now 0.9 or 90 percent of (or 10 percent below) its old value.

Exercise. If the annual requirement is cut to one-fourth of its old value, how would this affect the optimal lot size?

Answer: The optimal lot size would now be one-half the old value.

8.11 PROBLEM SET 8–5

1. A retail firm orders a product from a supplier Q units at a time. During a year, the firm will order $N = 2,400$ units. The cost per unit ordered is $u = \$4$, and the cost of preparing and handling is figured at $c = \$12$ cent of) the purchase cost of $Q/2$ units. What are the parameterized expressions for:
   a) The number of orders placed in a year?
   b) The total handling cost per year?
   c) The purchase cost of Q units?
   d) Inventory cost per year?
   e) $S(Q)$, the sum of the handling, purchase, and inventory cost per year?
   f) The order quantity, Q, that minimizes $S(Q)$?
   g) What is the optimal order quantity for the parameter values given in the problem statement?

2. A manufacturing process generates $W = 4,096$ cubic feet of waste per year. The waste is accumulated in a cubical container of side x feet (area = $6x^2$, volume = x^3), which lasts one year and is then disposed interior surface (also assumed to be $6x^2$ square feet) is decontaminated at a cost of $d = \$0.50$ per square foot. What are the parameterized expressions for:
   a) The cost of the container?
   b) The number of decontaminations per year?
   c) The yearly decontamination cost?
   d) The yearly sum, $C(x)$, of the container cost plus the decontamination cost?
   e) The container dimension, x, that minimizes $C(x)$?

   Finally,
   f) What is the optimum container dimension for the parameter values given in the problem statement?

FROM THEORY TO PRACTICE
The Inventory Cost Model

The inventory cost model we just studied is often called the **Economic Order Quantity (EOQ) Model.** There are four underlying assumptions in the EOQ Model:

1. Demand can be determined and is constant over time.
2. The lead time (time between reordering and receiving the order) is 0. (This is called the **instantaneous-receipt assumption.**)
3. Shipments are received in lots.
4. No shortages or back orders are permitted.

All these assumptions limit the basic EOQ Model to very special ideal situations. Most useful modeling starts by looking at a simplified ideal situation and then gradually customizing the model to real circumstances.

For example, if we were to relax the assumption that there are no back orders or shortages, our real inventory problem would be described by the graph in Figure 8–21.

The problem now is to determine the minimum-cost order quantity when shortages are allowed at a cost of s per unit. This cost would include the cost of special handling of customer relations and some factor for lost orders. Notice also that inventory now never rises above I_{max} since we assume that back orders are filled immediately upon receipt of a new lot of L items.

When these costs are included in our original model, the model becomes slightly more general but is somewhat more complex mathematically. Using more sophisticated techniques from the calculus, the resulting formulas (once solved) are

$$L = \sqrt{\frac{2NF}{i}} \times \sqrt{\frac{i+s}{s}},$$

$$C_{min} = \sqrt{2iNF} \times \sqrt{\frac{s}{i+s}}, \text{ and}$$

$$I_{max} = \sqrt{\frac{2NF}{i}} \times \sqrt{\frac{s}{i+s}}$$

where, as before, N is the number of units made in a year, F is the fixed setup cost per lot, and i is the average annual inventory carrying cost. Note that the present result for L is the old result multiplied by a factor of $\sqrt{(i+s)/s}$, resulting in an increased value of L. Similarly the present result for C_{min} is the old result multiplied by a factor of $\sqrt{s/(i+s)}$, resulting in a decrease in C_{min}. In addition, if i is large relative to s, the effect of shortages on L and C_{min} is significant. But if i is small relative to s, the effect will be small. This is due in part to the fact that average holding costs are reduced because of smaller average inventory balances when shortages are allowed. This reduction results in a large lot size needed to fill back orders and restore inventory levels. Hence annual preparation costs are reduced in addition to holding costs.

Let's consider two extreme cases. First, if s approaches ∞, the factors $\sqrt{(i+s)/s}$ and $\sqrt{s/(i+s)}$ approach 1 so that we have the original EOQ Model, which makes sense since no one in their right mind would allow shortages and back orders when the cost is infinite. On the other hand, if $s = 0$, we obtain an infinite lot size L, zero-cost C_{min}, and I_{max} of 0 as the solution. This implies a policy of infinite back ordering, just-in-time supply, or supply only on the basis of a special order.

(continued)

FIGURE 8-21

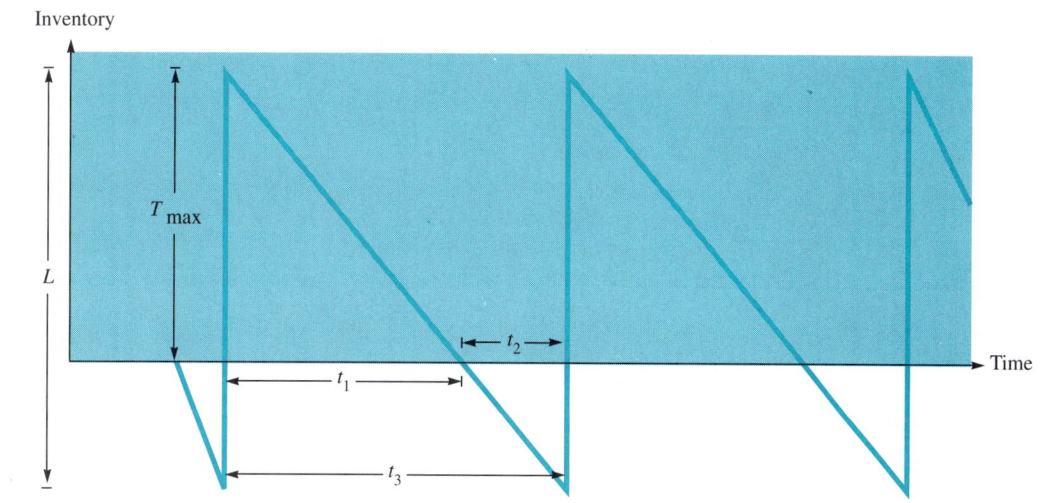

t_1 = Time when inventory is on hand.
t_2 = Time during which there is a shortage.
t_3 = Total time of one inventory cycle.
I_{max} = Maximum inventory level.

Other extensions of the original EOQ Model are possible. For example, we might want to take into account effects such as **quantity discounts** and **minimum-** and **upper-limit orders.** Also if we wish to relax the instantaneous-receipt assumption, product is being manufactured in house.

In many circumstances actual demand is uncertain or **stochastic** and we can build new models where demand is treated as a random variable. These models use the mathematics of probability and statistics (discussed in Chapters 11 and 12) to solve the problem of maintaining **buffer stocks,** which has widespread applications in practice.

The intent behind mathematical model building is not to find exact answers, but to develop a reliable collection of **predictive models** that enable managers to make informed decisions. Any mathematical model needs to be customized to the situation to which it is being applied, but many situations have a similar core nature such as inventory control problems. For this reason, it is useful to know how these basic core models work. One can then modify these models to a form that can be utilized to solve a specific problem or give guidance in determining certain strategies and operating guidelines.

8.12 SKETCHING GRAPHS OF POLYNOMIALS

In Sections 8.2 and 8.4 we saw how to use the first three derivatives to locate all local and endpoint optimum points and all points of inflection. We next present an example showing how to use these techniques to sketch graphs of polynomial functions.

Example. Sketch the graph of

$$f(x) = x^3 - 12x^2 + 50x - 60.$$

We begin by finding the first three derivatives, as usual:

$$f'(x) = 3x^2 - 24x + 50,$$
$$f''(x) = 6x - 24, \text{ and}$$
$$f'''(x) = 6.$$

Determining Local Optimum Points. We now look for stationary points by setting the first derivative equal to 0:

$$3x^2 - 24x + 50 = 0.$$

The quadratic last written cannot be factored so we shall apply the quadratic formula

$$x = \frac{-b \pm \sqrt{b^2 - 4ac}}{2a}$$

with $a = 3$, $b = -24$, and $c = 50$ to obtain

$$x = \frac{24 \pm \sqrt{576 - 600}}{6} = \frac{24 \pm \sqrt{-24}}{6}.$$

The square root of a negative number is not a real number so we conclude that $f(x)$ has no stationary points and hence has no local optimum points.

Determining Inflection Points. We next look for inflection points by setting the second derivative equal to 0:

$$6x - 24 = 0$$
$$x = 4.$$

Testing this point in the third derivative,

$$f'''(4) = 6,$$

so there is an inflection point when $x = 4$. The corresponding value of $f(x)$ is

$$f(4) = 12$$

so the inflection point is located at (4, 12).

Endpoints.   There are no endpoints.

At this point we know that there are no local or endpoint optimum points, but there is a single inflection point at (4, 12). If we knew the behavior of the curve to the left and right of the inflection point, we could sketch the entire curve. Recall that the first derivative told us when the function was increasing and/or decreasing. Thus we test to the left of $x = 4$,

$$f'(3) = 5 \uparrow,$$

indicating that the function is increasing, and to the right,

$$f'(5) = 5 \uparrow,$$

again indicating that the function is increasing. In summary, then, the function is increasing to the left of $x = 4$, has an inflection point at $x = 4$, and is increasing to the right of $x = 4$, with no other critical points. Since there are no local optima, we need to know the concavity profile of the curve to complete a sketch. Checking to the left of $x = 4$,

$$f''(3) = -6,$$

so the curve is concave down. Since $x = 4$ is an inflection point, we know that the curve must be concave up to the right of $x = 4$. This information leads us to

will find that you can draw the graph of almost any well-behaved function accurately and quickly. This is an important skill since cubics with no local optimum points play an important role in economic cost analyses. Our next example illustrates curve sketching of a fourth-degree polynomial, a **quartic,** on a restricted set of points.

graphed by focusing on local and endpoint optimum points and all inflection points.

Example.   Sketch the graph of $f(x) = x^4 - 8x^2 + 26$ on the interval $[-4, 6]$.

Following the procedure of the preceding example, we first find

$$f'(x) = 4x^3 - 16x,$$
$$f''(x) = 12x^2 - 16, \quad \text{and}$$
$$f'''(x) = 24x.$$

FIGURE 8-22
(not to scale)

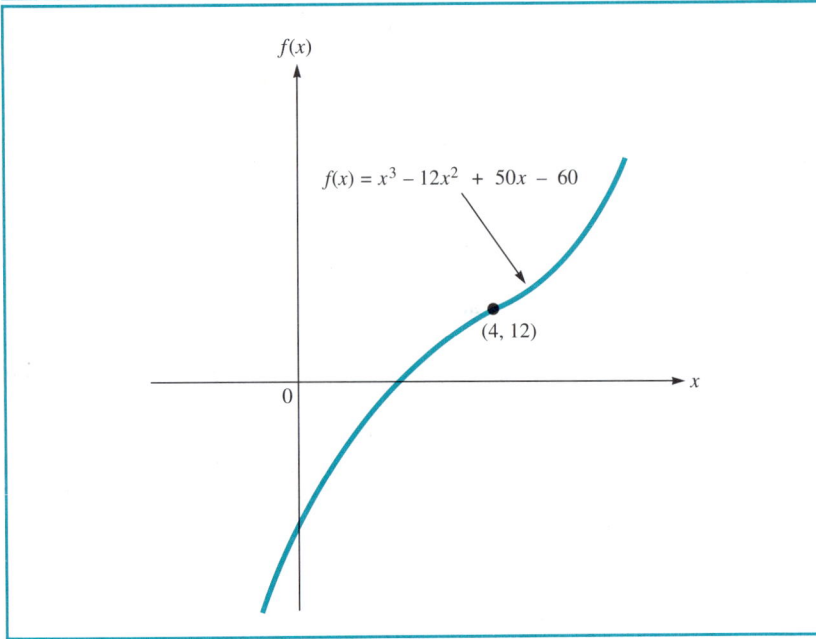

Determining Local Optimum Points. As usual, the stationary points occur where $f'(x) = 0$ so

$$4x^3 - 16x = 0$$
$$4x(x^2 - 4) = 0$$
$$4x(x - 2)(x + 2) = 0$$
$$x = 0, 2, -2.$$

Then checking the second derivative,

$$f''(0) = -16, \quad f''(2) = 32, \quad \text{and} \quad f''(-2) = 32,$$

so we have a local maximum at $x = 0$ and local minima at $x = 2$ and $x = -2$. The corresponding values of $f(x)$ are

$$f(0) = 26, \quad f(2) = 10, \quad \text{and} \quad f(-2) = 10.$$

Hence there is a local maximum at $(0, 26)$ and local minima at $(2, 10)$ and $(-2, 10)$.

Determining Inflection Points. The candidates for inflection point occur where $f''(x) = 0$ so

$$12x^2 - 16 = 0$$
$$12x^2 = 16$$
$$x^2 = \frac{4}{3}$$
$$x = \pm\sqrt{\frac{4}{3}}.$$

Then testing these points in the third derivative,

$$f'''\left(\sqrt{\frac{4}{3}}\right) = 24\sqrt{\frac{4}{3}} \quad \text{and} \quad f'''\left(-\sqrt{\frac{4}{3}}\right) = -24\sqrt{\frac{4}{3}}$$

so we have inflection points at both $x = \sqrt{4/3}$ and $x = -\sqrt{4/3}$. The corresponding values of $f(x)$ are

$$f\left(\sqrt{\frac{4}{3}}\right) = \frac{154}{9} \quad \text{and} \quad f\left(-\sqrt{\frac{4}{3}}\right) = \frac{154}{9}.$$

Hence there are inflection points at $(\sqrt{4/3}, 154/9)$ and $(-\sqrt{4/3}, 154/9)$.

Endpoints. There are endpoints at $x = -4$ and $x = 6$. Checking the first derivative to the right of the left-hand endpoint, $x = -4$, we have

$$f'(-3) = -60 \downarrow$$

so we have an endpoint maximum. The corresponding value of $f(x)$ at $x = -4$ is

$$f(-4) = 154$$

so there is an endpoint maximum at $(-4, 154)$. Next checking the first derivative to the left of the right-hand endpoint, $x = 6$, we have

$$f'(5) = 420 \uparrow$$

$$f(6) = 1{,}034$$

so there is an endpoint maximum at $(6, 1{,}034)$.

In summary, then, the function has a local maximum at $(0, 26)$, local minima at $(2, 10)$ and $(-2, 10)$, inflection points at $(\sqrt{4/3}, 154/9)$ and $(-\sqrt{4/3}, 154/9)$, and endpoint maxima at $(-4, 154)$ and $(6, 1{,}034)$. Note that the absolute maximum is 1,034, which occurs at the point $(6, 1{,}034)$, while the absolute minimum is 10, which occurs at both points $(2, 10)$ and $(-2, 10)$. This information leads us to sketch the graph as shown in Figure 8–23.

The procedure we have discussed can, in principle, be applied to sketch any polynomial. However as the degree of the polynomial rises above 4, problems arise in solving the equations $f'(x) = 0$ and $f''(x) = 0$ so we shall not discuss higher-

FIGURE 8-23
(not to scale)

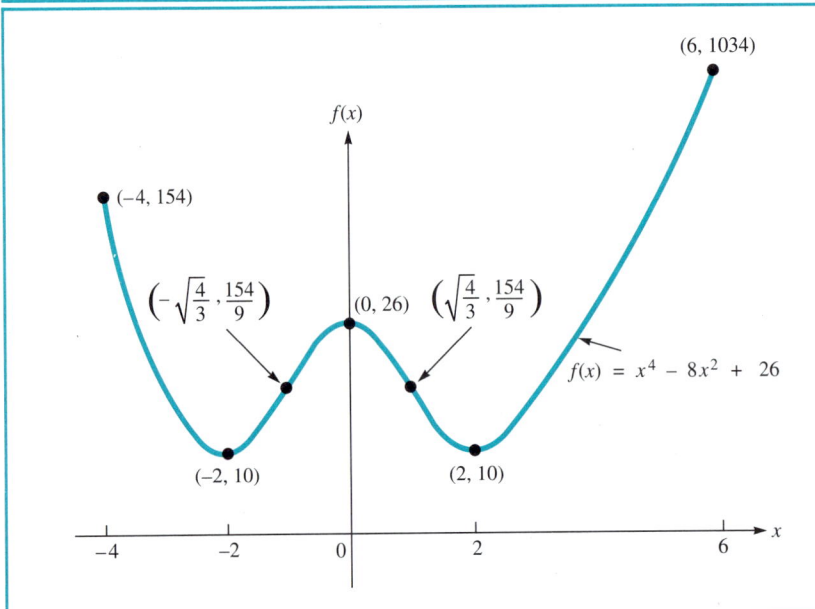

degree polynomials. Because our discussion has been quite detailed, it is worth noting that the procedures presented involved only finding and interpreting the first three derivatives.

8.13 PROBLEM SET 8-6

Graph the following polynomials.

1. $f(x) = x^3 - 18x^2 + 96x - 100$.
2. $f(x) = 9x^2 - x^3 - 15x$.
3. $f(x) = 5 - x^3$.
4. $f(x) = 0.2x^3 + 4$.
5. $f(x) = x^3 - 15x^2 + 80x - 70$.
6. $f(x) = -0.5x^3 + 6x^2 - 25x + 42$.
7. $f(x) = 50x^2 - x^4 - 100$.
8. $f(x) = x^4 - 18x^2 + 90$.
9. $f(x) = (0.001)(x - 10)^4 + 20$.
10. $f(x) = 0.01(6 - x)^4 + 0.32x + 0.56$.
11. $f(x) = x^4 - 8x^3 + 18x^2 - 27$.
12. $f(x) = 10 - 24x^2 - x^4$.

13. Consider the following test:

   Higher-order test for maximum, minimum, and stationary inflection points.

   1. Find $f'(x)$, set it equal to 0, and solve for candidates x (stationary points).

   2. a) If $f''(x) < 0$, then there is a local maximum at $(x, f(x))$.
      b) If $f''(x) > 0$, then there is a local minimum at $(x, f(x))$.
      c) If $f''(x) = 0$, then find $f''',f^{(4)}$, as needed.

8.13 PROBLEM SET 8-6 (concluded)

i) If the lowest derivative that is not 0 is of odd order, then there is a stationary inflection point at $(x, f(x))$.

ii) If the lowest derivative that is not 0 is of even order, then there is a local maximum (minimum) at $(x, f(x))$ if this derivative is < 0 (> 0).

Apply this test to graph the following functions:
a) Problems 1 through 12.
b) $f(x) = x^3 + 8$.
c) $f(x) = x^4 + 5$.
d) $f(x) = 6 - x^4$.
e) $f(x) = x^4 - 3x^3$.
f) $f(x) = x^5 + x^4$.
g) $f(x) = x^7 - x$.

8.14 SKETCHING RATIONAL FUNCTIONS

A rational function is a function that is the quotient, or ratio, of two polynomials. Examples are

$$f(x) = \frac{2x^2 - 3}{x + 5},$$

$$f(x) = \frac{x^3 - 3x^2 + 2x - 7}{x^2 + 3x}, \quad \text{and}$$

$$f(x) = \frac{x}{x - 5}.$$

We start with the last function,

$$f(x) = \frac{x}{x - 5},$$

and our first concern is the discontinuity at $x = 5$. Here the denominator becomes

$$f(5.1) = \frac{5.1}{0.1} = 51,$$

$$f(5.01) = \frac{5.01}{0.01} = 501, \quad \text{and}$$

$$f(5.001) = \frac{5.001}{0.001} = 5,001.$$

The closer x is to 5, the larger is $f(x)$. Thus the curve rises higher and higher as x becomes closer to 5, but x cannot equal 5. Similarly as x approaches 5 from the left through a sequence such as 4.9, 4.99, 4.999, and so on,

$$f(4.9) = \frac{4.9}{-0.1} = -49,$$

$$f(4.99) = \frac{4.99}{-0.01} = -499, \text{ and}$$

$$f(4.999) = \frac{4.999}{-0.001} = -4,999$$

so as x approaches 5 from the left, the curve falls further and further downward, but, again, x cannot equal 5. These characteristics are shown in the partial sketch of $f(x)$ in Figure 8–24, where the vertical line is $x = 5$. Coming in from the left of $x = 5$ the curve falls forever, **becoming closer to but never touching** $x = 5$. We describe this by saying $x = 5$ is an **asymptote** of $f(x)$ or that $f(x)$ falls, approaching $x = 5$ **asymptotically** from the left. Similarly $f(x)$ rises and approaches $x = 5$ asymptotically as the curve comes in from the right.

> If a curve approaches but never touches a vertical (horizontal) line, then that line is an asymptote of the curve.

The next questions concern what happens to $f(x)$ as x moves off indefinitely to the left and to the right. We shall use the symbols

$x \to -\infty$ to mean x decreases (moves off to the left) without limit.

$x \to \infty$ to mean x increases (moves off to the right) without limit.

The symbol ∞ (infinity) is not a number and to investigate $x \to -\infty$, we use a sequence such as $x = -100, -1,000, -10,000$ and so on, and similarly for $x \to \infty$. In

$$f(x) = \frac{x}{x - 5},$$

$$f(-1000) = \frac{-1,000}{-1,000 - 5} = \frac{1,000}{1,005} = 0.995, \text{ and}$$

$$f(-10,000) = \frac{-10,000}{-10,000 - 5} = \frac{10,000}{10,005} = 0.9995.$$

It does not take many such trials before it becomes clear that for very large values of x, the constant -5 in the denominator of

$$f(x) = \frac{x}{x - 5}$$

becomes almost, but not quite, inconsequential so $f(x)$ becomes almost, but not quite, x/x, which equals 1. A simple way to determine the limiting value of any rational function is to divide the numerator and denominator by the largest power of x that appears in the fraction of polynomials. In this case we are considering

$$\lim_{x \to \infty} \frac{x}{x - 5} = \lim_{x \to \infty} \frac{x/x}{(x - 5)/x} = \lim_{x \to \infty} \frac{1}{1 - 5/x} = \frac{1}{1} = 1$$

and

$$\lim_{x \to -\infty} \frac{x}{x - 5} = \lim_{x \to -\infty} \frac{1}{1 - 5/x} = \frac{1}{1} = 1.$$

Notice that as $x \to \infty$ or $x \to -\infty$, $5/x \to 0$.

FIGURE 8-24
(not to scale)

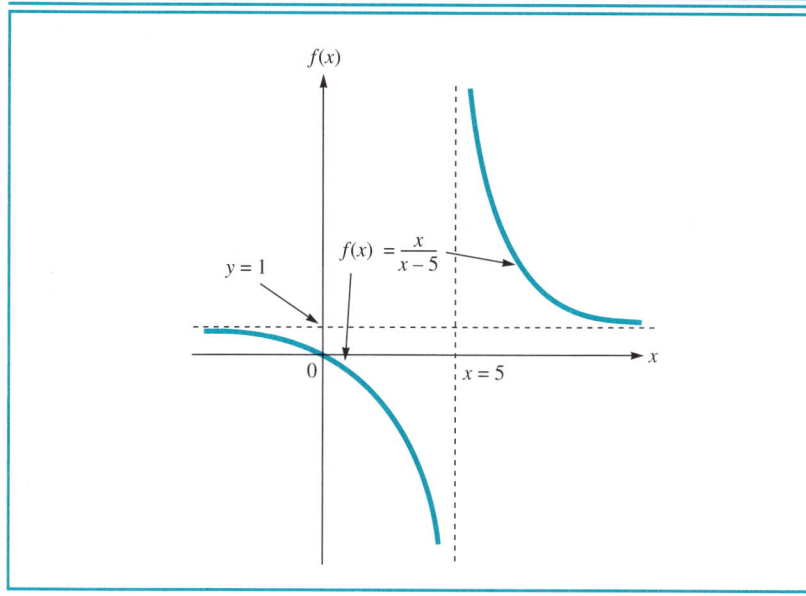

Now, as the preceding sequence shows, when $x \to -\infty$, $f(x)$ increases, but is always a bit less than 1. Hence $f(x)$ approaches the horizontal line one unit above the x-axis asymptotically as $x \to -\infty$. Figure 8–25 shows the asymptote as the constant function $A(x) = 1$. Verify by using a sequence such as 100, 1,000, 10,000, . . . that as $x \to \infty$, $f(x)$ approaches $A(x) = 1$ asymptotically from above, as shown in Figure 8–25. Separately the two branches are smooth curves, but the

$f'(x)$ is always negative (except at $x = 5$) so $f(x)$ is always decreasing (except at $x = 5$). This is consistent with Figure 8–25, which shows that tangents to the curve always slant downward to the right. The concavity (downward for $x < 5$ and upward for $x > 5$) can be verified by the second derivative, which is negative for $x < 5$ and positive for $x > 5$.

Example. Sketch the graph of

$$f(x) = 15x - \frac{100x}{60 - 0.5x}.$$

In the preceding example, we went immediately to the new idea of asymptotes. However, as we did when we sketched curves in Section 8.12, it is useful first to examine the function for local optimum points. To do so, we apply the quotient rule to find

FIGURE 8–25
(not to scale)

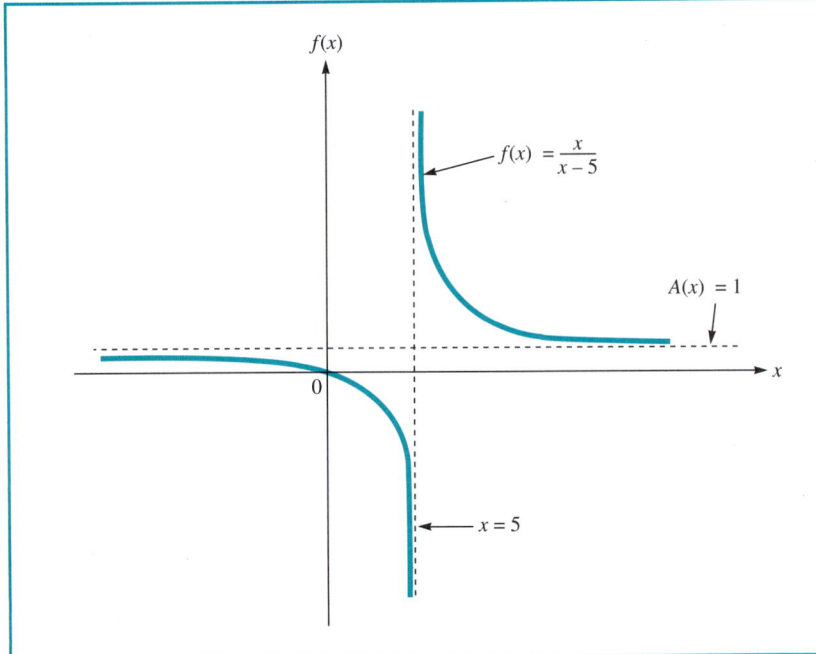

$$f'(x) = 15 - \frac{(60 - 0.5x)(100) - (100x)(-0.5)}{(60 - 0.5x)^2}$$

$$= 15 - \frac{6{,}000}{(60 - 0.5x)^2}$$

and then find

$$f''(x) = -\frac{6{,}000}{(60 - 0.5x)^3} \quad \text{and}$$

$$f'''(x) = -\frac{9{,}000}{(60 - 0.5x)^4}.$$

Next we set $f'(x) = 0$ to get

$$15 - \frac{6{,}000}{(60 - 0.5x)^2} = 0$$

$$\frac{6{,}000}{(60 - 0.5x)^2} = 15$$

$$(60 - 0.5x)^2 = \frac{6{,}000}{15} = 400.$$

Taking the square root of both sides yields ± 20 for the square root of 400 so

$$60 - 0.5x = +20, \quad x = \frac{40}{0.5} = 80, \quad \text{and}$$

$$60 - 0.5x = -20, \quad x = \frac{80}{0.5} = 160.$$

Then checking the second derivative, we get

$$f''(80) = -\frac{3}{4} \quad \text{and} \quad f''(160) = \frac{3}{4}$$

so we have a local maximum at $x = 80$ and a local minimum at $x = 160$. The corresponding values of $f(x)$ are

$$f(80) = 800 \quad \text{and} \quad f(160) = 3{,}200;$$

hence there is a local maximum at $(80, 800)$ and a local minimum at $(160, 3{,}200)$.

The second derivative is never 0, but is undefined at $x = 120$. Indeed, the original function is also undefined at $x = 120$ so this point could not be an inflection point.

Since there are no endpoints, we have only the local maximum at $(80, 800)$ and the local minimum at $(160, 3{,}200)$ together with the discontinuity at $x = 120$. As in the preceding example, $f(x)$ will approach $x = 120$ asymptotically. We now have sufficient information to sketch the graph of $f(x)$, as shown in Figure 8–26.

Note that the left branch falls forever and the right branch rises forever. Why? Let's examine

$$\lim_{x \to 120+} f(x) = \lim_{x \to 120+} \left(15x - \frac{100x}{60 - 0.5x} \right).$$

$$\lim_{x \to 120+} \left[\frac{15x}{(60 - 0.5x)/x} \right] \quad \lim_{x \to 120+} \left[\frac{\cdots}{60/x - 0.5} \right]$$

It is now fairly easy to see that this limit is $+\infty$ so the right branch does indeed rise forever.

Exercise. By looking at

$$\lim_{x \to 120-} \left(15x - \frac{100x}{60 - 0.5x} \right),$$

show that the left branch of Figure 8–26 does indeed fall forever.

FIGURE 8-26
(not to scale)

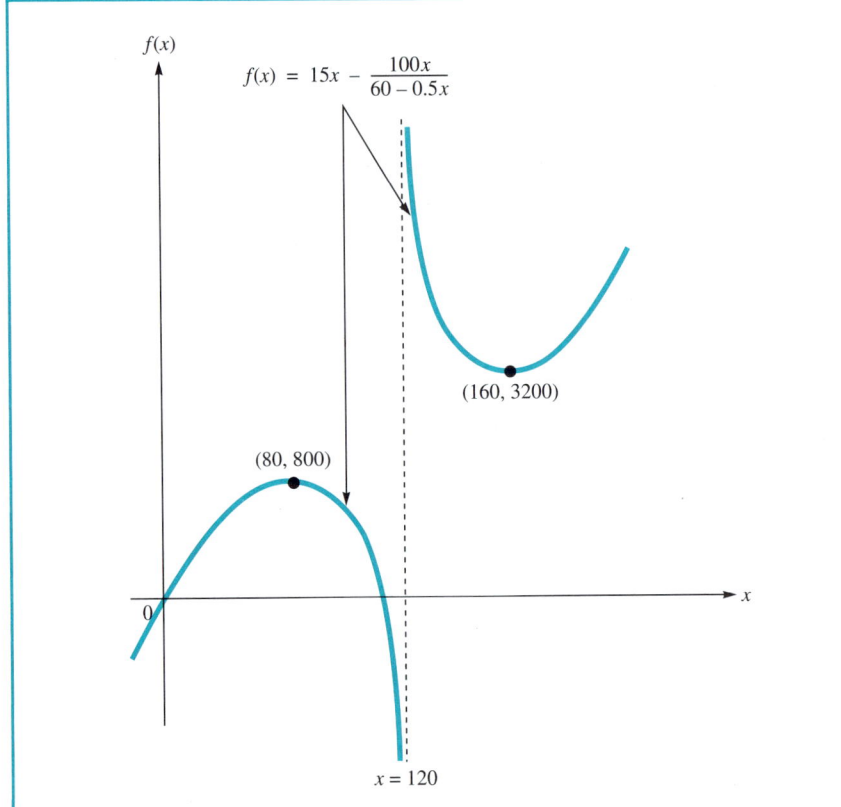

8.15 PROBLEM SET 8-7

Graph the following functions. Place coordinates of optimum points and inflection points on the sketch. If a curve has an asymptote, put it and its equation on the graph.

1. $f(x) = 1/x$.
2. $f(x) = 100/x^2$.
3. $f(x) = \dfrac{2x}{x-4}$.
4. $f(x) = \dfrac{x}{0.1x - 1}$.
5. $f(x) = 9x - \dfrac{48x}{3-x}$.
6. $f(x) = \dfrac{2x}{x-2} + x$.
7. $f(x) = \dfrac{x-1}{x+2}$.
8. $f(x) = x + 1/x$.

8.16 REVIEW PROBLEMS

For Problems 1 and 2, find the coordinates of all local optimum points and describe the graph of $f(x)$.

1. $f(x) = 0.5x^2 - 50x + 2{,}500$.
2. $f(x) = 10x - 0.2x^2 - 5$.

3. If the total cost of producing y yards of madras is, in dollars,
$$C(y) = 0.002y^2 + 5y + 100,$$
find the marginal cost at outputs of
   a) 2,000 yards.
   b) 2,500 yards.

4. If the total cost of producing t tons of coal is, in dollars,
$$C(t) = 0.001t^3 - 0.15t^2 + 10t + 100,$$
find the marginal cost at outputs of
   a) 10 tons.
   b) 50 tons.
   c) 60 tons.

For Problems 5 through 14, find the coordinates of all local and endpoint optimum points and all points of inflection.

5. $f(x) = 0.1x^2 - 4x + 50$.
6. $f(x) = 20x - x^2$.
7. $f(x) = 2x^3 - 3x^2 - 12x$.
8. $f(x) = 8x - x^3 - 5x^2 + 50$.
9. $f(x) = x^3 + x^2 + x - 4$ on $[-3, 4]$.
10. $f(x) = 2x^4 - 216x + 500$ on $[-1, 5]$.
11. $f(x) = 3x^4 - 16x^3 + 24x^2 + 10$.
12. $f(x) = 2x^3 - 9x^2 + 12x$.
13. $f(x) = 2x + 98/x$.
14. $f(x) = 96x^{1/2} - 6x$.

15. Interior and exterior walls of a rectangular 80,000-square-foot warehouse cost $90 per running foot. The warehouse is to be divided into 10 rooms by four interior walls in the x direction and one interior

16. A rectangular area is to be enclosed and then divided into thirds by two fences across the area parallel to one pair of the sides. If the area to be enclosed is 1,250 square feet, what dimensions will lead to the use of a minimum amount of fence?

17. (See Problem 16.) If the fence on the two ends costs $0.64 per running foot and the dividers and the sides cost $1 per running foot, what should be the dimensions if the cost of the fence is to be a minimum, and what is this minimum cost?

18. If a rectangular area is to be fenced in the manner of Problem 16, what is the maximum area that could be enclosed with 1,000 feet of fence?

19. A rectangular manufacturing plant with a floor area of 5,400 square feet is to be built in a location where zoning regulations require buffer strips 30 feet wide front and back, and 20 feet wide at either end. (A this minimum total area?

20. A box with square bottom and no top is to contain 32 cubic inches. Find the dimensions that will lead to a box of minimum area. What is the minimum area?

21. If the bottom material for the box in Problem 20 costs eight cents per square inch, and the side material costs one cent per square inch, what dimensions will lead to minimum cost? What is this minimum cost?

22. A box with no top is to be made from an 8-by 15-inch piece of cardboard by cutting equal-sized squares

8.16 REVIEW PROBLEMS (continued)

from the corners and then turning up the sides. What should be the dimensions of the squares if the box is to have maximum volume?

23. A parcel delivery service accepts cylindrical packages whose length, L, plus girth, $2\pi r$, does not exceed 120 inches. A shipper who uses cylindrical cartons, perforated, wishes to design a carton with maximum ventilation (area). What should be the length and radius of the carton?

24. An appliance service company is located centrally in a roughly square area x miles on a side. It charges $27 per call, not including parts and labor, and travel cost is figured at $1.50 per mile. The average distance traveled per call is $1.2x$ miles. In a month the average number of calls per square mile of service area is 30.
   a) What should x be if net travel income (which excludes parts and labor) is to be maximized?
   b) What is this maximum?

25. Following the inventory model of this chapter (Section 8.10), suppose it costs $250 to set up a plant to make a batch (lot) of a product and $2 for each unit made after setup. Inventory cost is $1.20 per year per unit in average inventory. The annual requirement for the product is 9,600 units.
   a) Write the expression for total annual cost as a function of the lot size, L.
   b) What lot size yields minimum cost?

26. A parcel delivery service picks up and delivers packages whose length plus girth does not exceed M inches. A shipper uses rectangular cartons with square ends. In terms of the parameter M, find the dimensions the carton should have if its volume is to be maximized.

27. Given the function
$$f(x) = 25(x^2 + 9)^{1/2} + 20(10 - x), \quad x \geq 0,$$
   a) Find the x-coordinate of the local optimum point.
   b) Determine whether the optimum point is a local maximum or minimum.

28. When x tons of magnesium are produced, the average cost per ton is $A(x)$, where
$$A(x) = \frac{4{,}000}{0.1x + 20} + 0.25x, \quad x > 0.$$
   a) Find the value of x at the local optimum point of $A(x)$.
   b) Prove that (a) is a local minimum.
   c) Compute the minimum average cost per ton.

29. Profit per tree grown and sold by a tree grower depends upon the height of a tree at the time of sale. Taking h as tree height in inches, the profit per tree, in dollars, is approximated by
$$p(h) = (10 + 2h)^{1/2} - 0.1h.$$
   a) What tree height provides maximum profit per tree?
   b) What is the maximum profit per tree?

30. Points B, C, and D are on a horizontal line with C between B and D. Point A is 4.2 miles vertically above B, and BD is 14 miles. Straight road sections are to be constructed from A to C, then from C to D. Along BD, construction cost is $200,000 per mile. Above BD, cost is $290,000 per mile.
   a) How far from B should the intersection at C be if construction cost is to be minimized?
   b) Compute the minimum construction cost.
   c) How much is saved by the two-section construction choice rather than a single road from A to D?

31. (Note: This problem is algebraically difficult so we shall give the answer, $x = 5/3$ mile.) Point $R(x, 0)$ is on the x-axis. To its left, and above, is point $P(1, 1)$; to its right, also above, is $Q(3, 2)$. A plant is to be built at R and the sum of its distances from points P and Q is to be minimized. Find the x-coordinate of $R(x, 0)$. Note that x is between 1 and 3, so x must be positive.

32. Given
$$f(x) = h(a^2 + x^2)^{1/2} + g(b - x),$$
where a, b, h, and g are all positive and $h < g$, find the expression for x if it is to mark a point where $f(x)$ has a local optimum point.

8.16 REVIEW PROBLEMS (concluded)

Find the coordinates of all local optimum points for Problems 33 through 35.

33. $f(x) = \dfrac{3x}{8 + 0.5x^2}, \quad x > 0.$

34. $f(x) = x(1 - x)^{1/2}, \quad x \leq 1.$

35. $f(x) = 2x + \dfrac{8x}{0.5x - 1}.$

For Problems 36 through 45, sketch the graphs of the functions.

36. $f(x) = 8x - 0.5x^2 - 20.$
37. $f(x) = x^2 - 10x + 35.$
38. $f(x) = x^3 - 6x^2 + 15x - 4.$
39. $f(x) = x^3 - 12x^2 + 21x + 100.$
40. $f(x) = 32x - (x + 7)^4 + 200.$
41. $f(x) = 0.04x^4 - 2x^2 + 30.$
42. $f(x) = x^4 - 16x^3 + 72x^2 - 128.$
43. $f(x) = 2x - \dfrac{50x}{1 - 0.2x} + 15.$
44. $f(x) = \dfrac{2x}{0.5x - 4}.$
45. $f(x) = 36/x.$

8.17 EXTENDED REVIEW PROBLEMS

1. A cattle rancher would like to fence an area of 180 square miles by first fencing the whole area and then running a fence across the middle from front to back. The rancher wants the exterior fence to be stronger than the interior fence and so will use fencing that costs $6 per mile along the outer perimeter and fencing that costs $3 per mile down the middle. What

2. Sketch the graph of the function
$$f(x) = x^6 - 6x^5 + 9x^4 + 4x^3 - 21x^2 + 18x + 15.$$

3. A metal box with a square bottom and top is to contain 768 cubic centimeters. The bottom material must be stronger than the rest of the box and costs four cents per square centimeter. Material for the sides and tops is less expensive and costs two cents per square centimeter. Find the dimensions of the box that satisfy the volume requirement at a minimum cost of materials. What is this minimum cost?

4. Find the coordinates of all local and endpoint optimum points and all inflection points of
$$f(x) = 3x^3 + 9x^2 - 27x$$
in the interval $[-5, 3]$.

5. Find the coordinates of all local optimum points and all inflection points of
$$f(x) = \dfrac{10}{3}x^3 - \dfrac{41}{2}x^2 + 21x.$$

lined decoration to place in the lobby of a new office building. Sam's sketch shows an eight-foot column whose cross section is a right triangle, so the column has three plane surfaces. The client commissions Sam to do the work, but stipulates that the hypotenuse of the triangle must be 40 inches and the triangular cross-sectional area is to be maximized. What dimensions should be used for the two sides of the right triangle if these stipulations are to be met? Recall that the area of a right triangle is one-half the product of the lengths of the sides, and the sum of the squares of the sides equals the square of the hypotenuse. State your answer to the nearest one-hundredth of an inch.

8.17 EXTENDED REVIEW PROBLEMS *(concluded)*

7. Find the coordinates of all local optimum points and all inflection points of
$$f(x) = x^4 - 4x^3 + 35.$$

8. Find the coordinates of all local and endpoint optimum points and all inflection points of
$$f(x) = 3x^4 - 4x^3 + 2$$
in the interval $[-2, 2]$.

9. Sketch the graph of the function
$$f(x) = 7x - \frac{20x}{30 - 0.3x} + 15.$$

10. Chicago Public Water and Sewer Department collects s cubic meters of sewerage annually. The sewerage is collected and treated in a cylindrical container sunken into the ground with a radius of r meters and a depth of h meters which lasts for one year before the metallic sides must be replaced. The top and bottom of the container are made of specially formulated materials which are never replaced. The metallic sides of the container cost m dollars per square meter to make. When full, the container is treated to neutralize the sewerage, then emptied, and the interior surfaces including the top and bottom are decontaminated at a cost of d dollars per square meter.
    a) What is the parameterized expression for the yearly container plus decontamination cost as a function of r?
    b) As a function of r, what dimensions and cost minimize the expression in (a)?
    c) If the total annual sewerage is 100,000 cubic meters, the depth is fixed at 50 meters, the cost of making the sides is $500 per square meter, and the cost of decontamination is $25 per square meter, what radius minimizes the cost? What is this minimum cost?

ADDITIONAL TOPICS IN DIFFERENTIAL CALCULUS

CHAPTER 9

9.1 INTRODUCTION

In Chapters 7 and 8, we learned the basic ideas of differential calculus and applied them to solve numerous problems involving maxima and minima of polynomial functions. Such problems arise in many situations where the appropriate formulation includes functions other than polynomial functions; so in the first part of this chapter, problem-solving ability is expanded by developing derivative rules for exponential and logarithmic functions and applying them to optimization problems. Then we provide a rule (the **chain rule**) that makes it possible to find the derivative when a functional form is implied, but not stated explicitly, and apply this rule to develop the formula for the **multiplier,** which is a fundamental determinant of the behavior of the economy. As we shall see, the derivative involved in the multiplier is a **rate,** and rate interpretations are a new application of the derivative, not necessarily related to maxima or minima. In the last part of the chapter we again expand our set of calculus tools by showing how optimization problems can be solved, and rate interpretations can be made, when a function has **two independent variables** rather than one, as has been the case up to this point. This introduction to multivariate calculus and its applications concludes our work in differential calculus.

The presentation in this chapter assumes that the reader is familiar with the basic ideas presented in Chapters 7 and 8. Additionally it is assumed that the reader is familiar with natural logarithms and the rules of logarithms presented in the first

9.2 DERIVATIVES OF EXPONENTIAL FUNCTIONS

If $1,000 is deposited in a bank account that earns interest at the rate of 8 percent compounded annually, the amount in the account after t years is

$$A(t) = 1,000(1.08)^t.$$

Observe that the independent variable, t, in the last expression is the exponent of the power of the constant base, 1.08. As we saw in Chapter 5, functions that have a constant base and a variable exponent are called **exponential functions**. Other examples are

$$f(x) = 2^x, \quad g(x) = e^{-0.1x}, \quad h(x) = 3e^{2x-5},$$

where, in $g(x)$ and $h(x)$, e is the base of the natural logarithm:

$$e \approx 2.7182818 \ldots .$$

Calculus applications involving exponential functions typically are expressed with e as the base because this choice leads to a remarkably simple derivative, which is

> **The derivative of e^x is e^x itself.**

$$\frac{d}{dx}(e^x) = e^x.$$

This says that **the derivative of the function e^x, is the function itself.** To show how the last statement comes about, we start as always with the definition of the derivative,

$$\frac{df(x)}{dx} = \lim_{h \to 0} \frac{f(x+h) - f(x)}{h}.$$

Hence

$$\frac{d(e^x)}{dx} = \lim_{h \to 0} \frac{e^{x+h} - e^x}{h}. \qquad (1)$$

Now, by a rule of exponents, we can write

$$e^{x+h} = e^x e^h$$

and use this to rewrite (1) as

$$\frac{d(e^x)}{dx} = \lim_{h \to 0} \frac{e^x e^h - e^x}{h}$$

and, by factoring,

$$\frac{d(e^x)}{dx} = \lim_{h \to 0} e^x \left[\frac{e^h - 1}{h}\right]$$

$$= e^x \lim_{h \to 0} \left[\frac{e^h - 1}{h}\right] \qquad (2)$$

where, in the last line, we have factored e^x outside the limit. This is permitted because x is to be thought of as being a coordinate of a fixed point that does not vary as h changes and approaches zero.

We cannot evaluate the limit needed in the preceding by any elementary procedure so, instead, we state and illustrate what happens to

$$\frac{e^h - 1}{h}$$

as h approaches zero. The important point, which can be proved rigorously, is that as h becomes smaller and smaller, approaching zero, e^h gets closer and closer to the value $(1 + h)$. To illustrate, for $h = 0.02$,

$$e^h = e^{0.02} = 1.0202 \text{ compared to } (1 + h) = 1.02.$$

and with a smaller h, $h = 0.01$,
$$e^h = e^{0.01} = 1.0101 \text{ compared to } (1 + h) = 1.01.$$
Continuing with an even smaller $h = 0.001$,
$$e^h = e^{0.001} = 1.0010005 \text{ compared to } (1 + h) = 1.001.$$
Note in the previous three arithmetic expressions that as h becomes smaller, e^h becomes closer to $(1 + h)$. Accepting the fact, then, that
$$e^h \text{ approaches } (1 + h) \text{ as } h \text{ approaches } 0,$$
the ratio in (2) approaches 1 as a limit. That is,
$$\frac{e^h - 1}{h} \text{ approaches } \frac{(1 + h) - 1}{h} = \frac{h}{h} = 1.$$
Hence (2) becomes
$$\frac{d(e^x)}{dx} = e^x \lim_{h \to 0} \left(\frac{e^h - 1}{h}\right) = e^x(1) = e^x.$$

Simple Exponential Rule, Base e

$$\frac{d(e^x)}{dx} = e^x.$$

The derivative of e^x is e^x itself; that is,
$$\frac{d(e^x)}{dx} = e^x.$$

The simple function, e^x, is not nearly as common as expressions such as

or, in general,
$$e^{f(x)},$$
where $f(x)$ is some function other than simply x itself. We have had much practice with the function power rule, which states
$$\frac{d[f(x)]^n}{dx} = n[f(x)]^{n-1} f'(x).$$
The procedure that led to this rule, when applied to
$$\frac{de^{f(x)}}{dx},$$
yields a corresponding result.

The derivative of $e^{f(x)}$ is $e^{f(x)}$ itself times $f'(x)$, the derivative of the exponent; that is,

$$\frac{d}{dx}[e^{f(x)}] = e^{f(x)} \cdot f'(x).$$

Exponential Function Rule, Base e

$$\frac{d}{dx}[e^{f(x)}] = e^{f(x)} \cdot f'(x).$$

Note that in the simple case where $f(x) = x$ so that $f'(x) = 1$ and $e^{f(x)} = e^x$, the Exponential Function Rule becomes

$$\frac{d}{dx}e^x = e^x \cdot 1 = e^x$$

which is precisely the Simple Exponential Rule.

Example. Find the first and second derivatives of

$$f(x) = e^{-0.5x}.$$

We have

$$f'(x) = \frac{d}{dx}(e^{-0.5x}) = e^{-0.5x} \cdot \frac{d}{dx}(-0.5x)$$
$$= e^{-0.5x}(-0.5)$$
$$= -0.5e^{-0.5x}$$

and so

$$f''(x) = \frac{d}{dx}[-0.5e^{-0.5x}]$$
$$= -0.5 \cdot \frac{d}{dx}e^{-0.5x}$$
$$= -0.5(-0.5e^{-0.5x})$$
$$= 0.25e^{-0.5x}.$$

To find the derivative of an exponential expression with base e, first write down the expression itself and then multiply by the derivative of the exponent.

Exercise. Find the first and second derivatives of

$$f(x) = e^{0.1x+2}.$$

Answer: $f'(x) = 0.1e^{0.1x+2}$. $f''(x) = 0.01e^{0.1x+2}.$

The important idea to be kept in mind is that the derivative of an exponential expression with base e consists of two factors. The first is the expression itself, and the second is the derivative of the exponent.

Example. Find the local optimum point of $f(x)$ and prove it is a local minimum if

$$f(x) = e^{0.2x} - 3x + 50.$$

We have

$$f'(x) = e^{0.2x}(0.2) - 3$$
$$= 0.2e^{0.2x} - 3.$$

Thus

$$f'(x) = 0 \quad \text{when} \quad 0.2e^{0.2x} - 3 = 0$$
$$0.2e^{0.2x} = 3$$
$$e^{0.2x} = \frac{3}{0.2}$$
$$e^{0.2x} = 15.$$

We next take the natural logarithm of both sides of the last equation and write

$$\ln(e^{0.2x}) = \ln 15.$$

By a rule of logarithms (see Chapter 5), this may be written as

$$0.2x \, (\ln e) = \ln 15$$
$$0.2x(1) = \ln 15$$

because $\ln e = 1$. Hence

$$x = \frac{\ln 15}{0.2} = \frac{2.708050201}{0.2} = 13.54025101$$

is a stationary point. There are no endpoints. To prove we have a local minimum, we return to

$$f''(x) = 0.2e^{0.2x}(0.2)$$
$$= 0.04e^{0.2x}$$

so that

$$f''(13.54025101) = 0.04e^{0.2(13.54025101)}.$$

There is no need to evaluate this because *e to any power is positive,* so $f''(x)$ is positive, proving there is at a local minimum at $x = 13.54025101$.

To evaluate the function

$$f(x) = e^{0.2x} - 3x + 50$$

at $x = 13.54025101$, recall that this was the solution to

$$e^{0.2x} = 15.$$

Thus we have

$$f_{min} = f(13.54025101) = 15 - 3(13.54025101) + 50$$
$$= 24.37924698$$

so that we have a local minimum at (13.540, 24.379), with three-decimal-place accuracy.

> **Exercise.** Given $f(x) = e^{2x} - 7x + 5.88467039$; a) Find the local minimum value of $f(x)$. b) Prove (a) is a local minimum.
>
> **Answer:** a) (0.626, 5). b) $f''(x) = 4e^{2x}$, which is always positive.

The Derivative of $f(x) = a^x$

The exponential rule we have used requires that the base of the exponential be e. We saw in Chapter 5 that there were bases other than e that are useful. How, then would we take the derivatives of exponential functions such as 10^x, 1.06^x, 3^{6x+5}, $(0.4)^{2x^2-3}$, and so on?

To generalize the exponential rule to cover all bases, a, where $a > 0$ but not equal to 1, we consider the function a^x. By a rule of logarithms,

$$\ln a^x = x \ln a.$$

Exponentiating both sides of the equation, we have

$$e^{\ln a^x} = e^{x \ln a}$$

or simply

$$a^x = e^{x \ln a}. \tag{3}$$

Here we have converted a^x into a form whose derivative we can take by applying the exponential function rule. Thus

$$\frac{d}{dx}(a^x) = \frac{d}{dx} e^{x \ln a}$$

$$= e^{x \ln a} \frac{d}{dx}(x \ln a)$$

$$\frac{d}{dx}(a^x) = e^{x \ln a} \cdot (\ln a). \tag{4}$$

Substituting from (3) into (4) we have

$$\frac{d}{dx}(a^x) = e^{x \ln a} \cdot (\ln a) = a^x \cdot (\ln a).$$

The derivative of a^x is a^x itself times $\ln a$, the natural logarithm of the base; that is

$$\frac{d}{dx}(u) = u \cdot (\ln u).$$

This says that for a base a, the exponential rule contains a conversion factor, $\ln a$. The same factor appears in the exponential function rule. Thus

Exponential Rules, Base a

$$\frac{d(a^x)}{dx} = a^x \cdot (\ln a).$$

$$\frac{d}{dx}[a^{f(x)}] = a^{f(x)} \cdot f'(x) \cdot (\ln a).$$

> To find the derivative of an exponential expression with base a, first write down the expression itself, then multiply by the derivative of the exponent and the natural logarithm of the base.

Note that these rules are consistent with our earlier rules for base e since $\ln e = 1$.

Example. Find the derivative of a) $f(x) = 2(3)^x$. b) $g(x) = 10^{-0.3x}$.

We have

a) $f'(x) = 2 \dfrac{d}{dx}(3)^x$

$= 2(3)^x \cdot (\ln 3)$

$= (2 \ln 3)(3^x)$

$= (2.197)(3^x).$

b) $g'(x) = \dfrac{d}{dx}(10^{-0.3x})$

$= 10^{-0.3x}(-0.3) \cdot (\ln 10)$

$= (-0.3 \ln 10)(10^{-0.3x})$

$= -(0.691)(10^{-0.3x}).$

Exercise Find the derivative of: a) $f(x) = 2^x$. b) $g(x) = 5 - (4^{1-2x})$.

Graphs of Exponential Functions

The characteristics of exponential functions were discussed in Chapter 5 and are illustrated in Figures 9–1 and 9–2 by the sketches of

$$f(x) = 2^x \quad \text{and} \quad g(x) = e^{-0.1x}.$$

Observe that the value $x = 0$, making the **exponent zero, yields the value 1** in the case of both $f(x)$ and $g(x)$. Also, **both functions approach the x-axis asymptotically.** In the case of $f(x) = 2^x$, we see that

$$\lim_{x \to -\infty} f(x) = 0,$$

> All exponential functions a^x pass through the point $(0, 1)$ and approach an asymptote.

FIGURE 9-1
(not to scale)

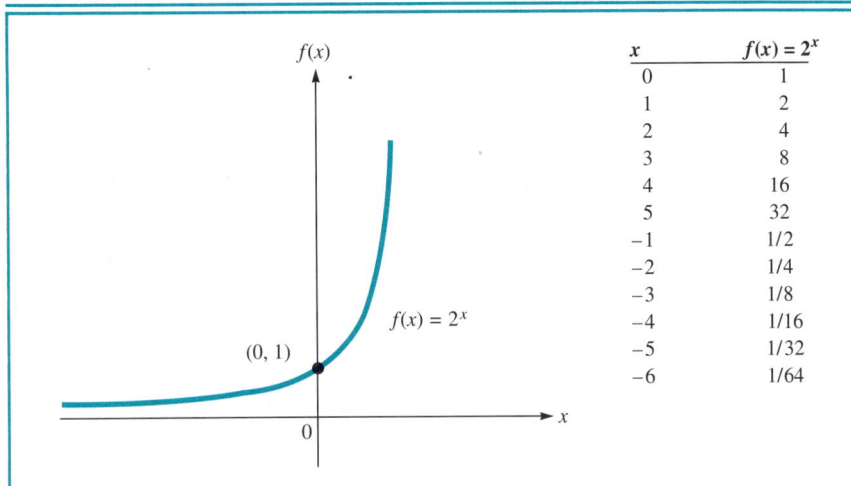

FIGURE 9-2
(not to scale)

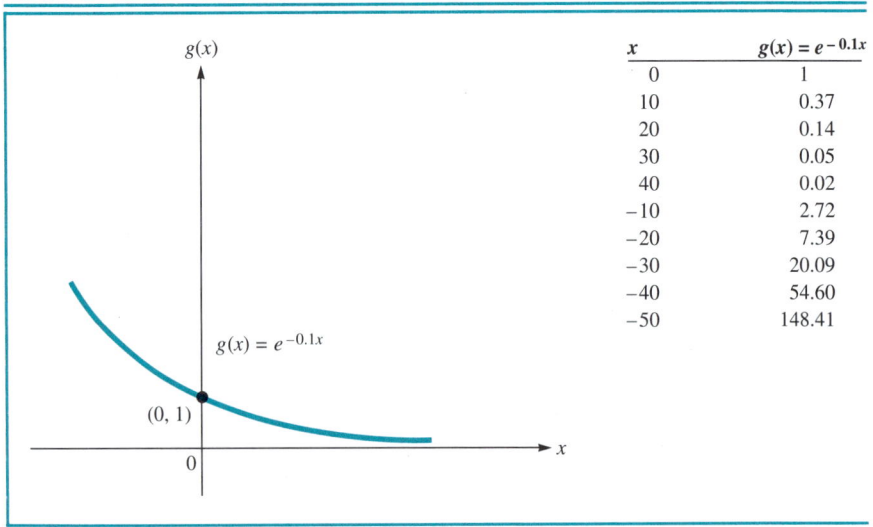

so this function approaches zero (the *x*-axis) as we move to the **left.** Conversely, $g(x)$ approaches 0 as we move to the **right,** as shown in the table accompanying Figure 9-2. It is important to remember that the base of an exponential function must be positive, but not 1, and **such a base to any power is always positive, never zero or negative.**

It follows from the preceding that an exponential can be sketched if we know what its **asymptote is,** in **which direction (to the left or right) it approaches the**

asymptote, and have one point, the **zero exponent point,** as a **starting point for the sketch.** The functions we will want to sketch consist of a constant term C, which may be zero, and an exponential term $Kb^{p(x)}$ as in

$$f(x) = C + Kb^{p(x)}.$$

An exponential function can be sketched knowing the asymptote, the approach direction, and the zero exponent point.

For example, consider

$$f(x) = 10 + 3(2^{1-x}).$$

Here $C = 10$, $K = 3$, $b = 2$, and $p(x) = 1 - x$, so that the constant term is 10 and the exponential term is

$$3(2^{1-x}).$$

Observe that the base of the exponential, 2, is greater than one and that the coefficient of x is negative. If we move to the right on the graph to larger values of x, such as $x = 100$, then

$$3(2^{1-x}) = 3(2^{-99}) = \frac{3}{2^{99}}$$

is a very small number, and becomes ever smaller as x increases. This means the curve approaches its asymptote to the right. Inasmuch as the exponential term approaches zero,

$$f(x) = 10 + 3(2^{1-x})$$

approaches 10, so the asymptote, which we shall symbolize as $A(x)$, is the horizontal line

$$A(x) = 10.$$

To obtain the zero exponent starting point, we note that the exponent $1 - x = 0$ where $x = 1$ and

Hence $(1, 13)$ is the starting point. [illegible]
Figure 9–3.

If the base of the exponential is greater than one and the coefficient of x in the exponent is positive, as in Figure 9–1, the curve approaches its asymptote to the left. Hence **for bases greater than one, the curve approaches its asymptote to the right (left) if the coefficient of x in the exponent is negative (positive).** If the base is between zero and one, its **reciprocal** is greater than one, and we can change to the reciprocal by changing the sign of the exponent. For example,

$$f(x) = (0.4)^x = \left(\frac{1}{0.4}\right)^{-x} = (2.5)^{-x},$$

and, by the right-left principle just stated for bases greater than 1, $f(x)$ **approaches its asymptote to the right.**

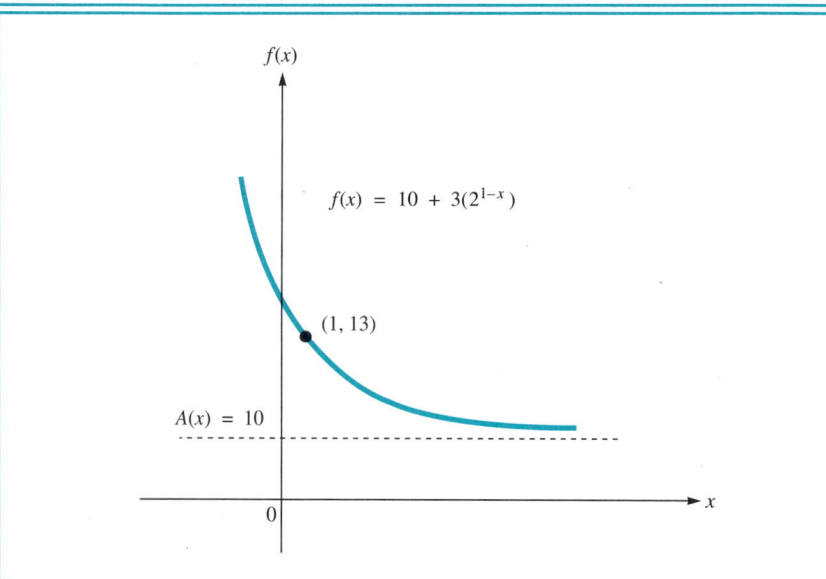

FIGURE 9-3 (not to scale)

Three-step procedure for sketching exponential functions using the horizontal asymptote, the zero exponent point, and the direction of approach indicator.

Procedure for Sketching Exponentials $f(x) = C + Kb^{p(x)}$

1. Draw the **horizontal asymptote,** which is $A(x) = C$ (the constant term).
2. Find the **zero exponent point** [the point where $p(x) = 0$] to locate on which side of the asymptote the curve will lie.
3. Find the **direction of approach indicator** to see how the curve approaches the asymptote by taking the sign of x in the exponent $p(x)$ for bases greater than one and the opposite sign for bases between zero and one. A positive (negative) indicator means the approach is to the left (right).

Note that at the zero exponent point,

$$f(x) = C + K.$$

Thus if $K > 0$, this point lies **above** the asymptote $A(x) = C$, and if $K < 0$, it lies **below.**

Example. Describe the characteristics of the graph of

$$f(x) = 20 - 9(2^{0.5x-3}).$$

Here

$$C = 20, K = -9, b = 2, \text{ and } p(x) = 0.5x - 3.$$

FIGURE 9-4
(not to scale)

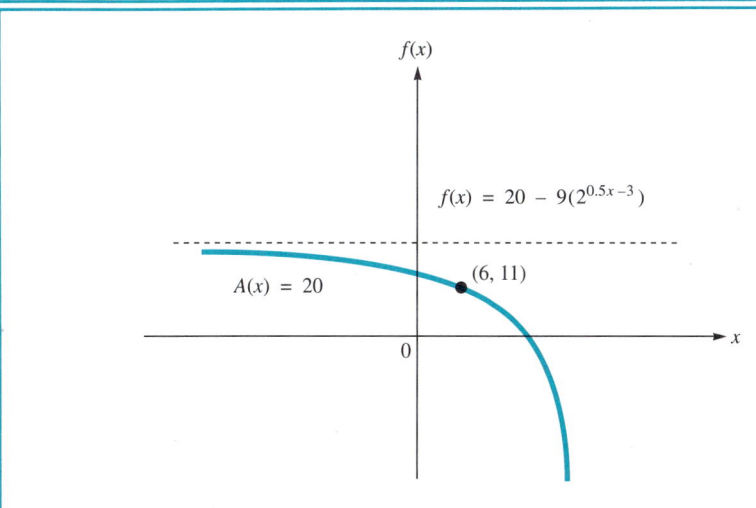

Applying the three-step procedure, then:

1. The asymptote is the horizontal line $A(x) = 20$.
2. The zero exponent occurs where

$$0.5x - 3 = 0$$
$$0.5x = 3$$
$$x = \frac{3}{0.5} = 6.$$

Thus

$$f(6) = 20 - 9(2^0) = 11$$

So $(6, 11)$ is a starting point located below the asymptote since the y-coordinate, 11, of the point is smaller than the y-coordinate, 20, of the asymptote. This is consistent with the fact that $K < 0$.

3. The base is greater than 1, so the positive coefficient of x means the curve approaches its asymptote to the left.

As shown in Figure 9-4, the curve rises to the left of $(6, 11)$ toward the asymptote and falls ever more steeply to the right of $(6, 11)$.

Exercise. Describe the graph of $f(x) = 20 + 10e^{3 - 0.5x}$.

Answer: Starting at $(6, 30)$ the curve falls to the right toward its asymptote, $A(x) = 20$. To the left of $(6, 30)$ it rises ever more steeply.

9.3 RESPONSE FUNCTIONS

Response functions measure the penetration or infiltration of a population over time.

Newprod Company is in the planning stages of a promotional effort to sell a new product. As a result of its market research, the company expects to penetrate at most 40 percent of the potential customers. So the company has decided to use the exponential function

$$r(t) = 0.40 - 0.40e^{-0.02t}$$

as an indicator of the proportion of all potential customers who will have responded to the promotion in its first t days of operation. Thus, for example, during the first 50 days

$$\begin{aligned} r(50) &= 0.40 - 0.40e^{-0.02(50)} \\ &= 0.40 - 0.40e^{-1} \\ &= 0.40 - 0.40(0.367879441) \\ &= 0.252848224 \end{aligned}$$

or 25.285 percent of potential customers are expected to respond. It follows from the discussion in the previous section that the exponential response function has $A(x) = 0.40$ as its asymptote and that the proportion responding rises as time goes on (t increases), but never reaches 0.40.

Newprod market research personnel estimate the total number of potential customers at 5,000,000 and that, on the average, one response will yield a revenue of $2. The cost of running the promotion consists of a fixed cost of $155,200 plus a variable cost of $24,000 each day the promotion is continued. In summary:

Proportion responding in t days: $r(t) = 0.40 - 0.40e^{-0.02t}$
Number of potential customers: 5,000,000.
Average revenue per response: $2.
Cost in t days: $C(t) = (155{,}200 + 24{,}000t)$ dollars.

Total revenue in t days, symbolized as $R(t)$, will be $2 times the number of responses, and the number of responses will be $r(t)$, the proportion responding, times 5,000,000. Thus

$$R(t) = \$2(\text{proportion responding})(5{,}000{,}000)$$
$$R(t) = 10{,}000{,}000(0.4 - 0.4e^{-0.02t}).$$

Profit at t days, $P(t)$, will be total revenue minus cost:

$$\begin{aligned} P(t) &= R(t) - C(t) \\ &= 10{,}000{,}000(0.4 - 0.4e^{-0.02t}) - (155{,}200 + 24{,}000t) \\ &= 4{,}000{,}000 - 4{,}000{,}000e^{-0.02t} - 155{,}200 - 24{,}000t \\ P(t) &= 3{,}844{,}800 - 4{,}000{,}000e^{-0.02t} - 24{,}000t. \end{aligned}$$

Newprod now wants to know how many days the promotion should be continued to maximize profit. Taking the derivative,

$$P'(t) = -4,000,000e^{-0.02t}(-0.02) - 24,000$$
$$= 80,000e^{-0.02t} - 24,000.$$

To have a local optimum point $P'(t)$ must be zero. Hence

$$80,000e^{-0.02t} - 24,000 = 0$$
$$80,000e^{-0.02t} = 24,000$$
$$e^{-0.02t} = \frac{24,000}{80,000}$$
$$e^{-0.02t} = 0.3.$$

Taking the natural logarithm of both sides yields

$$\ln(e^{-0.02t}) = \ln 0.3$$
$$-0.02t(\ln e) = \ln 0.3$$
$$-0.02t = \ln 0.3$$
$$t = \frac{\ln 0.3}{-0.02}$$
$$= \frac{-1.203972804}{-0.02}$$
$$t = 60.19864022$$

or 60.199 days. It may be verified that $P''(t)$ is negative for all values of t, so we have maximum profit if the promotion is continued for about 60 days. To compute the maximum, we find $P(t)$, remembering that $e^{-0.02t} = 0.3$. Thus

$$P_{max} = P(60.19864022) = 3,844,800 - 4,000,000(0.3)$$
$$- 24,000(60.19864022)$$
$$\approx \$1,200,000.$$

Exercise. Resolve the preceding example if the response function is changed to $r(t) = 0.50 - 0.50e^{-0.03t}$.

Answer: 60.086 days with a maximum profit of about $2,578,735.

9.4 PROBLEM SET 9-1

Find the first and second derivatives of each of the following functions:

1. $f(x) = 2e^x$.
2. $f(x) = 5^x$.
3. $f(x) = 7^x$.
4. $f(x) = 3e^x$.

9.4 PROBLEM SET 9-1 (concluded)

5. $f(x) = 5e^{-0.2x}$.
6. $f(x) = 2.5e^{-0.4x}$.
7. $f(x) = 20e^{3-0.1x}$.
8. $f(x) = 10e^{0.3x-6}$.
9. $f(x) = e^{x^2}$.
10. $f(x) = e^{-x^2}$.
11. $f(x) = (1/2)^{-3x}$.
12. $f(x) = (0.4)^{-0.3x}$.
13. $f(x) = 1{,}000(1.06)^x$.
14. $f(x) = 500(1.08)^{-x}$.

In Problems 15 through 22, sketch the curve. Show the starting point coordinates and the asymptote with its equation.

15. $f(x) = 5^x$.
16. $f(x) = 5^{-x}$.
17. $f(x) = 2^{3-0.5x}$.
18. $f(x) = 3^{0.5x-2}$.
19. $f(x) = (0.5)^x$.
20. $f(x) = (0.25)^{-x}$.
21. $f(x) = 15 - 10e^{3-0.1x}$.
22. $f(x) = 20 + 15e^{2-0.1x}$.

23. Find the slope of the line tangent to the following at the point where $x = 2$:
$$f(x) = e^{-0.1x^2 + 2x - 3}.$$

24. Newprod Company estimates the total potential number of customers for a new product is 1,000,000. It plans to operate a promotional campaign to sell the product and uses the response function
$$r(t) = 0.25 - 0.25e^{-0.01t}$$
as a measure of the proportion of total customer potential responding to the promotion after it has been in operation for t days. On the average, one response generates \$5 in revenue. Campaign costs consist of a fixed cost of \$15,000 plus a variable cost of \$1,000 per day of operation.
   a) How long should the campaign continue if profit (revenue minus cost) is to be maximized?
   b) Compute the maximum profit.

25. Solve Problem 24 if the response function is
$$r(t) = 0.25 - 0.25e^{-0.02t}$$
and other facts remain as given.

26. An oil deposit contains 1,000,000 barrels of oil, which, after being pumped from the deposit, yields a revenue of \$12 per barrel. The proportion of the deposit that will have been pumped out after t years of pumping is
$$0.9 - 0.9e^{-0.16t}.$$
Operating costs are \$345,600 per year.
   a) How long should pumping be continued to maximize profit?
   b) Compute the maximum profit.

27. Answer Problem 26 if revenue per barrel is \$15.

28. The revenue from, and cost of, operating an undertaking for t years are, respectively,
$$R(t) = 4e^{0.3t} \quad \text{and} \quad C(t) = 1.5e^{0.4t}$$
millions of dollars. How long should the undertaking be continued if profit is to be maximized?

In Problems 29 through 34, find the value of the function at its local optimum point and state whether this is a local maximum or minimum.

29. $f(x) = 25x - e^x$.
30. $f(x) = 0.1x + e^{-0.1x}$.
31. $f(x) = 0.02x + e^{-0.1x}$.
32. $f(x) = e^{x - 0.1x^2}$.
33. $f(x) = 10x - e^{0.2x}$.
34. $f(x) = 0.05x + e^{-0.1x} + 4$.

9.5 DERIVATIVES OF LOGARITHMIC FUNCTIONS

To obtain the simple logarithmic derivative rule, we start with

$$g(x) = \ln x. \qquad (1)$$

Applying the definition of a logarithm, equation (1) means

$$e^{g(x)} = x. \qquad (2)$$

Taking the derivative with respect to x by application of the Exponential Function Rule, we have

$$\frac{d}{dx}[e^{g(x)}] = \frac{d}{dx}(x)$$

$$e^{g(x)}g'(x) = 1$$

$$g'(x) = \frac{1}{e^{g(x)}}.$$

But from (2), the right side of the previous expression is $1/x$. Hence

$$g'(x) = \frac{1}{x}.$$

Thus

$$\frac{d}{dx}[g(x)] = g'(x) = \frac{1}{x},$$

and from (1), $g(x)$ is $\ln x$, so

$$\frac{d}{dx}(\ln x) = \frac{1}{x}.$$

Thus the simple logarithmic function, $\ln x$, has the reciprocal of x as its derivative. Moreover, as might by now be expected, the logarithm of $f(x)$, $\ln f(x)$, has as its

Logarithmic Rules, Base e

$$\frac{d}{dx}(\ln x) = \frac{1}{x}.$$

$$\frac{d}{dx}\ln[f(x)] = \frac{1}{f(x)} \cdot f'(x) = \frac{f'(x)}{f(x)}.$$

To find the derivative of the natural logarithm of an expression, first write down the reciprocal of the expression itself, and then multiply by the derivative of the expression.

Because of the simplicity of the derivative rules when the natural logarithm system is used, we shall not use base 10 (common) logarithms in our work with calculus. If we wish to find the derivative of $f(x) = \log_{10} f(x)$, we need only remember

$$\log_{10} f(x) = \frac{\ln f(x)}{\ln 10},$$

so

$$\frac{d}{dx}[\log_{10} f(x)] = \frac{1}{\ln 10} \cdot \frac{1}{f(x)} \cdot f'(x)$$

$$= 0.434294482 \, \frac{f'(x)}{f(x)}.$$

Example. Find $f'(2)$ if

$$f(x) = \ln(2x + 1) + \ln x.$$

We have

$$f'(x) = \frac{1}{2x + 1} \cdot 2 + \frac{1}{x}$$

$$= \frac{2}{2x + 1} + \frac{1}{x}.$$

Thus

$$f'(2) = \frac{2}{5} + \frac{1}{2} = 0.4 + 0.5 = 0.9.$$

Exercise. Find $h'(1)$ if $h(x) = \ln(x^2 + 3x + 1) + 2 \ln x$.

Answer: 3.

Sketching the Graph of $g(x) = \ln x$

The graph of $\ln x$ passes through the point $(1, 0)$, rises slowly to the right, and has the y-axis as a vertical asymptote to the left.

Inasmuch as $\ln 1 = 0$, the graph of this function passes through $(1, 0)$ as shown in Figure 9–5. The table accompanying the graph shows that to the right of $(1, 0)$ the curve rises, but not very rapidly, because $\ln x$ increases slowly as x increases. To the left of $(1, 0)$, where x is less than one, $\ln x$ is negative and the closer x is to zero, the further the curve drops below the x-axis. But note that x cannot be zero or negative because only positive numbers have logarithms. It follows that as x approaches zero, the curve falls and approaches the vertical axis asymptotically.

Exercise. Prove that $f(x) = \ln x$ is concave downward at all permissible values of x.

Answer: This is true because $f''(x) = -1/x^2$, which is negative for all values of x.

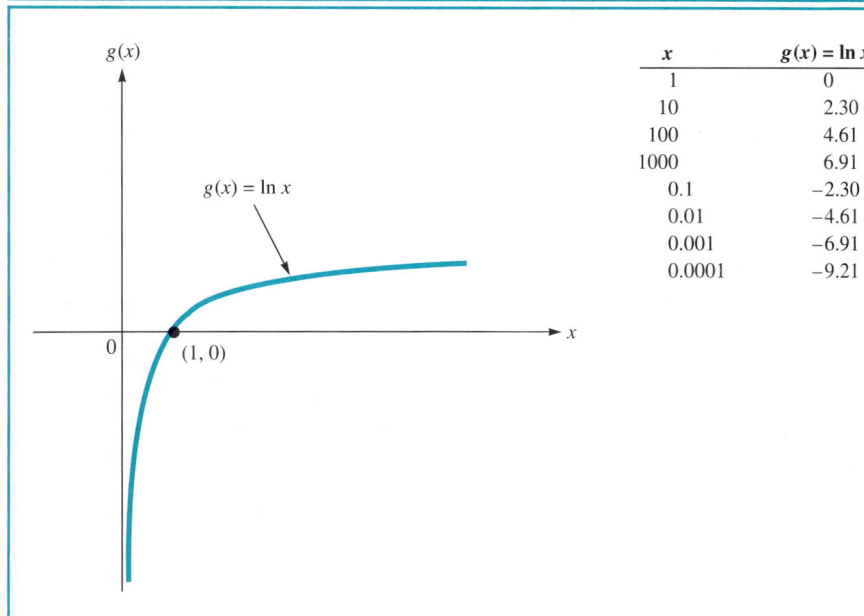

FIGURE 9-5
(not to scale)

x	$g(x) = \ln x$
1	0
10	2.30
100	4.61
1000	6.91
0.1	-2.30
0.01	-4.61
0.001	-6.91
0.0001	-9.21

9.6 PROBLEM SET 9-2

Find the derivatives of the following functions:

1. $f(x) = \ln x$.
2. $f(x) = 3 \ln(2x)$.
3. ~~$f(x) = \ln(2x + 3)$.~~
4. ~~...~~
5. ~~$f(x) = \ln e^x$.~~
6. $f(x) = \ln(2x + 5)^{1/3}$.
7. $f(x) = \ln(x^2 + 2x)$.
8. ~~$f(x) = \ln(2x^3 - 6x)$.~~

In Problems 10 through 15, find the value of $f(x)$ at its local optimum point and state whether this is a local maximum or minimum.

10. $f(x) = 20x - 10 \ln x$.
11. $f(x) = 100 \ln x - 0.5x^2$.
12. $f(x) = 3x - 12 \ln x$.
13. $f(x) = \ln(x^2 - 10x + 35)$.
14. $f(x) = 100x^2 - 72 \ln x$.
15. $f(x) = 0.5x^2 - 4x - 5 \ln x + 25$.

16. When x ounces of seed costing $2 per ounce are sown on a plot of land, the crop yield is $\ln(2x + 1)$ bushels worth $25 per bushel. How many ounces should be sown if the worth of the crop minus the cost of the seed is to be maximized?

17. Solve Problem 16 if seed cost changes to $2.50 per ounce and the crop is worth $30 per bushel.

18. Farmers use a certain plant food costing $4 per ounce to help them in growing oranges. It is estimated that when x ounces of the food are used on an acre of

9.6 PROBLEM SET 9-2 (concluded)

orange grove, the farmer is able to get $\ln(4x + 5)$ crates of oranges from that acre. If the farmer can sell the oranges at $20 per crate, how many ounces should be used per acre to maximize the orange crop's net value?

19. Repeat Problem 18 if the plant food costs $3 per ounce and the farmer can sell oranges at $24 per crate.

9.7 THE CHAIN RULE

The function power, exponential function, and logarithmic function rules are special cases of the **chain rule**.

The Function Power Rule, the Exponential Function Rule, and the Logarithmic Function Rule that we have developed and worked with are special cases of a general rule for taking derivatives called the **chain rule**. As an example of the chain rule, suppose we have a function

$$k(z) = z^5$$

and we wish to find

$$\frac{d}{dx} k(z) = \frac{d}{dx} z^5. \tag{1}$$

We must be careful not to confuse this with

$$\frac{d}{dz} z^5 = 5z^4 \tag{2}$$

because (1) asks for the **derivative with respect to** x whereas (2) asks for the **derivative with respect to** z. If we do not know exactly how z depends on x, we cannot find

$$\frac{d}{dx} z^5$$

in terms of x.

Suppose on the other hand that we do know that

$$z = x^3 + x^2. \tag{3}$$

Then

$$\frac{d}{dx} k(z) = \frac{d}{dx} z^5 = \frac{d}{dx} (x^3 + x^2)^5$$

$$= 5(x^3 + x^2)^4 \cdot (3x^2 + 2x) \tag{4}$$

by the function power rule. From (3), this last expression can be rewritten as

$$5z^4 \cdot \frac{dz}{dx}$$

so

$$\frac{d}{dx} k(z) = \frac{d}{dx} z^5 = 5z^4 \cdot \frac{dz}{dx}. \qquad (5)$$

Note that if we do not have an explicit expression for z as a function of x so we are unable to write the derivative in the form shown in (4), we can leave the derivative in the form shown in (5).

We can generalize the results of our preceding example to any function $k(z)$ where z is a function of x:

$$\frac{d}{dx} k(z) = \frac{d}{dz} k(z) \cdot \frac{dz}{dx}.$$

This last expression is an example of how the chain rule is used to find derivatives of **functions of functions,** otherwise known as **composite functions.**

> The chain rule enables us to take derivatives of **composite functions;** that is, functions of functions.

Chain Rule

If y is a function of z, say $y = f(z)$, and z is a function of x, say $z = g(x)$, then

$$y = f(z) = f(g(x))$$

and

$$\frac{dy}{dx} = \frac{dy}{dz} \cdot \frac{dz}{dx}$$

or

$$\frac{d}{dx} f(g(x)) = \frac{d}{dz} f(g(x)) \cdot \frac{d}{dx} g(x)$$

> To find the derivative of a function of a function by the chain rule, take the derivative of the first function with respect to the second function, and then multiply this by the derivative of the second function with respect to its independent variable.

Applied to the previous example of finding

$$\frac{d}{dx} z^5$$

so that $y = z^5$, the chain rule says **first take the derivative of the function of z** (which is z^5) **with respect to z** (which is what we would expect) **and then multiply this by the derivative of z with respect to x.** Thus

$$\frac{d}{dx} z^5 = \frac{d}{dz} z^5 \cdot \frac{dz}{dx} = 5z^4 \cdot \frac{dz}{dx},$$

which is precisely equation (5).

Now what about a problem like

$$\frac{d}{dx} e^{f(x)} = ?$$

If we think of $f(x)$ as a single variable z and apply the chain rule, then

$$\frac{d}{dx} e^{f(x)} = \frac{d}{dx} e^{z} = \frac{d}{dz} e^{z} \cdot \frac{dz}{dx} = e^{z} \cdot \frac{dz}{dx}$$

or, replacing z by $f(x)$,

$$\frac{d}{dx} e^{f(x)} = e^{f(x)} \cdot f'(x).$$

This is precisely the exponential function rule we presented in Section 9.2.

Again, to determine

$$\frac{d}{dw} e^{2y}$$

where y is a function of w, we must use the chain rule because the derivative is with respect to w, and the expression whose derivative is sought, e^{2y}, is a function not of w, but of y. Hence

$$\frac{d}{dw} e^{2y} = \frac{d}{dy} e^{2y} \cdot \frac{dy}{dw} \tag{6}$$

$$= e^{2y}(2) \cdot \frac{dy}{dw}.$$

Here we would need to have an explicit expression for y as a function of w to find dy/dw.

> To check that the chain rule is being used correctly, cover the denominator of the first factor and the numerator of the second factor.

Now there is a little trick we can use to be sure the chain rule has been applied correctly. Refer to (6) and, on the right, cover the denominator of the first factor with one finger and the numerator of the second factor with another finger. What remains in view should be the same as the expression on the left. Note that we avoided saying cancel dy on the right because d/dy does not mean d divided by dy but rather is an instruction meaning to take the derivative with respect to y, and we cannot cancel part of an instruction.

Example. Write the expression for the derivative with respect to w for the following, assuming y, w, and z are functions of x:

a) $2y^3$.   b) $e^{x^2} + 5w$.   c) $\ln(3z + 2)$.

We have

a) $\dfrac{d}{dw}(2y^3) = \dfrac{d}{dy}(2y^3) \cdot \dfrac{dy}{dw} = 6y^2 \cdot \dfrac{dy}{dw}.$

b) $\dfrac{d}{dw}(e^{x^2} + 5w) = \dfrac{d}{dw}(e^{x^2}) + \dfrac{d}{dw}(5w) = e^{x^2}(2x) \cdot \dfrac{dx}{dw} + 5.$

Notice that $\dfrac{d}{dx}(e^{x^2}) = e^{x^2} \cdot 2x$ by the chain rule.

c) $\dfrac{d}{dw}\ln(3z + 2) = \dfrac{d}{dz}\ln(3z + 2) \cdot \dfrac{dz}{dw} = \dfrac{3}{3z + 2} \cdot \dfrac{dz}{dw}.$

Notice that $\dfrac{d}{dz}\ln(3z + 2) = \dfrac{3}{3z + 2}$ by the chain rule.

Exercise. Assuming y, z, and w are functions of x, write the expressions for the derivative with respect to x of: a) $\ln y$. b) $2z^{3/2} + x^2$. c) e^{3w}.

Answer: a) $\left(\dfrac{1}{y}\right) \cdot \dfrac{dy}{dx}$. b) $3z^{1/2} \cdot \dfrac{dz}{dx} + 2x$. c) $3e^{3w} \cdot \dfrac{dw}{dx}$.

The next example and exercise reinforce the fact that the chain rule is a generalization of the Function Power, Exponential Function, and Logarithmic Function Rules.

Example. Find dy/dx if

$$y = 15\sqrt[3]{5x^4 + 7}$$

and verify the result by the Function Power Rule.

We first rewrite y as

$$y = 15(5x^4 + 7)^{1/3}. \tag{7}$$

$$y = 15z^{1/3}.$$

Now using the chain rule

$$\dfrac{dy}{dx} = \dfrac{dy}{dz} \cdot \dfrac{dz}{dx},$$

we get

$$\dfrac{dy}{dx} = 5z^{-2/3} \cdot \dfrac{dz}{dx}$$
$$= 5z^{-2/3} \cdot (20x^3)$$
$$= 5(5x^4 + 7)^{-2/3} \cdot (20x^3) \tag{8}$$
$$\dfrac{dy}{dx} = \dfrac{100x^3}{(5x^4 + 7)^{2/3}}.$$

If we had applied the Function Power Rule directly to (7), we would have the same result as in (8) and thus the same final result.

> **Exercise.** Use the chain rule to find a) dy/dx if $y = e^{-2.5x}$ and verify the result by the Exponential Function Rule. b) dy/dx if $y = \ln(4x^{1/4} - 8)$ and verify the result by the Logarithmic Function Rule.
> **Answer:** a) $-2.5(e^{-2.5x})$. b) $1/[x^{3/4}(4x^{1/4} - 8)]$.

9.8 MARGINAL PROPENSITY TO CONSUME AND THE MULTIPLIER

The major part of the income people have available for their use is spent on food, clothing, shelter, medical care, transportation, recreation, and so on, and the remainder is saved in one form or another. The amount spent is called **consumption expenditure** or, briefly, **consumption**. Consumption, of course, is a function of income. If we symbolize income by Y (as is conventional in economics) and consumption as the function $C(Y)$, then $C(Y)$ is called a **consumption function**. Suppose, for example, that

$$C(Y) = 30 + 0.6Y$$

and that Y and $C(Y)$ are in billions of dollars. At income level $Y = \$100$ billion,

$$C(Y) = C(100) = 30 + 0.6(100) = \$90 \text{ billion},$$

so that people having $100 billion of income available for use (referred to as **disposable income**) spend $90 billion on consumption, while the remaining $10 billion represents savings. Although aggregate numbers for consumption and savings are important numbers, the topic of this section is concerned with the **rate at which consumption changes per additional $1 of income received. This is the derivative of $C(Y)$ with respect to Y and is called the marginal propensity to consume,** MPC, as introduced in Section 1.2.

> *The marginal propensity to consume is the part of each extra dollar of income that is spent, and the marginal propensity to save is the part of each extra dollar saved; that is,*
>
> $MPC = \dfrac{dC(Y)}{dY}$
>
> $MPS = 1 - MPC.$

Definitions

$$\text{Marginal Propensity to Consume} = MPC = \frac{dC(Y)}{dY}.$$

$$\text{Marginal Propensity to Save} = MPS = 1 - MPC = 1 - \frac{dC(Y)}{dY}.$$

The second part of this definition means simply that if MPC is the part of an extra $1 of income going to consumption, the remaining part of the $1, 1 − MPC, goes to savings and is the marginal propensity to save, MPS.

For the preceding consumption function, we have

$$C(Y) = 30 + 0.6Y$$

$$\text{MPC} = \frac{dC(Y)}{dY} = 0.6$$

$$\text{MPS} = 1 - \text{MPC} = 1 - 0.6 = 0.4.$$

Thus of an additional $1 of income, $0.60 is spent on consumption and $0.40 is saved.

Exercise. For the consumption function $C(Y) = 20 + 0.75Y$: a) Find MPC and MPS. b) Interpret the answer to (a). c) What proportion (or percentage) of an income of $100 billion would be spent?

Answer: a) MPC = 0.75, MPS = 0.25. b) Of an additional $1 of income, 75 cents would be spent and 25 cents would be saved. c) 0.95 or 95 percent.

Note in part (c) of the previous exercise that

$$C(100) = 20 + 0.75(100) = 95,$$

so $95 billion of the $100 billion, or 95 percent, would be spent. The **proportion of income spent is not the same as the marginal propensity to consume** because in economics marginals always refer to the rate at which a function changes per increase of 1 in the independent variable. That is, marginals are slopes of lines

Be careful not to confuse MPC with the actual proportion of income spent.

At income level Y, $C(Y)$ is spent on consumption, and the difference

$$\text{Income} - \text{Consumption expenditure} = Y - C(Y)$$

is the amount saved. In our elementary analysis, we shall suppose that business investment opportunities exist, and all savings are put into these investments so **savings equal investment.** Letting I represent investment, we have

$$I = Y - C(Y).$$

Now, of course, investment by someone generates income for others. For example, a businessperson who invests $1,000 to pay the wages for two workers to build an addition on a building, using material the businessperson owns, generates a first round of a matching $1,000 of income to the workers. However, this is only the beginning round, and the important point we wish to demonstrate is that the $1,000

■ **The Multiplier**

investment initially generates a multiple of $1,000 of income, but the true multiplier is greater than one. To see this, we start with the $1,000 investment, which generates $1,000 of income to the workers. However the workers now spend (consume) part of the $1,000 income (remember MPC) on consumption, and this part becomes income to the suppliers of the consumption items. In turn, these suppliers spend part of their income on consumption, and so on and so on. Just how much income received at one link in this chain is spent on consumption and becomes income at the next link depends, of course, on the marginal propensity to consume, MPC. We now analyze the situation, starting with the algebraic expression

$$I = Y - C(Y).$$

What we want to know is by how much does income, Y, change per additional dollar of investment; that is, we want dY/dI. Taking the derivative of the last **with respect to I,** we have

$$\frac{d}{dI}(I) = \frac{d}{dI}(Y) - \frac{d}{dI}[C(Y)].$$

We must invoke the chain rule for the rightmost term. We have

$$1 = \frac{dY}{dI} - \frac{dC(Y)}{dY} \cdot \frac{dY}{dI}.$$

Remembering that dY/dI is sought, we proceed as follows:

$$1 = \frac{dY}{dI}\left[1 - \frac{dC(Y)}{dY}\right]$$

$$\frac{dY}{dI} = \frac{1}{1 - dC(Y)/dY}.$$

Next, remembering that $dC(Y)/dY$ is the marginal propensity to consume (MPC), we may write

$$\frac{dY}{dI} = \frac{1}{1 - \text{MPC}} = \frac{1}{\text{MPS}}.$$

The rate at which income increases per additional $1 of investment (Investment = Savings), dY/dI, is called the **multiplier**. Thus

The multiplier is the rate at which income increases for each extra dollar of investment (savings); that is,

$$\frac{dY}{dI} = \frac{1}{1 - \text{MPC}}.$$

$$\text{Multiplier} = \frac{dY}{dI} = \frac{1}{1 - \text{MPC}} = \frac{1}{\text{MPS}}$$

Returning to the consumption function at the beginning of this section,

$$C(Y) = 30 + 0.6Y$$

$$\text{MPC} = \frac{dC(Y)}{dY} = 0.6$$

$$\text{Multiplier} = \frac{1}{1 - \text{MPC}} = \frac{1}{1 - 0.6} = \frac{1}{0.4} = 2.5.$$

The multiplier here means that 2.5 dollars of income is generated by an additional $1 of investment. It is clear that MPC is a critical factor in income generation. When investment opportunities exist, **a high MPC generates new income in an amount that is a large multiple of the sum invested.**

Exercise. a) Find the multiplier if the consumption function is $C(Y) = 10 + 0.9Y$.
b) Interpret the answer to (a).

Answer: a) 10. b) An additional $1 of investment generates $10 of additional income.

We leave more extensive analysis of the topics introduced in this section for courses in economics. However our introduction serves to demonstrate the important contribution calculus can make to this analysis and also serves our purpose of illustrating a situation where the chain rule arises. We close the section by an example involving a consumption function that is not linear.

Calculus, and the chain rule in particular, make an important contribution to economic analysis.

Example. a) Suppose Y is family income in tens of thousands of dollars so that, for example, $Y = 2$ means $20,000, and suppose

$$C(Y) = 6 + 0.6Y - e^{-0.4Y}$$

b) Suppose Y is in trillions of dollars and the $C(Y)$ in part (a) represents the national income of a country. Find the multiplier at an income level of $0.8 trillion.

Here $C(Y)$ is not linear so MPC is a function of income that we shall symbolize as MPC(Y).
a) For

$$C(Y) = 6 + 0.6Y - e^{-0.4Y}$$

$$\text{MPC}(Y) = \frac{dC(Y)}{dY} = 0.6 - (e^{-0.4Y})(-0.4) = 0.6 + 0.4e^{-0.4Y}$$

$$\text{MPC}(1) = 0.6 + 0.4e^{-0.4(1)} = 0.6 + 0.4e^{-0.4}$$
$$= 0.6 + 0.4(0.670320046)$$
$$\approx 0.868.$$

$$MPC(2) = 0.6 + 0.4e^{-0.4(2)} = 0.6 + 0.4e^{-0.8}$$
$$= 0.6 + 0.4(0.449328964)$$
$$\approx 0.780.$$

Higher income tends to lead to smaller MPC.

Part (a) illustrates a common observation that the higher a family's income level, the smaller MPC tends to be. That is, at **a higher income, a smaller fraction of an additional dollar is spent on consumption and a larger fraction is saved.**

b) Here we have the same MPC function as in (a),

$$MPC(Y) = 0.6 + 0.4e^{-0.4Y}$$
$$MPC(0.8) = 0.6 + 0.4e^{-0.4(0.8)}$$
$$= 0.6 + 0.4e^{-0.32}$$
$$= 0.6 + 0.4(0.726149037)$$
$$\approx 0.89.$$

Then, from our earlier derivation,

$$\text{Multiplier} = \frac{1}{1 - MPC} \approx \frac{1}{1 - 0.89} = \frac{1}{0.11} = 9.1.$$

9.9 PROBLEM SET 9-3

For each of the following, find a) $f(g(x))$ and its derivative and b) $g(f(x))$ and its derivative:

1. $f(x) = x^{1/2}$ and $g(x) = 3x - 4$.
2. $f(x) = 2x + 5$ and $g(x) = 4x - 1$.
3. $f(x) = 2 - x$ and $g(x) = x^{1/3}$.
4. $f(x) = 5 - x^2$ and $g(x) = \sqrt{2 + x}$.
5. $f(x) = x^2 + 3$ and $g(x) = \sqrt{x - 2}$.
6. $f(x) = 3/\sqrt{x}$ and $g(x) = 5 - x$.
7. $f(x) = 4x + 3$ and $g(x) = x^2 + 1$.
8. $f(x) = 5x + 4$ and $g(x) = 3x^3 - 1$.
9. $f(x) = \sqrt{x + 3}$ and $g(x) = x + 3$.
10. $f(x) = 3 - x$ and $g(x) = \sqrt{3 - x}$.

Find dy/dx for each of the following and verify the result by either the function power rule, exponential function rule, or logarithmic function rule:

11. $y = 7(3x^3 + x^2)^{3/2}$.
12. $y = 5\sqrt{2x^3 - 1}$.
13. $y = 3\sqrt{7x + 2}$.
14. $y = 6x(2x^3 - 5)^4$.
15. $y = e^{-0.25x}$.
16. $y = e^{3x^2+1}$.
17. $y = e^{4x^3-9}$.
18. $y = e^{-1/(0.5x)}$.
19. $y = \ln(5x^{1/5} + 7)$.
20. $y = \ln(6 - 3x^{1/4})$.
21. $y = \ln(x^3 + 3x^2 + 14)^5$.
22. $y = \ln(2x^{3/2} + 6x^{4/3} + 3x + 7)$.

9.9 PROBLEM SET 9–3 (concluded)

Employ the chain rule to carry out each of the following:

23. $\dfrac{d}{dx}(y^4)$.

24. $\dfrac{d}{dy}(x^3)$.

25. $\dfrac{d}{dz}(e^{2w})$.

26. $\dfrac{d}{dq}(2e^{-0.5p})$.

27. $\dfrac{d}{dx}\ln(2y+3)$.

28. $\dfrac{d}{dw}\ln(z^2-3z)$.

29. $\dfrac{d}{dy}(xy)$.

30. $\dfrac{d}{dx}(x/y)$.

31. Find the expression for $\dfrac{dy}{dx}$ if y is a function of x and
$$x = y - g(y).$$

32. At income level Y, consumption expenditures are $C(Y)$ billion dollars, where
$$C(Y) = 34 + 0.68Y.$$
   a) Find the marginal propensity to consume.
   b) Interpret (a).
   c) How much income is generated by an additional dollar of investment?
   d) At income level 200, what proportion of total income is spent?

33. At income level Y, consumption expenditures are $C(Y)$ billion dollars, where
$$C(Y) = 54 + 0.63Y.$$
   a) Find the marginal propensity to consume.
   b) Interpret (a).
   c) How much income is generated by an additional dollar of investment?
   d) At income level 200, what proportion of total income is spent?

34. For the consumption function
$$C(Y) = 9 + 0.7Y - e^{-0.3Y},$$
find the multiplier at income level
   a) 3.   b) 10.

35. Find the consumption function
$$C(Y) = 6 + 0.8Y - e^{-0.2Y},$$
find the multiplier at income level
   a) 2.   b) 15.

9.10 CALCULUS OF TWO INDEPENDENT VARIABLES

All of our work in differential calculus thus far has involved functions having one independent variable. Thus, for example, if a producer makes only the product antifreeze, the cost of producing x gallons of antifreeze is $C(x)$, a function of the single variable x. However if the producer makes two products (x gallons of antifreeze and y gallons of windshield cleaner), production cost is a function of both x and y, which we symbolize as

$$C(x, y),$$

and C is now a function of two independent variables. Clearly the function concept can be extended to more than two independent variables and we refer to calculus

PART III INTRODUCTION TO APPLIED CALCULUS AND UNCONSTRAINED OPTIMIZATION

> Multivariate calculus is the calculus of two or more independent variables.

of two or more independent variables as **multivariate calculus.** This subject area is too extensive to treat in any detail in this book, but we can learn some of its important aspects and applications by considering the case of two independent variables.

Consider the function

$$f(x, y) = 3x^2 - 2xy - 8y + y^2 + 44.$$

A pair of numbers, one for x and the other for y, yield a value for $f(x, y)$. Thus at $x = 1$, $y = 2$, we find

$$f(1, 2) = 3(1)^2 - 2(1)(2) - 8(2) + (2)^2 + 44 = 31.$$

Exercise. Find $f(2, 6)$ for the preceding function.
Answer: 20.

> The partial derivative measures the rate of change with respect to one variable, keeping all other variables constant.

If we treat y in $f(x, y)$ as a constant and take the derivative of $f(x, y)$ with respect to x, the procedure is called taking the **partial derivative with respect to x** or, more briefly, the partial with respect to x. Among the symbols used to designate this procedure are

$$f_x; \quad \frac{\partial f(x, y)}{\partial x}; \quad \frac{\partial f}{\partial x}$$

where ∂ is called a **round delta.** Actually the large and small Greek deltas are Δ and δ; ∂ is really not a letter but is a symbol devised to represent taking a partial derivative. For

$$f(x, y) = 3x^2 - 2xy - 8y + y^2 + 44$$
$$f_x = 6x - 2y;$$

that is, if y is treated as a constant, then in the second term $(-2xy)$, $-2y$ is constant and the derivative of $(-2xy) = (-2y)x$ with respect to x is the constant, $-2y$. Similarly the derivatives with respect to x of $-8y$, y^2 and 44 are all zero. In round delta notation we would write

$$\frac{\partial}{\partial x} f(x, y) = \frac{\partial}{\partial x} (3x^2 - 2xy - 8y + y^2 + 44)$$
$$= 6x - 2y.$$

Next we find f_y, the partial of f with respect to y. This means to take the derivative of $f(x, y)$ treating x as a constant. We find

$$f_y = -2x - 8 + 2y.$$

The **second partial of $f(x, y)$ taken twice with respect to x** is symbolized as

$$f_{xx}; \quad \frac{\partial^2 f(x, y)}{\partial x^2}; \quad \frac{\partial^2 f}{\partial x^2},$$

and it means to **take the partial with respect to x, and then take the partial of this result again with respect to x.** For our example,

$$f_x = 6x - 2y,$$

so

$$f_{xx} = 6.$$

In round delta notation, we would write

$$\frac{\partial^2 f}{\partial x^2} = \frac{\partial}{\partial x}\left(\frac{\partial f}{\partial x}\right) = \frac{\partial}{\partial x}(6x - 2y) = 6.$$

Similarly we have

$$f_y = -2x - 8 + 2y$$
$$f_{yy} = 2.$$

Finally we may **take the partial with respect to x,**

$$f_x = 6x - 2y,$$

then take the partial of f_x with respect to y. This is symbolized as

$$f_{xy} \quad \text{or} \quad \frac{\partial f}{\partial y \partial x}$$

and is called the **second partial of $f(x, y)$, first with respect to x, then with respect to y** or simply the **mixed partial with respect to x, then y.** Thus with

For all functions in this book, we can obtain the same result by finding the mixed partial with respect to y and then x,

$$f_{yx} \quad \text{or} \quad \frac{\partial f}{\partial x \partial y};$$

that is, find the partial of $f(x, y)$ first with respect to y, and then take the partial of the result with respect to x. In our example,

$$f_y = -2x - 8 + 2y$$
$$f_{yx} = -2,$$

which is the same as f_{xy}. The equality of f_{xy} and f_{yx} is true wherever these derivatives are continuous, and will be true for all functions we shall deal with.

> **Exercise.** $f(x, y) = 2x + 3y + x^2y + 2xy^3 - 20$. Find: a) f_x. b) f_y. c) f_{xx}. d) f_{yy}. e) f_{xy}.
> **Answer:** a) $2 + 2xy + 2y^3$. b) $3 + x^2 + 6xy^2$. c) $2y$. d) $12xy$. e) $2x + 6y^2$.

Partial derivatives measure slopes or rates of change.

Partial derivatives, like derivatives of a function of one variable, can be interpreted as slopes or rates of change. For example, if the cost in dollars of making x gallons of antifreeze and y gallons of windshield cleaner is

$$C(x, y) = 3x + 2y + 10,$$

then

$$C_x = 3 \quad \text{and} \quad C_y = 2.$$

We can say that if production of windshield cleaner is held constant, cost increases at the rate of $C_x = 3$ dollars for each additional gallon of antifreeze made, whereas if production of antifreeze is held constant, cost increases at the rate of $C_y = 2$ dollars for each additional gallon of windshield cleaner made.

If, unlike the example just given, the partials are not constant, then the rate interpretation is made at a point; that is, a pair of values, (x, y).

Example. Total profit in dollars when x tons of oats and y tons of hay are produced and sold is given by

$$P(x, y) = 100x - x^2 - 2xy + 200y - 3y^2.$$

Find $P(15, 20)$, $P_x(15, 20)$, and $P_y(15, 20)$. Interpret the partials in rate terminology.

First we find

$$P(15, 20) = 100(15) - (15)^2 - 2(15)(20) + 200(20) - 3(20)^2 = \$3{,}475.$$

Next,

$$P_x(x, y) = 100 - 2x - 2y$$
$$P_x(15, 20) = 100 - 2(15) - 2(20) = 30.$$

Thus with hay production held constant (at $y = 20$), profit is increasing at the rate of $30 per additional ton of oats produced and sold. Similarly

$$P_y(x, y) = -2x + 200 - 6y$$
$$P_y(15, 20) = -2(15) + 200 - 6(20) = 50$$

and with production of oats constant (at $x = 15$), profit is increasing at the rate of $50 per additional ton of hay produced and sold.

Note in the preceding example that profit at the point where $x = 15$, $y = 20$, is $P(15, 20) = \$3{,}475$ and both partials indicate that profit can be increased by making and selling additional amounts of oats and hay. This suggests that production should be increased and raises the question of whether profit increases indefinitely or reaches a local maximum at some combination of outputs of oats and hay. We shall answer this question after the next set of problems.

> **Exercise.** For the profit function of the previous example, find: a) $P(26, 27)$. b) $P_x(26, 27)$. c) $P_y(26, 27)$. d) Interpret the answer to parts (b) and (c).
> **Answer:** a) $3,733. b) $P_x = -6$. c) $P_y = -14$. d) When hay (oat) production is held constant at 27 (26) units, profit is *decreasing* at the rate of $6 ($14) per additional unit of oats (hay) produced and sold.

9.11 PROBLEM SET 9-4

For the following find: a) f_x. b) f_{xx}. c) f_y. d) f_{yy}. e) f_{xy}.

1. $f(x, y) = 3x - 2y + 6$.
2. $f(x, y) = 2x + 5y - 10$.
3. $f(x, y) = x^2 + y^2 + 3x - 2y - 9$.
4. $f(x, y) = x^2 - y^2 - 5x + 4y + 7$.
5. $f(x, y) = 3x^2 - 2xy + y^2 + 4$.
6. $f(x, y) = 2x^3 + 3xy + 4y - 6$.
7. $f(x, y) = x^{1/2}y^{1/2}$.
8. $f(x, y) = x^{2/3}y^{1/3}$.
9. $f(x, y) = 2xy^{1/2} - 3x^{1/3}y$.
10. $f(x, y) = x^{3/2}y^2$.
11. $f(x, y) = xye^x$.
12. $f(x, y) = xy \ln y$.
13. $f(x, y) = \dfrac{x - y}{x + y}$.
14. $f(x, y) = \dfrac{x + y}{x - y}$.
15. $f(x, y) = \ln(3x + 2y)$.
16. $f(x, y) = e^{2x+3y}$.

Perform the following:

17. $\dfrac{\partial}{\partial z}(3z^2 - 2xz)$.
18. $\dfrac{\partial}{\partial w}(w^2 - 3z^2w)$.
19. $\dfrac{\partial^2}{\partial w^2}(w^2 - 3z^2w)$.
20. $\dfrac{\partial^2}{\partial z^2}(3z^2 - 2xz)$.
21. $\dfrac{\partial^2}{\partial w \partial z}(w^3 - 3zw)$.
22. $\dfrac{\partial^2}{\partial z \partial x}(z^3 + 3xz)$.

23. If $f(x, y) = 3x + 2y$, find:
    a) $f(1, 2)$.
    b) $f_x(1, 2)$.
    c) $f_{xx}(1, 2)$.
    d) $f_y(1, 2)$.
    e) $f_{yy}(1, 2)$.
    f) $f_{xy}(1, 2)$.

24. If $f(x, y) = 2x + 3y - 6$, find:
    a) $f(2, 3)$.
    b) $f_x(2, 3)$.
    c) $f_{xx}(2, 3)$.
    d) $f_y(2, 3)$.
    e) $f_{yy}(2, 3)$.
    f) $f_{xy}(2, 3)$.

9.11 PROBLEM SET 9-4 (concluded)

25. If $f(x, y) = x^2 + xy - 3y^2 + 5$, compute:
   a) $f(2, 1)$.
   b) $f_x(2, 1)$.
   c) $f_{xx}(2, 1)$.
   d) $f_y(2, 1)$.
   e) $f_{yy}(2, 1)$.
   f) $f_{xy}(2, 1)$.

26. If $f(x, y) = 2x^2 - 5xy + y^2 - 6$, compute:
   a) $f(3, 2)$.
   b) $f_x(3, 2)$.
   c) $f_{xx}(3, 2)$.
   d) $f_y(3, 2)$.
   e) $f_{yy}(3, 2)$.
   f) $f_{xy}(3, 2)$.

27. During a period of operation a producer makes and sells x tons of oats and y tons of hay at a cost in dollars of

$$C(x, y) = 3x^2 - 2xy + y^2 - 12x - 4y + 61.$$

Find $C_x(3, 5)$ and $C_y(3, 5)$ and interpret these numbers in rate terminology.

28. Using the cost function in Problem 27, find $C_x(3, 7)$ and $C_y(3, 7)$ and interpret these numbers in rate terminology.

29. A producer makes and sells x tons of oats and y tons of hay during a period of operation. Profit in dollars is

$$P(x, y) = 50x - 0.05x^2 + 110y - 0.10y^2.$$

Compute each of the following and interpret the result in rate terminology:
   a) $P_x(400, 500)$.
   b) $P_y(400, 500)$.
   c) $P_x(600, 500)$.
   d) $P_y(400, 600)$.

30. The total output of an industry, V million dollars, is a function of L (expenditure for labor) and C (dollars of capital invested in the industry). Suppose

$$V(L, C) = 8L^{1/3}C^{2/3}.$$

Compute the following and interpret the result in rate terminology:
   a) $V_L(64, 27)$.
   b) $V_C(64, 27)$.

9.12 MAXIMA AND MINIMA: TWO INDEPENDENT VARIABLES

Reviewing the example of Section 9.10, where $P(x, y)$ was the profit function for a producer who made and sold x tons of oats and y tons of hay,

$$P(x, y) = 100x - x^2 - 2xy + 200y - 3y^2, \qquad (1)$$

we found

$$P_x = 100 - 2x - 2y \quad \text{and} \quad P_y = -2x + 200 - 6y.$$

At $x = 15$, $y = 20$

$$P_x(15, 20) = 30 \quad \text{and} \quad P_y(15, 20) = 50,$$

so profit is increasing per additional unit of oats if production of hay is constant, and profit also is increasing per additional unit of hay if oats production is held constant. However the opposite (profit rates decreasing) occurs when $x = 26$ and $y = 27$ because

$$P_x(26, 27) = -6 \quad \text{and} \quad P_y(26, 27) = -14$$

are both negative. The change from increasing to decreasing rates suggest that a point of maximum profit exists. If such is the case at some pair of values (x, y), then for this pair of values profit must be neither increasing nor decreasing, so both

P_x and P_y must be zero. This is similar to the one-variable case condition that the first derivative must be zero at a local optimum point, except that with two independent variables, both first partial derivatives must be zero.

> **Condition**
>
> Both first partial derivatives must be zero at a local optimum point.

In the two-independent-variable case, both first partials must be zero at a local optimum; that is,
$$P_x = 0 \quad \text{and} \quad P_y = 0.$$

It may at first be hard to visualize what the maximum of a function of two independent variables looks like. Since $P(x, y)$ has two independent variables, x and y, then $z = P(x, y)$ is a third, dependent, variable in (1), which we can now rewrite as

$$z = 100x - x^2 - 2xy + 200y - 3y^2.$$

In this form, it is easy to realize that the graph of $P(x, y)$ must be drawn in three-dimensional space. We will not discuss graphing in three dimensions since it is very technical and sometimes very complex, but a few generic graphs are included in this section to help you see how maxima and minima appear in three dimensions.

The graph of a function of two independent variables is drawn in three-dimensional space.

For example, a minimum might appear as shown in Figure 9–6, where we see a local minimum at $z = P(0, 0)$. On the other hand, a maximum might appear, as shown in Figure 9–7. Here there is a local maximum at the point (x_0, y_0, z_0) and the value of this maximum is $P(x_0, y_0) = z_0$.

Now that we can visualize optima in three dimensions, how do we locate these optima? Our condition stated earlier in this section required that both first partial

equations e_1 and e_2.

$$e_1: \quad 100 - 2x - 2y = 0$$
$$e_2: \quad 200 - 2x - 6y = 0.$$

These equations are now solved simultaneously. The simplest procedure is to rewrite them and subtract, as follows:

$$\begin{aligned} e_1: \quad & 2x + 2y = 100 \\ e_2: \quad & 2x + 6y = 200 \\ \hline e_1 - e_2: \quad & -4y = -100 \end{aligned}$$

so that

$$y = 25.$$

FIGURE 9-6

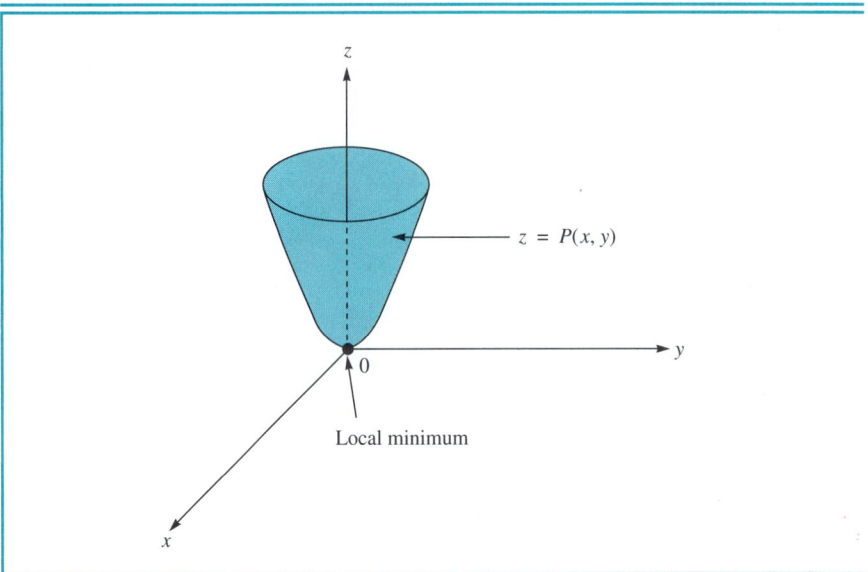

FIGURE 9-7

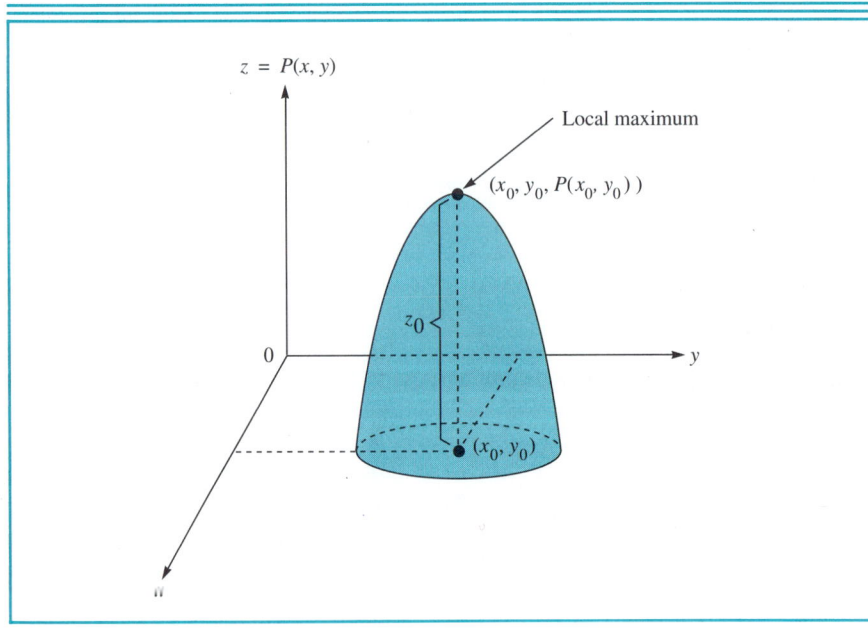

Substituting $y = 25$ into e_1, we find

$$2x + 2(25) = 100$$
$$2x = 50$$
$$x = 25,$$

and so $x = 25$, $y = 25$ marks a stationary point that may (or may not) be a local optimum point. In any event,

$$P(25, 25) = 100(25) - (25)^2 - 2(25)(25) + 200(25) - 3(25)^2$$
$$= \$3,750.$$

To determine whether we have a local optimum point and, if so, whether it is a maximum or minimum, we use a test that, as might be anticipated, involves the second partial derivatives. We shall not develop the source of this test because to do so would carry us too far afield.

To test a candidate for local optimum, we use a test involving all the second partial derivatives.

Test for Local Optima Points: Two Independent Variables

1. Find f_x and f_y, set both equal to zero, and solve the resultant equations simultaneously to obtain the candidate values x^* and y^*.
2. Compute $f_{xx}(x^*, y^*)$, $f_{yy}(x^*, y^*)$, and $f_{xy}(x^*, y^*)$.
3. Set $A = f_{xx}(x^*, y^*)$
   $B = f_{xy}(x^*, y^*)$
   $C = f_{yy}(x^*, y^*)$
   and
   $D = B^2 - AC.$
   D is called the **discriminant** of f.

if A or C is positive, there is a local minimum at (x^*, y^*).[1]

If $D > 0$: there is a saddle point (neither a maximum nor a minimum) at (x^*, y^*).

If $D = 0$: The test fails.

---

[1] It can be shown that when D is negative, A and C are either **both negative** or **both positive**, so that we need only test one of the two to determine whether the candidate point is a local maximum or local minimum.

In the example at hand, with $x = 25$, $y = 25$,

$$P_x = 100 - 2x - 2y, \quad \text{so} \quad P_{xx} = -2$$
$$P_y = -2 + 200 - 6y, \quad \text{so} \quad P_{yy} = -6$$
$$P_{xy} = -2.$$

Hence step (3) in the preceding test provides

$$A = -2, \quad B = -2, \quad C = -6$$
$$D = B^2 - AC = (-2)^2 - (-2)(-6) = -8.$$

So in step (4), we have $D < 0$. Since both A and C are negative, this proves we have a local maximum at the point (25, 25). Thus

$$\text{Maximum profit} = P_{\max} = P(25, 25) = \$3{,}750,$$

as previously computed. The producer should produce and sell 25 tons of oats and 25 tons of hay to achieve this maximum profit.

Exercise. a) Find the candidate optimum point for

$$f(x, y) = 3x^2 - 2xy + y^2 - 12x - 4y + 61.$$

b) Evaluate the function at this point. c) Show by test whether (b) is a local maximum or minimum.

Answer: a) $x = 4, y = 6$. b) $f(4, 6) = 25$. c) $D = -8$, $f_{xx} = 6$, $f_{yy} = 2$. Local minimum.

A saddle point is the three-dimensional equivalent of a two-dimensional inflection point.

If D, in the preceding test for optimum points, is positive we have a point that is the three-dimensional version of an inflection point. Such points are called **saddle points** and are neither maxima nor minima. Figure 9–8 is a clear demonstration of why such points are called saddle points.

As in the two-dimensional case, when $D = 0$ the test fails and an alternative test must be used.

However if D equals zero, the test fails and the point in question may not be a local optimum point. Situations where D is zero will not occur for the functions we shall deal with, but in passing we note that when D is zero it is possible to determine whether or not an optimum point occurs at (x, y). We do this by moving to nearby points, which we may symbolize as $[(x + h), (y + k)]$, where h and k are arbitrary small numbers. We then determine, either algebraically or by computation, whether the function values at the nearby points are greater than (less than) $f(x, y)$, thus making $f(x, y)$ a local minimum (maximum).

Example. Find the value of the function

$$f(x, y) = x^3 + x^2 + y^2 - xy + 8$$

FIGURE 9-8

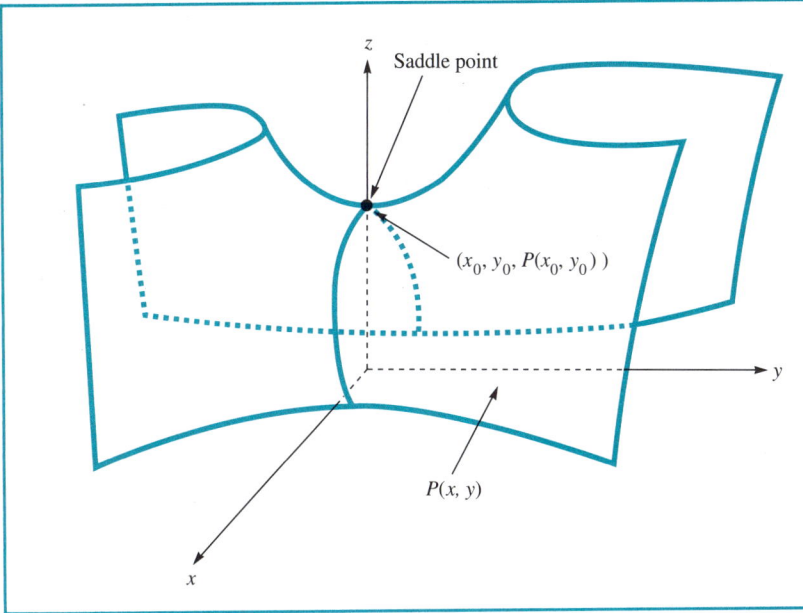

at its extreme and saddle point(s), if any exist. State whether each point is a local maximum, a local minimum, or a saddle point.

Since $f(x, y) = x^3 + x^2 + y^2 - xy + 8$, we have the partial derivatives

$$f_x = 3x^2 + 2x - y$$

$$f_{xy} = -1$$
$$f_{yy} = 2.$$

Setting $f_x = f_y = 0$, we get

$$e_1: \quad 3x^2 + 2x - y = 0$$
$$e_2: \quad 2y - x = 0.$$

To solve this system, we multiply e_1 by 2 and add the result to e_2, so

$$2e_1: \quad 6x^2 + 4x - 2y = 0$$
$$e_2: \quad \quad\quad -x + 2y = 0$$
$$\overline{2e_1 + e_2: \quad 6x^2 + 3x \quad\quad\quad = 0.}$$

Hence
$$x(6x + 3) = 0$$
so that
$$x = 0, -1/2.$$
Substituting these values back into e_2, we find
$$y = 0 \quad \text{and} \quad y = -1/4,$$
respectively. Thus in this case we have two points that are possible optimal:
$$(0, 0) \quad \text{and} \quad (-1/2, -1/4).$$
Beginning with $(0, 0)$,
$$A = f_{xx}(0, 0) = 2; \quad B = f_{xy}(0, 0) = -1; \quad C = f_{yy}(0, 0) = 2$$
so that
$$D = B^2 - AC = (-1)^2 - (2)(2) = -3 < 0.$$
Since A (and C) > 0, then $f(x, y)$ has a local minimum at $(0, 0)$, and the value of this minimum is
$$f(0, 0) = 8.$$
Now consider the point $(-1/2, -1/4)$. Here
$$A = f_{xx}(-1/2, -1/4) = 6(-1/2) + 2 = -1;$$
$$B = f_{xy}(-1/2, -1/4) = -1;$$
$$C = f_{yy}(-1/2, -1/4) = 2;$$
so that
$$D = B^2 - AC = (-1)^2 - (-1)(2) = 3 > 0.$$
We conclude that $f(x, y)$ has a saddle point at $(-1/2, -1/4)$ and the value of $f(x, y)$ at this saddle point is
$$f(-1/2, -1/4) = (-1/2)^3 + (-1/2)^2 + (-1/4)^2 - (-1/2)(-1/4) + 8$$
$$= 8 \, 1/16.$$

Example. A rectangular box with a volume of 16 cubic feet is to be manufactured from three different types of cardboard. The cost of the cardboard for the top and bottom is nine cents per square foot, the cost of the cardboard for the front and back is eight cents per square foot, and the cost of the cardboard for the other two sides is six cents per square foot. Find the dimensions of the box for which the cost of the materials is a minimum.

First we need to isolate an objective. In this problem, we see that we wish to minimize cost C for the box shown in Figure 9.9.

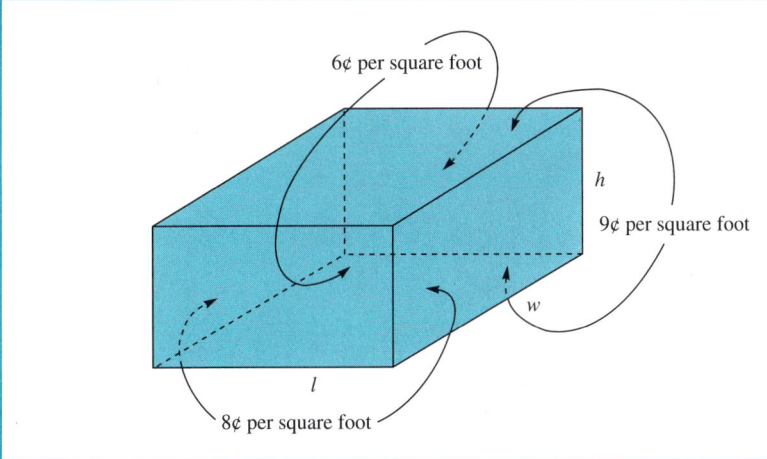

FIGURE 9-9

The cost function is then

$$C = (2)(6)\,lh + (2)(8)\,wh + (2)(9)\,lw$$
$$= 12lh + 16wh + 18lw. \qquad (2)$$

We know that the box must have a volume of 16 cubic feet, so

$$16 = lwh.$$

We can solve this equation for any one of the three variables, l, w and h in terms of the other two. Solving for h, we have

$$h = \frac{16}{lw}.$$

$$C(l, w) = 12l\left(\frac{16}{lw}\right) + 16w\left(\frac{16}{lw}\right) + 18lw$$

or

$$C(l, w) = \frac{(12)(16)}{w} + \frac{(16)^2}{l} + 18lw.$$

We can now test this function for local optima as usual by starting with the first partial derivatives,

$$C_l = -\frac{(16)^2}{l^2} + 18w$$

$$C_w = -\frac{(12)(16)}{w^2} + 18l,$$

and setting them equal to zero:

$$C_l = 0 \text{ when } \frac{(16)^2}{l^2} = 18w, \text{ or } l^2 = \frac{(16)^2}{18w}$$

$$C_w = 0 \text{ when } \frac{(12)(16)}{w^2} = 18l, \text{ or } l = \frac{(12)(16)}{18w^2}.$$

For both of these to be true, we must have

$$\left[\frac{(12)(16)}{18w^2}\right]^2 = \frac{(16)^2}{18w}$$

or

$$\left[\frac{(12)(16)}{18}\right]^2 \cdot \frac{18}{(16)^2} = w^3$$

or

$$\frac{(12)^2}{18} = w^3$$

$$8 = w^3$$

$$w = 2 \text{ feet.}$$

Substituting back into the equation for $C_w = 0$, we have

$$l = \frac{(12)(16)}{18(2)^2} = \frac{8}{3} \text{ feet}$$

and hence the only candidate local optimum point

$$(8/3, 2).$$

Computing the second partials, we obtain

$$C_{ll} = \frac{(16)^2 \cdot 2}{l^3}$$

$$C_{lw} = 18$$

$$C_{ww} = \frac{(12)(16)(2)}{w^3},$$

so

$$A = \frac{(16)^2(2)}{(8/3)^3} = 27; \quad B = 18; \quad C = \frac{(12)(16)(2)}{(2)^3} = 48$$

and

$$D = B^2 - AC = (18)^2 - (27)(48) = -972 < 0.$$

Since $D < 0$ and $A > 0$, we have a minimum cost when

$$l = 8/3 \text{ feet}, \quad w = 2 \text{ feet}, \quad \text{and} \quad h = \frac{16}{2 \cdot 8/3} = 3 \text{ feet}$$

The value of the minimum cost is

$$C(8/3, 2) = \frac{(12)(16)}{2} + \frac{(16)^2}{(8/3)} + 18(2)(8/3) = \$288.$$

Example. To meet customer demand for a product, the producer makes a batch, or **lot,** of L units of the product periodically. The producer's strategy is to establish the period of time between lot productions so that a new lot is not made until some time after current inventory has been exhausted. Thus there is an out-of-stock or stock-out interval. During this interval, orders received from customers are placed in **back order** status and are filled immediately when a new lot is made. Thus the producer makes L units, uses some to fill back orders, and places the remainder, I units, in inventory. Taking into account various costs, including a cost associated with being out of stock, the producer has developed the following cost-function model.

$$C(L, I) = \frac{1{,}350{,}000}{L} + \frac{20I^2}{L} + 15L - 30I.$$

What values of L and I will minimize this cost function?

We proceed by taking the first partial derivatives:

$$C_L = -\frac{1{,}350{,}000}{L^2} - 20\frac{I^2}{L^2} + 15$$

$$C_I = \frac{40I}{L} - 30.$$

If there is a local optimum point, the first partials must equal zero. Hence

$$\frac{40I}{L} - 30 = 0. \qquad (4)$$

The common solution of the pair of equations can be found by solving (4) for I in terms of L and substituting this into (3). Thus from (4)

$$\frac{40I}{L} - 30 = 0$$

$$40I - 30L = 0$$

$$40I = 30L$$

$$I = \frac{30L}{40} = 0.75L. \qquad (5)$$

Substituting (5) into (3), we have

$$-\frac{1{,}350{,}000}{L^2} - \frac{20(0.75L)^2}{L^2} + 15 = 0$$

$$-\frac{1{,}350{,}000}{L^2} - \frac{20(0.75)^2 L^2}{L^2} + 15 = 0$$

$$-\frac{1{,}350{,}000}{L^2} - 11.25 + 15 = 0$$

$$3.75 = \frac{1{,}350{,}000}{L^2}$$

$$3.75 L^2 = 1{,}350{,}000$$

$$L^2 = \frac{1{,}350{,}000}{3.75}$$

$$L^2 = 360{,}000$$

$$L = 600 \text{ units.}$$

With $L = 600$, we find from (5) that

$$I = 0.75 L$$
$$= 0.75(600)$$
$$I = 450 \text{ units.}$$

To prove the values found do minimize cost, $C(L, I)$, we find

$$C_{LL} = \frac{2(1{,}350{,}000)}{L^3} + 40 \frac{I^2}{L^3}$$

$$C_{LL}(600, 450) = \frac{2(1{,}350{,}000)}{(600)^3} + \frac{40(450)^2}{(600)^3} = 0.05.$$

$$C_{II} = \frac{40}{L} \quad \text{and} \quad C_{II}(600, 450) = \frac{40}{600} = \frac{1}{15}.$$

$$C_{LI} = -\frac{40 I}{L^2} \quad \text{and} \quad C_{LI}(600, 450) = -\frac{40(450)}{(600)^2} = -0.05.$$

Both C_{LL} and C_{II} are positive and

$$D = (C_{LI})^2 - (C_{LL})(C_{II}) = (-0.05)^2 - (0.05)\left(\frac{1}{15}\right) = -\frac{1}{1{,}200},$$

which is less than zero, so we have a minimum at

$$C(600, 450) = \frac{1{,}350{,}000}{600} + \frac{20(450)^2}{600} + 15(600) - 30(450) = \$4{,}500.$$

Hence the producer should make $L = 600$ units in each lot and place $I = 450$ units in inventory. This means that the remaining 150 units are used to fill back orders. The advantage the producer achieves by his out-of-stock strategy arises from the cost saving achieved by not having to carry these 150 units in inventory.

The previous example serves not only to illustrate a current application of multivariate calculus but also to bring out the point that the set of simultaneous equations encountered when first partials are set equal to zero may be very difficult to solve. The task was relatively easy in our example because we had only two variables and a relatively simple cost function. Typically when the function is more complicated and there are more than two variables, solutions of the set of simultaneous equations are approximated by specially prepared computer programs that also deal with the situation, earlier mentioned, where $D = 0$. Procedure for approximating solutions are treated in texts on **numerical analysis.**

> Often the equations resulting from setting the first partial derivatives equal to zero cannot be solved directly and require numerical analysis techniques.

FROM THEORY TO PRACTICE
Curve Fitting and Predicting

Whenever possible, scientists, economists, and business analysts strive to determine approximate relationships between known quantities in an effort to predict the value(s) of these quantities in the future. For example, the equation

$$y = a \cdot b^x$$

is frequently used to describe how a company's production or sales, y, grow with time, x. To find the equations describing such relationships, observed data is collected and then used to derive the mathematical equation for prediction. Such a procedure is called **curve fitting.**

One of the simplest and most commonly used curve fitting procedures is the **method of least squares.** To see what is involved, suppose that the observed data is as shown in Table 9–1. The x_i (number of units made) and y_i (corresponding total cost of making x_i units) can then be paired to generate the points (x_i, y_i) as shown in Figure 9–10.

Notice that the points scatter somewhat and do not fall on one straight line. The figure is called, aptly, a **scatter diagram.** To begin with, a straight line has been drawn **freehand** to describe the tendency for cost to rise as output increases. We do not yet have an equation for this line and, clearly, freehand drawing by different

line is to be judged to be the best-fitting line. In descriptive, but imprecise, terms, we want the line that comes **closest** to the points taken as a group. To make this more precise, look at Figure 9–10 and notice that for $x_i = 2$, the actual observed value, which is 3, has been labeled y_i. Now, denoting the as yet unknown value for y on the line when $x_i = 2$ as y_f (where y_f means the fitted value for y), the equation of the line is

$$y_f = mx_i + b,$$

and the **vertical deviation** of the observed point from the line is the difference of the vertical coordinates; that is,

$$\text{Deviation} = y_f - y_i$$
$$= mx_i + b - y_i.$$

(continued)

Moreover,
$$\text{Squared deviation} = (mx_i + b - y_i)^2.$$

The smaller this squared deviation, the closer is the line to the point. And the smaller the sum of the squared deviations for **all** observed points, the closer the line is to the group of points. Hence,

Least-Squares Best-Fitting Line Criterion

The line that best fits a set of observed points is the one whose slope and intercept, m and b, are such that the sum of the squares of the vertical deviations of the points from the line is a minimum.

If we write the sum of squares as

$$S(m, b) = \sum_{i=1}^{n} (mx_i + b - y_i)^2,$$

the problem then becomes finding the expressions for m and b that will minimize S.

Notice that $S(m, b)$ is a function of the two independent variables, m and b. Using the calculus of two independent variables, we are able to derive formulas for m and b that give the equation of the best line $y = mx + b$.

The method of least squares gives the best linear unbiased estimates for m and b, and hence a least squares line is an excellent predictor for data that behaves linearly. More sophisticated techniques are used to develop predictors for nonlinear circumstances. The most common technique used by economists and business analysts is **multiple regression,** a subject best left to a statistics textbook.

TABLE 9–1

Number of Units Made x_i	Total Cost y_i
1	4
2	3
3	8
4	11
5	10

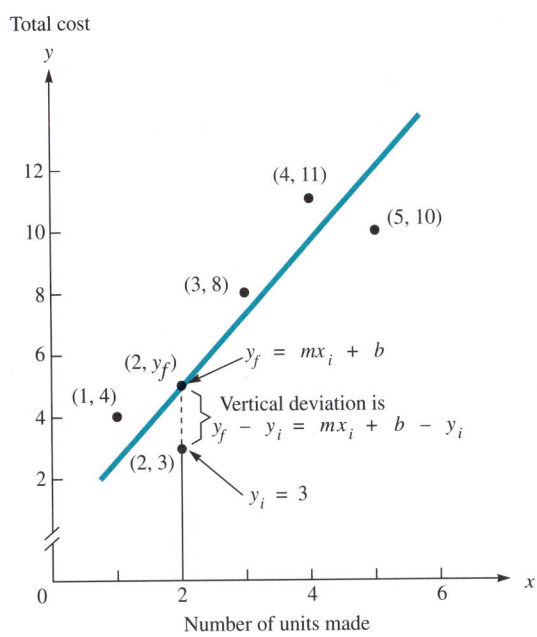

FIGURE 9-10

9.13 PROBLEM SET 9-5

Find the value of the function at its optimum and saddle points, if any exist. State whether each point is a local maximum, a local minimum, or a saddle point.

1. $f(x, y) = 2x^2 + 3y^2 + 10$.
7. $f(x, y) = xy - x - 2y + 2$.

4. $f(x, y) = 3x^2 + y^2 - 2xy - 12y + 104$.
5. $f(x, y) = x + y + 9/x + 4/y$ (x and y positive).
6. $f(x, y) = 4xy + 8x + 20y - 4x^2 - 4y^2$.

10. $f(x, y) = x^2 + 3y^2 - 4xy + 8x - 6y + 5$.
11. $f(x, y) = 10e^{-x^2} - y^2$.
12. $f(x, y) = 3x^2 - 5e^{-y^2}$.

13. Profit in dollars earned by making and selling x gallons of molasses and y gallons of maple syrup is

$$P(x, y) = 50x - 0.05x^2 + 110y - 0.10y^2.$$

   a) What number of units of each product will maximize profit?
   b) Prove (a) is a maximum.
   c) Compute the maximum profit.

14. One unit of product can be made by using Machine A for x hours and Machine B for y hours. The cost in dollars of making one unit is

$$C(x, y) = 3x^2 - 2xy + y^2 - 12x - 4y + 50.$$

   a) What numbers of hours on each machine will minimize the cost of making one unit?
   b) Prove (a) is a minimum.
   c) Compute the minimum cost.

9.13 PROBLEM SET 9-5 (concluded)

15. Assume a store's profit is dependent on the number of salespersons, s, and the amount of inventory, i (in hundreds of dollars). If the profit is given by

    $$P(s, i) = 1{,}400 - (12 - s)^2 - (40 - i)^2,$$

    then what values of s and i will maximize profit? Find the maximum profit.

16. A sporting goods store sells two kinds of lacrosse sticks, which are similar but are made by different manufacturers. The cost to the store of the first kind is $40, and the cost to the store of the second kind is $50. Experience has shown that if the selling price of the first kind is x dollars and the selling price of the second kind is y dollars, then the number sold monthly of the first kind is

    $$3{,}200 - 50x + 25y,$$

    and the number sold monthly of the second kind is

    $$25x - 30y.$$

    What should be the selling price of each kind of lacrosse stick for the greatest gross profit?

17. The inventory cost model discussed in the example near the end of the last section is to be applied to another product, and the cost function is

    $$C(L, I) = \frac{750{,}000}{L} + \frac{20I^2}{L} + \frac{25L}{2} - 25I,$$

    where L is the number of units to be made in each lot and I is the number to be placed in inventory each time a lot is made. The remaining part of the lot is used to fill back orders.
    a) Find the values of L and I that minimize $C(L, I)$.
    b) Compute the minimum cost.

18. Another company follows the strategy of the company in Problem 17, but uses the cost model

    $$C(L, p) = \frac{108{,}160}{L} + \frac{Lp^2}{2} + 2L(1 - p)^2,$$

    where $C(L, p)$ is in thousands of dollars, L is the lost size, and p is the **proportion** of a lot that is to be placed in inventory.
    a) Find the values of L and p that minimize $C(L, p)$.
    b) Prove (a) is a minimum.
    c) Compute the minimum cost.

19. (This problem is somewhat difficult, algebraically.) The cost model in Problem 17 is a special case of the general model

    $$C(L, I) = \frac{cd}{L} + \frac{(a + b)I^2}{2L} + \frac{bL}{2} - bI,$$

    where a, b, c, and d are parameters. Find the expressions for L and I that minimize cost in terms of these parameters.

9.14 REVIEW PROBLEMS

Find the first and second derivatives of each of the following functions:

1. $f(x) = 5e^{0.4x}$.
2. $f(x) = (1.09)^x$.
3. $f(x) = 4e^{0.5x-5}$.
4. $f(x) = e^{-0.5x^2}$.
5. $f(x) = e^{2x-x^2}$.
6. $f(x) = (1/4)^x$.

Find local optimum values, if any exist, and state which type of value has been found:

7. $f(x) = e^{2x} - 10x + 4$.
8. $f(x) = e^{0.5x} + 0.98x$.
9. $f(x) = xe^{-0.2x} + 3$.
10. $f(x) = 11 - x^4 - e^{x^2}$.

9.14 REVIEW PROBLEMS (continued)

Sketch graphs of the functions in Problems 11 and 12. Show the starting point coordinates and the asymptote with its equation.

11. $f(x) = 30 + 20e^{3+0.2x}$.

12. $f(x) = 30 - 20(0.5)^{x-10}$.

13. The revenue from, and the cost of, operating an undertaking for t years are, respectively, in millions of dollars,

$$R(t) = 3e^{0.05t} \quad \text{and} \quad C(t) = 1.5e^{0.08t}.$$

   a) How long should operations continue if profit is to be maximized?
   b) Compute maximum profit.

14. The total potential audience for a promotional campaign is 10,000 customers. Revenue averages $3 per response to the campaign. Campaign costs are a fixed amount of $500, plus $300 per day the campaign continues. The proportion of the total audience responding by time t days is

$$1 - e^{-0.25t}.$$

   a) How long should the campaign continue if profit is to be maximized?
   b) Compute maximum profit.

15. The total potential audience for a promotional campaign is 2,000 customers. Revenue averages $5 per response to the campaign. Costs are $105.36 per day plus a fixed cost of $100. The proportion of potential audience responding by time t days is

$$1 - (0.9)^t.$$

   a) How long should the campaign continue if profit is to be maximized?
   b) Compute maximum profit.

Find the derivatives of the following functions:

16. $f(x) = 2 \ln 3x$.
17. $f(x) = \ln(5x - 4)$.
18. $f(x) = \ln(1/(2x^2))$.
19. $f(x) = \ln(x^3 + x^2 + x - 5)$.
20. $f(x) = \ln(2x + 3)^{1/2}$.
21. $f(x) = \ln(xe^x)$.

Find the value of $f(x)$ at its local optimum points if any exists, and state whether this value is a local maximum or minimum.

22. $f(x) = 50 \ln x - x^2, \quad x > 0$.
23. $f(x) = x^2 - 4x - 16 \ln x + 30, \quad x > 0$.
24. $f(x) = 100(\ln 0.5x)/x, \quad x > 0$.
25. $f(x) = 0.5x^2 + 5x + 50 \ln x, \quad x > 0$.
26. $f(x) = 3 \ln(2x^2 - 16x + 40)$.

For each of the following find a) $f(g(x))$ and its derivative and b) $g(f(x))$ and its derivative:

27. $f(x) = x^3$ and $g(x) = \sqrt{x + 1}$.
28. $f(x) = x^2 + 3$ and $g(x) = x^3 - 2$.
29. $f(x) = x^2 - 1$ and $g(x) = x^{1/2}$.
30. $f(x) = x^3 + 4$ and $g(x) = x^{3/2}$.
31. $f(x) = 3(x^3 - 1)$ and $g(x) = 2x + 4$.
32. $f(x) = 4(x^2 - 2)$ and $g(x) = x^{3/2} + 1$.

Find dy/dx for each of the following and verify the result by either the function power rule, exponential function rule, or logarithmic function rule:

33. $y = 8\sqrt{3x^2 - 5}$.
34. $y = 3x(4x^5 + 6)^7$.

9.14 REVIEW PROBLEMS (continued)

35. $y = e^{5x^4 - 9}$.

36. $y = e^{-1/(0.9x)}$.

37. $y = \ln(2x^5 - 7x^3 + 4)^{4/3}$.

38. $y = \ln(5x^{7/5} - 2x^{5/2} + 2x - 9)$.

---

39. At income level Y, consumption expenditures are $C(Y)$ billion dollars, where

    $$C(Y) = 25 + 0.875Y.$$

    a) Find the marginal propensity to consume.
    b) Interpret (a).
    c) How much income is generated by an additional dollar of investment?
    d) At income level \$500 billion, what proportion of total income is spent?

40. For the consumption function

    $$C(Y) = 10 + 0.75Y - e^{-0.25Y}$$

    find the multiplier at income levels: a) 1. b) 4.

41. Find the expression for the multiplier if the consumption function is

    $$C(Y) = a + bY.$$

42. Find the expression for the multiplier if the consumption function is

    $$C(Y) = a + bY + e^{kY}.$$

For each of the following find: a) f_x. b) f_{xx}. c) f_y. d) f_{yy}. e) f_{xy}.

43. $f(x, y) = 2x^3 - 3xy + 4y^2 - 6$.

44. $f(x, y) = (x^2 + y^2)^{1/2}$.

45. $f(x, y) = 2y^5 - 6x^2y^3 + 3x - 2y$.

46. $f(x, y) = y \ln x$.

47. $f(x, y) = xe^y$.

48. $f(x, y) = \dfrac{x^2}{2y + 1}$.

Carry out the following:

49. $\dfrac{\partial}{\partial y}(x^2 - 3y^2)$.

50. $\dfrac{\partial^2}{\partial x^2}(x^3 y^2)$.

51. $\dfrac{\partial^2}{\partial x \partial y}(x^3 y^2)$.

52. $\dfrac{\partial^2}{\partial x^2}(xe^y)$.

---

53. If $f(x, y) = 5x - 4y$, compute:
    a) $f_x(1, 2)$.
    b) $f_{xx}(1, 2)$.
    c) $f_y(1, 2)$.
    d) $f_{yy}(1, 2)$.
    e) $f_{xy}(1, 2)$.

54. During a period of operations, a gasoline producer makes and sells x gallons of regular and y gallons of super at a cost, in cents, of

    $$C(x, y) = 2x^2 - 4xy + 3y^2 - 6x + 10y.$$

    Find $C_x(10, 15)$ and $C_y(10, 15)$ and interpret these numbers in rate terminology.

For the following, find the value of the function at its local optimum and saddle points, if any exist, and state whether a value found is a local maximum, a local minimum, or a saddle point:

55. $f(x, y) = xy - x^2 - y^2 + 15x$.

56. $f(x, y) = x + y + 25/x + 16/y$; x and y positive.

9.14 REVIEW PROBLEMS (concluded)

57. $f(x, y) = 3x^2 - 3xy + y^2 - 6x + 32$.
58. $f(x, y) = \ln x + \ln y - 0.2x - 0.5y + 5$.
59. $f(x, y) = \dfrac{1,600,000}{x} + 2xy^2 + \dfrac{x(1-y)^2}{2}$, $x > 0$.

9.15 EXTENDED REVIEW PROBLEMS

1. If $z = y^{1/2}$ and $y = x^2 + 2$, find dz/dx.

2. Find the local optimum and saddle points, if any exist, and the corresponding value of the function if
$$f(x, y) = 3x^3 - 12xy + 4y^2 + 18.$$

3. If $z = y^2$ and $y = x^{1/2} + 2$, find dz/dx.

4. Find the local optimum values, if any exist, and state which type of value has been found if
$$f(x) = x^2 e^{-0.5x} + 2.$$

5. The total potential audience for a new product is 50,000 customers. The product is projected to sell at $2 apiece. Advertising costs are estimated at $1,000 per day plus an initial design cost of $10,000. Marketing research has established that the proportion of the potential audience responding by time t days is
$$1 - (0.7)^t.$$
   a) How long should the advertising campaign continue if profit is to be maximized?
   b) What will the maximum profit be?

6. a) Find f_x, f_y, f_z, and f_{xy} if
$$f(x, y, z) = x^3 + y^2 z + z^2 x.$$
   b) Compute $f_z(0, 2, 3)$.

7. Find the first and second derivatives of
$$f(x) = \ln(x^2 e^{2x}).$$

8. Find the local optimum values, if any exist, and state which type of value has been found if
$$f(x) = 25(\ln x) - x^2, \quad x > 0.$$

9. Given
$$f(x, y) = \dfrac{ab}{x} + \dfrac{cxy^2}{2} + \dfrac{dx(1-y)^2}{2}$$
where x, y, and all parameters (a, b, c, and d) are positive:
   a) Find the expressions for x and y that minimize $f(x, y)$ in terms of the parameters a, b, c, and d.
   b) Prove (a) yields a minimum.

10. The total cost to manufacture b dozen ballpoint pens and p dozen pencils is given by
$$C(b, p) = 2bp + 3p^2 + b^2/2 - 44p - 17b + 191.5.$$
   a) Find the values of b and p that result in a minimum cost.
   b) What is this minimum cost?

10 INTRODUCTION TO INTEGRAL CALCULUS

10.1 INTRODUCTION

*The inverse operation to differentiation is **integration** and measures an area associated with the function in question.*

We have learned how to find the derivatives of functions and seen numerous applications of the derivative that stem from its interpretation as the slope of the curve representing the function. It is quite surprising to learn that if we start with a function, $f(x)$, carry out the process that is the **inverse** of taking the derivative, the result provides an area that has $f(x)$ as part of its boundary. The inverse process first entails taking the **antiderivative of** $f(x)$ then using the antiderivative to determine the **integral** of $f(x)$. Many of the applications of the inverse process stem from interpreting the result as an area that represents quantities such as dollars of profit or pounds of output.

Students generally find elementary integral calculus easy because, having had extensive practice in finding derivatives, the idea of doing the process in reverse, so to speak, is not hard to grasp. However, experience indicates that, at the beginning, students tend to get the two procedures mixed up. The need, therefore, is to concentrate on practicing integration until it is firmly fixed in mind.

In the first part of the chapter, only rational functions to a power are considered, and emphasis is placed on practicing integrating such functions; then attention turns to areas having these functions as part of their boundaries. Next, again using only rational functions to a power, applications involving area interpretations are presented. At this point, we will have learned most of the new ideas covered in the chapter. The last part of the chapter simply expands the list of integration rules to include exponential and logarithmic functions.

10.2 ANTIDERIVATIVES: THE INDEFINITE INTEGRAL

Addition and subtraction are examples of **inverse operations** where **one operation annuls the effect of the other.** Thus, if we start with the number 50, add 10 to it, then subtract 10, we have the original number 50. Similarly, multiplication and division are inverse operations. Cubing a number is annulled by the inverse operation of taking the cube root. Thus, starting with 2

$$2^3 = 8 \quad \text{and} \quad \sqrt[3]{8} = 2.$$

As a final example, recall that logarithms and antilogarithms (exponents) are inverse operations

$$\ln 5 = 1.609437912 \quad \text{and} \quad e^{1.609437912} = 5.$$

Now recall the Simple Power Rule for the operation of taking the derivative of x to a power n, that is, **multiply the function x^n by the power n and subtract one from the power to obtain a new power,** $n - 1$, thus getting

$$\frac{d}{dx}(x^n) = n \cdot x^{n-1}.$$

> In the Simple Power Rule for derivatives, we multiply by the power and then subtract one from the power; the inverse is to add one to the power and then divide by this new power.

Keeping this rule in mind, then, the correct inverse procedure would be to **add one to the power $n - 1$ to obtain a new power n and subsequently divide the entire expression by this new power** to get the original function x^n; i.e.,

$$\frac{n \cdot x^{(n-1)+1}}{(n-1)+1} = \frac{n \cdot x^n}{n} = x^n.$$

So if we take

$$\frac{d}{dx}(x^3) = 3x^2$$

and attempt to reverse the process of differentiation, we obtain

$$\frac{3x^{2+1}}{2+1} = \frac{3x^3}{3} = x^3,$$

as desired. However, the correct procedure just shown is still incomplete, because if we have

$$\frac{d}{dx}(x^3 + 10) = 3x^2,$$

and apply the above procedure to $3x^2$, we cannot recover the constant 10. What we can say is that $3x^2$ is the derivative of x^3 **plus an arbitrary constant,** C, and write

$$\text{antiderivative }(3x^2) = x^3 + C.$$

> An arbitrary constant should be added to an antiderivative since the derivative of any constant is zero.

The word **antiderivative** denotes the result of the operation that is the inverse of taking the derivative (just as antilogarithm is the inverse of the logarithm). Thus,

$$\text{antiderivative }(3x^2)$$

means **all expressions whose derivative is** $3x^2$. Again,

$$\text{antiderivative }(x^3) = \frac{x^{3+1}}{3+1} + C = \frac{x^4}{4} + C$$

and means that $x^4/4$ plus an arbitrary constant constitutes all expressions that have x^3 as their derivative.

> **Exercise.** a) Find antiderivative (x). b) What does the answer to (a) mean?
>
> **Answer:** a) $(x^2/2) + C$. b) $(x^2/2) + C$ constitutes all expressions that have x as their derivative.

For reasons that will become clear when we introduce interpretations of the antiderivative operation, we shall represent this operation by an elongated S; thus,

$$\int$$

is called the **integral symbol** and means the antiderivative of the expression following, as in

$$\int x^2 \, dx = \frac{x^3}{3} + C.$$

In general, we write

$$\int f(x) \, dx = F(x) + C$$

where $F(x)$ is an antiderivative of $f(x)$ so that

$$\frac{d}{dx} F(x) = f(x).$$

The dx is a **single** symbol and is called the **differential of** x. That is, just as Δx means the change in x and not Δ times x, so dx does not mean d times x. For the moment, we shall think of dx in the same sense as we did when we wrote

$$\frac{d}{dx}$$

The function to be integrated is the integrand, the result is the integral, and the arbitrary constant is the constant of integration.

to mean the derivative with respect to x. That is, **the dx means the independent variable is x and we are to integrate with respect to x.** Continuing with terminology, the function to be integrated is called the **integrand**, the outcome of the integration is called the **integral**, and the arbitrary constant is called the **constant of integration.** Thus, in

$$\int x^2 \, dx = \frac{x^3}{3} + C,$$

the integrand is x^2, the constant of integration is C, and

$$\frac{x^3}{3} + C$$

*Because the constant is arbitrary, the integral is called an **indefinite integral**.*

is the **indefinite** integral, where the word in bold is inserted because of the presence of the arbitrary constant, C.

The general rule for the indefinite integral of x to a constant power is

Simple Power Rule

$$\int x^n \, dx = \frac{x^{n+1}}{n+1} + C; \quad \text{if } n \neq -1.$$

In the Simple Power Rule for integration, we add one to the power and divide by the new power; i.e.,

$$\int x^n dx = \frac{x^{n+1}}{n+1} + C$$

as long as $n \neq -1$.

Observe that the rule is inapplicable if the power is $n = -1$ for then the divisor, $(n + 1)$, in the integral would be zero. We shall see later in this chapter that if $n = -1$, the integral is the natural logarithm of x.

Example. Integrate the following functions:

a) $f(y) = 1/y^2$. b) $f(x) = x^{1/2}$.

For part (a), we have

a) $\int \frac{1}{y^2} \, dy = \int y^{-2} \, dy = \frac{y^{-2+1}}{-2+1} + C = \frac{y^{-1}}{-1} + C = -\frac{1}{y} + C.$

For part (b), we obtain

b) $\int x^{1/2} \, dx = \frac{x^{1/2+1}}{1/2+1} + C = \frac{x^{3/2}}{3/2} + C = \frac{2}{3}x^{3/2} + C.$

Exercise. Integrate the following: a) z^5. b) $1/w^{1/2}$.

Answer: a) $\frac{z^6}{6} + C$. b) $2w^{1/2} + C$.

Note in the preceding example and exercise that we can check our answer by differentiating.

The following properties parallel those of the derivative operation. First, note that the derivative of x is 1, so that

$$\int 1 \, dx = x + C,$$

Properties of the Integration Operation

which is correct because

$$\frac{d}{dx}(x + C) = 1.$$

Conventionally, the factor 1 is not written, as is the case for example when we write x rather than one times x. That is,

$$\int dx = \int 1\, dx = x + C.$$

Similarly, we know that

$$\frac{d}{dx}(3x) = 3,$$

so that

$$\int 3\, dx = 3x + C$$

and, in general, for any constant k,

$$\int k\, dx = kx + C.$$

Note that this rule is really a special case of the Simple Power Rule when $n = 0$.

> The integral of any constant is simply the constant times the variable of integration; i.e.,
>
> $\int k\, dx = kx + C.$

Exercise. Find the following: a) $\int (-2)\, dx$. b) $\int dy/2$. c) $\int dz$.

Answer: a) $-2x + C$. b) $(1/2)y + C$. c) $z + C$.

> Constants can be factored out of integrals as with derivatives.

As was the case in taking derivatives, a constant factor may be placed inside or outside the operation symbol. For example,

$$\int 3x\, dx = 3\int x\, dx = 3 \cdot \frac{x^2}{2} + C.$$

We could have written

$$\int 3x\, dx = 3\int x\, dx = 3\left(\frac{x^2}{2} + C\right) = \frac{3x^2}{2} + 3C$$

but, inasmuch as C is an arbitrary constant, so is $3C$ an arbitrary constant, and **only one symbol is required for such a constant.** We shall follow convention and write the constant of integration as a single letter, which is usually C.

Again as in the case of taking derivatives, integration may be performed on an expression term-by-term. Thus,

$$\int (3z^3 + 2z + 5 + m)\, dz = \int 3z^3\, dz + \int 2z\, dz + \int 5\, dz + \int m\, dz$$

$$= 3\int z^3\, dz + 2\int z\, dz + 5\int dz + m\int dz$$

$$= 3\left(\frac{z^4}{4}\right) + 2\left(\frac{z^2}{2}\right) + 5z + mz + C$$

$$= \frac{3z^4}{4} + z^2 + 5z + mz + C.$$

Integrals can be done term-by-term as with derivatives.

In this example, note that m is to be considered as a constant because the symbol dz specifies the variable is z. Note also that, as stated earlier, we just have the single constant of integration C.

We summarize the last two properties as follows:

$$\int k f(x)\, dx = k \int f(x)\, dx$$

$$\int [f(x) \pm g(x)]\, dx = \int f(x)\, dx \pm \int g(x)\, dx.$$

Exercise. a) Write the symbols for integrating

$$6y - 10y^4 + b - 1$$

with respect to y. b) Write the integral.

Answer: a) $\int (6y - 10y^4 + b - 1)\, dy$. b) $3y^2 - 2y^5 + by - y + C$.

We shall have occasion from time to time to question whether an integral is correct. The answer, of course, is

An indefinite integral is correct if the derivative of the integral is the integrand.

One way to determine an indefinite integral is to check that the derivative of the integral is the integrand.

Example. Is the following correct?

$$\underbrace{\int (7x + 5)^2\, dx}_{\text{integrand}} \stackrel{?}{=} \underbrace{\frac{(7x + 5)^3}{3}}_{\text{integral}} + C. \qquad (1)$$

To check, we find the derivative of the integral,

$$\frac{d}{dx}\left[\frac{(7x+5)^3}{3} + C\right] = \frac{d}{dx}\left[\frac{(7x+5)^3}{3}\right] + \frac{d}{dx}(C)$$

$$= \frac{3(7x+5)^2(7)}{3} + 0$$

$$= (7x+5)^2(7)$$

by the Function Power Rule. Thus the integral is **incorrect** because its derivative contains the factor 7, which does not appear in the integrand. However, this tells us that we can obtain the correct result by dividing the integral in Equation (1) by 7. That is, the correct integral is

$$\int (7x+5)^2\,dx = \frac{(7x+5)^3}{3(7)} + C$$

where, again, we have chosen to use the symbol C rather than $C/7$, which would arise in dividing Equation (1) by 7.

Exercise. Is the following correct? Why or why not?

$$\int (2x+9)^{-1/2}\,dx \stackrel{?}{=} (2x+9)^{1/2} + C.$$

Answer: It is correct, because the derivative of $[(2x+9)^{1/2} + C]$, by the Function Power Rule, is the integrand, $(2x+9)^{-1/2}$.

= Integration Rule for Powers of a Linear Function

Returning to the correct integral in the preceding example,

$$\int (7x+5)^2\,dx = \frac{(7x+5)^3}{3(7)} + C,$$

the integrand is a **linear function**, $(7x+5)$, to a constant power. The integral can be obtained by proceeding first as we do for a simple power, that is, adding one to the power and dividing by the new power, to give

$$\frac{(7x+5)^3}{3}$$

provided that we **also divide by the coefficient of** x, which is 7, and write

$$\frac{(7x+5)^3}{3(7)} + C.$$

The reason for this is that in differentiating the last expression by the Function Power Rule, we would multiply by the coefficient 7 of x. Observe that the constant 5 in the linear expression $(7x + 5)$ has no effect on the result.

In this problem, we are treating $(7x + 5)$ as a single entity, just as we did in performing the chain rule. A standard technique used to handle integration problems like this is usually referred to as ***u*-substitution.** The basic idea is that $(7x + 5)$ is replaced by the letter u since it is treated as a **single entity,** and the problem is converted to a presumably simpler problem in the new variable u. Continued practice with the technique of *u*-substitution will help in simplifying complex problems. Let's illustrate the *u*-substitution technique by resolving our original problem

> A substitution often is helpful in transforming a complex integral into a simpler integral.

$$\int (7x + 5)^2 \, dx.$$

Step 1. Let $u = 7x + 5$.

Step 2. Take the derivative of u with respect to x:

$$\frac{du}{dx} = 7.$$

Step 3. Treating the derivative as the quotient of two differentials, solve Step 2 for dx:

$$dx = \frac{du}{7}.$$

Step 4. Substitute the appropriate *u*-expression for every term containing x in the original integral:

$$\int (7x + 5)^2 \, dx = \int (u^2) \left(\frac{du}{7}\right) = \frac{1}{7} \int u^2 \, du.$$

Step 5. Integrate the new problem with respect to u:

$$\frac{1}{7} \int u^2 \, du = \frac{1}{7} \left(\frac{u^3}{3} + C\right) = \frac{u^3}{3 \cdot 7} + C.$$

Step 6. Reverse the substitution process to obtain an answer in terms of the original variable x:

$$\frac{u^3}{3 \cdot 7} + C = \frac{(7x + 5)^3}{3 \cdot 7} + C,$$

so

$$\int (7x + 5)^2 \, dx = \frac{(7x + 5)^3}{3(7)} + C,$$

which is precisely the same result as before.

At first, this techique may appear to be a tremendous amount of effort for a simple problem. However, not only is it easier than memorizing formulas, but it even allows us to derive the rules themselves. Indeed if the linear function is expressed in general form as

$$mx + b,$$

we may write the following general rule:

> In the Power Rule for Linear Functions, we add one to the power, divide by the new power and also by the coefficient of the variable of integration.

Power Rule for Linear Functions

$$\int (mx + b)^n \, dx = \frac{(mx + b)^{n+1}}{m(n + 1)} + C; \quad n \neq -1.$$

Note that the power rule adds one to the power, divides the result by this new power, and also by the coefficient of x.

Exercise. a) What would u be substituted for in the Power Rule above? b) What is du?

Answer: a) $mx + b$. b) $m \cdot dx$.

We wish to emphasize that we could memorize formulas such as the power rule, but this can become cumbersome and is error prone. The u-substitution technique, on the other hand, works effectively in many situations, as we will see throughout this chapter.

Example. Integrate the following

$$\int \frac{dx}{(5x - 6)^3}.$$

We begin by choosing

$$u = 5x - 6$$

so that

$$\frac{du}{dx} = 5$$

and

$$dx = \frac{du}{5}.$$

Therefore,

$$\int \frac{dx}{(5x-6)^3} = \int \frac{1}{u^3} \cdot \frac{du}{5} = \frac{1}{5}\int u^{-3}\, du$$

$$= \frac{1}{5}\left(\frac{u^{-2}}{-2} + C\right) = -\frac{1}{10} \cdot \frac{1}{u^2} + C.$$

Resubstituting, we obtain

$$\int \frac{dx}{(5x-6)^3} = -\frac{1}{10} \cdot \frac{1}{(5x-6)^2} + C.$$

Exercise. Check the result of the preceding example using the Power Rule for Linear Functions.

Exercise. Find $\int (5-2x)^{-3/2}\, dx$ and write the answer with positive exponents.
Answer: $1/(5-2x)^{1/2} + C$.

Before turning to a practice problem set, it is worth noting that the product, quotient, and chain rules that applied in taking derivatives do not have general counterparts in integration. As a consequence, it is necessary to pay careful attention to the **form** of the expression to be integrated and be sure that it matches the form of the integration rule being applied. At the moment, we have only the two forms specified in

$$\int x^n\, dx = \frac{x^{n+1}}{n+1} + C; \quad n \ne -1$$

$$\int (mx+b)^n\, dx = \frac{(mx+b)^{n+1}}{m(n+1)} + C; \quad n \ne -1.$$

10.3 PROBLEM SET 10-1

Write the expression for the indefinite integral. Simplify results where possible. Express answers with positive exponents.

1. $\int dx$.
2. $\int dz$.
3. $\int 5\, dy$.
4. $\int (-7)\, dw$.

10.3 PROBLEM SET 10–1 (concluded)

5. $\int (1 + x)\, dx$.
6. $\int (3 - y)\, dy$.
7. $\int (2x^2 - 3x + 4)\, dx$.
8. $\int (3y^3 + 4y - 1)\, dy$.
9. $\int p\, dq$.
10. $\int q\, dp$.
11. $\int (pq)\, dp$.
12. $\int (pq)\, dq$.
13. $\int (x^3 + x^4 - 1)\, dx$.
14. $\int (y^2 + y^5 - 1)\, dy$.
15. $\int (3y^2 + 5y^4 + 1)\, dy$.
16. $\int (4x^3 - 6x^5 + 1)\, dx$.
17. $\int x^{-2}\, dx$.
18. $\int 7^{-3}\, dy$.
19. $\int \dfrac{dy}{y^3}$.
20. $\int \dfrac{dx}{x^4}$.
21. $\int (5 - 2y^{-3})\, dy$.
22. $\int (7 - 3x^{-4})\, dx$.
23. $\int \left(2x - \dfrac{1}{x^2} + 1\right) dx$.
24. $\int \left(y + \dfrac{2}{y^3} + 1\right) dy$.
25. $\int p^{1/2}\, dp$.
26. $\int q^{1/3}\, dq$.
27. $\int 3x^{-4/3}\, dx$.
28. $\int 5y^{-3/2}\, dy$.
29. $\int \left(2 - \dfrac{1}{x^2} - \dfrac{2}{3x^{5/3}}\right) dx$.
30. $\int \left(2x - \dfrac{2}{x^3} - \dfrac{1}{4x^{4/3}}\right) dx$.
31. $\int 12(x^2 + x^3)\, dx$.
32. $\int 3(x^2 + 2x)\, dx$.
33. $\int 16(2x - 9)^3\, dx$.
34. $\int 30(3x + 5)^5\, dx$.
35. $\int (3x - 9)^{-2}\, dx$.
36. $\int (2x + 3)^{-4}\, dx$.
37. $\int \dfrac{dx}{(5 - 3x)^{1/2}}$.
38. $\int \dfrac{dw}{(7 - 2w)^3}$.
39. $\int \dfrac{8\,dx}{(2x + 5)^{1/3}}$.
40. $\int \dfrac{12\,dx}{(3x - 7)^{1/2}}$.

10.4 AREA AND THE DEFINITE INTEGRAL

In differential calculus, we learned that, in geometric terms, the derivative of a function evaluated at a point is the slope of the line tangent to the curve at that point. In this section, we shall show that a form of the integral, in geometric terms, represents an *area* **having the integrand function as one of its boundaries.**

To better understand the connection between areas and integrals, consider the following simple example. Suppose we want to find the area under the curve $f(x) = x$ from $x = 0$ to $x = 4$ as shown in Figure 10–1. From the formula for the area of a triangle, we know that the desired area is

$$A = \dfrac{1}{2} \cdot b \cdot h = \dfrac{1}{2}(4)(4) = 8 \text{ square units.}$$

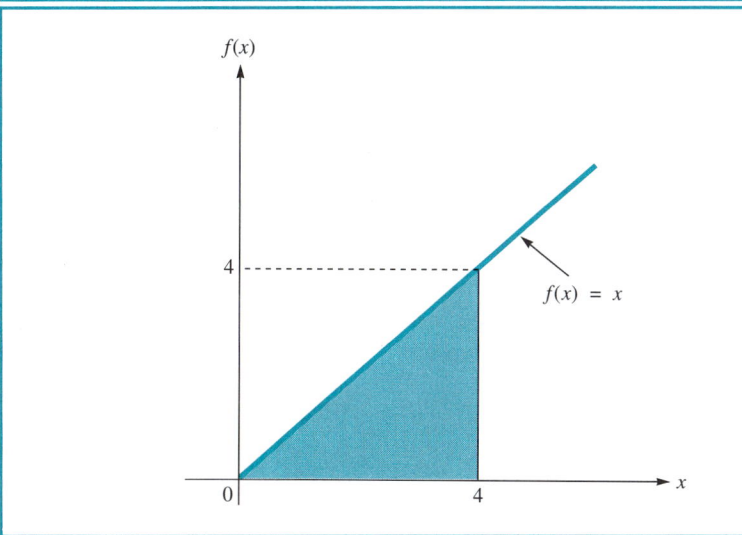

FIGURE 10-1

Now an alternative way to determine the area is by computing the value of the **definite integral**

$$\int_0^4 x \, dx.$$

This last expression is evaluated by first finding the antiderivative $x^2/2 + C$ of the integrand x, then finding the value of this antiderivative at the **upper limit** of $x = 4$, and lastly subtracting the value of the antiderivative at the **lower limit** of $x = 0$. This is the result of a famous theorem called the **Fundamental Theorem of Calculus** which states that the definite integral can be evaluated simply by computing the values of the antiderivative at the endpoints of the interval in question.

> The area under a curve between two limits can be evaluated by the definite integral; i.e., the difference between the value of the antiderivative at the upper and lower limits.

The Fundamental Theorem of Calculus

If a function $f(x)$ has an antiderivative $F(x)$ in an interval $[a, b]$, then

$$\int_a^b f(x) \, dx = F(x) \Big|_a^b = F(b) - F(a).$$

> A definite integral is the difference between the values of the antiderivative at the upper and lower limits.

Using the Fundamental Theorem of Calculus in our example, we have

$$\int_0^4 x \, dx = \left(\frac{x^2}{2} + C\right)\Big|_0^4$$

$$= \left(\frac{4^2}{2} + C\right) - \left(\frac{0^2}{2} + C\right) = 8 \text{ square units,}$$

which is the exact area under $f(x) = x$ from $x = 0$ to $x = 4$.

The constant of integration is not needed in a definite integral.

Note in this example, the constant of integration C is not needed since it is added in at the upper limit and then subtracted out at the lower limit. This will always be the case with a definite integral being evaluated by the Fundamental Theorem of Calculus, so henceforth we will omit the constant of integration C when computing definite integrals.

As another example suppose we want to find the area under the curve $f(x) = 5$ from $x = 2$ to $x = 6$ as shown in Figure 10–2. From the formula for the area of a rectangle, we know the desired area is

$$A = \ell \cdot w = (4)(5) = 20 \text{ square units.}$$

Using the definite integral approach as in the preceding example, we have

$$\int_2^6 5 \, dx = (5x)\Big|_2^6 = 5(6) - 5(2) = 20 \text{ square units.}$$

FIGURE 10-2

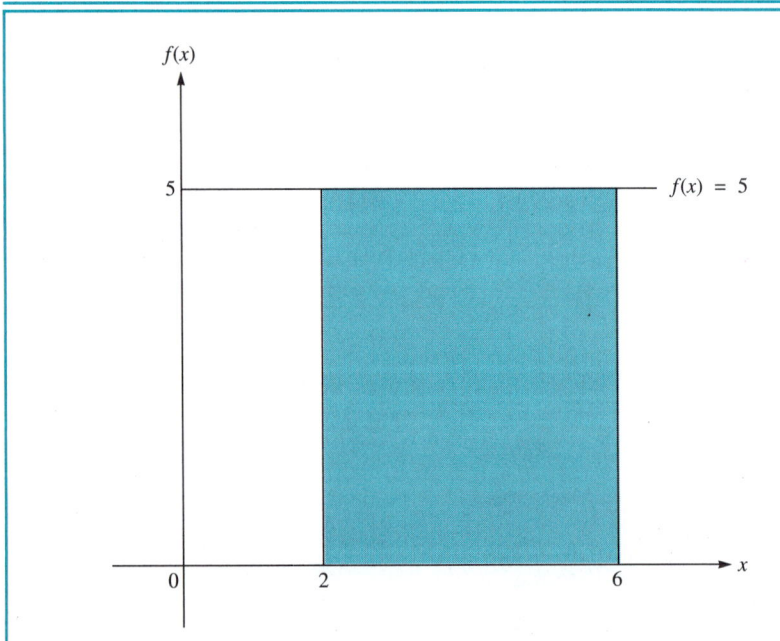

Now suppose we want to find the area under the curve $f(x) = x^2$ from $x = 1$ to $x = 3$ as shown in Figure 10–3. **This time there is no simple formula for the area.** But what if we were to use the definite integral technique of the previous two examples? Then we would guess that

$$A = \int_1^3 x^2 \, dx = \frac{x^3}{3} \Big|_1^3 = \frac{3^3}{3} - \frac{1^3}{3} = \frac{27}{3} - \frac{1}{3} = \frac{26}{3} \text{ square units}$$

which we will see is precisely the correct area.

We will now use something called **Riemann Sums** to illustrate why the definite integral really does represent the area under a curve $f(x)$ and above the x-axis. We saw in the preceding example that there was no simple geometric formula for computing the area under the curve $f(x) = x^2$ from $x = 1$ to $x = 3$. However, we can use a standard geometric figure, such as the rectangle, to approximate this area. For example, consider Figure 10–4A where we have used two rectangles to approximate the area. Here we see that

$$A \approx 1 + 4 = 5 \text{ square units.}$$

Clearly this is not a good approximation and **underestimates** the area because the nonshaded areas under the curve have been omitted. On the other hand, suppose that we had used the two rectangles in Figure 10–4B to approximate the area. In this case, we would have

$$A \approx 4 + 9 = 13 \text{ square units.}$$

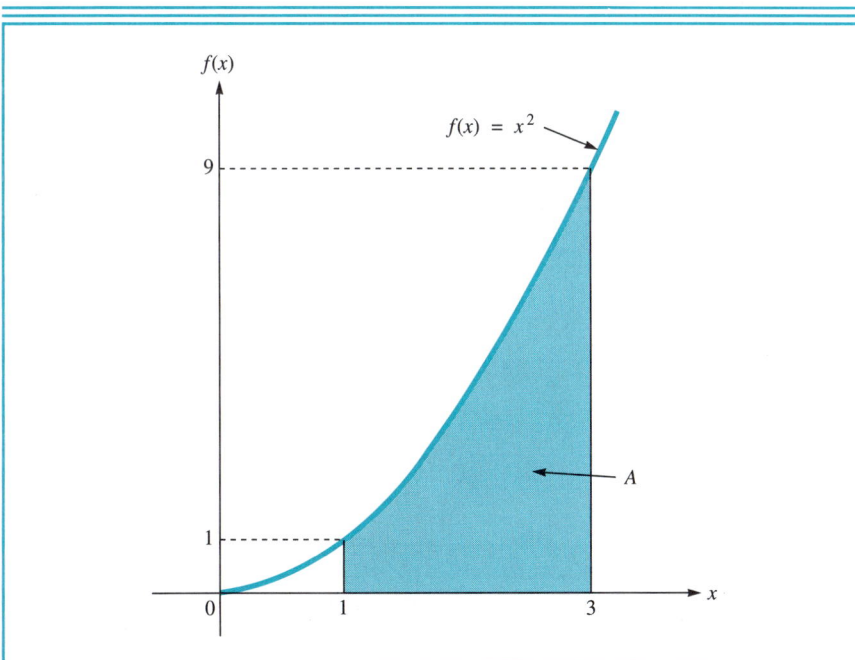

FIGURE 10–3

FIGURE 10-4A

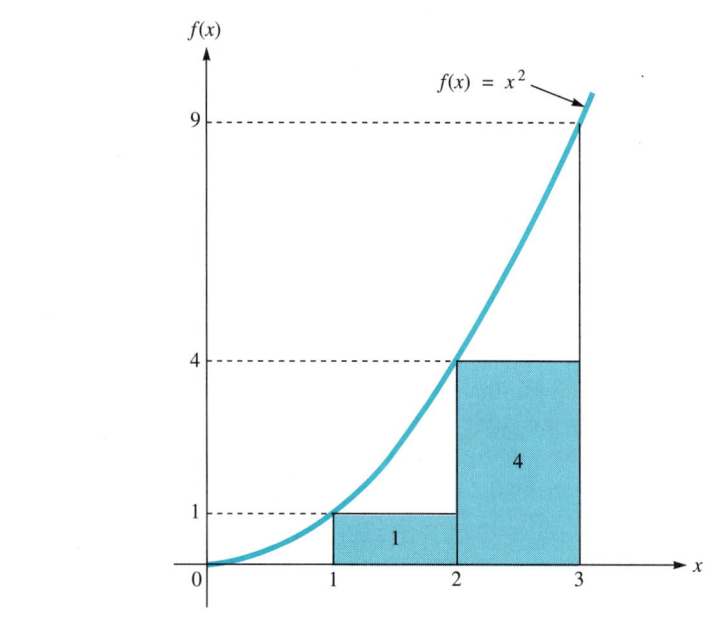

FIGURE 10-4B

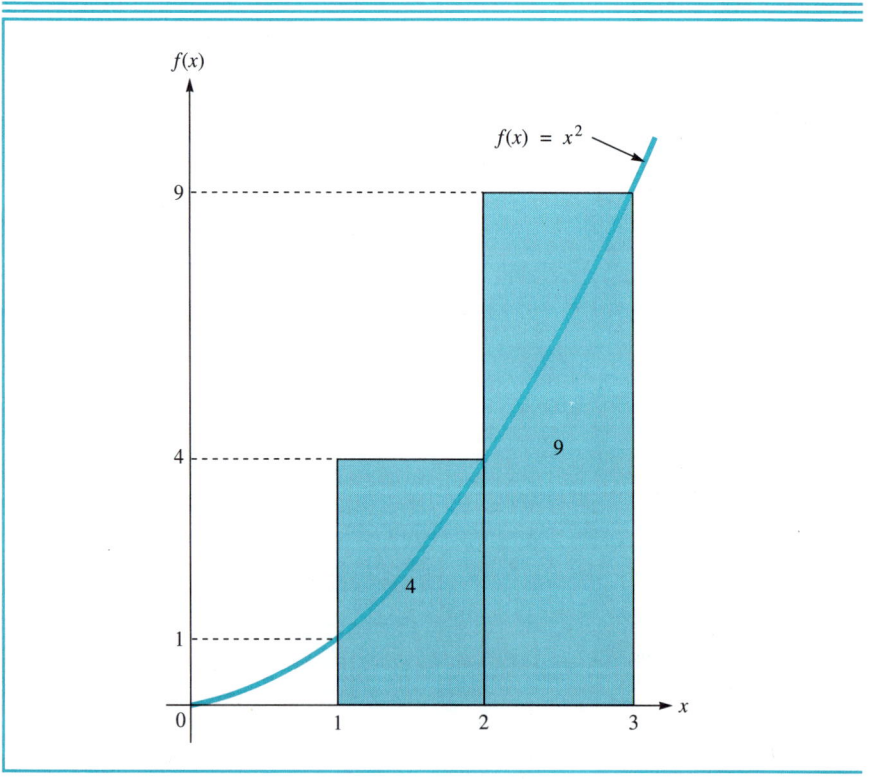

Again this is not a good approximation and, this time, **overestimates** the area because the shaded areas above the curve have been included. So we will have to use more rectangles to get a better approximation. By the way, the approximation from the rectangles in Figure 10–4A is an example of a **lower sum,** while that in Figure 10–4B is an example of an **upper sum.** Both are usually referred to as **Riemann Sums.**

Lower sums underestimate the area; upper sums overestimate the area.

Now suppose we use four rectangles to approximate the area as shown in Figures 10–5A and 10–5B. Then the lower sum is

$$A \approx \frac{1}{2} + \frac{9}{8} + 2 + \frac{25}{8} = 6\frac{3}{4} \text{ square units,}$$

while the upper sum is

$$A \approx \frac{9}{8} + 2 + \frac{25}{8} + \frac{9}{2} = 10\frac{3}{4} \text{ square units.}$$

Clearly, both this lower and upper sum are better approximations to the area than before, but they still are not very close to the correct area of 26/3 square units.

Suppose we next try approximating the area by eight rectangles as shown in Figures 10–6A and 10–6B. This time, the lower sum is

$$A \approx \frac{1}{4} + \frac{25}{64} + \frac{9}{16} + \frac{49}{64} + 1 + \frac{81}{64} + \frac{25}{16} + \frac{121}{64} = 7\frac{11}{16} \text{ square units,}$$

and the upper sum is

$$A \approx \frac{25}{64} + \frac{9}{16} + \frac{49}{64} + 1 + \frac{81}{64} + \frac{25}{16} + \frac{121}{64} + \frac{9}{4} = 9\frac{11}{16} \text{ square units.}$$

Once again, both the lower and upper sum are better approximations to the correct area of 26/3 square units, but they are still not close enough.

It seems clear from Figures 10–4 through 10–6 that if we were to keep increasing the number of rectangles used to approximate the area we would eventually be close enough to the actual area. Indeed, as we will see in the exercises and as was proven by Riemann, there is a unique number which is at one and the same time **larger than all lower sums and smaller than all upper sums,** and that number is both the **area** and the **definite integral.** Thus, **the definite integral must be precisely equal to the area.** Later on in this chapter we will introduce an alternative method known as the **Trapezoidal Rule** which will approximate the area more closely using a much fewer number of trapezoids than the number of rectangles needed with Riemann Sums.

In summary, then, we will henceforth use the definite integral technique developed to this point for evaluating areas; namely, **the area under a curve $f(x)$ in an interval $[a, b]$ when $f(x) \geq 0$ can be evaluated using the definite integral by**

$$A = \int_a^b f(x)\,dx = F(x)\Big|_a^b = F(b) - F(a).$$

The area under a nonnegative curve $f(x)$ in an interval $[a,b]$ is given by the definite integral.

FIGURE 10–5A

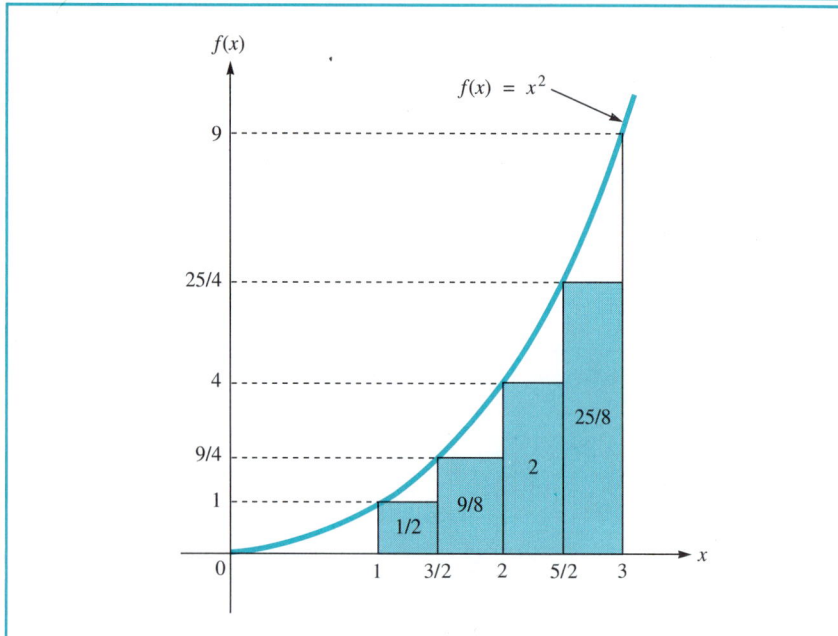

FIGURE 10–5B

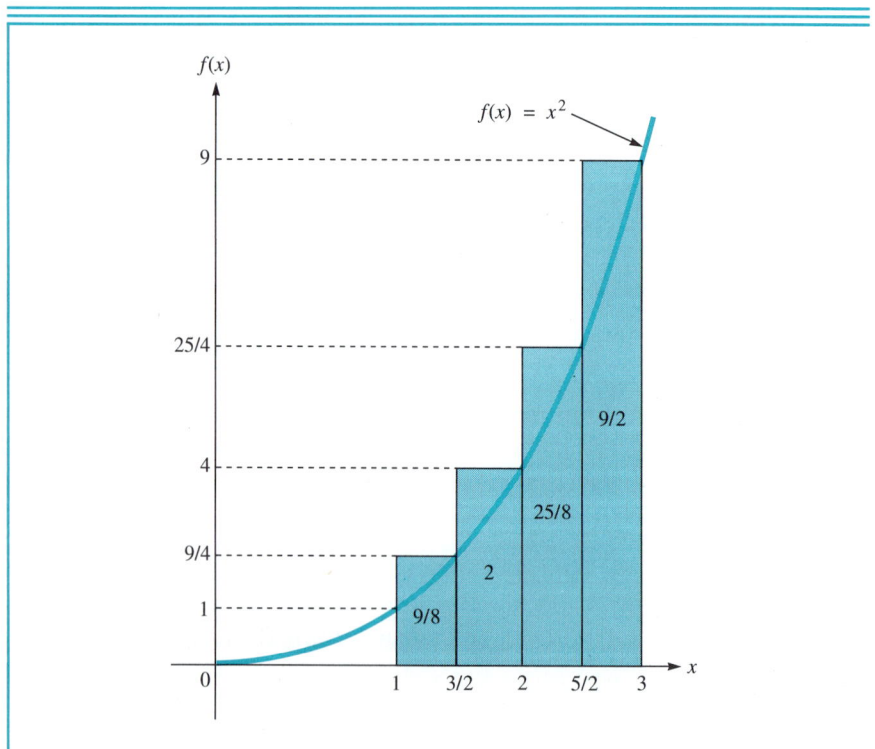

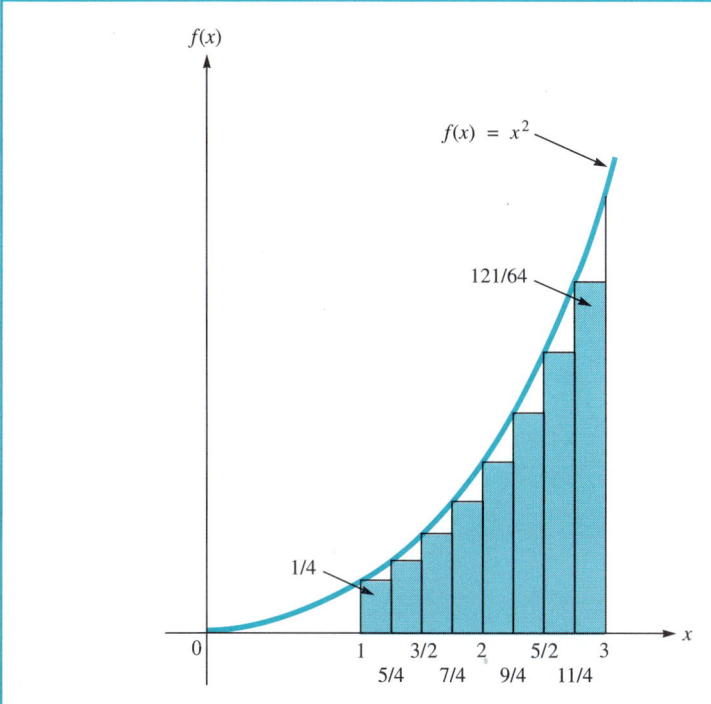

FIGURE 10-6A

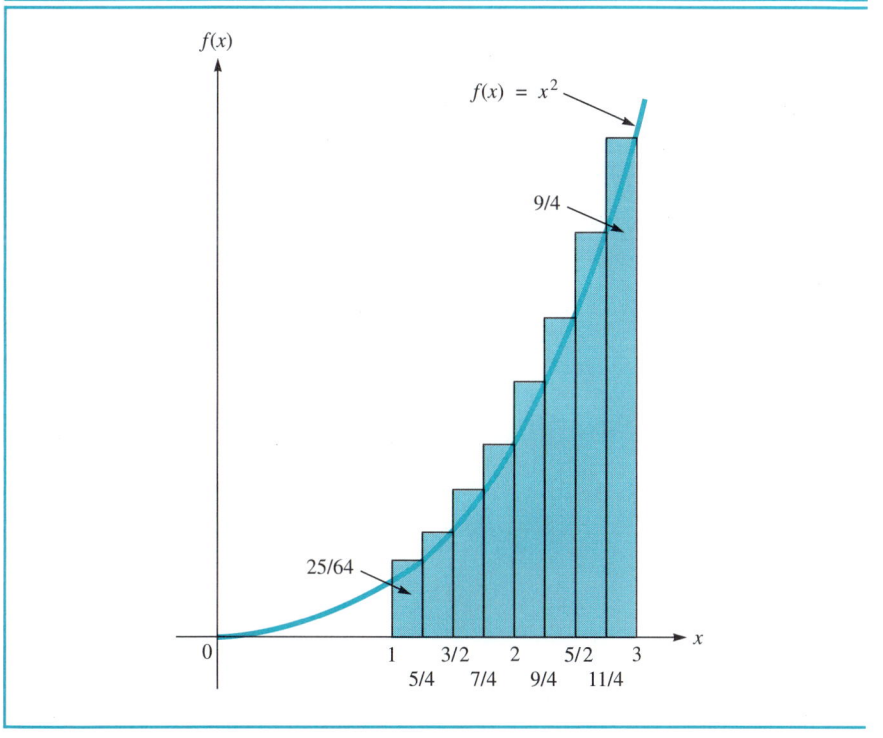

FIGURE 10-6B

Example. Find the area under $f(x) = x^{1/3} + 5$ over the interval $x = 1$ to $x = 8$.

The area sought is shown in Figure 10–7 and is computed by the definite integral as follows:

$$A = \int_1^8 (x^{1/3} + 5)\, dx = \left(\frac{3}{4} x^{4/3} + 5x\right)\bigg|_1^8$$

$$= \left[\frac{3}{4}(8)^{4/3} + 5(8)\right] - \left[\frac{3}{4}(1)^{4/3} + 5(1)\right]$$

$$= \left[\frac{3}{4}(16) + 40\right] - \left[\frac{3}{4} + 5\right]$$

$$= 12 + 40 - \frac{3}{4} - 5$$

$$= 46.25.$$

Exercise. Compute the area under $f(x) = 3x^{1/2} - 2$ over the interval $x = 4$ to $x = 16$.
Answer: 88.

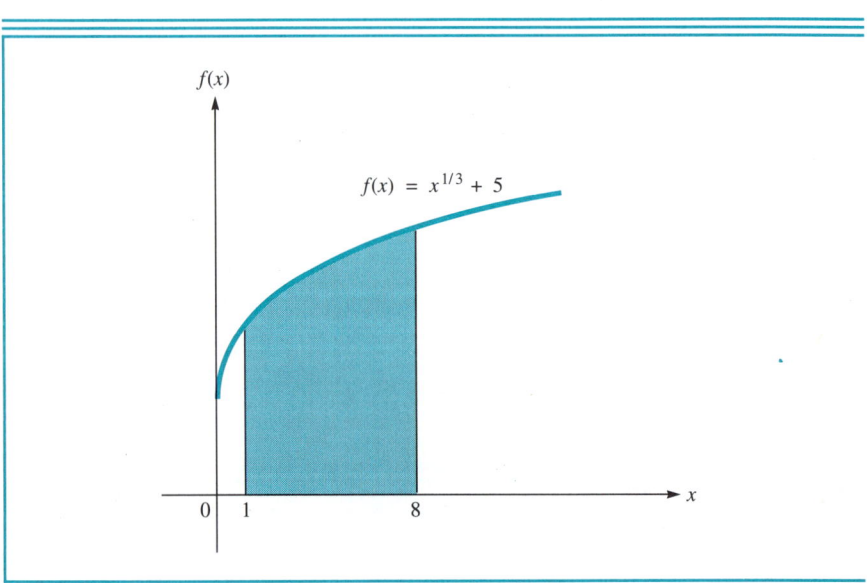

FIGURE 10–7
(not to scale)

Example. Sketch the function $f(x) = 10x - x^2$, then find the area bounded by the function and the x-axis.

From our work in Chapter 8, we know

$$f(x) = 10x - x^2$$

is a vertical parabola opening downward. The vertex is the local maximum that occurs where $f'(x) = 0$. Hence,

$$f'(x) = 10 - 2x, \quad \text{and} \quad f'(x) \text{ is zero when } x = 5, \quad f(5) = 25,$$

so (5, 25) is the vertex, as shown in Figure 10–8. The curve opens downward from the vertex and so must intersect the x-axis at two points. These points occur where $f(x) = 0$, and we find

$$f(x) = 0 \quad \text{when} \quad 10x - x^2 = 0$$
$$x(10 - x) = 0$$
$$x = 0, 10$$

so the intercepts are (0, 0) and (10, 0), as shown in Figure 10–8. The area sought is then computed as follows:

$$A = \int_0^{10} (10x - x^2) \, dx = \left(5x^2 - \frac{x^3}{3} \right) \Big|_0^{10}$$
$$= \left(500 - \frac{1000}{3} \right) - (0 - 0)$$
$$= \frac{500}{3}.$$

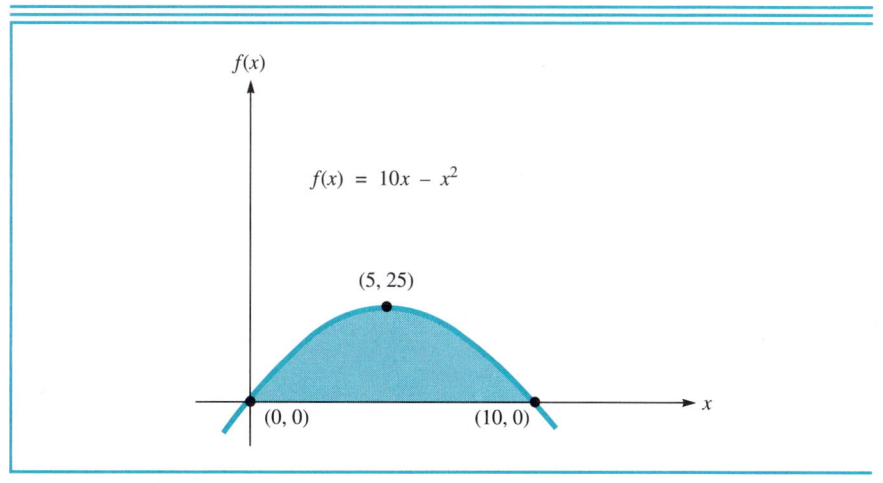

FIGURE 10–8
(not to scale)

When the interval endpoints are not explicitly stated, a sketch of the function is helpful in determining them.

When the endpoints of the interval over which an area is to be computed are given, the computation involves only integrating and evaluating the integral. But, as the last example shows, the problem specification may require that the interval endpoints be found and, in this case, a sketch of the function may be helpful.

> **Exercise.** Sketch the function $f(x) = 16 - x^2$ and compute the area bounded by the curve and the x-axis.
>
> **Answer:** The curve is a parabola with vertex at $(0, 16)$, opening downward, with intercepts $(-4, 0)$ and $(4, 0)$. The area is $256/3$.

Until now, we have only considered areas of the type shown in Figure 10–9 where the function is nonnegative so that it lies above the x-axis and the area is given by

$$A_1 = \int_a^b f(x)\, dx$$

When a function is nonpositive, the area is given by the negative of the definite integral.

What about areas of the type shown in Figure 10–10 where the function is nonpositive so that it lies below the x-axis?

$$A_2 = -\int_a^b f(x)\, dx$$

FIGURE 10–9

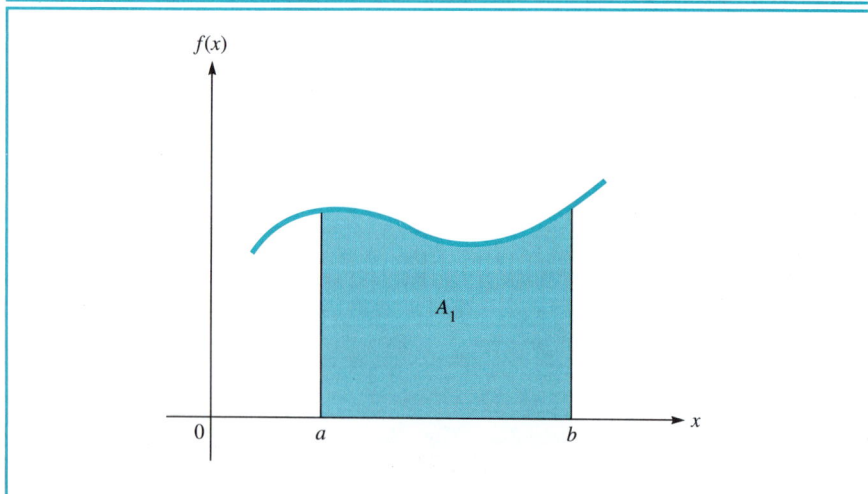

CHAPTER 10 INTRODUCTION TO INTEGRAL CALCULUS 661

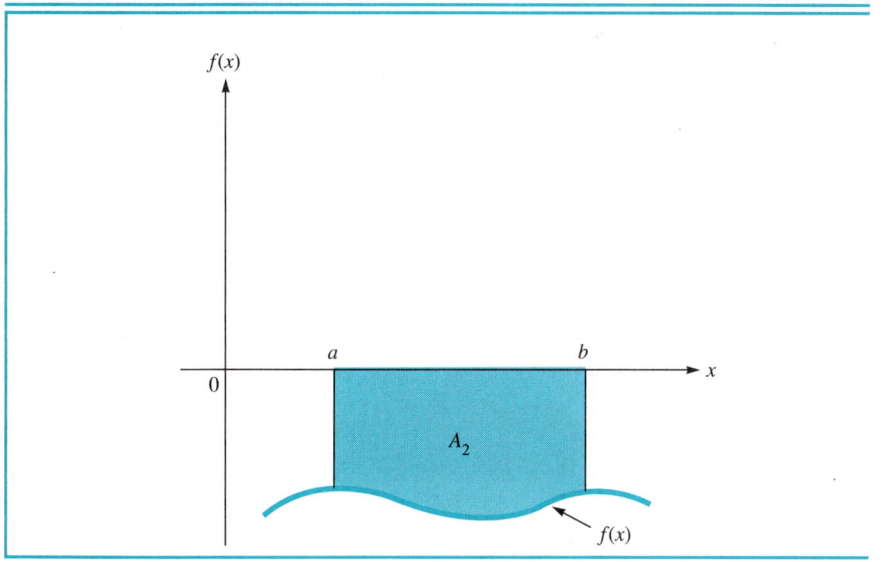

FIGURE 10-10

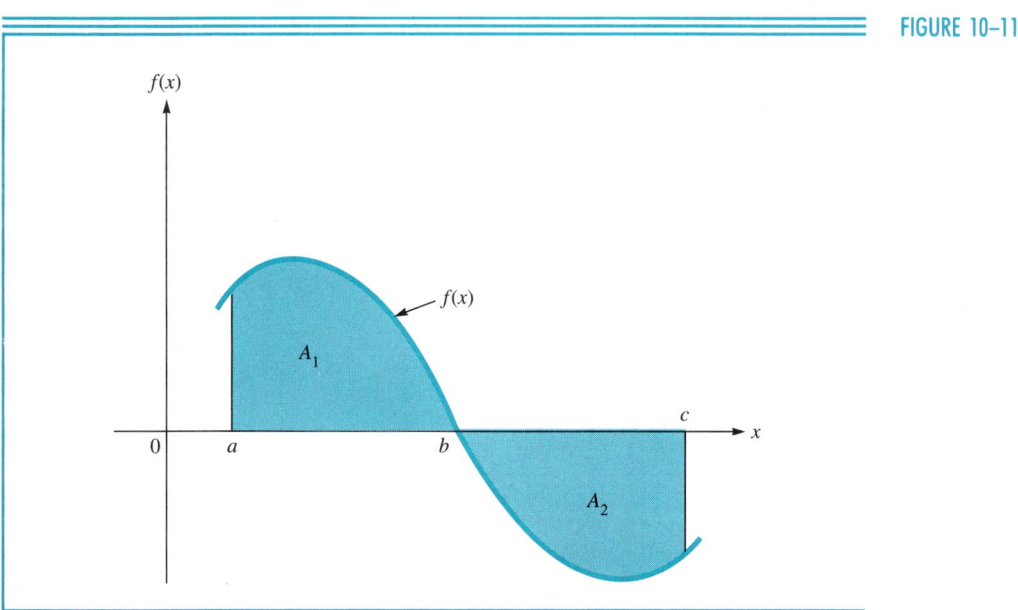

FIGURE 10-11

When a function is both nonnegative and nonpositive, the area is given by the definite integral of the nonnegative portion plus the negative of the definite integral of the nonpositive portion.

since **all the functional values will give negative heights and all area measurements must be positive.** In general, if we have an area such as shown in Figure 10–11, then the total area between $f(x)$ and the x-axis is given by

$$A = A_1 + A_2 = \int_a^b f(x)\, dx - \int_b^c f(x)\, dx.$$

Example. Find the area bounded by the curve $f(x) = x^3 - 3x^2 + 2x$ and the x-axis.

First, we draw a sketch, as shown in Figure 10-12. From this figure, we see that

$$A = A_1 + A_2 = \int_0^1 (x^3 - 3x^2 + 2x)\, dx - \int_1^2 (x^3 - 3x^2 + 2x)\, dx$$

$$= \left(\frac{x^4}{4} - x^3 + x^2\right)\bigg|_0^1 - \left(\frac{x^4}{4} - x^3 + x^2\right)\bigg|_1^2$$

$$= \left[\left(\frac{1}{4} - 1 + 1\right) - (0)\right] - \left[\left(\frac{16}{4} - 8 + 4\right) - \left(\frac{1}{4} - 1 + 1\right)\right]$$

$$= \frac{1}{4} - 0 - 0 + \frac{1}{4} = \frac{1}{2} \text{ square unit.}$$

Note that $A_1 = A_2 = 1/4$ square unit.

FIGURE 10–12

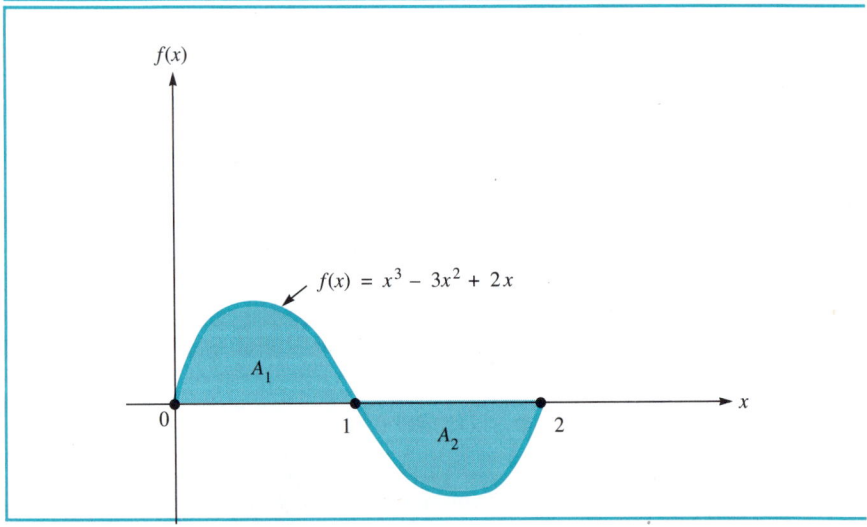

10.5 PROBLEM SET 10-2

Evaluate the following definite integrals:

1. $\int_2^5 2\,dx$.
2. $\int_1^3 3\,dx$.
3. $\int_{-1}^4 2x\,dx$.
4. $\int_{-3}^9 3x\,dx$.
5. $\int_2^6 (x+1)\,dx$.
6. $\int_{-1}^3 (2x-1)\,dx$.
7. $\int_0^8 x^{2/3}\,dx$.
8. $\int_0^9 x^{1/2}\,dx$.
9. $\int_1^2 (x^2 - 3x + 5)\,dx$.
10. $\int_0^3 (x^2 + 5x - 2)\,dx$.
11. $\int_1^9 (5 + y^{-1/2})\,dy$.
12. $\int_1^8 (1 + 2y^{-1/3})\,dy$.
13. $\int_2^6 (2x - 3)^{1/2}\,dx$.
14. $\int_1^8 (5x - 4)^{-1/2}\,dx$.
15. $\int_1^6 \dfrac{60\,dx}{(3x + 2)^2}$.
16. $\int_0^6 \dfrac{20}{(4x + 1)^{3/2}}\,dx$.
17. $\int_a^b 3x^2\,dx$.
18. $\int_c^d 4x^3\,dx$.
19. $\int_1^n (x + 1)\,dx$.
20. $\int_n^1 (2x - 1)\,dx$.

Find the area under the curve of the following functions over the given x-intervals:

21. $f(x) = 2x$; $x = 1$ to $x = 2$.
22. $f(x) = 3x$; $x = 1$ to $x = 5$.
23. $f(x) = 3x + 2$; $x = 1$ to $x = 2$.
24. $f(x) = 2x + 3$; $x = -1$ to $x = 1$.
25. $f(x) = \dfrac{6}{x^2}$; $x = 1$ to $x = 3$.
26. $f(x) = \dfrac{4}{x^3}$; $x = 1$ to $x = 2$.
27. $f(x) = \dfrac{40}{(2x + 1)^2}$; $x = 0$ to $x = 2$.
28. $f(x) = \dfrac{50}{x^{3/2}}$; $x = 1$ to $x = 25$.

Find the areas described in each of the following problems. (Sketches will be helpful.)

29. Find the area bounded by the axes and
$$f(x) = 10 - 0.5x.$$

30. Find the area bounded by the axes and
$$f(x) = 5 + x.$$

31. Find the area bounded by the x-axis and
$$f(x) = 30x - 3x^2.$$

32. Find the area bounded by the x-axis and
$$f(x) = 4x - x^2 + 21.$$

33. Find the area bounded by the x-axis and
$$f(x) = x^3 - 3x^2 - x + 3.$$

34. Find the area bounded by the x-axis and
$$f(x) = x^4 - 5x^2 + 4.$$

35. The technique of lower and upper Riemann sums illustrated in the preceding section can be generalized for finding the area under any nonnegative function $f(x)$. For example, as shown in Figure A on page 666, the lower sum rectangles are the product of the width Δx times the smaller of the two possible rectangle heights given by $\min[f(x_i), f(x_{i+1})]$. Using the sigma summation notation, then,

$$A \approx \sum_{i=0}^{n-1} \min[f(x_i), f(x_{i+1})] \cdot \Delta x$$

and the area is

$$A = \lim_{\Delta x \to 0} \sum_{i=0}^{n-1} \min[f(x_i), f(x_{i+1})] \cdot \Delta x.$$

10.5 PROBLEM SET 10–2 (continued)

FIGURE A

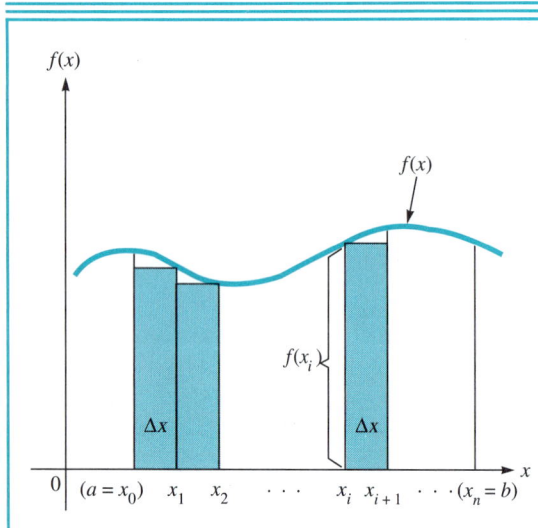

a) Find the approximation and the limit that represent the area using the upper sum rectangles.
b) For $f(x) = x^2$, find the lower and upper sum area approximations with $n = 10$ rectangles.

36. The QBasic program shown in Program 10–1 approximates the area under the curve $f(x) = x^2$ from $x = a$ to $x = b$ by n lower sum rectangles. Underneath is a computer run with $a = 1$, $b = 3$, and $n = 10$.
    a) Describe what the program is doing line-by-line.
    b) Run the program with $n = 10$ for Problems 1 through 28 and 31 through 34.

37. a) Modify Program 10–1 to approximate the area using upper sum rectangles.
    b) Run the program with $n = 10$ for Problems 1 through 28 and 31 through 34.

PROGRAM 10–1

```
REM PROGRAM 10-1
REM Approximation of Area under x^2 using Rectangles
CLS
INPUT "Enter limits a and b, and number of rectangles";
      a, b, n
PRINT
PRINT " Left", " Right", " f(x)", " SUM"
  interval = (b - a) / n
  FOR count = 0 TO n - 1
    left = a + count * interval
    right = a + (count + 1) * interval
    IF left ^ 2 < right ^ 2 THEN
      yvalue = left ^ 2
    ELSE
      yvalue = right ^ 2
    END IF
    sum = sum + interval * yvalue
    PRINT left, right, yvalue, sum
  NEXT count
PRINT
PRINT "The area is "; sum
```

PROGRAM 10-1
(concluded)

```
Enter limits a and b, and number of rectangles? 1, 3, 10
Left      Right     f(x)           SUM
1         1.2       1              .2
1.2       1.4       1.44           .488
1.4       1.6       1.96           .88
1.6       1.8       2.56           1.392
1.8       2         3.24           2.04
2         2.2       4              2.84
2.2       2.4       4.84           3.808
2.4       2.6       5.76           4.96
2.6       2.8       6.759999       6.312
2.8       3         7.84           7.88

The area is 7.88.
```

PROGRAM 10-2

```
REM PROGRAM 10-2
REM Approximation of Area under x^2 using 100 - 1000
Rectangles
CLS
INPUT "Enter lower limit a and upper limit b"; a, b
PRINT
FOR number = 100 TO 1000 STEP 100
 interval = (b - a) / number
 sum = 0
 FOR count = 0 TO number - 1
  left = a + count * interval
  right = a + (count + 1) * interval
  IF left ^ 2 < right ^ 2 THEN
   yvalue = left ^ 2
  ELSE
   yvalue = right ^ 2
  END IF
  sum = sum + interval * yvalue
 NEXT count
 PRINT "With "; number; " rectangles, the area is "; sum
NEXT number

Enter lower limit a and upper limit b? 1,3

With  100 rectangles, the area is 8.586799
With  200 rectangles, the area is 8.6267
With  300 rectangles, the area is 8.640016
With  400 rectangles, the area is 8.646671
With  500 rectangles, the area is 8.650676
With  600 rectangles, the area is 8.653337
With  700 rectangles, the area is 8.655238
With  800 rectangles, the area is 8.656668
With  900 rectangles, the area is 8.657781
With 1000 rectangles, the area is 8.658667
```

10.5 PROBLEM SET 10-2 (concluded)

38. The QBasic program shown in Program 10–2 approximates the area under the curve $f(x) = x^2$ from $x = a$ to $x = b$ using 100, 200, 300, . . . , 1,000 lower sum rectangles. A computer run with $a = 1$ and $b = 3$ follows.
    a) Describe what the program is doing line-by-line.
    b) Run the program for Problems 1 through 28 and 31 through 34.

39. a) Modify Program 10–2 to approximate the area using upper sum rectangles.
    b) Run the program for Problems 1 through 28 and 31 through 34.

10.6 THE AREA BETWEEN TWO CURVES

In Section 10.4, we discussed areas bounded by a function $f(x)$ and the x-axis. In this section we look at areas determined by two functions $f(x)$ and $g(x)$. We begin with an example.

Example. Find the area bounded by the functions

$$f(x) = 15 - 2x - x^2$$

and

$$g(x) = 9 - x.$$

Here, $f(x)$ is again a parabola opening downward. Its vertex is found in the usual manner to be $(-1, 16)$, as follows:

$$f'(x) = 0: \quad -2 - 2x = 0$$
$$x = -1,$$
$$f(-1) = 15 - 2(-1) - (-1)^2 = 16.$$

As shown next, the horizontal intercepts are at $x = -5$ and $x = 3$.

$$f(x) = 0: \quad 15 - 2x - x^2 = 0$$
$$(-x + 3)(x + 5) = 0$$
$$x = 3; \quad x = -5.$$

A sketch of $f(x)$ is shown in Figure 10–13. The function

$$g(x) = 9 - x$$

is a straight line that can be plotted from two points. As usual, the intercepts are the simplest points to find:

FIGURE 10-13
(not to scale)

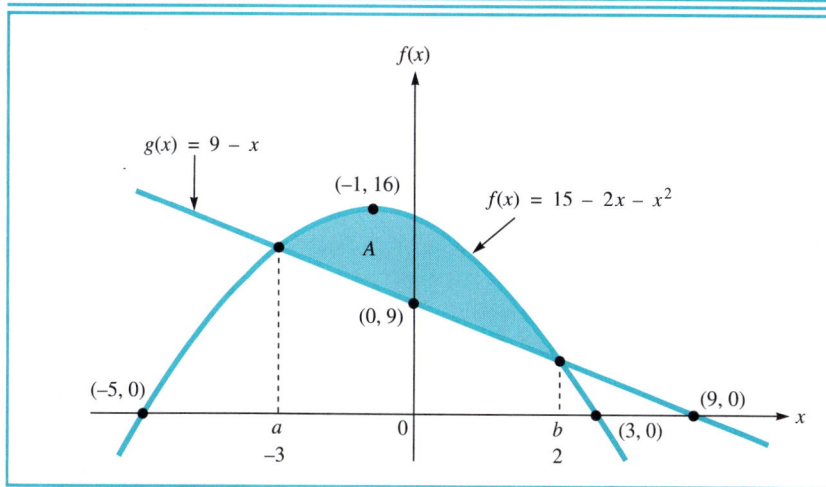

Horizontal (x) intercept ($y = 0$): $g(x) = 0$
$$0 = 9 - x$$
$$x = 9$$
Point is $(9, 0)$.

Vertical (y) intercept ($x = 0$): $g(x) = 9 - 0$
$$g(x) = 9$$
Point is $(0, 9)$.

After superimposing $g(x)$ on Figure 10–13, we see the specified (shaded) area extends over the interval $x = a$ to $x = b$, where dashed vertical lines have been drawn. We can find this area by taking the area under the **upper function** $f(x)$ over the interval from a to b, which would include also the area under the **lower function** (line) $g(x)$, and subtracting from this the area under the lower function $g(x)$. Thus,

$$A = \int_a^b f(x) \, dx - \int_a^b g(x) \, dx,$$

which is the same as

$$A = \int_a^b [f(x) - g(x)] \, dx.$$

The values of a and b are the x-coordinates of the points of intersection of $f(x)$ and $g(x)$. At these points,

The area between two functions $f(x)$ and $g(x)$ in an interval $[a, b]$ is the difference between the definite integral of the upper function and the definite integral of the lower function; i.e.,

$$A = \int_a^b [f(x) - g(x)] \, dx$$

where $f(x)$ is the upper function and $g(x)$ is the lower function.

$$g(x) = f(x)$$
$$9 - x = 15 - 2x - x^2$$
$$x^2 + x - 6 = 0.$$
$$(x + 3)(x - 2) = 0$$
$$x = -3; \quad x = 2.$$

Hence, $a = -3$ and $b = 2$, so the area is

$$A = \int_{-3}^{2} [f(x) - g(x)] \, dx$$

$$= \int_{-3}^{2} [(15 - 2x - x^2) - (9 - x)] \, dx$$

$$= \int_{-3}^{2} (6 - x - x^2) \, dx$$

$$= \left(6x - \frac{x^2}{2} - \frac{x^3}{3} \right) \Big|_{-3}^{2}$$

$$= \left[6(2) - \frac{(2)^2}{2} - \frac{(2)^3}{3} \right] - \left[6(-3) - \frac{(-3)^2}{2} - \frac{(-3)^3}{3} \right]$$

$$= \left[12 - 2 - \frac{8}{3} \right] - \left[-18 - \frac{9}{2} + 9 \right]$$

$$A = 19 - \frac{8}{3} + \frac{9}{2} = \frac{114 - 16 + 27}{6} = \frac{125}{6}.$$

It is important to note that when $f(x)$ is the upper function and $g(x)$ is the lower function,

$$A = \int_{a}^{b} [f(x) - g(x)] \, dx$$

but

$$A \neq \int_{a}^{b} [g(x) - f(x)] \, dx.$$

Why? Because

$$\int_{a}^{b} [g(x) - f(x)] \, dx = -A.$$

> In determining area between two functions, be careful to subtract the lower function from the upper function; treat a negative result as an error.

We always subtract the lower function from the upper function or else we would obtain a negative area. Treat a negative answer as a red flag indicating that you made an error and should go back and check your work carefully. Whenever possible, make a sketch before computing the area.

An alternative method for determining the upper and lower functions without sketching the graphs is as follows. **Evaluate each of the functions at a point in between intersection points. The larger value will represent the upper function, while the smaller value will represent the lower function.** Thus in the preceding example, we could test the two functions

$$f(x) = 15 - 2x - x^2 \quad \text{and} \quad g(x) = 9 - x$$

at $x = 0$, which lies in the interval $[-3, 2]$ to find

$$f(0) = 15 \quad \text{and} \quad g(0) = 9.$$

Since the value 15 for $f(0)$ is clearly larger than the value 9 for $g(0)$, we know (as we saw in the example) that $f(x)$ is the upper function and $g(x)$ is the lower function.

Now we saw in Section 10.4 that when determining areas associated with a single function the definite integral for a nonpositive function (below the x-axis) was the **negative** of that for a nonnegative function (above the x-axis). We do not have to worry about this when finding areas between two functions; that is, **regardless of whether the functions are nonnegative or nonpositive, the area between the functions is always the definite integral of the upper function minus the lower function.** The next example further illustrates this point.

Determination of the upper and lower function can be made by evaluating both functions at a point between intersection points.

Unlike areas associated with a single function, areas between two functions do not depend on whether the functions are above or below the x-axis.

Example. Find the area between the curves

$$f(x) = 3x^3 - 3x$$

and

$$g(x) = x.$$

First we sketch $g(x) = x$, as shown in Figure 10–14. Since $f(x) = 3x^3 - 3x = 3(x)(x - 1)(x + 1)$, $f(x) = 0$ when $x = -1, 0,$ and 1. With our knowledge of curve sketching, then, we can generate a rough sketch of $f(x)$, as shown in Figure 10–14.

To find the points of intersection of $f(x)$ and $g(x)$, we set $f(x) = g(x)$ so that

$$3x^3 - 3x = x$$
$$3x^3 - 4x = 0$$
$$x(3x^2 - 4) = 0$$
$$x = 0, \pm \frac{2}{\sqrt{3}}.$$

From Figure 10–14, then, we can see that in the interval $[-2/\sqrt{3}, 0]$ the upper function is $f(x)$ and the lower function is $g(x)$. On the other hand, in the interval $[0, 2/\sqrt{3}]$ the upper function is $g(x)$ and the lower function is $f(x)$. So, the total area consists of the sum of the two individual areas

FIGURE 10-14

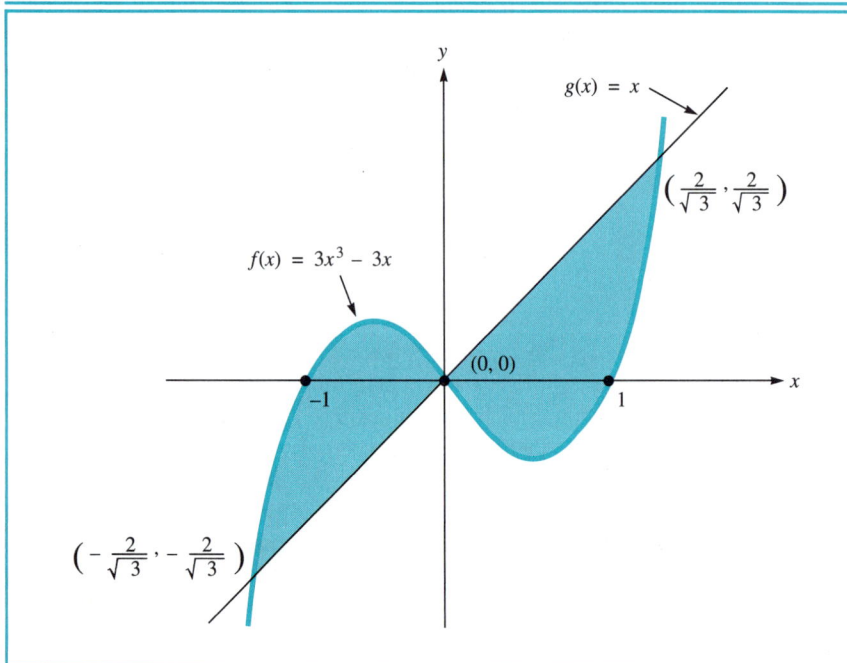

$$A = \int_{-2/\sqrt{3}}^{0} [f(x) - g(x)]\, dx + \int_{0}^{2/\sqrt{3}} [g(x) - f(x)]\, dx$$

$$= \int_{-2/\sqrt{3}}^{0} [(3x^3 - 3x) - x]\, dx + \int_{0}^{2/\sqrt{3}} [x - (3x^3 - 3x)]\, dx$$

$$= \int_{-2/\sqrt{3}}^{0} (3x^3 - 4x)\, dx + \int_{0}^{2/\sqrt{3}} (4x - 3x^3)\, dx$$

$$= \left(\frac{3x^4}{4} - 2x^2\right)\Bigg|_{-2/\sqrt{3}}^{0} + \left(2x^2 - \frac{3x^4}{4}\right)\Bigg|_{0}^{2/\sqrt{3}}$$

$$= (0) - \left(\frac{3}{4} \cdot \frac{16}{9} - 2 \cdot \frac{4}{3}\right) + \left(2 \cdot \frac{4}{3} - \frac{3}{4} \cdot \frac{16}{9}\right) - (0)$$

$$= -\frac{4}{3} + \frac{8}{3} + \frac{8}{3} - \frac{4}{3} = \frac{8}{3} \text{ square units.}$$

As stated earlier, an alternative method, without even sketching the graphs, is to find the points of intersection and then determine which is the upper function by testing each function at a point in between. For example, -1 lies between $-2/\sqrt{3}$ and 0; $f(-1) = 0$ while $g(-1) = -1$, so $f(x)$ is the upper function.

Exercise. a) What is a good test point between 0 and $2/\sqrt{3}$? b) Which is the larger function?

Answer: a) 1. b) $f(1) = 0$ and $g(1) = 1$, so $g(x)$ is the upper function.

Exercise. a) Sketch $h(x) = 8 - 2x$ and $g(x) = 16 - x^2$. b) Find the points where $g(x)$ and $h(x)$ intersect. c) Compute the area bounded by the functions.

Answer: a) $h(x)$ is a straight line passing through (0, 8) and (4, 0); $g(x)$ is a downward opening parabola with vertex at (0, 16) and intercepts $(-4, 0)$; (4, 0). b) $(-2, 12)$ and (4, 0). c) 36.

It will be useful to highlight a few important formulas before we move on to some problems.

1. $\int_a^b [f(x) \pm g(x)]\, dx = \int_a^b f(x)\, dx \pm \int_a^b g(x)\, dx.$

2. $\int_a^b f(x)\, dx + \int_b^c f(x)\, dx = \int_a^c f(x)\, dx.$

3. $\int_a^b f(x)\, dx = -\int_b^a f(x)\, dx.$

As with indefinite intervals, definite intervals can be done term-by-term.

The first formula follows directly from our discussion of indefinite integrals.

Exercise. Draw a graph to illustrate the second formula.

The third formula follows from the fact that

$$\int_a^b f(x)\, dx = F(b) - F(a)$$

and

$$-\int_b^a f(x)\, dx = -[F(a) - F(b)] = F(b) - F(a).$$

10.7 PROBLEM SET 10-3

1. For the functions

   $f(x) = 1 + x$ and $g(x) = 10 - 2x$,

   a) Find the first-quadrant area bounded by the functions and the y-axis.
   b) Find the first-quadrant area bounded by the functions and the axes.

2. Find the first-quadrant area bounded by the axes and the functions

   $f(x) = 0.5x + 2$; $g(x) = 2x - 4$.

3. Find the area bounded by the functions

   $f(x) = x^2 + 1$ and $g(x) = 10$.

4. Find the area bounded by the functions

   $f(x) = 34 - x^2$ and $g(x) = 9$.

5. Find the area bounded by the functions

   $f(x) = x^2 - 8x + 20$ and $g(x) = 14 - x$.

6. Find the area bounded by the functions

   $f(x) = 20 - 2x$ and $g(x) = 12x - 2x^2$.

7. [Note: $f(x)$ is the upper half of a **horizontal** parabola that opens to the right and has the origin as its vertex.] Find the area bounded by

   $f(x) = 8x^{1/2}$ and $g(x) = x^2$.

8. (See Note, Problem 7.) Find the area bounded by

   $f(x) = 6x^{1/2}$ and $g(x) = 0.4x$.

9. Find the area bounded by the functions

   $f(x) = x^3$ and $g(x) = x$.

10. Find the area bounded by the functions

    $f(x) = x^4 - 5x^2 + 4$ and $g(x) = 4$.

11. a) Modify Program 10–1 of Section 10.5 to find the area between two functions.
    b) Run the program in (a) for Problems 3 through 10.

12. a) Modify Program 10–2 of Section 10.5 to find the area between two functions.
    b) Run the program in (a) for Problems 3 through 10.

10.8 INTERPRETIVE APPLICATIONS OF AREA

The area of the rectangle shown in Figure 10–15A is

$$30(40) = 1{,}200.$$

If asked what this area represents, our reply depends upon what the 30 and 40 represent. Thus, if the rectangle is a piece of level land with dimensions 30 feet by 40 feet, then

$$(30 \text{ feet})(40 \text{ feet}) = 1{,}200 \text{ square feet}.$$

Here, the **unit of measure** is feet for both numbers, so the product of the numbers is square feet. However, if 30 means 30 gallons of gasoline and 40 means 40 miles per gallon of gasoline, then the first unit is **gallons** and the second is **miles per (divided by) gallon,** and we have

FIGURE 10–15A   **FIGURE 10–15B**

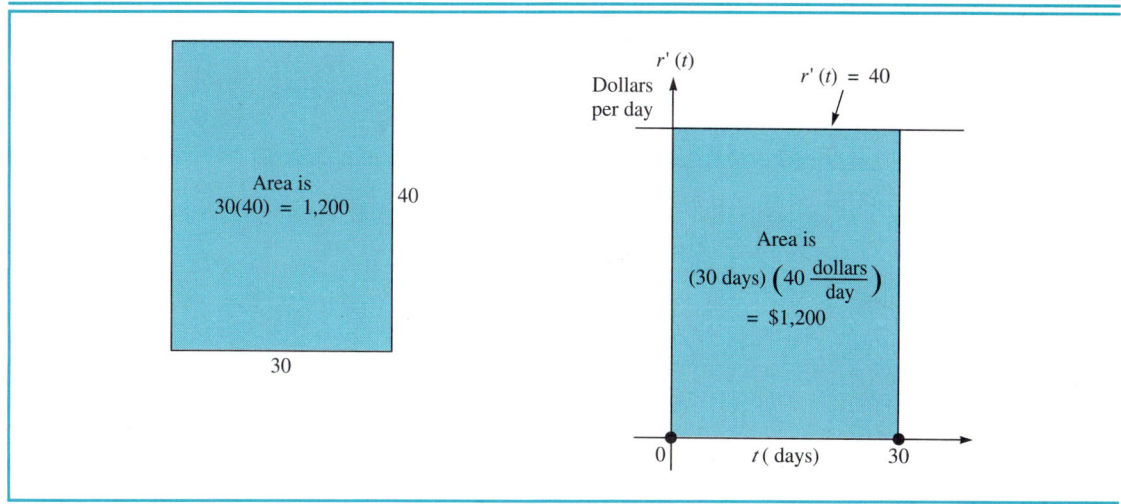

$$(30 \text{ gallons})\left(40 \; \frac{\text{miles}}{\text{gallon}}\right) = 1{,}200 \text{ miles},$$

so the gallon unit cancels and the area of the rectangle represents the 1,200 miles traveled by a car that consumes 30 gallons of gasoline and travels 40 miles per gallon consumed. Once again, if a person rents a motel room for 30 days (unit is **days**) and pays $40 per day (unit is **dollars/day**), we find

$$(30 \text{ days})\left(40 \; \frac{\text{dollars}}{\text{day}}\right) = 1{,}200 \text{ dollars},$$

and the area represents the $1,200 the person pays for the 30-day rental at $40 per day.

In the preceding, observe that miles per gallon and dollars per day are **rates**. The **derivative** of a function measures slope and so is also a rate. Thus, the **total** rent function in the last example is

Recall that the derivative of a function measures its slope (rate of change).

$$r(t) = (t \text{ days})\left(40 \; \frac{\text{dollars}}{\text{day}}\right)$$
$$r(t) = 40t$$

and

$$r'(t) = 40$$

is the rate at which rent changes per additional day's rental. We picture this as in Figure 10–15B, with the constant rate function plotted on the vertical axis. Then we can compute the area as

$$\int_0^{30} r'(t)\, dt.$$

Observe that the integrand, $r'(t)$, has the unit (dollars/day), whereas dt, which refers to the horizontal axis, has the unit (days). Hence,

$$r'(t)\, dt$$

or

$$\left(\frac{\text{dollars}}{\text{day}}\right)(\text{days}) = \text{dollars}$$

and

$$\int_0^{30} r'(t)\, dt = \int_0^{30} 40\, dt = 40t \Big|_0^{30} = 1{,}200 \text{ dollars}.$$

The point we wish to emphasize is that for

$$\int_a^b f(x)\, dx$$

> The area represented by the definite integral can be interpreted as the product of the units of the integrand times the units of the variable of integration.

an area interpretation is in terms of the product of the unit on the vertical, $f(x)$, axis times the units of dx, which is the unit on the horizontal axis. This point is important because it arises in numerous applications of integrals.

Example. The total amount of coal a country will consume in a period of years depends upon the rate of consumption, and this rate increases as time, t years, increases. Suppose it is estimated that the consumption rate, $r'(t)$, t years from now, will be

$$r'(t) = (20 + 1.2t) \text{ million tons per year}.$$

Compute the total amount of coal the country will consume in the next ten years.

Figure 10–16 shows the rate function, $r'(t)$, as a rising straight line. The total amount of coal consumed in the next ten years is represented by the shaded area, marked A, which is

$$\int_0^{10} (20 + 1.2t)\, dt = (20t + 0.6t^2) \Big|_0^{10}$$
$$= (200 + 60) - (0)$$
$$= 260.$$

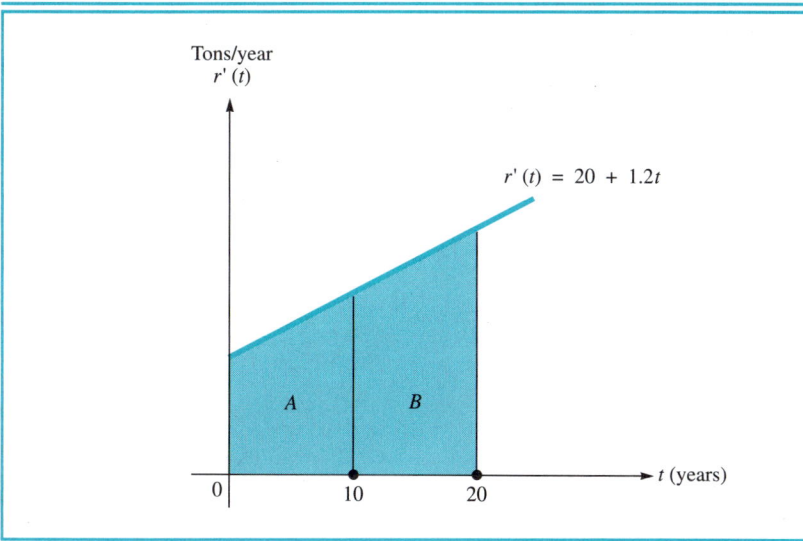

FIGURE 10-16 (not to scale)

The vertical axis has the unit (tons/year) and the horizontal axis has the unit (years). Hence, the number 260 has the unit

$$\left(\frac{\text{tons}}{\text{year}}\right)(\text{years}) = \text{tons}$$

and the area 260 represents 260 million tons consumed in the next 10 years.

Example. (See the preceding Example.) How much coal will be consumed in the following ten years, that is, during the second decade from now?

The answer here is the area marked as B in Figure 10–16. It is

$$\int_{10}^{20} (20 + 1.2t)\, dt = (20t + 0.6t^2)\Big|_{10}^{20}$$
$$= (400 + 240) - (200 + 60)$$
$$= 380 \text{ million tons.}$$

Example. (See the preceding two Examples.) If the total supply of coal available to the country now and in the future is 2,500 million tons, how long will it be until the total supply is exhausted?

Here, the total supply will be exhausted when the amount consumed, which is the value of the definite integral, equals 2,500. Thus we want to find an upper limit

T of the definite intregral so that

$$\int_0^T (20 + 1.2t)\, dt = 2{,}500.$$

Then T will represent the amount of time the coal will last. Evaluating this definite integral, we obtain

$$(20t + 0.6t^2)\Big|_0^T = 2{,}500$$

$$(20T + 0.6T^2) - (0 + 0) = 2{,}500$$

$$0.6T^2 + 20T - 2{,}500 = 0.$$

To solve the last equation, we rewrite it as

$$6T^2 + 200T - 25{,}000 = 0$$

or

$$3T^2 + 100T - 12{,}500 = 0.$$

Factoring, then, we have

$$(3T + 250)(T - 50) = 0$$

so

$$T = -\frac{250}{3} \quad \text{or} \quad T = 50.$$

The negative value for T is not in the permissible range, so $T = 50$, and the supply will be exhausted in 50 years.

Exercise. Maintenance cost on a new machine is at the rate of $100t$ dollars per year at time t years. a) Compute total maintenance cost for the first four years. b) How many years will it take for total maintenance cost to amount to $5,000?

Answer: a) $800. b) 10 years.

= **Accounting for a Fixed Component**

In the preceding exercise, it was assumed, reasonably, that maintenance cost at time $t = 0$ was zero and therefore it was not necessary to take this zero cost into account. Suppose, however, that a company spends $2,000 to have an advertising campaign prepared and then plans to run the campaign at a cost rate of $C'(t) = 900$ dollars per week at time t weeks. If we compute the total cost of running the campaign for 10 weeks as

$$\int_0^{10} C'(t)\, dt = \int_0^{10} 900\, dt = 900t \Big|_0^{10} = \$9{,}000,$$

the $9,000 does not include the fixed preparation cost of $2,000. The total cost would be

$$\text{Total cost} = \text{Fixed cost} + \int_0^{10} 900\, dt$$
$$= \$2{,}000 + \$9{,}000$$
$$= \$11{,}000.$$

Where does each of the terms on the right-hand side come from? Recall from the Fundamental Theorem of Calculus that

$$\int_0^{10} C'(t)\, dt = C(10) - C(0)$$

since $C(t)$ is an antiderivative of $C'(t)$. Hence

$$C(10) = C(0) + \int_0^{10} C'(t)\, dt.$$

Now $C(10)$ represents the total cost of the advertising campaign after 10 weeks. Since $C(0)$ represents the fixed cost, then

$$\int_0^{10} C'(t)\, dt$$

must represent the variable cost so that, as usual,

$$\text{Total cost} = \text{Fixed cost} + \text{Variable cost}.$$

It is important to realize, as we have just seen, that **if a total is obtained by integrating a rate, and a fixed element is present, this element must be added to the value of the definite integral to obtain the correct final value.**

Fixed elements (such as fixed cost) must be added to the value of the definite integral to obtain the total value.

Example. The fixed cost incurred when g gallons of paint are produced is $2,500 and marginal cost at g gallons of output is

$$C'(g) = 0.00045g^2 - 0.18g + 20.$$

Find the total cost of producing 100 gallons.

First we recall that **marginal cost at output level g gallons is the rate at which total cost is changing per additional gallon made.** That is, marginal cost has the unit (dollars/gallon) and dg has the unit (gallons). Hence,

$$\int C'(g)\, dg$$

has the unit

$$\left(\frac{\text{dollars}}{\text{gallon}}\right)(\text{gallons}) = \text{dollars}.$$

The total cost of making 100 gallons, fixed cost included, is

$$C(100) = \int_0^{100} C'(g)\, dg + C(0)$$

$$= \int_0^{100} (0.00045g^2 - 0.18g + 20)\, dg + 2{,}500$$

$$= (0.00015g^3 - 0.09g^2 + 20g)\Big|_0^{100} + 2{,}500$$

$$= [0.00015(100)^3 - (0.09)(100)^2 + 20(100)] - [0] + 2{,}500$$

$$= 1{,}250 + 2{,}500$$

$$= \$3{,}750.$$

> **Exercise.** Marginal cost at output level p pounds of nails is
> $$1 + (p + 1)^{-1/2}$$
> and fixed cost is \$400. Find the total cost of making 399 pounds of the product.
> **Answer:** \$837.

10.9 INTERPRETING THE AREA BOUNDED BY TWO FUNCTIONS

Suppose that an operation provided a company income at the **rate** of $I'(t)$ dollars per day at time t days, where

$$I'(t) = 110 + 4t^{1/2}.$$

The operation was started at an initial fixed expense of \$2,000. Variable expense at the **rate** of $E'(t)$ per day is incurred at time t days, where

$$E'(t) = 20 + 7t^{1/2}.$$

Profit is attained as long as the rate of income exceeds the rate of expense.

The income and expense rate functions are shown in Figure 10–17. From a profit maximization viewpoint, the operation should be continued as long as income per day exceeds expense per day; that is, as long as $I'(t)$ is above $E'(t)$ in Figure 10–17. This situation exists up until the intersection point, b, which we find by equating $E'(t)$ and $I'(t)$, thus

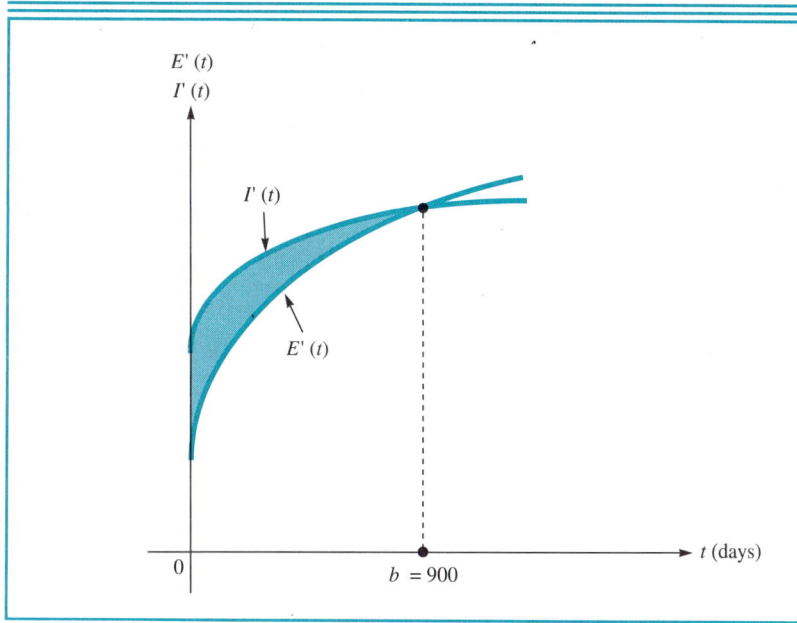

FIGURE 10-17
(not to scale)

$$20 + 7t^{1/2} = 110 + 4t^{1/2}$$
$$3t^{1/2} = 90$$
$$t^{1/2} = 30$$
$$t = (30)^2$$
$$t = 900 \text{ days},$$

which is the value shown for b in Figure 10–17. Thus

$$\text{Net profit} = \left[\int_0^{900} I'(t)\, dt + I(0) \right] - \left[\int_0^{900} E'(t)\, dt + E(0) \right]$$

or simply

$$\text{Net profit} = \int_0^{900} I'(t)\, dt - \int_0^{900} E'(t)\, dt - 2{,}000$$

since $I(0) = 0$ and $E(0) = 2{,}000$. Now, on the right, the **first term is total income** in 900 days, the **middle term is total *variable* expense**, and the **difference** in these two is the shaded area in Figure 10–17, which **represents profit before the fixed expense of $2,000.** The three terms therefore represent the net profit obtained, and this is the maximum profit, possible only if the operation is terminated at $t = 900$ days. Evaluating this net profit, then, we have

$$\text{Net profit} = \int_0^{900} I'(t)\,dt - \int_0^{900} E'(t)\,dt - 2{,}000$$

$$= \int_0^{900} [I'(t) - E'(t)]\,dt - 2{,}000$$

$$= \int_0^{900} [(110 + 4t^{1/2}) - (20 + 7t^{1/2})]\,dt - 2{,}000$$

$$= \int_0^{900} (90 - 3t^{1/2})\,dt - 2{,}000$$

$$= (90t - 2t^{3/2})\Big|_0^{900} - 2{,}000$$

$$= [90(900) - 2(900)^{3/2}] - [0] - 2{,}000$$

$$= 81{,}000 - 2(30)^3 - 2{,}000$$

$$= \$25{,}000.$$

Exercise. Income from an operation at time t months from its initiation is at the rate of $(10 + 0.2t)$ thousand dollars per month and variable expense is at the rate of $(5 + 0.3t)$ thousand dollars per month. If fixed start-up cost was \$5 thousand, find
a) The optimum time to terminate the operation. b) The maximum net profit that can be achieved.

Answer: a) 50 months. b) \$120 thousand (\$120,000).

10.10 CONSUMERS' AND PRODUCERS' SURPLUS

In the economic model of pure competition it is assumed that all consumers (buyers) of a product pay the **same** price per unit for a product. This price comes about by the interplay of competitive market forces and is the price per unit at which the quantity of product consumers are willing and able to buy (called **consumer demand**) is matched by the quantity producers (sellers) are willing and able to supply. The purpose of this section is to illustrate that this competitive situation benefits both consumer and supplier, and to develop a measure of these benefits.

Consumers' Surplus

Demand curves slope downward since consumers tend to buy more if prices drop.

Looking first at the consumer (buyer) side of the situation, it is a matter of observation that even though a product, say gasoline, sells competitively at 99 cents per gallon, there are buyers who would be willing to pay \$3 or more per gallon and, clearly, the lower price established by competition benefits these buyers. Economists use downward sloping curves, called **demand curves** (recall that we studied linear demand and supply functions in Chapter 1), to represent the observed relationship between the number of units, q, demanded by consumers and $p_d(q)$, the selling price per unit. The subscript d on $p_d(q)$ signifies that this is a **demand function** to distinguish it from the **supply function**, which will be introduced later and named $p_s(q)$. Figure 10–18A shows an illustrative demand curve. As the figure shows, low price is accompanied by high demand, and high price is accompanied by low demand. The point $E(q_m, p_m)$ is the **equilibrium point**; that is, the market price that matches the quantity consumers demand with the quantity producers will supply. The area under the curve,

> Equilibrium occurs when demand equals supply.

$$\int_0^{q_m} p_d(q)\, dq,$$

represents dollars because it is the product of price per unit times number of units. This area may be taken as a measure of what consumers might have had to pay for the q_m units if competition did not lead to the constant price, p_m, for all units; that is, if various consumers paid the higher prices on the demand curve to the left of (q_m, p_m). However, at equilibrium, consumers pay p_m dollars per unit for each of the q_m units demanded, so the total paid is $p_m q_m$ dollars, which is the area of the rectangle shown in Figure 10–18B. The amount paid, the rectangular area, is less than the whole area under the curve over the interval 0 to q_m, and the **difference** may be taken as a measure of the benefit to consumers of competitive forces that lead to the same unit price for all units sold. Hence, it is called **consumers' surplus** and, as shown by the shaded area in Figure 10–18B, it is the total area under the curve over the interval 0 to q_m, minus the area of the rectangle:

> Consumers' surplus is the amount of dollars left in the hands of consumers due to the market settling at an equilibrium point; it is the difference between what consumers expected to pay and what they actually paid.

FIGURE 10–18A   **FIGURE 10–18B**

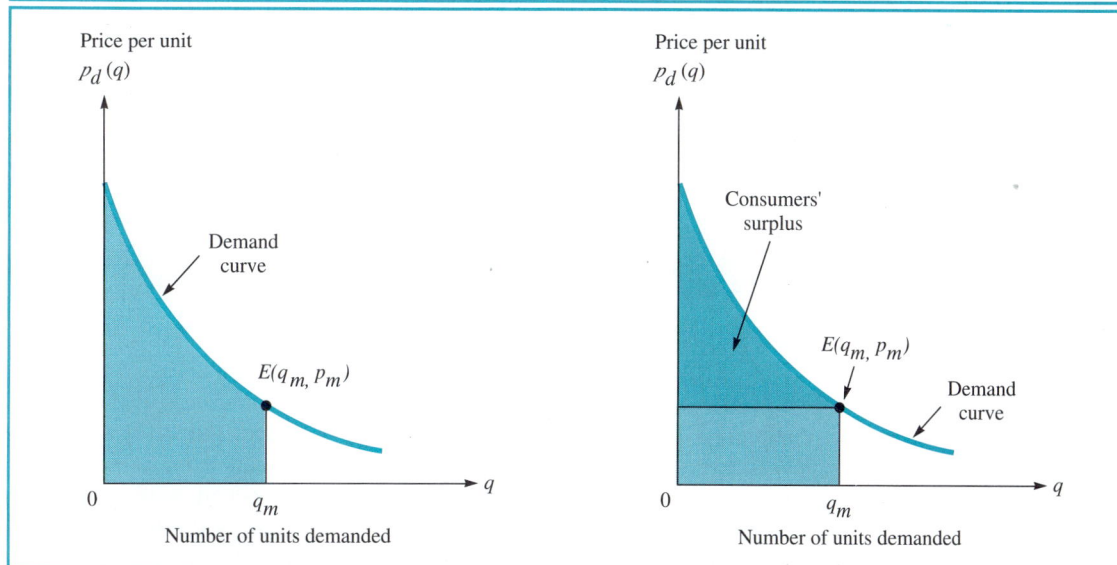

$$\text{Consumers' Surplus} = \int_0^{q_m} p_d(q)\, dq - p_m q_m.$$

Example. At market equilibrium, consumers demand 625,000 gallons of kerosene, which has the demand function

$$p_d(q) = 25 - 0.6q^{1/2},$$

where q is in thousands of gallons and $p_d(q)$ is in dollars per gallon. Compute consumers' surplus.

First we must determine the equilibrium point (q_m, p_m). We are given $q_m = 625$ thousand, so we compute p_m as

$$\begin{aligned} p_m = p_d(625) &= 25 - 0.6(625)^{1/2} \\ &= 25 - 0.6(25) \\ &= \$10 \text{ per gallon.} \end{aligned}$$

Then,

$$\begin{aligned} \text{Consumers' surplus} &= \int_0^{625} (25 - 0.6q^{1/2})\, dq - (10)(625) \\ &= (25q - 0.4q^{3/2})\Big|_0^{625} - 6{,}250 \\ &= [25(625) - 0.4(625)^{3/2}] - [25(0) - 0.4(0)^{3/2}] - 6{,}250 \\ &= [15{,}625 - 6{,}250] - [0] - 6{,}250 \\ &= \$3{,}125 \text{ thousand.} \end{aligned}$$

Exercise. At market equilibrium, consumers demand 100,000 tons of SAE 90 lubricating oil, which has the demand function $p_d(q) = 110 - 0.5q$, where q is in thousands of tons and $p_d(q)$ is in dollars per ton. Compute consumers' surplus.
Answer: $2,500 thousand ($2.5 million).

Producers' Surplus

Supply curves slope upward since producers tend to supply more if prices rise.

The relationship between the market price and the quantities producers are willing to supply is expressed as a supply function, $p_s(q)$. The supply curve slopes upward to the right as illustrated in Figure 10–19 because producers are willing to supply more at higher prices than at lower prices. Again, the equilibrium point $E(q_m, p_m)$ is at the price that matches the amount consumers demand with the amount producers

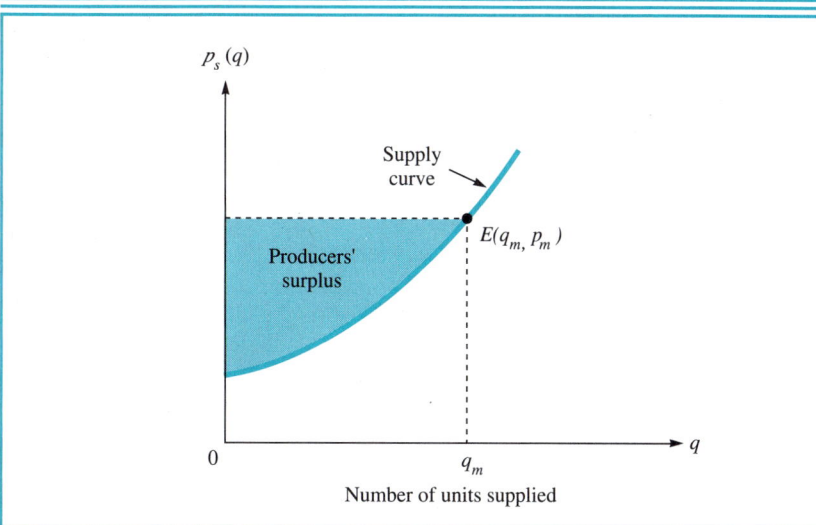

FIGURE 10-19

are willing to supply. However, producers receive the same unit price, p_m, for all q_m units they produce and sell, so the total received by producers is the product

$$p_m q_m$$

and this is the area of the rectangle shown in Figure 10-19. But, the supply curve implies that producers would have supplied some units of the product at prices lower than p_m, and the area under the supply curve may be taken as a measure of what producers might have received in the absence of an equilibrium price, that is, if various producers sold some units of the product at prices to the left (below) the equilibrium price on the curve. The **difference** between the area of the rectangle and the area under the curve then is a measure of the benefit to producers of market competition that leads to the equilibrium price, p_m, and is called **producers' surplus**. This is the shaded area in Figure 10-19, which is

Producers' Surplus $= p_m q_m - \int_0^{q_m} p_s(q) \, dq.$

Producers' surplus is the amount of additional dollars received by producers due to the market settling at an equilibrium point, and as the difference between what producers actually receive and what they expected to receive.

Example. At market equilibrium, consumers demand 625,000 gallons of kerosene, whose supply function is

$$p_s(q) = 2.5 + 0.3q^{1/2},$$

where q is in thousands of gallons and $p_s(q)$ is in dollars per gallon. Compute producers' surplus.

Again we begin by determining the equilibrium point (q_m, p_m). Since once more we are given $q_m = 625$ thousand, we can now compute p_m as

$$p_m = p_s(625) = 2.5 + 0.3(625)^{1/2}$$
$$= 2.5 + 0.3(25)$$
$$= \$10 \text{ per gallon.}$$

Then,

$$\text{Producers' surplus} = (10)(625) - \int_0^{625} (2.5 + 0.3q^{1/2})\, dq$$

$$= 6{,}250 - (2.5q + 0.2q^{3/2})\Big|_0^{625}$$

$$= 6{,}250 - [(2.5)(625) + 0.2(625)^{3/2} - (0 + 0)]$$

$$= 6{,}250 - [1{,}562.5 + 0.2(25)^3]$$

$$= 6{,}250 - [1{,}562.5 + 3{,}125]$$

$$= \$1{,}562.5 \text{ thousand.}$$

Exercise. At market equilibrium, consumers demand 100,000 tons of SAE 90 lubricating oil, whose supply function is

$$p_s(q) = 10 + 0.5q,$$

where q is in thousands of tons and $p_s(q)$ is in dollars per ton. Compute producers' surplus.

Answer: $2,500 thousand ($2.5 million).

Now that we have discussed both the demand function and the supply function for a product, we can see that the **equilibrium point $E(q_m, p_m)$ occurs at a price where the quantity consumers demand equals the amount producers are willing to supply.** That is, $E(q_m, p_m)$ is the intersection point of the supply and demand functions for the product. Thus, in our previous two examples, the product kerosene had supply and demand functions

$$p_s(q) = 2.5 + 0.3q^{1/2}$$
$$p_d(q) = 25 - 0.6q^{1/2}.$$

The equilibrium point occurs where $p_s(q) = p_d(q)$; that is, where

$$2.5 + 0.3q^{1/2} = 25 - 0.6q^{1/2}$$
$$0.9q^{1/2} = 22.5$$

The equilibrium point is the intersection of the supply and demand functions.

$$q^{1/2} = \frac{22.5}{0.9}$$
$$q^{1/2} = 25$$
$$(q^{1/2})^2 = (25)^2$$
$$q_m = 625.$$

Then, with $q_m = 625$

$$p_s(q) = 2.5 + 0.3(625)^{1/2}$$
$$= 2.5 + 0.3(25)$$
$$p_m = 10.$$

Thus, in the previous two examples the equilibrium point at demand $q_m = 625,000$ gallons and price $p_m = \$10$ per gallon were the same because they applied to the supply and demand functions for the same product, kerosene. It follows that if we have the supply and demand functions for a product, both producers' and consumers' surplus can be computed by first determining the equilibrium intersection point, then applying the formulas for producers' and consumers' surplus.

Exercise. The supply and demand functions for SAE 90 lubricating oil are

$$p_s(q) = 10 + 0.5q$$
$$p_d(q) = 110 - 0.5q,$$

where q is in thousands of tons and price is in dollars per ton. By review of the previous two exercises, or by starting anew, find: a) The equilibrium point, $E(q_m, p_m)$. b) Producers' surplus. c) Consumers' surplus.

Answer: a) (100, 60). b) $2,500 thousand ($2.5 million). c) $2,500 thousand ($2.5 million).

10.11 PROBLEM SET 10–4

1. Maintenance of newly purchased equipment is expected to cost $(2 + 0.1t)$ thousand dollars per year at time t years.
   a) Compute total maintenance cost during the first six years.
   b) Make a sketch showing what was computed in (a).
   c) Compute maintenance cost during the second six years.
   d) At what time, t, will the total spent on maintenance reach $60 thousand?

2. A currently new product is expected to be sold at the rate of $(20 - 0.4t)$ thousand dollars per year at time t years, $t < 50$.
   a) Compute total sales during the first 10 years.
   b) Make a sketch showing what was computed in (a).
   c) Compute total sales during the second 10 years.
   d) At what time, t, will total sales reach $375 thousand?

3. An industry consumes fuel at a rate of $(2 + 0.6t^{1/2})$ million barrels per year at time t years. How much fuel will the industry consume in 25 years?

10.11 PROBLEM SET 10-4 (continued)

4. An oil rig pumps oil from a well at the rate of $(360 - 72t^{1/2})$ barrels per year at time t years. How much oil will be pumped in the next nine years?

5. At time t years, an industry consumes fuel at the rate of $(2t + 9)^{1/2}$ million barrels per year. If the total supply of fuel available to the industry now and in the future is 63 million barrels, how many years will the supply last?

6. At time t years, sales of a currently new product are expected to be
$$\frac{10}{(0.5t + 16)^{1/2}}$$
million dollars per year. How many years will it take for total sales to amount to $40 million?

7. The population of a trading area is currently 100 thousand. At time t years from now population will be growing at the rate of
$$\frac{20}{(0.5t + 9)^{1/2}}$$
thousand per year. What will total population be 14 years from now?

8. A fixed cost of $2 thousand has been incurred in setting up an advertising campaign. Variable cost is expected to be at the rate of $(3 + 0.06t^{1/2})$ thousand dollars per month at time t months. Estimate total cost if the campaign runs 25 months.

9. When t tons of steel are produced, marginal cost in dollars per ton is
$$0.006t^2 - 1.2t + 50.$$
If fixed cost is $1,600, find the total cost of producing 100 tons.

10. When b barrels of whiskey are produced, marginal cost in dollars per barrel is
$$0.0045b^2 - 1.8b + 200.$$
If fixed cost is $4,000, find the total cost of producing 200 barrels.

11. A fixed cost of $50 thousand was incurred in setting up an operation. At time t months thereafter, the operation yields income at the rate of $(20 - 0.3t)$ and incurs expense at the rate of $(10 - 0.1t)$, where both rates are in thousands of dollars per month.
    a) What is the optimal time to terminate the operation?
    b) What will total profit be at the optimal time of termination?

12. A fixed cost of $4,100 was incurred in setting up an operation. At time t months thereafter, the operation yields income at the rate of $(2,000 - 100t^{1/2})$ and incurs expense at the rate of $(200 + 200t^{1/2})$ where both rates are in dollars per month.
    a) What is the optimal time to terminate the operation?
    b) What will total profit be at the optimal time of termination?

13. The demand function for a product is
$$p_d(q) = 75 - 0.6q,$$
where q is in millions of barrels and $p_d(q)$ is in dollars per barrel. Market equilibrium occurs at a demand of 100 million barrels.
    a) Compute consumers' surplus.
    b) Make a sketch showing what was computed in (a).

14. The supply function for a product is
$$p_s(q) = 5 + 0.2q,$$
where q is in millions of tons and $p_s(q)$ is in dollars per ton. Market equilibrium occurs at a demand of 50 million tons.
    a) Compute producers' surplus.
    b) Make a sketch showing what was computed in (a).

15. The supply function for a product is
$$p_s(q) = (4 + 0.2q)^{3/2}$$
where q is in thousands of truckloads and $p_s(q)$ is in dollars per truckload. Market equilibrium occurs at a demand of 60 thousand truckloads. Compute producers' surplus.

16. The demand function for a product is
$$p_d(q) = \frac{80}{(0.1q + 0.2)^2}$$
where q is in millions of tons and $p_d(q)$ is in dollars per ton. Market equilibrium occurs at a demand for 18 million tons. Compute consumers' surplus.

10.11 PROBLEM SET 10-4 (concluded)

17. The supply and demand functions for a product are

$$p_s(q) = 10 + 0.1q \text{ and}$$
$$p_d(q) = 100 - 0.2q,$$

where q is in thousands of tons and price is in dollars per ton.
a) Compute consumers' surplus.
b) Compute producers' surplus.

18. The supply and demand functions for a product are

$$p_s(q) = 1 + 0.02q \text{ and}$$
$$p_d(q) = 6 - 0.08q,$$

where q is in millions of pounds and price is in dollars per pound.
a) Compute consumers' surplus.
b) Compute producers' surplus.

10.12 THE INTEGRAL OF $(mx + b)^{-1}$

Recall from Section 10.2 that the Simple Power Rule and the Power Rule for Linear Functions were valid as long as the power $n \neq -1$. Now, what is the integral when $n = -1$? We first consider the Simple Power Rule, which is a special case of

$$\int (mx + b)^{-1} dx = \int \frac{1}{mx + b} dx = \int \frac{dx}{mx + b}$$

with $m = 1$ and $b = 0$; that is,

$$\int \frac{dx}{x} = \int \frac{1}{x} dx.$$

We know that

$$\frac{d}{dx}(\ln x) = \frac{1}{x},$$

and $1/x$ is the integrand of the integral. Hence,

$$\int \frac{1}{x} dx = \ln x + C, \quad x > 0$$

since the logarithm is defined only for positive numbers. Recalling the absolute value, we can rewrite the last integral as

$$\int \frac{1}{x} dx = \ln |x| + C. \tag{1}$$

Turning next to the general form,

$$\int \frac{1}{mx + b} dx,$$

we use the substitution

so
$$u = mx + b$$
and
$$du = m\,dx$$
$$dx = \frac{du}{m}.$$

Then,
$$\int \frac{1}{mx+b}\,dx = \int \frac{1}{u} \cdot \frac{du}{m} = \frac{1}{m} \int \frac{du}{u}.$$

Using (1) to evaluate the latter integral, we have
$$\int \frac{dx}{mx+b} = \frac{1}{m}(\ln|u| + C)$$

or

> The integral of a linear function with exponent $n = -1$ is the natural logarithm of the absolute value of the function, divided by the coefficient of the variable of integration.

$$\int \frac{dx}{mx+b} = \frac{1}{m}\ln|mx+b| + C;\quad m \neq 0. \qquad (2)$$

In words, the integral of one over a linear function to the first power is the natural logarithm of the absolute value of the function divided by the coefficient of the variable.

Example. Evaluate $\int_{-1}^{3} \frac{4\,dx}{2x+3}$.

If we have memorized (2), then we write the solution immediately, as follows:

$$4\left[\frac{\ln|2x+3|}{2}\right]\bigg|_{-1}^{3} = 2[\ln|2x+3|]\bigg|_{-1}^{3}$$
$$= 2(\ln 9 - \ln 1)$$
$$= 2(2.197224577 - 0)$$
$$= 4.394$$

to three-decimal-place accuracy. If on the other hand, we do not have (2) at our fingertips, we can then use *u*-substitution to solve the problem. Let

$$u = 2x + 3$$

so that

$$du = 2\,dx$$

and

$$dx = \frac{du}{2}.$$

Then

$$\int_{-1}^{3} \frac{4\,dx}{2x + 3} = \int_{1}^{9} \frac{4}{u} \cdot \frac{du}{2}.$$

Notice that the limits on the integral have changed. When we change the variable of integration from an x to a u, we must simultaneously change the limits of the integral. To find the new limits, we use the substitution equation

$$u = 2x + 3.$$

So, when $x = -1$, $u = 2(-1) + 3 = 1$; and when $x = 3$, $u = 2(3) + 3 = 9$. Therefore,

$$\int_{-1}^{3} \frac{4\,dx}{2x + 3} = \int_{1}^{9} \frac{2\,du}{u}.$$

When using *u*-substitution to evaluate a definite integral, remember to change the upper and lower limits to values in terms of *u*.

Now from Equation (1) on page 687

$$\int_{1}^{9} \frac{2\,du}{u} = 2(\ln |u|) \Big|_{1}^{9}$$

$$= 2(\ln 9 - \ln 1)$$

$$= 2(2.197224577 - 0)$$

$$= 4.394$$

to three-decimal-place accuracy, which is precisely the same result as before.

Exercise. Evaluate $\int_{1}^{3} \frac{6\,dx}{3x - 2}$.

Answer: $2\,(\ln 7) = 3.892$.

10.13 PROBLEM SET 10-5

Carry out the following; simplify results where possible.

1. $\int x^{-1}\, dx$.
2. $\int \dfrac{dx}{x}$.
3. $\int \dfrac{2\, dx}{x}$.
4. $\int 3x^{-1}\, dx$.
5. $\int x^{-2}\, dx$.
6. $\int \dfrac{dx}{x^2}$.
7. $\int \dfrac{dx}{5x+4}$.
8. $\int \left(\dfrac{1}{3-x}\right) dx$.
9. $\int \left(\dfrac{1}{3-0.2x}\right) dx$.
10. $\int 2(0.5x+1)^{-1}\, dx$.
11. $\int \dfrac{dx}{(2x-1)^2}$.
12. $\int \dfrac{10\, dx}{(5x+3)^2}$.
13. $\int_1^{10} \dfrac{dx}{x}$.
14. $\int_1^{e} x^{-1}\, dx$.
15. $\int_0^{2} \dfrac{dx}{0.5x+4}$.
16. $\int_5^{10} \left(\dfrac{1}{0.6x+1}\right) dx$.

17. If new reserves of a fuel are discovered at the rate of

$$\dfrac{100}{0.2t+1}$$

million barrels per year at time t years, find the total amount of fuel that will be discovered in the next 25 years.

18. The demand function for a product is

$$p_d(q) = \dfrac{50}{0.5q+1}$$

where q is millions of pounds and $p_d(q)$ is dollars per pound. Compute consumers' surplus if market equilibrium occurs at a demand of 18 million pounds.

10.14 INTEGRALS OF EXPONENTIAL FUNCTIONS

Inasmuch as the derivative of e^x is e^x, it follows that

$$\int e^x\, dx = e^x + C. \qquad (1)$$

If the exponent is the linear function $(mx+b)$, then, as in the case in Section 10.12, the integral has m as a divisor. Thus,

Exponential Rule, Base e

$$\int e^{mx+b}\, dx = \frac{e^{mx+b}}{m} + C; \quad m \neq 0. \tag{2}$$

An integral of e raised to a linear function is again e raised to that function, divided by the coefficient of the variable of integration.

Example. Evaluate

$$\int_0^{10} 30e^{0.06x}\, dx.$$

If we have memorized (2), then we can notice that the exponent has $m = 0.06$ and $b = 0$. Hence,

$$\int_0^{10} 30e^{0.06x}\, dx = 30\left(\frac{e^{0.06x}}{0.06}\right)\bigg|_0^{10}$$

$$= 500(e^{0.6} - e^0)$$

$$= 500(1.8221188 - 1)$$

$$= 411.059$$

to three-decimal-place accuracy. If we do not have (2) close at hand, we can again use the u-substitution technique to solve this problem. Let

$$u = 0.06x$$

so that

$$du = 0.06\, dx$$

and

$$dx = \frac{du}{0.06}.$$

Then

$$\int_0^{10} 30e^{0.06x}\, dx = \int_0^{0.6} 30e^u\, \frac{du}{0.06}.$$

Notice again that the limits have changed. As in Section 10.12, when we change the variable from x to u, we must change the limiting values in the definite integral from limiting values of x to limiting values of u. Since

$$u = 0.06x,$$

then when $x = 0$, $u = (0.06)(0) = 0$; and when $x = 10$, $u = (0.06)(10) = 0.6$. Thus, from (1),

$$\int_0^{0.6} 30e^u \frac{du}{0.06} = \frac{30}{0.06}(e^u)\Big|_0^{0.6}$$
$$= 500(e^{0.6} - e^0)$$
$$= 500(1.8221188 - 1)$$
$$= 411.059$$

to three-decimal-place accuracy, which is precisely the same result as before.

Exercise. Evaluate $\int_1^2 e^{2x-1} \, dx$. Note that $b = -1$ on this problem.

Answer. $0.5(e^3 - e^1) = 8.684$.

When taking the derivative of an exponential with base other than e, we multiplied by the natural logarithm of the base; so when taking the integral, we divide by the natural logarithm of the base.

Recall that the derivative of an exponential that has a base other than e requires a factor that is the natural logarithm of the base. That is,

$$\frac{d}{dx} a^x = a^x (\ln a).$$

It follows that in the inverse process we must divide by $\ln a$. That is,

$$\int a^x \, dx = \frac{a^x}{\ln a} + C.$$

Again, if the exponent is the linear function $(mx + b)$ we can derive a more general formula using u-substitution. In this instance, we obtain

The integral of any base a ($a > 0$ and $a \neq 1$) raised to a linear function is again a raised to that function, divided by the coefficient of the variable of integration and also the natural logarithm of the base.

Exponential Rule, Base a, $a > 0$, and $a \neq 1$

$$\int a^{mx+b} \, dx = \frac{a^{mx+b}}{m (\ln a)} + C; \quad m \neq 0. \tag{3}$$

Example. Evaluate

$$\int_1^2 (0.9)^{2x-1} \, dx.$$

Let

$$u = 2x - 1$$

so that

$$du = 2dx$$

and

$$dx = \frac{du}{2}.$$

Then

$$\int_1^2 (0.9)^{2x-1}\, dx = \int_1^3 (0.9)^u \cdot \frac{du}{2}$$

since at $x = 1$, $u = 2 \cdot 1 - 1 = 1$; and at $x = 2$, $u = 2 \cdot 2 - 1 = 3$. Thus,

$$\int_1^2 (0.9)^{2x-1}\, dx = \frac{1}{2} \int_1^3 (0.9)^u\, du$$

$$= \frac{1}{2}\left[\frac{(0.9)^u}{\ln 0.9}\right]\Big|_1^3$$

$$= \frac{(0.9)^3 - (0.9)^1}{2(\ln 0.9)}$$

$$= \frac{0.729 - 0.9}{2(-0.105360516)}$$

$$= 0.811$$

to three-decimal-place accuracy.

Exercise. Evaluate $\int_2^4 (6)^{0.5x}\, dx$.

Answer: 33.487.

Exponentials often arise in applied problems dealing with rates, as illustrated in the following:

Example. A company projects its cost of providing medical care to workers to be at the rate of

$$15e^{0.03t}$$

thousand dollars per year at time t years. a) Compute total medical care cost for the next 10 years. b) How long will it be until total cost amounts to $250 thousand?

The key word in this problem is the word **rate**. The total medical care cost for the next 10 years will be the area under the cost rate curve over the next 10 years.

If the cost rate were a constant, say $15 thousand per year, then the total cost over the next 10 years would be simply (10)(15 thousand) = $150 thousand. In this problem, however, the cost rate is not a constant, so we need to use the integral to compute the total cost.

Since this example makes no reference to fixed cost, we shall assume there is none, in which case the total cost sought in (a) is, by Equation (2) on page 691,

$$\int_0^{10} 15e^{0.03t}\,dt = 15\left(\frac{e^{0.03t}}{0.03}\right)\bigg|_0^{10}$$

$$= 500e^{0.03t}\bigg|_0^{10}$$

$$= 500(1.349858808 - 1)$$

$$\approx \$175 \text{ thousand.}$$

Part (b) of the example asks us to find the time, T years from now, such that

$$\int_0^T 15e^{0.03t}\,dt = 250.$$

By Equation (2), we find as before

$$500e^{0.03t}\bigg|_0^T = 250$$

$$500(e^{0.03T} - e^0) = 250$$

$$e^{0.03T} - 1 = \frac{250}{500}$$

$$e^{0.03T} = \frac{250}{500} + 1$$

$$e^{0.03T} = 1.5.$$

We solve for T by first taking the natural logarithm of both sides of the last expression. Thus,

$$\ln e^{0.03T} = \ln 1.5$$

$$0.03T\,(\ln e) = \ln 1.5$$

$$0.03T(1) = \ln 1.5$$

$$T = \frac{\ln 1.5}{0.03}$$

$$= \frac{0.405465108}{0.03}$$

$$\approx 13.5 \text{ years.}$$

To better understand the significance of the preceding example, note the cost rate

$$15e^{0.03t}$$

at $t = 0$ is

$$15e^0 = 15,$$

or $15 thousand per year. If this rate were **constant** over time, then total cost would accumulate to $250 thousand in $250/15 \approx 16.7$ years. However, the exponential factor in

$$15e^{0.03t}$$

indicates that the cost rate per year is increasing and this accounts for the fact that cost will accumulate to $250 thousand in 13.5 years rather than 16.7 years.

10.15 PROBLEM SET 10-6

Carry out the following. Simplify results where possible.

1. $\int e^x \, dx$.
2. $\int 2^x \, dx$.
3. $\int 3^{-x} \, dx$.
4. $\int e^{-x} \, dx$.
5. $\int e^{0.5x} \, dx$.
6. $\int 5^{0.2x} \, dx$.
7. $\int (0.5)^{1-0.4x} \, dx$.
8. $\int e^{2-0.5x} \, dx$.
9. $\int 2e^{3-0.1x} \, dx$.
10. $\int 4e^{5-0.2x} \, dx$.
11. $\int \dfrac{dx}{(0.8)^x}$.
12. $\int \dfrac{1}{e^{0.5x}} \, dx$.

Evaluate the following:

13. $\int_0^5 2e^{1-0.2x} \, dx$.
14. $\int_1^2 4e^{2-0.5x} \, dx$.
15. $\int_1^2 10(0.5)^x \, dx$.
16. $\int_0^2 5(0.9)^x \, dx$.

17. The total supply of a fuel available now and in the future is 1,000 million barrels. At time t years from now, fuel will be consumed at the rate of

$$10e^{0.05t}$$

million barrels per year.
a) How much fuel will be consumed in the next 20 years?
b) How long will the supply of fuel last?

18. At time t years, the cost of maintaining a facility is at the rate of $12e^{0.08t}$ thousands of dollars per year. Assuming there is no fixed cost involved,
a) Find total maintenance cost for the next 10 years.
b) How long will it take for total maintenance cost to reach $300 thousand?

19. At time t years, interest on a bank account is at the rate of $600e^{0.06t}$ dollars per year.
a) What will be total interest accumulation in 12 years?
b) How long will it take for total interest accumulation to reach $5,000?

20. Sales of a product are projected to be at the rate of $15e^{-0.2t}$ million pounds per year at time t years.

10.15 PROBLEM SET 10–6 (concluded)

a) Find total sales in the next five years.
b) How long will it take for total sales to reach 60 million pounds?

21. Sales of wheat at time t years are projected to be at the rate of $5 + 15e^{-0.2t}$ million pounds per year. Find total sales in the next five years.

22. Sales of milk at time t years are projected to be at the rate of $10 + 20e^{-0.4t}$ million gallons per year. Find total sales in the next five years.

23. The supply function for a product is

$$p_s(q) = 5 + e^{0.02q},$$

where q is in thousands of pounds and $p_s(q)$ is in dollars per pound. Market equilibrium occurs at a demand of 40 thousand pounds. Compute producers' surplus.

24. The supply function for a product is

$$p_s(q) = 10 + 2e^{0.05q},$$

where q is in thousands of gallons and $p_s(q)$ is in dollars per gallon. Market equilibrium occurs at a demand of 20 thousand gallons. Compute producers' surplus.

10.16 TABLES OF INTEGRALS

We saw in Sections 10.12 and 10.14 that having an integration formula close at hand can simplify the evaluation of definite integrals. Certain integrals should be fixed in your mind and require no reference. These include

$$\int x^n \, dx = \frac{x^{n+1}}{n+1} + C, \quad n \neq -1$$

$$\int \frac{1}{x} \, dx = \ln |x| + C$$

$$\int e^x \, dx = e^x + C$$

$$\int a^x \, dx = \frac{a^x}{\ln a} + C; \quad a > 0 \text{ and } a \neq 1.$$

Most of the problems in this text can be solved using these forms and the technique of u-substitution. Other forms that one might need to evaluate an integral are included in Table 10–1, which is part of the more extensive Table II at the end of the book.

Extensive lists of rules for integrals can be found in tables. Table II at the end of the book contains some of these rules.

An even more extensive list of rules can be found by consulting a recent edition of *Standard Mathematical Tables,* published by the CRC Press, Boca Raton, Florida. Before illustrating the use of a table of integrals, we should point out that the very general rules for taking derivatives (the chain, product, and quotient rules) do not have counterparts in integration. Consequently, rules presented in tables of integrals were developed by specialized procedures, some quite advanced. Even so, we would look in vain in a table to find a rule for

$$\int e^{x^2} \, dx.$$

TABLE 10-1
(Selected Integrals from Table II)

8. $\int (mx + b)^n \, dx = \dfrac{(mx + b)^{n+1}}{m(n + 1)} + C; \; n \neq -1.$

9. $\int (mx + b)^{-1} \, dx = \int \dfrac{dx}{mx + b} = \dfrac{\ln |mx + b|}{m} + C.$

10. $\int \dfrac{x \, dx}{mx + b} = \dfrac{x}{m} - \dfrac{b}{m^2} \ln |mx + b| + C.$

11. $\int \dfrac{x \, dx}{(mx + b)^2} = \dfrac{b}{m^2(mx + b)} + \dfrac{\ln |mx + b|}{m^2} + C.$

12. $\int \dfrac{dx}{x(mx + b)} = \dfrac{1}{b} \ln \left| \dfrac{x}{mx + b} \right| + C.$

15. $\int e^{mx+b} \, dx = \dfrac{e^{mx+b}}{m} + C.$

16. $\int a^{mx+b} \, dx = \dfrac{a^{mx+b}}{m(\ln a)} + C; \; a > 0 \text{ and } a \neq 1.$

17. $\int x e^{mx+b} \, dx = \dfrac{e^{mx+b}(mx - 1)}{m^2} + C.$

18. $\int x a^{mx+b} \, dx = \dfrac{x a^{mx+b}}{m(\ln a)} - \dfrac{a^{mx+b}}{(m \ln a)^2} + C; \; a > 0 \text{ and } a \neq 1.$

19. $\int x e^{ax^2+b} \, dx = \dfrac{e^{ax^2+b}}{2a} + C.$

20. $\int \dfrac{dx}{a + be^{mx}} = \dfrac{mx - \ln |a + be^{mx}|}{am} + C.$

21. $\int \ln x \, dx = x(\ln x - 1) + C; \; x > 0.$

22. $\int \log x \, dx = x\left(\log x - \dfrac{1}{\ln 10} \right) + C; \; x > 0.$

23. $\int \ln (mx + b) \, dx = \dfrac{(mx + b)[\ln(mx + b) - 1]}{m} + C; \; mx + b > 0.$

24. $\int \log (mx + b) \, dx = \left(\dfrac{mx + b}{m} \right) \left[\log (mx + b) - \dfrac{1}{\ln 10} \right] + C; \; mx + b > 0.$

(continued)

TABLE 10-1 (concluded)

25. $\int \dfrac{1}{x^2 - a^2}\,dx = \dfrac{1}{2a}\ln\left|\dfrac{x - a}{x + a}\right| + C; \quad x^2 > a^2.$

26. $\int \dfrac{1}{a^2 - x^2}\,dx = \dfrac{1}{2a}\ln\left|\dfrac{a + x}{a - x}\right| + C; \quad x^2 < a^2.$

27. $\int \dfrac{1}{x\sqrt{a^2 - x^2}}\,dx = \dfrac{-1}{a}\ln\left|\dfrac{a + \sqrt{a^2 - x^2}}{x}\right| + C; \quad 0 < x < a.$

Note: $a, b, k, m, n,$ and C are constants.

Some functions cannot be integrated directly, so their definite integrals are approximated by numerical integration.

There is no rule for this integral and, moreover, there are no integration rules for numerous functions that arise in practice. As a consequence, procedures for approximating values of definite integrals are important in solving applied problems. We shall introduce approximation procedures later in this chapter under the heading **numerical integration**.

To use a table of integral rules, it is necessary to study the **form** of the function to be integrated and, having determined this, the table is searched for the corresponding form. Then constants are matched and the integration is carried out, as illustrated next.

Example. Find

$$\int xe^{0.1x}\,dx.$$

Here the integrand has the form **x times e to a linear function of x.** Running through Table 10–1, we find the corresponding form in Rule 17, which states

$$\int xe^{mx+b}\,dx = \dfrac{e^{mx+b}(mx - 1)}{m^2} + C.$$

To match

$$xe^{0.1x} \quad \text{with} \quad xe^{mx+b},$$

it is necessary that

$$m = 0.1 \quad \text{and} \quad b = 0.$$

Therefore, with these values for m and b, we have

$$\int xe^{0.1x}\,dx = \dfrac{e^{0.1x}(0.1x - 1)}{(0.1)^2} + C$$

$$= \dfrac{e^{0.1x}(0.1x - 1)}{0.01} + C$$

$$= 100e^{0.1x}(0.1x - 1) + C.$$

Example. Find

$$\int \frac{8x\,dx}{(2x-3)^2}.$$

Here, the factor 8 remains in the integral and is not considered when determining the form of the function. This form

$$\frac{x}{(2x-3)^2}$$

is x over the square of a linear function of x, and Rule 11 of Table 10–1 states that

$$\int \frac{x\,dx}{(mx+b)^2} = \frac{b}{m^2(mx+b)} + \frac{1}{m^2}\ln|mx+b| + C.$$

Matching constants in

$$\frac{x}{(2x-3)^2} \quad \text{and} \quad \frac{x}{(mx+b)^2}$$

we see that

$$m = 2 \quad \text{and} \quad b = -3.$$

Consequently,

$$\int \frac{8x\,dx}{(2x-3)^2} = 8\left[\frac{-3}{(2)^2(2x-3)} + \frac{1}{(2)^2}\ln|2x-3|\right] + C$$

$$= \frac{-6}{2x-3} + 2\ln|2x-3| + C.$$

10.17 PROBLEM SET 10–7

Carry out the following using Table II at the end of the book. Simplify where possible.

1. $\int x(2^x)\,dx.$
2. $\int \frac{6x}{2x+1}\,dx.$
3. $\int \frac{2x}{(0.5x+1)^2}\,dx.$
4. $\int xe^x\,dx.$
5. $\int xe^{2-0.5x}\,dx.$
6. $\int \frac{9x\,dx}{(3x+4)^2}.$
7. $\int \frac{2\,dx}{x(0.5x+1)}.$
8. $\int 2xe^{0.4x-1}\,dx.$
9. $\int \frac{2x\,dx}{5x-3}.$
10. $\int \frac{6\,dx}{x(3x+2)}.$
11. $\int xe^{0.1x^2-2}\,dx.$
12. $\int \frac{dx}{1+e^{0.2x}}.$
13. $\int \frac{dx}{1+2e^{0.5x}}.$
14. $\int 2xe^{2-0.5x^2}\,dx.$

10.17 PROBLEM SET 10-7 (concluded)

15. $\int \dfrac{2}{x^2 - 9}\, dx.$

16. $\int \dfrac{-10}{x^2 - 16}\, dx.$

17. $\int \dfrac{3}{x\sqrt{1 - 9x^2}}\, dx, \quad 0 < x < \dfrac{1}{3}.$

18. $\int \dfrac{dx}{x\sqrt{1 - 16x^2}}, \quad 0 < x < \dfrac{1}{4}.$

10.18 ASYMPTOTIC AREAS: IMPROPER INTEGRALS

The expression

$$\int_1^\infty \dfrac{1}{x^2}\, dx \tag{1}$$

is called an **improper integral** because its upper limit, denoted by the infinity symbol, ∞, is not a number. We shall define (1) to mean the **limit** of

$$\int_1^b \dfrac{1}{x^2}\, dx$$

as the upper limit b approaches ∞; or

$$\int_1^\infty \dfrac{1}{x^2}\, dx = \lim_{b \to \infty} \int_1^b \dfrac{1}{x^2}\, dx.$$

With this definition, the improper integral may or may not have a value (be defined). In the case at hand, if we write

$$\lim_{b \to \infty} \int_1^b \dfrac{1}{x^2}\, dx = \lim_{b \to \infty} \left(-\dfrac{1}{x}\right)\Big|_1^b$$

$$= \lim_{b \to \infty} \left[-\dfrac{1}{b} - \left(-\dfrac{1}{1}\right)\right], \tag{2}$$

then we see that as b becomes larger and larger ($b \to \infty$), $1/b$ becomes smaller and smaller, approaching zero as a limit. Thus

$$\lim_{b \to \infty} \left(-\dfrac{1}{b}\right) = 0,$$

and (2) becomes

$$[0 - (-1)] = 1$$

so

$$\int_1^\infty \dfrac{1}{x^2}\, dx = 1.$$

Hence, this improper integral is defined and has the value of 1. On the other hand,

$$\int_1^\infty \frac{1}{x}\, dx = \lim_{b\to\infty} (\ln x) \Big|_1^b$$
$$= \lim_{b\to\infty} (\ln b - \ln 1)$$
$$= \lim_{b\to\infty} (\ln b)$$

since ln 1 is 0. Here, as b becomes larger and larger, ln b also becomes larger and larger and does not approach a finite limit. Thus

$$\int_1^\infty \frac{1}{x}\, dx$$

does not exist.

The preceding two examples lead us to the following general rule:

$$\int_a^\infty f(x)\, dx = \lim_{b\to\infty} \int_a^b f(x)\, dx. \qquad (3)$$

Now to see the area implication of the integral

$$\int_1^\infty \frac{1}{x^2}\, dx = 1,$$

we sketch the graph of the integrand,

$$f(x) = \frac{1}{x^2}.$$

> We evaluate an improper integral with ∞ as the upper limit by finding the limit of the definite integral as the upper limit goes to ∞.

The important facts to note are, first, that when x is close to zero, $f(x)$ has a large value. For example, with $x = 0.01$ (close to zero)

$$f(0.01) = \frac{1}{(0.01)^2} = \frac{1}{0.0001} = 10{,}000,$$

the closer x is to zero the larger $f(x)$ becomes, **but x cannot equal zero.** Second, if x becomes very large, $f(x)$ becomes very small. For example, at $x = 100$,

$$f(100) = \frac{1}{(100)^2} = \frac{1}{10{,}000} = 0.0001,$$

and the larger x is, the closer $f(x)$ gets to zero, **but $f(x)$ can never equal zero** no matter how large a number x is. Now refer to Figure 10–20, and note the right branch of the curve. As we move off to the right ($x \to \infty$), $f(x)$ approaches zero (the x-axis), but does not touch it, and we describe this behavior by saying $f(x)$ approaches the x-axis **asymptotically**, or that the x-axis is an **asymptote** of $f(x)$. Similarly, as we move to the left in the first quadrant, $f(x)$ rises higher and higher

FIGURE 10-20

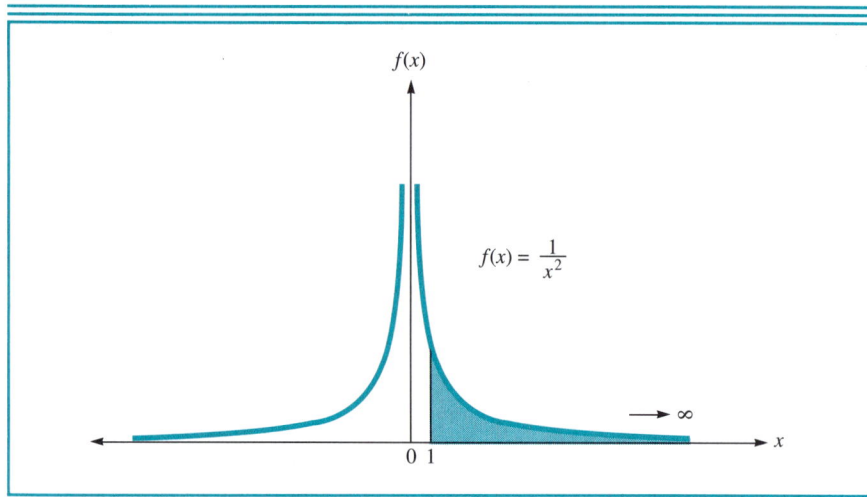

as x approaches zero, but x can never be zero, so the curve does not touch the vertical axis, but approaches it asymptotically as x approaches zero. The behavior exhibited by the left branch of Figure 10–20 follows from the fact that

$$f(x) = \frac{1}{x^2}$$

has the same value when x is a given number, whether the number be positive or negative.

As a consequence of the above, when we find

$$\int_1^\infty \left(\frac{1}{x^2}\right) dx = 1$$

we call this result, 1, the area under $f(x)$ over the interval 1 to ∞, even though the area is not completely enclosed by a finite boundary at the right. This idea of an **asymptotic area** is more than an exercise in applying the limit concept because there are numerous important applications of functions having areas in the asymptotic sense. Indeed, the **normal curve** in the study of probability and statistics (see Chapter 12) as shown in Figure 10–21, has the property under discussion.

Many real-world applications make use of asymptotic areas; for example, the normal curve in probability and statistics.

Example. Find the value, if one exists, of

$$\int_0^\infty \frac{30 \, dx}{(2x + 3)^2}.$$

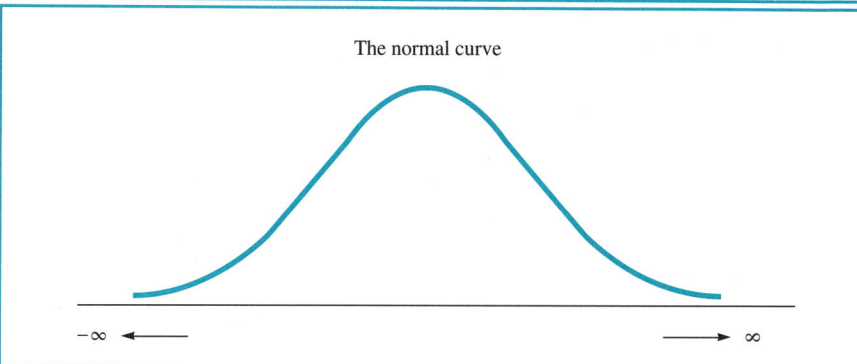

FIGURE 10-21

The normal curve

We write

$$\int_0^\infty \frac{30\,dx}{(2x+3)^2} = \lim_{b\to\infty} \int_0^b \frac{30\,dx}{(2x+3)^2}$$

$$= \lim_{b\to\infty} 30 \int_0^b (2x+3)^{-2}\,dx$$

$$= \lim_{b\to\infty} 30 \left[\frac{(2x+3)^{-1}}{2(-1)}\right]\Bigg|_0^b$$

$$= \lim_{b\to\infty} 30 \left[-\frac{1}{2}\left(\frac{1}{2b+3} - \frac{1}{3}\right)\right].$$

Now as $b \to \infty$, $\dfrac{1}{2b+3} \to 0$ so we have

$$= 30\left[-\frac{1}{2}\left(0 - \frac{1}{3}\right)\right]$$

$$= 30\left(\frac{1}{6}\right) = 5.$$

Exercise. Find the value of the following, if a value exists.

$$\int_6^\infty \frac{3\,dx}{(2x-10)^2}.$$

Answer: 3/4.

10.19 PROBLEM SET 10-8

Find the value of each of the following, if a value exists.

1. $\int_{1}^{\infty} 4x^{-3/2}\, dx.$

2. $\int_{2}^{\infty} \frac{6\, dx}{x^2}.$

3. $\int_{-3}^{\infty} \frac{dx}{(0.5x + 2.5)^2}.$

4. $\int_{3}^{\infty} 3(0.5x + 2.5)^{-3/2}\, dx.$

5. $\int_{1}^{\infty} x^{-1/2}\, dx.$

6. $\int_{1}^{\infty} x^{-2/3}\, dx.$

7. $\int_{0}^{\infty} 5e^{-0.2x}\, dx.$

8. $\int_{0}^{\infty} e^{-0.5x}\, dx.$

9. $\int_{25}^{\infty} \frac{-2}{\sqrt{x}}\, dx.$

10. $\int_{-\infty}^{-4} \frac{1}{x^4}\, dx.$

11. $\int_{-\infty}^{-1} x^2\, dx.$

12. $\int_{1}^{\infty} \frac{1}{x^{1.01}}\, dx.$

13. $\int_{1}^{\infty} \frac{1}{x^{.99}}\, dx.$

14. $\int_{-\infty}^{0} e^{4x}\, dx.$

Use Table 10-1 as necessary for the following:

15. $\int_{0}^{\infty} xe^{2x}\, dx.$

16. $\int_{-\infty}^{0} xe^{3x}\, dx.$

17. $\int_{1}^{\infty} \frac{4}{9x(x + 1)}\, dx.$

18. $\int_{2}^{\infty} \frac{2}{x(5x + 1)}\, dx.$

10.20 NUMERICAL INTEGRATION

Some integrals cannot be found directly and so definite integrals are often determined by approximation techniques.

Although extensive lists of integration rules are available in published tables, it frequently happens that a table does not have the counterpart of a form that arises in an applied problem. Sometimes it is possible to derive the integration rule for the form at hand either by applying a formal procedure such as the one to be discussed later in this chapter, or by some ingenious technique, but there are cases where formal procedures and ingenuity are to no avail. Thus, we note that while

$$\int e^x\, dx = e^x + C$$

is perhaps the simplest of all integration rules, no rule can be found to determine

$$\int e^{x^2}\, dx.$$

Lack of an integration rule poses no particular problem in applications where the value of a definite integral is sought because such values can be approximated quickly and with high accuracy on a computer that has been programmed to carry out **numerical** (approximate) **integration**. After the computer has been supplied with the program for numerical integration, we need only supply it with a statement specifying the function to be integrated and the values of the upper and lower limits of integration. The computer will then determine the desired value in less time than we spent supplying it with the problem. Lacking access to a computer, we can also approximate definite integrals easily on calculators. The procedure we shall develop for this purpose is called the **Trapezoidal Rule.** There are many other techniques that have been developed to approximate the value of definite integrals, but with the high internal speed of the modern computer more efficient procedures save only a negligible amount of actual run time.

We saw in Section 10.4 that Riemann Sums could be used to approximate areas under a curve (the definite integral) using upper and lower **rectangular** sums. The Trapezoidal Rule approximates this same area using **trapezoids**. For example, suppose as in Section 10.4, we want to find the area under the curve $f(x) = x^2$ from $x = 1$ to $x = 3$ as shown in Figure 10–22. We saw in Section 10.4 that the actual area given by the definite integral is

$$\int_1^3 x^2 \, dx = \frac{26}{3} \text{ square units.}$$

The Trapezoidal Rule uses trapezoids rather than rectangles to approximate the definite integral.

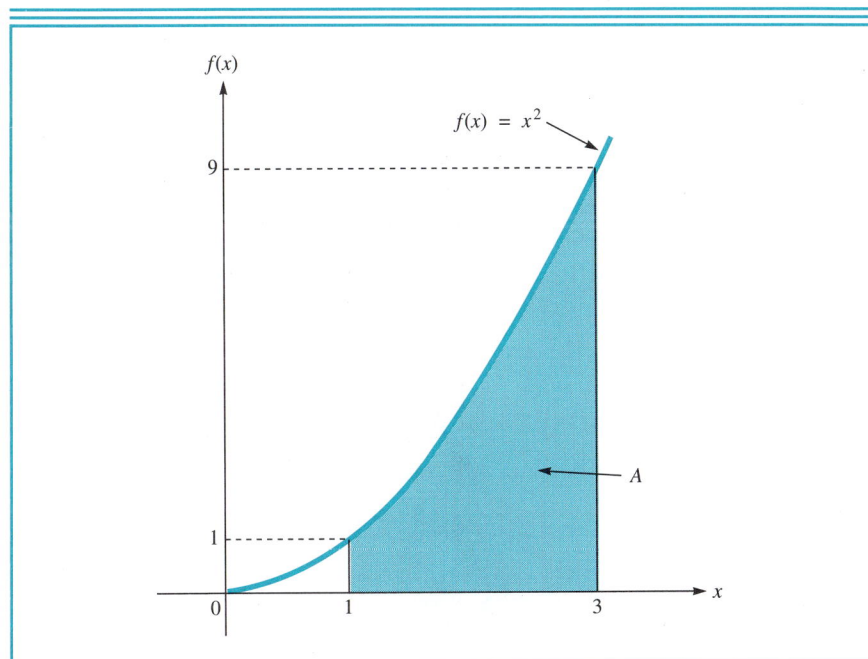

FIGURE 10–22

We also saw in Section 10.4 that using **two rectangles**, the lower sum approximation was 5 square units while the upper sum approximation was 13 units.

Now suppose we use **two trapezoids** to approximate the area as shown in Figure 10–23. This time, since the area of each trapezoid is one-half the base times the sum of the (parallel) sides

$$A = \frac{1}{2} b[s_1 + s_2],$$

The approximation of the definite integral using trapezoids is much more accurate than the approximation using the same number of rectangles.

the approximate area under the curve would be

$$A \approx \frac{1}{2}(1)\,[1 + 4] + \frac{1}{2}(1)\,[4 + 9] = \frac{5}{2} + \frac{13}{2} = 9 \text{ square units}, \quad (1)$$

which is much closer to the actual area of 26/3 square units than either Riemann Sum with two rectangles.

Next suppose we use four trapezoids to approximate the area as shown in Figure 10–24. Then the approximate area under the curve would be

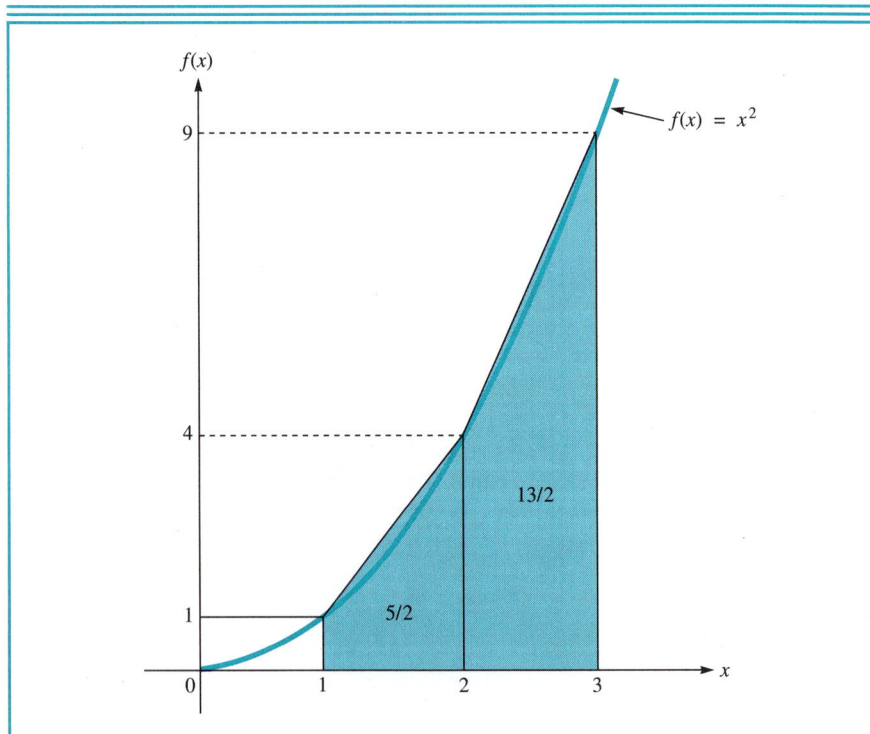

FIGURE 10–23

$$A \approx \frac{1}{2}\left(\frac{1}{2}\right)\left[1 + \frac{9}{4}\right] + \frac{1}{2}\left(\frac{1}{2}\right)\left[\frac{9}{4} + 4\right]$$
$$+ \frac{1}{2}\left(\frac{1}{2}\right)\left[4 + \frac{25}{4}\right] + \frac{1}{2}\left(\frac{1}{2}\right)\left[\frac{25}{4} + 9\right] = \frac{140}{16} \quad (2)$$

or 8.75 square units, which is very close to the actual area of 26/3 (approximately 8.667) square units. Recall that with four rectangles, the lower sum was 6.75 square units and the upper sum was 10.75 square units.

Before going on, it is helpful to take a closer look at Equations (1) and (2). We can rewrite (1) as

$$\frac{1}{2}(1)[1 + 4] + \frac{1}{2}(1)[4 + 9] = \frac{1}{2}(1)[1 + 2(4) + 9]$$

$$= \frac{w}{2}[f(a) + 2f(a + w) + f(b)]. \quad (3)$$

In this last equation, w represents the base of **all** of the trapezoids so that

$$w = \frac{b - a}{n} = \frac{3 - 1}{2} = 1$$

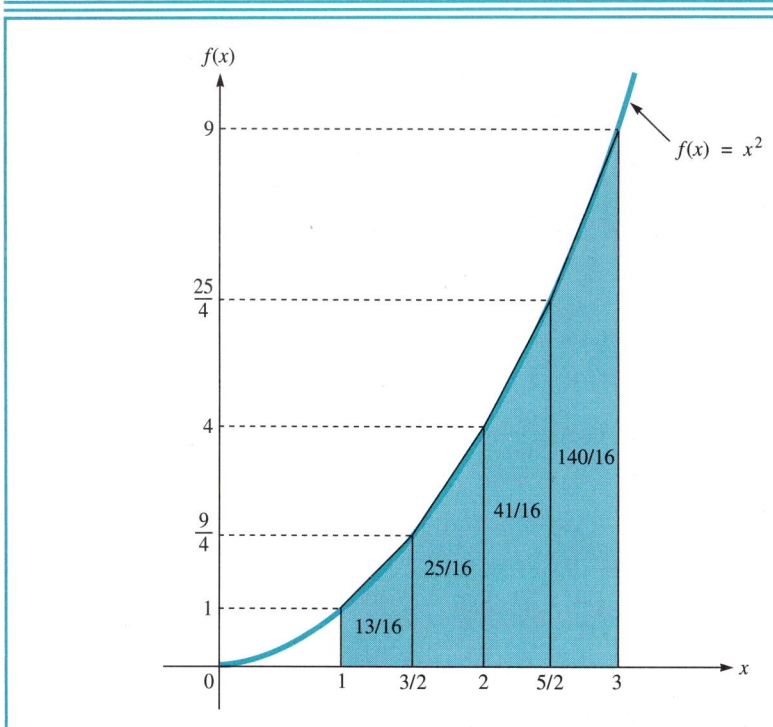

FIGURE 10-24

since the left endpoint is $a = 1$, the right endpoint is $b = 3$, and the number of trapezoids is $n = 2$. Also, $f(a) = f(1) = 1$ represents the length of the first side, $f(a + w) = f(2) = 4$ the length of the next side, and $f(b) = f(3) = 9$ the length of the last side. Note in Equation (3) that the value $f(a + w)$ is counted twice since it is a side in both trapezoids.

Similarly, we can rewrite Equation (2) as

$$\frac{1}{2}\left(\frac{1}{2}\right)\left[1 + 2\left(\frac{9}{4}\right) + 2(4) + 2\left(\frac{25}{4}\right) + 9\right]$$

$$= \frac{w}{2}[f(a) + 2f(a + w) + 2f(a + 2w) + 2f(a + 3w) + f(b)] \quad (4)$$

since here

$$w = \frac{b - a}{n} = \frac{3 - 1}{4} = \frac{1}{2}.$$

Note in (4) that all the values except at the endpoints are counted twice since they are all sides of two trapezoids. Now moving the 1/2 inside the square brackets in Equations (3) and (4), we have the general form of the Trapezoidal Rule:

The approximation of the definite integral by trapezoids is the product of the common base of the trapezoids times the sum of the values of the integrand function at each end of the trapezoids, where the first and last values are multiplied by 1/2.

Trapezoidal Rule

Using n trapezoids,

$$\int_a^b f(x)\, dx \approx w\left[\frac{f(a)}{2} + f(a + w) + f(a + 2w) + f(a + 3w) + \ldots + f(a + (n-1)w) + \frac{f(b)}{2}\right]$$

where the base of each trapezoid is given by

$$w = \frac{b - a}{n}.$$

Figure 10–25 illustrates the general Trapezoidal Rule for five trapezoids.

Suppose we next try approximating the area by eight trapezoids as shown in Figure 10–26. This time, since $n = 8$, the base is

$$w = \frac{b - a}{n} = \frac{3 - 1}{8} = \frac{1}{4} = 0.25$$

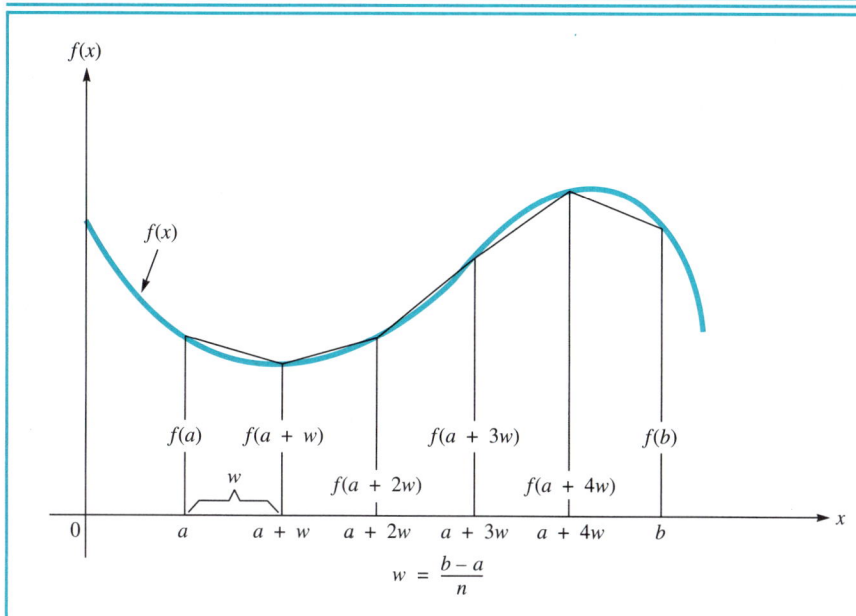

FIGURE 10–25

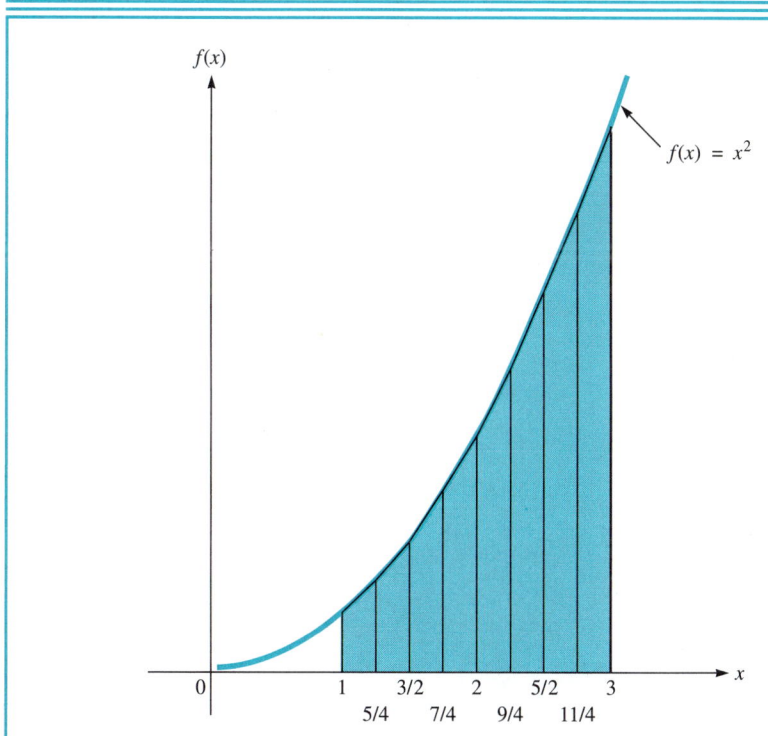

FIGURE 10–26

and we can calculate the approximation by the Trapezoidal Rule as shown in Table 10–2. From this table, we see that using eight trapezoids,

$$\int_1^3 x^2 \, dx = 8.6875$$

which once more is much closer to the actual area of 26/3 (approximately 8.667) than the lower and upper sums using eight rectangles. A final comparison of the Trapezoidal Rule with lower and upper sums for this example is given in Table 10–3.

Example. Approximate the following definite integral by the area of 10 trapezoids:

$$\int_0^1 e^{x^2} \, dx.$$

In this case, no rule can be applied to determine the correct value of the integral. The Trapezoidal Rule approximation with $n = 10$ leads to a subdivision width of

$$w = \frac{b - a}{n} = \frac{1 - 0}{10} = 0.1.$$

The calculations for the approximation are shown in Table 10–4, where the exponential values were determined on a calculator. The answer obtained,

$$\int_0^1 e^{x^2} \, dx \approx 1.467$$

TABLE 10–2

Point, x		Function Value, x^2		Numbers to Be Summed
a	$= 1$	1	(times 1/2)	0.5
$a + w$	$= 1.25$	1.5625		1.5625
$a + 2w$	$= 1.5$	2.25		2.25
$a + 3w$	$= 1.75$	3.0625		3.0625
$a + 4w$	$= 2$	4		4
$a + 5w$	$= 2.25$	5.0625		5.0625
$a + 6w$	$= 2.5$	6.25		6.25
$a + 7w$	$= 2.75$	7.5625		7.5625
b	$= 3$	9	(times 1/2)	4.5
				Sum = 34.75

Answer: w (Sum) $= 0.25(34.75) = 8.6875$.

to three-decimal-place accuracy, can also be obtained on a computer, as shown in the QBasic program of Table 10–5 on page 714. Note that the resultant area of 1.467175 is precisely the same as that in Table 10–4. Next we carried out approximations with $n = 10, 20, 30, \ldots, 100$ as shown in the QBasic programs of Table 10–6 on page 715. From this table, it appears that

$$\int_0^1 e^{x^2} \, dx \approx 1.463$$

to three-decimal-place accuracy.

TABLE 10–3

Comparison of Trapezoidal Rule and Riemann Sums for x^2 in the Interval [1, 3]

n	Lower Sum	Upper Sum	Trapezoidal Rule
2	5	13	9
4	6.75	10.75	8.75
8	7.6875	9.6875	8.6875

Correct Area = $26/3 \approx 8.667$.

TABLE 10–4

x	x^2	$f(x) = e^{x^2}$		Numbers to Be Summed
0.0	0.00	1.0000	(times 1/2)	0.
0.1	0.01	1.010050167		1.010050167
0.2	0.04	1.040810774		1.040810774
0.3	0.09	1.094174284		1.094174284
0.4	0.16	1.173510871		1.173510871
0.5	0.25	1.284025417		1.284025417
0.6	0.36	1.433329415		1.433329415
0.7	0.49	1.632316220		1.63231622
0.8	0.64	1.896480879		1.896480879
0.9	0.81	2.247907987		2.247907987
1.0	1.00	2.718281828	(times 1/2)	1.359140914
			Sum =	14.67174693

Answer: $w(\text{sum}) = 0.1(14.67174693) = 1.467174693$.

> **Exercise.** a) Modify Program 10-3 of Table 10-5 to approximate
>
> $$\int_1^2 \ln x \, dx$$
>
> with $n = 10$. b) Modify Program 10-4 of Table 10-6 to approximate the integral to three decimal places.
>
> **Answer:** a) 0.3858779. b) 0.386.

TABLE 10-5

```
REM PROGRAM 10-3
REM Approximation of Area under e^(x^2) using Trapezoids
CLS
INPUT "Enter limits a and b, and number of trapezoids";
         a, b, n
PRINT
PRINT " x", " x^2", " e^(x^2)", " SUM"
 interval = (b - a) / n
 FOR count = 0 TO n
   x = a + count * interval
   e = EXP (x ^ 2)
   IF x = a OR x = b THEN
     sum = sum + .5 * e
   ELSE
     sum = sum + e
   END IF
   PRINT x, x ^ 2, e, sum
 NEXT count
PRINT
PRINT "The area is "; sum * interval

Enter limits a and b, and number of trapezoids? 0,1,10

 x         x^2          e^(x^2)         SUM
 0         0            1               .5
 .1        .01          1.01005         1.51005
 .2        .04          1.040811        2.550861
 .3        .09          1.094174        3.645035
 .4        .16          1.173511        4.818546
 .5        .25          1.284025        6.102571
 .6        .36          1.433329        7.535901
 .7        .49          1.632316        9.168218
 .8        .64          1.896481        11.0647
 .9        .8100001     2.247908        13.31261
 1         1            2.718282        14.67175

The area is 1.467175.
```

TABLE 10-6

```
REM PROGRAM 10-4
REM Approximation of Area under e^(x^2) using 10 - 100 Trapezoids
CLS
INPUT "Enter lower limit a and upper limit b"; a, b
PRINT
FOR number = 10 TO 100 STEP 10
  interval = (b - a) / number
  sum = 0
  FOR count = 0 TO number
    x = a + count * interval
    e = EXP(x ^ 2)
    IF x = a OR x = b THEN
      sum = sum + .5 * e
    ELSE
      sum = sum + e
    END IF
  NEXT count
  PRINT "With "; number; " trapezoids, the area is "; interval * sum
NEXT number

Enter lower limit a and upper limit b? 0,1
With  10 trapezoids, the area is 1.467175
With  20 trapezoids, the area is 1.463784
With  30 trapezoids, the area is 1.463155
With  40 trapezoids, the area is 1.462935
With  50 trapezoids, the area is 1.462833
With  60 trapezoids, the area is 1.462778
With  70 trapezoids, the area is 1.462744
With  80 trapezoids, the area is 1.462723
With  90 trapezoids, the area is 1.462708
With 100 trapezoids, the area is 1.462697
```

10.21 PROBLEM SET 10-9

Approximate the following by the sum of the areas of n trapezoids. (Trapezoidal rule.)

1. $\int_1^4 \ln x \, dx; n = 6.$

2. $\int_1^4 e^{-x} \, dx; n = 6.$

3. $\int_0^{0.4} e^{-x^2} \, dx; n = 4.$

4. $\int_0^{0.8} e^{x^2} \, dx; n = 4.$

5. $\int_1^2 \frac{x-1}{x+1} \, dx; n = 5.$

6. $\int_2^3 \frac{x+1}{x-1} \, dx; n = 5.$

10.21 PROBLEM SET 10-9 (concluded)

7. $\int_1^3 \frac{\ln x}{x} dx; n = 5.$

8. $\int_0^{0.5} xe^{-x^2} dx; n = 5.$

9. $\int_1^3 \frac{x}{e^x} dx; n = 4.$

10. $\int_1^2 x \ln x \, dx; n = 5.$

The **normal curve** or, more precisely, the **standard normal probability density function**, is without question the most important function in probability and statistics. It is

$$f(z) = \frac{1}{\sqrt{2\pi}} e^{-z^2/2} \approx 0.398942 e^{-z^2/2}; \quad -\infty < z < \infty.$$

There is no rule for integrating this function to obtain areas, which, in applications, are probabilities. Consequently, to assist the millions of people who use normal probabilities (which includes nearly every student of management and economics), values have been computed and tabulated. Table V at the end of this book is a typical presentation. The entry next to $z = 1$ in Table V is 0.3413. This means that

$$\frac{1}{\sqrt{2\pi}} \int_0^1 e^{-z^2/2} dz = 0.3413$$

to four decimal places. Inasmuch as very few of the millions of users of tables such as Table V have any understanding of the source of the numbers, a reader who does problem 11 or 12 can properly claim to be "one in a million."

11. (See the preceding introduction.) Approximate the following integral by the sum of 10 trapezoids.

    $$0.398942 \int_0^1 e^{-z^2/2} dz.$$

12. Do Problem 11 using 20 trapezoids.

13. a) Modify Program 10–3 to solve Problems 1 through 11.
    b) Modify Program 10–4 to solve Problems 1 through 11.
    c) Using the results of (a) and (b), approximate the integrals in Problems 1 through 11 to four decimal places.

10.22 INTEGRATION BY PARTS

Integration by parts is based on the Product Rule for differentiation.

The purpose of this section is to illustrate one formal procedure called **integration by parts** that can be applied to integrate some functions whose integrals are not immediately obvious. There are other formal procedures that the reader can find in more extensive treatments of calculus under the headings of **trigonometric substitution**, **partial fractions**, and **reduction formulas**. But, it should be remembered that these procedures work only for functions of particular forms.

The method of integration by parts is based on the **Product Rule for derivatives**. If $f(x)$ and $g(x)$ are differentiable functions, then we know that

$$\frac{d}{dx}[f(x) \cdot g(x)] = f'(x) \cdot g(x) + f(x) \cdot g'(x). \tag{1}$$

Now let
$$u = f(x) \quad \text{and} \quad v = g(x)$$
so that
$$\frac{du}{dx} = f'(x) \quad \text{and} \quad \frac{dv}{dx} = g'(x).$$

Then (1) becomes
$$\frac{d}{dx}(uv) = v\frac{du}{dx} + u\frac{dv}{dx},$$
or rearranging the terms,
$$u\frac{dv}{dx} = \frac{d}{dx}(uv) - v\frac{du}{dx}. \tag{2}$$

Integrating both sides of (2) with respect to x, we have
$$\int \left[u\frac{dv}{dx} \right] dx = \int \left[\frac{d}{dx}(uv) \right] dx - \int \left[v\frac{du}{dx} \right] dx,$$
which can be restated as

Rule for Integration by Parts
$$\int u\, dv = uv - \int v\, du. \tag{3}$$

Equation (3), the formula for integration by parts, is applied as illustrated by the following examples:

Example. Find $\int \ln x\, dx$.

We first write down the integration-by-parts formula
$$\int u\, dv = uv - \int v\, du$$
and then try to make an appropriate choice for u and dv. Since the left-hand side of the formula must coincide with our problem statement, we choose
$$u = \ln x \quad \text{and} \quad dv = dx.$$

Then

$$du = \frac{1}{x} dx \quad \text{and} \quad v = \int dx = x.$$

Any constant may be added to v at this point, so for convenience we choose zero. Now, by Equation (3),

$$\int \ln x \, dx = (\ln x)(x) - \int x \cdot \frac{1}{x} dx$$
$$= x(\ln x) - x + C$$
$$= x(\ln x - 1) + C.$$

Note that the constant of integration is not necessary until the final step in the integration. Note also that the result is precisely Rule 21 in Table 10–1 of Section 10.16.

Even when integration by parts works, it may take trial and error to get started correctly. The trick is to make the proper selection of the parts.

When using integration by parts, we must carefully select u and dv.

Example. Integrate the following by parts.

$$\int (e^x) x \, dx.$$

Suppose we try taking $u = e^x$, so that

$$\frac{du}{dx} = \frac{d(e^x)}{dx} = e^x \quad \text{and} \quad du = e^x \, dx.$$

The remaining part is $dv = x \, dx$, and

$$\int dv = \int x \, dx$$
$$v = \frac{x^2}{2}.$$

We now have

$$u = e^x; \quad v = \frac{x^2}{2}$$
$$du = e^x \, dx; \quad dv = x \, dx.$$

Then, applying the rule,

$$\int u \, dv = \int (e^x) x \, dx$$
$$= uv - \int v \, du$$
$$= e^x \left(\frac{x^2}{2}\right) - \int \frac{x^2}{2} e^x \, dx,$$

and the integral on the right is **more difficult than the original problem.** Consequently we should start again and choose the parts **the other way around.** That is, let $u = x$ and $dv = e^x dx$. This leads to

$$u = x; \quad v = \int e^x \, dx = e^x$$
$$du = dx; \quad dv = e^x \, dx.$$

> If one particular selection of u and dv for integration by parts leads to a more complex problem, then choose the parts the other way around.

Hence,

$$\int u \, dv = uv - \int v \, du$$
$$= xe^x - \int e^x \, dx$$
$$= xe^x - e^x + C$$
$$= e^x(x - 1) + C,$$

which is Rule 17 in Table 10–1 of Section 10.16, with $m = 1$ and $b = 0$.

Exercise. Integrate by parts $\int x^2 (\ln x) \, dx$.

Answer: $\dfrac{x^3}{3} (\ln x) - \dfrac{x^3}{9} + C$.

10.23 PROBLEM SET 10–10

Carry out the following. Simplify where possible.

1. $\int 3 (\ln x) \, dx$.
2. $\int 2 (\ln x) \, dx$.
3. $\int (\ln 2x) \, dx$.
4. $\int (\ln 3x) \, dx$.
5. $\int \ln(2x + 1) \, dx$.
6. $\int \ln(3x + 5) \, dx$.
7. $\int 6 \ln(3x - 2) \, dx$.
8. $\int 4 \ln(2x - 1) \, dx$.

9. At time t years, the cost of electric power used by a plant is projected to be at the rate of $4 \ln(2t + 6)$ thousand dollars per year. Find total electric power cost for the next seven years.

10. At time t years, production of a food is projected to be at the rate of $9 \ln(3t + 5)$ million bushels per year. Find total production in the next five years.

Apply integration by parts and carry out the following:

11. $\int x (\ln x) \, dx$.
12. $\int x^3 (\ln x) \, dx$.
13. $\int \dfrac{\ln x}{x^2} \, dx$.
14. $\int \dfrac{x + \ln x}{x^2} \, dx$.
15. $\int x(x + 1)^5 \, dx$.
16. $\int \dfrac{4x}{\sqrt{8 - x}} \, dx$.
17. $\int x\sqrt{1 - x} \, dx$.
18. $\int \dfrac{x}{\sqrt{x - 1}} \, dx$.
19. $\int (x^2 + 8)e^x \, dx$.

10.23 PROBLEM SET 10-10 (concluded)

20. $\int_0^1 xe^{2x}\, dx.$

21. $\int_1^e x (\ln x)\, dx.$

22. $\int_0^1 \frac{(e^x + 2x)^2}{2}\, dx.$

10.24 DIFFERENTIAL EQUATIONS

A differential equation is an equation that contains a differential or a derivative.

Numerous problems earlier in this chapter start with given information about a **rate** and proceed to determine a desired quantity by integrating the rate. The methodology of **differential equations**, which we introduce in this section, is widely applied in solving such rate problems and, we should remark, such problems occur very frequently in practice.

A differential equation is one that contains a **differential** or a **derivative**. As examples, we write

$$y\, dy - x\, dx = 0$$

$$\frac{dy}{dx} = 2x + 1$$

$$\frac{d^2y}{dx^2} + 3\frac{dy}{dx} + x - 1 = 0.$$

The equation last written contains a second derivative and serves to illustrate the fact that differential equations may involve second and higher order derivatives and differentials. However, in this introduction we shall deal only with first-order equations. Before proceeding, we call attention to the use of differentials such as dy and dx as symbols having individual meanings. When these were introduced in differential calculus, it was emphasized that if

$$y = f(x)$$

then

$$\frac{dy}{dx} = f'(x)$$

and dy/dx was not a fraction with dy as numerator and dx as denominator, but a single symbol meaning the same as $f'(x)$. However, when we write

$$\int f'(x)\, dx,$$

The differentials dy and dx are treated as individual symbols with $dy = f'(x)\, dx$.

dx appears alone. To achieve consistency, we define dy to be $f'(x)dx$. That is, if

$$\frac{dy}{dx} = f'(x),$$

then

$$dy = f'(x)\,dx.$$

In terms of symbol manipulation, the last can be thought of as being obtained by multiplying both sides of the preceding equation by dx, and this is how we shall describe the procedure. Thus, for example, if

$$\frac{dy}{dx} = 2x$$

then

$$dy = 2x\,dx$$

is a differential equation that is solved by integrating the left with respect to y and the right with respect to x. That is,

$$\int dy = \int 2x\,dx$$
$$y + C_1 = x^2 + C_2$$
$$y = x^2 + C_2 - C_1.$$

Inasmuch as C_2 and C_1 are arbitrary constants, $C_2 - C_1$ is another arbitrary constant, which we may call C. **We shall follow the practice of writing only one constant for one integration step,** so the solution is

$$y = x^2 + C.$$

A solution such as this, which contains the constant of integration, is called the **general solution** of the differential equation, and each value for C yields a **particular solution** of the differential equation. Thus,

$$y = x^2 + 10$$

is one particular solution, and there are infinitely many particular solutions.

A solution that contains the constant of integration C is a general solution, and each value of C results in a particular solution.

If we are presented with a differential equation and with a pair of values that must satisfy the solution, the given values are called **initial conditions** or boundary values.

Initial Conditions

A pair of values that must satisfy the solution of a differential equation are called initial conditions.

Example. Solve the differential equation

$$dy = x^{1/2}\,dx$$

subject to the initial conditions that $y = 10$ when $x = 9$.

We write

$$\int dy = \int x^{1/2}\, dx$$

$$y = \frac{2}{3} x^{3/2} + C.$$

The point $x = 9$, $y = 10$ must satisfy the last equation. Hence,

$$10 = \frac{2}{3}(9)^{3/2} + C$$

$$10 = \frac{2}{3}(27) + C$$

$$10 = 18 + C$$

$$-8 = C,$$

so C must be -8, and the **particular solution** required is

$$y = \frac{2}{3} x^{3/2} - 8.$$

Exercise. Solve the differential equation

$$dy = 2x\, dx$$

subject to the initial condition that $y = 12$ when $x = 3$.
Answer: $y = x^2 + 3$.

A separable differential equation is one with dy times a function of y on one side and dx times a function of x on the other.

A differential equation that can be arranged in the form

$$g(y)\, dy = f(x)\, dx,$$

where one side is dy times a function of y and the other side is dx times a function of x, is called a **separable differential equation**. For example,

$$x \frac{dy}{dx} - 1 = 0$$

becomes

$$\frac{dy}{dx} = \frac{1}{x}$$

or

$$dy = \frac{dx}{x}.$$

The general solution of the last separated form is

$$\int dy = \int \frac{dx}{x}$$

$$y = \ln x + C, \; x > 0.$$

Exercise. Write the general solution of $\dfrac{dy}{dx} - 2x = 1$.

Answer: $y = x^2 + x + C.$

10.25 FORMS OF THE CONSTANT

The definition and rules of logarithms are applied frequently to obtain **explicit** solutions of differential equations. For reference, these are:

1. Definition: If $\ln a = b$, then $a = e^b$.
2. Product: $\ln(ab) = \ln a + \ln b$.
3. Quotient: $\ln(a/b) = \ln a - \ln b$.
4. Power: $\ln(a^b) = b(\ln a)$.

Example. Find the general solution of the following differential equation in **explicit form**.

$$\frac{dy}{dx} = \frac{y}{x}; \; x \neq 0.$$

First, multiplying by dx gives

$$dy = \frac{y}{x} dx.$$

Then dividing by y provides the separated form

$$\frac{dy}{y} = \frac{dx}{x}.$$

Integrating, we have

$$\int \frac{dy}{y} = \int \frac{dx}{x}$$

$$\ln y = \ln x + C.$$

This solves the equation in terms of $\ln y$, **but not explicitly in terms of** y. Proceeding, we write,

$$\ln y - \ln x = C$$

or

$$\ln \frac{y}{x} = C.$$

We next apply the definition of the natural logarithm and write

$$\frac{y}{x} = e^C.$$

Inasmuch as e is a constant and C is a constant, e^C is a constant, which may be denoted K. That is, there is no need for two constants in the solution. Hence, we have

$$\frac{y}{x} = K$$

$$y = Kx$$

as the **explicit general solution.** This surprisingly simple result is a straight line of slope K that passes through the origin, and a line through the origin is the only function whose slope can be found by dividing the y-coordinate of any one of its points by the x-coordinate; that is,

$$\text{Slope} = \frac{dy}{dx} = \frac{y}{x},$$

which is the initial differential equation. Observe, however, that x cannot equal zero, so the differential equation, and therefore the general solution, is not defined for $x = 0$. As a matter of convenience, we shall assume it to be understood that solutions we write exclude values of the independent variable where the differential equation and/or its solution are not defined.

Exercise. a) Write the following equation in separated form. b) Find the explicit general solution.

$$x\frac{dy}{dx} + y = 0.$$

Answer: a) $dy/y = -dx/x$. b) $y = K/x$.

As another example, consider the equation

$$x\, dy = 2y\, dx.$$

Dividing both sides by xy, we have

$$\frac{dy}{y} = \frac{2\,dx}{x}.$$

Integrating leads to

$$\int \frac{dy}{y} = 2 \int \frac{dx}{x}$$

$$\ln y = 2(\ln x) + C.$$

Now, applying logarithm rules,

$$\ln y = \ln x^2 + C$$
$$\ln y - \ln x^2 = C$$
$$\ln\left(\frac{y}{x^2}\right) = C$$
$$\frac{y}{x^2} = e^C = K$$

and we have

$$y = Kx^2$$

as the explicit general solution.

Finally, remember that the rule of exponents that says

$$e^x \cdot e^C = e^{x+C}$$

can be applied in reverse if an expression similar to the one on the right is encountered. That is

$$e^{x+C} = e^x(e^C) = Ke^x,$$

because if C is an arbitrary constant, so also is e^C an arbitrary constant.

Example. Find the explicit general solution of

$$2x(0.5y + 1)\,dx + dy = 0.$$

First we write

$$dy = -2x(0.5y + 1)\,dx.$$

Division by $(0.5y + 1)$ separates the variables, giving

$$\frac{dy}{0.5y + 1} = -2x\,dx,$$

$$\int \frac{dy}{0.5y + 1} = -2 \int x\,dx.$$

On the left we see a linear form whose integral we recall, or look up in Table 10–1 of Section 10.16, and have

$$\frac{\ln(0.5y + 1)}{0.5} = -2\left(\frac{x^2}{2}\right) + C_1$$

$$\ln(0.5y + 1) = 0.5(-2)\left(\frac{x^2}{2}\right) + 0.5C_1$$

$$= -0.5x^2 + C,$$

where, in the last statement, $0.5C_1$ has been written as another arbitrary constant, C. Application of the logarithm definition leads to

$$0.5y + 1 = e^{-0.5x^2 + C}$$

$$= (e^{-0.5x^2})(e^C)$$

$$= (e^{-0.5x^2})K_1,$$

where e^C has been replaced by another arbitrary constant, K_1. Continuing,

$$0.5y = (e^{-0.5x^2})K_1 - 1$$

$$y = \frac{K_1 e^{-0.5x^2} - 1}{0.5}$$

$$= \frac{K_1}{0.5} e^{-0.5x^2} - \frac{1}{0.5},$$

but $K_1/0.5$ is an arbitrary constant which we shall call K, and then write the explicit general solution,

$$y = Ke^{-0.5x^2} - 2$$

where -2 is *not* an arbitrary constant.

Exercise. Find the explicit general solution of

$$dy - (2y + 6)\, dx = 0.$$

Answer: $y = Ke^{2x} - 3$.

10.26 PROBLEM SET 10–11

Find the explicit general solution of each of the following:

1. $dy - dx = 0$.
2. $dy - 3x^2\, dx = 0$.
3. $x\, dy = dx$.
4. $dy = y\, dx$.

10.26 PROBLEM SET 10-11 (concluded)

5. $\dfrac{dy}{dx} = \dfrac{y}{x}$.

6. $\dfrac{dy}{dx} = \dfrac{y}{x^2}$.

7. $2\,dy - \dfrac{y\,dx}{x^{1/2}} = 0$.

8. $x\,dy + y\,dx = 0$.

9. $(0.2x + 3)\,dy = dx$.

10. $(0.5x + 2)\,dy = 2\,dx$.

11. $dy - (0.5y + 2)\,dx = 0$.

12. $dy = (0.2y + 3)\,dx$.

Find the explicit particular solution, using the stated initial conditions:

13. $dy = (x + 1)\,dx$; $y = 26$ when $x = 6$.

14. $\dfrac{dy}{dx} = 2x$; $y = 9$ when $x = 3$.

15. $\dfrac{dy}{dx} = y$; $y = 1.0874$ when $x = 1$.

16. $x\,dy + y\,dx = 0$; $y = 2$ when $x = 3$.

17. $dy = (0.2y + 3)\,dx$; $y = 4$ when $x = 0$.

18. $dy - (0.5y + 2)\,dx = 0$; $y = 1$ when $x = 0$.

19. $x\,dy - y\,dx - dx = 0$; $y = 2$ when $x = 1$.

20. $x\,dy + y\,dx + dx = 0$; $y = 3$ when $x = 2$.

10.27 APPLICATIONS OF DIFFERENTIAL EQUATIONS

In many applications, including the examples in this section, differential equations arise because the information available consists of an expression for a rate of change, together with initial conditions. When a rate expression is given, it will be helpful in setting up the associated differential equation to keep in mind the **units** associated with the differential and the rate.

Example. Smith owes Brown $100 now, at time $t = 0$, and the amount owed, y, is increasing at the rate of $10 per year at time t years. How much will Smith owe at time $t = 3$ years?

The answer is, of course, $100 + 3(10) = \$130$ because the rate of change is constant. However, we wish to use the example to illustrate the mode of thinking involved in setting up differential equations. To this end, we note that the rate of increase, $10 per year, has (dollars/year) as its unit of measurement. If this rate continued for dt years, where dt therefore has (years) as its unit of measurement, then

$$10\left(\dfrac{\text{dollars}}{\text{year}}\right) \cdot dt(\text{years}) = 10\,dt \text{ dollars},$$

so $10\,dt$ dollars represents the change in the amount owed in time dt years. Calling this change in amount owed dy, we write the differential equation

$$dy = 10\,dt$$

and its general solution is

$$\int dy = \int 10 \, dt$$
$$y = 10t + C$$
$$y(t) = 10t + C.$$

From the initial conditions, $y = 100$ at $t = 0$, we have

$$y(0) = 100 = 10(0) + C$$
$$100 = C$$

and the particular solution is

$$y(t) = 10t + 100.$$

Hence, at time $t = 3$ years, Smith will owe

$$y(3) = 10(3) + 100 = \$130.$$

Although the mode of thinking just illustrated is precise only when the rate function is linear, it will, nevertheless, lead to correct statements of differential equations, and we shall apply it in coming illustrations.

Example. A bank account contains \$5,000 now, at time $t = 0$, and yields interest at the rate of 6% (0.06) per year, compounded **continuously**. How much will the account contain at $t = 5$ years?

The consequence of continuous compounding is that at any point t in time, the amount in the account at that time $A(t)$ or A is increasing at the rate of 6 percent of that amount, or $0.06A$.

At a rate of

$$0.06A$$

per year, the change in the amount in the account, in dt years, is $0.06A \, dt$, and this change in A is dA. Thus,

$$dA = 0.06A \, dt.$$

We proceed to separate the variables and integrate.

$$\frac{dA}{A} = 0.06 \, dt$$
$$\int \frac{dA}{A} = 0.06 \int dt$$
$$\ln A = 0.06t + C$$
$$A = e^{0.06t + C}$$
$$A = e^{0.06t}(e^C)$$
$$A = Ke^{0.06t}.$$

The general solution of the differential equation is

$$A(t) = Ke^{0.06t}.$$

To evaluate K, we apply the initial condition $A(0) = \$5,000$.

$$A(0) = 5,000 = Ke^{0.06(0)}$$
$$5,000 = Ke^0$$
$$5,000 = K.$$

The particular solution is

$$A(t) = 5,000e^{0.06t},$$

so at $t = 5$, we have

$$A(5) = 5,000e^{0.06(5)}$$
$$= 5,000(e^{0.3})$$
$$= 5,000(1.349858808)$$
$$= \$6,749.29.$$

> **Exercise.** If the account in the preceding started with P dollars rather than \$5,000, and interest rate i instead of 0.06, what would be the expression for the particular solution?
>
> **Answer:** $A(t) = Pe^{it}$.

It should be noted that in Chapter 6 this formula was derived by much more laborious means.

Example. An oil company and a farmer upon whose land a well has been drilled agree that the farmer shall receive a royalty of \$2 per barrel of oil produced. The company wishes to pay for a year's output in a lump sum at the year's end. However, the farmer argues that a year's production does not occur all at once at the end of the year, but is spread out uniformly during the year. Consequently, asserts the farmer, his royalty income is generated **continuously** throughout the year but held by the company until the end of the year, and that he should receive interest. Because the flow is continuous, the company agrees to pay interest at the rate of 6 percent per year, compounded continuously, and consider the flow of royalty as being continuous. If the well produces 10,000 barrels in a year, what should the farmer's royalty be?

At the outset, we state that this example contains an idea that may be hard to grasp, and that is the idea of a continuous flow of royalties being compounded continuously. To sort the pieces out, we recall from the last example that whatever the amount A or $A(t)$ is in the account at time t years, that amount will grow at the rate of $0.06A$ dollars per year and in dt years will increase by $0.06A\,dt$ dollars. Next we note that 10,000 barrels per year at \$2 royalty per barrel is a royalty inflow at the rate of \$20,000 per year, which is $20,000\,dt$ dollars in dt years. Hence, there are two components of increase; $(0.06A)\,dt$ and $20,000\,dt$. The change in the royalty account in dt years is, therefore,

$$dA = (0.06A)\,dt + 20,000\,dt.$$

We proceed to solve the last differential equation:

$$dA = (0.06A + 20,000)\,dt$$

$$\frac{dA}{0.06A + 20,000} = dt$$

$$\int \frac{dA}{0.06A + 20,000} = \int dt$$

$$\frac{\ln(0.06A + 20,000)}{0.06} = t + C_1$$

$$\ln(0.06A + 20,000) = 0.06t + 0.06C_1$$

$$= 0.06t + C$$

$$0.06A + 20,000 = e^{0.06t + C}$$

$$= (e^{0.06t})(e^C)$$

$$= Ke^{0.06t}$$

$$0.06A = Ke^{0.06t} - 20,000$$

$$A = \frac{Ke^{0.06t} - 20,000}{0.06}$$

which is an explicit general solution. As to initial conditions, we recall that royalties accumulate from zero at the start of the year, $t = 0$, to the amount at the end of the year. Hence, $A = 0$ at $t = 0$, so

$$A(0) = 0 = \frac{Ke^0 - 20,000}{0.06}$$

$$0 = K(1) - 20,000$$

$$20,000 = K.$$

The particular solution is

$$A = A(t) = \frac{20,000e^{0.06t} - 20,000}{0.06}$$

$$= \frac{20,000(e^{0.06t} - 1)}{0.06}.$$

Consequently, at the end of the year, $t = 1$, the farmer should receive

$$A(1) = \frac{20{,}000(e^{0.06} - 1)}{0.06}$$

$$= \frac{20{,}000(1.061836547 - 1)}{0.06}$$

$$= \$20{,}612.18,$$

which is about \$612 more than a lump sum end-of-the-year payment of \$20,000.

If, in the last example, money flowed in at the rate of R dollars per year rather than \$20,000, and the interest rate was i rather than 0.06, the expression

$$A(t) = \frac{20{,}000(e^{0.06t} - 1)}{0.06}$$

would turn out to be

$$A(t) = \frac{R(e^{it} - 1)}{i},$$

which is the **formula for a continuous flow of money compounded continuously.**

Example. Suppose that a country has \$200 million worth of its old one-dollar bills in circulation and that an average of \$2 million worth of one-dollar bills flow through the country's banks each banking day. Starting today, $t = 0$ days, old bills appearing at banks are destroyed and replaced by new one-dollar bills. a) Find the expression for the amount of new currency in circulation at time t banking days. b) How much new currency will be in circulation after 50 banking days?

The key point to note in solving this problem is that even though two million one-dollar bills appear at banks each day, on the average, at any point in time except $t = 0$, not all of these bills will be old bills. For example, at the time when half the old bills have been replaced, only one million of the two million bills appearing will be old bills. Thus, the rate at which old bills appears is a function of t, and is a fraction of \$2 million per day. To construct this fraction, we let $N(t)$, or N, be the number (in millions) of **new** bills, in circulation at time t. Then, since we started with 200 million old bills, the number of old bills in circulation is $200 -$ (number of new bills),

$$\text{Number of old bills in circulation} = 200 - N.$$

The total number in circulation remains at 200 million. Hence,

$$\text{Proportion of old bills in circulation} = \frac{200 - N}{200}.$$

Taking this proportion of the total 2 million per day appearing at banks, we have for the rate of increase in the number of new bills, per day:

$$\frac{200 - N}{200} (2) \text{ million per day}$$

$$= \frac{200 - N}{100} \text{ million per day.}$$

Consequently, the change dN in new bills in dt days will be

$$dN = \frac{200 - N}{100} dt.$$

We now solve the last differential equation, as follows:

$$\frac{dN}{200 - N} = \frac{dt}{100} = 0.01\, dt$$

$$\int \frac{dN}{200 - N} = \int 0.01\, dt$$

$$-\ln(200 - N) = 0.01t + C$$

$$\ln(200 - N) = -0.01t - C$$

$$200 - N = e^{-0.01t - C}$$

$$= (e^{-C})(e^{-0.01t})$$

$$200 - N = Ke^{-0.01t}$$

$$-N = Ke^{-0.01t} - 200$$

$$N = 200 - Ke^{-0.01t}$$

or

$$N(t) = 200 - Ke^{-0.01t}$$

becomes the explicit general solution. At time $t = 0$, no new bills are in circulation, so the initial condition is $N(0) = 0$. Thus,

$$N(0) = 0 = 200 - Ke^0$$

$$0 = 200 - K$$

$$K = 200.$$

Hence,

$$N(t) = 200 - 200e^{-0.01t}$$

$$N(t) = 200(1 - e^{-0.01t})$$

is the explicit particular solution. To find the number of new bills in circulation at time $t = 50$ banking days, we compute

$$N(50) = 200[1 - e^{-0.01(50)}]$$

$$= 200(1 - e^{-0.5})$$

$$= 200(1 - 0.60653066)$$

$$\approx \$78.69 \text{ million.}$$

FROM THEORY TO PRACTICE
Dynamic Modelling and Difference Equations

Dynamic modelling is the process of translating situations involving changing quantities into mathematical relationships. In the case where we express these relationships as differential equations, we deal with continuous functions which have derivatives that express a **rate of change over time**. Another way to design the model is to assume that change occurs in **jumps**. When we make this assumption, we develop discrete models which involve equations called **difference equations**.

For example, the standard exponential growth model in differential equations is given by

$$\frac{dy}{dt} = r \cdot y.$$

This equation says that the rate of change of the population is a constant multiple, r, of the size of the population, y. Separating variables and solving, we obtain

$$\frac{dy}{y} = r \cdot dt$$

$$\ln y = rt + C$$

$$y = e^{rt+C} \quad \text{or} \quad y = ke^{rt}. \tag{1}$$

This equation is used to describe the unrestrained exponential growth of populations by biologists and sociologists.

Many populations, however, do not grow in a continuous manner. For example, plants which are seasonal would have a history of population growth that occurs in jumps. The same is true for animal species that breed at specified times during the year, or the growth of money when preagreed-to payments are made at specified times. In these cases, we would describe the model as

$$x_{n+1} - x_n = rx_n$$

where $x_{n+1} - x_n$ is the change in the population from generation n to generation $n + 1$. Again this change is a constant multiple, r, of the size of the population of generation n, namely x_n.

To solve a difference equation such as (1), we need an initial population size x_0. Then we find from (1) that

$$x_{n+1} = (1 + r) x_n$$

so

$$x_1 = (1 + r) x_0$$
$$x_2 = (1 + r) x_1 = (1 + r)^2 x_0$$
$$x_3 = (1 + r) x_2 = (1 + r)^3 x_0$$
$$\vdots$$
$$x_n = (1 + r)^n x_0. \tag{2}$$

(continued)

At first, Equations (1) and (2) look quite different. However, if we let $r = n/t$, we can rewrite (2) as

$$x_n = \left(1 + \frac{n}{t}\right)^{rt} x_0$$

$$x_n = \left[\left(1 + \frac{n}{t}\right)^t\right]^r x_0.$$

Now recall that

$$\lim_{t \to \infty} \left(1 + \frac{n}{t}\right)^t = e^n.$$

This indicates that the driving force of exponential growth is lingering in the background of the difference equation model.

The study of difference equations has received a great deal of attention in the last 25 years as ecologists, biologists, and mathematicians have become aware of the importance of understanding the interdependence and fragility of populations of the many species of living things on this earth. Difference equations enabled these scientists to develop a mathematical theory that describes the stability of various populations. More recently, new theories such as the **complexity theory** and the **chaos theory** have emerged, opening exciting new possibilities for modelling insights into the nature of the physical world in which we live.

All of the examples in this section have involved *time rates of change*, and while time rates are very common in practice and the coming problems will all involve time rates, we should not leave the impression that applications of differential equations are restricted to such rates. Thus, all of the marginals in economics (marginal cost, marginal propensity to consume, and so on) are rates not involving time and we could, if we wished to expand our examples, pose problems in terms of these marginals.

10.28 PROBLEM SET 10-12

1. Chris has just opened a sandwich shop and at time t days from opening expects to sell hamburgers at the rate of $150 + 6t$ per day.
   a) Represent total sales after t days by S or $S(t)$ and set up the relevant differential equation.
   b) What are the initial conditions?
   c) Find the particular solution of the differential equation.
   d) How many hamburgers will Chris sell in the first 50 days?
   e) How long will it take for Chris to sell 45,000 hamburgers?

2. (See Problem 1.) At time t days, Chris expects to sell hot dogs at the rate of $100 + 2t$ per day.
   a) Set up the relevant differential equation.
   b) What are the initial conditions?
   c) Find the particular solution of the differential equation.
   d) How many hot dogs will Chris sell in the first 50 days?

10.28 PROBLEM SET 10-12 (concluded)

e) How long will it take for Chris to sell 60,000 hot dogs?

3. Population of a town now, at $t = 0$ years, is 100,000. At any time t years, population grows at a per-year rate which is 10 percent of the population at that time.
   a) Set up the relevant differential equation, using $P(t)$ or P as population at time t years.
   b) Find the particular solution of the differential equation.
   c) Compute population 10 years from now.

4. Now, at time $t = 0$, $2,000 is deposited in a bank account that yields interest at 5 percent per year. Interest is compounded continuously, so that at any point t years in time, the amount in the account grows at an annual rate that is 5 percent of the amount in the account at that time. Let $S(t)$, or S, be the amount in the account at time t years.
   a) Set up the relevant differential equation.
   b) Find the particular solution of the equation.
   c) Compute the amount in the account 20 years from now.

5. A bank account now, at $t = 0$ years, contains $2,000. Interest, at an annual rate of 8 percent per year, is compounded continuously so that at any time t, the account will increase at the annual rate of 8 percent of the amount in the account at that time. Moreover, money is to be added to the account at a rate of $500 per year. The addition is to be thought of as a continuous flow so that $500 per year is $500 dt in dt years.
   a) Let A or $A(t)$ be the amount in the account at time t years and set up the relevant differential equation.
   b) Find the particular solution of the differential equation.
   c) How much will the account contain 10 years from now?
   d) How long will it take for the account balance to grow to $18,500?

6. (See Problem 5.) A bank account now, at $t = 0$ years, contains $5,000. Interest, at an annual rate of 8 percent, is compounded continuously. However, money is to be withdrawn from the account continuously at the rate of $500 per year.
   a) Set up the relevant differential equation.
   b) Find the particular solution of the equation.
   c) How much will the account contain 10 years from now?
   d) How many years will it take to reduce the account balance to zero?

7. The total supply of a fuel available now and in the future is 200 million barrels. At the present moment, $t = 0$, none of this total supply has been consumed. At time t years, the fuel is being consumed at the rate of
$$5e^{0.01t}$$
billion barrels per year. Let C, or $C(t)$, be the amount consumed at time t years.
   a) Set up the relevant differential equation.
   b) Find the particular solution of the equation.
   c) Compute the total amount of fuel which will be consumed in the next 10 years.
   d) How long will the fuel supply last?

8. Solve Problem 7 if annual consumption of the fuel at time t is at the rate of $5e^{0.02t}$ million barrels per year.

10.29 REVIEW PROBLEMS

Write the expression for the indefinite integral. Simplify results where possible. Express answers with positive exponents.

1. $\int dq$.
2. $\int dp$.
3. $\int k\, dx$.
4. $\int 5\, dz$.
5. $\int (1 + y^2)\, dy$.
6. $\int (2 + 3p^2)\, dp$.

10.29 REVIEW PROBLEMS (continued)

7. $\int (a + bx)\, dx.$
8. $\int (1 + cx)\, dx.$
9. $\int (12(2x^2 - x^3 + 3x + 2)\, dx.$
10. $\int 6(10x^4 - 8x^3 + 6x^2 + 4x + 3)\, dx.$
11. $\int (x^{2/3} + 2x^{-3/2})\, dx.$
12. $\int \left(x^2 - \dfrac{1}{x^2}\right) dx.$
13. $\int \left(1 + \dfrac{2}{x^3} + \dfrac{4}{x^{1/2}}\right) dx.$
14. $\int \left(1 - \dfrac{2}{x^{2/3}}\right) dx.$
15. $\int 30(3x - 5)^4\, dx.$
16. $\int \dfrac{15\, dx}{(7 - 5x)^2}.$
17. $\int \dfrac{6\, dx}{(8 - 3x)^{4/3}}.$
18. $\int 12(4x - 9)^{2/3}\, dx.$

Evaluate the following definite integrals:

19. $\displaystyle\int_1^5 dx.$
20. $\displaystyle\int_2^5 (1 + x)\, dx.$
21. $\displaystyle\int_1^{16} x^{3/4}\, dx.$
22. $\displaystyle\int_1^2 \left(3 + 4x + \dfrac{10}{x^2}\right) dx.$
23. $\displaystyle\int_2^3 \dfrac{12\, dx}{(3x - 5)^3}.$
24. $\displaystyle\int_0^6 \dfrac{dx}{(0.5x + 1)^2}.$

Express the definite integral in terms of its limits, simplifying where possible.

25. $\displaystyle\int_a^{2a} \left(\dfrac{x}{a} + \dfrac{a}{x^2}\right) dx.$
26. $\displaystyle\int_0^b \dfrac{ab}{(ax + b)^2}\, dx.$

Find the area under the curve of the following functions over the given x-intervals:

27. $f(x) = (8x + 4)^{1/2}$, $x = 0$ to $x = 4$.
28. $f(x) = \dfrac{20}{(0.5x + 4)^2}$, $x = 2$ to $x = 12$.

Find the areas described in each of the following problems. (Sketches will be helpful.)

29. Find area bounded by the axes and
$$f(x) = 10 - 0.2x.$$

30. Find the area bounded by an axis and
$$f(x) = 60x - 12x^2 - 48.$$

31. Find the area bounded by the x-axis and
$$f(x) = 3x - x^2 + 18.$$

32. Find the area bounded by
$$f(x) = 19 - x \quad \text{and} \quad g(x) = 25 - x^2.$$

33. Maintenance cost on newly purchased equipment is expected to be at the rate of $(1 + 0.2t)$ thousand dollars per year at time t years.

a) Compute total maintenance cost during the first five years.

10.29 REVIEW PROBLEMS (continued)

b) Make a sketch showing what was computed in (a).
c) Compute maintenance cost during the second five years.
d) At what time, t, will the total spent on maintenance reach $20 thousand?

34. At time t years, an industry consumes fuel at the rate of $(1 + 0.3t)$ million barrels per year. How much fuel will the industry consume in the next 9 years?

35. At time t years, sales of a currently new product are expected to be at the rate of

$$\frac{5}{(0.4t + 1)^{1/2}}$$

million dollars per year. How many years will it take for total sales to amount to $20 million?

36. Selling expense has a fixed component of $5,000 per year, each year, and a variable component estimated to be at the rate of $(10 + 0.1t)$ thousand dollars per year at time t years. Estimate total selling expense for the next four years.

37. Sales of a product are projected to be at the rate of $(81 - 3t)^{1/2}$ thousand tons per year at time t years. Find total sales during the next 24 years.

38. Sales of a product are projected to take place at the rate of $(0.9t + 9)^{1/2}$ thousand tons per year at time t years. Find total sales during the next 30 years.

39. When t tons of steel are produced, marginal cost in dollars per ton is

$$0.003t^2 - 0.4t + 25.$$

If fixed cost is $1,000, find the total cost of producing 200 tons.

40. A fixed cost of $20,000 was incurred in setting up an operation. At time t months thereafter, income and expense are at the rates, respectively, of $(4,100 - 100t^{1/2})$ and $(500 + 260t^{1/2})$ dollars per month.
a) What is the optimal time to terminate the operation?
b) What will total profit be at the optimal time of termination?

41. The demand function for a product is

$$p_d(q) = \frac{100}{(0.2q + 1)^2},$$

where q is in millions of gallons and $p_d(q)$ is in dollars per gallon. Market equilibrium occurs at a demand of 20 million gallons. Compute consumers' surplus.

42. The supply and demand functions for a product are

$$p_s(q) = 2 + 0.06q \text{ and}$$
$$p_d(q) = 10 - 0.02q.$$

a) Find the equilibrium market price.
b) Compute producers' surplus.
c) Compute consumers' surplus.
d) Sketch a graph containing both the supply and demand functions. Show by two different shadings which area represents producers' surplus and which represents consumers' surplus.

Carry out the following, simplifying where possible:

43. $\int \frac{3}{x} dx.$

44. $\int \frac{dx}{2x + 3}.$

45. $\int 2(5x + 4)^{-1} dx.$

46. $\int \left(\frac{1}{0.5x + 10}\right) dx.$

47. $\int_0^{10} 6(2x + 3)^{-1} dx.$

48. $\int_5^{50} \frac{dx}{0.2x + 1}.$

49. If new fuel reserves are discovered at the rate of

$$\frac{40}{0.25t + 1}$$

million tons per year at time t years, find the amount of fuel that will be discovered in the next 20 years.

10.29 REVIEW PROBLEMS (continued)

50. The demand function for a product is

$$p_d(q) = \frac{40}{0.2q + 3},$$

where q is in millions of gallons and $p_d(q)$ is in dollars per gallon. Market equilibrium occurs at a demand of 10 million gallons. Compute consumers' surplus.

Carry out the following, simplifying where possible:

51. $\int 6e^{2x+5} \, dx.$
52. $\int e^{-0.5x+1} \, dx.$
53. $\int 2^x \, dx.$
54. $\int 3^{0.5x} \, dx.$
55. $\int_5^{10} e^{0.2x-1} \, dx.$
56. $\int \frac{2 \, dx}{e^{0.5x-1}}.$
57. $\int 10(0.5)^x \, dx.$
58. $\int_1^2 10^x (\ln 10) \, dx.$

---

59. At time t years, interest on a bank account is accumulating at the rate of

$$800e^{0.08t}$$

dollars per year.
a) What will total interest accumulation be in five years?
b) How long will it take for interest accumulation to reach \$10,000?

60. The supply function for a product is

$$p_s(q) = 2 + e^{0.01q}$$

where q is in millions of pounds and $p_s(q)$ is in dollars per pound. Market equilibrium occurs at a demand of 100 million pounds. Compute producers' surplus.

Carry out the following, simplifying where possible:

61. $\int 5 (\ln x) \, dx.$
62. $\int \ln (5x) \, dx.$
63. $\int \ln (0.3x + 5) \, dx.$
64. $\int \ln (10x + 3) \, dx.$
65. $\int_1^5 10 (\ln x) \, dx.$
66. $\int_0^4 \ln (5x + 7) \, dx.$

---

67. At a rate t years from now, production of a food is projected to occur at a rate of $8 \ln (0.5t + 4)$ million bushels per year. Find total production during the next 12 years.

Carry out the following, simplifying results where possible:

68. $\int 4xe^{1-0.25x^2} \, dx.$
69. $\int \frac{6 \, dx}{3 + 5e^{2x}}.$
70. $\int \frac{4 \, dx}{x(0.4x + 3)}.$

10.29 REVIEW PROBLEMS (continued)

71. $\int \dfrac{2x\,dx}{0.5x + 9}$.

72. $\int 3xe^{5-0.1x}\,dx$.

73. $\int 3x(5^x)\,dx$.

74. $\int \dfrac{9x\,dx}{(3x + 2)^2}$.

75. $\int 5xe^{-0.4x}\,dx$.

76. $\int_0^{\infty} 10e^{-0.5x}\,dx$.

77. $\int_1^{\infty} 20x^{-5/4}\,dx$.

78. $\int_0^{\infty} \dfrac{2\,dx}{(0.2x + 1)^2}$.

79. $\int_1^{\infty} \dfrac{30\,dx}{x^3}$.

Approximate the following by the sum of the areas on n trapezoids. (Trapezoidal rule.)

80. $\int_0^3 \ln(x^2 + 1)\,dx$; $n = 6$.

81. $\int_0^2 e^{0.5x^2 - 0.3}\,dx$; $n = 5$.

Apply integration by parts and carry out the following:

82. $\int xe^x\,dx$.

83. $\int \dfrac{xe^x\,dx}{(1 + x)^2}$.

Find the explicit general solution of each of the following differential equations:

84. $dy + dx = 0$.

85. $3y^2\,dy - 2x\,dx = 0$.

86. $x^2\,dy - dx = 0$.

87. $x^2\,dy - y^2\,dx = 0$.

88. $x\,dy + 2\,dx = 0$.

89. $(2x + 3)\,dy = dx$.

Find the explicit particular solution for the following, using the stated initial conditions:

90. $dy - 2x\,dx = 0$; $y = 25$ when $x = 5$.

91. $x^2\,dy - y^2\,dx = 0$; $y = 1.8$ when $x = 18$.

92. $dy - y\,dx = 0$; $y = 10$ when $x = 0$.

93. $dy - (0.4y + 3)\,dx = 0$; $y = 2.5$ when $x = 0$.

---

94. Chris has just opened a pizza shop and at time t days from opening expects to sell pizzas at the rate of $50 + 2t$ per day.
   a) Represent total sales after t days by S or $S(t)$ and set up the relevant differential equation for $dS(t)$.
   b) What are the initial conditions?
   c) Find the particular solution of the differential equation.
   d) How many pizzas will Chris sell in the first 20 days?
   e) How long will it take for Chris to sell 3,600 pizzas?

95. A bank account now, at $t = 0$ years, contains \$1,000. Interest accrues at the annual rate of 6 percent per year, but is compounded continuously so that at any time t, the account will increase at the annual rate of 6 percent of the amount in the account at that time. Moreover, money is to be added to the account at the rate of \$300 per year. The addition is to be thought

10.29 REVIEW PROBLEMS (concluded)

of as a continuous flow, so that $300 per year is ($300 dt) in dt years.
a) Let A or $A(t)$ be the amount in the account at time t years and set up the relevant differential equation.
b) Find the particular solution of the differential equation.
c) How much will be in the account 10 years from now?

10.30 EXTENDED REVIEW PROBLEMS

1. Determine the following integral, simplify, and leave no negative exponents
$$\int \frac{5\, dx}{x\sqrt{16 - 25x^2}}, \quad 0 < x < 4/5.$$

2. Find the explicit general solution of the differential equation
$$dy - 0.4x(5y + 4)\, dx = 0.$$

3. Determine the following integral
$$\int \frac{5x\, dx}{\sqrt{7 - 2x}}.$$
   a) Using u-substitution.
   b) Using integration by parts.
   c) Show that the answers to (a) and (b) are identical.

4. Determine the following integral, simplify, and leave no negative exponents
$$\int \frac{3\, dx}{(9 - 2x)^{6/5}}.$$

5. Find the first-quadrant area bounded by an axis and the two functions
$$f(x) = x^2 \quad \text{and} \quad g(x) = \frac{x^2}{2} + 2.$$

6. Approximate the following definite integral by the area of 4 trapezoids
$$\int_0^2 \frac{dx}{\sqrt{4 + x^3}}.$$

7. The population of a trading area is currently 100 thousand. At time t years from now, population will be growing at the rate of
$$\frac{20}{(0.5t + 9)^{1/2}}$$
thousand per year. How long will it take for population to reach 260 thousand?

8. The total supply of a fuel available now and in the future is 200 billion barrels. At time t years from now, fuel will be consumed at the rate of
$$2e^{0.08t}$$
billion barrels per year.
   a) How much fuel will be consumed in the next 10 years?
   b) How long will the fuel supply last?

9. A trading area has 20,000 potential customers for a new product and an advertising promotion is planned to sell the product. $R(t)$ is the total number of potential customers who will have responded to the promotion at time t days. At time t days, responses occur at the daily rate of 2 percent of those who have **not** responded.
   a) Write the relevant differential equation for $dR(t)$.
   b) What are the initial conditions?
   c) Find the explicit particular solution of the differential equation.
   d) How many of the potential customers will have responded at $t = 10$ days?
   e) How many days will it take before 10,000 have responded?

10. Determine the following integral using integration by parts.
$$\int x^2 e^x\, dx.$$

INTRODUCTION TO PROBABILITY WITH APPLICATIONS

CHAPTER 11
Counting and Probability

CHAPTER 12
Probability Distributions

Managers and firms must make decisions on a regular basis. These decisions are made in one of two types of situations. In the first type, a **deterministic situation**, all the information is known and the final decision has a strong degree of certainty. The amortization schedule for a mortgage in Part II is clearly deterministic. The concept of constrained optimization using linear programming we studied in Part I and the concept of unconstrained optimization using differential calculus we studied in Part III are also deterministic, since in both cases we used known values to generate a result that would enable us to make the best decision.

The other type of decision-making situation is called a **stochastic situation.** In this case, decisions are made with a degree of **uncertainty. Probability theory** is extremely helpful in developing techniques for handling stochastic situations. In Chapters 11 and 12, we first develop the elements of probability theory and then show how probability can be used to help solve stochastic problems that commonly occur in decision-making situations.

PART IV

FROM THEORY TO PRACTICE
The Monty Hall Problem

The Monty Hall problem is an example of a decision-making situation that lends itself to solution using probability theory. The name arises from the popular television show "Lets Make a Deal" hosted by Monty Hall. The problem can be explained as follows. You are given a choice of selecting one of three doors. Behind one is a sports car, but behind the other two are worthless prizes. You pick door 1 and then Monty Hall, who knows what is behind each door, opens door 3 revealing a worthless prize. He next proceeds to ask if you want to change your selection to door 2. The problem is simple. Will switching your choice improve your chances of winning the sports car?

Everyone would agree that the chance of picking the correct door initially was 1/3. But after Monty Hall has revealed a worthless prize behind door 3, are the odds that door 1 contains the sports car still 1/3 or have they changed to 1/2? Analyses of this decision-making problem have been presented by statisticians, educators, the general public, and the press. As early as 1975, articles in *American Statistician* discussed this problem. Then in 1990 the question was posed and answered in *Parade's* "Ask Marilyn" column. Marilyn Vos Savant claimed that switching doubled the contestant's chances of winning. Educators from many colleges and universities disagreed with Marilyn's analysis, so she followed up with a simple example of the old "shell game" to show that the odds remain at 1/3 for the door initially selected. She then went on to list all the possibilities for the three doors and show that when you switch you win two out of three times and lose one time in three, but when you don't switch you win only one in three times and lose two in three. More articles appeared in *Bostonia* in 1991. In 1992 the full analysis of the problem using **tree diagrams** and **conditional probabilities** appeared in *Mathematics and Computer Education.**

*John C. Hegarty, "Expanded Monty Hall Problem." *Mathematics and Computer Education* (Spring 1992).

CHAPTER 11: COUNTING AND PROBABILITY

11.1 INTRODUCTION

One of the most conspicuous characteristics of the stock and bond markets is their unpredictability. No one has found a totally reliable technique for predicting the day-to-day or month-to-month fluctuations of the stock market, but repeated observations of the markets' behaviors over long periods of time reveal discernible patterns.

Many other events in the world exhibit the same random character. In this chapter we introduce the study of probability, which is the branch of mathematics concerned with making rational predictions about phenomena with seemingly random behavior or an element of uncertainty.

Before we can compute probabilities, however, we need to have some knowledge about counting problems. We will first study two different fundamental types of counting problems: the problem of counting the number of elements in a set and the problem of counting the number of rearrangements of a given set of elements. Then we will use these counting techniques to develop the rules for computing probabilities.

11.2 COUNTING TECHNIQUES

Suppose we have conducted a survey of financial analysts' views of various investment opportunities and found that of 150 analysts surveyed, 60 are bullish on computer stocks and 72 are bullish on general merchandise chains such as Wal-Mart and J.C. Penney. In addition, 19 of those analysts surveyed are bullish on both computer stocks and general merchandise chains. How many analysts would you expect to invest in either computer stocks or general merchandise chains? In neither of the industries surveyed?

To understand this problem it is helpful to restate it in terms of **sets**.[1] Suppose we let

$\mathcal{U}$ = The universe of the 150 analysts surveyed,
C = Analysts who are bullish on computer stocks, and
G = Analysts who are bullish on general merchandise chains.

---
[1] For a complete review of sets, read Appendix 3.

Then using set operations, we are interested in

$C \cup G$ = Analysts bullish on either computer stocks or general merchandise chains or both, and

$C' \cap G'$ = Analysts bullish on neither industry.

Exercise. Why does $C' \cap G'$ represent the analysts expected to invest in neither of the industries surveyed?

Answer: Since C' is the complement of C (those analysts in $\mathcal{U}$ but not in C) and G' is the complement of G (those analysts in $\mathcal{U}$ but not in G), the intersection $C' \cap G'$ represents those analysts in $\mathcal{U}$ that are not in C and not in G (i.e., in neither one).

The sets $C \cup G$ and $C' \cap G'$ can be portrayed visually by the *Venn diagrams* shown in Figure 11–1.

Now if we use the notation $n(S)$ for the number of elements in a set S, then the given data becomes

$$n(\mathcal{U}) = 150,$$
$$n(C) = 60,$$
$$n(G) = 72, \text{ and}$$
$$n(C \cap G) = 19.$$

Recall that $C \cap G$ is the intersection of the two sets C and G, which is the overlapping area of the two circles in Figure 11–1.

To answer our first query, we need to determine $n(C \cup G)$ from the given data. But is not

$$n(C \cup G) = n(C) + n(G)?$$

FIGURE 11-1

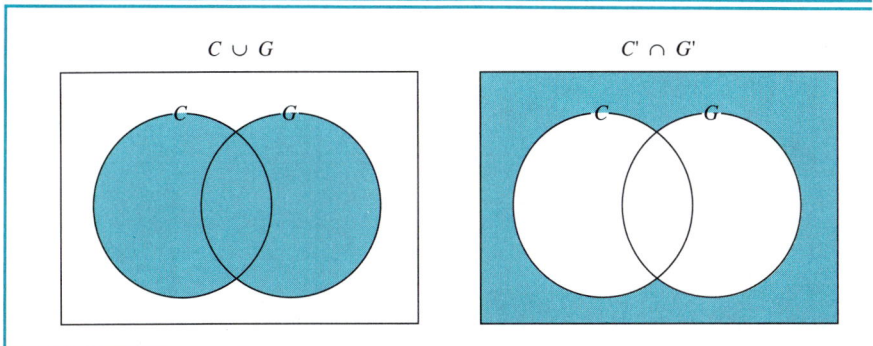

> When counting elements in a union of sets, be careful not to double count.

A closer look reveals that this expression does not take into account the fact that in counting $n(C)$ and $n(G)$, we have counted $n(C \cap G)$ twice. (A quick look at Figure 11–1 will help to confirm this.) To eliminate this double counting, we need to subtract the second counting of $C \cap G$.

> The number of elements in the union of two sets is the sum of the number in each individual set minus the number in their intersection.

Number of Elements in a Union of Two Sets

$$n(C \cup G) = n(C) + n(G) - n(C \cap G). \qquad (1)$$

Using Equation (1) for the given data, then,

$$n(C \cup G) = 60 + 72 - 19 = 113$$

so we would expect 113 analysts to invest in at least one of the two industries surveyed.

Now what about

$$n(C' \cap G')?$$

> The collection of elements in neither of two sets is the complement of the union of the sets.

A quick look at Figure 11–1 shows that $C' \cap G'$ is the complement of $C \cup G$ so that

$$n(C' \cap G') = n(\mathcal{U}) - n(C \cup G).$$

From the answer to our first query, then,

$$n(C' \cap G') = 150 - 113 = 37$$

so we would expect 37 analysts to invest in neither of the two industries surveyed.

An alternative approach to solving this example is by means of tables instead of Venn diagrams. A table gives a more complete picture than a Venn diagram and is especially helpful when more than two sets are involved. Another look at Figure 11–1 shows that the universal set is divided into four areas or **regions,** namely $C \cap G$ (the overlapping region of C and G), $C \cap G'$ (the left region of C), $C' \cap G$ (the right region of G), and $C' \cap G'$ (the region outside of both C and G). If we created a table to represent the number of elements in the universe $\mathcal{U}$ and its two sets C and G, it would appear as shown in Table 11–1. Note that this

> A Venn diagram for two sets divides the universe into four regions.

TABLE 11–1

	G	G'	Totals
C	$n(C \cap G)$	$n(C \cap G')$	$n(C)$
C'	$n(C' \cap G)$	$n(C' \cap G')$	$n(C')$
Totals	$n(G)$	$n(G')$	$n(\mathcal{U})$

table has **nine regions** in which to enter data, **five more than the Venn diagram** in Figure 11–1. Which five are these? They are the entries for the totals, namely the row totals $n(C)$ and $n(C')$, the column totals $n(G)$ and $n(G')$, and the grand total $n(\mathcal{U})$.

A table contains more regions than the corresponding Venn diagram. The extra regions of a table are for row and column totals.

Now returning to our given data for this example,

$$n(\mathcal{U}) = 150,$$
$$n(C) = 60,$$
$$n(G) = 72, \text{ and}$$
$$n(C \cap G) = 19,$$

we can insert all four values in Table 11–1 to arrive at Table 11–2.

Exercise. How many of the four given pieces of data could we insert in the Venn diagram of Figure 11–1? Where?

Answer: Only $n(C \cap G) = 19$ in the overlapping area of the two circles.

Now we can fill in the missing entries in Table 11–2 simply by subtracting the given entries from the given totals. For example, since $n(G) = 72$ and $n(C \cap G) = 19$,

$$n(C' \cap G) = 72 - 19 = 53.$$

Continuing in this way we get the results shown in Table 11–3.

TABLE 11–2

$\mathcal{U}$	G	G'	Totals
C	19		60
C'			
Totals	72		150

TABLE 11–3

$\mathcal{U}$	G	G'	Totals
C	19	41	60
C'	53	37	90
Totals	72	78	150

The missing tabular entries are determined by simple addition and subtraction of the given entries.

> **Exercise.** Verify the remaining entries in Table 11–3.

From Table 11–3 we see that

$$n(C \cup G) = n(C \cap G) + n(C \cap G') + n(C' \cap G)$$
$$= 19 + 41 + 53 = 113,$$

which is precisely the same result as before.

> **Exercise.** Using Table 11–3, verify that we also have
> $$n(C \cup G) = n(C) + n(G) - n(C \cap G) = 113.$$

Furthermore from Table 11–3 we can see directly that

$$n(C' \cap G') = 37.$$

A table gives more information than the corresponding Venn diagram.

This last result points out the advantage of the tabular approach. Also many other questions can now be answered directly. For example, if we wish to determine how many analysts would be expected to invest in computer stocks but not in general merchandise chains, we see from Table 11–3 that

$$n(C \cap G') = 41.$$

> **Exercise.** Determine the number of analysts that we would expect
> a) To invest in general merchandise chains but not in computer stocks.
> b) Not to invest solely in computer stocks.
> **Answer:** a) 53.   b) $19 + 53 + 37 = 109$.

Example. Suppose in the preceding survey of 150 analysts, 45 were found to be bullish on bank stocks. Of these 45, it was determined that 15 were also bullish on computer stocks and 22 were also bullish on general merchandise chains. Finally 24 analysts were not bullish on any of the three investments. How many analysts are bullish on all three investment opportunities?

First, we let

$$B = \{\text{Analysts bullish on bank stocks}\}.$$

Then the given data becomes

$$n(\mathcal{U}) = 150,$$
$$n(C) = 60,$$
$$n(G) = 72,$$
$$n(C \cap G) = 19,$$
$$n(B) = 45,$$
$$n(C \cap B) = 15,$$
$$n(G \cap B) = 22,$$
$$n(C' \cap G' \cap B') = 24,$$

and we wish to determine

$$n(C \cap G \cap B).$$

We could proceed with a Venn diagram as shown in Figure 11–2; but with the information available, we would only be able to fill in **one** region, namely

$$n(C' \cap G' \cap B').$$

Instead let's extend the tabular approach of Table 11–1 as shown in Table 11–4. Note that Table 11–4 allows us to identify 19 pieces of data rather than just the 8 in Figure 11–2.

If we enter the given data in Table 11–4 we get the results shown in Table 11–5. In this table the two circled bold entries are from

$$n(C \cap G) = n(C \cap G \cap B) + n(C \cap G \cap B') = 19,$$

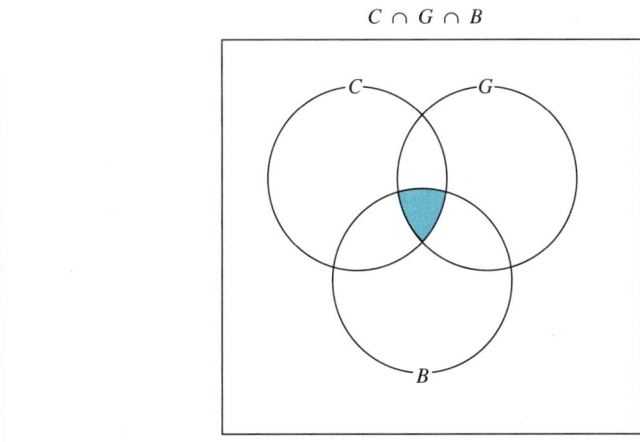

FIGURE 11–2

TABLE 11-4

$\mathcal{U}$	G		G'		Totals
	B	B'	B	B'	
C	$n(C \cap G \cap B)$	$n(C \cap G \cap B')$	$n(C \cap G' \cap B)$	$n(C \cap G' \cap B')$	$n(C)$
C'	$n(C' \cap G \cap B)$	$n(C' \cap G \cap B')$	$n(C' \cap G' \cap B)$	$n(C' \cap G' \cap B')$	$n(C')$
Totals	$n(G \cap B)$	$n(G \cap B')$	$n(G' \cap B)$	$n(G' \cap B')$	$n(\mathcal{U})$

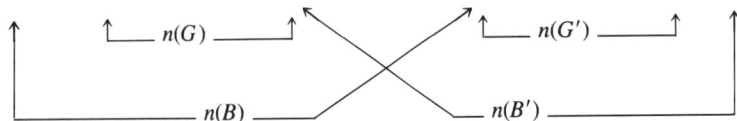

which is the sum of the first and second columns of the row for C, and

$$n(C \cap B) = n(C \cap G \cap B) + n(C \cap G' \cap B) = 15,$$

which is the sum of the first and third columns of the row for C. As before, we can fill in some of the missing entries of Table 11–5 by simple subtraction as shown in Table 11–6.

Now let's examine the C-row of Table 11–6. We see that

$$n(C) = 60,$$

the entry in the fourth column is

$$n(C \cap G' \cap B') = 31,$$

and the entries in the first and second columns sum to

$$n(C \cap G) = n(C \cap G \cap B) + n(C \cap G \cap B') = 19.$$

Thus the entry in the third column must be

$$n(C \cap G' \cap B) = 60 - (31 + 19) = 60 - 50 = 10.$$

> **Exercise.** What is the entry in the second column of the C-row?
> **Answer:** $n(C \cap G \cap B') = n(C) - [n(C \cap G' \cap B') + n(C \cap G')]$
> $= 60 - [31 + 15] = 14.$

Simple subtraction now yields the entry in the first column of the C-row

$$n(C \cap G \cap B) = 60 - (31 + 10 + 14) = 5.$$

TABLE 11-5

𝒰	G		G'		Totals
	B	B'	B	B'	
C	←⑲→		←⑮→		60
C'				24	
Totals	22				150

⌐ 72 ⌐
└── 45 ──┘

TABLE 11-6

𝒰	G		G'		Totals
	B	B'	B	B'	
C	←⑲→		←⑮→	31	60
C'				24	**90**
Totals	22	**50**	**23**	**55**	150

⌐ 72 ⌐
└── 45 ──┘

Filling in all the entries that have been generated so far gives us the results shown in Table 11–7 and the answer to the query of our example, namely five of the analysts are bullish on all three investment opportunities.

> **Exercise.** Fill in the missing entries of the C'-row of Table 11–7 and then determine the number of analysts who are bullish on a) General merchandise chains alone. b) Bank stocks alone. c) Either computer or bank stocks.
>
> **Answer:** 17, 36, 13. a) 36. b) 13. c) 90.

TABLE 11-7

$\mathcal{U}$	G		G'		Totals
	B	B'	B	B'	
C	5	14	10	31	60
C'				24	90
Totals	22	50	23	55	150

= **The Multiplication Principle**

Another very important counting technique is the so-called **multiplication principle** or **mn rule** for counting pairs of objects. Suppose, for example, you are considering the purchase of a microcomputer and printer. The microcomputer can have a monochrome or color monitor, while the printer can be either a dot-matrix, letter-quality, or laser printer. How many different configurations are there? Clearly we can put either of the two monitors together with any one of the three printers. This gives rise to

$$2 \cdot 3 = 6 \text{ configurations.}$$

This example illustrates the basic mn rule

The number of pairs of objects that can be formed taking the first object from a set with m objects and the second from a set with n objects is

$$m \cdot n.$$

The mn Rule

If we have two sets, the first with m objects and the second with n objects, then the number of pairs of objects that can be formed with one object from each set is

$$m \cdot n.$$

= **Exercise.** If in the preceding example there are additional choices of a high-resolution graphics monitor and a color laser printer, how many configurations are possible?

Answer: $3 \cdot 4 = 12.$

Tree diagrams, composed of branches extending from forks, are useful in visualizing counting problems.

A nice way to portray the preceding example visually is with a **tree diagram** as shown in Figure 11–3. In this figure there are 2 **branches** from the monitor **fork** and then 3 branches from each of the 2 printer forks, resulting in 6 branches corresponding to the 6 possible configurations.

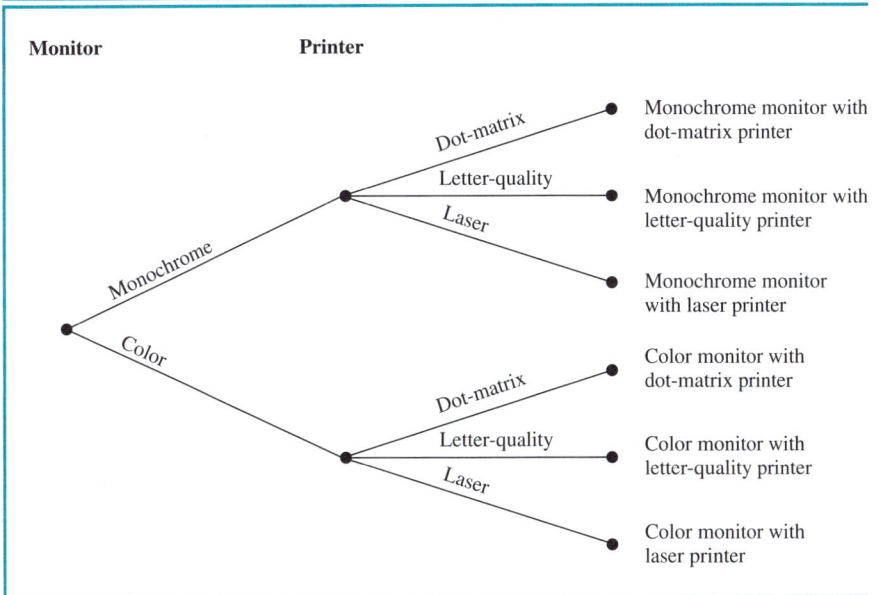

FIGURE 11-3

> **Exercise.** Draw the tree diagram associated with the preceding exercise.

Now the *mn* rule can be extended to three sets as is illustrated by the following example.

Example. In this expensive and competitive world of travel, there are many modes of travel we have to choose from. Usually we try to find the most efficient, comfortable, and economic choice. Suppose that the president of an import-export company wants to make a simple trip from the company's office in Boston to the office in Los Angeles. There are three ways to get from the Boston office to the airport: taxi, bus, and helicopter. Then there are three airlines that fly from Boston to Los Angeles. Finally, upon arrival in Los Angeles, there are two ways to travel to the office: limousine and taxi. How many different ways can the president's secretary arrange the trip?

The first leg of the trip (from the office to the airport in Boston) can be made in any one of three ways, the second leg of the trip (from the Boston airport to the Los Angeles airport) can be made in three ways, and the third leg of the trip (from the Los Angeles airport to the office) can be made in two ways. Thus the total number of possibilities is

$$3 \cdot 3 \cdot 2 = 18.$$

> **Exercise.** Draw the tree diagram associated with the preceding example.

The technique of the previous example can be generalized to any number of sets.

The number of objects that can be formed from k sets by taking the first object from a set with m_1 objects, the second from a set with m_2 objects, and so on, is

$$m_1 \cdot m_2 \cdot m_3 \cdot \ldots \cdot m_k.$$

> **Generalization of the mn Rule to k Sets**
>
> If we have k sets, the first with m_1 objects, the second with m_2 objects, the third with m_3 objects, and so on, then the number of objects that can be formed with one object from each set is
>
> $$m_1 \cdot m_2 \cdot m_3 \cdot \ldots \cdot m_k.$$

Example. How many different Social Security numbers can be issued by the U.S. government, excluding the number 000-00-0000?

A Social Security number consists of nine numbers, each of which can be any one of the **decimal digits** 0, 1, 2, . . . , 9. Thus there are

$$10 \cdot 10 \cdot 10 \cdot 10 \cdot 10 \cdot 10 \cdot 10 \cdot 10 \cdot 10 = 10^9$$

total possibilities. However, since we want to exclude the number 000-00-0000, there are precisely

$$10^9 - 1 = 999,999,999$$

possible Social Security numbers that can be issued.

> **Exercise.** Electronic garage door openers are coded by setting each of eight switches either on or off. How many different settings are possible if we exclude all switches being on or all being off?
> **Answer:** $2^8 - 2 = 254$.

11.3 PERMUTATIONS AND COMBINATIONS

In this section we will extend the techniques of the preceding section to counting the number of rearrangements of a given set of elements. We will investigate two different counting problems: in the first the order of the elements is important (commonly called **permutations**), while in the second the order it not important (commonly called **combinations**).

As a simple example of the difference between permutations and combinations, suppose we have two books, b_1 and b_2, and we place them on a bookshelf. If the order is important, then there are two ways of arranging the books:

$$b_1 b_2 \quad \text{or} \quad b_2 b_1.$$

On the other hand if the order is not important, then the two arrangements just specified are indistinguishable so that, for all practical purposes, there is only one way to place the two books on the bookshelf.

Now that we understand the distinction between permutations and combinations, we will develop counting rules for each. The following example will help us determine the counting rule for permutations.

Permutations are concerned with selections of objects where order is important; combinations are concerned with selections of objects where order is not important.

Example. A security system keypad has six keys labeled $a, b, c, d, e,$ and f. How many three-letter codes are possible if we do not allow any letter to be repeated? If repetition is allowed?

If no letters can be repeated, then by the generalized mn rule of the preceding section the first letter can be chosen in six ways, the second in five ways, and the third in four ways so we have

$$6 \cdot 5 \cdot 4 = 120$$

possible codes.

If the letters can be repeated, then this time by the generalized mn rule we have

$$6 \cdot 6 \cdot 6 = 216$$

possible codes.

Permutations are counted using the generalized mn rule.

> **Exercise.** Resolve the preceding example if four-letter codes are to be used.
> **Answer:** There are 360 codes if no repetition is allowed and 1,296 if repetition is allowed.

Determining the number of three-letter security codes with no repetitions in the preceding example is equivalent to determining the number of permutations of six objects taken three at a time. Generalizing the result of the example, we have the following definition and counting rule for permutations:

A permutation is a selection where order is important.

> **Definition**
> The number of **permutations** of n distinct objects taken r at a time is the number of all possible groups of r objects that can be selected from the original set of n objects with **order important** and is denoted by $P(n, r)$.

The number of permutations (arrangements) of n objects taken r at a time with order important is

$$P(n, r) = \frac{n!}{(n - r)!}$$

Counting Rule for Permutations

$$P(n, r) = n(n - 1)(n - 2) \cdots (n - r + 1) = \frac{n!}{(n - r)!}$$

where $n! = n(n - 1)(n - 2) \cdots (3)(2)(1)$ and $0! = 1$.

Using this counting rule for our preceding example, we have that the number of possible three-letter security codes with no letter repeated is

$$P(6, 3) = \frac{6!}{(6 - 3)!} = \frac{6!}{3!}$$
$$= \frac{(6)(5)(4)(3)(2)(1)}{(3)(2)(1)}$$
$$= (6)(5)(4) = 120,$$

which is precisely the same result as before.

Some calculators are preprogrammed with the $n!$ function. On such a calculator, the preceding example is solved as shown in Table 11–8.

Other calculators are preprogrammed with the statistical functions. On these calculators the preceding example is solved as shown in Table 11–9.

Exercise. Resolve the preceding exercise for four-letter security codes with no letter repeated using the counting rule for permutations.

Answer: $P(6, 4) = \frac{6!}{2!} = (6)(5)(4)(3) = 360.$

Now let's see what happens when the order is not important. For example, suppose that 6 members of a squash club have signed up to play for a league team to be comprised of 3 players. How many different teams can be chosen? If we designate the possible team players as a, b, c, d, e, and f, then a team will consist of selecting 3 distinct letters from this set of 6. As we saw with our security system example there are

$$6 \cdot 5 \cdot 4 = 120$$

ways to choose a team of 3, but some of these choices will constitute the same team. Specifically, if a, b, and c are chosen as a 3-member team, then

$$abc, \quad acb, \quad bac, \quad bca, \quad cab, \quad \text{and} \quad cba$$

are **6 possible permutations of this same three-member team.** Obviously the members of any 3-member team selected can be arranged in 6 different ways so

TABLE 11–8

Keystroke	Calculator Display
6, then n!	720
÷	720
3, then n!	6
=	120

TABLE 11–9

Keystroke	Calculator Display
6, then INPUT	6
3, then Pn,r	120

that there are

$$\frac{120}{6} = 20$$

possible different 3-member squash teams. Note in the last expression that the numerator is $P(6, 3) = 120$, the number of ways of selecting 3 objects from a group of 6 objects where order is important. The denominator is $P(3, 3) = (3)(2)(1) = 3! = 6$, the number of ways of rearranging the 3 objects.

Exercise. How many four-member squash teams could be selected from the six squash players?

Answer: $\frac{P(6, 4)}{P(4, 4)} = \frac{360}{4!} = \frac{360}{24} = 15.$

Generalizing the result of the preceding example, we have the following definition and counting rule for combinations:

Definition

The number of **combinations** of n distinct objects taken r at a time is the number of all possible selections of the n objects taken in groups of r with **order disregarded** and is denoted by $C(n, r)$.

A combination is a selection where order is not important.

The number of combinations of n objects taken r at a time with order disregarded is

$$C(n,r) = \frac{n!}{r!(n-r)!}.$$

Counting Rule for Combinations

$$C(n, r) = \frac{P(n, r)}{P(r, r)} = \frac{P(n, r)}{r!} = \frac{n!}{r!(n-r)!}.$$

Using this counting rule for our preceding example, we have that the number of possible 3-member squash teams is

$$C(6, 3) = \frac{6!}{3!(6-3)!} = \frac{6!}{3!3!} = \frac{(6)(5)(4)(3!)}{(3)(2)(1)(3!)} = \frac{(6)(5)(4)}{(3)(2)(1)} = 20.$$

On a calculator with preprogrammed statistical functions, we would solve the preceding example as shown in Table 11–10.

Exercise. Resolve the preceding exercise for 4-member squash teams using the counting rule for combinations.

Answer: $C(6, 4) = \dfrac{6!}{4!2!} = \dfrac{(6)(5)}{(2)(1)} = 15.$

Example. In the game of blackjack or 21, each player is dealt a hand with 2 cards. How many 2-card hands are possible from a standard deck of 52 cards?

Here we want to select any 2 cards from the deck of 52 and order is clearly not important. Thus the number of 2-card hands is

$$C(52, 2) = \frac{52!}{2!(52-2)!} = \frac{52!}{2!50!} = \frac{(52)(51)}{(2)(1)} = 1{,}326.$$

TABLE 11–10

Keystroke	Calculator Display
6, then INPUT	6
3, then Cn,r	20

Exercise. In the game of poker, each player is dealt a hand with 5 cards. How many 5-card hands are possible from a standard deck of 52 cards?

Answer: $C(52, 5) = \dfrac{52!}{5!47!} = \dfrac{(52)(51)(50)(49)(48)}{(5)(4)(3)(2)(1)} = 2{,}598{,}960.$

FROM THEORY TO PRACTICE
The Lottery Syndicate*

Many states have instituted lotteries as a means of generating revenues to help pay for growing state, city, and town expenses. Typically there will be a daily numbers game, instant card games, and weekly lotteries. The prize money is then distributed to the winner(s) over a 20-year period in equal installments—often taxes are withheld in advance. The dream of the everyday player is to buy a $1 ticket and win the $1 million jackpot.

When there are no winners for several weeks, the lottery jackpot continues to grow accordingly. The larger the jackpot, the more tickets are purchased. Many people have formed groups to purchase large numbers of tickets in the hope of getting a winning ticket. Sometimes the jackpot reaches a level—$25 million, $50 million, or $100 million—that draws national and even international attention.

On one such occasion in 1992, an international group known as the Lotto Fund attempted to buy every possible 6-number combination in an effort to win the lottery. The Lotto Fund was an Australian group which in a 1968 Australian lottery, had purchased all 3.8 million combinations on a lottery. What if it had accidentally missed the winning ticket? Soon after that Australia passed a law forbidding groups to resell lottery tickets for profit. For the February 15, 1992, drawing of the lottery in Virginia, the estimated jackpot was $27 million. The Lotto Fund picked Virginia because it has a 44-number lottery and 7,059,052 6-number combinations are possible, whereas 13,983,816 are possible in Florida's 49-number lottery. The group arranged with some retail chains to purchase bulk quantities of tickets. The sales began on February 12 and continued until five minutes before the drawing. Despite its efforts, the group was able to purchase only 5 million of the more than 7 million combinations. It did win the prize, but the payoff was delayed for several weeks due to numerous complaints of Virginia residents about the long lines created by the group's bulk purchases.

But was it worth an investment of $5 million on the **chance** of winning $27 million? There were 2,500 investors in the group, and each had put $3,000 into the fund. After taxes, each investor would get about $540 a year for each of the next 20 years—a 17.254 percent return on the $3,000 investment. However there were some risks. First of all, there was no guarantee that the group had been able to secure a winning ticket. Second, if there had been one other winning ticket, the annual return to each group member after taxes would have been about $270 or 6.395 percent on the $3,000 investment. Two other winners would have reduced the annual return to $180 (only 1.803 percent on the $3,000 investment). These clearly are not the returns a wise investor would want.

*Source: Based on articles in *The New York Times*, February 25, 1992, to March 11, 1992.

11.4 PROBLEM SET 11-1

1. Find $n(A \cup B)$ if
   a) $n(A) = 9$, $n(B) = 17$, and $n(A \cap B) = 6$.
   b) $n(A) = 117$, $n(B) = 13$, and $n(A \cap B) = 31$.
   c) $n(A) = 32$, $n(B) = 13$, and $n(A \cap B) = 0$.

11.4 PROBLEM SET 11-1 (continued)

2. The counting rule for unions can be extended to three sets:

$$n(A \cup B \cup C) = n(A) + n(B) + n(C)$$
$$- n(A \cap B)$$
$$- n(A \cap C)$$
$$- n(B \cap C)$$
$$+ n(A \cap B \cap C).$$

   a) Explain why this rule makes sense.
   b) Find $n(A \cup B \cup C)$ if
      $n(A) = 16$, $n(B) = 19$, $n(C) = 14$,
      $n(A \cap B) = 7$, $n(A \cap C) = 5$,
      $n(B \cap C) = 8$, and $n(A \cap B \cap C) = 3$.
   c) Find $n(A \cup B \cup C)$ if
      $n(A) = 36$, $n(B) = 22$, $n(C) = 26$,
      $n(A \cap B) = 12$, $n(A \cap C) = 7$,
      $n(B \cap C) = 5$, and $n(A \cap B \cap C) = 3$.

3. For each of the following, draw the Venn diagram and use the given information to determine the number of elements in each region:
   a) $n(\mathcal{U}) = 28$, $n(S) = 17$, $n(T) = 12$, and $n(S \cap T) = 4$.
   b) $n(\mathcal{U}) = 50$, $n(S) = 29$, $n(T) = 17$, and $n(S \cap T) = 11$.

4. For each of the following, use a table and the given information to determine the number of elements in each region:
   a) $n(\mathcal{U}) = 35$, $n(S) = 16$, $n(T) = 10$,
      $n(W) = 14$, $n(S \cap T) = 4$, $n(S \cap W) = 5$,
      $n(T \cap W) = 8$, and $n(S \cap T \cap W) = 3$.
   b) $n(\mathcal{U}) = 48$, $n(S) = 23$, $n(T) = 21$,
      $n(W) = 20$, $n(S \cap T) = 8$, $n(S \cap W) = 9$,
      $n(T \cap W) = 6$, and $n(S' \cap T' \cap W') = 6$.

5. A local automobile dealer has 589 cars on the lot. Of these, 384 have power steering, 264 have automatic transmissions, and 98 have both options.
   a) How many cars have at least one of the two options?
   b) Of the 589 cars, 61 have four-wheel drive. Among the four-wheel drive cars, 32 have power steering, 29 have automatic transmissions, and 25 have all three options. How many of the four-wheel drive cars have none of the options?

6. A survey of 1,000 registered voters found that 542 are Democrats and 405 are Republicans.
   a) How many voters registered as something other than Democrat or Republican?
   b) If 72 of those registered as Democrats or Republicans are undecided in their vote, how many Democrats and Republicans are decided as to their vote?

7. Of 28 students in a quantitative methods course, 12 are majoring in accounting, 8 in finance, and 12 in economics. Among the 28, there are 4 double majors in accounting and economics, 3 in finance and economics, 2 in accounting and finance, and no triple majors.
   a) How many students are majoring in something other than accounting, finance, or economics?
   b) How many students are majoring in accounting alone?
   c) In economics alone?
   d) In finance alone?

8. A survey of 150 college football coaches was conducted to determine how they kept abreast of sports developments. The results showed that 75 regularly read *Sports Illustrated* (*SI*), 92 regularly read the local newspaper, and 88 watched the evening news on TV. In addition 45 read both *SI* and the newspaper, 50 watched the TV news and read the newspaper, and 35 watched the TV news and read *SI*. Also 10 neither read *SI*, read the newspaper, nor watched TV news. How many
   a) Used all three sources to keep informed?
   b) Only watched the TV news?

---

9. How many two-letter words can be formed from the English alphabet if
   a) No repetitions are allowed?
   b) Repetitions are allowed?

10. A card is drawn from a standard deck of 52 cards and then replaced; then another card is drawn. How many sequences of 2 face-value cards (10, jack, queen, king) could occur if two face cards of the same denomination but different suits are
    a) Distinguishable?   b) Not distinguishable?

11. If 2 cards are drawn from a standard deck of 52 cards, how many sequences of 2 face-value cards

11.4 PROBLEM SET 11-1 (concluded)

could occur if two face cards of the same denomination but different suits are
a) Distinguishable?   b) Not distinguishable?

12. If there are four airlines that travel from New York to Washington and two that travel from Washington to Richmond, how many ways could a flight be booked from New York to Richmond through Washington? Draw the associated tree diagram.

13. A closet contains five hats, four coats, and two scarves. How many outfits can be assembled from the three items? Draw the associated tree diagram.

14. A coin is tossed five times and the sequence of heads and tails is recorded. How many sequences could there be?

15. If a true-false examination has 20 questions, how many different answer sheets could there be?

Evaluate each of the following:

16. a) $P(7, 2)$.   b) $P(32, 2)$.
17. a) $P(6, 3)$.   b) $P(4, 2)$.
18. a) $C(7, 2)$.   b) $C(32, 2)$.
19. a) $C(6, 3)$.   b) $C(4, 2)$.

20. Find the value(s) of p so that
    a) $C(9, 2) = C(9, p)$.   b) $C(8, 3) = C(p, 5)$.
21. Find the value(s) of p so that
    a) $C(7, 4) = C(p, 3)$.   b) $C(6, 1) = C(p, 5)$.
22. Show that
    a) $C(n, r) = C(n, n - r)$.
    b) $C(n, n - 1) = C(n, 1) = n$.
    c) $P(n, 0) = C(n, 0) = 1$.
    d) $P(n, 1) = C(n, 1) = n$.
    e) $P(n, n) = n!$.
    f) $C(n, n) = 1$.

23. How many different starting lineups of 5 basketball players can be chosen from a squad of 13 players?
24. How many different bridge hands of 13 cards can be dealt from a standard deck of 52 cards?
25. How many ways can three people sit in a minibus with nine seats?
26. How many different ways can 14 books be arranged on a shelf?
27. How many different ways can 5 books be chosen from a shelf containing 15 books?
28. How many different ways can 5 books be piled on a desk after being chosen from a shelf containing 15 books?
29. A student needs to choose 5 courses from a list of 23 electives. How many different selections can she make?
30. How many basketball games are played in the Ivy League of eight teams if every team plays every other team twice?
31. How many different ways can a committee of 7 be chosen from a school senate of 63?

32. The casino game of craps is played with two dice, each of which has six faces numbered 1 through 6. The two dice are thrown and the numbers appearing on the two upper faces are added together. On the first toss of the two dice,
    a) How many different sums are possible?
    b) For each sum, how many different ways can the sum be formed?
33. The daily lottery number consists of four sets of balls, each numbered 0, 1, 2, . . . , 9. Each set is placed in a rotating urn and a single ball is selected from each urn. How many different
    a) Four-digit numbers are there?
    b) Three-digit numbers can appear in the first three balls selected?
34. There are three semiweekly lotteries. How many different
    a) Five-number combinations are there in a lottery with 35 numbered balls?
    b) Six-number combinations are there in a lottery with 42 numbered balls?
    c) Six-number combinations are there in a lottery with 49 numbered balls?

11.5 MORE COUNTING PROBLEMS

Many real-world situations give rise to binary outcomes.

Now that we have had some experience with counting problems, we can investigate more sophisticated situations that require slightly more careful analysis. Although the examples may at first appear to be somewhat artificial, they are prototypes of real-world situations that give rise to **two-stage** (**binary**) outcomes. For example, managers are often faced with buy or sell, invest or do not invest, or hire or downsize decisions.

Example. A coin is tossed eight times and the sequence of heads and tails is recorded. Determine the number of a) Total outcomes possible. b) Outcomes with exactly four heads. c) Outcomes with at most three tails. d) Outcomes with at least four tails.

To solve this example, it helps to visualize what the sequences would look like. One possible outcome of tossing the coin eight times is

H	T	H	H	H	T	T	H

where H appears on the first toss, T on the second, H on the third through fifth, T on the sixth and seventh, and H on the eighth. From this possibility, it is clear that the total number of outcomes is equal to the number of ways of filling each of the preceding eight boxes with H or T. Using the mn rule of Section 11.2, this number is

$$2 \cdot 2 \cdot 2 \cdot 2 \cdot 2 \cdot 2 \cdot 2 \cdot 2 = 2^8 = 256,$$

so the answer to (a) is that there are 256 total outcomes possible.

For (b), we note that any outcome for the eight boxes that has exactly four heads must necessarily have exactly four tails. Thus once we have chosen the four boxes that contain H, the remaining four boxes must contain T. The answer to (b), then, is the number of ways that any four of the boxes can be chosen to be filled with an H or

$$C(8, 4) = \frac{8!}{4!(8-4)!} = \frac{8!}{4!4!} = 70.$$

Thus there are 70 outcomes with exactly four heads (and exactly four tails).

Next, for (c), the number of outcomes with at most three tails would be the sum of the number of outcomes with exactly 0, 1, 2, or 3 tails. Using the same analysis as in (b), this number is

$$C(8, 0) + C(8, 1) + C(8, 2) + C(8, 3) \tag{1}$$

or

$$\frac{8!}{0!8!} + \frac{8!}{1!7!} + \frac{8!}{2!6!} + \frac{8!}{3!5!} = 1 + 8 + 28 + 56 = 93.$$

Thus there are 93 outcomes with at most three tails.

Lastly, for (d), we could use an analysis similar to (c) to determine the number of outcomes with at least four tails as

$$C(8, 4) + C(8, 5) + C(8, 6) + C(8, 7) + C(8, 8). \qquad (2)$$

However a simpler way is to recognize that adding (2) to (1) would result in the entire set of possible outcomes. Thus (2) is simply the number from part (a) minus the number from part (c),

$$256 - 93 = 163,$$

so that there are 163 outcomes with at least four tails.

Sometimes it simplifies computation to use the complement of a set in solving counting problems.

> **Exercise.** In the preceding example, find the number of outcomes with a) At most two tails. b) At least three tails.
> **Answer:** a) 37. b) $256 - 37 = 219$.

Example. An urn contains 10 red balls and 5 black balls. Four balls are selected from the urn. How many ways can this be done if a) Color is not important? b) All four balls are to be red? c) All four balls are to be black? d) There are to be three red balls and one black ball?

Since color is not important in (a), we simply want the number of combinations of 15 objects taken 4 at a time,

$$C(15, 4) = \frac{15!}{4!(15-4)!} = \frac{15!}{4!11!} = 1,365.$$

Thus there are 1,365 total possible selections if color is not important.

For (b) all 4 balls must come from the 10 red balls. So now we have

$$C(10, 4) = \frac{10!}{4!(10-4)!} = \frac{10!}{4!6!} = 210,$$

meaning that there are 210 ways of selecting 4 balls all of which are red.

Similarly, for (c), all 4 balls must come from the 5 black balls. Thus this time we have

$$C(5, 4) = \frac{5!}{4!(5-4)!} = \frac{5!}{4!1!} = 5,$$

meaning that there are 5 ways of selecting 4 balls all of which are black.

Finally, for (d), we must determine the number of ways of selecting the 4 balls so that 3 of them are red and 1 is black. Using the *mn* rule of Section 11.2 again, this number is

$$C(10, 3) \cdot C(5, 1)$$

When two selection criteria are to be satisfied, the total number of ways is the product of the two individual numbers.

where $C(10, 3)$ is the number of ways of selecting 3 of the 10 red balls and $C(5, 1)$ is the number of ways of selecting 1 of the 5 black balls. Thus we have

$$C(10, 3) \cdot C(5, 1) = \frac{10!}{3!7!} \cdot \frac{5!}{1!4!}$$
$$= (120)(5) = 600,$$

so that there are 600 ways of selecting 4 balls with 3 being red and 1 being black.

> **Exercise.** In the preceding example, find the number of ways of selecting the 4 balls with   a) One red and 3 black.   b) Two of each color.
> **Answer:**   a) 100.   b) 450.

Lot acceptance sampling is often used to test a sample rather than an entire population of items.

Example. Now let's look at an example of **lot acceptance sampling.** Micros Unlimited assembles its own microcomputers using parts from various suppliers. When a shipment (**lot**) of hard disks arrives, it is impractical for Micros to test each and every one (the **population**).[2] A part of the lot (a **sample**) is randomly selected and tested. Based upon the test results Micros decides whether to accept the entire lot. One particular lot of 100 disks was received and, from past experience, it was known that ordinarily 5 percent are defective and 95 percent are nondefective. In a sample of 10 disks from this lot, however, there were 2 defective and 8 nondefective disks. How many different samples of 10 are possible with 2 defectives and 8 nondefectives?

The solution of this example is similar to the solution of part (d) of the preceding example. Specifically we want to determine the number of ways of selecting 10 disks from the lot of 100 with 2 of the disks being defective and 8 being nondefective. Since there are normally 5 defective and 95 nondefective in a lot of 100, we have

$$C(5, 2) \cdot C(95, 8) = \frac{5!}{2!3!} \cdot \frac{95!}{8!87!} = 1{,}215{,}509{,}316{,}450$$

so there are 1,215,509,316,450 samples of the 10 disks with 2 being defective and 8 being nondefective.

> **Exercise.** In the preceding example, how many samples are there with one defective and nine nondefective disks?
> **Answer:**   5,874,961,696,200.

---

[2]Populations and samples will be discussed in Section 11.8.

Example. A small U.S. college has a staff of 17 recruiters in its undergraduate admissions office. The director of admissions has broken the United States into 4 regions and has decided to assign 6 recruiters to the East, 4 to the South, 2 to the Midwest, and 5 to the West. How many different ways can the director assign the 17-member staff to the 4 regions?

Clearly the director can start by assigning any 6 of the 17 recruiters to the East. After this first assignment has been made, there will be 11 recruiters left from which the director can assign any 4 to the South. After this second assignment has been made, there will be 7 recruiters left from which the director can assign any 2 to the Midwest. After the third assignment has been made, there will be 5 recruiters left and the director will obviously assign all of them to the West. Using the generalized *mn* rule of Section 11.2, then, the number of ways the director can make these assignments

$$C(17, 6) \cdot C(11, 4) \cdot C(7, 2) \cdot C(5, 5) = \frac{17!}{6!\cancel{11!}} \cdot \frac{\cancel{11!}}{4!\cancel{7!}} \cdot \frac{\cancel{7!}}{2!\cancel{5!}} \cdot \frac{\cancel{5!}}{5!0!}.$$

When more than one selection criterion is to be satisfied, the total number of ways is the product of each individual number.

Note that we have not tried to compute each of the four combinations directly, but rather have simplified the last expression first by cancelling terms wherever possible. Specifically the 11! of the denominator of $C(17, 6)$ cancels the 11! of the numerator of $C(11, 4)$. Similarly the 7! of the denominator of $C(11, 4)$ cancels the 7! of the numerator of $C(7, 2)$. Also the 5! of the denominator of $C(7, 2)$ cancels the 5! of the numerator of $C(5, 5)$. Since we know that $0! = 1$, we can then evaluate the last expression as

$$\frac{17!}{6!4!2!5!} = 85,765,680,$$

so that the director has 85,765,680 different ways to assign the 15 recruiters to the 4 regions.

The preceding example illustrates situations that give rise to **multistage** or **multinomial** outcomes. The technique used to solve the example can be generalized to

Many real-world situations give rise to multistage or multinomial outcomes.

Multinomial Counting Rule

If we have n objects, then the number of ways to select n_1 objects of one kind, n_2 objects of a second kind, . . . , n_k objects of the last kind with

$$n_1 + n_2 + \cdots + n_k = n$$

is

$$\frac{n!}{n_1! \cdot n_2! \cdots n_k!}.$$

The number of ways to select n_1 objects of one kind, n_2 of a second kind, and so on, from a total group of n objects is

$$\frac{n!}{n_1! \cdot n_2! \cdots n_k!}.$$

> **Exercise.** In the preceding example, how many ways could the director assign 12 recruiters equally divided among the 4 regions? Use the multinomial counting rule.
>
> **Answer:** $\dfrac{12!}{3!3!3!3!} = 369,600$.

11.6 THE BINOMIAL THEOREM

The number $C(n, r)$ plays another important role in mathematics. To see this, consider the binomial expression

$$(x + y)^n.$$

As we know from Appendix 1, the expansion of this expression for $n = 0, 1,$ and 2 is

$(x + y)^0$ 1
$(x + y)^1$ $x + y$
$(x + y)^2$ $x^2 + 2xy + y^2.$

Continuing to multiply by $(x + y)$ gives us the next two expansions for $n = 3$ and 4:

$(x + y)^3$ $x^3 + 3x^2y + 3xy^2 + y^3$
$(x + y)^4$ $x^4 + 4x^3y + 6x^2y^2 + 4xy^3 + y^4.$

Note the pattern of coefficients of x and y in these five binomial expressions

```
              1
            1   1
          1   2   1
        1   3   3   1
      1   4   6   4   1
```

The coefficients of the binomial expansion of $(x + y)^n$ form Pascal's Triangle with 1 on the exterior and each interior number being the sum of the two numbers above to the left and right.

is a triangle with the exterior numbers all being 1, and each interior number being the sum of the two numbers to its left and right in the preceding row. This triangle is commonly called **Pascal's Triangle.**

> **Exercise.** What would be the numbers in the next row for the expansion of $(x + y)^5$? What is this expansion?
>
> **Answer:** 1, 5, 10, 10, 5, 1; $x^5 + 5x^4y + 10x^3y^2 + 10x^2y^3 + 5xy^4 + y^5.$

Now the first five rows of Pascal's triangle can be rewritten

$$C(0, 0)$$
$$C(1, 0) \quad C(1, 1)$$
$$C(2, 0) \quad C(2, 1) \quad C(2, 2)$$
$$C(3, 0) \quad C(3, 1) \quad C(3, 2) \quad C(3, 3)$$
$$C(4, 0) \quad C(4, 1) \quad C(4, 2) \quad C(4, 3) \quad C(4, 4).$$

Pascal's Triangle can be written in terms of combinations.

Exercise. Verify that the combinations in the preceding triangle are the same as in Pascal's Triangle. What would be the combinations in the sixth row?

Answer: $C(5, 0) \quad C(5, 1) \quad C(5, 2) \quad C(5, 3) \quad C(5, 4) \quad C(5, 5)$.

The preceding pattern of coefficients in the binomial expansion of $(x + y)^n$ holds for all n and leads to the **Binomial Theorem.**

The Binomial Theorem

If n is any positive integer, then

$$(x + y)^n = C(n, 0)x^n + C(n, 1)x^{n-1}y + C(n, 2)x^{n-2}y^2$$
$$+ \ldots + C(n, n-1)xy^{n-1} + C(n, n)y^n.$$

The Binomial Theorem gives the expansion of $(x + y)^n$ with the coefficients being the $(n + 1)$st row of Pascal's Triangle.

Example. Find the coefficient of x^3y^6 in $(x + y)^9$.

Using the Binomial Theorem with $n = 9$, the coefficient would be

$$C(9, 6) = \frac{9!}{6!3!} = 84.$$

Exercise. Find the coefficient of x^5y^7 in $(x + y)^{12}$.

Answer: $C(12, 7) = 792$.

Example. Expand the binomial expression $(x + 3y)^4$.

Here we treat 3y as a single variable so that this time by the Binomial Theorem, we have

$$(x + 3y)^4 = x^4 + 4x^3(3y) + 6x^2(3y)^2 + 4x(3y)^3 + (3y)^4$$
$$= x^4 + 12x^3y + 54x^2y^2 + 108xy^3 + 81y^4.$$

Exercise. Expand the binomial expression $(2x + y)^5$.
Answer: $32x^5 + 80x^4y + 80x^3y^2 + 40x^2y^3 + 10xy^4 + y^5$.

Example. Determine the number of subsets of a set with four elements.

The subsets will have either 0, 1, 2, 3, or 4 elements. The 0-element subsets (just the empty set itself) are obtained by selecting 0 elements from the universe of 4; that is, $C(4, 0) = 1$. The 1-element subsets are obtained by selecting any 1 element from the universe of 4; that is, $C(4, 1) = 4$. Clearly then, the total number of subsets will be

$$C(4, 0) + C(4, 1) + C(4, 2) + C(4, 3) + C(4, 4). \qquad (1)$$

But recall that the binomial expansion for $(x + y)^4$ was

$$(x + y)^4 = C(4, 0)x^4 + C(4, 1)x^3y^1 + C(4, 2)x^2y^2$$
$$+ C(4, 3)x^1y^3 + C(4, 4)y^4 \qquad (2)$$

and if we substitute $x = y = 1$ in (2), the result will be precisely (1). Thus we can calculate (1) simply by

$$(1 + 1)^4 = 2^4 = 16,$$

so that there are 16 subsets of a set with 4 elements.

Exercise. How many subsets are there of a set with 5 elements? With 8 elements?
Answer: $2^5 = 32$; $2^8 = 256$.

The preceding example and exercise lead to the following counting rule:

A set with n elements has 2^n subsets.

Number of Subsets of a Set

The number of subsets of a set with n elements is 2^n.

11.7 PROBLEM SET 11-2

1. A coin is tossed 10 times and the sequence of heads and tails is recorded. Determine the number of
   a) Total outcomes possible.
   b) Outcomes with at most three heads.
   c) Outcomes with at least four heads.
   d) Outcomes with exactly seven heads.
   e) Outcomes with at most seven heads.

2. A coin is tossed nine times and the sequence of heads and tails is recorded. Determine the number of
   a) Total outcomes possible.
   b) Outcomes with exactly five tails.
   c) Outcomes with at most six heads.
   d) Outcomes with at least three tails.
   e) Outcomes with at least three heads.

3. An urn contains eight white balls and three red balls. Six balls are selected from the urn. How many ways can this be done if
   a) Color is not important?
   b) All six balls are to be white?
   c) All six balls are to be red?
   d) There are to be four white balls and two red balls?
   e) At least two balls are to be red?

4. An urn contains 13 white balls and 12 blue balls. Six balls are selected from the urn. How many ways can this be done if
   a) Color is not important?
   b) All six balls are to be white?
   c) All six balls are to be blue?
   d) There are to be two white balls and four blue balls?
   e) At least three balls are to be white?

5. A shipment of 60 telephones has been received by a discount store and a sample lot of 12 is tested for performance. The manufacturer has stipulated that the defective rate is typically 10 percent. How many different samples of 12 are possible with
   a) Exactly zero defectives?
   b) Exactly one defective?
   c) Exactly two defectives?

6. The main distributor for a large retail store has received a shipment of 48 television sets. The manager has decided to take a sample of five sets from the lot and test them. The overall defective rate is expected to be 4 percent. How many different samples of two are possible with
   a) Exactly zero defectives?
   b) Exactly one defective?
   c) Exactly two defectives?

7. Each hand in the game of poker consists of 5 cards drawn from a standard deck of 52. Determine the number of
   a) Total poker hands possible.
   b) Poker hands with three aces and two kings.
   c) Poker hands with two aces and three kings.
   d) Poker hands with three of one kind and two of another kind (full houses). [Hint: Refer to (b) and (c).]
   e) Poker hands with four of a kind.
   f) Poker hands that are all the same suit (flushes).

8. Each hand in a version of the game of gin consists of 7 cards drawn from a standard deck of 52. Determine the number of
   a) Total gin hands possible.
   b) Gin hands with four aces and three jacks.
   c) Gin hands with three aces and four jacks.
   d) Gin hands with three of one kind and four of another kind. [Hint: Refer to (b) and (c).]

9. The faculty at a college of management consists of seven divisions: Accounting, Economics, Finance, Liberal Arts, Management, Marketing, and Quantitative Methods. A pool of 14 graduate assistants is to be assigned to the divisions. How many assignments are possible if
   a) Two assistants are assigned to each division?
   b) Three assistants are assigned to both Accounting and Management, one to both Economics and Liberal Arts, and the rest split equally among the remaining divisions?
   c) Two assistants are assigned to both Marketing and Management, three to Economics, four to Quantitative Methods, and the rest split equally among the remaining divisions?

10. The students at a university are housed in five dormitories. Dormitories 1 and 2 can each house 250 students, Dormitories 3 and 4 can each house 300 students, and Dormitory 5 can house 350 students. The student housing board is comprised of 12 students each assigned rooms in the dormitories they represent. How many ways can this be done if
    a) Two students are assigned to Dormitories 1, 2,

11.7 PROBLEM SET 11-2 (concluded)

and 3, and the rest are split equally between Dormitories 4 and 5?
b) Three students are assigned to Dormitories 4 and 5, and the rest split equally among the remaining dormitories?
c) Two students are assigned to Dormitory 1, one to Dormitory 2, and the rest split equally among the remaining dormitories?

11. Expand each of the following binomials:
   a) $(a + b)^7$.
   b) $(a + b)^8$.
   c) $(2x + y)^5$.
   d) $(x + 3y)^5$.
   e) $(3x + 2y)^4$.
   f) $(4x + 5y)^3$.
   g) $(3x - 2y)^5$.
   h) $(4x - 5y)^5$.

12. What is the coefficient of
   a) x^2y^3 in $(x + y)^5$.
   b) x^4y^3 in $(x + y)^7$.
   c) x^4 in $(x + y)^{10}$.
   d) y^4 in $(x + y)^{10}$.
   e) y^5 in $(3 + y)^6$.
   f) x^5 in $(x + 4)^6$.
   g) y^5 in $(x + y)^8$.
   h) x^5 in $(x + y)^8$.

13. How many different subsets can be chosen from a set
   a) With 6 elements?
   b) With 10 elements?
   c) With 25 elements?
   d) With 50 elements?

14. Use the technique of the last example of the preceding section to show that
   a) $C(5, 0) + C(5, 1) + C(5, 2) + C(5, 3) + C(5, 4) + C(5, 5) = 2^5 = 32$.
   b) $C(n, 0) + C(n, 1) + \ldots + C(n, n - 1) + C(n, n) = 2^n$.

15. A pizza shop offers cheese pizza with any combination of six other toppings: hamburger, onions, mushrooms, pepperoni, peppers, and sausage. How many different kinds of pizza can be ordered? (Hint: See Problem 14.)

16. How many different words (real or imaginary) can be formed using all the letters of the following words?
   a) Zephyr.
   b) Handicap.
   c) Bookkeeper.
   d) Mathematics.

11.8 PROBABILITY AND ODDS

In this section we show how to use the counting techniques we have learned to compute **probabilities** and **odds.** We will see not only that this is useful in its own right, but also that the probabilistic mode is characteristic of decision-making problems.

A weather forecaster may state in a radio broadcast that the probability of rain tomorrow is 60 percent and later, while playing poker, tell friends that the odds on rain tomorrow are 3 to 2. Other methods exist for expressing the degree of certainty or uncertainty. In mathematics we always express probabilities as numbers on a scale from 0 to 1, inclusive. Thus letting $P(R)$ represent the probability of rain, we convert 60 percent to its decimal equivalent and write

$$P(R) = 0.60.$$

Probabilities range between 0 and 1.

Odds are restatements of probabilities.

The odds statement 3 to 2 is viewed as meaning there are $3 + 2 = 5$ **chances** on tomorrow's weather, of which 3 are for rain, so

$$P(R) = \frac{3}{3 + 2} = \frac{3}{5} = 0.60$$

as before.

> **Exercise.** If the odds are 13 to 7 that the stock market will rise tomorrow, what is the decimal value of the probability of a rise?
> **Answer:** 0.65.

Odds are in common use, but suffer lack of comparability because they do not have a fixed base. Thus if the odds for a stock price rise are 11 to 7 while those for a rise in bond yields are 3 to 2, a conversion is needed to express the likelihood of rises in comparable form, and probabilities in decimal form are an appropriate conversion.

> **Exercise.** Convert the previous two odds statements into decimal probabilities.
> **Answer:** 0.611 and 0.600.

Statistical Inference

One of the most important areas in which comparability is fundamental is that of **statistical inference.** Many times in making important business decisions we need to know the profile of a certain **population.** This could be a population of consumers, a population of inventory items, or a population of numerical values.

> **Definition.** A **population** is the entire set or collection of elements associated with a particular study.

The population is the universal set of objects under study.

Since many populations are too large to yield to a total census, we frequently scrutinize a **sample** from the population.

> **Definition.** A **sample** is any subset of a population.

A sample is a subset of the population that is used to make inferences about the population.

Using the characteristics of a sample we make inferences about the characteristics of the entire population. For example, statisticians regularly predict the outcome of pending elections by polling a sample of voters out of the population of all voters. A statistical inference could be a decision, an estimate, or a prediction about a population that is based on information contained in a sample. Any statistical inference should be accompanied by a measure of reliability, which defines our confidence in the correctness of the inference. These measures of reliability depend heavily upon the theory of probability.

= Sources of Probabilities

If we plan to draw a card from a well-shuffled standard deck of 52 cards, we would find it natural to assess the probability that the card will be a spade as

$$P(S) = \frac{\text{Number of spades}}{\text{Total number of cards}} = \frac{13}{52} = \frac{1}{4} = 0.25.$$

What this implies is that if we repeat the experiment of drawing a card from a well-shuffled deck of 52 cards many times, we would expect the **proportion** or **relative frequency** of drawing a spade to approach 0.25 as a limit as the number of drawings increases. **Relative frequency over the long run under constant conditions** (e.g., drawing from a well-shuffled deck) is one source of probability measures. Most people feel confident in such probability assignments and refer to them as **objective probabilities** that can be verified by experiment. A novice in a poker game may feel that a pair of kings and a pair of aces should beat three deuces, but such is not the case. In poker, the more unusual (less probable) hand wins, and three of a kind is more unusual than two pairs—not because of intuition or any subjective factor, but because of mathematical computations that can be verified by experiment.

One source of probabilities is relative frequency that can be verified by experiment.

In general, if we perform an experiment with all outcomes equally likely to occur, then we assign the probability $P(E)$ to a particular outcome or **event** E following the rule

The probability of an event is the number of outcomes resulting in that event divided by the total number of outcomes possible.

$$P(E) = \frac{\text{Number of all favorable outcomes}}{\text{Number of all possible outcomes}} = \frac{n(E)}{n(\mathcal{U})}.$$

For example, if we were to toss two coins A and B, then there are four possible outcomes we could obtain as shown in Table 11–11.

TABLE 11–11

Coin A	Coin B
H	H
H	T
T	H
T	T

What is the probability of obtaining two tails?

$$P(2 \text{ tails}) = \frac{\text{Number of outcomes yielding 2 tails}}{\text{Number of all possible outcomes}} = \frac{1}{4}.$$

You should verify that

$$P(1 \text{ tail}) = \frac{2}{4} = \frac{1}{2}.$$

> **Exercise.** We toss three coins. a) List all the possible outcomes. b) What is the probability of obtaining exactly two heads?
>
> **Answer:** a) There are eight possible outcomes: HHH, HHT, HTH, HTT, THH, THT, TTH, and TTT. b) 3/8.

We should point out at once that objective probabilities, which arise as relative frequencies over the long run under constant conditions, are not as prevalent in management decision making as they are in games of chance. To see why, consider a firm that is deciding on whether to bid on a $5 million project, at a point in time, and in the competitive environment of that time. The firm knows it will cost about $100,000 to prepare the bid so naturally it will not prepare a bid unless the probability of winning the contract is sufficiently high to justify the cost. How does the firm assess the probability of winning? Past experience will be of some help, but it is unlikely that the circumstances surrounding this particular situation have occurred very often, if at all, in the past, so that a relative-frequency objective probability is not at hand. Nevertheless a decision based upon a probability assessment must be made. We may assume that the appropriate officials of the firm, drawing upon both quantified and nonquantified experience and projection, will make the assessment. We refer to the results as a **subjective probabilities.**

Management decision making is often based on experiential or subjective probabilities, not relative frequencies or objective probabilities.

In practice, probability assessments range from being highly objective to highly subjective. In this chapter we shall not distinguish between the two because probability theory is not concerned with the source of the probabilities we assign. The theory requires only that we consider **all of the different events** that may occur in a given situation and **assign to each event a nonnegative number between 0 and 1 in a manner such that the sum of all the probabilities is 1.** For example, in drawing a card from a deck, the events red card, spade, and club are one way to specify all the different events that can occur, and we may assign probabilities 0.5, 0.25, and 0.25, respectively, to these events.

Probabilities are assigned values between 0 and 1 so that their sum is 1.

11.9 ASSIGNING PROBABILITIES AND CONDITIONAL PROBABILITIES

Certain and Impossible Events. We assign a probability of 1 to an event that is certain to occur, such as the event of getting a red or a black card when drawing from a deck. The probability 0 is assigned to an impossible event, such as drawing a red spade from the deck. Again, a weatherman may assign a probability of 0 for rain tomorrow if he believes rain is impossible, or 1 if he believes rain is certain. In summary, if $P(E)$ is the probability of event E,

The probability of a certain event is 1; the probability of an impossible event is 0.

$$0 \le P(E) \le 1$$
$$P(\text{certain event}) = 1$$
$$P(\text{impossible event}) = 0.$$

We shall introduce probability terminology by reference to the data in Table 11–12. These data show the results of a poll of all 500 employees in a firm on the question of whether to change the work week from five 8-hour days to four 10-hour days.

The right margin shows there are 100 men in the group of 500 workers. If we were to draw an individual at random[3] from the 500, it would be natural to assign the probability of selecting a man $P(M)$, as

$$P(M) = \frac{100}{500} = 0.20.$$

Similarly the probability that the individual disfavors the change, $P(D)$, is

$$P(D) = \frac{160}{500} = 0.32.$$

Exercise. From Table 11–12 find: a) $P(W)$. b) $P(F)$.
Answer: a) 0.80. b) 0.48.

Joint events are the intersection or simultaneous occurrence of two events.

Joint Events: Intersection. In Table 11–12 draw a horizontal line across the M row and a vertical line down the F column. At the **intersection** of the two lines there are 70 people who are both men **and** in favor. Using the set terminology symbol

TABLE 11–12

	Favor (F)	Disfavor (D)	Neutral (N)	Totals
Men (M)	70	10	20	100
Women (W)	170	150	80	400
Totals	240	160	100	500

[3] The concept of random selection underlies all probability rules. In the case of card playing, randomness is sought by shuffling the cards before dealing a hand. In the case of Table 11–12, we could shuffle the 500 employee time cards or use other methods to ensure random selection.

∩ for intersection, the event at hand is M intersection F, or

$$M \cap F.$$

An alternative description refers to the intersection as the **joint event,** M and F. Clearly

$$P(M \cap F) = \frac{70}{500} = 0.14.$$

Similarly

$$P(W \cap N) = \frac{80}{500} = 0.16$$

is the probability that the selected individual is a woman **and** is neutral. Remember always that the intersection means **both** occur and is characterized by the word *and*.

Exercise. Write the symbols for the probability that a man who disfavors is selected. Compute this probability.

Answer: $P(M \cap D) = 10/500 = 0.02.$

Mutually Exclusive (Disjoint) Events. In Table 11–12 the intersection

$$F \cap D$$

is empty (has no elements) because an individual cannot both favor and disfavor the proposal. In set terminology, as we know, this means

$$F \cap D = \phi,$$

where ϕ is the **empty** or **null set.** We shall say F and D are **disjoint** or, more commonly, that they are **mutually exclusive.** Clearly

$$P(F \cap D) = 0$$

and, in general,

> Two events that cannot occur simultaneously are disjoint or mutually exclusive.

A and B are **mutually exclusive** if $A \cap B = \phi$ so that

$$P(A \cap B) = 0.$$

> The joint probability of two mutually exclusive events, A and B, is 0; that is,
>
> $P(A \cap B) = 0.$

> **Exercise.** If a card is drawn from a deck, what is the probability that it will be red and be a spade? Why?
>
> **Answer:** $P(R \cap S) = 0$ because red and spade are mutually exclusive.

Conditional Probabilities. Suppose next that an individual has been selected from the population of employees. We are told that the individual is a woman, but are not told her attitude toward the proposal. What now is the probability that this individual is in favor? Here it is **given** that we have a woman, so in Table 11–12 we consider only the 400 women and the 170 of these who are in favor. We find that

$$P(\text{in favor, given woman}) = P(F \mid W) = \frac{n(F \cap W)}{n(W)} = \frac{170}{400} = 0.425,$$

A conditional probability is the probability of an event occurring given the preoccurrence of some other event.

where the vertical line segment in $P(F \mid W)$ is read as **given,** and the whole symbol as the **probability of F, given W.**

Similarly if we are told the person selected disfavors the proposal and are asked to find the probability that the person is a man, we compute

$$P(M \mid D) = \frac{n(M \cap D)}{n(D)} = \frac{10}{160} = 0.0625.$$

> **Exercise.** If the person selected is in favor, write the symbols for, and compute the probability that, the person is a woman.
>
> **Answer:** $P(W \mid F) = \dfrac{n(W \cap F)}{n(F)} = \dfrac{170}{240} = 0.708.$

Dependent and Independent Events. Table 11–12 shows

$$P(M) = \frac{100}{500} = 0.200 \quad \text{but} \quad P(M \mid F) = \frac{70}{240} = 0.292.$$

We note that

$$P(M \mid F) \neq P(M)$$

Two events are dependent in the probability sense if the conditional probability is different from the unconditional probability.

and say that M and F are **dependent in the probability sense.** The idea is that the probability that the selected person is a male is related to, or depends on, whether the person is in favor. In this case, the **unconditional probability** that the selected person is a man is 0.200, but it is more likely (0.292) that the person is a man if we are given that the person is in favor.

On the other hand, we note that

$$P(M) = \frac{100}{500} = 0.20 \quad \text{and} \quad P(M \mid N) = \frac{20}{100} = 0.20$$

so that

$$P(M \mid N) = P(M)$$

which we translate by saying that the probability that the selected person is a male does not depend on (is independent of) whether the person is neutral. In general, we state that **in the probability sense,**

> **Definition**
>
> If $P(A \mid B) = P(A)$ or $P(B \mid A) = P(B)$, A and B are **independent**.
> If $P(A \mid B) \neq P(A)$ or $P(B \mid A) \neq P(B)$, A and B are **dependent**.

Events A and B are independent if

$P(A \mid B) = P(A)$ or $P(B \mid A) = P(B)$.

Events A and B are dependent if

$P(A \mid B) \neq P(A)$ or $P(B \mid A) \neq P(B)$.

> **Exercise.** See Table 11–12 (page 772). Are the following independent or dependent? Why?
> a) W and D. b) W and N.
> **Answer:** a) $P(W \mid D) = 0.9375$, which does not equal $P(W) = 0.8$, so W and D are dependent. b) $P(W \mid N) = 0.80 = P(W)$, so W and N are independent.

In the preceding definition of independence, we emphasized that independence as a mathematical concept is independence **in the probability sense.** We should note that events that we think or feel (intuitively) are independent or dependent may or may not prove to be so in the probability sense. Thus in the poll of workers under discussion, we might feel intuitively that women would tend not to be in favor of changing from an 8-hour to a 10-hour day because the longer workday would interfere with outside activities. That is, intuitively we might feel that women would be more likely not to favor a longer day than workers in general and, therefore, that Disfavor and Women are dependent. The test in the probability sense may or may not bear out this intuitive feeling, and the test is:

Probabilistic independence is not the same as intuitive independence.

If $P(D \mid W) = P(D)$, D and W are independent.
If $P(D \mid W) \neq P(D)$, D and W are dependent.

From Table 11–12 on page 772 we find

$$P(D \mid W) = \frac{150}{400} = 0.375 \text{ and}$$

$$P(D) = \frac{160}{500} = 0.32,$$

so D and W are dependent. Moreover the last two numbers confirm the intuitive feeling that women are more likely to disfavor a longer workday than workers in general. By way of contrast, we might feel intuitively that men would be less likely to be neutral on the question than workers in general. Here intuition is again suggesting dependence. However if we compute from Table 11–12

$$P(N \mid M) = \frac{20}{100} = 0.2$$

$$P(N) = \frac{100}{500} = 0.2,$$

we see that N and M are independent **in the probability sense,** and the data do not support intuition in this case.

Another matter worthy of special attention is the distinction between mutual exclusiveness and independence. The first point to note is that **if each of two events, A and B, has a nonzero probability and the events are mutually exclusive, they are necessarily dependent;** that is, they cannot be independent. To see why this is so, recall that

$$P(A \mid B) = \frac{P(A \cap B)}{P(B)}.$$

If A and B are mutually exclusive, then $P(A \cap B) = 0$ so

$$P(A \mid B) = \frac{0}{P(B)} = 0.$$

But since

$$P(A) \neq 0,$$

we have

$$P(A \mid B) \neq P(A)$$

and the events are dependent. The question of independence for mutually exclusive events thus always has the answer that the events are dependent in the probability sense.

On the other hand, **if A and B are not mutually exclusive, they may be independent or they may be dependent.** The last statement will be made clear in the next example.

> Mutually exclusive events with nonzero probabilities are always dependent.

> Events that are not mutually exclusive may be independent or dependent.

Example. An urn contains 200 small glass balls. Each ball has left and right halves of different colors. The left half may be R, W, or B (for red, white, or blue) and the right side may be G or Y (for green or yellow). A ball with red and yellow can be said to have some red (or some yellow). There are 80 balls with some red, 70 with white and green, 30 with white and yellow, 20 with blue and green, 140 with some green. Answer the following:

1. Are blue and green mutually exclusive? Why?
2. Are blue and green independent? Why?
3. Are white and yellow mutually exclusive? Why?
4. Are white and yellow independent? Why?
5. Are blue and yellow mutually exclusive? Why?
6. Are blue and yellow independent? Why?

The numbers given in this problem are summarized in Table 11–13A, and Table 11–13B provides the remaining numbers by using the counting techniques of Section 11.2. For example, the row sum for white must be 100, and because the column sum for green is 140, the red and green element must be 50. We turn now to questions 1 through 6 of the example statement, using completed Table 11–13B.

1. There are 20 balls that are both blue and green, so blue and green are not mutually exclusive; that is, $P(B \cap G) \neq 0$.
2. If we compute

$$P(B \mid G) = \frac{20}{140} = \frac{1}{7} \quad \text{and} \quad P(B) = \frac{20}{200} = \frac{1}{10},$$

TABLE 11–13A Given Data

	Green	Yellow	Totals
Red			80
White	70	30	
Blue	20	—	—
Totals	140		200

TABLE 11–13B Completed Table

	Green	Yellow	Totals
Red	50	30	80
White	70	30	100
Blue	20	0	20
Totals	140	60	200

we see that $P(B \mid G) \neq P(G)$, so blue and green are dependent, not independent. Or we could have computed

$$P(G \mid B) = \frac{20}{20} = 1, \quad P(G) = \frac{140}{200} = \frac{7}{10},$$

and $P(G \mid B) \neq P(G)$, showing again that blue and green are not independent.

3. There are 30 balls that are white and yellow, so white and yellow are not mutually exclusive; that is, $P(W \cap Y) \neq 0$.

4. If we compute

$$P(W \mid Y) = \frac{30}{60} = 0.5 \quad \text{and} \quad P(W) = \frac{100}{200} = 0.5,$$

we note that $P(W \mid Y) = P(W)$, so white and yellow are independent. Or, we could have computed

$$P(Y \mid W) = \frac{30}{100} = 0.3, \quad P(Y) = \frac{60}{200} = 0.3,$$

and $P(Y \mid W) = P(Y)$, showing again that yellow and white are independent.

Note: Observe in the answers to 1 through 4 that if two events are not mutually exclusive, they may be either dependent (as in 1 and 2) or independent (as in 3 and 4).

5. There is no ball with blue and yellow, so blue and yellow are mutually exclusive; that is, $P(B \cap Y) = 0$.

6. Mutually exclusive events with nonzero probabilities automatically are dependent, so blue and yellow are dependent. Numerically the dependence is exhibited by showing that $P(B \mid Y) \neq P(B)$. These probabilities are

$$P(B \mid Y) = \frac{0}{60} = 0 \quad \text{and} \quad P(B) = \frac{20}{200} = 0.1.$$

Summarizing the last example, we observe in the answer to 1 that if a ball has blue, it also can have green, so blue and green are not mutually exclusive; moreover the two demonstrations of the answer to 2 show that **if we know** one color is green (blue), this knowledge does affect the probability that the ball also has blue (green) because green and blue are dependent. Then in 3 we determine yellow and white also are not mutually exclusive, but 4 shows that **if we know** one color is yellow (white) this knowledge does not affect the probability that the other color is white (yellow) because yellow and white are independent. Finally 5 shows blue and yellow are mutually exclusive, so of necessity they are dependent; that is, as 6 shows, **if we know** one color is blue (yellow) this does affect the probability that the other color is yellow (blue); that is, this latter probability must be 0.

Exercise. If we draw two cards from a deck and let A_1 and A_2 represent the event that the first card is an ace and the event that the second card is an ace, respectively, are A_1 and A_2 mutually exclusive? Independent? Explain.

Answer: The events A_1 and A_2 (e.g., first card ace of spades, second card ace of clubs) both can occur, so $P(A_1 \cap A_2) \neq 0$ and the events are not mutually exclusive. However the probability that the second card is an ace **does** depend upon whether the first card was an ace. That is, because there are 4 aces in the deck of 52 cards, the probability that the first card is an ace is 4/52. If we know that the first card drawn was an ace, 3 aces remain in a deck of 51 cards and the probability of the second card being an ace, **given** that the first card is an ace, is 3/51.

Union of Events. Refer to Table 11–12 on page 772. As in sets, the union of W and F,

$$W \cup F,$$

means the set of individuals who are **either** women **or** in favor **or both**. The table shows there are 400 women in total and an additional uncounted 70 men in favor, for a grand total of 470 that are either women or in favor or both, so

$$P(W \cup F) = \frac{470}{500} = 0.94.$$

Recall from our counting techniques of Section 11.2 that another method is

$$P(W \cup F) = \frac{n(W) + n(F) - n(W \cap F)}{500}$$

$$= \frac{400 + 240 - 170}{500} = \frac{470}{500} = 0.94$$

as before.

On the other hand, F and D are mutually exclusive (the intersection is empty) so

$$P(F \cup D) = \frac{240 + 160 - 0}{500} = 0.8.$$

Exercise. From Table 11–12, find: a) $P(M \cup W)$. b) $P(F \cup N)$. c) $P(W \cup D)$. d) $P(M \cup F)$.

Answer: a) 1. b) 0.68. c) 0.82. d) 0.54.

Complementary Events

Recall from sets that the union of any set and its complement is the universal set. Now two events are said to be **complementary** if the sum of their probabilities is 1. As in sets, letting E' be the complement of E, we have

$$P(E) + P(E') = 1$$
$$P(E') = 1 - P(E).$$

The probability of the complement of an event is one minus the probability of the event that is,

$$P(E') = 1 - P(E).$$

E' may be read as **not** E. Similarly if R means rain, R' means not rain and if $P(R) = 0.40$, then

$$P(R') = 1 - P(R) = 1 - 0.40 = 0.60.$$

Again, if W means woman, W' is not woman (therefore man). In Table 11–12 (page 772)

$$P(W') = 1 - P(W) = 1 - \frac{400}{500} = 0.2.$$

> **Exercise.** From Table 11–12, a) What would constitute F'? b) What is $P(F')$?
> **Answer:** a) F' (not Favor) would include Disfavor and Neutral. b) $P(F') = 1 - P(F) = 1 - \frac{240}{500} = 0.52$.

The probability of the union of two events is 1 minus the joint probability of neither event.

For further practice with complements, recall that $F \cup D$ includes all joint events containing an F or a D (or both). The only remaining event is not F and not D; that is, $F' \cap D'$. $F' \cap D'$ is the complement of $F \cup D$ and we may write

$$P(F \cup D) = 1 - P(F' \cap D')$$

or

$$P(F' \cap D') = 1 - P(F \cup D).$$

Similarly

$$P(M \cup F) = 1 - P(M' \cap F')$$

or

$$P(M' \cap F') = 1 - P(M \cup F).$$

In this and the preceding section we have seen many examples of assigning probabilities and conditional probabilities. Before we collect our results into probability rules, further practice is provided in the following set of problems.

11.10 PROBLEM SET 11-3

1. The table shows for example that area A has 30 large stores and area C has 150 small stores.

   Store Size ($ Volume)

Geographic Area	Large L	Medium M	Small S
A	30	45	75
B	150	125	275
C	20	130	150

   Find the following probabilities:
   a) $P(M)$.
   b) $P(B)$.
   c) $P(M \cap S)$.
   d) $P(B \cap M)$.
   e) $P(A \cap C)$.
   f) $P(A \cap L)$.
   g) $P(L \cap A)$.
   h) $P(A \mid L)$.
   i) $P(L \mid A)$.
   j) $P(A \mid M)$.
   k) $P(S \mid B)$.
   l) $P(L \cup M)$.
   m) $P(B \cup S)$.
   n) $P(M \cup C)$.
   o) $P(B \cup C)$.
   p) $P(A')$.
   q) $P(M')$.
   r) $P'(L' \cap M')$.

   What event, joint event, or union of events is the complement of
   s) $M' \cap S'$?
   t) $B' \cap C'$?
   u) $A \cup C$?
   v) $A \cup M$?
   w) $B' \cap M'$?
   x) $L' \cap C'$?

2. See the table of Problem 1.
   a) Does $P(M \mid A) = P(M)$?
   b) What does the answer to (a) mean?
   c) Are A and L independent? Explain.
   d) Are B and L independent? Explain.
   e) What is $P(A \cap B)$? What does this mean?

3. a) Voters in an area are classified as Democrat, Independent, or Republican. If 48 percent are Democrats and 10 percent are Independents, what is the probability that a voter selected at random is a Republican?
   b) If the probability of rain tomorrow is 0.4, what is the probability that it will not rain?

4. An urn contains 600 glass balls. Each ball has a left half and a right half of different colors. The left may be G or Y (for green or yellow) and the right half may be R, W, or B (for red, white, or blue). The numbers of balls of various colors are shown in the table.

	R	W	B
G	30	42	138
Y	270	78	42

   a) Are white and blue mutually exclusive? Why?
   b) Are white and blue independent? Why?
   c) Are yellow and white mutually exclusive? Why?
   d) Are yellow and white independent? Why?
   e) Are yellow and red mutually exclusive? Why?
   f) Are yellow and red independent? Why?

5. An urn contains 400 small glass balls. Each ball has a left half and a right half of different colors. The left half may be R, W, or B (for red, white, or blue), and the right half may be Y, G, or T (for yellow, green, or tan). Each ball has R, W, or B on one side and Y, G, or T on the other, except that none of the balls has red on one side and green on the other. A ball that has, say, red and yellow can be said to have some red (or some yellow). There are 200 balls having some red; 40 are red and yellow; 10 are white and yellow, 50 are blue and yellow; 50 have some green; 20 are white and green; 120 have some blue. Construct a table having three rows labeled R, W, and B and three columns headed Y, G, and T. Place the given numbers in their proper position in the table. Then fill in the remaining elements and totals.

   A ball is selected at random. What is the probability that it has the following colors on it?
   a) Some red.
   b) Some green.
   c) White or green.
   d) Red and blue.
   e) Red and green.
   f) Both sides red.
   g) Some yellow.
   h) Red or green.
   i) Blue and tan.

   A ball that we cannot see has been selected. Answer the following according to the information provided
   j) If the ball drawn has some blue, what is the probability that the other color is green?
   k) If the ball drawn has some yellow, what is the probability that the other color is red?
   l) If the ball drawn is green, what is the probability that the other color is red?

11.10 PROBLEM SET 11-3 (concluded)

Answer the following:

m) Are white and yellow mutually exclusive? Why?
n) Are white and yellow independent? Why?
o) Are white and tan mutually exclusive? Why?
p) Are white and tan independent? Why?
q) Are red and green mutually exclusive? Why?
r) Are red and green independent? Why?

6. In the table, H, M, and L stand for high absenteeism, medium absenteeism, and low absenteeism, respectively. S stands for salaried worker and P for hourly paid worker. The table shows, for example, that there were 40 salaried workers who had high absentee records. Assigning probabilities as relative frequencies, show that method of pay and absenteeism (for these data) are independent in the probability sense.

	H	M	L
S	40	60	100
P	60	90	150

7. A plant has 300 workers, 200 of whom are females. Classified by H, M, and L absenteeism, there are 30 workers in the H class and 30 workers in the L class. Assuming independence of sex and absenteeism, how many workers should there be in each of the six possible classes?

8. Prove that, in general
   a) If $P(A \mid B) = P(A)$, then $P(B \mid A) = P(B)$.
   b) If $P(A \mid B) \neq P(A)$, then $P(B \mid A) \neq P(B)$.

11.11 PROBABILITY RULES

Table 11–12 (page 772) showed the numbers of people in each category, the marginal totals, and the grand total, 500. We now divide each number in Table 11–12 by 500 to yield the **probabilities** shown in Table 11–14.

From Table 11–12 we computed

$$P(W \cup F) = \frac{400 + 240 - 170}{500}$$

$$= \frac{400}{500} + \frac{240}{500} - \frac{170}{500}$$

$$= 0.80 + 0.48 - 0.34 = 0.94.$$

The corresponding calculation can be made directly from Table 11–14 as

$$P(W \cup F) = P(W) + P(F) - P(W \cap F)$$
$$= 0.80 + 0.48 - 0.34 = 0.94.$$

TABLE 11-14

	Favor (F)	Disfavor (D)	Neutral (N)	Totals
Men (M)	0.14	0.02	0.04	0.20
Women (W)	0.34	0.30	0.16	0.80
Totals	0.48	0.32	0.20	1.00

On the other hand, from Table 11–14

$$P(F \cup D) = P(F) + P(D) - P(F \cap D)$$
$$= 0.48 + 0.32 - 0$$
$$= 0.80$$

where, here, $P(F \cap D) = 0$ because F and D are mutually exclusive. Generalizing these results, we have the following rule:

Addition Rule

The probability that A or B occurs is the probability of A plus the probability of B, minus the probability of A and B. Thus

$$P(A \cup B) = P(A) + P(B) - P(A \cap B).$$

If A and B are mutually exclusive, then

$$P(A \cup B) = P(A) + P(B).$$

The probability of the union of two events is the sum of the two individual probabilities minus their joint probability; that is,

$P(A \cup B) = P(A) + P(B) - P(A \cap B).$

Exercise. From the Table 11–14 find: a) $P(M \cup N)$. b) $P(M \cup W)$. c) $P(D \cup N)$.

Answer: a) $0.20 + 0.20 - 0.04 = 0.36$. b) $0.20 + 0.80 - 0 = 1$. c) $0.32 + 0.20 - 0 = 0.52$.

As another example, suppose a political candidate runs for two offices: A and B. She assesses her probabilities of winning at 0.30 and 0.20 for A and B, respectively, and thinks she has an outside chance, probability 0.05, of winning both offices. The probability of winning A or B would then be

$$P(A \cup B) = P(A) + P(B) - P(A \cap B)$$
$$= 0.30 + 0.20 - 0.05$$
$$= 0.45.$$

Exercise. An investor thinks the probability that stock P will rise tomorrow is 0.70, and the probability that stock Q will rise is 0.80. He thinks there is a 50–50 chance that both will rise. What is his probability that P or Q will rise?

Answer: $0.70 + 0.80 - 0.50 = 1.00$.

If subjective probabilities lead to results with probabilities greater than 1 or less than 0, then the assignments must be reevaluated.

It is worth noting in the preceding exercise that the investor's subjective probability assignments lead logically to the conclusion that he is certain (probability 1) that P or Q will rise. Note also that if the investor had assessed the probability that both will rise at 0.4 (rather than 0.5), then $0.7 + 0.8 - 0.4 = 1.1$. **This would lead the investor to reassess probabilities because the probability of an event cannot exceed 1.** The last sentence illustrates a fundamental reason for understanding probability rules, namely to monitor probability assessments and ensure the internal logical consistency of such assessments.

Returning to Table 11–12 on page 772, recall that

$$P(F \mid M) = \frac{70}{100} = 0.70.$$

If we express the latter in the equivalent manner,

$$P(F \mid M) = \frac{70/500}{100/500} = \frac{0.14}{0.20} = 0.70$$

and relate the 0.14 and 0.20 to Table 11–14 on page 782, we observe that

$$P(F \cap M) = 0.14 \quad \text{and} \quad P(M) = 0.20.$$

It follows that

$$P(F \mid M) = \frac{P(F \cap M)}{P(M)}.$$

Thus the probability of F given M is the probability of the joint event, $F \cap M$, divided by the probability of M. Correspondingly

$$P(M \mid F) = \frac{P(M \cap F)}{P(F)}$$

which, from Table 11–14, is

$$P(M \mid F) = \frac{0.14}{0.48} = 0.292.$$

Exercise. Complete the following: a) $P(N \mid W) =$. b) $P(W \mid N) =$. Compute a) and b) from Table 11–14.

Answer: a) $P(N \mid W) = P(N \cap W)/P(W)$. b) $P(W \mid N) = P(W \cap N)/(P(N)$. The probabilities are a) 0.20 and b) 0.80.

The preceding examples and exercise lead to the following rule:

Conditional Probability Rule

The probability that B will occur, given that A has occurred, is the probability of $B \cap A$ divided by the probability of A. Thus

$$P(B \mid A) = \frac{P(B \cap A)}{P(A)} = \frac{P(A \cap B)}{P(A)}.$$

The conditional probability of event B given event A is the joint probability divided by the probability of A; that is,

$$P(B \mid A) = \frac{P(B \cap A)}{P(A)}$$
$$= \frac{P(A \cap B)}{P(A)}.$$

The rule just stated can be solved for $P(A \cap B)$ after multiplying both sides by $P(A)$. The result is

Joint Probability Rule

The probability of $A \cap B$ is the probability of A times the probability of B, given A, Thus

$$P(A \cap B) = P(A)P(B \mid A).$$

The joint probability of two events, A and B, is the probability of the first event, A, times the conditional probability of the second event, B, given A; that is,

$$P(A \cap B) = P(A) \cdot P(B \mid A).$$

As an example, suppose a box contains two defective and three good items, $DDGGG$. Two items are to be selected. We seek the probability, $P(GD)$, that the first is good and the second defective:

$$P(GD) = P(G)P(D \mid G).$$

The probability, $P(G)$, that the first is good is 3/5. We reason that if the first selected is G, the four remaining are $DDGG$, so the probability, $P(D \mid G)$, that the second is defective, given the first is good, is 2/4. Hence

$$P(GD) = \frac{3}{5} \cdot \frac{2}{4} = 0.30.$$

Observe that **order is significant** in the context of the last example. Thus GD means **first good, second defective.** Similarly GGD means first good, second good, third defective. Using a continuation of the joint probability rule,

$$P(GGD) = P(G)P(G \mid G)P(D \mid GG),$$

which means that $P(GGD)$ is the probability that the first is good times the probability that the second is good, given that the first is good, times the probability that the third is defective, given that the first two are good. Arithmetically

$$P(GGD) = \frac{3}{5} \cdot \frac{2}{4} \cdot \frac{2}{3} = 0.20.$$

> **Exercise.** For the preceding example, compute: a) $P(DD)$. b) $P(DDG)$. c) $P(DDD)$.
>
> **Answer:** a) 0.1. b) 0.1. c) 0.

Recalling that independence implies

$$P(B \mid A) = P(B),$$

when A and B are independent, we may substitute $P(B)$ for $P(B \mid A)$ in the joint probability rule and obtain $P(A \cap B) = P(A)P(B)$.

The joint probability of two independent events, A and B, is simply the product of the individual probabilities; that is,

$P(A \cap B) = P(A) \cdot P(B)$.

> **Joint Probability Rule, Independent Events**
>
> If A and B are independent in the probability sense, then the probability of the joint event $A \cap B$ is the probability of A times the probability of B. Thus
>
> $$P(A \cap B) = P(A)P(B).$$

We may use this rule as a test for independence. For example, in Table 11–14 on page 782, we note that

$$P(M) = 0.2, \quad P(N) = 0.2, \quad \text{and} \quad P(M \cap N) = 0.04.$$

Hence

$$P(M)P(N) = (0.2)(0.2) = 0.04 = P(MN),$$

so M and N are independent.

> **Exercise.** Refer to Table 11–14. Are W and D independent? Explain.
>
> **Answer:** $P(W) = 0.80, P(D) = 0.32$, whereas $P(W \cap D) = 0.30$. $P(W \cap D) \neq P(W)P(D)$, so W and D are not independent.

Independence in the probability sense has many real-world applications.

The assumption of independence underlies a multitude of probability applications. For example, suppose that, by test, a fire alarm functions successfully, S, in the presence of fire 90 percent of the time and fails, F, 10 percent of the time. For added protection, a store installs two alarms that operate independently. If there is a fire, what is the probability that both will fail? Here $P(F) = 0.1$ and, because of independence,

$$P(FF) = P(F)P(F) = (0.1)(0.1) = 0.01.$$

> **Exercise.** For the preceding example, find the probability that: a) Both will function successfully. b) The first will function and the second will fail.
> **Answer:** a) $P(SS) = (0.9)(0.9) = 0.81.$ b) $P(SF) = (0.9)(0.1) = 0.09.$

11.12 PRACTICE WITH PROBABILITY RULES

In this section we present a series of examples to provide further practice with probability rules and also illustrate how tree diagrams can be helpful in solving probability problems.

Example. A job applicant assigns probabilities as follows: The probability, $P(A)$, of being offered a job at company A is 0.6; the probability, $P(B)$, of being offered a job at company B is 0.5; the probability of being offered a job at both companies is 0.4. What is the probability of being offered a job with at least one of the two companies?

Here we shall apply a tabular approach to the problem. The given probabilities are entered in Table 11–15A; the entries in Table 11–15B follow as logical consequences. For example, the value $P(A \cap B') = 0.2$ is simply the difference between the row total 0.6 for $P(A)$ and the entry 0.4 in row A and column B for $P(A \cap B)$.

TABLE 11–15A
Given

	B	B'	Totals
A	0.4		0.6
A'	—	—	—
Totals	0.5		

TABLE 11–15B
Completed Table

	B	B'	Totals
A	0.4	0.2	0.6
A'	0.1	0.3	0.4
Totals	0.5	0.5	1.0

The event in question consists of the mutually exclusive events $A \cap B'$, $A' \cap B$, and $A \cap B$. By addition rule, then, we have

$$P[(A \cap B') \cup (A' \cap B) \cup (A \cap B)] = P(A \cap B') + P(A' \cap B) + P(A \cap B)$$
$$= 0.2 + 0.1 + 0.4$$
$$= 0.7.$$

<mark>Solving problems using the complementary event is often the simplest approach.</mark>

The complement of the event in question is $A' \cap B'$, so that the desired probability could alternatively have been found as

$$P[(A' \cap B')'] = 1 - P(A' \cap B')$$
$$= 1 - 0.3$$
$$= 0.7.$$

When only two events are at hand, problems often can be solved quite easily by construction of a two-by-two table as in the preceding example.

> **Exercise.** The probability of good weather, G, is 0.6 and the probability of accident, A, is 0.014. The probability of the joint event, accident and good weather, is 0.006. Find the probability of accident if the weather is not good. (Hint: Make a two-by-two table.)
>
> **Answer:** 0.02.

The completion of a two-by-two table may require application of the probability rule for joint events, as shown next.

Example. Ten percent of the workers in an area are accountants; 60 percent of accountants read the area paper *Goodnews*, and 30 percent of those who are not accountants read *Goodnews*. If a worker is selected at random, what is the probability that the worker reads *Goodnews*?

If we make a tabular format with A meaning accountant and G meaning a reader of *Goodnews*, the only direct entry that can be made from the given information is $P(A) = 0.10$, which follows from the fact that 10 percent are accountants. From the latter, we find $P(A') = 1 - 0.10 = 0.90$ and start the two-by-two table as shown in Table 11–16A.

In order to complete Table 11–16A we need joint probabilities. The key matter to think about is the meaning of a statement such as **60 percent of the accountants read *Goodnews***. The proper interpretation starts by observing that the statement is limited to accountants; that is, **accountant is given,** and the 60 percent is the probability of reading *Goodnews* given accountant,

$$P(G \mid A) = 0.60.$$

TABLE 11–16A

	G	G'	Totals
A			0.10
A'	—	—	0.90
Totals			1.00

TABLE 11–16B

	G	G'	Totals
A	0.06	0.04	0.10
A'	0.27	0.63	0.90
Totals	0.33	0.67	1.00

By similar reasoning, the meaning of **30 percent of those who are not accountants read *Goodnews*** is

$$P(G \mid A') = 0.30.$$

We can now determine the probabilities for the joint events $A \cap G$ and $A' \cap G$. These are

$$P(A \cap G) = P(A)P(G \mid A) = (0.10)(0.6) = 0.06$$
$$P(A' \cap G) = P(A')P(G \mid A') = (0.90)(0.30) = 0.27.$$

Completing Table 11–16A, we have the results shown in Table 11–16B. From Table 11–16B, we see that the answer to the question is the probability of G, which is

$$P(G) = 0.33.$$

■ **Tree Diagrams**

In Section 11.2 we saw that tree diagrams can be helpful in solving counting problems. Next we show that a tree diagram often is helpful in solving probability problems, especially when more than two events are involved.

Example. Solve the preceding example by a tree diagram.

We start by showing an initial node or **fork** (the oblong at the left of Figure 11–4A on page 790) and drawing two **branches** from the fork. One is A (for accountant) and the other A' (for not accountant). The respective probabilities for A and A' (0.1 and 0.9) are shown at the right ends of the two branches that end at the right-hand forks. Next Figure 11–4B shows two branches from each of the right-hand forks of Figure 11–4A. Each of the new pair of branches contains G and G', for those who are and are not readers of *Goodnews*. The new branch

FIGURE 11-4A

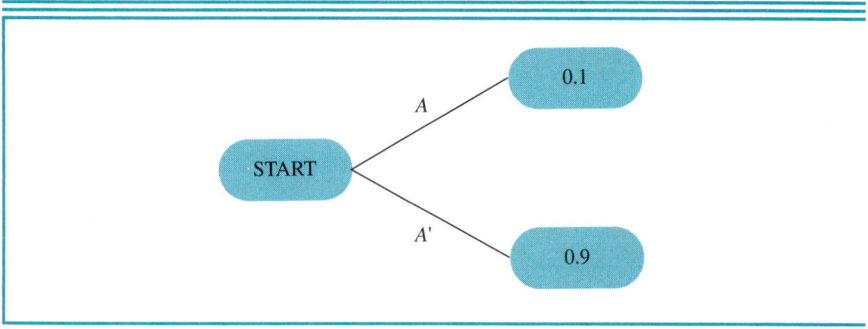

FIGURE 11-4B

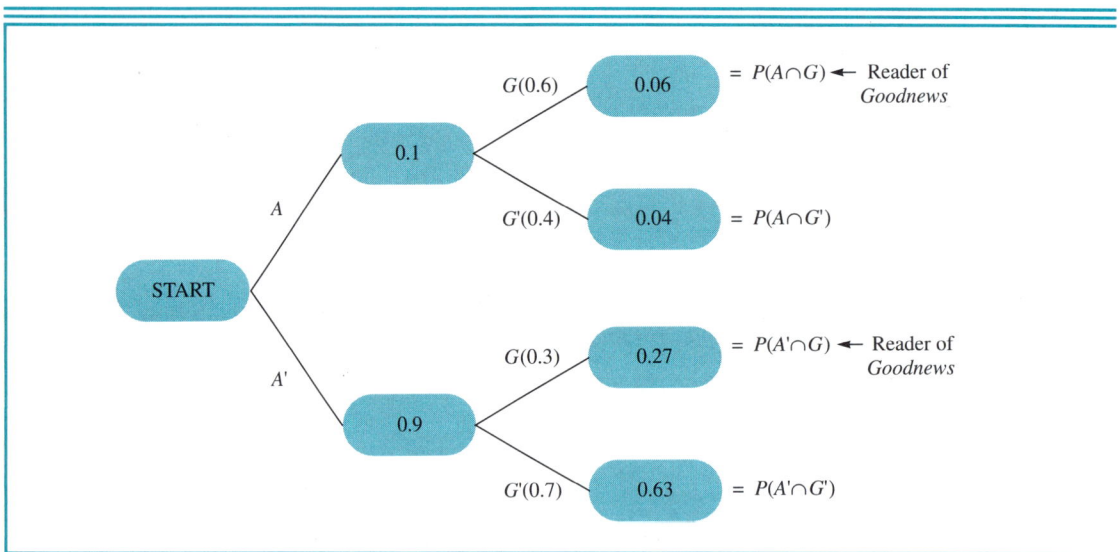

probabilities, indicated in parentheses, are **conditional probabilities.** Thus $G(0.6)$ on the top right branch of Figure 11–4B is the probability of G **given** A, as stated in the preceding example. Inasmuch as

$$P(G \mid A) + P(G' \mid A) = 1,$$

we have the conditional probability

$$P(G' \mid A) = 1 - P(G \mid A) = 1 - 0.6 = 0.4,$$

which is shown as $G'(0.4)$ in Figure 11–4B. Similarly, from the preceding example, $P(G \mid A') = 0.3$, so

$$P(G' \mid A') = 1 - 0.3 = 0.7,$$

as shown by $G(0.3)$ and $G'(0.7)$ on the bottom pair of branches of Figure 11–4B.

Finally the probability at the end of a branch is the probability at the beginning fork times the (conditional) branch probability. We complete the tree by filling in the conditional branch probabilities, then multiplying these by beginning fork probabilities to obtain the end probabilities, as shown in Figure 11–4B. The first and third joint events, $A \cap G$ and $A' \cap G$, represent readers of *Goodnews*, so

$$P(G) = 0.06 + 0.27 = 0.33,$$

as before.

Defining a **fork** as a point from which **branches** emerge, we may state the following rules each of which should be verified using the preceding example:

Rules for Trees

1. The sum of the probabilities on all branches from the initial fork is 1.
2. The probability at the end of a branch is the probability at the beginning fork multiplied by the (conditional) branch probability.
3. The sum of the probabilities at the ends of the branches from a fork equals the probability at the fork.
4. The probability at a fork is the joint probability of all events leading to the fork.
5. The probability of an event E is the sum of the probabilities of all joint events in which E appears.

Trees consist of branches extending from forks. By means of joint and conditional probabilities they can be helpful in visualizing and solving probability problems.

Example. To advertise the opening of a new store, management plans to hold one large outdoor display of fireworks on Thursday, Friday, or Saturday of the opening week if it does not rain. A meteorologist states that the probability of rain on Thursday is 0.6, but if it rains on Thursday, the probability of rain on Friday is 0.7, and if it rains on both Thursday and Friday, the probability of rain on Saturday is 0.10. What is the probability that the fireworks display will occur?

The tree in Figure 11–5 contains the given information, using R for rain and R' for not rain. We want only events containing R' (not rain) and, furthermore, if R' appears on a branch the fireworks display is held on the corresponding day and that part of the tree ceases at the end of that branch. Figure 11–5 presents the relevant branches of the tree and the given probabilities.

Exercise. Verify the probabilities in Figure 11–5. What is the probability that the fireworks display will be held?

Answer: $0.378 + 0.18 + 0.4 = 0.958$.

FIGURE 11-5

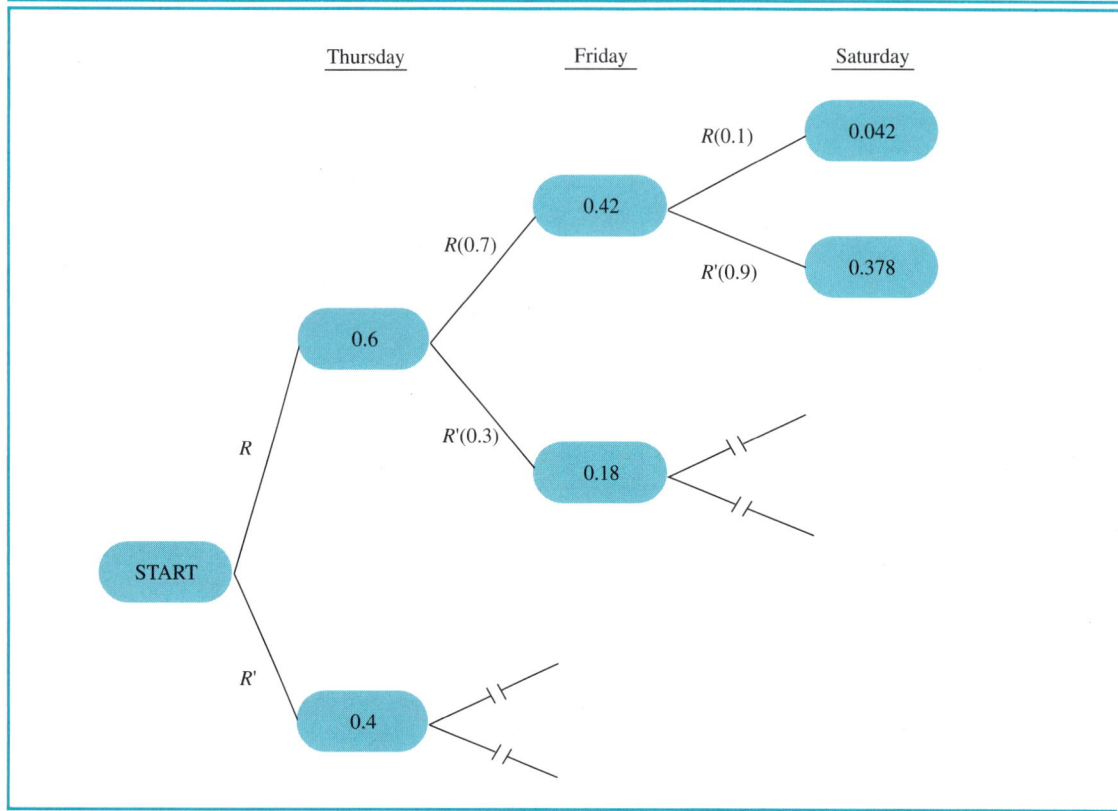

Now that we have done the problem the hard way, we can see that the only joint event that would result in the fireworks display **not** being held is rain on all three days. Hence the top path, *RRR*, with probability 0.042, is the **complement** of the desired event, so the answer to our problem is

$$1 - 0.042 = 0.958,$$

as shown in the exercise.

Situations often arise where events are, or are assumed to be, independent, and the complementary approach is the best way to solve the problem.

Example. In a lottery, a person buys a ticket containing four digits, and each digit is selected by a random procedure from the digits 0, 1, 2, . . . , 8, 9. The ticket holder wins a prize if the ticket held contains the same digit at least twice. What is the probability of having a winning ticket?

There are numerous ways of having a number occur at least twice. We have, as examples, 3537, 3339, and 3333. The **only** way for a digit not to appear at least twice is for every digit to be different. Thus **all digits different** is the **complement** of the event whose probability is sought. To compute the probability of this complement, we start with the observation that the first digit may be any digit, but the second digit must be different from the first. Hence whatever digit is drawn first in the lottery, there remain 9 different digits in the 10 that can appear when the second is drawn. Therefore

$$P(\text{Second different from first}) = \frac{9}{10}.$$

There are now eight digits different from the first and second remaining when the third digit is drawn. Hence

$$P(\text{Third different from first and second}) = \frac{8}{10}.$$

Similarly

$$P(\text{Fourth different from first, second, and third}) = \frac{7}{10}.$$

Because the outcome of the drawing of a digit does not depend on what happened in previous drawings, we have independent events, and the probability that all three occur is the product of the three probabilities:

$$P(\text{All digits different}) = \frac{9}{10} \cdot \frac{8}{10} \cdot \frac{7}{10} = \frac{504}{1,000} = 0.504.$$

Finally

$$P(\text{At least two digits same}) = 1 - P(\text{All digits different})$$
$$= 1 - 0.504 = 0.496.$$

11.13 PROBLEM SET 11-4

1. Convert the following to a probability table.

Store Size ($ Volume)

Geographic Area	Large L	Medium M	Small S
A	30	45	75
B	150	125	275
C	20	130	150

2. a) Complete the following probability table (Note: C' and F' are complements of C and F, respectively.)

	F	F'	Totals
C		0.24	
C'			0.60
Totals		0.40	

Find the following probabilities:
b) $P(C \cap F')$.
c) $P(C \cup F)$.
d) $P(C \cap C')$.
e) $P(F \mid C)$.
f) $P(C \mid F)$.

11.13 PROBLEM SET 11-4 (continued)

   g) $P(F \mid F')$.
   h) Are C and F independent? Why?
   i) Why is $P(F \cup F') = 1$?

3. A political candidate runs for two offices: A and B. She assesses her probabilities of winning at 0.6 and 0.2, respectively, and thinks she has only a probability of 0.01 of winning both.
   a) What is the probability that she wins one office *or* the other?
   b) If the candidate sets $P(A) = 0.7$, $P(B) = 0.4$, and $P(A \cap B) = 0.01$, what advice should she be given? Why?

4. A weatherman states that if it is colder tomorrow, the probability of snow is 0.7. He also states the probability that it will be colder is 0.5. What is the probability it will be colder *and* snow tomorrow? Why?

5. The probability that a student will graduate with honors and get a good job is 0.09, whereas the probability that a student will graduate with honors is 0.1. What is the probability that a student will get a good job if she graduates with honors?

6. A salesman has two prospective customers, A and B, to call on one day. He assigns the probability of making a sale to A at 0.4, of making a sale to B at 0.3, and the probability of making a sale to both at 0.1. What is the probability of making a sale to at least one of the customers?

7. In order to ensure that weather will not prevent making an air trip, an executive makes plane reservations for two successive days and assesses the probability of being able to fly either day at 0.95. What is the probability that the executive will be able to make the trip? (Assume independence.)

8. If $P(X \mid Y) = 0.7$, what is $P(X' \mid Y)$?

9. Given $P(X) = 0.6$, $P(Y) = 0.4$, and $P(X \cap Y) = 0.1$, find $P(X \mid Y)$ and $P(Y \mid X)$.

10. If $P(Y \mid X) = 0.4$, $P(X \mid Y) = 0.5$, and $P(X \cap Y) = 0.2$, find $P(X)$ and $P(Y)$.

11. If $P(Y \mid X) = 0.72$, $P(X \cap Y) = 0.18$, and $P(Y') = 0.4$, find $P(X \cup Y)$.

12. A candidate runs for two political offices: A and B. He assigns 0.4 as the probability of being elected to both, 0.7 as the probability of being elected to A if he is elected to B, and 0.8 as the probability of being elected to B if he is elected to A.
   a) What is the probability of being elected to A?
   b) What is the probability of being elected to B?
   c) What is the joint probability of being elected to neither?
   d) What is the probability of being elected to at least one of the offices?

13. The probability of snow is 0.4; of colder weather 0.5; and the conditional probability of snow if the weather turns colder is 0.7. Find the probability of
   a) Colder and snow.
   b) No snow.
   c) Either colder or snow.
   d) Neither colder nor snow.

14. Job candidates are screened by means of a preliminary interview. The probability is 0.6 that a screened candidate will be a good worker. Screened candidates are given a test. If the candidate is one who will prove to be a good worker, the probability of his passing the test is 0.8. If the candidate is one who will prove to be a poor worker, the probability of his passing the test is 0.4.
   a) What is the probability that a screened candidate will be a good worker and pass the test?
   b) What is the probability that a screened candidate will not be a good worker and will pass the test?

15. Fran plans to offer a new product for sale. In assessing the chances that the product will be successful, Fran has to take her competitor, Judy, into account because Judy may offer a competing new product for sale. Fran thinks that the chance of Judy competing is 0.4. Fran assesses the probability that she will be successful to be 0.85 if Judy does not compete, but only 0.25 if Judy does compete. Compute Fran's chance of being successful.

16. The first time an insurance salesman calls on a new client, he has a probability of 0.1 of selling a policy. *If* he does not sell the policy on the first call, he makes a second call and has a probability of 0.3 of making the sale. *If* he does not make the sale on either of the first two calls, he makes one final call and has a probability of 0.05 of making the sale. What is the probability that the insurance man will sell the policy to a client?

11.13 PROBLEM SET 11-4 (continued)

17. A company assesses the probability that its product will fail during the first month after sale as 0.01. The probability it will fail during the next 11 months if it did not fail during the first month is 0.001. The company guarantees the product for the first year. What is the probability that the product will fail in the first year?

18. See Problem 17. Suppose the probability of failure during the first month is 0.05, the probability of failure during the next five months (if the product did not fail in the first month) is 0.02, and the probability of failure for the remainder of the year if failure did not occur during the first noted time intervals is 0.01. What is the probability of failure during the first year?

19. Snow and colder weather are the events with $P(S) = 0.8$, $P(C) = 0.6$, $P(S' \cap C) = 0.1$.
    a) Show that the events are not independent in the probability sense.
    b) What probability would $S' \cap C$ have if the events were to be independent in the probability sense?

20. The probability that machine A will break down on a particular day is
    $$P(A) = 1/50.$$
    Similarly for Machine B,
    $$P(B) = 1/80.$$
    Assuming independence, on a particular day,
    a) What is the probability that both will break down?
    b) What is the probability that neither will break down?
    c) What is the probability that one or the other will break down?
    d) What is the probability that exactly one machine will break down?

21. A pair of dice is rolled, and a coin is tossed. Assuming independence, what is the probability of
    a) Heads on the coin and a 7 on the dice?
    b) Heads on the coin or a 7 on the dice?
    c) Heads on the coin and an even number on the dice?
    d) Heads on the coin or a sum greater than 8 on the dice?

22. Five parts go into the assembly of item X. The assembly is defective if any one of the parts is defective, and each part has a probability of 0.03 of being defective. Assuming independence, what is the probability that an assembly is defective?

23. Suppose an arena has two events, hockey and basketball, scheduled on Thursday and another two, hockey and track, on Friday. If two are selected to be played and two cancelled, calculate by probability rules the probability that there will be a hockey game on Thursday or on Friday.

24. Company A plans to bid on a contract. It does not know whether or not a competitor, Company B, will bid, but assesses the probability that it will bid at 0.6. A judges that it has a probability of winning of 0.8 if B does not bid, but only a probability of 0.4 if B does bid. What is the probability that A wins?

25. An arena has scheduled two events on Thursday and three on Friday of a particular week. To obtain time to carry out repairs, two of the events, selected at random, are to be postponed. Find the probability that there will be an event on Thursday and an event on Friday.

26. Five people at a party were born in the month of December. What is the probability that at least two of the five have the same birthday?

27. A mathematics class has 30 students. What is the probability that at least two have the same birthday (the same day of the same month)? Assume independence and assume a year has 365 days.

28. The casino game of craps is played with two dice, each of which has six faces numbered 1 through 6. The two dice are thrown and the numbers appearing on the two upper faces are added together. Determine the probability of each of the possible sums on the first toss of the dice.

29. The daily lottery number consists of four sets of balls, each numbered 0, 1, 2, . . . , 9. Each set is placed in a rotating urn and a single ball is selected from each urn. Determine the probability of matching.
    a) The first three numbers selected.
    b) All four numbers selected.

30. There are three semiweekly lotteries. What is the probability of matching
    a) A five-number selection in a lottery drawn from 35 numbered balls?

11.13 PROBLEM SET 11-4 (concluded)

b) A six-number selection in a lottery drawn from 42 numbered balls?
c) A six-number selection in a lottery drawn from 49 numbered balls?

31. Each hand in the game of poker consists of five cards drawn from a standard deck of 52. If five cards are dealt from the top of the deck, what is the probability that they are

a) Three aces and two kings?
b) Two aces and three kings?
c) Three of one kind and two of another kind (a full house)? [Hint: Refer to (a) and (b).]
d) Four of a kind?
e) All the same suit (a flush)?

11.14 BAYES' RULE

As a result of past hiring procedure, a company finds that 60 percent of its employees are good workers, G, and 40 percent are poor workers, which we shall designate by the complement, G'. The woman in charge of hiring believes that the proportion of good workers can be increased by designing a test to be administered to job applicants, and hiring only those who pass, P, the test. A consulting firm supplies the test and offers to administer it to applicants for a fee. Because of the cost, it is decided to determine how well the test discriminates between good and poor workers by trying it on current employees. It is found that 80 percent of the good workers and 40 percent of the poor workers pass the test. It is important to understand that these last two numbers are **conditional probabilities** because the first applies only to good workers and the second applies to poor workers. That is, *if* a worker is a good worker, the probability of passing is 0.80, so

$$P(P \mid G) = 0.80.$$

Similarly

$$P(P \mid G') = 0.40.$$

Note that

$$P(P \mid G) \neq 1 - P(P \mid G')$$

because there is no **necessary relationship** between a good worker's passing the test and a poor worker's passing the test.[4]

At first glance it may appear that the test functions well because it is twice as likely (0.80 versus 0.40) that an employee will pass if he is a good worker than if he is a poor worker. The important point to note, however, is that the real question at hand is whether the test should be used in selecting employees from job applicants.

For two events A and B,

$P(A \mid B) + P(A' \mid B) = 1$,

but $P(A \mid B)$ and $P(A \mid B')$ need not sum to 1.

---

[4]Similarly the probability that it will snow tomorrow if it is colder, $P(S \mid C)$, tells us nothing about $P(S \mid C')$, the probability that it will snow if it does not get colder. However **if the given is the same** as in $P(S \mid C)$ and $P(S' \mid C)$, then $P(S' \mid C) = 1 - P(S \mid C)$, which means simply that if it is colder it **must snow** or **not snow**, so $P(S \mid C) + P(S' \mid C) = 1$.

Thus the issue is not whether an employee will pass if he is a good worker, $P(P \mid G)$, but rather $P(G \mid P)$, which is the probability that an employee will be a good worker if he passes the test. Thus we know $P(P \mid G)$ and we seek the **inverse probability,** $P(G \mid P)$. We have given

$$P(G) = 0.60 \qquad P(G') = 1 - P(G) = 0.40.$$
$$P(P \mid G) = 0.80 \qquad P(P \mid G') = 0.40.$$

From the preceding we can compute

$$P(P \cap G) = P(G)P(P \mid G) = (0.60)(0.80) = 0.48.$$
$$P(P \cap G') = P(G')P(P \mid G') = (0.40)(0.40) = 0.16.$$

We now have the two-by-two table shown in Table 11–17.

Exercise. Fill in the P'-column of Table 11–17.

Answer: $P(G \cap P') = 0.12$, $P(G' \cap P') = 0.24$, and $P(P') = 0.36$.

It follows from Table 11–17 that

$$P(G \mid P) = \frac{0.48}{0.64} = 0.75.$$

To see the significance of the last result, recall that 60 percent of current employees are good workers. This means that past or prior employment procedures, without the test, had a probability of $P(G) = 0.60$, which we shall call the **prior probability**, of selecting a good worker. If we change the selection procedure and employ only those who pass the test, we **revise** the probability of hiring a good worker to $P(G \mid P) = 0.75$, and this revised probability is called the **posterior probability**. Management must decide whether the additional information provided by a test, which results in an increase in the probability of hiring good workers from 0.60 to 0.75, is worth the cost of administering the test.

To develop the formula (Bayes' Rule) for determining $P(G \mid P)$ from $P(P \mid G)$, refer to the preceding calculation of $P(G \mid P) = 0.75$,

$$P(G \mid P) = 0.75 = \frac{0.48}{0.64}.$$

Prior probabilities are unconditional probabilities based on past experience; posterior probabilities are revised conditional probabilities computed from additional information.

TABLE 11–17

	P	P'	Totals
G	0.48		0.6
G'	0.16		0.4
Totals	0.64	—	1.0

From Table 11–17 on page 799 we see that the numerator 0.48 on the right is

$$P(P \cap G) = 0.48$$

and the denominator 0.64 is

$$P(P \cap G) + P(P \cap G') = 0.48 + 0.16.$$

Hence

$$P(G \mid P) = 0.75 = \frac{0.48}{0.48 + 0.16}$$

$$P(G \mid P) = \frac{P(P \cap G)}{P(P \cap G) + P(P \cap G')}. \tag{1}$$

In the denominator of Equation (1) we have probabilities for the joint events $P \cap G$ and $P \cap G'$. The rule for joint probabilities allows us to write

$$P(P \cap G) = P(P \mid G)P(G)$$
$$P(P \cap G') = P(P \mid G')P(G').$$

Substituting this into Equation (1) yields

$$P(G \mid P) = \frac{P(P \mid G)P(G)}{P(P \mid G)P(G) + P(P \mid G')P(G')}. \tag{2}$$

Bayes' Rule for two events A and B computes the posterior probability $P(B \mid A)$ from the prior probabilities for B and B' together with the conditional probabilities for A given B and B'.

Bayes' Rule

$$P(B \mid A) = \frac{P(A \mid B)P(B)}{P(A \mid B)P(B) + P(A \mid B')P(B')}.$$

Bayes' Rule can be remembered easily if we note that in the numerator on the right we start with $P(A \mid B)$ which is simply the left side, $P(B \mid A)$ reversed. The numerator is completed in the manner of any joint probability by multiplying by $P(B)$ to give $P(A \mid B)P(B)$. The first term in the denominator repeats the numerator and the second term follows by replacing the B in the first term by B'.

Note that Bayes' Rule also comes directly from the two-by-two tables. Specifically if we examine Table 11–17 for our preceding example we see that the denominator of Equation (2) is precisely the column total for P, the **given event** in $P(G \mid P)$, and the numerator is precisely the row entry in the p-column for the desired event G.

Exercise. Use Table 11–17 to compute $P(G' \mid P)$.

Answer: $\dfrac{0.16}{0.64} = 0.25$.

To help fix in mind the inverse preceding probability concept expressed by Bayes' Rule, we shall review the example by constructing tree diagrams. Recall that the given information was

$$P(G) = 0.60 \quad \text{so} \quad P(G') = 0.40;$$
$$P(P \mid G) = 0.80 \quad \text{and} \quad P(P \mid G') = 0.40.$$

From these probabilities, we computed

$$P(G \cap P) = P(G)P(P \mid G) = (0.6)(0.8) = 0.48;$$
$$P(G' \cap P) = P(G')P(P \mid G') = (0.4)(0.4) = 0.16.$$

Figure 11–6A shows the probabilities now at hand. Note that this figure has **good** as given and shows the branch probability of passing the test, if good, is 0.8. Figure 11–6B is what we want because it shows **pass** as given, and the branch (conditional) probability $P(G \mid P)$ is the desired probability of good, given pass. To determine this, we use (3) and (4) together with Figures 11–6A and 11–6B to observe that the probabilities for the joint events $G \cap P$ and $G' \cap P$ are the same as the probabilities for $P \cap G$ and $P \cap G'$, respectively. Moreover the sum of these branch probabilities is the fork probability, 0.64, shown in Figure 11–6B, and, finally, following a tree rule,

$$(0.64)P(G \mid P) = 0.48.$$

From this, we have

$$P(G \mid P) = \dfrac{0.48}{0.64} = 0.75,$$

as before.

Exercise. Use Figure 11–6B to compute $P(G' \mid P)$.

Answer: $\dfrac{0.16}{0.64} = 0.25$.

The tree presentation just given serves well to show the inverse probability concept inherent in Bayes' Rule. For problem solving, one may use the symbolic formula, a table, or the tree approach.

FIGURE 11-6A

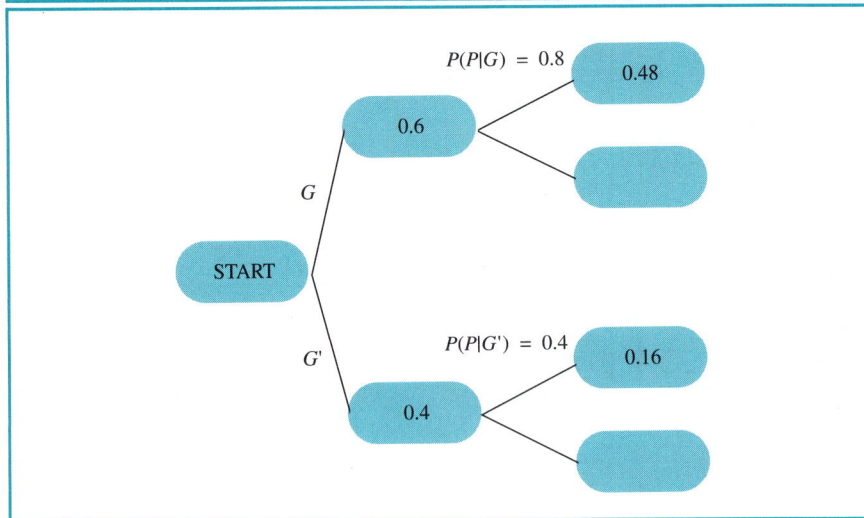

FIGURE 11-6B

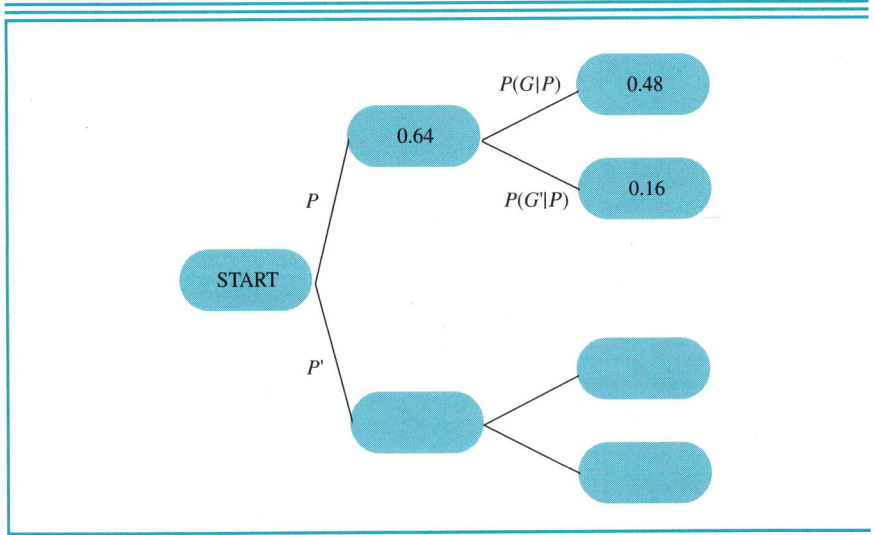

We now offer a second application of Bayes' Rule.

Bayes' Rule has many real-world applications.

Example. Suppose the probability that a person has disease D is

$$P(D) = 0.09.$$

The probability that medical examination will indicate the disease if a person has it is

$$P(I \mid D) = 0.6.$$

The probability that medical examination will indicate the disease if a person does not have it is

$$P(I \mid D') = 0.05.$$

What is the probability that a person has the disease if medical examination so indicates?

By Bayes' Rule:

$$P(D \mid I) = \frac{P(I \mid D)P(D)}{P(I \mid D)P(D) + P(I \mid D')(P(D'))}$$

$$= \frac{(0.6)(0.09)}{(0.6)(0.09) + (0.05)(0.91)}$$

$$= \frac{0.054}{0.0995} = 0.543.$$

The same result could be obtained by applying the two-by-two tabular analysis used earlier in this section. We see that the prior probability of the person having the disease, 0.09, has been revised to the posterior probability 0.543 as a consequence of the additional information that medical examination indicated the disease.

11.15 PROBLEM SET 11-5

1. Supervisors rate 87.5 percent of the workers as good workers. On a work-aptitude test, 64 percent of the good workers and 24 percent of the other (not good) workers obtained passing grades. If a worker passes the test, what is the probability that this is a good worker?

2. The probability that a person has disease D is 0.05. The probability that a medical test will indicate the disease is present is 0.80 if the person has the disease and 0.02 if the person does not have the disease. What is the probability that a person has the disease if the test so indicates?

3. A fellow notes that his girlfriend is happy on 60 percent of his visits to her home and that 40 percent of the times when she is happy she makes a drink for him. She makes drinks on 10 percent of the visits when she is not happy. If he arrives for a visit and finds her making drinks, what is the probability that she is happy?

4. The probability that a customer will be a bad debt is 0.01. The probability that he will make a large down payment if he is a bad debt is 0.20, and the probability that he will make a large down payment if he is not a bad debt is 0.60.
   a) Suppose that a customer makes a large down payment. Find the posterior probability that he will be a bad debt.
   b) What is the probability that a customer who does not make a large down payment will be a bad debt?

5. The probability that a machine is running properly is 0.95. From time to time, samples of output are selected and measured, and the sample average is computed. If the machine is running properly, the probability that the sample average will be in a certain range is 0.9. If the machine is not running properly, the probability that the sample average will be in this range is 0.04.
   a) A sample is selected, and its average is in the range. What is the probability that the machine is running correctly?
   b) What is the probability that the machine is running correctly if the sample average is not in the range?

11.5 PROBLEM SET 11-5 (concluded)

6. Two economic theories, T_1 and T_2, are proposed by two leading economists to predict the behavior of the GNP in the coming year. In the past, the two economists have been equally reliable, so we assign an equal prior probability of 0.50 to each theory. Let I be the event that the GNP increases, D the event that the GNP decreases, and S the event that the GNP is about the same as the previous year. Suppose that we have the following probabilities:

Theory	$P(T_i)$	$P(I \mid T_i)$	$P(D \mid T_i)$	$P(S \mid T_i)$
T_1	0.50	0.25	0.50	0.25
T_2	0.50	0.125	0.75	0.125

   a) Applying Bayes' Rule, find the probabilities that we would now assign to T_1 and T_2 if the GNP is actually the same or about the same as the previous year.

   b) Find the probabilities that we would now assign to T_1 and T_2 if the GNP has decreased from the previous year.

7. In Problem 6, assume that the two economic theories are not equally reliable from past experience, so that we assign $P(T_1) = 0.40$ and $P(T_2) = 0.60$. Find the probabilities that we would now assign to T_1 and T_2 if the GNP has increased over the previous year.

8. The following table is developed by a manufacturing firm indicating production by three machines: A, B, and C.

Machine	A	B	C
Percentage of total number of items produced	40%	25%	35%
Probability of a defective item	0.02	0.005	0.15

   If one item selected at random from the production line is defective, find the probability that the item was produced by
   a) Machine A.
   b) Machine B.
   c) Machine C.

9. The Business People Computer Company loses a shipment of its goods because of a mistake by one of its partners. The firm has three partners (John, Anne, and Sally) who could have made the mistake and it cannot tell with certainty which one was responsible. On the basis of past performance, it is known that the probability that John would make such a mistake is 0.001 (if he is responsible for the shipment), the probability for Anne is 0.002, and for Sally it is 0.001. If John is responsible for 50 percent of the shipments, and Anne and Sally share the rest of the responsibilities equally, what is the probability that each partner was responsible for the lost shipment?

11.16 REVIEW PROBLEMS

1. Persons are classified according to blood type and Rh quality by testing a blood sample for the presence of three antigens: A, B, and Rh. Blood is of type AB if it contains antigens A and B; A if it contains A, but not B; B if it contains B, but not A; and O if it contains neither A nor B. In addition, blood is classified as Rh positive ($+$) if the Rh antigen is present and Rh negative ($-$) otherwise. A national report stated that if 1,000 people were picked at random and their blood were sampled, then statistics indicated that 490 would contain antigen A, 515 would contain B, 430 would contain Rh, 205 would contain A and B, 140 would contain A and Rh, 160 would contain B and Rh, and 60 would contain all three.

   a) Use a table to determine the number of people who are of each of the eight blood classification types: $A+$, $A-$, $B+$, $B-$, $O+$, $O-$, $AB+$, and $AB-$.

   b) Which is the most plentiful blood classification?

   c) Which is the least plentiful blood classification?

11.6 REVIEW PROBLEMS (continued)

2. A group of 50 men and 50 women were involved in a test of a potential vaccine for the common cold. Each person was given an injection prior to the cold season, but not all received the actual vaccine. After the season had come and gone, the test results were reported as follows: 53 had been vaccinated, 48 had developed a cold, 26 men had been vaccinated, 23 men had developed a cold, 19 had been vaccinated and developed a cold, and 6 of the vaccinated men had developed a cold. Use a table to determine how many
   a) Vaccinated men had not developed a cold.
   b) Nonvaccinated men had developed a cold. Had not.
   c) Vaccinated women had developed a cold. Had not.
   d) Nonvaccinated women had developed a cold. Had not.
   e) On the basis of (a) through (d), what can be said about the effectiveness of the vaccine?

3. If three cards are drawn from a standard deck of 52 cards, how many sequences of three face-value cards could occur?

4. A multiple-choice examination consists of 10 questions, each with 3 choices for answers: A, B, and C. How many different answer sheets could there be?

5. How many different starting lineups of five basketball players can be chosen from a squad consisting of two centers, five guards (three point guards and two power guards), and five forwards?

6. How many different ways can 6 pairs of shoes be chosen from a closet containing 20 pairs of shoes?

7. How many different baseball games must be scheduled in the seven-team Eastern Division of the American League if every team plays every other team eight home and eight away games?

8. A garage entry system has 10 keys labeled 0, 1, 2, ..., 9. How many four-digit codes are possible if
   a) Repetitions are allowed?
   b) Repetitions are not allowed?

9. A coin is tossed 12 times and the sequence of heads and tails is recorded. Determine the number of
   a) Total outcomes possible.
   b) Outcomes with exactly four tails.
   c) Outcomes with at most three tails.
   d) Outcomes with at least three tails.
   e) Outcomes with at least five heads.

10. An urn contains six black balls and seven blue balls. Five balls are selected from the urn. How many ways can this be done if
    a) Color is not important?
    b) All five balls are to be black?
    c) All five balls are to be blue?
    d) There are to be three black balls and two blue balls?
    e) At least four balls are to be black?

11. The sports department of a discount store has received a shipment of 75 cartons of bungie cords. Each carton is supposed to contain 100 cords. Any carton with more or fewer cords must be sent back to the manufacturer. From past experience, the manager of the department knows that typically 8 percent of the cartons contain too many or too few cords. She has decided to test a sample of five cartons. How many different samples of five are possible with
    a) All five cartons containing the correct number of cords?
    b) One carton containing too many or too few?
    c) Two cartons containing too many or too few?
    d) No more than two cartons containing too many or too few?
    e) No more than four cartons containing too many or too few?

12. Currently 100 fourth-year medical students are training at University Hospital. Each student must rotate through the seven medical services. In a given month, 15 will be assigned to pediatrics, 20 to the emergency room, 12 to obstetrics, 8 to surgery, 17 to oncology, 10 to hematology, and 18 to orthopedics. In how many ways can the 100 students be assigned to the seven medical services?

13. Expand each of the following:
    a) $(2x + 3y)^7$.   c) $(2x - 3y)^7$.
    b) $(5x + 2y)^6$.   d) $(5x - 2y)^6$.

14. What is the coefficient of
    a) y^6 in $(2 + y)^9$.   c) y^6 in $(x + y)^{10}$.
    b) x^6 in $(x + 5)^9$.   d) x^6 in $(x + y)^{10}$.

15. The table shows, for example, that 40 cars of make Y had gear train malfunctions.

11.6 REVIEW PROBLEMS (continued)

Make of Car	Malfunction		
	Electrical (E)	Gear Train (G)	Carburetor (C)
X	17	60	23
Y	20	40	60
Z	15	48	117

Find the following probabilities:
a) $P(Y)$.
b) $P(E)$.
c) $P(C)$.
d) $P(X \cap G)$.
e) $P(G \cap X)$.
f) $P(E \cap G)$.
g) $P(Z \cap X)$.
h) $P(Y \cap C)$.
i) $P(X \mid C)$.
j) $P(C \mid X)$.
k) $P(E \mid Z)$.
l) $P(Z \mid G)$.
m) $P(X \cup Y)$.
n) $P(X \cup C)$.
o) $P(G \cup C)$.
p) $P(Y \cup G)$.

16. See the table of Problem 15.
   a) Are Z and C independent? Explain.
   b) Are Y and C independent? Explain.
   c) What is $P(X \cap Y)$? What does this mean?

17. a) In some areas, one may often predict tomorrow's weather correctly by stating it will be the same as today's weather. In such areas, is tomorrow's weather independent of today's weather? Explain.
   b) A card is to be drawn from a deck. Let B represent black card and D represent diamond. Are B and D mutually exclusive? Independent? Explain.
   c) Consider the physical traits of brown eyes, B, and dark hair, D. Are B and D mutually exclusive? Do you think B and D are independent?

18. a) Complete the following table if all event pairs such as A and X are independent.

	X	Y	Z	Totals
A				0.40
B				0.60
Totals	0.30	0.20	0.50	

Find the following probabilities from the completed table:
b) $P(A \mid X)$.
c) $P(X \mid A)$.
d) $P(X)$.
e) $P(A)$.
f) $P(A \cup X)$.
g) $P(X \cup Y)$.

19. a) Complete the following probability table. (Note: A' and B' are complements of A and B, respectively.)

	B	B'	Totals
A			0.70
A'		0.12	
Totals		0.34	

b) Are A and B independent? Explain. Compute
c) $P(B' \mid A')$.
d) $P(A \cup B')$.

20. An investor assesses the probability that the Dow-Jones stock market average will rise tomorrow as 0.65, and the probability that the price of stock S will rise if the Dow-Jones rises as 0.90. What is the probability that the Dow-Jones will rise and S will rise? Why?

21. A candidate runs for offices A and B, assessing the probability of winning both at 0.10 and the probability of winning B at 0.25. What is the probability of winning A if he wins B? Why?

22. An investor has funds in banks A and B. He assesses the probability that A will fail at 0.0001 and assigns the same failure probability to B. Further, he thinks the probability that both banks will fail is 0.00001.
   a) What is the probability that A or B will fail?
   b) Are the events A fails, B fails independent? Why?
   c) What is the probability that B fails if A fails?

23. A box of eight items contains six good and two defective items. If a sample of two items is selected, what is the probability that
   a) Both will be good?
   b) Both will be defective?
   c) Exactly one will be defective? (Note: Two events are involved.)
   d) If three items are drawn, what is the probability that at least one will be defective?

24. Graduation exercises are to be held outdoors on Friday if it does not rain. If it rains on Friday, the exercises will be postponed until Saturday and held outdoors if it does not rain and indoors if it rains. The probability that it will rain on Friday is 0.3, and

11.6 REVIEW PROBLEMS (continued)

the probability it will not rain on Saturday if it rains on Friday is 0.4. Find the probability that the exercises will be held outdoors.

25. A job applicant assigns probabilities as follows: The probability, $P(A)$, of being offered a job at company A is 0.4, the probability of being offered a job at B is $P(B) = 0.3$, and the probability of being offered jobs at both companies is 0.12. What is the probability of being offered a job at at least one of the two companies? At exactly one of the two companies?

26. Probability of colder weather is assigned at 0.7, probability of snow at 0.4, and probability of neither colder weather nor snow at 0.2. What is the probability
    a) That it will get colder and snow?
    b) That it will get colder but not snow?
    c) That it will snow but not get colder?

27. A test has two questions. A student assigns probability 0.6 of getting the first correct, 0.3 of getting the second correct, and 0.25 of getting both wrong.
    a) Show that with this assignment of probabilities, the outcome of the second question is not independent of the outcome of the first in the probability sense.
    b) What would the probability of getting both wrong be if the outcomes are to be independent in the probability sense?

28. The claim is made that whether or not an employee's attendance record is good depends upon the sex of the employee. On the basis of the table, using probability terminology, refute the claim.

	Number of Employees with	
Sex	Good Attendance Records	Poor Attendance Records
Male	40	10
Female	80	20

29. The probability that machine A will break down on a particular day is $P(A) = 1/100$; similarly, for machine B, $P(B) = 1/200$. Assuming independence, on a particular day,
    a) What is the probability that both will break down?
    b) What is the probability that neither will break down?
    c) What is the probability that one or the other will break down?
    d) What is the probability that exactly one will break down?

30. Five parts go into the assembly of item I. The assembly is defective if any one of the parts is defective, and each part has probability of 0.01 of being defective. Assuming independence, what is the probability that an assembly is defective?

31. There are five intersections between two cities where a driver can bear left or bear right. If, and only if, the proper turn is made at each intersection will a driver starting from one city arrive at the second city. Suppose that the driver flips a coin to choose each turn. What is the probability that he will arrive at the second city?

32. Given $P(X) = 0.5$, $P(Y) = 0.7$, and $P(X \cap Y) = 0.30$, find $P(X \mid Y)$ and $P(Y \mid X)$.

33. If $P(Y \mid X) = 0.80$, $P(X \mid Y) = 0.75$, and $P(X \cap Y) = 0.60$, find $P(X)$ and $P(Y)$.

34. If $P(Y \mid X) = 0.80$, $P(X \cap Y) = 0.20$, and $P(Y') = 0.30$, find $P(X \cup Y)$.

35. Job candidates are screened by means of a preliminary interview. The probability is 0.6 that a screened candidate will be a good worker. Screened candidates are given a test. If the candidate is one who will prove to be a good worker, the probability of her passing the test is 0.90. If the candidate is one who will prove to be a poor worker, the probability of her passing the test is 0.40.
    a) What is the probability that a screened candidate will be a good worker and pass the test?
    b) What is the probability that a screened candidate will not be a good worker and will pass the test?

36. A candidate runs for two political offices: A and B. He assigns 0.27 as the probability of being elected to both, 0.50 as the probability of being elected to A if he is elected to B, and 0.90 as the probability of being elected to B if he is elected to A.
    a) What is the probability of being elected to A?

11.6 REVIEW PROBLEMS (concluded)

b) What is the probability of being elected to B?
c) What is the probability of being elected to neither?
d) What is the probability of being elected to at least one of the offices?

37. Mr. M thinks his probability of winning an election is 0.9 if Ms. W does not run, but only 0.3 if Ms. W does run. Mr. M judges the probability that Ms. W will run to be 0.4. What is the probability that Mr. M wins the election?

38. Complete the Bayes' Rule formulation that starts with $P(A' \mid B) = $.

39. The probability that a customer will be a bad debt is 0.01. The probability that he will make a large down payment if he is a bad debt is 0.10, and the probability that he will make a large down payment if he is not a bad debt is 0.50. Suppose that a customer makes a large down payment. Find the posterior probability that he will be a bad debt.

40. Complete the tabular analysis for Problem 39 and find the probability that a customer will not be a bad debt if he does not make a large down payment.

41. The probability that a person has disease D is $P(D) = 0.008$. The probability that medical examination will indicate the disease if a person has it is $P(I \mid D) = 0.75$, and the probability that examination will indicate the disease if a person does not have it is $P(I \mid D') = 0.01$. What is the probability that a person has the disease if medical examination so indicates?

11.17 EXTENDED REVIEW PROBLEMS

1. A glass jar contains 500 marbles with one color on the left half and a different color on the right half. The left half may be orange (O), clear (C), or black (B), and the right half may be purple (P), aqua (A), or silver (S). Each marble has O, C, or B on one side and P, A, or S on the other, except that none of the marbles is clear on one side and purple on the other. A marble that is, say, orange and purple can be said to have some orange (or some purple). There are 240 marbles having some orange, 60 are orange and purple, 20 are orange and aqua, 60 are black and purple, 90 have some aqua, 40 are clear and aqua, and 140 have some black. Construct a table having three rows labeled O, C, and B and three columns labeled P, A, and S, and fill in all the entries.

   A marble is selected at random. Determine the probability that it has the following colors on it:
   a) Some clear.
   b) Some silver.
   c) Clear or aqua.
   d) Orange and black.
   e) Orange and silver.
   f) Some purple.
   g) Orange or aqua.
   h) Black and silver.

   Answer the following according to the information provided. A marble (which we cannot see) has been selected.
   i) If the marble drawn has some black, what is the probability that the other color is aqua?
   j) If the marble drawn has some purple, what is the probability that the other color is orange?
   k) If the marble drawn is aqua, what is the probability that the other color is orange?

   Answer the following:
   l) Are clear and purple mutually exclusive? Why?
   m) Are clear and purple independent? Why?
   n) Are clear and silver mutually exclusive? Why?
   o) Are clear and silver independent? Why?
   p) Are orange and aqua mutually exclusive? Why?
   q) Are orange and aqua independent? Why?

2. Two stock market theories, the fundamental analysis (S_1) and the technical analysis (S_2), are used to predict market behavior. In the past, the fundamental analysis has been 70 percent reliable and the technical analysis has been 30 percent reliable, so we assign the prior probabilities accordingly. Let I be the event that the stock market rises, D be the event that it falls, and S be the event that it is about the

11.7 EXTENDED REVIEW PROBLEMS (concluded)

same as in the past. Suppose we have the following probabilities:

Theory	$P(I\|S_i)$	$P(D\|S_i)$	$P(S\|S_i)$
S_1	0.375	0.425	0.200
S_2	0.350	0.365	0.285

a) Find the probability that we would now assign to S_1 and S_2 if the stock market is actually about the same as in the past.
b) Find the probabilities that we would now assign to S_1 and S_2 if the stock market has fallen.
c) Find the probabilities that we would now assign to S_1 and S_2 if the stock market has risen.

3. Fenway Park can seat 35,000 people in the bleachers (B), grandstand (G), and box seats (X). Five thousand seats are saved for the visiting fans (V) and the rest are left for the home fans (H). The park has 9,000 bleacher seats and 4,000 box seats. Assuming that seat location and fan preference are independent, how many seats are there in each of the six possible classes?

4. How many different ways can six pairs of shoes be stored on a shoe rack after being chosen from a closet containing 20 pairs of shoes?

5. There are three semiweekly lotteries. How many different
   a) Five-number combinations are there in a lottery with 39 numbered balls?
   b) Six-number combinations are there in a lottery with 45 numbered balls?
   c) Six-number combinations are there in a lottery with 64 numbered balls?

6. At the Indianapolis 500, Al Unser and Mario Andretti each have a race car entered. The probability that Unser's car (U) will break down is 1/40, while the probability that Andretti's car (A) will break down is 1/90. Assuming independence, on a particular day what is the probability that
   a) Both will break down?
   b) Neither will break down?
   c) One or the other will break down?
   d) Exactly one of the cars will break down?

7. In the game of hearts, all 52 cards in a standard deck are dealt. If there are four players, determine the number of
   a) Total hands possible.
   b) Hands with the queen of spades.
   c) Hands with the queen of spades and the ace of hearts.
   d) Hands with one or more suit missing.
   e) Hands with two or more suits missing.

8. A restaurant offers a salad bar with the following selections: lettuce, tomatoes, cucumbers, radishes, onions, green peppers, and croutons. There are also three salad dressings: Russian, French, and Italian. How many different kinds of salads with one dressing can be selected?

9. The faculty in the MIS division of a local university has been experiencing a recurring problem for several months. In a small faculty laboratory, a microcomputer is available for everyday use as well as printing directly to the resident laser printer. A faculty member typically takes a floppy disk with a word-processing file or a spreadsheet file into the laboratory, prints out the file, and edits it accordingly until the final result is satisfactory. Then the faculty member deletes the working files from the disk. Unfortunately someone is not careful in issuing the delete instruction and deletes not only the working files, but also all software resident on the microcomputer. This, of course renders the machine useless until all the system software has been restored. On one particular Monday morning, the microcomputer is discovered to be without any system software. The log in the laboratory indicates that three professors, Susan, Gordon, and John, were the only users on the previous day, with John using it 40 percent of the time, and Susan and Gordon sharing the rest of the time equally. From past experience, it is known that the probability that Susan would make such a mistake is 0.0015, the probability for Gordon is 0.0018, and the probability for John is 0.0012. What is the probability that each faculty member was responsible for deleting the software on the microcomputer?

10. Eight 2-megabyte chips go into the assembly of a 16-megabyte mother board for a particular microcomputer. The mother board is defective if any one of the chips is defective, and each chip has a probability of 0.02 of being defective. Assuming independence, what is the probability that the mother board is defective?

12 CHAPTER

PROBABILITY DISTRIBUTIONS

12.1 INTRODUCTION

In the past century, statistics and the gathering of statistical data have grown as rapidly as a forest fire spreads. Today, it is nearly impossible to read a newspaper or magazine without being confronted with statistical studies and polls revealing some new truth or prediction. Therefore it is important to understand how to collect, organize, and interpret data in a meaningful way and how to make appropriate decisions based on these interpretations.

In this chapter we study some basic topics from the branch of mathematics known as **statistics,** which deals with the collection, description, and analysis of data. We begin with applications illustrating the use of **discrete random variables** and **discrete probability distributions** or **discrete density functions.** Then we introduce applications involving **continuous probability distributions** or **continuous density functions.** In both the discrete and continuous cases we discuss the two most frequently used descriptive statistics: the **mean** and the **standard deviation.**

12.2 EXPERIMENT, EVENT, SAMPLE SPACE

The word **experiment** usually is associated with the natural sciences. However it is also used in a very broad sense in probability to specify what we plan to observe and measure. For example, one experiment may be to select 10 items from a continuous production line, examine them, and record the number of defectives. Another experiment may be to select a sample of 100 families and record the date at which they last purchased an automobile.

A formal definition of an experiment would be

The process of collecting observations or measurement is called an **experiment.**

> **Definition.** An **experiment** is the process of making an observation or taking a measurement to test or establish a hypothesis or to illustrate a known law.

An outcome of an experiment is called an **event.**

Definition. A **simple event** is an event that cannot be decomposed into two or more events. The collection of all simple events of our experiment is called a **sample space**.

*The collection of outcomes or events for an experiment is called a **sample space**.*

For example, consider the experiment of testing two fire alarms by subjecting them to fire and recording whether they worked or failed. One way to construct the space is to use ordered pairs such as *SF*, which means the first was successful and the second failed. The sample space would then be described by the events shown in Table 12–1. Observe that the occurrence of one of the events (say *SS*) excludes the possibility of occurrence of any of the others, so the events are mutually exclusive. Moreover every possible event is listed, so this is a proper sample space.

Often more than one sample space can be constructed for an experiment. In the case at hand, we could describe all possible events by listing the three mutually exclusive events; 0 fail, 1 fails, and 2 fail. This time the sample space would be described by the events shown in Table 12–2.

An experiment can often be described by more than one sample space.

Returning to Sample Space 1, suppose that $P(S) = 0.9$ and $P(F) = 0.1$. Then, assuming independence, we can compute $P(SS) = (0.9)(0.9) = 0.81$ and so on leading to the listing of the sample space and probabilities in Table 12–3. **The sum of the probabilities of the simple events in a sample space must be 1,** as indicated previously.

The probabilities of the simple events in a sample space must add to 1.

Turning now to probabilities for Sample Space 2, event **zero fail** is the event *SS*, so $P(0) = 0.81$. Similarly the event **two fail** is the event *FF*, so $P(2) = 0.01$.

TABLE 12–1
Events, Sample Space 1

SS
SF
FS
FF

TABLE 12–2
Events, Sample Space 2

Number Failing
0
1
2

TABLE 12–3
Sample Space 1, with Probabilities

Event	Probability
SS	0.81
SF	0.09
FS	0.09
FF	0.01
	1.00

However the event **one fails** occurs if *FS* or *SF* occurs. Keeping in mind that the latter two are mutually exclusive, we have

$$P(FS \cup SF) = P(FS) + P(SF) = 0.09 + 0.09 = 0.18.$$

We thus have the sample space and probabilities shown in Table 12–4.

A special way of constructing a sample space is to place each event in one or the other of two categories. In Table 12–4, for example, we could say *E* is the event **zero fail** and *E'* is the event **one or more fail.** We have

$$P(E) = 0.81$$
$$P(E') = 0.19$$
$$P(E) + P(E') = 1.00.$$

According to our earlier definition, *E'* is the complement of *E*. Clearly, complementary events constitute a sample space because they are mutually exclusive and the sum of their probabilities is 1. The rule for complementary events,

$$P(E') = 1 - P(E),$$

finds frequent application. Returning to the fire alarm example, the most important consideration is the probability that at least one of the two alarms functions in case of fire. This could be computed as

$$P(SS) + P(SF) + P(FS),$$

but the computation is simplified if we note that the event *FF* is the complement of the three just mentioned. Hence the desired probability is

$$1 - P(FF) = 1 - 0.01 = 0.99.$$

A sample space can be constructed by placing each event in one of two categories; that is, *E* and *E'* are mutually exclusive with

$P(E) + P(E') = 1.$

Exercise. If the store had three independent alarms with $P(S) = 0.9$ and $P(F) = 0.1$, what is the probability that at least one functions successfully?

Answer: $1 - P(0) = 1 - P(FFF) = 1 - (0.1)(0.1)(0.1) = 0.999.$

TABLE 12-4
Sample Space 2, with Probabilities

Number Failing	Probability
0	0.81
1	0.18
2	0.01
	1.00

Students are sometimes puzzled by the term **at least** and similar terms. Some equivalences are shown in the following to help make clear the meaning of terms that appear frequently. In reading the equivalences, assume x can be 0 or any positive whole number; that is, 0, 1, 2, 3, . . . and so on.

= Note on Terminology

Equivalences

x is at least 5;	x is 5 or more;	$x \geq 5$;	$x > 4$.
x is at most 4;	x is 4 or less;	$x \leq 4$;	$x < 5$.
x is exactly 3;	x is 3;	$x = 3$.	
x is less than 5;	x is 4 or less;	$x < 5$;	$x \leq 4$.
x is greater than 6;	x exceeds 6;	$x > 6$;	$x \geq 7$.

12.3 PROBLEM SET 12-1

1. A box contains seven good and three defective items. If a sample of two items is selected, what is the probability that
   a) Both will be good?
   b) Both will be defective?
   c) Exactly one will be defective? (Note: Two events are involved.)
   d) If a sample of three items is selected, what is the probability that at least one will be defective? (Hint: What is the complement of at least one defective?)

2. In the manufacture of an expensive product, each item is inspected independently by two women. The probability that either woman will correctly classify an item as defective is 0.95. If a defective item is inspected, what is the probability that
   a) Both will correctly classify the item?
   b) Neither will correctly classify the item?
   c) At least one will correctly classify the item?
   d) Exactly one will correctly classify the item? (Two events.)
   e) The second will correctly classify the item if the first did not? Why?

3. Three coins are to be tossed.
   a) Write the sample space in terms of *HHT* and so on where *HHT* means first coin heads, second heads, and third tails. (There are eight events.)
   b) Write the sample space in terms of the number of heads.
   c) Construct a probability table for (a).
   d) Construct a probability table for (b).

   What is the probability of
   e) At least one head?
   f) At least two heads?
   g) Exactly one head?
   h) Exactly two heads?

12.3 PROBLEM SET 12-1 (concluded)

4. An election results in a tie among two women (W_1 and W_2) and one man (M). It is decided to select two people at random from the three and appoint the first selected as president and the second selected as vice president.
   a) Construct a sample space using, for example, W_1M to mean woman 1 is president, and the man is vice president. Assign probabilities to each event in the sample space.

   Using the results of (a), what is the probability that
   b) The man will be president?
   c) The man will be either president or vice president?
   d) Women will occupy both offices?

5. See Problem 4, but do not refer to the sample space.
   a) Using W to represent either woman, write the symbol for the joint event that specifies the man is vice president.
   b) Compute the probability for the event in (a) using the conditional probability rule.
   c) Write the symbols for the event that a man is selected for neither office.
   d) Compute the probability for the event in (c) using the conditional probability rule.

6. A sample space consists of the five simple events: E_1, E_2, E_3, E_4, and E_5. The events E_1, E_2, E_3, and E_4 are equally likely, but $P(E_5) = 2P(E_2)$. Find
   a) $P(E_1)$.
   b) $P(E_2 \cup E_5)$.
   c) $P(E_3 \cup (E_1 \cap E_5))$.

7. Describe the associated sample space and state how many simple events are in it if the experiment is to
   a) Draw a poker hand of 5 cards from a standard deck of 52 cards.
   b) Toss a coin n times, and record the result (heads or tails).

12.4 DISCRETE RANDOM VARIABLES

In many situations, we are not interested in each simple event, but in some numerical value associated with each event. For example, if we toss two dice we are more interested in the sum of the value showing on the dice than the individual value on each die. In sampling 100 households for an election poll, we are more interested in the number of positive responses than in which households had a particular response. In each of these examples, we are considering a rule that assigns a numerical value to each simple event in an experiment. Such a rule or function is called a **random variable** and is usually denoted by the capital letter X.

A random variable assigns each simple event a numerical value.

Definition. A **random variable** is a rule that assigns one (and only one) numerical value to each simple event of an experiment.

Consider the experiment of tossing two coins. Let X be the random variable measuring the number of heads in each toss. From Table 12–5 we can see, for example, that there are two simple events, E_2 and E_3, that produce a random variable value of 1.

TABLE 12-5

Simple Event	Number of Heads, x	P(X = x)
E_1: HH	2	$\frac{1}{4}$
E_2: HT	1	$\frac{1}{4}$
E_3: TH	1	$\frac{1}{4}$
E_4: TT	0	$\frac{1}{4}$

We are really interested in the probability $P(X = x)$, abbreviated $p(x)$, of occurrence of each of the values x that X will take on. In the current example we have $p(0) = 1/4$ from E_4, $p(1) = 1/2$ from E_2 and E_3 and $p(2) = 1/4$ from E_1. Such a function $p(x)$ is called a **discrete probability density function** or **probability distribution** of the random variable X. We exhibit these probabilities for the current example of Table 12–5 in Table 12–6.

We can also present this same probability distribution on a graph called a **histogram**, as shown in Figure 12–1. A table and a histogram are the two customary ways of presenting a probability distribution of the random variable X.

There are two properties that a random variable must satisfy. The first property is the obvious one that the probability of each outcome must be between 0 and 1. The second is that the sum of the probabilities of all possible outcomes must be 1. Why? Because every time an experiment is performed, some event (i.e., some value of the random variable) must occur and the total probability must be distributed throughout these events so that their probabilities will sum to 1.

We can formalize these two properties as follows:

If we have any random variable X that has possible values $x_1, x_2, \ldots, x_n$, then

a) $0 \leq p(x_i) \leq 1, \quad i = 1, 2, \ldots, n$

and

b) $p(x_1) + p(x_2) + \cdots + p(x_n) = 1.$

In our coin-tossing example, it is easy to verify property (a). As for property (b), note from Table 12–6 that

$$p(0) + p(1) + p(2) = \frac{1}{4} + \frac{1}{2} + \frac{1}{4} = 1.$$

Example. Consider the tossing of two dice. What is the probability distribution of the random variable representing the sum of the faces of the two dice?

> A probability density function for a random variable is nothing more than a probability distribution for that variable.

> Histograms can be used to graphically represent probability distributions.

> The probability of each outcome of a random variable must be between 0 and 1, and the sum of the probabilities of all possible outcomes must be 1.

TABLE 12-6

Number of Heads, x	Probability of $X = x$, $p(x)$
0	$\frac{1}{4}$
1	$\frac{1}{2}$
2	$\frac{1}{4}$

FIGURE 12-1

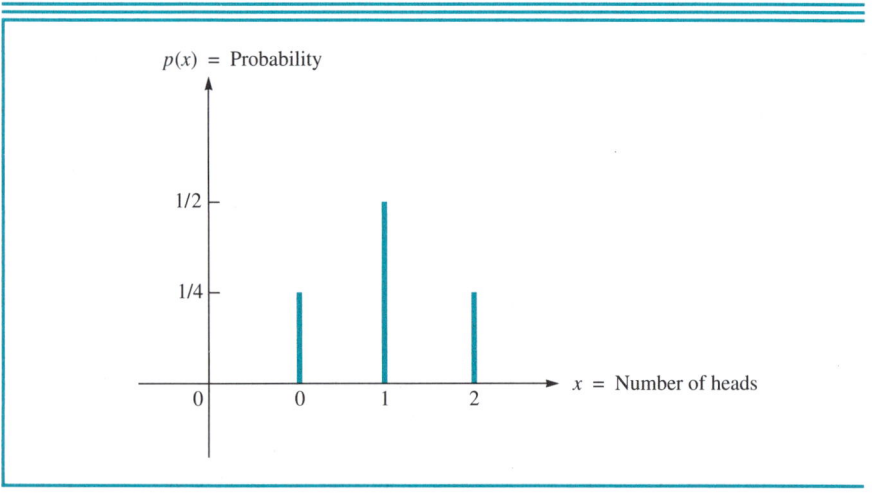

Let the random variable X be the sum of the two faces. We first need to list the possible outcomes x for X. Then we compute the probability of each outcome as shown in Table 12-7.

What do you suppose the average value of the sum of the dice is? We expect to toss two 1's for a sum of $x = 2$ one out of every 36 times. Also we expect to toss a sum of 3 two out of every 36 times, a sum of 4 three out of every 36 times, and so on. Verify these values by listing all possible ways of throwing a sum of 2, 3, and 4 out of the 36 possible rolls. Thus in the long run the **expected value of X**, which we write as $E(X)$, is

$$E(X) = 2\left(\frac{1}{36}\right) + 3\left(\frac{2}{36}\right) + 4\left(\frac{3}{36}\right) + \cdots + 12\left(\frac{1}{36}\right) = \frac{252}{36} = 7.$$

TABLE 12-7

Sum, $X = x$	2	3	4	5	6	7	8	9	10	11	12
Probability $p(x)$	$\frac{1}{36}$	$\frac{2}{36}$	$\frac{3}{36}$	$\frac{4}{36}$	$\frac{5}{36}$	$\frac{6}{36}$	$\frac{5}{36}$	$\frac{4}{36}$	$\frac{3}{36}$	$\frac{2}{36}$	$\frac{1}{36}$

Does this mean that we can expect with certainty to toss a 7 eventually? Absolutely not! It is very important to realize that the expected value of a random variable is the **weighted average value of the outcomes over a large number of experiments.** It is not a guaranteed outcome and indeed may not even be an actual outcome itself.

The expected value of a random variable is the weighted average value over a large number of experiments.

Exercise. Consider the experiment of tossing one die and let X equal the number of dots on the upper face. Compute $E(X)$.

Answer: 3.5.

Definition. If we have a random variable X with values $x_1, x_2, \ldots, x_n$ and corresponding probabilities $p_1, p_2, \ldots, p_n$, then

$$E(X) = p_1 x_1 + p_2 x_2 + \cdots + p_n x_n = \sum_{i=1}^{n} p_i x_i.$$

$E(X)$ is called the **expected value** or **mean value** of X.

In some sense, the mean value of X is the central balance point around which the actual X values occur. For this reason, the expected value or mean value of a random variable X is called **a measure of central tendency of X** and is frequently denoted by μ (the Greek letter mu) to denote the mean.

We will now look at a second important measure for X. To do this, let us assume we toss a single die 20 times and get two 1's, three 2's, four 3's, five 4's, four 5's, and two 6's; that is

1, 1, 2, 2, 2, 3, 3, 3, 3, 4, 4, 4, 4, 4, 5, 5, 5, 5, 6, 6.

The probability distribution for this experiment is shown in Table 12-8, and the histogram is shown in Figure 12-2. What do you think about this die? Would you

The expected or mean value of a random variable is a center of gravity or central balance point around which the actual values of the variable occur.

TABLE 12-8

x	1	2	3	4	5	6
$p(x)$	0.10	0.15	0.20	0.25	0.20	0.10

FIGURE 12-2

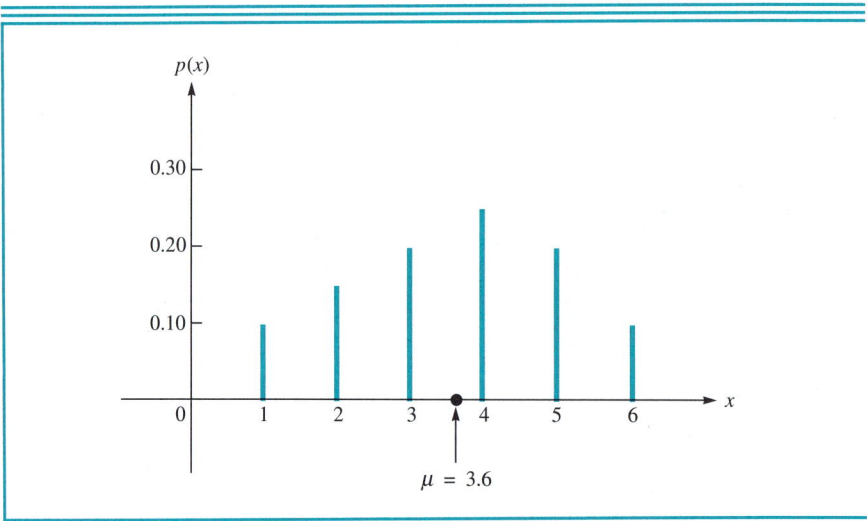

not have expected each face of the die to have come up about an equal number of times if the die were "fair"? This certainly should be the case in the long run, but we have only $n = 20$ outcomes in the current experiment. If such a probability distribution were to hold up in the long run, then the die would be called "unfair" or "loaded."

> **Exercise.** Find $\mu = E(X)$ for a loaded die with the same probability distribution as that given in Table 12-8.
>
> **Answer:** 3.6, as shown in Figure 12-2.

In addition to the central balance point μ of the distribution, it would be useful to see how scattered the distribution is. For this purpose, we obtain a **measure of** the **dispersion** or a **measure of the amount of spread** in the distribution of the probabilities about the central point μ. The two most common measures of dispersion are the **variance** denoted by σ^2 (σ being the Greek letter sigma) and the **standard deviation** σ of the random variable X.

> The variance and standard deviation measure the spread or dispersion of the data about their mean.

Definition. For a random variable X with values $x_1, x_2, \ldots, x_n$ and corresponding probabilities $p_1, p_2, \ldots, p_n$, the **variance** is defined as

$$\sigma^2(X) = (x_1 - \mu)^2 p_1 + (x_2 - \mu)^2 p_2 + \ldots + (x_n - \mu)^2 p_n$$

where

$$\mu = E(X) = x_1 p_1 + x_2 p_2 + \ldots + x_n p_n$$

is the mean of the distribution.

The **standard deviation of X** is the positive square root of the variance so

$$\sigma(X) = \sqrt{\sigma^2(X)}.$$

The standard deviation is the most frequently referred to measure of dispersion since it has the **same units as the values of X**.

> The standard deviation is the positive square root of the variance and has the same units as the values of the random variable.

As an example of how to compute the variance and standard deviation, let us reconsider the loaded die. We first compute

$$\begin{aligned}\sigma^2(X) &= (x_1 - \mu)^2 p_1 + (x_2 - \mu)^2 p_2 + (x_3 - \mu)^2 p_3 \\ &\quad + (x_4 - \mu)^2 p_4 + (x_5 - \mu)^2 p_5 + (x_6 - \mu)^2 p_6 \\ &= (1 - 3.6)^2(0.10) + (2 - 3.6)^2(0.15) + (3 - 3.6)^2(0.20) \\ &\quad + (4 - 3.6)^2(0.25) + (5 - 3.6)^2(0.20) + (6 - 3.6)^2(0.10) \\ &= 2.14.\end{aligned}$$

Thus the standard deviation is

$$\sigma(X) = \sqrt{2.14} = 1.463.$$

Exercise. Compute the variance and standard deviation for the random variable X = the number of dots on the face of a fair die.

Answer: $\sigma^2(X) = 2.917$, $\sigma(X) = 1.708$.

TABLE 12-9

```
                             Minitab

Worksheet size: 16174 cells
Press ALT + a highlighted letter to open a menu

MTB > set C1
DATA> 1, 1, 2, 2, 2, 3, 3, 3, 3, 4, 4, 4, 4, 4, 5, 5, 5, 5, 6, 6
DATA> end
MTB > histogram C1

Histogram of C1   N = 20

Midpoint      Count
    1           2  **
    2           3  ***
    3           4  ****
    4           5  *****
    5           4  ****
    6           2  **

MTB > describe C1

              N       MEAN      MEDIAN     TRMEAN     STDEV     SEMEAN
C1           20       3.600     4.000      3.611      1.501     0.336

            MIN        MAX         Q1         Q3
C1         1.000      6.000      2.250      5.000

MTB > stop
```

The computations involving the mean, variance, and standard deviation of a set of data from an experiment can become complex and tedious. However computer packages such as Minitab, SAS, and SPSS have been developed to help us compute the important descriptive statistical values. As an example, the computer output in Table 12-9 uses Minitab on a microcomputer (PC) to draw a histogram and find a set of measures including the mean and standard deviation of the 20 rolls of our loaded die. Notice that the standard deviation, STDEV, in this table is 1.501, whereas we earlier computed $\sigma(X)$ to be 1.463. The reason for the difference is that the computer package treats the data as a sample from a larger population, whereas we treated the data as an entire population. In general, the difference is $\sqrt{(n-1)/n}$ so that here, $1.501(\sqrt{19/20}) = 1.463$.

In addition to computer packages, some calculators have preprogrammed statistical function keys to simplify the computation of the mean, variance, and standard deviation of a set of data. On such a calculator, we would get the results shown in Table 12-10 for the mean and standard deviation of the 20 rolls of our loaded die.

TABLE 12-10

Keystroke	Calculator Display
Γ, then CLΣ	0
1, then Σ+	1
1, then Σ+	2
2, then Σ+	3
2, then Σ+	4
2, then Σ+	5
3, then Σ+	6
3, then Σ+	7
3, then Σ+	8
3, then Σ+	9
4, then Σ+	10
4, then Σ+	11
4, then Σ+	12
4, then Σ+	13
4, then Σ+	14
5, then Σ+	15
5, then Σ+	16
5, then Σ+	17
5, then Σ+	18
6, then Σ+	19
6, then Σ+	20
Γ, then $\bar{x}, \bar{y}$	3.600
Γ, then σ_x, σ_y	1.462873884

12.5 PROBLEM SET 12-2

In Problems 1 through 6, draw a histogram of the probability distribution and find the expected value and standard deviation of the random variable X.

1.

x	1	2	3	4	5	6
$p(x)$	0.1	0.2	0.2	0.2	0.2	0.1

2.

x	1	2	3	4	5	6
$p(x)$	0.1	0.2	0.2	0.3	0.1	0.1

3.

x	1	2	3	4	5	6
$p(x)$	0.4	0.3	0.1	0.1	0.05	0.05

4.

x	−1	0	1	2	3
$p(x)$	0.3	0.1	0.1	0.1	0.4

5.

x	−2	−1	0	1	2
$p(x)$	0.1	0.1	0.3	0.4	0.1

6.

x	−3	−2	−1	0	1
$p(x)$	0.3	0.4	0.1	0.1	0.1

12.5 PROBLEM SET 12-2 (concluded)

7. Explain why each of the following is or is not a valid probability distribution for a random variable X:

a)
x	$p(x)$
0	0.3
1	0.6
2	0.2

b)
x	$p(x)$
-1	0.25
0	0.30
1	0.20
2	0.25

c)
x	$p(x)$
3	-0.25
8	0.50
11	0.75

8. Given the following probability distribution for the random variable X,

x	10	20	30	40	50	60
$p(x)$	0.10	0.15	0.25	0.25	0.15	0.10

a) Find μ, σ^2, and σ.
b) Graph $p(x)$.
c) Locate μ and the interval $\mu \pm 2\sigma$ on your graph. What is the probably that X will fall within the interval $\mu \pm 2\sigma$, $\mu \pm \sigma$?

9. Given the following probability distribution for the random variable X,

x	1	2	3	4	5
$p(x)$	0.05	0.15	0.30	0.25	0.25

a) Find μ, σ^2, and σ.
b) Graph $p(x)$.
c) Locate μ and the interval $\mu \pm 3\sigma$ on your graph. What is the probability that x will fall within the interval $\mu \pm 3\sigma$, $\mu \pm \sigma$?

10. A local weekly newspaper receives orders for one-, two-, and three-year subscriptions, with probabilities 1/4, 1/2, and 1/4, respectively. For each subscription year, it receives $2. What is the expected return for each order received?

11. Use a calculator or computer package to solve Problems 1 through 6, 8, and 9.

12.6 THE BINOMIAL PROBABILITY DISTRIBUTION

We now look at a special discrete probability distribution called the **binomial probability distribution.** Let us assume that a basketball player is successful (hits) on 40 percent of his free-throw trials. Letting H represent *hit* and M represent *miss*, we assign

$$P(\text{Hit}) = P(H) = p = 0.40$$
$$P(\text{Miss}) = P(M) = q = 1 - p = 0.60.$$

We assume further that the outcome of one trial is **independent** of the outcomes of other trials and that p and q are the same on every trial. (This assumption, which is *required* in the development of the binomial distribution, may be subject to question in this case because players do have their ups and downs.) If we let $P(n)$ be the probability of n hits taking five shots and consider the probability of the five hits in a row, we find

$$P(5) = P(HHHHH) = (0.4)(0.4)(0.4)(0.4)(0.4) = (0.4)^5$$
$$= 0.01024.$$

Next consider $P(4)$, the probability of four hits in the next five trials. One way this can be done is *HHHHM*; that is, hit the first four trials and miss on the fifth. Another way is *HHHMH*. Writing all the events that constitute four hits and a miss, together with their probabilities, we get the sample space shown in Table 12–11.

The five events just written are mutually exclusive, so the total probability, $P(4)$, is the sum of the five probabilities. Moreover the five probabilities are equal so

$$P(4) = 5(0.4)^4(0.6)^1 = 5(0.01536) = 0.0768.$$

In the last statement, note that

$$P(4) = \text{(Number of ways of getting four hits and a miss)} \, p^4 q^1.$$

If we next ask for the probability of three hits in the next five trials, we would have

$$P(3) = \text{(Number of ways of getting three hits and two misses)} \, p^3 q^2.$$

One way to get three hits is *HHHMM*, another way is *HHMHM*, and if we persist we will find there are 10 different sequences in the event (three hits, two misses) in five trials. Fortunately we can compute this number by the formula

$$C(5, 3) = \frac{5!}{3!(5-3)!} = \frac{5!}{3!(2!)} = \frac{5(4)3!}{3!(2)(1)} = \frac{20}{2} = 10.$$

As we learned in Section 11.3, the symbol at the left in the preceding is read as **the number of combinations of five things taken three at a time.** In the present application, it is the number of different ways of arranging five things of which three are of one kind and the remaining $5 - 3 = 2$ are of another kind.

We now have

$$P(3) = C(5, 3) p^3 q^2$$
$$= 10(0.4)^3(0.6)^2 = 10(0.02304) = 0.2304.$$

TABLE 12–11

Components of Event Four Hits	Probability	
HHHHM	$(0.4)(0.4)(0.4)(0.4)(0.6)$	$= (0.4)^4(0.6)^1$
HHHMH	$(0.4)(0.4)(0.4)(0.6)(0.4)$	$= (0.4)^4(0.6)^1$
HHMHH	$(0.4)(0.4)(0.6)(0.4)(0.4)$	$= (0.4)^4(0.6)^1$
HMHHH	$(0.4)(0.6)(0.4)(0.4)(0.4)$	$= (0.4)^4(0.6)^1$
MHHHH	$(0.6)(0.4)(0.4)(0.4)(0.4)$	$= (0.4)^4(0.6)^1$

The binomial probability distribution is based on experiments that have precisely two possible outcomes.

> **Exercise.** Find the probability of two hits and three misses in the next five trials.
>
> **Answer:** $C(5, 2)\, p^2 q^3 = 10(0.4)^2(0.6)^3 = 10(0.03456) = 0.3456$.

We now generalize our demonstrations and state that if n dependent trials are made, where p is the probability of outcome A and $q = (1 - p)$ is the probability of the complementary outcome A' on any trial, then the probability that A will occur x times in the n trials is

---

The probability that an outcome A will occur x times in n independent binomial trials is

$$P(x) = C(n,x)p^x q^{n-x}$$

where p is the probability of A and $q = (1 - p)$ is the probability of A'.

Binomial Probability Rule

$$P(x) = C(n,x)\, p^x q^{n-x}.$$

Table 12–12 shows the Minitab printout for our previous example and exercise where $n = 5$ and $p = 0.4$ using the **pdf** command. Note that the probability for $X = K = 3$ is indeed 0.2304 as in the example, and the probability for $X = K = 2$ is 0.3456 as in the exercise.

TABLE 12–12

```
                Minitab

Worksheet size: 16174 cells

Press ALT + a highlighted letter to open a menu

MTB > pdf;
SUBC> binomial 5 .4.

   BINOMIAL WITH N =   5 P = 0.400000
       K            P( X = K)
       0             0.0778
       1             0.2592
       2             0.3456
       3             0.2304
       4             0.0768
       5             0.0102
MTB > stop
```

As an additional example, let us compute the probability that the basketball player hits exactly three times in his next 10 tries. We have

$$n = 10, \quad p = 0.4, \quad q = 0.6, \quad x = 3,$$

and

$$P(3) = C(10, 3)\, p^3 q^{10-3} = \frac{10!}{3!7!} (0.4)^3 (0.6)^7$$

$$= \frac{10(9)(8)}{3!} (0.4)^3 (0.6)^7$$

$$= 120(0.064)(0.0279936)$$

$$= 0.215$$

to three-decimal-place accuracy.

Exercise. Compute the probability that the player will hit exactly twice in his next six trials.
Answer: $15(0.16)(0.1296) = 0.311$.

If we seek the probability that $x = 0$ in $n = 7$ trials, it is clear that there is **only one** way, *MMMMMMM*, that can occur. The binomial rule states

$$P(0) = C(7, 0)(0.4)^0 (0.6)^7$$

$$= \frac{7!}{0!7!} (0.4)^0 (0.6)^7.$$

Recalling that $0! = 1$, we have

$$P(0) = 1(1)(0.6)^7$$

$$= 0.028.$$

One can compute the mean, variance, and standard deviation of the binomial probability distribution as we did in the last section. It turns out that some very nice formulas can be found for these values:

Mean: $\mu = np$
Variance: $\sigma^2 = npq$
Standard deviation: $\sigma = \sqrt{npq}$.

The mean, variance, and standard deviation of the binomial distribution turn out to be simply

$\mu = np$
$\sigma^2 = npq$
$\sigma = \sqrt{npq}$.

So the expected value for our basketball player in five free throws is

$$\mu = 5(0.4) = 2.0$$

hits; that is, in the long run he can expect to average two out of every five free throws.

> **Exercise.** Compute the mean, variance, and standard deviation of the binomial random variable for $n = 7$, $p = 0.4$.
> **Answer:** $\mu = 2.8$, $\sigma^2 = 1.68$, $\sigma = 1.296$.

Many real-world situations give rise to binomial distributions.

Binomial situations arise in many applications. For example, we may record an inspected item as good or defective, check male or female on a questionnaire, classify accounts receivable as active or bad debts, and so on. In some situations we apply the binomial rule even though the requisite constancy of probability from trial to trial is only approximately correct. For example, if we draw items from a batch of 100,000 items, of which 100 are defective, we would have

$$P(\text{First is defective}) = P(D_1) = \frac{100}{100{,}000} = 0.001.$$

The probability that the second is also defective, correctly computed, is not 0.001 but is

$$P(D_2 \mid D_1) = \frac{99}{99{,}999} = 0.00099.$$

The difference noted between 0.001 and 0.00099 would be lessened if we were drawing from a batch larger than 100,000. To call attention to this approximate use of the binomial, we shall indicate that selection is made from a (very) *large* group and *not* state the number in the group. For example, suppose that 35 percent of the people in a *large* area are independent voters. We select 10 people and compute the probability that exactly six are independents as approximately

$$P(6) = C(10, 6)(0.35)^6(0.65)^4$$
$$= 210(0.001838266)(0.17850625) = 0.069.$$

> **Exercise.** In a large batch of items, 10 percent are defective. If a sample of five is selected, what is the probability that exactly three will be defective?
> **Answer:** $C(5, 3)(0.1)^3(0.9)^2 = 10(0.001)(0.81) = 0.0081$.

Some applications require the computation of the probability of at least one occurrence. For example, suppose the assembly of a machine requires five independent operations, and the probability that any operation will result in a defect is 0.01. Further, the assembly is defective if one or more operations is defective; that is, if the number of defective operations is 1, 2, 3, 4, or 5. Hence we seek the probability of at least one defective operation, which is the complement of zero defective.

= **At Least One Occurrence**

Solving problems using the complementary event often simplifies the solution.

$$P(\text{At least one defective}) = 1 - P(0 \text{ defective})$$
$$= 1 - C(5, 0)(0.01)^0(0.99)^5$$
$$= 1 - 1(1)(0.99)^5$$
$$= 1 - 0.9509905$$
$$= 0.049.$$

= **Exercise.** A town has three ambulances for emergency transportation to the hospital. The probability that any one of the ambulances will be available at a point in time is 0.90. If a person calls for an ambulance, what is the probability that at least one will be available?

Answer: $1 - (0.1)^3 = 0.999$.

As a variation on the last example and exercise, consider a car salesman who makes telephone calls during the day to obtain prospective car buyers. He assesses the probability of obtaining a prospect on a given call as 0.10. How many calls should he make if his goal is to have a probability of 0.90 obtaining at least one prospect? Here we have

$$P(\text{At least one prospect}) = 1 - P(\text{No prospects}) = 0.90$$

or

$$1 - C(n, 0)(0.10)^0(0.90)^n = 0.90$$
$$1 - (0.90)^n = 0.90$$
$$-(0.90)^n = -0.10$$
$$(0.90)^n = 0.10.$$

As we learned in Chapter 5, we solve the latter expression for n by taking natural logarithms of both sides

$$n \ln (0.90) = \ln (0.10)$$
$$n = \frac{\ln (0.10)}{\ln (0.90)}$$
$$= \frac{-2.302585093}{-0.105360516} = 21.854,$$

which means about 22 calls.

> **Exercise.** A complicated computer program has a flaw ("bug") in it and will not execute properly. The program is to be sent to n experts, each of whom has a probability of 0.4 of finding the bug. What should n be if the probability that at least one expert will find that flaw is to be 0.99?
>
> **Answer:** 9.

12.7 CUMULATIVE BINOMIAL PROBABILITIES

Lot acceptance sampling uses the binomial rule on a sample to determine whether to accept the whole lot.

The binomial rule as applied in the preceding section computes the probability of **exactly** x occurrences in n trials. Thus in examples where we drew, say, five items from a large lot and recorded the number of defectives, the binomial rule calculates $P(2)$, the probability of exactly two defectives, or $P(1)$, and so on. In actual application the purpose of drawing the sample is to make a decision on whether or not to accept the whole lot on the basis of the sample evidence. Thus the quality control department may have a **sampling plan** that specifies that five items are to be drawn and inspected, and the whole lot is to be accepted if no more than one defective is found in the sample. That is, the lot is accepted if the sample contains zero or one defective; otherwise the lot is rejected. Hence if the *lot* is 10 percent defective,

$$P(\text{Acceptance}) = P(\text{None defective}) + P(\text{One defective})$$
$$= P(0) + P(1)$$
$$= C(5, 0)(0.1)^0(0.9)^5 + C(5, 1)(0.1)^1(0.9)^4$$
$$= (0.9)^5 + 5(0.1)(0.9)^4$$
$$= 0.59049 + 0.32805$$
$$= 0.91854.$$

The probability of acceptance is 0.919, so if lots 10 percent defective are submitted to this sampling plan, approximately 92 percent will be accepted and only 8 percent rejected.

> **Exercise.** If, in the preceding, lots submitted are 1 percent defective, what is the probability of acceptance and rejection?
>
> **Answer:** $(0.99)^5 + 5(0.01)(0.99)^4 = 0.999$ is the probability of acceptance and 0.001 is the probability of rejection.

If we consider 10 percent defective as poor quality and 1 percent defective as good quality, then the sampling plan at hand, with a sample of $n = 5$, has a high probability (0.999) of accepting good quality, but also an undesirably high probability (0.918) of accepting poor quality. We can easily see that the probability of accepting poor quality would be reduced by selecting a larger sample, say 20, and accepting the lot only if **none** of the 20 is defective. Now if lots are 10 percent defective,

$$P(\text{Acceptance}) = P(\text{None defective}) = C(20, 0)(0.1)^0(0.9)^{20} = 0.122.$$

This plan offers better protection against the acceptance of poor lots. On the other hand, a good lot (say 1 percent defective) now has

$$P(\text{Acceptance}) = P(\text{None defective}) = C(20, 0)(0.1)^0(0.99)^{20} = 0.818,$$

so in reducing the probability of accepting poor lots (from 0.919 to 0.122) we also lower the probability of accepting good lots (from 0.999 to 0.818). Clearly the choice of sampling plan (number in the sample to be inspected and the number of defectives permitted in the sample) can be adjusted to achieve a balance between the chances of accepting good and poor lots. For example, we may select 10 and accept the lot if it has no more than three defectives. If p is the proportion defective in a lot, then

> Cumulative binomial probabilities are frequently used to select between different sampling plans.

$$\begin{aligned} P(\text{Acceptance}) &= P(0, 1, 2, \text{ or } 3 \text{ defectives}) \\ &= P(0) + P(1) + P(2) + P(3) \\ &= C(10, 0)\, p^0 q^{10} + C(10, 1)\, p^1 q^9 + C(10, 2)\, p^2 q^8 + C(10, 3)\, p^3 q^7 \\ &= \sum_{x=0}^{3} C(10, x)\, p^x q^{10-x}. \end{aligned}$$

We refer to the last expression as a **cumulative binomial probability** and hasten to add that tables are available for these cumulative probabilities. Tables III ($n = 10$) and IV ($n = 25$) at the end of the book will be used in our examples and exercises. For the problem at hand, we find from Table III that for $p = 0.01$

$$\sum_{x=0}^{3} C(10, x)(0.01)^x (0.99)^{10-x} = 1.000.$$

The tabular entries have been rounded to three decimals and the last-written number, 1.000, does not mean exactly 1, but a number less than 1 that rounds to 1.000. We interpret this result by saying that if $n = 10$ items are selected from a lot that is 1 percent defective and three defectives are allowed in the sample, it is almost certain that the lot will be accepted.

Exercise. For the preceding find the probability of acceptance if the lot is 10 percent defective.

Answer: 0.987.

Table 12–13A shows the Minitab printout for our previous example where $n = 10$ and $p = 0.01$ using the **cdf** command. Note that the cumulative binomial probability for $K = 3$ is indeed 1.0000. Table 12–13B shows the complete Minitab table and accompanying graph of the cumulative binomial probability distribution.

To demonstrate an understanding of cumulative probabilities, we should be able to write summation expressions similar to the one we wrote in the preceding. Thus if we toss a coin 50 times and seek the probabilities of getting **at most** 10 heads, we have $n = 50$, $p = 0.5$. The probability of 0, 1, 2, . . . , 10 heads would be expressed as

$$\sum_{x=0}^{10} C(50, x)(0.5)^x(0.5)^{50-x}.$$

> **Exercise.** If a salesperson's probability of making a sale on any contact is 0.08, express in summation symbols the probability of making at most 15 sales in 100 contacts.
>
> **Answer:** $\sum_{x=0}^{15} C(100, x)(0.08)^x(0.92)^{100-x}.$

Now, for brevity, we shall express the cumulative probability for, say, 0, 1, 2, 3, 4, 5, as

$$\sum_{0}^{5}.$$

TABLE 12–13A

```
                 Minitab

Worksheet size: 16174 cells

Press ALT + a highlighted letter to open a menu

MTB > cdf;
SUBC> binomial 10 .01.

   BINOMIAL WITH N =  10  P = 0.010000
      K   P( X LESS OR = K)
      0         0.9044
      1         0.9957
      2         0.9999
      3         1.0000
MTB > stop
```

TABLE 12-13B

```
                    Minitab

Worksheet size: 16174 cells

Press ALT + a highlighted letter to open a menu

MTB > set C1
DATA> 0:10
DATA> end
MTB > cdf C1 C2;
SUBC> binomial 10 .01.
MTB > print C1 C2

ROW      C1          C2
 1        0      0.90438
 2        1      0.99573
 3        2      0.99989
 4        3      1.00000
 5        4      1.00000
 6        5      1.00000
 7        6      1.00000
 8        7      1.00000
 9        8      1.00000
10        9      1.00000
11       10      1.00000

MTB > plot C2 C1


           -
           -
C2         -           *   *   *   *   *   *   *   *
           -       *
    0.980+
           -
           -
           -
           -
    0.945+
           -
           -
           -
           -
    0.910+
           -       *
           -
              +-------+-------+-------+-------+-------+------ C1
             0.0     2.0     4.0     6.0     8.0    10.0

MTB > stop
```

Thus, from Table IV, with $n = 25$, $p = 0.4$,

$$\sum_{0}^{5} = 0.029$$

is the probability of **at most** five occurrences. If we seek the probability of *at least* five occurrences, which would be 5, 6, 7, ..., 25, it would be found as the complementary probability

$$1 - \sum_{0}^{4} = 1 - 0.009 = 0.991.$$

Again, the probability of 6 to 10 occurrences, inclusive, would be

$$\sum_{0}^{10} - \sum_{0}^{5} = 0.586 - 0.029 = 0.557.$$

Finally if we want the probability of **exactly** five occurrences, we compute

$$\sum_{0}^{5} - \sum_{0}^{4} = 0.029 - 0.009 = 0.020.$$

Exercise. For $n = 25$, $p = 0.3$, find the probability of a) Fewer than 8 occurrences. b) At most 5 occurrences. c) At least 10 occurrences. d) From 5 to 11 occurrences, inclusive. e) Exactly 8 occurrences.

Answer: a) 0.512. b) 0.193. c) 0.189. d) 0.866. e) 0.165.

Many real-world situations lend themselves to analysis by cumulative binomial probabilities.

As an application of Table IV, suppose a student takes a 25-question true-false test and determines the answer to each by flipping a coin so that the probability of getting the correct answer is $p = 0.5$ for each question. If 60 percent or more correct is passing, what is the probability of passing? We note that 60 percent or more is $25(0.6) = 15$ or more correct. Hence

$$P(\text{Pass}) = \sum_{15}^{25} = 1 - \sum_{0}^{14} = 1 - 0.788 = 0.212.$$

The student's probability of not passing is 0.788 (about 0.8). In other terminology, the odds are about 4 to 1 against passing.

> **Exercise.** If a student takes a 25-question four-choice multiple-choice examination and judges that her probability of getting any question correct is about 0.6, what is the probability that she will get 80 percent or more correct?
> **Answer:** 0.029.

12.8 PROBLEM SET 12-3

Compute the answers to Problems 1 through 8 using the binomial rule.

1. A basketball player has a probability of 0.3 of hitting on any shot from the foul line. What is the probability of
   a) Exactly one hit in three trials?
   b) At least one hit in three trials?
   c) Exactly two hits in five trials?
   d) More than two hits in four trials?

2. The probability that an inspector will properly classify an item is 0.8. If each item is inspected independently by three inspectors, what is the probability that at least one will properly classify the item?

3. A company has bid on five projects, assessing the probability of winning a contract at 0.6. To have a successful year, it must win at least two of the contracts. What is the probability for a successful year?

4. A sample of six items is selected from a large lot. The lot is accepted if the sample contains no more than one defective item. Find the probabilities of accepting and rejecting a lot if the proportion defective in the lot is   a) 0.1.   b) 0.2.

5. A department store employs four people who take orders over the telephone. Each person is busy taking an order 70 percent of the time. What is the probability that an operator will be free to take an order at the time of a call
   a) If one customer calls at a point in time?
   b) If three customers call at the same time?

6. See Problem 5. How many telephone operators should the store have if the probability that an operator will be free when a customer calls is to be 0.83?

7. A true-false examination has five questions, and a student guesses the answer for each question, assigning probability of 0.5 of being correct. Assuming independence, what is the probability that he gets
   a) All five correct?
   b) At least four correct?
   c) Exactly three correct?
   d) At least three correct?
   e) At least four incorrect?

8. A test has five four-choice questions, and a student guesses the answer to each question. Assuming independence, what is the probability of
   a) All five correct?
   b) At least four correct?
   c) Exactly three correct?
   d) At least three correct?

9. The probability that an item in a large group is defective is 0.05. Express the following by use of the summation symbol, but do not try to calculate the answer.
   a) The probability that at most 15 of 100 items purchased are defective.
   b) The probability that more than 10 of 200 items purchased are defective.

12.8 PROBLEM SET 12-3 *(concluded)*

Use Tables III and IV to answer Problems 10 through 15.

10. A sample of 25 items is selected from a large lot and the lot is rejected if the sample contains more than four defectives. Find the probability of acceptance if the proportion defective in a lot is a) 0.05. b) 0.20.

11. Repeat Problem 10 assuming the lot is rejected if more than one defective is found in the sample.

12. A test has 25 five-choice questions. A student gives answers at random. What is the probability that she gets
    a) Less than 40 percent correct?
    b) More than 40 percent correct?
    c) At least 20 percent correct?
    d) Exactly eight correct?
    e) Six to 10, inclusive, correct?
    f) At most five correct?

13. Repeat Problem 12 if the student assesses her probability of getting a correct answer at 0.5.

14. Ten percent of the (very large) supply of tires offered for sale around the country have faulty valves. If a person buys 10 of these tires (assumed to be a random selection), what is the probability that the buyer will get
    a) No faulty tires?
    b) Exactly one faulty tire?
    c) At least one faulty tire?
    d) Two or three faulty tires?

15. A company has 10 employees who, on the average, are absent from work on 5 percent of the working days. What is the probability that on a given day
    a) Exactly two are absent?
    b) Exactly nine are present?
    c) More than two are absent?
    d) One or two are absent?

12.9 EXPECTED MONETARY VALUE (EMV)

If we bet $1 that heads will appear on the toss of a coin for which we have assigned

$$P(H) = P(T) = \frac{1}{2},$$

we win $1 if heads appears and win $-$ $1 (lose $1) if tails appears. We compute the **expected monetary value (EMV) of the act** of tossing the coin as

EMV = (payoff if event H occurs) $P(H)$
    + (payoff if event T occurs) $P(T)$

$$= \$1\left(\frac{1}{2}\right) + (-\$1)\left(\frac{1}{2}\right) = 0.$$

The EMV of an act is the sum of the products of the payoff for each event times the probability of that event.

More generally the expected monetary value of an **act** is the sum of the products formed by multiplying the dollar payoff of each **event** by the probability of the event. It is assumed that the events constitute a sample space. For example, if we consider act A as having three events (E_1, E_2, and E_3) with probabilities 0.4, 0.5, and 0.1, respectively, and payoffs $10, $-$$8, and $2, then

EMV of act A = (0.4)(10) + (0.5)($-$8) + (0.1)(2) = $0.20.

Example. An urn contains five red, one white, and four green balls, and we assign probabilities

$$P(R) = 0.5$$
$$P(W) = 0.1$$
$$P(G) = 0.4.$$

A ball is to be drawn, and the payoffs are red ball, lose \$1; white ball, win \$3; green ball, win nothing. Compute the EMV of the act of drawing a ball.

First we build the payoff table shown in Table 12–14. From this table we have

$$\text{EMV} = (0.5)(-1) + (0.1)(3) + (0.4)(0)$$
$$= -\$0.20$$

or a loss of 20 cents.

Exercise. What is the expected monetary value of the act of tossing two coins if the payoffs are \$0 for zero heads, \$1 for one head, and −\$1 (loss of \$1) for two heads?
Answer: $(0)(1/4) + (\$1)(1/2) + (-\$1)(1/4) = \$0.25$.

Expected monetary value has been advanced as one criterion to aid decision making. The notion is that we list the various events that might arise in a certain situation and assign a probability to each event. In addition, we consider the payoffs that would occur for each event for each decision we might make, the decisions being the choice of act 1, act 2, and so on. Suppose that we use EMV to choose between act 1 and act 2 in Table 12–15. According to the EMV criterion, the decision maker would choose act 1 rather than act 2 because act 1 has the higher expected monetary value.

EMV is often referred to in real-world situations as a decision-making criterion.

$$\text{EMV, act 1} = (0.3)(2) + (0.4)(1) + (0.3)(8) = 3.4.$$
$$\text{EMV, act 2} = (0.3)(2) + (0.4)(3) + (0.3)(3) = 2.7.$$

TABLE 12–14

P	Event	Payoff
0.5	R	−1
0.1	W	3
0.4	G	0

**TABLE 12-15
Payoff Table**

		Act	
P	Events	A_1	A_2
0.3	E_1	$2.00	$2.00
0.4	E_2	1.00	3.00
0.3	E_3	8.00	3.00
1.0			

Example. Items are manufactured for sale. Each unit made and sold yields a profit of $3; each unit made but not sold yields a loss of $1. It is believed that zero, one, two, or three units might be demanded by customers, but the event four or more units demanded is considered impossible and assigned probability zero. Other probabilities are assigned by experience and judgment (Table 12–16). Use the expected monetary value to decide whether to make zero units (act 1), one unit (act 2), two units (act 3), or three units (act 4).

The payoff table can be filled in from the given information. For example, if two units are made and one unit is demanded, one of the two would yield a profit of $3 and the other a loss of $1, for a payoff of $2 net. Again, if one unit is made and two are demanded, the payoff is $3 on the single unit made. These and the remaining payoffs are shown in Table 12–17.

$$\text{EMV of } A_1 = 0.0.$$

$$\text{EMV of } A_2 = 2.2.$$

$$\text{EMV of } A_3 = 2.8.$$

$$\text{EMV of } A_4 = 2.2.$$

The decision would be to choose A_3, the act with the highest EMV, and so make two units.

EMV gives only one perspective on the monetary return from a decision. Other criteria should be considered.

EMV can be a useful criterion in some decisions. However it is easy to illustrate that this criterion does not have general applicability. For example, the EMV of A_1 in Table 12–18 is $2,500, compared to an EMV of $200 for A_2, and yet some persons would prefer A_2 to A_1.

$$\text{EMV of } A_1 = \$2,500.$$

$$\text{EMV of } A_2 = \$ \ 200.$$

The point here is that even though the EMV of A_1 is much larger than that of A_2, some people would not feel they could afford a loss of $5,000, which would arise if they chose A_1 and event E_2 occurred. Others would prefer A_2 on the ground that they cannot lose if they choose A_2, and have a 0.5 probability of gaining $400. Of course, a person possessing a large amount of money might well choose A_1 because

TABLE 12-16

Events (Number of Units Demanded)	Probability of Number of Units Being Demanded
0	0.2
1	0.4
2	0.3
3	0.1
4 or more	0.0
	1.0

TABLE 12-17
Payoff Table

P	Events (Units Demanded)	A_1 (Make 0)	A_2 (Make 1)	A_3 (Make 2)	A_4 (Make 3)
0.2	0	0	−1	−2	−3
0.4	1	0	3	2	1
0.3	2	0	3	6	5
0.1	3	0	3	6	9
0.0	4 or more	0	3	6	9
1.0					

TABLE 12-18

P	Event	A_1	A_2
0.5	E_1	$10,000	$400
0.5	E_2	−5,000	0

that person can afford to lose $5,000 and thinks a 50–50 gamble of winning $10,000 or losing $5,000 is sensible.

The last illustration shows that the act chosen depends upon the person making the decision and the amounts involved. EMV may or may not be a proper guide for action. A criterion applicable when EMV is not appropriate is **expected utility value (EUV)**, which allows a person to inject his or her own circumstances and inclinations into the analysis. Exploration of the EUV criterion would carry us beyond our immediate goals.

One-Time Decisions

The probability of heads when a coin is tossed, 0.5, means that as the number of tosses increases (approaches infinity in the limit sense), the proportion or relative frequency of heads approaches 0.5 as a limit. However if we toss a coin only once, heads or tails will appear and the 0.5 probability does not tell us which will occur. Similarly the EMV of an act is computed from probabilities and means the average payoff we would expect to arise if the act was performed an increasingly large number of times under constant conditions, but this EMV does not tell us what will occur if the act is performed only once. Consequently some people contend that it is not correct to apply the EMV criterion to a one-time decision. Other people, while agreeing with the long-run interpretation of EMV, contend that EMV may be applied to one-time decisions, arguing that if a person would choose act A over and over again in a repeated series of decisions, it would not be unreasonable to choose A if the decision circumstances occur only once. The latter group would also point out that management-administrative decisions typically are of the one-time variety because the circumstances under which actual decisions are made are not **constant over the long run.** The controversy between those who would and those who would not use probability considerations in one-time decisions really centers upon the question of what information a decision maker would choose to consider in making a one-time decision where the outcome is uncertain. Thus whether or not probabilities would be considered in chancy one-time decisions is a choice left to the decision maker. An informed manager or administrator should consider probabilities when making decisions where the outcome is uncertain, even if a one-time decision is at hand.

===
Business decision makers should consider probabilities when making decisions where the outcome is uncertain.
===

12.10 PROBLEM SET 12-4

1. A pair of dice is to be rolled. If the number appearing is even, you win that even number of dollars; if the number appearing is odd, you lose that odd number of dollars. Compute the EMV of the act of rolling the pair of dice.

2. An act is accompanied by three possible events with probabilities 0.2, 0.3, and 0.5, and payoffs $2, $3, and −$1, respectively. Compute the expected monetary value of the act.

3. Urn 1 contains four red, nine white, and seven green balls with payoffs $2, −$4, and $2, respectively. Urn 2 contains four red and six black balls with payoffs $3 and −$1.80, respectively. If act 1 is selecting a ball from Urn 1 and act 2 is selecting a ball from Urn 2, which act should be chosen according to the criterion of expected monetary value?

4. Which act should be chosen according to EMV?

Payoff Table

P	Event	A_1	A_2	A_3	A_4
0.2	E_1	$2	$1	$0	$0
0.1	E_2	2	2	−1	−3
0.4	E_3	2	3	3	3
0.3	E_4	2	2	4	5

5. If you make a unit of product and it is sold (demanded), you gain $5; if you make a unit that is not sold, you lose $2. You assign probabilities as follows:

12.10 PROBLEM SET 12-4 (concluded)

Number of Units Demanded	Probability of Number of Units Demanded
0	0.10
1	0.20
2	0.25
3	0.40
4	0.05
5 or more	0.00

According to the EMV criterion, how many units should you make?

6. In setting premiums to charge for protection against various hazards, insurance companies must start with a base figure (exclusive of overhead and profit), which represents their expected loss. A building is to be insured in the amount of $60,000 for fire damage. The probabilities of total, 75 percent, 50 percent, and 25 percent losses in a year are, respectively, 0.0001, 0.00015, 0.0005, and 0.001. Assuming these are the only losses to be considered,

a) What base figure should be used in computing the annual premium?
b) Why do the probabilities given not add up to 1?

7. Think seriously about your present circumstances, and then decide in each case whether you would choose act 1 or act 2. For example, in part (a), would you prefer a 0.6 probability of gaining $3 and 0.4 probability of losing $1, to a gamble with a 0.6 probability of gaining $1? (There are no correct answers to this question.)

a)

P	A_1	A_2
0.6	$3	$1
0.4	−1	0.

b)

P	A_1	A_2
0.6	$30	$10
0.4	−10	0.

c)

P	A_1	A_2
0.5	$3,000	$500
0.5	−1,000	0.

12.11 CONTINUOUS PROBABILITY DENSITY FUNCTIONS

The binomial probability distribution of Section 12.6 assigned probabilities to the **number of occurrences** of an event in a certain number of trials. As such, the events were counting numbers, 0, 1, 2, 3, and so on, with no event between a successive pair of these numbers. The set, 0, 1, 2, 3, . . . , is called a **discrete set** because its members are distinct. If we were to represent 0, 1, 2, 3, . . . graphically, it would consist of a set of separated points. We now introduce probability distributions for the **continuous** (as contrasted to discrete) **case**, and here graphical representation of the set of events consists of a continuous line or line segment.

Example. Fran, an executive in a company, is expecting a friend to arrive by ship one afternoon. Upon inquiry, Fran learns from a dock official that the ship will certainly arrive between 1 and 6 o'clock, but just when is a matter of chance. Fran decides to assign one (certainty) as the probability of arrival from 1 to 6 o'clock and assume that arrival is equally likely at any time in this interval. Fran has a business appointment that will prevent her from being at the dock from 2 to 3:30 and calculates the chance that she will not be there when her friend arrives is 0.30

because she will not be present for 1.5 hours in the five-hour interval from 1 to 6 o'clock; that is, 1.5/5 = 0.3.

Figure 12–3 shows a horizontal interval from 1 to 6 representing the time interval of arrival of Fran's friend. Because time is a **continuous variable,** the interval is a continuous line segment rather than a discrete (separated) set of points. A rectangle of height 1/5 has been drawn over the horizontal base, and its upper boundary is the constant function

$$p(x) = \frac{1}{5}; \quad 1 \le x \le 6.$$

The area of this entire rectangle is

$$A = 5\left(\frac{1}{5}\right) = 1,$$

and the 1 means it is **certain** (probability of 1) that the ship will arrive in this time interval. The shaded area over the horizontal interval from 2 to 3.5 (3:30 P.M.), which is

$$(3.5 - 2)\left(\frac{1}{5}\right) = 1.5\left(\frac{1}{5}\right) = 0.30,$$

represents the probability that the ship will arrive during this time period. The function $p(x) = 1/5$ is called a **continuous probability density function** or, more briefly, a **continuous density function.** Note carefully that a continuous density

FIGURE 12-3
(not to scale)

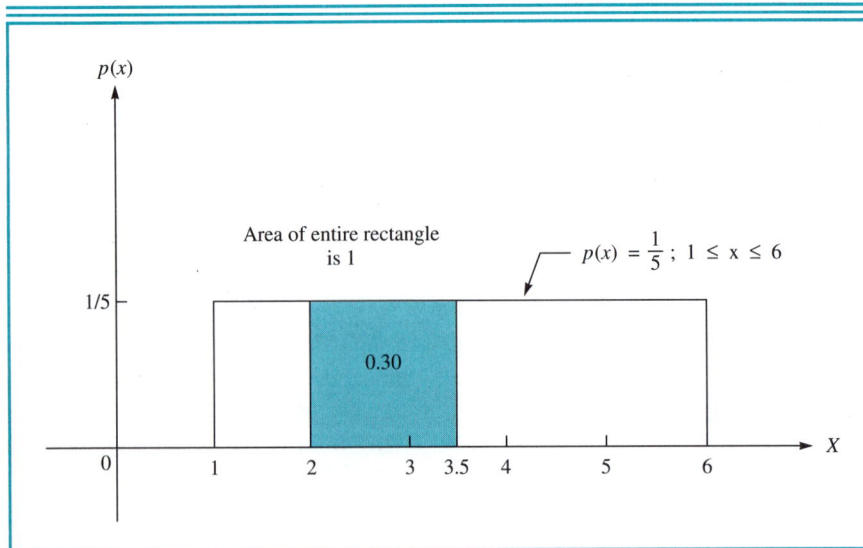

function does not provide probabilities. (Recall from Section 12.4 that discrete density functions do provide probabilities.) Rather, **areas under a continuous density function over a horizontal interval are probabilities assigned to the horizontal interval.** As stated in Section 12.4, density functions (discrete or continuous) are also called **probability distributions,** and we shall use the terms **density function** and **probability distribution** interchangeably.

Table 12–19A shows the Minitab printout for our previous example where we computed the probability of the ship arriving between 2 and 3:30 using a uniform distribution over the interval from 1 to 6. As in the example, the resulting probability of 0.3 is the difference between the probability 0.5000 for 3.5 and the probability 0.2000 for 2. An alternative way to arrive at this same result using Minitab is shown in Table 12–19B.

The density function of Figure 12–3 is called the **uniform density function** or **uniform distribution** because it is a contant function representing Fran's assumption that arrival of the ship is equally likely to occur anywhere in the interval. Inasmuch

> Areas are used to determine probabilities for continuous probability distributions.

TABLE 12–19A

```
                Minitab

Worksheet size: 16174 cells

Press ALT + a highlighted letter to open a menu

MTB  > cdf 3.5;
SUBC> uniform 1 6.
       3.5000      0.5000
MTB  > cdf 2;
SUBC> uniform 1 6.
       2.0000      0.2000
MTB  > stop
```

TABLE 12–19B

```
                Minitab

Worksheet size: 16174 cells

Press ALT + a highlighted letter to open a menu

MTB  > cdf 3.5 K1;
SUBC> uniform 1 6.
MTB  > cdf 2 K2;
SUBC> uniform 1 6.
MTB  > let K3 = K1 - K2
MTB  > print K1-K3
K1         0.500000
K2         0.200000
K3         0.300000
MTB  > stop
```

as probabilities are areas under a density function, the probability assigned to a horizontal interval is the definite integral of the density function between limits that are the interval endpoints. Thus in Fran's case the probability of arrival between 2 and 3.5 is

$$\int_2^{3.5} p(x)\, dx = \int_2^{3.5} \frac{1}{5}\, dx = \frac{1}{5} x \Big|_2^{3.5} = \frac{1}{5}(3.5 - 2) = \frac{1}{5}(1.5) = 0.3,$$

which is precisely the same result as before.

> **Exercise.** By integration find the probability that the ship will arrive between 3 and 3:30 if $p(x) = 1/5$.
>
> **Answer:** 0.10.

The probability associated with a point is 0 for any continuous probability distribution.

One consequence of area assignment of probabilities should be noted; namely, the **probability associated with a point is 0.** Thus in Fran's case the probability that the ship will arrive at exactly 2 o'clock is 0, where **exactly** means an instant (duration 0). This consequence arises because a point (instant) has 0 width and the area (probability) over a point necessarily is 0. In applications, of course, we shall be concerned with intervals, so the zero point probability causes no difficulty. However if we use the symbol

$$P(2 \leq x \leq 3.5) = 0.3$$

to represent Fran's probability assignment, we should realize that

$$P(2 \leq x < 3.5) = P(2 < x < 3.5)$$

because the probabilities for exactly 2 and exactly 3.5 are 0.

If we have a function $f(x)$ that is nonnegative over an interval, we can convert $f(x)$ to a continuous density function by dividing $f(x)$ by the total area under $f(x)$ over the interval so that the entire area is **normalized** (adjusted) to be 1.

Example. Convert $f(x) = 4x - x^2 - 3$, $1 \leq x \leq 3$, to a continuous density function.

First we find the total area under $f(x)$ by the methods of Chapter 10 to be

$$\int_1^3 (4x - x^2 - 3)\, dx$$

$$= \left(2x^2 - \frac{x^3}{3} - 3x \right) \Big|_1^3$$

$$= \left[2(9) - \frac{27}{3} - 9\right] - \left[2(1) - \frac{1}{3} - 3\right]$$

$$= 18 - 9 - 9 - 2 + \frac{1}{3} + 3$$

$$= \frac{4}{3}.$$

Then

$$p(x) = \frac{f(x)}{4/3} = \frac{3}{4} f(x)$$

$$p(x) = \frac{3}{4}(4x - x^2 - 3); \quad 1 \leq x \leq 3.$$

> To convert a continuous function into a continuous probability distribution over an interval, divide the function by the area over that interval (thus converting the total area to 1).

This function, $p(x)$, is a vertical parabola opening downward, with x-intercepts at $x = 1$ and $x = 3$, as shown in Figure 12–4. The conversion procedure simply changes $f(x)$, which has an area of 4/3 over the interval, to the density function, $p(x)$, which has an area of 1, as required. Once assured that we have a continuous density function, probabilities for intervals are computed as definite integrals.

Example. For the density function of Figure 12–4, find the probability that a randomly selected value of x will lie in the interval $2 \leq x \leq 2.5$.

FIGURE 12–4

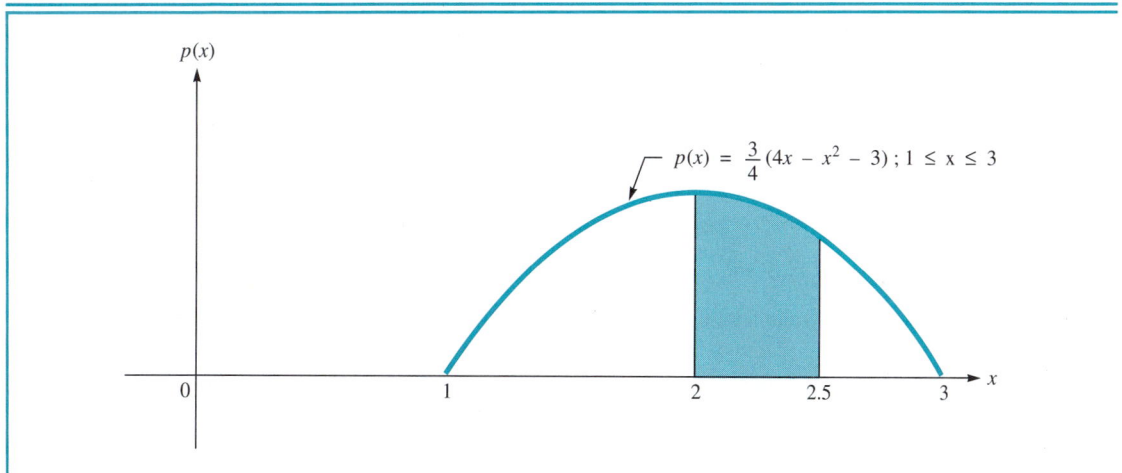

The desired probability is the shaded area in Figure 12–4. We compute it as

$$\int_2^{2.5} p(x)\,dx = \int_2^{2.5} \frac{3}{4}(4x - x^2 - 3)\,dx$$

$$= \frac{3}{4}\left(2x^2 - \frac{x^3}{3} - 3x\right)\Big|_2^{2.5}$$

$$= \frac{3}{4}\left[\left(-\frac{0.625}{3}\right) - \left(-\frac{2}{3}\right)\right]$$

$$= \frac{3}{4}\left(\frac{1.375}{3}\right) = \frac{1.375}{4} = 0.34375.$$

Exercise. For the density function of Figure 12–4, find the probability that a randomly selected value of x will lie in the interval from 1 to 2 inclusively.

Answer: 0.5.

12.12 PROBLEM SET 12–5

1. a) Convert $f(x) = 20$, $0 \le x \le 10$, to a density function.
   b) Compute the probability that a randomly selected x will lie in the interval $4 \le x \le 7$.

2. a) Convert $f(x) = x$, $0 \le x \le 10$, to a density function.
   b) Compute the probability that a randomly selected x will lie in the interval $4 \le x \le 5$.

3. a) Convert $f(x) = x^{1/2}$, $0 \le x \le 9$, to a density function.
   b) Compute the probability that a randomly selected x will lie in the interval $1 \le x \le 4$.

4. a) Convert $f(x) = 2 - x^{-2}$, $1 \le x \le 20$, to a density function.
   b) Compute the probability that a randomly selected x will lie in the interval $1 < x < 10$.

5. a) Convert $f(x) = 12x - 3x^2$, $0 \le x \le 4$, to a density function.
   b) Compute the probability that a randomly selected x will lie in the interval $0 < x < 2$.

12.13 EXPECTED VALUE

Recall that Fran assumed a ship was equally likely to arrive at any time during the interval from 1 to 6 o'clock. Now suppose the unlikely circumstance that Fran has repeated occasions to be faced with the same situation and that on each occasion she records the time at which the ship arrives and then computes the average of these times. Because all times in the interval 1 to 6 are equally likely to occur, we would expect that, on a sufficient number of repeated trials, the average time would be the midpoint of this interval, which is at 3.5 (3:30 P.M.). This average time is called the **expected** time of arrival. Thus as with discrete random variables in Section 12.4, **expected value** is an average value.

Since the definite integral for continuous probability distributions is analogous to the summation for discrete probability distributions, it seems likely that Fran's expected value for the time of arrival can be computed as

$$\int_1^6 xp(x)\, dx;$$

that is, the definite integral over the entire range of x's of x times the density function. For Fran's density function, $p(x) = 1/5$, we compute the expected value of x, symbolized by $E(x)$, as

$$E(x) = \int_1^6 x\left(\frac{1}{5}\right) dx$$
$$= \frac{1}{5}\left(\frac{x^2}{2}\right)\Big|_1^6$$
$$= \frac{36-1}{10} = \frac{35}{10} = 3.5,$$

which is the value anticipated earlier.

Definition. If $p(x)$ is a continuous probability distribution function, then the **expected value** of x is

$$E(x) = \int_{\text{all } x} xp(x)dx.$$

The expected value of a continuous probability distribution function $p(x)$ is the average value computed as

$$E(x) = \int_{\text{all } x} xp(x)dx.$$

In this definition, the "all x" on the integral sign means that the limits on the integral are the endpoints of the entire interval of permissible values of x.

As with the discrete case, the expected value of x, $E(x)$, is also referred to as the **mean** (or average) of the x values and is designated by μ:

$$E(x) = \mu.$$

The mean, μ, has another interpretation that aids understanding; namely, μ is the x-coordinate of the **center of gravity** of a graphical representation of the density function. (Recall from Section 12.4 that the expected value of a discrete probability distribution was also interpreted as a center of gravity.) To see what is meant here, suppose Figure 12–3 on page 840 was drawn on a piece of cardboard, then the rectangle was cut out with scissors and placed vertically across a knife edge, ($\wedge$),

The expected value of a probability distribution can be interpreted as the center of gravity.

as shown in Figure 12–5. The rectangle would just balance, not tipping down at one side, if the knife edge is at the center of gravity, $\mu = 3.5$.

By way of contrast, consider

$$p(x) = \frac{10 - x}{50}, \quad 0 \le x \le 10,$$

which is shown in Figure 12–6. If we cut this triangle out, it will not balance at the midpoint of the base, which is at $x = 5$, but at a point, μ, which is to the left of the midpoint. To see where μ is, we compute

$$\mu = E(x) = \int_0^{10} xp(x)\, dx$$

$$= \int_0^{10} x\left(\frac{10 - x}{50}\right) dx$$

$$= \int_0^{10} \frac{10x - x^2}{50}\, dx$$

$$= \frac{1}{50}\left(5x^2 - \frac{x^3}{3}\right)\Big|_0^{10}$$

$$= \frac{1}{50}\left[\left(500 - \frac{1{,}000}{3}\right) - 0\right]$$

$$= 10 - \frac{20}{3} = \frac{10}{3}.$$

Thus $\mu = 10/3$, as shown in Figure 12–6.

Exercise. Find the expected value of x, $E(x) = \mu$ if $p(x) = x/18$, $0 \le x \le 6$.
Answer: $\mu = 4$.

Example. Jon sells oil in amounts up to 20 gallons and uses

$$p(x) = 0.004x + 0.01, \quad 0 \le x \le 20$$

as the density function for amounts purchased by customers. a) Find the average (expected value) of the amounts purchased by customers. b) Estimate the amount that will be purchased by 30 customers.

FIGURE 12-5
(not to scale)

FIGURE 12-6
(not to scale)

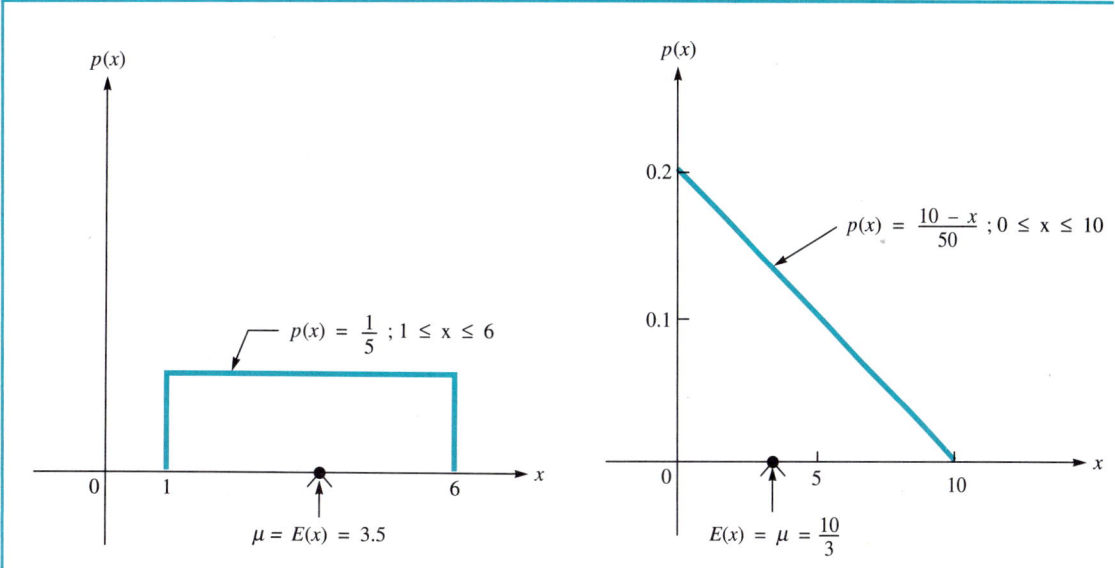

a) We compute the expected value as

$$\mu = \int_0^{20} xp(x)\, dx = \int_0^{20} x(0.004x + 0.01)\, dx$$

$$= \int_0^{20} (0.004x^2 + 0.01x)\, dx$$

$$= \left(\frac{0.004x^3}{3} + \frac{0.01x^2}{2} \right) \Big|_0^{20}$$

$$= \frac{0.004(20)^3}{3} + \frac{0.01(20)^2}{2} - 0$$

$$= \frac{32}{3} + 2$$

$$= \frac{38}{3} \text{ gallons per customer.}$$

b) With an average purchase of 38/3 gallons per customer, total purchases by 30 customers would be estimated at

(Number of customers)(Average purchased per customer)

$$= 30 \left(\frac{38}{3} \right) = 380 \text{ gallons.}$$

> **Exercise.** In the last example, estimate total sales to 90 customers.
> **Answer:** 1,140 gallons.

12.14 VARIANCE AND STANDARD DEVIATION

As in the discrete case, the standard deviation of a continuous probability distribution is denoted by σ. Its square, σ^2, is called the **variance**. Once again, using the definite integral analogy to the summation, we have

> **Definition**
>
> $$\text{Variance of } x = V(x) = \sigma^2 = \int_{\text{all } x} (x - \mu)^2 \, p(x) \, dx.$$

Example. Compute the variance and standard deviation of x if its density function is $p(x) = x/288$, $0 \le x \le 24$.

We must compute μ first. This is

$$\mu = \int_0^{24} x\left(\frac{x}{288}\right) dx = \frac{1}{288} \int_0^{24} x^2 \, dx = \frac{1}{288} \left(\frac{x^3}{3}\right)\Big|_0^{24}$$

$$= \frac{1}{288} \left(\frac{13{,}824}{3}\right) = 16.$$

Next we find

The variance and standard deviation of a continuous probability distribution are computed using definite integrals.

$$V(x) = \sigma^2 = \int_0^{24} (x - \mu)^2 \, p(x) \, dx$$

$$= \int_0^{24} (x - 16)^2 \left(\frac{x}{288}\right) dx$$

$$= \frac{1}{288} \int_0^{24} (x^2 - 32x + 256)(x) \, dx$$

$$= \frac{1}{288} \int_0^{24} (x^3 - 32x^2 + 256x) \, dx$$

$$= \frac{1}{288} \left(\frac{x^4}{4} - 32\frac{x^3}{3} + 256\frac{x^2}{2}\right)\Big|_0^{24}$$

$$= \frac{1}{288}(82{,}944 - 147{,}456 + 73{,}728)$$

$$= \frac{9{,}216}{288}$$

$$\sigma^2 = 32$$

$$\sigma = \sqrt{32} = 5.657.$$

Thus the variance is $\sigma^2 = 32$, and the standard deviation is the square root of the variance, which is approximately $\sigma = 5.657$.

Exercise. Find the mean, variance, and standard deviation of x if the density function is $p(x) = x/72$, $0 \le x \le 12$.

Answer: $\mu = 8$; $V(x) = \sigma^2 = 8$; $\sigma = 2.828$.

Figures 12–7 and 12–8 show the density functions of the last example and exercise. Note that the density function of Figure 12–7 spreads out over a wider interval than is the case in Figure 12–8, and it is the spread or variability that is measured by the variance or its square root, the standard deviation. We shall see the importance of σ in more understandable form when we introduce the **normal** probability density function in Section 12.16.

FIGURE 12–7
(not to scale)

FIGURE 12–8
(not to scale)

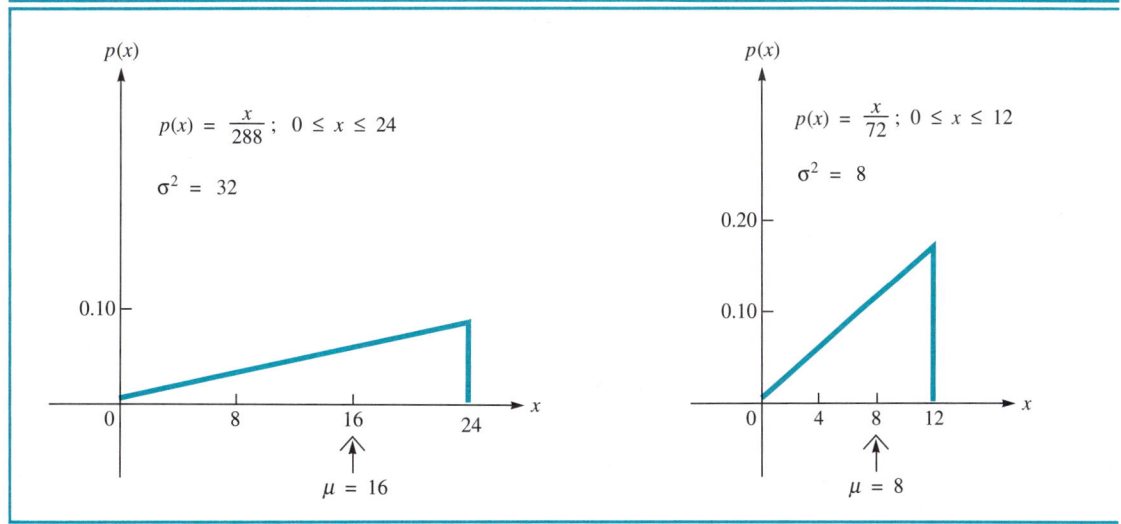

12.15 PROBLEM SET 12-6

1. Given $p(x) = 0.05$, $0 \le x \le 20$,
   a) Find μ. b) Find σ^2. c) Find σ.

2. Given $p(x) = 0.01$, $0 \le x \le 100$,
   a) Find μ. b) Find σ^2. c) Find σ.

3. Given $p(x) = \dfrac{x}{18}$, $0 \le x \le 6$,
   a) Find the expected value of x.
   b) Find the variance of x.
   c) Find the standard deviation of x.

4. Given $p(x) = (2x)/9$, $0 \le x \le 3$,
   a) Find the expected value of x.
   b) Find the variance of x.
   c) Find the standard deviation of x.

5. Fran sells oil to customers in amounts of x hundred gallons, x going from 0 to 5, with the density function
   $$p(x) = 0.04x + 0.1, \quad 0 \le x \le 5.$$
   a) Find average (expected) sales per customer.
   b) Estimate total sales to 72 customers.

6. Sam sells oil to customers in amounts of x thousand gallons, x going from 0 to 2 with the density function
   $$p(x) = 0.2x + 0.3, \quad 0 \le x \le 2.$$
   a) Find the average (expected) sales per customer.
   b) Estimate total sales to 90 customers.

7. The density function
   $$p(x) = \frac{3(1 - x^2)}{4}, \quad -1 \le x \le 1$$
   is a vertical parabola opening downward, with vertex at (0, 3/4) and intercepts at (−1, 0) and (1, 0).
   a) Sketch the density function.
   b) Why must μ equal zero?
   c) Verify that $\mu = 0$.
   d) Find the standard deviation of x.

8. The density function
   $$p(x) = \frac{3}{32}(4 - x^2), \quad -2 \le x \le 2$$
   is a vertical parabola opening downward, with vertex at (0, 3/8) and intercepts at (−2, 0) and (2, 0).
   a) Sketch the density function.
   b) Why must μ equal zero?
   c) Verify that $\mu = 0$.
   d) Find the standard deviation of x.

12.16 THE NORMAL DISTRIBUTION

The widely used normal distribution (normal density function) has the bell shape shown in Figure 12–9. The function that is the source of the normal distribution is

$$f(x) = e^{-\frac{1}{2}\left(\frac{x - \mu}{\sigma}\right)^2}, \quad -\infty < x < \infty.$$

Recall from Section 12.11 that to qualify as a density function it is necessary to determine k so that

$$k \int_{-\infty}^{+\infty} f(x)\, dx = 1.$$

By advanced methods, it can be proved that

$$k = \frac{1}{\sigma\sqrt{2\pi}}.$$

Hence the equation of the normal probability density function is

Normal Probability Density Function

$$p(x) = \frac{1}{\sigma\sqrt{2\pi}} e^{-\frac{1}{2}\left(\frac{x-\mu}{\sigma}\right)^2}.$$

> One of the most widely used density functions is the normal distribution.

The parameters in $p(x)$ are μ (the mean or expected value) and σ (the standard deviation). As shown in Figure 12–9 a normal distribution has symmetry with respect to a vertical line at μ; that is, in Figure 12–9, the curve has the same height at a point a units to the left or right of μ. The standard deviation measures the variability of x around the mean so that a distribution with a small value of σ concentrates a major proportion of the probability (area) over a small interval around μ. If σ is large, the major central proportion of the probability is spread over a wide interval around μ. Often we specify a normal distribution by $N(\mu, \sigma)$, meaning **normal, with mean mu and standard deviation sigma.** For example, $N(100, 5)$ specifies a normal distribution with mean 100, standard deviation 5 (variance 25). This specific distribution function is

> A normal distribution specified by $N(\mu, \sigma)$ means normal with mean mu and standard deviation sigma.

$$p(x) = \frac{1}{5\sqrt{2\pi}} e^{-\frac{1}{2}\left(\frac{x-100}{5}\right)^2}.$$

Normal curves may be described as being bell-shaped, symmetrical about the mean, and approaching the x-axis asymptotically in both directions.

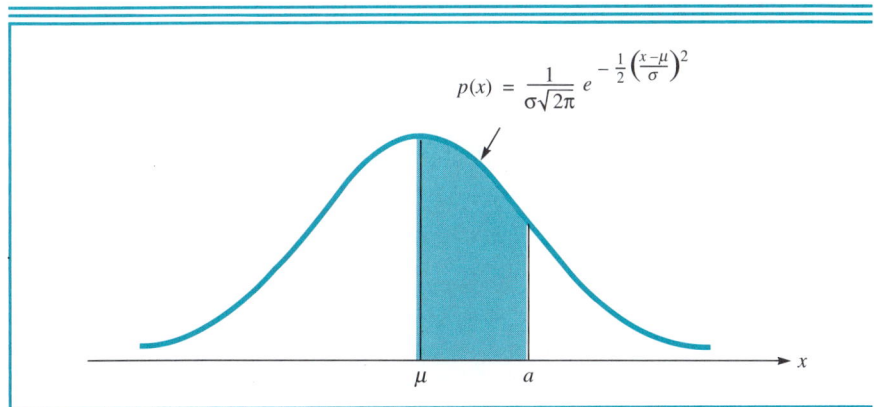

FIGURE 12–9

> **Exercise.** Write the equation of the normal distribution $N(40, 8)$. Geometrically, how would this distribution compare with $N(30, 2)$?
>
> **Answer:**
>
> $$p(x) = \left[\frac{1}{8\sqrt{2\pi}}\right]\left[e^{-\frac{1}{2}\left(\frac{x-40}{8}\right)^2}\right].$$
>
> This distribution would have its mean to the right of $N(30, 2)$ and would spread out more than $N(30, 2)$.

The integral for the normal distribution cannot be done directly and is approximated using numerical integration.

Starting from first principles to find the probability that a randomly selected x will lie in a specified interval, we would try to integrate the normal density function between the interval limits. As it happens, this function cannot be integrated exactly, but it is possible to make approximations using numerical integration. It seems natural to suggest that the approximations for various sets of limits be made and the outcomes tabulated, but this raises a problem. There is not just one normal distribution. There is a normal distribution for each of the combinations of μ and σ. Fortunately this latter problem can be handled by transforming each normal distribution to a **standard form.** To see how this is done, consider the problem of evaluating.

There are an unlimited number of normal distributions so we convert them to a standard form.

$$\frac{1}{\sigma\sqrt{2\pi}} \int_\mu^a e^{-\frac{1}{2}\left(\frac{x-\mu}{\sigma}\right)^2} dx.$$

(See Figure 12–9.) We introduce a new variable, z, called the **standardized normal deviate,** where

$$z = \frac{x - \mu}{\sigma}.$$

We must now make the following conversions:
If

$$z = \frac{x - \mu}{\sigma}$$

then

$$\frac{dz}{dx} = \frac{d}{dx}\left(\frac{x - \mu}{\sigma}\right) = \frac{1}{\sigma}$$

$$\sigma \, dz = dx.$$

This says we must replace dx in the integral by $\sigma \, dz$. Attention turns next to the limits on the integral. The limit $x = \mu$ becomes

$$z = \frac{x - \mu}{\sigma} = \frac{\mu - \mu}{\sigma} = 0.$$

Similarly the limit $x = a$ becomes

$$z = \frac{a - \mu}{\sigma}.$$

Substituting, we now have the expression

$$\frac{1}{\sqrt{2\pi}} \int_0^{\frac{a-\mu}{\sigma}} e^{-\frac{z^2}{2}} \, dz$$

in place of the original integral. See Figure 12–10.

To see what has been accomplished, consider the two normal distributions $N(50, 5)$ and $N(78, 2)$. Asked to integrate $N(50, 5)$ between the limits 50 (which is μ) and 55 (which is a), we find

$$z = \frac{55 - 50}{5} = 1$$

for the z corresponding to 55. The z corresponding to μ is, of course, always 0. Our problem here is to integrate the standardized normal distribution from $z = 0$ to $z = 1$.

Suppose, next, we are asked to integrate the second distribution, $N(78, 2)$, between the x limits 78 (which is μ) and 80 (which is a). We find again that the z limits are 0 and 1. Both problems lead to the evaluation of

$$\frac{1}{\sqrt{2\pi}} \int_0^1 e^{-\frac{z^2}{2}} \, dz.$$

Clearly the same evaluation arises if the transformation to z yields the interval from $z = 0$ to $z = 1$, no matter what normal distribution is at hand.

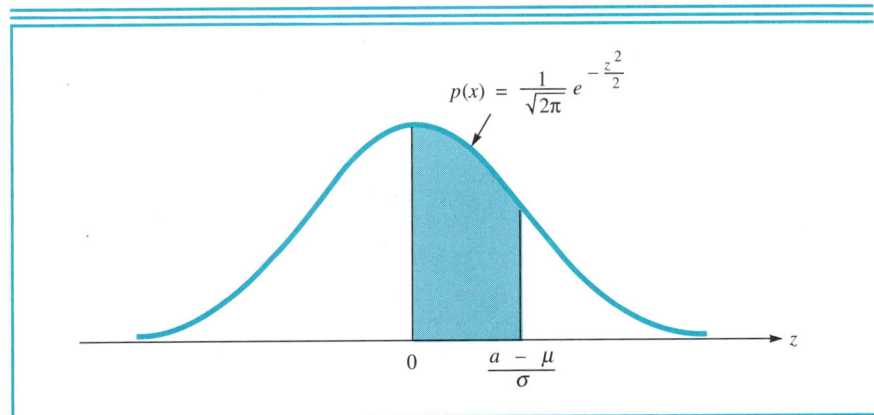

FIGURE 12–10

> **Exercise.** Given $N(20, 3)$, what z-values correspond to $x = 26$ and $x = 18.5$?
> **Answer:** $2; -1/2$.

Values of the definite integral

$$\frac{1}{\sqrt{2\pi}} \int_0^z e^{-\frac{z^2}{2}} \, dz$$

are given in Table V at the end of the book for various values of z. We find, for example, when $z = 1$, the tabulated probability is 0.3413.

Table 12–20A shows the Minitab printout for computing the standardized normal probability when $z = 1$. Since Minitab gives a cumulative probability from $-\infty$ to z, we must subtract .5 (the area in the left half of Figure 12–10 from $-\infty$ to 0) from the Minitab probability 0.841345 in $K1$ to get our desired result of 0.341345 in $K2$. This, of course, to four–decimal-place accuracy is the same 0.3413 we found in Table V.

Table 12–20B shows the same calculation done on a calculator with stored statistical function keys. In this case the calculator gives the probability from z to $+\infty$ so we must subtract the calculator probability 0.158655254 from .5 (the area

TABLE 12–20A

```
                    Minitab

Worksheet size: 16174 cells

Press ALT + a highlighted letter to open a menu

MTB > cdf 1 K1;
SUBC> normal 0 1.
MTB > let K2 = K1 - .5
MTB > print K1-K2
K1          0.841345
K2          0.341345
MTB > stop
```

TABLE 12–20B

Keystroke	Calculator Display
0.5	0.5
−	0.500000000
1, then ⌐ Q (z)	0.158655254
=	0.341344746

in the right half of Figure 12–10 from 0 to $+\infty$) to get our desired result of 0.341344746. Again, to four–decimal-place accuracy this is the same 0.3413 that we found in Table V.

The particular manner in which the normal probabilities are given in Table V must be kept in mind so that the problem at hand will be matched properly with the table. Frequently a sketch will lessen the chance of improper use of the table.

Example. Given a normal distribution with mean 50 and standard deviation 10, what is the probability that a randomly selected number will lie in the interval from 50 to 65?

The desired probability is shown in Figure 12–11 as the shaded area over the interval from 50 to 65. At the point 65

$$z = \frac{65 - 50}{10} = 1.5.$$

From Table V, with $z = 1.5$, we find the desired probability to be 0.4332.

Example. Given $N(50, 10)$, as in the preceding example, what is the probability that x will fall in the interval 42 to 50?

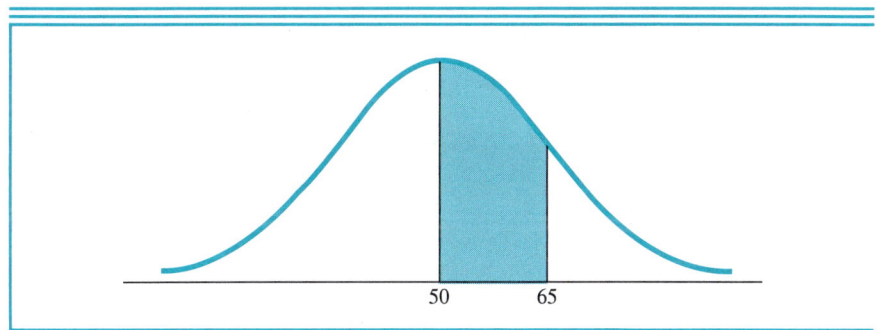

FIGURE 12–11

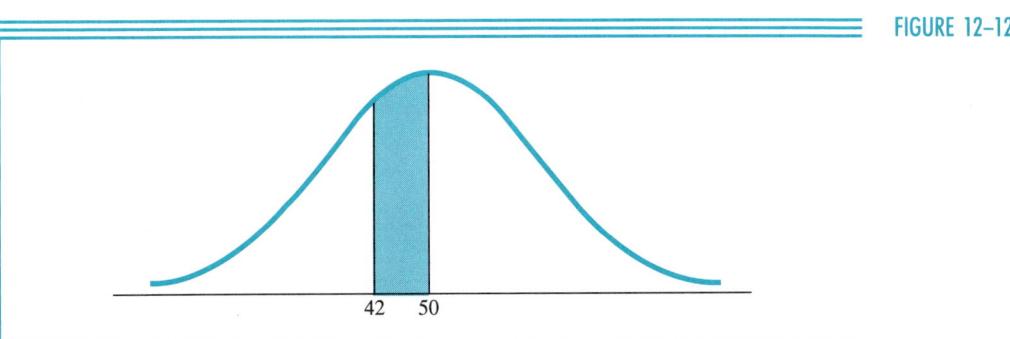

FIGURE 12–12

As Figure 12–12 on page 853 shows, 42 lies to the left of the mean. However the curve is symmetrical. The probability is the same for a given value of z, whether it be positive or negative. Here

$$z = \frac{42 - 50}{10} = -0.8.$$

The desired probability is found by entering Table V with z equal 0.8. It is 0.2881.

Table 12–21A shows the Minitab printout for the preceding example where $z = -0.08$. Since here we have a negative z-value, we want to subtract the Minitab probability 0.211855 in $K1$ from .5 to get our desired result of 0.288145 in $K2$.

Table 12–21B shows the same calculation done on a calculator with stored statistical function keys. In this case we want to subtract .5 from the calculator probability 0.78814460 to get our desired result of 0.288144601.

Exercise. Given $N(50, 10)$ as in the previous example, what is the probability that x will be in the interval a) 50 to 62? b) 45 to 50?

Answer: a) 0.385. b) 0.192.

TABLE 12–21A

```
                   Minitab

Worksheet size: 16174 cells

Press ALT + a highlighted letter to open a menu

MTB > cdf -.8 K1;
SUBC> normal 0 1.
MTB > let K2 = .5 - K1
MTB > print K1-K2
K1          0.211855
K2          0.288145
MTB > stop
```

TABLE 12–21B

Keystroke	Calculator Display
0.8, then +/−	−0.8
⌐ Q (z)	0.788144601
−	0.788144601
0.5	0.5
=	0.288144601

Example. Given $N(100, 20)$ what is the probability that x will be greater than 145?

The pertinent area is shown in Figure 12–13. It is a **right tail** area. Table V provides areas only for intervals that start at the mean (that is, at $z = 0$). We can find the desired area by applying the table and then subtracting from 0.5, inasmuch as the entire area to the right of the mean is 0.5.

$$z = \frac{145 - 100}{20} = 2.25.$$

The tabulated entry for $z = 2.25$ is 0.4878. Hence the desired area is

$$0.5000 - 0.4878 = 0.0122.$$

Exercise. How would we calculate the probability in the preceding example using a) Minitab? b) A calculator with statistical function keys?

Answer: a) Subtract the Minitab normal probability for $z = 2.25$ from 1. b) Use the calculator normal probability for $z = 2.25$ directly.

Example. Given $N(2, 0.1)$, what is the probability that x will lie in the interval 1.95 to 2.1?

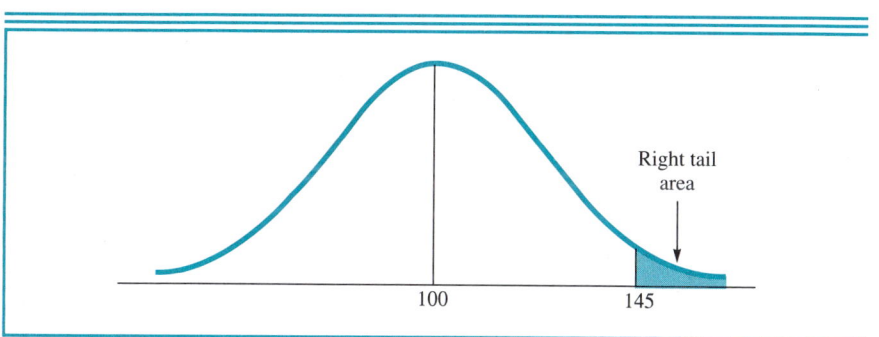

FIGURE 12–13

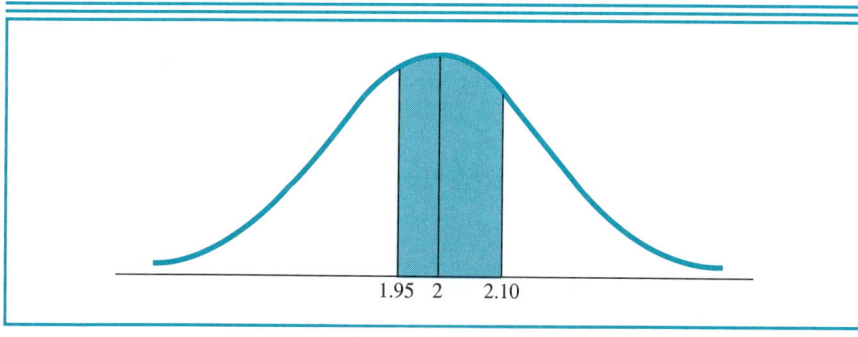

FIGURE 12–14

Figure 12–14 shows that we must add two tabulated entries.

At 1.95, z is -0.5 and the area is 0.1915.

At 2.1, z is 1 and the area is 0.3413.

Adding, we find the desired probability as

$$0.1915 + 0.3413 = 0.5328.$$

Exercise. How would we calculate the probability in the preceding example using a) Minitab? b) A calculator with statistical function keys?

Answer: a) Subtract the probability for $z = -0.5$ from that for $z = 1$. b) Subtract the probability for $z = 1$ from that for $z = -0.5$.

Example. Given $N(15, 2)$, find the probability that x will lie in the interval from 16 to 17.

Analysis of Figure 12–15 shows that the tabulated areas at $z = 1$ and $z = 0.5$ must be subtracted. Hence

$$0.3413 - 0.1915 = 0.1498.$$

Exercise. How would we calculate the probability for the preceding example using a) Minitab? b) A calculator with statistical function keys?

Answer: a) Subtract the probability for $z = 0.5$ from that for $z = 1$. b) Subtract the probability for $z = 1$ from that for $z = 0.5$.

FIGURE 12–15

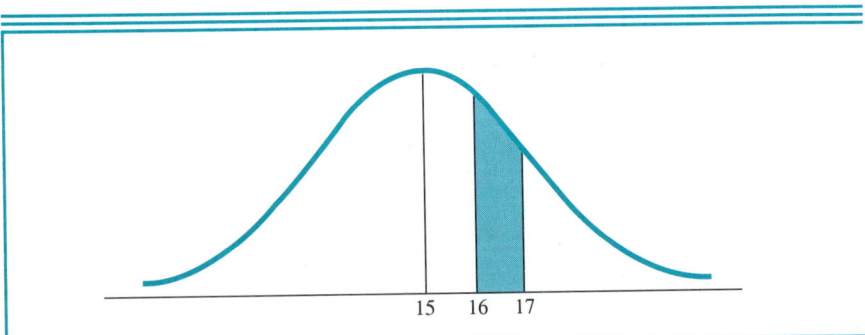

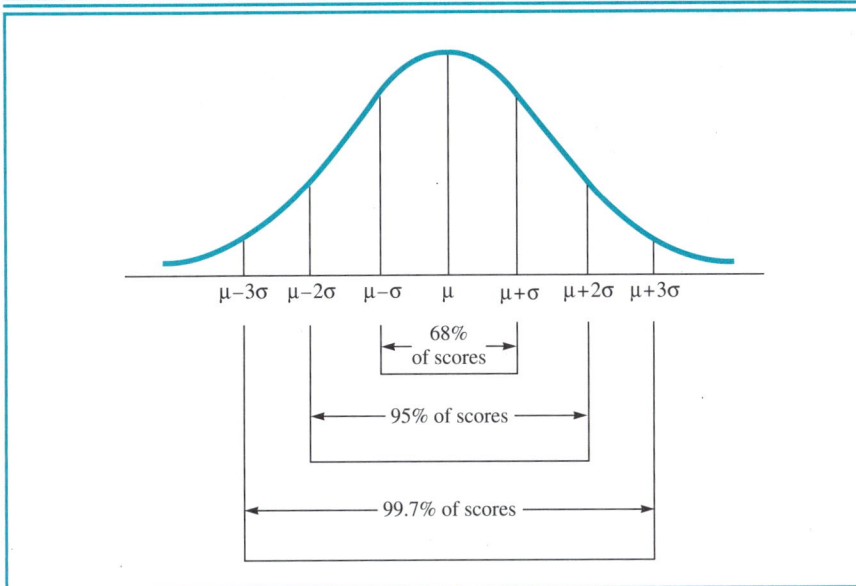

FIGURE 12-16

FROM THEORY TO PRACTICE
The Grading Game

Students are frequently told that their grades in a course will be curved or scaled according to a normal grading scheme. But just what does this mean? One way to do this would be to take all the students' final numerical scores, compute the average (μ) and standard deviation (σ), and then use the normal distribution for those particular values. Then the scores would be distributed as shown in Figure 12–16. Now suppose the instructor wants 5 percent of the grades to be *A* or *F*, 27 percent to be *B* or *D*, and 68 percent to be *C*. She then would assign an *A* to all students whose scores were two standard deviations or more **above** the mean, and an *F* to all students whose scores were two standard deviations or more **below** the mean. Similarly she would assign a *B* to all students whose scores were between one and two standard deviations **above** the mean, and a *D* to all students whose scores were between one and two standard deviations **below** the mean. Lastly she would assign a *C* all students whose scores were **within** one standard deviation of the mean. (Of course, pluses and minuses can be computed within each grade.)

The major advantage of this type of grading scheme is that instructors do not need to scale the raw scores to determine grades that adhere to a predetermined grading scheme. The reason for this is that by assuming that grades are normally distributed, the instructor can align the mean raw score with the mean of the grading scheme and assign the remainder of the grades accordingly.

(continued)

> But what about the assumption of normality for the grading distribution? If the class size is small (say 10 or so), grading on a normal curve is unjustifiable. But for a large class (say 100 or more), the assumption of normality is reasonable. So, for example, in a multisectioned course with 10 sections of 40 students each, any given section's grades may or may not be normally distributed. However the entire group of 400 grades can be expected to follow a normal distribution.

12.17 PROBLEM SET 12-7

1. Given a normal distribution with mean 150 and standard deviation 20, find the area over each of the following intervals:
   a) 150 to 160, inclusive.
   b) 150 up to but not including 160.
   c) Beyond 170.
   d) 160 to 170.
   e) Below 135.
   f) 145 to 165.
   g) 142 to 150.
   h) 138 to 146.

2. Given $N(50, 5)$ find the probability that a randomly selected x will lie in each of the following intervals:
   a) 45 to 65.
   b) 40 to 60.
   c) 35 to 65.
   d) Outside the interval from 40 to 60.
   e) Above 46.
   f) 44 to 48.
   g) Below 55.
   h) Above 56.

3. Given $N(10, 2)$, find the probability that a randomly selected x will lie in each of the following intervals:
   a) Above 6.
   b) 11 to 15.
   c) Below 9.
   d) 8 to 10.
   e) 8 to 9, excluding the end points.
   f) 8 to 12.
   g) Above 11.5.
   h) 9 to 13.
   i) Above 16.

12.18 ESTIMATING THE MEAN AND THE STANDARD DEVIATION

The normal distribution as a mathematical model can be related approximately to numerous real-world situations. Suppose, for example, that an automatic machine is adjusted to produce shafts that have a diameter of two inches. As shaft after shaft comes off the machine, it is not expected that each shaft will have a diameter of precisely two inches. Shaft diameters will vary somewhat, the amount of variability being dependent upon the precision of the machine. Quality control engineers often assume that the probability of various departures from the nominal figure, two inches, can be estimated by application of the normal distribution.

If we are to apply a normal distribution to a real-world problem, we must have numbers for the mean and standard deviation of the distribution. In the mathematical model, of course, these quantities represent the central point and the degree of spread of an infinite set of values of the variate x. In the real world, we work with a finite set of numbers and think of them as a **sample** of x's drawn at random from the infinite set. The numbers in the sample reflect the central tendency and variability of the infinite set. We estimate the mean and the standard deviation for the infinite set from the numbers in the sample. In the remainder of this section, we shall show how the estimates are made.

Suppose that we select a sample of 10 shafts from the output of a machine and measure the diameter of each shaft, obtaining the numbers shown in Table 12–22. Because we plan to use the sample to **estimate** μ and σ, we would prefer to have a sample of many more than 10 units. However our purpose is only to show how the estimates are made, and a small sample will suffice. The mean, μ, for the model is estimated by computing the mean (the ordinary average) of the sample. The procedure followed in estimating σ starts by estimating the variance, σ^2. Recalling that variance involves the squares of the amounts by which values differ from the mean, we proceed as follows:

> In most real-world situations, the mean and standard deviation are estimated from numbers in a sample.

1. Find the average of the sample data.
2. Subtract the average from a sample number, and square the difference.
3. Repeat Step 2 for each number in the sample, and then sum all the squares.
4. Divide the sum of squares in Step 3 by $n - 1$, where n is the number of values in the sample. The result of this step is the desired estimate of the variance.[1]

> The mean for a model is estimated by the mean of a sample; the variance for the model is estimated by dividing the sum of the squares of the differences from the mean for all numbers in a sample by $n - 1$, **not** n.

The steps are illustrated in Table 12–23. The difference between each value of x and the sample average, 2, is shown in the second column whose heading is $x - 2$; that is, sample value minus sample average. Note that this column sums to 0. This should always be the case; use this as a check on your arithmetic. The

TABLE 12–22

Diameters of 10 Shafts, in Inches

2.00	2.01	1.97	2.02	1.97
1.99	2.03	1.99	2.01	2.01

---

[1]Statisticians have proved that, for samples, the estimate is more accurate if we divide by $n - 1$ rather than n.

TABLE 12-23

Sample Value x	$x - 2$	$(x - 2)^2$
2.00	0.00	0.0000
1.99	−0.01	0.0001
2.01	0.01	0.0001
2.03	0.03	0.0009
1.97	−0.03	0.0009
1.99	−0.01	0.0001
2.02	0.02	0.0004
2.01	0.01	0.0001
1.97	−0.03	0.0009
2.01	0.01	0.0001
20.00	0.00	0.0036

squares of the differences are shown in the third column, whose heading is descriptive of the method for obtaining its entries. The sum of squares is 0.0036; dividing this sum of squares by one less than the number of values in the sample (that is, by $n - 1$ where n is 10), we obtain the variance estimate, 0.0004. The square root of the variance estimate, 0.02, is the estimated standard deviation.

$$\text{Mean estimate} = \text{Average} = \frac{20}{10} = 2; \quad n = 10.$$

$$\text{Variance estimate} = \frac{0.0036}{9} = 0.0004.$$

$$\text{Standard deviation estimate} = \sqrt{0.0004} = 0.02.$$

Table 12–24A shows the Minitab printout for the preceding example. Note that the MEAN is 2 and standard deviation (STDEV) is 0.02 just as in the example.

Table 12–24B shows the same calculations done on a calculator with stored statistical function keys. Again the results are the same as in the example.

The summation symbol, Σ, can be put to good use in summarizing instructions for computing estimates of the mean and standard deviation. Conventionally if the variate at hand is x and we wish to indicate the average of a sample of x's, we write the variate with a bar over it: $\bar{x}$. If we now let Σx represent the sum of a set of values of x, and n represent the number of values in the set, the average of the set is

$$\bar{x} = \frac{\Sigma x}{n}.$$

TABLE 12-24A

```
                        Minitab
Worksheet size: 16174 cells
Press ALT + a highlighted letter to open a menu

MTB > set C1
DATA> 2.00, 1.99, 2.01, 2.03, 1.97, 1.99, 2.02, 2.01, 1.97, 2.01
DATA> end
MTB > describe C1

              N       MEAN    MEDIAN   TRMEAN    STDEV   SEMEAN
C1           10     2.0000    2.0050   2.0000   0.0200   0.0063

            MIN        MAX        Q1       Q3
C1       1.9700     2.0300    1.9850   2.0125

MTB > stop
```

TABLE 12-24B

Keystroke	Calculator Display
┌, then CLΣ	0
2.00, then Σ+	1
1.99, then Σ+	2
2.01, then Σ+	3
2.03, then Σ+	4
1.97, then Σ+	5
1.99, then Σ+	6
2.02, then Σ+	7
2.01, then Σ+	8
1.97, then Σ+	9
2.01, then Σ+	10
┌, then $\bar{x}$, $\bar{y}$	2.00
┌, then S_x, S_y	0.02

Returning to Table 12–23, n is 10 and Σx is 20; hence

$$\bar{x} = \frac{20}{10} = 2.$$

Turning to the second column of Table 12–23, we express the operation of subtracting the average from each value of x by the instruction $x - \bar{x}$. In the third column, we square each difference, an operation denoted by $(x - \bar{x})^2$. The sum of the third column is expressed as $\Sigma(x - \bar{x})^2$. Finally, dividing the last expression by $(n - 1)$ provides the variance estimate, which we now label as s^2, so

$$s^2 = \frac{\Sigma(x - \bar{x})^2}{n - 1}.$$

The standard deviation estimate, s, is

The standard deviation estimate s is the nonnegative square root of the sum of the squares of the differences from the mean divided by $(n - 1)$.

Standard Deviation Estimate

$$s = \sqrt{\frac{\Sigma(x - \bar{x})^2}{n - 1}}.$$

Be careful not to confuse s^2 and s, the **estimated** variance and standard deviation from the sample, with σ^2 and σ, the **true** variance and standard deviation of the population.

Example. Compute $\bar{x}$ and s for the values of x given in the first column of Table 12–25.

$$\bar{x} = \frac{\Sigma x}{n} = \frac{36}{5} = 7.2.$$

$$s^2 = \frac{\Sigma(x - \bar{x})^2}{n - 1} = \frac{10.80}{4} = 2.7.$$

$$s = \sqrt{\frac{\Sigma(x - \bar{x})^2}{n - 1}} = \sqrt{\frac{10.80}{4}} = \sqrt{2.7} = 1.643.$$

TABLE 12-25

x	$x - \bar{x}$	$(x - \bar{x})^2$
5	-2.2	4.84
8	0.8	0.64
8	0.8	0.64
9	1.8	3.24
6	-1.2	1.44
36		10.80

12.19 PROBLEM SET 12-8

Compute $\bar{x}$ and s for each given set of x's:
1. 8, 8, 9, 6, 4.
2. 17, 15, 14, 20, 18, 16, 10, 12, 15, 13.
3. 8, 13, 12, 13, 10.
4. 2, 2, 6, 5, 1, 5.
5. 0.64, 0.58, 0.57, 0.57, 0.52, 0.58, 0.60, 0.58.

12.20 APPLICATIONS

In applications, the areas for the normal distribution are interpreted as percentages and proportions as well as probability, as we shall see in the examples that follow. In each example the mean and the standard deviation are presumed to have been estimated from sample data by the methods of Section 12.18.

Example. An automatic filling machine can be set to pour a certain number of ounces of fluid into containers. Data collected from runs of the machine show that the **average** amount of fill per container is, for practical purposes, equal to the machine setting. However the amount of fill per can varies, and the standard deviation of amount of fill per can has been estimated from sample data to be 0.4 ounces.

a) If the machine is set to pour 32 ounces, what is the probability that a container will receive less than 31.5 ounces?

We interpret this problem as one of finding the probability that x will be less than 31.5 in a normal distribution whose mean is 32 and whose standard deviation is 0.4. Figure 12–17 illustrates the probability sought.

$$\text{At } 31.5, \quad z = \frac{31.5 - 32}{0.4} = -1.25.$$

From Table V, with $z = 1.25$, the tabulated area is 0.3944. The shaded area in the sketch is

$$0.5000 - 0.3944 = 0.1056.$$

We estimate the probability that a can will receive less than 31.5 ounces to be 0.1056.

b) Given the circumstances in (a), what percentage of the containers will receive less than 31.5 ounces?

The probability, 0.1056, here is interpreted as the percent equivalent, 10.56 percent; that is, over the long run, about 10.56 percent of the containers will receive less than 31.5 ounces.

FIGURE 12-17

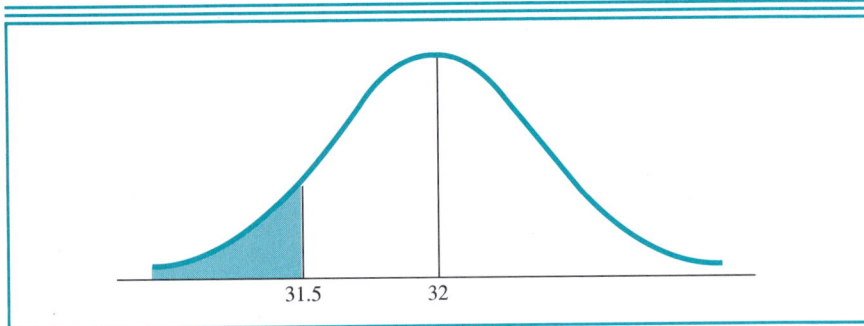

c) Given the circumstances in (a), if 1,000 containers are filled, approximately how many will contain less than 31.5 ounces?

Following the interpretation of (b), we find 10.56 percent of 1,000. This is

$$0.1056(1,000) = 105.6$$

or about 106 containers.

Exercise. How would we calculate the probability in (a) of the preceding example using a) Minitab? b) A calculator with statistical function keys?

Answer: a) Use the Minitab normal probability for $z = -1.25$ directly. b) Subtract the calculator normal probability for $z = -1.25$ from 1.

Example. Given the same machine as in the previous example, suppose that we wish to set the machine so that not more than 5 percent of the containers will receive less than 32 ounces. What should be the setting?

The nature of this problem is seen in Figure 12-18. We wish to find the mean (the setting) so that the probability below 32 is 0.05 (that is, the given 5 percent). This means, by subtraction, that the area over the interval from 32 to μ must be

$$0.5 - 0.05 = 0.45.$$

We can find, by **inverse** use of Table V, what value of z corresponds to the area 0.45.

Turning to Table V, we see in the field that 0.4500 is between the tabulated values 0.4495 and 0.4505. The corresponding marginal values, z, are 1.64 and 1.65, respectively. By interpolation, $z = 1.645$.

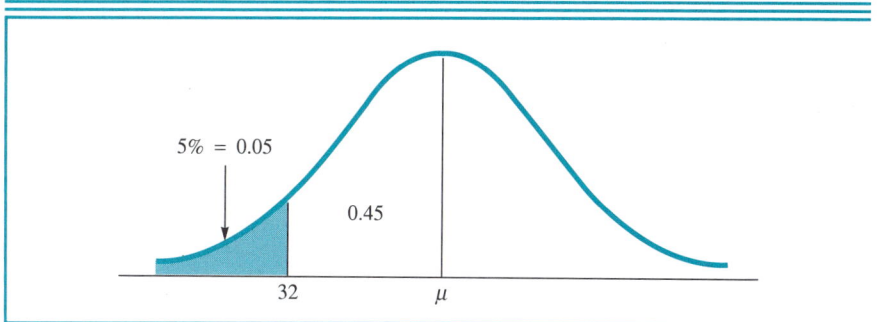

FIGURE 12-18

Now it is important to understand that in terms of the units of the original problem, **a value of z means z times the standard deviation.** In the present case, $z = 1.645$ means

$$1.645(0.4 \text{ ounces}) = 0.658 \text{ ounces}.$$

Hence the interval from 32 up to μ is 0.658 ounces, which tells us the machine should be set at

$$\mu = 32 + 0.658 = 32.658 \text{ ounces}$$

if not more than 5 percent of the containers are to receive less than 32 ounces.

The preceding bold-faced words refer to the definition

$$z = \frac{x - \mu}{\sigma}$$

from which it follows that

$$z\sigma = x - \mu.$$

The interval $x - \mu$ is the distance from x to the mean. It equals z (for the x in question) times the standard deviation. In passing, we note that the question of whether to add $z\sigma$ to x or to subtract $z\sigma$ from x to locate the mean depends upon which side of the mean our sketch shows x to be. In the present case the mean is to the right of 32, so we added $z\sigma$.

Table 12–26A shows the Minitab printout for the preceding example where we want to determine the z-value associated with a lower left tail area of 0.05. Remembering that Minitab gives a cumulative probability from $-\infty$ to z, we simply use the **invcdf** Minitab command with 0.05 as shown in the table to get $z = -1.6449$. The negative sign, of course, indicates that we are to the left of the mean, so this result agrees with that in the example where we found $z = 1.645$ from Table V.

Table 12–26B shows the same calculation done on a calculator with stored statistical function keys. In this case we remember that the calculator gives the

TABLE 12–26A

```
                          Minitab
Worksheet size: 16174 cells

Press ALT + a highlighted letter to open a menu

MTB > invcdf 0.05;
SUBC> normal 0 1.
   0.0500    -1.6449
MTB > stop
```

TABLE 12–26B

Keystroke	Calculator Display
0.95	0.95
⌐ z_p	−1.644853627

probability from z to $+\infty$, so we first subtract 0.05 from 1 to get 0.95 and then proceed as shown in the table. As with Minitab, the calculator result of -1.644853627 agrees with that in the example.

Example. If light bulbs of a certain type have an average burning life of 500 hours and a standard deviation of 40 hours, as estimated from experience, within what limits symmetrically located above and below 500 will the burning lives of half of such bulbs lie?

The desired limits are shown by question marks in Figure 12–19. If we want half (50 percent) of the numbers to fall between these limits, which are symmetrically located with respect to the mean, then 25 percent will be in each of the intervals 500 to ?. Table V tells us that the z corresponding to an area of 0.25 is 0.675. Hence the length of the interval from 500 to ? is 0.675 times the standard deviation:

$$0.675(40) = 27.$$

The desired limits are

$$500 \pm 27 \quad \text{or} \quad 473 \text{ to } 527 \text{ hours.}$$

Exercise. How would we calculate the z-value in the preceding example using a) Minitab? b) A calculator with statistical function keys?

Answer: a) Use the Minitab result for an area of $0.5 - 0.25 = 0.25$ (the left tail). b) Use the calculator result for $0.5 + 0.25 = 0.75$.

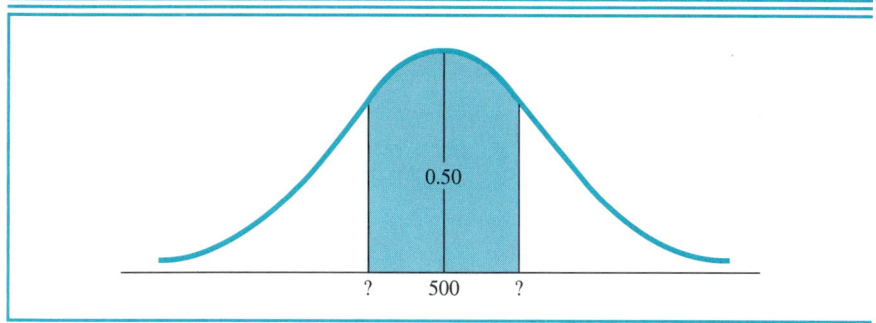

FIGURE 12-19

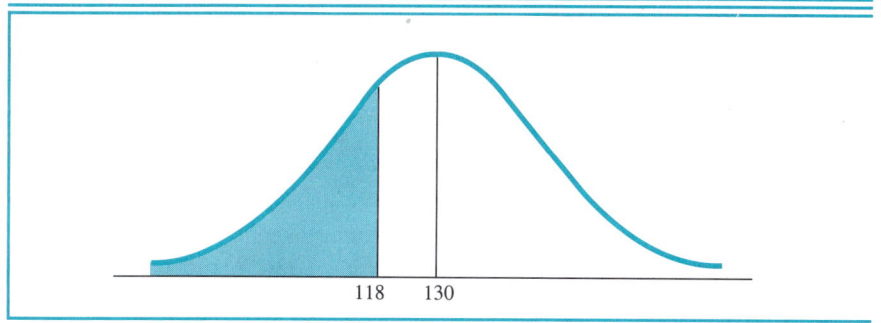

FIGURE 12-20

Example. A testing service reports the average score on a test as 130 points, and the standard deviation of test scores as 20 points. Jones takes the test and scores 118 points. What is Jones's percentile standing? See Figure 12-20.

We interpret percentile standing as the percentage scoring less than Jones, and estimate it as being the percentage below 118 in $N(130, 20)$:

$$z = \frac{118 - 130}{20} = -0.6.$$

From Table V, with $z = 0.6$, we obtain the area 0.2257. Figure 12-20 shows that the area **below** Jones's 118 points is found by the subtraction

$$0.5000 - 0.2257 = 0.2743 = 27.43\%.$$

Hence we estimate Jones's score as being at the 27th percentile.

FIGURE 12-21

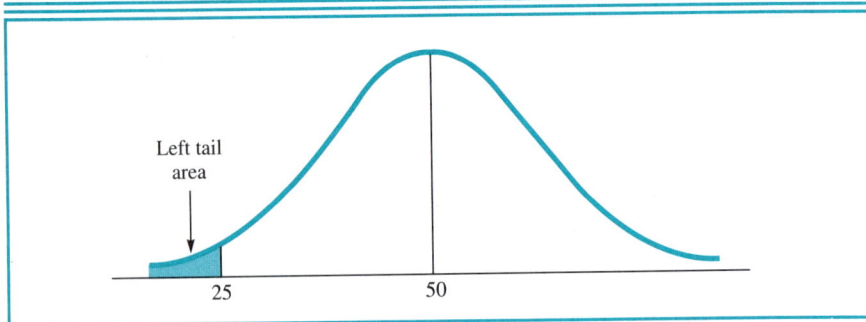

> **Exercise.** How would we solve the preceding example using a) Minitab? b) A calculator with statistical function keys?
>
> **Answer:** a) Use the Minitab normal probability for $z = -0.6$. b) Subtract the calculator normal probability for $z = -0.6$ from 1.

Example. Study of records of the number of units of item K3 in inventory day by day shows average inventory to be 50 units, and the standard deviation of the day-by-day numbers to be 10 units. Suppose that, during a day, 25 units are requested. What is the probability that there will not be enough units in inventory to meet this day's requests?

We interpret this problem as one of finding the probability that x is less than 25 in $N(50, 10)$.

$$z = \frac{25 - 50}{10} = -2.5.$$

From Table V, with $z = 2.5$, we obtain the area 0.4938. According to Figure 12-21, the desired area is

$$0.5000 - 0.4938 = 0.0062.$$

The probability of not being able to meet the requests is the small figure 0.0062; that is, the chances are only 6 in 1,000 that such requests could not be satisfied.

> **Exercise.** How would we solve the preceding example using a) Minitab? b) A calculator with statistical function keys?
>
> **Answer:** a) Use the Minitab normal probability for $z = -2.5$. b) Subtract the calculator normal probability for $z = -2.5$ from 1.

12.21 PROBLEM SET 12-9

All problems in this set are to be solved under the assumption that the normal distribution is applicable.

1. Given $N(50, 5)$,
   a) The probability is 0.17 that x will lie in the interval from 50 up to what number?
   b) The probability is 0.10 that x will exceed what number?
   c) The probability is 0.05 that x will be less than what number?
   d) The probability is 0.50 that x will lie in what interval symmetrically located above and below 50?
   e) The probability is 0.95 that x will be less than what number?

2. Assume that a machine will turn out parts whose average diameter is the figure at which the machine is set, and that the standard deviation has been estimated from sample data to be 0.001 inches.
   a) If the machine is set at 2.00 inches, what percentage of parts made will have diameters exceeding 2.001 inches?
   b) If the machine is set at 0.100 inch, what percentage of parts made will have diameters exceeding 0.098 inches?
   c) If the machine is set at 1.500 inches and 1,000 parts are made, approximately how many parts will have diameters less than 1.498 inches?
   d) Specifications state that parts are to have 2.000-inch diameter, tolerance plus or minus 0.002; that is, parts whose diameters differ by more than 0.002 from 2.000 are to be classified as defectives. What percent of the parts will be defective?
   e) Within what limits symmetrically located about a setting of 1.575 inches will the diameters of 95 percent of the parts lie?
   f) If the machine is set at 2.250 inches, 5 percent of the parts will have diameters less than what number of inches?
   g) A loss of 40 cents is incurred for every part that is scrapped because its diameter is too small. Specifications state that the part is to have diameter 1.500 inches, tolerance $\pm$ 0.0015 inches. The machine is set at 1.500 inches. If 2,000 parts are made, what will be the cost of the scrapped undersized parts?

3. The amounts poured by an automatic can-filling machine average out at the machine setting. Collected data indicate that the standard deviation of amounts of fill per can is 0.2 ounce.
   a) If the machine is set to pour 32 ounces, what is the probability that a can will contain less than 31.9 ounces?
   b) If the machine is set to pour 32 ounces, what percentage of the cans will contain at least 31.9 ounces?
   c) If the machine is set to pour 32 ounces and 2,000 cans are filled, approximately how many cans will contain less than 31.7 ounces?
   d) If the can label states the contents to be 32 ounces and the machine is set to pour 32.25 ounces, what percentage of the cans will be underfilled?
   e) If the can labels state contents to be 16 ounces, at what level should the machine be set if 99 percent of the cans are to contain at least 16 ounces?

4. The average breaking strength of certain connectors is 2,000 pounds, $s = 80$ pounds.
   a) Within what limits symmetrically located about 2,000 will the breaking strength of 75 percent of the connectors lie?
   b) What percentage of the connectors will have a breaking strength of more than 2,100 pounds?
   c) The breaking strength of 95 percent of the connectors will exceed what number of pounds?
   d) If a connector with breaking strength less than 1,800 pounds is classified as defective, what percentage of connectors will be defective?

5. A testing service reports the average score on a certain test to be 200 points. $s = 25$ points.
   a) What percentage of those taking the test score above 275?
   b) What percentage of those taking the test score below 160?
   c) Half of those taking the test make scores in what interval symmetrically located above and below 200?
   d) Ninety-five percent of those taking the test score above what number of points?
   e) What would be the percentile standing of a person who scored 260 points on the test?

12.22 REVIEW PROBLEMS

1. Let X be a random variable with the probability distribution given in the following table.

x	0	1	2	3
$p(x)$	.55	.35	.05	.05

   Find
   a) The expected value $E(X)$ of X.
   b) The variance $\sigma^2(X)$ of X.
   c) The standard deviation $\sigma(X)$ of X.

2. A multiple-choice examination consists of four questions, each of which has five possible answers. If a student guesses on all four questions,
   a) What is the probability distribution of the random variable X, the number of correct answers?
   b) What is the most likely number of correct answers?
   c) What is the expected value $E(X)$ of the random variable X?
   d) What are the variance $\sigma^2(X)$ and standard deviation $\sigma(X)$ of the random variable X?

3. During a 20-week tourist season, the number of vacancies after 6 P.M. on weekdays at the Roadside Motel was as follows:

Number of vacancies	0	1	2	3	4	5
Number of days	25	15	20	18	12	10

   a) Graph the probability distribution of vacancies.
   b) If two parties arrive after 6 P.M. on a weekday, what is the probability that they are accommodated?
   c) How many parties could arrive after 6 P.M. before the probability exceeded 0.75 that they could not all be accommodated?
   d) Find the expected number of vacancies on a weekday.
   e) Find the mean and variance of the probability distribution.

4. To save time and money, but still provide safeguards on the quality of incoming goods, buyers often inspect a portion of a shipment and judge the quality of the entire shipment on the basis of the quality of the inspected sample. Suppose a buyer has received a shipment of 10 microcomputer disk drives, 2 of which are defective. Three disk drives are selected at random from the shipment and tested. If d is the number of defective disk drives observed, then $d = 0, 1,$ or 2. Find the probability distribution for d and present the results graphically.

5. Simulate the experiment in Problem 4 using a computer simulation or a deck of cards with eight black cards (representing satisfactory disk drives) and two red cards (representing defective disk drives). Repeat this simulation 100 times so that 100 observations have been made of the value of d. Construct a relative frequency histogram for this sample and compare it to the graph of the probability distribution constructed in Problem 4.

Do Problems 6 through 15 using the binomial rule.

6. A baseball player assesses his probability of getting on base each time at bat at 0.20. What is the probability that he will get on base
   a) Exactly once in his next three times at bat?
   b) At least once in his next three trips?
   c) At least twice in his next three trips?
   d) Exactly twice in six trips?

7. The four engines of an airplane operate independently. On an overseas flight the probability that an engine will fail is 0.001. On such a flight, what is the probability that
   a) Exactly one will fail?
   b) More than one will fail?

8. A true-false examination has five questions. A student assigns probability of 0.7 of being correct on each question. Assuming independence, what is the probability that he gets
   a) All five correct?
   b) At least four correct?
   c) Exactly three correct?
   d) At least three correct?
   e) At least four incorrect?

12.22 REVIEW PROBLEMS (continued)

9. A test has five four-choice questions and a student assigns probability 0.8 of getting each one correct. What is the probability of getting
   a) All five correct?
   b) At least three correct?
   c) At least one correct?

10. The probability of success on a single trial of an event is 0.3. In 100 independent trials, write, but do not evaluate, the expression for the probability of
    a) At least one success.
    b) At most one success.
    c) Exactly five successes.
    d) At most three successes.

11. A test has 50 five-choice questions. A student guesses the answer to each question. Write, but do not evaluate, the expression for each of the following probabilities:
    a) Ninety percent or more correct.
    b) At least one correct.

12. The probability that any particular item is defective is 0.10. Using binomial probabilities, find
    a) The probability of at most one defective in 10 items.
    b) How many items would have to be selected to have a probability of 0.99 that the group would contain at least one good item.

13. A binomial experiment consists of m trials. Write the summation expression using m, p, q, r, and x for
    a) The probability of at most r occurrences in the m trials.
    b) The probability of more than r occurrences in the m trials.

14. A department store employs three people who take orders over the telephone. Each person is busy taking an order 80 percent of the time. What is the probability that an operator will be free to take an order at the time of the call
    a) If one customer calls at a point in time?
    b) If two customers call at a point in time?

15. See Problem 14. How many telephone operators should the store have if the probability that an operator will be free when a customer calls is to be approximately 0.6?

Do Problems 16 through 18 using Table IV.

16. A sample of 25 items is selected from a large lot, and the lot is rejected if the sample contains any defective items. Find the probability of acceptance if the proportion defective in the lot is
    a) 0.01.
    b) 0.10.
    c) 0.20.

17. Repeat Problem 16 assuming the lot is rejected if more than two defectives are found in the sample.

18. From past experience, a market research firm knows that 60 percent of the people contacted by telephone will agree to a telephone interview. If the firm calls 25 people, what is the probability of completing
    a) At most 10 interviews?
    b) At least 10 interviews?
    c) More than 15 interviews?
    d) From 15 to 20 interviews, inclusive?
    e) Exactly 10 interviews?

19. The act is to draw a card. If the card is a face card, you win $20; if it is not a face card, you lose $20. Compute the expected monetary value of the act. (Face cards are jack, queen, king, and ace.)

20. The act is rolling a pair of dice. If the dice come up 2, 7, or 11, you win $100; otherwise you lose $16. Compute the expected monetary value of the act.

21. Which act should be chosen according to the EMV criterion?

Probability	Event	Payoffs		
		A_1	A_2	A_3
0.5	E_1	$5	$4	$4
0.3	E_2	5	7	7
0.2	E_3	5	3	5

22. If you make a unit of a product and it is sold (demanded), you gain $10; if you make a unit and it is

12.22 REVIEW PROBLEMS (continued)

not sold, you lose $5. You assign probabilities as follows:

Number of Units Demanded	Probability of Number of Units Demanded
0	0.1
1	0.2
2	0.4
3	0.3
4 or more	0.0

According to the EMV criterion, how many units should you make?

23. A company offers insurance covering damage of 20 percent, 40 percent, 60 percent, 80 percent, or 100 percent. The owner of a particular property wishes to insure it for $200,000. The company assesses yearly damage probabilities (for the various respective damage percentages) at 0.0010, 0.0008, 0.0006, 0.0004, and 0.0002. What base figure (before overhead and profit) should the company use in establishing the annual premium to charge for insuring the property?

24. a) Convert $f(x) = x + 1$, $0 \le x \le 10$, to a probability density function.
    b) What is the probability that a randomly selected x will lie in the interval 0 to 1? The interval 5 to 6?

25. a) Convert $f(x) = x^{1/3} - 1$, $1 \le x \le 8$, to a probability density function.
    b) Find the probability that a randomly selected x will lie in the interval 1 to 27/8.

26. a) Convert $f(x) = 50$, $20 \le x < 45$, to a probability density function.
    b) Find the probability that a randomly selected x will lie in the interval 30 to 40.

27. Convert $f(x) = 10(x + 2)^{-3}$, $0 \le x < \infty$, to a probability density function.

28. Given that
$$p(x) = \frac{12x - 3x^2}{32}$$
is a probability density function over the interval $x = 0$ to $x = 4$, find the probability that x will lie in the intervals 0 to 1; 0 to 2; 2 to 3.

29. If $p(x) = kx^{3/2}$ is a probability density function over the interval 0 to 100, what must be the value for k?

30. Given the probability density function $p(x) = 0.02$, $0 \le x \le 50$,
    a) Find the expected value, μ.
    b) Find the variance, σ^2.
    c) Find the standard deviation, σ.

31. Given the probability density function
$$p(x) = 0.012x + 0.04, 0 \le x \le 10,$$

a) Find the expected value, μ.
b) Find the variance, σ^2.
c) Find the standard deviation, σ.

32. Find μ, the expected value of x, for the probability density function
$$p(x) = \frac{3}{x^4}, \quad 1 \le x < \infty.$$

33. Given a normal distribution with mean 30 and standard deviation 6, find the area over each of the following intervals:
    a) 30 to 33.
    b) 36 to 42.
    c) Less than 27.
    d) More than 48.
    e) 24 to 33.
    f) More than 21.

34. Given $N(100, 5)$, find the probability that a randomly selected x will lie in each of the following intervals:
    a) 90 to 105.
    b) 105 to 115.
    c) 92 to 96.
    d) Less than 103.
    e) More than 88.
    f) 112 to 115.

35. Compute the mean, $\bar{x}$, and the standard deviation, s, for each of the following:
    a) 3, 7, 7, 9, 14.
    b) 3, 5, 7, 7, 8.
    c) 15, 15, 15.
    d) 1.2, 0.7, 1.2, 1.3.

12.22 REVIEW PROBLEMS (concluded)

36. Given $N(20, 4)$,
    a) The probability is 0.20 that x will lie in the interval from 20 up to what number?
    b) The probability is 0.16 that x will exceed what number?
    c) The probability is 0.025 that x will be less than what number?
    d) The probability is 0.50 that x will lie in what interval symmetrically located above and below 20?
    e) The probability is 0.95 that x will be less than what number?

37. Assume that a machine will turn out parts whose average diameter is the figure at which the machine is set, and that the standard deviation has been estimated from sample data to be 0.002 inches.
    a) If the machine is set at 2.500 inches, what percentage of parts made will have diameters exceeding 2.503 inches?
    b) If the machine is set at 2.000 inches, what percentage of parts made will have diameters exceeding 1.999 inches?
    c) If the machine is set at 2.250 inches and 1,000 parts are made, approximately how many parts will have diameters less than 2.245 inches?
    d) Specifications state that parts are to have 2.500-inch diameter, plus or minus 0.003; that is, parts whose diameters differ by more than 0.003 from 2.500 are to be classified as defectives. If the machine is set at 2.500 inches, what percentage of parts will be defective?
    e) Within what limits symmetrically located about a setting of 3.000 inches will the diameters of 95 percent of the parts lie?
    f) If the machine is set at 2.500 inches, 10 percent of the parts will have diameters less than what number of inches?
    g) A loss of 50 cents is incurred for every part that is scrapped because its diameter is too small. Specifications state that the part is to have diameter 2.000 inches, tolerance ± 0.004 inches. If the machine is set at 2.000 inches and 5,000 parts are made, what will be the cost of the scrapped undersized parts?

38. If light bulbs of a certain type have an average burning life of 1,000 hours with a standard deviation of 100 hours.
    a) Within what limits symmetrically located above and below 1,000 will burning lives of 50 percent of the bulbs fall?
    b) If a large number of these bulbs burn continuously, how long will it be before 40 percent have burned out?
    c) How many bulbs out of 2,000 will have burning lives exceeding 1,250 hours?

39. A testing service reports the average score on a test to be 500 points with a standard deviation of 100 points.
    a) What percentage of those taking the test score above 600? Above 700?
    b) Seventy-five percent of those taking the test make scores in what interval symmetrically located about the average?

40. Inventory on hand for item X is brought up to 150 at the end of each day. Demand for X averages 100 units a day, with a standard deviation of 20 units. On a particular day, what is the probability that demand will exceed inventory on hand?

12.23 EXTENDED REVIEW PROBLEMS

1. a) Convert $f(x) = x^2$, $0 \le x \le 5$, to a probability density function.
   b) What is the probability that a randomly selected x will lie in the interval 0 to 1? 1 to 2? 1 to 3?

2. If 100 coins are tossed and the number of heads recorded, the number of heads, x, will be approximately normally distributed with mean 50 and standard deviation 5. Assuming $N(50, 5)$,

12.23 EXTENDED REVIEW PROBLEMS (concluded)

a) What percentage of the time would more than 65 heads appear in tossing 100 coins?
b) What is the probability that the number of heads will differ by more than 15, one way or the other, from 50?
c) What percentage of the time would the number of heads be between 40 and 60?

3. The quantity of fish brought to port varies from day to day and has the probability density function

$$p(x) = 0.003(x^2 - 20x + 100), 0 \le x \le 10,$$

where x is in thousands of pounds per day.
a) Find μ, the expected value of x.
b) Estimate the total quantity of fish that will be brought to port in a 30-day period.

4. The probability that a machine is running properly is 0.80. From time to time, samples of output are selected and measured, and the sample average is computed. If the machine is running properly, the probability that the sample average will be in a certain range is 0.95. If the machine is not running properly, the probability that the sample average will be in this range is 0.05. A sample is selected, and its average is outside the range. What is the probability that the machine is running properly?

5. A test has five five-choice questions. A student guesses the answer to each question. Assuming independence, what is the probability of
a) All five correct?
b) At least four correct?
c) Exactly three correct?
d) At least three correct?

6. Given $N(50, 3)$, find the probability that a randomly selected x will lie in each of the following intervals:
a) 54 to 58.
b) 44 to 48.
c) 45 to 55.
d) Less than 49.
e) More than 55.

7. From past experience, a college knows that 70 percent of student inquiries result in a personal interview on campus. The college is launching a special Honors Program and has received 25 inquiries. What is the probability that the admissions staff will personally interview

a) At most 15 candidates?
b) At least 15 candidates?
c) More than 20 candidates?
d) From 15 to 20 candidates?
e) Exactly 15 candidates?

8. One million tickets are sold at $1 each for a lottery. There is a first prize of $100,000, 2 second prizes of $50,000, 10 third prizes of $1,000, and 20 fourth prizes of $500. What is the (expected) value of a ticket?

9. The amounts poured by an automatic can-filling machine average out at the machine setting. Collected data indicate that the standard deviation of the amounts of fill per can is 1 percent of the machine setting; that is, for example, if the machine is set at 50 ounces, the standard deviation is 1 percent of 50 = 0.50 ounces.
a) If the machine is set to pour 20 ounces, what is the probability that a can will contain less than 19.7 ounces?
b) If the machine is set to pour 50 ounces, how many cans out of 1,000 will contain between 49 and 51 ounces?
c) If can labels state contents to be 48 ounces and the machine is set to pour 49 ounces, what percentage of the cans will be underfilled?
d) If specifications call for cans to contain at least 100 ounces, and the machine is set to pour 101 ounces, what percentage of cans will meet specifications?
e) In (d), if cans cannot hold any more than 102.3 ounces, what percent of cans will overflow?
f) If the maximum amount cans hold is 50.8 ounces and the machine is set at 50 ounces, some cans will overflow. Overflows are defectives and are removed from the batch under production. How many cans will have to be filled if the number left after removing defectives is to be 5,000?

10. Compute the mean, $\bar{x}$, and the standard deviation, s, for each of the following:
a) 1, 3, 3, 7, 5, 11, 2, 1.
b) 1/2, 2/3, 3/4, 4/5.
c) 1.2, 0.8, 1.1, 1.3.

ELEMENTS OF ALGEBRA

A1.1 INTRODUCTION

This appendix presents the basic definitions, conventions, and rules of algebra, together with discussions and illustrations of the fundamental properties of numbers. Each topic is accompanied by examples that will meet the needs of those who use isolated parts of the appendix for reference purposes. However topics are presented in logical order so that anyone seeking a substantial review may start at the beginning and move in an orderly fashion through the material. From time to time, the student may find it helpful to review relevant sections of this and the next two appendixes.

A1.2 THE REAL NUMBERS

The positive and negative whole numbers, with 0, form the set of **integers**. Combining the integers with the fractions, we have the set of **rational numbers**. Thus a rational number (**ratio** number) is a number that can be expressed in the form of a fraction that has integers as numerator and denominator. For reasons to be discussed soon, fractions with denominator 0 are excluded from our number system.

> **Exercise.** In what number set does 1.15 reside?
>
> **Answer:** This is a rational number because it can be expressed as 115/100, which is the ratio of the two integers, 115 and 100.

Numbers such as the square root of 2, the cube root of 6, and π cannot be expressed as a ratio of two integers; they serve as examples of **irrational numbers**. The set of all rational and irrational numbers is called the set of **real numbers**. Only real numbers will be used in this book. Numbers with an imaginary component (that is, a component involving the square root of -1) are called **complex numbers** and play no role in our discussions.

A1.3 RULES OF SIGN

The numbers $+2$ and -2 are opposites in the sense that each is the negative of the other. Think of $+2$ as \$2 of savings and -2 as \$2 of debt—positive and negative numbers play an important role in business applications. The statement that -2 is the negative of $+2$ is true by definition; the statement that the negative of -2 is $+2$ is a rule that can be derived from definitions and axioms. Thus

$$-(+2) = -2$$

and

$$-(-2) = +2.$$

Another derived rule justifies the statement

$$+(-2) = -(+2).$$

That is, the positive of the negative of a number is the same as the negative of the positive of the number. As a consequence of this rule, the true sign of a number is the same no matter what the **order** is of the signs immediately preceding the number. For example,

$$+[-(-5)] = -[+(-5)] = -[-(+5)].$$

The true sign is shown by working with the last expression to be

$$-[-(+5)] = -[-5] = +5.$$

Exercise. Write $-[-(-5)]$ with one sign.

Answer: -5.

Any sequence of signs immediately preceding a number can always be converted to a single sign, the true sign being **minus** if the sequence has an **odd** number of minus signs, and being **plus** if the sequence has an **even** number of minus signs. For example,

$$-[+(-3)] = +3$$

since there are two minus signs. However

$$-\{-[+(-3)]\} = -3$$

since here there are three minus signs.

A1.4 ADDITION AND SUBTRACTION OF SIGNED NUMBERS

If two numbers have the same sign, their sum is found by adding the two numbers and affixing the common sign. Thus

$$(+4) + (+3) = +7$$

and

$$(-3) + (-4) = -7.$$

> **Exercise.** Add $(-10) + (-4)$.
> **Answer:** -14.

The sum of a positive and a negative number is found by taking the difference between the two numbers, disregarding sign, and affixing the sign of the larger to the difference. For example,

$$(+7) + (-3) = +4.$$

Think of this as $7 of savings and $3 of debt resulting in $4 of net worth. In like fashion,

$$(-7) + (+3) = -4.$$

> **Exercise.** Add $(+5) + (-3)$.
> **Answer:** $+2$.

In terms of fundamentals, subtraction is addition of a negative number. Hence subtraction can be converted to addition by following the rule that states that subtracting a number is the same as adding its negative. This rule, together with the rule for adding two numbers already stated, permits us to write

$$+3 - (+4) = +3 + (-4) = -1.$$

As another example,

$$-3 - (-4) = -3 + (+4) = +1.$$

> **Exercise.** Write $+5 - (+11)$ as an addition problem and find the sum.
> **Answer:** $+5 + (-11) = -6$.

Observe that the minus symbol is used both to designate a negative number and to indicate the operation of subtraction. Again, the plus symbol designates both a positive number and the operation of addition. For example, we write $-(+2)$ to designate the **negative** of $+2$, but in the expression $+3 - (+2)$, the same symbol, $-(+2)$, means to **subtract** $+2$. Now to simplify life we will adopt two conventions. First, we will assume that an unsigned number is always positive; and second, we will indicate the subtraction of a number by a minus sign, rather than by addition of its negative. Thus instead of $+3 - (+2)$, we shall write the simplified statement, $3 - 2$. The conventions just stated, taken together with the rule for sign sequence, contribute to simplicity of expression, as illustrated next:

$$+1 + (+2) - (+3) + (-4) - (-5) - [+(-4)]$$

becomes

$$1 + 2 - 3 - 4 + 5 + 4 = (1 + 2 + 5 + 4) - (3 + 4) = 12 - 7 = 5.$$

Exercise. Simplify and evaluate $+(-1) + (-3) - (+2) + (+4) + [-(-6)]$.
Answer: 4.

The negative of the sum of two numbers is the same as the sum of the negatives of the numbers. Thus

$$-(7 + 5) = (-7) + (-5) = -7 - 5 = -12.$$

Once again, think of -7 as a $7 debt and -5 as a $5 debt resulting in a total debt of $12 or -12. Note that as we go from $-(7 + 5)$ to $-7 - 5$, the effect is to remove the parentheses and change the signs of the numbers inside the parentheses. This method applies generally; that is, parentheses preceded by a minus sign alone can be removed by changing the sign of each term inside the parentheses. As examples,

$$-(4 - 6) = -4 + 6$$

and

$$-(4 + 8) = -4 - 8.$$

Parentheses preceded by a plus sign alone (or no sign) serve no necessary purpose and may be omitted. Thus

$$+(8 - 6) = 8 - 6$$

and

$$(2 - 4 + 3) = 2 - 4 + 3.$$

> **Exercise.** Remove grouping symbols and evaluate $(2 + 3 - 5) - (5 - 2 + 4)$.
> **Answer:** $2 + 3 - 5 - 5 + 2 - 4 = 7 - 14 = -7$.

A1.5 MULTIPLICATION AND DIVISION OF SIGNED NUMBERS

As with addition and subtraction, multiplication is the basic operation with two numbers, while division is defined in terms of multiplication. One rule of sign suffices for both operations—namely, if two numbers have the **same** sign, their product (or quotient) is **positive**; if two numbers have **opposite** signs, their product (or quotient) is **negative**. In multiplication, for example,

$$(-4)(-2) = 8$$

and

$$2(-4) = -8.$$

Observe the use of parentheses in the last written expression to indicate multiplication. In the preceding expression, the absence of a symbol between the two sets of parentheses means that the numbers inside the parentheses are to be multiplied. We could have written $-4(-2)$ instead of $(-4)(-2)$ without confusion, but multiplication would not be indicated if the expression had read $(-4) - 2$. The last written number, -2, would be subtracted, not multiplied.

The division symbol, $\div$, is not used often in algebraic statements, but rather the fractional form of expression is easier to use. Thus 8 divided by 4 is written as $8/4$ or $\frac{8}{4}$. Moreover the general practice is to speak of the last expression as "8 over 4," not "4 into 8."

According to the rule for division of signed numbers,

$$\frac{8}{-4} = -2, \quad \frac{-8}{4} = -2, \quad \text{and} \quad \frac{-8}{-4} = 2.$$

> **Exercise.** Evaluate $-2(4)$; $3(6)$; $-(-3)(-5)$; $-4/-2$; $6/-3$; $-(6/-3)$; $-(-6/3)$; $-(-6/-3)$.
> **Answer:** -8; 18; -15; 2; -2; 2; 2; -2.

The sign of a term that involves only multiplications and divisions of numbers can be determined by counting the number of minus signs. If the count is **odd**, the true sign of the term is **minus**; if the count is **even**, the true sign of the term is **positive**. For example,

$$\frac{-4(2)(-3)}{-2(-1)(4)} = +\frac{4(2)(3)}{2(1)(4)} = 3$$

since there are four minus signs. However

$$\frac{-1(-4)(-5)}{2(-1)(-10)} = -\frac{4(5)}{2(1)(10)} = -1,$$

since here there are five minus signs.

Exercise. Write $\dfrac{-2(3)(6)(-10)}{12(-5)}$ as a single signed number.

Answer: -6.

A1.6 ORDER OF OPERATIONS

When an expression involves more than one operation, the order in which the operations are performed follows a very simple rule. Parentheses are the highest order of operation (expressions in parentheses are computed first), followed by multiplications and divisions together from left to right, and finally additions and subtractions together from left to right. (Later, in Section A1.28, we will discuss where exponents fit into this scheme.) For example,

$$4(1 - 3) + 5 \times 6 / 2 =$$
$$4(-2) + 5 \times 6 / 2 =$$
$$-8 + 30/2 =$$
$$-8 + 15 = 7.$$

Although problems in the text may not always appear in this form, it is useful to be familiar with this form since it is exactly how one would input such a problem into the computer. In like fashion,

$$9/3 - 2 \times 5 + 6 =$$
$$3 - 10 + 6 =$$
$$-7 + 6 = -1.$$

> **Exercise.** Evaluate (a) $6 \times 8 + 12 / 2 - 3$.
> (b) $7 / (10 - 11) \times (6 - 3) + (15 \times 2) - 9 + 4$.
> **Answer:** (a) 51. (b) 4.

To show how important parentheses are, consider the two expressions

$$(8 - 2) + 5 = 6 + 5 = 11$$

and

$$8 - (2 + 5) = 8 - 7 = 1.$$

Now compare these results with

$$8 - 2 + 5 = 6 + 5 = 11.$$

Note that the first and third values are the same, but the second value is different.

> **Exercise.** Which of the following expressions result in the same value: $12 \times (5 - 4)$, $(12 \times 5) - 4$, and $12 \times 5 - 4$?
> **Answer:** The values are 12, 56, and 56 so the second and third give the same value.

The proper use of parentheses and application of order of operations can be exemplified by the following application.

Example. Ace Sports Car Company purchases high-performance tires from National Rubber Corporation and receives a discount depending on volume. The basic cost is $150 per tire. However, if a customer purchases more than 50 tires, then these additional tires are discounted by $2 times the number of tires purchased in excess of 50. What is the cost to the company if 30 tires are purchased? 70 tires? 100 tires?

If the company purchases 30 tires, then the cost will be

$$(\$150 \text{ per tire})(30 \text{ tires}) = \$4,500.$$

On the other hand, if the company purchases 70 tires, the cost becomes

$$(\$150 \text{ per tire})(50 \text{ tires})$$

for the first 50 tires plus

$$[\$150 - (\$2)(70 - 50)] \text{ per tire} \times (70 - 50) \text{ tires}$$

for the remaining $(70 - 50)$ tires, or simply

$$(150)(50) + [150 - (2)(70 - 50)](70 - 50) =$$
$$7,500 + [150 - (2)(20)](20) =$$
$$7,500 + [150 - 40](20) =$$
$$7,500 + (110)(20) =$$
$$7,500 + 2,200 = 9,700$$

or, $9,700. In the same way, if the company purchases 100 tires, then the cost is

$$(150)(50) + [150 - (2)(100 - 50)](100 - 50) =$$
$$7,500 + (50)(50) =$$
$$7,500 + 2,500 = 10,000$$

or $10,000.

Although this is a good example of the use of parentheses, why would this be a bad business arrangement for the seller?

> **Exercise.** In normal operations a plant employs 100 workers working 8 hours per day for a total of $100(8) = 800$ labor-hours of work per day. In normal operations productivity averages 30 units per labor-hour worked. So in a normal day production is
>
> $$(800 \text{ labor-hours})(30 \text{ units per labor-hour}) = 24,000 \text{ units}.$$
>
> If the work level (labor-hours) is raised above 800, management estimates that average productivity per labor-hour worked falls off at a rate of 2 units for each 100 labor-hours in excess of 800. What would the total production level be if 900 hours are worked? 1,000 hours? 1,100 hours?
>
> **Answer:** 25,200 units; 26,000 units; 26,400 units.

A1.7 PROBLEM SET A1-1

Reduce to a single signed number or to 0:

1. $-2 + (-3) - [-(-4)] + (-5)$.
2. $-(-8) + 8 - (+3)$.
3. $-(+4) + (-4) - [-(-4)]$.
4. $6 - (+3) + (+5) - (-7) + (-2) - (+10)$.
5. $3.15 - (+1.08) - (-3.27)$.
6. $-4 - (3)(-2) + (-5)(-4)(-1) - (3)(2)$.
7. $-4(3) + (-1)(2)(-6)(-1) - (-1)(-1)(-1)$.
8. $-(-4 + 3) + [-1(-2)]$.
9. $14(-2) - (-13) + (-3)(-2) - (-5)$.
10. $(3 - 4) - (5 - 2)$.
11. $3 - (-2) - (7 - 5)$.
12. $-5 + (7 - 3) - (2 - 4)$.

A1.7 PROBLEM SET A1-1 *(continued)*

13. $+ (3 - 6) - (-5 + 4)$.
14. $-(-5 - 7) + (3 - 2)$.
15. $12 - (-3) + (-2) - (+2)$.
16. $-25 - (30 - 10)$.
17. $-5(8)$.
18. $9(-7)$.
19. $-(-6)(-10)$.
20. $\dfrac{-8}{2}$.
21. $\dfrac{-10}{-5}$.
22. $\dfrac{12}{-6}$.
23. $\dfrac{-3(20)}{-4}$.
24. $\dfrac{5(-2)(3)}{-4(-2.5)}$.
25. $\dfrac{-(-7)}{-2}$.
26. $\dfrac{6(-2)(-1)(-3)}{-(-12)-2}$.
27. $\dfrac{-(-26)(16)}{-[-(-13)]}$.
28. $\dfrac{4(-1)(-2)(3)(-7)}{(-5)(-3)(2)}$.
29. $\dfrac{-3 - (5 - 20)}{5 - (-2)}$.
30. $\dfrac{6 - (-7 + 3)}{-[-(-2 + 7)]}$.
31. $\dfrac{-(8 - 3)}{-2 + 3(-1)}$.
32. $\dfrac{40 - 2(-5)}{2 - (15 - 3)}$.

Evaluate the following:

33. $-3(2) + (3 - 7) - (2 + 4)$.
34. $-[-2 + (-3)] - 2(-3) + (-3)(-4)$.
35. $-(3 - 5) + (2 - 6)$.
36. $-[+(-3) + (-5)] + [-2 + (-3)]$.
37. $-[+(-5)] + [-(-3)] + (8 - 4) - (2 - 6)$.
38. $-(-3) + (-7) + (8) - (-6)$.

Evaluate the following:

39. $6 \times 3 + 4 / 1 - 7$.
40. $18 / 9 - 10 \times 5 + 3$.
41. $6 \times (3 + 4) / (1 - 7)$.
42. $18 / (9 - 10) \times (5 + 3)$.
43. $(24 - 8) + 12$.
44. $24 - (8 + 12)$.
45. $24 - 8 + 12$.
46. $(30 \times 6) / 3$.
47. $30 \times (6 / 3)$.
48. $30 \times 6 / 3$.

---

49. Midas Car Rental Corporation offers limousine service to the airport and the multiple locations of one of its valued client companies at special discount rates. If the company has 25 rentals or "runs" per day from Midas, then the cost per run is $20 for a total cost of ($20 per run)(25 runs) = $500. However the cost per run is increased by $5 for each run less than 25. So if only 24 runs are made, then the total cost will be ($20 + $5)(24) = $600. What is the total cost of 20 runs? Of 15 runs? Of 10 runs?

A1.7 PROBLEM SET A1-1 (concluded)

50. The local sports club has made an arrangement with Casino Weekends for a package deal including air transportation, hotel, and entertainment in Las Vegas. As an incentive to fill all 100 seats on the plane, the hotel has subsidized the cost of the flight with Eastwest Airlines so that the seats can be sold for $200 each, providing all 100 seats are filled. So if all 100 seats can be reserved by the sports club, their total cost for the flight will be ($200 per person)(100 seats) = $20,000. Now if there are any unsold seats, Casino Weekends has told the sports club that there will be a surcharge of $5 per person for each unsold seat. For example, if 8 seats are unsold, then each of the remaining 92 persons will have to pay $200 + $5(8) = $240 and the total cost will then be ($240 per person) (92 persons) = $22,080. What will be the total cost if 10 seats are unsold? 18? 30? 42?

51. Main Electric Company has the following charges for use of electricity: $7.50 flat charge for the first 10 kilowatt hours (kwh) of usage, 5 cents per kwh for the next 90 kwh, 3 cents per kwh for the next 300 kwh, and 1 cent per kwh in excess of 400 kwh. What is the charge for 5 kwh of usage? For 50 kwh? For 200 kwh? For 600 kwh?

A1.8 REPRESENTING NUMBERS BY LETTERS

Mathematics beyond arithmetic is characterized by its use of letter representation of numbers. The sum, difference, and quotient of two numbers in literal form, such as a and b, are written in the usual manner as, respectively, $a + b$, $a - b$, and a/b. The product conventionally is written as ab, the multiplication symbol being omitted. This convention is, of course, in conflict with the place system of decimal notation. For example, 34 means thirty-four, not 3 times 4. We would interpret $34a$ as thirty-four times a, not 3 times 4 times a. It follows that care must be exercised when writing numbers that have literal and numerical factors. Sometimes a dot is employed to indicate multiplication, as in $3 \cdot 4ab$. A more common practice, already introduced, is to use parentheses: $3(4)ab$ or $(3)(4)ab$.

The first advantage of literal representation of numbers is their utility in stating generalizations. For example, we may illustrate the point that the sum of any two real numbers is a real number by mentioning that the sum of 3 and 4 is 7, and 7 is a real number. To generalize the point and state it as a property of all real numbers, we need a statement that is not restricted to a particular pair of numbers. The statement desired is, **If a and b are any real numbers, then $a + b$ is a real number.** In this statement the word **any** means that the property applies to **all** real numbers. If someone asks if the statement applies to x and y, we inquire whether x and y are real numbers; if they are, the statement applies, and $x + y$ is a real number. The student will find it helpful to keep in mind the **all** implication of the word **any** in mathematical statements.

The fundamental properties we list for real numbers are formal statements of observations of arithmetic. The very fact that they seem obvious is a primary reason for stating them as fundamental properties. The fact that they seem obvious is not, however, justification for thinking time spent on them is wasted. Many questions that perplex beginning students arise simply because of failure to have in mind the

TABLE A-1

Property	Addition	Multiplication
1. Closure	If a and b are real, then $a + b$ is real.	If a and b are real, then $a \cdot b$ is real.
2. Identity	There exists a real number 0 such that $a + 0 = 0 + a = a$.	There exists a real number 1 such that $a \cdot 1 = 1 \cdot a = a$.
3. Commutative	If a and b are real, then $a + b = b + a$.	If a and b are real, then $a \cdot b = b \cdot a$.
4. Associative	If a, b, and c are real, then $(a + b) + c = a + (b + c)$.	If a, b, and c are real, then $(ab)c = a(bc)$.
5. Distributive	If a, b, and c are real, then $a(b + c) = a \cdot b + a \cdot c$.	

fundamental properties of numbers. Notice, for example, that the two associative laws allow us to write $a + b + c$ and abc without any parentheses.

We list four fundamental properties for addition and multiplication in Table A–1, together with a fifth property which combines both addition and multiplication.

A1.9 IMPORTANCE OF FUNDAMENTAL PROPERTIES

The **closure, identity, commutative, associative,** and **distributive** properties of the real numbers are important because they are the fundamental justifications for many of the steps taken in algebraic procedures. For example, the commutative law for multiplication tells us that $(a + b)c$ is the same as $c(a + b)$. But how do we multiply out $(a + b)c$—it is not listed in the accompanying box. Well, we know

$$c(a + b) = ca + cb$$

and so (commutative law for multiplication)

$$c(a + b) = ac + bc.$$

But we also know

$$c(a + b) = (a + b)c,$$

therefore

$$(a + b)c = ac + bc.$$

We now have derived a new property that we can use henceforth. For example, if we have an expression such as $(2 + a)b$, we can write

$$(2 + a)b = 2b + ab.$$

> **Exercise.** In $2a3 = (2a)(3) = (3)(2a) = 6a$, what justifies each of the three expressions following the equals sign?
>
> **Answer:** Associative law for multiplication; commutative law for multiplication; associative law for multiplication.

Carrying on one step further, let us learn how to expand

$$(a + b)(c + d).$$

We know by closure that $(a + b)$ is a real number, and the distributive law justifies writing

$$(a + b)(c + d) = (a + b)c + (a + b)d.$$

The right-hand side of the last expression can be expanded, leading to

$$(a + b)(c + d) = (a + b)c + (a + b)d = ac + bc + ad + bd.$$

A common mnemonic (memory-assisting technique) is the so-called **FOIL**, which stands for **First, Outside, Inside, Last**. So we get

$$(a + b)(c + d) = ac + ad + bc + bd.$$

Why is this last expression the same as the previous one? Note also that the expansion can be viewed as first distributing a through $(c + d)$ and then distributing b through $(c + d)$.

The distributive law works both ways. Writing it in reverse, we have

$$ab + ac = a(b + c).$$

Converting in this manner from the sum of ab and ac to the product of a multiplied by $(b + c)$ is referred to as **factoring**. Hence the distributive property is the fundamental property underlying factoring. When applied to obtain

$$2a + 3a = (2 + 3)a = 5a$$

the procedure is called **combining like terms**. As other examples,

$$2ab - 3ab + 5ab - 6 = 4ab - 6$$
$$4a - 2a + 5b - 2b = 2a + 3b.$$

In the last two examples the associative law for addition justifies the separate combinations of like terms. We may say in general that terms having the same literal factor can be added (subtracted) by adding (subtracting) their numerical coefficients. Thus in

$$3ab + 4ab - 2ab$$

each term has the same literal factor, ab. Combining the numerical coefficients, we have

$$(3 + 4 - 2)ab = 5ab.$$

> **Exercise.** Remove symbols of grouping and combine like terms for $a(2 - b) - 3(a - 2b)$.
>
> **Answer:** $a(2) - ab - 3a + 6b = 6b - ab - a$.

The following example shows how the fundamental properties come into play. Starting with the expression at the top left, we change to the expression on the next line, indicating on that next line, at the right, the justification for the step:

$$
\begin{aligned}
-2a(3b) + ab &= -2(3b)a + ab & \text{Commutative law, multiplication} \\
&= -6ba + ab & \text{Associative law, multiplication} \\
&= -6ab + ab & \text{Commutative law, multiplication} \\
&= -5ab. & \text{Distributive law (combining like terms, or factoring).}
\end{aligned}
$$

A similar example follows:

$$
\begin{aligned}
2 + ba + 3 &= 2 + 3 + ba & \text{Commutative law, addition} \\
&= 5 + ba & \text{Associative law, addition} \\
&= 5 + ab. & \text{Commutative law, multiplication.}
\end{aligned}
$$

We do not mean to suggest by these examples that the fundamental reason for every algebraic step should be cited. These steps usually remain behind the scenes and we call on them only when we need them. But we do mean to suggest strongly that understanding these fundamentals will help to avoid questions such as

"Is $(2 + 3b)(-c)$ the same as $-c(2 + 3b)$?"

> **Exercise.** What fundamental law specifies that the two last written expressions are equal?
>
> **Answer:** The commutative law for multiplication.

A1.10 PROBLEM SET A1-2

1. When we write ab or cxy, in what way does algebraic convention differ from the usual decimal notation?
2. What would abc mean in decimal notation?
3. What is the connotation of the word **any** in mathematical statements?
4. If we add the odd number 3 to the odd number 5, the sum is an even number, 8. State this odd-even relationship in a manner that shows it is a fundamental property of integers.
5. Explain the property of closure by using addition of clock numbers as an example.

A1.10 PROBLEM SET A1-2 (concluded)

6. Why does $3a + c$ not mean three times the sum of a and c?
7. How many specific numerical illustrations of the distributive property do you think you could devise?
8. Explain what is meant by the statement that the distributive property equates a product involving a sum to a sum of products.

What fundamental property or convention justifies each of the following?

9. $a(2) = 2a$.
10. $2 - a = -a + 2$.
11. $a(2 + 3) = a2 + a3$.
12. $a + 2 + b = a + b + 2$.
13. $+a = a$.
14. $a(b + c) = (b + c)a$.
15. $a + (-3) = a - 3$.
16. $a2 + a3 = 2a + 3a$.
17. $2 + 3 + b = 5 + b$.
18. $3a2 = 3(2)a$.
19. $3(2)a = 6a$.
20. $+b + (-a) = b - a$.
21. $5 - 4 + b = 1 + b$.
22. $2a + 2b = 2(a + b)$.
23. $a + 2 + b = a + b + 2$.
24. $a + (b + c) = (b + c) + a$.
25. $a(2)(4) = a(8)$.

Combine like terms:

26. $2b + (-3b)$.
27. $2a - 3b + 5a - 2b$.
28. $3abc - 2d - (-2abc)$.
29. $5 - (-3x) + 2 - (+2x)$.
30. $2abc - (-3abc) + 3abc$.
31. $3 + 2a - 3b + 5 - (-2b)$.

Name the fundamental property justifying each step:

32. $\quad -b + a$
    $= a - b$.

33. $\quad 2b(3a)$
    $= 2b3(a)$
    $= 2(3)ba$
    $= 6ba$
    $= 6ab$.

34. $\quad 3 + xy + 5 + 3(2ab)$
    $= 3 + 5 + xy + 3(2ab)$
    $= \quad 8 + xy + 3(2ab)$
    $= \quad 8 + xy + 6ab$.

35. $\quad 3 + a + 2$
    $= 3 + 2 + a$
    $= \quad 5 + a$.

36. $\quad a + 3 + c + 2$
    $= a + c + 3 + 2$
    $= a + c + 5$.

37. $\quad acdb$
    $= adcb$
    $= adbc$.

Write the following in algebraic form:

38. The sum of a and b.
39. To a, add the sum of b and c.
40. To the sum of a and b, add twice the product of c and d.
41. From twice the sum of a and b, subtract three times the sum of c and $2d$.
42. Multiply the sum of a, b, and c by the product of 2 and d.

A1.11 REMOVING GROUPING SYMBOLS

Instructions to remove grouping symbols are carried out by systematic application of the distributive property. Thus

$$a[b - c(d + 2)] = a[b - cd - 2c] = ab - acd - 2ac.$$

Observe that the innermost grouping symbols, the parentheses, were removed first. This order of attack lessens the chance of errors of omission. As another example,

$$\begin{aligned}a - \{-2 - 3[-4 + (5 - a)]\} &= a - \{-2 - 3[-4 + 5 - a]\} \\ &= a - \{-2 + 12 - 15 + 3a\} \\ &= a + 2 - 12 + 15 - 3a \\ &= -2a + 5.\end{aligned}$$

Exercise. Remove symbols of grouping and combine like terms in
$3x - 2[y - 4(x - 3y)]$.

Answer: $11x - 26y$.

Care must be exercised in the interpretation of grouping symbols. Thus

$$5 - 3(b + c) = 5 - 3b - 3c.$$

If we had wished to indicate that the difference of 5 and 3 was to be multiplied by the sum of b and c, the expression would have been

$$(5 - 3)(b + c) = 2b + 2c.$$

Extension of the distributive property justifies the expansions

$$(3 - a)(2b + 5) = 6b + 15 - 2ab - 5a$$

and

$$(a - b + 2)(c + d) = ac + ad - bc - bd + 2c + 2d.$$

A1.12 DEFINITIONS: EXPRESSION, TERM, FACTOR, PRODUCT

Any statement involving mathematical symbols may be referred to as a mathematical **expression**. When an expression consists of parts separated by plus or minus signs, or by an equal sign, the parts, together with their signs, are called **terms** of the expression. Thus in the expression

$$a + 2b - 3ac + 4$$

the terms are $+a$, $+2b$, $-3ac$, and $+4$.

Each term in an expression consists of one or more **factors**, a factor being one of the separate multipliers in a **product**. Thus in the expression $2a - 3bc$, the term $+2a$ consists of the two factors (2 and a); the term $-3bc$ consists of the three factors (-3, b, and c).

The words we have just defined make possible clear descriptions of mathematical statements. We shall provide illustrations for practice purposes. Consider the expression

$$(2a + b)(x + 2y).$$

As written, the expression is a single term consisting of the factors $(2a + b)$ and $(x + 2y)$. We may go on to say that the first factor is an expression containing the two terms $+2a$ and $+b$; the second factor is also an expression of two terms $+x$ and $2y$.

Exercise.   a) The expression $3ab + 4a - 3$ has how many terms?   b) What is the composition of the first term?   c) Do all the terms have a common factor other than 1?

Answer: a) Three.   b) The factors 3, a, and b.   c) No.

The distributive property assures us that

$$3(a - 2b + c) = 3a - 6b + 3c.$$

If we think of this last statement as multiplying the parenthetical expression by 3, we come to the general statement that to multiply an expression by a number, we must multiply **each term** of the expression by the number. On the other hand, if we think of

$$3(2a) = 6a$$

as multiplying the term $2a$ by 3, we come to the general statement that to multiply a term by a number, we multiply **one factor** of the term by that number.

According to the rule of sign from Section A1.3,

$$-(a - b + 2c) = -a + b - 2c.$$

If we think of this as changing the sign of the parenthetical expression, we see that to change the sign of an expression, we change the sign of every term of the expression.

On the other hand, the sign of a term is changed by changing the sign of any one of its factors. For instance, thinking of $-[a(-b)(c)(-2)]$ as changing the sign of the bracketed expression, the outcome of the sign change can be written as

$$-a(-b)(c)(-2)$$

or

$$a(b)(c)(-2)$$

or

$$a(-b)(-c)(-2)$$

or

$$a(-b)(c)(2).$$

Finally we may state that the sign of a term is unchanged if the signs of an even number of its factors are changed. For example,

$$-ab(-c) = a(-b)(-c) = abc$$

and

$$-3(4 - a) = 3(a - 4).$$

A1.13 ELEMENTARY FACTORING

We are assured by the distributive property that

$$ab + ac = a(b + c).$$

Thinking of this expression as changing from the form on the left to that on the right, we see that the sum of two terms has been converted to the product of two factors. Conversion from the sums and differences of terms to a single term with two or more factors is called **factoring** as we saw in Section A1.9. Observe that an expression in completely factored form has but one term.

When terms have a factor in common, factoring is carried out by writing the product of the common factor times an expression (in grouping symbols) whose terms are the remaining factors of each of the original terms, as shown in the following examples:

$$2xy + axy = xy(2 + a),$$
$$ax - bx = x(a - b),$$
$$6x + 2y - 4a + 8b = 2(3x + y - 2a + 4b).$$

It is conventional to omit the coefficient 1 when writing a term, but this convention must be kept in mind for frequently we reinsert the 1 as we factor. Thus

$$ab + b = b(a + 1)$$
$$abc - ab + abd = ab(c - 1 + d).$$

Exercise. Factor $xy + ax + x$.
Answer: $x(y + a + 1)$.

As another example, we note that each of the terms of

$$2aby - 6abyz - 12xaby$$

has 2, a, b, and y as factors so we write the factored form as

$$2aby(1 - 3z - 6x).$$

> **Exercise.** Factor $60xyz - 20axy + 5bxy$.
> **Answer:** $5xy(12z - 4a + b)$.

Thus far we have illustrated **monomial factoring,** that is, cases where the common factor has a single term. Sometimes the need for **binomial factoring** arises. As examples

$$a(b + 2) - 3(b + 2) = (b + 2)(a - 3),$$

since the common factor is the expression $(b + 2)$. Similarly,

$$(1 + i) + i(1 + i) = (1 + i)(1 + i),$$

because here the common factor is the expression $1 + i$.

> **Exercise.** Factor $bx + by - x - y$.
> **Answer:** $(x + y)(b - 1)$.

Finally consider the expression

$$(3x + 4)(2x - 1)$$
$$= 3x(2x - 1) + 4(2x - 1)$$
$$= 6xx - 3x + 8x - 4$$
$$= 6x^2 + 5x - 4$$

where, in the last line, xx is written as x^2 (read as x **squared**). Often we find it necessary to do problems like the last one, but in reverse; that is, start with a trinomial that contains a term in x^2, a term in x, and a constant, such as

$$6x^2 + 5x - 4,$$

and obtain the equivalent pair of binomial factors,

$$(3x + 4)(2x - 1).$$

We may do this by trial and error. As an example, let us factor

$$12x^2 + 7x - 10. \qquad (1)$$

First we write

$$(\quad)(\quad),$$

where each set of parentheses contains two terms: a **first** term and a **second** term. The product of the first terms must be $12x^2$ so the first terms could be x and $12x$, $2x$ and $6x$, $3x$ and $4x$, or any of these pairs with signs changed. The product of the second terms must be -10 so the second terms must have opposite signs and can consist of the pairs 1 and 10 or 2 and 5. Let us try x and $12x$ as first terms, 1 and -10 as second terms. We fill in the parentheses as follows:

$$(x + 1)(12x - 10).$$

The product of the first terms is $12x^2$, and the product of the second terms is -10, as required. The *test* of our trial is the product of the inner terms, $1(12x)$, plus the product of the outer terms, $x(-10)$, which is

$$12x - 10x = 2x.$$

Hence

$$(x + 1)(12x - 10) = 12x^2 + 2x - 10$$

and this does not have the same middle term, $7x$, as the original expression, Equation (1). So we try another set of first and second terms from our list. For example,

$$(3x + 2)(4x - 5).$$

All we need do at each trial is apply the test mentioned several lines back, and determine if the middle term in the expansion of the trial is the required $7x$. The test here yields

$$2(4x) + (3x)(-5) = 8x - 15x = -7x$$

which is the negative of the desired $7x$ so we need only change the signs of the second (or first) terms. Thus instead of $(3x + 2)(4x - 5)$ we write $(3x - 2)(4x + 5)$. The test term is now

$$-2(4x) + (3x)5 = -8x + 15x = 7x$$

so we have the desired factors of the original expression,

$$12x^2 + 7x - 10 = (3x - 2)(4x + 5).$$

With a little practice, the proper pairs of terms usually can be found quite rapidly if we take hints from the original expression and the results of a trial. Thus in

$$2x^2 - 13x + 20,$$

the second terms have the **positive** product 20, so both must be positive or both must be negative. Inasmuch as the middle term is negative, it follows that both second terms are negative. As a trial, we write

$$(2x - 4)(x - 5)$$

and the test term is $-14x$, which is not the desired $-13x$ in the original. However we will get the desired middle term if we interchange the second terms of the first trial. Thus

$$2x^2 - 13x + 20 = (2x - 5)(x - 4).$$

> **Exercise.** Factor $10x^2 + 26x + 12$.
> **Answer:** $(5x + 3)(2x + 4)$.

The expression

$$x^2 - 9$$

has a square term and a constant, but no middle term. The first term is the square of x and the second term is the square of 3 (that is, 3 times $3 = 3^2 = 9$) so the expression is called the **difference of two squares.** By trial and error we find

$$x^2 - 9 = (x + 3)(x - 3). \qquad (2)$$

Thus the difference of the squares of two numbers is the product of the sum of the numbers times the difference of the numbers. As another example, noting that $4a^2 = (2a)(2a)$ and $16b^2 = (4b)(4b)$, we have

$$4a^2 - 16b^2 = (2a + 4b)(2a - 4b). \qquad (3)$$

This type of expression occurs frequently so the factoring of Equations (2) and (3) should be committed to memory.

> **Exercise.** Factor a) $y^2 - 25$. b) $y^2 - 25x^2$.
> **Answer:** a) $(y + 5)(y - 5)$. b) $(y - 5x)(y + 5x)$.

A1.14 PROBLEM SET A1-3

Remove grouping symbols and combine like terms, if any, in the following:

1. $2ab(c - 2)$.
2. $(a - 2)(b + 1)$.
3. $2 - 3[1 - (+4)]$.
4. $(c + 2)(a - b + 3)$.
5. $-(-2) + 3[a - (1 - b)]$.
6. $10 - 3[4 - 5(-4 + a)]$.
7. $a - 2\{-3 - 2[5a - 2(a - 6)]\}$.
8. $(3x - 2)[a - 2(b + 3)]$.
9. $-(a - x - 2b)$.
10. $(2x + 3y)$.

A1.14 PROBLEM SET A1-3 (continued)

11. $(a - 2b) - b$.
12. $a + (3x + 2)$.
13. $b - 2b(a - 3)$.
14. $ab[c - 2(x - 5)]$.
15. $ax - 2b(a - 1)$.
16. $(a - bx)(3 - c)$.
17. $(a + b + 1)(x + y)$.
18. $(a - 1)(b + 1)$.

Reduce the following to a single signed number:

19. $-3(2) - 2(1 - 3)$.
20. $\dfrac{(-3)(2) - (-2)(4)}{-3(5) - 2.5(-4)}$.
21. $\dfrac{0.017(5 - 1.08) + 2.3[0.5 - 6.2(3.1)]}{-4(0.0025)}$.
22. $\dfrac{12 - (6 - 2)(3 - 1)}{(8 - 3)(-1 - 2) + 6}$.
23. $\dfrac{1.7 - [3 - 17(15.4 - 1.6)]}{-0.8(0.245 - 0.37)}$.

---

24. Define **expression**, **term**, and **factor**, giving an illustration in each instance.

Factor the following:

25. $ab - 2b$.
26. $3a + 5a$.
27. $4abc - 2ab + 6a$.
28. $ax - bx + x$.
29. $3ad - 5ac + a$.
30. $4uv - 2xv + 2$.
31. $abx + aby - ab$.
32. $2ax - 6ay + 4az$.
33. $2x + ax + bx$.
34. $-ab - 3ac - a$.
35. $a(x + 1) + b(x + 1)$.
36. $x + 1 + y(x + 1)$.
37. $2(x + y) - a(x + y)$.
38. $ax + bx + ay + by$.
39. $x^2 - x - 2$.
40. $2x^2 - 9x - 5$.
41. $12x^2 - 25x + 12$.
42. $10x^2 + 13x - 3$.
43. $x^2 - x - 6$.
44. $x^2 - 9$.
45. $x^2 - y^2$.
46. $4x^2 - 9y^2$.

Mark the following (T) for true or (F) for false:

47. ( ) The expression ab has only one factor.
48. ( ) The expression $a + 2b - c$ has three terms.
49. ( ) The expression $a(b - c)$, as written, is a single term.
50. ( ) Referring to $a(b - c)$, it would be proper to say that the expression has two factors.
51. ( ) If ab is to be doubled, both a and b must be doubled.
52. ( ) $(a - b)(-c) = c(b - a)$.
53. ( ) It is correct to state that "to multiply an expression by a number, every factor of each term in the expression must be multiplied by the number."

A1.14 PROBLEM SET A1-3 (concluded)

54. ( ) $-a(-b-c)(-d) = ad(b+c)$.
55. ( ) The sign of a term is changed if the sign of any one of its factors is changed.
56. ( ) The parentheses in $a + (b+c)$ are unnecessary.
57. ( ) $3 + 2(a+b) = 5(a+b)$.
58. ( ) $-a - b = +(-b) + (-a)$.
59. ( ) $(a+b) - c = -ac - bc$.
60. ( ) To change the sign of a term, it is sufficient to change the sign of one factor of the term.

A1.15 PROPERTIES OF THE NUMBERS 0 AND 1

The number 0 is unique in several respects. First,

$$a + (-a) = 0;$$

that is, the sum of any number and its negative is zero, and this property defines what we mean by the negative of any number. Another way to say this is that a number and its negative **cancel,** meaning their sum is 0; that is, $-a$ is the **additive inverse** of a. Second,

$$a + 0 = a - 0 = a;$$

that is, a number is not affected by adding 0 to it or by subtracting 0 from it. Another way to say this is that 0 is the **additive identity.** Third, for any number a

$$0(a) = 0;$$

that is, 0 times any number is 0. Finally

$$\frac{a}{0} \text{ is not defined.}$$

We shall find the last statement to be extremely important in our development of calculus. To understand why $a/0$ is not defined, we consider cases such as $6/0$ where $a \neq 0$, and $0/0$ where a is zero. What does $6/3$ mean? It means that it is equal in value to a number that when multiplied by 3 will yield 6. That is

$$6/3 = 2$$

since

$$6 = 2 \cdot 3.$$

This is the **definition** of division in terms of multiplication. Now what does $6/0$ mean? It means to find a number n such that

$$6/0 = n$$

or

$$6 \neq 0 \cdot n.$$

But $0 \cdot n = 0$ and $6 \neq 0$, so there is no such number n. Therefore we say that expressions such as 6/0 and $-5/0$ are not defined.

Next consider

$$\frac{0}{0}.$$

The temptation to say that this expression is 1 because $0(1) = 0$, which satisfies the definition of division. However we could say also the expression is 2, or 3.17, 0, or any number because

$$0(\text{any number}) = 0.$$

It follows that if 0/0 were permitted, the results of mathematical operations could be ambiguous or contradictory. To demonstrate the last statement, we would certainly agree that

$$2 \neq 1.$$

But clearly

$$2 \cdot 0 = 0$$

and

$$1 \cdot 0 = 0$$

so that

$$2 \cdot 0 = 1 \cdot 0.$$

In general, **except for a division of 0**, if two numbers are equal and we divide them by the same number, the results are equal. If we were to allow division by 0 and divide both numbers in the last equality by 0, we would have

$$\frac{2 \cdot 0}{0} = \frac{1 \cdot 0}{0}.$$

Cancelling the 0's (that is, letting $0/0 = 1$), we would then have

$$2 = 1,$$

which is clearly a contradictory result.

Remember: **Expressions such as 5/0, 0/0, or any number divided by 0 are not defined. We shall say alternatively that division by 0 is impossible or that it is not permitted.**

Summarizing the properties, we state that for any real number, a:

$$(0)a = 0$$
$$a + 0 = a - 0 = a$$
$$a + (-a) = 0$$

$a/0$ is not defined.

The unique properties of 1 exist for both multiplication and its inverse, division. Thus a number is unchanged if it is multiplied or divided by 1. We have

$$a = (1)a = \frac{a}{1},$$

and we call 1 the **multiplicative identity.** The equivalence of a and $1a$ is assumed conventionally in the writing of various algebraic expressions. Also, any term may always be assumed to have a factor of 1; recall the factoring of

$$ab - a = a(b - 1).$$

Exercise. A rational number is the quotient of two integers, yet the single number, 4, is rational. Explain.

Answer: 4 is the rational number 4/1.

Any number, 0 excepted, divided by itself yields a quotient of 1. This fact is employed often, as when we write

$$\frac{6}{6} = 1 \quad \text{or} \quad \frac{ab}{ab} = 1 \quad \text{or} \quad \frac{x - y}{x - y} = 1,$$

provided $a, b \neq 0$, and $x \neq y$. Circumstances arise also where we may wish to multiply an expression by

$$\frac{6}{6} \quad \text{or} \quad \frac{ab}{ab}$$

and this can be done without changing the expression because it is equivalent to multiplication by 1.

The words **cancel** and **cancellation** are frequently used with reference to 0 and 1. A number and its negative cancel each other, meaning their sum is 0. A number and its reciprocal cancel, meaning their product is 1. Thus

$$a + (-a) = 0 \quad \text{and} \quad a\left(\frac{1}{a}\right) = 1$$

where $1/a$ is called the reciprocal or **multiplicative inverse** of a. Often the latter type of cancellation is thought of in terms of division rather than multiplication of reciprocals. Thus in ab/a, we think of a over a as being 1, so that

$$\frac{ab}{a} = 1(b) = b$$

and we say that the a's cancel. An important rule to keep in mind when working with fractions is that cancellation (replacement by 1) can be performed **only for factors common to numerator and denominator.** We cannot cancel the a's in

$$\frac{a + 2}{a}$$

because a is not a factor of the numerator. On the other hand, the numerator of

$$\frac{ax + 2x}{x(b - 1)}$$

can be factored to permit cancellation; thus

$$\frac{x(a + 2)}{x(b - 1)} = \frac{a + 2}{b - 1},$$

provided $x \neq 0$.

Exercise. x is a factor of what parts of the expression

$$\frac{ax + 2}{x(b - c)}?$$

Can we cancel x?

Answer: x is a factor of the denominator and of the single term ax in the numerator; x is not a factor of the numerator. So no, we cannot cancel.

A1.16 PRODUCT OF FRACTIONS

The product of two fractions is the product of their numerators over (divided by) the product of their denominators. For example,

$$\left(\frac{2}{5}\right)\left(\frac{3}{7}\right) = \frac{6}{35}$$

$$\left(\frac{a}{2}\right)\left(\frac{3}{b}\right) = \frac{a(3)}{2b} = \frac{3a}{2b}$$

$$\left[\frac{a(b + 2)}{3}\right]\left(\frac{2}{b}\right) = \frac{a(b + 2)(2)}{3b} = \frac{2a(b + 2)}{3b}.$$

> **Exercise.** Express as a single fraction without grouping symbols:
> $$\left(\frac{3}{x+y}\right)\left(\frac{x-y}{2}\right).$$
>
> **Answer:** $\dfrac{3x-3y}{2x+2y}$.

Generally cancellation should be performed where it is possible to do so. For example

$$\frac{\cancel{a}(b+2)}{3}\left(\frac{2}{\cancel{a}}\right) = \frac{2(b+2)}{3},$$

$$\left(\frac{2a-2}{b}\right)\left(\frac{1}{2}\right) = \frac{\cancel{2}(a-1)}{b}\left(\frac{1}{\cancel{2}}\right) = \frac{a-1}{b},$$

$$\left(\frac{6ab}{5\cancel{a}}\right)\left(\frac{\cancel{a}}{3a}\right) = \left(\frac{6\cancel{a}b}{5}\right)\left(\frac{1}{3\cancel{a}}\right) = \left(\frac{6b}{5}\right)\left(\frac{1}{3}\right) = \frac{2b}{5}.$$

As another example, we start with

$$(x+y)\left[3 + \frac{a}{x+y}\right].$$

Any number can be expressed equivalently as the number divided by 1. Thus the last expression is the same as

$$\frac{(x+y)}{1}\left[\frac{3}{1} + \frac{a}{x+y}\right] = \frac{(x+y)}{1}\left(\frac{3}{1}\right) + \frac{\cancel{(x+y)}}{1}\left(\frac{a}{\cancel{x+y}}\right)$$

$$= \frac{(x+y)(3)}{1} + \frac{a}{1}$$

$$= 3(x+y) + a.$$

Similarly

$$3\left(\frac{a}{b}\right) = \left(\frac{3}{1}\right)\left(\frac{a}{b}\right) = \frac{3a}{b}$$

$$2\frac{(a-3)}{b} = \left(\frac{2}{1}\right)\frac{(a-3)}{b} = \frac{2(a-3)}{b}.$$

> **Exercise.** Carry out the multiplication, leaving the result as the sum of two fractions:
> $$2\frac{a}{b}\left[3 + \frac{x+2}{ax}\right].$$
>
> **Answer:** $\dfrac{6a}{b} + \dfrac{2x+4}{bx}.$

An equivalent expression is obtained if a given expression is multiplied or divided by -1 an even number of times because the net effect is multiplication or division by $+1$. For example, in

$$\frac{b-a}{-2}$$

we may change the sign of numerator and denominator to give

$$\frac{(-1)(b-a)}{(-1)(-2)} = \frac{-(b-a)}{-(-2)} = \frac{-b+a}{2} = \frac{a-b}{2}.$$

Keep in mind that three signs are associated with a fraction (the signs of the numerator and denominator and the sign of the fraction itself). So

$$-\frac{a}{b} = \frac{-a}{b} = \frac{a}{-b}.$$

Also, it is helpful to remember that an equivalent fraction results if any **two** of the three signs are changed. Thus the fraction

$$\frac{b-a}{-2}$$

has the three signs shown in parentheses:

$$(+)\frac{(+)(b-a)}{(-)2},$$

and we can change the signs of the numerator and denominator to yield

$$(+)\frac{(-)(b-a)}{+2} = +\frac{-b+a}{2} = \frac{a-b}{2}.$$

Similarly in

$$-\frac{2y-x}{3} = (-)\frac{(+)(2y-x)}{(+)3}$$

we may change the sign in front of the fraction and the sign of the numerator to give

$$+\frac{(-)(2y-x)}{+3} = +\frac{-2y+x}{+3} = \frac{x-2y}{3}.$$

It is important to remember that numerator and denominator are **expressions,** and to change the sign of an expression it is necessary to change the sign of every **term** in the expression, where the change of a term's sign is accomplished by changing the sign of **one** (or an odd number) of the term's **factors.** For example,

$$\frac{(-b-2)}{3(2a-5xy)} = (+)\frac{(+)(-b-2)}{(+)3(2a-5xy)},$$

where the expression at the right has the three fraction signs indicated in parentheses. Changing the sign of numerator and denominator gives

$$+\frac{(-)(-b-2)}{(-)3(2a-5xy)} = +\frac{b+2}{-6a+15xy} = \frac{b+2}{15xy-6a}.$$

After some practice, you will be able to use sign changes to simplify expressions or to reduce the number of negative signs that appear in expressions. While the latter use may seem inconsequential, it does occur frequently; and it helps to make life more simple. To show how sign change can lead to simplification, note that

$$3x - \frac{b-a}{a-b} = 3x - \frac{(+)(b-a)}{a-b}$$

$$= 3x + \frac{(-)(b-a)}{a-b}$$

$$= 3x + \frac{-b+a}{a-b}$$

$$= 3x + \frac{a-b}{a-b}$$

$$= 3x + 1.$$

However in

$$2x - \frac{a-y}{b} = 2x - \frac{+(a-y)}{b}$$

$$= 2x + \frac{-a+y}{b}$$

$$= 2x + \frac{y-a}{b},$$

the sign changes served only to reduce the original two negative signs in the beginning expression to one in the ending expression.

> **Exercise.** a) Simplify by sign changes $y + \dfrac{2x - z}{z - 2x}$.
>
> b) In $2x - \dfrac{a + 2}{10 - a} = 2x + \dfrac{a + 2}{a - 10}$ what sign changes were made?
>
> **Answer:** a) $y - 1$.   b) The sign of the fraction and the sign of its denominator were changed.

A final noteworthy point in the multiplication of fractions is the use of the word **of** to designate multiplication. Thus two-thirds **of** one-half means

$$\left(\frac{2}{3}\right)\left(\frac{1}{2}\right) = \frac{1}{3}.$$

A1.17 ADDITION AND SUBTRACTION OF FRACTIONS

Addition and subtraction of fractions is accomplished by changing each fraction to the same (common) denominator and then placing the sums (differences) of the resultant numerators over the common denominator. A common denominator can alway be found by forming the term that has each of the separate denominators as a factor. On the other hand, if all the factors of each denominator are set down and a term is constructed that contains each factor the maximum number of times it appears in any one denominator, this term is called the **lowest common denominator.** Consider

$$\frac{3}{5} + \frac{4}{15} - \frac{2}{3} + \frac{5}{18}.$$

Factors of 5 are 5 and 1.

Factors of 15 are 5, 3, and 1.

Factors of 3 are 3 and 1.

Factors of 18 are 3, 3, 2, and 1.

The lowest common denominator is $(5)(3)(3)(2) = 90$.

The mechanical procedure for changing each fraction to the common denominator is illustrated by reference to the fraction 3/5. Since the denominator contains only a 5, we divide the lowest common denominator by 5 to obtain the conversion factor $90/5 = (3)(3)(2)$, which is 18, and then multiply the numerator, 3, by the conversion factor to obtain 54. By this procedure, 3/5 is changed to 54/90. We have

$$\frac{3}{5} + \frac{4}{15} - \frac{2}{3} + \frac{5}{18} = \frac{54}{90} + \frac{24}{90} - \frac{60}{90} + \frac{25}{90} = \frac{43}{90}.$$

The mechanical procedure is efficient, but in the interest of emphasizing fundamentals, it should be made clear that the process derives from a fundamental property of the number 1; that is, a number is unchanged if it is multiplied by 1. For example, when converting 3/5 to a denominator of 90, we observe that 5 must be multiplied by 18 to yield 90, so we multiply 3/5 by 18/18; that is, in this instance the unit multiplier is 18/18. In the case of 4/15 the unit multiplier is 6/6. It follows that the mechanical procedure is a consequence of the more lengthy, but also more fundamental, process shown next:

$$\frac{3}{5} + \frac{4}{15} - \frac{2}{3} + \frac{5}{18} = \frac{3(18)}{5(18)} + \frac{4(6)}{15(6)} - \frac{2(30)}{3(30)} + \frac{5(5)}{18(5)} = \frac{43}{90}.$$

As another example, follow the conversion of each fraction in the next expression to the lowest common denominator, $a(2)(3)$:

$$\frac{2}{a} + \frac{b}{2} + \frac{2c}{3} + \frac{1}{6} = \frac{2}{a}\left(\frac{6}{6}\right) + \frac{b}{2}\left(\frac{3a}{3a}\right) + \frac{2c}{3}\left(\frac{2a}{2a}\right) + \frac{1}{6}\left(\frac{a}{a}\right)$$

$$= \frac{12 + 3ab + 4ac + a}{6a}.$$

Exercise. Add $5 + \dfrac{2}{y} + \dfrac{3}{4} + \dfrac{1}{2x}$.

Answer: $\dfrac{23xy + 8x + 2y}{4xy}$.

As a final example, consider

$$\frac{5}{3} + \frac{c}{2a} - \frac{c}{a(b+2)}.$$

The factors of the denominator are, in turn:

3 and 1,

2, a, and 1,

a, $(b + 2)$, and 1.

The lowest common denominator is $3(2)a(b + 2)$. Hence

$$\frac{5}{3}\frac{(2a)(b+2)}{(2a)(b+2)} + \frac{c}{2a}\frac{(3)(b+2)}{(3)(b+2)} - \frac{c}{a(b+2)}\frac{(3)(2)}{(3)(2)}$$

is equivalent to the original set of fractions. Notice that each term in this expression has the same (common) denominator. The numerator of the first term, $5(2a)(b + 2)$, can be viewed as 5 (the numerator of the first term of the original expression) times $(2a)(b + 2)$ [the common denominator, $3(2a)(b + 2)$, divided by the denominator, 3, of the first term of the original expression]. This insight should be used to verify the numerator of the second and third terms. By the associative and commutative properties, all of the denominators may be written as $6a(b + 2)$ so, placing all the numerators over this common denominator, we then simplify the expression

$$\frac{5(2a)(b + 2) + c(3)(b + 2) - c(3)(2)}{6a(b + 2)}$$

$$= \frac{10a(b + 2) + 3c(b + 2) - 6c}{6a(b + 2)}$$

$$= \frac{10ab + 20a + 3bc + 6c - 6c}{6a(b + 2)}$$

$$= \frac{10ab + 20a + 3bc}{6a(b + 2)}.$$

Exercise. Add $\dfrac{1}{x} + \dfrac{2}{y + 1} - \dfrac{2}{3}$.

Answer: $\dfrac{4x + 3y - 2xy + 3}{3x(y + 1)}$.

A1.18 DIVISION OF FRACTIONS

The division of the fraction a/b by the fraction c/d can be written in the form of a third fraction,

$$\frac{\dfrac{a}{b}}{\dfrac{c}{d}}.$$

This can be simplified if it is multiplied by a suitably chosen 1. The objective is to convert from the **complex fraction** (that is, a fraction whose numerator or denominator contains a fraction) to a **simple fraction** (which does not have a fraction in its numerator or denominator). Clearly we can cancel the c/d of the denominator if we multiply it by d/c. We must then also multiply the numerator by d/c so that the net effect is multiplication by 1. Thus

$$\frac{\dfrac{a}{b}}{\dfrac{c}{d}} = \frac{\dfrac{a}{b}\left(\dfrac{d}{c}\right)}{\dfrac{c}{d}\left(\dfrac{d}{c}\right)} = \frac{ad}{bc}.$$

The process often is described as **inverting the denominator and multiplying;** that is, invert c/d to give d/c and then multiply the numerator by d/c. This description is adequate when numerator and denominator are in completely factored form, but multiplication by a suitably chosen 1 not only is a more fundamental description, but also is somewhat more direct when numerator and denominator are not in factored form. Consider the problem of reducing the following to a simple fraction:

$$\frac{\frac{a}{2} + \frac{1}{3}}{\frac{1}{2} + b}.$$

We observe that the lowest common denominator of the terms in the numerator and denominator is 6, so we multiply the fraction by 6/6. Thus

$$\frac{6\left(\frac{a}{2} + \frac{1}{3}\right)}{6\left(\frac{1}{2} + b\right)} = \frac{3a + 2}{3 + 6b}.$$

Exercise. Convert to a simple fraction by multiplying numerator and denominator by 12:

$$\frac{\frac{1}{2} + \frac{1}{3}}{\frac{3}{4} + \frac{1}{3}}.$$

Answer: $\dfrac{10}{13}$.

In the next example the lowest common denominator of all terms in numerator and denominator is $3ab$. Hence we choose our 1 to be $3ab/3ab$:

$$\frac{\frac{2}{a} + \frac{1}{b}}{\frac{1}{3} + \frac{2}{b}} = \frac{\left(\frac{2}{a} + \frac{1}{b}\right)(3ab)}{\left(\frac{1}{3} + \frac{2}{b}\right)(3ab)} = \frac{6b + 3a}{ab + 6a}.$$

A1.19 PROBLEM SET A1-4

Mark (T) for true or (F) for false:

1. ( ) 0/0 equals 1.
2. ( ) 0/0 equals 0.
3. ( ) No matter what number a is, $a/0$ is meaningless.
4. ( ) If a is not 0, then $0/a$ equals 0.
5. ( ) The product of any number and 0 is 0.
6. ( ) The reciprocal of 4 equals 0.25.
7. ( ) The reciprocal of 3 equals 0.3.
8. ( ) In addition, it is said that a number and its reciprocal cancel.
9. ( ) In division, cancellation is the equivalent of substituting the factor 1 in place of the product of a number and its reciprocal.
10. ( ) Multiplying a number by its reciprocal gives the same result as dividing the number by itself.
11. ( ) **Inverting and multiplying** is equivalent to multiplying by a reciprocal.

12. What does it mean to say a number and its reciprocal cancel?

Simplify by cancellation where possible:

13. $\dfrac{-3a(-6)}{12c}$.

14. $\dfrac{2a - 3}{3}$.

15. $\dfrac{2a - 3a}{-a}$.

16. $\dfrac{2a + 6}{2}$.

17. $\dfrac{24acd}{4ad}$.

18. $\dfrac{x + y}{y}$.

19. $\dfrac{2xy + 6ax + x}{4xy}$.

20. $4(a + 2)\left(\dfrac{2x}{a + 2}\right)$.

21. State the rule for multiplication of fractions.

Multiply, leaving no grouping symbols in the answer:

22. $\dfrac{ab}{2}\left(\dfrac{3}{4}\right)$.

23. $\dfrac{a + b}{3}\left(\dfrac{2}{5}\right)$.

24. $\dfrac{-2}{3}\left(\dfrac{9a}{8}\right)$.

25. $(-2)\left(\dfrac{a}{3}\right)\left(\dfrac{b + 2}{-7}\right)$.

26. $(2)\left(-\dfrac{1}{3}\right)\left(\dfrac{1}{a + b}\right)$.

27. $3(a + 2)\left(\dfrac{1}{3} + \dfrac{2b}{a + 2}\right)$.

28. $6ab\left(\dfrac{2}{3b} - \dfrac{1}{a}\right)$.

A1.19 PROBLEM SET A1-4 *(concluded)*

Express with a single minus sign:

29. $\dfrac{-b(c-d)}{-2}$.

30. $-\dfrac{b-2}{-3-a}$.

31. $\dfrac{-2+(b-c)}{-2a}$.

32. $-\dfrac{-2+(b-c)-a}{2x(a+b)}$.

33. $-\dfrac{x+y}{x-y}$.

Reduce to one simple fraction:

34. $\dfrac{2}{3} - \dfrac{1}{2} + \dfrac{1}{6}$.

35. $\dfrac{a}{2} - \dfrac{3}{5}$.

36. $\dfrac{3}{2a} - \dfrac{1}{6} + \dfrac{2}{5b}$.

37. $\dfrac{2}{5} - \dfrac{2(a-10)}{5a} + \dfrac{1}{6}$.

38. $3\tfrac{1}{2} - 2\tfrac{1}{3}$.

39. $\dfrac{x}{a-2} + \dfrac{1}{b} - 2$.

40. $\dfrac{x}{2a} - b + \dfrac{3}{a}$.

41. $3x - \dfrac{1}{2} + \dfrac{2}{12ab}$.

42. $\dfrac{2a}{3(b-1)} - \dfrac{a-1}{4} + \dfrac{1}{6}$.

43. $\dfrac{7}{2(x+3)} - 3 + \dfrac{5}{4(x+3)}$.

---

44. Multiply $2\tfrac{1}{3}$ by $3\tfrac{1}{4}$, stating the product as a simple fraction.

45. Divide $1\tfrac{1}{8}$ by $7\tfrac{1}{3}$, stating the quotient as a simple fraction.

Reduce the following complex fractions to simple fractions by multiplying by a suitably chosen fraction equal to 1:

46. $\dfrac{\tfrac{1}{2} + \tfrac{1}{3} - \tfrac{1}{4}}{\tfrac{2}{3} - \tfrac{1}{6}}$.

47. $\dfrac{\tfrac{6}{a} + 2}{-\tfrac{3}{b} + \tfrac{5}{a}}$.

48. $\dfrac{\tfrac{ab}{2} - \tfrac{b-3}{c}}{\tfrac{b}{3} - 1}$.

49. $\dfrac{\tfrac{2a}{3b} - \tfrac{1}{c} + 2}{\tfrac{1}{6} - \tfrac{2}{bc}}$.

50. $\dfrac{\tfrac{a}{2} + \tfrac{b}{3} - \tfrac{c}{6}}{b - \tfrac{a}{4}}$.

A1.20 EXPONENTS

The product $(a)(a)(a)(a)(a)$ is denoted by writing a with a superscript of 5: a^5. It is called the fifth power of a. The number a is the **base**, and 5 is the **exponent** of the power. More generally if n is a positive integer, a^n is read as *a to the nth*, meaning the term has a as a factor n times. By convention we interpret absence of an exponent to mean the exponent is 1. We have

$$(a)(a) = a^2$$
$$(a)(a)(a) = a^3$$
$$a = a^1.$$

Since

$$(a^2)(a^3) = (a)(a)[(a)(a)(a)] = a^5,$$

we see that

$$(a^2)(a^3) = a^{2+3} = a^5.$$

Thus it follows that if two powers have the same base, their product is found by writing the common base with the sum of the exponents as its power. For example,

$$x^5(x)x^2 = x^{5+1+2} = x^8,$$
$$3a^2(2a^3) = 6a^5,$$
$$3^2(3) = 3^3 = 27,$$
$$(-2)^3(-2) = (-2)^4 = 16,$$
$$(-3)(-3)^2 = (-3)^3 = -27.$$

Exercise. Write $2x^2(3x^5)$ with a single exponent.

Answer: $6x^7$.

Turning to division, we have, for example,

$$\frac{a^5}{a^2} = \frac{(a)(a)(a)(a)(a)}{(a)(a)} = (a)(a)(a) = a^3$$

by cancellation. Alternatively the final exponent, 3, could have been obtained by the subtraction, $5 - 2$; that is, the numerator exponent (5) minus the denominator exponent (2). In general, if two powers have the same base, their quotient is the common base with an exponent found by the subtraction procedure just mentioned. As examples,

$$\frac{a^4}{a^2} = a^{4-2} = a^2,$$

$$\frac{a^2b^3}{ab} = ab^2,$$

$$\frac{(a+b)^3}{a+b} = (a+b)^2,$$

$$\frac{5^{12}}{5^{10}} = 5^2 = 25,$$

$$\frac{(-2)^5}{(-2)^2} = (-2)^3 = -8,$$

$$\frac{3^4(2a^6)}{3a^4} = 3^3(2a^2) = 54a^2,$$

$$\frac{(-3)^4(2x^5)}{-3x^2} = (-3)^3(2x^3) = -54x^3.$$

Exercise. Write $(5x^5)/3x^2$ with a single exponent.

Answer: $5x^3/3$.

A1.21 ZERO EXPONENT

Following the procedure of the last section we see that for any number a, not 0,

$$\frac{a}{a} = a^{1-1} = a^0.$$

Inasmuch as the beginning expression, a/a, equals 1, we conclude that any nonzero number to the 0 power equals 1. Thus

$$1^0 = 1, \quad (ab^3c^2)^0 = 1, \quad (14.6)^0 = 1, \quad (-x)^0 = 1.$$

Exercise. Evaluate $3^0 + (x+2y)^0$.

Answer: 2.

A1.22 NEGATIVE EXPONENTS

When exponents are subtracted, the difference may be negative. For example,

$$\frac{2^3}{2^6} = 2^{3-6} = 2^{-3}.$$

Alternatively we may evaluate the expression as

$$\frac{2^3}{2^6} = \frac{(2)(2)(2)}{(2)(2)(2)(2)(2)(2)} = \frac{1}{(2)(2)(2)} = \frac{1}{2^3}.$$

We see that

$$2^{-3} = \frac{1}{2^3}.$$

This leads to the general definition applying to a negative exponent that

$$a^{-n} = \frac{1}{a^n}.$$

As illustrations of the definition, we see that

$$2^{-1} = \frac{1}{2^1} = \frac{1}{2},$$

$$3^{-2} = \frac{1}{3^2} = \frac{1}{9},$$

$$ax^{-2} = \frac{a}{1}\left(\frac{1}{x^2}\right) = \frac{a}{x^2},$$

$$\left(\frac{2}{3}\right)^{-1} = \frac{1}{\left(\frac{2}{3}\right)} = 1\left(\frac{3}{2}\right) = \frac{3}{2},$$

$$\frac{1}{3^{-2}} = \frac{1}{\left(\frac{1}{3^2}\right)} = 1\left(\frac{3^2}{1}\right) = 3^2 = 9.$$

Note in the first equation how the 2^{-1} was brought from the numerator to the denominator and changed to 2^1. Similarly in the last equation the 3^{-2} was brought from the denominator to the numerator and changed to 3^2.

Exercise. Evaluate a) $\left(\frac{3}{4}\right)^{-2} + \frac{3^{-2}}{11^{-1}}$. b) $\frac{1}{2^{-2}} + 5(2^{-3})$.

Answer: a) 3. b) 37/8.

The following examples are self-explanatory and show how in some expressions we may avoid negative exponents by choice of procedure:

$$\frac{x^3}{x^5} = \frac{1}{x^{5-3}} = \frac{1}{x^2},$$

$$\frac{2x}{x^7} = \frac{2x^1}{x^7} = \frac{2}{x^{7-1}} = \frac{2}{x^6},$$

$$\frac{a^2 b^3}{a^4 b} = \frac{b^{3-1}}{a^{4-2}} = \frac{b^2}{a^2}.$$

> **Exercise.** Apply the laws of exponents to simplify the following expression and write the result without negative exponents:
> $$\frac{3x(x^{-2})y^5}{4x^4y^2}.$$
>
> **Answer:** $\dfrac{3y^3}{4x^5}.$

Finally we note that the expression

$$\frac{1 + x^{-n}}{2 + a}$$

is, in effect, a complex fraction because of the fractional nature of x^{-n}. Remembering that

$$x^{-n}(x^n) = x^0 = 1,$$

we may obtain a simple fraction by multiplying by x^n/x^n, as follows:

$$\frac{1 + x^{-n}}{2 + a} = \frac{(1 + x^{-n})x^n}{(2 + a)x^n} = \frac{x^n + 1}{(2 + a)x^n}.$$

As another example of the same procedure,

$$\frac{2 + 3^{-2}}{1 + 3^{-1}} = \left(\frac{2 + 3^{-2}}{1 + 3^{-1}}\right)\left(\frac{3^2}{3^2}\right) = \frac{18 + 1}{9 + 3} = \frac{19}{12}.$$

> **Exercise.** Remove negative exponents by multiplying numerator and denominator by x^n: $\dfrac{1 + x^{-n}}{x^{-n} + 2}.$
>
> **Answer:** $\dfrac{x^n + 1}{1 + 2x^n}.$

A1.23 POWER TO A POWER

The expression $(a^2)^3$ is an example of a power raised to a power; that is, the second power of a is indicated as being raised to the third power. According to definition,

$$(a^2)^3 = (a^2)(a^2)(a^2)$$

which is a^6 or $a^{(2)(3)}$. The procedure is generalized by stating that in raising a power to a power, exponents are multiplied. As other examples,

$$(2^2)^4 = 2^{(2)(4)} = 2^8 = 256,$$
$$(x^3)^2 = x^{(3)(2)} = x^6,$$
$$(x^{-1})^4 = x^{(-1)(4)} = x^{-4} = \frac{1}{x^4},$$
$$(5^{-2})^{-1} = 5^{(-2)(-1)} = 5^2 = 25.$$

Exercise. Evaluate $(2^{-2})^{-3}$.
Answer: 64.

A1.24 FRACTIONAL EXPONENTS

The number
$$8^{1/3}$$
may be read as **8 to the one-third power.** If we apply the rules discussed earlier for integral exponents to this rational fractional exponent, it follows that
$$(8^{1/3})(8^{1/3})(8^{1/3}) = 8^1 = 8$$
so that the number symbolized as $(8^{1/3})$ must be 2. That is,
$$(8^{1/3}) = 2.$$
Moreover
$$(8^{2/3}) = (8^{1/3})(8^{1/3}) = (2)(2) = 4.$$

Exercise. Express $8^{4/3}$ as an integer.
Answer: 16.

The number $8^{1/3}$ is also called the **cube root** of 8 and expressed by the **radical** symbol,
$$\sqrt[3]{8}.$$
The number appearing in the opening of the radical symbol is called the **index** of the root, and the number under the symbol, here 8, is called the **radicand.** We

note that the index of the root is the denominator of the fractional exponent. In similar fashion,

$$16^{1/2} = \sqrt[2]{16} = \sqrt{16}$$

is called the square root of 16 and, conventionally, the index 2 is not written. That is, if no index number appears on the radical, the index is assumed to be 2.

Both 4 and -4 are square roots of 16 because

$$(4)(4) = (-4)(-4) = 16.$$

Thus

$$16^{1/2} = \pm 4.$$

Exercise. What are the fourth roots of 16?

Answer: ± 2.

Even roots of positive numbers have both a positive and a negative value. However we shall generally follow the practice of using the radical symbol to indicate the principal or positive root. Thus

$$16^{1/2} = \pm 4,$$

but

$$\sqrt{16} = 4.$$

Even roots of negative numbers are not real numbers. For example, in

$$(-4)^{1/2}(-4)^{1/2} = (-4)^1 = -4$$

there is no real number for $(-4)^{1/2}$ that will make the statement true. This is so since there is no real number that, multiplied by itself, will yield -4, $(0)(0) \neq -4$, and the product of two nonzero numbers of like sign cannot be negative.

On the other hand, odd roots of negative numbers **can** be found, as in

$$(-8)^{1/3} = -2 \quad \text{and} \quad (-32)^{1/5} = -2.$$

If we write radical expressions at random, the desired root often is irrational and must be approximated. For example,

$$\sqrt{2} = 2^{1/2} = 1.414$$

to three decimal places. Irrational roots such as this can be found using a calculator, but in this appendix we consider only examples where roots are rational and can be determined by inspection. For example, inspecting

$$4^{3/2}$$

we first write the equivalent numbers

$$4^{3/2} = 4^{(1/2)(3)} = (4^{1/2})^3 = 2^3 = 8.$$

When expressions with fractional exponents are to be evaluated, we strongly urge that the fraction be written first. Thus in evaluating

$$64^{2/3}$$

we write

$$(64)^{2/3} = (64^{1/3})^2 = 4^2 = 16$$

rather than

$$64^{2/3} = (64^2)^{1/3} = (4{,}096)^{1/3} = 16.$$

The point is simply that the latter procedure, although correct, leads to $(4{,}096)^{1/3}$ and it is not easy to tell at a glance what this cube root is.

> **Exercise.** Evaluate $(27)^{2/3}$.
> **Answer:** 9.

Previous rules apply when exponents are fractional or negative, as shown by the following examples:

$$(3^{-2})(3^{-3}) = 3^{-2+(-3)} = 3^{-5} = \frac{1}{3^5} = \frac{1}{243},$$

$$\frac{5^{-6}}{5^{-8}} = 5^{-6-(-8)} = 5^{-6+8} = 5^2 = 25,$$

$$(2^{1/3})(2^{1/2}) = 2^{1/3+1/2} = 2^{2/6+3/6} = 2^{5/6},$$

$$\frac{a^{2/3}b^2}{ab} = \frac{a^{2/3}b^2}{a^1 b^1} = \frac{b^{2-1}}{a^{1-2/3}} = \frac{b}{a^{1/3}},$$

$$(a^{1/3})^2 = a^{(1/3)(2)} = a^{2/3}.$$

Fractional powers can be written with radical signs. Thus

$$16^{3/4} = (\sqrt[4]{16})^3 = 2^3 = 8.$$

It almost always makes life easier to use fractional exponents rather than radical signs.

A1.25 SUMMARY OF EXPONENT RULES

All the rules for exponents can now be stated in compact form:

If $a \neq 0$, then
$$a^m a^n = a^{m+n}$$
$$\frac{a^m}{a^n} = a^{m-n} = \frac{1}{a^{n-m}}$$
$$(a^m)^n = a^{mn}$$
$$a^0 = 1.$$

The rules of exponents are not restricted to terms having a single factor. We may raise a term to a power by raising each factor of the term to the power. Thus

$$(2a)^3 = 8a^3,$$
$$\left(\frac{a}{2}\right)^2 = \frac{a^2}{4},$$
$$(3x^2 y^{1/2})^3 = 27x^6 y^{3/2}.$$

Exercise. Express $(4y^4 x^3)^{1/2}$ without parentheses.
Answer: $2y^2 x^{3/2}$.

Observe, however, that in $3a^2$ the absence of parentheses means the exponent applies only to a, not to 3. Again,

$$3(2a^2)^3 = 3(8a^6) = 24a^6.$$

Exponents cannot be applied separately to terms of an expression. In the case of, say, $(a - b)^2$, we cannot simply raise each term to the second power. By definition,

$$(a - b)^2 = (a - b)(a - b),$$

and, using FOIL,

$$(a - b)(a - b) = a^2 - ab - ba + b^2 = a^2 - 2ab + b^2.$$

By way of numerical illustration,

$$(1 - 0.2)^2 = (0.8)^2 = 0.64$$

could be evaluated as

$$(1 - 0.2)(1 - 0.2) = 1^2 - 1(0.2) - 0.2(1) + 0.2^2 = 0.64.$$

This type of exercise is referred to as **squaring a binomial,** that is, raising the sum of two terms to the second power. We see in general that

$$(a + b)^2 = a^2 + 2ab + b^2.$$

This computation is often described as the **square of the first, plus twice the product of the two, plus the square of the second.** Verify that the cube of a binomial is given by

$$(a + b)^3 = a^3 + 3a^2b + 3ab^2 + b^3.$$

Before you work Problem Set A1–5, it will be helpful to practice by verifying the answer stated in each part of the following practice problem set.

A1.26 PRACTICE PROBLEM SET

Look at the following and justify each step by reference to the appropriate rule:

1. $a^{-3}a^5 = a^{-3+5} = a^2.$
2. $(4^{-1})(4^3) = 4^{-1+3} = 4^2 = 16.$
3. $(2^{-3})(2^{-2}) = 2^{-3+(-2)} = 2^{-5} = \dfrac{1}{2^5} = \dfrac{1}{32}.$
4. $\dfrac{5^2}{5^{-3}} = 5^{2-(-3)} = 5^{2+3} = 5^5 = 3{,}125.$
5. $125^{4/3} = (125^{1/3})^4 = 5^4 = 625.$
6. $16^{7/4} = (16^{1/4})^7 = 2^7 = 128.$
7. $27^{-1/3} = \dfrac{1}{27^{1/3}} = \dfrac{1}{3}.$
8. $125^{-2/3} = \dfrac{1}{125^{2/3}} = \dfrac{1}{(125^{1/3})^2} = \dfrac{1}{5^2} = \dfrac{1}{25} = 0.04.$
9. $27^{2/3} = (27^{1/3})^2 = 3^2 = 9.$
10. $9^{-3/2} = \dfrac{1}{9^{3/2}} = \dfrac{1}{3^3} = \dfrac{1}{27}.$
11. $8^{4/3} = 16.$
12. $\sqrt{-4}$ is not a real number.
13. $(2^{-2})(3^{-2}) = \dfrac{1}{4}\left(\dfrac{1}{9}\right) = \dfrac{1}{36}.$
14. $(2^{1/3})(2^{1/2})(2^{1/6}) = 2^{1/3+1/2+1/6} = 2.$
15. $(1 + 0.01)^2 = (1.01)^2 = 1.0201.$
16. $2^{-2} + 3^{-1} = \dfrac{1}{4} + \dfrac{1}{3} = \dfrac{7}{12}.$
17. $2^3(1 + 2^{-3}) = 2^3 + 2^0 = 8 + 1 = 9.$
18. $(15)^{12}(15)^{-10} = 15^2 = 225.$
19. $\dfrac{10^{-4}}{10^{-2}} = \dfrac{1}{10^{-2+4}} = \dfrac{1}{100}.$
20. $\dfrac{1}{3}(4^{-3/2}) = \dfrac{1}{3}\left(\dfrac{1}{4^{3/2}}\right) = \left(\dfrac{1}{3}\right)\left(\dfrac{1}{8}\right) = \dfrac{1}{24}.$
21. $\dfrac{5 + 2^{-2}}{3} = \dfrac{(5 + 2^{-2})2^2}{(3)(2^2)} = \dfrac{(5)2^2 + 2^0}{3(2^2)}$
    $= \dfrac{21}{12} = \dfrac{7}{4}.$

Combine exponents where possible, and simplify. If possible, do not leave grouping symbols, radical signs, or negative exponents in the result.

22. $a^2xa^3x^2 = a^5x^3.$
23. $2x^0 + (2x)^0 = 2 + 1 = 3.$

A1.26 PRACTICE PROBLEM SET (concluded)

24. $(a^2b)(a^{-1})b^3(ab)^{-1} = a^{2-1-1}b^{1+3-1} = b^3.$

25. $\dfrac{4x^2b}{(2b)^2} = \dfrac{4x^2b}{4b^2} = \dfrac{x^2}{b}.$

26. $\dfrac{a^3}{(a^x)^2} = \dfrac{a^3}{a^{2x}} = a^{3-2x}$ or $\dfrac{1}{a^{2x-3}}.$

27. $\dfrac{(2^3)(2^x)}{2^{1+x}} = 2^{3+x-(1+x)} = 2^2 = 4.$

28. $\dfrac{(x^{1/3})(y^{2/3})^2}{2(xy)^{1/2}} = \dfrac{x^{1/3}y^{4/3}}{2x^{1/2}y^{1/2}} = \dfrac{y^{5/6}}{2x^{1/6}}.$

29. $\dfrac{x^{1/3}\sqrt{b}}{b\sqrt{x}} = \dfrac{x^{1/3}b^{1/2}}{bx^{1/2}} = \dfrac{1}{b^{1/2}x^{1/6}}.$

30. $(a - 2b)^2 = a^2 - 4ab + 4b^2.$

31. $\dfrac{1}{3}(3x)^{-2/3} = \dfrac{1}{3(3)^{2/3}(x)^{2/3}} = \dfrac{1}{3^{5/3}x^{2/3}}.$

32. $\dfrac{1 + (1 + x)^{-n}}{x} = \dfrac{[1 + (1 + x)^{-n}](1 + x)^n}{x(1 + x)^n}$
$= \dfrac{(1 + x)^n + 1}{x(1 + x)^n}.$

A1.27 PROBLEM SET A1–5

Evaluate the following:

1. $2^4.$
2. $7(2)^0.$
3. $(1 - 0.02)^{-2}$ to three decimal places.
4. $\left(\dfrac{3}{4}\right)^{-1}.$
5. $(-3)^{-2}(2)^{-3}.$
6. $\dfrac{(10^{-3})(10^5)}{(10^3)(10^{-4})}.$
7. $\sqrt{-16}.$
8. $3^{-1} + \left(\dfrac{2}{3}\right)^{-2}.$
9. $3^{-2}.$
10. $(x - 3)^0.$
11. $16^{3/4}.$
12. $\left(\dfrac{1}{8}\right)^{1/3}.$
13. $\dfrac{10^{-4}}{10^{-5}}.$
14. $\dfrac{2}{3}(16)^{-3/4}.$
15. $\sqrt{\dfrac{25}{16}}.$
16. $5x^0 + (ax)^0.$
17. $(25)^4(25)^{-3}.$
18. $(1 + 0.05)^2.$
19. $(32)^{-3/5}.$
20. $\left(\dfrac{2}{3}\right)^{-1} + 2^{-3}.$
21. $\sqrt[3]{125}.$
22. $\left(\dfrac{8}{27}\right)^{-2/3}.$
23. $\dfrac{1 + 3^{-2}}{5}.$
24. $\dfrac{2^{-3} + 2^{-1}}{2^{-1}}.$
25. $3^{-2}(1 + 3^{-1}).$

A1.27 PROBLEM SET A1-5 *(continued)*

Combine exponents where possible, and simplify. If possible do not leave grouping symbols, radical signs, or negative exponents in the result.

26. $a^2 a$.
27. $(ab)(ac)(bc)$.
28. $a^2 b^3 (ab^4)$.
29. $(abc^2)(a^2 cb)$.
30. $(x^2 a)(x^2 b)$.
31. $\dfrac{a^2 b^3}{ab}$.
32. $\dfrac{a^4 b^2 c}{a^2 b^3 c^2}$.
33. $\dfrac{xy^3 b^3}{x^3 yb}$.
34. $\dfrac{a^3 (bxy)}{abx^2 y}$.
35. $\dfrac{x^3 y^2}{x^2 y^3}$.
36. $\dfrac{a(bc)^3}{ab^2}$.
37. $\dfrac{(ab)^2 ab}{a}$.
38. $\dfrac{a(bc)^3}{b(ac)^4}$.
39. $\dfrac{(-3b)^3 (2c)^2}{12 b^2 c}$.
40. $\dfrac{-2b^2 (-3c)^2}{-(-bc)^3}$.
41. $(xy^2)(ay^{-2})$.
42. $(ab^2 c^{-1})(a^2 b^{-1} c^2)$.
43. $a(ax)^{-2}$.
44. $\dfrac{2x^{-1} a^3}{(-ax)^2}$.
45. $\dfrac{x^{-2}}{ax}$.
46. $3a^{1/3} b^{1/2} a^2 b$.
47. $\dfrac{\sqrt{x}\sqrt[3]{y}}{x^{-1} y^{1/2}}$.
48. $\dfrac{a^{2/3} (b^3)^{1/2}}{\sqrt{a}\sqrt[3]{b}}$.
49. $\dfrac{2}{3}(3x)^{-1/2}$.
50. $\dfrac{2x^{-1/2}\sqrt{y^3}}{3y^{-1/3}\sqrt{x^3}}$.
51. $\dfrac{2 + x^{-2}}{x + 3}$.
52. $\dfrac{(1-x)^{-1} + 1}{x}$.
53. $\dfrac{x^{-1} + x^{-2}}{3}$.
54. $\dfrac{(ax)^2}{(a^x)^2}$.
55. $\dfrac{x^5 + 4}{x^2 + 2}$.
56. $a(a+b)$.
57. $(a-3b)^2$.
58. $a(a-b)^2$.
59. $(x-y)(x+y)$.
60. $a(a^{-1} + 1)$.
61. $(a^{1/2} - 1)^2$.
62. $\dfrac{a^{-1} + 2}{a}$.
63. $\dfrac{(3^2)(3^a)}{3^{a-1}}$.

Mark (T) for true or (F) for false:

64. ( ) $(2^3)(3^2) = 6^5$.
65. ( ) $ab^2 = a^2 b^2$.

A1.27 PROBLEM SET A1-5 (concluded)

66. ( ) $(2ab)^2 = 4a^2b^2$.
67. ( ) $\dfrac{a^2}{b^2} = \left(\dfrac{a}{b}\right)^2$.
68. ( ) $(a - b)^2 = a^2 - b^2$.
69. ( ) $(a + 1)^{1/2} = \sqrt{a} + 1$.
70. ( ) $\dfrac{\sqrt[3]{a}}{\sqrt[3]{b}} = \sqrt[3]{\dfrac{a}{b}}$.
71. ( ) $(1 + 0.1)^{-2} = \dfrac{1}{1.21}$.
72. ( ) An expression is raised to a power by raising each of its terms to the power.
73. ( ) The sum of the squares of two numbers is the same as the square of the sum of the two numbers.
74. ( ) $a^{-1} + b^{-1}$ is equivalent to the sum of the reciprocals of a and b.
75. ( ) $0^0 = 1$.
76. ( ) $5x^0 = 1$.
77. ( ) $(1 - 0.02)^{-5} = \dfrac{1}{(0.98)^5}$.
78. ( ) $2x^{-1/2} = \dfrac{2}{x^2}$.
79. ( ) $a^{2/3}$ is the cube root of a^2.
80. ( ) $\sqrt{x^2 + y^2 + z^2} = x + y + z$.
81. ( ) $\sqrt{2x} = 2^{1/2}x^{1/2}$.
82. ( ) $\sqrt{-12}$ is not a real number.
83. ( ) $\dfrac{2a^{1/6}}{b^{1/6}} = 2\left(\dfrac{a}{b}\right)^{1/6}$.
84. ( ) $a^{1/2}$ is called the square of a.
85. ( ) $(a - 2b)^2 = a^2 - 4ab + 4b^2$.

A1.28 ORDER OF OPERATIONS REVISITED

In Section A1.6 we stated the rule for the order in which the operations of parentheses, multiplication and division, and addition and subtraction are performed. When an expression also contains the operation of exponentiation (frequently denoted by the symbol ↑), a common mnemonic for remembering the order is

Please — Parentheses
Excuse — Exponentiation
My Dear — Multiplication/Division
Aunt Sally — Addition/Subtraction.

As before, multiplication and division are performed equally from left to right, and so are addition and subtraction. For example,

$$4 \uparrow 2 + 3 \times 5 - 8 =$$
$$16 + 3 \times 5 - 8 =$$
$$16 + 15 - 8 = 23.$$

Similarly

$$3(16 \uparrow 1/2 - 7 \times 2) + 5 \uparrow 3 =$$
$$3(16/2 - 7 \times 2) + 5 \uparrow 3 =$$

$$3(8 - 14) + 5 \uparrow 3 =$$
$$3(-6) + 5 \uparrow 3 =$$
$$3(-6) + 125 =$$
$$-18 + 125 = 107.$$

> **Exercise.** Evaluate (a) $27 \uparrow 1/3 - 4/2 + 6$. (b) $32 \uparrow 1/4 - (12 \times 3)/2$.
> **Answer:** (a) 13. (b) -10.

As another example, consider the two expressions
$$(2 \uparrow 3 \times 3)/4 + 15/5 = 9$$
and
$$2 \uparrow 3 \times 3/(4 + 15)/5 = 24/95.$$
Now compare these results with
$$2 \uparrow 3 \times 3/4 + 15/5 = 9.$$
The first and third values are the same, but the second value is different.

> **Exercise.** Which of the following expressions result in the same value: $5 \times 64 \uparrow (1/3)$, $(5 \times 64) \uparrow 1/3$, and $5 \times 64 \uparrow 1/3$?
> **Answer:** The values are 20, 320/3, and 320/3; so the second and third are the same.

The following application illustrates how exponentials can be useful in the solution of everyday problems and reemphasizes the proper order of operations.

Example. The real estate department of Primary Banking Company has determined through market analysis that the value of its commercial holdings has appreciated from $1.2 million to $1.26 million over the past year. If the value of real estate typically appreciates exponentially, what would be the expected value of the company's holdings in one more year? Two more years? Three more years? Ten more years?

The company's holdings have appreciated at a rate of
$$(1.26 - 1.2)/1.2$$
over the past year. Simplifying this expression, we have
$$0.06/1.2 = 0.05$$

or 5 percent. Assuming that this 5 percent appreciation will continue, the company's holdings after one more year will be worth

$$1.26 + 0.05 \times 1.26 = 1.26 + 0.063$$
$$= 1.323 \text{ million}$$

or $1,323,000. After two more years the worth will be

$$1.323 + 0.05 \times 1.323 = 1.323 + 0.06615$$
$$= 1.38915 \text{ million}$$

or $1,389,150.

Before going on, it is helpful to look at the last analysis in a different way. The 1.323 was calculated by adding 5 percent of $1.26 million to the original $1.26 million; that is, as we saw before, $1.323 = 1.26 + 0.05 \times 1.26$. So we can substitute $(1.26 + 0.05 \times 1.26)$ for 1.323 in the last calculation of

$$1.323 + 0.05 \times 1.323$$

to get

$$(1.26 + 0.05 \times 1.26) + 0.05(1.26 + 0.05 \times 1.26).$$

Now, factoring out the term $(1.26 + 0.05 \times 1.26)$, this last expression becomes

$$(1.26 + 0.05 \times 1.26)(1 + 0.05) =$$
$$[1.26(1 + 0.05)](1 + 0.05) = 1.26(1 + 0.05) \uparrow 2.$$

Exercise. Verify that $1.26(1 + 0.05) \uparrow 2$ results in 1.38915 million or $1,389,150.

Extending this last result, we find that after three more years the worth will be

$$1.26(1 + 0.05) \uparrow 3 = 1.4586075 \text{ million}$$

or $1,458,607.50.

In the same way, the value after 10 more years will be

$$1.26(1 + 0.05) \uparrow 10 = 2.05240723 \text{ million}$$

or $2,052,407.23.

Exercise. An automobile is purchased new in 1991 for $15,000. The typical rule of thumb is that the value will depreciate 25 percent each year.   a) What will be its value in 1992?   b) In 1993?   c) What is the exponential expression for the value in 1993?   d) What will be the value in 1994?   e) In 2001?

Answer: a) $11,250.00.   b) $8,437.50.   c) $15,000(1 - 0.25) \uparrow 2$.   d) $6,328.13.   e) $844.70.

A1.29 PROBLEM SET A1-6

Evaluate each of the following:
1. $3 \times 5 \uparrow 2 / 15 + 4 \times 2$.
2. $2 \uparrow 4 / 16 - 50 / 5 \uparrow 2$.
3. $(3 \times 5) \uparrow 2 / 15 + 4 \times 2$.
4. $2 \uparrow 4 / 16 - (50 / 5) \uparrow 2$.
5. $4 \uparrow 2 + 6 / 3 - 2 \times 3$.
6. $(4 \uparrow 2) + (6 / 3) - (2 \times 3)$.
7. $4 \uparrow (2 + 6 / 3) - 2 \times 3$.
8. $(4 \uparrow 2) + 6 / (3 - 2 \times 3)$.
9. $3 \times 2 \uparrow 3 / 14 / 2$.
10. $(3 \times 2) \uparrow 3 / (14 / 2)$.

11. The investment portfolio that financier Robert Q. Jones has accumulated currently has a value of $10.5 million. The firm investing Jones' holdings has established a record over the years of earning 15 percent on its investments. Jones is planning to live on $5 million of the money and wants to leave the rest in an estate for his children and grandchildren. How much will the estate be worth after one year? After two years? What is the exponential expression for the value after two years? What will the estate be worth in 10 years? In 25 years?

12. A luxury sailboat was purchased new in 1991 for $1.25 million. Typically these boats depreciate 10 percent each year. Estimate the value of the boat in 1992. In 1993. What is the exponential expression for the value in 1993? Estimate the value in 1994. In 2001.

13. The world population is approximately 5.04 billion. Last year it was about 4.8 billion. Using the ratio between this year and last year as the estimated growth rate, estimate what the population was two years ago. What is the exponential expression for this value? Estimate the population five years ago. What is the estimate for two years from now? What is the exponential expression for this value? What is the estimate for five years from now?

A1.30 REVIEW PROBLEMS

Reduce the following to a single signed number or 0:
1. $-4 + (-2) - [+(-3)]$.
2. $-(-8) + (-4) - (+4) + 2$.
3. $-2(3) + (-3)(-4) - (1)(-5)$.
4. $-(-3) + 2\{-[-3(2)]\} - (+10)$.
5. $-5(-2)(-3) + (3)(-2)(-5)$.
6. $\dfrac{-3(-2)(-4)}{8(-5)}$.
7. $\dfrac{-(5)(3)(-4)}{2(-6)}$.
8. $\dfrac{-(-5)(20)}{-\{-[-4]\}}$.
9. $\dfrac{3(2)(5)(-6)}{(-10)(-18)}$.
10. $\dfrac{(-1)(-2)(-3)(-4)}{(-5)(6)}$.

11. Evaluate the following:
   a) $20 \times 5 + 6 / 2 - 9$.
   b) $36 / 4 - 24 \times 3 + 2$.
   c) $8 \times (5 + 2) / (11 - 15)$.
   d) $12 / (10 - 11) \times (7 + 2)$.

A1.30 REVIEW PROBLEMS (continued)

12. Pure Gas Company has the following charges for use of natural gas: $9.75 customer service charge, 73 cents per therm for the first 120 therms of usage, 68 cents per therm for the next 180 therms, and 64 cents per therm in excess of 300 therms. What is the charge for 50 therms of usage? For 100 therms? For 200 therms? For 400 therms?

13. What fundamental property or convention justifies each of the following?
    a) $x2y = 2xy$.
    b) $4(3z) = 12z$.
    c) $+2 + (-a) = 2 - a$.
    d) $3x + 6y = 3(x + 2y)$.
    e) $3a + 2 + y = 3a + y + 2$.
    f) $(a + 2) + b = a + (2 + b)$.
    g) $1 + 2 + x = 3 + x$.
    h) $x2 + y3 = 2x + 3y$.
    i) $3 + (-x) = 3 - x$.
    j) $1a = a$.
    k) $2(a + b) = 2a + 2b$.
    l) $5 - xy = -xy + 5$.
    m) $3(x + y) = 3x + 3y$.
    n) $5a + 5b = 5(a + b)$.

14. Combine like terms:
    a) $2 + 5x - 4b + 7 - (-3b)$.
    b) $ab - a(2 - b) + 3a + 5$.
    c) $x(ay - 3) + 2x + 4axy - 7$.
    d) $xy - 2(2 - xy) + 5xy$.

15. Starting with $3x(2y) + 3 + x + 3x$, name the fundamental property that justifies each step:
    a) $3x(2y) + 3 + x + 3x = 3x(2y) + 3 + 4x$.
    b) $= 3(2)xy + 3 + 4x$.
    c) $= 6xy + 3 + 4x$.
    d) $= 6xy + 4x + 3$.
    e) $= (6xy + 4x) + 3$.
    f) $= 2x(3y + 2) + 3$.

16. Starting with $zy + 5 + 2(3 + 4y)$, name the fundamental property that justifies each step:
    a) $zy + 5 + 2(3 + 4y) = zy + 5 + 2(3) + 2(4y)$.
    b) $= zy + 5 + 6 + 2(4y)$.
    c) $= zy + 5 + 6 + 8y$.
    d) $= zy + 11 + 8y$.
    e) $= zy + 8y + 11$.
    f) $= yz + y8 + 11$.
    g) $= (yz + y8) + 11$.
    h) $= y(z + 8) + 11$.

17. Remove grouping symbols and combine like terms:
    a) $x - a[3 - 2(1 - x)]$.
    b) $5 - 3[2 - 4(-3 + z)]$.
    c) $3 - 2[a - x + 3(2x - a)]$.
    d) $(3 - a)(x - b + 2)$.
    e) $ax - a[-2x + 3(2x - 1)]$.

18. Reduce to a single signed number:
    $$-\frac{-3 + 2[-5 - (2 - 7)]}{5 + [2 - 3(2 - 3)]}.$$

19. Factor the following:
    a) $2x + ax$.
    b) $xy + 3xy + axy$.
    c) $2 + 4a + 6b$.
    d) $5xy + 4x$.
    e) $3ax + 6ay + 9a$.
    f) $2(x - 1) + a(x - 1)$.
    g) $a + b + ax + bx$.
    h) $x^2 + x - 2$.
    i) $10x^2 + 3x - 1$.
    j) $6x^2 + 7x - 20$.
    k) $8x^2 + 16x + 6$.

20. Simplify by cancellation where possible:
    a) $\dfrac{3(3 - a) + x}{2x}$.
    b) $\dfrac{3xy}{2x}$.
    c) $\dfrac{x - 2xy}{3x}$.
    d) $\dfrac{3}{x - y}[2(x + y)]$.

21. Multiply, leaving no grouping symbols in the answer:
    a) $\left(\dfrac{2x}{3}\right)\left(\dfrac{6a}{b}\right)$.
    b) $-2\left(\dfrac{x - 3}{a}\right)$.
    c) $2(x - y)\left(\dfrac{3a}{x - y} - \dfrac{1}{2}\right)$.
    d) $10xy\left(\dfrac{1}{5y} - \dfrac{a}{2xy}\right)$.

22. Express with a single minus sign:
    a) $\dfrac{-3x - 2y}{5 - a}$.
    b) $-\dfrac{2a - b}{x + b}$.
    c) $-\dfrac{a - b}{-5 - x}$.
    d) $\dfrac{a + b}{-5 - x}$.

23. Reduce to one simple fraction:
    a) $\dfrac{1}{3} - \dfrac{1}{6} + \dfrac{3}{4}$.
    b) $\dfrac{a}{b} + 1$.
    c) $\dfrac{3}{2x} - \dfrac{2}{x} + \dfrac{5}{4x}$.
    d) $\dfrac{y}{x} - 1 + \dfrac{y}{2a}$.

A1.30 REVIEW PROBLEMS (concluded)

e) $\dfrac{1}{12xy} + \dfrac{2}{3} - \dfrac{5}{x}$.

f) $\dfrac{1}{2x-3} + \dfrac{b}{3}$.

g) $\dfrac{a}{x+y} - \dfrac{b}{z} + 5$.

h) $\dfrac{3}{a} - \dfrac{b}{2} + \dfrac{c}{x+y} - d$.

i) Three-fourths of $2\frac{1}{2}$.

j) $5\frac{1}{4} - 2\frac{1}{3}$.

k) $1\frac{7}{8}$ divided by $2\frac{1}{2}$.

24. Reduce the following complex fractions to simple fractions by multiplication by a suitably chosen 1:

a) $\dfrac{\frac{2}{3} - \frac{1}{4}}{\frac{1}{6} + 1}$.

b) $\dfrac{\frac{x}{y} - 1}{\frac{2}{3} + \frac{3}{y}}$.

c) $\dfrac{x - \frac{y-4}{a}}{\frac{b}{2} + \frac{3}{a}}$.

d) $\dfrac{\frac{x}{x+y} - 1}{\frac{2}{x+y}}$.

25. Evaluate the following:
a) 3^3.
b) $2x^0$.
c) $(2x)^0$.
d) $(1 - 0.1)^{-2}$ to three decimals.
e) $\left(\dfrac{2}{3}\right)^{-2}$.
f) $(2)^{-2}(-2)^2$.
g) $(75)^{100}(75)^{-98}$.
h) $3^0 - (2x+1)^0$.
i) $\left(\dfrac{1}{16}\right)^{1/4}$.
j) $\left(\dfrac{1}{16}\right)^{-1/4}$.
k) $\dfrac{2}{5}(32)^{1/5}$.
l) $(27)^{2/3}$.
m) $(125)^{4/3}$.
n) $(8)^{-2/3}$.
o) $\left(\dfrac{2}{3}\right)^{-1}$.
p) $\dfrac{(10)^{-5}(10)^2}{(10)^3(10)^{-8}}$.
q) $2^{-3}(2^2 + 2^{-1})$.
r) $\dfrac{3^{-1} - 3^{-2}}{3^{-3}}$.
s) $\sqrt[3]{64}$.
t) $(1 + 0.03)^3$.
u) $\sqrt{-1}$.
v) $\left(\dfrac{2}{3}\right)^{-2}\left(\dfrac{3}{2}\right)$.
w) $\sqrt{\dfrac{4}{25}}$.
x) $(\sqrt[3]{27})^2$.
y) $\sqrt{16^3}$.
z) $\sqrt{9^{-3}}$.

26. Combine exponents, where possible, and simplify. If possible, do not leave grouping symbols, radical signs, or negative exponents in the final result:
a) $a(a^2)(a^3)$.
b) $xyz(x^2 y)$.
c) $xz(3xy)(2xz)$.
d) $(abc)^2(ab)$.
e) $\dfrac{a^2 b^3}{abc}$.
f) $\dfrac{a^2 yz^3}{ayz^2}$.
g) $\dfrac{(3ab)^2(2c)^3}{12ac^2}$.
h) $\dfrac{(-2x)^3 y^2}{4xy}$.
i) $\dfrac{(ab^{-1}c^2)^3}{2b^2 c^2}$.
j) $\dfrac{(3x^{-2}y)^2}{2x^3 y^{-3}}$.
k) $\dfrac{(-xy^2)^{-3}(2z^2)}{(-2yz)^4}$.
l) $[(x\sqrt{y})^{3/2}]^2$.
m) $\dfrac{ax^{1/3}y^{-1/2}}{bx^{1/2}y^{5/3}}$.
n) $(y^{1/2})^{-3/2}$.
o) $\dfrac{3}{4}(4y)^{-3/2}$.
p) $\dfrac{\sqrt[3]{ab}\sqrt{xy}}{9(ab)^{-1}(xy)^{3/2}}$.
q) $\dfrac{(2a^{1/2}b^{1/3}c)^3}{4abc}$.
r) $\dfrac{1 + a^{-1}}{1 - a^{-1}}$.
s) $\dfrac{(a-b)^{-1} - 1}{b^2}$.
t) $\dfrac{2a^{x-3}a^5}{a^2}$.
u) $\dfrac{x^{2a}}{x^a}$.
v) $a^2 b^3 (ab)^{-5}$.
w) $x(2-x)^2$.
x) $a^2(a^{-2} + a^{-3})$.
y) $a(a-b)(a+2b)$.
z) $(5^{x+1})(5a)^{-3}(5a^3)$.

27. Evaluate the following:
a) $6 \uparrow 2 \times 1 / 18 + 3 \times 5$.
b) $3 \uparrow 4 / 9 - 16 / 4 \uparrow 2$.
c) $6 \uparrow 2 \times 1 / (18 + 3) \times 5$.
d) $3 \uparrow 4 / 9 - (16 / 4) \uparrow 2$.

28. Commercial real estate has been appreciating at a rate of 8 percent each year. The current holdings of Jones Real Estate Trust have a value of $2.25 million. How much will the trust be worth after 1 year? After 2 years? What is the exponential expression for the value after 2 years? What will the trust be worth in 10 years? In 25 years?

Appendix 2

Formulas, Equations, Inequalities, and Graphs

A2.1 INTRODUCTION

The distributive property asserts that

$$a(b + c) = ab + ac.$$

Inasmuch as the assertion applies for *any* numbers, a, b, and c, it is called an **identity.** On the other hand, the statement

$$x + 5 = 7$$

is true only under the condition that x is 2, and for this reason is called a **conditional equality.**

A three-lined symbol, $\equiv$, can be used to denote an identity. In this book, however, the two-lined symbol, $=$, is used to denote both identities and conditional equalities because the context makes clear which interpretation of the symbol is relevant. Thus, in Appendix 1 the symbol $=$ means identically equal, whereas in most of the remainder of the book the symbol denotes conditional equality. We shall refer to conditional equalities briefly as equations.

In the equation $x + 5 = 7$, the letter x can be called the unknown, and the value of the unknown that makes the statement true (the number 2) can be called the root of the equation. We may also say that a number that makes the statement of equality true satisfies the equation.

The statement $y = x + 2$ is true for various pairs of values for x and y, and we shall call the letters x and y variables. A particular set of numbers, such as

$$x = -1, \quad y = 1,$$

that satisfy the equation, is a solution of the equation. In this book we use the **variable, solution** terminology (rather than unknown, root terminology) in the discussion of equations. Thus

$$y = x + 2$$

will be called an equation in two variables. It has an unlimited number of solutions. The equation

$$x + 5 = 7$$

is an equation in one variable. It has the unique solution $x = 2$.

To solve an equation for a variable means to perform whatever operations are necessary to put the equation in a form in which the stated variable appears by itself (with coefficient 1 and exponent 1) on one side of the equality sign, and the expression on the other side of the equality sign does not contain the stated variable. For example,

$$x - y = 3$$

is not solved for either x or y, but

$$x = y + 3$$

is solved for x, and the equation

$$y = x - 3$$

is solved for y.

Exercise. Fill in the blanks: The _____ $x + 10 = 4$ has a single _____, x. The _____ of the _____ is $x = -6$. On the other hand, the _____ $y - x = 7$ has two _____ and has an _____ number of solutions: if we write $y - x = 7$ in the alternate form $y = x + 7$, it is said to be _____ for _____.

Answer: Equation; variable; solution; equation; equation; variables; unlimited; solved; y.

We now turn to some elementary procedures employed when solving an equation for a variable.

A2.2 SOME AXIOMS

In mathematics, **axioms** are statements that we assume to be true and that we use as a foundation for our proofs and inquiries. For example, we assume that if equals are added to equals, the sums will be equal. Inasmuch as an equation is a statement of equality of the numbers on either side of the equal sign, the axiom says that if we add the same number to both sides of an equation, we shall obtain another statement of equality. For example, if we have the statement

$$x - 3 = 7$$

and we add 3 to each side, we obtain

$$x - 3 + 3 = 7 + 3$$

from which we find $x = 10$, and we have solved the equation for x.

In similar fashion, we assume that if equals are subtracted from equals, the differences are equal; if equals are multiplied by equals, the products are equal; and if equals are divided by equals (division by 0 excluded), the quotients are equal. In the context of equations, we say that the solutions of an equation are not altered if the same number is added to both sides, or if the same number is subtracted from both sides, or if both sides are multiplied or divided by the same number.

Examples.

$$x - 2 = 3$$
$$x - 2 + 2 = 3 + 2$$
$$x = 5.$$

Add 2 to both sides:

$$x + 2 = 3$$
$$x + 2 - 2 = 3 - 2$$
$$x = 1.$$

Subtract 2 from both sides:

$$\frac{x}{3} = 2$$
$$3\left(\frac{x}{3}\right) = (3)(2)$$
$$x = 6.$$

Multiply both sides by 3:

$$2x = 7$$
$$\frac{2x}{2} = \frac{7}{2}$$
$$x = \frac{7}{2}.$$

Divide both sides by 2:

Exercise. The solution $x = 4$ is obtained by applying which operation to each of the following: $6x = 24$; $x/2 = 2$; $x - 4 = 0$; $x + 2 = 6$?

Answer: Divide both sides by 6; multiply both sides by 2; add 4 to both sides; subtract 2 from both sides.

A2.3 SOLUTIONS BY ADDITION AND MULTIPLICATION, WITH INVERSES

The most direct way to solve an equation for a certain variable is to derive an expression that has that variable alone (coefficient 1 and exponent 1) on one side of the equal sign, and an expression not involving this variable on the other side of the equal sign. We apply axioms to accomplish this. If we are asked to solve

$$ax + b = c$$

for x, we may proceed by subtracting b from both sides to obtain

$$ax = c - b.$$

Next we divide both sides by a to obtain the desired solution

$$x = \frac{c - b}{a}.$$

The steps are justified by the axioms. However it is helpful to understand what steps are required, and this understanding is enhanced if we keep in mind the notion of **inverse** operation. Thus in solving

$$ax + b = c$$

for x, we wish to remove b from the left side. Inasmuch as b is **added** on the left, we apply the inverse operation and **subtract** b from both sides to obtain

$$ax = c - b.$$

We now observe that x is **multiplied** by a, so we apply the inverse operation and **divide** both sides by a to obtain

$$x = \frac{c - b}{a}.$$

Inverse operations are the tools we need to manipulate equations into desired form.

Be prepared to justify each step taken in the solution of an equation. For brevity, the phrase **both sides of the equation** may be omitted when citing justification for an operation. Thus, for example, **add 3** will be assumed to mean to add 3 to both sides of the equation. For uniformity, it is to be understood that the outcome of each operation performed is shown on the line following the description of the operation. For example,

$$x - 3 = 5 \quad \text{Add 3:}$$
$$x = 8.$$

Example. Solve for x, citing operations performed:

$$4x - 2 = 2x + 5 \quad \text{Subtract } 2x:$$
$$2x - 2 = 5 \quad \text{Add 2:}$$
$$2x = 7 \quad \text{Divide by 2:}$$
$$x = \frac{7}{2}.$$

> **Exercise.** Solve for x, citing operations performed:
> $$3 - 2x = -5x + 7.$$
>
> **Answer:**
>
> | | |
> |---|---|
> | $3 - 2x = -5x + 7$ | Add $5x$: |
> | $3 + 3x = 7$ | Subtract 3: |
> | $3x = 4$ | Divide by 3: |
> | $x = \dfrac{4}{3}.$ | |

Generally equations containing fractions can be handled most efficiently by finding the **lowest common denominator (l.c.d.)** of all the fractions in the equation, and then multiplying both sides by the l.c.d.

Example. Solve for x, citing operations performed:

$2x - \dfrac{1}{3} = \dfrac{x}{2}$	Multiply by 6 (the l.c.d.):
$6(2x) - 6\left(\dfrac{1}{3}\right) = 6\left(\dfrac{x}{2}\right)$	Carry out multiplications:
$12x - 2 = 3x$	Add 2:
$12x = 3x + 2$	Subtract $3x$:
$9x = 2$	Divide by 9:
$x = \dfrac{2}{9}.$	

Careful attention should be paid to the fact that each side of an equation is an expression; and **to multiply an expression by a number, we must multiply every term of the expression by that number.**

It is instructive to follow through the tactics of the last example. We observe fractions in the equation, and we know that the denominator of a fraction is canceled (replaced by 1, which need not be written) if the fraction is multiplied by a term having the fraction's denominator as a factor. Rather than treat each fraction separately, we make up a term (the lowest term) that has the denominators of all the fractions as factors. Then, when both sides are multiplied by this term, all denominators are canceled, and we are led to the statement

$$12x - 2 = 3x.$$

We decide to gather terms involving x on the left, with other terms on the right. The term -2 is removed from the left by the inverse operation of adding 2. Similarly the term $+3x$ on the right is removed by the inverse operation of subtracting $3x$ from both sides. We now have $9x = 2$. The 9 must be removed to obtain the desired solution. Inasmuch as 9 is multiplied by x, we apply the inverse operation and divide both sides by 9 to obtain

$$x = \frac{2}{9}.$$

Exercise. Solve for x, citing operations performed:

$$\frac{3x}{4} - 5 = \frac{x}{3}.$$

Answer:

$\frac{3x}{4} - 5 = \frac{x}{3}$ Multiply by 12:
$9x - 60 = 4x$ Subtract $4x$:
$5x - 60 = 0$ Add 60:
$5x = 60$ Divide by 5:
$x = 12.$

If the variable to be solved for is inside a grouping symbol, we remove the grouping symbol, citing the distributive property as justification, and then proceed with the solution. For example,

$3x - \frac{1}{4} = 2 - \frac{1}{6}[x - (2 - x)]$ Multiply by l.c.d. 12:
$36x - 3 = 24 - 2[x - (2 - x)]$ Distributive property:
$36x - 3 = 24 - 2[x - 2 + x]$ Distributive property:
$36x - 3 = 24 - 2x + 4 - 2x$ Add $4x$:
$40x - 3 = 24 + 4$ Add 3:
$40x = 31$ Divide by 40:
$x = \frac{31}{40}.$

In the next example, grouping symbols are introduced to emphasize proper procedure, and then are removed in due course.

$\frac{2}{3(x - 1)} - \frac{1}{2} = \frac{1}{4}$ Multiply by l.c.d. $3(4)(x - 1)$:

$3(4)(x - 1)\left[\frac{2}{3(x - 1)}\right] - 3(4)(x - 1)\left(\frac{1}{2}\right) = 3(4)(x - 1)\left(\frac{1}{4}\right).$

The last equation simplifies to

$$8 - 6(x - 1) = 3(x - 1) \quad \text{Distributive property:}$$
$$8 - 6x + 6 = 3x - 3 \quad \text{Add } 6x; \text{ add } 3:$$
$$17 = 9x \quad \text{Divide by } 9:$$
$$\frac{17}{9} = x.$$

The same procedures are followed when numbers are in literal form, but the next to the last step often requires factoring. Factoring is frequently just an inverse application of the distributive property, but we shall follow convention here and cite factoring rather than the distributive property when the need for justification arises.

Example. Solve for x, citing operations performed:

$$\frac{x}{a} - b = 2a(x - b) \quad \text{Multiply by } a:$$
$$x - ab = 2a^2(x - b) \quad \text{Distributive property:}$$
$$x - ab = 2a^2 x - 2a^2 b \quad \text{Subtract } 2a^2 x; \text{ add } ab:$$
$$x - 2a^2 x = ab - 2a^2 b \quad \text{Factor:}$$
$$x(1 - 2a^2) = ab - 2a^2 b \quad \text{Divide by } (1 - 2a^2):$$
$$x = \frac{ab - 2a^2 b}{1 - 2a^2}.$$

Exercise. Solve for x, citing operations performed:

$$\frac{2x}{a} + \frac{3}{b} = x + 4.$$

Answer:

$$\frac{2x}{a} + \frac{3}{b} = x + 4 \quad \text{Multiply by } ab:$$
$$2xb + 3a = abx + 4ab \quad \text{Subtract } abx:$$
$$2xb - abx + 3a = 4ab \quad \text{Subtract } 3a:$$
$$2xb - abx = 4ab - 3a \quad \text{Factor:}$$
$$x(2b - ab) = 4ab - 3a \quad \text{Divide by } (2b - ab):$$
$$x = \frac{4ab - 3a}{2b - ab}.$$

Example. Solve for x, citing operations performed:

$$a = \frac{x}{1 - nx} \qquad \text{Multiply by } (1 - nx):$$
$$a(1 - nx) = x \qquad \text{Distributive property:}$$
$$a - anx = x \qquad \text{Add } anx:$$
$$a = x + anx \qquad \text{Factor:}$$
$$a = x(1 + an) \qquad \text{Divide by } (1 + an):$$
$$\frac{a}{1 + an} = x.$$

Example. Solve for y, citing operations performed:

$$\frac{a}{y} - \frac{1}{b} = 2 \qquad \text{Multiply by } (by):$$
$$ab - y = 2by \qquad \text{Add } y:$$
$$ab = 2by + y \qquad \text{Factor:}$$
$$ab = y(2b + 1) \qquad \text{Divide by } (2b + 1):$$
$$\frac{ab}{2b + 1} = y.$$

The procedures presented in this section can be used to solve the types of problems illustrated by the following example.

Example. A cattle rancher has a rectangular grazing area with a fence around the entire perimeter so that the animals cannot wander off. The total perimeter is 500 feet. The length is 70 feet more than the width. What are the length and width?

A diagram of the grazing area is shown in Figure A2–1. Note that the length has been designated by $x + 70$ and the width by x since we are told that the length is 70 feet more than the width. Because the total perimeter is 500 feet, we have

$$\text{Total width} + \text{Total length} = \text{Total perimeter}$$
$$2x + 2(x + 70) = 500.$$

Solving this last equation results in

$$4x + 140 = 500 \qquad \text{Subtract 140:}$$
$$4x = 360 \qquad \text{Divide by 4:}$$
$$x = 90.$$

So the width is 90 feet and the length is 160 feet.

FIGURE A2-1

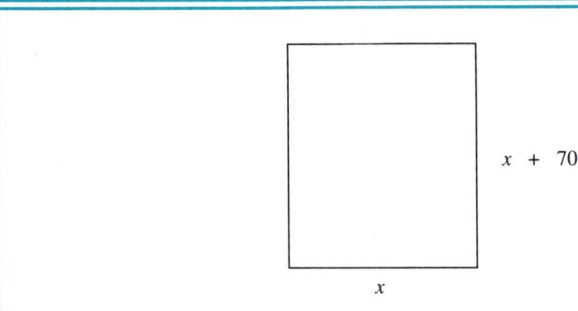

> **Exercise.** The sum of two consecutive even integers is 74. What are they?
> **Answer:** 36 and 38.

A2.4 PROBLEM SET A2-1

Solve each of the following for x, citing operations performed:

1. $2x - 3 = x + 4$.
2. $4x + 5 = 2x + 12$.
3. $3x - 7 = 2x + 4$.
4. $5 - 2x = 6$.
5. $7x - 5 = 3 - 4x$.
6. $3 - 2x = x - 4$.
7. $\frac{x}{3} + \frac{1}{2} = 3x$.
8. $\frac{x}{4} + \frac{x}{2} = 2 - \frac{5x}{8}$.
9. $\frac{2x}{5} - \frac{3x}{2} = 4$.
10. $1 - \frac{x}{3} + \frac{x}{2} = x - 4$.
11. $\frac{1}{7} - \frac{x}{3} = x$.
12. $1 - \frac{3x}{7} = 0$.
13. $\frac{x + 3}{2} = x - \frac{1}{4}$.
14. $\frac{5 - 2x}{3} + \frac{x}{2} = 1$.
15. $\frac{2x - 1}{3} - \frac{1 - x}{5} = 0$.
16. $\frac{x + 1}{2} - \frac{x - 1}{3} = 5$.
17. $bx + 2 = c$.
18. $ax + 2 - x = 0$.
19. $ax + b = cx$.
20. $ax + b = x - b$.
21. $a(x - a) = 2x$.

A2.4 PROBLEM SET A2-1 *(concluded)*

22. $\dfrac{x}{a} - \dfrac{1}{2} = 2x.$

23. $\dfrac{2}{a-x} + \dfrac{1}{3} = 4.$

24. $y = \dfrac{x}{b-cx}.$

25. $\dfrac{3}{4} - \dfrac{2x}{3} = 2x(a-1).$

26. $3(x-2) = 2 - a(x+2).$

27. $\dfrac{2}{3(x-2)} + \dfrac{3}{a} - \dfrac{1}{2} = 0.$

28. $ax - \dfrac{b}{2} = c + \dfrac{5[a - 2(b-x)]}{6}.$

29. $\dfrac{b}{a} - x = 2a(b-x).$

30. $x - a(b-x) = 2x - 3.$

31. $3(b-x) = 2 + b[x - (3-x)].$

32. $b(a+x) = a(b+x)$, where $a \ne b$.

---

33. A square office 500 feet by 500 feet is to be partitioned into two offices by a single interior wall. The difference between the perimeters of the resulting two offices is to be 200 feet. What are their dimensions?

34. The sum of three consecutive odd integers is 159. What are they?

35. a) Choose any number. Decrease the number by 7 and multiply the result by 3. Now add 21 and multiply this result by 5. Finally divide the last result by 15. What is your final result?
    b) Repeat (a) using the starting value x.

36. a) Take the year in which you were born, triple it, and then add 10. Now multiply this result by 100. Next add 3 times your age and subtract 1,000. Finally divide the last result by 300. What does the integral portion of this number represent? The decimal portion?
    b) Repeat (a) using b for year of birth and a for age.

A2.5 TRANSPOSITION

Problem Set A2–1 has afforded practice in citing fundamentals as justification for steps followed in the solutions of equations. From now on we shall lessen the writing burden by omitting step-by-step justification. The burden can be lightened further by applying the rule of **transposition**, which states that a term may be moved from one side of an equation to the other by changing its sign. For example,

$$x - 2a = b$$

becomes

$$x = b + 2a$$

by changing the sign of $-2a$ to $+2a$ and placing $+2a$ on the other side. Similarly

$$x + 7 = y$$

becomes

$$x = y - 7.$$

The transposition rule is a consequence of the axiom that states that the same number may be added to (subtracted from) both sides of an equation. That is, the change from

$$x + 7 = y$$

to

$$x = y - 7$$

is, in effect, subtracting 7 from both sides of the first equation. Transposition is a handy procedure, but we must keep in mind that it applies to *terms*. It would not be correct to say that any quantity can be moved to the other side by transposition. For example, the 2 in $2x = 6$ is not subject to the rule for transposition because 2 is only part of a term of the left member of the equation.

> **Exercise.** The change from $ax = b$ to $x = b/a$ is not accomplished by transposition. How is it accomplished?
>
> **Answer:** By dividing both sides of the equation by a.

A2.6 FORMULAS

Computational procedures are described efficiently by formulas employing the symbolism of algebra. Thus if x is the length and y the width of a rectangle, the area A of the rectangle is expressed by the formula $A = xy$. On the one hand, if we are told a rectangle has a length of eight inches and a width of five inches, we compute the area

$$A = (8)(5) = 40 \text{ square inches.}$$

On the other hand, if we are asked how wide a rectangle of 12 inches length should be if its area is to be 84 square inches, we substitute into the equation, obtaining $84 = 12y$ where y is a place holder for the width. Solving this equation, we find y, the desired width, is seven inches. The point here is that we may wish to use a formula to evaluate a variable other than the one for which the formula is solved, and to do so, we call upon the usual operations for solving equations. Actually the formula $A = xy$ leads easily to two other formulas:

$$x = \frac{A}{y} \quad \text{and} \quad y = \frac{A}{x}.$$

If we have the formula $A = xy$ and are given values for A and x, we can compute y by substituting the given values directly into the equation and solving for y, or we can solve the literal equation, obtaining

$$y = \frac{A}{x},$$

and then evaluate y by substituting the given values into this equation. Generally it is more efficient to substitute the given numbers directly into the formula if a single evaluation is to be made. If however several evaluations are to be made, the formula should be solved for the desired variable before substituting numbers. For example, suppose that we are given

$$y = 5 \quad \text{and} \quad a = 2$$

and are asked to evaluate x from the formula

$$y = 2(ax - 3).$$

Substituting the given numbers directly into the formula, we have

$$5 = 2(2x - 3)$$
$$5 = 4x - 6$$
$$11 = 4x$$
$$\frac{11}{4} = x.$$

On the other hand, if we are asked to carry out a whole series of evaluations of x for various values of y and a, it would be more efficient to solve the formula for x to obtain

$$x = \frac{y + 6}{2a}.$$

This formula permits rapid evaluation of x for given values of y and a.

Exercise. If $y = (1 + n)/2$, what would be an efficient way to compute n for many different values of y?

Answer: Substitute the values for y into the equation $n = 2y - 1$.

The techniques of this section can be further illustrated by the following example.

Example. The equation relating the cost, C, of an item to its retail price, R, is

$$C + pR = R,$$

where p is the percent markup on the retail price.

a) What percent markup on retail is achieved if an item costs $5.00 and sells at a retail price of $8.00?

Here we have $C = \$5.00$ and $R = \$8.00$. Substituting in the equation $C + pR = R$ results in

$$5.00 + p(8.00) = 8.00$$

or

$$5 + p(8) = 8.$$

Solving this last equation for *p* yields

$$8p = 3$$
$$p = 3/8 = 0.375$$

or 37.5 percent. Note that 37.5 percent of the $8.00 retail price results in a $3.00 markup, so that indeed the cost is $8.00 − $3.00 = $5.00.

b) How much can a merchant pay for an item that sells for $7.50 if the merchant wishes to achieve a markup that is 20 percent of the retail price?

This time we have $R = \$7.50$ and $p = 20$ percent or 0.20 so that

$$C + 0.20(7.5) = 7.5.$$

Solving now for *C*, we get

$$C = 7.5 - 1.5 = 6$$

or a cost of $6.00. Here 20 percent of the $7.50 retail price results in a markup of $1.50 to the cost of $6.00.

c) If a merchant seeks to achieve a markup of 40 percent on retail, at what price should an item sell that cost the merchant $2.70?

Now we have $p = 40$ percent or 0.40 and $C = \$2.70$ so

$$2.70 + 0.40R = R.$$

Solving here for *R* gives us

$$2.70 = R - 0.40R = 0.60R$$
$$4.50 = R$$

or a retail price of $4.50. Here 40 percent of the $4.50 retail price is $1.80 so indeed the cost is $4.50 − $1.80 = $2.70.

> **Exercise.** The amount of interest, I, earned on P dollars at simple interest of i percent per year for n years is
>
> $$I = Pin.$$
>
> Assume a year has 360 days.
> (a) How long will it take for $500 to earn $20 interest if the interest rate per year is 4 1/2 percent? (Hint: Let d be the number of days so that $n = d/360$.)
> (b) How many dollars must be invested at 10 percent per year if interest in the amount of $200 is to be earned in 50 days?
>
> **Answer:** a) 320 days. b) $14,400.

A2.7 EXACT EVALUATIONS

Evaluation by formulas often leads to approximations. Unless care is exercised, these approximations may not be accurate enough for the purpose at hand. Suppose, for example, that we wish to compute $3\frac{1}{3}$ percent of $1 million. If we change the stated percentage to 3.33 percent, and then to the decimal 0.0333, the computation is

$$0.0333(\$1,000,000) = \$33,300.00.$$

For most purposes the answer obtained would not be satisfactory. We can express the answer to any desired degree of accuracy by changing the stated percentage to its exact equivalent as follows:

$$3\tfrac{1}{3}\% = \frac{3\tfrac{1}{3}}{100} = \frac{10/3}{100} = \frac{10}{300} = \frac{1}{30}.$$

The computation with exact numbers would be

$$\left(\frac{1}{30}\right)(\$1,000,000) = \$33,333.33\ldots.$$

The point of this example is that if fractions are used up to the last step, the final answer can be carried accurately to as many places as desired.

> **Exercise.** Compute x exactly from $3x + 2 = 1/b$ if b is $2\frac{1}{7}$.
> **Answer:** $-23/45$.

As another example, let us evaluate y, given

$$y = \frac{a+b}{1-r}, \quad a = \frac{1}{3}, \quad b = \frac{1}{2}, \quad \text{and} \quad r = 1\frac{1}{3}\%.$$

To express all numbers in the same form, r is changed to its exact fractional equivalent, $1/75$. Substituting this value of r, we obtain

$$y = \frac{1/3 + 1/2}{1 - 1/75}.$$

This is an exact expression for y. If numerator and denominator are each multiplied by 150, we obtain

$$y = \frac{50 + 75}{150 - 2} = \frac{125}{148},$$

which again is an exact expression for y. This result could now be converted to an approximate decimal that is accurate to as many places as desired.

A2.8 PROBLEM SET A2-2

Given that $k = 12$, $m = 5$, $n = 4$, compute y from the following formulas:

1. $y = \dfrac{km}{n}$.

2. $y = \dfrac{k^2 m - n^3}{n^2}$.

3. $y = \dfrac{m}{n/k^2}$.

4. $y = \sqrt[3]{mn - k}$.

5. $y = (n - m)[n - k(m + n)]$.

6. $y = \dfrac{8m}{n^2/k}$.

7. $y = \left(\dfrac{kn}{3}\right)^{3/2}$.

8. $y = \left(\dfrac{4}{9k}\right)^{-2/3}$.

9. $y = \left(m^2 - \dfrac{3k}{4}\right)^{5/4}$.

10. $y = m^2 n + 3[4k - n(m^3 - k^2)]$.

In the following, find the exact value of y in the form of a fraction in lowest terms, given that

$$a = \frac{5}{3}, \quad b = \frac{1}{7}, \quad c = \frac{2}{9}, \quad d = \frac{5}{12}, \quad x = \frac{3}{8}, \quad z = \frac{1}{5}.$$

11. $y = \dfrac{x}{a}$.

12. $y = \dfrac{ab}{2}$.

13. $y = \dfrac{a(b + c)}{3}$.

14. $y = d - \dfrac{1}{a}$.

A2.8 PROBLEM SET A2.2 (continued)

15. $y = ax + bz$.

16. $y = ax^2 - \dfrac{2a}{b}$.

17. $y = \left(1 - \dfrac{a}{d}\right)^3$.

18. $y = \sqrt[3]{\dfrac{c}{2x}}$.

19. $y = \dfrac{a}{2} - b\sqrt{\dfrac{3d}{5}}$.

20. $y = \dfrac{a + 2c - d}{x - 4a}$.

---

21. Compute y to the nearest cent if
$$y = at + b(t - c),$$
$a = 16\tfrac{2}{3}\%$, $b = 15\%$, $c = \$75{,}000$, and $t = \$140{,}000$.

22. Given that $a = 0.52$ and $x = 4$, compute y to two decimal places if
$$y = \dfrac{a}{1 + x/100}.$$

23. Temperature in degrees Celsius, C, is related to temperature in degrees Fahrenheit, F, by the formula
$$C = \dfrac{5}{9}(F - 32).$$
Find the Fahrenheit temperature corresponding to the following Celsius readings:
a) 100.   c) -10.6.   e) -10.
b) 0.   d) 28.   f) 50.

24. A salesman's earnings, E, amount to 20 percent of his total sales, T, plus a bonus of $12\tfrac{1}{2}$ percent of any amount he sells in excess of $50{,}000$.
a) Write the equation relating earnings to sales if sales exceed $\$50{,}000$.
b) What must the man's sales be if he is to earn $\$10{,}000$? $\$15{,}000$? $\$20{,}000$?
c) How much must he sell if his earnings are to be 25 percent of total sales?

25. An executive is to receive compensation, B, amounting to x percent of his company's net profit after taxes. Taxes amount to y percent of net profits after deduction of the executive's compensation.
a) Letting P represent net profits before taxes, complete the following formula:
$$B = x[P - ?(? - ?)].$$

b) If the executive receives 25 percent of net profits after taxes, and taxes amount to 52 percent of net profits after deduction of the executive's compensation, how much must net profits before taxes be if the executive is to receive $\$50{,}000$?

26. A customer buys an article on the installment plan. The price of the article (or the amount she still owes after making a down payment) is B dollars. The seller adds a carrying charge of C dollars and requires that the debt be paid off by n equal payments. Letting y be the number of payments that would be made in a year (that is, if payments are weekly, y is 52; and if payments are monthly, y is 12), and letting r be the equivalent simple interest rate being paid by the customer, a formula states
$$r = \dfrac{2yC}{B(n + 1)}.$$
a) An article priced at $\$500$ is purchased. The customer pays $\$100$ down (so B is $\$400$). The seller adds $\$42$ as a carrying charge and requires that the debt be repaid in 10 equal monthly installments of $\$44.20$ each. What rate of interest is the customer paying? (Find r and convert it to percent form.)
b) If the simple interest equivalent of the installment rate is 15 percent, what should be the carrying charge on an article priced at $\$100$ (no down payment) if the debt is to be repaid in 20 equal weekly installments?

27. For each dollar of increase in sales, selling expense increases by $\$p$ where, it is hoped, p is less than 1. The sales level B at which the company will break even if its fixed expenses are $\$F$ is
$$B = \dfrac{F}{1 - p}.$$

A2.8 PROBLEM SET A2.2 (concluded)

a) Find B if $F = \$12,000$ and $p = 0.4$.
b) Fixed expenses are $10,000 and management wishes to control p so that break even will occur at $12,500. Find p.
c) Repeat (b) if fixed expenses are $20,000 and break even is to occur at $32,000.

28. The average cost per unit is $\$A$ when x units are made, and

$$A = \frac{100}{x} + 0.01.$$

Find the average cost per unit if
a) 10 units are made.
b) 20 units are made.
   How many units should be made if average cost per unit is to be
c) $1.01?   d) $0.41?   e) $0.21?

A2.9 COORDINATE AXES

An axiom of mathematics states that a correspondence exists between the real numbers and the points on a straight line called a **number line**; that is, for each real number, there is one and only one corresponding point on a number line, and each point on a number line corresponds to one and only one real number. Hence if we draw a straight line and mark upon it an arbitrary point, 0, all negative real numbers can be represented by points to the left of 0, while all positive real numbers can be represented by points to the right of 0. According to the axiom, each number corresponds to a unique point on the number line, and the totality of real numbers corresponds to the line itself. The number line enables us to determine location and measure distances in one dimension.

Often we need to work with information on locating distances in two dimensions. We use two number lines, perpendicular to one another, to set up a calibration of two-dimensional space. These lines are called **rectangular coordinate axes** and are obtained by drawing two intersecting perpendicular lines: one horizontal, the other vertical. Sometimes these axes are referred to as **Cartesian axes** since this approach was originally developed by the famous French philosopher René Descartes. The intersection of the horizontal and vertical axes so obtained is taken as the 0 point on the line and is called the **origin.** On the vertical, points above the origin are used to represent positive numbers, while points below represent negative numbers. On the horizontal axis, positive numbers are to the right of the origin, while negative numbers are to the left.

Any point in the plane of the axes can now be located by means of a number pair called the **coordinates** of the point. Conventionally, coordinates are written in the form (a, b), where the first number in the parentheses is the horizontal coordinate, or **abscissa,** and the second number is the vertical coordinate, or **ordinate.** Thus, the point (2, 3) is located by moving two units to the right of the origin, and then three units vertically upward. The procedure is analogous to the method of directing a person from a particular spot (origin) in a city by explaining that the point desired can be found by going two blocks east, and then three blocks north.

> **Exercise.** What are the abscissa and the ordinate of a point?
>
> **Answer:** The abscissa is the horizontal coordinate and the ordinate is the vertical coordinate of the point.

Figure A2–2 shows the point (2, 3) just mentioned, together with other aspects of the coordinate system. The axes divide the plane into **quadrants,** which we number counterclockwise I, II, III, and IV as shown in Figure A2–2. In quadrant I both abscissa and ordinate are positive. In II the abscissa is negative, the ordinate positive. In III both coordinates are negative. In IV the abscissa is positive, the ordinate negative.

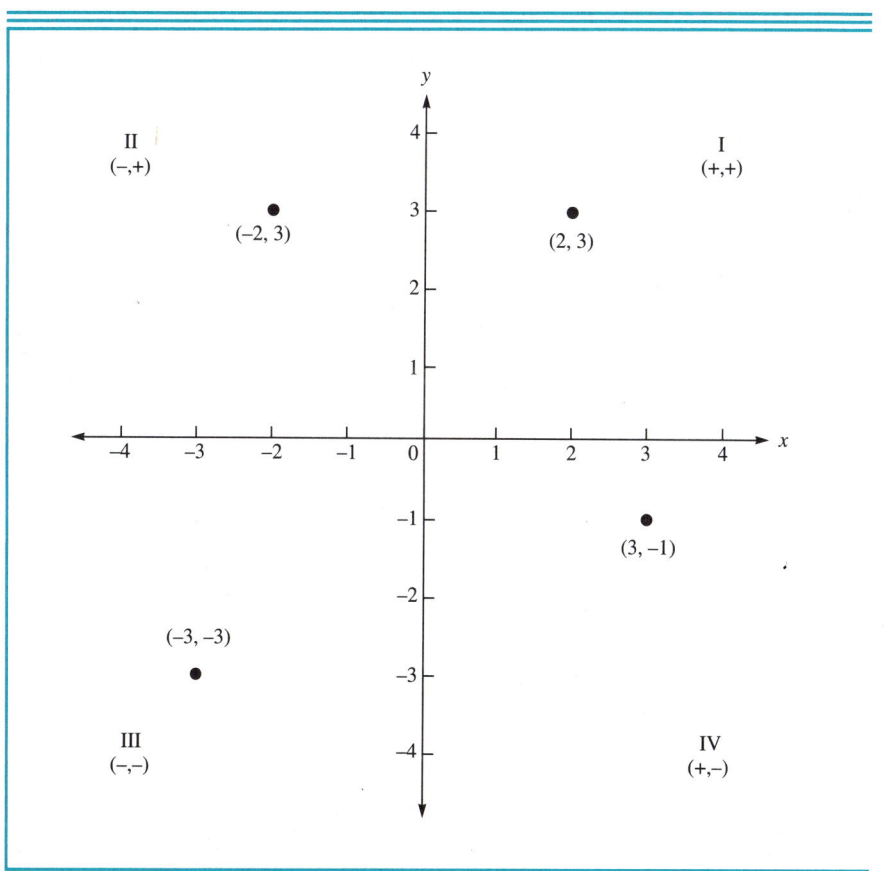

FIGURE A2-2

> **Exercise.** In which quadrants are the points $(-2, 3)$, $(3, 5)$, $(2, -3)$, and $(-5, -4)$?
>
> **Answer:** II, I, IV, III. See Figure A2–2 on page 943.

A2.10 PLOTTING OBSERVATIONAL DATA

By **observational data** we mean numbers collected in real situations—numbers such as costs, sales, units produced, and prices. Frequently we wish to display such data in a graphic manner, which helps to show relationships that may exist between two variables. Consider the data in Table A2–1.

Figure A2–3 is a graphic representation (or, more simply, a graph) of the data of Table A2–1. The numbers of units produced have been assigned the general designation x; the costs per unit have the general designation y. Following convention, the numbers x are assigned to the horizontal axis, the numbers y to the vertical. The vertical variable is conventionally called the **dependent** variable, and the horizontal variable is called the **independent** variable. In the present illustration, it is natural to think of production cost as depending on number of units produced so that cost would be the dependent variable and units produced the independent variable.

The interpretation of Figure A2–3 is simply that unit cost **tends** to decrease as the number of units made increases. It is a graphic illustration of the economies of mass production. We refer to this set of isolated points as a **discrete set.** If we wish to illustrate the relationship by means of a smooth curve, we may sketch in freehand a curve that comes close to the points, although it does not pass through all of the points. The points on the curve are not, of course, records of observations, because actual observations are limited in number, whereas a segment of a smooth curve has an unlimited number of points. However we might wish to use the smooth curve to estimate costs per unit for numbers of units other than those observed.

TABLE A2–1

Production Cost per Unit of Product

Lot Number	Number of Units in Lot (x)	Cost per Unit (y)
1	8	$11
2	20	4
3	5	13
4	10	9
5	15	8
6	25	5

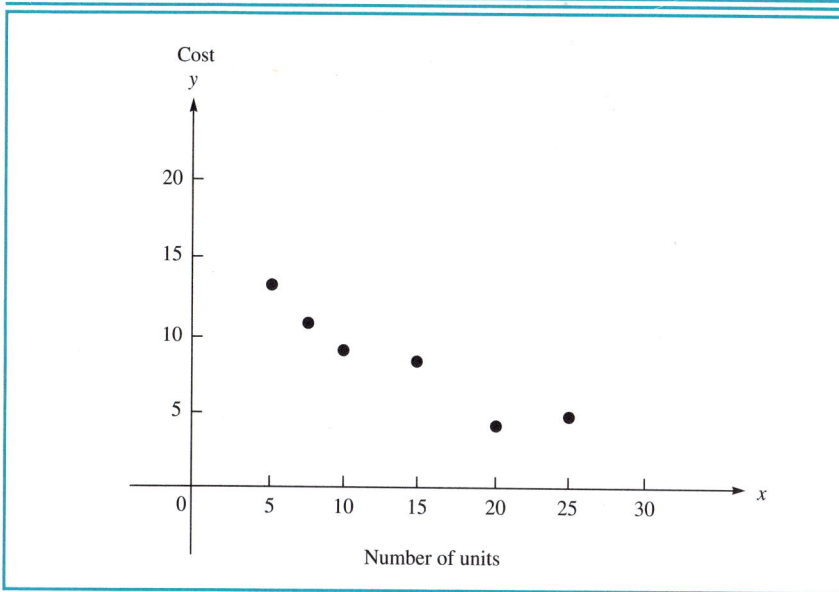

FIGURE A2–3

A2.11 PLOTTING EQUATIONS IN TWO VARIABLES: STRAIGHT LINES

Given the equation

$$y = x + 2,$$

we know that for every x, there is a number y such that the number pair (x, y) satisfies the equation. The entire solution set is an infinite set of ordered pairs. We can generate some members (obviously not all) of the solution set by arbitrarily assigning a value for x, and then computing the corresponding value for y. For example,

$$\text{if } x = 1, \quad \text{then} \quad y = 1 + 2 = 3$$

and $(1, 3)$ is a member of the solution set. Similarly if $x = 2$, then $y = 4$, and $(2, 4)$ is another member of the solution set.

Exercise. Find the points in the preceding solution set corresponding to $x = 0$ and $x = 5$.

Answer: $(0, 2)$; $(5, 7)$.

We **plot the graph** of an equation by finding and plotting points that satisfy the equation, then sketching in a smooth curve as suggested by the plotted points. In the case at hand, we may tabulate some of the points as in Table A2–2 where the x values are chosen arbitrarily.

The points of Table A2–2 are shown in Figure A2–4, where clearly all fall on the same straight line. We would also obtain a straight line if we made the graph of

$$y = 3x + 5 \quad \text{or} \quad y = -2x + 7.$$

In general, an equation that can be made into the form

$$y = mx + b,$$

where m and b are constant numbers, has a straight line as its graph and is called a **linear equation.** The graph of such an equation is easily sketched because **two points** determine a straight line.

> **Exercise.** How would you plot the graph of $y = 2x - 3$?
>
> **Answer:** Pick two arbitrary values of x and find the corresponding values of y to obtain two points. Plot the points and use a straightedge to draw a line through them.

A2.12 VERTICAL PARABOLAS

In the equation

$$y = x^2 - 5$$

if we let

$$x = 0, 1, 2, 3, 4, 5$$

in succession, we find the corresponding values of y to be $-5, -4, -1, 4, 11,$ and 20. In this equation the succession of negatives

$$x = -1, -2, -3, -4, -5$$

leads to the same last five values in the preceding sequence of y's. In tabular form, we have the points shown in Table A2–3 (page 948).

The general shape of the curve is shown in Figure A2–5 (page 948). It is clear that the curve will continue to rise at both ends because if we substitute x values of 6, 7, and so on (or $-6, -7,$ and so on), the term x^2 in

$$y = x^2 - 5$$

will overpower the number -5 and make y become larger and larger.

TABLE A2-2

$y = x + 2$	
x	y
0	2
1	3
2	4
3	5
4	6
5	7

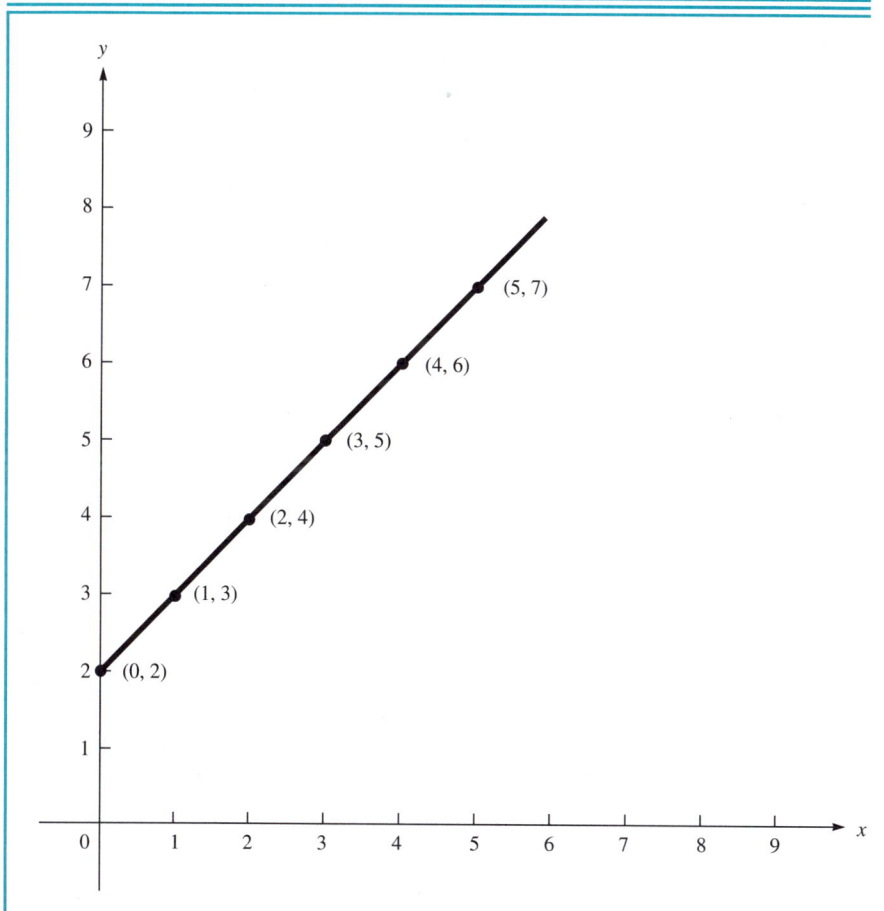

FIGURE A2-4

TABLE A2-3

\multicolumn{2}{c}{$y = x^2 - 5$}
x	y
−5	20
−4	11
−3	4
−2	−1
−1	−4
0	−5
1	−4
2	−1
3	4
4	11
5	20

FIGURE A2-5

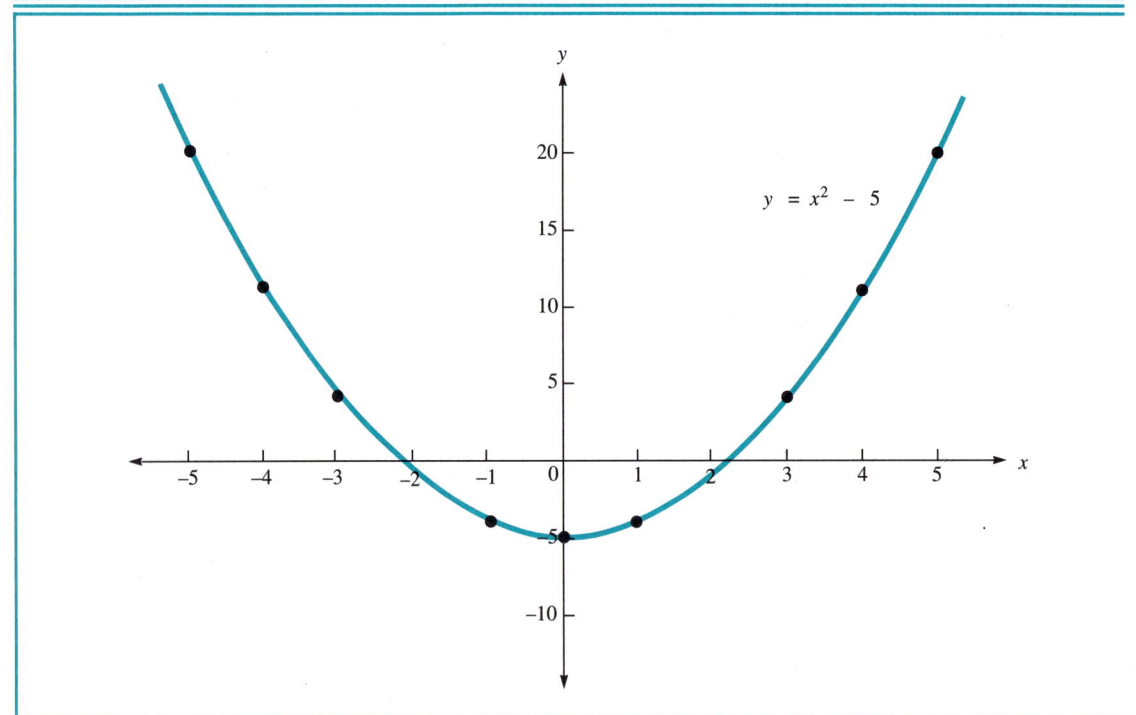

$y = x^2 - 5$

> **Exercise.** Find the coordinates of the points on $y = x^2 - 5$ where $x = 2.5$ and $x = -2.5$. Check the graph in Figure A2–5 by plotting these points.
>
> **Answer:** The points are $(2.5, 1.25)$ and $(-2.5, 1.25)$.

The graph shown in Figure A2–5 is known as a **vertical parabola.** If we plotted points for

$$y = -2x^2 + 5x - 6 \quad \text{or} \quad y = 3x^2 + 5x - 4,$$

we would again obtain vertical parabolas. In general, any equation that can be made into the form

$$y = ax^2 + bx + c,$$

where a, b, and c are constant numbers and $a \neq 0$, is a vertical parabola. The **nose** of the parabola is called the **vertex.** If $a > 0$, the parabola opens up; if $a < 0$, the parabola opens down. In the case of Figure A2–5, the vertex lies on the vertical axis. This is always the case if $b = 0$ in $y = ax^2 + bx + c$, as in the plotted equation

$$y = x^2 - 5.$$

Proper positioning of the vertex of a parabola is of key importance in drawing an accurate sketch. This can be done by use of the formula[1] that states that the x-coordinate of the vertex of a vertical parabola occurs at

$$x = -\frac{b}{2a}.$$

Thus comparing the parabola $y = x^2 - 5$ with $y = ax^2 + bx + c$, we have $a = 1, b = 0, c = -5$, so

$$x = -\frac{0}{2} = 0$$

is the x-coordinate of the vertex. The corresponding y is -5. The vertex is at $(0, -5)$, as shown in Figure A2–5. Why does the parabola open upward?

As another example, in

$$y = -2x^2 + 12x - 10$$

---

[1] Because a vertical parabola is symmetrical with respect to a vertical line through its vertex at $x = v$ (where v stands for vertex) it follows that the y value is the same at $x + v$ and $x - v$. That is, $a(x + v)^2 + b(x + v) + c = a(x - v)^2 + b(x - v) + c$. If we square, collect terms, factor, and solve, we find $x = -b/2a$.

we have $a = -2$ and $b = 12$. Since $a < 0$, the parabola will open down. Next we find the vertex from $x = -b/2a$:

$$x = -\frac{12}{-4} = 3$$

and

$$y = -2(9) + 12(3) - 10 = 8$$

so (3, 8) is the vertex in this case. Other points are computed in Table A2–4, and the graph of this parabola is shown in Figure A2–6.

Exercise. Find the coordinates of the vertex of $y = 3x^2 - 12x + 5$. Does the parabola open upward or downward?

Answer: (2, −7); up.

In general, peaks and valleys in curves are points of critical importance in sketching accurate graphs. We shall learn more about methods of determining such points and about important interpretations attached to them in Chapter 8. We shall now sketch the graph of the equation of the last exercise,

$$y = 3x^2 - 12x + 5.$$

We found the vertex to be (2, −7), and we may compute some other points as shown in Table A2–5 (page 952). The desired graph is shown in Figure A2–7 (page 952).

Exercise. Plot $y = x^2 - 8x + 15$.

Answer: This parabola rises on either side of the vertex at (4, −1), cutting the x-axis at 3 and 5. Other points include (2, 3), (6, 3), (0, 15), and (8, 15).

As another example, the parabola $y = -4x^2 + 7x - 3$ is found to have its vertex at (7/8, 1/16) and to fall on either side of the vertex (open downward). Again, $y = x^2$ is a parabola with vertex at the origin which rises on either side of the vertex (open upward).

TABLE A2-4

$y = -2x^2 + 12x - 10$	
x	y
0	−10
1	0
2	6
3	8
4	6
5	0
6	−10

FIGURE A2-6

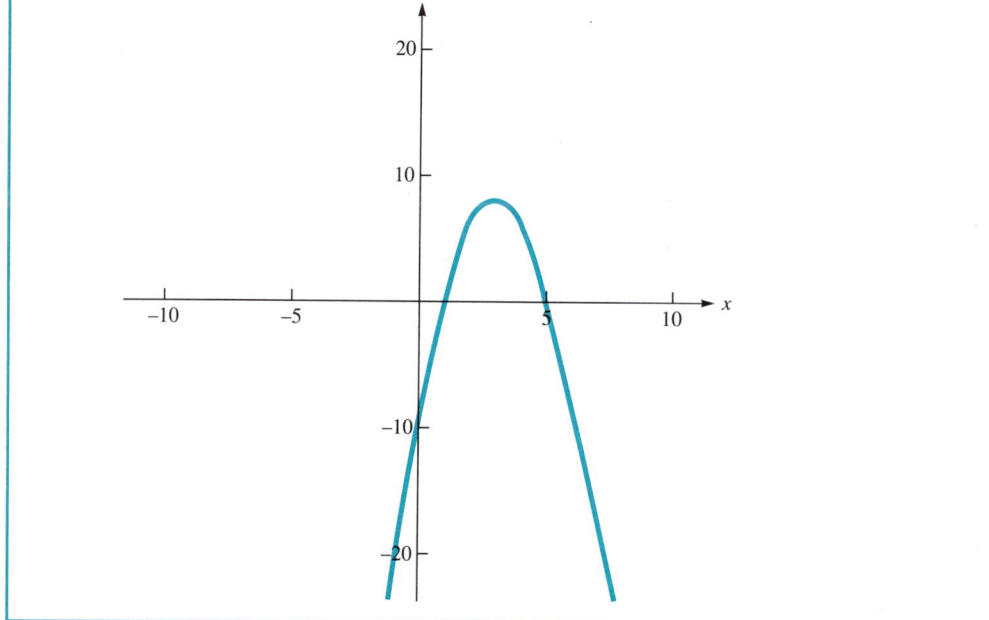

TABLE A2-5

$y = 3x^2 - 12x + 5$	
x	y
−1	20
0	5
1	−4
2	−7
3	−4
4	5
5	20

FIGURE A2-7

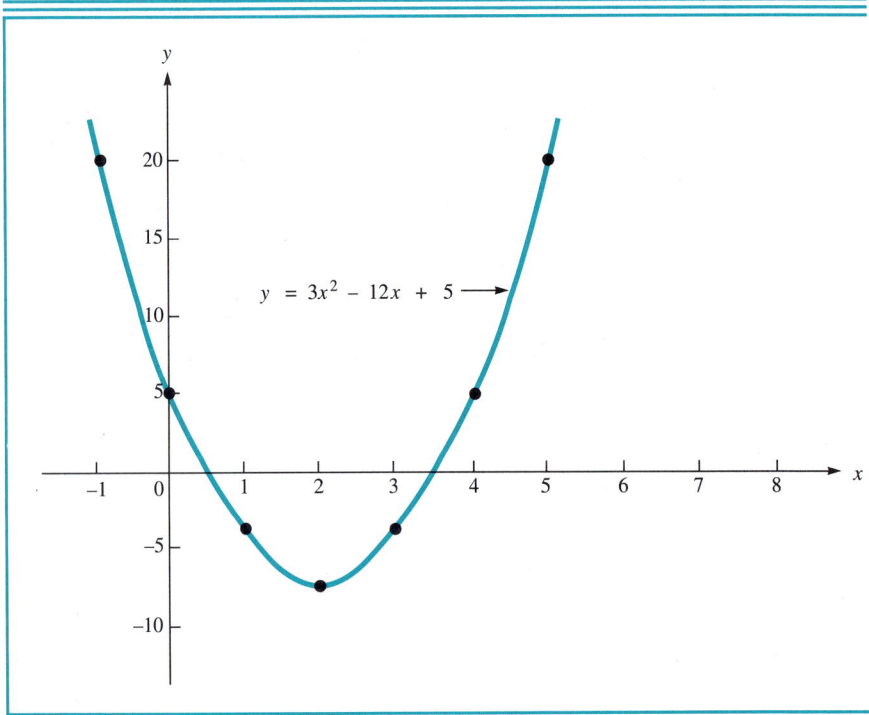

A2.13 QUADRATIC EQUATIONS

A quadratic equation is of the form

$$ax^2 + bx + c = 0,$$

where a, b, and c are constants, with $a \neq 0$. Thus

$$3x^2 - 12x + 5 = 0 \tag{1}$$

is a quadratic equation with $a = 3$, $b = -12$, and $c = 5$. The solution set consists of the values for x that make the equation a true statement. If we relate this equation to

$$y = 3x^2 - 12x + 5, \tag{2}$$

we see that the solution set of Equation (1) consists of the values of x that make y, in Equation (2), equal to 0. By reference to the graph in Figure A2–7, we see that the graph intersects the x-axis at about $x = 0.5$ and $x = 3.5$, and at these points y, or $3x^2 - 12x + 5$, is 0. An exact determination of the solution set can be found by the well-known **quadratic formula,** which states

$$x = \frac{-b \pm \sqrt{b^2 - 4ac}}{2a}.$$

In the present case

$$x = \frac{-(-12) \pm \sqrt{144 - 4(3)(5)}}{2(3)} = \frac{12 \pm \sqrt{84}}{6}.$$

Now $\sqrt{84}$ is about 9.17 so

$$x = \frac{12 \pm 9.17}{6}$$

$$= \frac{21.17}{6} \quad \text{or} \quad \frac{2.83}{6}$$

$$= 3.53 \quad \text{or} \quad 0.47,$$

and the solution set may be written as $x_1 = 0.47$, $x_2 = 3.53$ or as $\{0.47, 3.53\}$.

Three cases can arise in the solution of a quadratic. The graphical nature of these cases can be understood by reference to Figure A2–7. In its present state the graph shows **two different real solutions.** If now we hold the axes fixed and move the curve upward until the vertex is tangent to the x-axis (touches it at a single point), we have the case of **two equal real** solutions. Finally if we again move the parabola upward, it will not intersect the x-axis, and we have the case of **no real solutions.** Algebraically these cases relate to the quantity $b^2 - 4ac$ in the quadratic formula,

$$x = \frac{-b \pm \sqrt{b^2 - 4ac}}{2a}.$$

If $b^2 - 4ac$ is **positive** (greater than 0), we have a positive and a negative value for the square root so there are **two different real** solutions. If $b^2 - 4ac$ is 0, we have only one value for x and there are **two equal real solutions.** Finally if $b^2 - 4ac$ is **negative,** its square root is not a real number, and we have **no real solutions.**

> **Exercise.** Apply the quadratic formula to find the solutions for $x^2 - 9 = 0$.
>
> **Answer:** With $a = 1, b = 0, c = -9$, we find the two different roots: $x = 3$ and $x = -3$. The same result can be obtained by writing $x^2 = 9$ and noting that the square of $+3$ or -3 equals 9.

If we apply the formula to

$$3x^2 - 5x + 10 = 0,$$

we have

$$x = \frac{5 \pm \sqrt{25 - 120}}{6} = \frac{5 \pm \sqrt{-95}}{6}$$

and find that this equation has no real solutions.

> **Exercise.** Solve $x^2 - 4x + 4 = 0$ by the quadratic formula.
>
> **Answer:** $x_1 = x_2 = 2$. We have two real equal solutions.

Solution by Factoring

The equation

$$(x - 3)(x + 2) = 0$$

is true if either the factor $x - 3 = 0$ or the factor $x + 2 = 0$ because 0 times any number equals 0. Hence the solutions are $x_1 = 3, x_2 = -2$. Consequently we can easily find the solutions if the quadratic is factorable. For example,

$$2x^2 + 7x - 15 = 0$$

can be factored to yield

$$(2x - 3)(x + 5) = 0.$$

Setting $2x - 3 = 0$ and $x + 5 = 0$, we have the solutions

$$x_1 = \frac{3}{2}, \quad x_2 = -5.$$

> **Exercise.** Solve $6x^2 + x - 2 = 0$ by factoring.
>
> **Answer:** $x_1 = 1/2; x_2 = -2/3$.

Finally note that the factoring is elementary if the quadratic has no constant term. Thus

$$2x^2 - 5x = 0$$

factors to

$$x(2x - 5) = 0,$$

so the solutions are $x_1 = 0$ and $x_2 = 5/2$.

A2.14 PROBLEM SET A2-3

Graph each of the following:
1. $y = 3x - 1$.
2. $y = x$.
3. $y = -5x + 6$.
4. $2y - 3x = 6$.
5. $y = \dfrac{x}{2} + 3$.
6. $y = 3x^2$.
7. $y = x^2 - 7$.
8. $y = -2x^2 + 10$.
9. $y = 2x^2 - x$.
10. $y = x^2 + 2x - 6$.

Solve by the quadratic formula:
11. $x^2 - 10x + 3 = 0$.
12. $2x^2 + 5x - 2 = 0$.
13. $4x^2 - 12x + 9 = 0$.
14. $3x^2 + 2x + 5 = 0$.
15. $x^2 - 2x = 0$.

Solve by factoring:
16. $x^2 - 3x + 2 = 0$.
17. $3x^2 - 6x = 0$.
18. $6x^2 + 7x - 20 = 0$.
19. $x^2 - 25 = 0$.
20. $2x^2 + 5x - 7 = 0$.

A2.15 DEFINITIONS AND FUNDAMENTAL PROPERTIES OF INEQUALITIES

The symbols of inequality are $<$ and $>$. The first, $<$, means **is less than**; the second, $>$, means **is greater than.** Thus $3 > 2$ is the true statement that 3 is greater than 2, and $5 < 9$ is the true statement that 5 is less than 9. It may be of use to note that the symbols $>$ and $<$ point toward the smaller quantity. The statement $a < b$ is read *a* **is less than** *b*. If we wish to state that *a* **is less than or equal to** *b*, we combine the inequality sign with the equality sign and write $a \leq b$. For example,

$a \geq b$ means a is greater than or equal to b.
$a \leq 3$ means a is less than or equal to 3.
$b > 0$ means b is greater than 0; that is, b is positive.
$c < 0$ means c is less than 0; that is, c is negative.
$a \geq 0$ means a is not negative.

One of the fundamental properties of the real number system is the property of **order**. We say that the real numbers are ordered in the sense that either any two numbers are equal, or one is greater than the other. Thus given any two numbers, a and b, one and only one of the following must be true:

$$a < b$$
$$a = b$$
$$a > b.$$

Geometrically, to say that a first number is greater than a second implies that the first number lies to the right of the second on the number line. Arithmetically, to say that a first number is greater than a second implies that a positive number must be added to the second number to make the sum equal the first number. For example, $5 > 2$ implies that 5 lies to the right of 2 on the number line and that a positive number must be added to 2 to make a sum equal to 5. In general,

$$a > b \text{ implies that } a = b + c, \text{ where } c > 0.$$
$$a < b \text{ implies that } a + c = b, \text{ where } c > 0.$$

The last statement that **a is less than b** implies that a positive number ($c > 0$) must be added to a to make the sum equal b.

It is a consequence of the order property of the real numbers that $-5 < -2$ and $0 > -1$. That is, inasmuch as the positive number 3 must be added to -5 to make the sum equal -2, -5 is less than -2. Again, inasmuch as the positive number 1 must be added to -1 to make the sum 0, 0 is greater than -1.

Exercise. What argument leads to the conclusion that -10 is greater than -15? (See the immediately preceding paragraph.)

Answer: We see that -10 lies to the right of -15 on the number line; or $-15 + 5 = -10$.

The ordering of numbers is easiest to remember by referring to Figure A2–8. If the number a is to the left of the number b, then $a < b$. If the number a is to the right of the number b, then $a > b$. We see that $-1 < 0$, $0 < 1$, $-2 > -3$, $2 > -1$.

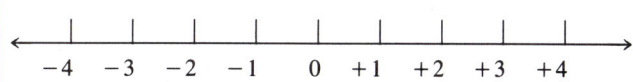

FIGURE A2-8

The direction in which an inequality symbol points is referred to as its **sense,** the particular use of the word being in phrases that describe inequalities as being of the **same sense** or of **opposite sense.** Thus $x < 3$ and $x < -1$ are of the same sense, and $x \leq 5$ and $x \geq 8$ are of opposite sense.

A2.16 FUNDAMENTAL OPERATIONS ON INEQUALITIES

As in the case with equalities, the same number may be added to or subtracted from both sides of an inequality, and both sides may be multiplied by, or divided by, the same *positive* (nonzero) number. However

multiplying or dividing both sides of an inequality by the same negative number changes the sense of the inequality.

For example,

$$-3 > -6$$

so multiplying both sides by -4 we have

$$12 < 24.$$

Thus the former inequality is the true statement that -3 is greater than -6. If we multiply both sides by -4, we change the sense to get the true statement that 12 is less than 24. It will be helpful to check the following sequence of operations:

$$
\begin{array}{ll}
2 > 1 & \text{Add 3:} \\
5 > 4 & \text{Multiply by } -6\text{:} \\
-30 < -24 & \text{Divide by } -3\text{:} \\
10 > 8 & \text{Subtract 12:} \\
-2 > -4 & \text{Read from } \textbf{right} \text{ to } \textbf{left:} \\
-4 < -2 & \text{Divide by } -2\text{:} \\
2 > 1.
\end{array}
$$

Ordinarily we read inequalities in the usual manner, from left to right. However, as shown in the preceding, we may, if we wish, read from right to left. For example, just as we can write

$$6 = x \quad \text{or} \quad x = 6,$$

so also we may write

$$6 < x \quad \text{or} \quad x > 6.$$

It may be helpful in the beginning to note that $>$ resembles an arrowhead and we read "greater than" when we read in the direction the arrow is pointing, and "less than" when we read against the arrow.

A2.17 SOLVING SINGLE INEQUALITIES

Keeping the fundamental operations in mind, we solve a single inequality as shown next.

Example. Solve the following for x:

$$3 - 2x \leq 7.$$

We proceed to get x alone on one side of the inequality

$$\begin{aligned} 3 - 2x &\leq 7 &&\text{Subtract 3:} \\ -2x &\leq 4 &&\text{Divide by } -2: \\ x &\geq -2. \end{aligned}$$

Exercise. Solve $7 - x \geq 3$ for x.
Answer: $x \leq 4$.

A single equation in two variables has a straight line as its geometric representation. A single inequality, on the other hand, is represented by all points on one side of a line, the line itself being included if the equality and inequality signs appear together ($\leq$, $\geq$). If we think of a straight line as dividing a plane in half, we may say that the solutions of an inequality in two-dimensional space consist of all points in a **half-space.** Consider the inequality

$$2x + 3y \leq 6.$$

Our first step in representing the inequality is to draw the line specified by the **equality**

$$2x + 3y = 6.$$

The intercepts are:

$$\begin{aligned} x &= 0; \quad y = 2; \quad \text{point is } (0, 2) \\ y &= 0; \quad x = 3; \quad \text{point is } (3, 0). \end{aligned}$$

The line is shown in Figure A2–9. Notice that the **origin** (0, 0) satisfies the inequality statement since

$$2x + 3y \leq 6$$
$$2(0) + 3(0) \leq 6$$
$$0 \leq 6.$$

Thus the origin, which is **below** the line, is in the solution space and **if one point below a line is in the solution space, then all points below the line are in the solution space** since the solution space for a linear inequality is a half-space. Hence the solution space consists of all points on the line, or below the line, as indicated in Figure A2–9 by the direction of the arrows on the line. Obviously the solution space contains an unlimited number of points.

To solve the inequality algebraically, we change the form of the inequality as follows:

$$2x + 3y \leq 6$$
$$3y \leq -2x + 6$$
$$y \leq -\frac{2}{3}x + 2.$$

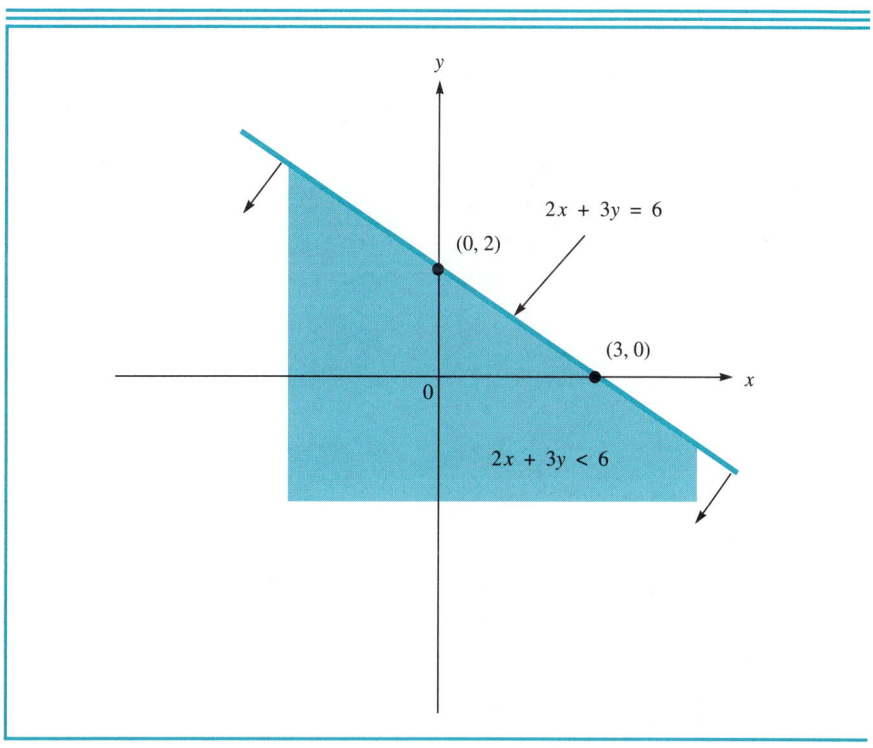

FIGURE A2–9

Here the equality part of

$$y \leq$$

means that points **on** the line are included in the solution space and the **less-than** part means points below the line are included. The algebraic solution then is

$$x \text{ arbitrary}$$
$$y \leq -\frac{2}{3}x + 2.$$

Thus if x is assigned any arbitrary value, the last expression states the permissible values for y. For example, if $x = -12$, then

$$y \leq -\frac{2}{3}(-12) + 2$$
$$y \leq 8 + 2$$
$$y \leq 10$$

and we have ($x = -12$, $y \leq 10$) as a specific (unlimited) set of solutions.

Example. a) Graph the solution space for the inequality

$$3x - 2y < -8.$$

b) Find the algebraic solution of the inequality.
c) Write the specific solution set if $x = 2$.

a) As before, we first draw the line

$$3x - 2y = -8$$

by finding the intercepts which are:

$$x = 0; \quad y = 4; \quad \text{point } (0, 4).$$
$$y = 0; \quad x = -8/3; \quad \text{point } (-8/3, 0).$$

This line is shown in Figure A2–10. This time checking the **origin** (0, 0), we have

$$3x - 2y < -8$$
$$3(0) + 2(0) < -8$$
$$0 < -8$$

which is obviously incorrect. Thus the origin, which is **below** the line, is **not** in the solution space so **all points on or above the line comprise the solution space.** This is indicated in Figure A2–10, as before, by the direction of the arrows. Once again the solution space contains an unlimited number of points.

FIGURE A2-10

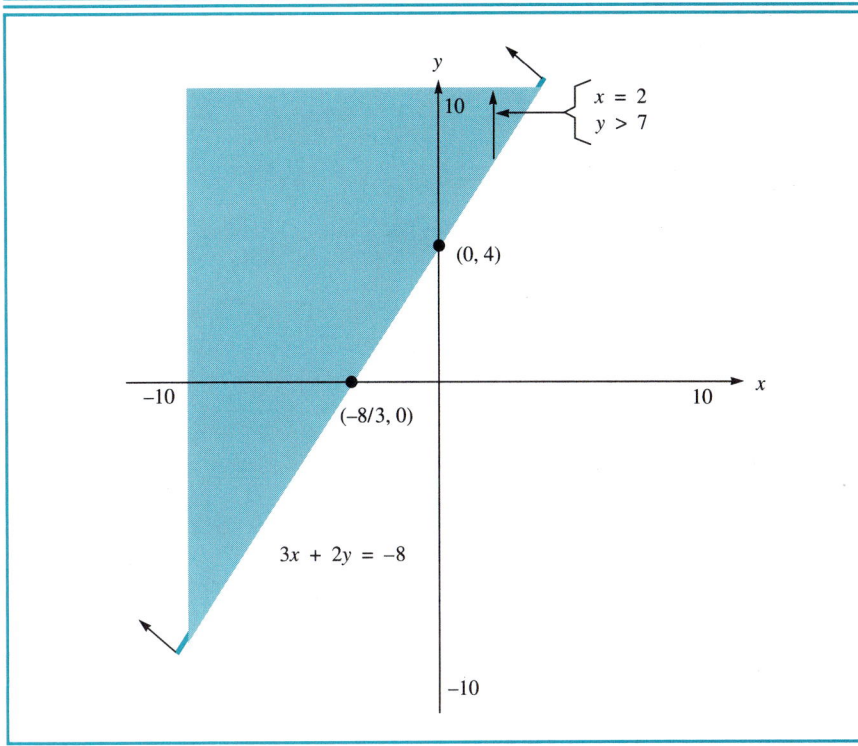

b) To solve the inequality algebraically, we isolate y on the left side as follows:

$$3x - 2y < -8$$
$$-2y < -3x - 8$$
$$y > \frac{3}{2}x + 4$$
$$y > 1.5x + 4.$$

The general solution is therefore

$$x \text{ arbitrary}$$
$$y > 1.5x + 4.$$

Here the strict inequality $>$ means that only points above the line are included in the solution space.

c) If $x = 2$, we have from the general solution

$$y > 1.5(2) + 4$$
$$y > 3 + 4$$
$$y > 7$$

so the specific solution set is ($x = 2$, $y > 7$). Note that $y = 7$ is not in this solution.

Exercise. Say $x - 3y \leq 12$. a) Write the general algebraic solution. b) On which side of the line does the solution space lie? c) Write the specific solution set if $x = 9$.
Answer: a) $y \geq (1/3)x - 4$. b) Above the line. c) ($x = 9$, $y \geq -1$).

To graph solution spaces, the line can be drawn from its intercepts or any two of its points and the side of the line on which the solution space lies indicated by arrows, as in Figures A2–9 and A2–10.

To determine the side of the line on which the solution space lies,

Either: a) Solve for y. Then $y >$ means above the line and $y <$ means below the line.

Or: b) Substitute the origin (0, 0) into the inequality. If the result is a true statement, the half-space is on the same side of the plotted line as the origin. If the result is a false statement, the half-space is on the side of the plotted line that does not contain the origin. Use a simple point other than (0, 0) [such as (1, 0) or (0, 1)] if the plotted line goes through the origin.

Every line whose equation has 0 as its only constant term passes through the origin. Both intercepts occur at the origin so to get a second point on the line we pick an arbitrary value of x and solve for y. For example,

$$3y + 2x = 0$$

passes through the origin (0, 0). If we give x an arbitrary value, say 3, then we can compute

$$3y + 2(3) = 0$$
$$3y = -6$$
$$y = -2.$$

The point just determined, $(3, -2)$, along with $(0, 0)$, determines the line shown in Figure A2–11. Substituting $(0, 0)$ into $3y + 2x \geq 0$ gives

$$0 + 0 \geq 0,$$

which is true, but it does not tell us on which side of the line the solution space lies because the origin is on the line. However if we take the point $(1, 0)$ and substitute this into the inequality, we find

$$3(0) + 2(1) \geq 0$$
$$2 \geq 0,$$

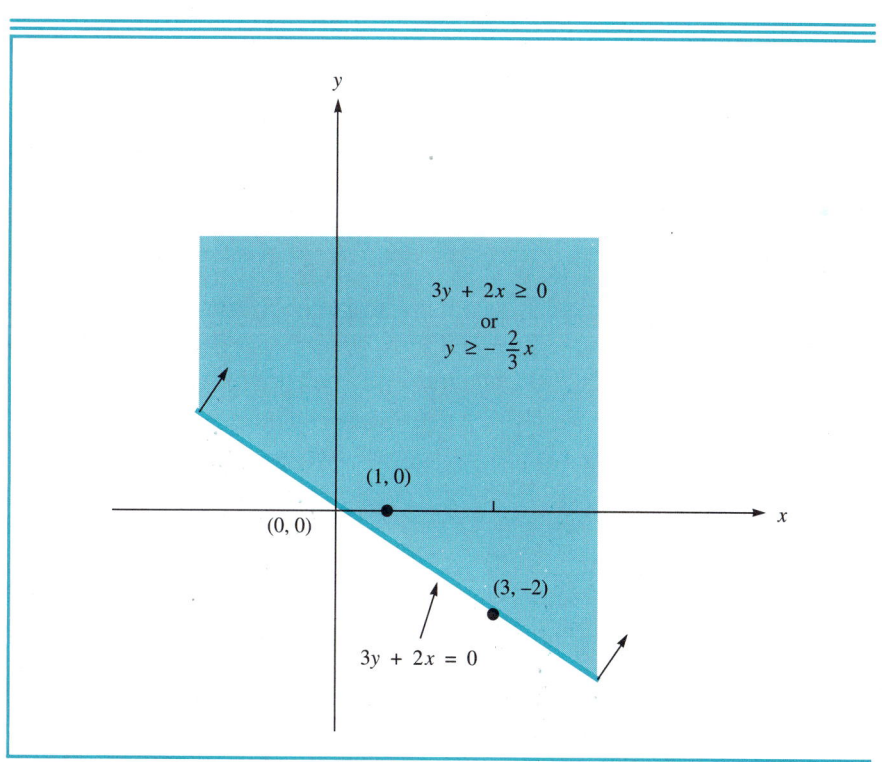

FIGURE A2–11

which is true. From Figure A2–11, we see that (1, 0) is above the line so all points in the solution space are above (or on) the line, as shown by the arrows on Figure A2–11.

The graph of the line

$$x = 6$$

is a **vertical** line through the point (6, 0), so the terms above and below cannot be applied to this case. However if we have

$$x < 6,$$

the **less than** sign, <, means the solution space is to the **left** of the vertical line $x = 6$. Similarly $x > 6$ means the solution space is to the **right** of the vertical line $x = 6$.

Exercise. What is the solution space of a) $y < 20$? b) $y > -12$?

Answer: a) The half-space below the horizontal line $y = 20$. b) The half-space above the horizontal line $y = -12$.

A2.18 PROBLEM SET A2–4

Mark (T) for true or (F) for false.
1. ( ) $-3 > -2$.
2. ( ) $a > b$ means a is greater than b.
3. ( ) If $4 < c$, then c could not equal 5.
4. ( ) $a \leq 0$ means a must be positive.
5. ( ) $a \geq 0$ means a must be positive.
6. ( ) If $a < b$, then $a = b + c$ for some positive number c.
7. ( ) If $a > b$, then b is less than a.
8. ( ) If $-a < 2$, then $a < -2$.
9. ( ) If $a - 2 > -5$, then $a > -3$.
10. ( ) If $x \leq y$, then $2x \leq 2y$.
11. ( ) The solution of $2 - 2x > -6$ is $x < 4$.
12. ( ) The origin is in the solution space of $2x + y \leq 8$.

Solve for x:
13. $3x - 2 \leq 4$.
14. $5x + 7 \geq 22$.
15. $5 - 2x > 11$.
16. $4 - 3x < 10$.
17. $4 \leq 3 + 2x$.
18. $5 \geq 6 + 4x$.

A2.18 PROBLEM SET A2–4 (concluded)

In the following, a) Write the general algebraic solution by solving for y. b) On which side of the line does the solution space lie? c) Write the specific solution space for the stated value of x.

19. $3x + 2y \le 12$; $x = 2$.
20. $2x + 5y \ge 35$; $x = 5$.
21. $7x - 5y \ge 45$; $x = 20$.
22. $3x - 2y \le 18$; $x = 10$.

State whether or not the origin is in the solution space of each of the following:

23. $3x - 7y \le 6$.
24. $2y - 3x \ge 4$.
25. $y - 2x \ge -1$.
26. $3x + 2y \le -5$.

Graph the following in two-space. Indicate by arrows the side of the line on which the solution space lies.

27. $3y - 2x \le 36$.
28. $2x - 10y \le 20$.
29. $5x + 2y \ge 40$.
30. $2x + 3y \le 60$.
31. $y \ge 5$.
32. $x \le 10$.
33. $x \ge 0$.
34. $y \ge 0$.
35. $y - 3x \le 0$.
36. $2x + 3y \le 0$.

A2.19 REVIEW PROBLEMS

Solve for x, citing the operations performed.

1. $3x - 2 = 2x + 5$.
2. $\dfrac{2x}{3} - 1 = 5x$.
3. $\dfrac{3 + 2x}{4} - 2 = x$.
4. $\dfrac{2(a - x)}{b} + 3x = c$.
5. $2a = \dfrac{x}{3 - cx}$.
6. $\dfrac{3}{a(x - 1)} + \dfrac{1}{2} - b = 0$.
7. $5(x - b) = a + b[3 - 2(x + 1)]$.
8. $\dfrac{2}{3} - \dfrac{3x}{4} = 4x(2 - b)$.
9. $x - \dfrac{c}{d} = a - \dfrac{3[2 - b(x - 1)]}{4}$.
10. $\dfrac{1}{1 - x} + 1 = b$.

---

11. A square office 1,000 feet by 1,000 feet is to be partitioned into two offices by a single interior wall. The difference between the perimeters of the resulting two offices is to be 400 feet. What are their dimensions?

12. The sum of three consecutive even integers is 156. What are they?

13. a) Choose any number. Add 8 to the number and

A2.19 REVIEW PROBLEMS (continued)

multiply the result by 4. Now subtract 32 and multiply this result by 6. Finally divide the last result by 24. What is your final result?

b) Repeat (a) using the starting value x.

14. a) Take the year in which you were born, quadruple it, and then add 20. Now multiply this result by 50. Next add twice your age and subtract 1,000. Finally divide the last result by 200. What does the integral portion of this number represent? The decimal portion?

b) Repeat (a) using b for year of birth and a for age.

In the following compute x, given that $a = 6$, $b = 2$, and $c = 10$.

15. $x = \dfrac{ab - c}{b}$.

16. $x = \dfrac{a^2b - b}{c}$.

17. $x = \dfrac{c^2/b}{a}$.

18. $x = \sqrt{c^2 - a^2}$.

19. $x = \left(3c - \dfrac{a}{2}\right)^{1/3}$.

20. $x = (3ab)^{-3/2}$.

21. $x = (c - a - b)[2b - a(c - 5b)]$.

22. $x = \dfrac{a^2/b - c}{b^2}$.

In the following, compute the exact value of y in the form of a fraction in the lowest terms, given that

$$a = \frac{2}{7}, \quad b = \frac{1}{3}, \quad c = \frac{4}{9}, \quad d = \frac{5}{12}, \quad x = \frac{1}{8}, \quad z = \frac{1}{5}.$$

23. $y = \dfrac{x}{a}$.

24. $y = \dfrac{ab}{2}$.

25. $y = d - \dfrac{1}{a}$.

26. $y = ax + bz$.

27. $y = \left(1 - \dfrac{b}{d}\right)^3$.

28. $y = (1 + 19x)^{1/3}$.

29. $y = \sqrt{c - b}$.

30. $y = \dfrac{b/2 + 3x}{1 + a}$.

---

31. Compute y to the nearest cent if

$$y = at + b(t - c),$$
$$a = 4\tfrac{1}{7}\%, \quad b = 22\%,$$
$$c = \$18{,}000, \text{ and}$$
$$t = \$28{,}000.$$

32. The equation relating the cost, C, of an item to its retail price, R, is $C + pR = R$, where p is the percent markup on the retail price.

a) What percent markup on retail is achieved if an item costs $10 and sells at a retail price of $15?

b) How much can a merchant pay for an item if he wishes to sell it for $20 and achieve a markup that is 30 percent of the retail price?

c) If the merchant seeks to achieve a markup that is 35 percent of the retail price, at which price should he sell an item that cost him $13?

33. Compute y accurate to three decimals if $x = 0.05$ and

$$y = \frac{(1 + x)^{-3} + 1}{x}.$$

A2.19 REVIEW PROBLEMS (continued)

34. The amount of interest, I, earned on P dollars at simple interest of r percent per year for t years is $I = Prt$. Assuming a year to have 360 days,
    a) How many days will it take for $2,000 to earn $50 interest at 4 percent?
    b) How many dollars must be invested at $5\frac{1}{3}$ percent if interest in the amount of $100 is to be earned in 90 days?

35. Temperature in degrees Fahrenheit, F, is related to temperature in degrees Celsius, C, by the formula
    $$F = \frac{9}{5}C + 32.$$
    Find the Celsius temperatures corresponding to the following Fahrenheit readings:
    a) 0.   b) 100.   c) 51.   d) -32.

36. When an asset is bought, its initial book value is $$A$. The book value will decline over the N years of the asset's life to the salvage value, $$S$. The ratio of salvage value to initial book value is $s = S/A$. In the straight-line method of computing book value from year to year, the appropriate formula is
    $$B = A\left[1 - \frac{t}{N}(1 - s)\right],$$
    where B is the book value after t years.
    a) An asset with an initial book value of $1,000 and a salvage value of $100 after 10 years of life will have what book value after three years?
    b) Solve the formula for s.
    c) If an asset with an initial book value of $1,000 and a life of 10 years is quoted as having a book value of $650 after 5 years, find the ratio of the salvage value to the initial value, and find the salvage value.
    d) What will the depreciation formula for book value be if the asset has no salvage value?

37. A customer buys an article on the installment plan. The price of the article (or the amount she still owes after making a down payment) is B dollars. The seller adds a carrying charge of C dollars and requires that the debt be paid off by n equal payments. Letting y be the number of payments that would be made in a year (that is, if payments are weekly, y is 52; and if payments are monthly, y is 12), and letting r be the equivalent simple interest rate being paid by the customer, a formula states
    $$r = \frac{2yC}{B(n + 1)}.$$
    a) An article priced at $200 is purchased. The customer pays $50 down. The seller adds a carrying charge of $28.50 and requires the debt to be repaid in 18 equal monthly installments. What is the amount of each installment and what is the interest rate being charged?
    b) If the simple interest equivalent of the installment rate is to be 30 percent, what should be the carrying charge on an article priced at $300 if the debt is to be paid off in 12 monthly installments and no down payment is made?

38. If D (demand) is the number of units of an item that can be sold when the item is priced at p cents per unit, and if
    $$D = \frac{20}{p - 1} - 1$$
    for values of p greater than 1 but less than 21, at what price will the demand be
    a) 19 units?
    b) 9 units?
    c) 3 units?
    d) 1 unit?

39. Graph the following equations:
    a) $y = 2x + 1$.
    b) $5y + 4x - 20 = 0$.
    c) $y = \frac{x}{3}$.
    d) $x - y = 1$.
    e) $y = 8 - x^2$.
    f) $y = x^2 - 10x + 15$.

40. Solve by the quadratic formula:
    a) $x^2 - 2x - 2 = 0$.
    b) $4x^2 - 4x + 1 = 0$.
    c) $x^2 + 2x + 5 = 0$.

41. Solve by factoring:
    a) $6x^2 - 5x + 1 = 0$.
    b) $16x^2 - 40x + 25 = 0$.
    c) $3x^2 - 48x = 0$.
    d) $x^2 - 100 = 0$.

A2.19 REVIEW PROBLEMS *(concluded)*

In Problems 42 through 47, a) Solve for y and write the general algebraic solution. b) On which side of the line does the solution space lie? c) Write the specific solution space for the stated value of x.

42. $x - y < 5; x = 10$.
43. $x + y > 3; x = 1$.
44. $2x - 3y < -5; x = 2$.
45. $-2x + 5y > 2; x = 4$.
46. $4x - 3y > -5; x = 7$.
47. $x - y \leq 0; x = 5$.

Solve for x:

48. $2 - 3x \leq 6$.
49. $2x + 7 \geq 4$.
50. $7 - 4x \leq 0$.
51. $3 \geq 5 - 2x$.
52. $0 \leq 2x + 3$.
53. $x - 4 \geq 0$.

SETS

APPENDIX 3

A3.1 INTRODUCTION

This appendix contains the basics of sets and set operations together with an introduction to relations and functions. This material provides helpful background material to Chapters 1 and 11.

A3.2 SET TERMINOLOGY

Some simple notions about groups or collections or **sets** are core ideas in mathematics. We use braces to indicate a set, and specify the **members** or **elements** of the set within the braces. Thus

$$\{\text{Boston, Wellesley, Newton}\}$$

is a set whose members (elements) are the cities Boston, Wellesley, and Newton. Again,

$$\{3, 4, 7, 8\}$$

is a set of numbers whose elements (members) are 3, 4, 7, and 8. The symbols ε and $\not\varepsilon$ are membership symbols. ε is read as "is a member of," $\not\varepsilon$ as "is not a member of." For example,

$$3 \; \varepsilon \; \{3, 4, 7, 8\}$$

says that 3 is a member (or element) of the $\{3, 4, 7, 8\}$ while

$$5 \; \not\varepsilon \; \{3, 4, 7, 8\}$$

says that 5 is not an element of this same set.

Each element of a set must be unique. For example, in set terminology, the numbers 1, 3, 4, 4 would be a set whose elements are 1, 3, and 4. A set may have no elements, a finite number of elements, or an unlimited number of elements. The set with no elements is called the **empty** (or **null**) **set** and is symbolized by ϕ, without braces. A set with an unlimited number of elements is said to be an **infinite set.** Two sets are **equal** if, and only if, they contain exactly the same elements. The expression

$$\{x | x \text{ is an integer between 5 and 6}\} = \phi$$

says the set of integers between 5 and 6 has no elements; it is the empty set. Note that the vertical line symbol is read **such that,** and the whole statement is read as: **The set of all x's such that x is an integer between 5 and 6 is the empty set.**

> **Exercise.** Read the following aloud:
> $$\{x|x \text{ is a red spade in a bridge deck}\} = \phi.$$
> **Answer:** The set of red spades in a bridge deck is the empty set.

The expression
$$\{x|x \text{ is an integer between 5 and 7}\} = \{6\}$$
says that the set of integers between 5 and 7 is the set with the single element 6. The next expression states that the set of integers between 5 and 10 is the set whose elements are 6, 7, 8, 9:
$$\{x|x \text{ is an integer between 5 and 10}\} = \{6, 7, 8, 9\}.$$

> **Exercise.** Express in set symbols that the numbers whose square is 25 are 5 and -5.
> **Answer:** $\{x|x \text{ is a number whose square is 25}\} = \{5, -5\}$.

The set specified by
$$\{x|x \text{ is an integer}\}$$
is an infinite set so we cannot completely list all its members.

> **Exercise.** Using braces and the symbols for set membership, express the facts that 1/2 is not an integer and 13 is an integer.
> **Answer:** $1/2 \notin \{x|x \text{ is an integer}\}$; $13 \,\varepsilon\, \{x|x \text{ is an integer}\}$.

It is conventional to use a capital letter, without braces, when an entire set is to be named by one symbol. For example, we might let E represent the (infinite) set of even integers; thus
$$E = \{x|x \text{ is an even integer}\}.$$
We may then refer to E by statements such as
$$3 \notin E \quad \text{and} \quad 4 \,\varepsilon\, E,$$
which say that 3 is not a member of E and 4 is a member of E.

Set terminology is not limited to collections of numbers. We may talk, for example, about the set of residents of New York, classifying residents as being members of the set and nonresidents as not being members of the set.

> **Exercise.** In set symbols, write the relationship of $ to L, and Q to L, if $L = \{x|x \text{ is a capital English letter}\}$.
> **Answer:** $ \notin L$. $Q \in L$.

A3.3 SET SPECIFICATION

A set is specified by identifying its elements. The **roster method** of specification lists each member of the set. The **descriptive method** states the rule or condition that distinguishes members of the set from nonmembers. Thus

$$S = \{1, 3, 5, 7, 9\}$$

specifies a set by the roster method. The same set could be specified by the condition that its members be odd numbers between 0 and 10; a descriptive specification therefore would be

$$S = \{x|x \text{ is an odd number between 0 and 10}\}.$$

In either specification it is clear whether an object is or is not a member of the set; for example,

$$3 \in S \quad \text{and} \quad 4 \notin S.$$

> **Exercise.** Specify $W = \{x|x \text{ is a day in the week}\}$ by the roster method.
> **Answer:** $W = \{\text{Sunday, Monday, Tuesday, Wednesday, Thursday, Friday, Saturday}\}$.

The set of positive integers, like any infinite set, cannot be listed completely. We may specify the set by the descriptive method as $P = \{\text{Positive integers}\}$ or by

$$P = \{1, 2, 3, \ldots\}$$

where the three dots are read **and so on.** We shall classify this last expression as being a roster specification, although in fact it is really a roster-like descriptive specification.

> **Exercise.** Specify the set of positive odd integers by the three-dot convention.
> **Answer:** $O = \{1, 3, 5, \ldots\}$.

A3.4 SOLUTION SETS FOR EQUATIONS

The statement, **two plus three equals five,** is a **sentence** that can be written as

$$2 + 3 = 5.$$

Similarly the sentence, **y plus three equals five,** can be expressed as

$$y + 3 = 5.$$

Sentences that use the equality symbol, $=$, are called **equations.** If we replace the symbol y by a number that makes the equation become a **true** sentence, the replacement number is a member of the **solution set** of the equation. In the case at hand, the solution set has only one element, 2. We may write

$$\{y|y + 3 = 5\} = \{2\}.$$

Exercise. a) Write the set symbols for $y + 1 = 6$. b) Translate the symbols $\{y|y - 2 = 10\} = \{12\}$.

Answer: a) $\{y|y + 1 = 6\} = \{5\}$. b) The set of y's such that y minus 2 is 10 is the set with the element 12.

A3.5 RELATIONS AND FUNCTIONS

A core concept in mathematics is defining the relationship, or correspondence, between the elements of *two* sets. One such relationship known as a **function** is of particular interest. To make clear the special nature of a functional relationship, think of the first set of elements as the set of all mothers and the second set as the set of all children. The set of mothers and the set of children are related, obviously, but there is a difference between the relationship of children to mothers and that of mothers to children. To see this difference, let children be the **starting set** and mothers be the **ending set.** If we now take a child from the starting set, there is one, **and only one,** corresponding mother in the ending set. This kind of correspondence is an example of a **functional correspondence.** If however mothers are taken as the starting set and children as the ending set, when we take a mother from the starting set, there can be **one or more** corresponding children in the ending set. Here we have a relationship that is not a functional relationship since each member of the starting set does not necessarily correspond to a unique member of the ending set.

One way to specify a function is to write pairs of elements in **order;** that is, the first element is the element from the starting set and the second is the corresponding element from the ending set. Thus, for example, the set of **ordered pairs**

$$\{(\text{child, mother})\}$$

is a function; however the set

$$\{(\text{mother, child})\}$$

is a relationship, but not a function. Similarly if we let x be any number whatsoever and $2x$ be twice whatever the number x is, the set of ordered pairs

$$\{(x, 2x)\}$$

is a function because for every first number, x, there is one, and only one, second number, $2x$. Clearly this set of ordered pairs is infinite. Some ordered pairs in the set are

$$(0, 0), \quad (1, 2), \quad \text{and} \quad (5/2, 5).$$

Usually we choose to represent functional correspondence by an equation if it is possible to do so. For example, the function

$$\{(x, 2x)\}$$

can be represented by the equation

$$y = 2x.$$

When it is necessary to specify which element is the starting element, this elment is specified in parentheses and is called the **independent variable.** For example, the last equation with functional specification would be

$$y(x) = 2x,$$

meaning x is the starting value **chosen independently** (arbitrarily). Thus taking x as 3, arbitrarily, we find the second element of the ordered pair, symbolized by $y(3)$, to be

$$y(3) = 2 \cdot 3 = 6$$

and the ordered pair

$$(3, 6)$$

is in the **solution set.** The complete (infinite) solution set is **the set of ordered pairs, (x, y), such that $y = 2x$** and we symbolize this by

$$\{(x, y) | y = 2x\}.$$

In the work we shall encounter in this book, it will be helpful to view a function as a **rule** stating how the member of the ending set is obtained for an arbitrarily selected member of the starting set. For example, if we have

$$f(x) = 5x + 1,$$

where $f(x)$ is read as **the f function of x or f of x,** the rule is

multiply 5 by x, then add 1.

Thus selecting x arbitrarily to be 20, we find

5 times 20, plus 1 = 100 plus 1 = 101.

The last is simple substitution. However, we shall have to work with expressions such as

$$f(a + 3),$$

and in such a case it is important to remember that the rule tells us that $f(a + 3)$ means

multiply 5 by $a + 3$, then add 1.

so

$$f(a + 3) = 5(a + 3) + 1$$

and if $a = 6$, then

$$f(6 + 3) = 5(6 + 3) + 1$$
$$= 46.$$

Exercise. Given $g(z) = 2z + 3$, a) How is $g(z)$ read? b) What is $g(4)$? c) State (write) the function rule. d) How would $g(a + b)$ be obtained?

Answer: a) **The g function of z or g of z.** b) 11. c) Multiply 2 by the value of z, and then add 3. d) Multiply 2 by $(a + b)$, and then add 3.

FIGURE A3–1   **FIGURE A3–2**

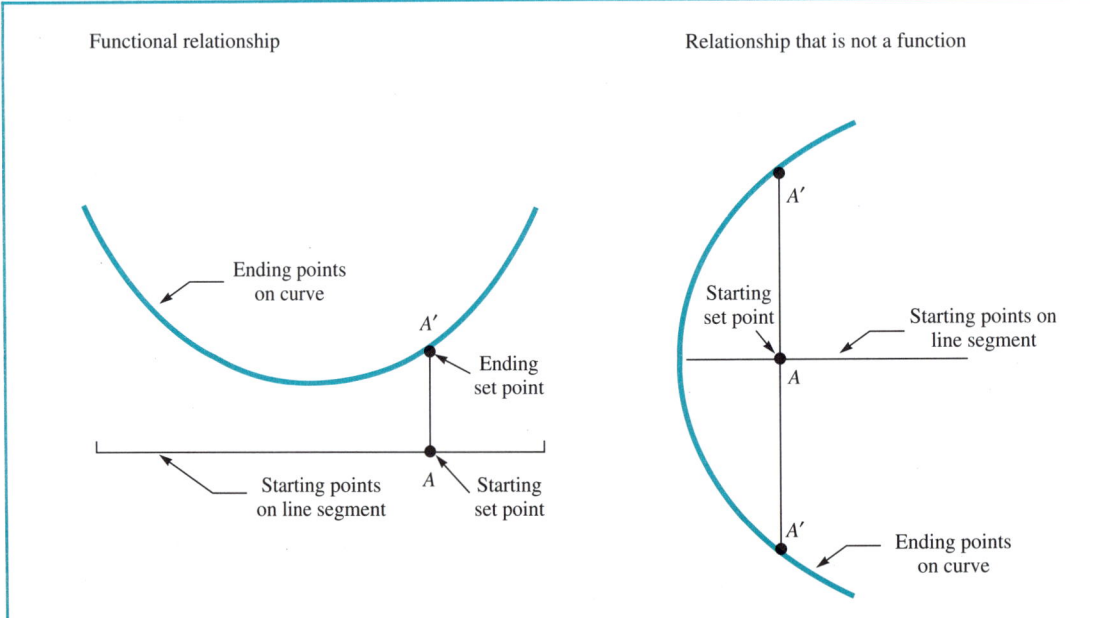

Functional relationship   Relationship that is not a function

We shall have frequent occasions to represent functions graphically, taking points on a horizontal line as being members of the starting set and a point on the graph **vertically** above or below the starting point as the corresponding member of the ending set. For example, Figure A3–1 represents a functional correspondence because for each point, such as A, in the starting set, there is one and only one point, A', in the ending set. However the relationship in Figure A3–2 is not a functional correspondence because a vertical line through a member of the starting set intersects the graph (the ending set) in two points.

A3.6 PROBLEM SET A3–1

1. Read the following aloud. For example, $A = \{5, 10, 15, \ldots, 100\}$ is read, **A is the set whose elements are 5, 10, 15, and so on, through 100.**
   a) $B = \{2, 4, 6\}$.
   b) $C = \{0\}$.
   c) $Q = \{1, 3, 5, \ldots, 29\}$.
   d) $F = \{a, e, i, o, u\}$.
   e) $L = \{$George, Charles$\}$.
   f) $K = \{2, 4, 6, \ldots\}$.

2. Specify each of the following sets by the descriptive method.
   a) $F = \{a, e, i, o, u\}$.
   b) $S = \{3, 6, 9, \ldots\}$.
   c) $P = \{1, 2, 3, 4, 5\}$.
   d) $G = \{A, B, C, D, E\}$.
   e) $R = \{100, 101, 102, \ldots\}$.
   f) $J = \{-1, -3, -5, \ldots, -101\}$.

3. Specify each of the following by roster:
   a) $\{x|x$ is an odd number less than 9$\}$.
   b) $\{x|x$ is one of the first four months of the year$\}$.
   c) $\{x|x$ is a positive even multiple of 7$\}$.
   d) $\{x|x$ is a positive number, less than 1,000, that is exactly divisible by 5$\}$.
   e) $\{x|x$ is a number representing the ratios formed by dividing integers by 0$\}$.
   f) $\{x|x$ is a square of the integers from 1 through 10$\}$.

4. Why is $\{0\}$ not equal to ϕ?

5. Using set membership symbols and the roster specification of the sets, write the following:
   a) 1/2 is not a positive integer.
   b) 64 is a multiple of 4.
   c) a is a lower-case vowel.
   d) 4 is not a positive odd number.
   e) $ is not a letter in the lower-case English alphabet.
   f) This problem does not have a part g.

6. Given $A = \{1, 3, 4, 7\}$, $B = \{3, 7, 12\}$, $C = \{1, 5, 8\}$, write the following sets:
   a) The set containing all elements that are members of A, or members of B, or members of both A and B.
   b) The set of elements that are members of both A and B.
   c) The set of elements that are members of both B and C.
   d) The set of elements that are members of A but not members of B.
   e) The set of elements that are members of both A and C.
   f) The set of elements that are members of all three sets.

7. a) Write the set symbols for $y + 2 = 10$.
   b) Translate the symbols
   $\{y|y + 5 = 8\} = \{3\}$.

8. a) Write the set symbols for $m - 6 = 4$ and its solution set.
   b) Translate the symbols $\{q|2q = 6\} = \{3\}$.

9. What is the solution set for $\{z|2z + 5 = 2z + 7\}$?

10. What is the solution set for $\{y|4y + 1 = 12\}$?

A3.6 PROBLEM SET A3-1 (concluded)

In Problems 11 through 14, the first mentioned set is the starting set.

11. Each state in the United States has two senators.
    a) Is the relationship between the set of states and the set of senators a functional correspondence? Why?
    b) Is the relationship between the set of senators and the set of states a functional correspondence? Why?

12. a) Is the relationship between the set of individual apples in an orchard and the set of individual apple trees in an orchard a functional correspondence? Why?
    b) Is the relationship between the set of apple trees and the set of apples a functional correspondence? Why?

13. Draw a horizontal line and a slant line intersecting the horizontal line. Then draw vertical lines intersecting the first two lines. Does the set of points at the intersection of such verticals and the horizontal line have a functional correspondence with the respective set of points at the intersection of verticals and the slant line? Why?

14. Draw a circle and a horizontal line that is a diameter of the circle. If vertical lines are drawn, does the set of points at the intersection of the vertical and the diameter have a functional correspondence with the respective set of points at the intersection of the vertical and the circle? Why?

15. If $h(z) = 4z + 7$,
    a) How is $h(z)$ read?
    b) What is $h(2)$?
    c) State the function rule.
    d) How would $h(x + 2)$ be obtained?

16. If $f(x) = 3x + 10$,
    a) How is $f(x)$ read?
    b) What is $f(5)$?
    c) State the function rule.
    d) How would $f(x + 1)$ be obtained?

17. If $y = 2x + 7$, write the symbolic expression for the solution set.

18. If $y = 5x$, write the symbolic expression for the solution set.

19. Does $y = 10x + 25$ represent a functional correspondence? Why?

20. If the starting set is 0 or any whole number and the elements of the ending set are obtained by dividing 5 by the starting element, is there a functional relationship between the sets? Why?

A3.7 SET OPERATIONS

= Subset

If every element of a set B is also an element of a set A, then B is called a **subset** of A. For example, if

$$A = \{1, 3, 6, 9\} \quad \text{and} \quad B = \{3, 6\},$$

then B is a subset of A. Moreover in this example, B is a **proper subset** of A because it does not contain all the elements of A. If

$$C = \{8, 9, 10\} \quad \text{and} \quad D = \{8, 9, 10\},$$

then D is an **improper subset** of C, and vice versa, because all the elements of one are elements of the other. It follows that if two sets are equal, they are improper subsets of each other. The empty set, ϕ, is by definition a proper subset of every set except itself. If $S = \{a, b, c\}$, then the proper subsets of S are

$$\phi, \ \{a\}, \ \{b\}, \ \{c\}, \ \{a, b\}, \ \{a, c\}, \ \text{and} \ \{b, c\}.$$

> **Exercise.** List all eight subsets of $K = \{2, 4, 6\}$.[1]
> **Answer:** ϕ, $\{2\}$, $\{4\}$, $\{6\}$, $\{2, 4\}$, $\{2, 6\}$, $\{4, 6\}$, K.

The **intersection** of two sets A and B is a set whose elements are elements of both A and B. The intersection symbol is like an inverted U. Thus

$$A \cap B$$

= Intersection

is read as **A intersection B** or **the intersection of A and B**. If we have

$$A = \{4, 8, 9, 11\} \quad \text{and} \quad B = \{8, 11, 14\} \quad \text{and} \quad C \{3, 5\},$$

then

$$A \cap B = \{8, 11\} \quad \text{and} \quad A \cap C = \phi.$$

The last expression says that the intersection of A and C is the empty set because the two sets have no common members. Sets with no common members also are said to be **disjoint sets.**

> **Exercise.** Given $A = \{a, b, c, d, e\}$ and $B = \{e, f, g, \ldots, z\}$, write $A \cap B$.
> **Answer:** $\{e\}$.

The **union** of sets A and B is a set containing those elements that are members of A or members of B, or members of both A and B. A U-like symbol represents the union; thus

$$A \cup B$$

= Union

is read **A union B** or **the union of A and B**. If

$$A = \{a, b, c, d, e\} \quad \text{and} \quad B = \{c, e, f, k\},$$

then

$$A \cup B = \{a, b, c, d, e, f, k\}.$$

> **Exercise.** Find $A \cup B$ if $A = \{2, 7, 8, 9, 13\}$ and $B = \{1, 8, 13, 22\}$.
> **Answer:** $\{1, 2, 7, 8, 9, 13, 22\}$.

---

[1] If a set has n elements, then the set will have 2^n subsets, counting the null set and the improper subset.

FIGURE A3-3

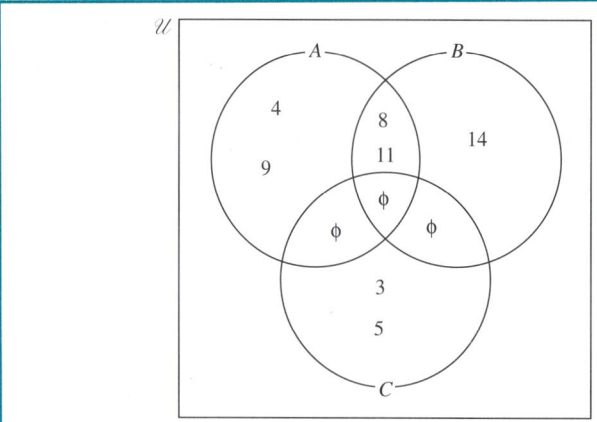

It is helpful to illustrate the ideas of intersection and union diagrammatically as in Figure A3-3. Returning to the earlier example with

$$A = \{4, 8, 9, 11\}, \quad B = \{8, 11, 14\}, \quad \text{and} \quad C = \{3, 5\},$$

if we think of A as a set containing all the points in circle A, and similarly for B and C, then $A \cap B = \{8, 11\}$ is the set of points indicated by the shaded area. In addition, $A \cup B$ is the set of points containing all the points in both circles A and B; $A \cup C$ contains all the points in circles A and C; and $A \cap C = \phi$ because A and C have no points in common so they are disjoint. Note we have adapted the convention of placing the empty set symbol ϕ in an area that has no elements.

= Complement

The **complement** of a set A is the set of all elements **not in set** A but in the **candidate set** from which the members of A were selected. The complement of A is denoted by A'. For example, if

$$A = \{\text{odd integers}\},$$

then the complement of A is

$$A' = \{\text{even integers}\}$$

since 0 is considered to be an even number. Similarly, if

$$A = \{\text{all nonnegative real numbers}\},$$

then the complement of A is

$$A' = \{\text{all negative real numbers}\}.$$

The candidate set from which members of all other sets are taken is frequently called the **universal set** and denoted by $\mathcal{U}$. For example, suppose

$$\mathcal{U} = \{1, 2, 3, 4, 5, 6, 7\}$$

and

$$A = \{1, 3, 5, 7\},$$

the odd members of $\mathcal{U}$. Then, the complement of A is

$$A' = \{2, 4, 6\},$$

the even members of $\mathcal{U}$. Note that

$$\mathcal{U} = A \cup A'.$$

In other words, the universal set is the union of the set A and its complement A'. This property will hold in general; that is, **the union of any set and its complement is the universal set.** Note also that

$$A \cap A' = \phi,$$

so that the intersection of the set A and its complement A' is the empty set. This property will also hold in general; that is, **the intersection of any set and its complement is the empty set.**

Diagrams such as the one in Figure A3–3 are usually called **Venn diagrams** after the English logician John Venn (1834–1883). The general Venn diagrams representing the set operations of subset, intersection, union, and complementation are shown in Figures A3–4A through A3–4D, respectively.

FIGURE A3–4A   **FIGURE A3–4B**

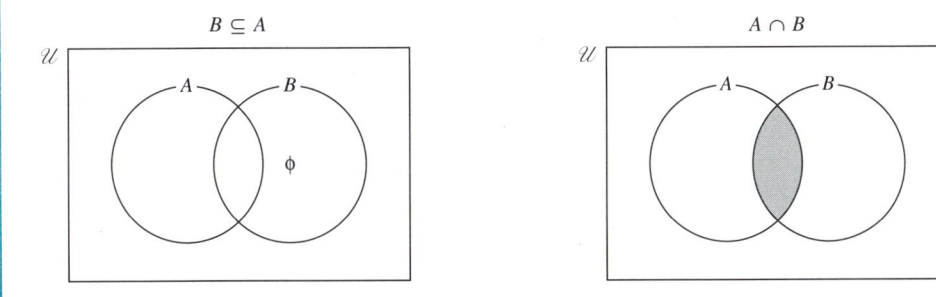

FIGURE A3-4C

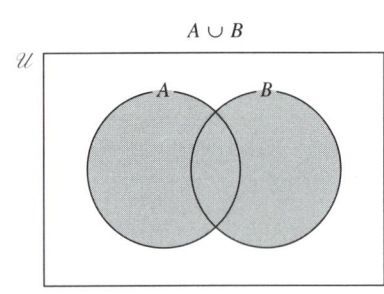

FIGURE A3-4D

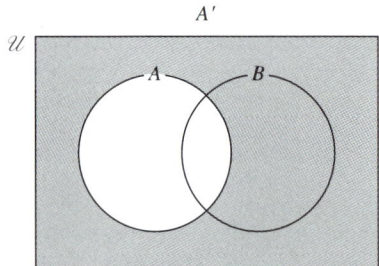

A3.8 PROBLEM SET A3-2

1. Figure A shows set R with points a, b, c, d, and e and similarly for sets S and T. Write the following sets by the roster method:
   a) $R \cup S$.
   b) $R \cup T$.
   c) $R \cap S$.
   d) $R \cap T$.
   e) $S \cup T$.
   f) $S \cap T$.

2. If $A = \{1, 3, 5, \ldots\}$, $B = \{0, 2, 4, 6, \ldots\}$, and $C = \{5, 7, 9\}$, write the following sets by the roster method:
   a) $A \cup B$.
   b) $A \cap B$.
   c) $A \cap C$.
   d) $B \cap C$.
   e) $A \cup C$.

3. If A is the set of face cards in a standard 52-card deck and B is the set of queens, what will be the elements of $A \cup B$ and $A \cap B$?

4. If A is the set of face cards in a standard 52-card deck, B is the set of red cards, and C is the set of nines, what will be the elements in $A \cup B$, $A \cap B$, $A \cap C$, and $B \cap C$?

5. If M represents the set of all points on one line in a plane, and N the points on a different line in the plane, what is $M \cap N$
   a) If the lines are parallel?
   b) If the lines are not parallel?

FIGURE A

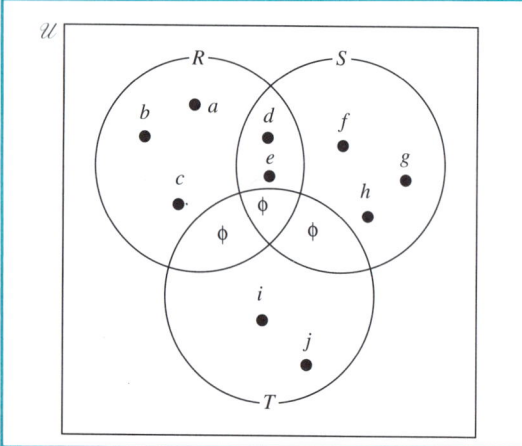

6. If R means rain tomorrow and W means warmer tomorrow, what do the following mean:
   a) $R \cup W$?
   b) $R \cap W$?

7. If $\mathcal{U} = \{$all positive integers$\}$ and $A = \{$all integers greater than 7$\}$, what is A'?

A3.8 PROBLEM SET A3-2 (concluded)

8. If $\mathcal{U}$ = {letters of English alphabet} and A = {a, b, c, d, y, z}, B = {d, e, f, u, v, w}, C = {g, h, i, r, s, t}, and D = {j, k, l, o, p, q}, list each of the following sets:
   a) $A \cup B$.
   b) $A \cap B$.
   c) $(A \cup B)'$.
   d) $(A \cap B)'$.
   e) $A' \cap B'$.
   f) $A' \cup B'$.
   g) $(A \cup B) \cup (C \cup D)'$.
   h) $(A \cap B) \cap (C \cap D)'$.

9. a) Compare the answers to Problems 8c and 8e. What general rule is suggested?
   b) Compare the answers to Problems 8d and 8f. What general rule is suggested?
   c) The rules in (a) and (b) are called **DeMorgan's Laws.** Verify these laws by drawing Venn diagrams shading the resultant sets on each side of the rules.

A3.9 REVIEW PROBLEMS

1. Read the following aloud. For example, A = {5, 10, 15, ... , 100} is read, "A is the set whose elements are 5, 10, 15, and so on, through 100."
   a) {5, 6, 7, 9}.
   b) B = {Amherst, Babson, Colgate, Dartmouth}.
   c) C = {1, 3, 5, 7, ... }.
   d) D = {A, B, C, ... , Z}.
   e) $E = \left\{1, \dfrac{1}{2}, \dfrac{1}{4}, \dfrac{1}{8}, \ldots\right\}$.
   f) F = {Tim, Dick, Harry}.

2. Specify each of the following sets by the descriptive method:
   a) A = {1, 3, 5, 7, 9, ... }.
   b) B = {5, 10, 15, ... }.
   c) C = {101, 102, 103, ... , 999}.
   d) D = {M, A, R, Y}.

3. Specify each of the following by the roster method:
   a) A = {$x|x$ is a letter in the word *Purdue*}.
   b) $B = \left\{\begin{array}{l}x|x \text{ is one of the first nine positive} \\ \text{prime numbers}\end{array}\right\}$.
   c) C = {$x|x$ is a positive odd multiple of 4}.
   d) $D = \left\{\begin{array}{l}x|x \text{ is one of the first five positive} \\ \text{even multiples of 3}\end{array}\right\}$.

4. Using set membership symbols and the roster method of specification of the sets, write
   a) The letter s is among the letters in the word *Texas*.
   b) 7 is not a positive integral multiple of 3.
   c) 3 is not a positive integral power of 2.
   d) 5 is not a lower-case English letter.

5. a) Write the set symbols for $t + 1 = 20$ and its solution set.
   b) Translate the symbols
      $\{y|3y + 5 = 11\} = \{2\}$.

6. Given the relation $y = x$,
   a) Is the relation a function? Explain.
   b) What is the function rule?
   c) What is meant by the **solution set** for the equation?
   d) How many elements are there in the solution set?
   e) What are the elements in the solution set corresponding to x = 1, 2, 3, 4?

7. What is the solution set for $\{t|t = t + 1\}$?

8. Suppose x is any positive whole number and y is any positive whole number that is an exact divisor of x. Is the relation between y and x a function? Explain.

9. Given A = {5, 10, 12, 13, 15}, B = {2, 10, 13, 14}, and C = {12, 16, 17}, write the following sets:
   a) The set containing all elements that are members of A or members of B or members of both A and B.
   b) The set of elements that are members of both A and B.
   c) The set of elements that are members of both B and C.
   d) The set of elements that are members of A but not members of B.

A3.9 REVIEW PROBLEMS (concluded)

e) The set of elements that are members of both A and C.
f) The set of elements that are members of all three sets.
g) The set of elements that are members of both A' and B'.
h) The set of elements that are members of both A' and C'.
i) The set of elements that are members of A', B', and C'.

10. Figure B shows set R with points p, q, r, s, and t, and similarly for sets S and T. Write the following sets by the roster method:
   a) $R \cup S$.
   b) $R \cup T$.
   c) $R \cap S$.
   d) $R \cap T$.
   e) $S \cup T$.
   f) $S \cap T$.
   g) $R' \cap T'$.
   h) $R' \cap S'$.
   i) $R' \cap S' \cap T$.

11. If $A = \{5, 10, 12, 15, 19\}$, $B = \{3, 10, 15\}$, and $C = \{7, 12\}$, write the following sets by the roster method:
   a) $A \cup B$.
   b) $A \cap B$.
   c) $A \cap C$.
   d) $B \cap C$.
   e) $A \cup C$.
   f) $B \cup C$.

12. Make a diagram showing sets R, S, and T (like the diagram in Problem 10) corresponding to the following requirements:
   a) $R \cap T = \{x\}$.
   b) $R \cap S = \{z\}$.
   c) $T \cap S = \phi$.
   d) $R \cup S = \{v, x, y, z\}$.
   e) $R \cup T = \{w, x, y, z\}$.

13. If sets M and N are, respectively, the sets of points on the perimeters of two concentric circles, what is $M \cap N$?

14. If P is the set of all cars with air conditioners, Q is the set with automatic shifting, and R is the set with manual (or stick) shifting, what are
   a) $P \cup Q$?
   b) $P \cap Q$?
   c) $Q \cap R$?
   d) $P \cap R$?

15. a) Write the set symbols for $y + 5 = 15$ and its solution set.
    b) Translate the symbols $\{x|x - 2 = 10\} = \{12\}$.

16. What is the solution set for $\{z|z + 7 = 30\}$?

FIGURE B

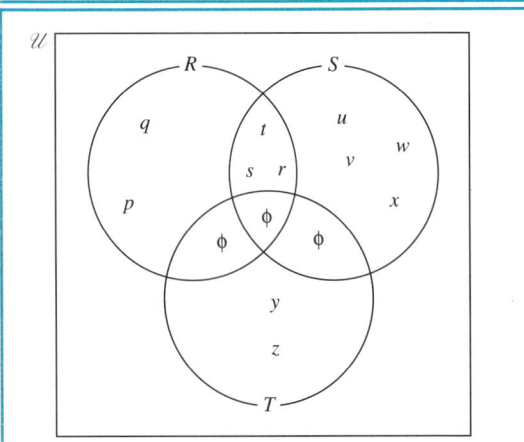

17. Is 5 in the solution set of $\{x|x < 10\}$? Why?

18. If x is a number in the starting set, and the corresponding number in the ending set is any number less than x, do the sets have a functional correspondence?

19. Each secretary in a company works for three executives, always the same three.
    a) Does the starting set of secretaries have a functional correspondence to the set of executives? Why?
    b) Does the starting set of executives have a functional correspondence to the set of secretaries?

20. If $f(x) = 20x + 50$,
    a) How is $f(x)$ read?
    b) What is $f(10)$?
    c) State the function rule.
    d) How would $f(x + 1)$ be obtained?

21. Write the symbolic expression for the solution set of $y = 12x + 6$.

22. Does $z = 3x + 5$ represent a functional correspondence? Why?

23. How many ordered pairs are there in the solution set for $y = x + 3$?

ANSWERS TO PROBLEM SETS

CHAPTER 1
Problem Set 1-1

1. a) The difference of the second (y) coordinates, $y_2 - y_1$.
    b) The difference of the first (x) coordinates, $x_2 - x_1$.
    c) The result in (a) divided by the result in (b).
2. a) The steepest line is vertical.
    b) As we go from one point to another on the line, the run is 0 (zero), so the slope ratio has a denominator of 0. A ratio with a denominator of 0 is not a number.
3. 2/3.
4. Vertical. The plane evidently crashed.
5. 1.
6. a) 8.   b) $8.
7. The slope is 0.96, and $1 - 0.96 = 0.04$. The first is the marginal propensity to consume; the second is the marginal propensity to save. The numbers 0.96 and 0.04 indicate that for an extra $1 of income, consumers spend $0.96 and save $0.04.
8. a) $16.   b) $12.   c) See Figure A.
9. 1.
10. -1.
11. $-1/8$.
12. Undefined.
13. 0.
14. 0.
15. Undefined.
16. 1.
17. 21/32.
18. -1.
19. $-11/9$.
20. Undefined.
21. 1.
22. $-1/13$.
23. See text.
24. $\dfrac{b-2}{a-3}, \dfrac{2-b}{3-a}$.

FIGURE A

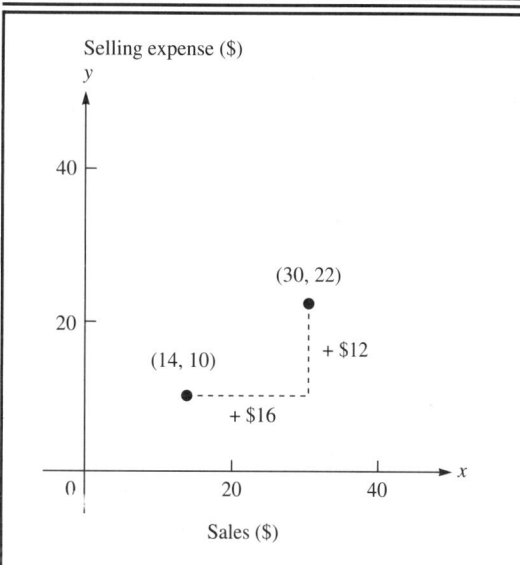

25. See Figure B (p. 986).
26. If a is not 0, there is no number x such that $a/0 = x$; if a is 0, x is ambiguous because it could have any value.
27. F.
28. T.
29. T.
30. T.
31. T.
32. T.
33. T.
34. F.
35. T.

Problem Set 1-1 (concluded)

FIGURE B

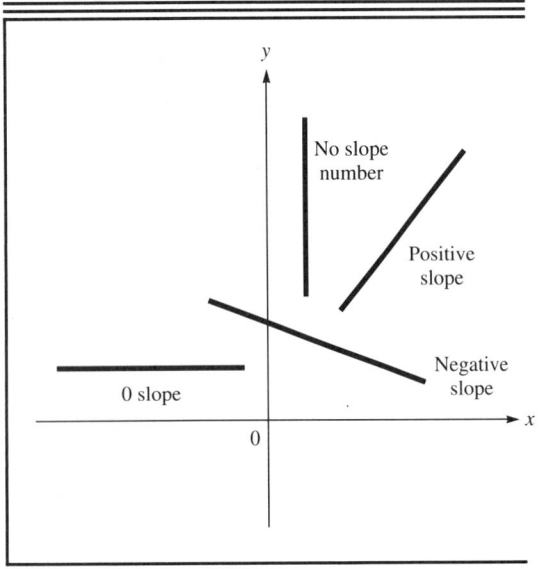

Problem Set 1-2

1. $y = 3x - 5$.
2. $y = -x + 1$.
3. $y = -\frac{2}{3}x + \frac{14}{3}$.
4. $y = \frac{1}{2}x - \frac{9}{2}$.
5. $y = -8$.
6. $y = -\frac{1}{6}x + \frac{22}{3}$.
7. $y = 13x + 57$.
8. $y = 0$.
9. $x = 5$.
10. $x = 0$.
11. $y = 4$.
12. $y = 5x - 23$.
13. $y = -\frac{1}{7}x + \frac{46}{7}$.
14. $y = \frac{6}{7}x + \frac{51}{7}$.
15. $y = x$.
16. $y = 9x + 14$.
17. $y = \frac{3}{2}x$.
18. $y = 4$.
19. $y = -\frac{3}{2}x$.
20. $x = -7$.
21. $y = \frac{1}{2}x + \frac{7}{2}$.
22. $y = 5$.
23. $y = 0$.
24. $y = -\frac{5}{7}x - \frac{29}{7}$.
25. $y = 0$.
26. $x = 0$.
27. $-24/7$.
28. -2.
29. $x = -6$.
30. a) $y = 3$.
    b) The tangent is the horizontal line $y = 500$ and shows the maximum (highest) profit is 500.
31. a) $y = 5$. b) $x = -10$.
32. $y = 0.25x + 50$.
33. $y = 3x + 50$.
34. $y = 3x + 10$.
35. a) $y = 0.8m + 0.5$.
    b) $E = 0.1V + 50$. The slope is the rate of commission.
36. F.
37. T.
38. T.
39. F.
40. F.
41. T.
42. See Figure C.
43. See Figure D.
44. See Figure E.
45. See Figure F.
46. See Figure G.
47. 3/2.
48. -1.
49. 1/3.
50. 1.
51. a) $8x + 12y = 96$.
    b) 1.5 pounds of A per pound of B.
    c) 2/3 pounds of B per pound of A.

Problem Set 1-2 (concluded)

52. $y = 2x - 6$.
53. If the equation is solved for y, the coefficient of x, which is the slope, turns out to be $-A/B$.
54. y/x is cost per unit; $y/x = 3$ or $y = 3x$ is the equation; slope is 3, and intercept 0 (line passes through the origin).
55. $2,200.

FIGURE C

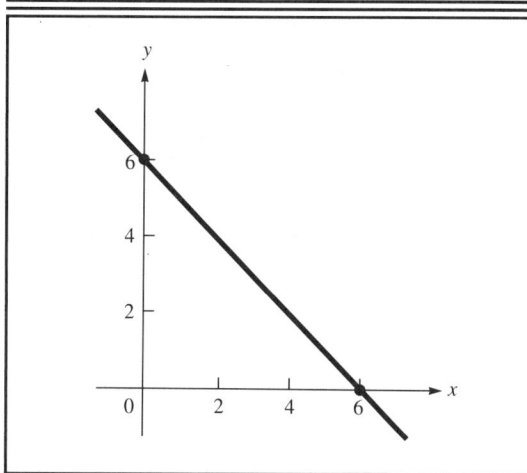

FIGURE D

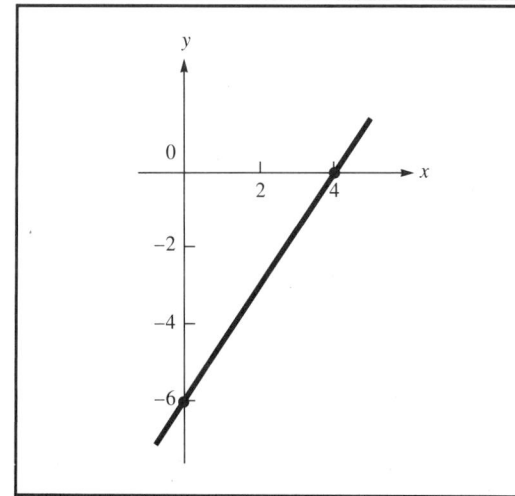

FIGURE E

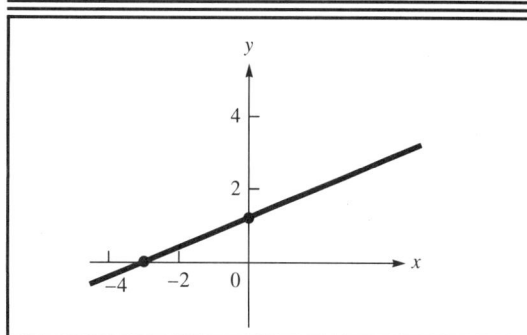

FIGURE F

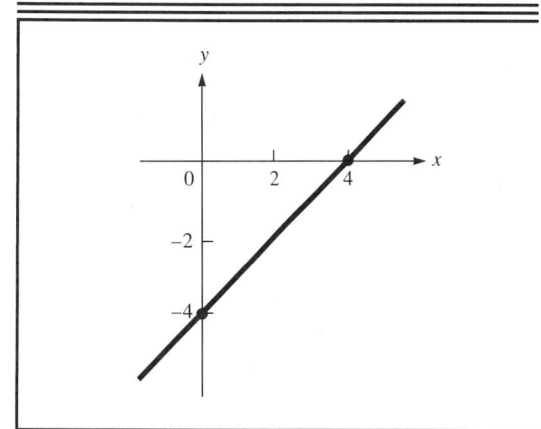

FIGURE G

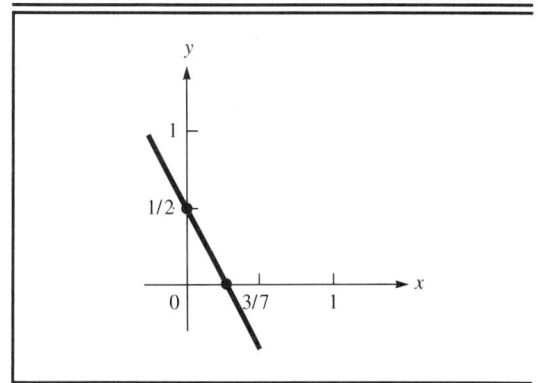

Problem Set 1-3

1. a) $y = 1.5x + 4$.   b) $y = -3x - 12$.
2. $y = 2x$.
3. $y = 0.8x$.
4. a) 1.25 miles to the right of the origin.
   b) Because the shortest distance from a point to a line is on a perpendicular to the line.
5. The coordinates of the origin, (0, 0), satisfy any equation of the form $Ax + By = 0$.
6. T.   8. T.   10. T.   12. T.   14. T.
7. T.   9. T.   11. T.   13. T.   15. T.
16. See Figure H.   18. See Figure J.
17. See Figure I.   19. See Figure K.
20. a) $C(u) = \begin{cases} 1.18u + 6.00, & 0 \le u \le 20 \\ 0.806u + 13.48, & u > 20. \end{cases}$

    See Figure L.

    b) $23.70; $1.58.   c) $53.78; $1.0756.   d) 75 units.

21. a) $C(k) = \begin{cases} 0.06021k + 6.00, & 0 \le k \le 2{,}300 \\ 0.02553k + 85.764, & k > 2{,}300. \end{cases}$

    See Figure M.

    b) $126.42; $0.06321.
    c) $187.88; $0.04697.
    d) 6,600 kwh.

22. a) $T(i) = \begin{cases} 0.15i, & 0 \le i \le \$19{,}450 \\ 0.28i - 2{,}528.50, & \$19{,}450 < i \le \$47{,}050 \\ 0.33i - 4{,}881.00, & \$47{,}050 < i \le \$97{,}620. \end{cases}$

    See Figure N (p. 990).

    b) $2,250.00.   d) $23,169.00.
    c) $7,271.50.   e) $45,000.00.

23. a) $T(i) = \begin{cases} 0.15i, & 0 \le i \le \$32{,}450 \\ 0.28i - 4{,}218.50, & \$32{,}450 < i \le \$78{,}400 \\ 0.33i - 8{,}138.50, & \$78{,}400 < i \le \$162{,}770. \end{cases}$

    See Figure O (p. 990).

    b) $2,250.00.   d) $19,911.50.
    c) $5,581.50.   e) $45,000.00.

24. a) $C(u) = \begin{cases} 2{,}495u, & 1 \le u \le 5 \\ 2{,}195u + 1{,}500, & 6 \le u \le 10 \\ 1{,}995u + 3{,}500, & u > 10. \end{cases}$

    See Figure P (p. 990).

    b) $7,485.00; $2,495.00.   e) 9 units.
    c) $19,060.00; $2,382.50.   f) 8 units.
    d) $33,245.00; $2,228.33.

25. a) $C(s) = \begin{cases} 325s + 125, & 1 \le s \le 50, \\ 275s + 2{,}625, & 51 \le s \le 100, \\ 195s + 10{,}625, & s > 100. \end{cases}$

    See Figure Q (p. 990).

    b) $9,875.00; $329.17.   d) $39,875.00; $265.83.
    c) $24,625.00; $307.81.   e) 200 suits.   f) 60 suits.

FIGURE H

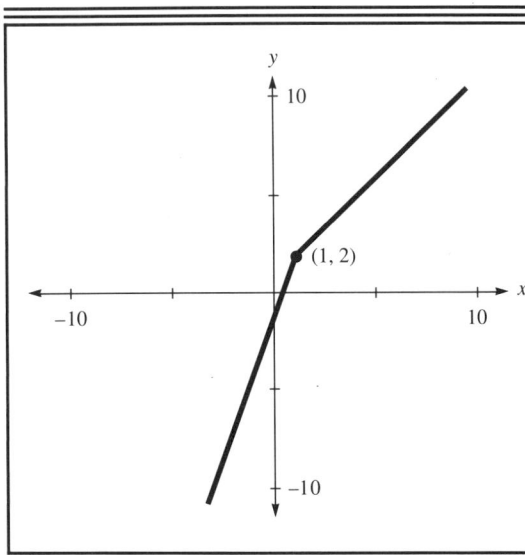

FIGURE I

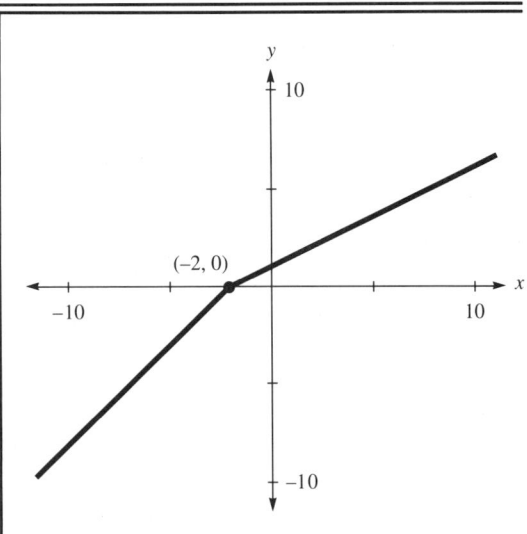

Problem Set 1-3 *(continued)*

FIGURE J

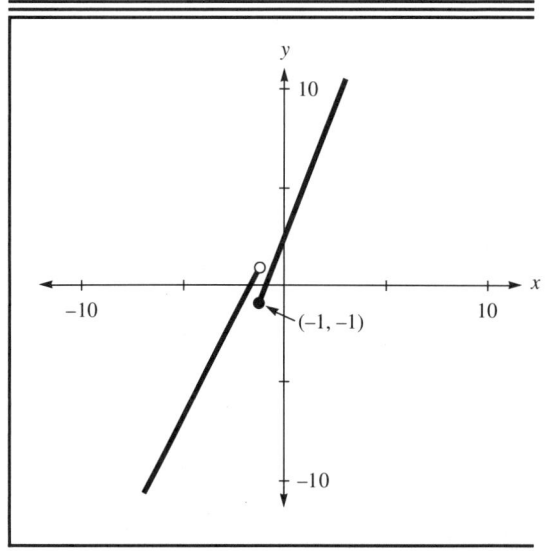

FIGURE K

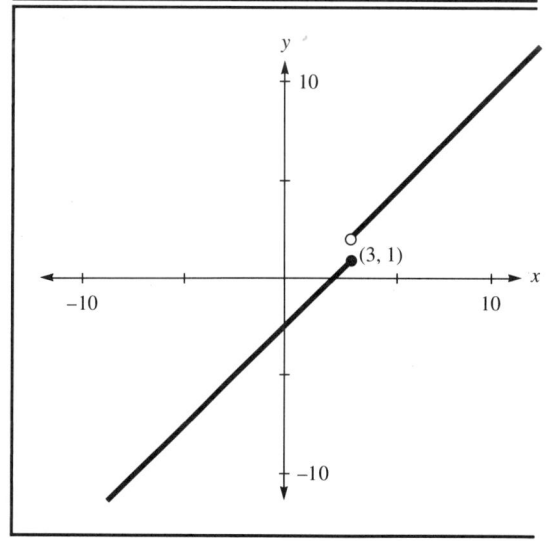

FIGURE L

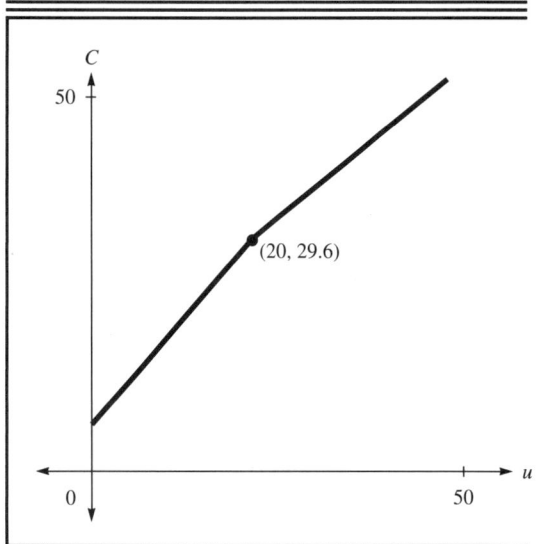

FIGURE M

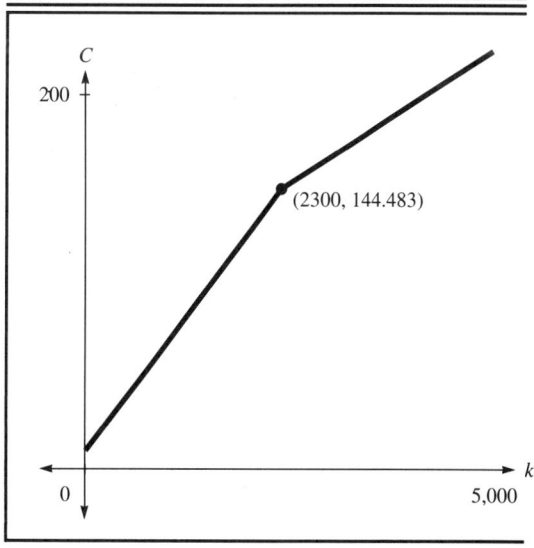

Problem Set 1-3 *(concluded)*

FIGURE N

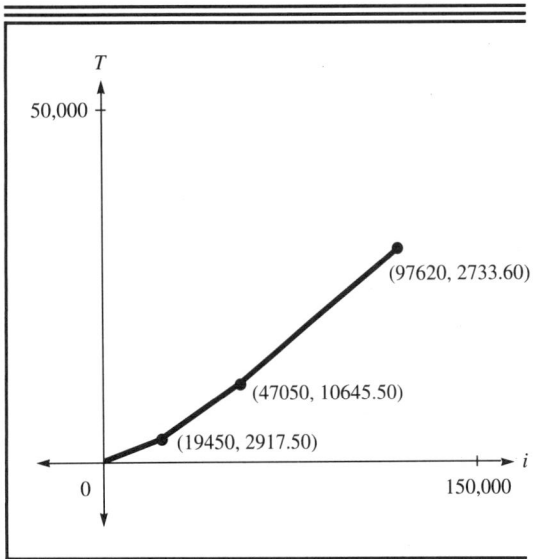

FIGURE P

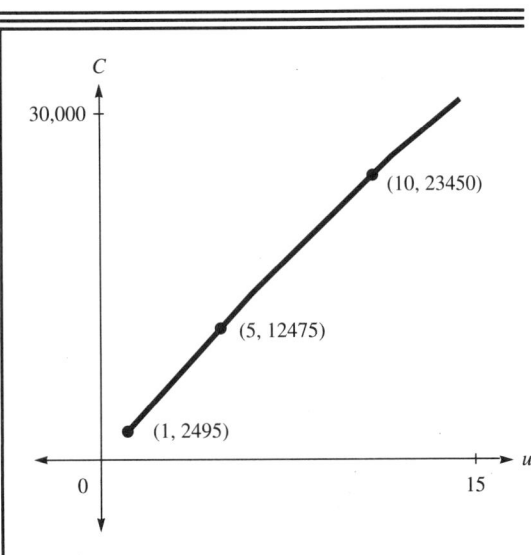

FIGURE O

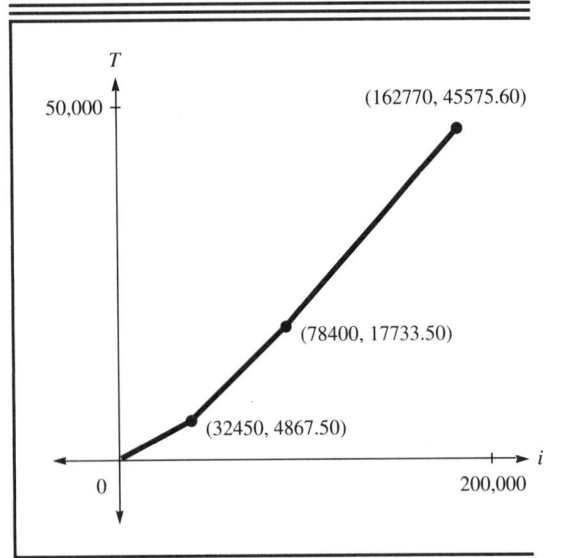

FIGURE Q

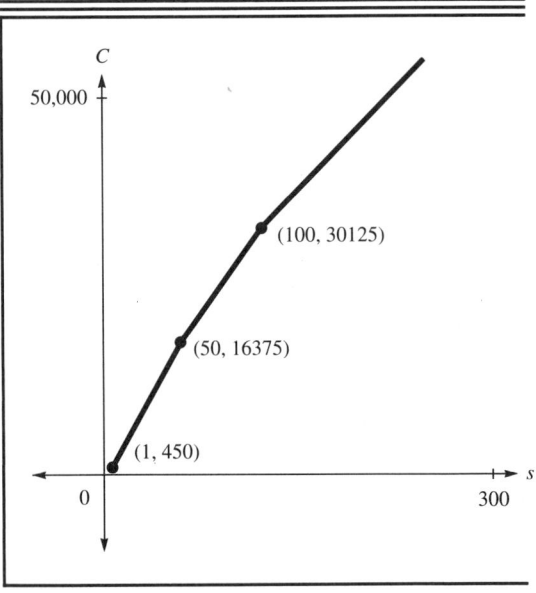

Problem Set 1-4

1. T. 3. F. 5. F. 7. T. 9. T.
2. T. 4. T. 6. T. 8. T. 10. T.
11. a) 150. b) 170. c) 3. d) 3.40. e) 3.
12. a) $10,000. c) $10.
    b) $10,500. d) $10.
13. a) $y = 5x + 2,500$. d) $5.
    b) $10,000. e) $6.25
    c) $2,500. f) $5.
14. a), b), c) See Figure R.
    d) $RS = 25$ = fixed cost; $ST = 20$ = variable cost for 10 units; $RT = 45$ = total cost for 10 units.
15. a) AB. d) BD/OA. g) EB.
    b) AD. e) AD/OA. h) BD/OA.
    c) BD. f) AB/OA.
16. a) Setup cost or fixed cost.
    b) Variable cost if OM units are made.
    c) Variable cost per unit.
    d) Average cost per unit if OM units are made.

Problem Set 1-5

1. T. 4. T. 7. T. 10. F.
2. F. 5. F. 8. F. 11. F.
3. T. 6. T. 9. T. 12. T.

13. a) $R(q) = 5q$; $C(q) = 2q + 60,000$; $P(q) = 3q - 60,000$.
    b) $15,000.
    c) Loss of $30,000.
    d) 20,000 units.
    e) $100,000.
    f) See Figure S.
14. a) $R(q) = 50q$; $C(q) = 20q + 120,000$; $P(q) = 30q - 120,000$.
    b) $180,000.
    c) Loss of $90,000.
    d) 4,000 units.
    e) $200,000.
    f) See Figure T (p. 992).
15. a) $R(q) = 180q$; $C(q) = 100q + 200,000$; $P(q) = 80q - 200,000$.
    b) $200,000.
    c) $100.
    d) 2,500 units.
    e) $450,000.
16. a) $R(q) = 5.5q$; $C(q) = 5q + 500,000$; $P(q) = 0.5q - 500,000$.
    b) $500,000.
    c) $5.
    d) $1,000,000 units.
    e) $5,500,000.

FIGURE R

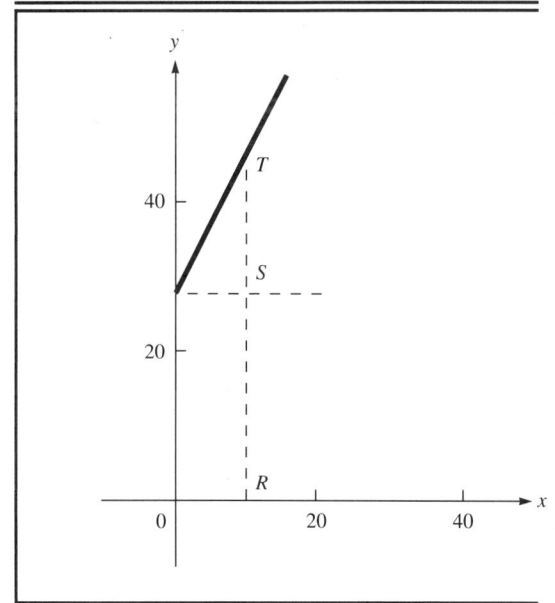

FIGURE S

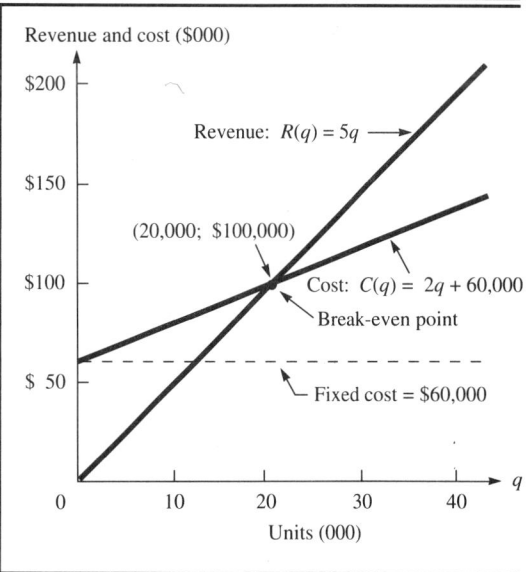

Problem Set 1-5 (continued)

FIGURE T

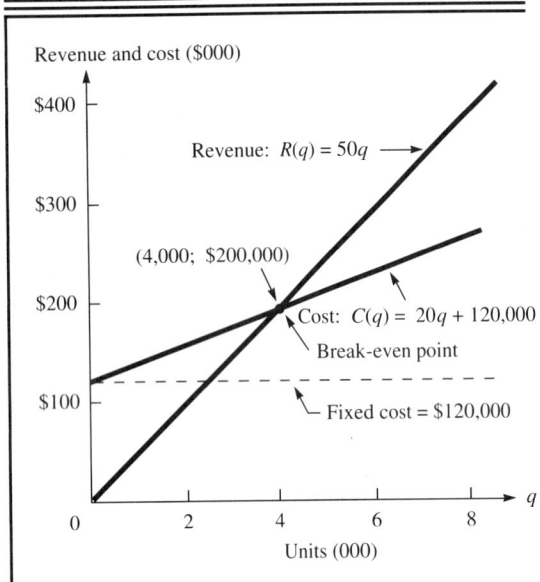

FIGURE U

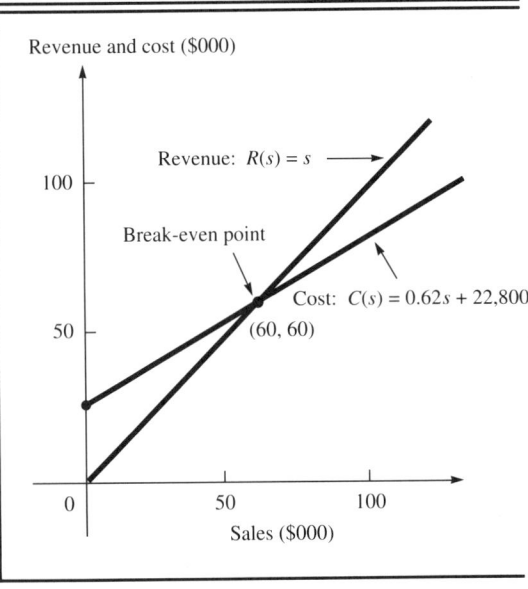

FIGURE V

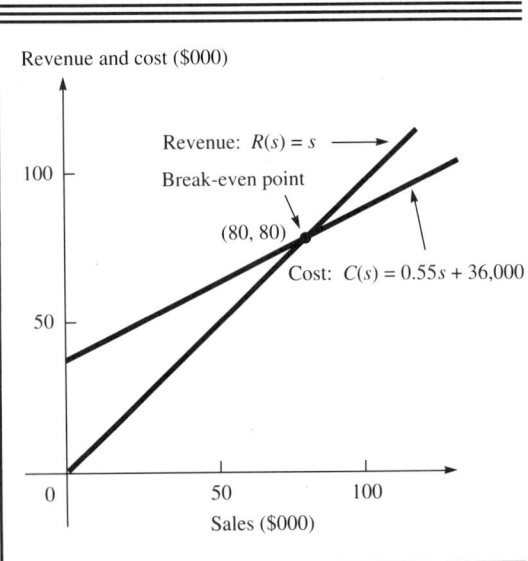

17. a) $200,000.
    b) The company should not shut down, because if it does the loss will be $200,000, but if it produces and sells 1,000 units the loss will be $120,000, which is a smaller loss than $200,000.

18. a) $500,000.
    b) The company should not shut down, because if it does the loss will be $500,000, but if it produces and sells 100,000 units the loss will be $450,000, which is a smaller loss than $500,000.

19. T.   21. T.   23. T.   25. F.   27. F.
20. T.   22. T.   24. T.   26. F.   28. T.

29. a) $R(s) = s$; $C(s) = 0.62s + 22,800$;
       $P(s) = 0.38s - 22,800$.
    b) $60,000.   c) $5,700.   d) See Figure U.

30. a) $R(s) = s$; $C(s) = 0.55s + 36,000$;
       $P(s) = 0.45s - 36,000$.
    b) $80,000.   c) $-$2,250.   d) See Figure V.

31. a) $R(s) = s$; $C(s) = 0.47s + 29,786$;
       $P(s) = 0.53s - 29,786$.
    b) $0.47   d) $33,840   f) $56,200
    c) $29,786   e) $63,626   g) $12,614.

32. a) $R(s) = s$; $C(s) = 0.32s + 23,800$;
       $P(s) = 0.68s - 23,800$.
    b) $0.32   d) $12,800   f) $35,000
    c) $23,800   e) $36,600   ) $3,400 loss.

33. $1,000.

34. a), b) See Figures W and X.

Problem Set 1-5 (concluded)

FIGURE W

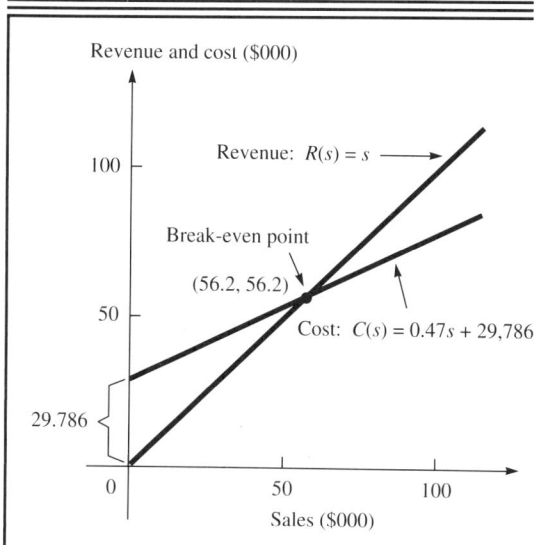

FIGURE X

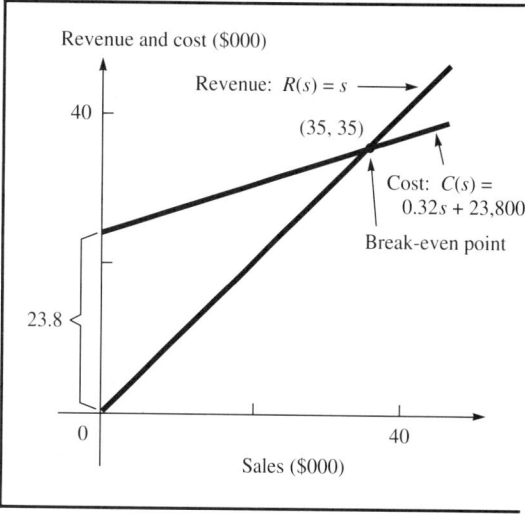

35. The shift is 50 to the left horizontally, so demand is 50 units less at every price level. The shift is 5 downward vertically, so price is $5 per unit less at every level of demand.

36. The shift is 200 to the right horizontally, so demand is 200 units greater at every price level. The shift is 10 upward vertically, so price is $10 per unit higher at every level of demand.

37. a) Demand is a constant number of units at every level of price per unit.
    b) Price per unit is constant at every level of demand.

38. Demand is the constant function $q = 100$ tons per week, a vertical line.

39. The demand function is a horizontal line, $p = $ a constant.

CHAPTER 2

Problem Set 2-1

1. (2, 3).
2. (−1, 4).
3. (1, 1).
4. (3/2, 2).
5. (1/2, 2/3).
6. (1/2, 3/2).
7. (−1, 4).
8. (1, 1).
9. (1/2, 2/3).
10. (1/2, 3/2).
11. (1/2, 1, 3/2).
12. (2/5, −3, 3/5).
13. (1, 2, 3).
14. (−2, −1, 6).
15. No solutions.
16. No solutions.
17. No solutions.
18. No solutions.
19. x arbitrary, $y = (-1/4)x - 3/4$.
20. x arbitrary, $y = (-5/3)x + 5$.
21. x arbitrary, $y = (-2/3)x + 5$.
22. x arbitrary, $y = (2/5)x + 1/5$.
23. No solutions.
24. No solutions.
25. No solutions.
26. No solutions.
27. x arbitrary, $y = x - 2, z = 5 - x$.
28. x arbitrary, $y = 3 - 2x, z = 5 - 3x$.
29. x arbitrary, $y = 17 - 17x, z = 22 - 9x$.
30. x arbitrary, $y = (1/3)x + 2, z = (-4/3)x + 8$.

Problem Set 2–2

1. 375 liters of regular and 625 liters of unleaded.
2. Invest $20,000 in Acme and $30,000 in Star.
3. Make 15 double-edged and 10 single-edged.
4. Make 5 captain's and 50 regular.
5. $x = 10, y = 15, z = 20$.
6. $x = 10, y = 15, z = 20$.
7. The solution is $0 \le y \le 3, x = 2 + y, z = 10 - 3y$.
8. $x = 2, y = 0, z = 10$.
9. The solution requires that $y = -2$, which is not permissible. The problem has no solution.
10. a) z units of C, $0 \le z \le 8$; x units of A, where $x = 80 - 10z$; y units of B, where $y = z - 5$.
    b) Maximum is $800, making 30 units of A, no B, and 5 units of C.
11. a) z units of C, $0 \le z \le 4$; y units of B, where $y = z$; x units of A, where $x = 40 - 10z$.
    b) Maximum is $800, making 40 units of A and no B or C.
12. a) z pounds of pecans, $0 \le z \le 2.5$; x pounds of macadamia nuts, where $x = (5 + z)/3$; y pounds of almonds, where $y = (10 - 4z)/3$.
    b) Minimum is $7.50, using 2.5 pounds of macadamia nuts, no almonds, and 2.5 pounds of pecans.
13. a) z pounds of pecans, $0 \le z \le 5$; x pounds of macadamia nuts, where $x = (10 + z)/3$; y pounds of almonds, where $y = (20 - 4z)/3$.
    b) Minimum is $15.00, using 5 pounds of macadamia nuts, no almonds, and 5 pounds of pecans.

Problem Set 2–3

1. a) See Figure A.   c) See Figure A.
   b) $E(70, 15)$.   d) $E'(40, 12)$.
   e) The decrease in demand was accompanied by a lower demand and a lower price per unit at equilibrium.
2. a) See Figure B.   c) See Figure B.
   b) $E(100, 30)$.   d) $E'(80, 38)$.
   e) The decrease in supply was accompanied by a lower supply but a higher price per unit at equilibrium.
3. $E'(125, 35)$. The increase in demand was accompanied by a higher demand and a higher price at equilibrium.
4. $E'(80, 10)$. The increase in supply was accompanied by a higher supply but a lower price at equilibrium.
5. The demand function shifted to the right. At the new equilibrium, both demand and price are higher.
6. The supply function shifted to the left. At the new equilibrium, supply is lower but price is higher.

FIGURE A

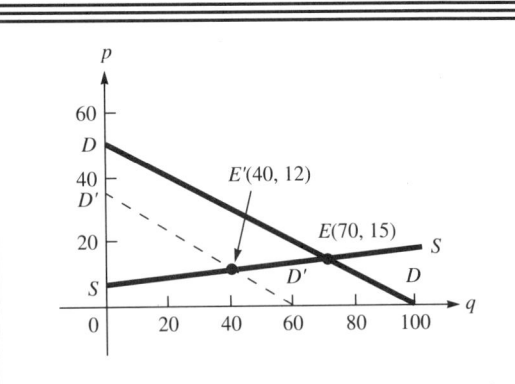

FIGURE B

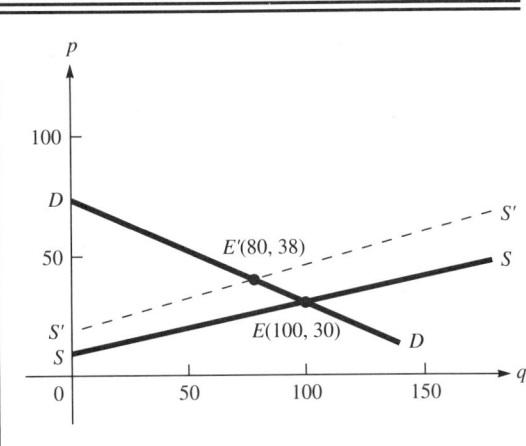

7. The supply function shifted to the right. At the new equilibrium, supply is higher but price is lower.
8. The demand function shifted to the left. At the new equilibrium, both demand and price are lower.
9. The supply function shifted to the right because a right shift of a supply function leads to a new equilibrium in which supply is *higher* but price is *lower*.
10. The demand function shifted to the left because with a left shift in demand, *both* demand and price are lower at the new equilibrium.
11. a) $p_1 = \$415, q_1 = 65$ units; $p_2 = \$445, q_2 = 65$ units.
    b) $p_1 = \$474, q_1 = 96$ units. $p_2 = \$472, q_2 = 64$ units.

Problem Set 2-3 (concluded)

12. a) $p_1 = \$800$, $q_1 = 100$ units.
    $p_2 = \$400$, $q_2 = 100$ units.
 b) $p_1 = \$740$, $q_1 = 60$ units.
    $p_2 = \$420$, $q_2 = 160$ units.

Problem Set 2-4

1. $(3 \quad 1 \quad 7)$.
2. $\begin{pmatrix} -2 \\ 2 \end{pmatrix}$.
3. $\begin{pmatrix} 10 \\ 13 \end{pmatrix}$.
4. $(8 \quad 0 \quad 4)$.
5. $\begin{pmatrix} 21 \\ 6 \end{pmatrix}$.
6. $(-10 \quad 18 \quad -6)$.
7. 41.
8. 5.
9. $\begin{pmatrix} 4 & -4 & 0 \\ -2 & 6 & 5 \end{pmatrix}$.
10. $\begin{pmatrix} 3 & 9 \\ 2 & -7 \end{pmatrix}$.
11. $\begin{pmatrix} -2 & -27 & 17 \\ 17 & -2 & -9 \end{pmatrix}$.
12. $\begin{pmatrix} 5 & -4 & 5 \\ 14 & -10 & 15 \end{pmatrix}$.
13. $(26 \quad 35)$.
14. $\begin{pmatrix} 3 & 18 \\ 3 & -30 \end{pmatrix}$.
15. $\begin{pmatrix} 13 & 16 \\ 8 & 7 \\ -5 & -9 \end{pmatrix}$.
16. $\begin{pmatrix} 7 & -1 & 5 & 6 \\ 11 & 3 & 8 & 13 \end{pmatrix}$.
17. $\begin{pmatrix} 1 & 4 \\ 2 & 5 \\ 3 & 6 \end{pmatrix}$.
18. $\begin{pmatrix} 1 & 2 & 3 \\ 3 & 2 & 1 \end{pmatrix}$.
19. a) $\begin{pmatrix} -6 & -47 \\ -49 & 38 \end{pmatrix}$.
    b) $\begin{pmatrix} 9 & 17 & 3 \\ 2 & 48 & 49 \end{pmatrix}$.
    c) $\begin{pmatrix} 2 & 24 \\ 94 & 23 \end{pmatrix}$.
    d) $\begin{pmatrix} 31 & 44 \\ 46 & -6 \end{pmatrix}$.
    e) $\begin{pmatrix} 150 & 206 & 204 \\ 205 & 124 & 102 \end{pmatrix}$.
    f) Cannot be done.
20. a) $\begin{pmatrix} -58 & -9 & -23 \\ -9 & 20 & -14 \\ 38 & -18 & -22 \end{pmatrix}$.
    b) $\begin{pmatrix} 25 & 64 & -43 \\ 14 & 43 & -6 \\ 51 & 60 & 0 \end{pmatrix}$.
    c) $\begin{pmatrix} -122 & -1 & 29 \\ 84 & 117 & 123 \\ 208 & 94 & 18 \end{pmatrix}$.
    d) $\begin{pmatrix} -55 & 300 & 210 \\ 72 & 98 & 2 \\ 17 & 12 & -30 \end{pmatrix}$.
    e) $\begin{pmatrix} 359 & 252 & -169 \\ 288 & 102 & -26 \\ -81 & -67 & 82 \end{pmatrix}$.
    f) $\begin{pmatrix} 190 & 38 & 84 \\ 139 & 48 & 56 \\ 302 & 371 & 305 \end{pmatrix}$.

21. $(0.06 \quad 0.07 \quad 0.08) \begin{pmatrix} 3000 \\ 2000 \\ 4000 \end{pmatrix} = \$640$.

22. a) $(10 \quad 20) \begin{pmatrix} 8 & 2 & 5 \\ 4 & 8 & 3 \end{pmatrix} = (160 \quad 180 \quad 110)$.

    The first component of the right vector, 160, is 10 batches of Superior times 8 pounds of beef per batch, plus 20 batches of Regular times 4 pounds of beef per batch, for a total of 160 pounds of beef to make the required number of batches. Similarly, we see that 180 pounds of pork and 110 pounds of lamb will be required.

    b) $\begin{pmatrix} 8 & 2 & 5 \\ 4 & 8 & 3 \end{pmatrix} \begin{pmatrix} 2.50 \\ 2.00 \\ 3.00 \end{pmatrix} = \begin{pmatrix} 39 \\ 35 \end{pmatrix}$.

    The component in the answer, 39, is 8 pounds of beef times \$2.50 per pound, plus 2 pounds of pork at \$2 per pound, plus 5 pounds of lamb at \$3 per pound, so the total cost of a batch of Superior is \$39. Similarly, the total cost of a batch of Regular is \$35.

23. a) $B = \begin{pmatrix} 50 \\ 40 \\ 25 \\ 10 \end{pmatrix}$ and $S = \begin{pmatrix} 75 \\ 55 \\ 30 \\ 15 \end{pmatrix}$.

    b) \$2,450, \$3,075, and \$2,875.
    c) \$2,975, \$3,725, and \$3,400.
    d) \$525, \$650, and \$525.

24. a) $(100 \quad 75)$.
    b) $\begin{pmatrix} 2 & 3 & 0 \\ 0 & 4 & 1 \end{pmatrix}$.
    c) $\begin{pmatrix} 50 \\ 25 \\ 30 \end{pmatrix}$.

Problem Set 2-5

1. $\begin{pmatrix} 1 & -3 \\ -2 & 7 \end{pmatrix}$.
2. $\begin{pmatrix} 1 & -4 \\ -2 & 9 \end{pmatrix}$.
3. $\begin{pmatrix} 5/4 & -1/2 \\ -3/4 & 1/2 \end{pmatrix}$.
4. $\begin{pmatrix} 2 & 1 \\ 1 & 1 \end{pmatrix}$.
5. Inverse does not exist.
6. Inverse does not exist.
7. $\begin{pmatrix} 0 & 1/2 \\ 1/3 & -1/6 \end{pmatrix}$.
8. $\begin{pmatrix} -4/7 & 5/7 \\ 3/7 & -2/7 \end{pmatrix}$.
9. $\begin{pmatrix} -3/2 & 1/2 \\ 1 & 0 \end{pmatrix}$.
10. $\begin{pmatrix} -5/6 & 1/2 \\ 1/3 & 0 \end{pmatrix}$.
11. $\begin{pmatrix} 1 & 2 & 1 \\ 4 & 5 & -3 \\ 3 & 4 & -2 \end{pmatrix}$.
12. $\begin{pmatrix} 3/2 & -3 & -1/2 \\ 2 & -3 & -1 \\ -2 & 4 & 1 \end{pmatrix}$.
13. Inverse does not exist.
14. $\begin{pmatrix} 2 & 2 & 3 \\ 0 & 1 & 1 \\ 1 & 1 & 1 \end{pmatrix}$.
15. $\begin{pmatrix} -4/9 & 5/9 & 2/9 \\ -7/9 & 2/9 & 8/9 \\ 2/3 & -1/3 & -1/3 \end{pmatrix}$.
16. Inverse does not exist.
17. a) $\begin{pmatrix} 1 & 0 & 0 \\ 0 & 1 & 0 \\ 0 & 0 & 1 \end{pmatrix}$.
    b) $\begin{pmatrix} 1 & 1 & 1 \\ 1 & 1 & 1 \\ 1 & 1 & 1 \end{pmatrix}$.
18. a) $7a + 3b = 1$
    $2a + b = 0$
    $7c + 3d = 0$
    $2c + d = 1$.
    b) $\begin{pmatrix} 1 & -3 \\ -2 & 7 \end{pmatrix}$.

Problem Set 2-5 (concluded)

19. See answers to Problems 2 through 10.

20. a) $2a + 8b - 11c = 1$
$-a - 5b + 7c = 0$
$a + 2b - 3c = 0$
$2d + 8e - 11f = 0$
$-d - 5e + 7f = 1$
$d + 2e - 3f = 0$
$2g + 8h - 11i = 0$
$-g - 5h + 7i = 0$
$g + 2h - 3i = 1.$

b) $\begin{pmatrix} 1 & 2 & 1 \\ 4 & 5 & -3 \\ 3 & 4 & -2 \end{pmatrix}.$

21. See answers to Problems 12 through 16.

Problem Set 2-6

1. a) $A = \begin{pmatrix} 8 & 5 \\ 3 & 2 \end{pmatrix}; \; x = \begin{pmatrix} x_1 \\ x_2 \end{pmatrix}; \; b = \begin{pmatrix} 2 \\ 1 \end{pmatrix}.$
   b) $(-1 \quad 2).$
   c) $A^{-1} = \begin{pmatrix} 2 & -5 \\ -3 & 8 \end{pmatrix}.$
   d) $\begin{pmatrix} x_1 \\ x_2 \end{pmatrix} = \begin{pmatrix} 2 & -5 \\ -3 & 8 \end{pmatrix}\begin{pmatrix} 2 \\ 1 \end{pmatrix}.$
   e) $(-1 \quad 2).$
   f) (1) $(2 \quad -3)$ (4) $(-14 \quad 23).$
      (2) $(-5 \quad 8).$ (5) $(-11 \quad 17).$
      (3) $(-3 \quad 5).$

2. a) $A = \begin{pmatrix} 4 & 3 \\ 9 & 7 \end{pmatrix}; \; x = \begin{pmatrix} x_1 \\ x_2 \end{pmatrix}; \; b = \begin{pmatrix} 2 \\ 3 \end{pmatrix}.$
   b) $(5 \quad -6).$
   c) $A^{-1} = \begin{pmatrix} 7 & -3 \\ -9 & 4 \end{pmatrix}.$
   d) $\begin{pmatrix} x_1 \\ x_2 \end{pmatrix} = \begin{pmatrix} 7 & -3 \\ -9 & 4 \end{pmatrix}\begin{pmatrix} 2 \\ 3 \end{pmatrix}.$
   e) $(5 \quad -6).$
   f) (1) $(7 \quad -9).$ (4) $(11 \quad -14).$
      (2) $(-3 \quad 4).$ (5) $(-13 \quad 17).$
      (3) $(4 \quad -5).$

3. a) $A = \begin{pmatrix} 6 & 8 \\ 2 & 3 \end{pmatrix}; \; x = \begin{pmatrix} x_1 \\ x_2 \end{pmatrix}; \; b = \begin{pmatrix} 3 \\ 1 \end{pmatrix}.$
   b) $(1/2 \quad 0).$
   c) $A^{-1} = \begin{pmatrix} 3/2 & -4 \\ -1 & 3 \end{pmatrix}.$
   d) $\begin{pmatrix} x_1 \\ x_2 \end{pmatrix} = \begin{pmatrix} 3/2 & -4 \\ -1 & 3 \end{pmatrix}\begin{pmatrix} 3 \\ 1 \end{pmatrix}.$
   e) $(1/2 \quad 0).$
   f) (1) $(-5/2 \quad 2).$ (4) $(-9 \quad 7).$
      (2) $(-4 \quad 3).$ (5) $(-11/2 \quad 4).$
      (3) $(3/2 \quad -1).$

4. $\begin{pmatrix} 1 & 7/5 \\ 1 & 8/5 \end{pmatrix}.$

5. a) $A = \begin{pmatrix} 3 & 0 & 5 \\ 2 & 2 & 5 \\ 0 & 1 & 1 \end{pmatrix}; \; x = \begin{pmatrix} x_1 \\ x_2 \\ x_3 \end{pmatrix}; \; b = \begin{pmatrix} 3 \\ 7 \\ 2 \end{pmatrix}.$
   b) $(6 \quad 5 \quad -3).$
   c) $A^{-1} = \begin{pmatrix} -3 & 5 & -10 \\ -2 & 3 & -5 \\ 2 & -3 & 6 \end{pmatrix}.$
   d) $\begin{pmatrix} x_1 \\ x_2 \\ x_3 \end{pmatrix} = \begin{pmatrix} -3 & 5 & -10 \\ -2 & 3 & -5 \\ 2 & -3 & 6 \end{pmatrix}\begin{pmatrix} 3 \\ 7 \\ 2 \end{pmatrix}.$
   e) $(6 \quad 5 \quad -3).$
   f) (1) $(-3 \quad -1 \quad 2).$ (4) $(7 \quad 6 \quad -4).$
      (2) $(-31 \quad -15 \quad 19).$ (5) $(34 \quad 21 \quad -20).$
      (3) $(7 \quad 3 \quad -4).$

6. a) $A = \begin{pmatrix} 7 & 3 & 0 \\ 0 & 3 & 5 \\ 1 & 1 & 1 \end{pmatrix}; \; x = \begin{pmatrix} x_1 \\ x_2 \\ x_3 \end{pmatrix}; \; b = \begin{pmatrix} 1 \\ 2 \\ 3 \end{pmatrix}.$
   b) $(37 \quad -86 \quad 52).$
   c) $A^{-1} = \begin{pmatrix} -2 & -3 & 15 \\ 5 & 7 & -35 \\ -3 & -4 & 21 \end{pmatrix}.$
   d) $\begin{pmatrix} x_1 \\ x_2 \\ x_3 \end{pmatrix} = \begin{pmatrix} -2 & -3 & 15 \\ 5 & 7 & -35 \\ -3 & -4 & 21 \end{pmatrix}\begin{pmatrix} 1 \\ 2 \\ 3 \end{pmatrix}.$
   e) $(37 \quad -86 \quad 52).$
   f) (1) $(16 \quad -37 \quad 22).$
      (2) $(-13 \quad 31 \quad -18).$
      (3) $(-34 \quad 79 \quad -47).$
      (4) $(-2 \quad 8 \quad -5).$
      (5) $(3 \quad -7 \quad 4).$

7. $\begin{pmatrix} 3/2 & -3 & -1/2 \\ 2 & -3 & -1 \\ -2 & 4 & 1 \end{pmatrix}.$

8. b) (1) $(-3 \quad 0 \quad 6).$ (2) $(0 \quad 3 \quad 0).$

9. b) (1) $(1 \quad 0 \quad 0 \quad 0).$ (2) $(2 \quad -2 \quad 2 \quad -1).$

10. a) $x_1 + 2x_3 = H_1$
    $x_2 + 3x_3 = H_2$
    $x_1 + 2x_2 = H_3.$

    b) $A = \begin{pmatrix} 1 & 0 & 2 \\ 0 & 1 & 3 \\ 1 & 2 & 3 \end{pmatrix}.$

    $A^{-1} = \dfrac{1}{8}\begin{pmatrix} 6 & -4 & 2 \\ -3 & 2 & 3 \\ 1 & 2 & -1 \end{pmatrix}.$

Problem Set 2-6 (concluded)

    c) (130   35   15).
    d) (200   100   100).
    e) (208   24   56).

11. No solutions.
12. No solutions.
13. No solutions.
14. No solutions.
15. x_2 arbitrary, $x_1 = -4x_2 - 3$.
16. x_2 arbitrary, $x_1 = -0.6x_2 + 3$.
17. x_2 arbitrary, $x_1 = -1.5x_2 + 7.5$.
18. x_2 arbitrary, $x_1 = 2.5x_2 - 0.5$.

Problem Set 2-7

1. (9, 4).
2. (−3, −5).
3. No solutions.
4. x_2 arbitrary, $x_1 = (-5/6)x_2 + 10/3$.
5. (3, 5, 4).
6. (−2, −1, 6).
7. No solutions.
8. x_2 and x_3 arbitrary, $x_1 = (-2/3)x_2 - (1/3)x_3 + 2$.
9. (7, 5, −3).
10. (8, 9, 2).
11. No solutions.
12. x_2 and x_3 arbitrary, $x_1 = (1/3)x_2 - (2/3)x_3 - 3$.
13. No solutions.
14. x_2 and x_3 arbitrary, $x_1 = (2/3)x_2 - (4/3)x_3 + 5$.
15. No solutions.
16. x_2, x_3 and x_4 arbitrary, $x_1 = (-5/3)x_2 + 2x_3 - (4/3)x_4 + 12$.
17. 3 dozens of Luscious Candy and 7 dozens of Delicious Candy.
18. 8 pounds of food X and 4 pounds of food Y.
19. Unlimited number of solutions given by

$$x_1 = \frac{1}{7}x_3 + \frac{17}{7}$$
$$x_2 = -\frac{5}{7}x_3 + \frac{55}{7}$$
x_3 arbitrary.

The only solutions with integral coordinates are (3, 5, 4) and (4, 0, 11).

20. Unlimited number of solutions given by

$$x_1 = -2x_4 + 10$$
$$x_2 = 9x_4 - 5$$
$$x_3 = -6x_4 + 8$$
x_4 arbitrary.

The only solution with integral coordinates is (8, 4, 2, 1).

Problem Set 2-8

1. a) 60% of customers who last purchased Lotus will purchase Lotus again, and 40% will switch to Microsoft.
   b) (0.55   0.45) and (0.555   0.445).
   c) (5/9 Lotus   4/9 Microsoft).
2. a) (0.29 spender   0.71 saver).
   b) (1/8 spender   7/8 saver).
3. a) (0.01099 users   0.98901 nonusers).
   b) This is an absorbing chain. The steady state is 100% users or the state vector (1   0).
4. a) (0.63994 owners   0.36006 nonowners).
   b) (0.9900 owners   0.0100 nonowners).
5. a) (0.8519 owners   0.1481 nonowners).
   b) (0.99992 owners   0.00008 nonowners).
6. a) 29% oil, 49.25% gas, 21.75% electric.
   b) 7.04%, 56.34%, 36.62%.
7. a) 14.925% rent, 26.625% own a condominium, 58.45% own a home.
   b) 10.959%, 23.288%, 65.753%.
8. a) 77.25% Babson, 27% Bentley, 25% Bryant.
   b) 73.19%, 22.45%, 19.15%.
9. a) 58.75% Democrats, 45% Republicans, 19.75% independents.
   b) 53.299%; 37.733%; 11.239%.
10. The new state vector is the original (a   b) because the ones in the transition matrix mean that all in state #1 remain in #1 and all in state #2 remain in #2.
11. (0.3   0.1   0.6); (0.1   0.6   0.3); (0.6   0.3   0.1).

CHAPTER 3

Problem Set 3-1

1. See Figure A.
2. See Figure B.
3. See Figure C.
4. See Figure D.
5. See Figure E.
6. See Figure F.
7. a) See Figure G.
   b) If $y \leq 10/7$, $-2x + 6 \leq y \leq (-1/4)x + 2$.
      Or
      if $x \geq 16/7$, $(-1/2)y + 3 \leq x \leq -4y + 8$.
8. a) See Figure H (p. 1000).
   b) If $y \geq 10/7$, $(-1/4)x + 2 \leq y \leq -2x + 6$.
      Or
      if $x \leq 16/7$, $-4y + 8 \leq x \leq (-1/2)y + 3$.
9. a) See Figure I (p. 1000).
   b) If $x \leq 16/7$, $y \geq -2x - 16$;
      if $x \geq 16/7$, $y \geq (-1/4)x + 2$. Or
      if $y \geq 10/7$, $x \geq (-1/2)y + 3$;
      if $y \leq 10/7$, $x \geq -4y + 8$.

FIGURE B

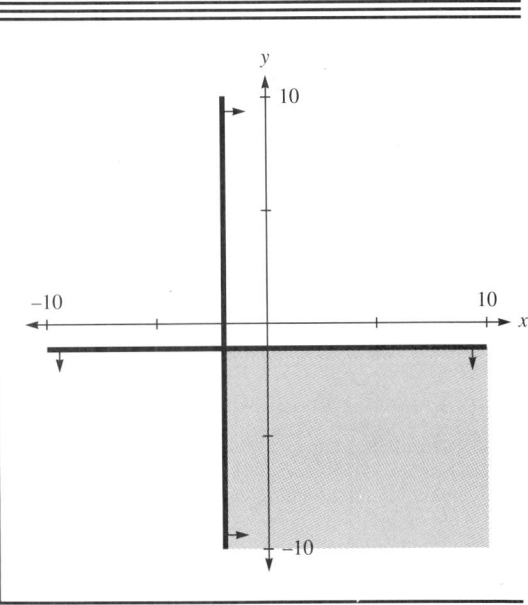

FIGURE A

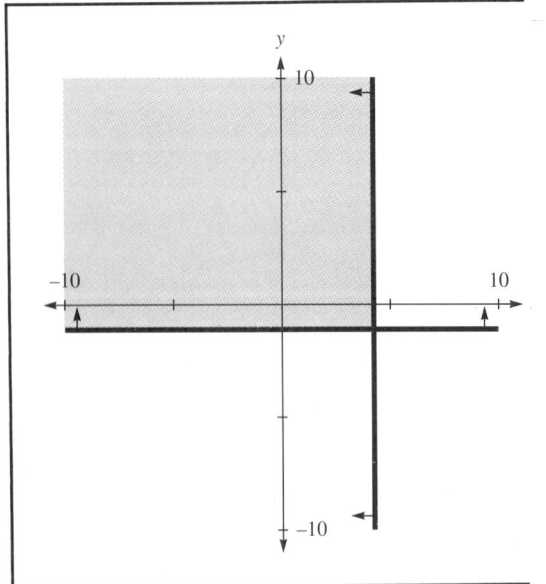

FIGURE C

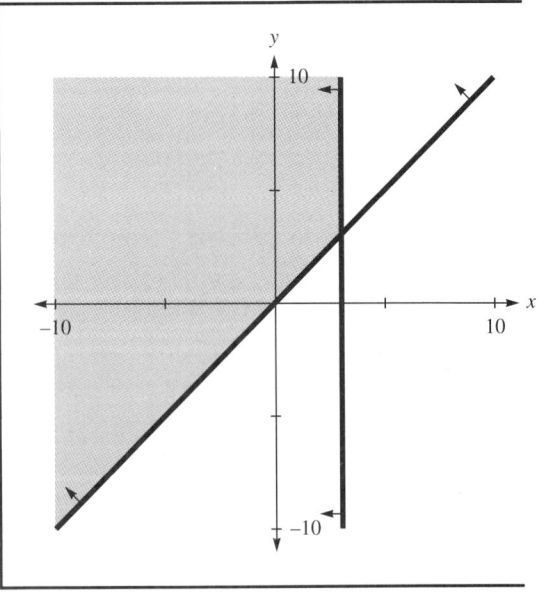

Problem Set 3-1 *(continued)*

FIGURE D

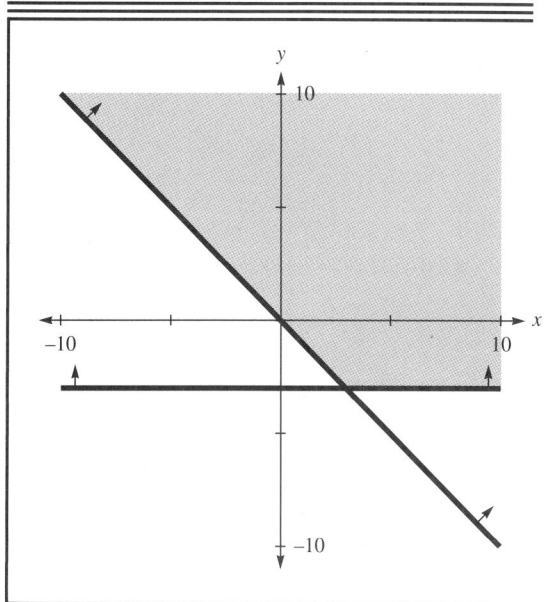

FIGURE F

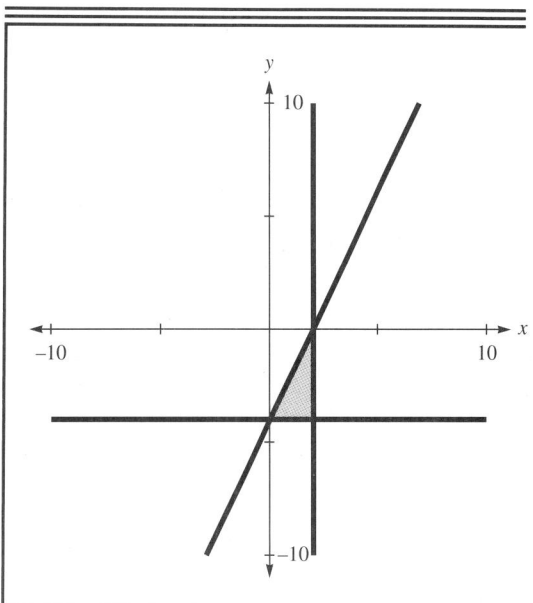

FIGURE E

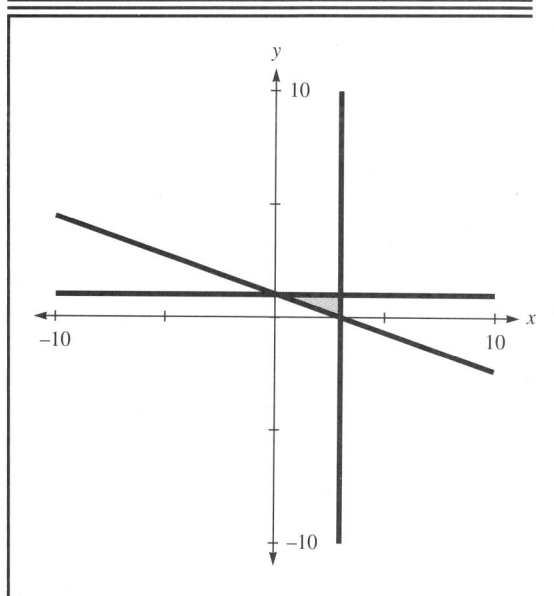

FIGURE G

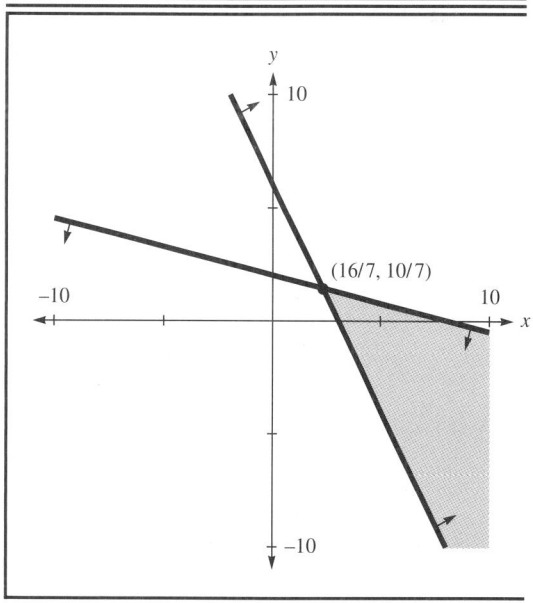

Problem Set 3-1 *(continued)*

FIGURE H

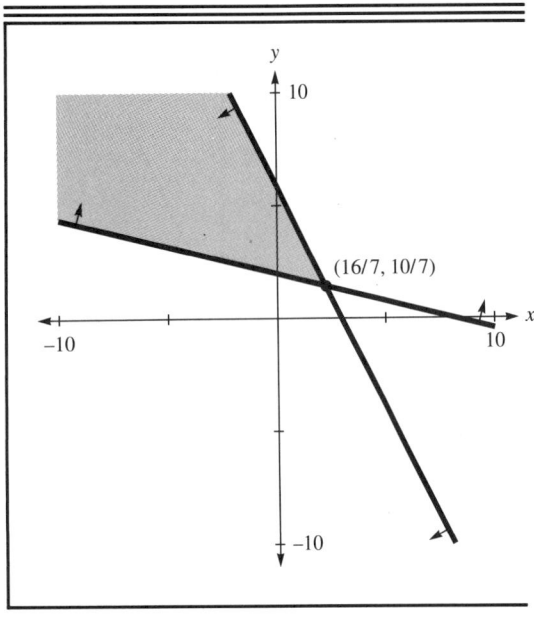

10. a) See Figure J.
    b) If $x \le 16/7$, $y \le (-1/4)x + 2$;
       if $x \ge 16/7$, $y \le -2x + 6$. Or
       if $y \ge 10/7$, $x \le -4y + 8$;
       if $y \le 10/7$, $x \le (-1/2)y + 3$.

11. a) See Figure K.
    b) If $y \ge -2$, $-x + 2 \le y \le (1/2)x - 4$.
       Or
       if $y \ge -2$, $-y + 2 \le x \le 2y + 8$.

12. a) See Figure L.
    b) If $y \le -2$, $(-1/2)x - 4 \le y \le -x + 2$.
       Or
       if $y \le -2$, $2y + 8 \le x \le -y + 2$.

13. a) See Figure M.
    b) If $y \ge -2$, $y \le -x + 2$;
       if $y \le -2$, $y \le (-1/2)x + 4$. Or
       if $y \ge -2$, $x \le -y + 2$;
       if $y \le -2$, $x \le 2y + 8$.

14. a) See Figure N.
    b) If $y \ge -2$, $y \ge (-1/2)x + 4$;
       if $y \le -2$, $y \ge -x + 2$. Or
       if $y \ge -2$, $x \ge 2y + 8$,
       if $y \le -2$, $x \ge -y + 2$.

FIGURE I

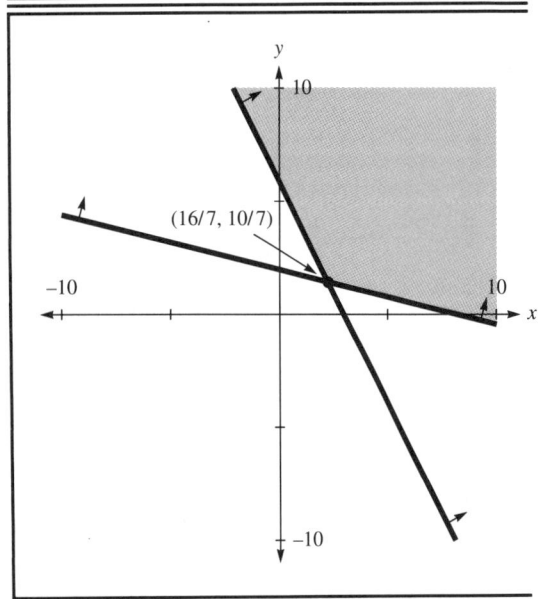

FIGURE J

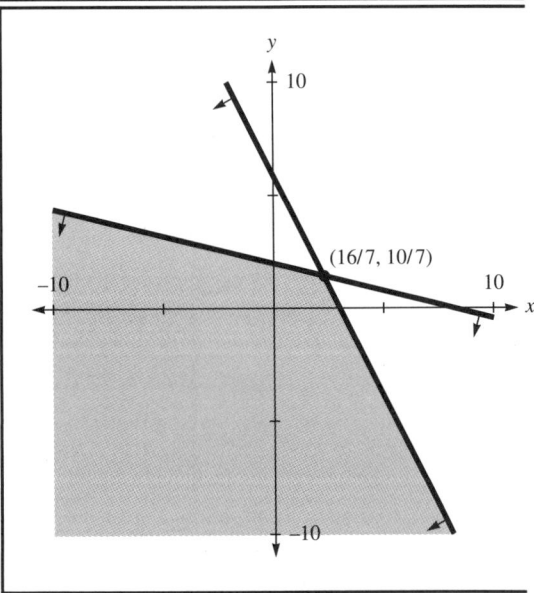

Problem Set 3-1 *(continued)*

FIGURE K

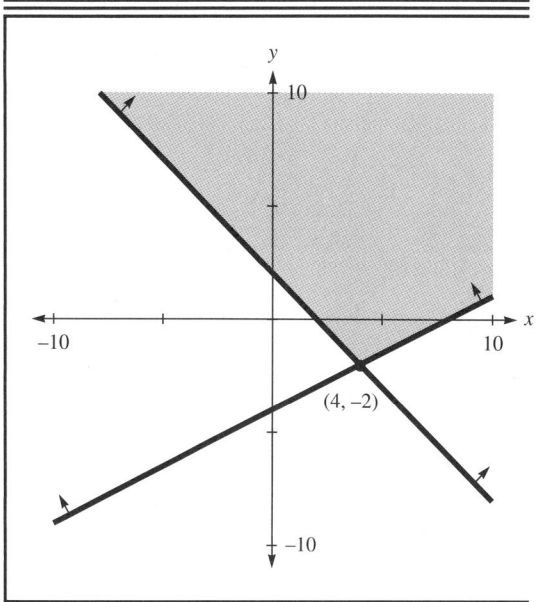

FIGURE L

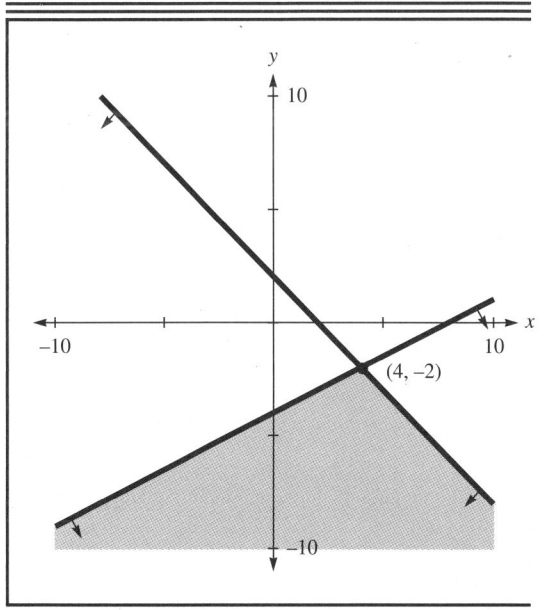

FIGURE M

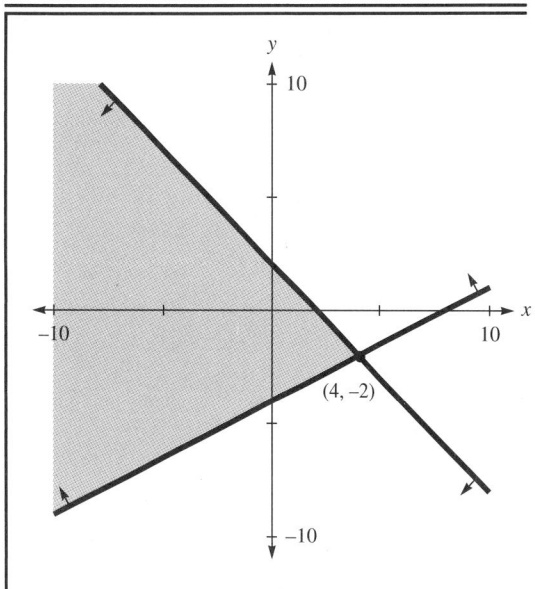

FIGURE N

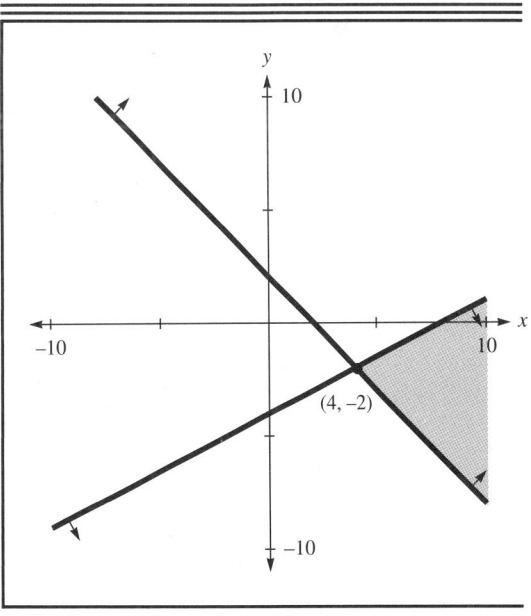

Problem Set 3-1 (continued)

15. a) See Figure O.
    b) If $5 \leq x \leq 10$,
    $(-4/9)x + 130/9 \leq y \leq (-2/3)x + 50/3$.
    Or
    if $10 \leq y \leq 40/3$,
    $(-9/4)y + 65/2 \leq x \leq (-3/2)y + 25$.

16. a) See Figure P.
    b) If $-10 \leq x \leq 10$,
    $(-1/2)x + 10 \leq y \leq (-3/2)x + 20$.
    Or
    if $5 \leq y \leq 15$, $-2y + 20 \leq x \leq (-2/3)y + 40/3$.

17. a) See Figure Q.
    b) If $2 \leq x \leq 30/7$, $y \geq (1/2)x - 1$;
    if $30/7 \leq x \leq 6$, $0 \leq y \leq (-2/3)x + 4$.

18. a) See Figure R.
    b) If $0 \leq x \leq 30/7$, $y \geq (-2/3)x + 4$;
    if $30/7 \leq x$, $8/7 \leq y \leq (1/2)x - 1$.

19. a) See Figure S.
    b) If $0 \leq x \leq 2$, $0 \leq y \leq (-2/3)x + 4$;
    if $2 \leq x \leq 30/7$, $(1/2)x - 1 \leq y \leq (-2/3)x + 4$.

FIGURE P

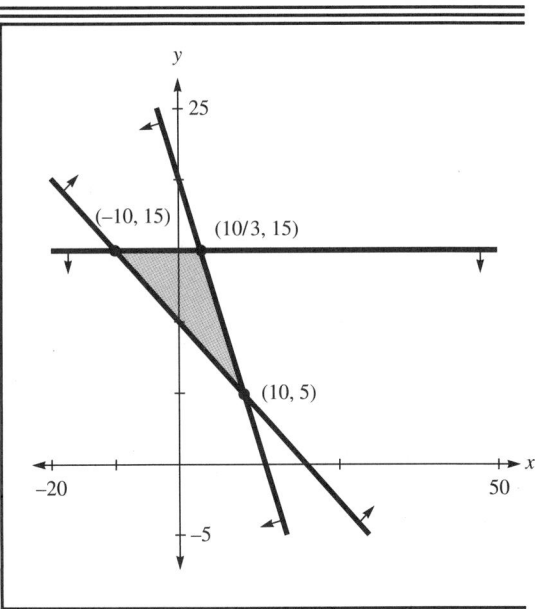

FIGURE O

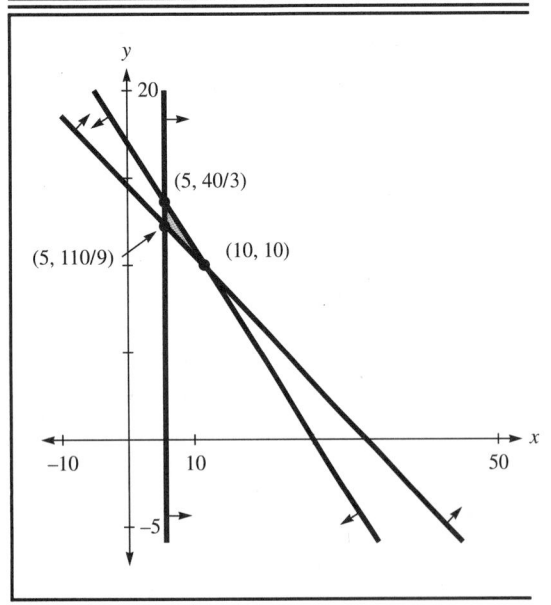

FIGURE Q

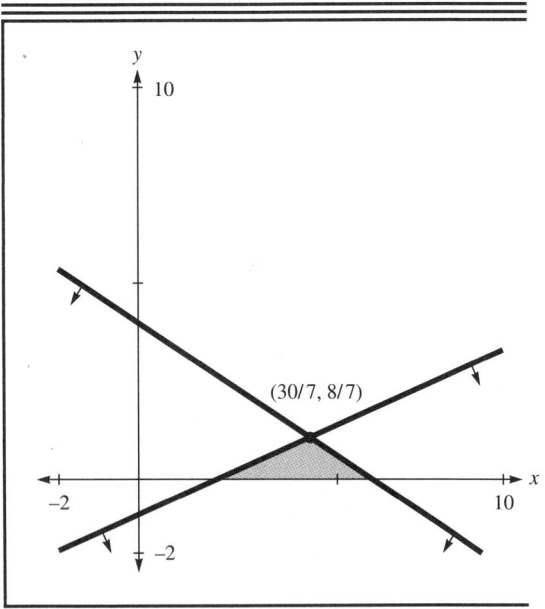

Problem Set 3-1 *(continued)*

FIGURE R

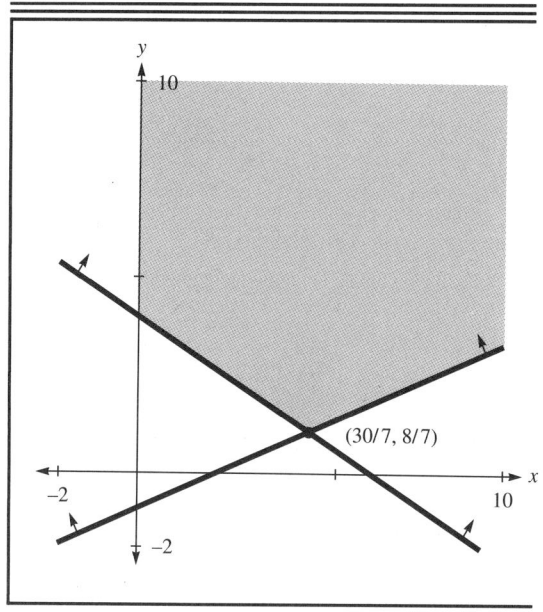

FIGURE S

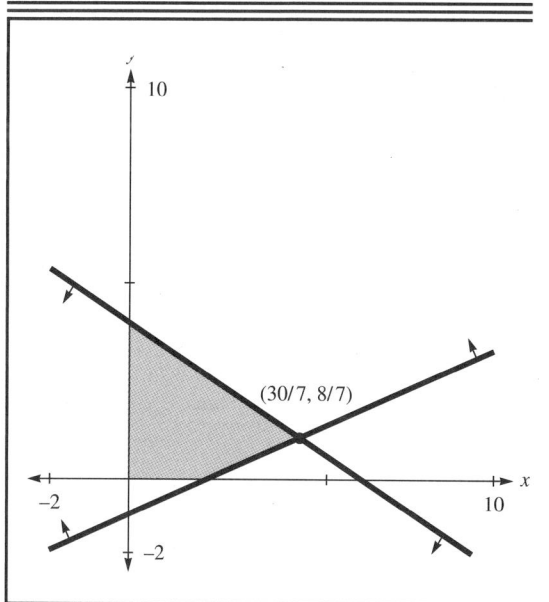

ANSWERS TO PROBLEM SETS 1001

20. a) See Figure T.
    b) If $30/7 \le x \le 6$, $y \ge (-2/3)x + 4$ and $y \ge (1/2)x - 1$; if $x \ge 6$, $y \ge 0$ and $y \ge (1/2)x - 1$.

21. a) See Figure U (p. 1004).
    b) If $52/19 \le x \le 3$, $-4x + 12 \le y \le (-1/5)x + 8/5$; if $3 \le x \le 8$, $0 \le y \le (-1/5)x + 8/5$.

22. a) See Figure V (p. 1004).
    b) If $0 \le x \le 52/19$, $0 \le y \le (-1/5)x + 8/5$; if $52/19 \le x \le 3$, $0 \le y \le -4x + 12$.

23. a) See Figure W (p. 1004).
    b) If $0 \le x \le 52/19$, $y \ge -4x + 12$; if $52/19 \le x \le 8$, $y \ge (-1/5)x + 8/5$; if $x \ge 8$, $y \ge 0$.

24. a) See Figure X (p. 1004).
    b) If $0 \le x \le 52/19$, $(-1/5)x + 8/5 \le y \le -4x + 12$.

25. a) See Figure Y (p. 1005).
    b) If $0 \le x \le 27$, $0 \le y \le (-6/7)x + 190/7$; if $27 \le x \le 30$, $0 \le y \le (-4/3)x + 40$.

26. a) See Figure Z (p. 1005).
    b) If $0 \le x \le 27$, $(-6/7)x + 190/7 \le y \le (-4/3)x + 40$.

FIGURE T

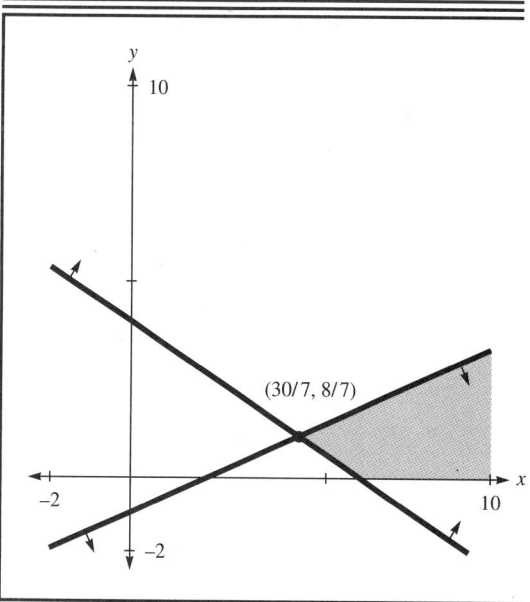

Problem Set 3-1 *(continued)*

FIGURE U

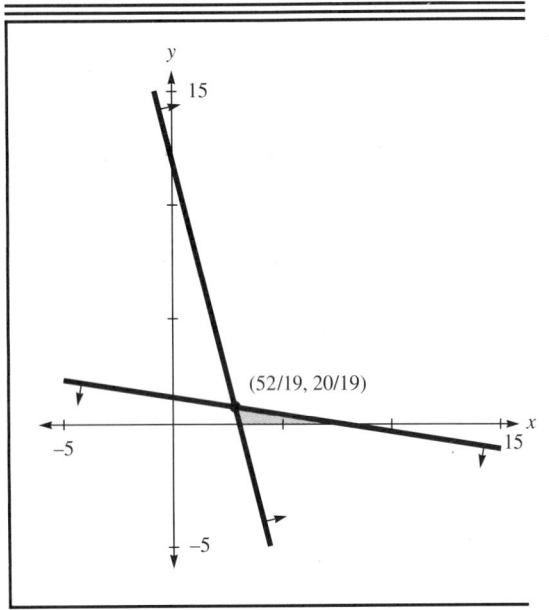

FIGURE V

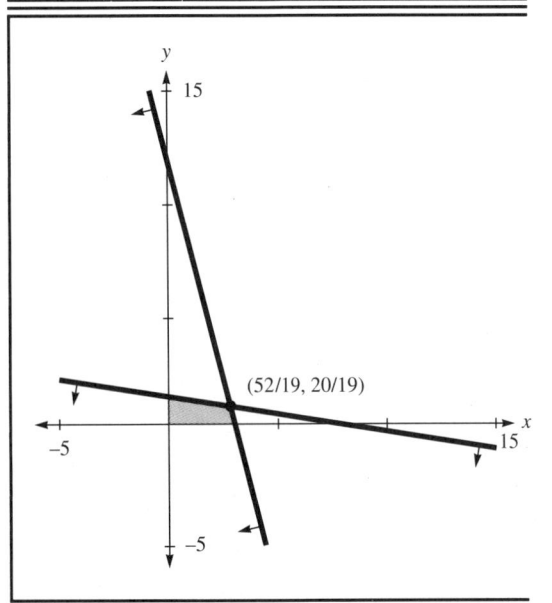

FIGURE W

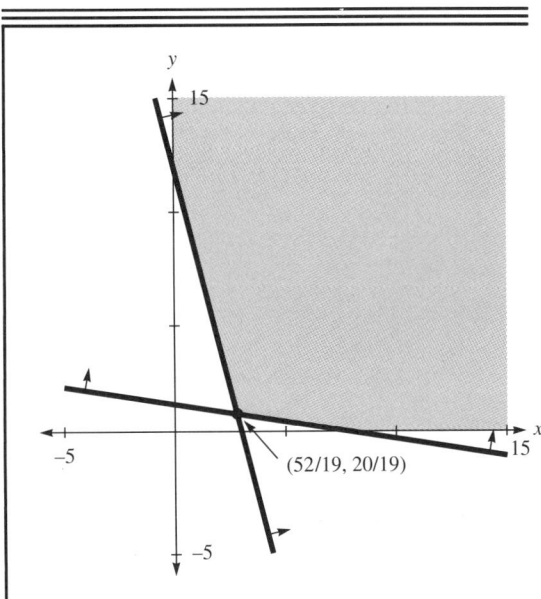

FIGURE X

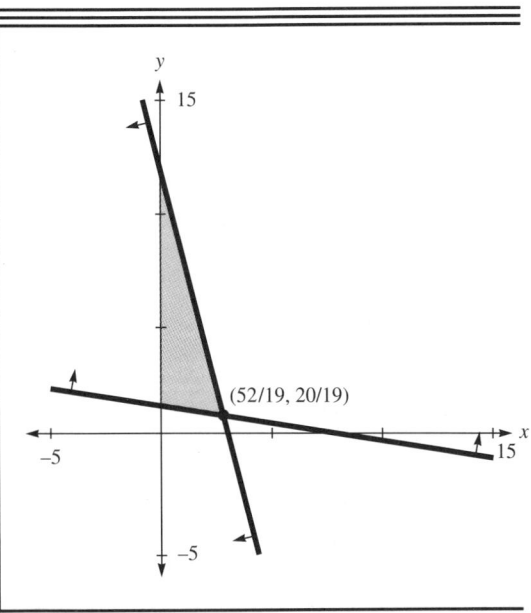

Problem Set 3–1 (concluded)

FIGURE Y

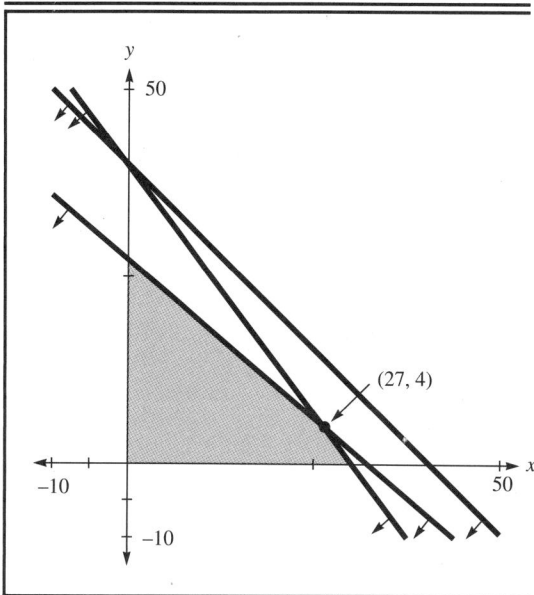

FIGURE Z

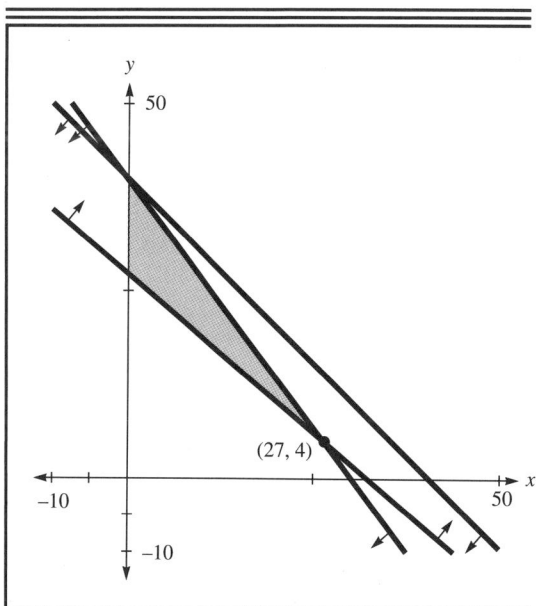

Problem Set 3–2

1. a) 7 at (3, 4).   c) 18 at (6, 0)
   b) 16.5 at (0, 5.5)
   d) 12 on line segment joining (6,0) and (3, 4).
2. a) 58 at (7, 3).   c) 44 at (0, 22/5).
   b) 28 at (14, 0).
   d) 21 on line segment joining (14, 0) and (7, 3).
3. a) 6 at (6, 0).   c) 17 at (0, 17).
   b) 29 at (3, 2).
   d) 17 on line segment joining (0, 17) and (3, 2).
4. a) 15 at (15/2, 0).   c) 14 at (5, 2).
   b) 19 at (0, 19/2).
   d) 60 on line segment joining (5, 2) and (15/2, 0).
5. a) 2.3 at (1, 4).   c) 15 at (3, 0).
   b) 7 at (2, 3).
   d) 15 on line segment joining (1, 4) and (2, 3).
6. a) 92 at (4, 9).   c) 77 at (0, 11).
   b) 16 at (4, 0).
   d) 110 on line segment joining (0, 11) and (4, 9).
7. a) 14 at (4, 10).   c) 36 at (0, 18).
   b) 46 at (4, 10).
   d) 104 on line segment joining (4, 10) and (12, 4).
8. a) 64/5 at (8/5, 48/5).
   b) 72/5 at (24/5, 24/5).
   c) 32 on line segment joining (8/5, 48/5) and (0, 16).
   d) 48 on line segment joining (24/5, 24/5) and (8/5, 48/5).
9. a) 30 at (10, 0) and 12 at (4, 0).
   b) 100 at (10, 0) and 136/7 at (10/7, 36/7).
10. a) 22 at (80, 40) and 20.5 at (80, 30).
    b) 20 at (80, 40) and 18 at (80, 30).
    c) 12 on line segment joining (60, 60) and (80, 40), and 11 at (80, 30).
11. a) 60 at (0, 12) and 45 at (0, 9).
    b) 48 at (6, 6) and 18 at (0, 9).
    c) 36 on line segment joining (0, 12) and (6, 6), and 27 at (0, 9).
12. a) 60 at (0, 12) and 45 at (0, 9).
    b) 40 at (4, 8) and 18 at (0, 9).
    c) 36 on line segment joining (0, 12) and (4, 8), and 27 at (0, 9).
13. See the answers to Problem 11.
14. The feasible solution set is empty, so there is no maximum or minimum.
15. a) 33 at (6, 4) and −7 at (0, 0).
    b) 43 at (3, 6) and −2 at (4, 0).
    c) 25 at (0, 0) and 4 at (3, 6).
    d) 50 on line segment joining (4, 0) and (6, 4), and 2 at (0, 4).

Problem Set 3-2 (concluded)

16. a) 36.75 at (120, 0) and 16.75 at (80, 40).
    b) -28.8 at (80, 40) and -72.8 at (120, 0).
    c) -67.5 at (100, 0) and -89.5 at (80, 40).
    d) 47.7 on line segment joining (120, 0) and (80, 40), and 39.7 at (100, 0).
17. $61 at (5, 2).
18. $44 at (7, 3).
19. $145 at (13,4). Machine B is not fully utilized.
20. $22 at (8, 4).
21. $22 at (8, 4).
22. a) $15,600 at (4, 10). No grades are overproduced.
    b) $36,000 on line segment joining (4, 10) and (24, 0). At (4, 10), no grades are overproduced. At all other points, AA and A are both overproduced.
23. $7 at (1, 3).
24. $7.25 at (1.25, 2.25).

Problem Set 3-3

1. a) 44 at (8, 2) and 42 at (6, 6).
   b) 48 at (6, 6) and 22 at (8, 2).
   c) Maximum and minimum are both 36 on line segment joining (6, 6) and (8, 2).
2. a) 60 at (4, 8) and 54 at (18/5, 36/5).
   b) 76 at (4, 8) and 342/5 at (18/5, 36/5).
   c) 32 at (4, 8) and 144/5 at (18/5, 36/5).
3. a) Maximum and minimum are both 43 at (7, 4).
   b) Maximum and minimum are both 35 at (7, 4).
   c) Maximum and minimum are both 36 at (7, 4).
4. a) Maximum and minimum are both 60 at (4, 8).
   b) Maximum and minimum are both 76 at (4, 8).
   c) Maximum and minimum are both 32 at (4, 8).
5. The feasible solution set is empty so there is no maximum or minimum.
6. The feasible solution set is empty so there is no maximum or minimum.
7. $0.90 at (3, 1).
8. $2.40 at any point on the line segment joining (6, 0) and (3, 6).
9. 580 at (520, 320, 0).
10. 228 at (120, 0, 360).
11. 9.5 at (11/3, 0, 2).
12. 30.5 at (1/2, 57/4, 0).
13. $2,000 at (0, 0, 1000).
14. $0.39 at (4/3, 7/3, 7/3).
15. $190 at (0, 40, 75).
16. $106 at (2, 3, 6).
17. $26 at (8, 4, 2).
18. $46 at (3, 5, 4).

Problem Set 3-4

1. 1,122,750 at (75, 15).
2. a) $165,000 at (1600, 400).
   b) $385,000 at (1000, 3000).
3. a) 23,250 at (50, 50). c) $5,700 at (30, 30).
   b) $9,500.
4. $26,000 at (4, 10).
5. Maximize
$$2x + y + 4z$$
subject to
$$\begin{aligned} x &\leq 50 \text{ (redundant)} \\ y &\leq 50 \\ z &\leq 10 \\ x + y + z &\geq 40 \\ x + y + z &\leq 60 \\ z &\geq 5 \\ -x + y &\geq 1 \\ -x + y - 2z &\geq 10 \\ x, y, z &\geq 0. \text{ (only } x \geq 0 \text{ needed)} \end{aligned}$$
56 corners.

6. Minimize
$$5.75x + 4.75y + 3.75z$$
subject to
$$\begin{aligned} x + y + z &\leq 10,000 \\ x + y + z &\geq 6,000 \\ z &\leq 2,000 \\ x, y, z &\geq 1,000 \\ x + y - 3z &\geq 0 \\ x, y, z &\geq 0. \quad \text{(redundant)} \end{aligned}$$
35 corners.

7. Maximize
$$18x + 23y + 15z$$
subject to
$$\begin{aligned} 4x + 5y + 3z &\leq 425 \\ x + 2y + z &\leq 140 \\ 3x + 4y + 3z &\leq 350 \\ 8x + 10y + 9z &\geq 500 \\ 7x + 8y + 4z &\geq 400 \\ 6x + 6y + 7z &\geq 300 \\ x, y, z &\geq 0. \end{aligned}$$
84 corners.

8. Maximize
$$0.08S_1 + 0.09S_2 + 0.07S_3 + 0.1B_1 + 0.11B_2 + 0.06N$$
subject to
$$\begin{aligned} S_1 + S_2 + S_3 - 0.4B_1 - 0.4B_2 &\leq 0 \\ N &\geq 2,500,000 \\ S_1 + S_2 + S_3 &\leq 3,500,000 \\ S_1, S_2, S_3, B_1, B_2 &\leq 3,000,000 \\ S_1 + S_2 + S_3 + B_1 + B_2 + N &= 10,000,000 \\ \text{All variables} &\geq 0. \end{aligned}$$

Problem Set 3-4 (concluded)

9. Maximize
$$30x_{1A} + 60x_{1F} + 100x_{1S} + 75x_{1T} + 5x_{2A} + 80x_{2F} + 65x_{2S} + 110x_{2T}$$

subject to

$$
\begin{aligned}
x_{1A} + x_{2A} &\leq 5{,}000 \\
x_{1F} + x_{2F} &\leq 3{,}000 \\
x_{1S} + x_{2S} &\leq 2{,}000 \\
x_{1T} + x_{2T} &\leq 1{,}000 \\
4x_{1A} + 4x_{1F} + 3x_{1S} &\leq 2{,}100 \\
8x_{1A} + 10x_{1F} + 6x_{1S} + 7x_{1T} &\leq 14{,}000 \\
x_{2A} + 5x_{2S} + 5x_{2T} &\leq 1{,}500 \\
3x_{2A} + 8x_{2F} + 6x_{2T} &\leq 2{,}400 \\
x_{2A} + x_{2F} + 11x_{2S} + 20x_{2T} &\leq 2{,}500 \\
\text{All variables} &\geq 0.
\end{aligned}
$$

10. a) Minimize
$$250x_{JR} + 350x_{JS} + 300x_{AR} + 375x_{AS} + 25x_1$$

subject to

$$
\begin{aligned}
x_{JR} + x_{JS} &\geq 600 \\
x_{AR} + x_{AS} + x_1 &\geq 500 \\
x_{JR} &\leq 650 \\
x_{JS} &\leq 200 \\
x_{AR} &\leq 450 \\
x_{AS} &\leq 150 \\
x_{JR} + x_{JS} - x_1 &= 600
\end{aligned}
$$

All variables ≥ 0.

b) Minimize
$$275x_{JRJ} + 275x_{JRA} + 375x_{JSJ} + 375x_{JSA} + 300x_{AR} + 375x_{AS} - 15{,}000$$

subject to

$$
\begin{aligned}
x_{JRJ} + x_{JSJ} &\geq 600 \\
x_{JRA} + x_{JSA} + x_{AR} + x_{AS} &\geq 500 \\
x_{JRJ} + x_{JRA} &\leq 650 \\
x_{JSJ} + x_{JSA} &\leq 200 \\
x_{AR} &\leq 450 \\
x_{AS} &\leq 150
\end{aligned}
$$

All variables ≥ 0.

If the first constraint is changed to an "=" then the objective function is changed to

$$250x_{JRJ} + 275x_{JRA} + 350x_{JSJ} + 375x_{JSA} + 300x_{AR} + 375x_{AS}.$$

11. Minimize
$$x_1 + x_2 + x_3 + x_4 + x_5 + x_6$$

subject to

$$
\begin{aligned}
x_1 + x_6 &\geq 12 \\
x_1 + x_2 &\geq 14 \\
x_2 + x_3 &\geq 16 \\
x_3 + x_4 &\geq 10 \\
x_4 + x_5 &\geq 6 \\
x_5 + x_6 &\geq 9
\end{aligned}
$$

All $x_i \geq 0$.

12. a) (6, 0, 0), 0; (4, 1, 0), 4; (3, 0, 1), 7; (2, 2, 0), 8; (2, 1, 1), 1; (1, 3, 0), 2; (1, 0, 7), 4; (0, 2, 1), 5.

b) Minimize
$$4x_2 + 7x_3 + 8x_4 + x_5 + 2x_6 + 4x_7 + 5x_8$$

subject to

$$
\begin{aligned}
6x_1 + 4x_2 + 3x_3 + 2x_4 + 2x_5 + x_6 + x_7 &\geq 50 \\
x_2 + 2x_4 + x_5 + 3x_6 + x_8 &\geq 75 \\
x_3 + x_5 + 2x_7 + x_8 &\geq 85
\end{aligned}
$$

All $x_i \geq 0$.

c) Minimize
$$60(x_1 + x_2 + x_3 + x_4 + x_5 + x_6) - 3{,}655$$

subject to the constraints in (b).

Problem Set 3-5

1. 8 at (0, 4).
2. 28 at (14, 0).
3. 92 at (4, 9).
4. 92 at (4, 9).
5. 55 at (35, 0, 5).
6. 60 at (30, 0, 0).
7. 125/2 at (3/2, 29/2, 1/2).
8. 35 at (0, 40/7, 5/7).
9. 27 at (0, 3, 1).
10. 54/5 at (0, 4, 2/5).
11. 335/12 at (0, 5/6, 95/12).
12. 22 at (2, 6, 0).
13. 9 at (0, 3, 3).
14. 79/7 at (61/7, 5/7, 13/7).

Problem Set 3-5 (concluded)

15. $61 at (5, 2).
16. $89 at (5, 8). Machines B and C are not fully utilized.
17. $2,000 at (0, 0, 1000).
18. $190 at (0, 40, 75).

Problem Set 3-6

1. 29 at (3, 2).
2. 58 at (7, 3).
3. 40 at (10, 0).
4. 29 at (3, 2).
5. 58 at (7, 3).
6. 32 at (8, 0).
7. 33 at (6, 4).
8. 0 at (0, 0).
9. 90 at (6, 0, 6).
10. 114 at (0, 12, 6).
11. 98 at (0, 12, 6).
12. 126 at (18, 0, 6).
13. 90 at (6, 0, 6).
14. 85 at (5, 5, 3).
15. 114 at (0, 12, 6).
16. 116 at (4, 6, 8).
17. 128 at (2, 3, 6).
18. $172 at (4, 6, 8).
19. $182,000 at (0, 0, 700, 1000, 0, 300, 200, 0).

Problem Set 3-7

1. 4/5 at (0, 22/5).
2. 5 at (0, 3).
3. 10 at (5, 15).
4. 54 at (0, 8).
5. 17 at (0, 11).
6. 26 at (0, 8).
7. 3 at (3, 6).
8. 4 at (0, 4).
9. $3 at (3, 6).
10. $10,000 at (5, 15).

CHAPTER 4

Problem Set 4-1

1. 28 at (14, 0).
2. 6 on line segment joining (4, 9) and (7, 6).
3. 38 at (6, 1).
4. 3 at (6, 1).
5. 27 at (9, 9).
6. 90 at (6, 0, 6).
8. 24 on line segment joining (0, 4) and (3, 2).
9. 21 on line segment joining (14, 0) and (7, 3).
10. 7 on line segment joining (5, 2) and (3, 4).
11. 4 on line segment joining (4, 0) and (5, 1).
12. 108 on triangle joining (0, 12, 6), (0, 0, 9), and (12, 0, 6).
13. Unbounded solution.
14. Unbounded solution.
15. Unbounded solution.
16. 27/10 at (0, 1/40, 9/40).
17. 22 at (0, 13, −6).
18. 9/10 at (1/20, 0, 3/20).

2. 11 to 14; 19 to 26; 17 with no upper limit.
3. a) 88 at (8, 6).
   b) s_3 would have a current value of −4.
4. a) 14 with no upper limit; 13 to 20; 9 to 12.
   b) 33 at (11, 0).
5. a) 9 to 54; 8 to 48.
   b) 110 at (6, 0, 8).
6. $138 at (9, 6).
7. 28 at (8, 2).
8. 28 at (8, 2).
9. a) $1,500 at (100, 0, 80).
   b) $30 per labor-hour of grinding time and $50 per labor-hour of polishing time.
   c) 38 and 45 for grinding time; 23 and 28 for polishing time.
10. a) $125 thousand at (4, 9, 0).
    b) 1/5 of $1 thousand, or $200, for land purchase and 1/20 of $1 thousand, or $50, for landscaping.
    c) $95 thousand and $103 thousand for land purchase; $38 thousand and $50 thousand for landscaping.
11. a) $58 at (10, 12, 0).
    b) 1/5 of $1, or 20 cents, for forming time and 2/5 of $1, or 40 cents, for painting time.
    c) 140 and 155 minutes for forming time; 60 and 75 minutes for painting time.

Problem Set 4-2

1. a) 94 at (6, 8).   c) 92 at (4, 9).
   b) 86 at (6, 7).

Problem Set 4-3

1. a) $193 at (13, 3, 4).
   b) $193 at (13, 3, 4).
   c) $1,050 at (12, 6, 0).

2. a) $365 at (5, 8).
   b) $374 at (5, 8).
   c) $406 at (0, 8).

3. Maximize
$$\theta = 20p_1 + 10p_2$$
   subject to
$$4p_1 + 6p_2 \le 5$$
$$2p_1 + p_2 \le 3.$$

Initial Tableau

Basic Variables	Coefficient of				Current Values	
	p_1	p_2	x_1	x_2		
x_1	[4]	6	1	0	[5]	5/4 →
x_2	[2]	1	0	1	[3]	3/2
(max) θ	−20	−10	0	0	0	

↑

4. Maximize
$$\theta = 10p_1 + 20p_2$$
   subject to
$$3p_1 + p_2 \le 4$$
$$2p_1 + 2p_2 \le 2.$$

Initial Tableau

Basic Variables	Coefficient of				Current Values	
	p_1	p_2	x_1	x_2		
x_1	3	[1]	1	0	[4]	4
x_2	2	[2]	0	1	[2]	1 →
(max) θ	−10	−20	0	0	0	

↑

5. Maximize
$$\theta = 2p_1 + 4p_2 + 6p_3$$
   subject to
$$3p_1 + 2p_2 + 4p_3 \le 1$$
$$3p_1 + p_2 + 2p_3 \le 1$$
$$p_1 \quad\quad + 2p_3 \le 1.$$

Initial Tableau

Basic Variables	Coefficient of						Current Values	
	p_1	p_2	p_3	x_1	x_2	x_3		
x_1	3	2	[4]	1	0	0	[1]	1/4 →
x_2	3	1	[2]	0	1	0	[1]	1/2
x_3	1	0	[2]	0	0	1	[1]	1/2
(max) θ	−2	−4	−6	0	0	0	0	

↑

6. Maximize
$$\theta = 10p_1 + 15p_2 + 20p_3$$
   subject to
$$p_1 + 2p_2 + 3p_3 \le 2$$
$$p_1 + 3p_2 + p_3 \le 3$$
$$p_1 + p_2 + 2p_3 \le 1.$$

Initial Tableau

Basic Variables	Coefficient of						Current Values	
	p_1	p_2	p_3	x_1	x_2	x_3		
x_1	1	2	[3]	1	0	0	[2]	2/3
x_2	1	3	[1]	0	1	0	[3]	3
x_3	1	1	[2]	0	0	1	[1]	1/2 →
(max) θ	−10	−15	−20	0	0	0	0	

↑

7. 16 at (0, 8).
8. 42 at (6, 3).
9. 600 at (0, 600, 0).
10. 36 at (0, 22/19, 6/19).
11. $22 at (8, 4).
12. $15,600 at (4, 10). No grades are overproduced.
13. $26 at (8, 4, 2).
14. $14,000 at (8, 4, 2).

Problem Set 4-4

1. 29 at (3, 2).
2. 15 at (15/2, 0).

Problem Set 4-4 (concluded)

3. 36 at (0, 18).
4. 50 at (10, 0, 5).
5. 56 at (6, 9, 0).
6. 57 on line segment joining (36, 0, 0) and (12, 0, 6).
7. 32 at (0, 6, 8).
8. 30 at (0, 18, 6).
9. $14,000 at (3, 5, 4).
10. $26 at (8, 4, 2).
11. 34 at (9, 6, 10, 0, 6, 3).
12. a)

Combinations							
10-inch	6	4	3	2	2	1	1	0
16-inch	0	1	0	2	1	3	0	2
23-inch	0	0	1	0	1	0	2	1
Waste	0	4	7	8	1	2	4	5

   b) 85 at (0, 0, 0, 0, 85, 0, 0, 0).
   c) 245 at (0, 0, 0, 0, 15, 0, 20, 30).

Problem Set 4-5

1. No feasible solutions.
2. No feasible solutions.
3. No feasible solutions.
4. No feasible solutions.
5. No feasible solutions.
6. No feasible solutions.
7. No feasible solutions.
8. 19 at (3, 2).
9. 60 on line segment joining (15/2, 0) and (5, 2).
10. 60 at (0, 12) and 45 at (0, 9).
11. 60 at (0, 12) and 45 at (0, 9).
12. 60 at (0, 12) and 45 at (0, 9).
13. No maximum; minimum is 36 at (6, 6).
14. 28 at (2, 8) and 20 at (4, 4).
15. 86 at (4, 11) and 62 at (4, 7).
16. 14 at (4, 6) and 12 at (6, 0).
17. 44 at (8, 2) and 42 at (6, 6).
18. 63 at (9, 3) and 54 at (6, 6).
19. 42 at (0, 12).
20. -48 at (0, 0, 12).

Problem Set 4-6

1. a) No lower limit with an upper limit of 54; 13 with no upper limit; no lower limit with an upper limit of 72.
   b) 40 at (0, 20).   c) 36 at (0, 18).
   d) p_3 would have a current value of -12.

2. a) 6 with no upper limit; 0 to 16; -4 to 12.
   b) 52 at (7, 9).   c) 36 at (6, 6).
   d) s_1 would have a current value of -22.

3. a) 10 with no upper limit; no lower limit with an upper limit of 12; 2 to 10.
   b) 16 at (4, 2).
   c) 32 at (16, 0).
   d) 12 at (6, 0).

4. a) 14 to 54; no lower limit with an upper limit of 12; 13 to 48.
   b) 46 at (6, 8).
   c) 38 at (2, 14).
   d) 44 at (8, 2).

5. a) 3 to 12; no lower limit with an upper limit of 12; 6 to 24.
   b) 72 at (8, 8).
   c) 54 at (6, 6).
   d) 54 at (6, 6). The column entries in (d) are 1/2 those in (c) because of the relationship between the two respective slack variables.

6. a) 2 to 4.   b) 1.5 to 3.
   c) No lower limit with an upper limit of 1.
   d) No lower limit with an upper limit of 1.

7. a) 202 at (14, 0, 8).
   b) 2 to 14.
   c) No lower limit with an upper limit of 49/3.
   d) 15/2 to 24.
   e) No lower limit with an upper limit of 8/3.
   f) No lower limit with an upper limit of 11/3.

8. a) 4 with no upper limit.
   b) 0 to 3.
   c) -2 to 8.

9. a) 777 at (0, 0, 15).
   b) 71/2 with no upper limit.
   c) 117/2 with no upper limit.
   d) No lower limit with an upper limit of 36.
   e) 23/2 with no upper limit.

10. a) $P \geq R_2 + R_3$.
    b) $4 or more.
    c) 4 units or fewer.
    d) None.

11. a) $C \leq 2R_2$.
    b) $6 or less.
    c) 7 units or more; unlimited; unlimited.

12. a) $3P \geq 8R_i + 11R_2$.
    b) $27 or more.
    c) 3 units or fewer.
    d) 3 units or fewer.

13. a) $2C \leq 24R_1 + 23R_2$.
    b) $94 or less.
    c) 3 units or more.
    d) 1 unit or more.

CHAPTER 5

Problem Set 5-1

1. 256.
2. 8.
3. 9.
4. 4.
5. 25.
6. 3.
7. 1/3.
8. $e^6 = 403.4288$.
9. $e^{-6} = 0.0025$.
10. $e^4 = 54.5982$.
11. See Figure A.
12. See Figure B.
13. See Figure C.
14. See Figure D (p. 1012).
15. See Figure E (p. 1012).
16. See Figure F (p. 1012).
17. See Figure G (p. 1012).
18. See Figure H (p. 1013).
19. See Figure I (p. 1013).
20. See Figure J (p. 1013).
21. See Figure K (p. 1013).
22. See Figure L (p. 1014).
23. See Figure M (p. 1014).
24. See Figure N (p. 1014).
25. See Figure O (p. 1014).
26. See Figure P (p. 1015).
27. See Figure Q (p. 1015).
28. See Figure R (p. 1015).
29. a) $1.28; $1.63.
    b)
Year	Value
1	$1.05
2	$1.10
3	$1.16
4	$1.22
5	$1.28
6	$1.34
7	$1.41
8	$1.48
9	$1.55
10	$1.63

FIGURE B

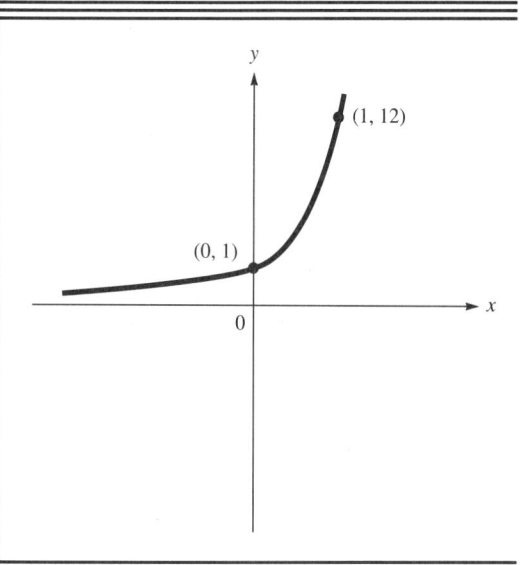

FIGURE A

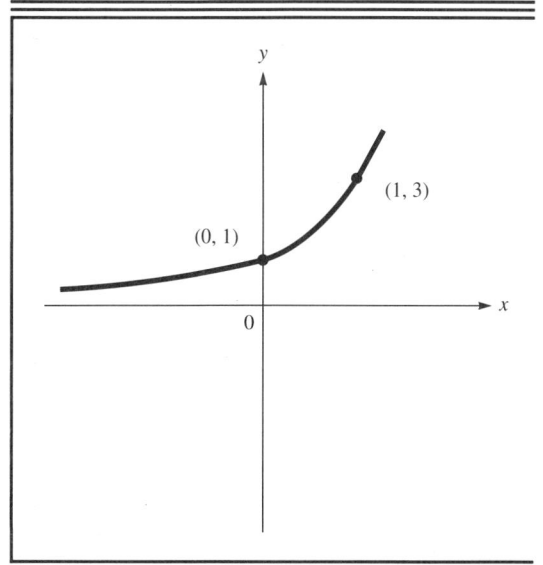

FIGURE C

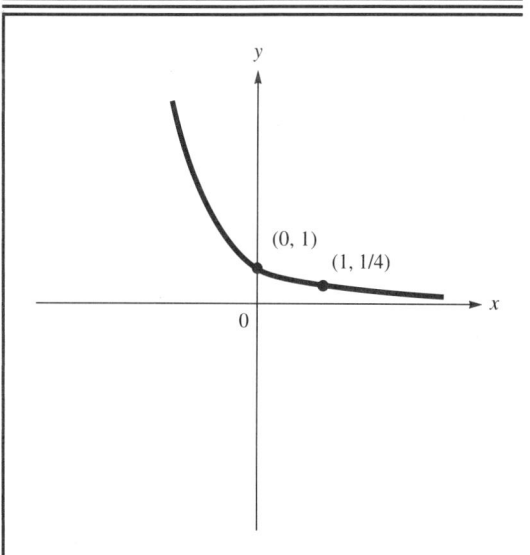

Problem Set 5-1 *(continued)*

FIGURE D

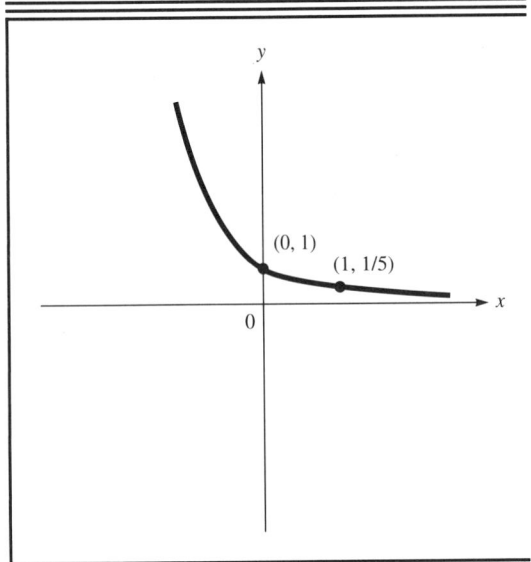

FIGURE F

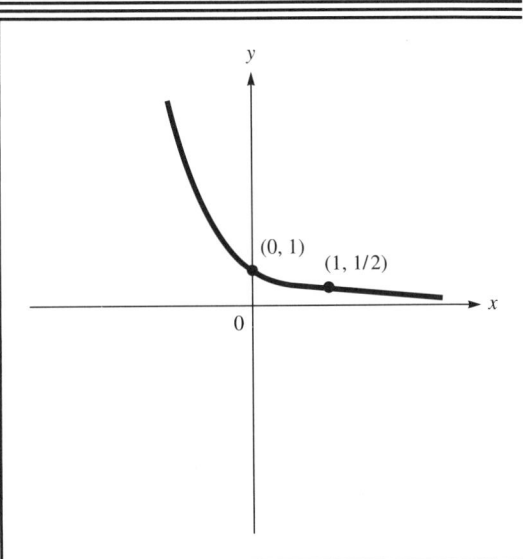

FIGURE E

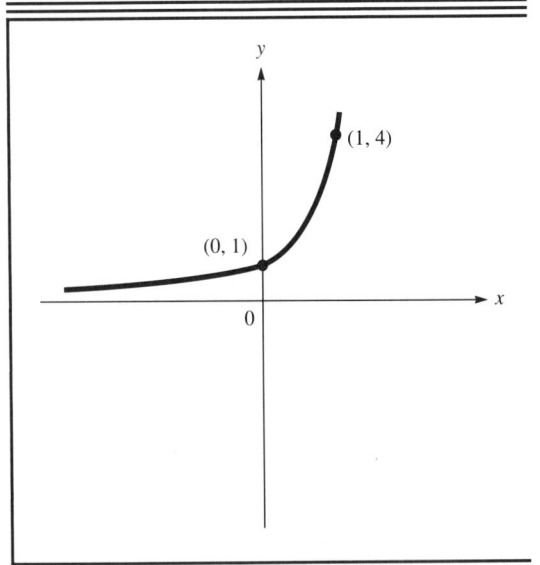

FIGURE G

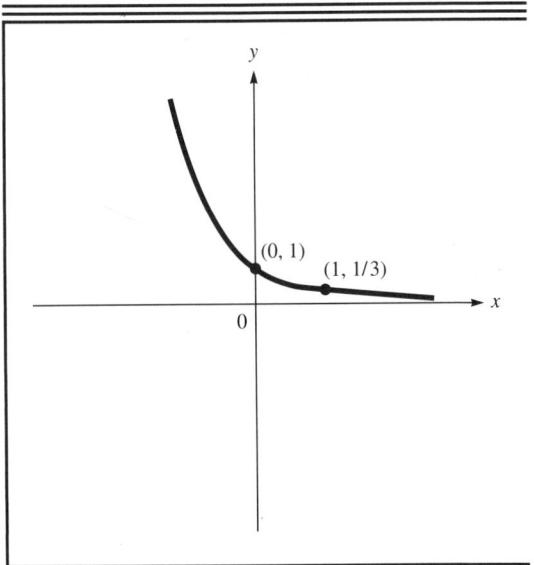

Problem Set 5-1 *(continued)*

FIGURE H

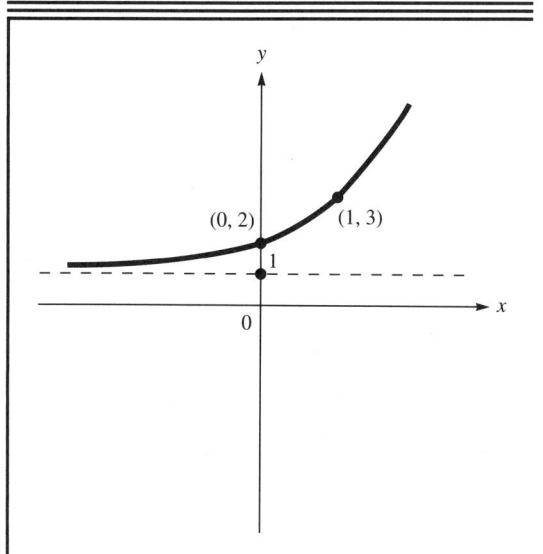

FIGURE J

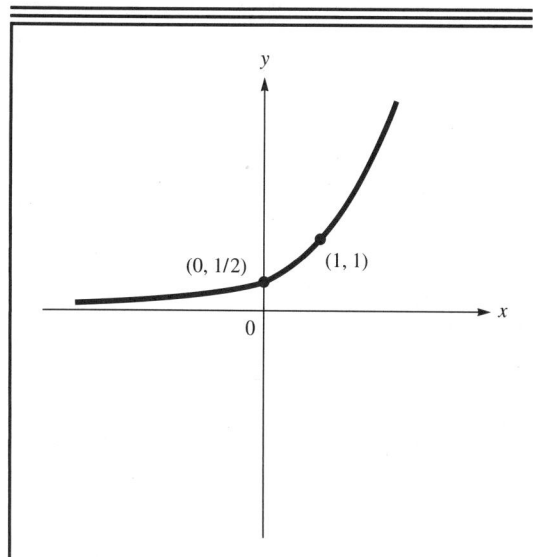

FIGURE I

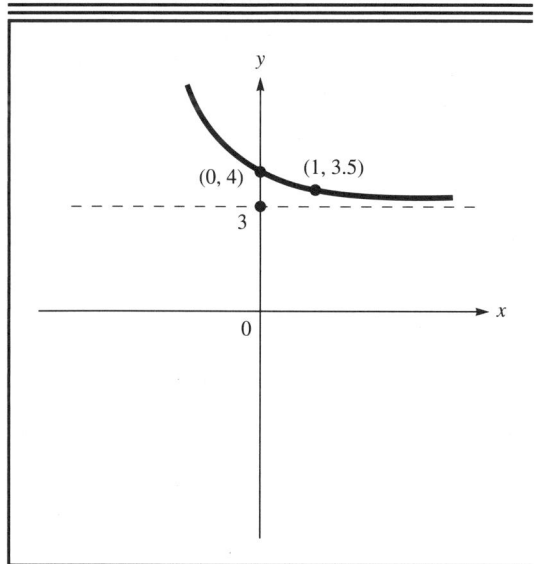

FIGURE K

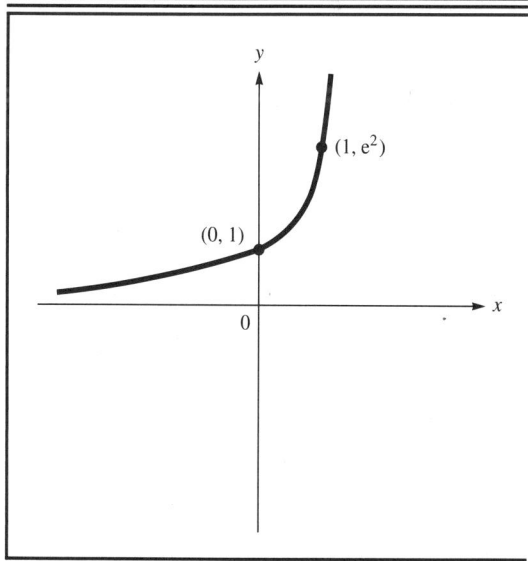

Problem Set 5-1 *(continued)*

FIGURE L
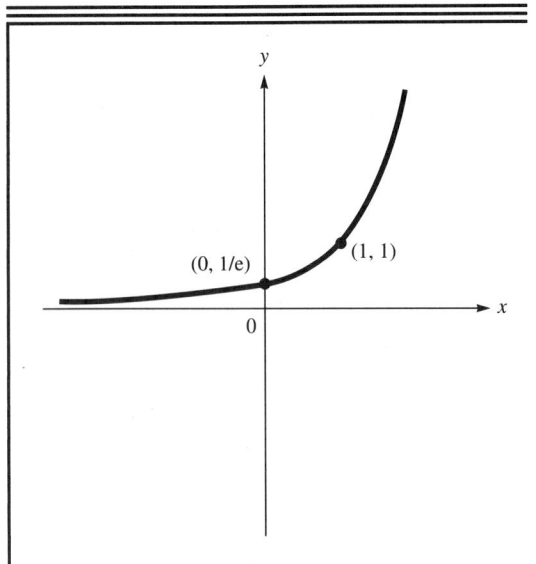

FIGURE N
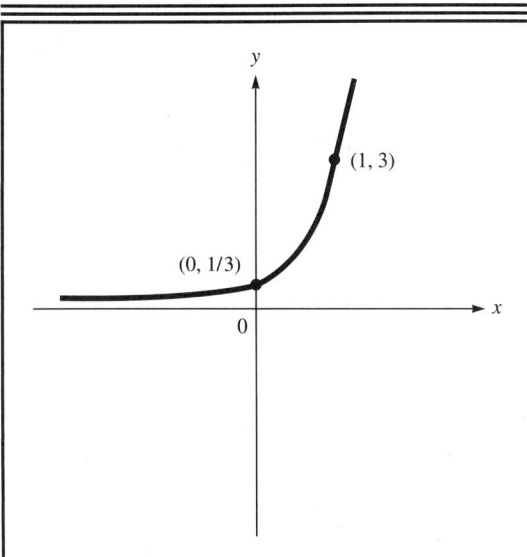

FIGURE M
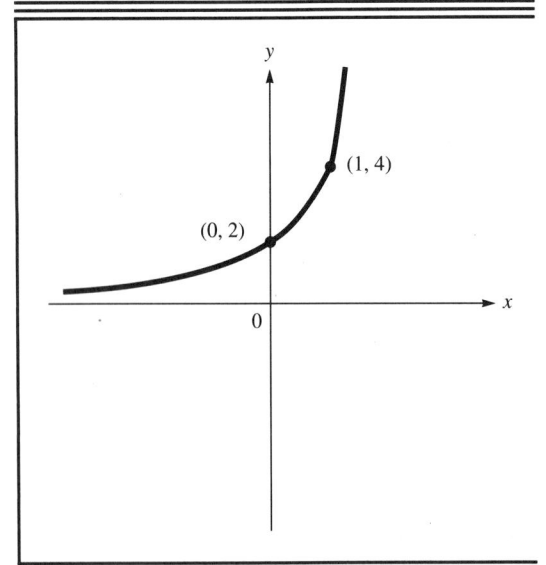

FIGURE O
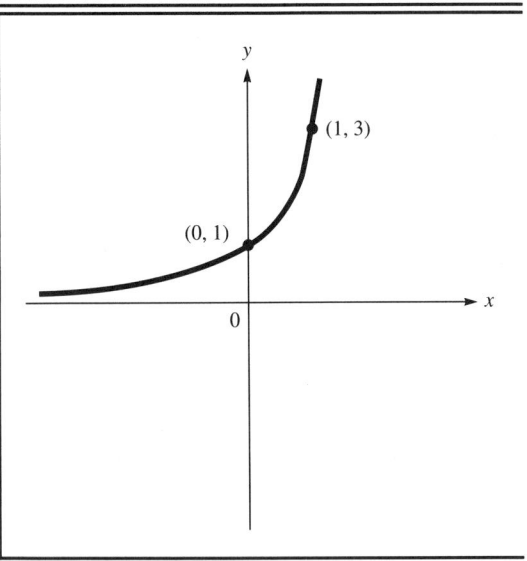

Problem Set 5-1 (concluded)

FIGURE P

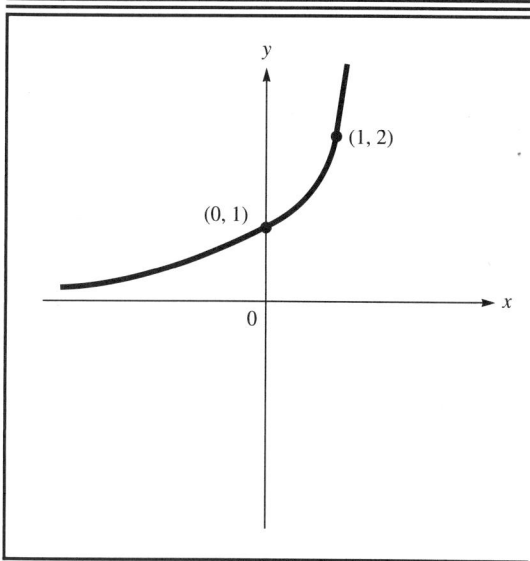

FIGURE Q

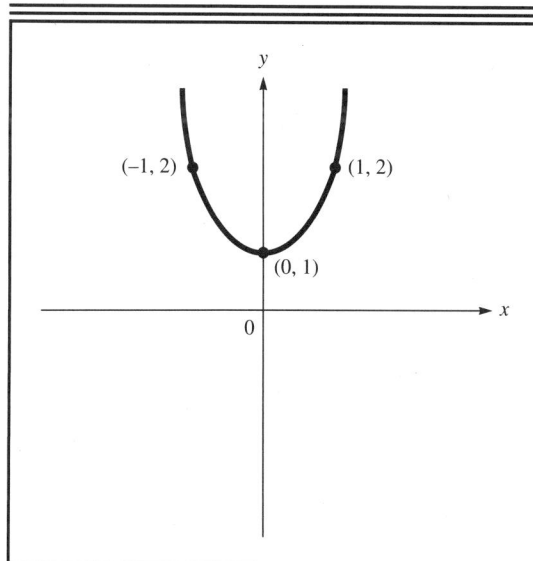

FIGURE R

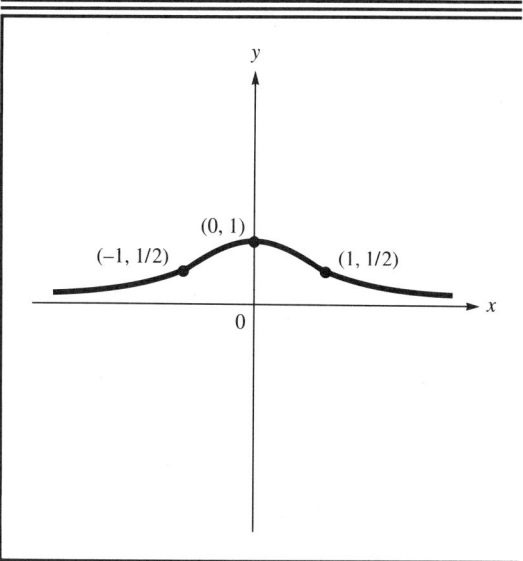

30. $30,626.08; $35,063.79.
31. 1.024 inches; 33,554.432 inches; 17,769,884.893 miles.
32. Linear growth can easily be predicted by extrapolating from the past since the slope of any line is constant. Exponential growth has changing slope and so requires more sophisticated analysis than linear growth.

Problem Set 5-2

1. $\log_3 9 = 2$.
2. $\log_2 32 = 5$.
3. $3^x = N$.
4. $2^y = N$.
5. $\log_{1/2} 0.125 = 3$.
6. $\log_{0.2} 0.04 = 2$.
7. $16^{1/2} = 4$.
8. $27^{1/3} = 3$.
9. $\log_2 0.125 = -3$.
10. $\log_3(1/9) = -2$.
11. $5^{-2} = 0.04$.
12. $2^{-4} = 0.0625$.
13. $e^{2.9957} = 20$.
14. $e^{2.3026} = 10$.
15. $10^{-0.3010} = 0.5$.
16. $e^{-0.6931} = 0.5$.
17. 1.
18. 1.
19. 2.
20. 3.
21. 1.
22. 1.
23. 1/2.
24. 1/3.
25. 4.4.
26. -0.6.

Problem Set 5–2 (concluded)

27. 5.4.
28. 6.8.
29. −1.8.
30. −2.4.
31. 2.8.
32. 1.
33. $\ln(x^2y^3)$.
34. $\ln(x^3/y^2)$.
35. $\ln x$.
36. $2 \ln x$.
37. $\ln y^{1/x}$.
38. $\ln x^{1/y}$.
39. $\ln(x^2z^3/y^2)$.
40. $\log(x^5y^{1/2}/z^2)$.
41. 1.585.
42. 0.631.
43. 0.699.
44. 0.111.
45. 0.012.
46. 18.854.
47. 9.006.
48. −3.000.
49. −1.661.
50. 14.275.
51. 54.449.
52. −4.596.
53. 5.815.
54. −0.926.
55. 3.092.
56. 18.854.
57. 23.791.

Problem Set 5–3

1. $\ln(e^{\ln x}) = \ln 2$
   $\ln x(\ln e) = \ln 2$
   $\ln x = \ln 2$
   antiln $(\ln x)$ = antiln $(\ln 2)$
   $x = 2$.
2. $\log(10^{\log x}) = \log 3$
   $\log x(\log 10) = \log 3$
   $\log x = \log 3$
   antilog$(\log x)$ = antilog$(\log 3)$
   $x = 3$.
3. 5.
4. 4.
5. 6.
6. 5.
7. 1.522.
8. 3.320.
9. 0.333.
10. 0.990.
11. 0.350.
12. 0.718.
13. 5.213.
14. 4.780.
15. 11.232.
16. 6.116.
17. 0.14870 or 14.870%.
18. 0.20112 or 20.112%.
19. 0.095.
20. 0.262.

CHAPTER 6

Problem Set 6–1

1. a) $35. b) $535.
2. a) $80. b) $1,080.
3. a) $45. b) $1,045.
4. a) $60. b) $2,060.
5. a) $12. b) $112.
6. a) $30. b) $530.
7. a) $36. b) $236.
8. a) $120. b) $620.
9. a) $3,600. b) $8,600.
10. a) $2,400. b) $6,400.
11. 15 months.
12. 18%.
13. 6.75%.
14. $714.29.
15. 30 months.
16. 20 months.
17. 16%.
18. 5%.
19. $400.
20. $854.70.
21. $904.98.
22. $869.57.
23. $1,640.
24. $466.25.
25. $2,580.65.
26. 12%.
27. 14.634%.
28. 9.651%.
29. 19.355%.
30. 8.802%.
31. 10.427%.
32. 13.483%.

Problem Set 6–2

1. $530.66.
2. $537.25.
3. $8,689.81.
4. $1,379.52.
5. $282.68.
6. $357.69.
7. $2,880.61.
8. $4,801.02.
9. 20.490 years.
10. 7.273 years.
11. 3.526%.
12. 11.248%.
13. $6,851.14.
14. $2,012.99.
15. 8.043 years.
16. 17.462%.

Problem Set 6-3

1. $214.55
2. $1,016.70.
3. $3,069.57.
4. $2,795.70.
5. $574.37.
6. $1,747.31.
7. 78.353 units per labor-hour.
8. $5,000.
9. $852.16.
10. $815.87.

Problem Set 6-4

1. 8.243%.
2. 10.25%.
3. 12.683%.
4. 16.986%.
5. 10.471%.
6. 7.186%.
7. 19.562%.
8. 9.308%.
9. 9.381%.
10. 9.416%.
11. 11%; 11.303%; 11.462%; 11.572%; 11.600%; 11.615%; 11.626%.
12. 14%; 14.490%; 14.752%; 14.934%; 14.981%; 15.006%; 15.024%.

Problem Set 6-5

1. $1,349.86.
2. $1,112.77.
3. $7,166.65.
4. $5,619.79.
5. $341.93.
6. $799.55.
7. $913.93.
8. $2,582.12.
9. 0.051.
10. 0.062.
11. 0.073.
12. 0.083.
13. 0.113.
14. 0.086.
15. 0.049.
16. 0.095.
17. $19,480.97.
18. $4,317.11.
19. $31,267.68.
20. $4,782.21.
21. About $2,598,119,706.
22. $5,444.39.
23. 8.220%.
24. 7.900%.
25. 8.010%.

Problem Set 6-6

1. $21,538.44.
2. $60,401.98.
3. $81,990.98.
4. $396,566.68.
5. $23,787.71.
6. $4,307.69.
7. $4,828.51.
8. $1,576.44.
9. $6,902.95
10. $687.30.
11. $312,232.31
12. $50,886.21.

Problem Set 6-7

1. $6,540.57.
2. $30,107.51.
3. $37,816.56.
4. $15,046.30.
5. a) $6,000.   b) $5,287.67.
6. a) $53,373.88.   b) $125,000.
7. $47.07.
8. $200.61.
9. a) $10,758.49.
   b) $6,000 for interest; $4,758.49 reduction of balance owed.
   c) $5,714.49 for interest; $5,044 reduction of balance owed.
10. a) $235.40.
    b) $120 interest; $115.40 reduction of balance owed.
    c) $117.69 interest; $117.71 reduction of balance owed.
11. a) $12,587.95.
    b) $11,250 interest; $1,337.95 reduction of balance owed.
12. a) $275.35.
    b) $255.21 interest; $20.14 reduction of balance owed.
13. $86,126.35.
14. $200,443.11

Problem Set 6-8

1. $1,146.39
2. $232.50.
3. $11,040.20.
4. $800.80.
5. $2,145.48.
6. $221,224.81.
7. 38,857.
8. $178.60.
9. $6,074.34.
10. $115,573.86.
11. $3,257.79.
12. $226.11.
13. $3,888.44.
14. $12,942.29.
15. $10,119.86.
16. $39,296.11.
17. $1,414.59.
18. $11,726.87.
19. $7,357.48.

Problem Set 6-9

1. 6.287%.
2. 6.933%.
3. 7.755%.
4. 5.723%.
5. 10; $33.
6. 29; $11.40.
7. 27; $15,633.
8. 163; $130,170.
9. $13,435.19.
10. $205.78.
11. $23,003.87.
12. $1,192.57.
13. $15,443.47.
14. $21,281.27.
15. $195.50.
16. $196.16.
17. $13,467.89.
18. $109.16.
19. $86,697.75.
20. $217.32.

CHAPTER 7

Problem Set 7-1

1. a) 7.
   b) -8.
   c) $3a - 2$.
   d) $(3a - 2)^2 = 9a^2 - 12a + 4$.
   e) $3ab - 2$.
   f) $9y + 10$.
   g) $3x + 1$.
   h) 3.

2. a) 10.   e) $x^2 + 4x + 1.75$.
   b) 0.   f) $a^2 + 5a + 4$.
   c) 1.75.   g) $a^2 + a - 2$.
   d) $(6a + 4)/a^2$. h) $2x + 2$.

3. a) $a^2y - y^2$.   b) $ax^2 - a^2$.
4. a) $2x + 15$.   b) $6 + 5y$.
5. a) 0.25.
   b) 1/3.
   c) $2/a - 3/a^2 = (2a - 3)/a^2$.
   d) $2/(x + 1) - 3/(x + 1)^2 = (2x - 1)/(x + 1)^2$.
6. a) 5.
   b) 131/16.
   c) 13.
7. a) Δx means the change in x.
   b) The value of $f(x)$ at the point $x + \Delta x$.
   c) $f(x + \Delta x) - f(x)$ means the change in $f(x)$ when x changes by Δx.
8. 0.75.
9. -0.98.
10. $-3h$.
11. mh.
12. a) $h(2x + h)$.
    b) $h(4x + 2h - 3)$.
13. a) $h(4x + 2h)$.
    b) $h(2x + h + 2)$.
14. a) $0.02 + 2.99$.
    b) $3.19.
    c) $3.99.
15. a) $0.2g + 0.9$.   b) $2.90.   c) $10.90.

Problem Set 7-2

1. 1.
2. -13.
3. ab^2.
4. a^4.
5. 0.
6. 1.
7. Limit does not exist.
8. Limit does not exist.
9. $(a - 1)^{1/3}$.
10. 5.
11. $8a$.
12. $4b$.
13. 6.
14. 10.
15. 0.
16. Limit does not exist.
17. Limit does not exist.
18. 0.
19. $2x$.
20. $3x^2$.
21. $-1/4$.
22. $-1/25$.
23. 3.
24. Limit does not exist.
25. 1.
26. 2.
27. Limit does not exist.
28. Limit does not exist.
29. 5/4.
30. 1.
31. Limit does not exist.
32. c) Limit does not exist.
33. c) -2.
34. c) 0.

Problem Set 7-3

1. None.
2. $x = 1$.
3. None.
4. $x = \pm 2$.
5. $x = 2$.
6. $x = 2; x = 3$.
7. $x = 1$.
8. None.
9. None.
10. None.
13. Continuous at all $x \geq 0$. See Figure A.
14. Continuous at all $x \geq 0$. See Figure B.

FIGURE A

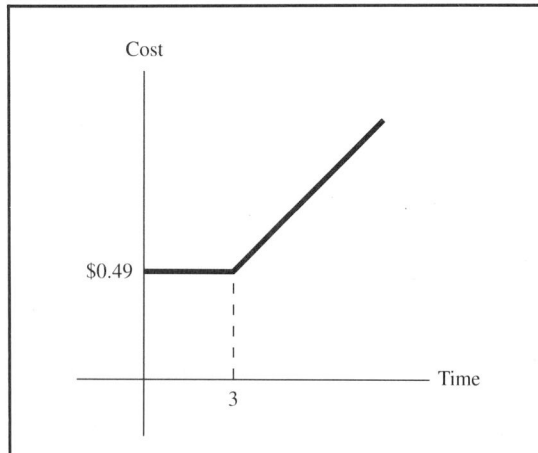

Problem Set 7-3 (concluded)

FIGURE B

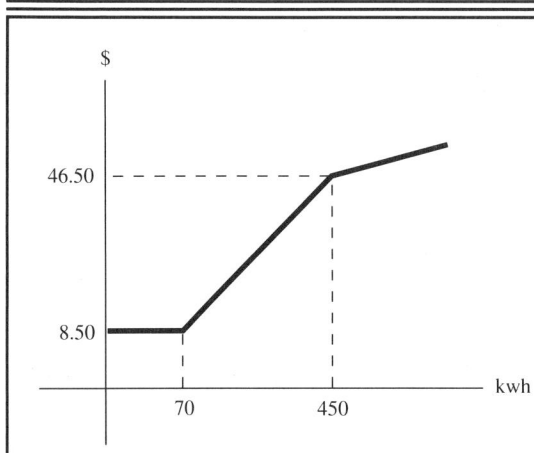

Problem Set 7-4

1. $f'(x) = 3; f'(1) = 3$.
2. $f'(x) = -0.5; f'(1) = -0.5$.
3. $f'(x) = 2x - 2; f'(1) = 0$.
4. $f'(x) = 6x - 12; f'(3) = 6$.
5. $f'(x) = -1/x^2; f'(2) = -1/4$.
6. $f'(x) = -2/x^3; f'(-1) = 2$.
7. $f'(x) = 3x^2 + 2; f'(2) = 14$.
8. $f'(x) = 3x^2 - x + 1; f'(-1) = 5$.
9. $f'(x) = 4x^3; f'(-1) = -4$.
10. $f'(x) = 1/(2\sqrt{x}); f'(1) = 1/2$.
11. $f'(x) = \lim\limits_{h \to 0} \dfrac{(x+h)^5 - 2(x+h)^4 - x^5 + 2x^4}{h}$.
12. $f'(x) = \lim\limits_{h \to 0} \dfrac{3(x+h)^6 + 2(x+h)^3 - 3x^6 - 2x^3}{h}$.
13. $f'(x) = \lim\limits_{h \to 0} \dfrac{(x+h)^{1/3} - x^{1/3}}{h}$.
14. $f'(x) = \lim\limits_{h \to 0} \dfrac{(x+h)^{1/2} - x^{1/2}}{h}$.

Problem Set 7-5

1. 0. 2. 1. 3. 1/2. 4. 2.

5. 1/3.
6. $-3/2$.
7. $6x + 2$.
8. $x^2 - x + 1$.
9. $0.02x + 2$.
10. $1.5x^2 - x$.
11. m.
12. $2ax + b$.
13. $(-2/x^2) + (2/x^3)$.
14. $-1/(2x^2) - (3/x^4)$.
15. $3x^{1/2} - (2/x^{1/2}) + (2/x^{1/3}) + 2$.
16. $2/(3x^{2/3}) + (4/3)x^{1/3} + 6x^{0.2} + 1$.
17. $-1/(3x^2) - (1/x^{3/2})$.
18. $(-1/x^{4/3}) + (3/x^{5/4})$.
19. $6x - 2$.
20. $20y$.
21. a.
22. 0.
23. $2kh - a/(3h^{2/3})$.
24. $(-a/m^2) - 6m$.
25. 0.
26. 0.
27. 2.
28. -4.
29. 1.
30. 0.
31. 0.
32. -1.
33. 5/3.
34. 1.
35. $x = 1/2$.
36. $x = 100$.
37. $x = 1/8$.
38. $x = 9/16$.
39. $x = 3$.
40. $x = 4$.
41. a) $4 per yard. b) $6 per yard.
42. a) $55 per ton. b) $40 per ton. c) $55 per ton.

43. $\dfrac{d}{dx}[f(x) + g(x)] = \lim\limits_{h \to 0}\left[\dfrac{f(x+h) + g(x+h) - f(x) - g(x)}{h}\right]$

$= \lim\limits_{h \to 0}\left[\dfrac{f(x+h) - f(x) + g(x+h) - g(x)}{h}\right]$

$= \lim\limits_{h \to 0}\left[\dfrac{f(x+h) - f(x)}{h} + \dfrac{g(x+h) - g(x)}{h}\right]$

$= \lim\limits_{h \to 0}\left[\dfrac{f(x+h) - f(x)}{h}\right] + \lim\limits_{h \to 0}\left[\dfrac{g(x+h) - g(x)}{h}\right]$

$= f'(x) + g'(x)$.

Problem Set 7-6

1. $30(6x - 5)^4$.
2. $10(2x + 6)^4$.
3. $6(2x)^2 = 24x^2$.
4. $2/(6x)^{2/3}$.
5. $2/(4x)^{1/2} = 1/x^{1/2}$.
6. $12(9x)^{1/3}$.
7. $12(8x - 3)^{1/2}$.
8. $20(12x - 9)^{2/3}$.

Problem Set 7-6 (concluded)

9. $15(x - 1)(3x^2 - 6x + 2)^{3/2}$.
10. $4(x^2 - 2x + 2)(x^3 - 3x^2 + 6x)^{1/3}$.
11. $1/(2x - 3)^{1/2}$.
12. $4x/(3x^2 + 5)^{1/3}$.
13. $-8/(2x - 3)^2$.
14. $-18/(3x - 5)^2$.
15. $(-2/x^2)(1/x - 2)$.
16. $(6/x^3)(5 - 1/x^2)^2$.
17. $-54/(3x - 5)^3$.
18. $-72/(2x + 10)^4$.
19. $5 - 30/(3x + 2)^2$.
20. $0.1 + 1/(5 - 0.2x)^2$.
21. $3 - 1/(5 + 2x)^{3/2}$.
22. $-2 - 3/[2(3x - 7)^{3/2}]$.
23. $28/3$.
24. $13/2$.

Problem Set 7-7

1. $12x + 11$.
2. $19 - 42x$.
3. $9x^2 - 10x + 6$.
4. $3(5 - 4x - 5x^2)$.
5. $4x(x - 1)^3 + (x - 1)^4 = (x - 1)^3(5x - 1)$.
6. $3x^2(x + 5)^2 + 2x(x + 5)^3 = 5x(x + 5)^2(x + 2)$.
7. $\dfrac{3x^2(x + 3)^{1/2}}{2} + 2x(x + 3)^{3/2} = x(x + 3)^{1/2}\left(\dfrac{7x}{2} + 6\right)$.
8. $\dfrac{4x^3}{(6x - 1)^{1/3}} + 3x^2(6x - 1)^{2/3} = \dfrac{x^2(22x - 3)}{(6x - 1)^{1/3}}$.
9. $\dfrac{4x^2}{(3x^2 + 7)^{2/3}} + 2(3x^2 + 7)^{1/3} = \dfrac{2(5x^2 + 7)}{(3x^2 + 7)^{2/3}}$.
10. $\dfrac{9x^3}{(2x^3 + 5)^{1/2}} + 3(2x^3 + 5)^{1/2} = \dfrac{15(x^3 + 1)}{(2x^3 + 5)^{1/2}}$.
11. $-\dfrac{1}{(x - 1)^2}$.
12. $\dfrac{3}{(x + 1)^2}$.
13. $\dfrac{2x(x + 3)}{(2x + 3)^2}$.
14. $\dfrac{3x^2(2x + 5)}{(3x + 5)^2}$.
15. $\dfrac{3 - 2x^2}{(3 + 2x^2)^2}$.
16. $\dfrac{3(2x^2 + 1)}{(1 - 2x^2)^2}$.
17. $\dfrac{(3x + 2)^{1/2} - \dfrac{3x(3x + 2)^{-1/2}}{2}}{3x + 2} = \dfrac{3x + 4}{2(3x + 2)^{3/2}}$.
18. $\dfrac{2(2x + 3)^{1/2} - 2x(2x + 3)^{-1/2}}{2x + 3} = \dfrac{2(x + 3)}{(2x + 3)^{3/2}}$.
19. $\dfrac{2(x^2 + 5)^{1/3} - \dfrac{2x(2x + 1)(x^2 + 5)^{-2/3}}{3}}{(x^2 + 5)^{2/3}} = \dfrac{2(x^2 - x + 15)}{3(x^2 + 5)^{4/3}}$.
20. $\dfrac{-5(x^3 + 2)^{1/3} - x^2(3 - 5x)(x^3 + 2)^{-2/3}}{(x^3 + 2)^{2/3}} = -\dfrac{3x^2 + 10}{(x^3 + 2)^{4/3}}$.

CHAPTER 8

Problem Set 8-1

1. (2.5, 6.25) is a local maximum.
2. (3, 2) is a local minimum.
3. (0, 3) is a local maximum.
4. (0, 20) is a local minimum.
5. (5, 85) is a local maximum.
6. (0.5, 0.75) is a local minimum.
7. (0, 12) is a local maximum; (8, −244) is a local minimum.
8. (0, 2) is a local maximum; (2, −2) is a local minimum.
9. (0, 27) is a stationary inflection point.
10. (0, 14) is a stationary inflection point.
11. (5, −5) is a local maximum; (2, −32) is a local minimum.
12. (3, 0) is a local maximum; (1, −4) is a local minimum.
13. (4, −8) is a local minimum.
14. (27, 27) is a local maximum.
15. (4, −16) is a local minimum.
16. (125, 25) is a local maximum.
17. (4, 32) is a local minimum; (−4, −32) is a local maximum.
18. (5, 30) is a local minimum.
19. (3, 27) is a stationary inflection point; (−1, −37) is an endpoint minimum; (6, 54) is an endpoint maximum.
20. (−5, −125) is a stationary inflection point; (−8, −152) is an endpoint minimum; (2, 218) is an endpoint maximum.

Problem Set 8-1 (concluded)

21. (2, 52) is a local minimum. Endpoint maxima at $(-2, 180)$ and $(4, 228)$.
22. $(3, 243)$ is a local maximum. Endpoint minima at $(-1, -109)$ and $(5, -85)$.
23. $(1, 5)$ is a local maximum; $(0, 4)$ is a stationary inflection point. Endpoint minimum at $(-1, -3)$.
24. $(3, 3)$ is a local minimum; $(0, 30)$ is a stationary inflection point. Endpoint maximum at $(-2, 78)$.
25. a) 50 gallons.   c) $5 per gallon.
26. a) $x = 25$ feet.
    c) 25 feet by 25 feet, a square.
    d) 625 square feet.
27. a) $p = 0.50$.   c) $V(0.5) = 0.025$. $V(0.1) = 0.009$.
28. a) 2,000 gallons.   c) $20,000.

11. Local minimum at $(2, -1)$.
12. Local minimum at $(-5, -34)$.
13. Local maximum at $(1, 5)$; local minimum at $(3, 1)$; inflection point at $(2, 3)$.
14. Inflection point at $(0, 0)$.
15. Local maximum at $(-2/3, 121/27)$; local minimum at $(2, -5)$; inflection point at $(2/3, -7/27)$.
16. Local maximum at $(-3, 24)$; local minimum at $(1, -8)$; inflection point at $(-1, 8)$.
17. Local maximum at $(-3, 56)$; local minimum at $(-5, 52)$; inflection point at $(-4, 54)$.
18. Local minimum at $(0, 0)$.
19. Local minimum at $(14, 8)$.
20. Local minimum at $(0, 27)$; inflection point at $(1, -16)$; stationary inflection point at $(3, 0)$.

Problem Set 8-2

1. $f'(x) = 5x^4 - 8x^3 + 3x^2$.
   $f''(x) = 20x^3 - 24x^2 + 6x$.
   $f'''(x) = 60x^2 - 48x + 6$.
2. $f'(x) = 3x^2 - 2x - 1$.
   $f''(x) = 6x - 2$.
   $f'''(x) = 6$.
3. $f'(x) = 24x^2 - 4x$.
   $f''(x) = 48x - 4$.
   $f'''(x) = 48$.
4. $f'(x) = 6x^5 - 4x^3 + 6x$.
   $f''(x) = 30x^4 - 12x^2 + 6$.
   $f'''(x) = 120x^3 - 24x$.
5. $f'(x) = 12x^3 - 15x^2 + 4x$.
   $f''(x) = 36x^2 - 30x + 4$.
   $f'''(x) = 72x - 30$.
6. $f'(x) = (5/2)x^{3/2} - 10x + 1$.
   $f''(x) = (15/4)x^{1/2} - 10$.
   $f'''(x) = (15/8)/x^{1/2}$.
7. $f'(x) = 3(x + 5)^2$.
   $f''(x) = 6x + 30$.
   $f'''(x) = 6$.
8. $f'(x) = x(x^2 + 1)$.
   $f''(x) = 3x^2 + 1$.
   $f'''(x) = 6x$.
9. $f'(x) = -13/(x - 3)^2$.
   $f''(x) = 26/(x - 3)^3$.
   $f'''(x) = -78/(x - 3)^4$.
10. $f'(x) = -4/(x - 2)^2$.
    $f''(x) = 8/(x - 2)^3$.
    $f'''(x) = -24/(x - 2)^4$.

Problem Set 8-3

1. a) 50 by 66 feet.
   b) $33,000.
2. a) 75 by 99 feet.
   b) 7,425 square feet.
3. a) $C(x) = \left(2x + 2\dfrac{A}{x}\right)e + ix$.
   b) $x = \sqrt{\dfrac{2Ae}{i + 2e}}$.
4. a) $A(x) = x\left(\dfrac{D - 2ex - ix}{2e}\right)$.
   b) $x = \dfrac{D}{2(2e + i)}$.
5. a) 90 by 150 feet.
   b) $90,000.
6. $210.
7. 500 square feet.
8. 18 by 12 inches; area = 216 square inches.
9. 1,100 by 660 feet; increase would be 10,000 square feet.
10. a) $A = 2x^2 + 4xL$.
    b) $A(x) = 432x - 14x^2$.
    c) $x = 108/7$; $A''(x) = -28$ is always negative, proving we have a maximum.
    d) 108/7 by 108/7 by 3(108/7), or about 15.4 by 15.4 by 46.3 inches.
11. $x = \dfrac{M}{7}$; $L = \dfrac{3M}{7}$.
12. A cube 4 by 4 by 4 inches; area = 96 square inches.

Problem Set 8-3 (concluded)

13. 10 by 10 by 5 inches; area = 300 square inches.
14. 5 by 5 by 10 inches; minimum cost = $300.
15. $2.785.   16. One-inch squares.
17. 10/3 by 10/3 inches.
18. $r = 20$ feet; $h = 40$ feet.
19. $r = 24$ feet; $h = 250/9 = 27.8$ feet.
20. Maximum group charge $1,512.50 for 55 persons or more.
21. a) $80r^2$.   d) $r = 8$ miles.
    b) $24 - 2r$.   e) $40,960.
    c) $T(r) = 80r^2(24 - 2r)$.
22. $175; $24,675.

Problem Set 8-4

1. a) $y = 400$ barrels.
   b) $164 per barrel.
2. a) $x = 200$ barrels.
   b) $150 per barrel.
3. a) $x = 52.5$ thousand gallons.
   b) $14.5 thousand.
4. a) $t = 10$ hours.
   b) 2.5 hundred pounds.
5. Q is $Q(0, 125)$.
6. Q is $Q(0, 25)$.
7. a) 4 miles.
   b) $24.5 hundred thousand, or $2,450,000.
   c) $160,007.
8. a) 8 miles.
   b) $47.64 hundred thousand or $4,764,000.
   c) $221,639.
9. a) $x = \dfrac{(ab/k)^{1/2} - c}{b}$.
   b) $f''(x) = \dfrac{2ab^2}{(bx + c)^3}$ is positive, so we have a local minimum.
10. a) $x = \dfrac{[a/(2k)]^2 - b}{a} = \dfrac{a}{4k^2} - \dfrac{b}{a}$.
    b) $f''(x) -\dfrac{a^2}{4(ax + b)^{3/2}}$ is negative, so we have a local maximum.
11. a) $x = (k_1/k_2)^{1/2}$.   b) 35 miles per hour.
12. a) $x = \left(\dfrac{p + k_1 d}{k_2 d}\right)^{1/2}$.   b) 74.5 miles per hour.

13. 11,664 cubic inches.
14. 40 miles per hour.
15. 30 miles per hour.
16. $(k_1/k_2)^{1/2}$ miles per hour.
17. $p = 0.10$ yields a maximum because $C'(0.1) = 0$ and $C''(0.1)$ is negative.
18. $p = 1/n$.
19. a) $x = 200$ pounds.   b) $1,000.
20. a) $x = 800$ pounds.   b) $8,000.

Problem Set 8-5

1. a) N/Q.
   b) cN/Q.
   c) uQ.
   d) $p(uQ)/2$.
   e) $S(Q) = cN/Q + uN + p(uQ)/2$.
   f) $Q = \sqrt{\dfrac{2cN}{pu}}$.
   g) 240 units.
2. a) Kx^2.
   b) W/x^3.
   c) $(W/x^3)(6x^2d) = \dfrac{6Wd}{x}$.
   d) $C(x) = 6Kx^2 + \dfrac{6Wd}{x}$.
   e) $x = \sqrt[3]{\dfrac{Wd}{2K}}$.
   f) $x = 8$ feet.

Problem Set 8-6

1. See Figure A.   7. See Figure G.
2. See Figure B.   8. See Figure H.
3. See Figure C.   9. See Figure I (p. 1024).
4. See Figure D.   10. See Figure J (p. 1024).
5. See Figure E.   11. See Figure K (p. 1024).
6. See Figure F.   12. See Figure L (p. 1024).
13. b) Inflection point at $(0, 8)$.
    c) Local minimum at $(0, 5)$.
    d) Local maximum at $(0, 6)$.
    e) Inflection point at $(0, 0)$; local minimum at $(9/4, -2187/256)$.
    f) Inflection point at $(0, 0)$; local maximum at $(-4/5, 256/3125)$.
    g) Local minimum at $(\sqrt[6]{1/7}, (-6/7)\sqrt[6]{1/7})$.

Problem Set 8-6 *(continued)*

FIGURE A

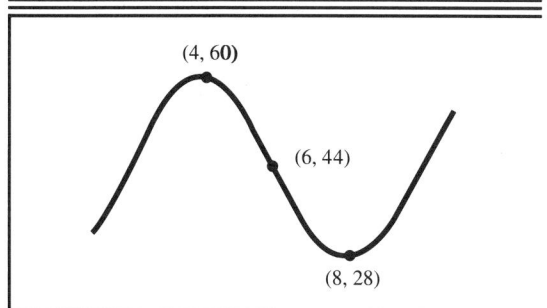

FIGURE B

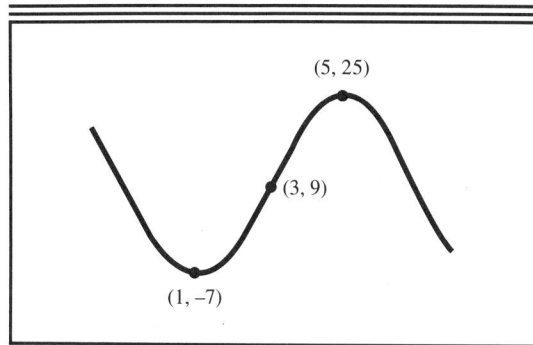

FIGURE C

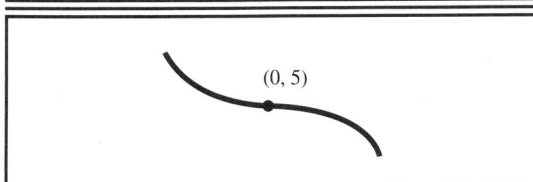

FIGURE D

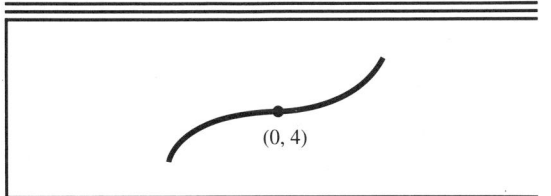

FIGURE E

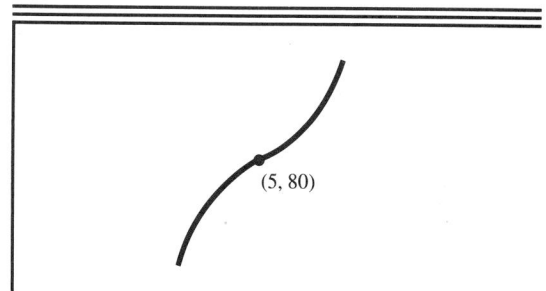

FIGURE F

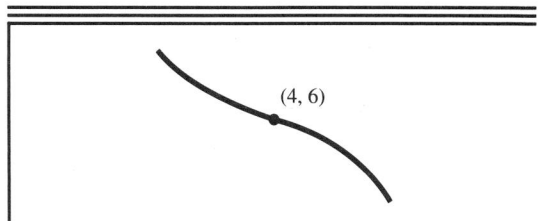

FIGURE G

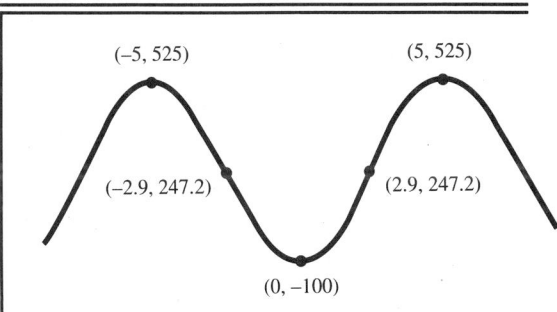

FIGURE H

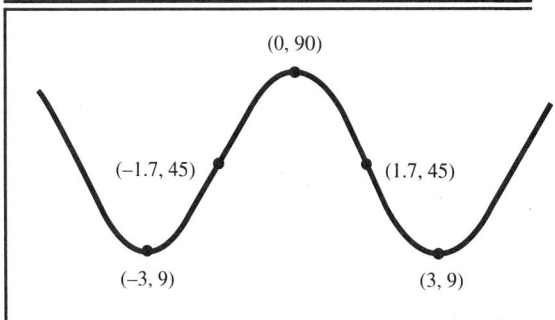

Problem Set 8–6 *(concluded)*

FIGURE I

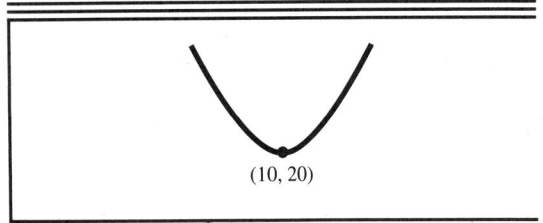

FIGURE L

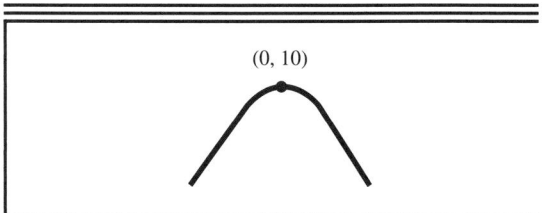

FIGURE J

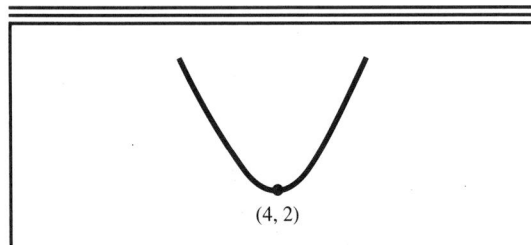

Problem Set 8–7

1. See Figure M.
2. See Figure N.
3. See Figure O.
4. See Figure P.
5. See Figure Q.
6. See Figure R (p. 1026).
7. See Figure S (p. 1026).
8. See Figure T (p. 1026).

FIGURE M

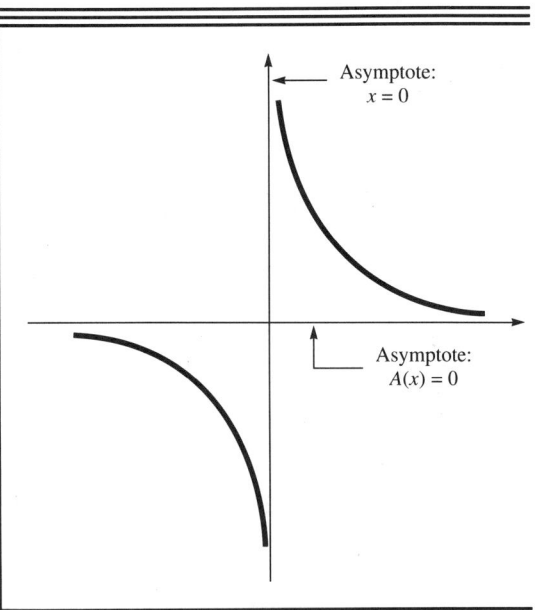

FIGURE K

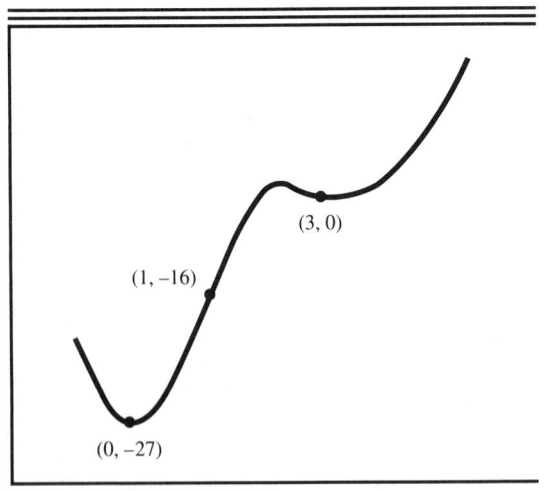

Problem Set 8-7 *(continued)*

FIGURE N

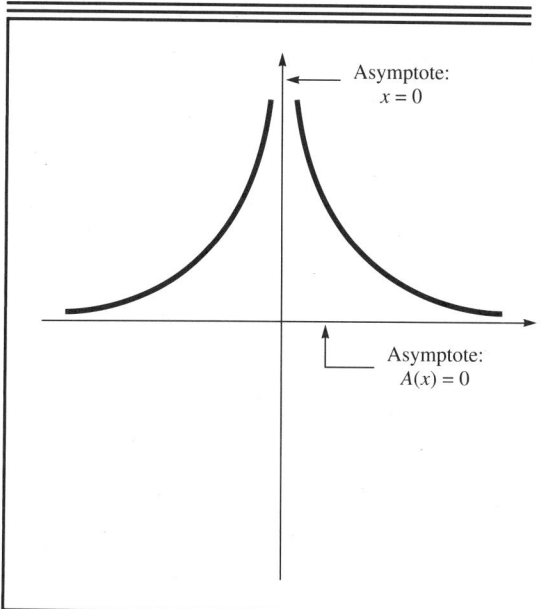

FIGURE P

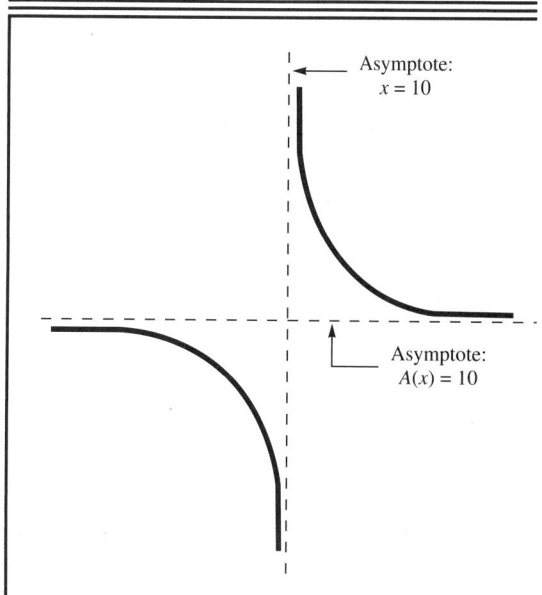

FIGURE O

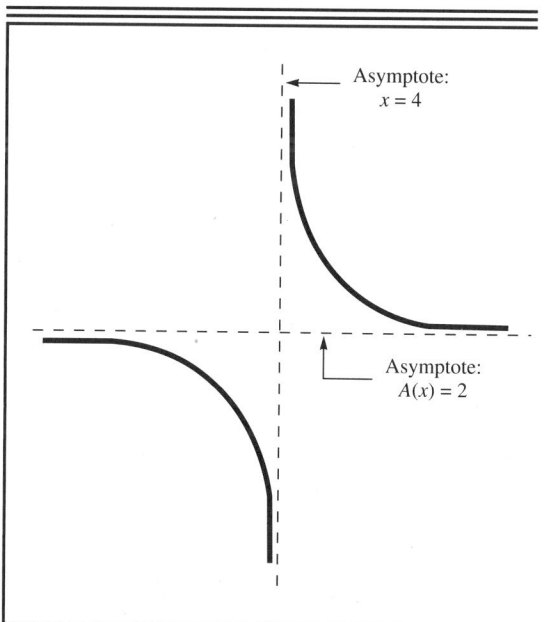

FIGURE Q

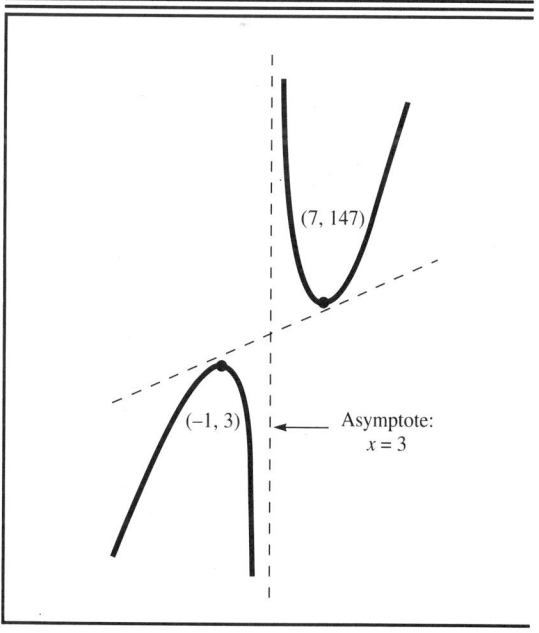

Problem Set 8-7 *(concluded)*

FIGURE R

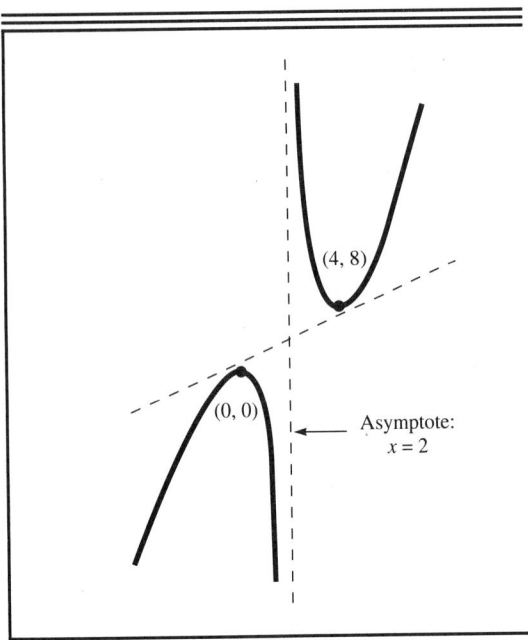

FIGURE T

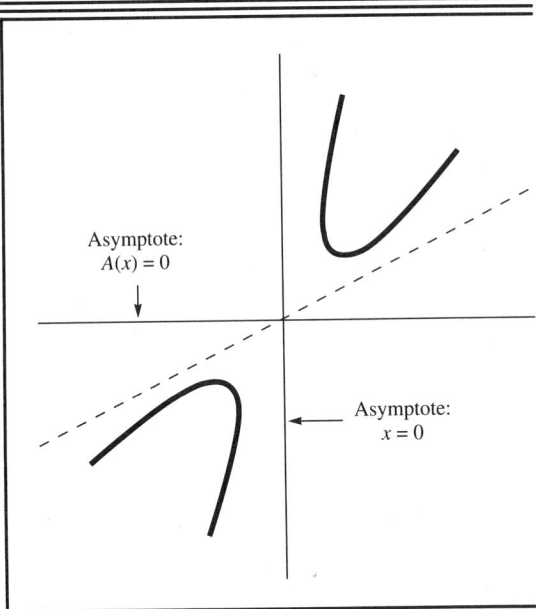

FIGURE S

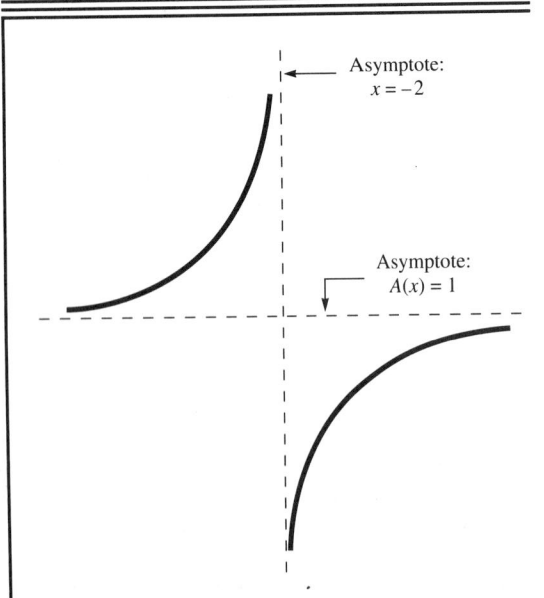

CHAPTER 9

Problem Set 9-1

1. $f'(x) = 2e^x$. $f''(x) = 2e^x$.
2. $f'(x) = 5^x \ln 5$. $f''(x) = 5^x(\ln 5)^2$.
3. $f'(x) = 7^x \ln 7$. $f''(x) = 7^x(\ln 7)^2$.
4. $f'(x) = 3e^x$. $f''(x) = 3e^x$.
5. $f'(x) = -e^{-0.2x}$. $f''(x) = 0.2e^{-0.2x}$.
6. $f'(x) = -e^{-0.4x}$. $f''(x) = 0.4e^{-0.4x}$.
7. $f'(x) = -2e^{3-0.1x}$. $f''(x) = 0.2e^{3-0.1x}$.
8. $f'(x) = 3e^{0.3x-6}$. $f''(x) = 0.9e^{0.3x-6}$.
9. $f'(x) = 2xe^{x^2}$. $f''(x) = 2xe^{x^2}(2x^2 + 1)$.
10. $f'(x) = -2xe^{-x^2}$. $f''(x) = 2e^{-x^2}(2x^2 - 1)$.
11. $f'(x) = 2.079(1/2)^{-3x} = 2.079(2)^{3x}$.
    $f''(x) = 4.324(1/2)^{-3x} = 4.324(2)^{3x}$.
12. $f'(x) = 0.275(0.4)^{-0.3x}$.
    $f''(x) = 0.076(0.4)^{-0.3x}$.
13. $f'(x) = 58.27(1.06)^x$. $f''(x) = 3.395(1.06)^x$.
14. $f'(x) = -38.48(1.08)^{-x}$.
    $f''(x) = 2.962(1.08)^{-x}$.
15. See Figure A.
16. See Figure B.
17. See Figure C.
18. See Figure D.
19. See Figure E (p. 1028).
20. See Figure F (p. 1028).
21. See Figure G (p. 1028).
22. See Figure H (p. 1028).

FIGURE A
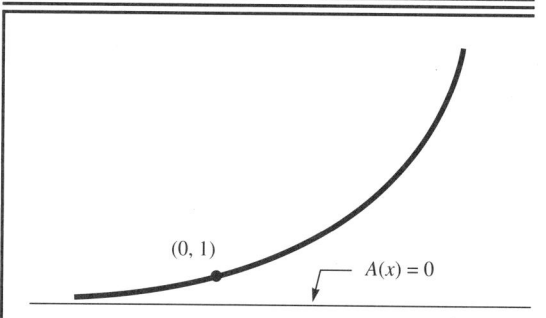

FIGURE B
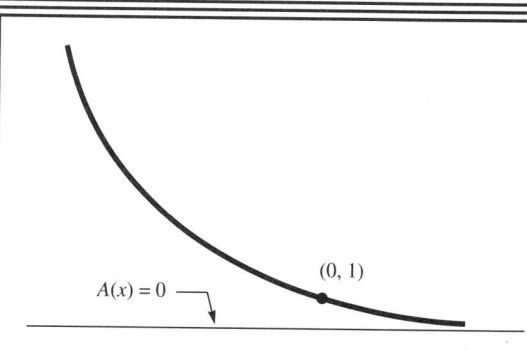

FIGURE C
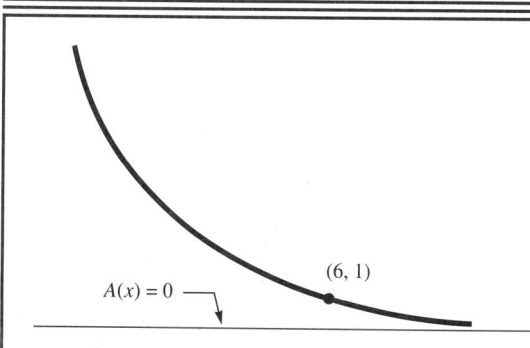

FIGURE D
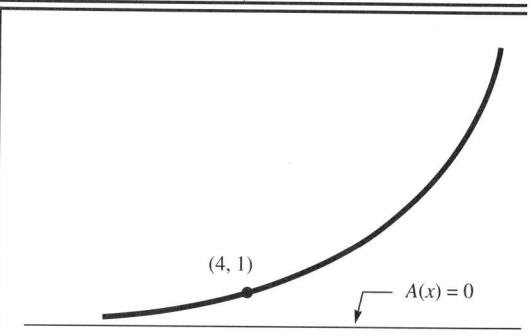

Problem Set 9-1 (concluded)

FIGURE E

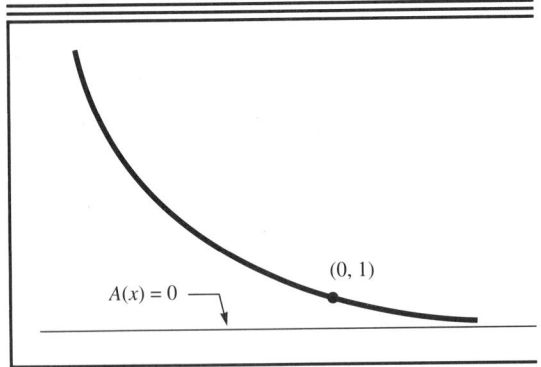

FIGURE F

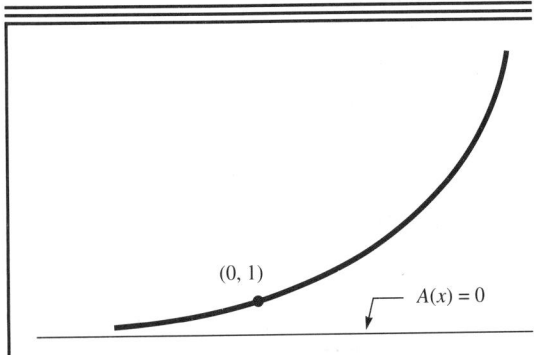

FIGURE G

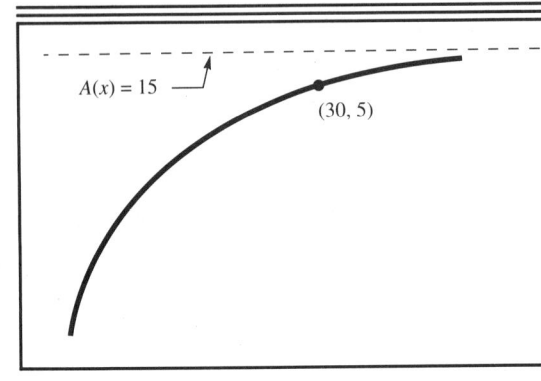

FIGURE H

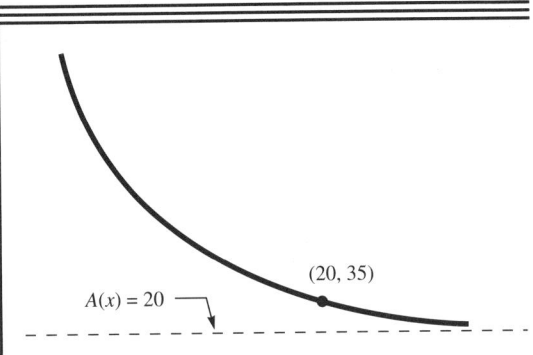

23. 2.915.
24. a) $t = 252.573$ days. b) $882,427.
25. a) $t = 160.944$ days. b) $1,024,056.
26. a) $t = 10.059$ years. b) $5,163,614.
27. a) $t = 11.454$ years. b) $7,381,624.
28. $t = 6.93$ years.
29. Maximum is 55.47.
30. Minimum is 1.
31. Minimum is 0.52.
32. Maximum is 12.18.
33. Maximum is 145.60.
34. Minimum is 4.85.

Problem Set 9-2

1. $1/x$.
2. $3/x$.
3. $2/(2x + 3)$.
4. $-1/x$.
5. 1.
6. $2/[3(2x + 5)]$.
7. $2(x + 1)/[x(x + 2)]$.
8. $\dfrac{6x^2 - 6}{2x^3 - 6x} = \dfrac{3(x^2 - 1)}{x(x^2 - 3)}$.
9. $3/[2(3x + 2)]$.
10. Minimum is (1/2, 16.932).
11. Maximum is (10, 180.259). (Note x cannot be negative.)
12. Minimum is (4, $-$ 4.636).
13. Minimum is (5, 2.303).
14. Minimum is (3/5, 72.779). (Note x cannot be negative.)
15. Minimum is 9.45. (Note x cannot be negative.)
16. 12 ounces.
17. 11.5 ounces.
18. 3.75 ounces.
19. 6.75 ounces.

Problem Set 9–3

1. $\sqrt{3x-4}$, $3/[2(3x-4)^{1/2}]$; and $3\sqrt{x}-4$, $3/(2\sqrt{x})$.
2. $8x + 3$, 8; and $8x + 19$, 8.
3. $2 - x^{1/3}$, $-1/(3x^{2/3})$; and $(2-x)^{1/3}$, $-1/[3(2-x)^{2/3}]$.
4. $-x + 3$, -1; and $\sqrt{-x^2 + 7}$, $-x/\sqrt{x^2+7}$.
5. $x + 1$, 1; and $\sqrt{x^2 + 1}$, $x/\sqrt{x^2+1}$.
6. $3/\sqrt{5-x}$, $3/[2(5-x)^{3/2}]$; and $5 - 3/\sqrt{x}$, $3/(2x^{3/2})$.
7. $4x^2 + 7$, $8x$; and $16x^2 + 24x + 10$, $32x + 24$.
8. $15x^3 - 1$, $45x^2$; and $375x^3 + 900x^2 + 720x + 191$, $1{,}125x^2 + 1{,}800x + 720$.
9. $\sqrt{x+6}$, $1/(2\sqrt{x+6})$; and $\sqrt{x+3}+3$, $1/(2\sqrt{x+3})$.
10. $3 - \sqrt{3-x}$, $1/(2\sqrt{3-x})$; and $\sqrt{x}$, $1/(2\sqrt{x})$.
11. $(21x/2)(9x + 2)\sqrt{3x^3 + x^2}$.
12. $15x^2/\sqrt{2x^3 - 1}$.
13. $21/(2\sqrt{7x+2})$.
14. $6(2x^3 - 5)^3 (26x^3 - 5)$.
15. $-0.25e^{-0.25x}$.
16. $(6x)e^{3x^2 + 1}$.
17. $(12x^2)e^{4x^3 - 9}$.
18. $[2e^{-1/(0.5x)}]/x^2$.
19. $1/(5x + 7x^{4/5})$.
20. $-1/(8x^{3/4} - 4x)$.
21. $[5(3x^2 + 6x)]/(x^3 + 3x^2 + 14)$.
22. $(3x^{1/2} - 8x^{1/3} - 3)/(2x^{3/2} - 6x^{4/3} - 3x + 7)$.
23. $4y^3 \cdot \dfrac{dy}{dx}$.
24. $3x^2 \cdot \dfrac{dx}{dy}$.
25. $2e^{2w} \cdot \dfrac{dw}{dz}$.
26. $-e^{-0.5p} \cdot \dfrac{dp}{dq}$.
27. $\dfrac{2}{2y + 3} \cdot \dfrac{dy}{dx}$.
28. $\dfrac{2z - 3}{z^2 - 3z} \cdot \dfrac{dz}{dw}$.
29. $x + y \cdot \dfrac{dx}{dy}$.
30. $\left(y - x \cdot \dfrac{dy}{dx}\right)/y^2$.
31. $\dfrac{1}{1 - \dfrac{dg(y)}{dy}}$.
32. a) 0.68.
    b) 68 cents of an additional dollar of income is spent.
    c) $3.125.
    d) 0.85, or 85%.
33. a) 0.63.
    b) 63 cents of an additional dollar of income is spent.
    c) $2.70.
    d) 0.90, or 90%.
34. a) 5.62.   b) 3.51.
35. a) 15.17. b) 5.26.

Problem Set 9–4

1. a) 3.
   b) 0.
   c) -2.
   d) 0.
   e) 0.
2. a) 2.
   b) 0.
   c) 5.
   d) 0.
   e) 0.
3. a) $2x + 3$.
   b) 2.
   c) $2y - 2$.
   d) 2.
   e) 0.
4. a) $2x - 5$.
   b) 2.
   c) $-2y + 4$.
   d) -2.
   e) 0.
5. a) $6x - 2y$.
   b) 6.
   c) $-2x + 2y$.
   d) 2.
   e) -2.
6. a) $6x^2 + 3y$.
   b) $12x$.
   c) $3x + 4$.
   d) 0.
   e) 3.
7. a) $y^{1/2}/(2x^{1/2})$.
   b) $-y^{1/2}/(4x^{3/2})$.
   c) $-x^{1/2}/(2y^{1/2})$.
   d) $-x^{1/2}/(4y^{3/2})$.
   e) $1/(4x^{1/2}y^{1/2})$.
8. a) $(2y^{1/3})/(3x^{1/3})$.
   b) $(-2y^{1/3})/(9x^{4/3})$.
   c) $(x^{2/3})/(3y^{2/3})$.
   d) $(-2x^{2/3})/(9y^{5/3})$.
   e) $2/(9x^{1/3}y^{2/3})$.
9. a) $2y^{1/2} - y/x^{2/3}$.
   b) $(2y)/(3x^{5/3})$.
   c) $(x/y^{1/2}) - 3x^{1/3}$.
   d) $-x/(2y^{3/2})$.
   e) $(1/y^{1/2}) - (1/x^{2/3})$.
10. a) $(3x^{1/2}y^2)/2$.
    b) $(3y^2)/(4x^{1/2})$.
    c) $2x^{3/2}y$.
    d) $2x^{3/2}$.
    e) $3x^{1/2}y$.
11. a) $ye^x(x + 1)$.
    b) $ye^x(x + 2)$.
    c) xe^x.
    d) 0.
    e) $e^x(x + 1)$.
12. a) $y (\ln y)$.
    b) 0.
    c) $x(1 + \ln y)$.
    d) x/y.
    e) $1 + \ln y$.
13. a) $2y/(x + y)^2$.
    b) $-4y/(x + y)^3$.
    c) $-2x/(x + y)^2$.
    d) $4x/(x + y)^3$.
    e) $2(x - y)/(x + y)^3$.
14. a) $-2y/(x - y)^2$.
    b) $4y/(x - y)^3$.
    c) $2x/(x - y)^2$.
    d) $4x/(x - y)^3$.
    e) $-2(x + y)/(x - y)^3$.
15. a) $3/(3x + 2y)$.
    b) $-9/(3x + 2y)^2$.
    c) $2/(3x + 2y)$.
    d) $-4/(3x + 2y)^2$.
    e) $-6/(3x + 2y)^2$.
16. a) $2e^{2x+3y}$.
    b) $4e^{2x+3y}$.
    c) $3e^{2x+3y}$.
    d) $9e^{2x+3y}$.
    e) $6e^{2x+3y}$.
17. $6z - 2x$.
18. $2w - 3z^2$.
19. 2.
20. 6.
21. -3.
22. 3.
23. a) 7.   d) 2.
    b) 3.   e) 0.
    c) 0.   f) 0.

Problem Set 9–4 (concluded)

24. a) 7.
    b) 2.
    c) 0.
    d) 3.
    e) 0.
    f) 0.

25. a) 8.
    b) 5.
    c) 2.
    d) −4.
    e) −6.
    f) 1.

26. a) −14.
    b) 2.
    c) 4.
    d) −11.
    e) 2.
    f) −5.

27. At the production level of 3 tons of oats and 5 tons of hay, cost is decreasing at the rate of $4 per additional ton of oats and cost is not changing (is stationary) with respect to a change in hay.

28. At the production level of 3 tons of oats and 7 tons of hay, cost is decreasing at the rate of $8 per additional ton of oats and cost is increasing at the rate of $4 per additional ton of hay.

29. At 400 tons of oats and 500 tons of hay,
    a) Profit is increasing at the rate of $10 per additional ton of oats.
    b) Profit is increasing at the rate of $10 per additional ton of hay.
    c) At 600 tons of oats and 500 tons of hay, profit is decreasing at the rate of $10 per additional ton of oats.
    d) At 400 tons of oats and 500 tons of hay, profit is decreasing at the rate of $10 per additional ton of hay.

30. When labor expenditure and capital investment are, respectively, $64 and $27 million,
    a) Output is increasing at the rate of $1.50 per additional $1 of labor expenditure.
    b) Output is increasing at the rate of $7.11 per additional dollar of capital investment.

Problem Set 9–5

1. Minimum at $f(0, 0) = 10$.
2. Maximum at $f(2, 3) = 23$.
3. Maximum at $f(12, 10) = 120$.
4. Minimum at $f(3, 9) = 50$.
5. Minimum at $f(3, 2) = 10$.
6. Maximum at $f(3, 4) = 52$.
7. Saddle point at $f(2, 1) = 0$.
8. Saddle point at $f(0, 0) = 0$.
9. Maximum at $f(14, 26) = 175$.
10. Saddle point at $f(6, 5) = 14$.
11. Maximum at $f(0, 0) = 10$.
12. Minimum at $f(0, 0) = -5$.
13. a) 500 gallons of molasses and 550 gallons of maple syrup.
    b) Both P_{xx} and P_{yy} are negative and $D = (0)^2 - (-0.1)(-0.2)$ is negative, so we have a maximum.
    c) $P_{max} = \$42,750$.
14. a) Use Machine A for 4 hours and Machine B for 6 hours.
    b) Both C_{xx} and C_{yy} are positive and $D = (-2)^2 - 6(2)$ is negative, so we have a minimum.
    c) $C_{min} = \$14$ per unit.
15. $1,400 for 12 salespeople and $40 hundreds of inventory.
16. $74.86 for the first kind and $70.71 for the second kind.
17. a) $L = 400, I = 250$.
    b) $C_{min} = \$3,750$.
18. a) $L = 520, p = 0.8$.
    b) $C_{LL} = 0.0015, C_{pp} = 2,600$, and $C_{pL} = 0$. Hence, $D < 0$ and both partials are positive, so we have a minimum.
    c) $C_{min} = \$416,000$.
19. $L = \left[\dfrac{2cd(a + b)}{ab}\right]^{1/2}$.

    $I = \dfrac{bL}{a + b} = \left[\dfrac{2bcd}{a(a + b)}\right]^{1/2}$.

CHAPTER 10

Problem Set 10–1

1. $x + C$.
2. $z + C$.
3. $5y + C$.
4. $-7w + C$.
5. $x + \dfrac{x^2}{2} + C$.
6. $3y - \dfrac{y^2}{2} + C$.
7. $\dfrac{2x^3}{3} - \dfrac{3x^2}{2} + 4x + C$.
8. $\dfrac{3y^4}{4} + 2y^2 - y + C$.
9. $pq + C$.
10. $qp + C$.
11. $\dfrac{qp^2}{2} + C$.
12. $\dfrac{pq^2}{2} + C$.
13. $\dfrac{x^4}{4} + \dfrac{x^5}{5} - x + C$.
14. $\dfrac{y^3}{3} + \dfrac{y^6}{6} - y + C$.
15. $y^3 + y^5 + y + C$.
16. $x^4 - x^6 + x + C$.

Problem Set 10-1 (concluded)

17. $-\dfrac{1}{x} + C.$
18. $\dfrac{y}{343} + C.$
19. $-\dfrac{1}{2y^2} + C.$
20. $-\dfrac{1}{3x^3} + C.$
21. $5y + \dfrac{1}{y^2} + C.$
22. $7x + \dfrac{1}{x^3} + C.$
23. $x^2 + \dfrac{1}{x} + x + C.$
24. $\dfrac{y^2}{2} - \dfrac{1}{y^2} + y + C.$
25. $\dfrac{2p^{3/2}}{3} + C.$
26. $\dfrac{3q^{4/3}}{4} + C.$
27. $-\dfrac{9}{x^{1/3}} + C.$
28. $-\dfrac{10}{y^{1/2}} + C.$
29. $2x + \dfrac{1}{x} + \dfrac{1}{x^{2/3}} + C.$
30. $x^2 + \dfrac{1}{x^2} + \dfrac{3}{4x^{1/3}} + C.$
31. $4x^3 + 3x^4 + C.$
32. $x^3 + 3x^2 + C.$
33. $2(2x - 9)^4 + C.$
34. $\dfrac{5(3x + 5)^6}{3} + C.$
35. $-\dfrac{1}{3(3x - 9)} + C.$
36. $-\dfrac{1}{6(2x + 3)^3} + C.$
37. $-\dfrac{2(5 - 3x)^{1/2}}{3} + C.$
38. $\dfrac{1}{4(7 - 2w)^2} + C.$
39. $6(2x + 5)^{2/3} + C.$
40. $8(3x - 7)^{1/2} + C.$

Problem Set 10-2

1. 6.
2. 6.
3. 15.
4. 108.
5. 20.
6. 4.
7. 96/5.
8. 18.
9. 17/6.
10. 51/2.
11. 44.
12. 16.
13. 26/3.
14. 2.
15. 3.
16. 8.
17. $b^3 - a^3.$
18. $d^4 - c^4.$
19. $\dfrac{n^2}{2} + n - \dfrac{3}{2}.$
20. $n - n^2.$
21. 3.
22. 36.
23. 13/2.
24. 6.
25. 4.
26. 3/2.
27. 16.
28. 80.
29. 100.
30. 25/2.
31. 500.
32. 500/3.
33. 8.
34. 8.

Problem Set 10-3

1. a) 27/2.
   b) 23/2.
2. 8.
3. 36.
4. 500/3.
5. 125/6.
6. 9.
7. 64/3.
8. 3,375.
9. 1/2.
10. $20\sqrt{5}/3 = 14.907.$

Problem Set 10-4

1. a) $13.8 thousand.
   b) See Figure A.
   c) $17.4 thousand.
   d) 20 years.
2. a) $180 thousand.
   b) See Figure B.
   c) $140 thousand.
   d) 25 years.
3. 100 million barrels.
4. 1,944 barrels.
5. 13.5 years.
6. 18 years.
7. $100 + 80 = 180$ thousand.
8. $80 + 2 = \$82$ thousand.
9. $2,600.
10. $20,000.

FIGURE A

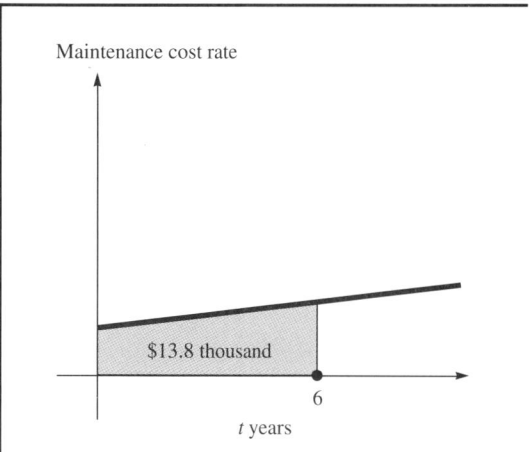

FIGURE B

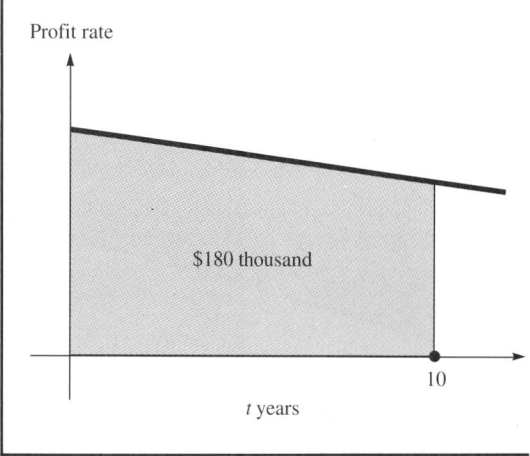

Problem Set 10-4 (concluded)

11. a) 50 months.   b) $200 thousand.
12. a) 36 months.   b) $17,500.
13. a) $3,000 million.   b) See Figure C.
14. a) $250 million.   b) See Figure D.
15. $1,856 thousand. 16. $3,240 million.
17. a) $9,000 thousand.   b) $4,500 thousand.
18. a) $100 million.   b) $25 million.

FIGURE C

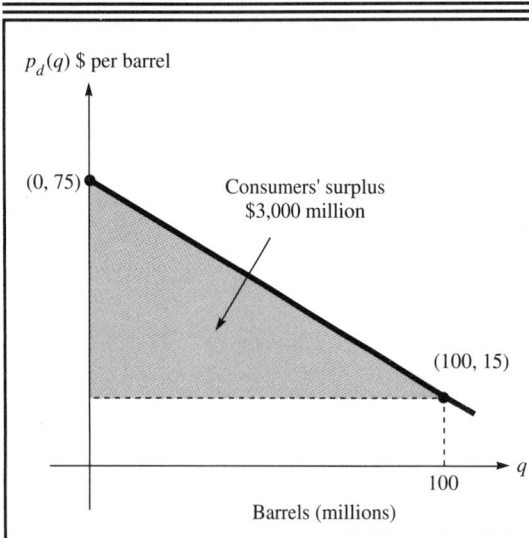

FIGURE D

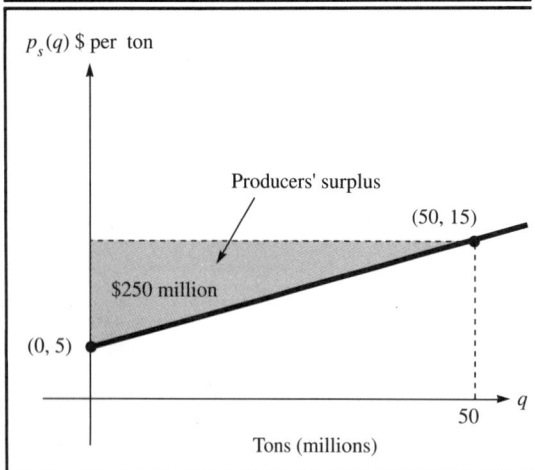

Problem Set 10-5

1. $\ln|x| + C$.
2. $\ln|x| + C$.
3. $2 \ln|x| + C$.
4. $3 \ln|x| + C$.
5. $-\dfrac{1}{x} + C$.
6. $-\dfrac{1}{x} + C$.
7. $\dfrac{\ln|5x + 4|}{5} + C$.
8. $-\ln|3 - x| + C$.
9. $-5 \ln|3 - 0.2x| + C$.
10. $4 \ln|0.5x + 1| + C$.
11. $-\dfrac{1}{2(2x - 1)} + C$.
12. $-\dfrac{2}{(5x + 3)} + C$.
13. 2.303.
14. 1.
15. 0.446.
16. 0.933.
17. 895.880 million barrels.
18. $140.256 million.

Problem Set 10-6

1. $e^x + C$.
2. $\dfrac{2^x}{\ln 2} + C$.
3. $-\dfrac{3^{-x}}{\ln 3} + C$.
4. $-e^{-x} + C$.
5. $2e^{0.5x} + C$.
6. $\dfrac{5(5^{0.2x})}{\ln 5} + C$.
7. $\dfrac{-2.5(0.5)^{1-0.4x}}{\ln(0.5)} + C$.
8. $-2e^{2-0.5x} + C$.
9. $-20e^{3-0.1x} + C$.
10. $-20e^{5-0.2x} + C$.
11. $\dfrac{-1}{(0.8)^x \ln(0.8)} + C$.
12. $-2/e^{0.5x} + C$.
13. 17.18.
14. 14.11.
15. 3.61.
16. 9.02.
17. a) 343.656 million barrels.   b) 35.835 years.
18. a) $183.831 thousand.   b) 13.733 years.
19. a) $10,544.33.   b) 6.758 years.
20. a) 47.409 million pounds.   b) 8.047 years.
21. 72.409 million pounds.
22. 93.233 million gallons.
23. $27.745 thousand.
24. $40 thousand.

Problem Set 10-7

1. $\dfrac{x(2^x)}{\ln 2} - \dfrac{2^x}{(\ln 2)^2} + C$.
2. $3x - (3/2)\ln|2x + 1| + C$.
3. $8\left[\dfrac{1}{0.5x + 1} + \ln|0.5x + 1|\right] + C$.
4. $e^x(x - 1) + C$.
5. $-4e^{2-0.5x}(0.5x + 1) + C$.

Problem Set 10-7 (concluded)

6. $\dfrac{4}{3x+4} + \ln|3x+4| + C.$

7. $2\ln\left|\dfrac{x}{0.5x+1}\right| + C.$

8. $12.5e^{0.4x-1}(0.4x - 1) + C.$

9. $2\left[\dfrac{x}{5} + \dfrac{3}{25}\ln|5x - 3|\right] + C.$

10. $3\ln\left|\dfrac{x}{3x+2}\right| + C.$

11. $5e^{0.1x^2-2} + C.$

12. $5[0.2x - \ln(1 + e^{0.2x})] + C.$

13. $x - 2\ln(1 + 2e^{0.5x}) + C.$

14. $-2e^{2-0.5x^2} + C.$

15. $(1/3)\ln\left|\dfrac{x-3}{x+3}\right| + C.$

16. $(-5/4)\ln\left|\dfrac{x-4}{x+4}\right| + C.$

17. $3\ln\left|\dfrac{1 + \sqrt{1-9x^2}}{3x}\right| + C.$

18. $\ln\left|\dfrac{\sqrt{1-16x^2}-1}{x}\right| + C.$

Problem Set 10-8

1. 8.
2. 3.
3. 2.
4. 6.
5. Does not exist.
6. Does not exist.
7. 25.
8. 2.
9. Does not exist.
10. 1/192.
11. Does not exist.
12. 100.
13. 1/98.
14. 1/4.
15. Does not exist.
16. $-1/9.$
17. $(4/9)\ln 2 = 0.308.$
18. $2\ln 1.1 = 0.191.$

Problem Set 10-9

1. 2.53.
2. 0.366.
3. 0.379.
4. 1.019.
5. 0.188.
6. 2.391.
7. 0.590.
8. 0.110.
9. 0.535.
10. 0.639.
11. 0.341.
12. 0.341.

Problem Set 10-10

1. $3x(\ln x - 1) + C.$
2. $2x(\ln x - 1) + C.$
3. $x(\ln 2x - 1) + C.$
4. $x(\ln 3x - 1) + C.$
5. $\dfrac{(2x+1)[\ln(2x+1) - 1]}{2} + C.$
6. $\dfrac{(3x+5)[\ln(3x+5) - 1]}{3} + C.$
7. $2(3x - 2)[\ln(3x - 2) - 1] + C.$
8. $2(2x - 1)[\ln(2x - 1) - 1] + C.$
9. $70.33 thousand.
10. 110.6 million bushels.
11. $\dfrac{x^2 \ln x}{2} - \dfrac{x^2}{4} + C.$
12. $\dfrac{x^4 \ln x}{4} - \dfrac{x^4}{16} + C.$
13. $-\dfrac{\ln x + 1}{x} + C.$
14. $\ln x - \dfrac{\ln x}{x} - \dfrac{1}{x} + C.$
15. $\dfrac{(x+1)^6 (6x - 1)}{42} + C.$
16. $(-8/3)(8 - x)^{1/2}(x + 16) + C.$
17. $(-2/15)(1 - x)^{3/2}(3x + 2) + C.$
18. $(2/3)(x - 1)^{1/2}(x + 2) + C.$
19. $e^x(x^2 - 2x + 10) + C.$
20. $\dfrac{e^2 + 1}{4} = 2.097.$
21. $\dfrac{e^2 + 1}{4} = 2.097.$
22. $\dfrac{3e^2 + 29}{12} = 4.264.$

Problem Set 10-11

1. $y = x + C.$
2. $y = x^3 + C.$
3. $y = \ln x + C.$
4. $y = Ke^x.$
5. $y = Kx.$
6. $y = Ke^{-1/x}.$
7. $y = Ke^{x^{1/2}}.$
8. $y = K/x.$
9. $y = 5\ln(0.2x + 3) + C.$
10. $y = 4\ln(0.5x + 2) + C.$
11. $y = Ke^{0.5x} - 4.$
12. $y = Ke^{0.2x} - 15.$
13. $y = 0.5x^2 + x + 2.$
14. $y = x^2.$
15. $y = 0.4e^x.$
16. $y = 6/x.$
17. $y = 19e^{0.2x} - 15.$
18. $y = 5e^{0.5x} - 4.$
19. $y = 3x - 1.$
20. $y = 8/x - 1.$

Problem Set 10-12

1. a) $dS = (150 + 6t)\,dt.$
   b) $S = 0$ when $t = 0.$
   c) $S(t) = 150t + 3t^2.$
   d) 15,000.
   e) 100 days.

2. a) $dS = (100 + 2t)\,dt.$
   b) $S = 0$ when $t = 0.$
   c) $S(t) = 100t + t^2.$
   d) 7,500.
   e) 200 days.

Problem Set 10-12 (concluded)

3. a) $dP = 0.1 P dt$.
   b) $P(t) = 100e^{0.1t}$.
   c) 271.8 thousand.
4. a) $dS = 0.05S dt$.
   b) $S(t) = 2{,}000e^{0.05t}$.
   c) \$5,436.56.
5. a) $dA = 0.08A dt + 500\, dt$.
   b) $A(t) = 8{,}250e^{0.08t} - 6{,}250$.
   c) \$12,110.71.
   d) 13.733 years.
6. a) $dA = 0.08A dt - 500\, dt$.
   b) $A(t) = 6{,}250 - 1{,}250e^{0.08t}$.
   c) \$3,468.07.
   d) 20.118 years.
7. a) $dC = 5e^{0.01t}\, dt$.
   b) $C(t) = 500(e^{0.01t} - 1)$.
   c) 52.586 million barrels.
   d) 33.647 years.
8. a) $dC = 5e^{0.02t}\, dt$.
   b) $C(t) = 250(e^{0.02t} - 1)$.
   c) 55.351 million barrels.
   d) 29.389 years.

CHAPTER 11

Problem Set 11-1

1. a) 20.   b) 99.   c) 45.
2. a) As with the union of two sets, the intersection of each pair is counted twice and so must be subtracted out. In so doing, the intersection of all three sets is subtracted out three times and must be added back in once.
   b) 32.   c) 63.
3. a) See Figure A.
   b) See Figure B.
4. a) See Table A.
   b) See Table B.
5. a) 550.   b) 18.
6. a) 947.   b) 875.
7. a) 5.   b) 6.   c) 5.   d) 3.
8. a) 15.   b) 18.
9. a) 650.   b) 676.
10. a) 256.   b) 16.
11. a) 240.   b) 16.
12. 8.
13. 40.
14. 32.
15. 1,048,576.
16. a) 42.   b) 992.
17. a) 120.   b) 12.
18. a) 21.   b) 496.
19. a) 20.   b) 6.
20. a) 2; 7.   b) 8.
21. a) 7.   b) 6.
23. 1,287.
24. 635,013,559,600.
25. 504.
26. 87,178,291,200.
27. 3,003.
28. 120.
29. 33,649.
30. 56.
31. 553,270,671.

FIGURE A

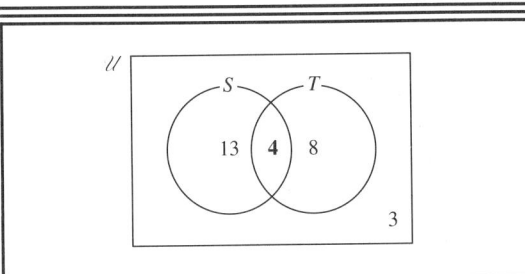

FIGURE B

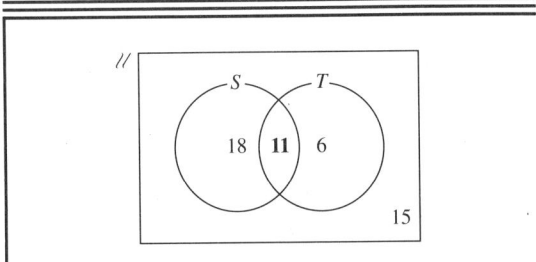

Problem Set 11-1 *(concluded)*

TABLE A

$\mathcal{U}$	T		T'		Totals
	W	W'	W	W'	
S	3⁴	1	⁵2	10	**16**
S'	5	1	4	9	19
Totals	8	2	6	19	**35**

└─10─┘
└──14──┘

TABLE B

$\mathcal{U}$	T		T'		Totals
	W	W'	W	W'	
S	1	⁸7	⁹8	7	**23**
S'	5	8	6	**6**	25
Totals	**6**	15	14	**13**	**48**

└─21─┘
└──20──┘

32. a) 11.
    b)

Sum	2	3	4	5	6	7	8	9	10	11	12
Ways	1	2	3	4	5	6	5	4	3	2	1

33. a) 10,000.   b) 1,000.
34. a) 324,632.   b) 5,245,786.   c) 13,983,816.

Problem Set 11-2

1. a) 1,024.   b) 176.   c) 848.   d) 120.   e) 968.
2. a) 512.   b) 126.   c) 466.   d) 466.   e) 466.
3. a) 462.   b) 28.   c) 0.   d) 210.   e) 266.
4. a) 177,100.   c) 924.   d) 38,610.   e) 127,270.
   b) 1,716.
5. a) 343,006,888,770.   c) 5,143,103,331,550.
   b) 574,337,116,080.
6. a) 1,712,304.   b) 389,160.   c) 17,296.
7. a) 2,598,960.   c) 24.   e) 624.
   b) 24.   d) 3,744.   f) 5,148.
8. a) 133,784,560.   b) 4.   c) 4.   d) 624.

9. a) 681,080,400.   b) 403,603,200.   c) 151,351,200.
10. a) 1,663,200.   b) 1,663,200.   c) 1,108,800.
11. a) $a^7 + 7a^6b + 21a^5b^2 + 35a^4b^3 + 35a^3b^4 + 21a^2b^5 + 7ab^6 + b^7$.
    b) $a^8 + 8a^7b + 28a^6b^2 + 56a^5b^3 + 70a^4b^4 + 56a^3b^5 + 28a^2b^6 + 8ab^7 + b^8$.
    c) $32x^5 + 80x^4y + 80x^3y^2 + 40x^2y^3 + 10xy^4 + y^5$.
    d) $x^5 + 15x^4y + 90x^3y^2 + 270x^2y^3 + 405xy^4 + 243y^5$.
    e) $81x^4 + 216x^3y + 216x^2y^2 + 96xy^3 + 16y^4$.
    f) $64x^3 + 240x^2y + 300xy^2 + 125y^3$.
    g) $243x^5 - 810x^4y + 1,080x^3y^2 - 720x^2y^3 + 240xy^4 - 32y^5$.
    h) $1,024x^5 - 6,400x^4y + 16,000x^3y^2 - 20,000x^2y^3 + 12,500xy^4 - 3,125y^5$.
12. a) 10.   c) $210y^6$.   e) 18.   g) $56x^3$.
    b) 35.   d) $210x^6$.   f) 24.   h) $56y^3$.
13. a) 64.   b) 1,024.   c) 33,554,432.   d) 2^{50}.
15. 64.
16. a) 720.   b) 20,160.   c) 151,200.   d) 4,989,600.

Problem Set 11-3

1. a) 0.30.   i) 0.20.   q) 0.70.
   b) 0.55.   j) 0.15.   r) 0.50.
   c) 0.   k) 0.50.   s) $M \cup S$.
   d) 0.125.   l) 0.50.   t) $B \cup C$.
   e) 0.   m) 0.775.   u) B or $A' \cap C'$.
   f) 0.03.   n) 0.47.   v) $A' \cap M'$.
   g) 0.03.   o) 0.85.   w) $B \cup M$.
   h) 0.15.   p) 0.85.   x) $L \cup C$.
2. a) $P(M|A) = 0.3 = P(M)$.
   b) M and A are independent in the probability sense.
   c) Independent because $P(A|L) = 0.15 = P(A)$, or $P(L|A) = 0.20 = P(L)$.
   d) Not independent because $P(B|L) = 0.75$ and $P(B) = 0.55$, so $P(B|L) \neq P(B)$.
   e) $P(A \cap B) = 0$. A and B are mutually exclusive.
3. a) 0.42.   b) 0.60.
4. a) Yes. $P(WB) = 0$.
   b) No $P(W|B) = 0$ does not equal $P(W)$, which is 0.20.
   c) No. $P(YW) \neq 0$.
   d) Yes. $P(Y|W) = 78/120 = 0.65$, and $P(Y) = 390/600 = 0.65$.
   e) No. $P(YR) \neq 0$.
   f) No. $P(Y|R) = 270/300 = 0.9$ but $P(Y) = 390/600 = 0.65$, so $P(Y|R) \neq P(Y)$.
5. a) 0.50.   d) 0.   g) 0.25.
   b) 0.125. e) 0.   h) 0.625.
   c) 0.275. f) 0.   i) 0.10.

Problem Set 11-3 *(concluded)*

j) 0.25.   k) 0.40.   l) 0.
m) No. $P(YW) \neq 0$.
n) No because $P(W|Y) = 10/100 = 0.10$ does not equal $P(W) = 80/400 = 0.20$.
o) No. $P(WT) \neq 0$.
p) Yes. $P(W|T) = 50/250 = 0.2$ equals $P(W) = 80/400 = 0.20$.
q) Yes. $P(RG) = 0$.
r) No. $P(R|G) = 0$, which does not equal $P(R) = 0.50$.

6. $P(S) = 0.4$, and $P(S|H) = P(S|M) = P(S|L) = 0.4$.
   $P(P) = 0.6$, and $P(H|P) = P(M|P) = P(L|P) = 0.6$.

7.

	H	M	L
Female	20	160	20
Male	10	80	10

Problem Set 11-4

1.

Area	L	M	S	
A	0.03	0.045	0.075	0.15
B	0.15	0.125	0.275	0.55
C	0.02	0.130	0.150	0.30
	0.20	0.30	0.50	1.00

2. a)

	F	F'	
C	0.24	0.36	0.60
C'	0.16	0.24	0.40
	0.40	0.60	1.00

b) 0.36.   d) 0.   f) 0.60.
c) 0.76.   e) 0.40.   g) 0.
h) $P(CF) = 0.24$ and $P(C)P(F) = 0.60(0.40) = 0.24$. Hence, $P(CF) = P(C)P(F)$, so C and F are independent.
i) F and F' are complementary events.

3. a) 0.79.
   b) As a consequence of these probability assignments, $P(A \cup B) = 1.09$, which is greater than 1, so the candidate should be advised to reassess her subjective probabilities.

4. $P(CS) = 0.35$ because $P(CS) = P(C)P(S|C) = 0.5(0.7) = 0.35$.

5. $P(G|H) = 0.90$, where G means good job and H means honors. This follows from the rule $P(G|H) = P(GH)/P(H) = 0.09/0.10 = 0.90$.

6. 0.6

7. 0.9975.
8. 0.3.
9. $P(X|Y) = 1/4; P(Y|X) = 1/6$.
10. $P(X) = 1/2; P(Y) = 2/5$.
11. 0.67.
12. a) 1/2.   b) 4/7.   c) 23/70.   d) 47/70.
13. a) 0.35.   b) 0.60.   c) 0.55.   d) 0.45.
14. a) 0.48.   b) 0.16.
15. 0.61.
16. 0.402.
17. 0.011.
18. 0.078.
19. a) $P(SC) = 0.5; P(S)P(C) = 0.48$; $P(SC) \neq P(S)P(C)$.
    b) 0.12.
20. a) 1/4,000.
    b) 3,871/4,000.
    c) 129/4,000.
    d) 128/4,000.
21. a) 1/12.   b) 7/12.   c) 1/4.   d) 23/36.
22. 0.141.
23. 5/6.
24. 0.56.
25. 0.9.
26. 0.288.
27. 0.706.
28.

Sum	2	3	4	5	6	7	8	9	10	11	12
Prob.	1/36	1/18	1/12	1/9	5/36	1/6	5/36	1/9	1/12	1/18	1/36

29. a) 1/1,000.   b) 1/10,000.
30. a) 1/324,632.   b) 1/5,245,786.   c) 1/13,983,816.
31. a) 1/108,290.   c) 6/4,165.   e) 33/16,660.
    b) 1/108,290.   d) 1/4,165.

Problem Set 11-5

1. 0.949.
2. 0.678.
3. 0.857.
4. a) 0.003.   b) 0.020.
5. a) 0.998.   b) 0.664.
6. a) 0.5; 0.5.   b) 0.667; 0.333.
7. 0.308; 0.692.
8. a) 0.13.   b) 0.02.   c) 0.85.
9. 0.4 for John; 0.4 for Anne; 0.2 for Sally.

CHAPTER 12

Problem Set 12-1

1. a) $7/15 = 0.467$.
   b) $1/15 = 0.067$.
   c) $7/15 = 0.467$.
   d) $1 - P(0 \text{ defective}) = 1 - P(GGG) =$
      $1 - (7/10)(6/9)(5/8) = 0.708$.

2. a) 0.903.
   b) 0.003.
   c) 0.998.
   d) 0.095.
   e) 0.95 because of independence.

3. a) $HHH, HHT, HTH, HTT, THH, THT, TTH, TTT$.
   b) 0, 1, 2, 3.
   c)
Event	HHH	HHT	HTH	HTT
Probability	0.125	0.125	0.125	0.125
	THH	THT	TTH	TTT
	0.125	0.125	0.125	0.125

   d)
Event	0	1	2	3
Probability	0.125	0.375	0.375	0.125

   e) 0.875.   g) 0.375.
   f) 0.50.   h) 0.375.

4. a)
Event	W_1M	W_2M	W_1W_2	MW_1	MW_2	W_2W_1
Probability	1/6	1/6	1/6	1/6	1/6	1/6

   b) 1/3.   c) 2/3.   d) 1/3.

5. a) WM.
   b) $P(WM) = P(W)P(M|W) = (2/3)(1/2) = 1/3$.
   c) WW.
   d) $P(WW) = P(W)P(W|W) = (2/3)(1/2) = 1/3$.

6. a) 1/6.   b) 1/2.   c) 1/6.

7. a) $\binom{52}{5} = 2{,}598{,}960$.   b) 2^n.

Problem Set 12-2

1. 3.5; 1.5.
2. 3.4; 1.428.
3. 2.25; 1.445.
4. 1.2; 1.720.
5. 0.3; 1.1.
6. -1.7; 1.269.
7. a) No because $\Sigma p(x) > 1$.
   b) Yes.
   c) No because -0.25 is not a valid probability.
8. a) 35; 205; 14.318.
   b) See Figure A.
   c) 1; 0.5.
9. a) 3.5; 1.35; 1.162.
   b) See Figure B.
   c) 1; 0.55.
10. $4.

FIGURE A

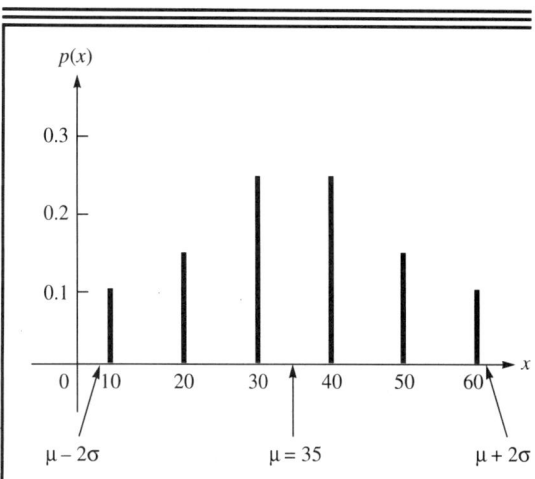

FIGURE B

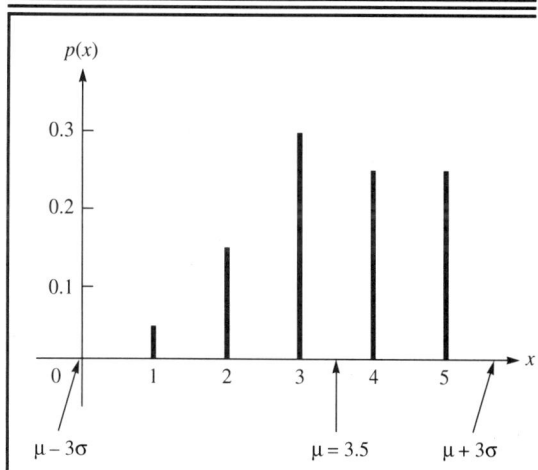

Problem Set 12-3

1. a) 0.441.   b) 0.657.   c) 0.309.   d) 0.084.
2. 0.992.
3. 0.913.
4. a) 0.886.   b) 0.655.

Problem Set 12-3 (concluded)

5. a) 0.760.   b) 0.084.
6. 5.
7. a) $1/32 = 0.03125$.   d) $1/2 = 0.50$.
   b) $3/16 = 0.1875$.   e) $3/16 = 0.1875$.
   c) 5/16, 0.3125.
8. a) $1/1,024 = 0.001$.   c) $45/512 = 0.088$.
   b) $1/64 = 0.015625$.   d) $53/512 = 0.104$.
9. a) $\sum_{x=0}^{15} C_x^{100}(0.05)^x(0.95)^{100-x}$.
   b) $\sum_{x=11}^{200} C_x^{200}(0.05)^x(0.95)^{200-x}$.
10. a) 0.993.   b) 0.421.
11. a) 0.642.   b) 0.027.
12. a) 0.983.   c) 0.579.   e) 0.377.
    b) 0.006.   d) 0.062.   f) 0.617.
13. a) 0.115.   d) 0.032.
    b) 0.788.   e) 0.210.
    c) 1.000.   f) 0.002.
14. a) 0.349.   b) 0.387.   c) 0.651.   d) 0.251.
15. a) 0.075.   b) 0.315.   c) 0.012.   d) 0.390.

Problem Set 12-4

1. 0.   3. Act 2.
2. $0.80.   4. A_4.
5. Make three. EMV = $8.35.
6. a) $42.75.
   b) $P(0 \text{ loss}) = 0.99825$ is not stated.
7. Choose A_1 in each case, even though A_2 presents no chance of loss. At first glance, the choice of A_1 may not seem appropriate, especially in (c) where there is a 50 percent chance of a loss of $1,000. However, $E(A_1)$ in (c) is $1,000, compared to $E(A_2) = \$250$.

Problem Set 12-5

1. a) $p(x) = 0.1$.   b) 0.3.
2. a) $p(x) = x/50$.   b) 0.09.
3. a) $p(x) = x^{1/2}/18$.   b) 0.259.
4. a) $p(x) = \dfrac{2 - x^{-2}}{37.05}$.
   b) 0.462.
5. a) $p(x) = \dfrac{12x - 3x^2}{32}$.
   b) 0.5.

Problem Set 12-6

1. a) $\mu = 10$.
   b) $\sigma^2 = 100/3$.
   c) $\sigma = 5.774$.
2. a) $\mu = 50$.
   b) $\sigma^2 = 2,500/3$.
   c) $\sigma = 28.87$.
3. a) $\mu = 4$.
   b) $\sigma^2 = 2$.
   c) $\sigma = 1.414$.
4. a) $\mu = 2$.
   b) $\sigma^2 = 0.5$.
   c) $\sigma = 0.707$.
5. a) 35/12 hundred gallons.
   b) 210 hundred gallons.
6. a) 17/15 thousand gallons.
   b) 102 thousand gallons.
7. a) See Figure A.
   b) The function is symmetrical, so its center of gravity is at the midpoint of the x-interval, which is 0.
   c) $\displaystyle\int_{-1}^{1} x\left[\dfrac{3(1 - x^2)}{4}\right] dx = \dfrac{3}{4}\left(\dfrac{x^2}{2} - \dfrac{x^4}{4}\right)\bigg|_{-1}^{1} = 0$.
   d) $(0.2)^{1/2} = 0.447$.

FIGURE A

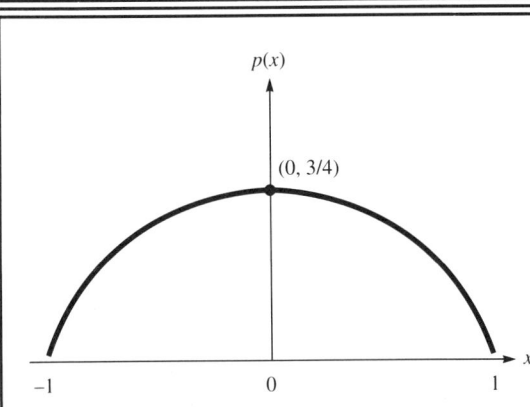

FIGURE B

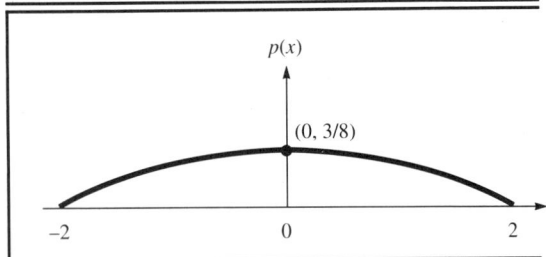

ANSWERS TO PROBLEM SETS 1037

Problem Set 12-6 *(concluded)*

8. a) See Figure B.
   b) The function is symmetrical, so its center of gravity is at the midpoint of the x-interval, which is 0.
   c) $\int_{-2}^{2} x \left[\frac{3(4 - x^2)}{32} \right] dx = \frac{3}{32} \left(2x^2 - \frac{x^4}{4} \right) \Big|_{-2}^{2} = 0.$
   d) 0.894.

Problem Set 12-7

1. a) 0.1915.   c) 0.1587.   e) 0.2266.   g) 0.1554.
   b) 0.1915.   d) 0.1498.   f) 0.3721.   h) 0.1464.
2. a) 0.8400.   c) 0.9974.   e) 0.7881.   g) 0.8413.
   b) 0.9544.   d) 0.0456.   f) 0.2295.   h) 0.1151.
3. a) 0.9772.   d) 0.3413.   g) 0.2266.
   b) 0.3023.   e) 0.1498.   h) 0.6247.
   c) 0.3085.   f) 0.6826.   i) 0.0013.

Problem Set 12-8

1. $\bar{x} = 7, s = 2.$
2. $\bar{x} = 15, s = 2.94.$
3. $\bar{x} = 11.2, s = 2.17.$
4. $\bar{x} = 3.5, s = 2.07.$
5. $\bar{x} = 0.58, s = 0.03.$

Problem Set 12-9

1. a) 52.2.
   b) 56.410.
   c) 41.775.
   d) 46.6 to 53.4.
   e) 58.225.
2. a) 15.87 percent.
   b) 97.72 percent.
   c) 23 parts.
   d) 4.56 percent.
   e) 1.5730 to 1.5770.
   f) 2.2484.
   g) $53.44.
3. a) 0.3085.
   b) 69.15 percent.
   c) 134 cans.
   d) 10.56 percent.
   e) 16.465.
4. a) 1,908 to 2,092.
   b) 10.56 percent.
   c) 1,868.
   d) 0.62 percent.
5. a) 0.13 percent.
   b) 5.48 percent.
   c) 183 to 217.
   d) 159.
   e) 99th percentile.

APPENDIX 1

Problem Set A1-1

1. −14.
2. +13.
3. −12.
4. +3.
5. +5.34.
6. −24.
7. −23.
8. +3.
9. −4.
10. −4.
11. +3.
12. +1.
13. −2.
14. +13.
15. +11.
16. −45.
17. −40.
18. −63.
19. +60.
20. −4.
21. +2.
22. −2.
23. +15.
24. −3.
25. −7/2.
26. +3/2.
27. −32.
28. −28/5.
29. +12/7.
30. +2.
31. +1.
32. −5.
33. −16.
34. 23.
35. −2.
36. 3.
37. 16.
38. 10.
39. 15.
40. −45.
41. −7.
42. −144.
43. 28.
44. 4.
45. 28.
46. 60.
47. 60.
48. 60.
49. $900; $1,050; $950.
50. $22,500; $23,780; $24,500; $23,780.
51. $7.50; $9.50; $15.00; $23.00.

Problem Set A1-2

1. *ab* means *a* times *b*; *cxy* means *c* times *x* times *y*.
2. $100a + 10b + c.$
3. All.
4. If *a* and *b* are any odd integers, then $a + b$ is an even integer.
5. Whenever we add two clock numbers (in the time sense), the sum is another clock number.
6. By convention, it is agreed that three times the sum of *a* and *c* will be indicated by parentheses; thus, $3(a + c).$
7. Any (whole) number.
8. In $a(b + c)$, we have the product of the number *a* by the number $(b + c)$. The distributive property says this product equals the sum of *ab* and *ac*.
9. Commutative, multiplication.
10. Commutative, addition.
11. Distributive.
12. Commutative, addition.
13. Convention; no sign means assume a plus sign.
14. Commutative, multiplication.
15. Definition; indicate addition of negative by minus sign.

Problem Set A1-2 (concluded)

16. Commutative, multiplication.
17. Associative, addition.
18. Commutative, multiplication.
19. Associative, multiplication.
20. Convention; b means $+b$; definition; indicate addition of negative by minus sign.
21. Associative, addition.
22. Distributive property.
23. Commutative, addition.
24. Commutative, addition.
25. Associative, multiplication.
26. $-b$.
27. $7a - 5b$.
28. $5abc - 2d$.
29. $7 + x$.
30. $8abc$.
31. $8 + 2a - b$.
32. $-b + a$
    $= a - b$ Commutative, addition.
33. $2b(3a)$
    $= 2b3(a)$ Associative, multiplication
    $= 2(3)ba$ Commutative, multiplication
    $= 6ba$ Associative, multiplication
    $= 6ab$ Commutative, multiplication.
34. $3 + xy + 5 + 3(2ab)$
    $= 3 + 5 + xy + 3(2ab)$ Commutative, addition
    $= 8 + xy + 3(2ab)$ Associative, addition
    $= 8 + xy + 6ab$ Associative, multiplication.
35. $3 + a + 2$
    $= 3 + 2 + a$ Commutative, addition
    $= 5 + a$ Associative, addition.
36. $a + 3 + c + 2$
    $= a + c + 3 + 2$ Commutative, addition
    $= a + c + 5$ Associative, addition.
37. $acdb$
    $= adcb$ Commutative, multiplication
    $= adbc$ Commutative, multiplication.
38. $a + b$.
39. $a + (b + c)$.
40. $(a + b) + 2(cd)$.
41. $2(a + b) - 3(c + 2d)$.
42. $2d(a + b + c)$.

Problem Set A1-3

1. $2abc - 4ab$.
2. $ab + a - 2b - 2$.
3. 11.
4. $ac - bc + 3c + 2a - 2b + 6$.
5. $3a + 3b - 1$.
6. $15a - 62$.
7. $13a + 54$.
8. $3ax - 6bx - 18x - 2a + 4b + 12$.
9. $x + 2b - a$.
10. $2x + 3y$.
11. $a - 3b$.
12. $a + 3x + 2$.
13. $7b - 2ab$.
14. $abc - 2abx + 10ab$.
15. $ax - 2ab + 2b$.
16. $3a - ac - 3bx + bcx$.
17. $ax + bx + x + ay + by + y$.
18. $ab + a - b - 1$.
19. -2.
20. $-2/5$.
21. $+4{,}298.936$.
22. $-4/9$.
23. $+2{,}333$.
24. See text.
25. $b(a - 2)$.
26. $a(3 + 5) = a(8) = 8a$.
27. $2a(2bc - b + 3)$.
28. $x(a - b + 1)$.
29. $a(3d - 5c + 1)$.
30. $2(2uv - xv + 1)$.
31. $ab(x + y - 1)$.
32. $2a(x - 3y + 2z)$.
33. $x(2 + a + b)$.
34. $-a(b + 3c + 1)$.
35. $(x + 1)(a + b)$.
36. $(x + 1)(1 + y)$.
37. $(x + y)(2 - a)$.
38. $(x + y)(a + b)$.
39. $(x - 2)(x + 1)$.
40. $(2x + 1)(x - 5)$.
41. $(4x - 3)(3x - 4)$.
42. $(5x - 1)(2x + 3)$.
43. $(x - 3)(x + 2)$.
44. $(x + 3)(x - 3)$.
45. $(x - y)(x + y)$.
46. $(2x + 3y)(2x - 3y)$.
47. F.
48. T.
49. T
50. T.
51. F.
52. T.
53. F.
54. F.
55. T.
56. T.
57. F.
58. T.
59. F.
60. T.

Problem Set A1-4

1. F.
2. F.
3. T.
4. T.
5. T.
6. T.
7. F.
8. F.
9. T.
10. T.
11. T.
12. The product of a number and its reciprocal is 1.
13. $\dfrac{3a}{2c}$.
14. Cancellation is not possible as the expression stands.
15. 1.
16. $a + 3$.
17. $6c$.
18. Cancellation is not possible as the expression stands.
19. $\dfrac{2y + 6a + 1}{4y}$.
20. $8x$.
21. See text.
22. $\dfrac{3ab}{8}$.
23. $\dfrac{2a + 2b}{15}$.
24. $\dfrac{-3a}{4}$.
25. $\dfrac{2ab + 4a}{21}$.
26. $\dfrac{-2}{3a + 3b}$.
27. $a + 6b + 2$.
28. $4a - 6b$.
29. $\dfrac{b(c - d)}{2}$.
30. $\dfrac{b - 2}{a + 3}$.
31. $\dfrac{2 + (c - b)}{2a}$.
32. $\dfrac{2 + (c - b) + a}{2x(a + b)}$.
33. $\dfrac{x + y}{y - x}$.
34. $1/3$.
35. $\dfrac{5a - 6}{10}$.
36. $\dfrac{45b - 5ab + 12a}{30ab}$.
37. $\dfrac{a + 24}{6a}$.
38. $7/6$.
39. $\dfrac{a - 2ab + 4b + bx - 2}{b(a - 2)}$.
40. $\dfrac{x - 2ab + 6}{2a}$.
41. $\dfrac{18abx - 3ab + 1}{6ab}$.
42. $\dfrac{11a + 5b - 3ab - 5}{12(b - 1)}$.
43. $\dfrac{-(12x + 17)}{4(x + 3)}$.
44. $91/12$.
45. $27/176$.
46. $7/6$.
47. $\dfrac{6b + 2ab}{5b - 3a}$.
48. $\dfrac{3abc - 6b + 18}{2bc - 6c}$.
49. $\dfrac{4ac - 6b + 12bc}{bc - 12}$.
50. $\dfrac{6a + 4b - 2c}{12b - 3a}$.

Problem A1-5

1. 16.
2. 7.
3. 1.041.
4. 4/3.
5. 1/72.
6. 1,000.
7. Not a real number.
8. 31/12.
9. 1/9.
10. 1.
11. 8.
12. 1/2.
13. 10.
14. 1/12.
15. 5/4.
16. 6.
17. 25.
18. 1.1025.
19. 1/8.
20. 13/8.
21. 5.
22. 9/4.
23. 2/9.
24. 5/4.
25. 4/27.
26. a^3.
27. $a^2b^2c^2$.
28. a^3b^7.
29. $a^3b^2c^3$.
30. x^4ab.
31. ab^2.
32. $a^2/(bc)$.
33. y^2b^2/x^2.
34. a^2/x.
35. x/y.
36. bc^3.
37. a^2b^3.
38. $b^2/(a^3c)$.
39. $-9bc$.
40. $-18/(bc)$.
41. ax.
42. a^3bc.
43. $1/(ax^2)$.
44. $2a/x^3$.
45. $1/(ax^3)$.
46. $3a^{7/3}b^{3/2}$.
47. $x^{3/2}/y^{1/6}$.
48. $a^{1/6}b^{7/6}$.
49. $2/(3^{3/2}x^{1/2})$.
50. $2y^{11/63}/(3x^2)$.
51. $\dfrac{2x^2 + 1}{x^3 + 3x^2}$.
52. $\dfrac{2 - x}{x - x^2}$.
53. $\dfrac{x + 1}{3x^2}$.
54. $\dfrac{x^2}{a^{2x-2}}$.
55. Exponents in this expression can't be combined.
56. $a^2 + ab$.
57. $a^2 - 6ab + 9b^2$.
58. $a^3 - 2a^2b + ab^2$.
59. $x^2 - y^2$.
60. $1 + a$.
61. $a - 2a^{1/2} + 1$.
62. $\dfrac{1 + 2a}{a^2}$.
63. 27.
64. F.
65. F.
66. T.
67. T.
68. F.
69. F.
70. T.
71. T.
72. F.
73. F.
74. T.
75. F.
76. F.
77. T.
78. F.
79. T.
80. F.
81. T.
82. T.
83. T.
84. F.
85. T.

Problem Set A1-6

1. 13.
2. -1.
3. 23.
4. -99.
5. 12.
6. 12.
7. 250.
8. 14.
9. 6/7.
10. 216/7.
11. $6,325,000.00$; $7,273,750.00$; $5.5(1 + 0.15)^2$ million; $22,250,567.55$; $181,054,239.50$.

Problem Set A1–6 *(concluded)*

12. $1,125,000.00$; $1,012,500.00$; $1.25(1 - 0.10)^2$; $911,250.00$; $435,848.05.

13. 4.57 billion; $5.04/(1 + 0.05)^2$ billion; 3.95 billion; 5.56 billion; $5.04 (1 + 0.05)^2$ billion; 6.43 billion.

APPENDIX 2

Problem Set A2–1.

1. $2x - 3 = x + 4$ — Add 3
   $2x = x + 7$ — Subtract x
   $x = 7$.

2. $4x + 5 = 2x + 12$ — Subtract 5
   $4x = 2x + 7$ — Subtract $2x$
   $2x = 7$ — Divide by 2
   $x = 7/2$.

3. $3x - 7 = 2x + 4$ — Add 7
   $3x = 2x + 11$ — Subtract $2x$
   $x = 11$.

4. $5 - 2x = 6$ — Subtract 5
   $-2x = 1$ — Divide by -2
   $x = -1/2$.

5. $7x - 5 = 3 - 4x$ — Add 5
   $7x = 8 - 4x$ — Add $4x$
   $11x = 8$ — Divide by 11
   $x = 8/11$.

6. $3 - 2x = x - 4$ — Subtract 3
   $-2x = x - 7$ — Subtract x
   $-3 = -7$
   $x = 7/3$. — Divide by -3

7. $\dfrac{x}{3} + \dfrac{1}{2} = 3x$ — Multiply by 6
   $2x + 3 = 18x$ — Subtract 3
   $2x = 18x - 3$ — Subtract $18x$
   $-16x = -3$ — Divide by -16
   $x = 3/16$.

8. $\dfrac{x}{4} + \dfrac{x}{2} = 2 - \dfrac{5x}{8}$ — Multiply by 8
   $2x + 4x = 16 - 5x$ — Add $5x$
   $2x + 4x + 5x = 16$ — Combine like terms
   $11x = 16$ — Divide by 11
   $x = 16/11$.

9. $\dfrac{2x}{5} - \dfrac{3x}{2} = 4$ — Multiply by 10
   $4x - 15x = 40$ — Combine like terms
   $-11x = 40$ — Divide by -11
   $x = -40/11$.

10. $1 - \dfrac{x}{3} + \dfrac{x}{2} = x - 4$ — Multiply by 6
    $6 - 2x + 3x = 6x - 24$ — Subtract 6
    $-2x + 3x = 6x - 30$ — Subtract $6x$
    $-2x + 3x - 6x = -30$ — Combine like terms
    $-5x = -30$ — Divide by -5
    $x = 6$.

11. $\dfrac{1}{7} - \dfrac{x}{3} = x$ — Multiply by 21
    $3 - 7x = 21x$ — Subtract 3
    $-7x = 21x - 3$ — Subtract $21x$
    $-28x = -3$ — Divide by -28
    $x = 3/28$.

12. $1 - \dfrac{3x}{7} = 0$ — Multiply by 7
    $7 - 3x = 0$ — Subtract 7
    $-3x = -7$ — Divide by -3
    $x = 7/3$.

13. $\dfrac{x + 3}{2} = x - \dfrac{1}{4}$ — Multiply by 4
    $2(x + 3) = 4x - 1$ — Apply distributive property
    $2x + 6 = 4x - 1$ — Subtract 6
    $2x = 4x - 7$ — Subtract $4x$
    $-2x = -7$ — Divide by -2
    $x = 7/2$.

14. $\dfrac{5 - 2x}{3} + \dfrac{x}{2} = 1$ — Multiply by 6
    $2(5 - 2x) + 3x = 6$ — Apply distributive property
    $10 - 4x + 3x = 6$ — Subtract 10
    $-4x + 3x = -4$ — Combine like terms
    $-x = -4$ — Divide by -1
    $x = 4$.

Problem Set A2-1 (continued)

15. $\dfrac{2x-1}{3} - \dfrac{1-x}{5} = 0$ Multiply by 15
    $5(2x - 1) - 3(1 - x) = 0$ Apply distributive property
    $10x - 5 - 3 + 3x = 0$ Add 8
    $10x + 3x = 8$ Combine like terms
    $13x = 8$ Divide by 13
    $x = 8/13.$

16. $\dfrac{x+1}{2} - \dfrac{x-1}{3} = 5$ Multiply by 6
    $3(x + 1) - 2(x - 1) = 30$ Apply distributive property
    $3x + 3 - 2x + 2 = 30$ Subtract 5
    $3x - 2x = 25$ Combine like terms
    $x = 25.$

17. $bx + 2 = c$ Subtract 2
    $bx = c - 2$ Divide by b
    $x = (c - 2)/b.$

18. $ax + 2 - x = 0$ Subtract 2
    $ax - x = -2$ Factor
    $x(a - 1) = -2$ Divide by $(a - 1)$
    $x = -2/(a - 1).$

19. $ax + b = cx$ Subtract cx
    $ax - cx + b = 0$ Subtract b
    $ax - cx = -b$ Factor
    $x(a - c) = -b$ Divide by $(a - c)$, multiply by $-1/-1$
    $x = b/(c - a).$

20. $ax + b = x - b$ Subtract b
    $ax = x - 2b$ Subtract x
    $ax - x = -2b$ Factor
    $x(a - 1) = -2b$ Divide by $(a - 1)$
    $x = -2b/(a - 1)$ Multiply by $-1/-1$
    $x = 2b/(1 - a).$

21. $a(x - a) = 2x$ Apply distributive property
    $ax - a^2 = 2x$ Add a^2
    $ax = 2x + a^2$ Subtract $2x$
    $ax - 2x = a^2$ Factor
    $x(a - 2) = a^2$ Divide by $(a - 2)$
    $x = a^2/(a - 2).$

22. $(x/a) - 1/2 = 2x$ Multiply by $2a$
    $2x - a = 4ax$ Add a
    $2x = 4ax + a$ Subtract $4/ax$
    $2x - 4ax = a$ Factor
    $x(2 - 4a) = a$ Divide by $(2 - 4a)$
    $x = a/(2 - 4a).$

23. $2/(a - x) + 1/3 = 4$ Multiply by $3(a - x)$
    $6 + a - x = 12(a - x)$ Apply distributive property
    $6 + a - x = 12a - 12x$ Add $12x$
    $6 + a + 11x = 12a$ Subtract $(6 + a)$
    $11x = 11a - 6$ Divide by 11
    $x = (11a - 6)/11.$

24. $y = x/(b - cx)$ Multiply by $(b - cx)$
    $y(b - cx) = x$ Apply distributive property
    $yb - ycx = x$ Add ycx
    $yb = x + ycx$ Factor
    $yb = x(1 + yc)$ Divide by $(1 + yc)$
    $yb/(1 + yc) = x$
    or
    $x = yb/(1 + yc).$

25. $(3/4) - (2x/3) = 2x(a - 1)$ Multiply by 12
    $9 - 8x = 24x(a - 1)$ Apply distributive property
    $9 - 8x = 24ax - 24x$ Add $8x$
    $9 = 24ax - 16x$ Factor
    $9 = x(24a - 16)$ Divide by $(24a - 16)$
    $9/(24a - 16) = x$
    or
    $x = 9/(24a - 16).$

26. $3(x - 2) = 2 - a(x + 2)$ Apply distributive property
    $3x - 6 = 2 - ax - 2a$ Add ax
    $3x + ax - 6 = 2 - 2a$ Add 6
    $3x + ax = 8 - 2a$ Factor
    $x(3 + a) = 8 - 2a$ Divide by $(3 + a)$
    $x = (8 - 2a)/(3 + a).$

27. $2/[3(x - 2)] + 3/a - 1/2 = 0$ Multiply by $6a(x - 2)$
    $4a + 18(x - 2) - 3a(x - 2) = 0$ Apply distributive property
    $4a + 18x - 36 - 3ax + 6a = 0$ Subtract $10a$
    $18x - 36 - 3ax = -10a$ Add 36
    $18x - 3ax = 36 - 10a$ Factor
    $x(18 - 3a) = 36 - 10a$ Divide by $(18 - 3a)$
    $x = (36 - 10a)/(18 - 3a).$

Problem Set A2-1 (concluded)

28.
$$ax - b/2 = c + 5[a - 2(b - x)]/6 \quad \text{Multiply by 6}$$
$$6ax - 3b = 6c + 5[a - 2(b - x)] \quad \text{Apply distributive property}$$
$$6ax - 3b = 6c + 5[a - 2b + 2x] \quad \text{Apply distributive property again}$$
$$6ax - 3b = 6c + 5a - 10b + 10x \quad \text{Subtract } 10x$$
$$6ax - 10x - 3b = 6c + 5a - 10b \quad \text{Add } 3b$$
$$6ax - 10x = 6c + 5a - 7b \quad \text{Factor}$$
$$x(6a - 10) = 6c + 5a - 7b \quad \text{Divide by } (6a - 10)$$
$$x = \frac{6c + 5a - 7b}{6a - 10}.$$

29.
$$b/a - x = 2a(b - x) \quad \text{Multiply by } a$$
$$b - ax = 2a^2(b - x) \quad \text{Apply distributive property}$$
$$b - ax = 2a^2 b - 2a^2 x \quad \text{Add } 2a^2 x$$
$$2a^2 x + b - ax = 2a^2 b \quad \text{Subtract } b$$
$$2a^2 x - ax = 2a^2 b - b \quad \text{Factor}$$
$$x(2a^2 - a) = 2a^2 b - b \quad \text{Divide by } (2a^2 - a)$$
$$x = (2a^2 b - b)/(2a^2 - a).$$

30.
$$x - a(b - x) = 2x - 3 \quad \text{Apply distributive property}$$
$$x - ab + ax = 2x - 3 \quad \text{Subtract } 2x$$
$$-x - ab + ax = -3 \quad \text{Add } ab$$
$$-x + ax = -3 + ab \quad \text{Factor}$$
$$x(-1 + a) = -3 + ab \quad \text{Divide by } (-1 + a)$$
$$x = (-3 + ab)/(-1 + a) \quad \text{Use commutative property}$$
$$x = (ab - 3)/(a - 1).$$

31.
$$3(b - x) = 2 + b[x - (3 - x)] \quad \text{Apply distributive property}$$
$$3b - 3x = 2 + b(x - 3 + x) \quad \text{Apply distributive property again}$$
$$3b - 3x = 2 + bx - 3b + bx \quad \text{Subtract } 2bx$$
$$3b - 3x - 2bx = 2 - 3b \quad \text{Subtract } 3b$$
$$-3x - 2bx = 2 - 6b \quad \text{Factor}$$
$$x(-3 - 2b) = 2 - 6b \quad \text{Divide by } (-3 - 2b)$$
$$x = (2 - 6b)/(-3 - 2b) \quad \text{Multiply by } -1/-1$$
$$x = (6b - 2)/(2b + 3).$$

32.
$$b(a + x) = a(b + x) \quad \text{Apply distributive property}$$
$$ba + bx = ab + ax \quad \text{Subtract } ax$$
$$ba + bx - ax = ab \quad \text{Subtract } ba$$
$$bx - ax = 0 \quad \text{Factor}$$
$$x(b - a) = 0 \quad \text{Divide by } (b - a)$$
$$x = 0.$$

33. 500 feet by 200 feet and 500 feet by 300 feet.
34. 51, 53, and 55.
35. a) The original number. b) x.
36. a) Year of birth; age. b) b; a.

Problem Set A2-2

1. 15.
2. 41.
3. 180.
4. 2.
5. 104.
6. 30.
7. 64.
8. 9.
9. 32.
10. 472.
11. 9/40.
12. 5/42.
13. 115/567.
14. −11/60.
15. 183/280.
16. −4,435/192.
17. −27.
18. 2/3.
19. 16/21.
20. −122/453.
21. $33,083.33.
22. 0.50.

Problem Set A2-2 (concluded)

23. a) 212°F.   c) 12.92°F.   e) 14°F.
    b) 32°F.   d) 82.4°F.   f) 122°F.
24. a) $E = 0.2T + 0.125(T - 50,000)$.
    b) $50,000; $65,384.62; $80,769.23.
    c) $83,333.33.
25. a) $B = x[P - y(P - B)]$.   b) $362,500.
26. a) 22.9 percent.   b) $3.03.
27. a) $20,000.   b) 0.2.   c) 0.375.
28. a) $10.01.   c) 100.   e) 500.
    b) $5.01.   d) 250.

Problem Set A2-3

Problems 1 through 10: See Figures A through J (pp. 1045–1047).

11. $x_1 = 9.69; x_2 = 0.31$.
12. $x_1 = 0.35; x_2 = -2.85$.
13. $x_1 = x_2 = 3/2$.
14. No real solutions.
15. $x_1 = 0; x_2 = 2$.
16. $x_1 = 2; x_2 = 1$.
17. $x_1 = 0; x_2 = 2$.
18. $x_1 = -5/2; x_2 = 4/3$.
19. $x_1 = 5; x_2 = -5$.
20. $x_1 = -7/2; x_2 = 1$.

Problem Set A2-4

1. F.
2. T.
3. F.
4. F.
5. F.
6. F.
7. T.
8. F.
9. T.
10. T.
11. T.
12. T.
13. $x \leq 2$.
14. $x \geq 3$.
15. $x < -3$.
16. $x > -2$.
17. $x \geq 0.5$.
18. $x \leq -0.25$.
19. a) $y \leq 6 - 1.5x$.
    b) On and below the line.   c) $y \leq 3$.
20. a) $y \geq 7 - 0.4x$.
    b) On and above the line.   c) $y \geq 5$.
21. a) $y \leq -9 + 1.4x$.
    b) On and below the line.   c) $y \leq 19$.
22. a) $y \geq -9 + 1.5x$.
    b) On and above the line.   c) $y \geq 6$.
23. Yes.   24. No.   25. Yes.   26. No.
27. See Figure K.   32. See Figure P.
28. See Figure L.   33. See Figure Q.
29. See Figure M.   34. See Figure R.
30. See Figure N.   35. See Figure S.
31. See Figure O.   36. See Figure T.

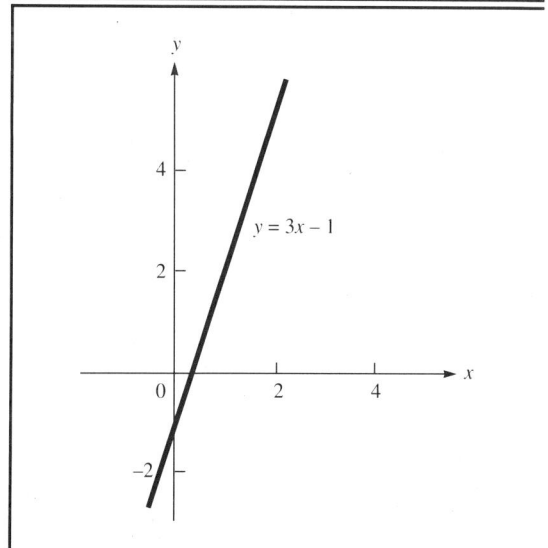

FIGURE A

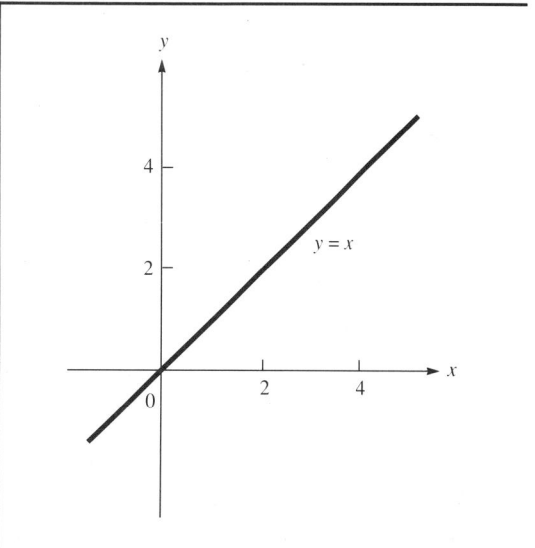

FIGURE B

Problem Set A2-3 *(continued)*

FIGURE C

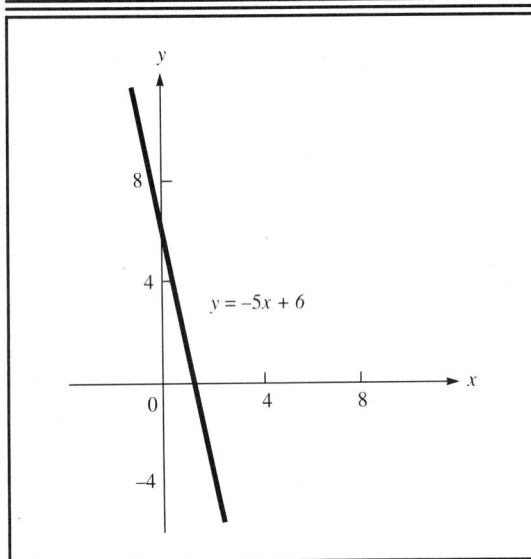

FIGURE D

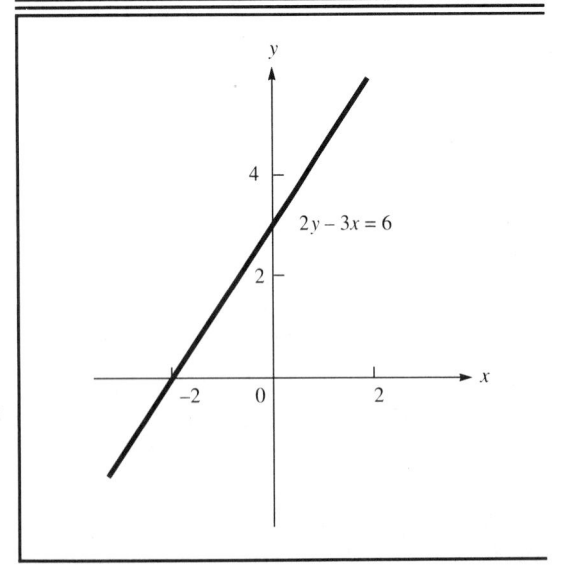

FIGURE E

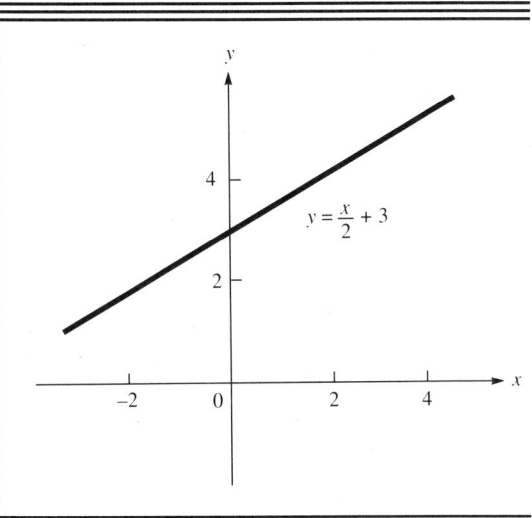

FIGURE F

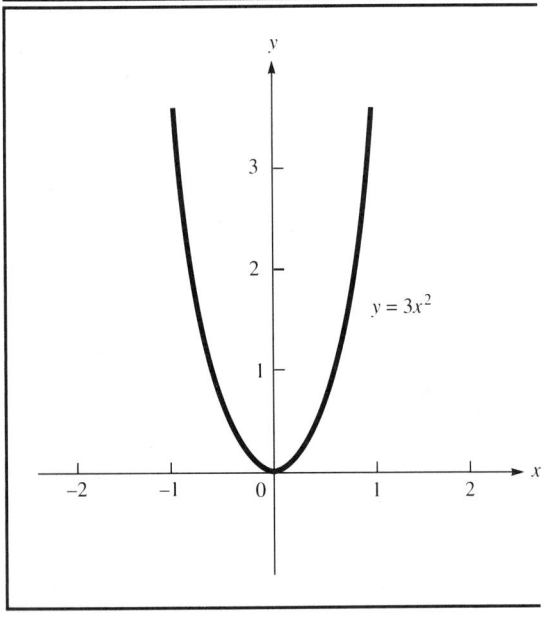

Problem Set A2-3 *(concluded)*

FIGURE G

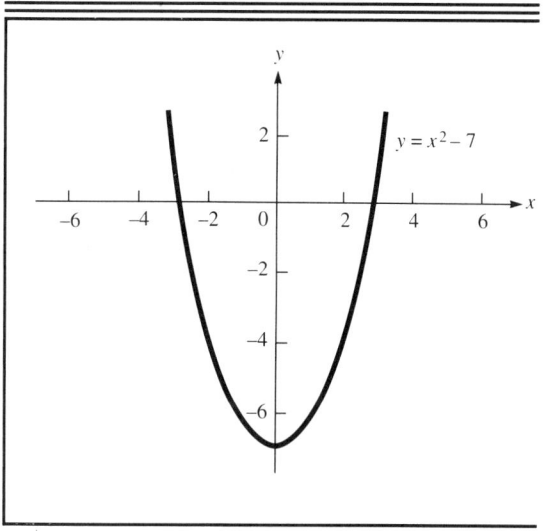

FIGURE H

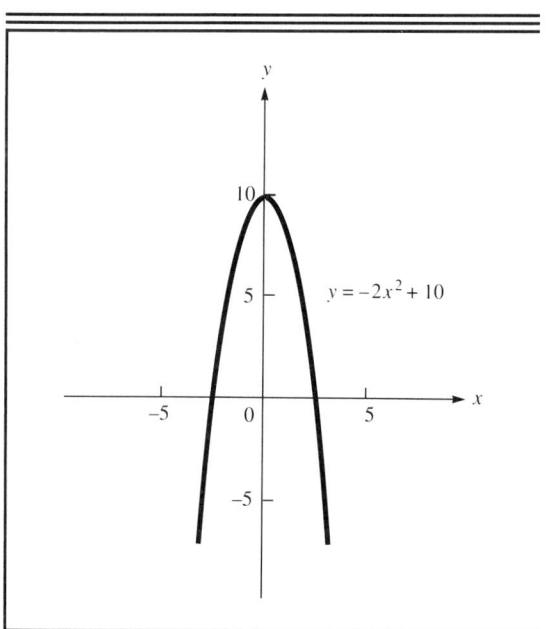

FIGURE I

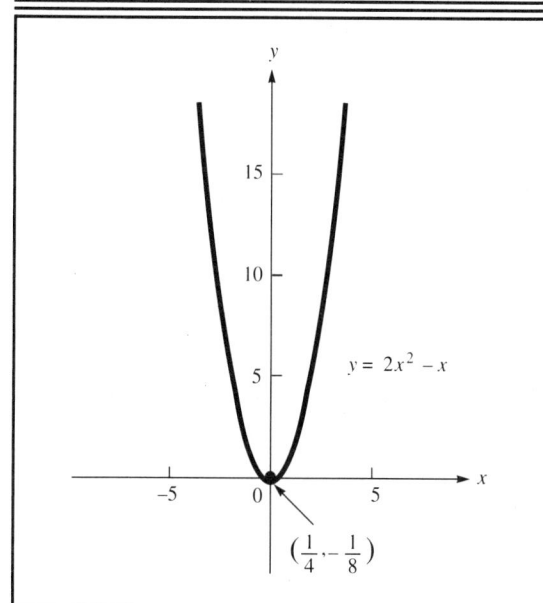

FIGURE J

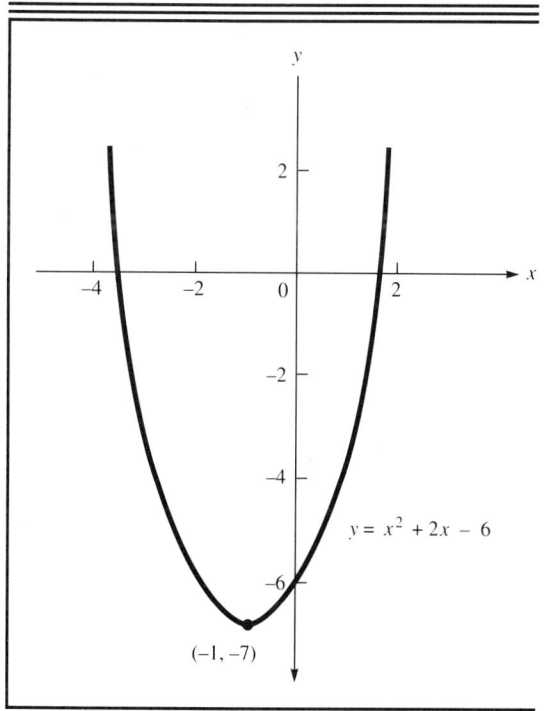

FIGURE K

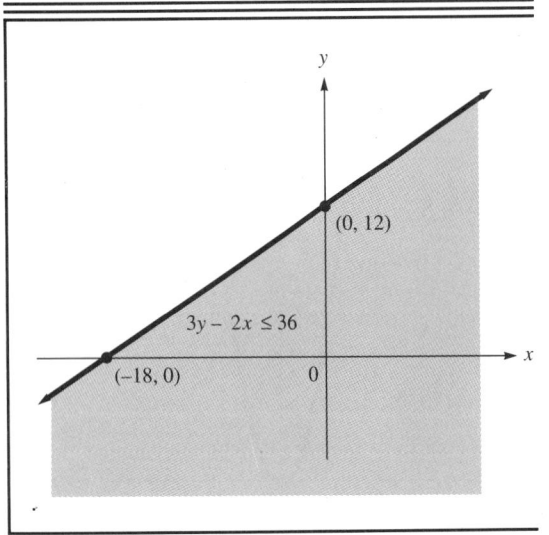

FIGURE M

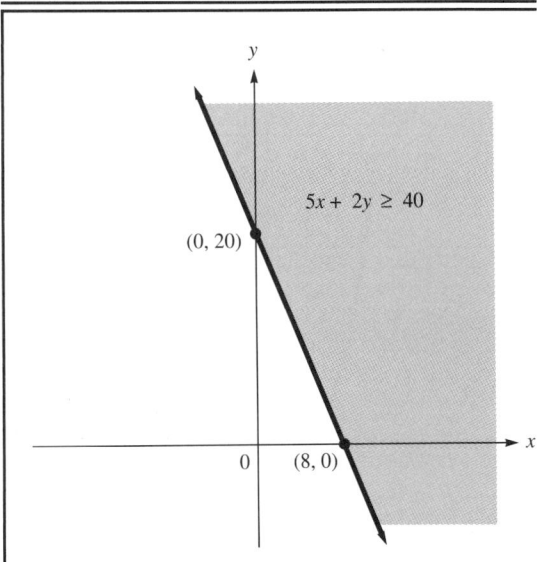

FIGURE L

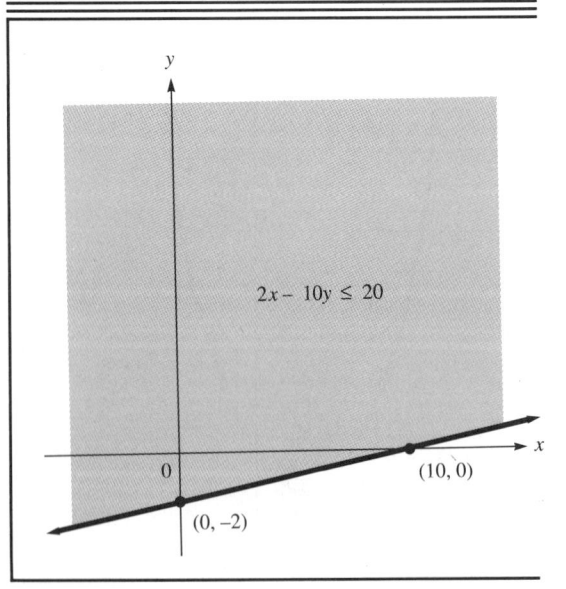

FIGURE N

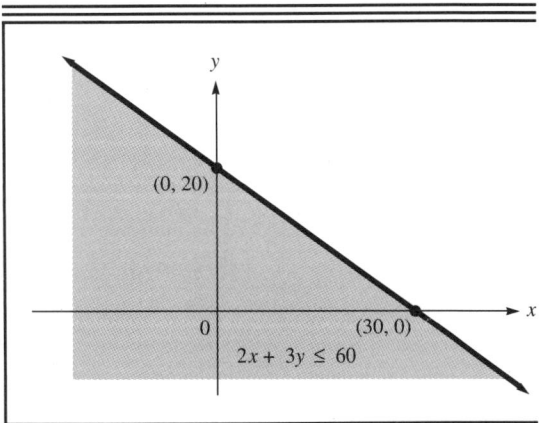

ANSWERS TO PROBLEM SETS   1047

FIGURE O

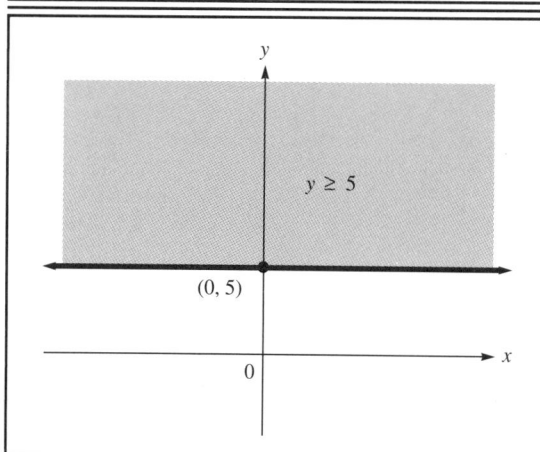

FIGURE P

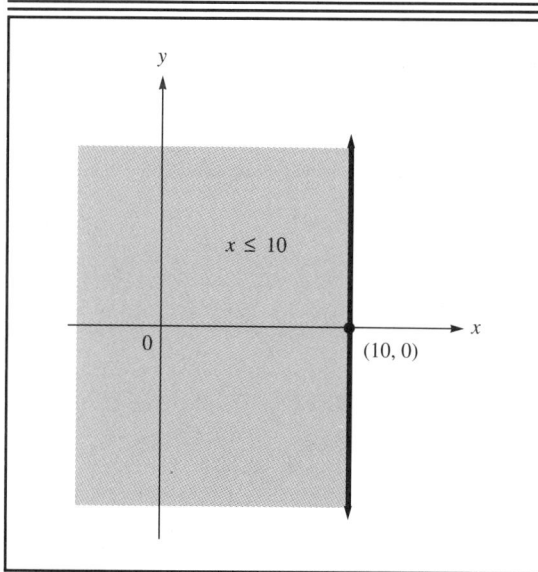

FIGURE Q

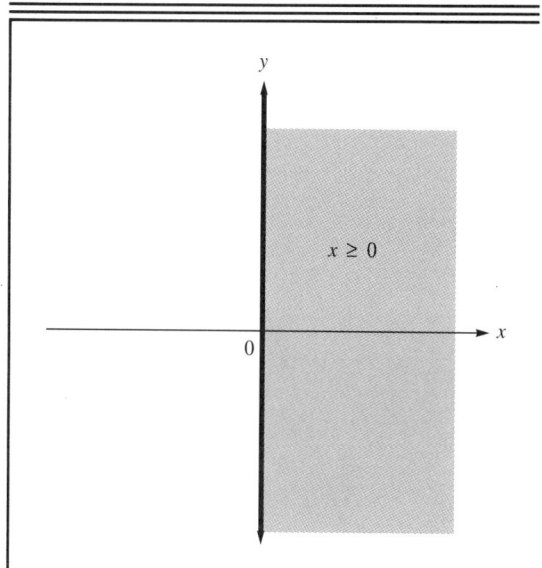

FIGURE R

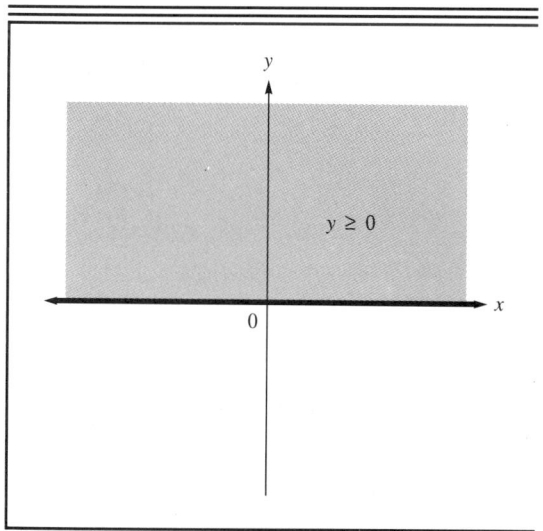

Problem Set A2-4 *(continued)*

FIGURE S

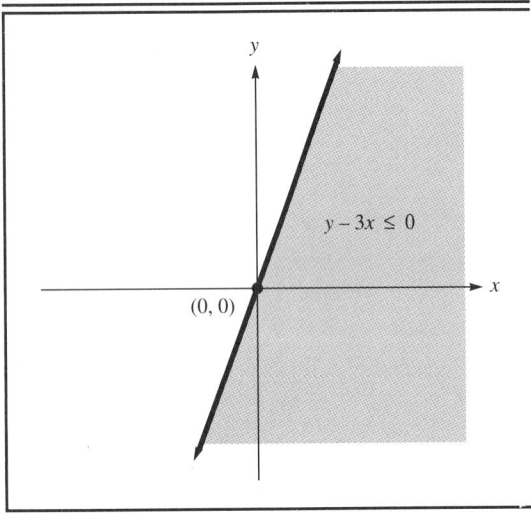

FIGURE T

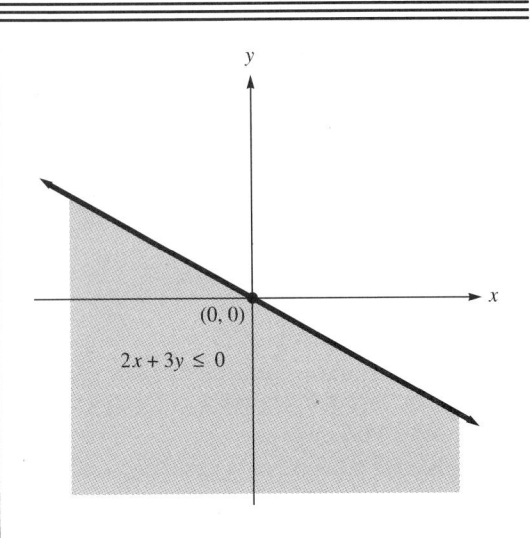

APPENDIX 3

Problem Set A3-1

1. a) "B is the set whose elements are 2, 4, and 6."
    b) "C is the set whose element is 0."
    c) "Q is the set whose members are the odd numbers 1 through 29."
    d) "F is the set whose elements are the lowercase English vowels."
    e) "L is the set whose members are George and Charles."
    f) "K is the set of positive even integers starting with 2."

2. a) $F = \{x \mid x$ is a lowercase English vowel$\}$.
    b) $S = \{x \mid x$ is a positive integral multiple of 3$\}$.
    c) $P = \{x \mid x$ is a first one of five positive integers$\}$.
    d) $G = \{x \mid x$ is a first one of five uppercase English letters$\}$.
    e) $R = \{x \mid x$ is an integer greater than 99$\}$.
    f) $J = \{x \mid x$ is a negative odd integer from -1 through $-101\}$.
    $= \{x \mid x$ is a negative odd integer greater than $-102\}$.

3. a) $\{1, 3, 5, 7\}$.
    b) $\{$January, February, March, April$\}$.
    c) $\{14, 28, 42, \ldots\}$.
    d) $\{5, 10, 15, \ldots, 995\}$.
    e) ϕ. f) $\{1^2, 2^2, 3^2, \ldots, 10^2\}$.

4. ϕ has no elements, whereas $\{0\}$ is the set with the single element 0.

5. a) $1/2 \notin \{1, 2, 3, \ldots\}$.
    b) $64 \varepsilon \{4, 8, 12, \ldots\}$.
    c) $a \varepsilon \{a, e, i, o, u\}$.
    d) $4 \notin \{1, 3, 5, \ldots\}$.
    e) $\$ \notin \{a, b, c, \ldots, z\}$.
    f) $g \notin \{a, b, c, d, e, f\}$.

6. a) $\{1, 3, 4, 7, 12\}$.   c) ϕ.   e) $\{1\}$.
    b) $\{3, 7\}$.   d) $\{1, 4\}$.   f) ϕ.

7. a) $\{y \mid y + 2 = 10\} = \{8\}$.
    b) The set of y's such that y plus 5 equals 8 is the set with the single member 3.

Problem Set A3-1 (concluded)

8. a) $\{m \mid m - 6 = 4\} = \{10\}$.
   b) The set of q's such that 2 times q is 6 is the set with the single member 3.
9. ϕ, the empty set.
10. $\{11/4\}$.
11. a) No, because for each state there are two senators.
    b) Yes, because for each senator there is one and only one state.
12. a) Yes, because each apple grows on one and only one tree.
    b) No, because one tree may have 0, 1, or more than 1 apple.
13. Yes, because for each point on the horizontal line there is one and only one point on the slant line.
14. No, because for each point on the diameter there are two points on the circle.
15. a) The h function of z, or h of z.   b) 15.
    c) Multiply 4 by the value of z and add 7.
    d) Multiply 4 by $(x + 2)$ and add 7.
16. a) The f function of x, or f of x.   b) 25.
    c) Multiply 3 by the value of x and add 10.
    d) Multiply 3 by $(x + 1)$ and add 10.
17. $\{y \mid y = 2x + 7\}$.
18. $\{y \mid y = 5x\}$.
19. Yes, because for each value of x there is one and only one value for y.
20. No, because for the starting element 0 there is no ending element; that is, 5/0 is undefined. See Appendix 1, Section 15.

Problem Set A3-2

1. a) $\{a, b, c, d, e, f, g, h\}$.
   b) $\{a, b, c, d, e, i, j\}$.   c) $\{d, e\}$.
   d) ϕ.   e) $\{d, e, f, g, h, i, j\}$.   f) ϕ.
2. a) $\{0, 1, 2, 3, \ldots\}$.   c) $\{5, 7, 9\}$.   e) $\{1, 3, 5, \ldots\}$.
   b) ϕ.   d) ϕ.
3. $A \cup B = \{\text{face cards}\}$; $A \cap B = \{\text{queens}\}$.
4. Assuming an ace is a face card, and using the notation 3D, jC to represent the three of diamonds and the jack of clubs, and so on:
   $A \cup B = \{\text{Face card}, 2H, 3H, \ldots, 10H, 2D, 3D, \ldots, 10D\}$.
   $A \cap B = \{jH, qH, kH, aH, jD, qD, kD, aD\}$.
   $A \cap C = \phi$.
   $B \cap C = \{9H, 9D\}$.
5. a) ϕ.
   b) $M \cap N$ is the point at which the lines intersect.
6. a) Rain tomorrow, or warmer tomorrow, or rain and warmer tomorrow.
   b) Rain and warmer tomorrow.
7. $\{1,2,3,4,5,6,7\}$.
8. a) $\{a, b, c, d, e, f, u, v, w, y, z\}$.
   b) $\{d\}$.
   c) All letters except $a, b, c, d, e, f, u, v, w, y$, and z.
   d) All letters except d.
   e) All letters except $a, b, c, d, e, f, u, v, w, y$, and z.
   f) All letters except d.
   g) $\{a, b, c, d, e, f, m, n, u, v, w, x, y, z\}$.
   h) $\{d\}$.
9. a) $(A \cup B)' = A' \cap B'$.
   b) $(A \cap B)' = A' \cup B'$.

TABLES

TABLE I
Rules for Derivatives

1. $\dfrac{d}{dx}[f(x) + g(x)] = \dfrac{d}{dx}f(x) + \dfrac{d}{dx}g(x)$.

2. $\dfrac{d}{dx}[f(x) - g(x)] = \dfrac{d}{dx}f(x) - \dfrac{d}{dx}g(x)$.

3. $\dfrac{d}{dx}(a) = 0$.

4. $\dfrac{d}{dx}(x) = 1$.

5. $\dfrac{d}{dx}(ax) = a; \dfrac{d}{dx}af(x) = a\dfrac{d}{dx}f(x)$.

6. $\dfrac{d}{dx}(x^n) = nx^{n-1}$.

7. $\dfrac{d}{dx}[f(x)]^n = n[f(x)]^{n-1}f'(x)$.

8. $\dfrac{d}{dx}(e^x) = e^x$.

9. $\dfrac{d}{dx}(a^x) = a^x (\ln a), a > 0$.

10. $\dfrac{d}{dx}[e^{f(x)}] = e^{f(x)}f'(x)$.

11. $\dfrac{d}{dx}[a^{f(x)}] = a^{f(x)}[f'(x)](\ln a), a > 0$.

12. $\dfrac{d}{dx}(\ln x) = \dfrac{1}{x}, x > 0$.

13. $\dfrac{d}{dx}(\log x) = \dfrac{1}{x(\ln 10)} = \dfrac{0.43429}{x}, x > 0$.

14. $\dfrac{d}{dx}[\ln f(x)] = \dfrac{1}{f(x)}[f'(x)] = \dfrac{f'(x)}{f(x)}, f(x) > 0$.

15. $\dfrac{d}{dx}[\log f(x)] = \dfrac{f'(x)}{f(x)(\ln 10)} = \dfrac{(0.43429)f'(x)}{f(x)}, f(x) > 0$.

16. $\dfrac{d}{dx}f[g(x)] = \dfrac{d}{dg}[f(g)] \cdot \dfrac{d}{dx}g(x)$.

17. $\dfrac{d}{dx}[f(x)g(x)] = f(x)g'(x) + g(x)f'(x)$.

18. $\dfrac{d}{dx}\left[\dfrac{f(x)}{g(x)}\right] = \dfrac{g(x)f'(x) - f(x)g'(x)}{[g(x)]^2}$.

Note: a and n are constants;
$$\dfrac{d}{dx}f(x) = f'(x); \dfrac{d}{dx}g(x) = g'(x).$$

TABLE II
Rules for Integrals

1. $\int [f(x) + g(x)]dx = \int f(x)dx + \int g(x)dx.$
2. $\int [f(x) - g(x)]dx = \int f(x)dx - \int g(x)dx.$
3. $\int kf(x)dx = k\int f(x)dx.$
4. $\int dx = \int 1 dx = x + C.$
5. $\int k dx = kx + C.$
6. $\int x^n dx = \dfrac{x^{n+1}}{n+1} + C;\ n \neq -1.$
7. $\int x^{-1}dx = \int \dfrac{1}{x}dx = \int \dfrac{dx}{x} = \ln|x| + C.$
8. $\int (mx + b)^n dx = \dfrac{(mx+b)^{n+1}}{m(n+1)} + C;\ n \neq -1.$
9. $\int (mx+b)^{-1}dx = \int \dfrac{dx}{mx+b} = \dfrac{\ln|mx+b|}{m} + C.$
10. $\int \dfrac{x\,dx}{mx+b} = \dfrac{x}{m} - \dfrac{b}{m^2}\ln|mx+b| + C.$
11. $\int \dfrac{x\,dx}{(mx+b)^2} = \dfrac{b}{m^2(mx+b)} + \dfrac{\ln|mx+b|}{m^2} + C.$
12. $\int \dfrac{dx}{x(mx+b)} = \dfrac{1}{b}\ln\left|\dfrac{x}{mx+b}\right| + C.$
13. $\int e^x dx = e^x + C.$
14. $\int a^x dx = \dfrac{a^x}{\ln a} + C,\ a > 0\ \text{and}\ a \neq 1.$
15. $\int e^{mx+b}\,dx = \dfrac{e^{mx+b}}{m} + C.$
16. $\int a^{mx+b}dx = \dfrac{a^{mx+b}}{m(\ln a)} + C,\ a > 0\ \text{and}\ a \neq 1.$
17. $\int xe^{mx+b}dx = \dfrac{e^{mx+b}(mx-1)}{m^2} + C.$
18. $\int xa^{mx+b}dx = \dfrac{xa^{mx+b}}{m(\ln a)} - \dfrac{a^{mx+b}}{(m\ln a)^2} + C,\ a > 0\ \text{and}\ a \neq 1.$
19. $\int xe^{ax^2+b}dx = \dfrac{e^{ax^2+b}}{2a} + C.$
20. $\int \dfrac{dx}{a + be^{mx}} = \dfrac{mx - \ln|a+be^{mx}|}{am} + C.$
21. $\int \ln x\,dx = x(\ln x - 1) + C,\ x > 0.$
22. $\int \log x\,dx = x\left(\log x - \dfrac{1}{\ln 10}\right) + C,\ x > 0.$
23. $\int \ln(mx+b)dx = \dfrac{(mx+b)[\ln(mx+b) - 1]}{m} + C,\ mx+b > 0.$
24. $\int \log(mx+b)dx = \left(\dfrac{mx+b}{m}\right)\left[\log(mx+b) - \dfrac{1}{\ln 10}\right] + C,\ mx+b > 0.$
25. $\int \dfrac{1}{x^2 - a^2}dx = \dfrac{1}{2a}\ln\left|\dfrac{x-a}{x+a}\right| + C,\ x^2 > a^2.$
26. $\int \dfrac{1}{a^2 - x^2}dx = \dfrac{1}{2a}\ln\left|\dfrac{a+x}{a-x}\right| + C,\ x^2 < a^2.$
27. $\int \dfrac{1}{x\sqrt{a^2 - x^2}}dx = -\dfrac{1}{a}\ln\left|\dfrac{a+\sqrt{a^2-x^2}}{x}\right| + C,\ 0 < x < a.$

Note: a, b, k, m, n and C are constants.

TABLE III

Cumulative Binomial Distribution for $n = 10$ (Tabulated values are $\sum_{0}^{x} C_x^{10} p^x q^{10-x}$)

Values of x	\multicolumn{13}{c|}{Values of p}												
	0.01	0.05	0.10	0.20	0.30	0.40	0.50	0.60	0.70	0.80	0.90	0.95	0.99
0	.904	.599	.349	.107	.028	.006	.001	.000	.000	.000	.000	.000	.000
1	.996	.914	.736	.376	.149	.046	.011	.002	.000	.000	.000	.000	.000
2	1.000	.988	.930	.678	.383	.167	.055	.012	.002	.000	.000	.000	.000
3	1.000	.999	.987	.879	.650	.382	.172	.055	.011	.001	.000	.000	.000
4	1.000	1.000	.998	.967	.850	.633	.377	.166	.047	.006	.000	.000	.000
5	1.000	1.000	1.000	.994	.953	.834	.623	.367	.150	.033	.002	.000	.000
6	1.000	1.000	1.000	.999	.989	.945	.828	.618	.350	.121	.013	.001	.000
7	1.000	1.000	1.000	1.000	.998	.988	.945	.833	.617	.322	.070	.012	.000
8	1.000	1.000	1.000	1.000	1.000	.998	.989	.954	.851	.624	.264	.086	.004
9	1.000	1.000	1.000	1.000	1.000	1.000	.999	.994	.972	.893	.651	.401	.096
10	1.000	1.000	1.000	1.000	1.000	1.000	1.000	1.000	1.000	1.000	1.000	1.000	1.000

TABLE IV

Cumulative Binomial Distribution for $n = 25$ (Tabulated values are $\sum_{0}^{x} C_x^{25} p^x q^{25-x}$)

Values of x	\multicolumn{13}{c|}{Values of p}												
	0.01	0.05	0.10	0.20	0.30	0.40	0.50	0.60	0.70	0.80	0.90	0.95	0.99
0	.778	.277	.072	.004	.000	.000	.000	.000	.000	.000	.000	.000	.000
1	.974	.642	.271	.027	.002	.000	.000	.000	.000	.000	.000	.000	.000
2	.998	.873	.537	.098	.009	.000	.000	.000	.000	.000	.000	.000	.000
3	1.000	.966	.764	.234	.033	.002	.000	.000	.000	.000	.000	.000	.000
4	1.000	.993	.902	.421	.090	.009	.000	.000	.000	.000	.000	.000	.000
5	1.000	.999	.967	.617	.193	.029	.002	.000	.000	.000	.000	.000	.000
6	1.000	1.000	.991	.780	.341	.074	.007	.000	.000	.000	.000	.000	.000
7	1.000	1.000	.998	.891	.512	.154	.022	.001	.000	.000	.000	.000	.000
8	1.000	1.000	1.000	.953	.677	.274	.054	.004	.000	.000	.000	.000	.000
9	1.000	1.000	1.000	.983	.811	.425	.115	.013	.000	.000	.000	.000	.000
10	1.000	1.000	1.000	.994	.902	.586	.212	.034	.002	.000	.000	.000	.000
11	1.000	1.000	1.000	.998	.956	.732	.345	.078	.006	.000	.000	.000	.000
12	1.000	1.000	1.000	1.000	.983	.846	.500	.154	.017	.000	.000	.000	.000
13	1.000	1.000	1.000	1.000	.994	.922	.655	.268	.044	.002	.000	.000	.000
14	1.000	1.000	1.000	1.000	.998	.966	.788	.414	.098	.006	.000	.000	.000
15	1.000	1.000	1.000	1.000	1.000	.987	.885	.575	.189	.017	.000	.000	.000
16	1.000	1.000	1.000	1.000	1.000	.996	.946	.726	.323	.047	.000	.000	.000
17	1.000	1.000	1.000	1.000	1.000	.999	.978	.846	.488	.109	.002	.000	.000
18	1.000	1.000	1.000	1.000	1.000	1.000	.993	.926	.659	.220	.009	.000	.000
19	1.000	1.000	1.000	1.000	1.000	1.000	.998	.971	.807	.383	.033	.001	.000
20	1.000	1.000	1.000	1.000	1.000	1.000	1.000	.991	.910	.579	.098	.007	.000
21	1.000	1.000	1.000	1.000	1.000	1.000	1.000	.998	.967	.766	.236	.034	.000
22	1.000	1.000	1.000	1.000	1.000	1.000	1.000	1.000	.991	.902	.463	.127	.002
23	1.000	1.000	1.000	1.000	1.000	1.000	1.000	1.000	.998	.973	.729	.358	.026
24	1.000	1.000	1.000	1.000	1.000	1.000	1.000	1.000	1.000	.996	.928	.723	.222

TABLE V
Areas under the Standardized Normal Distribution from the Mean to z

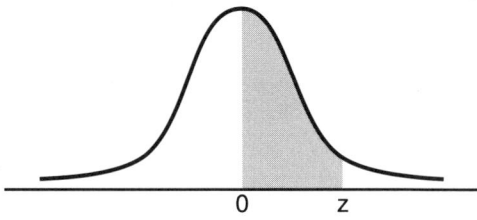

Normal Deviate, z	.00	.01	.02	.03	.04	.05	.06	.07	.08	.09
0.0	.0000	.0040	.0080	.0120	.0160	.0199	.0239	.0279	.0319	.0359
0.1	.0398	.0438	.0478	.0517	.0557	.0596	.0636	.0675	.0714	.0753
0.2	.0793	.0832	.0871	.0910	.0948	.0987	.1026	.1064	.1103	.1141
0.3	.1179	.1217	.1255	.1293	.1331	.1368	.1406	.1443	.1480	.1517
0.4	.1554	.1591	.1628	.1664	.1700	.1736	.1772	.1808	.1844	.1879
0.5	.1915	.1950	.1985	.2019	.2054	.2088	.2123	.2157	.2190	.2224
0.6	.2257	.2291	.2324	.2357	.2389	.2422	.2454	.2486	.2517	.2549
0.7	.2580	.2611	.2642	.2673	.2704	.2734	.2764	.2794	.2823	.2852
0.8	.2881	.2910	.2939	.2967	.2995	.3023	.3051	.3078	.3106	.3133
0.9	.3159	.3186	.3212	.3238	.3264	.3289	.3315	.3340	.3365	.3389
1.0	.3413	.3438	.3461	.3485	.3508	.3531	.3554	.3577	.3599	.3621
1.1	.3643	.3665	.3686	.3708	.3729	.3749	.3770	.3790	.3810	.3830
1.2	.3849	.3869	.3888	.3907	.3925	.3944	.3962	.3980	.3997	.4015
1.3	.4032	.4049	.4066	.4082	.4099	.4115	.4131	.4147	.4162	.4177
1.4	.4192	.4207	.4222	.4236	.4251	.4265	.4279	.4292	.4306	.4319
1.5	.4332	.4345	.4357	.4370	.4382	.4394	.4406	.4418	.4429	.4441
1.6	.4452	.4463	.4474	.4484	.4495	.4505	.4515	.4525	.4535	.4545
1.7	.4554	.4564	.4573	.4582	.4591	.4599	.4608	.4616	.4625	.4633
1.8	.4641	.4649	.4656	.4664	.4671	.4678	.4686	.4693	.4699	.4706
1.9	.4713	.4719	.4726	.4732	.4738	.4744	.4750	.4756	.4761	.4767
2.0	.4772	.4778	.4783	.4788	.4793	.4798	.4803	.4808	.4812	.4817
2.1	.4821	.4826	.4830	.4834	.4838	.4842	.4846	.4850	.4854	.4857
2.2	.4861	.4864	.4868	.4871	.4875	.4878	.4881	.4884	.4887	.4890
2.3	.4893	.4896	.4898	.4901	.4904	.4906	.4909	.4911	.4913	.4916
2.4	.4918	.4920	.4922	.4925	.4927	.4929	.4931	.4932	.4934	.4936
2.5	.4938	.4940	.4941	.4943	.4945	.4946	.4948	.4949	.4951	.4952
2.6	.4953	.4955	.4956	.4957	.4959	.4960	.4961	.4962	.4963	.4964
2.7	.4965	.4966	.4967	.4968	.4969	.4970	.4971	.4972	.4973	.4974
2.8	.4974	.4975	.4976	.4977	.4977	.4978	.4979	.4979	.4980	.4981
2.9	.4981	.4982	.4982	.4983	.4984	.4984	.4985	.4985	.4986	.4986
3.0	.4987	.4987	.4987	.4988	.4988	.4989	.4989	.4989	.4990	.4990

Adapted by permission from Ernest Kurnow, Gerald J. Glaser, and Frederick R. Ottman, *Statistics for Business Decisions* (Homewood, Ill.: Richard D. Irwin, 1959), p. 501. © 1959 by Richard D. Irwin, Inc.

INDEX

A

Absolute maximum/minimum, 523
Acceleration, 503
Algebra
  refresher, 2–12
  review, 2–12, 874–984
Alternative optimal
  points, 166–67, 248
  solutions, 246–48
Amortization
  with calculators, 434–35
  definition of, 432
  and mortgage payments, 436–37
  schedules, 437–39
Annuity; *see also* Ordinary annuities
  certain, 424
  complex, 424
  due, 424
  simple, 424
Antiderivatives, 640–42
Antilogs, 374
Arbitrary variable, 86–88
Artificial variable, 293, 308
Area
  and the definite integral, 650–52
  between two curves, 666–71
Associative property, 102, 106, 887
Asymptote, 598–601
Asymptotic integrals, 700–703
Augmented matrix, 114

B

Bank discount, 395–97
Banker's rule, 389
Basic variable, 205, 212
Basis, 205, 207
Bayes' rule, 796–801
Binding constraint, 260

Binomial probability
  distribution, 820–26
  rule, 822
Binomial theorem, 764–66
Break-even
  analysis, 50–61
  chart, 54–59
  quantity, 56
  sales, 60
Burgi, J., 362

C

Cartesian coordinate system, 8, 944–46
Chain rule, 608–12
Charnes, A., 242
Closure property, 887
Coefficient, 6–7
Coefficient matrix, 111
Column vector, 100
Combinations, 752–57
Common logarithm, 367–68
Commutative property, 102, 105–6, 887
Complement, 11–12, 743, 761, 780, 978
Compound
  discount factor, 410
  interest, 401–15
Computers; *see also by individual program*
  and linear relationships, 14
  matrix inversion on, 118
Concavity, 527, 540–41
Conditional equality, 466, 928
Conditional probability, 774–76
Consistent system, 82
Constant function, 501
Constant of integration, 642, 676–78
Constraints
  binding, 260
  conversion, 203, 283, 308
  degeneracy in, 241–42
  equality, 184–86, 306–12

Constraints—*Cont.*
 linear, 151
 linearly independent, 191
 mix of, 179–81
 nonnegative, 155–59
 in program formulation, 173
 redundant, 181
Consumers' surplus, 680–85
Consumption function, 612
Continuity, 483–86
Continuous
 compounding, 416–23, 450–51
 density function/distribution, 838–42
Conversion period, 404–6
 with calculators, 405
Cooper, W. W., 242
Coordinate axes, 944–46
Corners
 in linear programming, 163
 nonpermissible, 186–87
Cost
 fixed, 49
 marginal, 49–50, 469, 503–6
 variable, 49–50, 571
Cost-output analysis, 47–49
Counting techniques, 742–64
Critical points, 523
Cumulative binomial
 distribution tables, 979
 probability, 826–31
Current values column, 206
Curve sketching, 576–86
Cusps, 523

D

Decimal rate, 393
Definite integral,
 definition of, 650–52
 properties of, 671
Degeneracy, 241–42, 311
Delta notation, 467–70
Demand function
 and consumers' surplus, 680–81
 horizontal, 63
 linear, 61–63
 two-product, 96–97
 vertical, 63
Dependent variable, 8
Derivatives; *see also by function*
 definition of, 491–93
 endpoint test, 532–38

Derivatives—*Cont.*
 of exponential functions, 591–602
 first test, 522–38
 function power rule for, 507–11
 higher-order test, 580–81
 of logarithms, 605–6
 partial, 617–21
 product rule for, 511–15
 quotient rule for, 515–17
 rules for, 501–2, 979
 second test, 540–44
 simple power rule for, 498–500
 third test, 544–48
 with respect to x, 500–503
Difference quotient, 487–91
Differential calculus
 derivatives in, 493–97
 limits in, 471–80
 multivariate, 617–35
 notation for, 464–67, 500
Differential equations
 applications of, 718, 725–32
 definition of, 718
 explicit solutions to, 719
 general solutions to, 719
 initial conditions, 719–21
 particular solutions to, 720
 separable, 720
Discriminant, 625
Disjoint sets, 11, 773, 979
Distribution
 binomial, 820–26
 continuous, 838–42
 normal, 714, 848–58, 863–68
 probability, 813
Distributive property, 4, 887
Dual problem
 definition of, 282–83
 formation, 282–84
 minimizing primal by maximizing, 282–89
 solving, 284–89
Dual theorem, 284

E

e
 with calculators, 374
 computation of, 380–82
 with computers, 381
 definition of, 368
Effective rate, 397–99, 413–15, 420–23
Elasticity of demand, 63–64

Element of a set, 11–12, 971
Empty set, 11–12, 980
Endpoints, 523, 532–38
Equations
 definition of, 3
 graphs of, 16–18, 28–29, 72, 947–54
 quadratic, 7–8, 954–57
 solving, 6–7, 928–42
Equilibrium point, 94, 681, 684
Events (probabilistic)
 certain and impossible, 771–72
 complementary, 780
 definition of, 771
 dependent, 774–76
 independent, 774–76
 joint, 772–73
 mutually exclusive, 773–74, 776
 simple, 809
 union of, 779
Expected
 monetary value, 832–36
 utility value, 835
 value, 815, 843
Experiment, 808
Exponential functions
 definition of, 354–62
 derivatives of, 591–97
 graphs of, 357, 597–601
 rules, 593, 594, 597, 691–92, 918–19
Exponents
 definition of, 5–6, 911–12
 fractional, 6, 915–17
 multiplying, 6, 914–15
 negative, 5, 912–14
 properties of, 5–6, 355
 rules for, 5–6, 918–19
 zero, 6, 912
Expression, 891

F

Factor, 891
Factorial, 754
Factoring, 4, 888, 893–97
Feasible solutions, 163
First derivative test, 528
Fixed cost, 49, 61
Functional notation, 19, 464–67
Function power rule, 507–11; *see also* Chain rule
Functions
 area interpretations, 650–85
 concavity of, 527, 540–41

Functions—*Cont.*
 consumption, 612
 continuity in, 483–86
 decreasing, 523, 525
 definition of, 19–20, 464–67, 975
 density
  continuous, 838
  normal, 714, 848–58, 863–68
  uniform, 839
 exponential, 354–62
  derivatives of, 591–97
  graphs of, 355, 597–601
  integrals of, 690–95
  properties of, 355
  rules for, 593, 594, 597, 691–92; *see also* Chain rule
 increasing, 523, 525
 linear, 19–20, 40–43
 logarithmic, 605–7
 maxima of, 523–38
 minima of, 523–38
 polynomial, 475, 486, 576–80
 power rules for, 464–67
 rational, 581–82
 response, 602–3
 value of, 20
Fundamental theorem of calculus, 651
Future value
 at compound interest
  calculation of, 401–3
  with calculators, 402–3
  with continuous compounding, 418–20
  QBasic program for, 403
  time diagram for, 402
 of ordinary annuities
  calculation of, 424–27, 441, 443, 445–46
  with calculators, 426–27
  time diagram of, 425, 427, 441–43, 446
 at simple interest
  calculation of, 391–93
  QBasic program for, 392
  time diagram of, 391

G–H

Gauss-Jordan method
 definition of, 113–17
 row operations in, 123
 solving m by n linear systems, 132–38
 solving n by n linear systems, 121–30
 zeroes-first variation of, 117–19
Global maximum/minimum, 523

Half plane, 153
Hanna, S., 324
Henderson, A., 242
Higher-order test, 580–81
Hillier, F. S., 274
Histogram, 813–14
Horizontal
 lines, 34–35
 asymptote, 598–601
 axis, 8, 944

I

Identity
 additive, 888
 law, 103, 108, 887
 matrix, 107–8
 multiplicative, 900
Improper integrals, 700–703
Inconsistent system, 82, 152
Indefinite integral
 definition of, 642
 properties of, 643–46
Independent
 events, 786
 variable, 8, 464–65, 975
Inequalities
 definition of, 3, 959–60
 inconsistent, 152
 linear, 152–55, 960–66
 redundant, 152
 solving, 7–8, 960–66
Inflection point, 527–28, 544
Inner product, 104
Integers, 1
Integral calculus
 determining correctness in, 645–46
 versus differential calculus, 641
 fundamental theorem of, 651
 notation for, 642
 properties of, 643–46
Integrals; *see also* Integration by parts
 area interpretations, 650–62
  applications of, 672–85
  with two functions, 666–71
 definition of, 642, 671
 definite, 650–62; *see also* Numerical integration
 of exponential functions, 690–95
 improper, 700–702
 indefinite, 642
 of linear functions, 646, 687–88

Integrals—*Cont.*
 power rule for linear functions, 643
 rules for, 696–99
 symbol for, 642
 tables of, 696–99
 u-substitution, 647, 688–89
Integrand, 642
Integration by parts, 714–17
Intercepts, 28–29
Interest
 compound, 401–15
  conversion period for, 404–6
  continuous, 416–23
  defined, 401
  effective rate of, 413–15
  future value, 401–3
  present value, 410–12
  QBasic program for, 403, 412
 simple, 388–99
  bank discount, 395–97
  deducted-in-advance, 396
  exact, 389–91
  future value, 391–92
  maturity value, 395
  ordinary, 389–91
  present value, 393–95
  proceeds, 395–96
  QBasic program for, 392, 395
Interest rates
 with calculators, 408–9
 conversion period, 404–7
 decimal equivalents of, 393
 determination of, 408–9
 effective, 388–99
Intersection symbol, 9–10, 979
Interval notation, 522
Inventory model, 570–75
Inverse
 additive, 888
 of a function, 374
 of a matrix, 112–13
 multiplicative, 112, 900
Irrational numbers, 1, 877
Isocost line, 176
Isoprofit line, 164

K–L

Keller, B.R., 238
Kurnow, Ernest, 633–35

Least squares, 633–35
Leibnitz, Gottfried Wilhelm, 459

Leibniz notation, 500
Lieberman, G. J., 274
Limits
　concept of, 471–74
　definition of, 474
　of integration, 651
　theorems for, 480–82
　uses for, 474–80
LINDO computer program
　alternative optimal solutions, 249
　constant term, 278
　equality constraints, 311–12
　introduction to, 218–20, 227–28
　minimizing constraints, 222–28
　negative decision variables, 257–58
　no feasible solution, 305–6
　sensitivity analysis, 259–74, 318–19, 320–22
　unbounded solutions, 252
　using, 218–20, 227–28
Linear equations
　definition of, 16
　expression of, 19–20
　graphs of, 17–18, 28–29, 947–48
　matrix representation, 121–22
　point-slope form, 32–33
　slope-intercept form, 26–29
　systems of
　　applications, 89–92
　　consistent, 82
　　definition of, 71
　　elimination procedure, 75–88
　　graphs for, 72
　　inconsistent, 82
　　m by n, 73
　　matrix representation, 110–11, 121–22
　　matrix solution of, 121–30, 132–38
　　number of solutions, 73
　　optimization in, 90–92
　　row operations, 73–75
　　solutions of, 71–88
　　2 by 2, 73, 82
　　3 by 2, 79
　　3 by 3, 80, 84
　　two-point form, 33–34
Linear function, 19–20, 42–45
Linear inequalities
　nonnegative constraints, 155–59
　solution of, 960–66
　systems of, 152–55
Linear programming
　alternative optimum points, 166–67, 248
　corners in, 163
　definition of, 151
　equality constraints, 184–86, 306–12

Linear programming—*Cont.*
　isolines, 164
　maximization problems, 161–73
　minimization problems, 174–81, 222–28
　multivariate, 187–91
　no feasible solutions, 302–6
　pivot column, 207
　pivot row, 208
　problem formulation, 169–73, 194–98
　simplex method; 202–6, 237–328; *see also* LINDO computer program
　　alternative optimal solutions, 246–50; *see also* Sensitivity analysis
　　basic variables, 205
　　conversion of constraints and objective function, 202–4, 283, 293, 308
　　definition of, 202
　　entering variable, 206–7
　　feasible solutions, 205
　　grand summary, 313–15
　　initial solution, 204–6
　　leaving variable, 207–8
　　matrix techniques in, 206–16
　　maximizing problems, 206–16
　　minimizing problems, 174–81, 222–28
　　negative ratios, 208, 226
　　negative decision variables, 253–58
　　no feasible solutions, 302–6
　　nonbasic variables, 205
　　outline, 211
　　solutions, 164
　　tie for entering variable, 237–41
　　tie for leaving variable, 241–46
　　unbounded solutions, 179, 250–53
　　use of tableaus, 206–16
　three-step graphical procedure, 178–79
Linear systems; *see* Linear equations, systems of
Lines, 16–63; *see also* Linear equations
　parallel, 38–39
　perpendicular, 39–40
　through the origin, 41–42
Local Maximum/Minimum, 523–25
Logarithmic function rule, 605–6; *see also* Chain rule
Logarithms
　base, 363
　with calculators, 369–70, 372, 374, 377, 380–81
　common, 367
　with computers, 384
　natural
　　computation of, 382–83
　　definition of, 368

Logarithms—*Cont.*
  natural—*Cont.*
    graph of, 377–80
    inverse, 373–77
    need for, 362–64
    rules of, 364–67
Lot acceptance sampling, 762
Lowest common denominator, 905, 932

M

Margin, 57
Marginal cost, 49–50, 469, 503–6, 677–78
Marginal propensity to consume
  definition of, 24, 612
  and the multiplier, 612–16
Marginal propensity to save, 25, 612–13
Markov chains, 139–43
Markup, 57–58
Mathematical models, 573–75
Matrices; *see also* Gauss–Jordan method
  adding, 101–3
  associative laws, 102, 106
  augmented, 114
  commutative laws, 102, 105–6
  conformable, 104
  definition of, 99
  dimension of, 99
  element, 98
  forms of, 110–11
  identity, 107–8
  identity laws for, 103, 108
  inverses of, 112–13
  multiplying, 103–7
  n by n, 101, 107, 113
  order of, 99
  row operations on, 110–12
  scalar product for, 101
  singular, 119
  square, 101
  subtracting, 101–3
  symbols for, 99
  transition, 140
  zero, 107
Maturity value, 395
Maxima and minima
  absolute/global, 523–25
  applications, 549–58, 561–67, 570–75
  local, 523–25, 528, 625
  with two independent variables, 622–35
Maximizing profit, 151
Mean
  with calculators, 860

Mean—*Cont.*
  definition of, 815, 823, 859
  estimating, 858–62
Minimizing cost, 151
MINITAB computer program, 818, 822, 828–29, 852, 854, 860–61
mn rule, 750–52, 764
Multinomial counting rule, 763
Multiplication principle, 750–52
Multiplicative inverse, 112–13
Multivariate function, 618

N–O

Napier, John, 362
Nauss, R.M., 238
Negative decision variables, 253–58
Newton, Isaac, 459
New product analysis, 326–27
Nominal rate, 404–5
Nonbasic variable, 205
Nonnegative constraints, 155–59
Normal distribution, 714, 848–58, 863–68
Numerical integration
  with calculators, 710–11
  definition of, 704–12
  QBasic program for, 712–13

Objective function
  linear, 151, 161
  maximization of, 161–72
  minimization of, 174–81
  and optimum values, 151
  in problem formulation, 169–73, 194–98
  sensitivity analysis on, 323–27
  in simplex method, 202–3
Odds as probabilities, 768–69
One, 900–902
Order
  of operations, 1–2, 882–84, 922–24
  properties, 3, 957–59
Ordinary annuities
  and amortization, 433–39, 442–43
  with calculators, 426–27, 429, 434–35, 449–50
  with continuous compounding, 450–51
  definition of, 424
  future value of, 424–27, 441–43, 445–46
  present value of, 431–33, 440–45
  sinking funds, 428–30, 443–44
  time diagram of, 425, 427, 441, 444–45
  with unknown interest rates, 449–50
  with unknown time elements, 449

P

Parameters, 55, 464
Particular solutions, 720
Pascal's triangle, 764
Payoff tables, 833–35
Percent rate, 393
Permutations, 752–57
Piecewise linear functions, 42–45
Phase I–Phase II method
  advantages of, 291
  equality constraints, 306–12
  no feasible solutions, 302–6
  using, 291–300
Pivot column, 207
Pivot row, 208
Point of inflection, 527–28
Point-slope form, 30–31
Polynomial; see also Maxima and minima
  functions, 475, 486
  graphs of, 576–80
Population (statistical), 762, 769
Postoptimality analysis; see Sensitivity analysis
Present value
  compound interest
    calculation of, 410–12
    with calculators, 411
    with continuous compounding, 420
    QBasic program for, 412
  of ordinary annuities
    calculation of, 431–33, 440–41, 444–45
    with calculators, 432–43
    time diagram of, 441
  simple interest
    formula for, 393–94
    time diagram for, 394
    QBasic program for, 395
Primal problem
  definition of, 282–83
  solving, 284–89
Principal, 388
Probabilities
  addition rule for, 783
  binomial, 820–26
    cumulative, 826–31
  conditional, 774
  conditional rule for, 785
  joint rules for, 785–86
  objective and odds, 768–69
  posterior, 797
  prior, 797
  sources of, 770–71
  subjective, 771
  unconditional, 774

Probability distribution; see also Functions, density
  area assignment of, 714
  binomial
    cumulative, 826–31
    definition of, 820
    mean of, 823
    standard deviation of, 823
    variance of, 815
  central tendency of, 815
  with calculators, 822, 854
  continuous, 838–42
  definition of, 813
  normal, 714, 848–58, 863–68
  and standard deviation, 817
  and variance, 817
Proceeds, 395–96
Producers' surplus, 680–85
Product rule, 511–15
Proportion, 41–42

Q–R

Quadratic
  equations, 8–9, 954–57
  formula, 7, 955
Quadratics, 7–9, 948–54
Quotient rule, 515–17

Radical, 1, 7, 915
Radicand, 915
Random sample, 859
Random selection, 772
Random variable
  definition of, 812
  expected value of, 815, 843
  mean value of, 815; see also Probability distribution
  properties of, 813
  standard deviation of, 817, 823, 846
  variance of, 817, 823, 846
Rational
  expressions, 4
  functions, 581–86
  numbers, 1, 877
  operations, 5
Rates
  bank discount, 396
  of change, 489, 678, 731
  of interest, 388, 395
Real numbers
  definition of, 1, 877, 886–87
  fundamental properties of, 887

Reference functions, 602–3
Reliability (statistical), 770
Relative frequency, 770
Riemann sums
   definition of, 653–55, 663
   QBasic program for, 664–65
Row operations
   linear systems, 73–75
   on a matrix, 110–12
Row vector, 100

S

Saber, J., 324
Saddle points, 626–28
Sample (statistical), 762, 769
Sample space, 809–11
SAS computer program, 818
Scalar, 101
Scalar product, 101
Schrage, L., 238
Secant line, 489, 491
Second derivative test, 541
Sensitivity analysis
   binding constraint, 260
   on equality constraints, 320–23
   on greater than constraints, 318–20
   on less than constraints, 259–74
   with LINDO computer program, 270–71
   on minimizing constraints, 318–20
   on objective function, 323–27
   purpose of, 259
   right-hand-side ranges, 268–70
   through vector relationships, 262
Separable differential equations, 720
Sets
   complement of, 10, 980
   continuous, 837
   definition of, 9, 971
   discrete, 837
   disjoint, 9, 773, 980
   empty, 9–10, 980
   intersections of, 9–10, 979
   object of, 9–10, 971
   member of, 9–10, 971
   solution, 974–77
   specification, 973
   subsets of, 10, 766, 978
   terminology for, 971–73
   unions of, 9–10, 979
   universal, 10, 979

Shadow price, 267
Shao, Stephen P., 424
Simple
   discount, 393–95
   event, 809
   fraction, 907
   interest, 388–399
   power rule, 498–500
Simplex method; *see* Linear programming
Singular matrices, 119
Sinking fund, 428–30, 443–44
Slack variable, 203
Slope, 20–23
Slope-intercept form, 26–29
Solution
   feasible, 163
   particular, 720, 928
   set, 974–77
   of a system, 71–88
SPSS computer program, 818
Square matrix; *see also* Identity matrix
   definition of, 101
   Gauss-Jordan computation, 121–30
   inverses of, 112–13
   zeros-first computation, 117–19
Standard deviation
   with calculators, 860–61
   definition of, 817–19, 846–47
   estimating, 858–62
   Minitab calculation of, 818, 861
State vector, 140–43
Stationary points, 523–32
Statistical inference, 769–70
Subscript notation, 21
Subset, 12, 766, 978
Substitution rate, 31
Sum or difference of matrices, 101–3
Sum or difference rule
   for derivatives, 502
   for integrals, 645, 671
Supply functions
   linear, 93–95
   and producers surplus, 681–82
   two-product, 96–97
Surplus variable, 283
System of equations
   consistent, 82
   inconsistent, 82
   solution of, 71–88
System of inequalities
   bounded and unbounded solutions, 152–59
   corner point, 163
   solution by graphing, 152–59

T–U

Tableaus, 206–16
Tangent line, 463, 491
Third derivative test, 544
Three-step graphical procedure, 178–79
Time value of money, 238, 353, 360, 395
Transition matrix, 140
Trapezoidal rule
   with calculators, 710–11
   definition of, 705–9
   QBasic program for, 712
Tree diagrams, 741, 750–52, 789–93, 799–801
Two-point form, 33–34

Uniform distribution, 839
Union symbol, 11–12, 979
Unit gain, 239
Unit matrix; *see* Identity matrix
Universal set, 12, 980
u-substitution technique, 646–49

V–Z

Van Cor, 117
Variable cost, 49
Variables; *see also* Random variable
   artificial, 293, 308
   basic, 205
   continuous, 838
   definition of, 3
   dependent, 8
   entering, 206–7, 237–41

Variables—*Cont.*
   independent, 8, 464–65, 975
   leaving, 207–9, 241
   negative decision, 253–58
   nonbasic, 205
   slack, 203
   solution, 928–42
   surplus, 283
Variance, 817, 823, 846
Vectors
   column, 100
   components of, 100
   row, 100
   state, 140–43
Velocity, 505
Venn Diagram, 743, 980
Vertex, 9, 951
Vertical
   asymptote, 582–86
   axes, 8, 944
   lines, 35–36
   parabola, 8, 948–54

Wagner, H. M., 274
Weingarter, H. M., 238
Word problems, 10–11

x-axis, 8–9, 942
x-intercept, 29

y-axis, 8–9, 944
Years to double, 408
Yield, 389
y-intercept, 29

Zero, 3–4, 888–900
Zero exponent, 6, 912
Zero matrix, 107

ALGEBRA

Rational Operations (p.5)

$$\frac{A}{B} \pm \frac{C}{D} = \frac{AD \pm BC}{BD}.$$

$$\frac{A}{B} \times \frac{C}{D} = \frac{AC}{BD}.$$

$$\frac{A}{B} \div \frac{C}{D} = \frac{A}{B} \times \frac{D}{C} = \frac{AD}{BC}.$$

Properties of Exponents ($a, b > 0$) (p. 355)

1. $a^0 = 1$.
2. $a^x \cdot a^y = a^{x+y}$.
3. $a^x/a^y = a^{x-y}$.
4. $(a^x)^y = a^{xy}$.
5. $(ab)^x = a^x b^x$.
6. $(ab)^x = a^x/b^x$.
7. $a^{-x} = 1/a^x$.

STRAIGHT LINES

$$\text{Slope} = m = \frac{\text{Difference of } y\text{'s}}{\text{Difference of } x\text{'s}} = \frac{y_2 - y_1}{x_2 - x_1}. \quad (p. 21)$$

Slope-Intercept Form (p. 28)

$$y = mx + b.$$

Point-Slope Form (p. 33)

$$\frac{y - y_1}{x - x_1} = m, \quad \text{or} \quad y - y_1 = m(x - x_1).$$

MATHEMATICS OF FINANCE

Compound Interest

Future value (p. 402)

$$F = P(1 + i)^n = P\left(1 + \frac{j}{m}\right)^{mt}.$$

Present value (p. 410)

$$P = F(1 + i)^{-n}.$$

Effective Rate of i Compounded m Times a Year (p. 414)

$$r_e = (1 + i)^m - 1; \quad i = \frac{j}{m}.$$

Continuous Compounding

Future Value with Continuous Compounding (p. 419)

$$F = Pe^{jt}.$$

Present Value with Continuous Compounding (p. 420)

$$P = Fe^{-jt}.$$

Effective Rate of Nominal Rate j (p. 421)

$$r_e = e^j - 1.$$

Ordinary Annuities

Future Value of Ordinary Annuity (p. 425)

$$F = R\left[\frac{(1 + i)^n - 1}{i}\right].$$

Sinking Fund Payment (p. 428)

$$R = F\left[\frac{i}{(1 + i)^n - 1}\right].$$

Present Value of Ordinary Annuity (p. 431)

$$P = R\left[\frac{1 - (1 + i)^{-n}}{i}\right].$$

Amortization Payment (p. 434)

$$R = P\left[\frac{i}{1 - (1 + i)^{-n}}\right].$$

INTEGRALS

Simple Power Rule (p. 643)

$$\int x^n\, dx = \frac{x^{n+1}}{n + 1} + C; \quad \text{if } n \neq -1.$$

$$\int x^{-1}\, dx = \int \frac{1}{x}\, dx = \ln |x| + C.$$

Power Rule for Linear Functions (pp. 648, 688)

$$\int (mx + b)^n dx = \frac{(mx + b)^{n+1}}{m(n + 1)} + C; \quad n \neq -1.$$

$$\int \frac{dx}{mx + b} = \frac{1}{m} \ln |mx + b| + C; \quad m \neq 0.$$

Exponential Rule (pp. 691, 692)

$$\int e^{mx+b}\, dx = \frac{e^{mx+b}}{m} + C; \quad m \neq 0.$$

$$\int a^{kmx+b}\, dx = \frac{a^{kmx+b}}{m (\ln a)} + C; \quad m \neq 0.$$